THE PHOTOSHOP CS3 CS4 "WOW!" BOOK

LINNEA DAYTON   CRISTEN GILLESPIE

Peachpit Press

The Photoshop CS3/CS4 Wow! Book

Linnea Dayton & Cristen Gillespie

Wow! Series Editor: Linnea Dayton

Peachpit Press
1249 Eighth Street
Berkeley, CA 94710
(510) 524-2178
(510) 524-2221 (fax)

Find us on the Web at www.peachpit.com

To report errors, please send a note to errata@peachpit.com

Peachpit Press is a division of Pearson Education.

Cover design: Donal Jolley

Book design: Jill Davis; revised by John Odam

Production and prepress: Jonathan Parker

Direct-to-plate printing: CDS Publications / Medford, Oregon

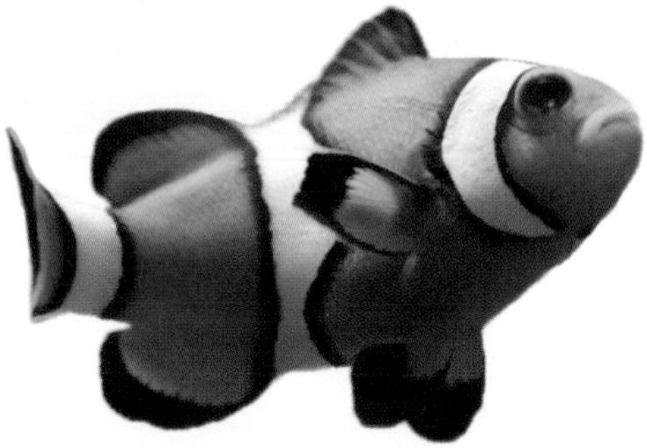

ISBN 13: 978-0-321-51495-0
ISBN 10: 0-321-51495-5

0 9 8 7 6 5 4 3 2 1

Printed and bound in the United States of America

To 20 years of Adobe Photoshop, and 19 years of Photoshop Wow!
— *Linnea*

To Nancy Carroll for constantly asking me hard questions about Photoshop, and to my cat Willie for being willing to share the keyboard with me — thank you.

— *Cristen*

Acknowledgments

Although Jack Davis has gone on to other endeavors, evidence of his larger-than-life talent, no-nonsense methodology, and generous collaboration are still found throughout the book and on the DVD-ROM. Like the previous ones, this edition would not have been possible without him.

We've had a great deal of support from others as well — photographers, designers, illustrators, and fine artists who have so generously allowed us to include their work and reveal their secrets. In this edition we are fortunate to have some who have been a part of the book since work began on the first edition in 1991. We feel so grateful for the others who have joined along the way, and for those who are brand-new contributors with this edition. The "Artists & Photographers" appendix lists their names and contact information and tells where in the book their work can be found. Special thanks go to Donal Jolley, who once again designed and produced a wonderful cover, as well as some fantastic new tutorial examples. Even more than that, his knowledge and accessibility have added depth to the book's content.

Many thanks, as always, to Jonathan Parker, an absolutely essential part of the team, who once again made room in his design studio's schedule — more room than he bargained for! — to do the production and prepress, taking on more for this edition than ever before.

We appreciate the support of Adobe Systems, Inc., who allowed us to participate in the Photoshop beta program for authors. Our heartfelt thanks also go especially to Val Gelineau of PhotoSpin.com, who generously gave us access to the PhotoSpin collections of stock photography, illustrations, video clips, and fonts to use in our tutorials. And we'd like to thank Ben Willmore for his *Photoshop Up to Speed* books, which helped us make sure we hadn't overlooked anything in the new versions of Photoshop.

Thank you to our friends and colleagues at Peachpit Press, who have now supported us through 11 editions of *The Photoshop Wow! Book*. They have the patience of Job and the enthusiasm of a cheerleading squad, and we appreciate it. In particular, we thank publisher Nancy Ruenzel, managing editor Becky Morgan, executive editor Victor Gavenda (Adobe Press), production editor Hilal Sala, designer Mimi Heft, and media producer Eric Geoffroy. Thanks also to freelance proofreader extraordinaire Scout Festa.

Over the course of this project, the day-in and day-out support of our families and friends   and *their* families and *their* friends — has been remarkable, and we feel extraordinarily lucky.

Finally, heartfelt thanks to those readers of previous editions who have let us know that *The Photoshop Wow! Book* has inspired as well as educated them, and to those who have just quietly used and appreciated it. Thanks also for pointing out where we could improve the book so all of us can continue to get the most "Wow!" from our favorite tool — Photoshop, and now Photoshop Extended.

— *Linnea Dayton & Cristen Gillespie*

Contents

9 Putting It All Together 570

Composition Methods • Elements in a Photoshop File • Choosing & Preparing Components • Fitting an Element to a Surface • Creating Panoramas • Operating on Several Layers at Once • Reordering Layers • Merging & Flattening • Layer Comps

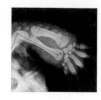

Welcome to
The Photoshop CS3/ CS4 Wow! Book

Two Versions — and Extended

Because this book covers two versions of Photoshop — CS3 and CS4 — we've included some guideposts to make it clear when we're talking about CS3 or about both versions (black type) and when we're talking about something that's different in CS4 (blue type). Also, watch for the symbol at the right, which identifies illustrations or techniques that are CS4-specific.

CS3 and CS4 also come in two versions apiece: Photoshop and Photoshop Extended, which has all the features of Photoshop and several more. Most of the information in this book applies to both types. Where we show and tell about features exclusive to Extended, we make that clear.

Adobe Photoshop is one of the most powerful visual design and production tools ever to appear on the desktop. For print, for the web, or for anywhere else where photos or graphics appear, Photoshop is the standard for professional design, production, and organization. Included in the several different varieties of **Adobe Creative Suite**, Photoshop is also still available as a separate product. ("Separate" isn't the same as "alone." Even when sold separately, Photoshop comes with some powerful companion products; two of them, Bridge and Camera Raw, are especially helpful.) Many of the most important changes in Photoshop CS3 and CS4 are introduced in "What's New?" starting on page 5.

The aim of *The Photoshop CS3/CS4 Wow! Book* is to provide the kind of inspirational examples and practical "nuts-and-bolts" info that will help you maximize the performance of Photoshop and boost your own creativity with it. Its goal is to help you produce work that's better and faster, and easier to change or repurpose if you need to later. The book provides version-accurate instructions for both CS3 and CS4, and if you're still using CS3, the book will give you a look at what's to be gained from an upgrade.

ORIGINAL PHOTO: YURI ARCURS / PHOTOSFIN.COM; ORIGINAL GRAPHICS: FRED FRASCO / PHOTOSPIN.COM

Before you set sail on Photoshop's ocean, you might want to take a look at the first four chapters. They provide a crash course in how Photoshop thinks.

PICTURE THIS...

Photoshop is launched and looking at you from your computer screen — a virtual *ocean* of tools, menu choices, and panels. Rest assured that you don't have to navigate the entire ocean to get the professional results you want. If you understand some *Photoshop basics*, you'll be able to cruise off to any of the fabulous creative destinations in this book and beyond. (***Note:*** In CS3 the **panels** are called **palettes**, but rather than bother you every two sentences with "palettes/panels," we'll call them all "panels." All of the other programs in Adobe Creative Suite had "panels" in version CS3, so we'll boldly "update" Photoshop CS3 as well.)

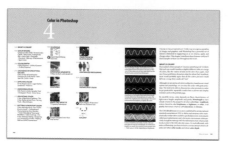

In the chapter introductions, learn the basics of how Photoshop works.

Each "Quick" section, such as the six-page "Quick Integration" in Chapter 9, provides a short introduction and then several easy-to-grasp solutions. Many of the examples are supplied as layered files on the Wow DVD-ROM so you can learn by deconstructing them.

For more complex techniques, or to find out the "why" behind each step of the instructions, try the longer tutorials. Each one starts with an overview of the technique.

Like Photoshop itself, this book is an ideal tool for:

- **Photographers,** who need faster, easier ways to do the retouching, resizing, cropping, and basic color correction of their daily production work, and who, knowing Photoshop, can plan their photo shoots thinking of Photoshop as an extension of their camera equipment.

- Print-oriented **designers, illustrators,** and **fine artists,** whose professional horizons have been broadened by Photoshop and by advances in digital imagery, now including 3D models and DICOM radiographs.

- **Information architects** and **budding animators and videographers** who are forging ahead, designing and creating on-screen imagery for the web and other interactive digital delivery systems, or presenting information visually.

Beyond that, *The Photoshop CS3/CS4 Wow! Book*, along with its Wow DVD-ROM, supports creative people of all kinds who want to use the Photoshop laboratory for synthesizing textures, patterns, and all kinds of visual effects — from subtle to flamboyant — that can be applied to photos, graphics, type, or video. And it helps you automate many of these tasks — from routine production to complex special effects.

DIVE IN!

If you're new to Photoshop, you'll benefit from learning the "basics" in Chapters 1 through 4 of this book. Even if you're already experienced with Photoshop, you might want to at least *skim* these first four, just to see if there are any new methods, tools, or techniques that you might not have encountered before.

Feel free to jump in anywhere in the book that grabs your interest. The directions you need to get where you're going will be supplied in the step-by-step instructions for the technique, though we recommend that you use the opening pages of the chapter you're working in as a resource.

Throughout the book, pointers like this one ▼ and their **"Find Out More"** boxes will direct you if you want more information about something basic. But they're designed to be easy to ignore if you've mastered the basics and don't want to be interrupted.

FIND OUT MORE

▼ Using Smart Filters
page 72

If there's a deadline pressing, or if you simply want a *short* excursion into Photoshop, take a look at the techniques in the **"Quick" sections**, where even beginners can get great results

Each "Exercising" tutorial explores an especially useful part of the Photoshop interface, to familiarize you with its remarkable and specialized capabilities.

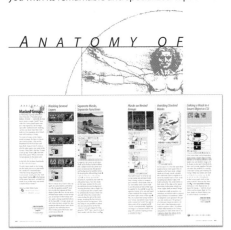

Each "Anatomy" section explores some kind of Photoshop construction. For instance, "Anatomy of Masked Groups" on page 620 shows how to construct masked groups in order to apply the same mask to a number of images or to apply more than one mask to a single layer.

"Is It 'Real'? Or Is It Photoshop?" sections relate Photoshop to more traditional approaches to art and photography. And in "Secrets of the Universe Revealed" sections, look for novel approaches to using Photoshop.

really quickly. On the other hand, when you have more time and you want to delve deeper, the longer **step-by-step tutorials** and the **"Exercising"** and **"Anatomy" sections** are designed to help you explore some of the most useful, sometimes nearly hidden, gems in Photoshop, and to learn to "think like Photoshop," to become an expert at analyzing each Photoshop challenge that comes your way, and building the file you need to meet it.

You can also find **tips** throughout the book, like the one at the right, with the gray title bar on top. (The title bar is blue for tips that relate to Photoshop CS4 only.) The tips are nuggets of information that relate to the text nearby, but each one also stands on its own. You can quickly pick up a lot of useful information simply by flipping through the book and reading the tips.

> **TOGGLING THE PREVIEW**
>
> In many of the dialog boxes for Photoshop's filters and Adjustments commands, you can quickly toggle the document-window Preview on and off simply by typing "P" while the dialog is open. This works for Adjustment layers in Photoshop CS3 (they use dialog boxes) but not in CS4's Adjustments panel.
>
> ☑ **Preview**

You'll find a different kind of insight in **"Secrets of the Universe Revealed"** and **"Is It 'Real'? Or Is It Photoshop?"** These "sidebars" provide the discoveries, some of them a bit off the beaten path, of Photoshop artists who have been kind enough to share them with us.

Each chapter ends with a **"Gallery"** of inspirational real-world examples of outstanding work by Photoshop professionals. Extensive captions are packed with useful information about how the artwork was produced.

At the very back of the book, you'll find **"Appendix" sections,** with visual examples of the wealth of goodies found in Photoshop itself or on the Wow DVD-ROM that comes with this book, along with tips and instructions for putting them to work. "Appendix E" has contact information for the exciting and generous artists and photographers whose work appears in the book.

DON'T MISS THE WOW DVD-ROM!

The Wow DVD-ROM has **"before"** and **"after" files** for the step-by-step techniques, as well as finished files for many of the "Quick," "Exercising," and "Anatomy" sections, so you can compare as you build or deconstruct the projects in the book.

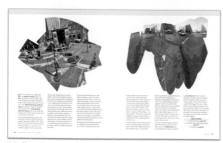

"Gallery" pages display the artwork large, and show how the artists arrived at their inspiring results.

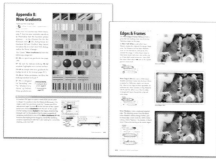

For catalogs of the Adobe filters, the Wow Layer Styles, and other goodies from the Wow DVD-ROM that comes with this book, look in the "Appendix" sections at the back of the book.

The Wow Layer Styles, Tool Presets, Gradients, Patterns, and Actions are designed to make your work easier — not to mention more spectacular. You'll find complete sets in the PS CS3-CS4 Wow Presets folder on the Wow DVD-ROM.

The DVD-ROM also holds the **Wow presets and Actions**:

- **Styles** that instantly transform photos, graphics, type, and web buttons with effects from subtle to spectacular

- **Tools** crafted especially for painting, image-editing, and cropping

- **Patterns** and **Gradients** to use as fills or in your own Styles

- **Actions** that automate many of the creative and production techniques covered in the book

We've removed some material from the previous edition of the printed book, just to make room for new techniques. Still useful, the old techniques are provided as **Outtakes** in the Wow Goodies folder on the DVD-ROM.

BON VOYAGE!

This book will get you started "thinking like Photoshop" and using the tools if you're new at it, and it will give you some new insight and ideas if you're an old hand. Try out the tips, techniques, Styles, and Actions, and use them to set forth fearlessly toward your own Photoshop destinations. 〰

INSTALLING WOW STYLES, PATTERNS, TOOLS & OTHER PRESETS

In Photoshop CS3 and CS4, installing presets couldn't be easier: **Drag the Wow Presets folder** from the Wow DVD-ROM **into the Presets folder** within your installed Adobe Photoshop CS3 or CS4 folder. Now whenever you launch Photoshop, the program will load the Wow presets into the menus of the panels and dialog boxes where they can be used.

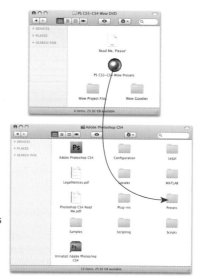

What's New in Photoshop CS3/ CS4?

THIS SECTION INTRODUCES some impressive new features in Photoshop CS3 and CS4, as well as important improvements to old ones. Many of these updates will make a big difference to almost anyone who uses the program. We'll start with the most exciting, then briefly describe other useful changes in Photoshop CS3 and CS4, and finally look at the new Photoshop Extended.

REALLY "WOW!"

Many small improvements in CS3 and CS4 add up to increased efficiency, productivity, and power. But among the big changes — the ones that will wow anyone who uses Photoshop — are the following:

- The new **Smart Filter** technology, first available in CS3, allows us to apply most of Photoshop's filters to Smart Objects, keeping the filters "live." With Smart Filters the filter settings can be changed at any time, along with the blend that combines the filtered image and the unfiltered. For the first time, two color-and-contrast adjustments — Shadows/Highlights and Variations — can be applied "live," as Smart Filters. Smart Filters are introduced in Chapter 2.

- CS4's **Adjustments panel** makes color and tone adjustments much easier to work with. Now when you add an Adjustment layer to your file, you don't lose access to the rest of Photoshop. With modal dialog boxes, which are standard in CS3 and earlier versions (and even in CS4 if you apply an adjustment via the Image > Adjustments command rather than as an Adjustment layer), your activity is restricted as long as the dialog is open. If you'd like to see what the adjustment would be like if you reduced layer Opacity or switched to Luminosity mode, the modal dialog has to be closed before you can change these layer settings. With the Adjustments panel, on the other hand, you're free to change any layer

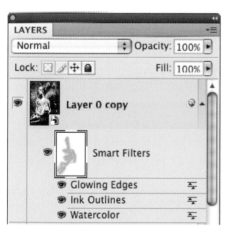

With access through the Layers panel, you can change the settings for a **Smart Filter** you've applied, change the way the filtered image blends with the original, or target the filter effects with a mask. "Exercising Smart Filters" on page 72 introduces this important new feature and explains how it works in CS3 and CS4. You'll find other examples also, especially in Chapters 5 and 9.

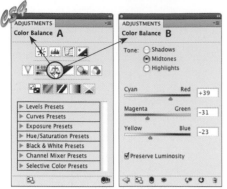

The **Adjustments panel** in Photoshop CS4 offers the full menu of Adjustment layers, some with useful presets. Rolling the cursor over any button in the panel puts the name of that adjustment at the top of the panel **A**. When you click the button to add the Adjustment layer, the panel changes to show the appropriate dialog **B**. The dialog will stay open, with "live" settings, anytime that layer is targeted in the Layers panel.

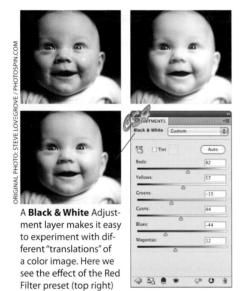

A **Black & White** Adjustment layer makes it easy to experiment with different "translations" of a color image. Here we see the effect of the Red Filter preset (top right) and a custom setting.

The **Black & White** adjustment can be useful for graphics also. See "Quick Black & White Graphics" on page 490.

settings, paint the layer mask to target the adjustment, move the Adjustment layer up or down the layer stack, clip it to the layer below it, or turn your attention to another layer entirely, all while adjustment dialog settings remain available in the Adjustments panel.

- The new **Black & White adjustment** makes it so much easier to "translate" photos from color to black-and-white. With separate controls for six different divisions of the color spectrum, you can decide, for example, whether the blues in your image will be dark or light grays, and the same for each of the other five "color families." Use any of the six color sliders, or use the targeted-adjustment "scrubber" 👆 to click on a particular color in the image and move it toward a lighter or darker gray. "From Color to Black & White" (page 214), as well as "Tinting with Black & White" (page 204) and "Tinting with Masking" (page 206) show this new adjustment in action.

- Photoshop CS3 and CS4 show significant new approaches to **selecting and masking**, the two processes essential for isolating elements so you can work on them.

  The **Quick Selection tool** 🖌, introduced in Photoshop CS3, makes selections based on a combination of color, texture, and edge detection. Often one or two strokes with the Quick Selection cursor will do what would take a lot of addition and subtraction with other selection tools. The Quick Selection tool is introduced in Chapter 2.

  Starting in Photoshop CS3, the **Refine Edge** dialog (opened from the Select menu or from a button on the Options bar when a selection is active and a selection tool is chosen) can expand or contract an active selection, or harden or soften its edge. This self-contained "toolkit" also works on layer masks.

  In CS4 the Select > **Color Range command** has been improved with the addition of the **Localized Color Clusters** option. It lets you limit the Color Range you're selecting in two important ways: You can now make a selection based on two (or more) colors without also selecting all the colors in-between. For instance, you can select blue and yellow areas without also selecting green. And you can limit how far your selections can extend outward from the sampling point.

  From CS4's new **Masks panel** you can now **Feather** (soften) the edges of a vector mask while still keeping its sharp-edged nature waiting in the wings in case you want to reshape the outline or try a different degree of feather later on. You can

A single stroke with the **Quick Selection tool** in its default "Add to selection" mode can often isolate most of a subject, leaving most of the background unselected. You can then add to or subtract from the selection using Quick Selection or another selection tool. See page 49.

You can use **Refine Edge** to improve the selection of wispy hair. An approach that often works is to set the **Radius** high **A**, increase the **Contrast B**, and then eliminate "bumps" in the edge with the **Smooth** setting and add a small amount of **Feather** to help the selected area blend with a new background **C**. Contract just enough to get rid of a fringe of the old background, or **Expand** enough to pick up the subject all the way to its edges **D**. See page 58 for more detail.

also reduce the **Density** (hiding power) of a layer mask or vector mask so that masked-out areas of a layer are allowed to show through to some degree. See page 63 for more.

- **Photomerge technology** (designed for assembling a series of images into a panorama) has not only been improved, both in CS3 and again in CS4, but has also been "opened up": Its component parts have been made available separately for collecting a photo series into a single file, aligning the components, and then masking and adjusting them to blend together seamlessly. The three separate parts are the File > Scripts > **Load Files into Stack** command, the Edit > **Auto-Align Layers** command, and the Edit > **Auto-Blend Layers** command. If you plan ahead and take several shots, Auto-Align and Auto-Blend can eliminate unwanted "foot traffic" from a scene (page 327), coax an ideal group photo from several not-quite-perfect tries, increase depth of focus by combining a series of photos focused at different distances (page 344), or even help eliminate digital noise (page 325). The separation of the three photo-merging functions also allows more options for piecing together panoramas. Multishot techniques with Auto-Align and Auto-Blend are covered in Chapter 5, and panoramas and other uses of Photomerge are covered in Chapter 9.

- CS4's **Content-Aware Scale** is another example of Photoshop's power to analyze images. This command is designed to

The improved **Color Range** command gives better control of which colors are selected. With **Localized Color Clusters** turned on, we could select blue and yellow without also picking up green. See page 51 for more.

The **Masks panel** lets you adjust the overall **Density** (hiding power) of a mask and the **Feather** (softness) of its edge, both nondestructively, so you can always get back to the original mask. This panel has three other buttons: **"Mask Edge"** opens the Refine Mask dialog (this works for layer masks only); the **"Color Range"** button opens that dialog so you can make a selection to define a mask; and **"Invert"** creates the negative of the current mask ("Color Range" and "Invert" work on layer masks and Smart Filter masks).

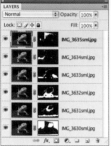

Load Files Into Stack, Auto-Align Layers, and **Auto-Blend Layers** were originally available only as part of the hidden magic of Photomerge. Now you can use them as independent commands. Here we aligned and blended a series of close-ups so that all parts of the subject are in focus. See page 344.

PHOTO: KAVRAM / PHOTOSPIN.COM

Photoshop CS4's Edit > **Content Aware Scale** command "condenses" or expands an image while automatically preserving features that seem to be important. We used it here without protecting any parts of the photo. Often you'll want to do some "rough" masking to keep particular areas from changing. See examples on pages 243 and 419.

scale unimportant parts of an image without changing texture or distorting the important image content. For instance, it can change a portrait's aspect ratio by stretching only the background, or condense a bucolic landscape, keeping the farmhouse and barn the same while shrinking the stretches of grass and sky in between. It can be great for expanding a product shot with a studio background to fit the column inches available in a brochure or catalog.

- **Improvements to Camera Raw** have made it the "interface of choice" for many photographers for starting the process of adjusting tone and color in their photos. In fact, in some cases the entire image-adjusting process can be carried out in Camera Raw. Starting with the version that comes with Photoshop CS3, Camera Raw works well not only on cameras' raw-format files but also on JPEGs and TIFFs. The tools for global corrections in the Camera Raw interface (including some, such as Clarity and Post-Crop Vignetting, that aren't found in Photoshop itself) are organized in a way that leads you through the correction process logically. And Camera Raw is set up to apply changes to an entire photo shoot if you like, once you've corrected one image. Beyond global changes, local retouching is introduced in the Camera Raw that comes with CS3 and greatly expanded in CS4. You'll find an introduction to Camera Raw in Chapter 3 and applications of its features in Chapter 5.

OTHER USEFUL NEW FEATURES & IMPROVEMENTS

Here are some less spectacular but nevertheless noteworthy changes in versions CS3 and CS4, starting with the interface (the new interfaces for CS3 and CS4 are examined on pages 20–24):

- Those of us who enjoy working in relative chaos, with many files and panels piled up, can probably benefit from the attitude adjustment encouraged by the changes in the Photoshop interface. But if you absolutely can't get used to the degree of organization now available, you can resort to changing things back via the Preferences menu (Ctrl/⌘-K).

  Starting in Photoshop CS3 the **palettes/panels can be grouped** together, with one fully visible "on top" and only name tabs showing for the others in the group. Single panels or groups can also be joined head-to-tail and even docked to the edges of the screen. Panels can be reduced to small icons or to icons with name labels. Then when you open one, it will close again as soon as you click somewhere else.

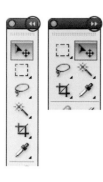

The new **single-column Tools panel** takes up less horizontal space on your monitor, and if you routinely choose tools by typing their keyboard shortcuts (shown on page 21) rather than mousing to the Tools panel, you may find this layout ideal. But you can toggle to the more compact two-column format, if you like, by clicking the double-arrow button at the top.

OPENGL DRAWING

In Photoshop CS4, **OpenGL accelerated video processing** gives you smooth, continuous control of brush-tip size and hardness while you operate brush-based tools. OpenGL also makes panning and zooming smooth and dynamic. And in Photoshop CS4 Extended it significantly improves performance when you open, move, or edit 3D models.

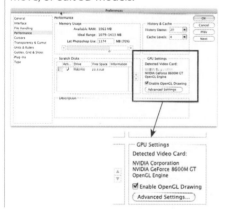

☑ Animated Zoom
☑ Zoom Resizes Windows
☐ Zoom with Scroll Wheel
☐ Zoom Clicked Point to Center

Controls for zooming can be set in General Preferences (Ctrl/⌘-K). In Photoshop CS4 with **OpenGL Drawing** enabled, Animated Zoom is added to the list of zooming options (see page 19).

But if you find it annoying to have the Layers panel, for instance, disappearing from your workspace every time you turn your back on it, you can turn off **Auto-Collapse** Icon Palettes/Auto-Collapse Iconic Panels in the Interface section of Preferences (Ctrl/⌘-K).

The Tools panel has changed to a single-column format, starting in CS3.

CS4 adds the **Application bar,** with convenient placement of the Extras from the View menu and the navigation tools (Hand 🖐, Zoom 🔍, and Rotate View 🖐) as well as document-arrangement options and screen mode, which is no longer available in the Tools panel. Also added on the Mac is the **Application frame**, a Windows-like environment that hides all other programs while you work in Photoshop.

Once you have a **custom workspace** set up with the panels where you want them, along with any customized keyboard shortcuts and menus, you can save it (and call it up again) with the Workspace menu at the right end of the Options bar in CS3 or the right end of the new Application bar in CS4.

If you have an up-to-date video card, one that supports **OpenGL/GPU acceleration**, there are several changes in CS4 that can make working in Photoshop more fun. When you open the **Preferences** dialog (Ctrl/⌘-K) and choose **Performance** from the list on the left, you'll see **GPU Settings** in the lower-right corner of the dialog; if **Enable OpenGL Drawing** is available and turned on, you can take advantage of these and other performance improvements:

Smooth zooming allows you to see a sharp, smooth display at any percentage enlargement, even 33.47% if you like. And with **Animated Zoom** turned on in General Preferences, zooming in or out is a smooth change in magnification, rather than a series of jumps. "Zooming & Panning" on page 19 tells more about it.

When you **interactively resize a brush tip** or change its hardness, the change is previewed in the brush-tip cursor (as shown on page 71), so you get a better idea of what your changes are doing.

The **Rotate View tool** 🖐 allows you to turn your active document to any angle you like on-screen, to make painting and drawing more comfortable. Using the Rotate View tool affects only the view, not the file content.

• Having the histogram right there as part of the **improved Curves display** makes it possible to see where you can "bor-

With the **Rotate View tool** ✋ you can change the working position of a painting or drawing. If you turn on the **Rotate All Windows** option in the Options bar, rotating one document will rotate all open documents to the same angle, regardless of the angle they started at.

The **Curves dialog** now includes the histogram. In CS4's Adjustments panel (shown here), choose Curves Display Options from the panel menu ▾≡ to access the controls for grid size and for using light or inks as the axes.

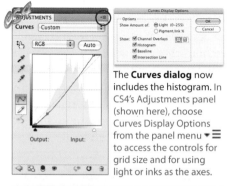

A negative **Vibrance** setting was used to desaturate (right), especially the strongest colors. Pages 205, 255, and 290 show examples of using Vibrance.

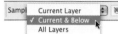

The Sample: **Current & Below** choice for the Clone Stamp 🖋 and Healing Brush 🩹 lets you keep your repairs on a separate layer (always a good idea in case you decide to change the repair) without having to include layers *above* the repair in your sampling. That means you can add an empty "repairs" layer just above the layer you want to touch up and the Clone Stamp or Healing Brush will ignore any Adjustment layers above the repair when it samples cloning or healing material. That way, the repairs will always match the original in tone and color.

row" from tonal ranges that aren't important in the image to boost contrast in ranges that *are* important.

- The **Vibrance** adjustment appears in Camera Raw in CS3 and was also added to Photoshop in CS4. It can boost color saturation while protecting highly saturated colors from becoming oversaturated, so that images don't become garish and lose detail in the heavily saturated areas. Vibrance is also designed to protect skin tones from becoming oversaturated.

- For retouching, the addition of **Current & Below** to the sampling options for the Healing Brush 🩹 and Clone Stamp 🖋 make it much easier in a file that includes Adjustment layers to sample cloning or "healing" material that has the same tone and color as the image you're repairing. And the **Clone Source panel** gives you more options for these two tools than in previous versions of the program. You can set up multiple clone or healing sources, and you can scale and rotate clone source material.

- Starting in CS3, significant improvements have been added to **Vanishing Point,** the "megafilter" that lets you establish perspective in your image and then paste or paint into that perspective. For instance, you can now generate an attached perspective plane, connected to an existing plane, at other than a right angle. And you can slide a pasted element from plane to plane, even wrapping it around corners. "Exercising Vanishing Point" on page 612 puts this megafilter through its paces.

- Photoshop CS3 and CS4 introduce several new color features.

It's just one small button, but **"Add to Swatches"** in the Color Picker shortcuts the process of assembling a custom color palette for a project. Develop a color in the Picker and then simply click this button to add it to the Swatches panel.

New **Lighter Color** and **Darker Colo**r blend modes make it easier to predict the outcome of blending than it is with the Lighten and Darken modes; the difference is explained on pages 182–184.

The **kuler** extension (Window > Extensions > kuler) provides a way to develop a color scheme from an image or share color schemes that you and others post online (see page 172).

You can now see a representation of how your image will look to people with reduced color sensitivity. Turn on one of the **Color Blindness** options available through View > Proof Setup and then turn on the View > Proof Colors option.

Three large flowers from another image were sampled as clone sources and scaled to different sizes before they were added to the greenery. See page 257 for more about using the **Clone Source panel**.

Using the improved **Vanishing Point**, it's easy to create the attached planes you need and wrap graphics to fit them. See page 612 for more.

The new **Lighter Color** mode (right) blends colors differently than Lighten does (left).

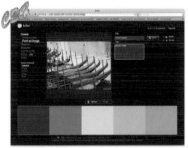

With Photoshop CS4's **kuler extension** you can upload an image directly from Photoshop to Adobe's kuler site online and automatically generate color "themes" to match the image. For more about kuler, see page 172.

Previews for two common types of color blindness, protanopia (center) and deuteranopia

- Both CS3 and CS4 advance the number of adjustments and filters that can be applied to **32-bit images**. So if you open or create a 32-bit HDR image, you can now do more editing before you reduce it to 16-Bit or 8-Bit mode. The filter examples in Appendix A show which filters work on 32-bit images.

- In CS3 and CS4 (shown below) the option to preview printed color, including ink and paper colors, was added to the **Print dialog**.

- The File > Export > **Zoomify** command (shown on page 12) allows you to make large images available for efficient zooming and panning in a Web browser.

- **Bridge,** the file management program that comes with Photoshop, has undergone significant changes in the arrangement of its commands, buttons, and panels. With CS3 came more freedom to move and group the panels; a context-sensitive **Filter panel** for sorting files; **Loupe view,** a magnifier for zooming in on an image; **virtual collections** for organizing related images without changing where they're kept on your hard drive; and **Stacks** for compact display of parts of a panorama series, bracketed exposures, or other related shots. **Photo Downloader** can collect photos from a camera's memory card, via a connection to the camera itself or through an adapter (click File > Get Photos from Camera or click the 📷 button at the top left of the Bridge CS4 interface,

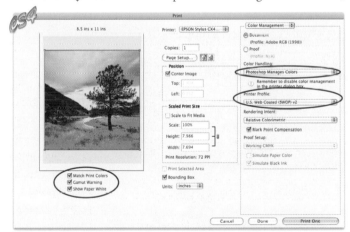

To preview the printed color and paper color in the File > **Print dialog**, choose **Photoshop Manages Colors** and choose the **Printer Profile** for the printing method you will use. In Photoshop CS3, choosing **Match Print Colors** will preview both the ink and paper colors. In Photoshop CS4 (shown here) you can preview the inks with or without the paper color, and you can also choose to see what colors in your image may not print well because they are out of gamut for the printer you've chosen. You can find a description of the paper that goes with a particular printer profile by choosing that profile in the Working Spaces section of the Color Settings dialog (Edit > Color Settings) and reading about the paper in the Description section at the bottom of the dialog.

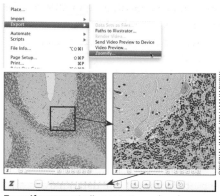

Zoomify automatically generates and packages all the files a browser needs for close-up examination of a high-res image without downloading delays. This includes the Zoomify viewer, which can be operated with the simple control bar shown here or with keyboard shortcuts. See page 130 for another example, explained step-by-step..

 **Histology Zoomify**

Device Central can show you what your graphics will look like on various mobile devices under different light conditions.

This 3D model of a globe was created with a 2D world map and the 3D > New Shape From Layer command in Photoshop CS4 Extended. In either CS3 or CS4, layers containing 3D models can be stacked and masked like standard layers. Here two copies of the same 3D models were stacked, one rendered in Solid mode and one in Wireframe, with a layer mask applied to the Wireframe layer.

or set it to launch automatically). CS4 further refines the Bridge interface, improves its performance and speed, adds new methods for reviewing and sorting images, and adds an **Output module** with updated versions of PDF Presentation, Contact Sheet II, and Web Photo Gallery, functions that used to be in Photoshop itself. Bridge is covered in Chapter 3.

- **Device Central** helps with designing and testing files to be displayed on cell phones and other mobile devices. You can open Device Central through Photoshop's File > Open or File > Save for Web & Devices commands (see page 146).

PHOTOSHOP EXTENDED

CS3 is the first version of Photoshop to be available in an Extended version that includes a collection of features designed to expand Photoshop's usefulness in **animation, video,** and **3D**, and in professional and scientific applications in which **measurement** and **simple statistical analysis** are important.

Compared to 3D applications and video editing programs, the features in Photoshop Extended are limited. But they make it easier to apply color, pattern, and texture to 3D models, and to enhance video clips. Chapter 10, "3D, Video & Animation," covers some of these features that designers, illustrators, fine artists, and photographers will find useful, and others are introduced throughout the book. The **Animation panel** becomes more functional in Photoshop Extended. Besides the Frame mode found in Photoshop, it also has a **Timeline mode** that lets you control animation with keyframes and add video and 3D to animations. **Video clips and 3D constructions can now be integrated** into layered Photoshop files, which makes it easy to apply filters and tone and color adjustments to all or part of an entire video clip, as shown in "Quick Video Techniques" on page 687. And the ability in Photoshop CS4 to convert an image or type into a 2D object that can be manipulated in 3D space makes it easier for designers to experiment with perspective distortion and with animated graphics. "Quick Sources of 3D Material" on page 668 provides some examples.

Chapter 11, "Measurement & Analysis," introduces Photoshop Extended's counting and measuring functions, located in the **Analysis menu**. Photoshop has always stored a wealth of color data for each image file and provided a variety of ways, with different degrees of automation, to compare color and to select areas that are similar. Now Photoshop Extended can mine some of this data to measure **linear dimensions**, **perimeters**,

To count features in a photo in Photoshop Extended, you can place dots by hand with the **Count tool**, as we did here (page 725), or make a selection and automatically count the number of separate areas selected (page 728).

Adobe Photoshop CS3\MATLAB

```
Adobe Photoshop toolbox.
Version 1.0 13-Dec-2006

General.
    psconfig          - Get and set the current
    psjavascript      - Execute the given text
    pslaunch          - Launch Photoshop or att
    psquit            - Quit the Photoshop appl

Document functions.
    psclosedoc        - Close the active docume
    psdocinfo         - Return information for
    psdocnames        - Return the names of all
    pshistogram       - Return the histogram fo
```

```
000                    psunsharpmask.m
function [] = psunsharpmask(a, r, t)
%PSUNSHARPMASK    Run the Unsharp Mask filter.
%  PSUNSHARPMASK() runs the Unsharp Mask filter with the default
%  parameters.
%
%  PSUNSHARPMASK(A) A for amount is a percent in the range of 1 -> 500,
%  default is 50.
%
%  PSUNSHARPMASK(A,R) R for radius is in pixels in the range 0.1 -> 250.0,
%  default is 1.0
%
%  PSUNSHARPMASK(A,R,T) T for threshold is the levels in the range of 0 ->
%  255, default is 0.
%
%  Example:
%  psunsharpmask()
%  psunsharpmask(65)
%  psunsharpmask(65, 2.2)
%  psunsharpmask(65, 2.2, 34)
%
%  See also PSADDNOISE, PSAVERAGE, PSBLUR, PSBLURMORE, PSBOXBLUR,
%  PSCUSTOM, PSDUSTANDSCRATCHES, PSGAUSSIANBLUR, PSHIGHPASS, PSLENSBLUR,
%  PSMAXIMUM, PSMEDIAN, PSMINIMUM, PSMOTIONBLUR, PSOFFSET, PSRADIALBLUR,
%  PSSHAPEBLUR, PSSHARPEN, PSSHARPENEDGES, PSSHARPENMORE, PSSMARTBLUR,
%  PSSURFACEBLUR

%  Thomas Ruark, 2/3/2006
%  Copyright 2006 Adobe Systems Incorporated

if nargin < 1
    a = 50;
end
if nargin < 2
    r = 1.0;
end
```

The installation of Photoshop CS3 Extended or Photoshop CS4 Extended includes commands for calling Photoshop functions from MATLAB.

and **areas**, and to calculate **means**, **medians**, and other useful statistics. Measurements can be set to reflect a custom scale. The statistical comparisons can be useful not only for scientific and technical applications, but also for addressing some problems that crop up in photography all the time. For instance, with the ability to do pixel-by-pixel comparisons of several versions of an image, stacked as layers, the **Median** command can partially (or sometimes completely) eliminate unwanted distractions from a photo taken in a public place (see page 327), and the **Mean** command can help reduce noise (see page 325).

MATLAB, a computing environment for data analysis and visualization, can now include Photoshop image-editing features in MATLAB commands. From MATLAB, the **pslaunch** command connects to Photoshop, and **psquit** disconnects. The **psfunctionscat.html** file, found in the Adobe Photoshop CS3 (or CS4) > MATLAB > Required > English folder, lists Photoshop functions that can be called from MATLAB and provides examples. MATLAB's Help system also has examples of using Photoshop with MATLAB.

DICOM (Digital Imaging and Communications in Medicine) is the current standard for various kinds of medical imaging techniques, including X-ray, mammography, ultrasound, PET (positron emission technology), and MRI (magnetic resonance imaging) scans. Besides improving contrast and bringing out detail in such images, Photoshop Extended can assemble a series of cross-sections into a 3D volume or animate a range-of-motion series for a joint into an animation for analysis or presentation, while protecting confidential patient information.

WHAT'S MISSING?

As new features have been added to Photoshop CS3 and CS4, some old ones have been abandoned rather than updated. ImageReady has been discontinued, so interactivity for the Web is no longer directly within Photoshop's realm. In CS4, Extract and Pattern Maker are no longer found in the Filter menu, and Picture Package is also missing, although these features can be added back with the Optional Plug-ins download from Adobe.com (see page 120).

Fundamentals of Photoshop

1

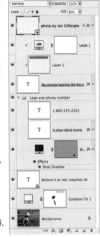

Photoshop's Layers panel shows how the elements of a file stack up. Layers are important in almost every aspect of Photoshop work, as you'll see in the techniques throughout the book. The different kinds of layers and how they relate to one another are explored in "Anatomy of a Photoshop File" on page 34.

PALETTES TO PANELS

In this book we've used **_panel_** when referring to both CS3 and CS4. In Photoshop CS3 they were still officially called _palettes_ (the old name), even though the equivalent items were panels in the other Creative Suite programs. In CS3, you'll need to use the term "palette" to find information about one of these in Photoshop's Help.

On screen a gray and-white checkerboard pattern represents transparent areas of the image file, so you can see where the pixels are and what parts of each visible layer are transparent.

THIS CHAPTER IS AN OVERVIEW of how Photoshop works — how the program organizes information when you create or edit an image, how you interact with the program, and what it takes to keep Photoshop working smoothly.

HOW PHOTOSHOP THINKS

Back when Photoshop was born (late in the 20th Century), the answer to the question "What is a Photoshop file?" was a lot simpler than it is now. It was a digital picture made up of a monolayer of **_picture elements_**, or **_pixels_** for short — tiny square dots of color, like microscopic tiles in a really precise mosaic. Today the program is a lot more powerful than it was then, and most Photoshop files are more complex.

Layers, Masks, Modes & Styles

You can think of a typical Photoshop file as a stack of **layers**, kind of like an open-face sandwich. The image you see on-screen or in print is what you would see if you looked down at the sandwich from directly above. The Layers panel — an example is shown at the left — is a dynamic "diagram" of the stack.

Several different kinds of layers can comprise the stack:

- There can be a **_Background_** at the bottom of the stack, completely filled with pixels.

- Like the _Background_, **regular layers** can also hold pixels. But _unlike_ the _Background_, these layers can also have areas that are completely or partly transparent, so that any pixels from the layers underneath can show through.

- **Adjustment layers** don't contribute any pixels to the image at all. Instead, they store instructions for how to change the color or tone of the pixels in layers below.

- **Type layers** hold — you guessed it — type, in a "live," or _dynamic_, form that can be edited if you need to change the

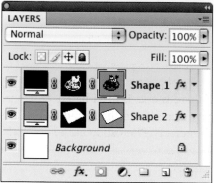

A smooth-edged vector mask and a filtered, rough-edged layer mask work together to shape the graphics and type for this logo. A Layer Style adds dimension and surface texture. You'll find this example on page 517.

Organizing layers isn't the only thing Groups are good for. Even a single layer can benefit from being in a Group (or even a Group within a Group) because it provides a way to add another mask (or masks), independent of any mask on the layer itself, as in this composition from page 595.

wording or spelling, the spacing of the characters, the font or the color, or any other characteristics of the type.

- **Fill layers** and **Shape layers** are also dynamic. Instead of including *pixels* of color, they include *instructions* for what color (solid, gradient, or pattern) the layer should hold.

- A **Smart Object** is a "package" of elements, like a file within a file. It protects its content by accumulating the instructions about what's to be done to it, such as rotating, scaling, or applying Photoshop filters, and automatically boiling those instructions down to the form that will minimize the damage that could be done if the changes were applied one by one and the content was worked and reworked. (What this damage is and how to protect against it are described in "Pixels or Instructions?" below.) Smart Objects can be created entirely in Photoshop, pasted from Adobe Illustrator, or opened into Photoshop from Camera Raw.

Each kind of Photoshop layer, except the *Background,* can include two kinds of **masks** — a pixel-based **layer mask** and an instruction-based **vector mask**. Each mask can hide part of the layer so it lets the layers below show through. Other ways to control how a layer blends into the image are its **opacity** (how transparent the layer content is), its **blend mode** (how its colors combine with the rest of the image), and its other **blending options** (which of its tones or colors may be excluded from blending at all).

All layers, again with the exception of the *Background,* can also include a **Layer Style**. A Style is a "kit" of instructions for creating special effects like shadows, glows, and bevels, or for simulating materials with characteristics like translucency, shine, color, and pattern. "Exercising Layer Styles" on page 80 shows how versatile and efficient Layer Styles can be.

Besides the basic "stacking order" of layers and their masks, the Layers panel provides various ways of relating layers to one another. Layers can be collected in **Groups**, represented in the Layers panel by **folder** icons. Folders can be open (to show a list of their contents) or closed (to make the Layers panel more compact). The layers in a Group can be moved and scaled together. Masking to a folder masks all the layers in the Group.

Pixels or Instructions?

In the "layer sandwich" of the Photoshop file, the difference between the **pixel-based elements** and the **instruction-based elements** is an important one. We might think of the pixel-based layers as, for example, the bread, lettuce, and tomatoes put

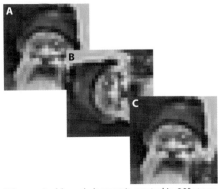

When a pixel-based element is rotated in 90° steps (or multiples of 90°), only the position and orientation of the perfectly square pixels change, and the image is not degraded. This "dramatic re-enactment" shows a very tiny detail **A** (27 by 27 pixels) from the upper left corner of the original color photo used for "Tinting with Masking" on page 206 rotated 90° to the left **B**, and then rotated 90° back to the right **C** — there's no difference between **A** and **C**.

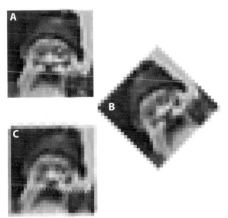

Changes such as scaling or non-90°-angle rotations, can change the image because of rounding errors. Applied one by one, each transformation can take it farther from its original form. When the elf **A** is rotated 45° to the left **B**, Photoshop has to interpolate, or *resample*, the tilted pixels, averaging colors to create pixels that fit into its straight-up-and-down grid. When the element is rotated 45° back to the right, more color-averaging occurs, and the "softening" of the image is obvious, as you can see by comparing **A** and **C**.

together in the sandwich. Then we could think of the instruction-based elements as little notes that say "put some mustard here between the tomato and cheese, but on the left side only" or "put Swiss cheese here, or cheddar if you want." Instruction-based elements don't have any tiny mosaic squares — only instructions. Magically, in a Photoshop "sandwich" the computer translates the instructions and pixels into an on-screen "preview" that shows us what the complete result will look like.

Most Photoshop files rely heavily on pixel-based elements, usually scanned images or digital photos. In a layered Photoshop file, the *Background,* if there is one, is pixel-based. So are the regular layers with image material on them, and so are layer masks. For pixel-based elements, Photoshop has to work with and perhaps change the position and color of each pixel in the mosaic grid — potentially *billions* of pixels.

Pixel-based elements can suffer from rounding errors. Here's an example of how that works. If you rotate a pixel-based image 90°, Photoshop can handle that with no problem. Each square pixel just changes position and turns onto another edge, and Photoshop notes the new grid positions now that the image has been turned on its side. If, however, you rotate the image some number of degrees (say 45) that isn't a whole-number multiple of 90, there isn't a direct correspondence between the old pixels and the new ones. Photoshop will do its best to make the new image look the same as it did before the rotation, but the program is going to have to do some *interpolation* of the color information, as it averages the colors of the "tilted pixels" to come up with a color for each square in the non-tilted grid. Rotating is just one example of changes that lead to interpolation. Each time interpolation happens, the image gets a little more different from what it was originally.

On the other hand, for instruction-based elements and operations, Photoshop just thinks in terms of math formulas. For

An instruction-based element like this Shape layer is only translated into dots of ink or pixels of color when it's printed on the page or displayed on the screen. It can be rotated or scaled many times without the cumulative wear and tear that happens to a pixel-based element. This Shape layer (rasterized here at 24 by 24 pixels each time) was rotated 45° to the left and back twice, but it didn't get progressively "softer" as a pixel-based element would. We've enlarged it here to show the pixels.

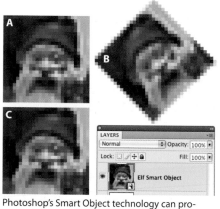

Photoshop's Smart Object technology can protect pixel-based elements from damage due to repeated rotating, scaling, and other forms of distortion. Here we turned the elf from page 17 into a Smart Object **A** (Layer > Smart Objects > Group into New Smart Object) and rotated it 45° left **B**; Photoshop still had to interpolate because of the tilt. But when we rotated it 45° back **C**, there was no further damage (compare to page 17) because the Smart Object could go back to the *original image data* and apply the combined rotations left and right into one instruction, which left the elf as it was, rather than carrying out one transformation and then the other, accumulating rounding errors along the way.

shapes, color or tonal changes, and overall opacity, for example, Photoshop can simply change a few numbers to change the instructions, without having to process and reprocess all those pixels. One advantage of using instructions instead of pixels wherever possible is that it's a lot easier and "cleaner" to change things if you change your mind. In the Photoshop sandwich, you can decrease the mustard to half a tablespoonful or swap mayonnaise for mustard, or trim the cheese to the edges of the bread. If these elements had already been locked into the "sandwich" in *pixel* form, it would be a lot messier to "revise" the sandwich without leaving telltale traces behind, just as it would be to take off the mustard or restore the trimmed-away edges of the cheese. Changing the *instructions* is a clean operation that doesn't leave behind a residue or make us wish later that we hadn't cut something off. The instructions can be changed right up until the "sandwich is served" — in other words until the layered file is translated into a monolayer of pixels to be printed on paper or viewed on a web page. "Anatomy of a Photoshop File" on page 34 explores the components that can make up a file.

Photoshop's **Smart Object** layers provide a way to scale or reshape pixel-based elements without subjecting them to rounding errors. That's because a Smart Object layer "remembers" its original content from when it was made, along with the instructions for each transformation (scaling, reshaping, or rotating) that has been done to it since. Each time a Smart Object is scaled or reshaped, it goes back and uses that original information and combines all the transformation instructions up to that point into a single change, to arrive at its new form. So you can scale or reshape a Smart Object layer several times, each time building on the previous transformations, without degrading the image more with each change.

Channels & Paths

At the same time that Photoshop is keeping track of an image as layers in a stack, it also thinks about file content in another way — as **color channels**. If we imagine the layers as the stacked sandwich components, then we might think of the color channels as the nutrients in the food — proteins, carbohydrates, fats, and vitamins and minerals. Same sandwich, but a different way of

HANG ONTO THOSE LAYERS!

For maximum flexibility, so you can make changes in the future, keep your Photoshop files in layered form. If you need a flattened file (single-layer, without transparency) to put into a page layout or web program, you can make a duplicate file (Image > Duplicate) and flatten it (Layer > Flatten Image) and save this *flattened*, or *Background*-only duplicate.

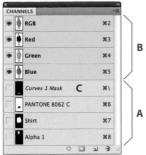

Alpha channels are listed at the bottom of the Channels panel **A** (opened by choosing Window > Channels, for instance). They aren't really related to the color channels that appear at the top of the panel. Instead alpha channels mainly store masks that can be activated to select different areas of the image. If the currently active layer has a layer mask, the mask is a "transient" resident in the Channels panel **C**, appearing only as long as that particular layer is active. Its name appears in italics.

The Paths panel stores vector-based outlines. The *Work Path* is the path that's currently being drawn and hasn't been saved yet. The vector mask of the currently active layer also appears in the Paths panel. Because the vector mask and the *Work Path* are transient, their names appear in italics.

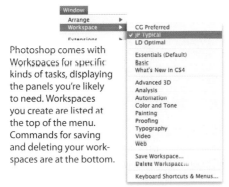

Photoshop comes with Workspaces for specific kinds of tasks, displaying the panels you're likely to need. Workspaces you create are listed at the top of the menu. Commands for saving and deleting your work-spaces are at the bottom.

The Navigation panel shows what area of the image currently appears in the work-ing window. Drag the frame **A** to move to another part of the image. Zoom with the slider at the bottom of the panel **B**.

analyzing its content, and one that's also important for the way Photoshop works. There's much more about color channels in Chapter 4, "Color in Photoshop."

In addition to the layers (with masks and Styles) and the color channels, Photoshop files can also have:

- *Alpha channels*, which are pixel-based masks stored perma-nently in the Channels panel, and
- *Paths*, which are instruction-based outlines or curves that are listed in the Paths panel when you add them; paths are covered extensively in Chapter 7.

THE PHOTOSHOP INTERFACE

On the next four pages is a "tour" of some of the important parts of Photoshop's interface, complete with updates on how the commands, tools, and panels (remember they're "palettes" in CS3) have changed in versions CS3 and CS4.

Workspaces

Photoshop comes with Workspaces designed for efficiency when you're working on particular kinds of projects, such as painting, or color and tone correction. You can customize workspaces even further, to save your panels the way you want them arranged on your screen for particular tasks. You can even change the menus, to hide commands you seldom use or add color to certain com-mands so they catch your eye. You can save and load workspaces from the Workspace menu on CS3's Options bar or at the right end of CS4's new Application bar.

Navigation

When you're zoomed in enough so only part of your document shows in the working window, you can drag with the Hand tool 🖑 to pan, moving a different part of the document into the window. The Navigator panel provides another way to get around. A red rectangle shows you what part of the image is framed in the window, and moving the rectangle frames a new area. You can use the slider underneath the Navigator image to zoom in or out.

ZOOMING & PANNING

With Enable OpenGL Drawing turned on (see page 9) it's easy to choose your next location when you're zoomed in. **Press and hold the H key** as you click and hold the mouse button (you'll zoom out for a "bird's eye view"), and then drag the cursor to the location where you want to work next, and **release the mouse button** to zoom in again. You can let go of the H key anytime after you start dragging.

PHOTOSHOP'S WORKING WINDOW

In both CS3 and CS4 (CS4 Extended is shown here) you can save Workspaces that you've set up for a particular task or job, and even customize the main menu and panel menus. Whatever size monitor you have, it's now easier to keep most of the panels handy but out of the way, as shown below. Panels can be *docked* (anchored) to the left or right edge of the screen, attached or nested together, and reduced to icons to save space. Page 23 tells how to manage panels.

The **Options bar** (see page 22) offers the choices appropriate for the tool or command that's active.

Photoshop CS4's **Application bar** (see page 22) provides access to commonly used viewing commands, and a "Launch Bridge" button.

Panels can be **"nested"** to form a **group**. And single panels or groups can be attached "head to toe" in **stacks**, or side-by-side (page 23 has more about how panels operate and how to manage them for efficiency).

The **Tools panel** can be displayed as a single or double column. New tools include Quick Selection and Rotate View; 3D Scale and 3D Orbit tools occur in CS4 Extended.

The **"zoom" box** in the lower left corner is "live" — you can type in a percentage; see "What Percentages Mean" on page 24.

Open a **pop-up menu** to view the size or color profile associated with the document, how much RAM or scratch space the file requires, or how long it takes for your computer to carry out the commands you're using on the file. A Reveal in Bridge command locates the file for you on your hard drive. For more about this menu, see "Efficiency Indicators" on page 32.

Right-click/Ctrl-click on almost anything in Photoshop's interface to open a **context-sensitive menu** of choices that are specific to the tool you're using (here the Quick Selection tool) or the element you've clicked on.

PHOTOSHOP'S TOOLS PANEL

In Photoshop's Tools panel the smaller fly-out panels name the tools and present the keyboard shortcuts, which, when used with the Shift key, toggle through tools that share a space. The Tools panel from **Photoshop CS3 Extended** is shown below. The Count tool, highlighted here in pink, occurs only in the Extended version.

In **Photoshop CS4**, the Crop tool and Slice tools share a space; the Blur, Sharpen, and Smudge tools have no keyboard shortcut, since "R" has been assigned to the new Rotate View tool; the Audio Annotation tool is gone; and the Note tool now shares a space with the Eyedropper and other information tools. The screen mode controls have been moved out of the Tools panel and onto the Application bar (see page 22), though they have the same shortcut (F) as before. Tools that occur only in the Photoshop Extended version are highlighted here in pink.

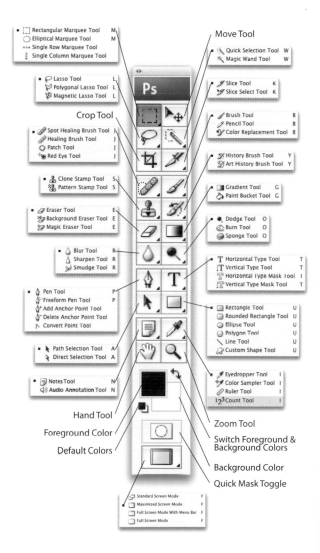

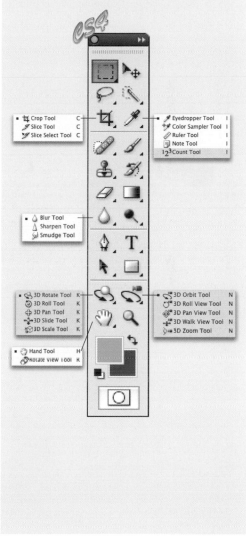

OPTIONS BAR

Photoshop's **Options bar**, which appears at the top of the working window by default, has buttons and entry fields for the current tool or command.

The Options bar in CS3 has a button for opening **Bridge** for managing files. It also has an easily accessible **Workspace** menu.

Clicking the buttons marked with **tiny arrows** will pop out more options in the form of menus, pickers, or slider bars. (**Pickers** are arrays of choices, such as type styles, brush tips, patterns, or gradients that can be used with the currently active tool.)

For some operations, such as setting type with the Type tool T or rotating with the Move tool ▸⊕, the Options bar has **"Cancel"** ⊘ and **"Commit"** ✔ buttons for canceling or accepting the current changes.

CS4 APPLICATION BAR

In Photoshop CS4 the tools that affect how you view your document (Hand, Zoom, and Rotate View) are repeated in the new **Application bar**, which sits above the Options bar by default. The Application bar also houses the Bridge button (which has moved from the Options bar), the screen modes (which have moved from the Tools panel), a picker for how documents are arranged, and a menu where you can choose what Extras (Guides, Grids, and Rulers) are showing. The name of the currently active Workspace appears on the far right, with quick access to the Workspace menu.

Float All in Windows
New Window
Actual Pixels

Click an icon in the **Arrange Document picker** to choose a display arrangement.

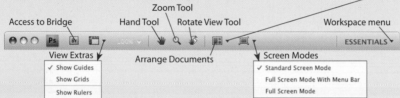

Access to Bridge   Zoom Tool   Hand Tool   Rotate View Tool   Workspace menu

View Extras
✓ Show Guides
Show Grids
Show Rulers

Arrange Documents

Screen Modes
✓ Standard Screen Mode
Full Screen Mode With Menu Bar
Full Screen Mode

CS4 TABS & WINDOWS

In Photoshop CS4 your documents can appear in free-floating windows as they did in earlier versions (shown below on the right) or in a tabbed view. Your settings in Preferences determine how Photoshop opens your images, tabbed or floating (Open Documents as Tabs), and whether a floating window will become tabbed if you drag it near other tabbed windows (Enable Floating Document Window Docking). See "Panel & Document Display Preferences" on page 24 for more about these preferences.

ORIGINAL PHOTOS: DARREN GREEN / PHOTOSPIN.COM

For the tabbed view the default is to display a single image with the others as tabs at the top of the window. To change the view, choose one of the layouts form the Arrange Documents pop-out. Shown here is the 3 Up arrangement with the Application Frame turned on (Window > Application Frame).

Floating windows can overlap one another, as shown here, or they can be tiled (Window > Arrange > Tile). A floating window can be resized by dragging on any side of the window.

PANELS

Photoshop panels are designed for convenience — to make their contents easily available when you need them, without getting in your way. The key color for combining panels is blue — a blue line appears when you've positioned one panel to **group** (nest) or **stack** with another, or when a panel, group, or stack is in position to **dock**, or attach to an edge of your screen. You can set Preferences to have docked panels appear only if you move your cursor to the edge (see page 24).

Drag a side edge of an icon or stack of icons to show the panel names.

No dark bar between icons means they will open as a nested group.

Drag the double row of dots at the top of an icon to drag that panel away from others.

COLOR

STYLES

SWATCHES

Drag the dark bar at the top to move an entire nested group or stack.

Click the **"Close" button** to make a single panel, nested group, or stack disappear from your workspace. To close one panel in a group or stack, use the Close command in that panel's menu, or in CS3 click the X on the panel's tab.

Drag the **name tab** of an open panel to move it out of the stack or nested group.

The **"Create new. . ."** button at the bottom of a panel makes a new swatch, layer, channel, or whatever the panel houses.

Click the dark bar or double arrow to toggle between a full display and icons.

Open the **panel menu** by clicking on this button. If the Panel Options command appears in the menu, it offers choices for changing the panel's appearance.

To group, or nest, one panel with another, drag the panel's tab to the tab of the panel you want to nest it with. When you see the blue line, let go and it will nest.

To stack a panel below another, drag its tab to the bottom of the other panel. When the blue line appears between them, let go and the panels will "lock together."

COLOR STYLES

R   255
G   255
B   255

SWATCHES

If a panel can be lengthened, it will have a triangle of dots in its lower right corner. Hover over the bottom edge until the cursor turns into a double-headed arrow. If the arrow is at a 45° angle, you can both lengthen *and* widen the panel by dragging.

If the width of a panel or stack of panels can be changed, hovering your cursor over a side edge will turn the cursor into a double-headed arrow; drag to change the width.

TITLE BAR PUNCTUATION

An * **(asterisk)** at the very end of the title bar information shows that the file hasn't been saved since you last took some action with it.

The # **(pound) sign** next to the color mode/bit depth indicators shows there's a profile mismatch between your working space and the file itself. The file may not have a profile, or it may be in a different working space. (For more on working spaces, see "Color Management" on page 187.)

DRAG AND DROP WITH A TABBED VIEW

A tabbed arrangement helps control clutter and can make it easier to find the document you're looking for, but it makes dragging and dropping between documents a little different than if windows are free-floating (as described on page 33). In a tabbed arrangement, if you can see only the tab of the destination image, drag and drop this way: Make sure the layer, channel, selection, or path you want to move is targeted and visible in its document window and drag from that window onto the destination window's tab. Only an outline will show what you are dragging. Hover over the tab until the window "springs open," and drag the outline into the window.

The gray vertical lines are part of the outline — all that shows of the item you're dragging. When the tab "lights up," the window opens to receive it.

PANEL & DOCUMENT DISPLAY PREFERENCES

To set Photoshop's **Interface Preferences**, press **Ctrl/⌘-K**, then choose Interface from the list on the left side of the Preferences dialog. The Interface section of Preferences offers options for panel behavior, and in CS4 (shown here) for whether documents will open in tabbed view or in floating windows.

Panels & Documents
- ☐ Auto-Collapse Iconic Panels
- ☑ Auto-Show Hidden Panels
- ☑ Remember Panel Locations
- ☑ Open Documents as Tabs
- ☑ Enable Floating Document Window Docking

If this option is turned on, when you open a panel that's displayed as an icon, the panel will then close down to an icon again as soon as you click away from the panel.

If you use the Tab key shortcut (which hides all panels except the Tools panel), moving your cursor to the edge of the screen will reveal any panels that you've docked there. (Docking is described on page 23.)

Photoshop will remember and use your panel arrangement from one session to another. (For a permanent arrangement, save a Workspace.)

Documents will tab together when opened if you enable this.

Floating document windows can be dragged to tab together if this option is enabled. Holding down the Ctrl key while dragging toggles this preference.

DIALOGS

Photoshop's dialog boxes vary widely, but most of them have certain attributes in common.

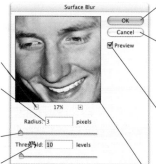

Click the + and – buttons to zoom the dialog preview.

Click in a number field and use the arrow keys (↑ and ↓) to raise and lower values. For increments of 10 instead of 1, add the Shift key.

Or move a slider to change the setting.

If you pause the cursor over the name associated with a slider, the cursor turns to a "scrubber" . "Dab" left or right to lower or raise the value in the number field. This may offer finer control than the slider.

Pressing the **Enter key** is like clicking **"OK."**

Pressing the **Escape key** is like clicking **"Cancel."** Holding down the **Alt/Option key** changes the "Cancel" button to **"Reset,"** to restore the default or previous settings.

Click this checkbox (or type **P**) to toggle the Preview in the document window off and on. You might turn it off so you don't have to wait for a large image to redraw every time you make a minor adjustment.

Click and hold on the dialog preview to compare the "before" version.

WHAT PERCENTAGES MEAN

Changing the view (displayed in the file's title bar and editable in the lower left corner of the working window) doesn't change your image file — it just changes your on-screen view of it.

- When you view an image at **100%**, it doesn't mean you're seeing it at the dimensions it will print. It means that every pixel in the image file is represented by 1 pixel on-screen.

- **Higher percentages** mean that more than 1 screen pixel is being used to represent 1 pixel of the image file. For instance, at 200% each pixel in the image file is represented by a 2 x 2-pixel block on-screen.

- **Lower percentages** mean just the opposite: 1 on-screen pixel represents more than 1 image pixel. For instance, at 50% each pixel on-screen represents a 2 x 2 block of pixels in the file.

In Photoshop CS4 if you have OpenGL Drawing enabled in Preferences (see page 9), you can zoom smoothly at any percentage. Without OpenGL Drawing the views at 100% (above, left), 50%, and 25% look much smoother and are more accurate for on-screen editing than odd settings like 33.3%, 66.7%, or the 104% view shown here (above, right). Without OpenGL Drawing, odd views can give you the impression that your image has been somehow corrupted, when in fact it's fine.

With an Adjustment layer you can explore tone and color options as we did to restore this antique portrait. The Adjustment layer stays "live" and editable so you can change its settings or change the blend mode or Opacity of the layer.

The Masks panel lets you soften the edges of a mask by using the Feather slider. You can also adjust the mask's overall Density, or hiding power. You can access the Color Range dialog for selecting the area you want to mask, based on its color. You can also open the Refine Edge dialog from here, for further mask edge modifications. Or invert your mask to conceal what the mask revealed, and vice versa.

WORKING SMART IN PHOTOSHOP

The *Wow!* approach to Photoshop has always emphasized working quickly and with as much flexibility as possible, in case you want to make changes later.

Maintaining Flexibility

Keeping your options open is an important part of developing a Photoshop file. By planning ahead and using instruction-based methods such as Layer Styles, Adjustment layers, Smart Objects, and Smart Filters, you can build flexibility into your files, making your work easier and your workflow more efficient.

Working with Adjustment layers. If you apply color or contrast corrections with Adjustment layers instead of menu commands, it's easy to readjust without starting over or degrading the image by changing your changes. For more, see "Color Adjustment Options" starting on page 180 and "Working with Adjustment Layers" starting on page 245.

Protecting pixels. You can achieve some of the benefits of using instruction based elements, even if you're working with pixel-based images, by making use of **Camera Raw** and **Smart Objects**. If your image file is a photo in a camera's raw format, Photoshop will automatically open it in Camera Raw, where you can make a variety of tone and color adjustments interactively and then apply these changes in one operation before opening the file in Photoshop. And you can always get back to the original raw data — it's retained in the file. (Camera Raw also works with JPEG or TIFF files, but you have to be careful not to save over your original.) Within Photoshop itself, Smart Objects can provide a similar kind of protection from "pixel fatigue" due to repeated scaling or rotating, for instance, or filter effects. Find an introduction to Smart Objects on page 75 and to Smart Filters (filters applied live to Smart Objects) on page 72, and learn about Camera Raw in Chapter 3.

Saving selections as you work. When you use the selection tools or commands (see page 47) to build a complex selection, save it periodically in an **alpha channel** (Select > Save Selection). Be sure to save the selection one last time when it's finished, either by turning it into a layer mask or by using an alpha channel, so you can reselect exactly the same area if you need to later. Saving selections and masks is covered in Chapter 2.

Keeping selections "live." Photoshop CS4's new **Masks panel** allows you to set the softness of the edge of a layer mask, or even a vector mask, or the "hiding power" of the mask, keeping these

Keeping image edits or stages of a painting on separate layers allows flexibility — you can modify the way your changes interact with each other. Rather than use the Dodge and Burn tools, which are tricky to use and can't work on a separate layer, we used a "dodge and burn" layer to brighten and add contrast. We could then adjust the effect by lowering Opacity or changing the blend mode. The technique is described on page 339.

When a Layer Style is applied to a layer and then the layer's content is changed, the Style automatically conforms to the new content. Here the font was changed for the "Hot Rods" type layer, and the Drop Shadow and Bevel and Emboss effects changed along with it.

settings "live" in the file. You can change the Feather (softness) or Density (hiding power) later, even returning to the original selection used to make the mask. Learn more about the new masks controls in Chapter 2.

Making a "repairs" or "painting" layer. When you use the Sharpen/Blur/Smudge tool ◊ △ ⏦, or the Clone Stamp ♣, Healing Brush ✐, or Spot Healing Brush ✐, to retouch an image, you can add the repairs to a separate, transparent top layer, keeping the repairs isolated so the new work doesn't actually get mixed into the original image. That way, if you want to undo or modify part of your retouching, you can erase, or select and delete, that part from the repairs layer, leaving the rest of the repairs intact. You can also change the opacity or blend mode of the layer to change its contribution to the image.

Using a separate layer is also a practical approach for dodging and burning, or for adding brush strokes to a painting without risking the work you've already done. When you're sure you like the new brush strokes you've added, you can merge them with the layer below (Ctrl/⌘-E), then add another empty layer and experiment with more strokes.

Using Layer Styles. When you add a drop shadow, a beveled edge, or other special-effects treatments by means of a Layer Style, you can make repeated changes to the effects themselves without degrading the image. And you can apply the Style to one or more other layers in the same file or even in other files. You can even change the content of the layers you've applied them to and the effects will automatically and instantly "rewrap" themselves to fit the new content. For a demonstration of the flexibility of Layer Styles, see page 80. To learn how to put them to work, see "Working with Layer Styles" (page 498) and the Chapter 8 sections that follow, especially the "Anatomy" sections.

Duplicating a layer. When you want to make changes to a particular layer but you also want an "escape hatch" to get back to the previous version if the changes don't work out, copy the layer (Ctrl/⌘-J) and work on the copy. A duplicate layer can also be helpful if you want the flexibility of combining the changed version with the original.

Making a merged copy. Say you've built a layered file and now you want to apply a change to the entire image — maybe sharpening it or applying an artistic effect with a filter. One way is to use a Smart Object. Another is to make a layer at the top of the layer stack that's a "merged" copy of everything visible in

Many of the commands in Photoshop's menus have keyboard shortcuts for quick application. The shortcut appears to the right of the entry in the menu.

A context-sensitive menu offers commands appropriate in the context of what you're doing currently.

THE "MAKE ONE" BUTTON

In a preset picker, such as the one for choosing patterns, the "Create a new. . ." button ▣ lets you name the current element and add it as a new preset. This gives you a way to create a Pattern preset from a Pattern Overlay that's included in a Style, for instance.

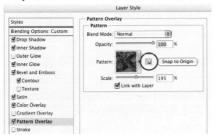

your file. Then, because it's a single layer, you can easily modify it, experimenting freely, since you still have all the separate layers right below it in the layer stack if you need to backtrack. To make a merged copy, hold down Ctrl-Shift-Alt-E (Windows) or ⌘-Shift-Option-E (Mac).

Keyboard Shortcuts

To help you manage all of its panels, commands, and tools, Photoshop has built-in keyboard shortcuts for choosing tools and carrying out commands quickly, so you don't have to move the cursor around the working window. The Edit > **Keyboard Shortcuts** command lets you add your own shortcuts. In the Wow Goodies folder on the Wow DVD-ROM, you'll find the **Wow Shortcuts.pdf** file, a collection of the shortcuts we find most useful beyond those for choosing tools. *Note:* When we use keyboard shortcuts in this book, we use Photoshop's defaults.

Context-Sensitive Menus

Right-click/Ctrl-click in your working window — in the document, on a thumbnail in the Layers panel, or on just about any other part of the interface — and a **context-sensitive menu** will appear with choices related to the task you're working on, the tool you've chosen, or the layer, mask, or selection that's active. These context-sensitive menus save time because they appear right where you're working, with exactly what you need — no need for a trip to the main menu or a panel menu. And they work even if you've modified the menus, forgotten which menu a particular command resides in, or changed the keyboard shortcut associated with a particular menu item.

Working with Several Files at Once

If you have enough RAM, it's easy to open and manage as many files as you need to work with. Adobe Bridge, which comes with Photoshop, lets you select and open or automatically process several files at once. We cover both versions of Bridge (CS3 and CS4) in Chapter 3. Because it's so easy to sort and search in Bridge, it's a great entry to Photoshop.

The **Automate** and **Scripts** commands in Photoshop's File menu include some useful automated production tasks for working with several files at once. And you can run **Actions** (which carry out a prerecorded series of operations) on **batches** of files. You'll find more about automation in Chapter 3.

Managing Presets

Photoshop gives you tremendous freedom to collect or make your own brush tips, specialized tools, Layer Styles, patterns,

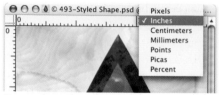

You can change the ruler units by right-clicking/
Ctrl-clicking on one of the rulers.

Double-click on a ruler to open the Units & Rulers
section of the Preferences dialog box, so you can
see or change the Column Width or Gutter. Photoshop can use Column Width as a unit of measure
for creating a new file or resizing an image. If you
specify a width of more than one column, the Gutter width is included.

Smart Guides can be useful for lining up elements
"by eye." A Smart Guide appears when the center,
top, bottom, or side of an element lines up with
another element. Here Smart Guides are used to
align elements in a pattern tile (see page 76).

The same options available in Photoshop's **Align
Linked** and **Distribute Linked** commands from
the Layer menu are also provided as buttons in
the Options bar when the Move tool is chosen.
They let you line up or evenly space the contents
of several layers. Simply Ctrl/⌘-click or Shift-click
the layers in the Layers panel whose content you
want to align, and then choose the command or
click the button.

gradients, swatches of color, and more, and save them as **presets**,
so you won't have to reinvent them when you want to use them
again later. To save presets permanently, they need to be included
in named sets and the sets have to be saved. Directions for using
the Preset Manager for saving Layers Styles can be found in the
"Saving Styles" tip on page 82. The same process works for the
other kinds of presets as well: First you use the "Create new. . ."
option to add your new preset (see "The 'Make One' Button" on
page 27). Then you can choose Edit > Preset Manager, choose
the appropriate Preset Type, and save a new set.

Taking Advantage of Precision Tools

Photoshop is equipped for precision. You can toggle the **rulers**
on and off by typing **Ctrl/⌘-R**, and change the ruler units by
right-clicking/Ctrl-clicking on a ruler to open a context-sensitive
menu of units. Double-clicking on a ruler opens the Units &
Rulers section of the Preferences dialog box, where you can see
and reset the column size.

You can also create **Guides** simply by dragging from either the
top or the side ruler. Or set up a custom **Grid** by opening the
Preferences dialog (Ctrl/⌘-K) and clicking on Guides, Grid
& Slices in the list on the left side of the box. You can toggle
visibility on and off for these Guides (**Ctrl/⌘-'**) and Grid (**Ctrl-
Alt-'** in Windows **or ⌘-Option-'** on the Mac), and make them
"magnetic" by choosing the Snap options in the View menu. (For
more about Guides and Grid, see The "Drawing on the Grid" tip
on page 454 and "Exercising Drawing Tools" on page 471.)

Smart Guides are transient guidelines you can turn on by
choosing **View > Show > Smart Guides**. Then, as long as **Extras**
is turned on in the View menu, these handy "outriggers" will
appear as you reposition a layer with the Move tool ▸⊕, to show
you when an edge or the center of the element you're moving is
precisely aligned with the edge or center of another element such
as a shape or the content of a transparent layer. "Exercising Smart
Objects" on page 75 shows how useful Smart Guides can be.

The **Options bar for the Transform and Free Transform commands** allows you to enter precise specs for angles and distances
(as described in "Transforming & Warping" on page 67).

When the **Move** tool ▸⊕ is selected, the **Align** and **Distribute**
commands from the Layer menu automatically align the content
of selected layers or distribute layer contents evenly over the
span you specify.

You need to find the middle of your image. You turn on the rulers (Ctrl/⌘-R). But maybe you're not good at dividing 7¹³/₁₆ inches by 2 and remembering the answer long enough to drag a Guide to that point on the ruler to mark the halfway point. Here's a quick and easy way to find the **center of a document**:

Right-click/Ctrl-click on either ruler and choose **Percent** from the context-sensitive menu. Then just drag a Guide in from the left ruler until it lines up with 50% on the top ruler, and drag one down from the top to 50% on the vertical ruler. The intersection of the Guides marks the center.

And here's a way to find the **geometric center of the content of a layer** that doesn't extend to the edges of the document. For this one it doesn't matter what units the ruler is set to: Target the layer by clicking its thumbnail in the Layers panel. Choose the Move ▶⊕ tool and in the Options bar turn on Show Transform Controls. The Transform frame will appear, with a handle in the center of each of its four sides. Drag a Guide from the top ruler to line up with the side handles, and drag a guide from the side ruler to line up with the top and bottom handles. The intersection of the Guides marks the center.

The **Ruler tool** ✎ can measure the distance between two points or an angle you draw; these measurements appear in the Info panel. Photoshop Extended adds the **Count tool** ₁₂³ and the **Analysis menu**, with other kinds of support for establishing scale in an image and measuring or counting selected areas. Measurement data are stored in the **Measurement Log**, a panel that can accumulate and export many kinds of measurements useful in science for comparing one sample to another. Photoshop Extended's Vanishing Point "megafilter" even allows measurement in perspective; see Chapter 11.

Recording What You Do

Recording an Action doesn't take extra time or RAM as you carry out a process in Photoshop, and the Action can help you recall and apply the steps in a technique you've developed or one you've found in a tutorial. There are some processes that Actions don't record — for instance, brush strokes with painting, toning, and retouching tools. To get a start on recording and applying Actions, see "Automating with Actions" in Chapter 3.

Another way to record what you're doing is to use the **Edit History Log**. Unlike an Action, this log doesn't let you replay what you've done, but it can keep a record (in text form) of what has been done to the file; you can choose the level of detail you want to record by selecting from the Edit Log Items menu in the General Preferences dialog box (Ctrl/⌘-K). The Edit History Log stays with the file. It continues when the file is reopened, and it goes along if you duplicate the file or save a copy. You can go back and read through the text in the log by choosing File > File Info and clicking on History, which can be helpful if there's no other way to recall what has been done to a file.

RECOVERING FROM MISTAKES

Even if you use Layer Styles, Adjustment layers, Smart Objects, and other instruction-based methods to give yourself as much flexibility as possible, if you're at all adventurous, you're eventually going to do something in Photoshop that you want to undo. Luckily, Photoshop has you covered — with enough options so you can feel free to experiment.

Undoing

Photoshop's **Ctrl/⌘-Z** (for Edit > **Undo**) will undo your last operation, and if you change your mind again immediately, you can use **Ctrl/⌘-Z** to "redo." The **History panel** can be set up to let you go much further back. You can either click one of the states in the panel (for more, see "Using the History Panel" next) or use

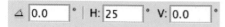

The Options bar for the Transform commands reflects any changes you make by manipulating the center point or handles of the Transform box. Or you can enter numbers for the parameters you want to change, such as the rotation angle and horizontal or vertical skew, in the part of the Options bar shown here.

THE HISTORY PANEL

The History panel records step-by-step **states** at the bottom. **Snapshots**, made when you choose to, are stored at the top of the panel. The History Brush icon ✎ in the **source column** shows the current source for any tool or command that uses History.

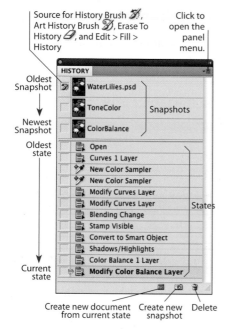

Source for History Brush ✎, Art History Brush ✎, Erase To History ⬛, and Edit > Fill > History

Click to open the panel menu.

Oldest Snapshot

Newest Snapshot

Oldest state

States

Current state

Create new document from current state   Create new snapshot   Delete

The settings in the History Options dialog box determine how the History panel operates.

Edit > Step Backward (**Ctrl-Alt-Z** in Windows or **⌘-Option-Z** on the Mac) to backtrack through your most recent changes. The History States setting in General Preferences (Ctrl/⌘-K) determines how far back you can undo. You can also **use "Undo" inside dialog boxes** that have more than one entry box or slider, pressing **Ctrl/⌘-Z** to undo the last setting you changed.

Using the History Panel

The **History panel** (Window > History) is a kind of interactive "chain of events" that lets you go back to an earlier state of your file. The panel lists the most recent **states,** or steps, of your current work session — work you've done since opening the file — and allows you to undo state by state. In practice, the History panel's "memory" can be quite limited. In order to keep from tying up too much RAM, by default the panel retains only the last 20 steps. You can increase the number of steps (Ctrl/⌘-K), but this increases the amount of RAM used and potentially slows down all Photoshop operations. History disappears when you close the file. So the current states and any Snapshots you've made won't be there when you open the file again.

More than just a step, a **History Snapshot** is a stored stage of the file. It persists even after its equivalent state has disappeared from the panel to make room for more recent states. You can make a Snapshot by Alt/Option-clicking the "Create new snapshot" button ⬛ at the bottom of the History panel. Typically, it's a good idea to make a **"Merged Layers" Snapshot**.

You can go back to a previous stage of the file by clicking on the thumbnail for a state or Snapshot in the History panel. Another way to restore part of an earlier version of an image is to choose the History Brush ✎ and then click in the column to the left of the thumbnail for the state or Snapshot you want to use as a source, and then paint. Or click to set the source and use the Edit > Fill command.

If you click the History panel's ▾☰ button to pop out the panel menu and choose History Options, you can set History to create a new Snapshot as soon as you open a file (the **Automatically Create First Snapshot** option is turned on by default) and whenever you save the file as you work (the **Automatically Create New Snapshot When Saving** option automatically names the Snapshot with the time you saved the file). With **Allow Non-Linear History** you can also go back to an earlier state of the file (by clicking its thumbnail in the panel) and make changes at that point, without throwing away all the states since then. The

Besides providing multiple undo's, History can serve as a source for painting with the Art History Brush ✍. This tool generates brush strokes that automatically follow the color and contrast contours in an image, using a Snapshot or state from the History panel as a source. With carefully chosen settings, you can produce a pleasing Art History Brush "painting." The lower apple was painted with a Wow Art History Brush preset that simulates pastels. You can see more Art History examples on page 414 and in "Art History Pastels" on page 407.

FADING

Immediately after you apply a filter, a color adjustment command, or a brush stroke — before you do anything else — you can use the **Edit > Fade** command to reduce the effect or change the blend mode. The Fade command used to be more important before Photoshop had Adjustment layers and Smart Filters for maintaining "live" control of color and tone adjustments and filters. Now it's probably most useful for blending a painted stroke into surrounding paint.

Show New Snapshot Dialog by Default option automatically opens the New Snapshot box when you click the 📷 button at the bottom of the History panel, so you're always offered the chance to name the Snapshot and choose "From: Merged Layers." Ordinarily, making a layer visible or invisible by clicking in the 👁 column of the Layers panel is not recorded as a state in the History panel. However, if you turn on the **Make Layer Visibility Changes Undoable** option, History records a state whenever you turn a layer's visibility off or on, and the Edit > Undo/Redo and Edit > Step Backward/Foreward commands can also undo/redo the visibility.

Remember that History disappears when you close the file. For a more permanent record of changes to the file, use the Edit History Log.

Resetting a Dialog Box

In any dialog box that lets you enter at least one value and that has a "Cancel" button, holding down the **Alt/Option** key changes the "Cancel" button to **"Reset"**; clicking this button leaves the dialog open but returns all the settings to the state they were in when you first opened the box.

Reverting

The File > **Revert** command takes the file back to its condition the last time it was saved.

KEEPING PHOTOSHOP HAPPY

Photoshop files tend to be large — the number of layers is limited only by your computer's capacity to keep track of them. And a great deal of information has to be stored to record the color of each of the thousands or billions of pixels that can make up an image. Simply opening a file, which brings that information into the computer's working memory, or RAM, can take quite a bit of computer processing. And applying a special effect can involve complicated calculations for evaluating and changing the color of every pixel in the image. Here are some suggestions for making sure Photoshop will have the large block of space it needs to do all this work efficiently.

Add Power & RAM

The system requirements that Adobe lists for Photoshop CS3 and CS4, including 512MB of RAM, can be considered minimums. The faster your computer is and the more RAM it has, the faster Photoshop will work. Photoshop, especially CS4, will work better with an up-to-date video card and **OpenGL**/GPU acceleration (described in "What's New" on page 9).

In **Scratch Sizes** mode the box near the lower left corner of the working window shows roughly how much RAM is available for Photoshop to use (right) and how much memory is currently tied up by all open Photoshop files plus the clipboard, Snapshots, and so on (left). If the left-hand figure is higher, Photoshop is using virtual memory.

Would more RAM help? You can watch the **Efficiency** indicator to see how much Photoshop is using RAM alone, rather than swapping data with the scratch disk.

A value near 100% means the scratch disk isn't being used much, so adding more RAM probably wouldn't improve performance. A value less than about 75% means that assigning more RAM would probably help. Scratch Size and Efficiency options are accessed by clicking the arrow and choosing Show from the menu.

Choosing Edit > **Purge** > **Histories** or Edit > **Purge** > **All** affects not only the currently active file but *all files* open in Photoshop. *Note:* Purge cannot be undone.

To purge the History *from the active file only,* in the History panel click the ▾≡ button and choose **Clear History**.

Use a Bigger Scratch Disk

If Photoshop doesn't have enough room to handle a file entirely in RAM, it can use hard disk space to extend its memory — that's *virtual memory,* or in Photoshop parlance *scratch disk*. In that case, two factors become important. The first is how much **empty hard disk space** you keep clear for Photohop's use, beyond the 1 GB (Windows) or 2 GB (Mac) required for running Photoshop. You'll want at least as much space as you have RAM *plus* at least five times the size of any file you might work on.

The second factor is the *transfer rate* of the disk drive, or the speed at which data can be read off the disk. Consider dedicating an entire fast multi-gigabyte hard disk drive as a scratch disk. Disk space is relatively cheap these days, and this will give Photoshop plenty of "elbow room." Second best would be to dedicate a multi-gigabyte partition of a hard disk as the scratch disk. Either way, because you won't be storing anything on it permanently, the drive or partition won't become *fragmented,* with the free space broken up into small pieces; so Photoshop can run in top-notch form.

Free Up RAM

If you find that Photoshop is slowing down or that its efficiency is consistently well below 100% (see "Efficiency Indicators" at the left), there are some things you can do to free up RAM or to operate Photoshop in ways that don't require as much memory.

Close other programs. Even if you aren't doing anything with them at the moment, open applications can tie up RAM.

Reduce the number of presets. Loading a file of Layer Styles, color Gradients, Brushes, or other presets can use a significant amount of RAM and scratch disk. Keeping presets organized so they're easy to find and load, but loading only those you need at the time, can reduce the drain on RAM. "Installing Wow Styles, Patterns, Tools & Other Presets" on page 4 tells how to make presets accessible for easy loading.

Purge. As Photoshop works, it accumulates a lot more information in RAM than just what it needs to carry out the command you've given it most recently. In the clipboard it remembers the last thing you copied or cut from a file, and in History it remembers a certain number of your most recent steps in working with a file, as described in "Using the History Panel" on page 30. Since you can have more than one file open at a time in Photoshop and the program keeps track of the History for every open file, all that remembering can tie up quite a bit

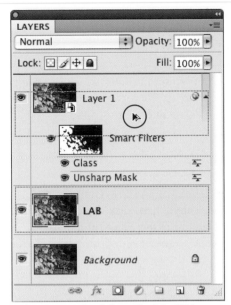

Rather than use the clipboard (and the RAM involved) to copy and paste a layer from one position in the file to another, hold down the Alt/Option key and drag the layer you want to copy. The double arrow, instead of a grabbing fist, shows that you are copying, not just moving, the layer.

When you copy a file by using the Image > Duplicate command or the History panel's "Create a new document from current state" button 🔲, the new file is named (as shown above) but not saved. As soon as you duplicate a file, it's a good idea to choose File > Save (Ctrl/⌘-S) so you can rename and permanently save the document.

of memory. There are certain commands that Photoshop can carry out only in RAM, not by using the scratch disk, so it's good strategy to release RAM by clearing out a large clipboard selection or purging History that you no longer need. If you choose Edit > Purge, any choices that aren't grayed out indicate that something is stored and can be purged. When you choose Purge Histories, the History states (step-by-step changes) will be deleted, but any Snapshots you've made will remain.

Use "low-overhead" alternatives for copying. If RAM is limited, there are several ways you can "copy and paste" without using the clipboard and tying up RAM:

- **To duplicate a targeted layer (or a selected area of it) as another layer just above it in the same file**, press Ctrl/⌘-J (for Layer > New > Layer via Copy).

- **To duplicate a layer in the same file**, Alt/Option-drag its thumbnail in the Layers panel to the position in the panel's stack of layers where you want the duplicate to be.

- **To duplicate a selected area to another open file**, drag and drop the selection with the Move tool ▶⊕ from the one document's working window to the other. To center the selection in the new file, press and hold the Shift key as you drag. (In CS4, if you use tabbed documents, be sure to read the "Drag and Drop with a Tabbed View" tip on page 23 for how to drag between documents.)

- **To duplicate a layer, channel, or Snapshot from one file to another**, drag it from the Layers, Channels, or History panel of the source file into the working window of the file you want to add it to. (In CS4 with tabbed documents, where this isn't possible, instead target the Layer, Channel, or Snapshot in the appropriate panel, but drag from the document window itself. See the tip on page 23 for full instructions.)

- **To copy an entire image as a new file**, either with all layers intact or merged into a single layer, choose Image > Duplicate.

GETTING AN OVERVIEW

The "Anatomy of a Photoshop File" section that follows is designed to familiarize you with some of the options available for constructing a flexible Photoshop file. Then enjoy the "Gallery" of inspirational artwork, demonstrating a variety of Photoshop approaches, before you go on to Chapter 2 for an introduction to essential Photoshop skills. *Wow!*

ANATOMY OF
a Photoshop File

The picture we see when we look at a Photoshop file in print or on-screen is often a combination of elements. The Layers panel provides one way to look at the makeup of the file and also to access its individual components.

Here we use the finished file for "Adding Type to an Image" from Chapter 9 as an example of how the components found in a typical Photoshop file are represented in the Layers panel.

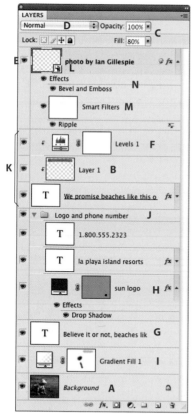

The layers that make up the **Add Type-After.psd** file

Background

ORIGINAL PHOTO: IAN GILLESPIE

A **BACKGROUND A** is a pixel-based layer without the potential for transparency or for having a Layer Style applied. Locked in place, it can't be moved, rotated, or scaled. Scans and digital photos typically consist of a *Background* only. A *Background* can be given the potential for transparency by double-clicking its name. Not every layered Photoshop file has a *Background,* but if it's present, it's the bottom layer in the stack.

Transparent Layers

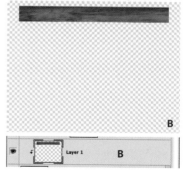

REGULAR PIXEL-BASED LAYERS that aren't a *Background* have the potential for **transparency**, which Photoshop represents on-screen as a gray checkerboard pattern. In this file, layer **B** holds a copy of a part of the *Background*. Besides parts of images, transparent layers can also hold pixels applied with Photoshop's painting, drawing, and image-editing tools.

ORIGINAL PHOTO: IAN GILLESPIE

If you'd like to open the file and follow along, you can find it on the DVD-ROM that comes with this book in Wow Project Files > Chapter 9 > Add Type.

 Add Type-After.psd

Opacity, Blend Mode & Visibility

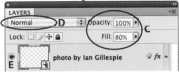

FOR ANY LAYER other than the *Background,* you can adjust **Opacity** and **Fill opacity C** (the difference is explained on page 573), and also change the **blend mode D** (how the colors in a layer interact with the rest of the image). Opacity and blend mode can be changed repeatedly without damage to the layer. You can also turn off a layer's visibility completely by clicking its ☉ icon **E**, and turn it back on whenever you like.

Adjustment Layers

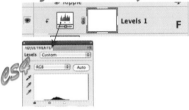

AN **ADJUSTMENT LAYER** is instruction-based. It contributes to the image by changing the tone or color of layers below it in the stack. For instance, the role of the Levels Adjustment layer in this file **F** is to lighten the image in the layer just below it. An Adjustment layer has a built-in mask, ready to be edited to limit the adjustment to a specific area (see "Masks," at the right). The dialog box for the adjustment can be reopened at any time and the adjustment changed, so it's a very flexible way to control tone and color. Each kind of Adjustment layer (Levels, Curves, Invert, and so on) is identified in the Layers panel by a specific symbol, although a generic symbol ◑ is used if the file is much wider than it is tall.

Type Layers

A **TYPE LAYER**, represented by a "T" symbol in the Layers panel, holds "live" (editable) type. So, for instance, if we wanted to change the wording of the text in this layer **G**, we could select and edit the type; we could also change the type's font, size, or other characteristics, or reshape the area it fills. On each type layer, type can be set either one line at a time or as an automatically wrapping paragraph. Type can also be enclosed within a shape or set to follow a path like the type around the circular logo in this file.

Shape & Fill Layers

SHAPE AND FILL LAYERS are instruction-based. They tell what solid color, gradient, or pattern should be applied to the layer; these instructions can be changed without disturbing any pixels. Built-in masks can be used to control where the color, gradient, or pattern is revealed. In this file the sun logo in the lower right corner is a shape layer **H**, and a Gradient Fill layer (shown in "Masks" at the right) is used to lighten the right side of the image to make the block of type easier to read.

Masks

WITH A MASK you can hide part of a layer without actually removing that part, so you can easily bring back the hidden component if you want to, just by changing the mask. Each layer (except *Background*) can have two masks — a pixel-based layer mask and an instruction-based vector mask. In this file the **layer mask** on the Gradient Fill layer **I** protects the face, the arm, and an area behind the headline from being lightened by the white gradient that makes a background for the paragraph type. The **vector mask** on the shape layer (shown at the left) defines the shape of the logo; a vector mask can be scaled and rotated without any "softening" of its crisp edges.

Groups

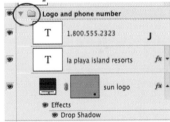

A **GROUP** IS USED HERE simply to help organize the Layers panel and make it more compact **J**. Shown open here, the Group can be toggled closed or open by clicking the arrow to the left of the folder icon ▭. When a mask is applied to a Group, it affects all the layers within the Group.

Clipping Groups

A **CLIPPING GROUP** is a construction that uses one layer as a kind of mask for the layers above. For instance, a clipping group is used in this file to "fill" the headline type with an image **K**. The type is the clipping layer; it masks, or "clips," both the image layer and the Adjustment layer, allowing them to show only within the "footprint" created by the type. Like layer masks and vector masks, clipping groups are "nondestructive." (Page 65 has more about clipping groups.)

Smart Objects

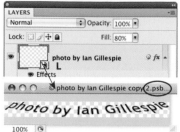

A **SMART OBJECT** is a "package" **L**, a file-within-a-file that protects one or more layers (the contents of the Smart Object) from damage from repeated scaling, rotation, or other transformations. It accumulates transformation instructions and converts them into a single transformation operation to apply to the package. It also contains a copy of the original file, which allows you to get back to the pre-transformation original. To change the contents of the package, the Smart Object can be opened to make the change, then saved again, and the previously applied transformations will automatically be applied to the new content. Here the content is the photo credit.

Smart Filters

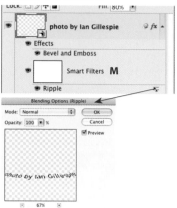

A **FILTER** can be applied to a Smart Object as a Smart Filter **M**. Smart Filter settings stay "live," and the filter can be removed or the settings changed, instantly and without leaving behind any "residue" of the filter's former effects. In this file, because the Ripple filter was applied as a Smart Filter, the filter settings are available to be changed. The blend mode and opacity of the Smart Filter's effect can also be modified. It's as if the filter had been applied to a copy in a layer above and then the blend mode and Opacity of that layer were changed. For the Smart Filters (there can be more than one) that are added to one Smart Object, there's just one mask. It can be used to limit how much of the Smart Object is affected by the combined Smart Filters.

A CLOSER VIEW

If your layers include small items and you'd like to see them larger in the Layers panel, click the panel menu button ▾☰ and choose Panel Options. In the Panel Options dialog, click the Layer Bounds button in the Thumbnail Contents section.

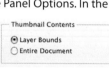

Layer Styles

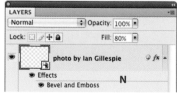

A LAYER STYLE can supply color, texture, dimension, and lighting for any layer except a *Background*. "Exercising Layer Styles" on page 80 is an introduction to working with Layer Styles. In the Layers panel a Style is represented by the *fx* symbol on the layer. You can open a list to view the components of the Style, or close the list to make the Layers panel more compact, by clicking the tiny triangle ▼ next to the *fx*. In this image Layer Styles provide drop shadows for the headline type and the logo elements, and a Style also supplies the "carved" look for the photo credit **N**.

For publisher Haddad's Fine Arts, illustrator **Michael L. Kungl** created *Retro Tea, Deco Tea,* and *Espresso Fresco* in a style that combined the hard edges and gradients of Art Deco with the earthy and loose textures of traditional art media. Kungl began each poster as a pencil sketch and then moved the artmaking process to Adobe Illustrator, to Photoshop, to Corel Painter, and back to Photoshop. In Illustrator he drew the hard-edged curves that he then quickly converted into alpha channels in Photoshop. (The process is described in more detail on page 155.) He saved the files in Photoshop (.psd) format and opened them in Painter. There he used the alpha-channels as "friskets" for masking, to control the color and textures as he applied them to several layers with Painter's outstanding brushes and gradient fills. Finally, he saved the layered files (again in PSD format) and returned them to Photoshop to make color adjustments and to convert the files to CMYK for printing.

BLEND MODE COMPATIBILITY

While Photoshop and Painter share many layer blend modes, each program also includes unique modes that may not "travel" when files are opened in the other program. This may require combining some layers to preserve the color relationships before moving from one application to the other.

To complete his painterly **Hills of Tuscany**, **Mark Wainer** used a quick and easy dodge-and-burn finishing system he's developed. The technique is invaluable for bringing out color and contrast exactly where you want it, either for paintings or for photos.

Wainer started with an original photo **A** and applied a "simplifying" filter to create a painterly effect. His approach was very similar to the one used for *Boats in Fog, Northhampton*, described on page 424.

Next, to tone down the green hills in the background and grass in the foreground, Wainer applied a Selective Color Adjustment layer,▼ adjusting only the Greens range, by adding the opposite color (Magenta) to neutralize the green.

He cloned the window on the small building several times to add more windows to both structures. He then enhanced the composition by selecting the buildings and stretching them taller (Edit > Transform > Scale) and used the History Brush ✎ set to the pre-transformed state to repair the areas around the stretched buildings.▼ He also cloned trees into the skyline and elsewhere.

Wainer selected the sky, pasted in a sky he had selected and copied from another photo, and cloned some of the clouds.▼ He used a large soft Brush ✎ and white paint at a low Opacity to add fog to the hillsides.▼ He made final adjustments to overall contrast and color using several masked Adjustment layers▼ with different blend modes **B**.▼ He had

worked on separate layers as he built the composition, but then he combined the layers into a single *Background* (Layer > Flatten Image).

Wainer uses an Action he recorded▼ to add the layers he needs for dodging and burning, so he can then do the loose brushwork needed to bring out color and contrast. The Action adds three Curves Adjustment layers, each with a black (hide-all) mask and each in a different blend mode: One layer is in Multiply mode (for darkening), another in Screen mode (for lightening), and one in Hard Light mode (for increasing color intensity as well as contrast).▼ If you were to do it without an Action, you might Alt/Option-click the "Create new fill or adjustment layer" button ◑ at the bottom of the

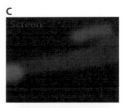

C

Screen

Hard Light

Multiply

A

A

B

B

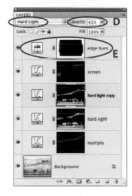

Layers panel and choose Curves to add the first layer; using Alt/Option creates the Adjustment layer with a black-filled mask. Duplicate the layer twice (type Ctrl/⌘-J twice), and change the blend modes for the three layers. Depending on your image and the kind of color you want, you might want to try a different contrast mode, such as Overlay or Soft Light, rather than Hard Light. The three Curves layers, without any adjustments to the Curves, have the same effect as stacking three more copies of the image itself, in each of the blend modes chosen.

The black masks in Wainer's file completely hid the darkening, lightening, and color effects of the Curves layers. But now he could use a soft Brush 🖌 and white to paint the

masks very loosely **C** to reveal those effects exactly where he wanted them. When he wanted more color enhancement than a single Hard Light layer could give him, Wainer targeted the Hard Light layer in the Layers panel and duplicated it (Ctrl/⌘ J); the effect was now too strong, so he reduced the new layer's Opacity and also painted over some of the light areas of the mask with black paint and used a low Opacity to reduce the effect of the new layer in those areas **D**.

To complete the image, Wainer added an "edge burn" layer at the top of the layer stack (the process is detailed on page 279) and painted its mask with black to remove the darkening from the foggy parts of the edges **E**.

LAYERS
Hard Light — Opacity: 41% ▸ **D**
Lock: Fill: 100%
edge burn **E**
screen
hard light copy
hard light
multiply
Background

FIND OUT MORE

▼ Selective Color **page 253**
▼ Restoring with History **page 30**
▼ Clone Stamp **page 256**
▼ Using brush tips **page 71**
▼ Adjustment layers **page 245**
▼ Blend modes **page 181**
▼ Recording Actions **page 120**

Photoshop was essential in the development of **Betsy Schulz's** award-winning architectural mosaics for nine street-level columns for the ***Sapphire Tower*** residential condominium development in downtown San Diego, California. After extensive research on the history of San Diego and consultation with the San Diego Historical Society, the Sycuan Band of the Kumeyaay Nation, the Barona Band of Mission Indians, and others, Schulz identified nine historical periods, collected photos and other artwork, and drafted text to characterize each period. In Photoshop she made a file for each column with a top-layer "frame" that represented the hardware that would be used to mount the mosaics on the column **A**. Then she developed a collage **B**, viewing the artwork through the template to see each of the four faces of the column **C**. Schulz kept the type live throughout the project, so she could easily change the wording in response to the comments from reviewers or change size or typeface if the design required it.

When the design was ready for review, Schulz produced flat color prints and small folded-card-stock column mockups for the client. To confirm that the designs would work at full size and in three dimensions, Schulz's team built a full-size column out of plywood. When the design for the first column was completed and approved, she had full-size prints of the four column faces output at FedEx Kinko's and taped them to the dummy column for inspection.

Two sets of black-and-white "template" sheets were produced (again at FedEx) for each column, one set at column size, and one set 12.5% bigger in all dimensions, and laid out on

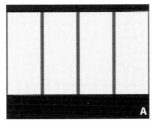

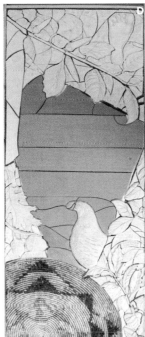

large tables built in Schulz's studio. The larger sheets, placed on drywall in wooden frames, served as a base **D** for assembling the rolled and sculpted elements of the mosaic, allowing for shrinkage during firing. Sheets of clay produced with a slab-roller could be placed on the templates and cut to fit the design. Some of the artwork and scanned photos in the collages were output from the Photoshop file by a photographic process onto 100- to 300-mesh screens to be used for printing underglaze directly onto wet clay to which a background color had already been

applied with a brush **E**. Schulz describes the screening process as similar to printing on fabric. She chose to use Duncan Concepts CC and CN underglazes because their refined texture worked well with the screens, they would shrink along with the clay as it dried, they met the high-firing requirements for architectural ceramics, and they offered a broad spectrum of colors. With experience Schulz learned how to set Photoshop's Curves adjustment to get the high contrast she needed to produce the right coverage of underglaze. As a final control on the underglaze

density, she could vary the angle of the squeegee as she drew it across the screen. She used an X-Acto knife to cut the clay into freeform tiles.

When all the pieces had been printed or sculpted and fired, they were assembled over the smaller set of templates in Schluter aluminum frames attached to cement board. The tile was glued with thinset mortar and grouted **F**, **G**, **H**, and the panels were then transported to the building site and installed on the columns with thinset, and the frames were secured with construction-grade epoxy **I**.

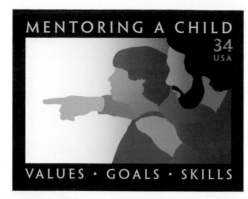

Lance Hidy's design and illustration techniques combine traditional methods with Photoshop and Adobe Illustrator. When he was commissioned by the U. S. Postal Service to design the *Mentoring stamp*, and later the *Special Olympics commemorative*, he began with photography. Having decided on the gesture he wanted to capture for the mentoring stamp, he shot dozens of photos, asking the models to make adjustments and shifting his camera angle slightly between shots. "For me, photography is more than a reference," says Hidy. "I've come to think of my art *as* photography. True, I manipulate the photograph by flattening the shapes and eliminating details, but the essence of the photograph is still there."

Reviewing the photo shoot, he chose a photo that was almost exactly what he wanted in terms of content and composition **A**. Hidy outlined the important shapes (one way to do this is to open the photo in Photoshop and use a pressure-sensitive tablet and stylus with the Pencil tool on a separate transparent layer above the photo). Hidy turned off visibility for the photo, and with only the line work visible **B**, he used Photoshop's selecting and filling tools to develop the scanned file into his stamp design. He added an empty layer for the background of his illustration and used the Gradient tool to fill it with a custom white-to-yellow-to-violet gradient that introduced light to symbolize the child's future. For an early draft

he used solid-color fills everywhere else **C**. To fill the areas surrounded by the black line work, he clicked with the Paint Bucket, with Contiguous turned on to limit the selection to one line-enclosed area at a time, and Anti-alias turned off, to prevent creating partially filled pixels at the edges. Without antialiasing, the edges look pixelated, or stairstepped, if you zoom in for a close look. But the pixels aren't obvious in the printed illustrations. That's because Hidy works at full finished size or larger, at a resolution approximately twice the halftone screen resolution that will be used for printing, so it's the halftone screen rather than the pixels that will determine the smoothness of the printed edges. (For an alternative method for developing color fills and gradient fills, see "Advantages of Fill Layers" on page 421.)

After completing the color fills, Hidy selected the black line work using the Magic Wand with Anti-alias turned off, to prevent partially selected pixels at the edges. He could then invert the selection to contain the color as he refined the edges, using the Pencil to slightly expand one or both color-filled shapes where two colors met.

In the final version of the stamp (shown on the facing page) Hidy reinforced the effect of the implied light source by adding gradients to all shapes except the boy's shirt, whose vivid hue emits a light of its own.

He completed the stamp design by adding type in the Adobe Penumbra

typeface, which he had designed. Using an Adobe Illustrator template that the Postal Service had provided, Hidy also set type for the pane (the sheet of stamps), confining the type to the selvedges, outside the block of stamps. The same process was used later for the Special Olympics commemorative.

FIND OUT MORE

▼ Isolating line work on a transparent layer **page 483**

▼ Resolution for halftone printing **page 105**

Bruce Dragoo's *Chief* began as a "pencil sketch" of the cigar-smoking rooster. "My favorite medium to work with is graphite," says Dragoo, who has worked in a wide range of art media. "But it isn't my favorite medium to look at."

Inspired by the quality of the prints from a friend's wide-format Epson printer, Dragoo began scanning his pencil drawings and using Photoshop to add color. He puts the scanned artwork in Multiply mode and adds layers underneath.

Dragoo used the Magic Wand to select the background,▼ inverted the selection (Ctrl/⌘-Shift-I) to select the rooster, and filled the selection with white, to act as a base for the color. For the color layer, he made a "frisket" to contain the color he applied

next (one way is to duplicate the white base layer by pressing Ctrl/⌘-J and then lock the new layer's transparency by clicking the ⊠ at the top of the Layers panel).

To apply the color, he chose the Gradient tool ▭, clicking the Radial Gradient button in the Options bar. Choosing the Spectrum gradient from the pop-out Gradient picker, he dragged outward from the center of the eye.▼

He used the Brush tool 🖌 with the Airbrush option turned on in the Options bar to paint highlights on the color layer. To break up the smooth airbrushed look of the color, he also scribbled with a very small, hard brush tip and white paint, and added thin strokes of other colors on the neck.

To color his scanned graphite sketches, Dragoo works with bright colors at full intensity. "It makes it easier to see what I'm doing," he says. To get the more subdued color that he wanted for *Chief,* he then added a Hue/Saturation Adjustment layer above the color, reducing the Saturation and increasing Lightness.▼

FIND OUT MORE

▼ Using the Magic Wand 🪄 **page 50**

▼ Using the Gradient tool ▭ **page 174**

▼ Adjustment layers **page 245**

Essential Photoshop Skills

2

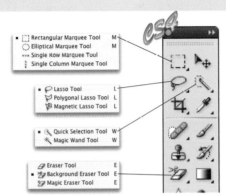

The tools labeled here and the commands in the Select menu are important for isolating part of an image — isolating it so you can change it or protect it from change. In addition, the Pen tools can be used to create paths that can then be converted to selections ("The Pen Tools" on page 454 tells how these tools operate).

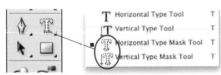

The **Type Mask** tools can be used to set type in layer masks and alpha channels, where live type isn't possible. All the normal Type tool controls are available as you type with these tools, but when you finish, the type turns into an active selection and is no longer editable. Chapter 7 tells about using the Type tools, and page 639 has an example of using a Type Mask tool.

Certain skills are at the heart of most Photoshop operations: working with brush-based tools, selecting, masking and blending, and transforming and resizing images. Other skills that are important to have in your command in order to get the most from Photoshop are using Smart Objects and Smart Filters, and applying Layer Styles. All of these skills are introduced in this chapter.

THE ESSENTIAL SKILLS

Selecting, masking, and transforming are covered in these introductory pages and in tutorials later in the chapter. Tutorials also introduce brushes, Smart Objects, Smart Filters, and Styles, and these are then explored more fully throughout the book. For example, sophisticated brush tip design and operation are covered in Chapter 6, "Painting," and designing your own Layer Styles is covered in "Styling a Photo" in Chapter 5 and in Chapter 8, "Special Effects for Type & Graphics."

SELECTING

Most of what we do in Photoshop starts with telling the program which part of the image you want to affect. And this often starts with targeting a layer or its mask, simply by clicking on its thumbnail in the Layers panel. To limit changes to a particular area within a targeted layer or mask, you can *select* part of it. Knowing the ins and outs of making, cleaning up, storing, and recalling selections is at the heart of successful image editing and compositing.

A good general approach to selecting is as follows:

1 **Make a selection,** doing your best to define the edge all the way around the area you want to isolate.

2 **Repair the edge** as needed, and fill any "holes" in the interior. Quick Mask mode (page 60) can be helpful here.

When you make a selection some hard-to-select areas may be missed, as shown in this detail.

You can clean up edges and holes by painting or erasing the red Quick Mask overlay to subtract from or add to the selection.

Using the Refine Edge command to improve the quality of the edge

After the edge is smoothed and slightly feathered with Refine Edge, the selection can be stored for safekeeping as a grayscale mask, either in an alpha channel or as a layer mask.

3 **Refine the edge** with the Select > Refine Edge command (page 59) or with Photoshop CS4's **Masks panel** (page 63), making it smoother, sharper, softer, or slightly larger or smaller.

4 **Store the selection** in a more permanent form. You can save it as an **alpha channel** (as described on page 60). Or the selected area can be turned into a **layer mask** that limits how much of a particular layer is hidden or revealed (page 62) or a **layer** of its own (page 66).

Making Selections

Selections of pixel-based layers and masks can be made with commands from the **Select menu**, with **selection tools**, or with the **Extract command** (in Photoshop CS3 Extract is in the Filter menu, but in CS4 you'll need to add it if you want to use it; see "Extract in CS4" on page 57). You can also select with the **Blend If** options in the Layer Style dialog or by modifying a copy of one of the file's **color channels** — for instance, the Red, Green, or Blue Channel of an RGB image.

Some tools and commands make selections **procedurally** — basing the selection on color or brightness information in the image. With others, you draw a selection boundary **by hand**. Procedural methods are often faster and more accurate. Sometimes the best way to select is to use one selection method to start and then add to or subtract from the selection with another tool or command. "Modifying Selections" on page 58 tells how to accomplish these changes.

The edges of a selection can be abrupt and "stairstepped" (each pixel is either fully selected or not selected at all); **antialiased** (sharp with just a little transparency in the edge pixels to make the edge smooth), or **feathered** (soft-edged with obvious partial transparency).

An **active selection** is represented on-screen by a pulsating dashed border. If you click outside the selection boundary with a selection tool, the pulsating dashes disappear — and the selection is gone. If you accidentally drop a selection and miss the opportunity to undo,▼ sometimes by acting quickly you can **recover a lost selection** by choosing Select > Reselect before you make another selection. But a more permanent way to preserve a selection is to store it.

FIND OUT MORE
▼ Undoing recent steps **page 29**

Each of the selection tools and commands has its own advantages and disadvantages. To decide which tool or command to use, you need to analyze the area you want to select. Is it organic or

A continuous, curving stroke with the Quick Selection tool in its default "Add to selection" mode selected most of the man, leaving most of the background unselected.

Clicking in a few spots with a smaller brush tip added the hair that had been missed, and then the tool could be used in its "Subtract from selection" mode (shown here) to delete parts of the background that had accidentally been included in the selection. The selection was now ready for Refine Edge, as shown on page 59.

geometric? Is it fairly uniform in color, or is it multicolored? Does it contrast with its background or blend into it, or do some parts of it contrast and others blend in? Does it have a different texture than its background? Will it be easier to select the part you *don't* want to target and then invert the selection? This kind of analysis will help you choose the tool, command, or combination of techniques that will do the best job. You can select by color, by shape, or by shape *and* color. And then there's the new Quick Selection tool.

Selecting by "Magic": The Quick Selection Tool

The **Quick Selection tool** doesn't really work by magic, but it can seem to. It's so good that it's almost always worth a try for isolating a subject from its background. If it doesn't work, you can drop the selection (Ctrl/⌘-D) and try another method.

You operate the Quick Selection tool by hand, but loosely — "painting" the area you want to select, dabbing and stroking with the tool to expand the selection. (To control whether the selection is based on the color of only a single layer or on all visible layers combined, turn off or on **Sample All Layers** in the Options bar before you click or drag.) With each additional stroke or dab the tool expands the selection border to include contiguous (touching) areas that match the color and texture in the area you've already selected, and it stops when it recognizes an edge. It seems to "learn" as you add to the selection, getting better at recognizing what you want to select.

The tool's footprint is circular, with crosshairs in the middle of the circle. To use the tool, position the cursor so the crosshairs are on something you want to select. Before you click or drag, make sure the circular footprint is *entirely inside* the area you want to select. If you need to shrink the size of the cursor in order to make that happen, use the left bracket key [, or use CS4's dynamic resizing. ▼ Then click or drag to make a stroke over the area you want to select, without letting the circular cursor cross any boundary you want to preserve. Now that there's an active selection, the Quick Selection tool will assume that you want to add to the selection rather than start over. Continue to add to the selection by clicking or dragging. If you accidentally select something you don't want, you can use the **Alt/Option** key with the tool **to deselect** that area.

FIND OUT MORE
▼ Resizing brush tips **page 71**

Turning on the **Auto Enhance** option tends to make more extensive selections with smoother edges, doing some of the

You can use the Magic Wand ✎ to check a silhouetted image to make sure the solid-color background is spot-free, or check a vignette, drop shadow, or glow to see exactly how far it extends: In the Magic Wand's Options bar, set the Tolerance to 0 and make sure Anti-aliased is deselected. Turn on the Contiguous option and then click on the background. The pulsating boundary will show where the edge of the color change is, and any stray "sparkles" will indicate spots in the background.

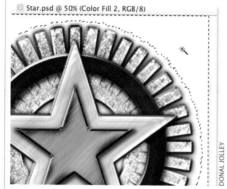

Star.psd @ 50% (Color Fill 2, RGB/8)

DONAL JOLLEY

The **Magic Wand** ✎ can help you see the extent of soft-edged effects, as shown here. It can also help you detect unwanted spots in a solid-color background.

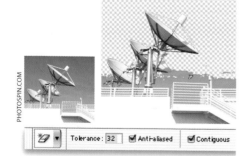

PHOTOSPIN.COM

The Options bar for the **Magic Eraser** ✐ looks very much like the Magic Wand's. In fact, this tool works like a Magic Wand that doesn't select but instead "clears" the area. It's "destructive" in that it removes pixels and replaces them with transparency. But for a nondestructive way to use destructive selecting tools, see page 51.

refining that could otherwise be done later with the Refine Edge command (described on page 59).

You may notice that the Quick Selection tool seems to get more confident about what you want to select as you continue to use it to build a selection, that it selects larger, more diverse patches than at the beginning. As it seems to think along with you, it may recognize that you've made a mistake if you accidentally let the cursor stray slightly over an edge you've been preserving. Whereas if you'd done that on the first click the tool would have selected on both sides of that edge (not what you wanted, but how could it know), if you do it later in the process, the tool may see it as unintentional, based on what you've been selecting and deselecting so far.

If your selection goes wrong and you want to start over completely, you can click the "New selection" (leftmost) button in the Options bar to drop the current selection. If you find that you're deselecting, reselecting, and even starting over a lot and it's getting frustrating because it's hard to predict exactly what will happen when you click or drag with this tool, it may be that there are too many shared colors and textures between subject and background for the tool to be effective, and a different, more directly controlled tool for drawing the selection boundary will do a better job (see "Selecting by Shape" on page 54). Or it may be easier to leave the selection a little rough and use Quick Mask or Refine Edge to clean it up (see page 58). Or maybe it's simply a case of practice makes perfect — making the cursor the right size, choosing whether it will be easier to select the area you want, or select the area you don't want and invert the selection, and starting each selection (or deselection) in the right place.

Selecting by Color: Magic Wand ✎, Magic Eraser ✐, Color Range & Color Channels

To make a selection of all the pixels of a similar color, Photoshop has the **Magic Wand** tool ✎ and the **Select > Color Range** command. Unlike the Quick Selection tool, which "grows" the selection by adding areas contiguous to where you click, the Magic Wand and Color Range can select noncontiguously. A selection can also be developed from one of the **color channels**.

The Magic Wand ✎. Using the **Magic Wand** is a quick and easy way to select one uniformly colored area or a small number of similarly colored areas in an image where there are other spots of the same color but you don't want to select them all — for instance if you wanted to select several purple flowers in a field of green leaves, but not all the purple flowers. Just click the Magic

The Magic Eraser 🔲 and Background Eraser 🔲 tools, and the Extract filter, do their "selecting" by erasing the parts of the image outside the area you want to keep, rather than by making a mask to hide that part, nevertheless preserving it in case you change your mind and want it back later. For these methods, though, you can avoid destruction:

1 Make a duplicate of the layer from which you want to select.

2 Turn off visibility for the original and use the destructive method on the duplicate.

3 When the selection is complete in the duplicate layer, Ctrl/⌘-click on its thumbnail in the Layers panel.

4 Turn on visibility for the original layer, target it by clicking its name in the Layers panel, and add a layer mask by clicking the "Add a mask" button 🔲 at the bottom of the Layers panel.

5 Turn off visibility for the duplicated (erased) layer.

You can now refine the layer mask if you like. You'll have the refined selection stored in the layer mask and the original selection stored in the transparency of the duplicate layer.

In the Color Range dialog with Sampled Colors chosen and Fuzziness at the default 40 (and Localized Color Clusters off), clicking on a blue balloon with the dialog's Eyedropper tool and then dragging over the one balloon with the "Add to Sample" tool selects all three blue balloons.

Wand on a pixel of the color you want to select. By default the Wand is in **Contiguous** mode, so it selects the pixel you clicked and all similarly colored pixels for as far as that color continues without interruption. You can add separate areas to the Magic Wand selection by Shift-clicking. Or you can use the Wand to **select *all* pixels of the same color** in the entire image by clicking in the Options bar to turn off the Contiguous option.

To specify how broad a **range of color** the Magic Wand should include in a selection, set the **Tolerance** value in the Options bar to a number between 0 and 255. The lower the number, the smaller the range of colors. To control whether the selection is based on the color of only a single layer or of all visible layers combined, turn **Sample All Layers** off or on in the Options bar. By default, Magic Wand selections are **antialiased**, or smooth-edged, but you can turn that option off if you like.

The Magic Eraser 🔲. The Magic Wand's "cousin," the **Magic Eraser** 🔲, does the same kind of selecting as the wand, except that the process is destructive — it erases everything it "selects."

Color Range. The **Select > Color Range** command is more complex than the Magic Wand, but it **shows the extent of the selection more clearly**, and it **offers more control** of what's selected. By default, the little preview window in the Color Range dialog box shows a grayscale image of the selection. White areas are selected; gray areas are partially selected, and black indicates areas that are completely outside the selection. With its many levels of gray, this picture is much more informative than the pulsating border you see when you use the Quick Selection tool or the Magic Wand. The Selection Preview menu at the bottom of the dialog lets you choose how to view the selected area in the larger document window.

The **Fuzziness** setting in the Color Range dialog box is like the Magic Wand's Tolerance setting, but it's easier to work with, since the entire range is spread out on a slider scale and the preview window instantly shows the effect of changing it. Keeping the setting above 16 will usually prevent jagged edges in the completed selection. And if you have to go below 16, you can smooth things out later with Refine Edge.

The **Select** field at the top of the Color Range dialog box lets you choose the color selection criteria. **To select based on colors you sample from the image,** choose **Sampled Colors**. (What's visible to the Color Range sampling function will be the same as what's visible to you on-screen. If you want Color Range to

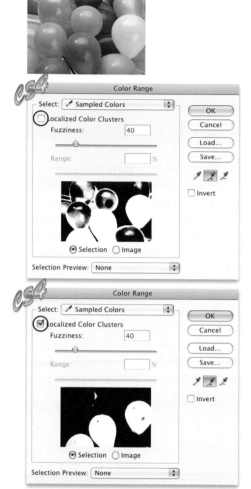

After the blue balloons are selected (see previous page), in Photoshop CS3, or in CS4 with Localized Color Clusters turned off **A**, clicking on the yellow balloon with the "Add to Sample" tool adds not only the yellow but also parts of the green balloons to the selection, since green is between blue and yellow in the spectrum. In CS4 with Localized Color Clusters turned on **B**, a second color range (such as yellow) can be added without selecting intermediate colors.

ignore the contribution of some layers, turn off their visibility by clicking their 👁 icons in the Layers panel.) In CS4 you can decide whether you want the Localized Color Clusters option turned on or off, since the result of clicking will depend on whether its checkbox is checked:

- **If Localized Color Clusters is not checked**, the selection will extend throughout the image (as if you had clicked with the Magic Wand with Contiguous turned off).

- **If Localized Color Clusters is checked,** the Range setting will determine how far from the click point Color Range will look for the sampled color. The Range setting is a percentage of the bigger dimension of the document — either width or height; it defines a soft-edged circular area around the click point where Color Range will look for the sampled color.

To extend or reduce the range of colors in the current selection, click or drag with the + Eyedropper or – Eyedropper to add new colors or to subtract colors. Or click or drag with the plain Eyedropper, with Shift (to add) or Alt/Option (to subtract). Again, in CS4 the Localized Color Cluster setting has an effect: The setting affects not only the radius around the click point, but also whether only the two colors you've clicked are selected (Localized Color Clusters on) or whether all the colors in the spectrum between the ones you've sampled are also included in the selection (Localized Color Clusters off). So,

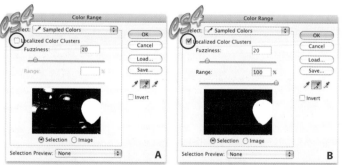

Starting from scratch, we used Color Range's Eyedropper tool and "Add to Sample" tool to select the yellow balloon, with Fuzziness set to 20 to reduce the range of other colors selected. In CS3 or with Localized Color Clusters turned off in CS4, some of the oranges and light greens were also selected **A**. Simply turning on the Localized Color Clusters option **B** limited the selection, even without reducing the Range to limit the area. Reducing the Range would also eliminate the partly selected area at the left edge.

In Photoshop CS3's Color Range, without the Localized Color Clusters option, you can still limit a Color Range selection: Before you choose Select > Color Range, restrict the area that Color Range will act on. Here we used the Rectangular Marquee to make a quick selection of the yellow balloon's locale and then used Color Range.

To isolate the butterfly **A** from its background, designer Wayne Rankin inspected the color channels in the Channels panel. He chose the Blue channel as having the best definition of the edge between butterfly and background, so he copied it to make an alpha channel. After using the Image > Adjustments > Levels and Invert commands on the alpha channel **B**, he viewed it along with the RGB composite **C** and painted it with the Brush tool and white paint to eliminate internal "holes" in the butterfly silhouette, and with black paint to patch light areas in the background **D**, **E**. Ctrl/⌘-clicking on the altered alpha channel selected the butterfly **F**. For more about Rankin's selecting and masking processes, see page 94.

for instance, clicking the Eyedropper on a red pixel and then clicking the "Add to Sample" tool on yellow will select only red and yellow (Localized Color Clusters on) or red, orange, and yellow (Localized Color Clusters off). You can also expand or contract the color range in the selection by adjusting the Fuzziness, of course.

To select a family of colors instead of sampling color, choose from the color ranges offered in the dialog box's "Select" menu. The color families are predefined — you can't change the Fuzziness or use the Eyedroppers to expand or shrink these ranges, and the Localized Color Clusters option isn't available. **To select only the light, medium, or dark colors,** choose Highlights, Midtones, or Shadows. Again, there's no opportunity to make adjustments to the range.

The **Invert** box provides a way **to select a multicolored subject on a plain background:** Use the Color Range eyedropper to select the background, and then click the Invert box to reverse the selection.

Color channels. Though it's less likely to be the best choice now that the Quick Selection tool has been added to Photoshop, a color channel can sometimes be a good starting point for a selection. Often one of the color channels (Red, Green, or Blue in an RGB file, for instance) shows better contrast between a subject and its surroundings than the other channels do. Look for a channel where there's a distinct light-dark boundary between subject and background. Then copy that channel to make an alpha channel by dragging the color channel's name to the "Create new channel" button at the bottom of the Channels panel. You can apply choices from the Image > Adjustments menu to increase the contrast even more, or click on the new alpha channel's thumbnail in the Channels panel and paint with white to add to the area that will be selected, or with black to add to the area that will be unselected. Finally, load the alpha channel as a selection by Ctrl/⌘-clicking on the channel's thumbnail in the Channels panel.

"Selecting" with the "This Layer" slider. "Blending" on page 66 tells how to use the "Blend If" sliders in the Layer Style dialog box as a kind of masking method for blending layers. "Making a Selection from 'This Layer'" on page 66 describes a way to turn the "Blend If" settings into a selection. It's a unique color-and-tone-based selection method that's worth knowing about.

In earlier versions of Photoshop, many more selections had to be made with the Lasso tools 🔾 🎮 🎮. When the subject and background shared colors, the selection boundary had to be drawn by hand. Now many of these selections can be made with the sophisticated Quick Selection tool 🔧 instead. In this example, you can drag the Lasso around the edge as shown here, or simply use the Quick Selection tool on the background.

Beginning a selection with either the Lasso 🔾 or the Polygonal Lasso 🎮 and then adding the Alt/Option key lets you switch between dragging the Lasso in its freeform mode and clicking it as the Polygonal Lasso.

With the Alt/Option key held down, you can drag the Lasso 🔾 outside the boundaries of the image, to make sure your selection doesn't miss any pixels at the edges.

Selecting by Shape: Geometric or Custom Shapes & Irregular Shapes

If the area you want to select is not distinctly different in tone or color from its surroundings, outlining its shape by hand may be the best way to select it. In that case the Marquees, Shapes, Lassos, and Pens are the tools to choose from.

Selecting geometric or custom shapes. To "frame" a selection, you can use the Rectangular or Elliptical Marquee tool, as explained next, or use one of the Shape tools. The Marquees offer a variety of options for selecting:

- The default mode for the Marquee tools ⬚ ⬭ is to position the cursor where you want one "corner" of the selection to be and then drag diagonally. But many times you have better control of exactly what you select if you draw from the center. **To draw a selection outward from the center,** press and hold the **Alt/Option** key at any time while you're dragging.

- **To select a square or circular area,** constrain the Marquee by holding down the **Shift** key after you start to drag.

- **To make a selection of a particular width-to-height ratio,** choose **Constrained Aspect Ratio** for the Style in the Options bar and set the ratio.

- **To make a selection of a specific size,** choose **Fixed Size** for the Style in the Options bar and enter the Width and Height measurements in pixels (adding "px" to the number), inches (add "in"), or centimeters (add "cm").

In addition to the Marquees, the vector-based **Shape tools** offer many more preformed shapes, both geometric and custom, that you can use for selecting. First drag to draw the shape (the same Alt/Option and Shift modifiers apply as for the Marquees), and then convert the path you've drawn to a selection by Ctrl/⌘-clicking its thumbnail in the Layers panel or in the Paths panel. ▼

Selecting irregular shapes. To select a subject from a background of a very similar color, you may need to "hand-draw" the selection border with a Lasso or Pen tool. If the element you want to select has smooth, curved edges, use a Pen. ▼ If the boundary is complex with detailed "ins and outs," try out one of the Lasso tools:

- For **very detailed edges,** drag the standard **Lasso** 🔾.

- For fairly smooth edges, clicking a **series of short line segments with the**

FIND OUT MORE

▼ Working with Shape tools
page 451

▼ Working with Pens
page 454

ORIGINAL PHOTO: CARLA GILBERT

The Magnetic Lasso 🖰 can automatically follow a distinct edge such as the shoulder of the shirt **A**. (Before you begin, be sure the Feather is set to 0 in the Options bar.) If necessary, you can click to anchor the selection border in a spot where the edge is ambiguous, such as the highlight on the dark band crossing the collar **B**. In areas where the Magnetic Lasso can't follow the edge, you can hold down the Alt/Option key and then drag to use the Lasso 🖰 **C** or click to use the Polygonal Lasso 🖰.

Polygonal Lasso 🖰 is often easier and more accurate than trying to trace the edge by dragging the Lasso. Holding down the **Shift key** as you use the **Polygonal Lasso** restricts its movement to **vertical, horizontal, or 45° diagonal.**

- Holding down the **Alt/Option key** lets you **operate either tool as** the Lasso 🖰 or the Polygonal Lasso 🖰, switching back and forth between them simply by dragging 🖰 or clicking 🖰.

There are other advantages to holding down the Alt/Option key: First, it **keeps the selection from closing up** if you accidentally let go of the mouse button before you've finished selecting. Second, if you make a mistake, you can **"unravel" the selection boundary** you're drawing, by repeatedly pressing the Delete key while you also hold down Alt/Option until you get back to the "good part." And if you want **to make sure your Lasso selection extends all the way to the edges** of the image without missing any pixels, you can hold down Alt/Option and click or drag the tool outside the image. Finally, you can even switch between these two tools and the Magnetic Lasso 🖰, described next.

Selecting by Shape *and* Color: Magnetic Lasso, Background Eraser & Extract

Some of Photoshop's selecting tools are designed to let you take advantage of distinct color differences where they exist, but then also select by hand in areas where this contrast breaks down. These tools include the Magnetic Lasso 🖰 and Magnetic Pen 🖰, the Background Eraser 🖰, and the Extract command. The Background Eraser and Extract command are "destructive" selection methods — removing rather than just isolating the pixels they select. But see "'Destructive' Doesn't Have To Be" on page 51 for a nondestructive workaround.

The Magnetic Lasso 🖰. To operate the Magnetic Lasso 🖰, you click the center of the circular cursor somewhere on the edge you want to trace and then "float" the cursor along, moving the mouse or stylus without pressing its button or moving the stylus without touching it to the tablet. The tool automatically follows the edge. Parameters that can be set in the Options bar include **Width, Frequency, Edge Contrast,** and **Feather,** and if you have a graphics tablet, you can turn on the **Stylus Pressure** option.

Here are some pointers for using the Magnetic Lasso 🖰:

- If you're tracing a **well-defined edge**, use a large Width and move the tool quickly. **To increase the contrast at the**

No matter what selection method you use, selecting can be made easier if you exaggerate the color or tone contrast between the area you want to select and its surroundings before you try to make the selection. For instance, a Levels Adjustment layer can be added above the image layer to make color differences more obvious than they were in the original. Then you may be able to select by color, or at least have a better view of an area you're selecting by hand. After the selection is made, the Adjustment layer can be deleted, or its visibility 👁 can be turned off.

This image was lightened overall by moving the Levels dialog's gamma slider, to make the colors more obvious than they were in the shadows.

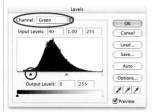

In this example, the Levels adjustment was made to the Green channel only, to increase the color difference between the leaves and the rock; see page 549 for details.

edge, and thus make the tool easier to operate, you can use a temporary Adjustment layer as described in the "Easier Selecting" tip at the left. **If there are other distinct edges nearby**, use a small Width and keep the cursor carefully centered on the edge you're tracing. **If the edge is soft** with little contrast, use a smaller Width and trace carefully. **Where there is no contrast** for the Magnetic Lasso to follow, you can operate the tool like the Polygonal Lasso, clicking from point to point. **Or hold down the Alt/Option key to have access to all three Lassos**, switching between the Magnetic Lasso (by floating), the Polygonal Lasso (by clicking), and the Lasso (by dragging).

- As for most other tools whose cursor size can vary, you can use the left and right **bracket keys** — [and] — to change the Width as you operate the Lasso, as described below, or use a graphics tablet and turn on **Stylus Pressure**. With increasing pressure the Width becomes smaller.

- Increase the **Frequency** to put down more fastening points, which determine how far back the selection border will "unravel" each time you press the Delete key.

- The **Edge Contrast** determines how much contrast the tool should be looking for to find the edge. Use a low setting for a low-contrast edge.

The Background Eraser 🩹. The Background Eraser tool 🩹, which shares a spot with the other Erasers in the Tools panel, erases the pixels you drag it over, leaving transparency instead. The "+" in the center of the tool's cursor is the "hot spot," and the circle around it defines the tool's "reconnaissance area." When you click, the Background Eraser samples the color under the hot spot. And as you drag the tool, it evaluates the color of pixels within the reconnaissance area, to see which ones should be erased. Which pixels get erased depends on the settings in the Options bar.

Tolerance affects the range of colors to be erased. With a setting of **0**, pixels of only a **single color** are erased — the specific color under the hot spot when you click. **At higher Tolerance** settings the tool erases a **broader range of colors**.

Use the three **Sampling** buttons to control how the "hot spot" is used in choosing the color to erase:

- Choose **Sampling: Once** to **erase only the color that's under the hot spot when you first push the button down** on your mouse or stylus. The Background Eraser will erase this color

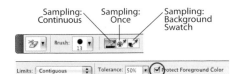

Sampling: Continuous | Sampling: Once | Sampling: Background Swatch

Limits: Contiguous | Tolerance: 50% | ☑ Protect Foreground Color

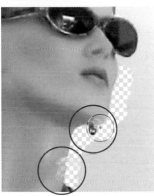

The Protect Foreground Color option for the Background Eraser makes this a very powerful selection tool. It lets you sample a color that you want to protect from being erased, even though that color falls within the range of colors you're erasing. For instance, it's used here to protect the mannikin as the multi-tone gray of the background is erased. Compare the top image, where Protect Foreground Color is turned on to protect the chin and neck, and the bottom image, with it turned off.

EXTRACT IN CS4

The Extract filter is not installed with Photoshop CS4; if you want to use it, you'll need to put the **ExtractPlus.plugin** file in the Filters folder (Adobe Photoshop CS4 > Plugins > Filters) and restart Photoshop. ExtractPlus.plugin is in the Goodies folder on the Adobe Photoshop CS4 DVD-ROM. Or you can download it as part of the Optional Plugins package (see page 120).

as you drag, until you release the mouse button. When you push the button down again, it will sample again, choosing the new color that's now under the hot spot.

- **To set a single specific color or color family to be erased,** regardless of when you press and release the mouse button, choose **Sampling: Background Swatch** and click the Background square in the Tools panel; then either specify a color in the Color Picker or click in your image to sample a color.

- **Sampling: Continuous** repeatedly updates the color to be erased, so the tool **erases every color you drag the hot spot over,** unless it's protected (see below).

For the **Limits,** you can choose Discontiguous, Contiguous, or Find Edges.

- **To erase any occurrence of the color anywhere within the circular cursor** as it moves along, choose **Discontiguous.**

- To erase **only pixels whose color continues uninterrupted** from the hot spot, choose **Contiguous.**

- **Find Edges** is like Contiguous, but it pays special attention to **preserving sharp edges.**

What really sets the Background Eraser apart from other selecting tools, both destructive and nondestructive, is the **Protect Foreground Color** option in the Options bar. It lets you sample and protect any one color at a time as you erase. This is useful for preserving an element that's within the range of the colors you want to erase. Even if you drag the cursor over it, that color won't be erased.

The Extract Filter. The Extract command (located in the Filter menu in Photoshop CS3) isolates a part of an image by erasing all other pixels on that layer, leaving transparency in their place. The Extract interface is complex, but the intelligent masking it does can be very useful. "Exercising Extract" on page 90 outlines a fairly direct way to proceed.

Although the Background Eraser or the combination of the Quick Selection tool and Refine Edge (page 58) can do a good job of isolating many subjects, the more sophisticated Extract command may work better on an image like this one, in which the curls in the hair enclose pockets of the background colors. The Extract process for this image is detailed in "Exercising Extract" on page 90.

The **Transform Selection** command is great for angling and skewing selections. Here it's used to shape a shadow for the lipstick, which was already isolated on a transparent layer. With a new layer added below the lipstick layer to hold the shadow, we Ctrl/⌘-clicked the lipstick layer's thumbnail to load its outline as a selection. Then we chose Select > Transform Selection. Ctrl/⌘-dragging the top center handle down and to the right **A** allowed us to lay the selection down where we wanted the shadow. Then we Ctrl/⌘-dragged the top left corner handle to the right **B** to distort the selection so it got narrower as it receded into the distance. Pressing the Enter key accepted these changes. We filled the selection with gray, and dropped the selection (Ctrl/⌘-D). We then softened the edge with the Gaussian Blur filter.

The Options bar for selection tools includes four buttons for specifying whether the selection you are about to make will be (left to right) a new selection, an addition to the current selection, a subtraction from it, or the intersection.

MODIFYING SELECTIONS

When you've completed a selection boundary, there are several ways you can modify it if you need to. Quick Mask (page 60) provides a stable, easy-to-use "painting" environment for adding to or subtracting from the selection. And the Select > Refine Edge command can improve edge quality or expand or contract the selection. But first, here are some other ways to manipulate the selection boundary:

- To **move the boundary** without moving any pixels, drag inside the selection with any selection tool.

- To **skew**, **scale**, **distort**, or **flip the selection boundary**, choose **Select > Transform Selection**. Then right/Ctrl-click in the document window to bring up a menu of kinds of transformation. Drag or Shift-drag the handles of the Transform frame, and press Enter (or double-click inside the frame) to complete the transformation.

- To **invert the selection**, deselecting the selected area and vice versa, type Ctrl/⌘-Shift-I or choose **Select > Inverse**.

- To **add to**, **subtract from**, or make an **intersection with** the current selection, click one of the buttons at the left end of the selection tool's Options bar, and then make the new selection.

- To **add pixels anywhere in the image that are similar in color** to the pixels in the current selection, choose **Select > Similar**.

- To **add pixels that are similar in color** *and adjacent* **to the current selection**, you can choose **Select > Grow**. Each time you use Grow, the range of colors selected gets larger.

> **TOLERANCE VALUES**
>
> The Tolerance for the Magic Wand ✦ also controls the range of Select > Similar and Select > Grow. If the original selection shows high color variation and contrast, Grow or Similar may not produce the results you expect. You can try again by undoing (Ctrl/⌘-Z), resetting the Tolerance lower, and choosing Grow or Similar again.

Using Refine Edge

The Select > Refine Edge command, also available as a button in the Options bar when any selection tool is active, is a great tool for improving a selection edge. The adjustments in the Refine Edge dialog — which include expanding, contracting, smoothing, and softening — are interactive, and you can preview the results, checking the edge quality against various kinds of backgrounds. When you've finished improving the edge, clicking "OK" closes the dialog and returns the "marching ants."

REFINE EDGE

With the Refine Edge dialog you can modify the edge of a selection or a mask while evaluating the result in your document window. (This dialog is called **Refine Mask** when you use it on a mask rather than an active selection.) The dialog's settings — for smoothing, softening, contracting, or expanding selection edges, or for making detailed edges more accurate — are interactive, and there are five live preview options. A "Refine Edge" button is available on the Options bar whenever a selection tool is chosen, and the command is available in the Select menu whenever there's an active selection; in Photoshop CS4 it's also available in the Masks panel whenever a mask is targeted.

The **Default** settings provide a small amount of smoothing and an even smaller amount of feather, or edge softening. Because the Refine Edge dialog opens with its previous settings, click the "Default" button to return to this suggested starting point for refining the edge.

Radius determines how far from the current selection edge Photoshop looks to refine the accuracy of the edge. For wispy hair, increase the Radius. For a hard edge, keep the Radius low.

Increasing **Contrast** "pushes" any partially selected pixels (including those in the band defined by the Radius setting) toward full selection or non-selection; it can resolve "halos" of partly selected pixels that appear with a high Radius. The trick is to strike a balance between Radius and Contrast to get the edge detail you want.

Smooth evens out the bumpiness, or kinks, in a detailed edge. **Feather** adds an even amount of blur all around the selected area's edges, extending partly inward and partly outward, softening the edge so the edges of the selected area will blend with whatever is below in the stack of layers that make up an image file.

Contract/Expand lets you modify the overall area in the selection, contracting inward from the edge or expanding outward. The preview makes it easy to see when you've contracted enough to get rid of a "fringe" of background, or expanded enough to pick up the subject all the way to its edge.

With the **Preview** box checked (above, upper right), pressing the **F** key cycles through the five Preview modes.

Standard shows the image and "marching ants." Press **X** to toggle the marching ants off and on.

Mask previews the selection as a grayscale mask.

Quick Mask shows the selection as a clear area in a red overlay over the image. To change from red to a different color, double-click this icon.

On Black previews the selected area over a black background, a good way to see a "fringe" of light pixels at the edge.

On White previews the selected area over a white background, a good way to see a "fringe" of dark pixels at the edge.

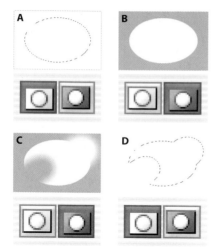

Making a selection in Standard mode **A**, converting to Quick Mask mode **B**, removing from the selection with black paint and adding to the selection with white paint **C**, and turning the altered mask back into a selection **D**

Using Quick Mask

If you make a selection and then click the Quick Mask button ▣ (at the bottom of the Tools panel), the selection appears as a clear area in a mask; you can then modify the mask with Photoshop's painting and other tools. In Quick Mask mode you see the mask as a partly transparent red overlay on the image; because you can see both at once, you can do some fairly precise and subtle editing. As you edit, Quick Mask remains stable, preserving the selection while you work on it. When you've finished modifying the mask, you can turn it back into a selection boundary by clicking the Standard mode button ▣.

SAVING & LOADING SELECTIONS

After you've invested the time and effort to make a selection, it makes sense to preserve it so you can load it back into the image if you need to later. One way to do that is with an **alpha channel**. When a selection is stored in an alpha channel, white shows areas that can be recalled as an active selection, black areas won't be selected, and gray areas will be partially selected, proportionally to the lightness of the gray.

To make an alpha channel from an active selection (pulsating border), choose Select > Save Selection, choose New Channel,

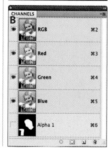

In this "hand-tinting" project we saved the skin selection **A** in an alpha channel **B**. Then we made a rough selection of the dress, without tracing the neck or arm **C**. We Ctrl-Alt-clicked (Windows) or ⌘-Option-clicked (Mac) the alpha channel in the Channels panel to subtract it from the rough selection so we could color the dress only **D**.

Here are two tips that make it easier to edit layer masks or alpha channels:

• Use a Quick Mask-like view with an overlay that represents the mask. In the Channels panel, target the thumbnail of the alpha channel (or the layer mask for the active layer). Make sure its visibility is turned on (click to the left of the thumbnail to turn on the 👁), and then tap the tilde key ⌐, and edit. Tapping ⌐ again shows the mask alone.

Making an alpha channel to use with Lens Blur. The default mask overlay is red and 50% transparent.

• To switch quickly between black paint and white for adding to or subtracting from the mask, set the Foreground and Background colors to black and white (type D, then X if needed) and then just tap the B and E keys to switch between the Brush (to paint with black) and the Eraser (to paint with white). With this method you can set separate brush tips, Opacity, and Flow in the Options bar for the two tools.

and click "OK." Or in the Channels panel (opened by choosing Window > Channels) simply click the "Save selection as channel" button 🔲 at the bottom of the panel.

To make an active selection from an alpha channel, Ctrl/⌘-click on the alpha channel's thumbnail in the Channels panel. Another option is to choose Select > Load Selection, and in the Load Selection dialog box, choose the document and channel you want to load. With this command you can load an alpha channel from any open document that has the same pixel dimensions as the one you're working on.

MASKING

Each layer in a Photoshop file, except a *Background* at the bottom of the stack, can have two kinds of "masks" for hiding or revealing parts of the layer. These masks are invaluable because they hide without permanently changing the content of the layer. Instead of erasing or cutting away part of an image, you can leave it intact but block it with a ***layer mask*** or a ***vector mask***. Masks are often used to combine images, but they're equally useful for combining two different versions of the same image, or for targeting a tone or color adjustment to a particular area. Layer masks and vector masks can also be applied to Groups of layers, ▼ and masks can help determine the outline to which a Layer Style is applied (see "Masks & Layer Styles" on page 64).

FIND OUT MORE
▼ Layer Groups
page 583

Masks are cataloged in the Layers panel, where they appear to the right of the image thumbnail for the layer. If a layer has both

One way to mask an element inside part of an existing image is to use the **Paste Into** command: Select and copy (Ctrl/⌘-C) the element you want to paste, then activate the layer you want to paste into (by clicking its name in the Layers panel). Make a selection of the area where you want to paste, and choose Edit > Paste Into. The pasted element will come in as a new layer, complete with a layer mask that lets it show only within the area you selected. If you hold down the Alt/Option key as you choose Paste Into, the effect will be to **Paste Behind** the selected area instead.

Typically, when you add a layer mask, the image and mask are linked, so moving or transforming the image moves or transforms the mask, too. But when you use **Paste Into** (left) or **Paste Behind** (below), the mask and image are unlinked by default. That way if you move the image around, resize it, or make other transformations, the mask stays in the right position relative to the image below.

To make changes to a layer mask, click the mask thumbnail, or use the  button in the Masks panel. An outline around the thumbnail will show that the mask is active. You'll still be viewing the image rather than the mask, but any painting, filtering, or other changes you make will affect the mask, not the layer.

To make a *layer mask* visible instead of the image, Alt/Option-click the mask thumbnail. Alt/Option-click again to make the image visible again.

To see and edit the outline of a *vector mask* at the same time you're viewing the layer *or* the layer mask, click the thumbnail for the vector mask, or use the  button in the Masks panel. An outline appears around the thumbnail and the path appears on-screen. You can then change the path with the Shape or Pen tools or with one of the Transform commands. Click the thumbnail or button again to turn off the outline.

To turn a layer mask or vector mask off temporarily so it has no effect, Shift-click the mask thumbnail, or click the 👁 at the bottom of the Masks panel. An "X" on the thumbnail shows that the mask is turned off. Shift-click again to turn it back on.

a layer mask and a vector mask, the vector mask is farther right. If a layer has a layer mask, its mask thumbnail also appears in the Channels panel anytime the layer is targeted; if the layer has a vector mask, it appears in the Paths panel when the layer is targeted. There are some important differences between layer masks and vector masks.

Layer Masks

A **layer mask** is a pixel-based grayscale mask that can have up to 256 shades of gray, from white to black. Where the mask is white, it's transparent, and it allows the image or adjustment on its layer to show through and contribute to the composite. Where the mask is black, it's opaque, and the corresponding portion of the image is blocked (masked out). Gray areas are partly transparent — the lighter the gray, the more transparent — and the corresponding pixels in the layer's image (or adjustment) make a semitransparent (or partial) contribution to the composite. You can **create a layer mask by clicking the "Add layer mask" button**  at the bottom of the Layers panel or in CS4 near the top of the Masks panel. If there's a selection active when you add a layer mask, the selected area becomes the white (revealing) area of the mask; or if you Alt/Option-click the  button, the reverse mask is produced and the selected area becomes the black (hiding) area of the mask. ("Quick Masking & Blending" on page 84 will quickly get you up to speed on using masks.)

Vector Masks

As the name implies, a **vector mask** is vector-based. It's resolution-independent so it can be resized, rotated, skewed, and otherwise transformed repeatedly without deterioration. And it creates a smooth outline when the file is output to a PostScript printer, regardless of the resolution (pixels per inch) of the file. Since it's vector-based, it has crisp edges. In Photoshop CS3 it doesn't have the capacity for softness or partial transparency in the parts of the layer it reveals, but in CS4 the new Masks panel makes it possible to vary the density of a vector mask and assign a feather to its edge.

You can **create a "reveal all" vector mask by holding down the Ctrl/⌘ key and clicking the**  at the bottom of the Layers panel (the Ctrl/⌘ key turns it into the "Add vector mask" button); or if the layer already has a layer mask, the button changes automatically, and you don't need the Ctrl/⌘ key. For a "hide all" mask, add the Alt/Option key. If a path is active when you add the mask, the mask will reveal the area inside the path, unless you use the Alt/Option key to hide it instead.

In Photoshop CS4 the new **Masks panel** gathers the mask controls in one convenient interface (as shown below). It also makes available some new features: When applied with the easy-to-use **Density** and **Feather** controls of the Masks panel, the hiding power of a layer mask and the overall softness of its edge are "live" — these changes are instruction-based rather than permanently changing the pixels of a layer mask.

PHOTO: SUSAN HELLER

Before

Density (in Photoshop CS4's Masks panel) is a new "live" control for masks. Here we wanted to make the raccoon more distinct from its environment. After using the Quick Selection tool to select the background, we added a Photo Filter Adjustment layer to warm it up; the selection automatically became a mask for the Adjustment layer. We then decided to apply some of the warming effect to the raccoon as well, so we lowered the **Density** slightly so the black part of the mask wouldn't hide the color change completely, and we added a small **Feather** to ensure that the edge of the masked raccoon would blend well with the background (our settings are shown in "The Masks panel" below).

After

Mask Density and Feather.psd

THE MASKS PANEL

Scattered throughout Photoshop are commands for creating and modifying layer masks. Photoshop CS4 has gathered several of the most useful commands into a single Masks panel and added some great new mask-related features.

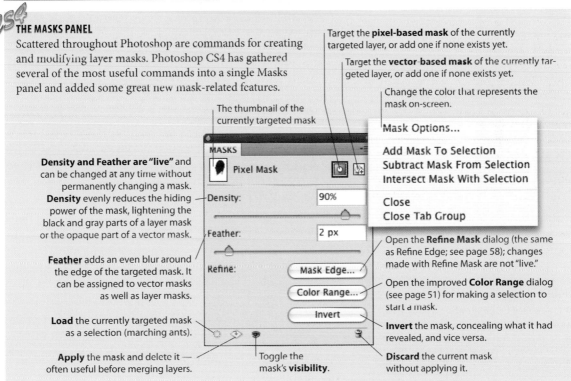

The thumbnail of the currently targeted mask

Target the **pixel-based mask** of the currently targeted layer, or add one if none exists yet.

Target the **vector-based mask** of the currently targeted layer, or add one if none exists yet.

Change the color that represents the mask on-screen.

Mask Options...

Add Mask To Selection
Subtract Mask From Selection
Intersect Mask With Selection

Close
Close Tab Group

Density and Feather are "live" and can be changed at any time without permanently changing a mask. **Density** evenly reduces the hiding power of the mask, lightening the black and gray parts of a layer mask or the opaque part of a vector mask.

Feather adds an even blur around the edge of the targeted mask. It can be assigned to vector masks as well as layer masks.

Load the currently targeted mask as a selection (marching ants).

Apply the mask and delete it — often useful before merging layers.

Toggle the mask's **visibility**.

Open the **Refine Mask** dialog (the same as Refine Edge; see page 58); changes made with Refine Mask are not "live."

Open the improved **Color Range** dialog (see page 51) for making a selection to start a mask.

Invert the mask, concealing what it had revealed, and vice versa.

Discard the current mask without applying it.

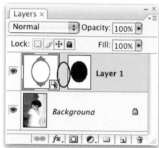

In Photoshop CS3 a layer mask can be applied to a Smart Object layer, but layer and mask can't be linked, so they can't be transformed together.

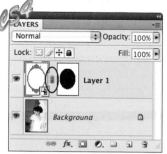

In Photoshop CS4, A Smart Object layer and its mask can be linked.

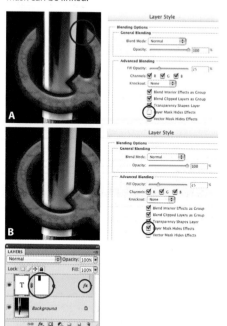

With the Layer Mask Hides Effects option turned off **A** the Bevel and Emboss effect in the Layer Style on the "Q" layer follows the edges of the mask, which interferes with the illusion of the brush handle passing through the "Q." With the Layer Mask Hides Effects option turned on **B**, the illusion is preserved.

Masks on Smart Objects

In both Photoshop CS3 and CS4, Smart Objects can have layer masks and vector masks, just like any standard layer. But the masks work a little differently in the two versions:

In CS3 a mask you apply to a Smart Object is not linked to the image — in fact, it *can't* be linked. So if you resize or rotate the Smart Object, the mask isn't transformed with it. In CS4 the mask *is* linked by default, and like masks on other layers it can be unlinked by clicking the 🔗 next to it in the Layers panel. The ability to link the mask makes a layer mask more useful in CS4, but here's something to keep in mind: A Smart Object can be repeatedly transformed without deterioration, because its "Smart Object-hood" protects it. But the Smart Object's layer mask *isn't* protected. So if you repeatedly transform the mask along with the Smart Object, as is possible in CS4, the mask edge may be degraded, and consequently the mask may no longer work as well as it did originally.

A WORKAROUND FOR SMART OBJECT MASKS IN PHOTOSHOP CS3

In Photoshop CS3, where a Smart Object and its mask can't be linked, you can still **apply the same transformation to a Smart Object and its layer mask**: Target the Smart Object by clicking its thumbnail in the Layers panel; choose Edit > Transform and carry out the transformation you want. Then click the layer mask (or vector mask) thumbnail by clicking its thumbnail in the Layers panel; choose **Edit > Transform > Again**. The danger in applying the same transformations to a Smart Object and its mask is that the mask can be degraded by the repeated transformations, so it may no longer "fit" as well as it did originally.

Masks & Layer Styles

By default, a mask on a layer that has a Style applied to it will help define the shape the Style conforms to. As illustrated at the left, edges created by the mask are treated with any edge effects that are part of the Style. For instance, if the Style includes a Bevel and Emboss effect, the edges created by the mask will also be beveled. If you want to avoid this, change your Blending Options settings for the "styled" layer: Open the Blending Options section of the Layer Style dialog (Ctrl/⌘-click on the image thumbnail for the layer, or choose Layer > Layer Style > Blending Options). Then, in the Advanced Blending section, click the appropriate checkbox to exempt the mask edges from the Style: For a layer mask, turn on "Layer Mask Hides Effects"; for a vector mask, turn on "Vector Mask Hides Effects."

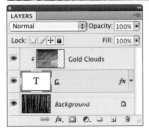

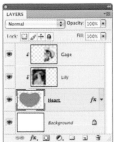

A clipping group provides a way to mask a photo or painting inside live type, leaving open the option of changing the font or editing the text.

With a clipping group you can mask more than one image in a single shape. And you can apply a Layer Style to the clipping element, such as the dark Inner Glow used here or the Drop Shadow and Pattern Overlay applied to the type at the top of the page,. The Style applies to the enclosed images.

Clipping Groups

Another nondestructive kind of "masking," a **clipping group**, is a series of layers, the bottom layer of which acts as a mask. The outline of the bottom layer — including image pixels and masks — "clips" all the other layers in the group so only the parts that fall within the outline can contribute to the image.

You can make a clipping group by Alt/Option-clicking on the borderline between the names of two layers in the Layers panel.

Sometimes, despite your best efforts, you may find yourself with an isolated element with a tinge of the original background visible around the edge. You may be able to get rid of this unwanted "fringe" quickly and simply with a command from the **Layer > Matting** submenu. The Matting commands include **Remove White Matte** (for replacing white with transparency in the edge pixels of an element selected from a white background), **Remove Black Matte** (for replacing black with transparency in the edge pixels of an element selected from a black background), and **Defringe** (for dealing with obvious "edging" in an element selected from a multicolor background; an example is shown at the left below). Note that these commands work only *after* the selected material has been separated from its surrounding pixels and put on a transparent layer of its own.

If you notice a narrow "fringe" of background pixels surrounding a silhouetted subject when you layer it over a new background, try Layer > Matting > Defringe. The Defringe command pushes color from the inside of the selection outward into the edge pixels, thus eliminating the fringe.

Another option is to **trim away the fringe**. Make a selection based on the layer's content outline (also called its *transparency mask*) by Ctrl/⌘-clicking the layer's thumbnail in the Layers panel. Next choose the Select > Modify > Contract command to shrink the selection. Then type Ctrl/⌘-Shift-I to invert the selection and press the Delete key to remove the fringe; or you can **trim nondestructively** by Ctrl/⌘-clicking the layer thumbnail as described, shrinking and inverting, and then clicking the "Add a layer mask" button ▣ at the bottom of the panel. "Quick Integration" on page 624 has other pointers for fitting a selected and silhouetted subject into a new background.

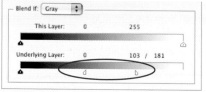

Using the "Blend If" sliders can be an important step in developing a composite. Here the pixels of the can layer are hidden where they overlap the light pixels in the flame image. Each slider can be split (by Alt/Option-dragging) to make a smooth transition. Here splitting the white slider smooths the blend of the flames and the can. The Blending Options process for compositing is described in "'Blend If' Tonality" on page 85 and other examples in "Quick Masking & Blending."

MAKING A SELECTION FROM "THIS LAYER"

To turn what you've done with the **This Layer** slider into a selection, first add a new layer (Ctrl/⌘-Shift-N). Then turn off visibility for all layers except the one you've been using as This Layer (you can do this by Alt/Option-clicking its 👁 icon in the Layers panel). Now turn the new layer into a copy of This Layer (Ctrl-Shift-Alt-E in Windows; ⌘-Shift-Option-E on the Mac). Finally, Ctrl/⌘-clicking the thumbnail for the new layer will load a selection based on the visible content of the new layer.

The "This Layer" slider was used to drop out the dark reds and blues in Layer 0, and the layer was copied. The copy shows transparency where the colors were dropped out.

The lower layer becomes the **clipping mask**, and its name is now underlined in the panel. The other layer is clipped; its thumbnails are indented, and a down-pointing arrow points to the clipping layer below. To add more clipped layers to the group, you can just work your way up the Layers panel, Alt/Option-clicking more borderlines. (To be members of a clipping group, layers have to be together in the stack. You can't add one, skip one, add the next, and so on.)

A clipping group can also be set up (or added to) when a layer is first added to the stack. To do this, Alt/Option-click the "Create a new layer" button 🔲 at the bottom of the Layers panel; in the New Layer dialog box, check the **Use Previous Layer to Create Clipping Mask** box.

BLENDING

In the Blending Options section of the Layer Style dialog box, you'll find the "Blend If" sliders (shown at the left). With these sliders you can control how the pixels of the targeted layer (called "This Layer") and the image underneath will combine. To get to the Blend If sliders, target a layer by clicking its thumbnail in the Layers panel, and click the "Add a layer style" button *fx* at the bottom of the panel.

The sliders of the **"This Layer"** bar determine what range of colors in the targeted layer will be allowed to contribute to the composite image. So, for instance, if you want only the dark colors of the targeted layer to contribute, move the white slider for "This Layer" inward so the light colors are outside the range. Holding down the Alt/Option key as you drag a slider will allow you to split the slider. This lets you smooth the transition by defining a range of colors that are only partially visible.

The sliders of the **"Underlying Layer"** bar define what range of colors in the underlying image are available to be affected by the active layer. So, for instance, if you wanted only the medium-to-dark pixels to be affected, you would move the white "Underlying Layer" slider inward so the lightest tones are outside the range and thus can't be affected.

By default, the Blend If sliders use the overall tonal range (dark to light). But you can also limit them to a single color channel — for instance, Red, Green, or Blue in an RGB image — by choosing something other than Gray in the Blend If: pop-out menu.

Turning on **Show Transform Controls** in the Move tool's ▶⊹ Options bar automatically brings up the Transform frame on the targeted layer whenever the Move tool is chosen in the Tools panel, without choosing from the Edit menu or typing Ctrl/⌘-T.

TRANSFORMING & WARPING

To scale, rotate, skew, distort, create perspective, warp, or flip a selected element, you can choose **Edit > Transform** or **Free Transform** from the Edit menu to open the Transform frame. Another way is to use the **Ctrl/⌘-T** keyboard shortcut, or use the **Show Transform Controls** checkbox in the Move tool's

TRANSFORM OPTIONS

Choosing the Transform or Free Transform command brings up a Transform frame whose handles you can move to scale, rotate, skew, or distort the content of a layer. Instead of using the handles, you can set parameters in the Options bar.

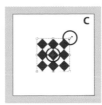

The **Transform** Options bar offers a way to enter precise position, scale, and skew factors, and angle of rotation. It also has a "Commit" button ✔ (the Return/Enter key is the shortcut) and a "Cancel" button ⊘ (the Escape key is the shortcut).

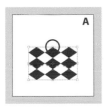

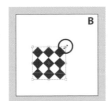

Once the Transform frame is on-screen, **dragging any handle will resize** the layer contents A. **Shift-dragging** a corner handle will keep the image in proportion as you scale it B. Adding the **Alt/Option key**, with the Shift key as shown here, or without it — scales from the center point C.

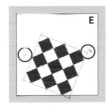

If you move the cursor outside the Transform frame, the cursor will become a **double-headed curved arrow**, and dragging will **rotate** the image D. To change the center of rotation, before you rotate, drag the center point icon to a new position E.

To **Skew, Distort** by moving a single corner, or transform in **Perspective**, first choose one of those options from the Transform menu F (right/Ctrl-clicking opens it), or use a keyboard shortcut.

With **Distort** chosen, you can move a single corner independently I, or drag a side handle to skew, scale, and flip. The shortcut for performing Skew or Distort transformations is to hold down the **Ctrl/⌘** key as you drag.

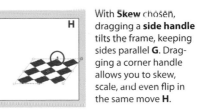

With **Skew** chosen, dragging a **side handle** tilts the frame, keeping sides parallel G. Dragging a corner handle allows you to skew, scale, and even flip in the same move H.

With **Perspective** chosen, moving one corner causes an equal but opposite move in its horizontal or vertical mate J. The keyboard shortcut for Perspective is to hold down **Ctrl-Alt-Shift** (Windows) or **⌘-Option-Shift** (Mac) and drag a corner handle.

THE WARP COMMAND

Photoshop's Transform Options bar has a button near the right end of the bar for switching between the standard Transform controls and the Warp controls.

Choosing Edit > Transform > **Warp** or clicking the toggle in the Options bar brings up the Warp mesh, with more shaping controls than the Transform frame.

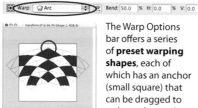

The Warp Options bar offers a series of **preset warping shapes**, each of which has an anchor (small square) that can be dragged to reshape the mesh.

Preset warping shapes can also be customized by entering values in the **Bend** and **H**orizontal and **V**ertical distortion fields.

For more control of the warping mesh, choose **Custom**. Then you can change the bend by dragging on the mesh itself, or on the direction lines that control its curves.▼

FIND OUT MORE

▼ Operating direction lines
page 450

Options bar. Once the frame is open, right-clicking/Ctrl-clicking inside the Transform frame opens a context-sensitive menu, where you can choose the kind of transformation you want to make. (The Distort and Perspective options aren't available for live type or in Photoshop CS3 for Smart Objects, though they've been added in CS4 for Smart Objects.) "Transform Options" on page 67 and "The Warp Command" at the left show how these transformations work.

Transformations can be carried out "freehand" by dragging on the handles of the Transform box or with numeric precision by typing numbers into the appropriate fields in the Options bar. While the Transform frame is open, you can work back and forth between the different transformations, previewing the changes until you get exactly what you want. Finally, press the Enter key (or double-click inside the frame) to complete the transforming "session." Only when the session ends does Photoshop actually "redraw" the image, making a single change that combines all the transformations you've made since opening the Transform frame.

After you've completed a Transform session, you can repeat the transformation on the same element by using the Edit > Transform > Again command or pressing Ctrl/⌘-Shift-T. Or make a duplicate and transform it by also holding down the Alt/Option key in addition when you transform again.

New in Photoshop CS4 is the **Edit > Content-Aware Scale** command. When you drag a handle of the Transform frame to scale the image, Photoshop does its best to scale the unimportant parts (large expanses of similar color and texture), leaving the important parts untouched. Like magic, Content-Aware Scale maintains the texture of the parts it scales, rather than obviously stretching or compressing the texture. The Options bar offers a way for you to help Photoshop with its analysis. There's a button for turning on or off the "protect skin tones" function, especially useful for changing the aspect ratio of a portrait, for example, by stretching or shrinking the background without distorting the subject. In addition, the Protect menu lets you provide input into what Photoshop protects from scaling. You can add an alpha channel, paint it with white in the areas you want to protect from scaling, save the alpha channel, and choose it from the Protect menu. You'll find more about Content-Aware Scale on page 243 in Chapter 5, "Enhancing Photos."

UNDERSTANDING RESAMPLING

As explained in Chapter 1 (page 17), each time you transform a pixel-based element, you risk degrading the image a bit, making details a little softer or less distinct. This happens because of *resampling*: Additional pixels are "filled in" if the transformation made the element bigger. Or the colors of adjacent pixels are averaged and the new colors assigned to fewer pixels if the element got smaller. When an element is rotated, the tilted pixels have to be remapped to the square pixel grid. So rather than making a series of separate transformations, each time pressing the Enter key and then starting another one, do all the transforming operations you can in a single session, so the image is redrawn only once. For vector elements such as Shapes and type and for Smart Objects, transforming causes no degradation (as

THE IMAGE SIZE DIALOG BOX

Choosing Image > Image Size opens the Image Size dialog box, where you can see and change the dimensions and resolution of the file. ▼

In the **Pixel Dimensions** section, you can see or change the Width and Height of the document in pixels or as a percent of the size you started with. You can also see the size of the flattened file these dimensions will produce. (Not included in these numbers are any parts of layers that extend beyond the document bounds, or any alpha channels.)

In the **Resolution** field you can set the number of pixels per inch (or centimeter) that you need for output.

When you resize a file, turn on the **Scale Styles** option if you want to scale effects such as drop shadows, bevels, and glows along with the file. Leaving Scale Styles unchecked will make these effects look relatively bigger or smaller after the file is scaled down or up.

When **Constrain Proportions** is checked, changing **Width** or **Height** automatically changes the other dimension, to keep the original proportions.

If **Resample Image** is checked, changing Width, Height, or Resolution will change the file's Pixel Dimensions, causing resampling. **Uncheck the Resample Image box** if you want to change Width, Height, or Resolution but you don't want to change the number of pixels in the file.

If the **Resample Image** box is checked, you can choose from a menu of resampling options. **Bicubic Smoother** was designed for resampling up (making the file larger), and **Bicubic Sharper** was designed for resampling down (making the file smaller).

Clicking the **"Auto"** button opens the **Auto Resolution** dialog box, where you can enter the line screen to be used for printing and choose Good or Best to prepare the image for print. The Good option produces a smaller file but the Best option may produce a better print.

The link icon is a reminder that **Constrain Proportions** is turned on.

Auto Resolution

Screen: 133   lines/inch   OK

Quality   Cancel

○ Draft   ● Good   ○ Best

Image Size

Pixel Dimensions: 2.29M

Width: 1000   pixels   OK

Height: 800   pixels   Cancel

Document Size: Auto...

Width: 4.444   inches

Height: 3.556   inches

Resolution: 225   pixels/inch

☑ Sca   Nearest Neighbor (preserve hard edges)
☑ Co   Bilinear
☑ Re   Bicubic (best for smooth gradients)
    Bicubic Smoother (best for enlargement)
  ✓ Bicubic Sharper (best for reduction)

FIND OUT MORE

▼ Pixel dimensions or Resolution required for output   **page 110**

Before

After

MARK WAINER

The new Content-Aware Scale command isn't just for changing the aspect ratio of photos. After finishing his painterly treatment of Hamaroy lighthouse, Mark Wainer decided he wanted to change the composition. Rather than recomposing the original photo and repainting, he used Content-Aware Scale; see page 419 for more about the process.

explained on page 18), but it's still more efficient to do all the transformations that you can in the same session.

SIZING UP OR SIZING DOWN

Regardless of how well you plan, there are likely to be times when you need to make an entire file smaller (*resample down*) or make it bigger (*resample up*). You might resample down because you have more information than you need for printing and you want to reduce the bulk of the file. You might resample up if the original you scanned isn't available to be scanned again at the resolution you need for the screen frequency or display size you want. Or your original may have been a digital photo, and there's no way to go back and reshoot the picture.

To resample, you can use the **Image Size dialog box** as shown on page 69. Make sure that **Constrain Proportions** is checked (so the image stays in proportion as it's resized). The **Resample Image** box should also be checked.

- From the Resample Image menu, **choose Bicubic Smoother for enlarging** (resampling up). The **Bicubic Sharper** option is designed **for reducing the size** (sampling down).

- **To change the size at which the image will print,** in the Document Size section, enter a new value in the Height or Width field. The other dimension will change automatically, the Resolution will stay the same, and so the file size will change.

- **To keep the print dimensions the same but change the resolution,** in the Document Size section, set Height and Width units to anything but pixels. Then enter a new value in the Resolution field. The size at which the image will print will stay the same but file size will change with the change in resolution.

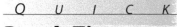
Brush Tip Controls

In Photoshop, painting isn't the only operation that depends on brushes. Many of Photoshop's other hand-operated tools — for toning, cloning, or retouching, for instance — are brush-tip-based. Each of these tools has its own specialized settings related to the tasks it performs. But whatever you're doing with a brush-tip-based tool, you'll want to be able to quickly adjust two of its properties — the stroke width, or size (small, to get into nooks and crannies, or large, to cover a lot of territory in a hurry) and the hardness (for crisp, hard-edged strokes or softer edges that blend the stroke into the surroundings). On this page are some quick options for simply changing brush size and hardness.

Context-Sensitive Panels

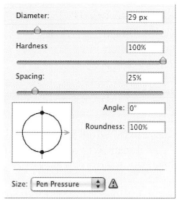

RIGHT-CLICK/CTRL-CLICK wherever your cursor is in the document window to open a context-sensitive panel with size controls, along with other brush-tip-related options appropriate for the tool you're using, Shown here is the context-sensitive panel for the Healing Brush or Spot Healing Brush .

Bracket Keys

To SIMPLY CHANGE SIZE or hardness, release the mouse button to stop painting, then use the bracket keys — [**to reduce size,**] **to enlarge,** in preset steps — then release the key and paint again with the newly sized brush tip. Use the **Shift key** with [or] to decrease or increase the **hardness** of the tip.

Interactive Control

In PHOTOSHOP CS4 with OpenGL-Drawing enabled (in the Performance section of the Preferences dialog), you can change **size** simply by releasing the mouse button to stop painting, then holding down the right mouse button and Alt key (Windows) or the Ctrl and Option keys (Mac) and dragging **left to scale down** the brush tip or **right to scale up**, smoothly and continuously; then release the keys and drag to continue to paint.

To control **hardness** instead of size, add the Shift key in Windows (**right-Alt-Shift**) or the ⌘ key on the Mac (**Ctrl-Option ⌘**); drag **left to soften**, **right to harden**.

When you resize or change hardness interactively in this way, the cursor also shows the softness of the edge as you make the change.

SETTING PREFERENCES FOR BRUSH TIP CURSORS

The appearance of the cursor for brush-based tools is set by opening the Preferences dialog (Ctrl/⌘-K), choosing Cursors, and making choices in the Painting Cursors section (shown below). A practical strategy is to choose the Normal Brush Tip or Full Size Brush Tip with the Show Crosshair in Brush Tip option turned on, and use the **Caps Lock** key to toggle to the Precise cursor if you want it.

The cursor is the **tool's icon** from the Tools panel.

The cursor -¦- is **crosshairs alone**, marking the center of the brush footprint — precise but hard to see as you reposition the cursor. If you choose Precise, the Caps Lock key toggles to the Normal Brush Tip with small crosshairs marking the center.

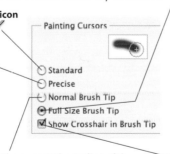

The cursor is the **outline of the brush footprint** — that is, the shape a single dab will make. For tools that can produce soft-edged strokes, the cursor shows only the areas where the dab is **50% opaque or more.**

The brush footprint shows the outline of the entire dab, including areas of every opacity, from 0% to 100%. So **for soft-edged brush tips, this cursor is bigger** than the Normal Brush Tip cursor.

Small crosshairs are added at the center of the Normal or Full Size Brush Tip.

EXERCISING

Smart Filters

From sharpening to artistic effects, the "subprograms" chosen from Photoshop's Filter menu play an important role in enhancing images. Before Smart Filters, new in Photoshop CS3, to protect the original image when we applied a filter, we duplicated the image layer and ran the filter on the copy. To blend the filter's effect with the original, we adjusted the Opacity or blend mode of the filtered layer. To keep track of the filter settings we had used, we gave the layers complex names, like Watercolor-Plastic Wrap-FadeSoftLight50. And if we needed to change the filter settings, we started over, making and filtering a new copy.

Now with Smart Filter technology we can run filters without permanently changing any pixels in the process. The filter settings stay "live," so we can come back later and see exactly what settings we used, and we can change them. Also, the Smart Filter acts like a duplicate layer — we can adjust its blend mode or Opacity to change how the filter effect interacts with the original.

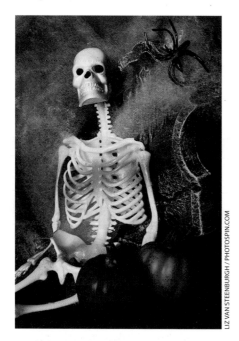

LIZ VAN STEENBURGH / PHOTOSPIN.COM

YOU'LL FIND THE FILES

in (wow) > Wow Project Files > Chapter 2 > Exercising Smart Filters:
- Halloween-Before.psd
- Halloween-After.psd

FIND OUT MORE
▼ Smart Objects
page 75

1 Applying a Filter

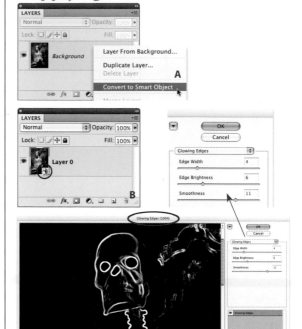

OPEN **HALLOWEEN-BEFORE.PSD** (shown at the left) In order to apply a Smart Filter, you have to convert the layer (or a series of layers) to a Smart Object. ▼ The quickest way is to target the layer(s) and right-click/Ctrl-click to bring up the context-sensitive menu, then choose Convert to Smart Object **A**. You could instead choose Filter > Convert for Smart Filters or choose Convert to Smart Object from the Layer > Smart Objects menu or the Layers panel's menu ▼≡. Whichever way you choose, the result is exactly the same. Smart Object status protects the original. In the Layers panel the thumbnail will display the Smart Object icon **B**.

Now apply the Smart Filter: Choose Filter > Stylize > Glowing Edges, choosing settings that keep the glow on the skeleton, not the background **C**, and click "OK."

TWO "SMART ADJUSTMENTS"

Shadows/Highlights and Variations (both from the Image > Adjustments menu) can't be applied as Adjustment layers, but they *can* be applied as Smart Filters. Like other Smart Filters, they will be fully editable at any time.

2 Changing the Blend

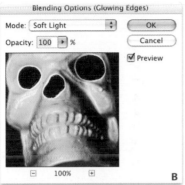

We wanted to make the skeleton visible again, along with the glow. To do that, right-click/Ctrl-click on the filter's entry in the Layers panel and choose **Edit Smart Filter Blending Options A**. When the Blending Options dialog opens, experiment with other Blend modes (and Opacity settings if you like, though we didn't); we liked the edge glow that Soft Light produced **B**.

3 Editing the Filter Settings

We wanted a stronger glow now that the skeleton was visible again. Right-click/Ctrl-click the "Glowing Edges" entry in the Layers panel and choose **Edit Smart Filter** to reopen the filter dialog. We increased the Edge Brightness to make the glow stronger. Notice that you can't see a preview of Glowing Edges (and the same is true of many other filters) in the main document window while you're working in the dialog box. This makes it especially nice to be able to keep the filter live and adjustable as a Smart Filter.

4 Adding Other Filters

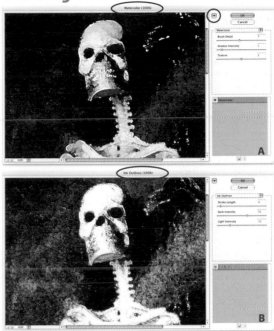

A Smart Object isn't limited to having just one Smart Filter. You can add others. We added Filter > Artistic > Watercolor. The preview in the Watercolor dialog showed the effect of applying the Watercolor filter to the image in its current condition, with Glowing Edges in Soft Light mode **A**. Next we applied Filter > Brush Strokes > Ink Outlines, and the preview showed the effect of Ink Outlines on the image with Glowing Edges and Watercolor **B**. Each new filter appears "above" the previous ones in the Layers panel **C**.

Now you can edit the individual filters' settings and change their blend modes. You can also toggle off or on the visibility for any filter (use the 👁).

STACKING ORDER AND SMART FILTER PREVIEWS

When you reopen the filter dialog or Blending Options dialog for a Smart Filter, the effects of any filters "below" it in the stack will show up in the filter preview, but the effects of any filters "above" it are "disabled" and don't show up. After you close the dialog, their effects are recalculated and will show up again.

5 Changing Filter Order

A

B

BECAUSE FILTER RESULTS ARE CALCULATED in their stacking order, just like regular layers, you can change the results of combined filters by changing their order in the stack. This isn't something you're likely to want to do when you're correcting images with Shadows/Highlights or Unsharp Mask, for instance, but for artistic effects it's nice to have the freedom to experiment. Starting with the image from step 4 **A**, copy the Smart Object layer (Ctrl/⌘-J) to experiment with a different arrangement (as we did), or even with different filters. (Making a copy will preserve the current filtered image while you experiment further.) We dragged the Glowing Edges filter from the bottom of the stack to the top and the whole image brightened as if lit by a full moon **B**.

6 Masking

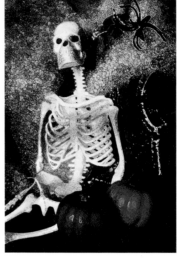

THE EFFECTS OF THE FILTERS can often be just right in some areas of the image, but not everywhere. To tone down the skeleton, which was losing detail now that Glowing Edges was on top of the stack, we used the built-in Smart Filter mask. You get only one mask for all the Smart Filters on a Smart Object, so masking the filter results for Glowing Edges also masks Ink Outlines and Watercolor. To prevent taking away too much of the filters' effects, use the Brush tool 🖌 with a very soft brush tip and low Opacity chosen in the Options bar; paint over the skeleton. ▼ (In CS4, you can paint at 100% Opacity; then preview the effect as you reduce the mask's Density in the Masks panel.) ▼

Once you're finished, if you want to see the original image (before) and then the filtered results, you can toggle the visibility icon next to the mask to turn on or off all the filter effects at once.

FIND OUT MORE
▼ Brush tool 🖌 basics **page 71**
▼ Masks panel **page 63**

ENABLING ADDITIONAL FILTERS

Some filters, such as Liquify and many non-Adobe filters, aren't set up to run as Smart Filters. But there's a script called **EnableAllFiltersForSmartFilters.jsx** that will allow them to be applied as Smart Filters. Copy it from Application > Scripting > Sample Scripts into Photoshop's Presets > Scripts folder, restart Photoshop and run it by choosing File > Scripts. It stays active from then on. Note that not all filters can retain "live" settings, even when run as Smart Filters.

EXERCISING

Smart Objects

A **Smart Object** is like a file within a file. Once you make a Smart Object (or import one from Adobe Illustrator or Camera Raw), you can carry it along as a "package" in your larger file, treating it as a single layer — you can scale, distort, warp, or filter the entire "package," copy it, apply a Layer Style to it, or integrate it into the file with masks, Adjustment layers, clipping groups, and so on.

You can also open the package — by double-clicking its thumbnail in the Layers panel. This opens the Smart Object as a separate file (launching Illustrator or Camera Raw if necessary) so you can get back inside the package and edit its contents as you would any Photoshop (or Illustrator or Camera Raw) file. When you save the edited file, the changes are automatically carried through to the larger (parent) file.

Here are some of the reasons Smart Objects are so useful:

- A Smart Object **protects pixel-based contents** from deteriorating (as explained on page 18) if you repeatedly scale, rotate, distort, or filter them. For instance, you can copy a Smart Object, scale and rotate the copy, make another copy from that one and scale and rotate some more, and so on, with no more deterioration than a single scale-and-rotate operation would cause.

- If your larger file includes several copies (or *instances*) of a Smart Object, **you can edit all the instances of a Smart Object at the same time**, simply by opening, editing, and saving just one of them.

- With a Smart Object and instances, **file size is smaller** than with standard layer copies, since the Smart Objects *refer to* the original rather than actually duplicating it in the file.

- You can **"spin off" one or more instances** into a new Smart Object, which breaks the editing link. You can then change just the instances in the *new* Smart Object, without changing the other instances, or vice versa.

YOU CAN FIND THE FILES

in **wow** > Wow Project Files > Chapter 2 > Exercising Smart Objects:

- Exercising SO-Before.psd (to start)
- Dancers.psd (for step 5)
- Exercising SO-After.psd (to compare)

THIS SECTION INTRODUCES the mechanics of working with Smart Objects by using them to build and then modify a pattern tile. Whether or not you're an avid user of patterns, the exercise will show you the potential of Smart Objects and provide some important tips about how to create and work with them.

First you'll make and arrange several copies of a Smart Object to create the pattern used on the wall in the illustration above. Then you'll convert the pattern tile to a new pattern (used here for the dress): You'll edit the Smart Object to substitute a dancing couple for the leaping lady and then create a new Smart Object to substitute "JOY" for some of the copies of the dancing couple. At the end of the process, you'll have a working knowledge of Smart Objects, as well as a file you can use to generate your own patterns if you like.

1 Setting up the File

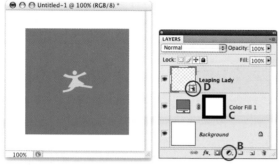

To start the pattern tile, we made a new file (File > New) 300 pixels square **A**, which was slightly larger than the tile we wanted to design. To make the tile base, we Shift-dragged diagonally with the Rectangular Marquee tool ⬚ to make a square selection, leaving space at the edges of the document so our pattern elements could extend outside the tile. With the selection active, we clicked the "Create new fill or adjustment layer" button ◑ at the bottom of the Layers panel **B** and added a Solid Color Fill layer **C** by choosing Solid Color from the menu, and picking a color.

In a separate layer we added the graphic element for the pattern — a rasterized version of a character from the Pedestria font (from MVBFonts.com). This completed the **Exercising SO-Before.psd** file; open it to follow along, or create your own similarly structured file.

Turn your pattern element layer into a Smart Object by holding down the right mouse button/Ctrl key, clicking on the layer's name in the Layers panel, and choosing **Convert to Smart Object** from the context-sensitive menu. In the Layers panel, a little notch in the thumbnail for the layer will show that the layer is now a Smart Object **D**. Creating this "file within a file" will protect the graphic from deteriorating as we transform copies of it (in step 3). The Smart Object also sets the stage for changing the entire pattern by changing a single layer (in steps 5 and 6).

2 Making & Copying a Smart Object

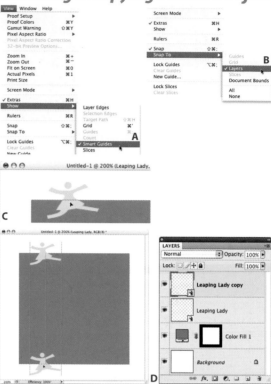

Another "smart" technology, **Smart Guides**, will make it easy to align graphics "on the fly" so they cross the edges of the tile seamlessly, to help hide our pattern's "repeat." Choose View > Show, and turn on Smart Guides **A**; also in the View menu, turn on Snap, then choose **Snap To** and turn on **Layers B**.

Choose the Move tool ▸⊕ and drag your pattern element so it overlaps the top edge of the tile. When the element is centered on the edge, you'll see a Smart Guide running through the center of it **C**.

The next step is to arrange a perfectly paired element on the opposite edge of the tile, so any overhang on the top is balanced on the bottom. This will make a seamless transition from tile to tile when you define the pattern in step 4. Duplicate the Smart Object layer (type Ctrl/⌘-J) to make a copy; this copy, or instance, is tied to the original so that if *either* Smart Object is opened, edited, and saved, *both* Smart Object instances will be updated with the changes. With the Move tool ▸⊕, hold down the Shift key, and in the document window drag the copy down to the bottom edge of the tile **D**. The Shift key will keep the copy aligned with the original, and a "snap" will let you know when the copy is centered on the edge.

3 Making More "Instances"

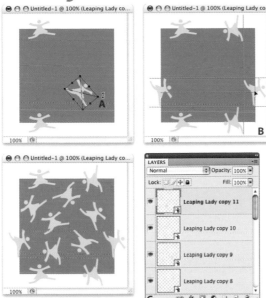

TO MAKE OTHER EDGE-CROSSING PAIRS, first make another instance of the Smart Object: With either Smart Object layer targeted, type Ctrl/⌘-J again. For variety, tilt the new element (type Ctrl/⌘-T, move the cursor outside the Transform box until it turns into a curved, double-headed arrow, and drag to rotate; then press the Enter key) **A**. With the Move tool ▸⊕, drag this transformed element to an edge; again rely on the Smart Guides and the "snap" to center the element on the edge. Make the second half of the pair (Ctrl/⌘-J) and Shift-drag until it's centered on the opposite edge.

(Once an edge pair is aligned, you can move the pair around, as long as you move both elements together: Click on the thumbnail for one element in the Layers panel, then Ctrl/⌘-click the other's thumbnail and use the Move tool ▸⊕ in the document window to drag them into position.)

Make any additional edge elements you want **B**. Then go back to the View menu and turn off Smart Guides and Snap To > Layer, so they don't interfere as you fill in the rest of the tile. Duplicate the current Smart Object again (Ctrl/⌘-J), and drag this copy to a position fully inside the tile. Rotate the element. Then repeat the process (duplicate, drag, and transform) until you have as many elements as you want on your tile **C**. Because they were produced as copies of the original Smart Object layer, all the Smart Object instances are tied — editing any one will change all of them.

4 Defining a Pattern

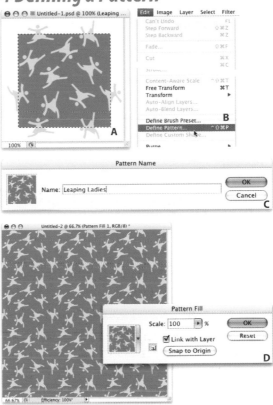

WITH YOUR PATTERN ELEMENTS ARRANGED on the tile, define your first pattern: Make a selection **A** by Ctrl/⌘-clicking on the layer mask thumbnail for the Fill layer in the Layers panel. Then choose Edit > Define Pattern **B**, name the pattern, and click "OK" **C**.

To try out your new pattern, make a new file (File > New) more than twice the dimensions of the tile. Add a Pattern Fill layer by clicking the "Create new fill or adjustment layer" button ⊘, and choosing Pattern. In the Pattern Fill dialog, choose your new pattern **D** (it will be the last swatch in the pop-out Pattern picker); finally, click "OK."

Examine the pattern fill in your new file. If you see any misalignment in the pattern (where two halves of one element don't match up exactly) or if you want to change the spacing of the elements, go back to the tile-development file and adjust alignment of the appropriate elements. You can also move any edge pairs or single internal elements to improve spacing in the pattern if you need to. Then select the pattern square again (by Ctrl/⌘-clicking its mask thumbnail) and choose Edit > Define Pattern to make a new version.

5 Editing a Smart Object

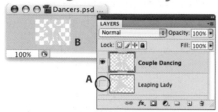

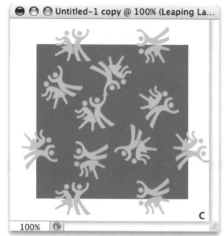

Now the *real fun begins.* With Smart Objects the possibilities for variations on the pattern tile are endless. Because we built the pattern using copies of a Smart Object, we can simply change one element to change them all. Double-click any of the Smart Object thumbnails in the Layers panel (a shortcut for Layer > Smart Objects > Edit Contents). When the file-within-a-file opens, change the graphics by turning off visibility for the existing graphics layer (click its 👁 in the Layers panel **A**) and adding new graphics or type on a new layer. *Note: Make your replacement element no taller and no wider than the original element; scale it proportionately if necessary*▼ (otherwise it will be cropped in your pattern tile; see "Understanding the Package" on page 79). To follow along with this example, open the **Dancers.psd** file (another rasterized character from the Pedestria font) and use the Move tool ▸ to drag and position it **B**.

Save the Smart Object file (Ctrl/⌘-S). Then click in the window of your tile-development file to make it the active file; you'll see that the new character is substituted everywhere the Smart Object occurs, complete with the previously applied rotations **C**.

FIND OUT MORE

▼ Transforming
page 67

6 Creating a New Smart Object

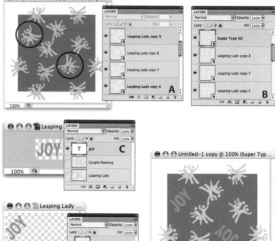

It's also possible to break the updating ties between instances of a Smart Object, so that changing one of them *doesn't* change all the others. This is done by creating a new Smart Object. In the Layers panel for your tile-development file, target the elements you want to change by clicking on the thumbnail for one of them and Ctrl/⌘-clicking the other thumbnails. (If you choose an element that crosses an edge, select its paired element also.) We targeted two internal elements **A**.

Then choose Layer > Smart Objects > **Convert to Smart Object, or right-click/Ctrl-click on the name** of one of the targeted Smart Objects in the Layers panel to open a context-sensitive menu and choose **Convert to Smart Object.** This brand-new "super" Smart Object **B** remembers any transforming you've done to the Smart Objects it contains (in this case rotating them to different angles). But you can now change the graphics in your new Smart Object *without changing the other graphics in the file.*

In the Layers panel double-click the thumbnail for your new Smart Object. When the file opens, double-click one of its component Smart Objects, and change the graphics; we added a type layer with the word "JOY" in the Arial Black font in orange **C**. Save the file (Ctrl/⌘-S) to update your new Smart Object **D**. And finally, save the new Smart Object .psb file (Ctrl/⌘-S) to update the tile-development file **E**.

7 Applying Styles to Smart Objects

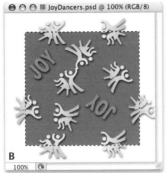
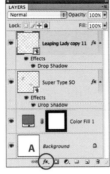

A Smart Object provides a way to apply a Layer Style to several layers at once. The **Exercising SO-After.psd** file includes the nested Smart Objects (from step 6) and the Layer Styles described next.

With the Smart Object for "JOY" targeted in the Layers panel of the tile-development file (as shown above), we added a Drop Shadow effect — we clicked the "Add a layer style" button *fx* at the bottom of the Layers panel **A**, chose Drop Shadow from the pop-out list, and adjusted the Distance (offset), Size (softness), and Angle (where the light seems to come from) to create the kind of Drop Shadow we wanted. We saved this edited Smart Object (Ctrl/⌘-S), which updated the tile-development file.

An efficient way to then add the same Drop Shadow to the dancing couples was to first turn them into another new "super" Smart Object by targeting their layers in the Layers panel and choosing Layer > Smart Objects > Convert to Smart Object (or right-clicking/Ctrl-clicking on the name of one of the targeted layers and choosing Convert to Smart Object), then copying the Drop Shadow for the "JOY" super Smart Object and pasting it onto the new Smart Object layer, so the shadows matched.▼

To recolor one of the individual dancing-couple Smart Objects nested within this new Smart Object, we double-clicked the thumbnail for one of them, then clicked the *fx* at the bottom of the Layers panel and added a Gradient Overlay effect. When we saved the edited Smart Object file, all the dancing couples in the new Smart Object file were updated. And when we saved the Smart Object file, the tile-development file was updated.

Now we selected the tile **B** and defined another pattern (as in step 4), and applied our two patterns to our illustration,▼ shown on page 75.

FIND OUT MORE

▼ Copying & pasting Layer Styles **page 82**

▼ Applying patterns **page 176**

UNDERSTANDING THE PACKAGE

We can think of a Smart Object as consisting of two distinct parts — a *package* and its *contents*.

The **contents** are the graphics, type, or photo material that you import from Camera Raw or Illustrator, or that you put into the Smart Object (by targeting layers in the Layers panel and choosing Convert to Smart Object from the Layer > Smart Objects menu or the context-sensitive menu that opens if you right-click/Ctrl-click on the layer's name).

The **package** is essentially a bounding box — the smallest rectangle that's big enough to surround the nontransparent contents of a Smart Object.

The green (nontransparent) area is the contents. The "package" is the smallest rectangle that will hold the contents.

Once a Smart Object is created, Photoshop lets you change the contents (for instance, by choosing Edit Contents from the context-sensitive menu described above). When you save the edited Smart Object file, the larger "parent" file it resides in is updated with the changes.

But the Smart Object's package, or bounding box, is permanently "locked" at the size and shape it was when you first set up the Smart Object. This means that if you edit the Smart Object in a way that makes the new contents bigger than the original contents, the new contents will automatically be cropped to fit within the original package unless you scale the new contents down (Ctrl/⌘-I and Shift-drag on a corner handle).

If you anticipate needing to edit a Smart Object you create in Photoshop, you may be able to avoid cropping or scaling by making your original Smart Object big enough so the package can accommodate any likely edits. For instance, in Photoshop you can include a rectangle on a "placeholder" layer (with its visibility turned off) to hold some space for later changes.

A Smart Object imported from Illustrator works a little differently. Instead of being cropped, the enlarged contents may be disproportionately scaled. For more about Smart Objects from Illustrator, see page 462.

EXERCISING
Layer Styles

With Photoshop's Layer Styles you can instantly turn flat type and graphics into glowing, textured, dimensional objects, or add elegant styling to photos. From simple drop shadows to translucency to colorful bumpy surfaces, the possibilities are virtually unlimited. These three pages will give you an idea of the range of what Styles can do, and inspire you to make them part of your own Photoshop toolkit if you haven't already. There's more about how Styles are constructed and how to modify them or design your own in Chapter 8 and in "'Styling' a Photo" on page 265.

Adobe Photoshop
Some text layers might need to be updated before they can be used for vector based output. Do you want to update these layers now?

Update   No

☐ Don't show again

Because the Hot Rods files include live type, we've chosen faces that most people have (Arial Black and Trebuchet). If you see a warning when you open a Hot Rods file, you may have a slightly different version of one or more of the fonts. We suggest you click "Update" and ignore any small differences in how your file looks compared to the illustrations here.

YOU'LL FIND THE FILES

in 🔘 > Wow Project Files > Chapter 2 > Exercising Styles:
- Hot Rods-Before.psd (to start)
- Hot Rods-Asphalt.psd (to compare at step 2)
- Hot Rods-Antique.psd (to compare at step 5)
- Wow Exercising Styles.asl (a Styles preset file)

1 Preparing the File

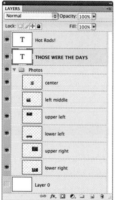

ORIGINAL PHOTOS: PHOTOSPIN.COM

To START, open the **Hot Rods-Before.psd** file and take a look at the Layers panel. Because there can be only one Layer Style per layer, for maximum flexibility each element is on a separate layer. To tidy up the Layers panel, we clicked the "Create a new group" button 🗀 at the bottom of the panel and dragged the photo layers' thumbnails into the folder thumbnail this created.

The *Background* is the only kind of layer than can't accept a Style, so we turned it into a standard layer (Layer 0) by Alt/Option-double-clicking its thumbnail. (Here Layer 0's visibility has been toggled off by clicking its 👁 icon.)

2 Applying Styles

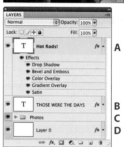

A
B
C
D

To ADD the **Wow Exercising Styles** to the Styles panel, choose Load Styles from the Styles panel's menu, opened by clicking the ▾☰ button in the upper right corner of the panel. Target each layer in turn by clicking its thumbnail in the Layers panel, and apply a Style to it by clicking a thumbnail in the Styles panel. For the Group, see "'Styling' Several Layers" on the next page.

A Wow Hot Rod (a Bevel and Emboss effect shapes the metal letters)

B Wow Red Letter* (the coloring comes from the combination of a Color Overlay and a Pattern Overlay)

C Wow Edge Glow (the Style consists of a Drop Shadow in a light color and Screen mode)

D Wow Asphalt* (the bumpy surface comes from Texture in the Bevel and Emboss effect)

It's easy to apply a Style from the Styles panel to several layers at once. In the Layers panel, you can simply click the name of the top or bottom layer of a series you want to apply the Style to, then Shift-click the name of the layer at the other extreme (bottom or top); if there are layers you don't want to style in between the ones that you do, Ctrl/⌘-click the names of the layers you want to style. With the layers targeted, click the Style you want in the Styles panel.

If you want to apply a Style to all the layers in a Group, it's even easier. In the Layers panel, click the Group's folder icon 🗀 and then click the Style in the Styles panel.

In the Styles panel, an **asterisk** in the name of a Wow Style means that a pixel-based texture or pattern is used in this Style, so care should be taken when scaling it. Such a pattern or texture may look pixelated if you scale it up too much. And it can look fuzzy when it's scaled down, especially to a percentage other than 50% or 25%.

3 Scaling a Style

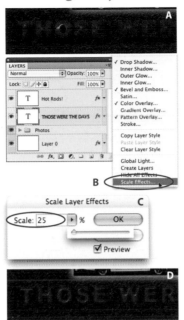

WHENEVER YOU APPLY a preset Layer Style, the first thing to do is to check the scale. If the Style was designed at a different resolution or for a larger or smaller element, it may look entirely different than it was designed to look until you resize it. This is the case with the **Wow Red Letter** Style on the lower line of type in this file **A**.

You can scale all the effects in a Style together easily, by right-clicking (Windows) or Ctrl-clicking (Mac) on the *fx* icon next to the name of the "styled" layer in the Layers panel and choosing Scale Effects from the context-sensitive menu when it opens **B**. To change the scale, use the slider, or type an entry, or hold down the Ctrl/⌘ key and "scrub" (drag left or right) over the number field. Scaling the **Wow Red Letter** Style to 25% **C** brings out the bevel and pulls the drop shadow under the type **D**.

4 Instant Style Changes

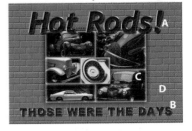

A LAYER STYLE can be changed instantly. With the layer targeted in the Layers panel, you can either assign a different Style by clicking in the Styles panel as we did here, or scale an entire Style to change its look as described at the left, or change any component effect. ▼

A Wow Brass Edge (a Bevel and Emboss effect shapes the metal letters)

B Wow Brass Edge scaled to 50% to fit the smaller type

C Wow Antique (the Style tints the photos with a brown Color Overlay)

D Wow Painted Brick* (the same pattern used as a Pattern Overlay to define the bricks is also used as the Texture in Bevel and Emboss to create the dimensional effect)

Note: For a layer styled with **Wow Painted Brick** it's possible to keep the dimensional brick surface but remove the bevel from the edges of the layer, so the wall looks like it extends beyond the edges of the image. The "Pattern, Texture & Bevel" tip on page 765 in Appendix C tells how to do this.

FIND OUT MORE

▼ Layer Style components
page 502

5 Changing Content

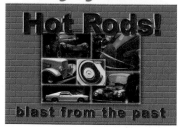

IF YOU CHANGE the content of a layer, as we did here for both the large and the small type, the Style instantly conforms to the new content.

To change the font for the entire top line of type, target its layer in the Layers panel and choose the Type tool T. Then, *without clicking in the document window*, change the Font in the Options bar to Arial Black.

To change the wording for the small type, in the Layers panel double-click the T thumbnail for the layer to select all the type, and in the Options bar choose the Arial Black font (or a similar bold face) and type the new wording.

6 Scaling a "Styled" File

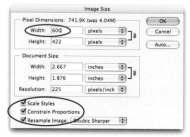

IF YOU WANT TO RESIZE a styled file, first duplicate it so you can keep the original: Choose Image > Duplicate. In the new file choose Image > Image Size. Make sure all three boxes in the lower left corner are checked, including Scale Styles. Then in the Pixel Dimensions section at the top of the box, type in a new Width or Height, whichever is the more important dimension (we used 600 pixels for Width) and click "OK."

A Style from one layer can be copied and pasted to another layer, either in the same file or a different one. This can be especially handy if you've built a Style or changed one you applied from the Styles panel but you haven't yet given the new version a name and saved it.

1 In the Layers panel, right-click/Ctrl-click on the *fx* for the layer that has the Style you want to copy. In the menu that opens, choose **Copy Layer Style**.

2 Then for the layer where you want to apply the Style, right-click/Ctrl-click to the right of the layer's name, and choose **Paste Layer Style** from the menu.

SAVING STYLES

Whenever you modify a Layer Style or create a new one, it's a good idea to name the new Style and save it as part of a set of presets so it's easy to find and use again later.

To add the Style that's on a layer to the current Styles panel and to Styles pickers elsewhere in Photoshop, first target the "styled" layer in the Layers panel. Then click the "Create new style" button at the bottom of the Styles panel, name the Style, and click "OK."

To save the Style *permanently* as part of a presets file so you can always load it and use it later, first add it to the Styles panel as described above. Then open the Styles panel's menu (click the ▾☰ button) and choose Preset Manager; the Preset Manager will open to its Styles section.

To save a set with just a few of the current Styles, Shift-click or Ctrl/⌘-click those few Styles and click the "Save Set" button. But if you want to *save* more Styles than you want to *exclude*, it's faster to Shift-click or Ctrl/⌘-click on the few you *don't* want to save and click the "Delete" button. Then select all of the remaining Styles (Ctrl/⌘-A) and click "Save Set." Name the set, choose where to save it, and click "Save."

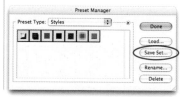

Every Layer Style "remembers" its "design resolution" — the resolution (pixels per inch, or ppi) of the file in which it was originally created. Most of the Styles on the Wow DVD-ROM were designed in files at 225 ppi for printing; the exceptions are the Wow-Button Styles, which were designed at 72 ppi for use on-screen.

Whenever you apply a Style to a file whose resolution is different from the Style's design resolution, Photoshop automatically scales the Style. This scaling can make the Style look out of proportion. And if the Style includes a texture or pattern, it can also degrade the pattern.

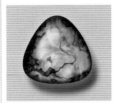  

Wow-Gibson Opal Style, (designed at 225 ppi) applied to a file whose resolution is 225 ppi

Wow-Gibson Opal Style applied to a file whose resolution is 72 ppi

To avoid unwanted automatic scaling, before you apply the Style, temporarily and nondestructively change your file to the Style's design resolution by taking these three steps:

1 To temporarily and nondestructively change a file's resolution to 225 ppi, for instance, choose Image > **Image Size** and **make sure Resample Image is turned off. Note the file's Resolution**. Then **change the Resolution** to 225 ppi to match the Style's "design resolution," and click "OK" to close the Image Size dialog box.

2 Now in the Layers panel click the thumbnail for the layer where you want to apply the Style, and click a thumbnail in the Styles panel to apply the Style.

3 Finally, you can nondestructively **change the file's resolution back to what it was**: Choose Image > Image Size, make sure Resample Image is still turned off, and type in the original resolution that you noted in step 1. **Nothing about the appearance of the Style will change.**

Before the **Wow-Gibson Opal** Style was applied to a 72 ppi file, the file's resolution was temporarily changed to 225 ppi (as in step 1 above). Afterwards the resolution was changed back (as in step 3).

If one Layer Style in your file includes an effect that you'd like to use for another layer, you can add it or substitute it. To illustrate, we'll use the **Hot Rods-Asphalt.psd** file (page 80), "borrowing" the glow from the photo layers and adding it to the "Hot Rods!" type:

1 In the Layers panel, find the layer with the effect you want to borrow. Then locate the specific effect, expanding the list of effects, if it isn't expanded already, by clicking the tiny arrow next to the *fx* for the layer.

In **Hot Rods-Asphalt.psd** the glow around the outer photos is created by the Drop Shadow effect, which uses a light color in Screen mode.

2 Alt/Option-drag the name of the effect to the layer you want to add it to. The signal that you're in the right place to drop the effect is a heavy border around the entire entry for the layer.

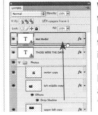 

When we added the Drop Shadow borrowed from the photo layer, it replaced the Drop Shadow that had already been applied to the "Hot Rods!" layer.

Masking & Blending

Layer masks, Blending Options, and clipping groups provide a variety of options for blending images, as shown by the examples on these four pages. Files for some of the examples are provided on the Wow DVD-ROM so you can experiment or "dissect" them.

A blend of two photos can be quite seamless and convincing if one of the images is fairly amorphous and fluid, such as a photo of clouds, fire, ocean surf, or vegetation at a distance. But masking and blending techniques are also excellent for seamlessly blending two versions of the same image (filtered and original, for example) or for targeting a tone or color change to part of an image.

Throughout the book you'll find examples of carefully made selections, turned into masks. But the examples on the next four pages show that in many situations you can do a fine job of blending *without* painstaking selection, using a quickly made mask, or the premade silhouette that comes with many stock photos, or a quick Blending Options adjustment.

FIND OUT MORE

▼ Using the Gradient tool ▦ **page 174**

▼ Using the Brush tool ✐ **page 71**

YOU'LL FIND THE FILES
in ⓦⓞⓦ > Wow Project Files > Chapter 2 > Quick Masking and Blending

Gradient Mask

To FADE the bottom of the can into the flames while keeping both originals intact, add a layer mask (by targeting the "Can" layer and clicking the "Add layer mask" button ▣). To fill the mask with a black-to-white gradient, choose the Gradient tool ▦ , and in the Options bar, click the little arrow to the right of the gradient sample **A** and choose the "Black, White" gradient (it's the third one in the default set that comes with Photoshop); make sure the Linear option is chosen **B**. Then be sure the mask is targeted (click its thumbnail in the Layers panel). Hold down the Shift key so the gradient will be drawn straight up as you drag from a point just above the bottom edge of the can to the point where you want the can to completely emerge from the flames. ▼

Painted Mask

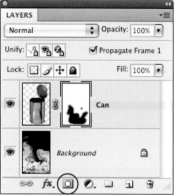

BY HAND-PAINTING a layer mask you can precisely control how the two images are blended. Target the "Can" layer and add a layer mask by clicking the ▣ button, then choose the Brush tool ✐ and in the Options bar choose Photoshop's soft 100-pixel brush tip; we left the Opacity for the Brush at 100%. (The Opacity needed will vary with the images and the kind of blend you want.) ▼

In the Layers panel make sure the layer mask is targeted (click its thumbnail) and set the Foreground color to black (typing X once or twice will do it). To help in painting the mask, reduce the Opacity for the "Can" layer to about 60% so you can see through the can to the flames you want to reveal. After painting the mask, restore the layer's Opacity to 100%.

 **Can and Flames-Before.psd**

ORIGINAL PHOTOS: PHOTOSPIN.COM

Blurred Mask

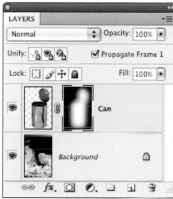

To make a layer mask that fades a silhouetted subject at its edges, in the **Can and Flames-Before.psd** file start by Ctrl/⌘-clicking on the subject's thumbnail in the Layers panel; this creates a selection based on the silhouette. Then click the "Add layer mask" button ▢ at the bottom of the panel to make a mask that reveals the selected area and hides the rest of the layer (you won't see any difference in your image at this point, since the rest of the layer is transparent and so there's nothing to hide). Now blur the mask: Choose Select > Refine Edge; in the Refine Mask dialog, set all sliders to 0 to start, and then increase the Feather as you watch the image; we used a Feather of 70 pixels. ▼ The can's reflective surface plays a part in the end result of this blend. A more general, nonreflective example is shown at the right.

FIND OUT MORE

▼ Using the Refine
Mask dialog   **page 59**

Blurred & Painted

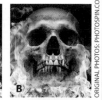

If you use the method shown at the left, the edge becomes partly transparent, but it can still be clearly seen **A**. Here are two approaches to making the edge less distinct:

- Before you leave the Refine Mask dialog, move the Contract/Expand slider to the left to make the mask smaller all around **B**.

- Paint the edges of the mask with black (as on page 84) **C, D**; we used the Brush ✎ with a soft 100-pixel tip and Opacity set to 50%.

🅦 **Skull and Flames.psd**

"Blend If" Tonality

Starting with **Can and Flames-Before.psd**, double-click the thumbnail for the "Can" layer in the Layers panel to open the Blending Options section of the Layer Style dialog box **A**. In the "Blend If" area, adjust the sliders (as described next) to blend the layers based on their tonality. ▼

Here we set up the "Blend If" sliders **B** so the "Can" layer would *not* cover up the light colors in the *Background*. Any colors lighter than the tone set by the white slider for "Underlying Layer" will show through from the *Background*. Separating the two sliders (by holding down the Alt/Option key as you drag) makes the tones between the two brightness values show through partially for a smooth blend. Any tones darker than that set by the left half will be totally hidden by the layer above.

Notice that the Layers panel shows no evidence of any work you do in the "Blend If" section.

FIND OUT MORE

▼ Using the "Blend
If" sliders   **page 66**

"Blend If" & Mask

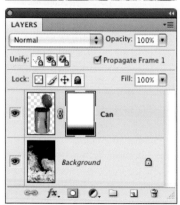

ADJUSTING THE "BLEND IF" sliders (as in "'Blend If' Tonality" on page 85) can be combined with a layer mask (such as the one from "Gradient Mask" on page 84). Notice that the Layers panel looks the same as the one in "Gradient Mask," since "Blend If" changes don't show up in the panel.

Mode & Mask

ORIGINAL PHOTO: PHOTOSPIN.COM

WHEN THESE TWO IMAGES are layered, putting the "Lightning" layer in Screen mode removes the black, since black has no effect in Screen mode.▼ Reducing the layer's Opacity will tone down the lightning a bit, and a painted layer mask hides the otherwise obvious edges of the "Lightning" layer; to paint the mask, we applied black paint using the Brush 🖌 with a soft 100-pixel brush tip at 100% Opacity with the Airbrush option turned on in the Options bar.

FIND OUT MORE

▼ Using blend modes **page 181**

▼ Using the "Blend If" sliders **page 66**

Mode, Mask & "Blend If"

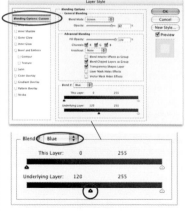

ORIGINAL PHOTO: JOHN CALIHAN / PHOTOSPIN.COM

TO PUT THE LIGHTNING at the top of the rocks, or behind them, you can use the "Blend If" sliders for the Blue channel.▼ Open the Blending Options section of the Layer Style dialog box by double-clicking at the right side of the layer's entry in the Layers panel. Then choose Blue (instead of the default Gray) from the "Blend If" menu. Dragging to the right on the black point for the "Underlying Layer" slider makes the lightning disappear from areas that contain almost no blue, such as the reddish-brown rock (with Blend If: Blue chosen, the black end of the bar represents colors with no blue component). Again, working with the "Blend If" sliders makes no change to the Layers panel.

 Lightning Landscape.psd

Masking a Filter

ORIGINAL PHOTO: PHOTOSPIN.COM

To PROTECT part of an image from a change, first turn the layer into a Smart Object (one way is to choose Filter > Convert for Smart Filters). Then apply the change (we used the Radial Blur filter in Zoom mode, with the zoom centered on the biker's head). In the Layers panel click the thumbnail for the Smart Filter mask to target it. For this example, choose the Gradient tool ▭ and choose the Radial style in the Options bar. Use the "Black, White" gradient, dragging outward from the center of the area you want to protect. To show other parts of the original (sharper) image, such as the sign and the biker's hands, paint the mask with black (as in "Painted Mask," page 84).

ⓦⓞⓦ **Masked Smart Filter.psd**

Filtering a Mask

PHOTOSPIN.COM

A LAYER MASK treated with a filter can artistically frame one image against another. For such a custom-edged vignette treatment, you can make a selection (we used the Rectangular Marquee ⬚), turn it into a layer mask, and then modify the mask to create some gray at its edges and run a filter on the mask. See page 268 for the technique and pages 272 and 273 for filter ideas.

Here we added an edge texture to show beyond the mask by filling the *Background* with the **Wow Weave 03** pattern, first clicking the *Background* thumbnail in the Layers panel to target it, then selecting all (Ctrl/⌘-A), and finally choosing Edit > Fill > Pattern and choosing from the pop-out Pattern picker.

FIND OUT MORE

▼ Using Adjustment layers
page 245

Masking an Adjustment

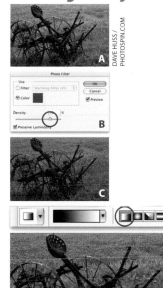

DAVE HUSS / PHOTOSPIN.COM

ADJUSTMENT LAYERS, which make changes in tone and color, have their own built-in layer masks. So you can set up your adjustment and then mask it to target the effect, leaving some areas of your image "unadjusted." ▼ Starting with a photo of antique farm equipment **A**, we clicked the "Create new fill or adjustment layer" button ◉ at the bottom of the Layers panel and chose Photo Filter; in the Photo Filter dialog **B** we clicked the color square and chose a red, increased the Density to 75% for stronger color, and clicked "OK" to tint the photo **C**. Then we faded the tint by Shift-dragging up with the Gradient tool ▭ using a "Black, White" Linear gradient **D**, **E**, **F**.

ⓦⓞⓦ **Masked Adjustment.psd**

Marie Brown Thinks "Fuzzy"

SELECTING A BROWNISH-GRAY RACCOON from a grayish-brown background posed a challenge for Marie Brown. After trying various selection methods and refining the mask, she still didn't have an isolated subject that could go over a light or dark background. So she tried a different approach, involving the Dune Grass brush tip and a stroked path.

 Fur Mask.psd

FIND OUT MORE

▼ Selecting by color **page 50**

▼ The Extract filter **page 90**

▼ The Lasso tools ⬭ ⬭ ⬭ **page 54**

▼ Pen tool ⬭ and paths **page 454**

▼ Refine Edge/Refine Mask **page 59**

▼ Saving brush-tip presets **page 402**

A method that selects by color (such as Select > Color Range) or by color and texture combined (like the Quick Selection tool ✎) wasn't going to work in this case, because it wouldn't be able to tell the difference between the raccoon's fur and the dry grass and leaves around her.▼

PHOTO: SUSAN HELLER

The selecting challenge

Marie gave the Extract filter a quick try, both with and without Smart Highlighting, but neither worked.▼ "I didn't think the Magnetic Lasso would be able to follow the edge if Extract's Highlighter hadn't been able to," says Marie. "The straight segments of the Polygonal Lasso weren't ideal for the rounded lines of the animal. And I knew better than to try to follow the edge with the Lasso."▼

M arie chose the Pen tool ⬭ and drew a path to follow the smooth curves of the animal's body.▼ Then she converted the path to a selection by targeting it in the Paths panel and clicking the "Make selection from path" button ⊙ at the bottom of the panel.

The path (shown above) was loaded as a selection.

With the selection active, she added a layer mask to the raccoon layer by clicking the ⬚ button at the bottom of the Layers panel.

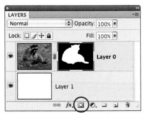

The selection was turned into a layer mask.

The raccoon looked like it had been cut out with scissors. With the mask targeted in the Layers panel, Marie chose Select > Refine Edge and worked with the settings in the Refine Mask dialog to make the edge better able to blend with a new background.▼ "But it still didn't look good," Marie reports.

A nd that's when she thought of the Dune Grass brush. The single blade of grass in Dune Grass could just as easily be a hair. By

modifying the brush and stroking the path around the raccoon, she could build a fuzzy edge.

Marie chose the Brush tool ✐, chose Dune Grass from the pop-out picker in the Options bar, and opened the **Brushes panel** by clicking the ⬚ button at the right end of the bar. She could tell that the "hair" was too big; so in the Brushes panel she reduced the **Master Diameter** from 112 to 25 px.

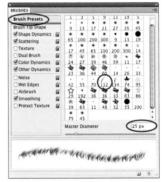

Reducing the size of the brush tip

She wanted the fur to be smoother than this brush tip would paint, so she opened the **Scattering** section (by clicking its name on the left side of the Brushes panel) and lowered the Scatter to 20%. She also reduced the **Count Jitter**, which would reduce the "patchiness" of the hairs.

In the **Color Dynamics** section she turned the Foreground/Background Jitter to 0 since she wanted to paint the mask with white only.

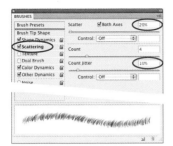

Reducing the Scatter and Count Jitter to arrange the "hairs" more uniformly

In the **Shape Dynamics** section, she set the **Angle Control** (under the Angle Jitter slider) to **Direction**. That would align the "hair" so it maintained a constant orientation relative to the path when she stroked the path.

Setting the Angle Control to Direction orients the brush footprint according to the direction of the path.

"Now I was ready to give it a try," Marie says. She duplicated the raccoon layer (Ctrl/⌘-J) and targeted the layer mask on the new layer. She set Foreground and Background colors to white and black and filled the new layer mask with black (press D, then Ctrl-Backspace in Windows, ⌘-Delete on the Mac). She clicked the "Stroke path" button ○ at the bottom of the Paths panel. The hairs appeared, but they were oriented in the wrong direction.

Stroking the path created a mask edge with hairs, but not at a realistic angle.

To change the direction of the fur, she undid her previous stroking of the path (Ctrl/⌘-Z) and went to the **Brush Tip Shape** section of the Brushes panel to experiment. When she turned on Flip Y, changed the Angle to 20° and the Spacing to 35%, and stroked the path again, she met with success.

Reorienting the brush footprint by changing the angle, and spreading out the hairs a bit with Spacing

The new mask created a smooth coat.

Marie turned her custom brush into a preset by choosing New Brush Preset in the Brushes panel's menu ▾☰, naming it "furbrush1." She went on to make two more brush-tip presets, one for the raccoon's left leg (she turned on Flip X as well as Flip Y and changed the Angle to –30°) and one for

smoother areas with shorter fur (with a size of 10 px, Flip X, Flip Y, Angle –30°, and spacing increased to 75%). She saved the brushes with the Preset Manager. ▼ She made a total of three fur-edge layers, each with a mask with a different kind of fur stroke.

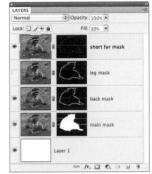

The Layers panel showing the refined path-based mask and three masks made by stroking the path with "fur" brushes

To finish the masking, she painted each of the fur-edge masks with black to hide each type of fur everywhere except where she wanted it.

The silhouetted raccoon

DODGING & BURNING MASKS

The Dodge 🔍 and Burn ✋ tools, with their ability to target changes to the Highlights, Midtones, or Shadows, can make local changes to mask density. Making these changes when the silhouetted image is over its new background lets you gauge the effect of your edits.

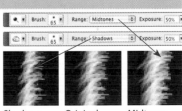

Shadows burned   Original   Midtones dodged

Extract

The combination of a selection tool (or more than one) and the Refine Edge command (to clean up the selection's edges, see page 58) does a great job of selecting in many cases. But what the Extract command adds is the ability to vary the width of the edge band where Photoshop looks to separate subject from background. You can set only one Radius (edge band width) in the Refine Edge dialog box, but with Extract you can vary the width. (Extract doesn't appear in the Filter menu in Photoshop CS4 unless you install the plug-in; see page 120.)

PHOTO: CORBIS ROYALTY FREE

YOU'LL FIND THE FILES
in 🔵 > Wow Project Files >
Chapter 2 > Exercising Extract:
 • Extract-Before.psd
 • Extract-After.psd

1 Starting to Extract

USING THE **EXTRACT** COMMAND (Filter > Extract) is a "destructive" process — it permanently removes pixels. So before you Extract, duplicate your image layer for safekeeping (type Ctrl/⌘-J). Then click the 👁 icon of the bottom image layer to turn off its visibility so you'll be able to see the result of your extraction **A**.

Open the Extract dialog box (Filter > Extract). With the Edge Highlighter tool ✎ chosen **B**, set the Brush Size in the Tool Options section **C**. A large brush works well for soft or fuzzy edges. Some edges may be "fuzzy" because they are partly out of focus or partly transparent, or because they include highlights or shadows that have picked up color from the background. Typical edges of this kind include wisps of hair, or tree leaves or blades of grass against the sky. On first inspection, the contrast between the green background and black hair looks strong. But some of the hair is out-of-focus and soft, and the background has created green highlights in the hair.

To highlight fuzzy edges, use a large Brush Size setting. Choose a size that's big enough so you can easily drag it around the edge of the area you want to isolate (the subject), drawing a highlight that overlaps both the subject and the background where they meet, without veering off the edge. This highlight defines the band where the Extract function will look for the edge when it selects the subject. But keep in mind that anything the Edge Highlighter paints is fair game for Extract to make fully or partially transparent. We set Brush Size at 40 and dragged along the edge of the hair **D**.

2 Smart Highlighting

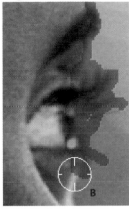

A SMALLER BRUSH is better for highlighting a distinct, hard edge (keeping the brush small will prevent it from being confused by anything near the edge) or if there are two edges close together (with a small brush you can highlight only the one you want). But instead of resetting Brush Size, you can click the **Smart Highlighting** checkbox **A** or hold down the Ctrl/⌘ key. When you switch to Smart Highlighting, the brush becomes "magnetic," automatically clinging to the edge as you drag the cursor and automatically narrowing the brush as much as possible to hug the edge **B**. When contrast gets low again, turn off Smart Highlighting.

In our portrait there are two high-contrast edges on the woman's profile — the green-against-white edge between background and highlight (this is the edge we want) and the white-against-brown edge between highlighted and normal skin tones (the edge we don't want). We zoomed in (Ctrl/⌘-spacebar) to follow the edge. On the shoulders we switched back to manual operation of the Edge Highlighter (by holding down the Ctrl/⌘ key), and reduced Brush Size to 10. Smart Highlighting would have followed the higher-contrast edge between the white highlight and darker skin, cutting off the highlight.

CHANGING BRUSH SIZE

The control keys for resizing the brush tip for the tools in the Extract dialog box are the bracket keys, the same as for Photoshop's painting tools: Press [to shrink the brush, or] to enlarge it.

NAVIGATING WHILE HIGHLIGHTING

To temporarily turn on navigation tools in the Extract dialog box without dropping the Edge Highlighter ✎, use these keyboard shortcuts:

Hold down the **spacebar** for the **Hand tool** ✋, to scroll around the image.

Hold down **Ctrl/⌘-spacebar** for the Zoom tool 🔍 and click to magnify the image.

Hold down **Ctrl-Alt-spacebar** (Windows) or **⌘-Option-spacebar** (Mac) and click to zoom out.

REPAIRS "ON THE FLY"

If you make a mistake with the Edge Highlighter ✎, you can:

- Add to the highlight by dragging the tool back over an area you missed.

- Remove highlight material (as shown here) by holding down the Alt/Option key to erase.

THE DUMB/SMART TOGGLE

Unfortunately, "Smart Highlighting" is really only smart about sharp, high-contrast edges. So as you drag from an area with a high-contrast edge to an area of low contrast, you'll need to turn off Smart Highlighting and operate the Edge Highlighter ✎ "by hand." Holding down the **Ctrl/⌘** key automatically switches out of Smart Highlighting if you have it turned on, or switches into it if you have it turned off. Release the key to toggle back again.

3 Completing & Previewing

B

CONTINUE TO DRAG the Edge Highlighter around the edge until you've outlined the entire subject. The highlighting is complete when the subject is entirely enclosed within the highlight, except that you don't have to drag along the outside edges of the image — you can draw just to the edge.

In order to be able to preview your "extraction," choose Extract's own **Fill** tool ⬦ to click inside the highlight-bordered subject area **A**. Then click the **"Preview"** button to see the extracted subject. Changing the Smooth setting can affect the edge quality. If you change the setting, you'll need to press "Preview" to see the change. You can zoom in for a closer look at the edge with Extract's own **Zoom** tool 🔍, or change the preview's background color by choosing from the pop-out **Show** list in the Preview section of the dialog box; we chose a red background **B** to contrast with any green edges that remained. You can also toggle the view to compare the extracted subject with the original by choosing from the **View** settings.

4 Cleaning Up

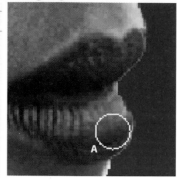

IF YOU DON'T LIKE what the Preview shows you about the edge quality, you have several choices for making corrections. As you touch up the extraction, keep in mind that **it's better to leave too much material at the edge than not enough** (you can remove any excess later, but it won't be easy to restore any missing material once you leave the Extract dialog box).

- If there are extra pixels outside the edge, use the **Cleanup tool** 🖌 **A to erase excess** material. Or if there's semitransparency where the subject's edge should be solid, use the **Cleanup tool with Alt/Option held down to restore** edge material.

- Use the **Edge Touchup tool** 🖌 **B to consolidate and remove "pixel debris"** at the edge.

- If the edge itself looks good but there are areas completely inside the edge that need to be eliminated — such as **small patches** of sky showing through the leaves of a tree you've selected — you don't need to highlight the edge of each patch. Instead, click "OK" to close the Extract dialog box and then use the **Background Eraser** (see page 56).

(see page 56)

"THICKENING" HAIR

If too much hair seems to have disappeared in the selection process, with Extract or with another selecting or masking method, you may be able to restore it by adding a copy of the layer (Ctrl/⌘-J). This will build opacity in partly transparent areas; areas that were already fully opaque won't change. If the thickening effect is too strong, lower the new layer's Opacity.

There are no parameters to set in the Find Edges filter, but it can be used with artistry nevertheless. The art is in the choice of photo and in choosing the right blend mode (and sometimes Opacity) for combining the filtered image and the original. **Marv Lyons** finds that particularly with images with strong light-dark contrast and neutral colors like this one, Find Edges produces dark outlines and enhances small texture. Applied in Overlay mode, the filtered version brightens the light areas as it applies the dark edges.

Lyons created *Tehachapi Snowbirds* before there were Smart Filters, by duplicating the image to a new layer (Ctrl/⌘-J), then filtering the duplicate (Filter > Stylize > Find Edges), and changing the filtered layer's blend mode to Overlay. In Photoshop CS3 or CS4, instead of duplicating the layer, Lyons could have applied Find Edges as a Smart

Filter. What are the advantages of each method?

• The working file size is smaller (about half the size) with Smart Filters, so if working memory is limited, a Smart Filter may be the way to go. (In our tests, there wasn't a great deal of difference between the two options in the saved file size, especially if we chose the Maximize Compatibility option when saving. ▼)

• Both methods allow you to change the Opacity and blend mode of the filter effect, one through the settings for the layer, and the other by clicking the 🔀 button.

• Smart Filters allow you to alter your settings, keeping the filter "live," but when there are no settings to alter, using a Smart Filter doesn't add anything to future edibility.

• With normal layers, a quick glance at the Layers panel shows you what blend mode and Opacity a filtered

layer uses **A**. With a Smart Filter, you have to dig deeper (double-click the 🔀 icon) **B** to figure it out.

Original

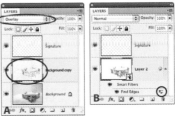

FIND OUT MORE

▼ Maximize Compatibility **page 127**

The **Rainforest Butterflies** set is part of the **Nature of Australia** series of stamps designed by **Wayne Rankin** and issued by Australia Post. For the rainforest environment backgrounds, Rankin combined photos from several sources, using the Move tool to drag them into the composite file he had set up for each stamp. He then used layer masks to blend them together. For the background of the large $2 stamp, for instance, Rankin used three photos of the Daintree Rainforest. He started with the largest of the three photos **A** and then filled in the extra width in his stamp format by copying a selection from

the right side of this image to a new layer (Ctrl/⌘-J) and using the Move tool to slide the new layer over to the left. In the final composition the tree with buttresses **B** would hide the top part of this copy, and the waterfall image **C** would hide the

ALIGNING IMAGE LAYERS

To see how the layer you're working on lines up with the image underneath, temporarily reduce the upper layer's Opacity using the slider in the Layers panel. Once the layer is in place and any masks are painted, restore the Opacity to 100%.

lower right side of the original, so there would be no obviously repeating elements.

While he worked, Rankin clicked 👁 icons to toggle on and off the visibility for layers that held the vignette edges, the color-filled rectangle for the denomination of the stamp, the type elements, and the layout of the stamp outline. The type and outline had been created in Adobe Illustrator, then copied and pasted into Photoshop as separate layers so Rankin could develop his design in relation to these standard elements.

To blend the images together, he added a layer mask to each of the

A © LIK HOTSTOCK.

B © PETER WALTON

C © LIK HOTSTOCK

D © STANLEY BREECON

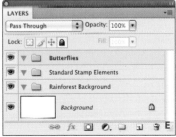

LAYERS

Pass Through ⬦ Opacity: 100% ▼

Lock: ☐ ✐ ✛ 🔒 Fill: 100% ▼

👁 ▼ 📁 **Butterflies**

👁 ▼ 📁 **Standard Stamp Elements**

👁 ▼ 📁 **Rainforest Background**

👁 ☐ *Background* 🔒

🔗 *fx* 🔲 🌑 ☐ 🗑 E

image layers except the bottom one, by clicking to make a white-filled "reveal all" mask, or Alt/Option-clicking to make a black-filled "hide-all" mask. Working on the layer masks, he used the Brush tool ✐ to paint, or made selections and filled them with white or black and then modified them by painting soft edges, watching the composite as the masks blended the images. Rankin added Adjustment layers (such as Curves) with painted masks to direct their tone and color changes where they were needed for a seamless blend.▼

To isolate each of the butterflies **D** from its background so he could drag it into the composite, Rankin developed a selection based on one of the color channels. For each butterfly photo he chose the channel with the best definition of the edge between butterfly and background and duplicated it as an alpha channel by dragging its thumbnail in the Channels panel to the "Create new channel" button 🔲 at the bottom

of the panel. Then he used various Image > Adjustments commands to enhance the edge definition. The process Rankin used to develop the butterfly selections is shown on page 53.

Once selected, each butterfly could then be dragged with the Move tool ▶⊕ into the composite file to make its own transparent layer. Rankin invoked the Edit > Free Transform command (Ctrl/⌘-T) to scale each butterfly layer and rotate it into place.▼

For final output, visibility for the type and outline layers was turned off **E** before the flattened file was made (Image > Duplicate > Duplicate Merged Layers Only). The final layout, with live type, was assembled in Illustrator.

FIND OUT MORE

▼ Using Adjustment layers **page 245**

▼ Transforming **page 67**

Jeff Irwin's image-transfer work, seen in **Fall** (above) and **Songs** (on the facing page) combines his environmental photos with scans and with elements added in Photoshop. Some of the layering of the image elements is done in Photoshop, but much of it happens on the ceramic tiles themselves.

To start, a photo or scan can be quickly cropped and resized in one operation with Photoshop's Crop tool 🔲. Width, Height, and Resolution can be set in the Options bar; then the crop is completed by dragging to select the area to preserve and pressing the Enter key. Irwin starts the process with a high-res photo or scan, enlarging it to the size of the finished piece at about

200 pixels per inch. The files for *Songs* and *Fall* were sized for a three-by-three arrangement of 8-inch-square tiles with a border around the outside. Irwin displayed the rulers (Ctrl/⌘-R) and dragged horizontal and vertical Guides to mark the edges of the individual tiles.

The *Fall* file started with a photo, and *Songs* started with a scan of plywood. For *Songs* Irwin added musical notation photographed from a songbook, enlarged, and treated with Photoshop's Stamp filter (Filter > Sketch > Stamp) to add weight to the lines and smooth the edges.

When transferred to ceramics and fired, iron oxide, which is a component of the black toner used in laser printers and photocopiers, can

produce a range of colors. Darker tones will fire as sepia; medium tones as intense orange, and light tones as light orange. One way Irwin controls the color is with Photoshop's Brightness/Contrast adjustment in Legacy mode, adjusting first Contrast and then Brightness. (In Legacy mode increasing Brightness works as it did in earlier versions of Photoshop, lightening all tones in the image; with a strong enough adjustment, highlight detail is eliminated. In Normal mode, with Use Legacy unchecked, Brightness can be increased without losing as much highlight detail.)

Irwin added white shapes to each image. For *Songs* he used the Elliptical Marquee ⬭ (Shift-M) to select

the ovals. For *Fall* he drew several leaf shapes with the Pen tool ♦, then copied, pasted, and reshaped them with Image > Transform > Scale and Distort.

Next he used the Guides he had set up (with View > Snap To > Guides chosen) and the Rectangular Marquee ⬚ (Shift-M) to select the artwork for each of the nine tiles in each composition. For each square he copied the selected square (Ctrl/⌘-Shift-C for Edit > Copy Merged makes a composite copy), made a new file from the clipboard contents (Ctrl/⌘-N, then Enter), and then pasted (Ctrl/⌘-V).

Irwin printed on Bel Laser Decal paper (www.beldecal.com) using a laser printer. He typically transfers

onto white glazed Dal tiles he buys at Home Depot. After cleaning the tiles, cutting the edge pieces, and arranging all in a wooden frame to hold them in position for the transfer, he put each decal sheet in turn into water to separate the decal from the backing sheet. He put the decal onto the tile, squeegeed the water off, and let it dry overnight.

When he fired the tiles, Irwin had another chance to affect the color. Firing at cone 03 (1987°F) produces more orange, at cone 04 (1945°F) more dark sepia. Packing the kiln, which reduces air circulation during firing, can also affect color. For instance, in *Songs*, the tiles on the top left are a darker

brown than the others because of how they were packed in the kiln.

Irwin often adds black elements after the initial firing. The birds were added by applying black glaze in the overall shape, then sketching the composition on the glaze with white pencil, and finally scratching away the glaze (the *sgraffito* technique) to create the detail. Then the tiles were fired again at the same temperature as the first firing, or lower. For the edges, Irwin used the same sgraffito technique on the cut tiles to create the woodgrain borders.

For each composition the tiles were mounted with Silicone seal on a sheet of plywood about an inch-and-a-half smaller all around than the assembled tiles.

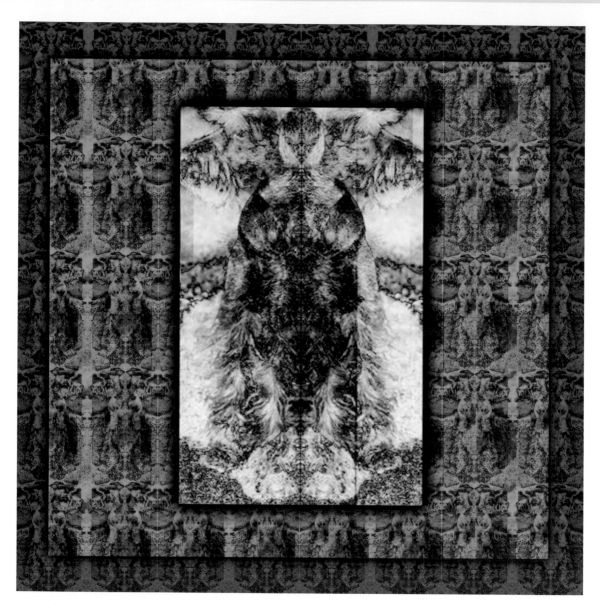

The organic geometry of lines and colors that emerges in the images of **Laurie Grace's** *Intrusions* series comes from the interaction of repeated instances of a photo or painting, arranged in a grid and flipped, with several copies layered together and combined by changing the blend modes of the layers. ▼ For *Intrusion 2*, shown here, Grace made a new Photoshop file (File > New, with the default choices of RGB Color for the Color Mode and White for the Background Contents) and used the Move tool ▶⊕ to drag-and-drop a grayscale version of a photo of a dog **A** into the new file. She aligned the photo with the upper right corner, and scaled it down (Ctrl/⌘-T brings up the Transform frame, and Shift-dragging a corner handle of the frame inward will shrink the image, keeping its original proportions). ▼

Grace made a duplicate of most of this imported image, right beside the original **B**. One way to do that is to drag with the Rectangular Marquee ⬚ to select the part of the image you want and then Ctrl-Alt-drag

FIND OUT MORE

▼ Blend modes **page 181**

▼ Transforming **page 67**

▼ Adding a drop shadow **page 506**

(Windows) or ⌘-Option-drag (Mac) sideways to make a duplicate of the selected part of the image; adding the Shift key after starting to drag keeps the motion horizontal so the copy stays aligned with the original and the two together form a rectangular unit.

Next Grace selected and repeated her entire two-image unit in the same way, to make a four-image unit, and then selected and repeated the four-image unit to complete a row of eight. She selected the row of eight and repeated the row four times, moving each copy down, to complete her grid of images **C**.

She duplicated the layer of images (Ctrl/⌘-J), and then flipped this new layer (Edit > Transform > Flip Horizontal) **D**. When she put this layer in Difference mode (by choosing from the blend mode menu in the upper left corner of the Layers panel), the grids of dog images interacted to become something entirely different **E**.

Adding a blue-filled layer, also in Difference mode, turned the black in her composite blue, and colored the white with the opposite color, an orange **F**.

Next Grace layered another grid of images made from selections from the same original photo **G**, making this grid a little smaller than the other layers **H**. She put the new layer in Soft Light mode **I** and added a drop shadow, which can be seen in the final montage on the facing page. ▼ Finally she added an enlarged copy of a detail made from the grid of **E**. She put the layer in Normal mode and added a drop shadow.

When a selection is active, the result you get when you drag depends on what keys you're holding down:

- Dragging while any selection tool is chosen, without any helper keys, will reposition the selection boundary only — no pixels are moved.

- If you hold down the Ctrl/⌘ key and drag, the selection tool turns into the Move tool temporarily, and the pixels are moved along with the selection boundary, leaving behind a hole.

- If you hold down both Ctrl/⌘ and Alt/Option and drag, you make a *copy* of the selected area on the same layer.

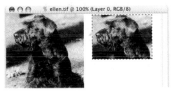

- To make a copy on a separate layer so you can move it and still keep the original layer intact, type Ctrl/⌘-J, and then hold down the Ctrl/⌘ key to turn the selection tool into the Move tool temporarily so you can drag the copy.

A

B

C

D

E

F

G

H

I

Cristen Gillespie's *Fireworks Celebration II* blends two images (shown at the right) by using a blurred layer mask made with Photoshop's Transparent Stripes gradient. Using a striped mask would reveal the Capitol building in the center and create the illusion of multiple bursts of fireworks coming from within. Before layering the images, though, Gillespie needed to make some minor adjustments to the Capitol building.

Because she could see that the dark shadows of the building needed to be lit up (as if the fireworks were brightening the night), and that the photographer's perspective had the building tilting back a little, she decided to convert the image layer to a Smart Object. Then she could run both the Shadows/Highlights adjustment and the Lens Correction filter as Smart Filters (and tinker

with them later if need be). She right-clicked/Ctrl-clicked on the *Background* layer and chose Convert to Smart Object from the context-sensitive menu. When she next chose Image > Adjustments > Shadows/Highlights, the default settings seemed like they added enough light, so she clicked "OK" to let the filter run. ▼ Next Gillespie chose Filter > Distort > Lens Correction. She used the Move Grid Tool to align the vertical grid lines with the columns in the image. A small amount of Vertical Perspective straightened the dome, and choosing Background Color for the Edge setting filled in the edge with Black, which in this case would be fine **A**. ▼

Since the Capitol building image has so much black, Gillespie wanted to be sure that it was a rich black, that it didn't have a significant color cast, and that it wouldn't exceed the ink

limits of the printing process. She found out from the printer that she should use the North American Pre-press 2 color profile, and not allow her rich blacks to exceed 300%. First she placed a Color Sampler 🖉 on a solid black area of the background. In the Info panel, she clicked on the triangle beside the Eyedropper 🖉 icon in the top section (which tracks actual color values) and chose Total Ink from the menu. Next, she chose CMYK from the pop-up menu in the lower section that tracks color sampler values. Gillespie added a Selective Color Adjustment layer by clicking the "Create new fill or adjustment layer" button ◑ at the bottom of the Layers panel and choosing from the pop-up list. She chose Blacks from the Colors menu in the Selective Color dialog and adjusted the sliders for a neutral Black until she could see in the Info panel that Magenta and Yellow were about equal, with Cyan about 8 to 10 points higher. (A higher percentage of Cyan is needed to balance Magenta and Yellow and make the black neutral.) She then checked to see if the total ink coverage was within

the prescribed limits by moving the Eyedropper tool over various black areas and checking the readout at the top of the Info panel. To reduce the Total Ink value below 300%, she lowered the amount of Black **B**, **C**.

With the Capitol building image ready, Gillespie opened the Fireworks image and used the Move tool ▶₊ to drag it on top of the Capitol. She wanted the fireworks to cover the entire building, so she moved the layer to center the fireworks over the dome, and then used Free Transform (Ctrl/⌘-T) to slightly enlarge the "bloom." She added a layer mask to the Fireworks image, chose the Transparent Stripes gradient, and Shift-dragged horizontally with the Gradient tool ▦ . (With this gradient, the width of the bars is determined by how far you drag with the Gradient tool, so a very short drag produces very thin bars, with a wide black area on one side and a wide white area on the other; a long drag, on the other hand, makes wide bars across the entire mask.) In the Layers panel she clicked on the link icon 🔗 between the layer mask and image thumbnail to unlink the two,

then dragged in the image window to move the layer mask until the bars revealed the dome. She clicked between the thumbnail and mask again to relink them so she couldn't accidentally move one without the other.

To blend the two images so the fireworks would seem to come from inside the dome, she targeted the gradient-filled layer mask and in CS3, used Filter > Blur > Gaussian Blur, increasing the amount until the Preview showed the edges of the mask had disappeared and the document window showed the Capitol building revealed through the fireworks **D**. Another option is to choose Select > Refine Edge▼ and set the Feather slider, with all the other sliders set to 0. In CS4 there's a third possibility: She could use the Feather slider in the Masks panel to achieve the same result, and the feather would remain "live" and editable, in case she later wanted to reveal more or less of the building **E**.▼ When she was satisfied with the blend **F**, she dragged with the Crop tool 🔲 to crop the image, focusing the viewer's attention on the dome.▼

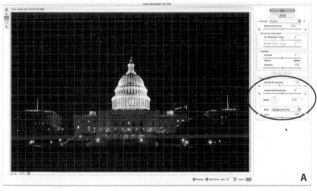

A

B

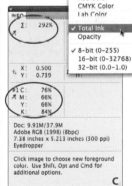

C

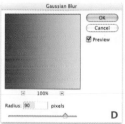

D

E

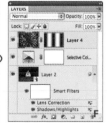

F

Getting In, Going Fast & Getting Out

3

The File > Open command is the oldest way to locate files and bring them into Photoshop, and it still works perfectly. But Photoshop CS3 and CS4 also offer more efficient browsing (through Bridge ▼) and "protective packaging" (through Open As Smart Object ▼).

FIND OUT MORE

▼ Using Bridge **page 133**

▼ Smart Objects **page 75**

SCANNING IN 3D

By placing small objects on a flatbed scanner, you may be able to capture their dimensionality. One or more sides of an object may show, depending on where on the bed you place it. The farther off-center you move the object (toward an edge or corner of the scan bed), the more the depth of its sides will show.

THIS CHAPTER COVERS THE BEST ways to get images into and out of Photoshop. It also has some hints for organizing your files so you can find them easily, and suggests ways to shift some of your work to Photoshop's Actions and other automation skills.

GETTING IN: INPUT

Looking first at input, or acquiring images, the quality of the images you put into Photoshop can have a big impact on the quality of the output, and also on the amount of work you'll need to do in Photoshop. As a rule of thumb, collect more information in your input file than you think you will need for output — billions of colors instead of millions in an RGB scan or a digital camera photo, for instance, or twice the resolution (pixels/inch) you need for final output for scanned line art. With more color depth and higher resolution, you can get smoother color transitions and cleaner edges. Even when you ultimately reduce the number of colors or the resolution, the image or line art will look better than if you had started with less information.

Scanning

With a **flatbed scanner**, you can capture photographic prints, drawings and paintings, and even some three-dimensional objects, as files you can work with in Photoshop. The more *color depth* your scanner offers — that is, the more colors it can distinguish — the more shadow and highlight detail it will be able to record. You and Photoshop can use this extra information to help make finer color and tone adjustments. While many flatbed scanners now come with adapters for scanning slides or film negatives, if you have a lot of slides or negatives that you want to scan, a dedicated **film scanner** is worth considering. The model you choose depends partly upon the film format you need to scan. Not all film scanners can handle medium format or APS in addition to 35mm, but some can. And some

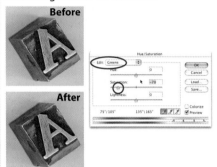
also have an attachment for feeding entire rolls of negative film. Another input option is to have your film scanned by a photo service and delivered on CD-ROM, in which case the quality of the scan will depend on the optical and mechanical precision of the scanner and the skill of the person operating it.

Prescanning. Scanners let you *prescan* your image so you can identify the area you want to scan. Then, as described on these next two pages, you can specify the dimensions and color mode you want for your scanned image, and enter a scan resolution. The goal is to collect all the information you need for the way you want to use the file in Photoshop, without collecting an inconveniently large amount.

Setting the dimensions of the scan. When your scanner shows you a preview of your image, use the scanning software's cropping tool to identify the area you want to scan. Then tell the scanner whether you want your scanned image to be the same linear dimensions as the original or some other size. Most scanners will let you set a new height or width, and then will automatically adjust the other dimension. Or you can set the new dimensions as a percentage of the original size.

SETTING UP A SCAN

Your scanning software's interface has the input fields you need to tell the scanner how much information to collect.

For a color scan, set the scan to capture at least 24-Bit color.

Choose (or type in) the resolution you need for your image file.

Choose to make the scan the same dimensions as the original or one of the standard sizes offered, or customize the settings.

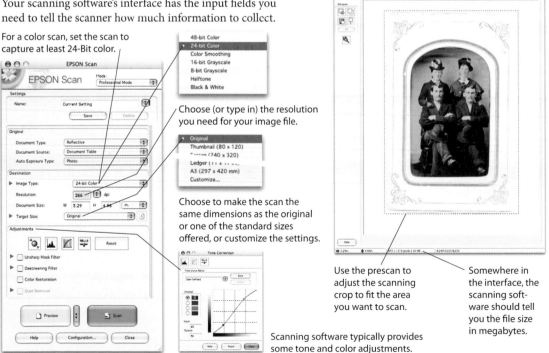

Use the prescan to adjust the scanning crop to fit the area you want to scan.

Somewhere in the interface, the scanning software should tell you the file size in megabytes.

Scanning software typically provides some tone and color adjustments.

Setting the color mode of the scan. Color mode also affects file size. ▼ For example, a full-color scan records at least three times as much information as a grayscale scan (one with black and white and 254 shades of gray in between). Here are some criteria for choosing the color mode for scanning:

- **For color images**, even if you plan to convert them to "black-and-white" (Grayscale) for output, ▼ scan in full color. Your scanner may call this, its best color mode, "millions of colors," "billions of colors" (for 16 Bits/Channel mode), or "true color."

- **Grayscale images,** such as black-and-white photos, often turn out better if you scan in color and then convert to Grayscale mode in Photoshop.

- **Black-and-white line art** usually has smoother, more consistent lines if it's scanned in Grayscale mode, or even in color, and then perfected in Photoshop, using an Adjustment layer, as in the example at the left. For even more control of line quality, you can take advantage of the **Refine Edge** command (see page 108).

Setting the scan resolution. Scanner software typically asks for the scan resolution you want as *pixels per inch (ppi)*. To figure out the scan resolution you need in order to print the image on a press, you can multiply the print resolution (number of lines

Scanning line art in color or Grayscale mode produces smooth lines and allows the "ink" to be lightened or darkened — with a Levels or Brightness/Contrast adjustment, for instance. Tommy Yune used a Levels adjustment layer (added by clicking the ⬤ at the bottom of the Layers panel and choosing from the menu) to smooth the lines in this ink drawing, which he had scanned in Grayscale mode. For such a Levels adjustment, move the gamma (gray, midpoint) slider for Input Levels **A** to the left to thin the lines, or to the right to thicken them. Use the Input Levels white point slider **B** to brighten a gray background to white, and the black point slider **C** to darken the ink.

TOMMY YUNE

FIND OUT MORE

▼ Color modes **page 164**

▼ Converting from color to grayscale **page 214**

SCANNING SEVERAL IMAGES AT ONCE

If you put several photos side-by-side on your flatbed scanner, with a little space in between, Photoshop will separate the images into individual files, straightening them in the process, when you choose **File > Automate > Crop and Straighten Photos.**

Four photos were scanned at once (left), and the Crop and Straighten Photos command was run to separate them, producing four files with the same name, followed by the word "copy" and a sequence number.

When you scan an image that was printed on a press, the halftone screen pattern used for printing can interact with the scanner's sampling scheme to produce an unwanted *moiré* (interference pattern). Many desktop and other scanners have built-in descreening algorithms for reducing the moiré. More work may be needed to finish the job.

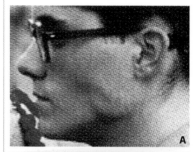

These screen captures show an enlarged detail of a photo scanned from a book, without descreening **A** and with the descreening built into the scanning software **B**. Enable Descreening and select the source (such as a magazine, a newspaper or fine art), which tells the software how much to blur the halftoned pixels. A Surface Blur ▼ was then applied to the descreened image **C** to smooth it more.

FIND OUT MORE
▼ Surface Blur filter
page 321

per inch, or lpi, in the halftone screen that the printer will use) by 1.5 to 2. The 1.5 multiplier (for example, 1.5 ppi/lpi x 150 lpi = 225 ppi for the file) works well for photos of natural scenery without stark geometric patterns, sharp color boundaries, or ultra-fine details (most of the images in this book, including the cover, fit in this category). For photos of manmade structures, which tend to have straight lines and sharp color breaks, or for close-up "beauty" photography with details like fine eyelashes, a multiplier of 2 is a safer choice (for example, 2 ppi/lpi x 150 lpi = 300 ppi for the file). A multiplier greater than 2 increases the file size without making the picture look significantly better. *Note:* The difference in file size between a file that's 1.5 and 2 times the line screen is almost double, which is a lot of extra weight to carry around if you don't really need it.

Inkjet printers may use dpi or ppi to indicate their print-quality resolutions, or they may only use words like "Good" and "Best." For files that will be printed on an inkjet, scanning at a resolution between 225 and 300 ppi and choosing "Best" in the printer setup dialog will come close to photo-quality prints on most recent inkjets. Fine-art inkjet printers typically require 200 to 400 dpi, for a print whose resolution (as viewed with our eyes or through a loupe) looks much higher. If you will be sending a file out to be printed on a high-quality commercial inkjet, ask the printer what resolution or file size will be needed for the size and kind of print you want.

Double-checking. Once you've chosen image size, color mode, and resolution, your scanner will tell you how big (in megabytes, MB) the file will be when your image is scanned. As a check, the chart on page 110 shows some typical files sizes and print dimensions.

JUST BECAUSE YOU CAN . . .
Just because you *can* successfully scan printed material, descreening it to get rid of a moiré, doesn't mean it's OK to scan and appropriate anything that's in print. Most recently printed material is (or was) copyright-protected. "Corinna Buchholz Researches Copyright" on the facing page provides tips for finding material that's in the public domain (available for unrestricted use, unprotected by copyright). And you can find information about U. S. copyright law and fair use at www.copyright.gov.

Corinna Buchholz Researches Copyright

THE SUCCESS of Corinna Buchholz's business, **piddix.com,** depends not only on finding wonderful artwork to scan, scanning it well and cleaning it up in Photoshop, and arranging it in digital collage sheets, but also on being absolutely sure the images she scans are copyright-free.

You'll find a **piddix.com Sampler** of royalty-free scans in the Wow Goodies folder on the DVD-ROM that comes with this book.

"How does that copyright thing work?" is by far the number one question Corinna is asked about digital images and collage sheets, she says. She isn't a lawyer, but in the course of building Piddix LLC she has worked with her lawyer and educated herself on copyright laws.

For works published in the United States from 1923 through 1963 to be copyright-protected, Corinna tells us, the copyright notice had to appear on the work the first time it was published, and the copyright would have had to have

been renewed 28 years later. So one of several ways she researches copyright status for a book, for instance, that she would like to scan, is to check a web site that provides page images for Library of Congress copyright renewals, cataloged by year and then alphabetically by author:

http://onlinebooks.library. upenn.edu/webbin/gutbook/ lookup?num=11800

Knowing the year of the original publication and copyright, she checks to see whether the copyright was renewed 28 years later. "And 26, 27, 29, and 30," says Corinna, "just to be safe." Then she

often locates an original copy in a bookstore or on eBay, buys it, and personally scans the art.

We found Corinna's written explanation of copyright and related topics, such as terms of usage, derivative works, and right of publicity, to be both thorough and easy to understand. We found it on her blog, along with links to other good resources, at:

http://piddix.blogspot. com/2008/03/copyright-and- digital-collage-sheets.html

Almost everything that was published in the United States before 1923 is in the public domain in the United States. This is why, in part, so many of the images you see for sale are "vintage," such as this portrait taken by St. Louis photographer F. W. Guerin at the beginning of the 20th century. (In the public domain means the copyright is no longer owned by anyone — it's owned by the public — and you can use the images almost any way you like.)

A published item from the 1920s through 1978 may be in the public domain because it didn't have the © copyright symbol on it when it was published, as is the case with this lithographed cleaning product label. But the name or logo of the product may be protected by trademark or other intellectual property law.

On the Trail of The Space Pirates by Carey Rockwell (a pseudonym for a group of writers hired by publisher Grosset & Dunlap) was illustrated by Louis Glanzman. It was copyrighted in 1953 but the copyright was not renewed. Copyright status for items like these, originally published under copyright between 1923 and 1978, is more difficult to confirm than works that originated before 1923.

We Explore the Refine Mask Dialog as a "Line-Art Cleanup" Studio

WHEN WE FIRST SAW THE REFINE MASK DIALOG BOX, we thought it looked like an ideal "studio" for cleaning up scanned black-and-white line art, whether the scans were of printed material or pencil or ink drawings. We knew Refine Edge was designed to work on selections and masks, but we were pretty sure we could coax it into working with the line art scans, and we did. Corinna Buchholz of **piddix.com** (a master of scanning and scan cleanup) kindly allowed us to use some of her raw scans to experiment.

The **Space Pirates.psd** file is provided on the Wow DVD-ROM (in the Wow Goodies folder).

1 The first step is the scan. Corinna, who collects hundreds of examples of printed imagery, has developed a scanning method that works best for the scanner she carries with her, producing scans that take as little Photoshop work as possible (described on page 156). The scan we've used here is from an out-of-print book, whose copyright status Corinna thoroughly researched, as described on page 107.

The RGB scan from the book *The Revolt on Venus,* illustrated by Louis Glanzman and published in 1954, shows a stain or two on slightly yellowed pages, and the type also shows through from the back of the page.

2 To begin the clean-up, open the scan file in Photoshop and open the Channels panel (Window > Channels). Load the luminosity of the line work as a selection by Ctrl/⌘-clicking the thumbnail at the top of the Channels panel. (For an RGB file like this one, it's the composite RGB channel; for a Grayscale file, there's just the one channel.) Any smudges, stains, or bleeding type will be included along with the art, but we'll fix that later.

Click the RGB thumbnail to load the luminosity of the artwork as a selection. The light areas are selected and the dark areas unselected.

3 Add a new empty layer (click the 🔲 button at the bottom of the Layers panel) and then add a layer mask to it (click the 🔘 button). Because you have the active selection, the line art will be reproduced in the layer mask.

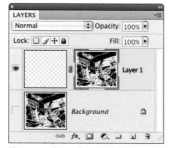

The artwork as a layer mask.

4 Now that you have a mask, you can use Refine Edge. With your new layer mask targeted in the Layers panel, turn off visibility for the original scan layer by clicking its 👁 in the Layers panel, and choose **Select > Refine Edge** to open the **Refine Mask** dialog. Make sure the **Preview** box is checked, and click on the Mask icon (the rightmost of the five preview mode icons near the bottom of the box). To start, move all the sliders to 0.

With all sliders set to 0, the type "bleed" is visible and the lines are a bit "soft."

5 Now increase **Contrast** until any smudging or gray on the paper — in this case the "ghost type" — disappears.

The bleeding type is gone, but some detail has been lost and the line edges look a little rough.

Use the **Radius** slider to regulate the amount of detail showing in the finest line work, and use the **Contract/Expand** slider to thicken or thin the lines. Readjust the Contrast if needed. If lines look jagged, increase **Smooth** a little. Leave **Feather** at 0. Marks that aren't part of the original artwork, such as the stain below the man's nose, are best removed later with Photoshop's Eraser tool rather than trying to finesse the repair in the Refine Mask dialog at the expense of the line work itself. When you have a look that you're happy with — there isn't one perfect

"right answer," just what appeals to you as clean line work and the right balance of ink and paper — click "OK" to close the dialog.

With these final settings the lines are a little thinner and smoother, and more white spaces have opened up.

6 To retrieve the line work from the layer mask, target the mask in the Layers panel, Select All (Ctrl/⌘-A) and Copy (Ctrl/⌘-C); then add a new layer (click ▣) and Paste (Ctrl/⌘-V). The result is shown at the bottom of the page.

In the finished file only the cleaned-up artwork in Layer 2 is visible. Though we haven't done it here, you can create paper color by adding a Solid Color Fill layer (click ⬤, choose Solid Color, and pick a color), dragging the new layer below Layer 2 in the Layers panel, and putting Layer 2 in Multiply mode (from the list at the top of the Layers panel).

JHDAVIS

A high-quality digital camera can capture an image with enough detail for successful enlargement.

FIND OUT MORE

▼ Bridge **page 133**

▼ Photo Downloader **page 134**

Digital Cameras

Digital cameras bypass film and record images directly as digital files. Digital cameras provide instant feedback — you can see the picture as soon as you take it, or even *before* you take it, with an accurate preview of the framing and lighting. This feature encourages experimentation and lets you know right away if you've captured the right shot or if you should try again. Also, the media card where the camera stores the photos can be re-used. Failed images can be erased immediately to make room for more successful ones.

Many digital cameras come with USB or FireWire connections for downloading images directly to your computer's hard drive or importing them into Photoshop as if the camera itself were a hard drive. Bridge (the file-management program that comes with Photoshop)▼ can recognize many digital cameras and automatically download images.▼ To save the camera's battery life, inexpensive card readers (USB and FireWire) are available for all types of camera storage media.

Comparing digital cameras to film cameras, digital files often have more noise at high speeds (ISO 200 and up) than film has grain. Most digital cameras are slower to respond. Pre-focusing and panning, two film photography techniques for capturing action, can be tricky for many digital cameras. Apertures (lens

MEGAPIXELS, MEGABYTES & PRINT SIZE

This chart is an enlargement guide for images from digital cameras (at their rated megapixel size) and scans of various file sizes (in megabytes). Or you can read the chart from the other direction — choose the print size you want and the printing method you plan to use, and see how big a file you will need. The numbers in the chart are conservative — for a given enlargement size, you will have plenty of resolution at the number of megapixels, megabytes, or pixel dimensions listed, without enlarging the image in Photoshop— which is always an option if you need it!

			Enlargement Size (to the nearest half-inch)		
Megapixels	Megabytes	Pixel Dimensions	Inkjet Printer (300 ppi)*	Halftone Press (133 lpi)**	Poster/Billboard (72 ppi)***
4	11.1	2272 x 1705	7.5" x 5.5"	8.5" x 6.5"	31.5" x 23.5"
5	14.4	2592 x 1944	8.5" x 6.5"	10" x 7"	36" x 27"
8	22.9	3264 x 2448	11" x 8"	12" x 9"	45" x 34"
10	28.6	3648 x 2736	12" x 9"	14" x 10"	50" x 38"
12	34.3	4000 x 3000	13.3" x 10"	15" x 11.3"	56" x 42"

*   Inkjet printers produce high-quality prints between 225 and 300 pixels/inch.

**   Halftone printing requires 1.5 to 2 pixels per inch for every line per inch in the halftone screen. For these enlargements, at 133 lpi, the ratio of ppi to lpi is high (2 ppi to 1 lpi); for the same enlargements at 150 lpi, the ratio is 1.77 to 1; at 175 lpi, the ratio is 1.52 to 1.

*** Billboards may require less resolution. Posters benefit from higher resolutions at closer viewing distances.

Card readers with slots for several kinds of media cards make it easy to download photos without connecting your camera directly to your computer, and they work with Bridge's **Get Photos from Camera** command.

openings) are not in the same relationship to the "film" plane as in film cameras, which means it's harder to use depth of field as creatively, keeping the subject in focus and blurring the background.▼ Aperture sizes in fixed-lens digital cameras usually lack the range of good film camera lenses, and shutter speeds are often neither as fast nor as slow as the extremes of the average 35mm camera. This limits stop-action photography or shooting in very bright or dim lighting.

FIND OUT MORE

▼ Simulating a shallow depth of field in Photoshop **page 309**

Choosing a digital camera. If you're trying to choose a digital camera, it can be helpful to make a list of your own priorities before you begin shopping — just so you don't succumb to "feature lust" and get sidetracked by features you'll seldom use. To prioritize, think about what type of photography you're most interested in. Following is a brief list of features to consider when trying to find a digital camera that fits your budget. Keep in mind, too, that there's no substitute for some in-store hands-on practice before you choose.

Very compact cameras are convenient to carry. Medium-size cameras have more controls available on the body; this one also has an LCD screen that swivels so you can preview shots at odd angles. Digital single-lens reflex cameras, which allow you to change lenses, are larger, often with even more controls on the body.

- **Megapixels.** The chart on page 110 shows that the more megapixels in a photo, the bigger the print you can make without having to enlarge the file in Photoshop. If your photo file isn't large enough, you may be left with too few pixels for the print size you want if you need to crop the image.

- **Size and shape.** Be sure to handle various styles and try out the controls to see which camera suits you. A **very compact** camera fits in a shirt pocket, but features may be limited. Few camera controls can fit on the body, and changing settings can mean scrolling through a number of menus. **Medium-sized** cameras, bigger and slightly heavier, often have a comfortable camera grip and more controls on the body, and they have room for more features. **SLR-type** bodies and full **DSLRs** (*digital single-lens reflex* cameras, with interchangeable lenses and the ability to view directly through the lens without waiting for the camera to project the image on an LCD screen) are bigger and bulkier, though they still may be small and lightweight compared to many film SLRs. They often have more features and more of their controls on the body.

- **Viewfinders.** The LCD screens on digital cameras come in various styles and sizes. A few cameras have LCDs that tilt and swivel, making it easier to take pictures at unusual angles, to be less obtrusive doing "street" photography, or simply to reduce glare on the screen. (This flip-and-swivel feature is harder to find today than it was a few years ago.)

One advantage of an LCD preview screen that flips out and swivels is that you can put the camera under things — such as live, growing flowers — and shoot without looking through the viewfinder. That's how Katrin Eismann shot *Poppy Underbelly*.

You can take advantage of the easy-to-use Camera Raw interface and keep color and tone adjustments "live," not only if you shoot in your camera's raw format, but even if you start with JPEG or TIFF files. If you start with a JPEG, you'll be limited to working in 8 Bits/Channel mode,▼ but Camera Raw can save time and file size in adjusting tone and color, compared to doing the same in Photoshop with Adjustment layers. "Camera Raw" on page 141 introduces this adjunct to Photoshop, and "Adjusting Tone & Color in Camera Raw" on page 297 has an example.

FIND OUT MORE

▼ 8 Bits/Channel mode **page 168**

▼ 16 Bits/Channel mode **page 169**

▼ Using Camera Raw **page 149**

On a real SLR, the mirror that allows direct viewing through the lens has to flip out of the way at the last instant as you take the picture. For this reason the LCD on some DSLRs can only be used for accessing menus and reviewing images after they've been taken, not for previewing them; other DSLRs now use another sensor to allow the screen to show you exactly what you'll get, before you take the picture. Non-SLR digital cameras have the LCD preview capability. Some LCDs have features to assist viewing in very dim or bright conditions, and some can be fitted with a hood to shield the screen from bright light.

Many cameras also have an **optical viewfinder**. It provides a continuous live view of the subject, but it usually shows less of the image than is being captured (sometimes a *lot* less) and can be partially blocked by a zoom lens. However, an optical viewfinder coupled with a short lag time (with the LCD turned off) between pressing the shutter and recording the image can be important for action photography.

Some digital cameras have an SLR-type **electronic viewfinder** (EVF) instead of an optical viewfinder. These generally show more of the image than an optical viewfinder, but like LCDs they have some lag in viewing. If controlling depth of field will be important when you shoot, make sure your camera's EVF will preview this.

- **File formats.** Digital cameras save photos in JPEG format, usually with at least two JPEG options (roughly Fine and Normal) — plenty for those occasions when storage space is at a premium. Some cameras also offer TIFF, and some also support their manufacturer's own raw format, which will have its own file suffix (.CRW and .NEF for Canon and Nikon are examples). Saving photos as TIFFs avoids compression artifacts that may happen with JPEGs, but often a camera's raw format is compressed (without JPEG artifacts) and faster to save than TIFF. For Photoshop users, the raw format is the most versatile. Raw files can be color-rich, taking advantage of Photoshop's 16 Bits/Channel mode.▼ A second advantage is that each image is stored in two separate parts: image data (the light information the camera collects) and the camera settings (the processing instructions, based on how you have the camera set). When you view a raw file in Photoshop's Camera Raw interface▼ or with the camera manufacturer's own software, you'll see the image as if the camera's settings had been applied to the image data, but you can quickly and easily apply alternate settings without changing the raw data and without throwing away the original settings. This

A digital camera takes the White Balance setting into account when processing the image data to make the picture. These color photos were taken under incandescent light at night without a flash. For the one at the top, the White Balance was set to Tungsten, so the camera corrected the image to "ignore" the yellow in the light. The bottom image shows what can happen if the White Balance is set for Daylight under the same circumstances.

means you can get back to the raw data again later and try different settings. It would be like sending your film back to be processed another way, or redoing exactly the same photo shoot but with a different type of film or lighting.

- **Metering and focusing.** If you plan to do your metering by pointing the camera at the subject, **center-weighted metering,** which computes an average exposure for the scene but by weighting the central 60–80%, is adequate only for evenly lit scenes and for flash photography. **Matrix,** or **pattern, metering** averages exposure of several light and dark areas, often weighting the exposure at the auto-focus point, and using a database of stored patterns to choose the pattern that best fits the scene. The addition of **spot metering** allows you to meter a smaller area (typically only 5–10% of the scene, so you can precisely expose for a specific subject whose lighting is atypical for the rest of the scene, letting the exposure for the rest of the image fall where it may. **Face detection** is a kind of spot metering that uses a pattern-recognition system (looking for two eyes, for instance) to find a face and then exposes for the face it has found; it can be useful for capturing the face of a backlit subject, or for "guerrilla" photography, unobtrusively taking quick shots of people. The more metering options you have, and the better you understand when to turn them on or off, the easier it will be to handle any kind of lighting.

Some cameras offer various **program modes,** such as portrait, landscape, sports, and night scenes, to set an optimal aperture and shutter speed for you, based on the camera's metering system. Several cameras offer more options to let you take control, including white balance, saturation and contrast controls, bracketing, manual exposure (only sometimes with aperture and shutter priority modes), and exposure lock (so you can recompose your shot for a small subject after using a larger, similarly lit area to set the exposure). The ability to control auto focus and auto exposure separately, now available on some digital cameras, lets you combine the advantages of automation with the control of manual operation, regulating exposure and focus separately for artistic lighting and depth of field.

White balance is the digital-camera equivalent of changing your film to suit the lighting. You've probably seen the orange- or green-tinged skin typical of tungsten or fluorescent lighting shot with daylight-balanced film. Unless you want the color cast for creative reasons, you can choose to have the camera adjust the "white" values to make the image look like it was taken in normal daylight. Some cameras will even

While bracketing is often used for exposure, with some digital cameras you can also bracket other image characteristics. These three shots resulted from bracketing saturation.

FIND OUT MORE

▼ Merging to HDR **page 260**

▼ Dealing with red-eye **page 318**

"program" a custom correction if you shoot a white target in the scene first.

Saturation and *contrast* controls allow you to choose vivid colors for landscapes and softer colors for portraits.

With *autobracketing*, all you need to do is select what to alter (exposure or saturation, for instance), and the camera typically will set up three shots — at normal, overexposed (or oversaturated), and underexposed (or undersaturated). Exposure bracketing is especially useful if lighting conditions are extreme and might fool the meter into over- or under-exposing (for photographing a big black dog or a sunset, for instance).

Photoshop can merge several exposures of the same shot into a single high-dynamic-range (HDR) file. ▼ To take advantage of the extra highlight and shadow detail this offers, you'll need a camera that can autobracket in steps of at least 0.5 EV (EV stands for *exposure value*, which is an aperture change of one f/stop or a doubling or halving of the shutter speed), or that offers aperture priority or manual mode so that you can do your own exposure bracketing.

Focus options range from *autofocus* to *focus lock* (on a sub-ject that can be off-center), to *continuous focus* (on moving subjects). Many cameras also provide *autofocus assist*, which is a beam of light that the autofocusing system can use to continue to work in dim light.

- **Zoom.** If it's important to you to have a camera that can zoom in on a subject, the criterion to pay attention to is the **optical zoom** capability. **Digital zoom** does one of two things, nei-ther of which is true lens zooming. In some cases a cropped version of the image is recorded; there is no loss of quality but no real advantage over using Photoshop for cropping. In other situations the camera's software enlarges the picture, but not as well as you can do it in Photoshop.

- **Wide angle.** Wide angle lenses span a wider field of view than our normal vision. Wide angle is essential for photographing room interiors and vast landscapes successfully in a single shot. A few very compact cameras offer the equivalent of 28mm or even 24mm in a film camera. But in general you'll need a larger camera for wider angles.

- **Flash.** Most cameras come with a small built-in flash unit that works in **Auto** mode, has **red-eye reduction** (which it offers because the flash is typically mounted very close to the lens, where the subject is likely to be looking), ▼ and can be turned off. Some also offer **fill flash** and **slow**, or **rear**, **sync**

If you plan to do much flash photography, you'll want to be sure to have extra batteries on hand. A flash uses lots of battery power.

If you find that your built-in flash is too bright for a particular situation, and you don't have easy-to-use software control of its brightness, try this: Cut a small rectangle of single- or double-ply toilet paper just big enough to cover and slightly overlap the flash. Moisten one edge and stick it onto the camera so it hangs down in front of the flash unit.

Several manufacturers of very compact cameras make waterproof models that also have features such as image stabilization and video (see page 118). An underwater camera housing is another option.

JHDAVIS / PENTAX OPTIO W60

for taking long exposures in low ambient light while freezing the subject in sharp focus. These flashes work only over short distances and rarely work well with wide-angle lenses. Some cameras offer a **hot shoe** for attaching a bigger, more flexible flash system. If you think you'll want that option, be sure to check that the camera will work with all the features of these expensive flash units.

- **Image stabilization (IS).** Mechanical stabilization in the camera or the lens helps minimize camera shake with video, low light, long lenses, and light cameras that can be hard to stabilize. Even if you can hold your breath when you shoot and brace your camera arm against something stable, IS may be helpful.

- **Macro.** If you plan to take photos of small objects at close range, a close-up, or *macro*, capability can be important. Pay attention to the range of focus. If there aren't several inches between the minimum and maximum focusing distances, your macro photography will be limited. Macro settings that engage only at the wide-angle setting can also be limiting, since there might not be enough magnification for the subject until you're so close that perspective is distorted. Check also to see if the camera can be equipped with a flash unit designed for macro mode — good lighting at close range can be difficult, and the built-in flash may not work at all.

- **Video.** Many still cameras now shoot short video clips as well, so you can have video and still get to take a still from it. "Jack Davis Gets the Shot He Wants" on page 118 shows an interesting use of the video feature.

Other features that are nice to have and that may be worth considering include:

- Weather resistance, an obvious consideration if you'll be shooting under exposed conditions.

- Long-lasting, rechargeable **battery** systems, the option to use batteries that are easy to find in most stores, and the ability to set the camera to turn off automatically if it's inactive for a period of time.

- Adapters or lens threads for filters and other accessories, such as macro, telephoto, and wide-angle lenses; you're more likely to find these in medium-size, SLR-like, and DSLR cameras.

- Diopter adjustments on viewfinders so people who wear glasses for distance correction can still see if they take off their glasses to keep them from bumping the viewfinder.

Digital Infrared

INFRARED-SENSITIVE black-and-white film, shot with a very dense filter, produces results that are spectacular, evocative, and always a bit of a surprise. The photographer can't preview the photo because the near infrared wavelengths the film records are just beyond what we can see. Infrared-capable digital cameras (see the tip at the right) offer certain advantages over film cameras. First, a digital camera with an LCD preview can give you an idea of how the shot will look before you take it. Second, you can see your results immediately. And you can also shoot infrared in color.

"Real" (mostly) The digital infrared examples on these two pages were created primarily in the camera — with help after the fact from Photoshop or Camera Raw. We hope they'll inspire you to experiment.

To block the visible light so it doesn't overwhelm the infrared, you'll need an infrared filter. Some infrared filters pass no visible light. The Hoya R72 filter, which is less expensive than some others, passes near infrared and some deep red light also.

If you can't mount a filter directly on your camera, you may be able to buy a conversion lens adapter (or tube adapter) designed for that purpose. For most infrared photography, you'll need a long exposure to pick up enough infrared "light" to make an image. So you may want to steady the camera with a tripod. Also, before you shoot, you'll want to make sure your flash is turned off.

The "real" part For the example at the right, photographer Rod Deutschmann shot a color image for reference **A** with a Canon PowerShot S45 in Program mode at 1/1000s at f/7.1. Next he turned on the camera's black-and-white effect and attached his infrared filter. He switched to the camera's Manual mode and watched the LCD monitor as he adjusted the exposure to 0.5s at f/3.2. To hold the camera still for the long exposure, he set it on a custom bean-bag and used a time delay **B**.

The Photoshop part Digital black-and-white infrared images are often low in contrast. One way to fix that is with a Levels or Curves Adjustment layer in Photoshop. Rod clicked the "Create new fill or adjustment layer" button ⬤ at the bottom of the Layers panel and chose Levels, then moved the black point and white point Input Levels sliders inward to adjust contrast **C**.▼

Experimenting with infrared in color Inspired by Deutschmann's infrared work, we tried some experiments of our own, shooting infrared in color. Our Auto snapshot of the duck pond looked quite ordinary **D**. Our infrared version **E**, taken after we added a Hoya R72 filter and set the exposure at 0.8s at f/2.0, was somewhat soft and grainy, like many infrared photos taken with film. Color was in the magenta/red range.

We opened the image file in Camera Raw▼ so we could use its convenient interface to experiment.

ROD DEUTSCHMANN

Compared to a color photo **A**, in infrared photographs (**B** and **C**), green leaves generally look white and luminous because of the way they reflect and refract infrared energy. Skies often look black because the infrared is absorbed, or sometimes they look silvery, depending on what's in the air. Shadow patterns are often different than in a standard photograph, and water surfaces tend to look smoother and less reflective.

To follow along with the Camera Raw adjustments, open the **Infrared duck pond.psd** file in Photoshop CS4 (or CS3, but you'll need Camera Raw 4.2 or later for the Clarity adjustments below▼). Double-click the Smart Object thumbnail in the Layers panel to open Camera Raw.

In Camera Raw we set the view to 100% (in the lower left corner of the Camera Raw interface) for an accurate look as we adjusted settings. In the **Basics panel** we expanded the tonal range by clicking **Auto**, which increased the Blacks (resetting the black point) and the Contrast. We raised the **Fill Light** value to lighten the shadows to show more detail there, set **Clarity** to the maximum value to sharpen up the trees, and increased **Vibrance** to intensify some of the more neutral colors.

From there we went to the **HSL/Grayscale panel.** In the **Hue tab** we moved the **Purples** and **Magentas** sliders far to the left to shift these colors toward blue. Our color changes had increased the color noise, so we worked in the **Details panel** to increase Color noise suppression to the maximum 100%. In the **Lens Corrections panel** we set a negative value for the Amount of **Lens Vignetting**, darkening the edges to "frame" the scene.

Our last Camera Raw adjustment was made with the **Adjustment Brush** 🖌, available in CS4"s Camera Raw. When we chose it from the tool bar at the top of the interface, the **Adjustment Brush panel** opened, showing all the adjustments that can be made with this tool. We set **Clarity** at 100 and all other sliders at 0, chose a large brush size, and softened the edge of the brush by setting the Feather. We painted over the trees, reduced the size of the brush, and dabbed the duck, essentially giving them a "second dose" of Clarity by adding to the 100% maximum we had set in the Basics tab; we didn't paint the sky or water because we didn't want to bring back the noise **F**.

We Shift-clicked to change the "Open" button to "Open Object" and open the file in Photoshop as a Smart Object. We added a Hue/Saturation Adjustment layer▼ and moved the Hue and Saturation sliders **G**. (A Hue shift on a normal color image is risky, since it can distort color relationships. But here we didn't worry about that.)

 Wow Goodies > Infrared pond.psd

FIND OUT MORE

▼ Opening JPEGs & TIFFs in Camera Raw **page 141**

▼ Updating Camera Raw in Photoshop CS3 **page 142**

▼ Using Adjustment layers **page 245**

Jack Davis Gets the Shot He Wants

WHERE THERE'S A WILL THERE'S A WAY. Not everyone wakes up one morning wanting to shoot photos from a surfboard. But Jack Davis's approach to that challenge highlights the advantages of knowing the capabilities of your equipment and feeling free to stretch the limits and try out something new.

Jack started with a camera that could capture the vastness of the nearshore Pacific *and* withstand the rigors of moving through the surf — waterproof, coldproof, and wide-angle. Davis could paddle out on his surfboard and shoot photos, then go back to his studio and enhance color, contrast, and clarity in Camera Raw, and add vignette edges.▼ From there he could open the photos in Photoshop for any additional work he might want to do.

Shot with the Pentax Optio W60

ALL PHOTOS: JACK DAVIS

FIND OUT MORE
▼ Using Camera Raw **page 141**

But for real action shots he would need to mount the camera on the surfboard so it could operate hands-free while he surfed. Using a Sticky Pod suction cup and knuckle, he could secure the camera without putting holes in the board, and he could set up in landscape or portrait orientation.

Camera mounted with a Sticky Pod suction cup and knuckle (www.stickypod.com), in landscape orientation, facing forward. (Images shown here were actually shot with the camera in portrait orientation.)

Now, how would he trigger the shot? It wasn't as if he could set the self-timer and count on a perfectly framed shot when the shutter clicked. Many compact digitals can shoot short videos, some at a high enough resolution to use the individual frames as stills. Davis would shoot HD 720p (1280 x 720) AVI at 15 frames per second and choose frames for stills afterwards.

He was ready. He could now paddle his board into position, turn the camera on in movie mode, and catch the wave. With the constant wave motion and the single rubber suction-cup mount, "the video," Jack says, "won't work as video." As stills, though, the individual frames would work fine. Back at his computer later, Jack reviewed the video and picked out any

frames he wanted as stills; "Stills from Video" in Chapter 10 tells one way to do this, and two examples of Jack's results are shown below.

An image extracted from video shot with a surfboard-mounted camera. Davis aimed the board to aim the camera.

Shot with a surfboard-mounted camera facing backwards to capture the photographer

Cher Threinen-Pendarvis used Photoshop with a Wacom Intuos tablet and a laptop computer to draw sketches (top two) for her *Alps Study* on location, then completed the painting on her desktop computer, also with the Intuos. To optimize Photoshop's performance while working on location and the "natural media" feel of the painting tools, she painted on a single layer and purged History often.

When you choose File > Open and then choose a .pdf file, the Import PDF dialog opens, and you can choose whether to open one or more images or one or more entire pages. If you choose Pages, you can set the size, color mode, and resolution of the file that opens.

Digital Stock

In addition to the images you scan yourself or capture with a digital camera, there's a wealth of stock images, patterns, textures, and illustrations downloadable from the web or available on CD-ROM, with a variety of arrangements for use and payment. As an alternative to per-image fees, some stock photo sources offer subscriptions that allow you to pay in advance for a number of images at a reduced rate and then download files as you need them. Sources of stock photos include those that provided some of the images used in this book — PhotoSpin.com, Corbis Royalty Free, iStockphoto, and PhotoDisc. Another great source is Stock.XCHNG (www.sxc.hu), self-described as "a friendly community of photography addicts who generously offer their works to the public free of charge"; some Stock.XCHNG images require attribution to and notification of the photographer.

Pressure-Sensitive Tablets

For imitating traditional art media such as the paintbrush, pencil, airbrush, or charcoal, a pressure-sensitive graphics tablet with stylus — for example, any of those in Wacom's Intuos or less expensive Graphire line — has a more familiar feel than a mouse and also provides much better control. Photoshop's painting tools (see Chapter 6) are "wired" to take advantage of pressure sensitivity for controlling brush size, how thick or thin the paint is and how fast it flows, how much paint the brush can hold, and how much the color of the paint varies. You can simply paint or sketch on the tablet surface and the strokes respond to the subtle movements of the hand. Such variations are natural, even unavoidable in traditional media, and they also bring a hand-painted look to painting on the computer.

Acquiring Images from PDFs

Choosing File > Open and choosing a PDF file opens the **Import PDF** dialog box, where you can choose to import full Pages or individual Images; click to identify the image or page you want to open (or Ctrl/⌘-click or Shift-click for more than one) and click "OK." Alternatively, you can import from PDFs via Bridge. With one PDF file targeted in **Bridge**, choose **File > Open With > Adobe Photoshop CS3/CS4** to bring up the Import PDF dialog, and open pages or images as described above. ***Note:*** Opening PDF pages can result in files that include transparency, so they may not look exactly as you would expect from looking at the original PDF pages. Add a layer filled with white at the bottom of the stack of layers if you want to view the PDF the way it would look when printed on white paper.

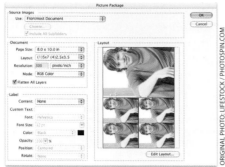

ORIGINAL PHOTO: LIFESTOCK / PHOTOSPIN.COM

Useful for arranging multiples of an image in the most compact layout for cutting them apart efficiently, Picture Package can also be used to assemble several images in a custom layout, as shown on page 646. Picture Package is not installed with Photoshop CS4. To add it to the File > Automate menu, download the Optional Plug-ins package from the Adobe web site: We found it at (Mac) http://www.adobe.com/support/downloads/detail.jsp?ftpID=4047 or (Windows) http://www.adobe.com/support/downloads/detail.jsp?ftpID=4048. Picture Package is installed as part of the Contact Sheet II installation.

Actions provide a way to automate effects that are more complex than applying a single filter or Layer Style. Find examples of Wow Actions for painting on page 415 and for special effects on page 553.

GOING FAST: AUTOMATING

Many filters and Layer Styles, shown and discussed in detail throughout this book, "automate" complex dimensional or tone-and-color effects. Beyond the filters and Styles, two menus — **File > Automate** and **File > Scripts** — offer several options for automating tasks in Photoshop, with some of them moving to Bridge in CS4. And the **Actions panel** is one of the most useful automation tools found in the program.

Actions

The Actions panel offers a way to **record** a whole series of Photoshop operations and **play them back** in order, on a single file or a whole batch. An Action can be a great way to automate routine production tasks that you find yourself repeating often, or just to record your creative process as you work out some phenomenal Photoshop treatment, so you have an operational record of what you did.

In a nutshell the process of creating and using an Action is this: You open a file of the kind you want to operate on, turn on Photoshop's recording apparatus, carry out the operations you want to record, and stop recording. You can then go back into the Action and add pauses where you want the routine to wait for user input, or where you want to insert directions or an explanation. Save your Action. Now you can play back the Action on another file whenever you want to.

Actions are listed by name in the Actions panel, where they are grouped in **sets**, with each set indicated by a folder icon ▢. Sets make it possible to assemble "toolkits" of Actions for particular jobs, and you can include the same Action in several different sets, or even within other Actions.

NO ACTION STANDS ALONE

It used to be that an Action could be "naked" — separate and independent of a set. But now each Action has to be in a set, even if it's the set's only member. To record a new Action, you first have to choose or create a set for it to belong to.

To run an Action on more than one file at a time, use the File > Automate > **Batch** command, or incorporate the Action in an Image Processor or Script Events Manager routine (described on pages 125 and 126). Or turn an Action into a *Droplet*, a stand-alone "mini program" with its own icon that sits on the Desktop and runs the Action on any files whose icons are dragged onto it, as described on page 125.

continued on page 122

THE ACTIONS PANEL

Actions are listed in **sets** in the Actions panel. The control strip at the bottom has buttons for recording and playing Actions, while the panel's menu ▾☰ offers most of the commands you need for editing, controlling playback, saving and loading Actions, and assigning keyboard shortcuts. Each Action is made up of a series of recorded **steps**, and each Action is part of a set.

A **black check mark** next to the name of a **set**, an **Action**, or an individual **step** shows that it's active and will play if you click or Ctrl/⌘-click on its name and click the "Play" button ▶ at the bottom of the panel.

A **red check mark** alerts you to the fact that **some steps** in a set or an Action are **currently not active** and won't play.

A **black modal control icon next to an Action or set** means there will be a stop at *every* step that involves a dialog box or an Enter/Return option.

A **red modal control icon next to an Action or set** means there is *at least one* stop-and-wait-for-input step included.

A **black modal control icon next to a step** indicates that this step will stop and wait for input via a dialog box or the Enter/Return key.

If **no check mark** appears, that particular set, Action, or step is **currently turned off** and will not be carried out if you try to play it.

Stop: Click to stop recording or playing.

Record: Click to begin recording. When the button is red, recording is in progress.

Play: Click to run a selected Action or to play from a selected step onward. **Ctrl/⌘-click** to play only the selected step and then stop.

Click to **expand or close the listing**.

Action **set**

Action

Step

Create new set

Create new action

Delete: Remove the targeted step, Action, or set.

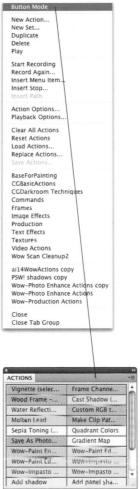

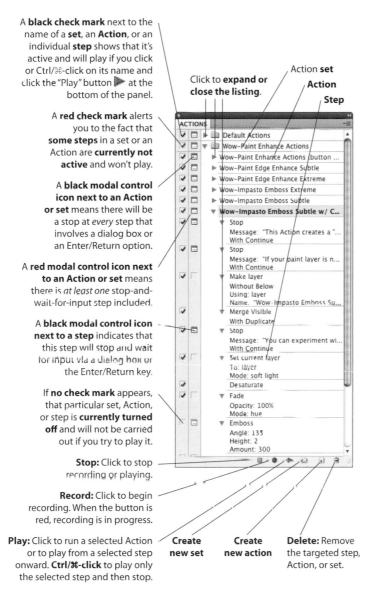

If you put the Actions panel in **Button mode** (as shown here), you can use a multi-column layout: Simply drag the lower right corner to widen the panel to two or more columns; the individual buttons will get narrower. Also, you can color-code Actions, making it easier to find them again in Button mode. **Color coding** an Action can be done in the New Action dialog box when an Action is recorded, or by choosing **Action Options** from the Actions panel's menu ▾☰ when the panel is in List mode. (If you have the panel in Button mode, you can toggle back to List mode by choosing Button Mode again from the panel menu.)

Besides Photoshop's main menu and panel menus, choices from context-sensitive menus can also be recorded in Actions.

PHOTO: YURI ARCURS / PHOTOSPIN.COM

Right-clicking/Ctrl-clicking opens a context-sensitive menu with "recordable" choices appropriate for the element you're working on or the tool you're using.

In an Action the effect of a **toggle command** like Snap To Guides or Show/Hide Guides will depend on the state of the file when the Action plays the command. In other words, even though the command you recorded when you made the Action was Show Guides, if guidelines are already showing when the Action plays the Show Guides command, it will *Hide Guides* instead.

Choices from the Actions panel itself are among the things that can be recorded in an Action. That means you can nest an existing Action within the one you're currently recording. Here's how: As you record, click in the Actions panel to target the Action you want to include, then press the "Play" button ▶. This Action will be added as a step in the one you're recording. Being able to nest Actions means that you can easily run several nested Actions with one application of the File > Automate > Batch command or with File > Scripts > Image Processor.

Recording an Action. To record an Action so you'll be able to apply the whole series of steps again, start by opening a file like the ones you want the Action to work on. Then do one of the following:

- **To record your Action as the first in a brand-new set,** click the "Create new set" button ▭ at the bottom of the Actions panel, name the set, and click "OK." Then click the "Create new action" button ▣ next to it, name the Action, and click "Record." Start performing operations, tailoring your choices within the limitations of "actionable" operations, as described in "What's 'Actionable,'" below.

- **To record your Action as part of an existing set,** do as described above, except skip the "Create new set" step, instead clicking on the name of the set you want to add it to.

The "Record" button ● at the bottom of the Actions panel will stay red (indicating that recording is in progress) until you press the "Stop" button ■ to end the recording session.

What's "Actionable." Many of Photoshop's **commands** and **tool operations** are "actionable" — each is recorded as a step in the Action as you carry out the command or use the tool. Also recorded are choices made in the **Layers, Channels, Paths, History, Animation, Adjustments, Masks, 3D,** and other panels, as well as the **Actions panel** itself (see the "Nesting Actions" tip at the left).

For other commands and operations that can't be recorded directly, there are workarounds.

- **Paths drawn "by hand" with the Pen tools** ✑ ✒ **won't be recorded as you draw them,** but you can include a path as part of an Action by drawing the path, saving it in the Paths panel with a unique name,▼ then selecting the path in the Paths panel, clicking the Actions panel's ▾☰ button to open the panel menu, and choosing the **Insert Path** command. When the Action is played on another file, the original path will be added to the new file's Paths panel as the *Work Path*, and further commands in the Action can use that path.

  FIND OUT MORE
  ▼ Working with paths **page 448**

- **The strokes of brush-based tools aren't recorded.** These are strokes made with the Brush ✐, Pencil ✐, Healing Brush ✐, Spot Healing Brush ✐, Clone Stamp ♨, Pattern Stamp ♨, Erasers ⌫⌫⌫, Smudge ✋, Sharpen △, Blur ⬭, Dodge 🔍, Burn ✋, and Sponge ⬭. Instead you can insert a pause, complete with directions for what to do during the pause, so the

There are a few dialog box and panel settings that are recorded *only if they are changed* from an existing setting. Examples are the Layer Properties, Color Settings, and Preferences dialogs. So if you want to record current settings, you have to *change to other settings before recording* so you can then record the process of *changing* to the desired settings. As a check, after you've recorded the use of a dialog box or panel, you can tell which settings have been recorded by expanding the Actions panel's listing for the recorded step to see what it includes.

The Insert Menu Item dialog is a little unusual, in that it requires you to work outside the dialog while it's open. When the dialog opens, choose the item you want to insert from one of Photoshop's menus and then click "OK" to close the box.

When you choose **Insert Stop** from the Actions panel's pop-out menu so that your Action will stop running and display a message or give the user some instructions or a chance for input, you have the opportunity to "Allow Continue." If you check this box, the message that's displayed when the Action stops will include a "Continue" button to make it easier to continue the Action if the user doesn't need to do anything. The user can simply click "Continue" to close the dialog and go on. Without a "Continue" button, it would be necessary to click the next step in the Actions panel and then click the "Play" button at the bottom of the panel.

user can stop and do the necessary work with these tools. To put a pause in the Action, choose the **Insert Stop** command from the Actions panel's menu ▾☰, as described below.

- Some of the choices made in the **Options bar**, **panels**, and **dialog boxes** are recorded, and others are not. (To tell which choices are recorded, watch the Actions panel as you record to see whether your choice adds a step to the Action.) Again, you can include the **Insert Stop** command for a choice that isn't recorded, with directions so the person playing the Action can make the appropriate settings.

It's helpful to insert a Stop at the beginning of an Action to tell what the Action does, how the file needs to be set up to run it, or how to handle any error messages that might appear. Be sure to include the option to Continue after reading.

- Some commands can't be recorded directly as you carry them out. Instead this kind of command can be recorded by choosing **Insert Menu Item** from the Actions panel's menu ▾☰. When the Insert Menu Item command opens, go outside the dialog to choose the menu command you want, and then click "OK" inside the dialog. *Note:* When you use Insert Menu Item, *the inserted command won't be carried out during your recording session.* So if you need a nonrecordable command to be carried out in order for the rest of the Action to be recorded correctly, you'll have to both **carry out the operation in its nonrecordable form** (to do the job in the file you're recording from) *and* **use the Insert Menu Item command** (to get the operation recorded so that it will be carried out when the Action is played).

- Of course, once your Action is recorded, it will work only if the **conditions of the file** you're working on will allow it to work. For instance, if your Action includes a step to add a layer mask, that won't happen if the layer that's active when that step is played is the *Background* layer, which can't have a mask. So you have to be sure that you include in the Action all the steps necessary to prepare the file for each next step of the Action — or choose **Insert Stop** from the panel's menu ▾☰, and type a message that explains the requirements so the user can pause and get the file ready. Select the **Allow Continue** option if you want the user to be able to proceed with the Action without doing anything more than reading the message. As a safeguard, you can leave the Allow Continue box unchecked if some input is *required* before the Action can proceed. When you've finished making entries in the Record Stop dialog box, click "OK."

Here are some things that are worth thinking about almost any time you record an Action:

• As soon as you start recording, **make a copy of the file's "pre-Action" state** with the Image > Duplicate command, so you have a way to recover your original if you don't like the "actioned" result.

• For some Photoshop operations the file has to be in a certain mode. For instance, the Lighting Effects filter runs only on RGB Color files. If your Action requires that the file be in a specific mode, record choosing the **File > Automate > Conditional Mode Change** command.

Turning on all the Source Mode options and setting the Target Mode to RGB Color ensures that the Conditional Mode Change command will convert a file in any other color mode to RGB Color.

• Whenever your Action creates a new layer or channel, make sure to give it a **unique name** rather than leaving it at the default "Layer 1" or "Alpha 1," for instance. That way you'll avoid problems that can arise from running the Action on a file that already has a "Layer 1" or "Alpha 1."

Editing an Action. If you want to modify an Action you've recorded, here are some easy methods. Start by expanding the list of steps in the Action by clicking the ▶ to the left of the Action's (or set's) name in the Actions panel, so you can see all the steps.

• To make the Action **pause within a step** so the user can make choices in a dialog box, click in the **modal control column** just to the left of the step's name. A **modal control icon** ⊡ will appear in the column to show that the Action will pause with the dialog box open. Clicking again in this column toggles the pause function off; the ⊡ disappears.

The modal control works not only for dialog boxes but also for operations that require pressing the Enter/Return key (or double-clicking) to accept the current settings, such as using the Free Transform command or the Crop tool ⛏.

• **To change settings** for a step that involves a dialog box, double-click the step in the expanded listing to open the dialog, then enter new settings, and click "OK."

• **To remove a step** (or even an entire Action or set), drag it to the "Delete" button 🗑 at the bottom of the panel.

• **To temporarily disable a step** so it isn't carried out when you play the Action, click the step's check mark in the farthest left column of the Actions panel. Click in this column again to bring back the check mark and re-enable the step. (This also works for disabling or re-enabling an Action without permanently removing it from the set.)

• **To insert a new step** (or steps) in an Action, click the step you want the new step to come after. Then click the "Record" button ●, record the new step, and click "Stop" ■.

• **To change the order of steps,** drag their names up or down to new positions in the list of steps for the Action.

• **To duplicate a step,** hold down the Alt/Option key and drag the step's name to the point where you want the copy.

Saving Actions. A new or changed Action set can (and should!) be permanently saved. You can do this by clicking on the set's name in the Actions panel, then clicking the ▾≡ button in the top right corner of the panel, and choosing Save Actions. (If you don't want to replace the old version, give the new one a new name.)

The **Playback Options** command from the Actions panel's menu ▾ ≡ can be used to make Actions run speedily (Accelerated, the default) or one step at a time so you can see the result of each step before the Action continues (good for diagnosing a problematic Action) or with a defined pause.

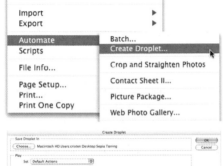

If you click on the name of an Action in the Actions panel's list mode and then choose the File > Automate > **Create Droplet** command, the Create Droplet dialog box opens, where you can choose how your processed documents will be named. Here the word "_sepia," a sequence number, and the file-type extension (such as .tif or .psd) are added to the document name for files processed by a Sepia Toning Droplet so it's easy to tell, just from the name, that the file has been sepia-toned. Adding a sequence number creates a unique filename in case there are identically named images in the subfolders.

When you click "OK" in the Create Droplet box, the Action is exported as a standalone macro. You can run the Action saved in the Droplet by dragging a file or folder icon onto the Droplet icon.

Loading Actions. You can load any saved Actions set as an *addition* to the current panel (choose **Load Actions** from the panel's pop-out menu ▾ ≡), or you can load it *instead of* the Actions currently in the panel (choose **Replace Actions**). *Note:* Before you replace Actions, make sure you've saved the current set so you'll be able to retrieve it again.

Playing an Action. Once you've recorded and saved an Action or loaded an Action that was recorded by someone else, you have several playback options:

- **To run an entire Action (or even a series of nested Actions),** click its name in the Actions panel and click the "Play" button ▶ at the bottom of the panel.

- **To play an Action from a specific step** forward, click on that step in the Actions panel and simply click the "Play" button ▶.

- **To play a single step** of an Action, click on that step to select it, and then **Ctrl/⌘-click** the "Play" button ▶.

Automating Actions. To run an Action on a whole batch of files, put the files into a folder and use the File > Automate > **Batch** command. Or create a standalone **Droplet,** an application made from the Action, by choosing File > Automate > **Create Droplet**. In the Batch or Create Droplet dialog box, choose the Action you want to play. In designating a Destination for the files after they've been treated with the Action, **if you choose "Save and Close," the old files will be overwritten** by the altered ones. If you choose to save the files to a designated Folder, you have tremendous flexibility in naming them. You can choose from the pop-up File Naming lists, or type in your own choices. This makes it possible, for instance, to create a numbered or lettered series of files with the same basic name.

Once you've made a Droplet, you can drag a file or a folder of files onto the Droplet's icon on the Desktop to launch Photoshop (if necessary), run the Action on the file(s), and save the results in the folder you chose.

The process of running Actions can also be automated through the File > Scripts menu with the Image Processor command or with Script Events Manager, as described on page 126.

Scripts

Even if you don't care to do your own script-writing, you're likely to find the scripts provided with Photoshop, through

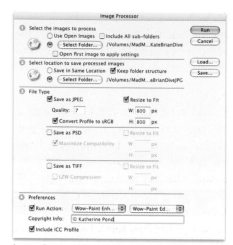

Image Processor is a quick and easy way to convert multiple files to any of three different common formats for print and web publishing, and archiving.

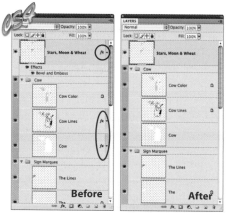

The Flatten All Layer Effects command and the Flatten All Masks command are new in CS4. They take all the Layer Styles and masks applied anywhere in your file and rasterize them, merging their effects into their respective layers as pixels. It's a "one-click" way to help ensure that other programs that can't "read" Layer Styles can still work with your file. These two commands also provide a way to pass on a file to someone else without giving the recipient access to changing the Styles or masks. Both commands can be found in the File > Scripts menu.

SCRIPTING GUIDES

Adobe provides references for writing your own scripts for Photoshop, installed along with the program. Find them in the Scripting Guide folder inside the Adobe Photoshop CS3 (or CS4) folder if you're so inclined.

the File > Scripts command, worth exploring. Both CS3 and CS4 have scripts to export all the layers or layer comps in a file as a series of separate files, to import files as layers in a single file, and (in Photoshop Extended) to perform statistical comparisons on color data from layer to layer, as well as other more specialized commands such as Load Multiple DICOM Files. The File > Scripts menu also accesses two very practical file-management scripts, **Image Processor** and **Script Events Manager**.

Image Processor. If you want to save a group of files in a particular format, at a particular size, or after performing the same set of operations on each file, Image Processor can speed up the process. Open the dialog box (File > Scripts > Image Processor), choose the folder or open files you want to process, and choose the file formats (TIFF, PSD, or JPEG) and sizes you need. Choose to add copyright data if you like, or run an Action of your choice. If this process is one you use often, save your Image Processor settings to load and use again. You can also run Image Processor through Bridge's Tools > Photoshop > Image Processor command.

Script Events Manager. The Script Events Manager could be called the Script and Action Events Manager. With this command you can set up Photoshop to invoke a Script (or an Action) of your choice whenever the *event* you specify happens. An event can be the startup of Photoshop, or opening, creating, or saving a file, for instance.

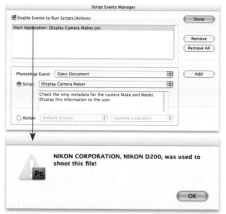

Here the **Script Events Manager** was used to display the EXIF data for the camera maker whenever a file is opened. Processing several images from different cameras, you might want to run different Actions "calibrated" to the camera model, and running this script is easier than opening File > Info for each image. When you're processing other types of files, however, the info box just gets in the way. The Script Events manager makes it easy to turn on these automatic "mini programs" (with the "Add" button) or turn them off (with "Remove").

The Photoshop Format Options dialog box appears when you save a file in PSD format. If you know that you always want to include the composite, you can avoid having the dialog box appear: Choose Preferences > File Handling (from the Edit menu in Windows, the Photoshop menu on the Mac) and choose from the Maximize Compatibility pop-up menu.

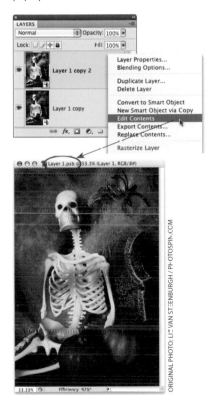

A PSB file that holds the contents of a Smart Object is stored as part of the Photoshop (PSD) file the Smart Object resides in. You can open the PSB file by right-clicking/Ctrl-clicking the Smart Object's thumbnail in the Layers panel and choosing Edit Contents from the context-sensitive menu.

GETTING OUT: OUTPUT

Photoshop can save files in dozens of formats. The one to choose will depend on how you want to use the file. Here are some suggestions.

Photoshop (PSD) Format

Photoshop (PSD) is a very conservative and flexible format that makes it easy to change or repurpose a file later. It preserves all the layers, masks, channels, paths, live type, Layer Styles and animation, as well as annotations added with the Notes/Note tool 📝 (or with the Audio Annotation tool 🔊 in CS3; audio annotation is gone from CS4). Whenever you plan to open and work on a file in Photoshop again, the PSD format is an ideal way to save it. The PSD format works well for files that you want to take into other programs in the Adobe Creative Suite, such as Adobe InDesign (see below), and Adobe Illustrator (see page 459).

By default, when you save in PSD format, you can save with or without the composite, as shown at the left. Saving **without the composite** makes the file size smaller. But if you save **with the composite**, the image can be displayed in programs that accept Photoshop files but don't necessarily support all the features of Photoshop CS3/CS4 — programs like earlier versions of Photoshop, as well as InDesign CS and Illustrator CS, which need the composite in order to work with 16 Bits/Channel PSD files. Another good reason to opt for PSD is that Adobe recommends **PSD with "Maximize compatibility"** turned on as the format with the most compatibility with future versions of Photoshop.

Very Large Files & Smart Objects (PSB)

If you need to create an image that's bigger than the 2 gigabyte limit that PSD and other file formats allow, you can use Large Document Format (PSB), which supports documents up to 300,000 by 300,000 pixels. Like PSD, it preserves all the layers, channels, paths, live type, Layer Styles, and annotations you can create in Photoshop. Also, a PSB file is automatically created when a Smart Object is created, to store the information protected by the Smart Object. **Note:** PSB files can be opened in Photoshop CS and later versions, but not in earlier versions.

Formats for Page Layout Programs & Output Services

Photoshop (PSD) files can be placed directly into **Adobe InDesign** CS and later versions with transparency maintained. This means that a silhouetted or partly transparent element will let the InDesign page show through. And you can fine-tune, or even completely change, the placement of the elements of your

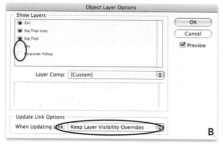

Our original layout was designed in Photoshop using five layers, an alpha channel for silhouetting, and type converted to Shape layers with Layer Styles applied; it was saved in PSD format. To put three different versions of the file on this Adobe InDesign page, we first placed it, using InDesign's File > Place command **A**. We then Alt/Option-dragged with InDesign's Selection tool to make another copy. Right-clicking/Ctrl-clicking on the copy brought up a context-sensitive menu; we chose Object Layer Options to open a dialog box where we could choose which layers to show **B**. We clicked the 👁 for each layer whose visibility we wanted to turn off to produce a version with the logotype and silhouetted girl **C**. For the third version **D**, we made three more copies and set visibility for each — one showing the logotype, one with the girl, and one with the sky. We stacked the three, stretched the one with the sky, and rearranged the girl and logotype.

 Jog Togs.psd

Photoshop file to suit the page layout. You can specify which layers (or layer comps if you've made them) should be displayed and which should be hidden, so that you can work with the separate parts of your file, as shown at the left.

For page layout programs that don't support PSD files, the formats of choice are TIFF, Photoshop EPS, and Photoshop DCS 2.0. **Photoshop EPS** files can include sharp-edged type and clipping paths, to silhouette the image so it appears without a background or a block of white space around it. **TIFF** files can use lossless compression, making the file smaller for storage and transport without degrading the image at all; they can also include clipping paths, but type is rasterized (converted to pixels at the resolution of the image), so it may not look as sharp as in the PSD or EPS format. Because not all programs support all TIFF and EPS features, it's a good idea to check your page layout program or ask your imagesetting or printing service to find out what formats and features they accept or prefer.

For files that include **spot colors** (custom inks that are used instead of or along with the standard CMYK printing inks), PSD format works with InDesign CS and later versions. For QuarkXPress or earlier versions of InDesign, save spot-color files in the Photoshop EPS, PDF, or DCS 2.0 format. Again, check your page layout program or ask your output service.

PDF for Communicating with Others

When you need a file format that's **readable by others who may not have Photoshop, Photoshop PDF** is a very flexible choice. It's the option of choice for many print service providers. All that's needed to display the image and to read any notations you may have added with Photoshop's Notes/Note tool 📝 is the free Adobe Reader software. In CS4 you can choose **Preserve Photoshop Editing Capabilities** in the Save Adobe PDF dialog box. Checking this box allows Notes added or edited in Acrobat to be preserved when the file is opened again in Photoshop (you'll need the full Acrobat program for this, not just the Reader).

Besides saving a single file as a PDF, you can create a slide show in PDF format of several Photoshop images with a choice of transitions between the slides. In CS3 use File > Automate > **PDF Presentation**. In CS4 use the output module in Bridge's Workspace menu, a pop-out in the Applications bar (page 136).

Formats for Compact Storage & Transfer

Some file formats are more compact than others. When file size is important, the format you use to compress your file will depend on how you want to use that file:

By default, when the File > Save As command makes a JPEG file, it includes an icon and thumbnails, which help you identify the file on your hard drive, but which also add to the file size. If you want to be able to really pare down files for the web, you can choose Preferences (the shortcut is Ctrl/⌘-K) > File Handling and set the Image Previews option to Ask When Saving, so you can choose not to include these items.

The standard JPEG file format is "lossy." This means that the image may be degraded each time it's "JPEGed." To minimize image degradation don't "re-JPEG" a file. Instead save your file in PSD or TIFF as you work, and convert a copy to the compact JPEG format just before you post or send it.

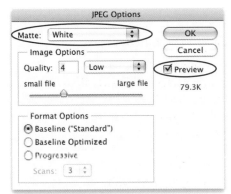

Photoshop's JPEG Options dialog, which opens when you choose JPEG as the Format in the Save As dialog box, lets you preview the effect that JPEG compression will have on your image, so you can adjust the Quality until you get the balance you want between quality and file size. If your file doesn't have a *Background*, you can choose what background color (Matte) will be used to fill in for transparency.

FIND OUT MORE

▼ 16 Bits/Channel & 32 Bits/Channel modes **page 169**

▼ Camera Raw **page 141**

- For maximum flexibility, keeping layers, editable type, and other Photoshop features intact, use PSD or PDF.
- For on-screen viewing and printing, use JPEG (described next) or PDF.
- To send via email for on-screen viewing only, use JPEG, but first reduce the file's size (see "Preparing an Image for Emailing" on page 132).
- For display on the web, use JPEG or GIF, as described in "Choosing a File Format for Static Web Graphics" on page 131.

JPEG can be great for embedding or attaching to an email as a quick way to let someone look at an image. JPEG is popular because it can be so compact, but its file compression can be "lossy" — that is, it throws away some color detail information in the process of reducing the file's bulk. The File > Save As > JPEG command gives you 12 choices for degree of compression. In general, the more you increase compression to decrease file size, the more you reduce image quality. JPEG was designed to start its compression by throwing away the kinds of color detail data that would be lost in the printing process anyway. So a high-quality JPEG file may not show a loss of quality when the file is printed.

File Formats for 16 & 32 Bits/Channel

Photoshop offers several file formats that support 16 Bits/Channel mode.▼ Photoshop (PSD), Large Document Format (PSB), Photoshop PDF, and TIFF preserve all the layers, channels, paths, live type, Layer Styles, and annotations that Photoshop supports. Photoshop 32 Bits/Channel images can be saved in PSB, as well as PSD, TIFF, HDR, and PBM (portable bitmap, a format used for transferring files between programs). In addition, Photoshop can save flattened 16 Bits/Channel files in specialty formats such as Cineon, PNG, Photoshop RAW, and Dicom (a medical format; in Photoshop Extended only).

Digital Negative Format for Camera Raw Files

Adobe's **Digital Negative (DNG)** is a format for archiving any camera's raw files, or any JPEG or TIFF files that you open in Camera Raw and want to maintain in a raw format. (Recall that raw formats store photos in two parts, as the raw data recorded by the camera's sensors and the *metadata* that describes the camera settings to be used to produce an image from the raw data.) DNG is one of the formats that you can save directly from Camera Raw▼ (along with TIFF, JPEG, and PSD), without opening the file in Photoshop. If you save a raw file in DNG format, it's a good idea to also keep the original file in the camera's own

Zoomable

The **Zoomify** command is extremely easy to use, especially considering the scope of what it does. To turn a high-resolution image **A** into a navigable, smoothly zoomable image, economically packaged for use on the web, choose File > Export > Zoomify. In the Zoomify Export dialog box **B**, choose a Template, with or without a Navigator element in the interface; the Zoomify Navigator is similar to Photoshop's Navigator window. Choose a Base Name and a location for saving the Zoomify output. Choose a Quality level for the JPEG tiles that Zoomify will make (the higher the Quality, the longer each tile will take to display). Set the size you want the image to appear in the browser; we found that the Width needed to be at least 350 pixels to provide room for all the buttons on the navigation bar. Make sure the Open in Browser checkbox is checked, and click "OK." Now marvel at the result **C**. In the Output Location you chose, find the image files and html file to upload to the web server **D**. Double-clicking the .html icon will load the interactive image into your browser.

raw format, just in case the original metadata from the camera includes something that isn't supported in DNG.

Formats for Display on the Web

Photoshop's File > **Save for Web & Devices** command opens a dialog box where you can choose a file format: JPEG (provides effective compression but doesn't support transparency), GIF (supports transparency but fewer colors), WBMP (with only black pixels and white pixels), and PNG (described at the right). Here you can also balance image quality and file size, as shown on page 152. The "Device Central" button opens a window where you can test an image or animation as it will display on various mobile devices.

> **WHAT IS PNG?**
> PNG is a file format for web graphics that does a better job than JPEG for text, line art, and images with sharp transitions. Lossless so it can be edited and resaved without worry, it was conceived as an alternative to GIF, with better compression, transparency, and color depth. It's now supported by the major browsers.

To import your Photoshop work into Flash, save your layered file in PSD format. In Flash, start a new file (File > New) and import the PSD file (File > Import > Import to Stage). You can decide whether to keep each layer as vector, type, or bitmap, and layers can be animated individually in Flash.

A new addition to Photoshop is the File > Export > **Zoomify** command, which turns your image into a navigable, zoomable file. Designed to make high-resolution images quickly accessible in a browser, Zoomify tiles the image file, dividing it into numerous small files that can be individually displayed by the browser as needed. In addition to the folder of tiles, Zoomify provides an .html file as well as the .xml file and Zoomify viewer — everything needed to incorporate this interactive image into a web page.

3D, Video & Animation

Photoshop Extended can import and export files in several formats used for 3D and video. And Photoshop's Animation panel, even without the capability added by the Extended version, can produce animation files to be saved in GIF and PSD formats. These formats are covered in Chapter 10.

DICOM & MATLAB

Photoshop extended can process DICOM (Digital Imaging and Communication in Medicine) files and can also interface with the MATLAB program. See Chapter 11 for more.

CHOOSING A FILE FORMAT FOR STATIC WEB GRAPHICS

Choosing a format for web graphics is a matter of analyzing the content of the file and knowing a bit about how the different file types handle compression. **JPEG** (.jpg) excels at compressing photos and other continuous-tone images because it supports a **full range of colors** and makes a very compact file. For **flat-color art**, **GIF** (.gif) and **PNG-8** are great, and they offer **transparency** options that make them worth considering even for silhouetted photos.

For **color graphics** such as logos or drawings, GIF or PNG-8 allows you to reduce the file size by reducing the number of colors, as described in "Quick Optimizing for the Web" on page 152. These formats allow for transparency, so your artwork doesn't have to be rectangular.

For a **rectangular photo** or other continuous-tone image that doesn't have any areas that need to be transparent, plan to use JPEG. Try several Quality settings, comparing image quality and loading time. Often Low quality works for photos, while Medium may be needed for color gradients.

If your photo or **continuous-tone image** has a shape **other than rectangular** — especially if it has a soft, feathered edge or internal transparency, JPEG is still an option if your web-page background consists of a seamless, randomized texture that doesn't require precise alignment. The same randomized pattern that was used to make the seamlessly tiled web-page background was incorporated into each of the graphics on this web page. The graphics were saved as JPEG files with the same compression settings used for the background tile.

If your **continuous-tone non-rectangular** image is **small and silhouetted,** you may want to use the GIF or PNG-8 format. This is true especially if you can't match the web-page background as described above. For gradual transparency on rounded corners PNG-24 may be the best option.

WBMP (Wireless Bitmap) is a standard format used for mobile devices. In this **black-and-white-only** format (1-bit, no gray tones) the distribution of black and white pixels is controlled by the type of dither. When Diffusion Dither is chosen, the relative amounts of black and white can be adjusted to produce the tonal balance you want.

When you want to make an image file smaller so you can send it as an email attachment, choosing the right file format is only part of the solution. Before you even address the file format question, you can save on file size by making a flattened, low-res version of the file. Suppose, for example, you want to email a copy of a 7.5-by-9.25-inch book cover illustration for someone to look at on-screen. Your original file is composed of several layers and designed at an appropriate resolution for printing, with some extra resolution in case we want to print a small poster — 350 pixels per inch. Our layered example file in PSD format **A** started out at 400 MB. Let's look at what happens to the closed file size (since the closed size is what's important for transport) as we make the file smaller:

1 We can **start by making a single-layer copy** (Image > Duplicate > Duplicate Merged Layers Only) so the full-size, full-resolution layered file will be preserved separately as we reduce the copy **B**. Saved in PSD format, our closed single-layer example file is 26.2 MB.

2 Using the copy, we **reduce the resolution to 72 ppi** for viewing on the screen (choose Image > Image Size, make sure Resample Image is turned on in the Image Size dialog box, change the Resolution setting to 72, and click "OK") **C**. The closed size is now 1.12 MB.

3 Now we can put the 72 ppi file in JPEG format (File > Save As > JPEG, using a Quality setting of 10, which looked fine on-screen even at 200% view), to produce a 486 KB file **D**.

Every file is different, and the savings varies according to the file structure, image content, and degree of compression. For our particular test image, if we had made our JPEG after step 1 — before reducing the resolution of the file — we could have used a lower Quality setting (8), but at 1.4 MB the file still would have been almost three times as "bulky" as the file we ended up with, and potentially less convenient because of its large display size.

Original multi-layer file

Copy flattened to a single layer

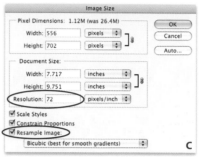

Reducing the resolution to 72 ppi

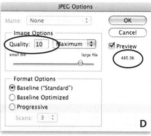

Saving as a high-quality JPEG

DONAL JOLLEY

Ready to email at 486K, the file will appear on-screen at its 7.5-by-9.25-inch size if screen resolution is 72 ppi.

PHOTOSHOP'S COMPANIONS

There are three programs that come along with Photoshop: Bridge, Camera Raw, and Device Central all increase Photoshop's efficiency. **Bridge** (described next) helps organize and locate files. It allows direct access to some of Photoshop's automated image-processing functions, such as Photomerge and Image Processor, and it also provides direct access to a second copy of Camera Raw — you can open files in Camera Raw without interrupting your work in Photoshop.

Camera Raw itself is a great "front end" for image files on their way into Photoshop. Originally Camera Raw was designed to quickly and easily adjust tone and color in 16-bits/channel raw-format photos and to deal with a few adjustments specifically related to digital cameras, such as noise and chromatic aberration. With the latest versions (used with Photoshop CS3 and CS4) many files, even JPEGs or TIFFs, can be fully edited in Camera Raw without the photographer ever needing to open Photoshop. You'll find an overview of Camera Raw for CS3 and CS4 on page 141 and a Camera Raw "entry" workflow on page 149.

You can work back and forth between Photoshop and **Device Central** to design and adapt images for the screens of handheld devices such as cell phones. You'll find an introduction to Device Central on page 146.

Bridge

Bridge is a central location for organizing, viewing, and manipulating image and graphics files, audio, and video. Many of the commands in Bridge's File menu — Open, Move, Rename, and New Folder — can also be performed by your operating system. But there are advantages of doing these things in Bridge: You can see the content of more kinds of files; you can "cross select" files from several locations at once; and you have more Search options — including keywords, lens focal length, and copyright information — generally not available as criteria in your operating system's search functions. With Bridge you can also:

- Download camera files using **Photo Downloader** (see page 134).

- **Drag and drop** files from one folder to another, even from one hard drive to another.

- Gather files into **virtual stacks** and **collections** without disrupting your hard drive organization.

- Add a **copyright notice** to protect your files.

Bridge's Preferences dialog (Ctrl/ ⌘-K), lets you decide how dark you want your interface to be, whether you want to open raw-format image files in Camera Raw whenever you double-click on one, how large a file has to be before Bridge doesn't take the time to generate and store a thumbnail for it, and so on.

LAUNCHING CAMERA RAW FROM BRIDGE

The advantage of opening raw files from Bridge, rather than through Photoshop's File > Open command, is that when you open from Bridge, Camera Raw doesn't "take over" Photoshop, so you can have both Photoshop and Camera Raw open and working independently. You can select a file in Bridge's Content panel and choose File > Open in Camera Raw (in CS4 you can also click the ⬤ icon in the Applications bar). Or you can choose to always launch Camera Raw from Bridge rather than Photoshop when you double-click a raw-format file — simply turn on the "Double-click edits Camera Raw settings in Bridge" option in the General panel of Preferences (Ctrl/⌘-K).

Photo Downloader (Standard version). Click the "Advanced" button for more options (shown below).

- Add **keywords** to make it easy to search for specific files long after their file names have been forgotten.
- Act on **multiple files** preselected in Bridge — for example, to process files in Camera Raw, to convert one file format to another, or to piece together a panorama in Photoshop.
- Create **contact sheets**, **slide shows**, and **web sites**.

Using Bridge workspaces. To customize Bridge for tasks you perform often — such as adding keywords — you might want to start by selecting a workspace that ships with Bridge: Choose Window > Workspace and choose one, or click one of the workspace buttons in the bottom right corner of the Bridge interface (see page 135). In CS4 you can choose from the menu or choose a workspace in the Applications bar (see page 136). In

continued on page 137

BRIDGE'S PHOTO DOWNLOADER

Choosing **File > Get Photos from Camera** or clicking on the 📷 button in CS4 opens the **Photo Downloader**, to give you many more options for quickly organizing, converting, and copying files and adding metadata. The Standard version of Photo Downloader is shown above. Shown here is the version that appears when you click the "Advanced "button.

Before downloading, see that the camera or card is detected, and that the files you want to download are checked for downloading.

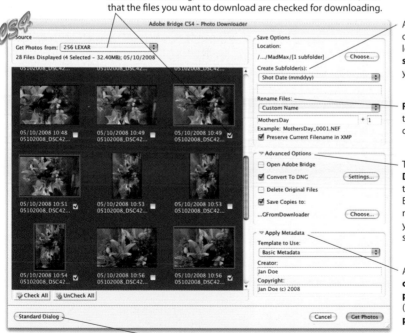

After you choose or create a folder on your hard drive, Photo Downloader can automatically create **subfolders** according to criteria you choose.

Rename files to make them easier to search for. Use preset options or custom text.

Take this opportunity to save in the **DNG** (digital-negative) format or to save a **copy** to another folder. Be careful not to delete the original files from the camera before you make sure the download was successful.

Add just the basic information for **copyright,** or add a metadata **template** with customized image info (find the **Create Metadata Template** in Bridge's Tools menu).

Toggle between the much simpler **Standard** dialog (at the top of this page) and the **Advanced** interface shown here.

THE BRIDGE CS3 INTERFACE

In the Bridge CS3 interface you can customize most of Bridge's features to suit your needs for viewing, arranging, and managing your files. Create workspaces for different tasks, put "smart" Collections and frequently used folders within easy reach, sort files according to date or other criteria, or limit the files displayed to just the content you want to see at the moment. The default interface is shown here, unmodified except for the darkness setting and the choice of highlight—in this case, Amber.

Drag and drop folders you access frequently to your **Favorites** tab. Or in the context-sensitive menu right-click/ Ctrl-click on a folder to choose **Add to Favorites** (or Remove From Favorites).

Navigate quickly to recently accessed folders or favorite folders using the **Recent Folders Menu**.

Or click on the **Folders** tab for the familiar directory tree view of your drives.

Use the icons for **New Folder**, **Rotate 90°**, **Delete Item**, and **Compact Mode** for quick access to often used operating system functions.

In the **Preview** panel, you can view up to nine selected files. Use a Loupe (just click in the image) for close inspection. Use the playback controls that appear below the pre-view when multi-page PDFs or video or audio files are selected.

In the **Filter** panel (*filter* is Bridge's term for *sort*), choose to limit the files displayed, or to **sort** by date, by your rating, by color profile, or by other criteria.

Click here to dis-play all the files in a folder in the Content section as if there were no **subfolders**.

View just the types of files and folders you need at this moment by choosing criteria from the **File Type** list. For efficiency, Bridge will display only criteria that apply to the current folder's contents.

You can **Lock** your filtering criteria, to keep them the same as you navigate through different folders.

Quickly **hide or show** all panels; the Content panel remains visible even when the others are hidden.

The **status bar** lets you know when Bridge is busy writing metadata or caching, as well as the size and number of files you have selected and the number hidden.

Select and group related Images into **Stacks** to simplify your view. More than nine images in a stack reveals "**flip book**" and scroll bar controls for view-ing images within the stack.

In the **Content** panel, you can see **previews** of files, although to preview some files, such as an InDesign file, you need to save a preview with the file in the originat-ing application.

Use the slider to scale the **size** of your thumbnails. You can set the quality of your thumbnail display in Bridge's Preferences menu (Ctrl/⌘-K).

Assign up to three **workspaces** to these quick-switching icons, or choose a preset from one of their drop-down lists.

In this panel, view **metadata** that iden-tifies a selected file, and add **keywords** to the metadata. The metadata you add can be read by an increasing num-ber of programs.

THE BRIDGE CS4 INTERFACE

In CS4, many features that people use often have been made accessible through icons. Because it's so helpful to tailor Bridge to your specific workflow, Workspaces figure prominently in CS4.

At the left end of the **Applications bar** are icons (left to right) for accessing your Favorites list ▼, Recent Files & Folders ↺ Photo Downloader 📷, Refine 📄 (for reviewing, batch renaming, and other file-management functions), Open in Camera Raw ⟳, and Output 📄◆ (to Web, PDF, and other options).

The names of some of Bridge CS4's **workspaces** appear on the right side of the Applications bar, along with a down-arrow ▼ to access a list of all workspaces.

In **Compact Mode** a simpler Bridge window floats above other application windows. Bridge commands are limited, but you can drag-and-drop files into other applications as you need them.

The **Path bar** provides a "breadcrumb" navigation trail for the item(s) currently select-ed in the **Content** panel.

Enter a filename, folder name, or keyword, and **Quick Search** will search currently selected files or folders.

Other useful options include **thumbnail quality** (▦ for standard, which is quick, or ▦ to set pre-view options), the ability to sort (or "filter" in Bridge terminology) by **rating** ☆, sort by **criteria you choose**, **rotate** ⟳, access **recently open files** 📁, create a **new folder** 📁, and **delete** the currently selected file(s) 🗑.

The **Preview** panel shows up to nine selected files — multi-page PDFs, video, and audio, even some 3D for-mats (if your video card supports 3D rendering).

Playback controls allow you to pre-view multimedia files.

In the **Metadata** panel, view the metadata associ-ated with a select-ed file, and add **keywords**. The metadata you add can be read by an increasing number of programs.

Bridge **Filter** catego-ries are now closed by default. Your choice to open or close a cat-egory persists between sessions. The **pushpins** make filter choices "sticky" during a ses-sion, retaining your filter choices, such as your selected rating, from folder to folder.

The **status bar** lets you know when Bridge is busy writing metadata or caching. It also tells the size and number of files you have selected and the number hidden.

In the Content window, besides showing indi-vidual files and folders, Bridge CS4 can identify and **auto-stack** images for panoramas or HDR series (Stacks > Auto-Stack Panorama/HDR).

Scale the size of the thumbnails in the Content window.

Choose the type of **view** you want— thumbnails, thumb-nails with additional data, or list view, and lock or unlock a **thumbnail grid** that constrains the size of the thumbnails.

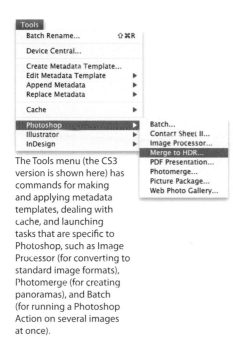

The Tools menu (the CS3 version is shown here) has commands for making and applying metadata templates, dealing with cache, and launching tasks that are specific to Photoshop, such as Image Processor (for converting to standard image formats), Photomerge (for creating panoramas), and Batch (for running a Photoshop Action on several images at once).

Choose Tools > Create Metadata Template and add personal information, such as a Copyright Notice. Save your template. Now using Photo Downloader, the Tools menu, or Bridge's context-sensitive menu, add your copyright to each image.

the workspace you've chosen, change which panels are open or closed, drag them into new locations, resize them, and choose the thumbnail view you prefer. Save any custom workspace with a descriptive name to add it to the workspace list (Window > Workspace > Save Workspace/New Workspace). In CS4 a newly saved workspace will appear first in the list in the Applications bar (you can drag it to a different position in the list if you like). On-the-fly changes to your workspace automatically persist from session to session. But you can also get back to your workspace as you originally defined and saved it: In CS3 select it again from the Window > Workspace menu, or in CS4 Ctrl/⌘-click on the workspace name in the Applications bar or click on its name and choose Window > Workspace > Reset Workspace.

Processing files. Bridge's processing power lies mainly in the **Tools** menu and the **context-sensitive menu** that appears when you right-click/Ctrl-click on the element you want to affect. The Tools menu puts **Batch Rename** at the top of the list, then follows with ways to handle *metadata* and *cache.* (Metadata includes camera settings and the non-image data you add to the file, such as keywords and copyright notice, and the cache contains thumbnail images and metadata lists, stored and ready to go so they don't need to be re-created from the files in a folder each time Bridge displays the folder's contents.) The **Tools** menu also lets you run some Photoshop functions on the files selected in Bridge's Content panel.

Gathering files: stacks and collections. Beyond the basic file maneuvers, Bridge allows you to group files virtually, in *stacks* and *collections* for further manipulation. Think of **stacks** as representing piles of slides grouped on your table by date, content, location, or some combination of criteria that works for you. A stack, which is "local" to a single folder, can be useful for gathering various shots of a single subject or an image sequence from a video segment, so you won't have to sift through all the files in the folder to find them each time you want them. By selecting and grouping these files in stacks (Ctrl/⌘-G), you organize the files and clear out some visual clutter. If there are more than nine images in a stack, a scroll bar appears so you can look through the stack. *Note:* Stacks don't move to other folders, but within a folder you can drag and drop files to add them to or remove them from the stack.

CS4 has added one more feature to stacks. Now if you choose Stacks > **Auto-Stack Panorama/HDR,** Bridge will go to work selecting all images within a folder whose camera metadata suggests that you shot a sequence of images for either a panorama or

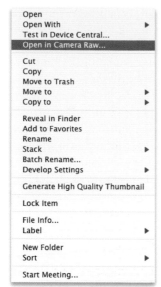

When you right-click/Ctrl-click on a thumbnail in Bridge, a **context-sensitive menu** appears with all the usual file commands as well as commands for sorting files, creating stacks (files you want to visually group together on-screen), or revealing the file location on your computer. The **Develop Settings** command allows you to copy, paste, or clear a Camera Raw setting or preset from a selected image file without ever opening Camera Raw.

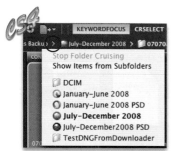

From CS4's Path bar, you can navigate anywhere. To reveal a list of all folders contained within a folder, click on the arrow (>) to the right of that folder. If you want to see the contents of all the subfolders at once (as if there *were* no subfolders), click Show Items from Subfolders.

a bracketed exposure. Bridge looks for images taken sequentially over a short timespan, either with different exposures and a lot of content overlap (HDR) or with similar exposures with less content overlap (panorama). The Auto-Stack command can take some time, depending on your computer's power and how large a folder you're sorting, but the results are remarkably accurate. If you choose Tools > Photoshop > Process Collections in Photoshop, Bridge will process **all** the stacks in the current folder. So for large folders, you may want to select a particular stack and then choose Photomerge or Merge to HDR from the Tools > Photoshop menu instead.

If you like to keep your files on your hard drive in folders according to their creation date or client name, but you want to work with them according to genre, for example, you can create virtual collections, to show just the files you need, regardless of where they're stored on your system. In CS3 you make a **Collection** by performing a search using the Find dialog (Ctrl/⌘-F, or Edit > Find), where you select the criteria used to gather files, and choose a name for the Collection and where to store it; the search can be in a single folder, across several folders, or on your entire hard drive. Then every time you open the Collection to view its contents, Bridge will perform the search and gather the files again based on the Collection's saved criteria. Any files that you've added since you made the search and that meet your original search criteria will also be added to the Collection that opens on-screen. And if you've deleted any of the files you originally collected, or moved them to locations outside the search parameters you chose originally, they *won't* appear in the Collection.

In CS4 the kind of collection described for CS3 in the previous paragraph has been renamed **Smart Collection**. It can be made with the Find command or by using the **New Smart Collection** button ▣ at the bottom of the **Collections panel**, naming the collection, and choosing criteria. The name of your new Smart Collection is added to the top list on the Collections panel.

The **Find** dialog lets you establish criteria for Bridge to use when it searches your chosen folder(s) every time you open a Collection. In CS3 (shown here) you save a Collection to a location of your choice.

You can let Bridge CS4 scan a folder for you to collect your panorama shot and multi-exposure images in individual stacks. Showing here is the Collection log after a scan has been completed, resulting in two auto-stacks of five images each. The 12-image stack on the right was created from hand-picked files and shows both the **Play button** (▶) that turns a Stack into a "flip book," useful primarily when you've saved a sequence of video frames, and the **scroll bar,** which lets you move through the stack at your own speed.

In CS4, open the **Collections** panel and click on the New Smart Collection Icon ▣ to open the Smart Collection dialog. Data for collections is automatically saved to one location on your hard drive; for instance, on the Mac it's in the *.user/* Application Data/Adobe/Bridge CS4 folder.

Choose whether to preview your files quickly, or at a high quality. With CS4, saving 100% Previews lets you more quickly check focus and details later on.

Besides these Smart Collections, there's another kind of collection in CS4, and this one has inherited the old name of "**Collection**." (So . . . a CS3 "Collection" is the same as a CS4 "Smart Collection," and a CS4 "Collection" is something a little different, which doesn't exist in CS3.) To make one of these "hand-picked" Collections in CS4, you assemble files in the Content panel, select them, and then click the New Collection button ▣, which is just to the left of the New Smart Collection button. Hand-picked Collections are listed below Smart Collections in the Collections panel. The advantage of a Collection (over a Smart Collection), is that you can add any files you want, without specifying search criteria. If you want a collection of all files from the Jan Doe account, all pictures of poodles from anywhere on your hard drive, and all photos you ran the Twirl filter on, you can drag and drop those pictures into your Collection.

Reviewing and evaluating images: Slideshow and Review modes. When you're searching for files, speed is great. But when you're evaluating images to include in a project, being able to see the most image detail with the least distraction is more helpful. Bridge lets you choose the quality you need for each occasion. In CS3, choose to set Preferences (Ctrl/⌘-K) for Quick Thumbnails, High Quality Thumbnails, or Convert to High Quality When Previewed. Even when your Preference is set for Quick Thumbnails, a right-click/Ctrl-click on the thumbnail lets you choose to display a high-quality thumbnail. In CS4, buttons to the right of the Path bar give you immediate access to your choices for **thumbnails** and **preview display**, and a new option has been added: You can choose to store the full-size image (a **100% Preview**) in your cache, rather than a smaller thumbnail. This increases the size of your cache file, but loading files to view at 100% when you need to check details and focus can take time, so it may be more convenient to give up disk space to store the large previews so you can work faster.

Bridge CS3's main ways to review and evaluate images are Slideshow and the Preview panel. Use **Slideshow** to show images singly, without any distracting interface. Images can be rated and labeled right in the Slideshow. In the **Preview** panel (shown in the upper right corner of the Bridge interface on pages 135 and 136) you can view up to nine files at a time, and each file can have its own **Loupe** for enlarging details to 100% or more. Ctrl/⌘-dragging on a Loupe drags all the Loupes at once, making it possible to check focus on the same detail in all the images, for instance.

In CS4, a new **Review Mode** has been added. What if you need to perform a quick-and-dirty edit of a folder full of images? For

PHOTOSPIN.COM

Use the keyboard shortcut **H** to show or hide all the options and shortcuts you can use in Slideshow. Pressing **Esc** returns you to Bridge.

In CS4 enter Review Mode (Ctrl/ ⌘-B) in carousel view, where you can quickly sort through many images, check focus in the active image with the Loupe **A**, and even save your picks to a Collection **B**.

When you open four or fewer images in Review Mode (Ctrl/⌘-B), they appear "N-up" rather than in carousel format. This mode is good for reviewing images carefully, comparing attributes such as composition, color, and focus. Every image can have its own Loupe — just click on the spot you want to enlarge.

that, select all the images you want and use the shortcut **Ctrl/⌘-B** to bring them all into Review Mode. If you've selected more than four images, they will appear in a **"carousel"** view (think 35 mm slide projectors). In carousel mode the active image is the largest, appearing front and center. The rest are arranged in a ring behind. Using left and right arrow keys (← and →) you can move around the circle. The down arrow key ↓ removes an image from the carousel. You can add labels and ratings as in Slideshow, use a Loupe as in Preview, and when you've eliminated all you don't want from the carousel, you can save the remainder as a Collection using the New Collection button ⊞₊ at the bottom of the Collections panel.

Entering Review Mode (**Ctrl/⌘-B**) when you have four or fewer images selected opens the files in **N-up** mode (two-up or three-up, for instance) rather than in carousel mode. Now you can quickly compare composition or check focus with multiple Loupes. If you want to simply review **one image** without distraction, you can get into a type of Review Mode even more quickly—with your file selected, press the **spacebar** to enter or to exit.

Making files easier to find: ratings, labels, and keywords.
Bridge has several different schemes for making it easier to find the files you need. You can **color-code them with Labels** or give them **star ratings through Bridge's Labels menu** or **add**

Enter this special Review mode with the spacebar shortcut. To zoom, click once and, if the file hasn't already been cached at 100%, you will see "Loading 100%" at the top of your screen. To zoom back out to the "Fit in Screen" view, click once again. To pan when you're looking at the full-size image, simply click-and-hold until the cursor becomes the hand icon 🖑; then drag.

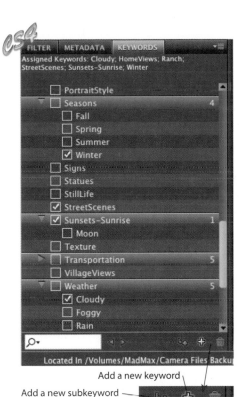

Add a new keyword

Add a new subkeyword

Keywords can be subsets of larger categories, and each can be assigned with or without its parent category; simply select the files in the Content panel (they must be file formats able to accept XMP data), and click on the checkboxes for the keywords. Add a new keyword or "subkeyword" to the list by clicking one of the "plus" icons at the bottom of the panel.

keywords (terms you associate with the content of a file and might use to search for it later); **use the Search field to find files based on keywords** (in CS4 you can also use the New Search button 🔎). In addition, Bridge can read (and search) the metadata stored in the file by the camera or by other programs.

Bridge CS4 comes with a **Metadata workspace**, available as a button in the top right corner of the interface (see page 136). The Metadata panel that's displayed with this interface is very pliable — you can display or hide categories of metadata via a context-sensitive menu, widen or narrow the data columns by dragging on the breaks between them, and order your selected files by clicking on a column title, clicking again to reverse the order. In the Keywords panel you can add or remove words, editing your entire Keywords list or for individual files.

> **WORKING WITH METADATA IN CS4**
> Adobe.com has a good video on using the Metadata workspace in Bridge CS4. We found it at **http://tv.adobe.com/watch/ learn-bridge-cs4/working-with-metadata-and-keywords/**

CS4's **Filter** panel displays lists of any Labels, Ratings, Keywords, and other criteria assigned to the files in the Content panel. You can use the Filter panel to put displayed files in the order you want, or to change the display criteria.

Camera Raw

The Camera Raw interface is an elegant and efficient entry into Photoshop for working with a camera's raw-format files. You may even find that its flexible, easy-to-use one-stop interface makes you want to do most of your color and tone correcting and enhancing in Camera Raw, not only for raw files but also for JPEGs and TIFFs, without taking your photo into Photoshop at all.

A digital camera's raw-format file has two separate parts — (1) the image information that comes through the lens and is captured (raw data) and (2) the camera settings at the time the picture was taken (recorded as processing instructions the camera uses to turn this data into the image we see). Camera Raw acts on the camera settings only. As you experiment with its tools, menus, and sliders, Camera Raw shows you an on-screen preview, but it doesn't actually process the image until you click the "Open," "Save," or "Done" button.

Working with raw files in Camera Raw offers some huge advantages over opening the files directly into Photoshop. For

When this photo (the original is at the top) was taken with a Minolta Dimage A1 digital camera, the light from the white clouds fooled the camera into using a fast shutter speed ($\frac{1}{3200}$ sec) and a small aperture (f/10), which resulted in an underexposed image. Because the camera was set to record in raw format, when the file was opened from Photoshop, it was intercepted by Camera Raw **A**. In the Adjust panel, White Balance, Temperature, and other controls could be changed **B** and quickly viewed. Clicking the dialog box's "Open Image" button opened the file in Photoshop.

one thing, you can work quickly and painlessly with large files in 16 Bits/ Channel mode, preserving all their extra color depth without slowing the processing of the image with each change. The more you can do in Camera Raw, the less "heavy lifting" you'll need to do in Photoshop.

For another thing, with raw files you gain tremendous power from Camera Raw's ability to change the **white balance**, which is like being able to go back and reshoot with different lighting. For instance, if you meant to capture the warm yellow light of a cozy interior but the camera's automatic white balance didn't take that into account, you can put back the yellow and restore the mood.

Even if you rename or move the raw-format file, the next time you open it, Camera Raw will bring it up with your most recent settings, and it will also offer the choice of using the original camera settings. By default, your Camera Raw settings are stored in *sidecar* (.xmp) files that Camera Raw creates. These sidecar files can be moved off the computer with the raw files, and can be read by other applications that support metadata.

When you take a file from Camera Raw into Photoshop as a Smart Object, you have instant access to the Camera Raw interface and settings at any time. All you have to do to reopen the file in Camera Raw is double-click the Smart Object thumbnail in the Layers panel.

The next three pages provide an overview of Camera Raw's interface, including its panels and tools. "Quick Camera Raw as a 'Front End'" on page 149 outlines an efficient approach to using Camera Raw for raw files, JPEGs, and TIFFs. You'll also find Camera Raw in action in "Adjusting Tone & Color in Camera Raw" and "Bringing Out Detail," both in Chapter 5.

KEEPING UP WITH CAMERA RAW

Camera Raw is updated more often than Photoshop is, with new features and more cameras supported. Check at Adobe.com for the latest Camera Raw: **www.adobe.com/products/photoshop/cameraraw.html**

(For Photoshop CS3, the **4.6 update**, which added some significant new features, is provided in the Wow Goodies folder on the DVD-ROM that comes with this book.)

THE CAMERA RAW INTERFACE

Shown here, for Camera Raw 5.0, which shipped with Photoshop CS4, is the interface you'll see if you open several photos at once from Bridge. Shown here (under the histogram) is the **Basic** panel, the place to start for adjusting color and contrast. Additional panels of the Camera Raw interface are shown on page 144.

This "filmstrip" of thumbnails appears when you open more than one file at a time in Camera Raw. Selecting thumbnails and then clicking the **"Synchronize"** button lets you apply some or all settings for the current image (the large central one) to those files.

Bridge settings, such as labels and ratings, are retained or can be set here (click the dots to add stars).

The histogram graph gives a detailed picture of color and tone distribution from the darkest tones (on the left) to the lightest (on the right). Toggle the Shadow clipping warning and Highlights clipping warning on to see a warning color if your image (as currently adjusted) is losing detail because the shadows have been pushed to black or the highlights to white.

To retroactively change the lighting under which the photo was taken, use the **Temperature** and **Tint** sliders.

To adjust **exposure** (how light or dark an image is) and **contrast** (how much difference there is between the light and dark tones), use **Exposure** to set the white point (pushing the lightest tones to white) and use **Blacks** to set the darkest tones to black. Use **Recovery** to bring out detail in the highlights, and **Fill Light** to lighten the shadow tones to show more detail. Change the **Brightness** to make the midtones lighter or darker, and change **Contrast** to get more or less contrast in the midtones.

Clarity increases local contrast to bring out fine detail (see page 249). Or at negative settings it can be used to suppress detail for cosmetic purposes, for instance (see page 323).

Increasing **Saturation** increases color intensity. **Vibrance** does the same, except that it protects colors from becoming so intense that you can't see color detail anymore, and it protects skin tones.

Save options include PSD, TIFF, JPEG, and DNG. The dialog allows you to select a destination and naming convention for the files. Your Save settings persist, so you can skip the dialog by Alt/Option-clicking to apply the settings you used last.

Viewing (magnification) options

To open the **Workflow Options** dialog, click on the button that looks like a link. Choose your profile, bit depth, resolution, and file size for saving the file or opening it in Photoshop. Your most recent choices are displayed in the button itself.

Click here to open the file in Photoshop. The button will say **"Open Image"** or **"Open Object,"** depending on whether you've turned on the Smart Object option in the Workflow Options dialog. Shift-click to toggle to the other option. Or Alt/Option-click to open the file without saving your current Camera Raw settings to the file's metadata — this could be useful for opening a black-and-white version, for instance, when you want to retain the color metadata.

"Done" applies the adjustments to the metadata, but doesn't open the image in Photoshop.

CAMERA RAW PANELS

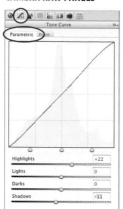

The **Tone Curve** panel lets you adjust contrast in the parts of the tonal range that you choose. The **Point** curve operates like Photoshop's Curves adjustment (see page 246). The **Parametric** curve offers a different way of working, dividing the tonal range into four parts (see page 249).

The **Detail** panel's **Sharpening** compensates for the softness that's characteristic of raw-format files. The **Noise Reduction** settings correct for the "digital grain" (**Luminance**) and **Color** artifacts that can occur in low light or at a high ISO setting.

The HSL phase of the **HSL/Grayscale** panel lets you control the hue, saturation, and lightness of any of eight color "families" independently. So you can, for instance, make the oranges a little redder (**Hue**), lighten up the blues (**Lightness**), or remove all color except the reds (**Saturation**); there's an example on page 300.

Or, as shown here, you can make a black-and-white version of the image by clicking the **Convert to Grayscale** checkbox. Then you can use the sliders to retroactively determine how light or dark a gray each original color becomes in the conversion (see page 300).

The **Split Toning** panel lets you tint **Highlights** one color and **Shadows** another. The **Balance** value determines, for tinting purposes, how much of the tonal range is considered highlights and how much is considered shadows. Move the slider left to apply your Shadows tint to more tones, or right to apply the Highlights tint to more.

In the **Lens Corrections** panel you can fix color fringing (**Chromatic Aberration**) or darkening of the edges (**Lens Vignetting**), two problems associated with camera lenses. Instead of *removing* a vignette, you also have the option of *adding one*. In Camera Raw 4.2 and later, **Post-Crop Vignetting** allows you to apply a vignette to the cropped edges of the image (see page 280).

The **Camera Calibration** panel is designed to allow you to fine-tune the camera profiles built into Camera Raw. In the **Name** menu you may be able to choose from several profiles made for your model of camera. For JPEG and TIFF files (as shown here) the camera has already embedded its profile in the color data of the file.

The **Presets** panel lists presets you've saved in the Settings folder (by using the button at the bottom of the panel, for instance).

In Camera Raw 5.2 and later, a new **Snapshots** panel allows you to save and recall more than one set of Camera Raw settings with the file. For example, you could save a tinted and a black-and-white version as well as the optimized color version. The panel lists the Snapshots available for the currently open file.

CAMERA RAW TOOLS

To correct a color cast in the photo, if you know of something in your image that should be neutral in color, try clicking on it with the **White Balance** tool.

"Floating" the **Color Sampler** cursor over the image gives you a read-out of color composition (it appears under the histogram); or click to set up to four permanent sampling spots (read-outs appear under the toolbar).

If you click the **Preferences** button, you can reset Camera Raw Preferences without going to Bridge.

Navigation tools include **Zoom** and **Hand** (for panning).

Drag with the **Crop** tool to reframe the image. Drag with the **Straighten** tool along a line in the image that should be horizontal to set up a crop that will straighten the image; then adjust the crop if needed.

CS4 adds tools for applying any adjustment you can set in any of the panels, but locally instead of globally: The **Adjustment Brush** applies the change to the specific spot you paint, and the **Graduated Filter** tool effectively applies it through a gradient mask you draw with the tool.

THE TARGETED ADJUSTMENT TOOL

The Targeted Adjustment tool (or TAT) is new, added to Camera Raw 5 updates.

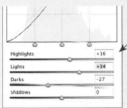

The click samples the color you clicked on. If Parametric Tone Curve (the default) is chosen in the menu, the drag up or down increases or decreases the setting for the part of the curve the clicked color falls in.

You operate the TAT by choosing from its pop-out menu and clicking in the image and then dragging up or down.

If the HSL/Grayscale panel is open, or if you choose anything other than Parametric Curve from the tool's pop-out menu, Camera Raw adjusts Hue, Saturation, or Lightness, depending on which panel is active. Or if Convert to Grayscale is turned on, the TAT adjusts the Grayscale Mix, determining how light or dark a gray the sampled color is converted to.

SHARPENING IN CAMERA RAW

Camera Raw offers two different kinds of sharpening:

- **Capture sharpening** (controlled in the **Details** panel) corrects for the softness created by the digital capture apparatus in your camera. Capture sharpening is useful for raw files. For JPEGs and TIFFs the camera has already made a correction when it combined the capture information with the camera settings to arrive at the JPEG or TIFF. Depending on how you have your Camera Raw Preferences set, input sharpening either becomes part of the metadata that's stored with the file or is only previewed and not stored with the metadata. The preview option allows you to evaluate how your other Camera Raw settings will look on a sharpened image, whether you opt to apply Camera Raw's sharpening or sharpen later in Photoshop.

- **Output sharpening,** offered only in the most recent Camera Raw 5 updates (5.2 and later), is designed to provide final sharpening if you don't plan to open your image in Photoshop and sharpen there. In the **Workflow Options** dialog you can choose from three sharpening presets, for **Screen**, **Glossy**, or **Matte** output.

Adobe Device Central: the Mobile Web

Today web content is moving to hand-held devices — cell phones, PDAs, and other small, internet-capable units. With their tiny screen sizes, and viewing conditions ranging from outdoors and sunny to candlelit restaurants, graphics and the web sites they enrich need to be designed for on-the-go web interactivity. If your target audience is likely to have Flash Lite–enabled devices, Adobe Device Central, introduced with Photoshop CS3, will help you preview your design, while simulating common viewing conditions and the controls the user will have to navigate with. Although you can launch Device Central as a separate application, it makes sense to use File > **Save for Web & Devices**, optimizing your graphics for the web (see page 152), and then clicking on the **"Device Central" button** to view them inside Device Central. There you can download models and their individual specifications for the Emulator to work with; you can store these specs in your local library, and even create sets of models to help you organize and test for a particular project. Device Central is a complete application in itself, and outside the scope of this book, but it can emulate the orientation (how the cell phone is being held, for instance) and the light it's being used in. It can run scripts that put your design and interactivity through their paces, and allow you to choose how to scale your design. All in all, it's a versatile application for helping you design for the new way people are interacting with the web.

Testing a graphic in Device Central for visibility in bright sunlight with reduced backlighting, paying attention to size and orientation

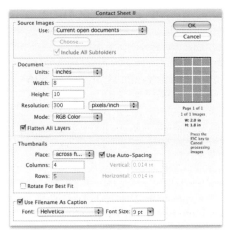

Setting up Contact Sheet II output in **Photoshop CS3**

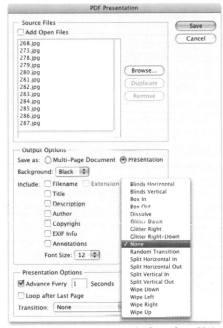

Making a PDF Presentation with **Photoshop CS3**'s File > Automate > **PDF Presentation** command

2-UP Greeting Card
2*2 Cells
4 Wide
✓ 4*5 Contact Sheet
5*8 Contact Sheet
Fine Art Mat
Maximize Size
Triptych

These templates are included with Bridge CS4 for PDF Presentations and Contact Sheets.

SPECIALIZED OUTPUT OPTIONS

In **Photoshop CS3** three specialized output options — **Contact Sheet II**, **PDF Presentation**, and **Web Photo Gallery** — are available through the **File > Automate** menu. In CS4 these options have moved from Photoshop to Bridge's Output workspace. Although there are fewer options to choose from in Photoshop CS3, the interface in each case (shown at the left) is simpler and quite self-explanatory. In a single dialog box, you choose the files you want to include, set up the document format, and click the "Save" button.

In **Bridge CS4** you can create these three kinds of specialized output without involving Photoshop. Select the files you want in Bridge, select **Output** from the pop-out Workspace menu, and make the choices you want in the **Output panel**. *Note:* If you don't see the Output panel, drag left on the right-hand border of the large **Output Preview panel** to make room for it; you can also drag the bars on the left side to conceal the Favorites and Folders panels if you want more room for the Output Preview and Output panels.

Contact Sheet in CS4

At the top of the Output panel on the right, click on the **"PDF" button**, choose a **Template**, and click the **"Refresh Preview" button**. (As you work, you'll need to click "Refresh Preview" again to see the changes you make.) Move down to the **Document** section of the Output panel (click its ▶ button to open it if necessary), and choose the type of paper and the background color you want, as well as any security settings. In **Layout**,

To make a Contact Sheet in CS4, choose Output from Bridge's Workspace menu and click the "PDF" button. Then make choices from the Output panel, clicking "Refresh Preview" to update the Output Preview panel

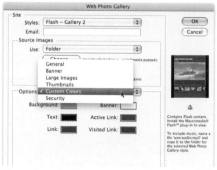

Choose from the Options menu in Photoshop CS3's Web Photo Gallery dialog to display appropriate choices in the panel below the menu. Shown here is the interface for choosing colors for the various non-image elements of the Gallery.

When you make a Web Photo Gallery in Bridge CS4, the Template menu offers several choices **A**. Styles are available for each of the templates. Shown here are the styles for the Lightroom Flash Gallery template **B**, along with the resulting Gallery **C**.

FLASH DETECT UPDATE

If you have Flash galleries you already created, or you want to use Web Photo Gallery to create new ones, search on the Adobe site for the "WPG Flash Detect Update." It includes instructions and new presets for making the Web Photo Gallery's Flash Player detection work correctly with the Flash Player 10 plug-in.

the next section down, you can change the paper size and the number and arrangement of images. (Notice that you can even repeat a single photo over the entire page. In this case, you get a "contact sheet" for each of the photos you've selected.) Add and style any text you want in the **Overlays** and **Watermark** sections of the panel. Then click "Refresh Preview" one last time, turn on the **View PDF After Save** option if you want to open the contact sheets right away, and click **"Save."**

PDF Presentation in CS4

To put together a slide show as a PDF Presentation, start by clicking the **"PDF" button** in the Output panel. In the **Template** section, you'll probably want to choose the Fine Art Mat or Maximize Size option. Click the **"Refresh Preview" button** now and as you work to see the results of each choice. In the **Document** section choose a **Page Preset** and **Size** that produce a nice aspect ratio for your slide show. In the **Layout** section, you'll probably want to make sure **"Rotate for Best Fit" is turned off,** so all your images will appear right-side-up. Add and style any text you want in the **Overlays** and **Watermark** sections. In the **Playback** section, decide whether you want full-screen presentation or looping. Choose a time for slides to appear and a style of transition; you're limited to one kind of transition per slide show, unless you choose Random Transition, so you may want to choose None to keep the transitions from being distracting. Turn on **View PDF After Save**, and click **"Save."**

Web Photo Gallery in CS4

From the images you choose for your gallery, Web Photo Gallery will create the JPEGs needed for thumbnails and display images, as well as all the support files needed to operate the gallery in a browser. At the top of the Output panel, click the **"Web Gallery"** button. Choose a **Template** and click **"Refresh Preview"** to see the result; as you make other choices for your gallery, click "Refresh Preview" again to see each change. In the **Site Info** section you can enter a gallery title and description, and contact and copyright information. In the **Color Palette** section, choose colors for buttons, text, background, and borders. In the **Appearance** section, choose what sizes of thumbnails you want and where you want them to appear (on the left or below, for instance; if you don't want thumbnails, choose **Slideshow Only**). Finally, in the **Create Gallery** section, click the **Save to Disk** or **Upload** option. To upload to your web site, enter your FTP server information and click on the **"Upload"** button at the bottom of the panel. Or to save to disk, click **"Save"** (or "Browse" to choose a new location).

Camera Raw as a "Front End"

Originally, Camera Raw was designed as a basic means to manipulate the data from a camera's raw-format files, to play the role the camera itself plays in the case of a JPEG or TIFF image, converting the captured information to an image you can open in Photoshop for further work. Today Camera Raw's well-organized and easy-to-approach interface makes it popular for adjusting tone and color, both globally (overall) and locally (in particular spots), in JPEGs and TIFFs as well as raw files. You'll find examples of Camera Raw used in this way in "Quick Vignetting," "Adjusting Tone & Color in Camera Raw," and "Bringing Out Detail," all in Chapter 5. Here we look at Camera Raw as an efficient way to prepare raw-format images from a photo shoot to be brought into Photoshop for further work.

When you have several images that all need the same kind of global adjustment of color and tone, it makes sense to open them in Camera Raw all together. Then you can either select all of them and make the changes to all as you work on one, or you can simply make the changes to one and then use Camera Raw's **Synchronize** function to apply those changes to all the rest. The advantage of the second approach is that you won't have to wait for Camera Raw to work through each change on all of your images before you can move on to the next change. The time-consuming multiple-application process can be left until the end, and you can walk away and do something else while Camera Raw finishes the job.

When you plan to Synchronize, you don't want to leave anything undone that you could effectively synchronize, but on the other hand, you don't want to make work for yourself by synchronizing adjustments that work well on one image but may have to be reversed in other images. The strategy we follow here is to review images in Bridge and choose which ones look similar enough to benefit from the same changes, open those files together in Camera Raw and make changes, and then select all and Synchronize, leaving the more image-specific changes to be done to single files or smaller groups. (Another approach would be to adjust first and sort later — open a larger batch of images in Camera Raw, make all the changes you want to one of them, and then select only the similar images to Synchronize, applying only a subset of the changes you made to the one image.)

1 Setting Up

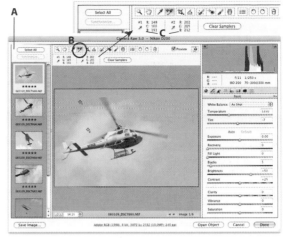

In Bridge, select all of the images you want to process together — similar subject matter under similar lighting conditions from one camera in a single photo shoot, for instance. Choose **File > Open in Camera Raw** (**Ctrl/⌘-R**). Opening multiple files this way will open a filmstrip arrangement in the Camera Raw window **A**. ▼ The images will open with your Default settings for color and contrast — either Camera Raw's built-in defaults, or new ones you've saved through Camera Raw's panel menu ≔ ◢. For instance, some photographers like to start with all sliders set to 0, so they change to those settings and choose Save New Camera Raw Defaults.

Quickly preview each of the images in Camera Raw by clicking its thumbnail in the filmstrip and looking at its histogram. Choose a single photo whose histogram looks "average" for this group, so adjusting it first and applying those adjustments to the rest of the images isn't likely to result in extreme settings.

Although you can work in Camera Raw in any order you like, if you work through the first six tabs in left-to-right order, and top-down in each tab, you're working in a logical order for the features to build on each other. You can always go back later and adjust earlier settings.

In addition to the histogram for monitoring overall tone and color, Camera Raw's Color Sampler tool ✒ lets you watch the color in as many as nine spots in the image. In the example shown above, we set two samplers **B** by choosing the tool in the bar at the top left of the interface and clicking on sky and cloud, so we could watch the RGB readouts **C** to monitor the blue of the sky, and keep the clouds a bluish white.

FIND OUT MORE

▼ Using Bridge **page 133**

2 Basic Tone & Color Adjustments

WORKING IN BASIC (the first tab), we started at the top with **White Balance A.** With White Balance set to As Shot, we didn't see any obvious color shift we would need to address. But to look at another option, we chose Daylight from the menu of White Balance settings. For raw images this menu provides a way to reset the lighting for the photo shoot. We felt that Daylight gave us a more balanced blue; we used the Temperature and Tint sliders to adjust it further, which turned the menu choice to Custom. *Note:* If the histogram shows that your image is very underexposed (with all the data at the left end), or very overexposed (with all the data at the right end), it makes sense to start by adjusting exposure and contrast and *then* do White Balance, because sometimes a big change in exposure can create a color shift.

Moving down to the next section of the Basic panel, you can choose to go right to the sliders or try **Auto,** which is Adobe's best guess at adjusting exposure and contrast, given the image data in the file. Since you can always go back to your **Default** settings, it doesn't hurt to try Auto; then make finer adjustments with the sliders. **Exposure** resets the white point; avoid big moves if you can. **Recovery** brings out detail in highlights. **Fill Light** brings out detail in the shadows. After using Fill Light, you may want to adjust **Blacks** if the histogram no longer reaches the left end. **Brightness** and **Contrast** act mostly on the midtones. **Clarity** (in Camera Raw 4.2 and later ▼) controls local contrast in the midtones, to bring out detail. **Vibrance** controls saturation in nonsaturated colors, and **Saturation** controls saturation in all colors. We increased Clarity **B** to sharpen details and also increased Vibrance **C** to make the sky bluer without oversaturating the bright colors of the heli-copter. (Step 1 of "Bringing Out Detail" on page 332 has more about the Basic tab.)

FIND OUT MORE

▼ Updating Camera Raw
page 142

3 Sharpness and Noise

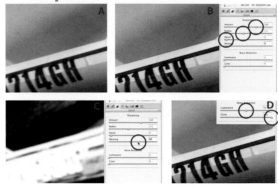

IN THE DETAIL TAB the **Sharpening** sliders are for *capture sharpening.* Digitally acquired images are slightly soft, whether a camera lens or a scanner is used, and the Sharpening in Camera Raw has been designed to address this. For capture sharpening to take effect, you'll need to choose **Apply Sharpening To: All Images** in the Camera Raw **Preferences** dialog, which you can open by clicking the ☰ button in the tool bar. Otherwise, Camera Raw only *previews* the sharpening it would apply but leaves it to you to sharpen in Photoshop, for instance. Sharpening only the preview is designed to give you an idea of how your later sharpening will interact with your Camera Raw settings. By setting the Preferences to apply the sharpening, you can always set the Amount to 0 whenever you don't want it — for instance, when you're working with a JPEG, since some sharpening has already been done in the camera. To preview the sharpening, set your view to 100% (Ctrl-Alt-0 for Windows, ⌘-Opt-0 for Mac) or higher; we used 200% **A.** Hold down the Alt/Option key while dragging on a slider to see a gray-scale preview of the effect. Adjust the **Amount** (how much the local contrast is increased when Camera Raw detects an edge) and the **Radius** (how many pixels on each side of the edge the increase in contrast is applied to) **B**; larger Radius settings can lead to obvious halos. **Detail** affects the prominence of the halo, with 0 showing almost no halo. **Masking C** controls how much the sharpening is hidden in smoother areas of the image. It provides a way to avoid unwanted sharpening of skin or sky, for instance. With the default setting of 0, the entire mask will appear white (with Alt/Option held down), and all areas will be sharpened.

To reduce noise (light-dark or color speckling) without reducing real detail in the image, zoom in on an area with both real detail and smooth color and in the **Noise Reduction** section adjust the **Luminance** and **Color** sliders to produce the noise/detail balance you want **D**.

4 Spot Removal

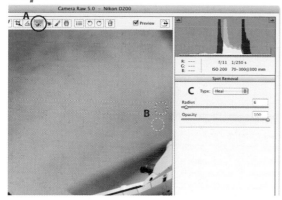

Dust on your camera's lens or sensors can cause spots on your images. A dust spot will appear in the same place on each image until the dust is removed from the camera. Because the problem is consistent from image to image, it can be a good candidate for fixing in a synchronized workflow, especially for expanses like sky or a studio backdrop. To remove the dust spot, choose the **Retouching/Spot Removal tool** ✒ **A** and drag the cursor over the spot. The result will be a red-and-white dashed circle surrounding the spot. Camera Raw immediately chooses and samples a source area of the same size (indicated by a green-and-white circle), and uses material from that source to hide the spot **B**. If you don't like the result, you can move the green-and-white source circle by putting the cursor inside it and dragging. *Note:* Although the dust spot stays in the same place from image to image because it's stuck to the lens or sensors, the source used for repair may not. Left to its own devices when you Synchronize, Camera Raw will automatically detect what it considers a good repair source in each separate image for each spot you've marked. But *if you've moved the repair source* (green-and-white circle) from its original automatic position, *Camera Raw will use that same custom source location* in all of the images.

While the Retouching/Spot Removal tool is chosen, the tabs on the right side of the dialog are replaced by controls for the way the repair blends with the spot you're trying to remove **C**. The **Heal** option blends the repair with the texture of the area you're repairing. The **Clone** option doesn't.

To remove a repair, click its circle and press the Backspace/Delete key. Use the "Clear All" button at the bottom of the tab to remove all current repairs. When you've finished spot removal, you can bring back the tabs by choosing a different tool (for instance, press the H key for the Hand tool).

5 Synchronizing, Saving & Opening

Before you Synchronize, make any other global adjustments you want to apply to all the images you've opened. For instance, you may want to adjust a particular color that seems either dull or oversaturated or convert the entire batch to grayscale (in the **HSL/Grayscale** tab), or apply a particular tinting scheme (in the **Split Toning** tab), or remove vignetting introduced by your camera (in the **Lens Corrections** tab).

When you've made all the global changes that all your open images can benefit from, apply them: Click the "**Select All**" button above the filmstrip **A**. (If you want to apply the changes to some of the images, but not all, you could Shift-click or Ctrl/⌘-click to select the ones you want.) Next click the "**Synchronize**" button **B**. When the Synchronize dialog box opens **C**, you can choose one of the subsets of settings from the menu at the top and then click in the checkboxes to add or delete particular options. Click "OK" to close the dialog.

If you think you might want to apply some or all of these settings to other images in the future, you can save the settings so they'll appear in the list in Camera Raw's **Presets** tab. To do that, click ▤ ◢ to open the panel menu and choose **Save Settings**. In the Save Settings dialog (which is basically identical to the Synchronize dialog), make your choices and click the "**Save**" button. Give the preset a name that will remind you of what it is. If you save it in the Settings folder, the preset will be listed on the Presets tab whenever Camera Raw is open.

Finally, click or Shift-click the "**Open**" button to take your selected images into Photoshop **D**. Or save the files without opening them in Photoshop by clicking the "**Save Images**" button **E**.

Optimizing for the Web

The challenge in *optimizing* a file for use on a web site or mobile device is to balance image quality with fast downloading, to reduce the file size but keep the artwork looking good. While it's not as important today as it was before broadband connections, keeping files small without sacrificing image quality can still be worth the time and effort. This is done in Photoshop's Save for Web & Devices dialog. With a photo or graphics file open in Photoshop, choose File > **Save for Web & Devices**. In the working area, click the **2-Up** or **4-Up** tab to compare the original with the optimized version(s) you'll make.

Below each window are the file size and download time **A**. In CS3 you can click the ⊙ just above the top right preview to open a menu of download speeds; in CS4 each preview has its own ▾≡ menu **B**. Choose the speed that's typical of the audience you're designing for.

If your artwork is bigger than you need it, start by reducing its dimensions. In the **Image Size** section, make sure **Width and Height are linked C**, so the artwork will be scaled proportionately. Specify a particular width or height, or a percentage of the original dimensions **D**. For Quality, try the **Bicubic Sharper** option, which will keep the image crisp as it's sized down **E**.

Once you've reduced image dimensions, choose an appropriate file format (see page 131), and then follow the directions for that format on the next three pages. When you're happy with the color and file size, click the **"Save"** button (not shown here) at the bottom of the dialog.

YOU'LL FIND THE FILE

in 🅦🅞🅦 > Project Files > Chapter 3 > Quick Optimizing

JPEG

ORIGINAL PHOTO: DAREN GREEN / PHOTOSPIN.COM

TO COMPARE THREE DIFFERENT DEGREES of JPEG compression for a photo, click the **4-Up** tab. Then click on each of the three optimized previews in turn and make choices for the JPEG settings, comparing the three versions and the original.

• Choose **JPEG** for the file format **A**.

• Set a level of quality; choose from the menu of **presets B** and then fine-tune with the **Quality** slider **C**.

• Adding a bit of **Blur D** often allows compression to a smaller file size; you may be able to save on file size without reducing image quality noticeably. Adobe recommends a setting of 0.1 to 0.5.

• Choose **Progressive** or **Optimized E**. Progressive is designed to download the image first as a low-res version (to assure the viewer that something is happening), and then build to higher resolution. Choosing this option adds to the overall file size, and for small files it isn't needed. Optimized reduces file size.

• To ensure that the image will look the same in all browsers, turn on **Convert to sRGB Color**, which is the color that browsers use by default. (In Photoshop CS3, the Convert option is in the ⊙ menu for the dialog.)

• The choices in the **Preview** menu in Photoshop CS4 allow you to see how your file will look on monitors like yours and on Mac and Windows platforms.

• Leaving out some of the **Metadata** reduces file size.

AUTOMATIC ALTERNATIVES

As you work, if you have an optimization that you like best of the three but you want to see if you can get the file size even smaller, choosing **Repopulate Views** from the ⊙/▾≡ menu at the top right corner of the dialog will replace the other two optimized previews with files with the Quality setting reduced to half and to a quarter, so you can compare them; all other settings remain the same.

GIF: 1 Setup

IF YOU WANT TRANSPARENCY in your artwork so it can appear silhouetted on a web page, **GIF** and PNG-8 are good options. Open the background image or tile in Photoshop and use Photoshop's Eyedropper tool 🖋 to click on the color, making it Photoshop's Foreground color. With your artwork file open, choose File > Save for Web & Devices. For the **Matte** color (which fills in for transparency) choose Foreground. Make sure **Transparency is turned on**, and set **Colors** at the maximum number (256). In the Color Table's menu ⊙ /▾ ☰ choose **Sort by Popularity** (this will put the colors that occur most at the top of the chart). Set Lossy to 0.

GIF: 2 Reduction Algorithm

For the **Colors** setting, start with 256 (the maximum number) **A**. Choose one of the color-reduction algorithms (Adaptive, Perceptual, or Selective) **B**, based on the nature of the art:

- An **Adaptive** palette is optimized to reproduce the colors that occur most often in the image.

- A **Perceptual** palette is like an Adaptive palette, but it also takes into consideration the parts of the spectrum where the human eye is most sensitive.

- A **Selective** palette — often a good choice — is like the Perceptual but also favors colors that occur in large areas of flat color.

For this art we chose **Selective**.

 **Spaceman-Before.psd**

GIF: 3 Color Reduction

TO REMOVE SOME OF THE COLORS (and thus decrease file size) **watch the changes** in the optimized version **A** as you **reduce the Colors** number (as described below). Colors will be eliminated starting at the bottom of the Color Table. As you work, experiment with Dither settings also **B**, **C** (see below).

To reduce the number of colors in large steps, use the pop-up Colors menu **D** (each choice is half the one below it). Keep going with the color reduction until the image quality doesn't look good to you anymore. Then increase the number of Colors by one large step.

Now decrease by 10 colors at a time: Click in the Colors field, hold down the Shift key, and tap the down arrow key ↓ on your keyboard. Again, keep going until the image quality doesn't look good anymore **E**. If the last step degrades the image too much, release the Shift key and raise the number of colors again ↑ until you reach a good compromise between quality and speed. Click the "Preview in browser" button **F** to preview. If necessary, back in the Save for Web & Devices dialog, adjust your Optimize settings, preview again, and so on until you like the result.

DITHER

Dither intersperses dots of two different colors to create the illusion of a third color. It can prevent "banding" (distinct color breaks in what should be a smooth transition). But because Dither can interfere with compression, it sometimes *increases* the size of a GIF file even though it allows you to reduce the number of colors. Balancing Dither with color reduction is a matter of experimenting.

GIF: 4 Transparency

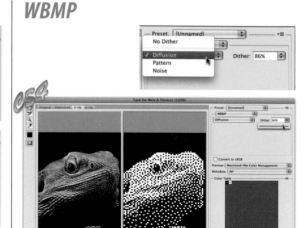

WBMP

In a GIF (or PNG-8) file, transparency is different than in Photoshop in general — we can think of it as just one of the colors in the Color Table. Each pixel in a GIF file has to be either fully transparent or a fully solid color — it can't be partly transparent. But there are ways to "fake" partial transparency — to keep the antialiased edges of your artwork smooth, or to allow soft edges to fade into the web page background. If you didn't select a Matte color in step 1, set one now.

If you turn **Transparency off**, all the full transparency in your artwork will be replaced with the Matte color **A**, which will also be blended with existing semi-transparent color at the edges of your artwork to give each partly transparent pixel a solid color in the GIF. On the other hand, if you turn **Transparency on**, the Matte color will still be blended into the partly transparent pixels (such as those in the antialiasing here), but any fully transparent pixels will stay transparent **B**.

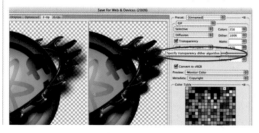
WBMP is a standard format for use on mobile devices such as cell phones. This format uses 1-bit color — each pixel is either white or black. Of the four **Dither** choices for the WBMP format, **Diffusion** provides the most opportunity for controlling the overall tone of the image and the level of detail. To "translate" a color or grayscale image, choose WBMP for the file format. You might look at the No Dither, Pattern, and Noise options, just in case one of those looks great for your particular image. Then try **Diffusion** dither, moving the Dither slider to adjust the light-to-dark ratio and "grain" of the result.

WORKING TO A PARTICULAR FILE SIZE

If you have a target size you'd like your file to be reduced to, you might want to try the Save for Web & Devices dialog's **Optimize to File Size** option. Click on one of the Optimized previews and choose from the menu ⊙/▾≡ at the upper right corner of the dialog box to open the Optimize to File Size dialog. With the **Auto Select GIF/JPEG** option, Photoshop will choose GIF or JPEG based on image content and produce a file of the target size. If you choose to start with **Current Settings** instead, the current **file format** for the Optimized preview will be maintained as the file is compressed to the target size; **JPEG** and **GIF** are the only formats for which this choice is available.

Commissioned by Resorts Casinos in Atlantic City, New Jersey, **Mike Kungl's *Taste of Style*** was applied to everything from matchbook covers to billboards. Kungl began with a pencil sketch, scanned it, and used it as a template in Adobe Illustrator, where he drew shapes and filled them with flat colors to make a design comp, shown at the right. When he finished in Illustrator, Kungl copied the artwork to the clipboard and pasted it as paths into a Photoshop file.

Working in Photoshop, Kungl turned each subpath into an alpha channel by clicking it with the Path Selection tool, then clicking the "Load path as a selection" button at the bottom of the Paths panel, and finally clicking the "Save selection as channel" button at the bottom of the Channels panel. When he had converted all the paths, he had a file with a single empty layer and many channels. He saved the file in Photoshop (PSD) format and opened it in Corel Painter, where he turned the

channels into selections and used them as friskets to limit gradient fills, paper textures, and brushwork.

When he had finished in Painter, Kungl saved the file in PSD format again and reopened it in Photoshop, where the layer hierarchy created in Painter was preserved. In this layered file, he touched up the artwork, made color adjustments with Levels, Hue/Saturation, and Selective Color, and changed layer Opacity to blend the elements.

piddix digital collage sheet no. 380 – Dogs 2-inch squares five – © 2008 piddix llc –

piddix digital collage sheet no. 285 – Hand-Colored Eggs 2.75x4 inches – © 2009 piddix llc – www.piddix.com

© 2007 www.piddix.com

Collecting photos and graphics in the public domain from around the world, **Corinna Buchholz** of **piddix.com** assembles related items to produce her *digital collage sheets* in PDF or JPEG format. Many of her customers use the images in jewelry, cards, and other hand-crafted products.

Buchholz obtains some images from the U. S. Library of Congress web site (www.loc.gov), a rich source of imagery, and she also photographs some antique artwork with a digital camera. But most of her work consists of scanning (typically at 600 pixels per inch, saved as TIFFs), meticulously cleaning up the scans and restoring color, and making sure the artwork is copyright-free (see "Corinna Buchholz Researches Copyright" on page 107).

At her home office she uses an Epson GT-20000 scanner, often taking advantage of the Epson Scan software to begin the cleanup. She typically scans in 24-bit color, even if the original art is "black-and-white," so she can pick up subtle paper colors, and she often uses the software's Unsharp Mask and the Descreen filter setting for fine prints. She usually chooses the Photo option, or for black-and-white art on matte paper, the Document option.

"But when I visit archives and use my travel scanner (an Epson Perfection 4990 Photo)," she says, "I bring back the unfiltered 'raw' scan, since I won't be able to rescan if something doesn't turn out to my liking."

With the scan in hand Buchholz next continues the cleanup in Photoshop.

If she needs to descreen, ▼ she uses Filter > Noise > Despeckle. (With Smart Filters in Photoshop CS3 and CS4, this descreening can be kept live and changed later if necessary.) ▼

Often Buchholz uses the Clone Stamp 🖈 and the Healing Brush 🩹, ▼ along with Adjustment layers such as Levels and Curves. ▼ When working with a series of similar scans, she often records an Action ▼ as she edits one scan and then runs the Action on the rest of the scans in the series.

piddix digital collage sheet no. 496 – Wizard of Oz 1.5 in Squares – © 2007

piddix digital collage sheet no. 520 – Stained Glass Windows – © 2009 piddix

piddix digital collage sheet no. 1029
1x1.5 in Vintage Hawaii Hula & Surf
© 2009 piddix llc · www.piddix.com

The degree of cleanup required depends not only on the condition of the original but also on the look she wants to achieve. For instance, her goal was clean, rich color in **Vintage Dogs and Puppies** (scanned directly from fine art prints, posters, photos, and cards from the 1850s to the 1930s) and in **Wizard of Oz** (scanned from crisp woodblock prints from a first edition of The Wonderful Wizard of Oz, illustrated by W. W. Denslow). But for **Hand-Colored Vintage Bird Eggs** (scanned from a dusty, dilapidated volume from 1890) and **Stained Glass Windows** (scanned from a chromolithograph in an 1880s German encyclopedia), Buchholz sharpened the images and removed the larger stains and creases but intentionally kept the original vintage look of the labeling and the color and grain of the paper.

Once the scans are cleaned up, she selects the images she wants to use on a sheet. "I've tried many different ways to shorten the process," she says, "including clipping groups and other ways to automate it, but none of them has suited me so far. Each sheet of images is different." So she uses fixed-size and fixed-ratio Rectangular Marquee ⌐ and Elliptical Marquee ◯ tools, ▼ in several sizes often used for crafts, to isolate parts of an original image, copying and pasting into her developing page document. Smart Guides and the Align and Distribute commands can be useful for positioning imported elements on a page. ▼

"My own personal 'template' is simply a blank 8.5-by-11-inch file with a white background, a type layer with my information on it, and a reduced-opacity layer with a 'watermark' for protecting the images when they're advertised on the web." She also produces some sheets in a 4-by-6-inch format, such as **Japanese Nature** (scanned Japanese woodblock prints from the mid-1800s) and **Vintage Hawaii Hula & Surf** (scanned and photographed from Japanese woodblock prints from 1919, antique postcards, and vintage travel posters and ads). These smaller sheets are designed for output on a photo printer or at a photo kiosk.

FIND OUT MORE

▼ Selecting with Marquee tools **page 54**

▼ Smart Guides **page 28**

▼ Align & Distribute **page 28**

To decorate her ceramic **Tea Party Chez Zandra** with images of fashion designer Zandra Rhodes, **Irene de Watteville** started with her own photos of Rhodes **A** and in Photoshop developed them into medallions for the teapot and its base. She used transfer sheets printed with black Versa*Ink* (www.g7ps.com), which contains a magnetic component (iron oxide) for printing bank-readable checks on inkjet printers. Printed in reverse

on a glue-treated transparency, a Versa*Ink* image can be transferred to the surface of fresh clay and fired.

To begin the project, Watteville opened the photo files in Photoshop and converted each one to Grayscale (Image > Mode > Grayscale); she would do her brightness and contrast adjustments in black-and-white. For each of the designs for the teapot, she used the Lasso tool to select the area

of the photo she wanted to use ▼ and copied it (Ctrl/⌘-C). She then started a new Grayscale image file (File > New) at 8.5 by 11 inches (the size of the transparent acetate sheets she would use for printing) and pasted in the copied photo. She lightened the pasted image and increased contrast using Image > Adjust > Brightness/Contrast. ▼ She then selected the hair with a feathered Lasso and lightened it even more, as she planned to color

A

B

C

it with a red glaze. She used Edit > Transform to scale the image (by Shift-dragging a corner handle). ▼ Then she duplicated the image to a new layer (Ctrl/⌘-J) as many times as she needed copies. For the side of the teapot shown above, she made one duplicate and used Edit > Transform > Flip Vertical to change its orientation **B**. To each of the developing medallions for the teapot and its base, she added clip art scanned from Dover's *Catchpenny Prints*.

Watteville knows from experience that the image she prints needs to be quite a bit denser and darker than she wants the design to be on the fired ceramic piece.

To make each transfer sheet, she started by writing the word "glue" with a permanent marker on one corner of an inkjet transparency. She then applied a dollop of mucilage the size of a quarter coin to the marked side of the sheet, and spread it evenly over the sheet with moistened fingers. (Mucilage is the brownish liquid glue people used before glue sticks; Ross Mucilage is available at several arts-and-crafts retailers via the internet.) She let the glue dry overnight. Then, after testing her print on plain paper, she printed her Photoshop image in Ver-sa*lnk* black on the glue side of the sheet. "Be sure to set your printer's software to print in Photo mode and in Black only," says Watteville, since it's the black ink that contains the iron oxide. "Let the transparency dry a few hours after printing, or use a hair-dryer on low for a few minutes."

Starting with a very smooth low-fire clay (Raku-K White EM345), Watteville used a slab roller to flatten it to half a centimeter thick (a rolling pin works for small pieces), and used a knife to cut the clay into the exact shapes she would need to assemble the teapot and base. Looking through the transparency to position the art, she applied the printed side to the damp clay. "I smooth it on with fingers first," says Watteville, "then horizontal strokes with the edge of a credit card, for even application. The moisture in the clay liquefies the glue enough to transfer the image.

But you have to work quickly, making the transfer in less than a minute, or you can end up with a mess."

Watteville assembled the pieces and fired at cone 06 (1828°F) to produce a black image on the white clay **C**. As she expected, the image was quite a bit less dense than in the print. After this first (bisque) firing Watteville applied color with Duncan E-Z Strokes for translucent watercolorlike colors and a light coat of clear glaze. (At this point in the process, she could also touch up lines in the print with black underglaze if needed.) She fired again at cone 06, added the red for the hair, and fired again. "The clear glaze has to be applied as a very thin coat," says Watteville, or the black lines will get murky. And the additional firings have to be at the same temperature as the first or lower."

Note: Watteville doesn't print with her Versa*lnk* cartridge every day, or even every week, so it can get a bit clogged between projects. If her test print is incomplete or fuzzy, she follows this routine, suggested by the manufacturer, to revitalize the cartridge: Stand the cartridge ink-side-down in a half-inch of lukewarm water for 15 minutes. Then put a wet paper towel in the microwave oven for 1 minute. Carefully remove the hot towel from the oven and stand the cartridge on it for 2 minutes. Pat the cartridge dry and reinstall it in the printer.

FIND OUT MORE
▼ Using the Lasso 🔎 **page 54**
▼ Using Brightness/Contrast **page 250**
▼ Transforming **page 67**

When **Donal Jolley** photographed the model for ***Red-Striped Couch***, he didn't hesitate to use a fast shutter speed and a low ISO setting (100), to capture a sharp image with little noise. Because he knew he could adjust the exposure as much as two f-stops later in Camera Raw, he could concentrate on getting the pose and the angle exactly as he wanted them.

Viewing his photo shoot in Adobe Bridge, Jolley chose an image **A** and double-clicked its thumbnail. It was automatically recognized as a raw image and opened in Camera Raw. There the Auto settings instantly adjusted color and tone, making corrections based on the data in the raw file itself **B**. Camera Raw is fast, and because its many controls work interactively, the adjustment routine is fluid. Jolley altered the Shadows

and Brightness settings slightly, increasing the contrast **C**. When he had the color and lighting set, he clicked the "Open" button to open the file in Photoshop, where he saved it in the native PSD format.

Jolley opened the file in Corel Painter and used the Tracing Paper feature to view the image as he blocked in the figure, couch, and floor and created the drapery and the wall. With his reference photo

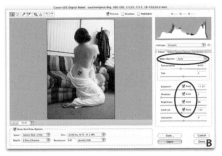

A   B   C   D

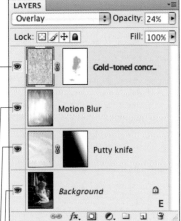

LAYERS

Overlay ▾   Opacity: 24% ▸

Lock: ☐ ◢ ✛ 🔒   Fill: 100% ▸

Gold-toned concr...

Motion Blur

Putty knife

Background

E

fx. ◯ 🔲 ⊿ 🗑

on the screen next to his developing painting, he sampled color as he worked to add detail. When he had finished painting **D**, he saved the file and opened it in Photoshop again.

To build up a "lacquer finish," Jolley drew from his "texture library," adding three texture layers, as shown in the final Layers panel **E**.

The first texture layer was a photo of an old putty knife, which Jolley desaturated (Image > Adjustments > Desaturate) and lightened (Image > Adjustments > Levels, moving the Output Levels black point slider inward to lighten and reduce contrast). He changed the layer's blend mode to Overlay ▾ and added a layer mask, using the Gradient tool 🔲 to create a divided mask that allows

Open the **Red Couch Detail.psd** file (in the Wow Goodies folder) to see how the layers, masks, and blend modes interact.

the layer to contribute in the upper right corner of the image only. ▾

The middle texture layer was a photo of a concrete garage floor, blurred (Filter > Blur > Motion Blur at 90° at a high Distance setting to make long vertical streaks). He put the layer in Overlay mode and reduced the Opacity to 34%, using the more pronounced streaking that the Motion Blur filter creates at the "front" and "back" edges of the blur to add a slight vignetting effect at the top and bottom edges of the painting. Using the Brush tool ◢ with a soft brush tip, a low Opacity setting, and the Airbrush option, Jolley painted the motion-blurred layer with white. This protected the figure from the texture (as a layer mask would have); with the layer in Overlay mode, it had the added advantage of brightening the skin tones.

The top texture layer started as a shot of Jolley's concrete driveway, which he tinted (Image > Adjustments > Hue/Saturation, moving the Hue slider). In Overlay mode and with Opacity reduced to 24%, the light olive-gold layer completed the surface texture of the painting as it lightened and warmed the image overall. Jolley added a layer mask and airbrushed it with gray paint to mostly eliminate the texture from the torso. ▾

FIND OUT MORE

▾ Blend modes **page 181**

▾ Gradient masks **page 84**

▾ Painting layer masks **page 84**

Color in Photoshop

4

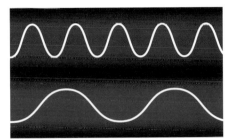

The wavelength of light, which determines hue, is the distance from one peak of the wave to the next. Of the colors we can see, violet light has the shortest waves and red has the longest.

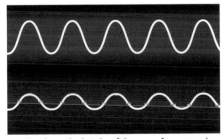

Amplitude, or the height of the wave from trough to peak, determines the brightness of a color. The greater the amplitude, the more energy in the wave and therefore the brighter, or lighter, the color.

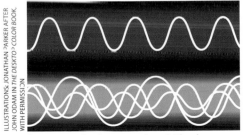

A pure, completely saturated, or vivid, color contains light of only one wavelength. As varied wavelengths are mixed, the result is a more neutral color — black, gray, or white, depending on brightness.

COLOR IS VITALLY IMPORTANT TO the way we express ourselves in images and graphics, and Photoshop has a powerful set of features dedicated to supporting us as we choose, apply, and change colors. This chapter introduces these features, and you'll find examples of their use throughout the book.

WHAT IS COLOR?

If you asked a dozen people to "picture something red," it's likely that each one would visualize a slightly different color, or a range of colors, like the variety of reds on the skin of an apple. And yet, if you could show all parties what the others had visualized, most would probably agree that all the colors pictured would fall into a range they could call "red."

Although our perception of color is subjective, based on our visual system and psychology, we *can* describe color with great precision. We need to be able to characterize color precisely in order to get predictable, repeatable results from scanners and display monitors and on the printed page.

In scientific terms, color depends on three characteristics of light waves: length, amplitude, and purity. **Wavelength** is most closely related to the property of color called **hue**. **Amplitude** comes closest to color **brightness**, or **lightness,** or **value**. And **purity** determines what we call **saturation**, or **chroma**.

The CIE **Lab color** space is a system established by an international standards committee in 1931 to define and measure color mathematically so that colors could be specified precisely. Instruments called *spectrophotometers* and *colorimeters* can measure color precisely enough to come up with the information that will precisely locate a color in the CIE Lab color space. To work efficiently with color in Photoshop, you have to know a certain amount about Lab color and other **color modes** and about **color depth**.

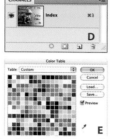

In most color modes the first listing in the Channels panel represents the combined channels (often referred to as the "composite" channel). In some modes, such as RGB Color **A** and CMYK Color **B**, the Channels panel shows the primary colors. In Lab Color mode **C** we see the Lightness (gray) channel and two channels that supply the other color ingredients. In Indexed Color mode (in which the color palette is reduced to 256 or fewer colors), a single "channel" appears in the Channels panel **D**; the colors are stored in the Color Table **E**, which can be accessed through File > Save for Web & Devices or Image > Mode > Color Table.

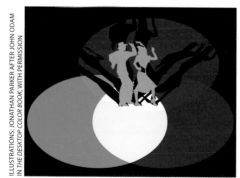

In an additive color model (represented by this illustration) red, green, and blue light combine on-screen to make white light.

COLOR MODES

Photoshop uses several different systems, or **modes**, of color representation, as shown at the left. Most of these can be chosen through the Image > Mode menu. In some of the color modes (such as RGB and CMYK) the *primary colors* are the basics from which all other colors are mixed, and Photoshop stores the color data for each of the primary colors in a *color channel*. These channels are shown in the Channels panel.

In other modes, color is defined not in terms of primaries but as **brightness** (in Grayscale mode) or **brightness with color components** added (in Lab Color mode). And in Indexed Color mode, color is not broken down into its elements at all, but is delivered instead as a limited number of specific "swatches" stored in a **color table**.

Creative Color: RGB

Computer monitors, digital cameras, and scanners display or record colors by mixing the primary colors of light — red, green, and blue, or **RGB**. When all three of these *additive primaries* are at full intensity, the result is white light; when all are turned off, black results. The three colors, at various brightnesses, mix visually to make all the colors of the RGB spectrum. Unless your work in Photoshop requires another color mode for some specialized purpose, RGB is often the best mode for creative work, since it offers the most function and flexibility. All of Photoshop's tools and commands work in this mode, whereas other modes have a more limited set. RGB also has a broader *gamut*, or range of colors, than most other modes, with the exception of Lab.

Within the RGB mode, as in other modes, there can be many different *color spaces*, or subsets of the overall gamut, that different scanners, digital cameras, and monitors can reproduce. Photoshop can use ICC *profiles*, which are descriptions of these color spaces, in its color management system. ("Color Management," starting on page 187, tells more about profiles.)

MISSING MODES

If certain color mode choices are "grayed out" (unavailable), it's because those color modes aren't directly accessible from the mode the file is in currently. For instance, to get to Bitmap or Duotone mode, you have to go through Grayscale.

In subtractive color (above) cyan, magenta, and yellow inks combine to make a dark, nearly black color.

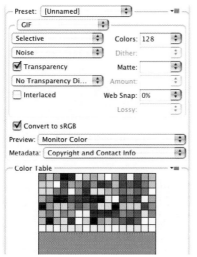

Photoshop's Save For Web & Devices dialog, part of which is shown here, has more options for reducing the number of colors in an image than the Image > Mode > Indexed Color command offers.

"The Yellow Shirt (Working in Lab Color Mode)" starting on page 221 provides a great example of where Lab mode excels at changing color while preserving highlight and shadow detail.

Printed Color: CMYK

CMYK, or **four-color process**, is the type of commercial printing most often used for reproducing photos, illustrations, and other works. The CMYK inks (called **subtractive primaries**) are cyan, magenta, and yellow, with black added to intensify the dark colors and details. Adding black makes dark colors look crisper than darkening with a heavier mix of cyan, magenta, and yellow. Darkening with black also requires less ink; this can be important because there's an upper limit to the amount of ink a press can apply before the ink will no longer adhere to the paper cleanly.

Web Color: Indexed (for GIF)

The process of assigning 256 or fewer specified colors to represent the millions of colors in a full-color image is called *indexing*. Indexing, most often done in the preparation of graphics destined for the web or a handheld device, is usually worked out in Photoshop's Save For Web & Devices dialog box. "Quick Optimizing for the Web" on page 152 provides an example.

For **Indexed Color** you can choose from **Perceptual**, **Selective**, and **Adaptive** palettes, each of which uses different criteria to choose the colors (anywhere from 2 to 256) that best represent the color in the currently active image. The **Color Table** choice at the bottom of the Image > Mode menu lets you view and edit the colors used in an Indexed Color image. You can also name and save the colors in the Color Table, and load colors from previously saved Color Tables and from Swatches. ▼

FIND OUT MORE

▼ Swatches panel
page 171

Lab Color

Photoshop's Lab Color mode represents color as a brightness component and two hue-saturation components. "L" (lightness) values fall between 0 (black) and 100 (white). The "a" component goes from yellow (positive) to blue (negative), and "b" values go from magenta (positive) to green (negative). For "a" and "b" a 0 value is neutral, or colorless. Because its gamut is large enough to include both the CMYK and the RGB gamuts, and because it can characterize colors precisely, Lab Color mode serves as an intermediate step when Photoshop converts from RGB to CMYK. Working on the "L" (or lightness) channel of a Lab file is an easy way to modify the light/dark information in the image without affecting hue and saturation. Conversely, working on the "a" and "b" channels is a good way to alter color dramatically without affecting tonal range. Also, slightly blurring the "a" and "b" channels is a great way to reduce color noise without affecting image detail.

With a Black & White Adjustment layer you can use the sliders to control how much brightness each of six colors will contribute to a monochrome version of the image. In addition, you can pick out a color in the image and "scrub" to make it lighter or darker in the black-and-white.

Photoshop's Duotone mode provides curves that store information for printing a grayscale image like the one shown on the left above in one to four ink colors. The program comes with several sets of preset duotone, tritone, and quadtone curves to load. Or you can shape the curves yourself.

Grayscale

An image in **Grayscale** mode, such as a black-and-white photo, includes brightness values, but no data for the hue or saturation characteristic of color images. For the best reproduction of a color photo in black-and-white, you can get more control and flexibility by using a Black & White Adjustment layer (new in Photoshop CS3). "From Color to Black & White" on page 214 covers several ways to convert.

Duotone

With two colors of ink (or even one color of ink applied in two passes through the printing press) it's possible to get more shades and tones than you could get with a single pass of a single ink, and thus you can deliver more of the detail in your image onto the printed page. As an example, adding a second color in the highlights increases the number of tones available for representing the lightest tones in an image. Besides extending tonal range, the second color can "warm" or "cool" a black-and-white image, tinting it slightly toward red or blue, for example. Or the second color may be used for dramatic effect or to visually tie a photo into a series of images or to other design elements.

In Photoshop's Duotone mode, a set of *curves* determines how the grayscale information will be represented in each of the ink

HSB COLOR

There's one approach to color classification that you won't find in the Image > Mode menu but that's very important in Photoshop. The **HSB** system (Hue, Saturation, and Brightness) is found in Photoshop's tools for choosing, evaluating, and adjusting colors. Look for it, for instance, in the Color Picker, the Info panel, and the Hue/Saturation Adjustment layer, whose values are used here.

In terms of our visual perception, some hues look brighter than others; here the green shirt looks lighter than the blue. Also, it's harder to distinguish the hue when saturation is reduced and colors go toward neutral gray, or when colors are very light (pastel) or very dark.

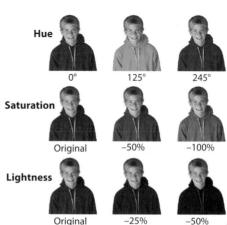

Photoshop's Presets > Duotones folder includes settings for tritones and quadtones as well as duotones. Or you can specify your own colors. By drastically reshaping curves as in this quadtone, you can make different colors predominate in highlights, midtones, and shadows. This quadtone incorporates a custom green ink, available because it was used elsewhere in the color publication.

To convert the color graphics from page 479 to a stylized black-and-white, we chose Image > Mode > Grayscale, then Image > Mode Bitmap. In the Bitmap dialog, we set the Output Resolution the same as the input and chose Halftone Screen for the method, and then we chose Cross for the Shape of the dot.

colors. Will the second color in the duotone be emphasized in the shadows but omitted from the highlights? Will it be used to color the midtones?

Photoshop's Duotone mode also includes tritone and quadtone options, for producing printing plates for three or four ink colors. A Duotone image is stored as a grayscale file and a set of curves that will act on that grayscale information to produce the printing plates, as shown in the "Duotones" technique on page 199.

GETTING BACK TO GRAYSCALE

In a Duotone file, you can always get back to the Grayscale image you started with: Choose Image > Mode > Duotone, and choose Monotone for the Type. If the Ink 1 graph in the Duotone Options dialog isn't the default 45° diagonal, click it to open the Duotone Curve dialog. Then simply drag any points you see on the curve off one edge of the graph to restore the diagonal.

Bitmap

Like Grayscale, Bitmap mode uses only brightness data, no hue or saturation. But in Bitmap mode each pixel is either fully OFF or fully ON, producing a gamut of two "colors" — black and white, with no grays in between. Bitmap mode can be effective as an artistic style or for creating graphics for single-color displays.

OVERPRINT COLORS

A button **A** in the Duotone dialog box opens the Overprint Colors dialog, where you adjust the on-screen display of your duotone to look more like it will when it's printed with custom inks. To do this you need a printed sample that shows your custom inks overprinted solid. Clicking any of the color squares in the Overprint Colors dialog **B** opens the Color Picker so you can change the display of that color mixture to match your printed sample. The settings in the Overprint Colors dialog are reflected in the color bar at the bottom of the Duotone Options dialog **C**.

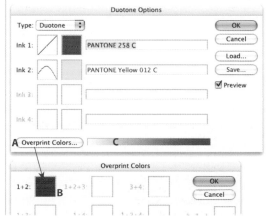

Expressions

Spot colors can be added at full strength or as tints overlaid on a photo. See page 226.

Multichannel

Multichannel is a *subtractive* color mode, so if you convert an RGB file, the Multichannel document has cyan, magenta, and yellow channels rather than red, green, and blue. If you delete one or more of the channels from a color image (either CMYK or RGB), its color mode automatically becomes Multichannel.

Spot Color

You won't find a Spot Color mode in the Image > Mode menu, but **spot colors**, also called **custom colors**, can be added to files in any color mode except Bitmap. Spot colors are often special color mixes formulated to a particular ink system, such as the Pantone Matching System.

In Photoshop you can add spot colors by clicking the Channels panel's ▾☰ button and choosing New Spot Channel. A spot color channel is a good choice when an absolute color standard has to be met for printing a corporate color or logo — the custom ink is premixed to the standard, so the printed color always looks the same. Spot colors are also used to print colors that are outside the CMYK printing gamut, such as certain oranges or blues, fluorescents, or metallics, or to apply a clear varnish. "Adding Spot Color" on page 226 shows how to apply custom color.

HI-FI PRINTING

The Pantone Hexachrome™ printing process, developed to provide a bigger color range and better color accuracy than standard four-color process printing, uses brighter CMYK inks than those used in standard printing, and also adds vivid orange and green inks. For accurate conversion to the Hexachrome color system, Pantone supplies the Hex-Image® plug-in for Photoshop.

COLOR DEPTH

Besides the color *mode*, the Image > Mode menu also shows the color *depth*, or **bit depth** — how many bits per pixel Photoshop is using to store the color data in each color channel of a file. The more bits available for this storage, the more color and tone distinctions an image can include.

8 Bits/Channel

The standard for color in Photoshop, for print and for the screen, is still 8 Bits/Channel, which offers millions of colors and tones. All of Photoshop's functions work in 8 Bits/Channel mode, whereas not all of them work in the modes with more colors.

---

8 BITS? 16 BITS? 24 BITS? 32 BITS?

The terminology used for color depth, or **bit depth**, has evolved as monitors, scanners, and digital cameras have become more capable. Here are some of the most commonly used terms and what they mean:

8-bit color has 256 (or 2^8) levels of brightness for each primary color. So for Grayscale mode there are 256 shades of gray, including black and white. In RGB color there are 256 x 256 x 256 = more than 16 million possible colors. (Previously, the term "8-bit color" was used to describe color on monitors that could display only 256 colors.)

16-bit color has more than 65,000 (or 2^{16}) levels of brightness for each primary color. That's 65,000+ grays in Grayscale, and billions of colors in RGB mode.

24-bit color is an older term, which is still sometimes used to mean the same as 8-bit RGB (8 bits per channel x 3 channels = 24 bits).

32-bit color is used when several photos of the same scene are taken at different exposures, and then combined in an HDR (High Dynamic Range) file to make the image look more like what the human eye-brain visual system perceives when looking at the scene. Photoshop's 32 Bits/Channel mode is currently limited, compared to what the program can do in 8-bit or 16-bit files.

Before | After

Adjusting tone and color in Camera Raw (see page 297) or in Photoshop in 16 Bits/Channel mode can sometimes produce better results than working in 8 Bits/Channel mode. Especially for an image file with a limited dynamic range (a dark or low-contrast photo, for example), adjusting tone and color in 16 Bits can help prevent posterization when you expand the dynamic range.

Many of the filters that might be important to run on information-rich files are available in 16 Bits/Channel mode, including the Liquify and Vanishing Point "megafilters," and the Smart Filters feature can keep them live. The filter samples in Appendix A of this book indicate which filters work in 16 Bits/Channel mode.

16 Bits/Channel

Most of Photoshop's core functions — including layers, masks, Adjustment layers, and Smart Filters — are available in 16-bit mode. If you have a scanned image or a digital photo captured with more than 8 bits per channel of color information (as in the "billions of colors" option offered by some scanners or by the raw format offered by many digital cameras), you can open it in Camera Raw ▼ or in Photoshop in 16 Bits/Channel mode and make tone and color adjustments using this extra information.

FIND OUT MORE
▼ Camera Raw
page 141

The wealth of extra image information in 16 Bits/Channel mode provides some very practical payoffs. First, it's much easier to coax good looking shadow and highlight detail from an image, in whatever part of the tonal range is troublesome, because you have many more tones to work with. If you've ever tried to bring out detail in an underexposed photo in 8 Bits/Channel mode, you know the challenge. With 16 Bits/Channel you have 256 possible tonal steps for every one step you have in 8 Bits/Channel mode. Second, color transitions are smoother with billions of potential color combinations. And third, because you have a potential 65,000+ shades of gray instead of just 256, you can also get a better monochrome result when you convert an image from color to Grayscale in 16 Bits/Channel mode.

So why would you ever work in 8 Bits/Channel mode? One reason is that 16 Bits/Channel files are twice as large as 8-bit ones, and if you start with a relatively big file and begin adding layers, at some point your work may get painfully slow. Also, many photos start out as 8-bit files and have to end up as 8-bit files for printing. And although theoretically you can get better results with color adjustments if you convert to 16 Bits/Channel temporarily to make the adjustments and then switch back, the increase in color detail may very well be imperceptible when the image is printed.

32 Bits/Channel

High Dynamic Range (HDR, or 32-bit) files allow even finer distinctions in color and tone than 16-bit. Since HDR allows a bigger dynamic range (or number of tones between pure white and pure black) than most cameras can capture or than any printer or monitor can achieve, you might wonder why you would want to work with this bigger file format. The reason is that with all that information available, you can pick and choose where in the image you want to expand the dynamic range, without losing printable or displayable tones in other areas. In

Photoshop's 32-bit color and **HDR** (high dynamic range) format can provide a good start for combining several exposures of the same image, without selecting or masking. It can produce realistic or surrealistic results. You'll find a step-by-step example of combining bracketed exposures to accurately represent the wide range of tones we see in an image in Chapter 5, on page 292. For an example of extending dynamic range with bracketed exposures "by hand" (without HDR), see Loren Haury's work on page 366.

Besides blending bracketed exposures, you can use Photoshop's HDR feature with a single image for artistic expression. You'll find an example on page 212.

a way, the ability to use the extra information in a 32-bit image when you convert it to 16-bit or 8-bit mimics the eye's ability to accommodate to different light levels in the shadows and bright areas of a scene, seeing detail in both.

Photographers can use Photoshop's Merge to HDR command (from the File > Automate menu) to blend together several bracketed exposures of the same scene. With HDR, for example, you can combine three photos of the interior of a room, one exposed for the sunny window, one for the deepest shadows, and one for the lighting in between. (There are some restrictions on how the photos must be taken and combined. ▼)

FIND OUT MORE
▼ Taking photos for merging to HDR
page 293

The 32 Bits/Channel mode has some options for editing images — Photoshop Extended even allows painting on layers and provides an HDR-specific Color Picker. But to display or print the file, you'll need to convert your image to 16 or 8 Bits/Channel. The HDR Conversion dialog box lets you try out different methods of compressing the dynamic range, comparing them to find the solution you like best, although Local Adaptation is the most commonly used.

SAVE IN 32-BIT MODE!

When you convert an HDR file to an 8-bit or a 16-bit file, some of the original data is necessarily "thrown away" in the compression process and can't be recovered later. But saving the HDR file in 32 Bits/Channel mode first and then converting a *copy* of it allows you to keep all the data intact, so you can come back to the saved HDR file as many times as you like, make another copy, and alter exposure for different parts of the image, producing a different result each time.

CHOOSING OR SPECIFYING COLORS

The **Foreground** and **Background color squares** in the Tools panel in Photoshop show what color you'll get when you paint on any layer (the Foreground color) or erase on the *Background* layer (the Background color). Black and white are the default colors, but it's easy to choose new ones.

Color Picker & Eyedropper

You can choose a new Foreground or Background color simply by clicking on one of the Tools panel's two color squares to open the **Color Picker**;

FOREGROUND/BACKGROUND

To restore the Default Foreground and Background colors (black and white), type **D**. To e**X**change the Foreground and Background colors, type **X**.

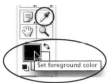

Click the Foreground or Background color swatch in the Tools panel to open the Color Picker. Or click with the Eyedropper tool ✐ to pick a new Foreground color. Alt/Option-click to choose a new Background color.

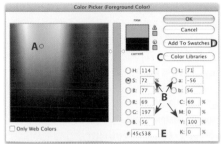

Photoshop's **Color Picker** lets you simply click a color you choose by eye **A**. Or you can enter numeric values to mix colors in the RGB, CMYK, Lab, or HSB model **B**. Click one of the round radio buttons to switch between color models. Clicking the "Color Libraries" button **C** lets you choose from several custom color-matching systems. And the new "Add To Swatches" button **D** lets you add the current color to the Swatches panel and then returns you to the Color Picker. Near the bottom of the dialog box is the hexadecimal code for the current color **E**, which you can copy and paste into an HTML document. Or enter a new number here to choose exactly that color.

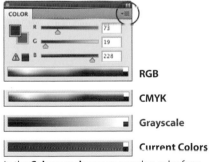

In the **Color panel** you can sample a color from the spectrum bar at the bottom; choose the color mode of the spectrum bar by clicking the panel's menu button ▾☰ and picking from the list, or **right/Ctrl-click** on the bar to display the bar for a different color mode. **Shift-clicking** repeatedly on the bar will step through the options. You can also choose in the panel menu to display the sliders in other color modes besides the ones available in the spectrum bar, such as HSB or Lab.

then click on a color, inside the dialog box or outside it, or "mix" a color by typing numeric values to specify components. Another way to choose a new Foreground color is to sample with the **Eyedropper** tool ✐ (type I) from the Tools panel: Click on a color in any open Photoshop document; Alt/Option-click to sample a new Background color.

Swatches & Color Panel

The **Color panel**, with its different modes, has sliders for mixing colors by eye, and number fields for mixing them scientifically. It also has a spectrum bar for sampling color.

By default, the **Swatches** panel shows a set of 125 color samples. You can click a swatch to make it the Foreground color or Alt/Option-click to select a Background color. You can add to this scrollable panel by sampling a new Foreground color and clicking on the "Create new

SAMPLING COLOR FROM ANYWHERE

See a color you like in an icon on your desktop? Or in a document that's open in another program? Clicking with the Eyedropper cursor ✐ in any open Photoshop document samples color where you click. But if you then *drag outside the document before releasing the mouse button,* you can sample color from anywhere on the screen.

MAKING CHANGES "ON THE FLY"

Right/Ctrl-clicking with the Eyedropper tool ✐ opens a context-sensitive menu that lets you choose the sample size. You can also copy a color's hexadecimal code to the clipboard — for instance, COLOR="#B80505" — so it can be inserted into an HTML document without changing Photoshop's Foreground color.

Point Sample
✓ 3 by 3 Average
5 by 5 Average
11 by 11 Average
31 by 31 Average
51 by 51 Average
101 by 101 Average
Copy Color as HTML

QUICK, ANONYMOUS SWATCHES

If you want to add a sampled color to the Swatches panel but you don't care about naming it, press Alt/Option as you click in the empty area at the bottom of the panel.

In the Swatches panel's menu ▾☰ you can choose Save Swatches for Exchange, to save all the swatches in the panel so they can be used in Adobe Illustrator and InDesign. (To save only some of the swatches, select and save them in the Preset Manager and choose Save Swatches for Exchange from its pop-out menu ▶.) This can be a big time- and work-saver and helps ensure that colors are consistent and available to everyone who works on a project.

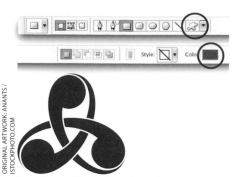

You can set a fill color for a Shape that's independent of the current Foreground color and that can be saved as part of a tool preset. Thus you can make a Custom Shape for a logo and save it as a tool preset, already "loaded" with the "corporate color." This process is outlined step-by-step on page 453.

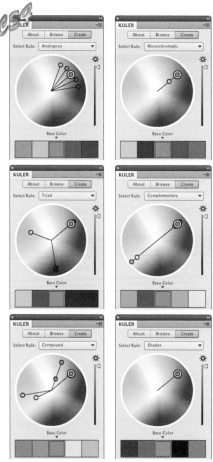

Kuler's six "rules" produce five-color themes from a base color you choose. Colors go from intense (fully saturated) at the edge of the color wheel to neutral in the center. A separate vertical slider lets you choose shades of a color.

swatch from foreground color" button, or the empty space, at the bottom of the panel. Or you can add an entire set of colors by choosing from the panel's fly-out menu. From this menu you can also save a custom set of Swatches or load one.

Tool-Specific Colors

Certain tools can have their own assigned colors, which can be changed without changing the overall Foreground and Background colors. For instance, for the drawing tools (Pens and Shapes), color can be set in the Options bar, and for the Type tools in the Options bar or the Character panel.

kuler

Adobe's **kuler** (pronounced "cooler") is one of several Web-based applications for creating and sharing color themes. Photoshop CS4 has a built-in link to connect with kuler. Photoshop CS3 has no direct link to kuler, but you can get there with a browser: http://kuler.adobe.com; register to use the site and download the color themes you create as well as those others have posted to share, just as you can in CS4. An AdobeTV link at the site provides a tutorial video on using kuler.

In CS4 choosing **Window** > **Extensions** > **Kuler** opens Photoshop's kuler panel. With an Internet connection, clicking the panel's "Browse" button lets you explore the color themes posted on the site, sorting by popularity, newness, or even subject tags added by the themes' originators. If you see something you want to capture for your own use in Photoshop, click the "Add selected theme to swatches" button at the bottom of the kuler panel, to add the colors at the end of your current Swatches panel. Then you can save them if you like, with or without the others in the panel.▼

FIND OUT MORE
▼ Saving sets of Swatches **page 402**

Even when you're not connected to the Internet, you can create your own color themes inPhotoshop CS4's kuler panel. Clicking the "Create" button brings up a color wheel and a menu of six "rules" for making color themes, a great resource for putting together an Analogous, Complementary, or Triad palette, for instance. There's also a Custom option for total freedom in assembling your theme of five or fewer colors.

For designers especially, a second Create option that exists only online can be helpful for developing a palette of colors for graphics and type to go with an image. In Photoshop's kuler panel, click the "About" button to bring up the **kuler** link, and click it to connect. At the site, choose Create from the menu on the left, and then choose From an Image; click the "Upload" button and upload your image (for your use only). Kuler will come up with five different theme moods. Circles on the image show you where the colors are sampled from, and you can create a custom theme by moving any of the circles to new sampling points. Give each new theme a name and save it; then you can download it and later load it into your Swatches panel.

THE KULER PANEL IN PHOTOSHOP CS4

Choosing Window > Extensions > Kuler opens a three-part panel for downloading and creating color themes.

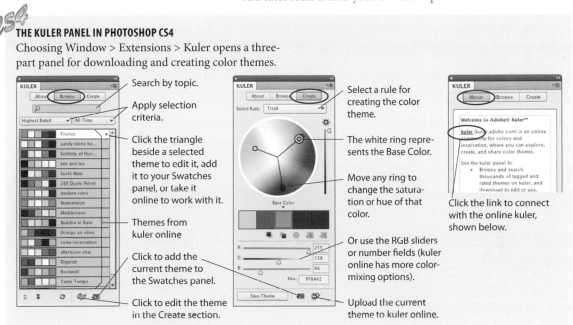

Search by topic.

Apply selection criteria.

Click the triangle beside a selected theme to edit it, add it to your Swatches panel, or take it online to work with it.

Themes from kuler online

Click to add the current theme to the Swatches panel.

Click to edit the theme in the Create section.

Select a rule for creating the color theme.

The white ring represents the Base Color.

Move any ring to change the saturation or hue of that color.

Or use the RGB sliders or number fields (kuler online has more color-mixing options).

Upload the current theme to kuler online.

Click the link to connect with the online kuler, shown below.

KULER ONLINE

At the kuler site you can create a color theme to match an image.

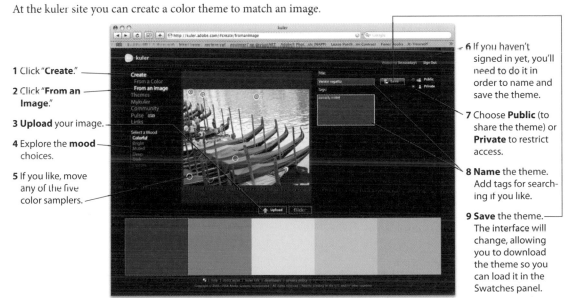

1 Click "**Create**."

2 Click "**From an Image**."

3 **Upload** your image.

4 Explore the **mood** choices.

5 If you like, move any of the five color samplers.

6 If you haven't signed in yet, you'll need to do it in order to name and save the theme.

7 Choose **Public** (to share the theme) or **Private** to restrict access.

8 **Name** the theme. Add tags for searching it you like.

9 **Save** the theme. The interface will change, allowing you to download the theme so you can load it in the Swatches panel.

Three kinds of Fill layers offer the advantage of easy experimentation and changes, as described in "Adding Type to an Image" on page 587.

APPLYING COLOR

In Photoshop, color can be applied with the **painting** and **filling tools**; these are covered in Chapter 6, "Painting." You can also apply color with the **Edit > Fill command**, or with a Fill layer or a Shape layer, or with the effects in a Layer Style (page 265 has a step-by-step example).

Fill & Shape Layers

Add a **Fill layer** by clicking the "Create a new fill or adjustment layer" button ◐ at the bottom of the Layers panel and choosing a type of fill — Solid Color (for the current Foreground color or another color of your choice), Pattern, or Gradient. The color in a Fill layer is shaped by its built-in layer mask that hides or reveals parts of the color layer. A **Shape** layer provides the same kind of color-filled layer, but the built-in mask is a vector-based *layer clipping path*. Shape layers are covered in Chapter 7. Both Fill layers and Shape layers are easy to change — you can change the color simply by clicking the layer's thumbnail in the Layers panel and choosing a new color.

Layer Styles

Still another way to apply color is with a **Layer Style**, that portable combination of effects you can save and apply to other elements and in other files. Layer Styles are introduced on page 80 and are used in step-by-step techniques throughout the book, but especially in Chapter 8.

Gradients

In Photoshop a gradient is a sequence of transitions from color to color. Some gradients include changes in transparency as well as color. Gradients are supplied as presets that you can choose and apply, or modify to make new ones using the Gradient Editor, shown on page 176. When you design a Solid gradient, you control all the color and opacity changes. On the other hand, if you create a Noise gradient, ▼ Photoshop puts colors together somewhat randomly, but within limits you define. To apply a gradient you can use the Gradient tool ▦, a Fill or Adjustment layer, or a Layer Style.

FIND OUT MORE

▼ Noise gradients
pages 197 & 198

The Gradient tool ▦**.** Photoshop's original Gradient tool ▦ (Shift-G) is a hands-on, direct approach — you simply drag the cursor where you want to apply the color blend. There are five kinds of gradients you can apply with the Gradient tool — Linear, Radial, Angle, Reflected, and Diamond. For the Linear gradient you drag across the span where you want the gradient to go,

This photo's color comes mainly from a Color Overlay effect in a Layer Style, so it's easy to change the hue or the degree to which the tint replaces the original color (see page 265 for the technique).

Wow-Gradient 09 is a Solid gradient without transparency. (You'll find samples of all the Wow Gradients on pages 750 and 751).

Wow-Gradient 06 is a Solid gradient with transparency built in.

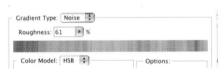

Wow-Gradient 25 is a Noise gradient.

from where you want it to start to where you want it to stop. For the other four kinds of gradients, you drag outward from where you want the center to be. Because we can use transparency in gradients, we can make several swipes with the Gradient tool to create complex shading or coloring on a single layer. There are other more flexible ways to apply gradients (these "nondestructive," or editable, methods are described next), but for creating a graduated layer mask or creating gradients in color channels, the Gradient tool can be ideal.

Gradient Fill. A Gradient Fill layer can apply the same five types of gradients as the Gradient tool. But using a Fill makes editing easier — at any time after you've set it up, you can double-click its thumbnail in the Layers panel to reopen its dialog box and change the gradient or choose another. To add a Gradient Fill layer, click the "Create new fill or adjustment Layer" button ◔ at the bottom of the Layers panel and choose Gradient.

Gradient Map. The Gradient Map is an Adjustment layer that contains instructions for replacing the tones in an image with the colors of the gradient you choose. The starting color of the gradient (at the left end) replaces black, the ending color replaces white, and the intermediate colors of the gradient replace the range of tones in between.

Layer Style. In a Layer Style you can use a gradient as an Inner Glow, an Outer Glow, a Stroke, or a Gradient Overlay. Find examples in "Exercising Gradients" on page 196 and in "Neons & Glows" on page 767.

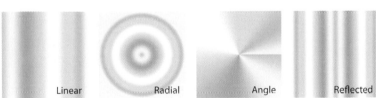

Linear   Radial   Angle   Reflected   Diamond

In the Gradient tool's ▣ Options bar or in any of the gradient-related dialog boxes, you can choose the type of gradient.

45°   80°

A Linear gradient's orientation is set by the direction you drag the Gradient tool ▣ or the Angle you set in a gradient dialog.

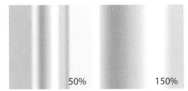

50%   150%

To change the span of the color transitions, change the drag distance for the Gradient tool, or change the Scale in a dialog

☑ Reverse

Choosing the Reverse option for applying a gradient reverses the order of the colors.

Patterns

Like gradients, Photoshop's pattern presets can be used as pixel-based fills (through the Edit > Fill command or the Pattern Stamp tool 🖌️) or in Fill layers or Layer Styles. As part of a Layer Style a pattern can apply both surface color (through the Pattern Overlay effect) and surface texture (through the Texture section of the Bevel and Emboss effect). Patterns are used throughout the book, "Quick Backgrounds & Textures" (page 556) has loads of suggestions for creating your own, and don't miss the patterns in the Presets folder on the Wow DVD-ROM.

THE GRADIENT EDITOR

Controls for **applying gradients** are found in the Options bar for the Gradient tool 🔲 and in the dialog box that opens when you choose any of the other gradient-application methods (such as the Gradient Fill dialog, shown at the right). If you want to change a **gradient's composition**, that's done through the Gradient Editor, shown below.

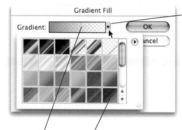

Click the **arrow** to open a panel of preset gradients, as shown here.

Click the **gradient preview bar** itself to open the Gradient Editor (shown below).

Click a swatch to choose a gradient. **Double-click** to open a dialog where you can rename the gradient. **Alt/Option-click** to remove it from the picker.

Build a new gradient by clicking one of the swatches in the Presets section and then changing any or all of the settings below the Presets.

A **Solid** gradient (shown here) blends between colors and opacities whose positions you control. The other choice is a **Noise** gradient; Photoshop generates a randomized series of colors within limits you set (see page 197).

Click below or above this gradient preview bar where you want to add a new color or transparency stop.

When you click on a stop, you can set the Opacity (if it's a transparency stop as shown here) or change the Color (if it's a color stop).

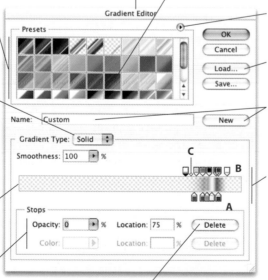

Load other gradients into the picker by clicking the ▶ button and choosing from the pop-out list, or by clicking the "Load" button and navigating to the set of gradients you want.

If you make a gradient you might want to use again, type a Name and *then* click the "New" button to add it to the current picker of presets.

"Stops" below the gradient bar control color **A**. Stops above the gradient bar control opacity **B**. When you click on a stop to choose it, a midpoint "diamond" appears between it and the next stop **C**. Drag a stop or midpoint to change the color transitions.

Remove the currently selected stop by clicking its "Delete" button, or by dragging it off the edge of the dialog box.

The Wow DVD-ROM includes many custom patterns; you'll find printed samples in Appendix D. Some of these patterns are also used in Layer Styles as both Pattern Overlay (for color and surface design) and Texture (for dimensionality). The **Bricks*** Style is shown above with the Texture effect turned off (left) and turned on (right, its default).

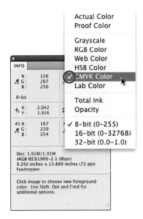

Choosing Palette Options/Panel Options from the Info panel's menu opens the Info Options dialog box. The panel options, with the addition of 16- and 32-Bits/Channel readouts, can also be accessed by **clicking and holding on one of the** 🖉 **icons** in the panel. In the menu you can choose to display composition readouts for two different color modes if you like. For each of the two readouts you can choose from a variety of useful kinds of information to display, including Opacity and Total Ink coverage.

ASSESSING COLOR

Photoshop has some excellent tools, including the Info panel and the Histogram panel, that report on the current tone and color in your image. These tools can be set to also report statistics for how tone and color will change as you adjust the image.

Info Panel & Color Sampler Tool 🖋

When you want to know the composition of a color in your image, you can use the Info panel and the Color Sampler tool 🖋 (Shift-I). The **Info panel**, shown at the left, provides a dynamic display of color composition — as you move any cursor over your image, the panel shows the color composition for the pixel(s) currently under the cursor's "hot spot." As you apply a color or tonal adjustment such as Levels or Hue/Saturation, the Info panel displays the color composition both *before* and *after* the change.

You can also set up as many as four "permanent" color-sampling sites in your image, each with its own separate readout in the Info panel. To set up the samplers, choose the **Color Sampler** tool 🖋 (Shift-I) — it's nested in the Tools panel with the Eyedropper 🖋 — and click as many as four locations where you want readouts. Once the points are established, you can use the tool to drag them around, or Alt/Option-click on a point to remove it. The Info panel also shows document size information and hints for using tools.

Histogram Panel

Photoshop's Histogram panel shows how colors and tones are distributed in your image, in a panel you can leave open so you can preview what will happen as you make changes to the image. Open the panel by choosing **Window > Histogram**. Then enlarge the panel to show the individual color channels (along with the composite histogram) by clicking the ▾≡ button in the upper right corner of the panel and choosing Show All Channels from the fly-out menu. The Histogram offers a range of helpful viewing options:

- Choose **Show Color Channels in Color** from the panel's menu ▾≡ to show the individual graphs in color.

- Choose **Colors** from the panel's Channel menu to show colors in the *composite* histogram.

- When you activate an Adjustment layer or a Filter dialog box that includes a Preview option, choose **Adjustment Composite** to see both "before" and "after" versions of the

You can establish as many as four stationary samplers with the Color Sampler tool ✨ (Shift-I), to feed color information to the Info panel. Color samplers let you pinpoint important areas of an image and watch how their color composition changes as you adjust tone and color. The same Sample Size (set in the Options bar) is shared by the Eyedropper 🖋; changing the setting for either tool will also change it for the other, and for the eyedroppers in the Levels, Curves, and Exposure dialog boxes. When sampling color from a textured area, such as the woven fabric of this dress, use a sample size large enough to average any color variation due to texture.

Before **After**

E. A. M. VISSER

The **Histogram** provides a wealth of information about how colors and tones are distributed in an image, and, as shown here, how their distribution will be changed by a color adjustment. The intense colors show the distribution after the adjustment; paler colors show the pre-adjustment condition.

histograms. Although the histogram also appears in both the Curves and the Levels dialog boxes (described on page 247), the Histogram panel itself is the only one that shows both before and after values.

When you use the Histogram panel, clicking on the ⚠ when it appears will make sure the Histogram displays the most complete and accurate information. "The Histogram & Color Samplers" in Chapter 5 shows some common histogram configurations and explains what they tell you about tone and color in the image.

Color Views

In the View menu you'll find three commands that relate to color. These commands let you "soft proof" your image on-screen, previewing it as closely as possible to the way it will look when it's output. Accurate soft proofing only works if you have accurate profiles for your monitor and for the device on which the image will be displayed or printed. Before you can see an on-screen proof, you need to specify what kind of output you want to proof by choosing **View > Proof Setup**. For instance, you can choose to see the **Working CMYK**, which uses the CMYK specifications in the Color Settings dialog box, ▼ or choose to preview how the color will look when viewed in the standard **RGB Macintosh** or **RGB Windows** color space. In CS4 you can also preview for two types of color blindness, especially useful if you're creating information graphics. Choose View > Proof Setup > Custom to open the Proof Setup dialog box and load the profile for a specific output device, such as your desktop printer. Here you can select Simulate Paper White (duller than on-screen white). Or choose Simulate Ink Black to view the grayer "black" of your target printer. (These options are not available for all printers.)

FIND OUT MORE
▼ Color Settings
page 190

The **View > Proof Colors** command is the toggle for turning the soft proof on and off. Unlike choosing Image > Mode > CMYK Color to convert the file from RGB to CMYK, the Proof Colors option doesn't actually convert the file — it just gives you a preview — so you don't lose the RGB color information as you would if you converted it.

The **Gamut Warning**, also chosen from the View menu, identifies the colors in your RGB image that may be outside

TOGGLING VIEWS

Press **Ctrl/⌘-Y** (for View > Proof Colors) to toggle your view back and forth between your working color space and the color space chosen with the View > Proof Setup command.

Photoshop's out-of-gamut warning lets you know if a color in an RGB file might not print as you expect in the CMYK color space you've chosen with View > Proof Setup:

- In the **Info panel**, the warning shows up as exclamation points beside the CMYK values, which represent the closest printable color mix to the specified RGB color.

- In the **Color picker** and **Color panel** the warning is a caution sign ⚠ with a swatch of the nearest CMYK match. Clicking the swatch **A** changes the chosen color to the printable match.

Note: Photoshop's out-of-gamut warning is conservative — some "out-of-gamut" colors may actually print fine.

The "not Web safe" warning (for colors outside the 216-color Web palette) is a small cube. Clicking the accompanying swatch **B** chooses the Web-safe color, although with today's monitors, Web-safe color isn't as important.

the printable or viewable color range that you've chosen with the Proof Setup command.

ADJUSTING COLOR

Photoshop's powerful tools for adjusting tone and color are found in the Tools panel, the Image > Adjustments menu, and the list of Adjustment layers that pops up if you click the "Create a new fill or adjustment layer" button ⊘ at the bottom of the Layers panel. In Photoshop CS4 the new Adjustments panel, with a button and presets for each kind of Adjustment layer, is a one-stop source for nondestructive, editable tone and color adjustments. Perhaps a bigger advantage of the panel over Adjustment layers in previous versions is that it allows you to work with other layers, including other Adjustment layers, while keeping the dialog open. You can work back and forth seamlessly between making the adjustment and masking it, for instance, or changing the opacity or blend mode of any layer in the file.

For some of Photoshop's adjustments, you can target your color changes to specific color families or to a particular brightness range — highlights, midtones, or shadows. "Color Adjustment Options" (page 180) points out the special advantages of each type of adjustment.

When you can, it's generally better to use an *Adjustment layer* rather than the corresponding *command* from the Image > Adjustments menu. An Adjustment layer has at least four advantages: It doesn't change the pixels of the image themselves; it has a built-in layer mask for targeting the adjustment; it can easily be changed later if needed; and it can modify all layers below it in

Photoshop's on-screen "proofing" of files, available through the **View > Proof Colors** command, shows what will happen when the file is converted from the RGB Color mode as displayed by your monitor to another RGB color space or to CMYK printing colors.

To watch the gamut changes as you work, you can open one window for your working color space and a second one to use for proofing, like the smaller window at the right. With View > Gamut Warning turned on, the view will show flat gray (or a user-selectable color such as the lime green we've chosen here) where there are colors that may change when the file is converted.

To change the warning color for the View > Gamut Warning command from flat gray to a color that contrasts better with your image, choose Photoshop > Preferences > Transparency & Gamut, click the Color swatch at the bottom of the dialog box, and choose a new color.

Ctrl/⌘-Shift-Y is the toggle to turn on or off View > Gamut Warning. When the Color Picker is open, this command shows you a conservative view of the colors available in CMYK — maybe a little more conservative than absolutely necessary. But by dragging the slider up and down the Hue bar, you can get an animated lesson about which color families are most likely to lose their punch when you change from RGB to CMYK.

The Color Picker will stay "CMYK-safe" until you turn this mode off — for instance, by pressing **Ctrl/⌘-Shift-Y** again when the Color Picker is open.

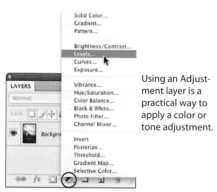

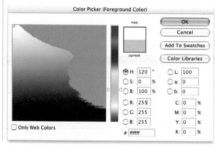

Using an Adjustment layer is a practical way to apply a color or tone adjustment.

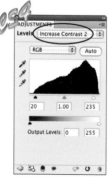

The Adjustments panel in Photoshop CS4 can stay open and "live" while you work on other layers. It also offers preset choices for the Adjustment layers.

the layer stack, or it can be restricted to one layer or a few layers. Some of the commands in the Image > Adjustments menu don't exist as Adjustment layers, although two — Shadows/Highlights and Variations — can be run nondestructively on a Smart Object layer. ▼ For Adjustments commands, which *do* change the pixels, it's best to protect your previous work by merging the visible layers into a new layer and then running the adjustment on that new layer.

FIND OUT MORE

▼ "Smart Filter" adjustments **page 72**

Color Adjustment Options

One of the most challenging things about making color adjustments in Photoshop is deciding which is the right tool for the job among the dozens of commands found in the Image > Adjustments menu, the Adjustments panel, and Adjustment layers. Since these commands are most often used to improve or apply special effects to photos, you'll find them covered in the introductory pages of Chapter 5, with short descriptions that point out the special talents of each command. In addition, "Quick Tone & Color Adjustments" on page 281 provides some practical applications of Adjustment layers for "quick fixes" for photos.

The Color Replacement Tool 🖌

With the Color Replacement tool 🖌 you can **brush on a color change just where you want it** without losing light-dark detail. The tool applies the color that's currently showing in the Foreground color swatch. In the Options bar you can control the tool's **Sampling** process — whether it chooses the color to be replaced the first time you click in the image and then replaces only that color, or whether it continuously samples as you drag it, or whether it replaces only a pre-chosen color. The **Tolerance** setting determines how wide a range of color is replaced. The **Mode** determines what qualities of color will change as you paint — hue or saturation or both, or luminosity. And the Limits setting helps control how widespread the change is. See an example in "Quick Attention-Focusing Techniques" on page 301.

Toning Tools

The toning tools — Dodge 🔍 and Burn ✊ — are designed to change brightness and contrast, and thus detail, with independent control in the highlights, shadows, and midtones. The other tool that shares the same spot on the panel — Sponge 🟤 — increases or decreases saturation. With all their powerful variables, the toning tools can be difficult to control for correcting exposure problems (see page 339 for a more flexible method for pinpoint control of contrast, brightness, and detail). But they can

Before

After

With the Color Replacement tool ![tool icon], you can paint a color change while preserving shading details, as the tool's Limits settings help you "stay inside the lines." You'll find an example of using this tool on page 308 in "Quick Attention-Focusing Techniques."

Dodge Tool	O
Burn Tool	O
Sponge Tool	O

The Burn tool ![icon] is useful for shading color in artwork, as described on page 487. And both Dodge and Burn can be helpful for refining masks (page 89).

be very useful for **highlighting and shading flat-color artwork**. In CS4 the Dodge and Burn tools have been improved so they produce more natural-looking results by preserving hue while they lighten or darken. The results, especially for the Dodge tool, can be more subtle than before. Besides increasing or reducing saturation, CS4's Sponge tool can also act on Vibrance.▼ (The Options bar offers the opportunity to Use Legacy if you want these tools to perform as they did in the past.)

Blend Modes

Blend modes control how the colors in a layer, in paint, or in a Smart Filter▼ interact with the existing image. Blend modes are powerful for **combining images**. Sometimes just layering an identical copy of an image over the original and applying a different blend mode to the top one can be exactly what's needed to improve color and contrast.

The blend modes are available as a pop-up menu in the Layers panel, in the Options bar for the painting and toning tools, and in several of Photoshop's dialog boxes, including various panels in the Layer Style dialog and the Blending Options dialog for Smart Filters. In the menus the blend modes are organized in groups according to the way they affect color, and the blend modes in most of these groups share the same "neutral" color (actually a neutral tone — black, white, or 50% gray) that will have no effect when applied in those blend modes.

FIND OUT MORE
▼ Vibrance **page 254**
▼ Smart Filters **page 72**

BLEND MODE MENU

A blend mode can be applied to a layer by targeting the layer in the Layers panel and then choosing from a pop-up menu. Blend modes are grouped in this menu according to a shared effect, and in some cases a shared neutral color. If black is the neutral color, white has the strongest effect, and vice versa. If 50% gray is neutral, the effect is strongest for both black and white, and weaker for the intermediate tones. See page 182 for descriptions of the individual blend modes.

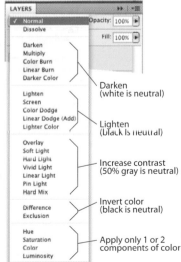

Darken (white is neutral)

Lighten (black is neutral)

Increase contrast (50% gray is neutral)

Invert color (black is neutral)

Apply only 1 or 2 components of color

Layered graphics

An image layered over itself

ORIGINAL PHOTO: CORBIS ROYALTY FREE

Modes that blend only if Opacity is reduced

Normal

Dissolve (75% Opacity)

BLEND MODES & COLOR MODES

For some blend modes, there's a noticeable difference in the effect you get in RGB Color and in CMYK Color.

RGB   CMYK

To preserve the look you've achieved with blend modes in RGB when you convert to CMYK, duplicate the file (Image > Duplicate) and flatten this copy (Layer > Flatten Image), and *then* convert the flat file (Image > Mode > CMYK).

Following are descriptions of the individual blend modes and their groups, with suggestions for how they can be useful. Examples to the left of the descriptions show how the modes blend two different images, as well as an image layered over itself. Blending was done with files in RGB mode; the overlying layer was at 100% Opacity, except in the case of Dissolve mode. The **blend color** is the color that's applied in the blend mode, the **base color** is the original color in the image, and the **result color** is the combined color after blending.

At full opacity, the first two modes in the menu, Normal and Dissolve, don't really blend at all. They simply **cover up** what's underneath. It's when Opacity is reduced that the difference between the two becomes apparent when you look close-up.

Normal. A layer or paint at 100% Opacity in Normal mode covers up the layers below it. As Opacity is reduced in Normal mode, the layer or paint becomes partly transparent, allowing the color below to show through.

Dissolve. At full opacity, Dissolve mode is just like Normal. But reducing the Opacity setting makes a dither (randomized dot) pattern, instead of making the layer or paint partly transparent. In the dither, some pixels become completely transparent (they disappear) and the others remain at full opacity. **The lower the Opacity setting, the more pixels disappear.**

Two blend modes, Behind and Clear, occur **only for painting and filling tools and with the Edit > Fill command.**

Behind. Behind allows color to be applied only to transparent (or partly transparent) areas of a layer. Any opaque pixels are protected.

Clear. In **Clear** mode a painting tool or the Fill command acts like an eraser, replacing color with transparency.

The next four blend modes darken, but in some cases only where the blend color is dark. **White is the neutral color** for these modes — that is, white has no effect on the image below.

Darken. Darken mode compares each pixel in the overlying layer (or the paint that you're applying) and the pixel underneath, channel by channel. So for instance, for an RGB image it compares the Red channels of both, the Blue channels, and the Green channels, **chooses the darker channel component** in each case, and "mixes" these components to get the result

Darken

Multiply

Color Burn

Linear Burn

Darker Color

color. So it's possible for the result to be a third color, different from either the blend or base color. Of course, Darken has no effect when an image is blended with itself.

Multiply. In **Multiply** mode white paint, or any white on the overlying layer, has no effect on the image below. Colors darken the image below, with dark colors darkening the most. Multiply mode is good for **applying shadows without completely eliminating the color of the shaded areas** in the layers underneath, and for layering line work over color or vice versa, as in "Watercolor Over Ink" on page 389. Multiply mode can also be helpful for increasing the density of a badly faded photo, as in "Quick Tone & Color Adjustments" on page 285.

Color Burn. Working channel by channel, **Color Burn intensifies the color** of the image underneath as it darkens. The darker the blend color, the greater the effect it has on the image below. Because of this, when you blend an image with a duplicate of itself, the composite changes only slightly in the light colors and highlights, but it begins to darken dramatically as values approach the midtones. This makes Color Burn a good blend mode to use at very low Opacity settings if, for example, you want to give pale lips in a portrait more color and definition, without "blowing out" the highlights. You'll find an example in "Quick Cosmetic Changes" on page 317.

Linear Burn. Linear Burn darkens what's underneath by decreasing the brightness component. Linear Burn can be useful for adding definition to, say, a washed-out sky with clouds. The darker edges of the clouds will be darkened more with Linear Burn than with Multiply, giving them a more three-dimensional appearance. With Linear Burn, **color is not as intensified (saturated) as it is with Color Burn.**

Darker Color. Darker Color, added in CS3, **compares the blend color pixel and the base color pixel and uses the one that's darker overall.** The result, for each pixel, is either the blend color or the base color. You can't get a third color as you can with Darken mode.

The next four blend modes lighten, but in some cases only where the overlying layer or paint is light. Black is the neutral color for these modes — that is, black has no effect on the image below.

Lighten. Like Darken mode, Lighten **compares pixels in the paint or the overlying layer and the image underneath, channel by channel**; it chooses the lighter component for each

Modes that lighten (black has no effect)

Lighten

Screen

Color Dodge

Linear Dodge

Lighter Color

A BLEND MODE FOR GROUPS ONLY

Pass Through is the default mode for layer Groups. ▼ It allows each individual layer in the Group to keep its own blend mode when it acts on the layers below the Group. If you choose any other blend mode for the Group, it's as if the layers of the Group (with their individual blend modes) had been merged to form a single layer and then the Group's blend mode had been applied to that layer. For instance, switching to **Normal** instead of Pass Through can keep the effect of an Adjustment layer "local," within the Group only.

FIND OUT MORE

▼ Groups **page 583**

channel to make the result color, which can consequently be different than either the blend color or the base color. Unlike Screen mode (below), Lighten will have no effect if you try to blend an image with itself. Like Darken, Lighten mode can be useful in achieving subtle blends and natural-looking textures.

Screen. The counterpart of Multiply mode, Screen has an effect similar to overlapping colored spotlights. The result is to lighten the composite. Screen mode is good for **applying highlights to an image**, or for lightening a too dark image by blending it with itself.

Color Dodge. Color Dodge **lightens and makes colors more vivid.** Light colors are lightened a lot more than dark colors, so there is more contrast than with Screen mode. At low Opacity, Color Dodge can add sparkle to the eyes in portraits by both intensifying the color and increasing the contrast. You can find an example in "Quick Cosmetic Changes" on page 317.

Linear Dodge. Linear Burn's counterpart, Linear Dodge, increases brightness. It **lightens the lightest colors more intensely than Screen mode does**, **but acts more evenly than Color Dodge**.

Lighter Color. Lighter Color, added in CS3, **compares the blend color pixel and the base color pixel and uses the color that's lighter overall** for the result. For each pixel, the result is either the blend color or the base color. You can't get a third color as you can with Lighten mode.

The next seven modes increase contrast in various ways. For these modes **50% gray is neutral**.

Overlay, Soft Light & Hard Light. Overlay, Soft Light, and Hard Light provide three different complex combinations of Multiply and Screen. All three increase contrast. Of the three, **Soft Light** has the least effect on deep shadows and bright highlights, **Hard Light** affects these extremes the most, and **Overlay** is intermediate. A 50%-gray-filled layer in Overlay or Soft Light mode can be an easy and flexible substitute for the **Dodge and Burn** tools. By painting the layer with white or black at low opacity, you can dodge out or burn in areas to balance the lighting and make the image look "sharper." Page 339 has an example.

Vivid Light. Vivid Light mode **burns and dodges on a channel-by-channel basis**. The farther the overlying color is from 50% brightness, the more Vivid Light increases contrast. At full or

Overlay

Soft Light

Hard Light

Vivid Light

Linear Light

Pin Light

Hard Mix

close-to-full Opacity settings, both Vivid Light and Linear Light (described next) are great for modern-looking intense blends of image layers. Try Vivid Light or Linear Light at reduced Opacity to bring out color in sunrise and sunset skies; there's an example on page 341.

Linear Light. Linear Light is similar to Vivid Light, but it doesn't increase contrast as much at the extremes. As a result, Linear Light can produce a more **subdued, gradual change in contrast**.

Pin Light. Pin Light is a complex combination of Lighten and Darken. Like these modes it compares the blend and base colors channel by channel. For each channel, if the blend color is lighter, it lightens the base color to produce the result channel, and if the blend color is darker, it darkens the base color. The closer the blend color is to 50% brightness in a particular channel, the less effect it will have in that channel. Like Lighten and Darken modes, Pin Light has no effect when an image is blended with itself (as shown at the left). But it offers some fairly subdued alternatives for blending image layers or as a blend mode used in Layer Styles.

Hard Mix. Hard Mix applies the Threshold filter to each channel in an image. The result of blending one image layer with another (or itself) at 100% Opacity is to **posterize** the resulting image, though with a different set of colors than a Posterize Adjustment layer would produce. In a very different application, used at low Opacity settings, applying a duplicated image layer in Hard Mix mode increases contrast evenly over the range from shadows through midtones to highlights. The other contrast-enhancing modes tend to affect shadows and highlights more than midtones.

For the next two modes, **black is neutral,** having no effect, and **white inverts** the color underneath, producing its opposite. Besides having some very practical applications, these modes are also good for creating special effects.

Difference. Difference mode does complex calculations to compare the overlying color and the color underneath. If there is **no difference in pixel color, black results.** Where the colors are different, Difference produces intense, and sometimes surprising, colors. Since this mode will show any difference between two images, it's useful for aligning parts of an image that was too large for the flatbed scanner or that was torn. It's also useful for seeing what changes occur when you apply an Adjustment layer

Difference

Exclusion

Modes that apply color attributes

Hue

Saturation

Color

Luminosity

or a Smart Filter: Apply the Adjustment layer or Smart Filter and make the changes you want; then put the changed layer in Difference mode temporarily. The differences will show up in color; solid black means no difference.

Exclusion. In Exclusion mode, as in Difference mode, black produces no effect and white produces the opposite color. At high Opacity settings, Exclusion mode can be used to blend an image with itself to produce results like Filter > Stylize > Solarize (shown in Appendix A) but lighter and more muted. **At very low Opacity settings, a duplicate layer in Exclusion mode will reduce contrast and saturation.** Another interesting use for this mode, and for Difference, is in adding color to black and white graphics, as shown on page 187.

The last four blend modes apply one or two of the three color attributes — **hue**, **saturation**, and **brightness** (or **luminosity**). There is no neutral blend color. Hue, Saturation, and Luminosity modes each apply only one of the three color attributes of the blend color. Color mode applies two out of three (hue and saturation). When two copies of the same image are layered, none of these modes produces a change.

Hue. Hue mode is good for **shifting color without changing how intense or neutral the color is, or how light or dark**. Hue mode has no effect if the base color is black, white, or gray, because these "colors" have no hue to change.

Saturation. In Saturation mode, **the saturation of the blend color becomes the saturation of the result color.** Neutral blend colors make the underlying colors neutral, and more intense blend colors boost the intensity of colors underneath, in each case without changing their hue or how light or dark they are. Saturation mode has no effect on underlying black or white.

Color. In Color mode, the **hue and saturation of the overlying color replace those of the underlying color,** but the light-dark detail remains. Underlying black and white are not changed.

Luminosity. Luminosity is the mode to use if you want **to transfer only the light-and-dark information** from a texture, graphic, or grayscale image onto an image underneath without changing the underlying colors. It can also be useful in sharpening — duplicate the image layer, apply the Unsharp Mask filter, and then put the sharpened layer in Luminosity mode, to eliminate color shifts the filter might have produced.

To replace black and white with a color and its complement, put the file in RGB mode and add a color-filled layer. Put the new layer in Exclusion mode, or for a richer palette, in Difference mode.

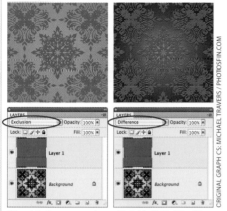

ORIGINAL GRAPH CS: MICHAEL TRAVERS / PHOTOSFIN.COM

We added an empty layer (Ctrl-Alt-Shift-N in Windows or ⌘-Option-Shift-N on the Mac) and filled it with the Foreground color, a medium blue (Alt-Backspace in Windows or Option-Delete on the Mac). Another option would be to use a Solid Color Fill layer.

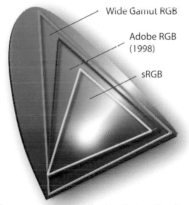

Wide Gamut RGB

Adobe RGB (1998)

sRGB

The **gamut,** or range of colors that can be displayed or printed, varies for different RGB working spaces. For instance, the sRGB space that Adobe recommends as part of its General Purpose and Web/Internet Settings in the Color Settings dialog box is smaller than the Adobe RGB (1998) color space recommended for Photoshop files destined for print. The Wide Gamut RGB color space, available at the bottom of the pop-out list of RGB options in the Color Settings dialog box, is bigger still. Click the "More Options" button in the Color Settings dialog to see the expanded list that includes Wide Gamut RGB and others.

GETTING CONSISTENT COLOR

There are several fundamental factors that make on-screen and printed color look different from each other. First of all, monitor color, because it's lit up, looks brighter than printed color. Second, the *gamut,* or range of colors that can be displayed or printed, is different for RGB than for CMYK — not all the colors that can be displayed on-screen can be printed, and vice versa. Third, when you convert RGB colors to CMYK for printing, you're moving from a three-color to a four-color system in which black can partially substitute for mixes of the other three colors (cyan, magenta, and yellow). Because of this fourth "primary color," there are many ways to represent a particular RGB color in the CMYK system, and because of the way ink pigments interact, the results of all these ways can look slightly different from each other. Finally, variations in printing methods, paper, and ink also affect the color in the final printed product.

Color Management

As if the differences between on-screen and printed color weren't enough, the various scanners and digital cameras record colors in slightly different ways, and various monitors display them differently also. Different kinds of input and display devices operate in different *color spaces,* or subsets of the full range of RGB color. To compensate for the variability in color spaces, Photoshop offers a color management system to translate color accurately between devices and printing processes. The **Color Settings** dialog box (Shift-Ctrl/⌘-K) is where you can choose how to configure Photoshop to produce consistent color from input to output.

In a perfect world — one in which every component of every computer graphics system was calibrated to a universal benchmark, stayed consistent over time, and had a known *ICC profile* — the color-management system built into Photoshop could work perfectly, and color would stay consistent no matter what device or graphics program was used to display or print Photoshop documents. (An ICC profile is a component's color characteristics according to the CIE Lab standard designed to help reproduce colors accurately.) ▼

FIND OUT MORE
▼ CIE Lab standard
page 163

Some Photoshop users, especially designers or photographers working alone who **don't share their Photoshop files as they're creating them,** prefer to choose the "Off" options in the Color Management Policies section of the Color Settings dialog box. This choice avoids any complications that might arise because

Through Bridge, which is part of all the Adobe Creative Suites, you can coordinate Color Settings so that all the programs in the Suite use the same settings. Shown here is part of the expanded list of color space choices.

You can use Mac OS X's built-in Display Calibrator Assistant to walk you through the process of creating a color profile for your monitor.

the file was passed from or to another graphics program that doesn't include the same color management functions, such as many Web page applications, HTML editors, or video-editing programs. But by also **turning *on* the Embed Color Profile option** when a file is saved (File > Save As), you can still include information about the color space *you* were using when the file was developed, in case it's useful for the next person in the workflow — or to jog your own memory later on.

On the other hand, if your workflow involves passing files from one system to another for different stages of the creative process, it can be worthwhile to implement a color management system within the work group and to share the profiles. Setting up and using the color management system will involve searching out or creating the ICC profile for each scanner, digital camera, monitor, and output device (with various settings for different resolution and paper settings) to be used in the workflow; and keeping each component in the workflow calibrated so the ICC profile is meaningful for that component.

To keep color consistent between Photoshop and other Adobe Creative Suite applications, you can synchronize their color settings. First go to Bridge (you can do this by clicking the "Go to Bridge" button on Photoshop's Options bar). In Bridge choose Edit > Creative Suite Color Settings. In the Suite Color Settings dialog box (shown at the left), choose from the short list, or choose from more options made available by clicking the "Show Expanded List of Color Settings Files" checkbox or the "Show Saved Color Settings Files" button, and make a choice. Finally, click the "Apply" button.

Your "Color Environment"

To get consistent color, it's important to keep not only your monitor but also your viewing environment constant, because changes in lighting conditions can change your perception of colors. Here are some ways to keep environmental color conditions from interfering with your on-screen color work:

- If your Desktop is visible while you're working in Photoshop, use a neutral Desktop color (medium gray works well), with no bright colors or distracting pictures.

- Position the room's light source above and in back of the monitor, and keep it dimmed and constant. If your room lighting is controlled by a rheostat, mark the knob and the base plate so you can always restore the lighting to the same level.

Profiling services such as ColorValet offer target files you can print and send in, and the service then creates profiles for you.

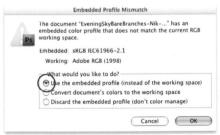

With the "Ask When Opening" options turned on in the Color Settings dialog box, when you open a file (or paste from a file) that has an embedded profile that's different from your current working space, you can choose to use the embedded profile. Whenever the embedded profile of a file is a different color mode than the workspace you chose in the Color Settings dialog, Photoshop places an asterisk (for example, RGB/8*) in the document title bar to remind you of the difference.

- If your screen is reflective, the wall behind you should be neutral in color, with no bright posters or other images. Wear neutral colors when doing color-critical work, to minimize color reflection from your clothes onto the screen.

Calibrating & Characterizing Your Monitor

In order for your computer monitor to show you consistent color — so a file displayed on the screen today looks the same as it did last week and as it will next week — the monitor has to be calibrated periodically to bring it into compliance with the standards it was designed to meet. Some monitors come with special calibration software. If yours didn't, you may want to try a hardware-software combination package (a colorimeter) that either actually adjusts your monitor or tells you which settings need correcting so you can manually adjust it; after the adjustment the software creates a profile that describes how your monitor is currently representing color. That way, the color management system can accurately translate color between your monitor and various input and output devices.

If you don't use a colorimeter, you can use software to calibrate and profile your monitor visually. Even if the results are subjective, it might be all you need for personal work. On the Mac, you can use the **display calibrator** interface that opens when you choose System Preferences from the Apple menu, click on Displays, and then click on the Color tab and the "Calibrate" button. This utility uses the factory calibration settings to calibrate the monitor and then build a profile for your particular device. There are also calibration utilities available for the various versions of Windows that can run Photoshop CS3 or CS4.

"Color-Managing" Your Local Workflow

Once your monitor is calibrated and its profile has been built, consistent color management requires that other devices in your workflow — such as your scanner and desktop color printer used for proofing — also be calibrated, or at least have ICC-compliant profiles, so color can be accurately translated from one device to the next. Your scanner or printer (and the paper you use) may vary from the profile created by the manufacturer of your equipment, and there may not be an easy way to bring the equipment into compliance with the profile. A better solution is to generate custom profiles for the specific scanner and printer you own. One option is a profiling service such as ColorValet (**www.chromix.com/colorvalet**), which offers a money-back guarantee.

This screen capture shows what this photo looked like when we opened it by choosing "Use embedded profile (instead of the working space)" in the Embedded Profile Mismatch dialog. The photo had been taken with a digital camera, which had embedded the sRGB IEC61966-2.1 profile. Photoshop was showing us what the image looked like to the photographer working in that sRGB color space. But only the display was translated; the color data was not affected. Once we saw the image and decided what we wanted to do, we could choose Edit > Convert to Profile and pick Adobe RGB (1998), our current working color space; this changed the color data in the file, without changing how the file looked on-screen. We could have done the translating and converting in a single step by choosing "Convert document's colors to the working space" in the Embedded Profile Mismatch dialog, but by using the method we chose, we could see how the image looked and then decide whether to convert.

This screen capture shows how the same file as shown above looked when we opened it by choosing "Discard the embedded profile (don't color manage)" in the Embedded Profile Mismatch dialog. Originally in the sRGB IEC61966-2.1 color space, the image looks more saturated and "contrasty" when the profile is ignored and Photoshop assumes that the color data for the file were generated in our working color space, Adobe RGB (1998). Assuming that we wanted to start with what the photographer intended and go on to make other changes, we would have had more work to do on this version of the image than on the one above it.

Color Settings

In the Settings section of the Color Settings dialog box, you can choose one of the predefined color management options for producing consistent color in the most widely used on-screen and print workflows. The Color Settings dialog is opened by choosing Edit > Color Settings. Each setting can be used "as is" or you can modify it. Adobe recommends that you leave all the "Ask When Opening" options turned on (as shown on page 191), so Photoshop will alert you whenever you open a file that has no embedded profile or that has a profile that doesn't match the working color space in your Color Settings dialog box.

Assigning or Converting a Profile

Let's suppose that you open an RGB file that came from a working color space other than the one you're using. If you've turned on all the "Ask When Opening" options as Adobe recommends, one of two things will happen, depending on whether the file has an embedded profile:

Embedded profile. If the file has a color profile embedded but it isn't the same as your working space, the **Embedded Profile Mismatch** dialog box (shown on page 189) will open. Adobe recommends that you choose "Use the embedded profile (instead of the working space)" to open the file. The advantage of using the embedded profile is that you'll be starting your image-editing with the image displayed as your source intended it to look. Now you can decide whether to stay with this "foreign" profile (for instance, if you're not doing much editing, you're not relying on your monitor to give you an accurate preview, and the file is going right back to the system in which it originated) or use the Edit > Convert to Profile command to convert the file to your own RGB working space.

No profile embedded. On the other hand, if no color profile was embedded in the file — the person who created it may not have had their software set up to embed a profile when the file was saved, or the image may have come from a scanner that couldn't embed profile information — Photoshop can't know how to display the color that the originating source intended. In that case, Photoshop will display the **Missing Profile** dialog box. Here are some options:

- If you have a pretty good idea of what working space the file originated in (your friend always works in Apple RGB, for instance, or the digital camera was most likely sRGB), you can choose the **"Assign profile"** option. This may change the file's appearance on your monitor, in order to show you what the

continued on page 192

THE COLOR SETTINGS DIALOG

Clicking the "Options" button in the Color Settings dialog offers a broad array of options for managing color. The choices you make here will affect the result you get when you choose Gamut Warning or Proof Colors from the View menu.

Adobe recommends starting with the Settings that best describe the output process that will be used to produce your images — typically, **Web/Internet,** or regional **General Purpose** or **Prepress** defaults. Then you can change individual Working Spaces settings to match your actual workflow. For instance, you can change the CMYK working space according to custom CMYK Setup settings provided by the printer who will be producing a specific job. The printer may also provide Custom Dot Gain settings for a black-only or spot color printing job. As soon as you change any settings in the Color Settings dialog box, the Settings entry changes to **Custom.**

If you have chosen Edit > Creative Suite Color Settings in Adobe Bridge, Photoshop's Color Settings dialog will indicate that your color settings are currently the same for all programs in the Creative Suite.

Clicking the "More Options" button allows you to create or load profiles other than those listed in the pop-out Working Spaces menus. To do this, choose Custom in the Settings menu or click the "Load" button.

With the **"Save"** button you can save different Color Settings preferences to accommodate different job requirements, and then **"Load"** them as you need them.

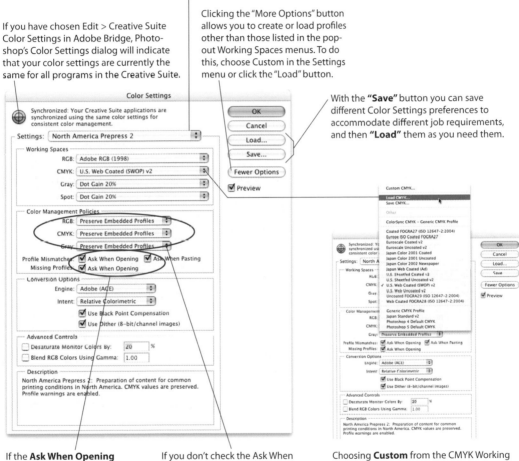

If the **Ask When Opening** boxes are checked, as Adobe recommends, you are offered the opportunity to override the Color Management Policies whenever you open a file or paste an element whose profile doesn't match the current working space.

If you don't check the Ask When Opening boxes, your choice of **Color Management Policies** will determine what happens if you open a file that doesn't have an embedded profile or whose profile isn't the same as the current working space.

Choosing **Custom** from the CMYK Working spaces menu opens the CMYK Setup dialog box, where you can choose Separation Options. (Instead of choosing Custom, you can choose **Load CMYK** to load a CMYK profile — for instance, one supplied by the printer who will be producing a specific job.)

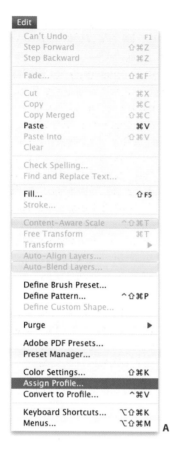

There's an advantage to using the Assign Profile command from the Edit menu **A** rather than assigning a profile in the Missing Profile box when you first open the file: With Preview checked in the Assign Profile dialog box **B**, using the command lets you preview the change in the file's appearance as you test different profile assignments before you commit to one.

file looked like in the working space in which it was created. The advantage is that you'll be starting your image-editing with the image as your source intended it to look.

- If you choose **"Leave as is (don't color manage)"** or **"Assign working RGB"** in the Missing Profile dialog box, the color data will be interpreted for your display as if it came from your working color space. For example, if you open an sRGB file into the Adobe 1998 working space, it will look "hotter" ("contrastier" and more saturated) than it looked on the system where it was created. So you will be starting with an image that will take more work to edit: Your edits will need to address the increased contrast and saturation as well as whatever else you want to do.

Regardless of whether you choose a working space from the **Missing Profile** dialog box or choose "Leave as is (don't color manage)," once the file is open in Photoshop, you can use the more flexible **Edit > Assign Profile** command. Even if you can't guess what working space the file originated in, this command may save you some work. Choosing Edit > Assign Profile opens the Assign Profile dialog box. Unlike the Embedded Profile Mismatch or the Missing Profile dialog, the Assign Profile box lets you "audition" different color profiles in the Profile menu to see how they will affect your on-screen display of the file, to find a profile that improves the way the image looks on your screen. You can then choose Edit > Convert to Profile to convert the file to your working RGB space. Using the Convert to Profile command changes the actual color data in the file. With the profile converted, you do whatever work is necessary to complete the image, and then embed your working profile when you save the file and pass it on. The next person to get the file won't have to do any detective work to assign a profile, because you will have already assigned it by embedding it in the file. If your file is headed for the web (only a few browsers can use ICC profile information) or for some other application that doesn't use profiles, after you finish your editing you may want to duplicate the image and convert the copy to sRGB; again the look of the image will stay the same but the color data will change, this time so that the image will look as you intended when it's displayed on an sRGB system. Embed that profile when you save the copy.

Making RGB-to-CMYK Conversions

If you're preparing an image for print, in most cases the image will eventually need to be turned into CMYK ink colors. This can be done at any of several different stages in the development of the image:

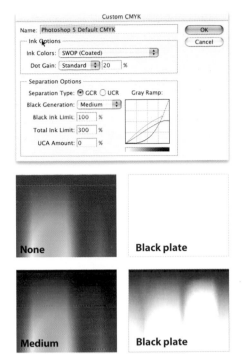

The parameters for converting RGB to CMYK color can be customized in the Custom CMYK dialog box (top). There are several options for Black Generation, which controls how much of the dark colors is contributed by black ink and how much is contributed by a mix of cyan, magenta, and yellow. Shown here are results of converting from RGB to CMYK color using each of three different Black Generation settings in the CMYK Setup dialog box.

- You can choose CMYK Color mode when you first create a new Photoshop file (File > New > Mode: CMYK Color) or in some cases during the scanning operation.

- If, on the other hand, you start in RGB, you can choose Photoshop's Image > Mode > CMYK Color at any point in the development of an image to convert from the RGB working space to the CMYK working space chosen in Photoshop's Color Settings dialog box. Or you can choose Image > Mode > Convert to Profile to choose a CMYK separation, to match a profile your press operator gave you, for instance. But once you make the conversion, you can't regain the original RGB color by choosing Image > Mode > RGB Color. Instead, if you don't like the result, you may be able to undo (Ctrl/⌘-Z), or go back to a previous state or Snapshot from the History panel made before the conversion, ▼ or choose File > Revert to go back to the last saved version of the file.

FIND OUT MORE

▼ Using the History panel **page 30**

- You can keep the file in RGB Color mode until it reaches a page layout program or color separation utility (for the press). Typically, for desktop printing, your printer's driver will convert your RGB document into the CMYK inks it uses.

How do you decide which one of these options is best for converting from RGB to CMYK? Here are some tips to help you choose when to convert:

- **The single advantage of working in CMYK from the beginning** is that it prevents last-minute color shifts, since it keeps the image within the printing gamut during the entire development process. But there's a risk — if you're working in CMYK mode and your printing specifications change (a different paper may be chosen for the job, for instance), the CMYK working space you chose may no longer apply.

- Working in RGB and putting off the CMYK conversion until the last possible moment allows more freedom, so you can get just the color you want on-screen and then work with Photoshop's Hue/Saturation, Selective Color, Levels, or Curves adjustments to tweak out-of-gamut colors to get CMYK alternatives that are as close as possible to your original colors.

- Another very significant advantage of working in RGB is that some of Photoshop's finest functions (for example, the Black & White and Vibrance adjustments) and half the filters in the Filter menu (including Vanishing Point and Lens Correction) don't work in CMYK.

- With Photoshop's Proof Color and Gamut Warning available, it makes sense to work in RGB and preview CMYK in a second window. Choose Window > Arrange > New Window for *<filename>*. Then choose View > Proof Setup > Working CMYK. Choose Window > Proof Colors for just one of the two windows. Then do the actual RGB-to-CMYK conversion at the end of the process. Or work in just one window and toggle between RGB and CMYK previews as needed (Ctrl/⌘-Y).

- You may be able to bow out of the conversion process altogether for many jobs. The commercial printer you work with may have a separation utility, "tweaked" to do an excellent job of converting RGB to CMYK for that particular printing environment. If that's the case, this method may save you some time and angst if you carefully check the printer's proofs (although there may be an additional charge for conversion).

At whatever point you make the conversion, the specifications in Photoshop's Color Settings dialog box and the profiles that support those settings will affect the final result. *wow*

BOOST SATURATION IN CMYK

Photoshop's Gamut Warning is designed to let you identify the colors in your image that may not translate successfully from the RGB working space to CMYK. For some CMYK printing processes, the Gamut Warning is conservative, "predicting" more color problems than will actually be encountered. Instead of reducing saturation or shifting colors in RGB to eliminate all the problem areas indicated by the Gamut Warning, try making the conversion to CMYK and then using the Saturation slider in a Hue/Saturation Adjustment layer to restore color intensity, either overall, as shown here, or by targeting the adjustment to a particular color range that has become dull in the conversion.

Before

After

YURI ARCURS / PHOTOSPIN.COM

Inspecting & Mixing Channels

THE DOCUMENT IS REAL, BUT THE CLEANUP IS PHOTOSHOP. Faced with the challenge of "restoring" a 1937 newspaper clipping that had been glued to a board and matted with an equally pulpy and acidic stock, artist and author Sharon Steuer scanned the clipping and began the search for a color channel clean enough to use as a starting point for redeeming the discolored document.

FIND OUT MORE
▼ Converting from RGB to CMYK
page 192
▼ Working with Color Settings
page 190

1 The clipping was an article about the successful defense of the *New York American,* a Hearst newspaper, in a libel suit.

In the RGB scan, William Randolph Hearst's hand-written congratulations to the lawyer didn't look too bad, but the glue had streaked the clipping itself, and in some places the type showed through from the back of the page.

2 Sharon viewed the individual Red, Green, and Blue channels of the scan, looking for a relatively clean starting point for her restoration, but to no avail. She made a copy of the file to experiment with (Image > Duplicate).

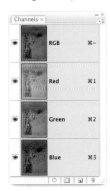

The Red, Green, and Blue channels all showed the dark stains.

3 Next Sharon converted the duplicate to CMYK mode, ▼ to see if she could generate a better channel. The results you get when you translate an image from RGB to CMYK depend on what CMYK Working Space and Intent you use. (Some Intent settings preserve as many of the original colors as possible. Others try to preserve the *relationship between colors,* even if it means changing more colors.) ▼ By turning on Advanced Mode in the Color Settings dialog box, Sharon could set a Working Space and Intent combination, click "OK," make the conversion (Image > Mode > CMYK Color), and check the result. Then she could undo the mode change (Ctrl/⌘-Z), try other settings, and convert again, repeating the process until she found a clean channel.

Using US Web Coated (SWOP) v2 for the CMYK Working Space and Perceptual for the Intent in the Color Settings box produced a Cyan channel with little streaking.

4 Sharon made a new CMYK file from the Cyan channel. One way to do this is to click the channel's name in the Channels panel to make it the only channel visible, then select all (Ctrl/⌘-A) and copy (Ctrl/⌘-C). Start a new file (Ctrl/⌘-N, choosing RGB or CMYK Color for Mode in the New File dialog box, and click "OK"); then paste (Ctrl/⌘-V). Sharon added a Levels Adjustment layer, working with the Input Levels sliders for the individual Cyan, Magenta, and Yellow channels to improve contrast and add a tint. She stacked up several copies of the Levels layer in Multiply mode to darken the type. To fix particular problem areas, she added other Levels layers, using blend modes and layer masks to target the changes.

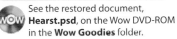
See the restored document, **Hearst.psd,** on the Wow DVD-ROM in the **Wow Goodies** folder.

Gradients

Photoshop's versatile gradients are introduced on page 174. To supplement that introduction, these four pages have examples of gradients in use, with files for dissecting or re-creating the gradients.

You can apply a gradient with the **Gradient tool** ▭ (via the Tools panel **A**), as part of a **Layer Style** (via the "Add a layer style" button *fx* at the bottom of the Layers panel **B**), or with a **Gradient Fill** or **Gradient Map** layer (via the "Create new fill or adjustment layer" button ◐ **C**).

Some of the examples in this section use **Wow-Gradients**, supplied on the Wow DVD-ROM that comes with this book. If you loaded them along with the other Wow presets, ▽ you can add them to any panel of gradient swatches in Photoshop by clicking the panel's ▼☰ button and choosing them from the menu that pops out. If you haven't already loaded them, and therefore they don't show up in the pop-out menu, you may want to simply load the gradients you need for this "Exercising" section — choose Load Gradients in the pop-out menu and navigate to the **Wow-Exercising.grd** file, located as described below. Once you've loaded the Wow Gradients, ▽ they become available anywhere in Photoshop that the Gradient swatches panel appears. Appendix B shows the Wow Gradients.

FIND OUT MORE
▽ Loading the Wow presets **page 4**

YOU'LL FIND THE FILES
in ⬤ > Wow Project Files > Chapter 4 > Exercising Gradients

Orienting a Gradient Fill

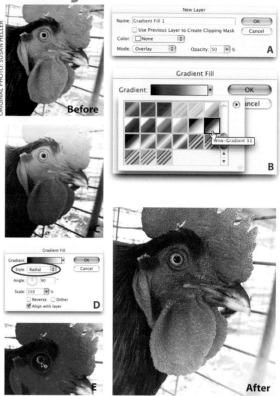

ORIGINAL PHOTO: SUSAN HELLER

Before

After

IN ANY OF THE GRADIENT-RELATED DIALOG BOXES, you can change a gradient's geometry, its orientation, and its scale. To demonstrate, start with a "black-and-white" image in RGB mode and add color by applying Wow-Gradient 33 in a Gradient Fill layer: Alt/Option-click the ◐ button and choose Gradient; using the Alt/Option key opens the New Layer dialog box **A**, where you can set the Mode and Opacity for the new layer. Try Overlay for the Mode so the gradient will both tint the image and increase contrast; then click "OK."

In the Gradient Fill dialog, click the triangle to the right of the gradient preview bar to open the panel of Gradient swatches **B**. Double-click the **Wow-Gradient 33** swatch (the first click chooses the gradient and the second closes the panel). In the Gradient Fill dialog, change the Style to **Radial**, and "reach into" the working window for the image (your cursor will turn into the Move tool ▶⊕) and **drag the gradient** to center it on the eye **D**, **E**. This will leave the lower right corner of the image without color, but you can increase the **Scale** to spread the color. Click "OK" and adjust the layer's Opacity; we set it at 65%.

 Chicken Gradient.psd, Wow-Exercising.grd

Changing the Color Transitions

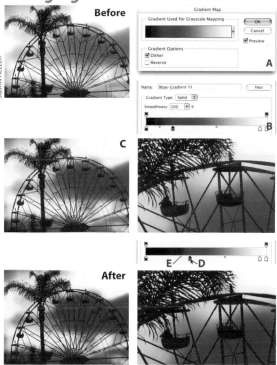

Before

C

E / D

After

SUSAN HELLER

A GRADIENT MAP, with a gradient whose colors progress from dark to light (such as **Wow-Gradient 32**, **33**, or **34**), can add color to your image and still maintain some of the photo's original tonality. Here we start with an image with very little color — though you can use a more colorful one if you like. Add a brilliant sunset: Click the "Create new fill or adjustment layer" button ⬤ at the bottom of the Layers panel (or open the Adjustments panel) and choose Gradient Map. In the Gradient Map dialog box **A** choose a gradient — open the panel and double-click the **Wow-Gradient 33** swatch (to choose the gradient and close the panel). Open the **Gradient Editor** by clicking the gradient preview bar in the Gradient Map dialog and inspect the Gradient Editor's expanded gradient preview bar **B**, **C**. To improve the silhouetting by taking the red "bloom" off the people and gondolas, "remap" the red so it doesn't tint the darker tones: Drag the **Color stop** for the red color to the right, farther from the black stop, just until the red-orange-yellow balance begins to change too much, and then drag the stop back slightly **D**. To shift more of the dark shades from red to black, without affecting the red-orange-yellow balance, drag the black-red midpoint diamond to the right **E**.

WOW Sunset Gradient.psd, Wow-Exercising.grd

Noise Gradients

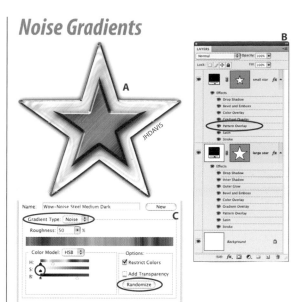

JHDAVIS

MOST OF THE WOW GRADIENTS are of the **Solid** type, but **Wow Gradients 19 through 26** are **Noise** gradients. To enhance a streaked-metal look, we used **Noise gradients** in the Gradient Overlay effects applied to these two stars **A**. To see the first gradient, in the Layers panel double-click on Gradient Overlay in the list of Effects for the "small star" layer **B**. When the Layer Style dialog box opens to the Gradient Overlay panel, click on the gradient preview bar to open the Gradient Editor **C**. For a Noise gradient, the ranges you set by moving the sliders on the Color Model bars will determine the "outside" limits of the colors that *can* appear in the gradient, but the gradient will often include a much narrower range of colors. Working with the **HSB Color Model**, we moved the **Saturation** slider all the way to the left to remove all color to get a gradient of grays. With Saturation at 0, the **Hue** range is unimportant. We set a fairly broad **Brightness** range. Setting **Roughness** at 50% made streaks that are distinct but not too sharply defined. A high Roughness setting makes more and sharper color bands; at lower Roughness there are fewer bands and smoother transitions. It isn't a concern in this gray example, but you can also turn on the **Restrict Colors** option, so the gradient wouldn't include any colors too saturated to be printed with CMYK inks.

To see the Noise gradient for the large star, double-click its Gradient Overlay entry in the Layers panel as you did for the small star. This gradient uses exactly the same settings as the other one. But we made and saved a different gradient by clicking the **Randomize** button until Photoshop generated the version we wanted.

WOW Star Gradients.psd

Gradients & Transparency

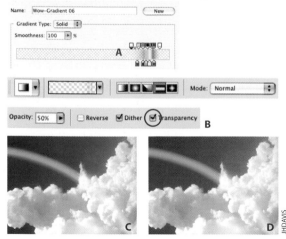

C   D

JHDAVIS

Wow Gradients 4 through 6 and 43 through 47 have transparency built in. You can build transparency into a gradient by using Opacity stops in the Gradient Editor **A**. This built-in transparency is treated differently in the different methods of applying the gradient:

- For the **Gradient tool** ▣, you can use the built-in transparency or not, simply by clicking the Transparency checkbox in the Options bar **B**.

- The **Gradient Fill layer** and the **Gradient effects** that use gradients in a Layer Style have no transparency controls. Whatever transparency is built into the gradient is expressed.

- The **Gradient Map** ignores transparency, using only the information provided by the Color stops.

Here the **Wow-Gradient 06** rainbow gradient with transparency built-in is applied with the Gradient tool ▣ at 50% Opacity in Screen mode (set in the Options bar). For the first example **C**, the Transparency option is turned on. With Transparency turned off **D**, the "outside" colors of the gradient extend to fill the transparent areas.

NOISE GRADIENTS & TRANSPARENCY

To add transparency to a **Noise gradient**, you *can* introduce random variations in opacity with the **Add Transparency** checkbox in the lower right corner of the Gradient Editor dialog box. But if you've generated a Noise gradient that you like, random transparency will probably introduce more variability than you want to cope with. To control the transparency of your Noise gradient, it's often more effective to use a layer mask when you apply it.

Shape Burst Gradients

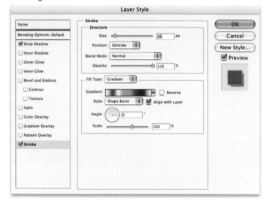

The **Stroke**, one of the effects in Photoshop's Layer Styles, offers some exciting options — especially when you choose Gradient for the **Fill Type**. Like the Gradient found elsewhere in the program, this one offers the usual Linear, Radial, Angle, Reflected, and Diamond options. But it also offers **Shape Burst**. The Shape Burst is like a Radial gradient that conforms to the shape of the element instead of spreading out from a single center point. Here we've applied a **Shape Burst Gradient Stroke** effect to the type using **Wow-Gradient 05**, with Position set to **Outside** for an inline/outline effect. You can find other examples of Shape Burst gradients in "'Outlining' with Neon" on page 552.

🔵 **Shape Burst Gradient.psd, Wow-Exercising.grd**

SAMPLING FROM THE GRADIENT

When you **double-click a Color stop** in the Gradient Editor, you can choose from the "Select stop color" dialog or sample color by clicking in the Swatches panel or in any open Photoshop file. Or, instead of double-clicking the stop, you can **single-click to sample from the gradient preview bar** itself. This makes it easy to repeat a color you've already used in the gradient.

Duotones

YOU'LL FIND THE FILES

in <wow> > Wow Project Files > Chapter 4 > Duotones:

- Duotone-Before.psd (to start)
- Wow Duotone (Duotone presets files)
- Duotone-After files (to compare)

OPEN THESE PANELS

(from the Window menu, for example)

- Layers • Adjustments

OVERVIEW

Convert a color file to Grayscale mode and then to Duotone mode • Choose a custom color to use with black for making duotones • Adjust the Duotone curves • Make adjustments to the image if you like

FOR MANY two-color design projects, the two inks are black and a custom color added for headings, rules, and other accents. With the second color available, Photoshop's Duotone mode can subtly but effectively extend the range of tones the printing press can produce in a photo, or it can add an obvious color accent, or even an "edgy" look. For a project printed with CMYK process inks, as this book was (or with an inkjet or photo printer), you may want to use Duotone mode to develop a tint, and then convert to CMYK (or RGB) for printing.

Thinking the project through. A Photoshop Duotone is actually a Grayscale image with special printing instructions stored with it. You can adjust the Ink Curves in Photoshop's Duotone Options dialog box, then change your mind later and go back to Duotone Options, to find your current duotone settings intact and ready to be altered. Here we start with a subtle use of the second ink color and move on to more colorful tints, like the one above.

1a

The original grayscale photo

1b

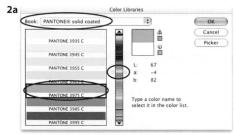

Choosing Image > Mode > Duotone opens the Duotone Options box, where you can choose Duotone for a two-color treatment. Clicking the "Load" button lets you open preset Duotone curves. Alternatively, clicking the Ink 2 color square opens a dialog box where you can choose a color to build your own Duotone settings.

2a

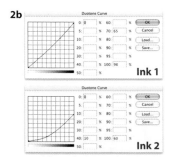

Choosing the color for Ink 2

2b

Modifying the curves for Ink 1 (black) and Ink 2 (gold) to warm the image and extend the tonal range with gold ink

(For other approaches to tinting, see "Quick Tint Effects" on page 203 and "Styling a Photo" on page 265.)

1 Converting to Duotone mode. Photoshop's Duotone mode lets you control how each of your two inks is printed across the range of tones in your image. This is done through the curves for Ink 1 and Ink 2 in the Duotone Options dialog box. We started with a Grayscale file **1a**. If your image is in color, convert it to Grayscale,▼ because the only way to Duotone mode is through Grayscale. Now convert your Grayscale file to Duotone mode (Image > Mode > Duotone). In the Duotone Options dialog box **1b**, choose Duotone from the Type menu. You can then set up the curves for your two colors, as described in step 2 below, or click the "Load" button and choose one of the Duotone color sets that Adobe supplies with Photoshop, or choose the **Wow Warming.ado** preset supplied for this technique.

FIND OUT MORE
▼ Converting from color to grayscale **page 214**

2 Warming up the photo. To make your own set of Duotone curves as we did, leave Ink 1 set to black. When you click the color square for Ink 2, the Color Libraries dialog box will open. (If the Color Picker opens instead, click its "Color Libraries" button.) In the Color Libraries dialog, choose a color system from the Book menu **2a** and pick a color: To warm the photo, we chose Pantone® Solid Coated, then moved the slider on the vertical bar to a gold range and clicked the Pantone 3975 C swatch. Click "OK" to get back to the Duotone Options dialog box.

Once you've chosen the Ink colors, click the curve box to the left of one of the color squares in Duotone Options to open the Duotone Curve dialog. On the Duotone Curve, the horizontal axis represents the tones in the image, from highlights on the left to 100% black shadows on the right. The vertical axis represents the tint of ink, from none at the bottom to 100% coverage at the top. So a point on the graph determines what tint of the ink will be printed for any particular tone in the image. You control the tinting either by clicking on the curve to make a new point (the point will snap to a vertical line) and dragging the point to a new position, or by typing the tint you want into any of the 13 fields for tone percentage.

Clicking and dragging to change the curve will modify the color treatment, and you can watch the image change as you adjust the curves. The Overprint Colors bar at the bottom of the Duotone Options dialog box (shown in figure 1b) shows how the ink colors will mix over the range of tones.

2c

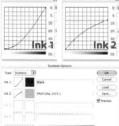

With the settings in figure 2b, the gold tint (Ink 2) barely shows in the image and in the Overprint preview bar at the bottom of the Duotone Options dialog box.

3a

Lowering the black curve (Ink 1) and raising the curve for Ink 2 makes the color more obvious in the image and in the Overprint preview bar at the bottom of the Duotone Options box.

3b

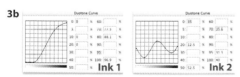

To try these ink curves, set them up "by hand" or click the "Load" button in the Duotone Options box and choose **Wow Duotone FX2.ado**.

For a subtle use of color to expand the number of tones available for midtones and shadows, we set the curve to add Ink 2 slowly, building to only 10% coverage in the light midtones and then to 60% coverage in the darkest shadows. We reduced the amount of black (Ink 1) in the midtones just slightly by changing the 70% value to 65% **2b**. Click "OK" to return to Duotone Options **2c**. (If you want to save the Duotone Options settings as a preset so you can load them again later, click the "Save" button. And if you close the Duotone Options dialog box, you can reopen it at any time by again choosing Image > Mode > Duotone.)

3 Adding a tint. Now modify the curves to try a setting that allows Ink 2 to come through as a distinct tint. Or load the **Wow Gold Tint.ado** settings; here the contribution of the black ink is reduced, especially in the highlights and light midtones, by pulling the Ink 1 curve down to a 5% tint at the 20% point in the tonal range. Reducing the black in this way allows more of the gold to show when we increase the contribution of the Pantone 3975 by pulling the middle of the Ink 2 curve up. You can now see the gold in the image and also in the Duotone Options color bar **3a**.

To produce an edgy look, try an oscillating curve for Ink 2. Here we modified the Ink 1 curve to remove black from the highlights, and we drew the Ink 2 curve to add gold in the lightest tones and in various other parts of the tonal range **3b**, **3c**.

To try a different color ink, click the Ink 2 color square and choose another color **3d.** We changed to Pantone 7522 by typing 7522 quickly (if you hesitate between digits, the Color Libraries box will think you've started over). Choosing a color that's darker or lighter, or more or less saturated than your original Duotone swatch can make big changes in the look of the image.

4 Making adjustments. Recall that a Photoshop Duotone is really just a Grayscale image with instructions for printing with two or more inks. That means you can make changes to your original Grayscale image, even *after* you've picked out your ink curves. For instance, we were happy with the Duotone curves for Ink 1 and Ink 2 and the new color chosen in step 3d. But we had lost the catchlight and most of the other detail in the eye. To bring them back, we added a "dodge and burn" layer: Add a gray-filled layer in Soft Light mode by Alt/Option-clicking the "Create a new layer" button ⬛ at the bottom of the Layers panel. In the New Layer dialog box, name the layer, choose Soft Light for the Mode and click the checkbox in front of "Fill with Soft-Light-neutral color (50% gray)" **4a**. Then use the Brush ✏ (Shift-B), with a soft brush tip and Opacity set low in the Options

3c

With the settings in figure 3b, the gold tint (Ink 2) is distributed less evenly over the tonal range, producing this effect.

3d

Clicking the Ink 2 color square in the Duotone Options dialog box opens the Color Libraries box, where you can change the color.

4a

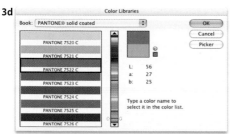

Adding a "dodge and burn" layer

4b

In a Duotone file the "neutral gray" of the "Dodge & Burn" layer shows up in the Layers panel as the 50:50 Overprint color of the inks used for the Duotone. The result of changing the color to Pantone 7522 (in step 3d) and dodging the eye is shown in the opening image on page 199.

bar, to paint with white over the eye **4b**; we used a 50-pixel brush with Hardness 0 and Opacity 15%.▼

To experiment further, try adding a Levels Adjustment layer (click the "Create new fill or adjustment layer button" ◕ at the bottom of the Layers panel and choose Levels, or use the ⛰ button in the Adjustments panel in CS4) and move the Input Levels gamma (middle) slider to the right **4c**.▼

Preparing to print. If your Duotone will be printed with a custom color, discuss with your printer which plate (black or color) will be printed first and whether you or the prepress operator will take responsibility for setting the screen angles. Often the color ink is printed first, to keep it from interfering with the black where the halftone dots overlap, regardless of how opaque the color ink is. Generally, pastel colors (which contain opaque white), dark shades (which contain black), and metallics are more opaque. For screen angles, consult your prepress operator or refer to Adobe's suggestions in the "Printing duotones" and "Selecting halftone screen attributes" from Photoshop's Help menu.

If your Duotone file will be placed in a page layout program for two-color printing, Adobe recommends using Photoshop EPS or Photoshop PDF format when you save the Duotone (File > Save As). If you add a spot color channel to your Duotone, however, Adobe recommends converting the file to Multichannel mode and saving in Photoshop DCS 2.0 format.

To convert the Duotone to CMYK for printing as we did for these pages (or to RGB for an inkjet or photo printer, or for the web), make a copy (Image > Duplicate, "Duplicate merged layers only") and choose Image > Mode > CMYK Color (or RGB Color). If the image will be used in a page layout file, save the converted file in a compatible format, such as TIFF (File > Save As). *Wow!*

FIND OUT MORE

▼ Setting up the Brush tool ✎
   page 71

▼ Adjusting Levels **page 246**

4c

After adding a Levels Adjustment layer, we painted its built-in mask with black to protect the eye.

Tint Effects

Whether you're tinting a single image that will stand alone, coordinating a series of photos for a publication, or recoloring graphics or a pattern, Photoshop CS3/CS4 has some great options. "Hand-Tinting a Black & White Photo" on page 351 takes you step-by-step through a process that imitates traditional photo-tinting with brushes and inks. But when you don't need a hand-painted look for your tinting, one of the simpler techniques shown on the next nine pages can produce great results quickly. Some start with a color image, while others start with a "black-and-white." But in order to color a black-and-white, the file has to be in a color mode. Most of the techniques use RGB Color, although one (on page 210) relies on working in the color channels of a CMYK or Spot Color file. (To convert a Grayscale image to color so you can add a tint, choose Image > Mode > RGB Color or CMYK Color.)

Many tinting techniques can start with clicking the "Create new fill or adjustment layer" button ⬤ in either CS3 (above left) or CS4. In Photoshop CS4 you also have the option of clicking one of the buttons in the Adjustments panel (above right).

In addition to the methods shown here, Camera Raw provides a number of easy-to-use options for tinting single-layer files that are in raw, JPEG, or TIFF format. An example can be found in "Adjusting Tone & Color in Camera Raw" in Chapter 5.

For a tinting treatment that includes custom edges, a drop shadow, or even a surface texture, see "Styling a Photo" on page 265 and check out the Wow Styles for photos, provided on the Wow DVD-ROM and shown in Appendix C.

YOU'LL FIND FILES FOR MOST OF THESE EFFECTS

In 🔵 > Chapter 4 > Quick Tint Effects

OPEN THESE PANELS

from the Window menu, for example:

• Tools • Layers • Adjustments

Tinting with a Custom Color

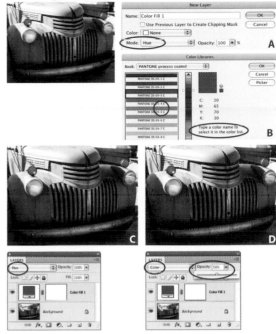

A SOLID COLOR FILL LAYER is a great way to tint with a specific color, such as the Pantone DS 69-3C used here. To start, hold down the Alt/Option key as you click the "Create new fill or adjustment layer" button ⬤ at the bottom of the Layers panel and choose Solid Color from the list. In the New Layer dialog box **A**, which opens because you used the Alt/Option key, choose Hue for the Mode (in the default Normal mode, the Solid Color would simply cover up the image); click "OK." In the "Pick a solid color" dialog, click the Color Libraries button. In the Color Libraries dialog **B** choose the color Book you want, and type the number of the color you're after, or locate the color by using the sliders; click "OK" to close the dialog.

In the Layers panel you can vary the tint effect by choosing from the menu near the upper left corner of the panel. While Hue mode **C** leaves neutrals (black, white, and grays) untinted, Color mode **D** tints all the colors or tones in the photo except pure black and white. (A layer in Hue mode has no effect on a black-and-white photo.)

🔵 **Solid Color Fill.psd**

"TITRATING" THE COLOR

With a Fill or Adjustment layer you can tweak the color simply by using the Opacity slider for the layer to blend the color change with some of the "pre-adjustment" color.

Colorizing with Hue/Saturation

PHOTO: BEVERLY GOWARD

IF YOU DON'T HAVE A PARTICULAR CUSTOM COLOR in mind (as in "Tinting with a Custom Color"), a Hue/Saturation Adjustment layer makes it easy to experiment to find a color you like. To add the tinting layer, click the "Create new fill or adjustment layer" button ⬤ at the bottom of the Layers panel and choose Hue/Saturation from its menu. In the Hue/Saturation dialog box, first click the Colorize checkbox. Black and white will remain black and white, but colors and grays will be tinted. Experiment by moving the Hue and Saturation sliders until you like the color and intensity of the tint; click "OK" to close the dialog box. Try using Color (as shown) or Hue for the Adjustment layer's blend mode.

 Hue-Saturation.psd

TAKE THE PHOTO IN COLOR

Many digital cameras offer a Sepia setting that records the image in sepiatone rather than full color. With the variety of tinting methods available in Photoshop, it makes sense to keep your options open by shooting in full color and then converting to sepiatone using a Solid Color Fill, Hue/Saturation, or Photo Filter layer, or a Gradient Map.▼

FIND OUT MORE
▼ Tinting with a Gradient Map **page 208**

Tinting with Black & White

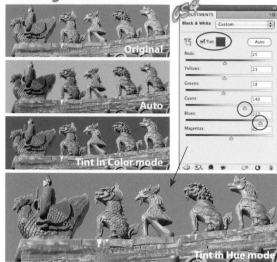

THE BLACK & WHITE ADJUSTMENT LAYER, new in Photoshop CS3, includes a "Tint" option. Start by clicking the "Create new fill or adjustment layer" button ⬤ at the bottom of the Layers panel and choosing Black & White from the list. Here we simply clicked the "Auto" button for the adjustment to arrive at the conversion.

Then click the Tint option, click the color swatch, choose a color, and click "OK" to close the "Select target color" box. (In CS3 at this point you'll need to click "OK" to close the Black & White dialog; in CS4 the dialog remains open in the Adjustments panel.) Put the layer in Hue or Color mode by choosing from the list of blend modes at top of the Layers panel. In CS3 reopen the Black & White dialog box (double-click the Adjustment layer's thumbnail in the Layers panel); in CS4 there's no need — it's still open. Now you can interactively experiment with the sliders or scrubbers for the Black & White adjustment to arrive at the optimal conversion to go with your tint.

 Black-and-White.psd

TINTING A SERIES

Once you've used an Adjustment layer to achieve a tint effect you like for one image, you can apply the same effect to a whole series by dragging and dropping your Adjustment layer to the working window of other open images. ▼

PHOTOS: PHOTOSPIN.COM

FIND OUT MORE
▼ Dragging-and-dropping layers **page 33**

Partial Desaturation: Vibrance

SOMETIMES JUST "TURNING DOWN" THE COLOR in a photo can produce the tinted look you're after. A Vibrance Adjustment layer makes it easy to produce pale or muted color. Starting with a fairly saturated, high-contrast image, as we have here, click the Vibrance button ▽ on the Adjustments panel **A**. Move the Vibrance slider to the left **B**. You'll find that even if you move it all the way to the left (at –100 %), some color remains. You could use the Saturation slider instead or in addition, but Vibrance has the advantage of differentially preserving the intense colors as it fades the more neutral colors.

If you want to do something similar in Photoshop CS3, which lacks a Vibrance adjustment, add a Black & White Adjustment layer at reduced Opacity (as in "Tinting with Masking" on page 206). Or use a Hue/Saturation layer, moving the Saturation slider to the left to get the overall color reduction you want, and then masking to bring back the intense colors more than the neutrals.

 **Partial Desaturation.psd**

Tinting by Tonal Range

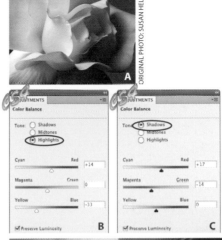

TO TINT THE HIGHLIGHTS ONE COLOR and the shadows another, use a Color Balance Adjustment layer. Start with an image that has little or no color (like this rose) **A**. Click the "Create new fill or adjustment layer" button ◐ at the bottom of the Layers panel and choose Color Balance from the list. Then click the Highlights button and move the sliders toward the colors you want to add more of **B**. Do the same for the Shadows and Midtones if you like **C**.

To tint this rose in RGB Color mode, we added Red and Yellow to the Highlights and Red and Magenta to the Shadows **D**. With a Color Balance adjustment, the three tonal ranges (Highlights, Midtones, and Shadows) overlap somewhat. This ensures smooth color transitions. But it also means that a color change in one part of the tonal range will interact with changes in the other two parts of the range. So tinting with Color Balance is, true to its name, a balancing act.

 **Color Balance.psd**

Retaining Specific Colors

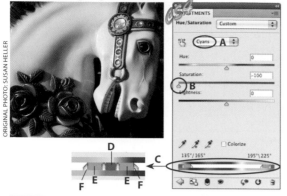

ORIGINAL PHOTO: SUSAN HELLER

Tinting with Masking

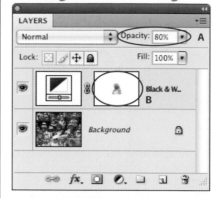

To remove all but one or two colors from an image, add a Hue/Saturation Adjustment layer (as in "Colorizing with Hue/Saturation" on page 204, but put the layer in Normal mode). Then do the following for each of the colors in the menu, *except* the color(s) you want to retain: In the Hue/Saturation dialog, click on "Master" to open the list of colors. Choose a color from the menu **A** and drag the Saturation slider all the way to the left **B**. Here we desaturated all colors except Reds. You can move the markers on the spectrum bar at the bottom of the Hue/Saturation dialog **C** in order to redefine the section of the spectrum that constitutes the Hue you're working with. You can move the range to a different hue (drag the dark gray middle of the bar **D**), expand or reduce the range of colors (drag one of the lighter outer bars **E**), or change how abrupt the transition is between colors that are included in the range and those that aren't (move an outer slider **F**).

The Saturation panel in Camera Raw's HSL/Grayscale tab allows the same kind of adjustment, with two additional sliders: Oranges, which can be very useful for working with skin tones, and Purples.

 **Specific Colors.psd**

If you'd like some parts of your image to be tinted more intensely than others, or you want the original color to show through, you can use an Adjustment or Fill layer's built-in mask to put the color where you want it. With the Adjustment or Fill layer targeted (by clicking its thumbnail in the Layers panel), choose the Brush tool 🖌 (or type B) and also choose black for the Foreground color (tap the X key once or twice, until the Foreground color swatch in the Tools panel is black). In the Options bar choose a soft brush tip and set the Opacity low. Then paint loosely over the part of the image whose original coloring you want to restore. This darkens the mask in this area, protecting this part of the image from the Adjustment or Fill layer's effect.

Here we started with a color image and added a Black & White Adjustment layer by clicking the ⬤ button at the bottom of the Layers panel and choosing from the list. We restored a little color throughout the image by reducing the Adjustment layer's Opacity to 80% **A**, and then painted the mask **B**, using one of Photoshop's default brushes (Airbrush Soft Round 100).

 **Tinting-Masking.psd**

Tinting a "Photo Graphic"

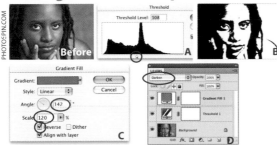

THIS TINTING TECHNIQUE starts with reducing a photo to black and white pixels only — no color and no grays. To do that, add a Threshold Adjustment layer by clicking the "Create new fill or adjustment layer" button ⊘ at the bottom of the Layers panel and choosing from its menu, or by clicking ▮ in the Adjustments panel. In the Threshold dialog box move the slider to balance the black and white to taste **A**, **B**.

Next add a Gradient Fill layer in a way that will let you color the white areas while leaving the black intact: Alt/Option-click the ⊘ button and choose Gradient for the type of layer. When the New Layer dialog box opens, choose Darken for the Mode and click "OK." (Or choose Lighten instead of Darken to tint the black instead of the white.) When the Gradient Fill dialog box opens, click the downward arrow to the right of the Gradient swatch and choose a gradient (to use a Wow Gradient, we clicked the ▾≡ button to open the panel menu, chose Wow-Gradients, and then double-clicked on **Wow-Gradient 15**). ▼ In the Gradient Fill dialog box, experiment with the Angle, the Scale, and the Reverse option. We settled on 142° for the Angle and 120% for the Scale, with Reverse turned on **C**; with the Gradient Fill dialog open we dragged in the image to reposition the gradient and clicked "OK" to close the dialog **D**.

FIND OUT MORE

▼ Installing the Wow Gradients
page 4

 Photo Graphic.psd

Gradient Tints for Landscapes

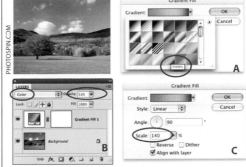

A COLOR GRADIENT can even change the time of day or the season. To apply a Gradient Fill layer, click the "Create new fill or adjustment layer" button ⊘ at the bottom of the Layers panel and choose Gradient from the list. In the Gradient Fill dialog box, click the tiny arrow to the right of the gradient swatch and choose a gradient; we double clicked the Wow-Violets gradient swatch and used the default Angle (90° vertical) and default gradient Style (Linear) **A**. The gradient will completely cover up the image, but you can fix that next with the blend mode controls for the layer, so go ahead and click "OK" to close the Gradient Fill dialog.

In the Layers panel **B** experiment with the Opacity of the Gradient layer and try different blend modes from the list in the upper left corner of the panel; the Color mode and 45% Opacity seemed to provide the best change in color from Summer to Fall. But we wanted to make some adjustments to the gradient.

To adjust the gradient in a Gradient Fill layer, in the Layers panel double-click the thumbnail for the layer to reopen the Gradient Fill dialog box. There you can scale the gradient; we set Scale to 140% **C**, enlarging the transparent section in the middle to blend more of the original color with the gradient color in that area of the image. With the dialog box open, you can also adjust the gradient's position by "reaching into" the working window and dragging; we dragged the gradient up a little, extending the warm colors farther up.

 Gradient Fill Layer.psd

Using a Gradient Map Layer

A Gradient Map Adjustment layer recolors an image by "remapping" the brightness values to the colors of a gradient of your choice. Using a gradient that goes from a dark color on the left through to a light color on the right (going only to *near* white to preserve an old photo look), you can roughly maintain the lights and darks of your image, especially if you put the Gradient Map layer in Color mode, which lets the original tonal values of the image come through.

To add a Gradient Map, click the "Create new fill or adjustment layer" button ⊘ at the bottom of the Layers panel and choose Gradient Map from the list. In the Gradient Map dialog, click the tiny triangle to the right of the gradient swatch and choose a gradient (to use a Wow Gradient▽ we clicked the ▾☰ button to open the menu of Gradient presets and chose Wow Gradients; then we clicked the swatch for the **Wow-TintypeBrown1 gradient**). Adjust the gradient sliders to suit the image. Changing the blend mode to Color (as we did) preserves the tonal range of the original black-and-white photo (in CS3 you'll need to close the dialog before changing the blend mode).

 **Gradient Map.psd**

FIND OUT MORE

▽ Installing the Wow Gradients **page 4**

Creating a Mock "Split-tone"

In days gone by when all film was black-and-white, photographers who did their own printing observed that with certain papers, processes, and chemical toners a black-and-white print would show color, with the colors "splitting out" according to the tonal values. Darkroom artists began to deliberately create this somewhat unpredictable effect. There are many techniques for split-toning in Photoshop, but this one is easy and involves nothing more than using a Gradient Map.

Start with a "black-and-white" photo in RGB color mode; if your photo is in color, remove the color▽ but stay in RGB mode. ▽ In the Layers panel, click on the "Create new fill or adjustment layer" button ⊘ and choose Gradient Map. When the dialog opens, click on the gradient to open the Gradient Editor. For a traditional look, choose a gradient that's divided between warm and cool colors. To "tone" the image, the colors on the left should be dark, becoming increasingly lighter as you move to the right **A**. Watch your image as you adjust the color stops and intermediate triangles to "split" the colors among the tones as you like **B**. ▽

 **Split-Tone.psd**

FIND OUT MORE

▽ Converting to black-and-white **page 214**

▽ Changing color transitions in gradients **page 197**

Tinting with a Photo Filter

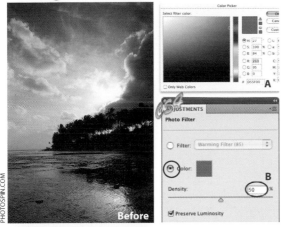

Before

Tinted

PHOTOSPIN.COM

PHOTOSHOP'S PHOTO FILTER Adjustment layers simulate the effect of taking a photo with the equivalent traditional color filter mounted on the camera lens. To add
a Photo Filter, click the "Create new fill or adjustment
layer" button ⊘ at the bottom of the Layers panel and
choose Photo Filter. In the Photo Filter dialog box both
options — Filter and Color — apply color in exactly the
same way. The difference between the two options is
that Filter offers a menu of the traditional color filters
used on camera lenses, while Color opens the "Select
filter color" dialog to a broader choice of tints. For the
tint shown here, choose Color and pick a red-orange **A**.
Increase the Density to 50% for a stronger tint than you
would get with the traditional 25% **B**, leave Preserve
Luminosity turned on (so the filter won't darken the image), and click "OK" to close the dialog box.

 **Photo Filter Tint.psd**

Combining Photo Filters

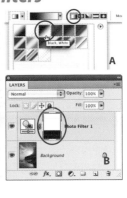

A

Tinted & masked

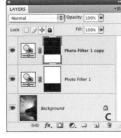

Double-tinted

YOU CAN COMBINE PHOTO FILTER LAYERS to get the
effect of a dual filter, or two graduated filters mounted
together on the camera lens. Starting with the tinted image file from "Tinting with a Photo Filter" at the left, use
the Photo Filter's built-in layer mask to limit the color
to the sky: Choose the Gradient tool ▭ (or type G). In
the Options bar click the tiny arrow to the right of the
gradient swatch; from the picker that opens, choose the
"Black, White" gradient and make sure the Linear Gradient style is chosen **A**. Now move the cursor just below the
horizon in the image, hold down the Shift key, and drag
upward a very short distance across the horizon. This will
create a mask that's white on top and black on the bottom, allowing the orange tint to show only at the top **B**.
To add the second tint, duplicate the Photo Filter layer
(Ctrl/⌘-J), invert the mask (Ctrl/⌘-I) **C**, and double-click
the new layer's Photo Filter thumbnail to open the Photo
Filter dialog; click the color swatch and choose a purple.

 **Photo Filters Combined.psd**

Using Three Photo Filters

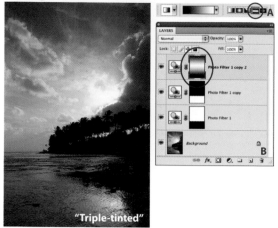

"Triple-tinted"

WANT TO TRY A THIRD FILTER? To add a glow centered at the level of the sun, start with the dual-tinted image file from "Combining Photo Filters" on the previous page. Duplicate your second Photo Filter layer (Ctrl/⌘-J). Then change the layer mask on this new layer: In the Gradient tool's Options bar, with the "Black, White" gradient still chosen, click the "Reflected Gradient" button for the gradient style **A**; also click the Reverse box so the gradient you're about to draw will go from white to black. Hold down the Shift key again and drag upward from just below the level of the sun in the image to the point where you want the red-orange sky tint you applied earlier to be at full strength. With the new mask now in place **B**, double-click the Photo Filter thumbnail and choose the color and density for this third tint; we clicked the Filter button and chose Deep Yellow from the list, leaving the density at 50%.

With three tinting filters in place, you now have all kinds of options if you want to experiment further:

• You can double-click the thumbnail for any one of the Photo Filters and change its color or density.

• You can also control color density with the Opacity slider for any of the Photo Filter layers.

• You can redirect a tint by painting the Photo Filter's layer mask with the Brush tool 🖌 and a soft brush tip. Or redraw its gradient with the Gradient tool ⬛. Or stretch its mask: Type Ctrl/⌘-T and drag a top or bottom handle up or down beyond the top or bottom edge of the image. Double-click inside the box to complete the transformation.

 **3 Photo Filters Combined.psd**

"Painting" in the Ink Channels

Before

After

ORIGINAL PHOTO: BEVERLY GOWARD

IN CMYK COLOR MODE (and Spot Color also) the thumbnails in the Channels panel represent ink colors; the black shows where each ink will print, and white represents the absence of ink. A quick tinting technique involves painting loosely with black in the individual color channels to apply tints of the ink colors. Here we started with a "black-and-white" in RGB color mode and converted the file to CMYK (Image > Mode > CMYK Color).

The first step is to duplicate the image to a new layer (Ctrl/⌘-J) **A** so you can tint a copy and still protect the original. Then choose the Brush tool 🖌 (or type B) and in the Options bar choose a large soft brush tip and lower the Opacity of the paint to less than 10%. In the Channels panel (Window > Channels) target one of the color channels (we clicked the thumbnail for the Yellow channel) **B**. So you'll be able to see the color developing as you work, click in the 👁 column for the composite CMYK at the top of the Channels panel. With black as the Foreground color (tap the X key once or twice), paint quick strokes on the face, hair, and background.

Then paint the other channels. We targeted the Magenta channel (Ctrl/⌘-2 or Ctrl/⌘-4), reduced the Brush tool's Opacity even more in the Options bar (because magenta is a stronger color), and again painted with black; we chose a smaller brush tip for the lips. For the Cyan channel (Ctrl/⌘-1 or Ctrl/⌘-3), we used the small brush tip and increased Opacity to paint the eyes, then went back to a larger brush and lower Opacity for the hair and background.

 **Painting in Channels.psd**

Channel Mixer Pastels

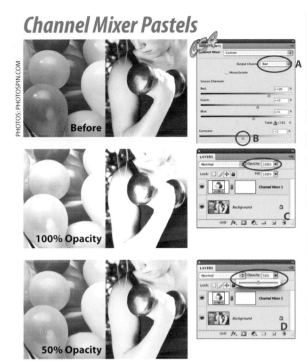

Before

100% Opacity

50% Opacity

PHOTOSHOP'S CHANNEL MIXER CAN GENERATE some interesting color tint effects. Open an RGB image and add a Channel Mixer Adjustment layer by clicking the ⊘ button at the bottom of the Layers panel and choosing Channel Mixer from the list, or in the Adjustments panel, click the Channel Mixer button ⬥.

When it opens, the Channel Mixer dialog offers the sliders for the Red channel. As a first step toward making pastels, move the sliders so the Red channel includes all the brightness information it originally contained (Red 100%) plus the brightness information from the Green channel at half strength (Green 50%) and some of the brightness information from the Blue channel as well (we used Blue 31%) **A**. Now choose Green from the Output Channel menu at the top of the Channel Mixer box and make similar boosts to the brightness values, and then do the same for Blue. For Green we used Red 13%, Green 100%, and Blue 68%; and for Blue we used Red 28%, Green 23%, and Blue 100%. The overall effect is to lighten all the colors, producing pastels. You can reduce the Constant **B** to counteract some of the lightening by slightly darkening the image overall; we used a setting of –11.

Experiment with the Channel Mixer layer's Opacity **C**, **D** to get the effect you want.

Channel Mixer Pastels.psd

Patch Tool Tinting

Before

After

WE STUMBLED UPON THIS TINTING approach while experimenting with the Patch tool ⬥. For a "black-and-white" image in RGB Color mode, it produces a subtle glow at high-contrast edges.

First use the entire image to make a pattern by choosing Edit > Define Pattern **A**. Then add a new layer (Ctrl/⌘-Shift-N, or click the ▣ button at the bottom of the Layers panel). Fill the new layer with the color you want for the tint. (One way to choose the color is to choose Edit > Fill > Color and choose from the "Choose a color" dialog.)

Next choose the Patch tool ⬥. The Patch requires an active selection, but the selection doesn't have to be made with the tool itself, so simply select all (Ctrl/⌘-A). In the Patch tool's Options bar click the Pattern swatch (to the right of the "Use Pattern" button) to open a picker showing the currently available patterns **B**. Navigate to the bottom of the picker to find your newly defined pattern, and click on it. Then click the "Use Pattern" button and have a cup of tea while Photoshop works on "healing" to blend the color and the image.

Patch Tool Tinting.psd

Cristen Gillespie Turns Real into Surreal

PHOTOSHOP'S MERGE TO HDR FUNCTION was designed to combine different exposures of the same image in a way that matches what the human eye can see, better than any single shot from a camera can do. ▼ But its HDR Conversion dialog, combined with Camera Raw, ▼ has a "hidden talent." Here Cristen Gillespie uses Camera Raw and HDR Conversion with a single image, to recast a scene in surrealistic color, using a method that's highly flexible and easy to control.

The **Surreal-Before.tif** file is provided in the Wow Project Files, Chapter 4 folder on the Wow DVD-ROM.

FIND OUT MORE

▼ Merge to HDR **page 294**

▼ Camera Raw **page 141**

1 In order to make use of features found only in Camera Raw, the image must be in raw, TIFF or JPEG format.

Images shot in a camera's raw format will automatically open in Camera Raw when you try to open them in Photoshop. For a JPEG or TIFF file, in Photoshop simply choose File > Open, locate and highlight your image file, then choose Camera Raw from the Open dialog's Format menu, and click the "Open" button.

The original image

2 Once the image is open in Camera Raw, the key features for preparing heightened, even surreal color are on the Basic panel. Begin by dragging the sliders for Recovery, Fill Light, Contrast, Clarity, and Vibrance

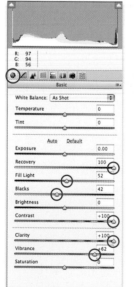

Moving the sliders in Camera Raw's Basic panel started the journey toward surreal by brightening the colors. (The HSL/Grayscale tab can also be useful in developing surreal color, but it wasn't used in this case.)

all the way to the right. Immediately color will probably be both extreme and much lighter than you want. To restore some darker tones, drag the Blacks slider toward the right, and if you like, readjust some of the other sliders you moved earlier. You can use the other sliders also — Exposure, Brightness, and Saturation — but be careful, because a little goes a long way and these can quickly push an image too far; it's often easier to make these adjustments at the end of the process in Photoshop. When you've approximated the surreal color you want, open the image in Photoshop: Click Camera Raw's "Open Image" button (if you see "Open Object" instead, hold down Alt/Option to get "Open Image" or "Open Copy").

3 In Photoshop choose Image > Mode > 32 Bits/Channel to move into a mode that provides a lot more subtlety and "stretch" in adjusting tone and color. Right away, choose Image > Mode > 16 Bits/Channel to open the **HDR Conversion** dialog. From the Method list, choose **Local Adaptation** and click the ▾ button to open the Toning Curve and Histogram section of the dialog. At this point your image will probably become too bright or washed-out-looking.

When you choose Local Adaptation, the image becomes very light and bright.

To restore your developing color, with the graph set up in the default mode (as shown here) with the black end of the Input gradient at the left, bend the **Curve** line to match the gradual curve at the left-hand side of the histogram, by dragging the Curve down. (You may also find it helpful to move the left endpoint to the right to get the right bend, though it wasn't necessary here.) What you've just done is to tell Photoshop where the tones are in your image, so it can roughly map them to the 32-Bit space.

A simple curve begins to restore the image closer to the appearance it had when first opened in Photoshop.

4 Now you can make adjustments within that huge 32-Bit space to lighten or darken particular tonal ranges: Click on a place in the image that you'd like to lighten or darken; a corresponding marker will appear on the Curve; click in that spot on the Curve and drag up to lighten that color or down to darken it. In this 32-Bit space you can make wild, wiggly humps in the Curve without posterizing the image (breaking the colors and tones into obvious "steps") as would happen in 8-Bit or 16-Bit color modes, because here in 32-Bit you have many more in-between tones to work with—the colors can "bend" without breaking.

For even more control, go ahead and "break" the color in places if you like: After placing an anchor point, click on the **Corner** checkbox to turn the anchor into a cusp. "Cusps in the curve allow for more abrupt changes in tonal values," says Gillespie. "I use smooth curves when I want very realistic results from HDR. But for an unreal look, when I'm not aiming for the smoothest possible transition in values, I use corner points to put darks and lights where I want them."

Turn your attention now to the **Radius** and **Threshold** sliders. For the purposes of this technique, note that a higher Radius setting creates larger areas of a similar

brightness, clumping more of the pixels into similar values. Highlight regions, for instance, become larger and more noticeable, and halos might appear. Low Radius settings produce a more natural, but flatter appearance. If you want to soften the transition between adjacent colors, increase the Threshold. If you want to make color boundaries crisper or eliminate halos caused by a high Radius, lower the Threshold. Working between your Curve and the Radius and Threshold settings, you can produce almost any look from natural to surreal, from brightly colored like this image to "grunge," like the example on page 364.

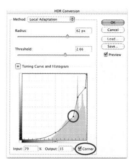

The final curve with its many cusp anchors, along with high Radius and Threshold settings, produced the bright "summer sunshine" colors, complete with halos, to emphasize a slightly unreal quality in this Southern California scene.

From Color to Black & White

OPEN THESE PANELS
from the Window menu, for instance:
- Tools • Layers • Adjustments

OVERVIEW
Add a Black & White Adjustment layer • Use a Default, Auto, or custom conversion to "translate" the image from color to black-and-white • If needed, add another Black & White layer and use a layer mask to target each conversion where you want it in the image • Convert to Grayscale

ORIGINAL PHOTO: PHOTOSPIN.COM

MANY WAYS TO BLACK & WHITE

You'll find examples of specialized black-and-white conversions throughout the book. For instance:

"Inspecting & Mixing Channels" on page 195 tells how to mix color channels to revive a damaged image.

"Retaining Specific Colors" on page 206 and other sections of "Quick Tint Effects" tell how to combine black-and-white with some of the original color.

"Tinting a 'Photo Graphic'" on page 207 includes a method for converting to black and white only, no grays.

"Quick Black-and-White Graphics" on page 490 takes conversion beyond photos, to converting color graphics.

THERE ARE PROBABLY A DOZEN WAYS to convert a color image to black-and-white in Photoshop. But these days the method of choice will almost always be either an HSL/Grayscale adjustment in Camera Raw, if you're adjusting a single-layer photographic image and you're working in Camera Raw anyway,▼ or Photoshop's Black & White adjustment, added in CS3. There are other options you might use under specific conditions (see "Many Ways to Black & White" at the left), but for most conversions a Black & White Adjustment layer is an effective and easy solution.

FIND OUT MORE
▼ Black-and-white in Camera Raw **page 300**

Thinking the project through. Turning a color image to black-and-white involves two distinct operations. The first is interpreting the color in terms of black, white, and a range of grays, and the other is converting the file from a color mode (usually RGB) to Grayscale so it will print in just one ink. The first operation involves a huge amount of personal choice. Conversion is less about finding "the one" perfect black-and-white conversion than about arriving at a result that expresses the meaning you want the photo to convey.

The second operation is cut-and-dried, and very simple. After you've chosen a black-and-white conversion for your color image, the photo *looks* black-and-white but it's actually still in a color mode. To reduce it to a one-ink file, choose Image > Mode > Grayscale. But first things first.

1 Adding a Black & White Adjustment layer. Open an RGB image such as **Plants-Before.psd 1a**. Click the "Create new fill

The original color photo

Black & White is one of the tone and color adjustments that can be applied through the Layer > New Adjustment Layer command, the Layers panel's "Create new fill or adjustment layer" button ⬮, or CS4's Adjustments panel (shown here).

1d

Default interpretation   "Auto" interpretation

Applying the Blue Filter from the menu of presets. As you experiment, you can always restore the Default by choosing it from the menu of presets; click the "Auto" button again to restore Auto.

1f

In addition to reducing the Yellows value, we reduced the Cyans and Magentas slightly to restore the streak in the middle of each petal. *Note:* Clicking the "Switch panel to Extended View" button ⬚ at the bottom of the Adjustments panel widens the sliders for easier control.

or adjustment layer" button ⬮ at the bottom of the Layers panel and choose Black & White from the list of options, or in CS4 you can click the ▰ button in the new Adjustments panel **1b**. Immediately you'll see a Default black-and-white version based on the colors in your image **1c**. Click "Auto" in the Black & White dialog to see a second interpretation, this one maximizing the number and distribution of different grays **1d**. Now experiment in the Black & White dialog with the presets, color sliders, and scrubber ✋, translating some colors to lighter grays and other colors to darker shades:

- Many of the **presets** in the menu at the upper right of the dialog simulate filters one might use on a camera lens for shooting in black-and-white.

- Moving any **slider** left darkens the gray that represents that color in the image; moving it right lightens.

- In CS3, clicking on the image shows you which of the six colors represented by the sliders predominates in the spot you clicked: The color swatch for the predominant color's slider is highlighted; or if you hold down the Alt/Option key as you click, its number field is highlighted. In CS4, you first click the scrubber button ✋ in the Black & White dialog; then when you then click in the image, the number field is highlighted. When you've seen which color predominates, you can lighten or darken by moving that slider or typing a number.

- Clicking the **scrubber** ✋ button and then dragging in the image lightens or darkens the gray that represents the color where the drag began. Dragging left darkens, and dragging right lightens.

We wanted more contrast between the flowers and the leaves than either Default or Auto provided. Since the flowers are blue, we tried the Blue Filter preset **1e**; it lightened the blue and darkened some of the other colors. (Note that when you choose the Blue Filter, not only does the Blues slider move to the right, but also the Cyans and Magentas sliders; mixing cyan and magenta makes blue.)

Next we customized the settings: Clicking on a green leaf (in CS4 you have to click the scrubber button ✋ first) highlighted the Yellows slider to show that the predominant color in the leaf is yellow. We could either simply drag left from our position on the leaf, or use the Yellow slider. We opted for the slider, since it seemed easier to control. When we had the conversion we wanted **1f**, we duplicated the file (Image > Duplicate > Merged Layers Only) and chose Image > Mode > Grayscale.

We see grass, trees, and other plants as green. But in many cases Photoshop sees them as primarily yellow. In a Black & White adjustment, often moving the Green slider does less to lighten or darken plants than moving the Yellow slider. To see which color predominates, click the plant in the image and see which slider "lights up" (in CS4, click Black & White's scrubber 👆 before clicking in the image).

2a  **2b**

Original photo · Auto conversion

2c

The Red Filter setting reduces shadows on the face.

2d

ORIGINAL PHOTO: STEVE LOVEGROVE / PHOTOSPIN.COM

Reducing the Reds value brought back some shading to the face. Reducing Blues and Magentas kept the eyes dark, in contrast to the skin, but increasing Cyans brought back detail and made the eyes brighter and more lively. Minor adjustments were made to other sliders to keep the transitions smooth.

2 Looking at options. Sometimes the goal in converting to black-and-white is to bring out a certain feature in the photo. In our black-and-white interpretation of a portrait **2a**, we wanted to focus attention on the baby's eyes. To follow along with what we did, open the **Portrait-Before.psd** file and add a Black & White Adjustment layer, as in step 1. Look at the Default conversion, and click "Auto" to check the Auto conversion **2b**. We found that in both instances the detail in the skin tones and shadows on the face interfered with the look we wanted. We tried the Red Filter from the menu of presets at the top of the dialog **2c**. It was the direction we wanted to go, but it was too strong. So we scrubbed (as described on page 215), to the left on the baby's forehead to arrive at a compromise we liked (scrub right if you go too far and need to recover). To increase contrast between the eyes and the face, we clicked on the iris of one eye and scrubbed left, dragging and adjusting sliders until the eyes contrasted nicely **2d**. To finish, duplicate the file and convert to Grayscale, as at the end of step 1.

3 Combining two translations. When two elements in your photo share the same predominant color, but in your black-and-white interpretation you want one element to be light and the other dark, consider making two conversions and combining them with a layer mask. For example, open **Still Life-Before.psd 3a**. Add a Black & White Adjustment layer (as described in step 1 on page 214) and in the Black & White dialog, click "Auto" **3b**. We liked this version, but we wanted to try another one, with the flowers light and the leaves and vase dark in contrast. To lighten the red in the tulips, use the scrubber 👆 (its operation in CS3 and CS4 is described in step 2); click on the red in one of the tulips and drag to the right to lighten. When the tulips are as light as you want **3c**, click on the leaves and drag to the left to darken. We had to balance the darkening of the leaves with the increasing noise this generated (see "Avoiding Noise" on page 217).

Next duplicate the Black & White Adjustment layer (Ctrl/⌘-J) **3d**. *Note:* When you add a second Black & White layer, even if its

When you use the scrubber in the Black & White dialog, color is sampled only where you click to start your drag to the left or right; it isn't resampled continuously as you drag. So you can click on an eye, for instance, and drag across the hair or the face to darken or lighten the eye, without the face or hair being changed in the process.

When you "scrub" the part of an image you want to lighten or darken, the color you start the scrub on will be changed throughout the image, not just where you scrubbed.

3a

Original photo

3b

The Auto interpretation

3c

Clicking with the scrubber and dragging to the right lightens all the reds in the image.

3d

A second Black & White layer is added.

3e

Selecting the vase with the Quick Selection tool

3f

Masking the lower Black & White layer (shown with visibility turned off for the upper layer)

3g

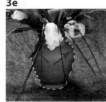

When we clicked the scrubber on the vase and dragged left, some vertical streaking began to appear as the vase darkened. So we moved the Reds slider back to the right a bit and then moved the Magentas slider left to darken more without streaking

settings are wildly different from the first, you won't see a change in your image when you add it. The top layer has no effect, because the image it "sees" is already black-and-white, rather than color, so there's nothing for it to interpret. However, if you turn off visibility for the lower Black & White layer, or mask it to block its effect in some areas, you'll be able to see the interpretation applied by the upper layer.

It isn't hard to create a mask on the lower Black & White layer that will block its effect on the vase and thus allow the upper Black & White layer to act on it. Target the photo layer by clicking its thumbnail in the Layers panel, and make a selection of the area you want to mask. The vase is a solid color; it shares color with the mottled background, but the texture of vase and background are very different. So we used the Quick Selection tool ▼ dragging out and up from the center of the vase, first to the upper right edge and then to the upper left **3e**. We didn't bother to deselect the leaves that overlap the vase; in the duplicate Black & White layer we wouldn't change the tone that represented the green leaves, so the leaves would be treated the same in both conversions.

With your selection complete, target the lower Black & White layer by clicking its thumbnail in the Layers panel and fill it with black (Edit > Fill > Black). The mask will block this layer's effect on the vase **3f**. Target the upper Black & White layer, and darken the vase; we used the scrubber to drag left, and then moved the Magentas slider left to darken more without creating artifacts **3g**. Duplicate the file and change its mode to Grayscale. The final Grayscale result is shown at the top of page 214.

FIND OUT MORE

▼ Choosing the right selection tool **page 48**

AVOIDING NOISE

A few simple "rules of thumb" can help minimize noise and other artifacts in a Black & White adjustment:

• In a noisy image, reduce noise in the color file before you begin. Use Lens Corrections in Camera Raw or Photoshop's Reduce Noise filter, for instance.

• Keep color transitions smoother by arranging the Black & White sliders so a line drawn through them would form a smooth curve, rather than a wild zigzag. Remember that the series of colors is really "circular" like the traditional color wheel, so the Magentas at the bottom are as much "next to" the Reds as the Yellows are.

• Watch the image at 100% view on-screen as you work, so you can detect noise developing and adjust the sliders to head it off.

Controlled Recoloring

YOU'LL FIND THE FILES
in (wow) > Wow Project Files > Chapter 4 >
Controlled Recoloring:
  • Red Shirt-Before.psd (to start)
  • Green Shirt-After.psd (to compare)
  • Yellow Shirt-After.psd (to compare)

OPEN THESE PANELS
from the Window menu, for instance
  • Tools • Layers • Channels • Info

OVERVIEW
Add a swatch of your custom color
• Select the element you want to recolor
CMYK : Add a Solid Color Fill layer in
Hue mode in your custom color • Adjust
luminosity and saturation if necessary
until the color matches the swatch
Lab : Convert to Lab Color • Add Color
Samplers • Add a Curves layer and adjust
to match colors "by the numbers"

For many Photoshop print applications it makes sense to work in RGB color, then make a duplicate file in CMYK mode at the end when you need to save the image for printing. But if your goal is to match a particular custom color — for a clothing catalog, for example — it works better to tackle the project in CMYK from the beginning. That way the swatch you're trying to match is a stable target — one that you can check with a process color chart and that won't have a chance to change during an RGB-to-CMYK conversion.

Another option that can often produce better results with less work is to go from CMYK to Lab Color for the color changes and then back to CMYK for printing. Lab Color is the most versatile mode for changing colors because it makes it so easy to control luminosity (lightness or darkness) independently of hue and saturation.

Thinking the project through. For this project we'll first change the shirt color from red to green in CMYK Color mode. **CMYK works well for colors that are about equal in intensity (lightness and saturation), even if they are very different in hue.** Then we'll start with the red shirt again, this time changing it to yellow using Lab Color. **Lab Color works much better than other color modes when there's a marked difference in**

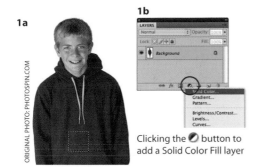

1a

1b

Clicking the ⊘ button to add a Solid Color Fill layer

Making a selection for the swatch

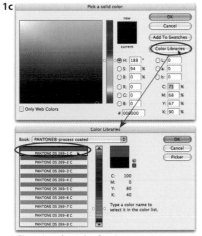

1c

Choosing the color for the swatch layer

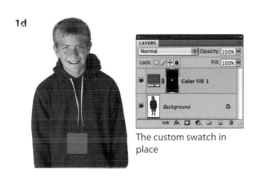

1d

The custom swatch in place

2a

The Options bar for the Quick Selection tool. We used a 30-pixel brush tip.

saturation or lightness between the original and the new color. For this kind of color change, the Lab Color process is so much easier and more successful than trying to work in CMYK or RGB that it's well worth the venture into a less familiar color space!

THE GREEN SHIRT (WORKING IN CMYK MODE)

1 Making an on-screen swatch. Open the photo you want to recolor; in the **Red Shirt-Before.psd** file we wanted to change the color of the sweatshirt to a custom green. Duplicate the file (Image > Duplicate) and then close the original; this way you know you won't lose your original file no matter what you do. If the file isn't yet in CMYK mode, choose Edit > Color Settings and *pick the CMYK settings given to you by the printer.* Close the Color Settings dialog and choose Image > Mode > CMYK Color. For this project we'll suppose we received the CMYK file from the client.

Use a Fill layer to make a swatch to use for comparison as you change the shirt color, as follows: Make a selection in the size you want the swatch in an area that's neither heavily shaded nor strongly highlighted; we used the Rectangular Marquee ⬚ **1a**. Then click the "Create new fill or adjustment layer" button ⊘ at the bottom of the Layers panel and choose **Solid Color 1b**. When the "Pick a solid color" dialog opens, choose the color you want to match; we needed to match Pantone Process 269-1, so we clicked on the "Color Libraries" button **1c**, chose "PANTONE® process coated" from the Book menu, scrolled to 269 1 and clicked it, then clicked "OK" to finish adding the Fill layer **1d**.

2 Selecting the element to recolor. Next select the item you want to recolor. ▼ There's a selection for the shirt stored as an alpha channel in the **Red Shirt.psd** file; we made it as described next and as adjusted in step 4. (You can shortcut the selecting and masking process if you like by simply Ctrl/⌘-clicking the thumbnail for the "Shirt" channel in the Channels panel to load it as a selection, and then skip to step 3.)

We targeted the *Background* by clicking its thumbnail in the Layers panel. Because our subject — the shirt — was distinct from the colors that surrounded it — the white background, the boy's skin, and the gray shorts — we chose the Quick Selection tool ✎, turned on Auto-Enhance in the Options bar to get good edges, and turned off Sample All Layers to use only the *Background* image **2a**. ▼ We clicked near the center of the shirt front and

FIND OUT MORE

▼ Choosing a selection method **page 48**

▼ Using the Quick Selection tool **page 49**

2b

With **Sample All Layers turned off,** we clicked the Quick Selection tool near the middle of the shirt front and dragged almost to the edge at the shoulder.

2c

With the Alt/Option key held down, the + inside the Quick Selection cursor turned into a –, ready to click on the hand and subtract it from the selection.

2d

Use the Refine Edge dialog to preview the selected area against a contrasting background.

2e

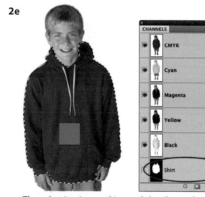

The selection is saved in an alpha channel.

3a

Adding a Solid Color Fill layer in Hue mode to color the shirt

dragged up and outward toward one shoulder **2b**. (If your first click-drag leaves part of the shirt unselected, click-drag again, from the center toward the other shoulder, for instance.) Our selection included one hand, so we held down Alt/Option and clicked on the hand to subtract it **2c**.

When you've made your selection, choose Select > Refine Edge to check its accuracy. In the Refine Edge dialog, first click the "Default" button to reset all parameters. Then click a button that contrasts with the background of your original image (we clicked "On Black" to contrast with white) **2d**. You may want to refine the selection now if you see overall problems with the edges. ▼ We saw just a few problem areas (two small triangles of white showed below the hood, and part of a thumb was still selected. Since these were local rather than general problems, we would wait to correct them "by hand" in the mask we were about to make. Click "OK" to close the Refine Edge dialog. Store the selection in an alpha channel (Select > Save Selection) ▼ so you won't have to build it again if you make a mistake **2e**.

3 Recoloring in CMYK. With the selection active and the image layer targeted in the Layers panel, add another Solid Color Fill layer in your custom color as in step 1, but this time, hold down the Alt/Option key as you click the ⊘ button and choose Solid Color, to open the New Layer dialog box **3a**, where you can name the layer and choose the blend mode — Hue — and then click "OK." Choose the same custom color as in step 1 **3b**.

4 Checking the mask. At this point it will be easy to see whether your mask is a perfect fit. In this example, if you see red at the edges of the green shirt, or if you see green extending beyond the shirt, click the mask thumbnail for the custom color layer in the Layers panel and adjust the mask **4**.▼

3b

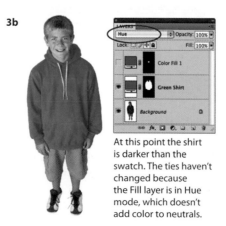

At this point the shirt is darker than the swatch. The ties haven't changed because the Fill layer is in Hue mode, which doesn't add color to neutrals.

FIND OUT MORE

▼ Refining selection edges **page 59**

▼ Saving selections **page 60**

▼ Cleaning up masks **page 59**

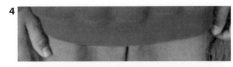

To remove the green from the thumb, we targeted the mask and painted the thumb with black, using the Brush with a soft brush tip and reduced Opacity, both set in the Options bar. A thin red line remained at the bottom of the shirt (top). We loaded the mask for the "Green Shirt" layer as a selection (by Ctrl/⌘-clicking its thumbnail in the Layers panel) and nudged the selection down slightly with the ↓ key. Then Alt/Option-Shift-dragging with the Rectangular Marquee selected the intersection of the shirt selection and the rectangle (bottom), and we filled this selected part of the mask with white.

5a

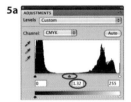

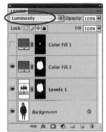

Adding a Levels Adjustment layer in Luminosity mode just above the original image and adjusting gamma until the green shirt matches the custom color swatch

5b

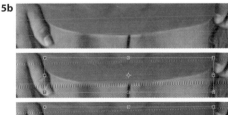

With the Levels layer's mask targeted in the Layers panel as in figure 5a, we selected the bottom of the shirt, pressed Ctrl/⌘-T (for Edit > Free Transform) and dragged the bottom handle of the Transform frame up "just a hair" to shrink the Levels layer's mask and eliminate the light streak.

5 "Tweaking" the recoloring. Now compare your custom color swatch to the new color of the element you selected (the shirt). If your recolored element is just a little lighter or darker than the swatch (as ours was; refer to 3b), you'll need to make a change to the luminance. To fix the problem of the green shirt being too dark, we used a simple Levels adjustment to lighten the original red of the underlying shirt: We loaded the shirt selection by Ctrl/⌘-clicking the thumbnail for its mask in the Fill layer. Then we clicked on the *Background* thumbnail in the Layers panel so the Adjustment layer we were about to add would come in just above the *Background,* where it would act on the original photo only. We Alt/Option-clicked the ⬤ button at the bottom of the panel and chose Levels, putting the new layer in Luminosity mode so that it would adjust only brightness when we changed its settings. (In CS4 the Alt/Option assist isn't necessary, because you can set the new layer's blend mode even after the Levels dialog is open. With the Adjustments panel open (Window > Adjustments), you can simply click on the ⟰ icon to open the Levels dialog; put the new layer in Luminosity mode using the Layers panel's blend mode list, and adjust Levels settings to taste.) In the Input Levels section of the dialog box, we dragged the center (gray, gamma) slider to the left to lighten the shirt **5a** and clicked "OK." We now had a light streak at the bottom of the shirt — the mask for the shirt, as altered in step 4, needed to be changed again for the Levels layer; we shortened it **5b**. The results are shown at the top of page 218.

If, after lightening or darkening, your recolored element still looks just a little "hotter" (more saturated) or duller (less saturated) than your swatch, you can add a masked Hue/Saturation Adjustment layer in Saturation mode below the swatch layer and adjust the Saturation slider. *Note:* "Tweaking" the color with a Saturation adjustment works well only for minor changes; with larger changes it may be hard to keep neutral highlights and shadows from picking up color. If your recoloring requires fairly big changes in tone or changes in saturation, the Lab Color method (next) is likely to work better.

THE YELLOW SHIRT (WORKING IN LAB COLOR MODE)

For making a color change, Lab Color mode excels at preserving smooth transitions of color and shading. Lab is a huge space, encompassing more colors than any monitor can display or any press can print. But the feature that makes Lab especially useful for a drastic color change is that it lends itself so well to controlling luminosity separately from hue and saturation. You

When it isn't necessary to match a specific custom color, a quick way to change the color of a selected area of an image is to use the Hue slider in a Hue/Saturation adjustment. With Colorize turned on in the Hue/Saturation dialog box, you can ensure that all the colors in the original will change toward the particular color you choose, which shows up in the bottom color bar. Without the Colorize option, all colors would simply shift a certain amount around the color wheel. This would mean that if highlights or shadows in the original image had their own color cast, the color-shifted highlights and shadows might end up looking the wrong color, both in relation to the new color and in relation to the highlights and shadows elsewhere in the image.

The Pantone 309-6 swatch added to **Red Shirt-Before.psd**

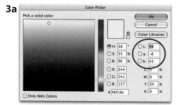
Converting from CMYK to Lab Color mode

Finding the Lab numbers for Pantone 309-6

can make big changes in color (from a dark red to a light yellow, for instance) while maintaining detail in the shadows and highlights, and keeping neutral colors neutral.

Although you can try using the "matching by eye" method we used for CMYK, there's an advantage to "doing it by the numbers" in Lab — you can count on a stable color match, no matter what inks are used to print the piece or what light it's viewed under (see "When To Do It by the Numbers" on page 225). As you'll see, in Lab mode it's really easy to use the numbers.

1 Making a swatch. Open the photo you want to recolor; again we started with the **Red Shirt-Before.psd** file. Follow step 1 for "The Green Shirt" (starting on page 219) to duplicate the file for safekeeping and make a swatch of the custom color **1**; our custom yellow was Pantone process color 309-6.

2 Converting to Lab Color. To convert the image from CMYK to Lab Color, choose Image > Mode > Lab Color **2**. Choose "Don't flatten" in the warning box that opens — the layers of this file are image layers in Normal mode, and this causes no problem in the conversion, despite the warning.

Since the Lab color space was designed to encompass all the colors of all RGB and CMYK color spaces and then some, you won't need to worry about losing image data in the conversion to Lab. And since you'll be working in a very limited range of prescribed colors, you won't generate any colors that might cause a difference between your Lab image and the CMYK space when you convert back to CMYK.

3 Finding the Lab numbers. To gain the advantages of an exact match "by the numbers" as we're doing here, you need to know the Lab composition for your custom color. In the Layers panel, double-click on the thumbnail for the swatch layer to open the Color Picker. Read the "L," "a," and "b" values and make a note of them **3a** — for our yellow, "L" is 94, "a" is –8, and "b" is 43.

Before going further, a brief explanation of what Lab numbers represent might help **3b**. In Lab Color mode, **"L" values (for Luminosity)** range from 0 to 100, with 100 being white. The "a" and "b" components each represent an axis with opposite colors at the ends. The **"a" continuum is from Green to Magenta,** and the **"b" axis goes from Blue to Yellow**. The **"warm" colors Magenta and Yellow are denoted by positive numbers;** the **"cool" colors Green and Blue are negative numbers**. The full range of "a" and "b" values is from –128 to +127. But most of the colors in the CMYK gamut have values between –80 and +80. As you

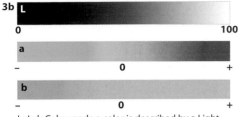

3b

L
0   100

a
–   0   +

b
–   0   +

In Lab Color mode a color is described by a Lightness value between 0 and 100 and by positive or negative values for the "a" and "b" color channels.

3c Sample Size: 3 by 3 Average

Setting up the Color Sampler tool

3d

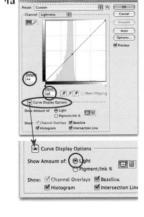

Color Samplers are added to mark a spot on the shirt and one on the tie, so the same two spots can be sampled repeatedly for adjusting Curves.

4a

Ctrl/⌘-click on the spot on the red shirt that's marked by Color Sampler #1 to mark this color on the l ightness curve. Since you haven't changed the curve yet, the Input and Output values are the same. To match our curves, make sure Curves Display Options is set to Show Amount of Light. In CS3 (shown here) this is done by clicking the arrow next to Curve Display Options to expand the dialog and clicking the "Light" button.

proceed along each axis from one color extreme to its opposite, you pass through the point where the opposites cancel each other out; this point, **zero (0) on the "a" or "b" axis, is neutral** (colorless — white, black, or gray, depending on whether the "L" value is 100, 0, or in between).

After you click "OK" to close the Color Picker, take a look at some examples of Lab numbers: Choose the Color Sampler tool (find it sharing a space in the Tools panel with the Eyedropper, or type Shift-I); in the Options bar's Sample Size menu **3c** choose "3 by 3 Average" or "5 by 5 Average" (to get a typical color sample), not "Point Sample" (which could pick up color from an off-color pixel). Click on a "flat color" area of the red shirt to place one Sampler there; then click on one of the ties to place a second Sampler in this neutral area **3d**. If we click on the *Background* thumbnail in the Layers panel and look in the Info panel at the numbers for the red shirt (Color Sampler #1), we see that the "L" value is 44, slightly darker than the middle tone (your value may differ if you put your Sampler in a slightly different place). The "a" channel (53) is quite positive, which means the color has a strong Magenta component. The "b" value is also quite positive (37), or quite Yellow, but somewhat less than Magenta, the two channels making the sweatshirt an intense red. To make the sweatshirt yellow to match our Pantone 309-6 swatch, we need to make the Luminosity value much lighter (94, from page 222), the "a" channel somewhat Green (–8), and the "b" channel even more Yellow (43). The gray ties (Color Sampler #2) are nearly neutral in color ("a" is 0 and "b" is 1), but the Luminosity is darker than white (83). Our client's yellow sweatshirts have near-white ties, so this will need to be lightened.

4 Using Curves in Lab. To make the color change, we'll use a Curves Adjustment layer. In order to restrict your color change to the sweatshirt, in the Channels panel Ctrl/⌘-click on the "Shirt" channel to load the premade selection. Then click on the "Create new fill or adjustment layer" button at the bottom of the Layers panel and choose Curves. Move your cursor over to the marker for Color Sampler #1 on the red shirt and Ctrl/⌘-click on it to set a point on the Lightness curve **4a, 4b**. If the bottom gradient has black on the left and white on the right as ours does, the Curves you are about to make will match ours, with darker values (lower numbers) on the left and bottom. If you are set up the opposite way, to change settings so you can follow our example, follow the directions in figure **4a** for CS3 or **4b** for CS4. Now, for the anchor point you set on the Lightness curve, you'll keep the Input number the same

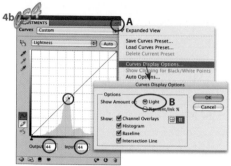

In Photoshop CS4 you set the Curves Display Options a little differently than in CS3: Choose Curves Display Options from the Adjustments panel's menu **A**, and then click the Light button in the Curves Display Options dialog **B**.

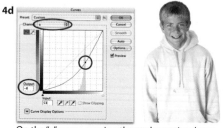

Typing "94" (the Lightness value for Pantone 309-6) into the Output field lightens the shirt and the ties.

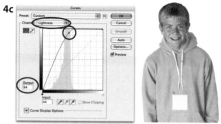

On the "a" curve, moving the anchor point downward removes magenta from the shirt color.

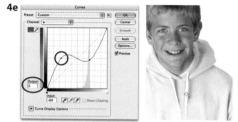

Adding a second point for the ties and adjusting it to keep the ties neutral

but change the Output value to 94; an easy way to do this is to type 94 into the Output field **4c**. Notice that the ties have also lightened, which is fine.

PRECISE CURVES ADJUSTMENTS

To change the Output value of an anchor point in Curves, while keeping the Input value the same:

- If you know the precise Output value you want, type it into the Output field.
- If you don't know exactly what Output value you're aiming for, use the ↑ or ↓ arrow key to nudge the value up or down (add the Shift key for bigger moves).

Next choose "a" from the Curves dialog's Channel menu. Set the anchor point as you did for the "Lightness" channel, and change the Output number to –8, which we noted in step 3 as the "a" component of our custom color **4d**. This change has moved the ties away from neutral. Set another anchor point, for the ties, by clicking on the spot marked by Color Sampler #2, and change the Output value to 0 (neutral, since we don't want a magenta or green cast) **4e**. Straight lines in the Curves dialog are best for maintaining smooth transitions between colors, so drag the ends of the "a" curve to straighten the line **4f**.

Already we can see that the sweatshirt is yellow, but we need it to be Pantone 309-6 yellow. Select the "b" channel in the Curves dialog's Channel menu, set an anchor point for the shirt, and change the "b" Output value to 43 (more Yellow). Again set the anchor point for the ties and adjust to near neutral (we tapped the ↑ key to change the Output value to 2), and move the two endpoints to straighten the line **4g**.

With the color change complete — we can compare "by eye" using the swatch and also "by the numbers" in the Info panel. Check the highlights and shadows. We felt the shadows were too deep for this light, soft yellow. Fortunately, in Lab we can lighten the shadows without disturbing the color at all. We returned to the "L" channel and moved the black point anchor (bottom left in our setup) straight up using the ↑ key until the shadows lightened enough to look more realistic to us **4h**.

5 Checking the mask. Check the masking as in step 4 in "The Green Shirt" (page 220). The Curves layer had washed out the detail in the grommets and ties. We painted the layer mask with black to restore the grommets. We clicked the *Background* thumbnail in the Layers panel and selected the ties by clicking one with the Magic Wand (Tolerance 32, Contiguous and Anti-alias on, Sample All Layers off) and Shift-clicking the other.

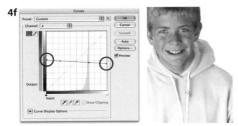

4f

Moving the end points to straighten the "a" curve maintains a smooth color transition from the intense to the neutral colors. In this instance, it takes a green tinge out of the shadows.

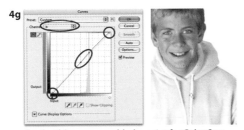

4g

For the "b" curve we added a point for Color Sampler #1 and increased its Output value from 37 to 43. We added a point for Color Sampler #2 and changed its Output value from 1 to 2. We moved the endpoints to straighten the line. Our "b" curve was now steeper than it had been before we started. A steep color channel curve in Lab improves color definition.

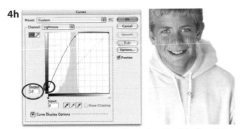

4h

In the Lightness channel, moving the black point anchor straight up makes the shadows lighter.

5

Painting the Curves layer's mask with black restores the grommets. The ties are selected and filled (Edit > Fill, Use: Black at 10% Opacity).

Then we targeted the Curves mask again and filled the selection with light gray **5**.

Saving and converting. To keep your Lab Color file in case further changes are required, save the file in PSD format while you're still in Lab mode. Then turn off visibility for the swatch layer (by clicking its 👁 icon in the Layers panel) and choose Image > Duplicate, turning on the Duplicate Merged Layers Only option in the Duplicate dialog. (Adjustment layers don't always convert neatly between Lab and RGB or CMYK, and merging before converting avoids that complication.) If you were working in your target CMYK color space before you converted to Lab at step 2, simply choose Image > Mode > CMYK Color to get back to it. Otherwise, choose Edit > Convert to Profile and pick the profile you need according to instructions from the printer. Our result is shown at the top of page 218. 🖋

WHEN TO DO IT BY THE NUMBERS

When your goal is to match a particular CMYK process color, much of the "art" of the match is in choosing the right area to compare to your custom color — a well-lit area, not shadowed but also not blown out. This can be difficult in a photo of clothing, with folds, drapes, or a pronounced weave, or in an image of a shiny car. Since choosing the right area is subjective — there's no practical way around it — doesn't it make sense to do the entire process by eye, as in "The Green Shirt" starting on page 219? Often, this is a great way to go.

But an argument can be made for moving into Lab Color mode and matching the numbers, as in "The Yellow Shirt," starting on page 221, even when the color change isn't terribly drastic. An example would be if the item whose color you're changing has to match something that appears near it on the printed page. Here's why: There are many ways to formulate the "same" color using CMYK inks, as explained on page 193. So the color you arrive at by eye may have a slightly different CMYK composition than the one you're trying to match, even though it looks the same on-screen, especially given the tonal variations in cloth or metal.

However, the difference may be noticeable on the page, especially if the standard color is printed nearby. To add to the risk, some CMYK inks look different under different lighting conditions. If the color you arrive at "by eye" has a different CMYK composition than the "same" color that appears nearby, differences in the ink proportions might become apparent under different lighting conditions. For instance, a change in lighting may make a bigger change in how the cyan ink looks than it does in the magenta, so if the two "matched" colors contain different proportions of cyan and magenta, they will become *more* different from each other when the lighting is changed. But if the color formulas for the two instances of the color are exactly the same, both instances will make exactly the same shift and will still match in any light

Adding Spot Color

YOU'LL FIND THE FILES
in  WOW > Wow Project Files > Chapter 4 > Adding Spot Color:
- Spot Color-Before.psd (to start)
- Spot Color-After.psd (to compare)

OPEN THESE PANELS
from the Window menu, for instance:
- Tools • Layers • Channels

OVERVIEW
Prepare a Grayscale or color image • Create knockouts in the image where you want custom colors to print at full intensity without overprinting the image • Create a spot color channel for each custom color you want to include • To overprint a tint of spot color, select the area and in the spot color channel fill it with Black at reduced opacity • Prepare a comp from the on-screen preview • Consult your printer and make any necessary changes

ORIGINAL IMAGES: PHOTOSPIN.COM

1a

We started with an assembled grayscale background image and added the logotype as a Shape layer.

Custom color — or spot color — can be a great option when you need to exactly match a standard branding color or to prepare a file for screen printing a T-shirt or a poster. It's the way to go when you want a fluorescent or metallic accent, or that brilliant hue or solid pastel that you can't reliably achieve with process inks. And of course, if a project already includes spot color, you can take advantage of it to enhance your illustrations without adding to the printing cost.

Thinking the project through. For a hang-tag for a clothing company (shown above), we'll add the brand's colors to a black-and-white image. (You can use a similar approach for adding spot color to a full-color image.) The two inks from the Pantone Solid Coated series (Pantone 708, a pink, and Pantone 266, a blue-violet) will be used as spot tints in the photo itself. In those areas the inks will print at partial intensity (a screen tint), to color the black-and-white image.

In addition, the logotype will appear in Pantone 266 with a white glow around it, and we'll use Pantone 708 for a band at the edge of the tag. We'll make knockouts (white areas free of black ink) in the grayscale image for the logotype and the edge, so the spot inks will print at full strength in those areas. We'll also need knockouts anywhere custom-color elements overlap each other, so the colors won't overprint — the pink will be knocked out where the purple logotype overlaps the pink gradient.

1b

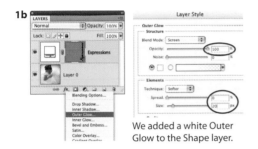

We added a white Outer Glow to the Shape layer.

2a

Adding a "reveal all" layer mask to the image layer

2b

Setting options for the Gradient tool

2c

With the layer mask targeted, we dragged the Gradient tool from right to left across the logotype.

1 Preparing the artwork. Create your background image. For the **Spot Color-Before.psd** file, we selected the child from a color photo.▼ We added an abstract background, then used a Black & White Adjustment layer to "translate" the image to black-and-white and a Curves layer to lighten the image overall; we flattened the file (Layer > Flatten Image) and chose Image > Mode > Grayscale to finish the conversion. (With Black & White, you can control how light or dark a gray each color becomes when the file is "translated" to black-and-white.)▼ The type was set in the Bickham Script font, then converted to a Shape layer (Layer > Type > Convert To Shape) and rotated to vertical (Edit > Transform Path > Rotate 90° CCW) **1a**. To create the white glow around the logotype, we clicked the "Add a layer style" button *fx* at the bottom of the Layers panel, chose Outer Glow, and set up the Glow, changing Opacity to 100% and Size to 20 px **1b**.▼

2 Creating knockouts in the grayscale image. The white Shape layer will automatically knock out the grayscale image to create white space for the custom-color logotype. To create the knockout for the pink edge of the tag, target the photo layer and add a "reveal all" layer mask by clicking the "Add layer mask" button at the bottom of the Layers panel **2a**. Then choose the Gradient tool and in the Options bar **2b** choose the Black, White Gradient (by default it's the third swatch in the pop-out Gradient picker that opens when you click the tiny triangle to the right of the gradient bar).

To make a transition on the mask from black (to hide the image and create the knockout for the edge) to white (where you want the image to show), click the layer mask's thumbnail in the Layers panel to target it. Then position the cursor approximately on the (vertical) baseline of the type (the point where you want the solid pink to begin to fade into the image), and Shift-drag to the left, stopping at about the top of the letter "s" **2c**, **2d**.

3 Creating the first spot color channel. You now have white or transparency in your image everywhere the solid custom inks will print at full strength, and also in the glow, where no ink will print. You can use these knockouts to build the spot color channels. First we made the channel for the purple logotype: Load the logotype as a selection by Ctrl/⌘-clicking the logotype layer's thumbnail in the Layers panel **3a**. With the selection active, in the Channels panel, click the menu button ▼≡ in the upper right corner and choose

FIND OUT MORE

▼ Selection methods
  page 47

▼ Converting to grayscale **page 214**

▼ Adding Glow effects
  page 506

2d

The soft-edged black band in the layer mask clears the edge for the Pantone 708 ink. On-screen, the gray checkerboard represents transparency.

3a

The logotype is loaded as a selection by Ctrl/⌘-clicking the thumbnail for the Shape layer in the Layers panel.

3b

With the selection active, a custom color channel is added to the file.

3c

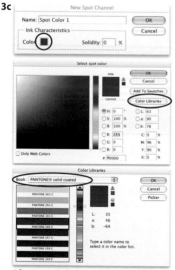

After you click the color swatch (top) and the "Color Libraries" button (middle), choose the PANTONE® solid coated series of colors. Choose a color for the new Spot channel; you can do this by quickly typing the number code; we used 266.

New Spot Channel **3b**. Choose a custom color by clicking the swatch in the New Spot Channel dialog box to open the Color Picker (labeled "Select spot color:"), then clicking the "Color Libraries" button and choosing a color (we chose the PANTONE® Solid Coated series and Pantone 266) **3c**; click "OK" to close the Color Picker. In the New Spot Channel dialog box you can set the Solidity; we left it at 0% since the printer told us this ink was quite transparent, allowing other inks to show through it **3d** (see the "Previewing Spot Colors" tip on page 232). Click "OK" to close the New Spot Channel dialog box. Since there was an active selection when you chose New Spot Channel, its shape was used in making the channel, and the selection filled with black. Black in a Spot Color channel represents where the custom ink will print at 100% coverage.

4 Tinting some areas of the spot color channel. With both the Gray and Pantone 266 channels now visible and the Pantone 266 channel targeted in the Channels panel, select the area you want to tint; we used the Lasso ⌀ to select the scalloped hair clip **4a**.▼ Add the tint to the spot channel by choosing Edit > Fill > Use: Black and adjusting the Opacity setting; we used 40% Opacity and clicked "OK." We used a combination of tools to select the second clip and filled it with 40% Black also **4b**.

FIND OUT MORE
▼ Selection methods
page 47

5 Adding the second spot color channel. For the Pantone 708 (pink) channel, we would need to put down the ink for the edge panel but cut out the area where the logotype and its glow overlapped the panel; that way the purple ink for the type wouldn't have to overprint the pink of the edge, and the white

3d

With the selection active, a custom color channel is added to the file.

4a

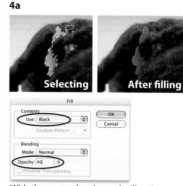

With the spot color channel still active, we used the Lasso ⌀ to select one part of the clip (top left), then held down the Shift key as we selected the second part of the clip. Filling the selection with Black at 40% Opacity tinted the clip with 40% Pantone 266.

The Solidity value you set in Photoshop's New Spot Channel dialog box is designed to simulate on-screen how the color will look when it's printed. At 100% Solidity the spot color will appear to cover other inks virtually completely; at 0% the color will appear quite transparent. The Solidity setting doesn't actually affect the density of the printed ink; it's just for preview purposes. Generally, pastel colors (which contain opaque white), dark inks (which contain black), and metallics are more opaque; purer colors and, obviously, varnish are more transparent. As you start your spot color project, an experienced printer can help you make the best educated guess about Solidity settings for an accurate preview.

Setting Solidity at 0% works well for previewing many PANTONE® solid coated inks. For the PANTONE® metallic and pastel series, using a high Solidity gives a more accurate preview.

4b

For the second clip we clicked with the Elliptical Marquee ⬭ in the center of one large bead, starting to drag and then pressing Shift (to select a perfect circle) and Alt/Option (to center the selection on the starting point). To add the second bead, we held down the Shift key, began to drag from the center of the second bead, then released the Shift key momentarily and pressed Shift and Alt/Option again to finish the second circular selection as shown above. We then used the Lasso ⬭ (with the Shift key) to add other parts of the clip to the selection before filling with a 40% tint.

5a

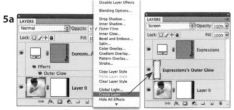

Using the *fx* context-sensitive menu for the logotype layer (left), to separate the Outer Glow (right) and make it available for selecting

glow would remain white. To make this knockout we could load the edge as a selection, then subtract the logotype and its glow, and fill what remained of the selection with black in a new Spot channel.

The glow is currently an effect in a Layer Style. If you Ctrl/⌘-click the logotype layer's thumbnail in the Layers panel, the logotype will be loaded as a selection, but without the glow; we saw this in step 3. To turn the glow into pixels so its thumbnail can be Ctrl/⌘-clicked to load it as a selection, choose Layer > Layer Style > Create Layer **5a**.

Now create a selection for the second (pink) Spot channel: Ctrl/⌘-click the layer mask thumbnail for the photo layer to load the mask as a selection, and then invert (Ctrl/⌘-Shift-I) to select the edge **5b**. Then depress the Alt/Option key as you Ctrl/⌘-click on the logotype layer, and continue holding Alt/Option down as you Ctrl/⌘-click on the glow layer (the added Alt/Option key will subtract the logotype and then the glow from the edge selection). Now when you choose New Spot Channel and set up the new pink channel (Pantone 708), it will automatically include a knockout for the logotype and glow **5c**.

To tint the rose, zoom in and select it (we used the Lasso ⬭). Fill the selection with a tint; we used a 40% tint here, using the same method as for the clips in step 4 (Edit > Fill, using Black at 40% Opacity) **5d**.

6 Proofing. A reliable way to produce a comp for your client or a guide for the printer is to use the screen-capture function built into your System software to capture your on-screen preview **6**:

5b

With the layer mask targeted, make a selection based on the layer mask (left), then subtract the logotype (center) and the glow (right).

5c

A detail of the Pantone 708 channel, viewed alone (left) and with the other channels

5d

Selecting and filling the rose with a 40% tint in the Pantone 708 channel

6

Before making this screen capture as a comp for the printer, we added a Solid Color Fill layer below the image layer by using the "Create new fill or adjustment layer" button at the bottom of the Layers panel and then dragging this new layer's thumbnail down below the image layer (if your image is a *Background,* you'll first need to turn it into a regular layer by double-clicking its name in the Layers panel and clicking "OK" in the New Layer box).

7a

With the layer mask targeted, we selected and stretched the black edge to hide more of the background image so the pink would print cleanly.

7b

We viewed the Gray and the Pantone 708 channels, targeted the Pantone 708 channel, and used the Eraser to lighten the tint in the darkest and lightest areas of the rose, to bring out the petals. In the Eraser's Options bar we chose the Brush option, picked a small soft brush tip, and set the Opacity to 15%.

- On a Windows-based system, press **Alt-Print Screen** to copy the active window to the clipboard. In Photoshop create a new file (File > New) and paste (Ctrl-V).

- On a Mac, press ⌘-**Shift-4** and drag to highlight the area you want to capture. The file will be saved to your Desktop as "Picture number" using the lowest number not already in use in another Picture file name.

7 Tweaking the file. Once your custom-color Photoshop file is set up and you've produced a comp, your printer may be able to help you improve the result. We showed our screen-capture comp and our Photoshop file to the printer, who suggested that we "push" the black ink farther back from the edge, to get a "cleaner" fade for the pink. We targeted the layer mask for the photo layer and used the Rectangular Marquee [ ] to select an area from the edge inward beyond the fade. Then we pressed Ctrl/⌘-T (for Edit > Free Transform) and dragged the left side handle of the Transform frame to the left to expand the knockout for the edge **7a**. We double-clicked inside the frame to complete the Transform.

Another suggestion was to partially erase some of the pink rose, "to let the black ink 'shape' the flower," he said. Working on the Pantone 708 (pink) channel, we used the Eraser ⌀ with a small, soft brush tip and a low Opacity setting in the Options bar, to take away some of the pink in the darkest and lightest areas of the rose **7b**.

Printing. When a comp has been approved, the file can be output directly from Photoshop. Or place it in a page layout program; one way is to save a copy of the file in Photoshop DCS 2.0 format; turn on the As a Copy and Spot Colors options, but turn off the Alpha Channels and Layers options. Ask your printer for advice on the other settings. *wow!*

PREVIEWING OPAQUE INKS

In a Grayscale file with Spot channels added, Photoshop's on-screen preview is designed to show how the printed piece will look if the inks are laid down in the order they appear in the Channels panel — that is, if the black ink in the top channel prints first, then the ink in the next channel down, and so on. To preview the effect of laying down a spot color before the black, you'll need to convert the file from Grayscale to Multichannel (Image > Mode > Multichannel), so you can freely drag Spot channel thumbnails above the Black ink channel.

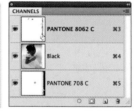

When you want to preview an opaque metallic ink (for instance, Pantone 8062) that will print before the other inks, convert from Grayscale to Multichannel mode and reorder the channels. A screen capture of the preview shows how the inks should knock out or overprint.

Bruce Dragoo "Airbrushes" with the Gradient Tool

WITH A BACKGROUND IN CLASSICAL PAINTING and drawing techniques, Bruce Dragoo didn't pick up an airbrush until his career as a fine artist was well under way. "I was discouraged from using the airbrush," Bruce reports. "It just wasn't considered a fine arts tool. I held off until I just absolutely *had* to use it. And when I did, I found it was exactly the tool I needed."

FIND OUT MORE
▼ Using Gradients **page 174**
▼ Blend modes **page 181**
▼ Adjustment layers **page 245**

Bruce uses Photoshop's Gradient tool in a way that's reminiscent of airbrushing, layering gradients to produce backgrounds for his scanned graphite sketches. Here he shares some of his gradient-layering techniques. The finished illustrations can be seen larger on pages 422 and 423.

As a background for **Rhino Sketch** (below) Bruce started with a Linear "landscape" gradient **A**. ▼ Then he added a pronounced vignette: He Shift-dragged with the Rectangular Marquee tool to select a square area and filled this selection with a Radial Foreground-to-Transparent gradient with Reverse checked in the Options bar. Then he used the Free Transform command (Ctrl/⌘-T), dragging a side handle until the gradient was as wide as the canvas, and put the layer in

Multiply mode **B**. ▼ He pushed the colors toward neutral by adding a Hue/Saturation Adjustment layer and reducing Saturation **C, D**. ▼

In **Faru and Mom** (below) a single Radial gradient creates the background. Centered at the horizon to the right of center in the image, the gradient defines the sky with the sun low on the horizon **A**. In the final illustration, the addition of a few airbrushed streaks of cloud shifts the viewer's impression from "cool Photoshop gradient" to "beautiful light" **B**.

For **Sleeping** (below) Bruce started with a slightly altered version of the Chrome gradient that comes with Photoshop **A**, layering it over a white background and reducing its Opacity to 83%. To create a "purple haze," he added a Radial gradient from yellow through pink to violet, centered near the bottom of the canvas **B**. He put the layer in Multiply mode at 51% Opacity **C**. After adding and coloring the scanned sketches for the rhinos and plants, he added another copy of the purple haze in a layer above to unify the composition **D**. Finally, he used a Hue/Saturation layer to neutralize the color somewhat **E**.

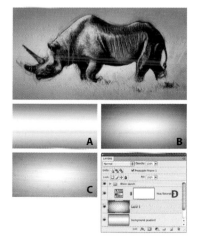

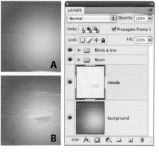

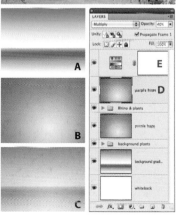

For this portrait of *Rachel*, **Jack Davis** started with a color photo of his model in dance recital makeup to develop a high-key image that captures her glowing personality. In Photoshop Davis converted the original RGB photo **A** to a CMYK color space — Edit > Convert to Profile > U.S. Web Coated (SWOP) v2. This conversion, which uses Medium Black Generation and GCR, produced a Black channel that defined the important features in the portrait, along with the three other black-and-white versions of the image in the Cyan, Magenta, and Yellow channels **B**.

Next Davis added a Channel Mixer Adjustment layer to make the conversion from color to black-and-white. In the Channel Mixer dialog **C** he chose the Black channel as his starting point, and clicked the Monochrome button. Then, using the sliders, he added a contribution of 30% from the Magenta channel, which added density to the lips and skin tones. He also added 20% from the Cyan channel, which showed good detail in the hair and eyes because of the overhead blue lighting and eye makeup in the original photo. This addition also somewhat reduced the density of the skin tones that had been added with the Magenta channel **D.**

The next step was to make the image glow with softened highlights, without changing the dark detail in the eyes and hair. Davis started this process by duplicating the developing image in a new layer (Ctrl-Shift-Alt-E in Windows; ⌘-Shift-Option-E on the Mac). Before he blurred the duplicate using the Gaussian Blur filter, he put the layer in Screen mode **E** so he could preview the glowing highlight effect as he experimented in the Gaussian Blur dialog; he watched the effect on the highlights and midtones until he saw what he wanted, ignoring changes in the darkest tones because he planned to protect them, next. After clicking "OK" to close the Gaussian Blur dialog, Davis clicked the *fx* button at the bottom of the Layers panel **F** and chose Blending Options.

In the Blending Options dialog he went to work with the Blend If sliders▼ to limit the contribution of the blurred layer **G**. For This Layer he moved the black point slider inward to eliminate any contribution from the blurred layer's darker tones, then Alt/Option-clicked the slider to split it, and moved the left half back to the left; this smoothed the transition between the tones from this layer that contributed to the image and the tones that didn't.

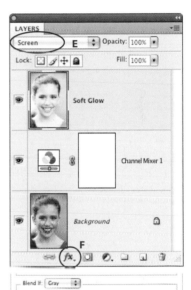

Davis finished the image with a white vignetted edge, adding a new empty layer (Ctrl/⌘-Shift-N) and using the Brush tool ✐ with a large soft brush tip and white paint (type D, then X) to hide distracting detail at the edges and corners of the photo.

FIND OUT MORE

▼ Using the Blend If sliders **page 66**

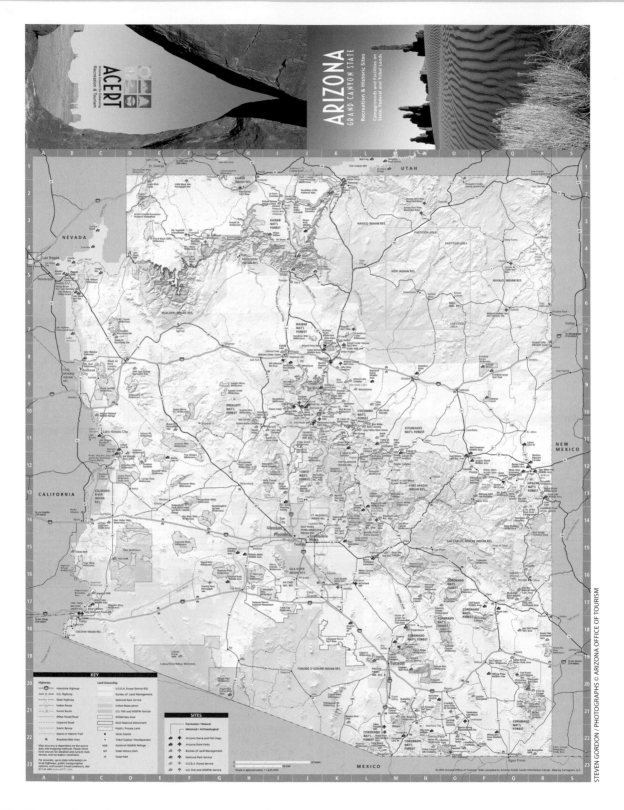

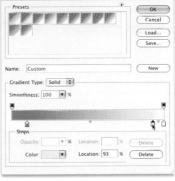

For the **Arizona Recreation and Historical Sites** map, cartographer **Steven Gordon** built a terrain image with colors signifying the federal agencies and tribal nations that own public land in Arizona. He began the terrain image in Natural Scene Designer, software that imports real geographic-elevation data, lets you set the sun angle and other parameters, and turns the data into an image (**www.naturalgfx.com**). After opening the resulting RGB TIFF in Photoshop, he converted the image to gray tones in a CMYK file (Image > Mode > Grayscale, then Image > Mode > CMYK) so he could color it using the CMYK specifications in government publication guidelines for map colors representing federal agency lands.

To prepare for coloring, Gordon placed Illustrator files (File > Place) that he had created earlier from geographic data for each class of public land, using MAPublisher plug-ins (**www.avenza.com**). He decided to use Gradient Map Adjustment layers for coloring the map because each gradient could maintain the unique color for a class of public land while allowing natural variations of color in the terrain shadows and highlights.

Gordon first built each of the Adjustment layers: He made a selection from each layer of the placed Illustrator artwork by Ctrl/⌘-clicking the layer's thumbnail in the Layers panel. Then he clicked the ⊘ button at the bottom of the Layers panel and selected Gradient Map from the pop-up menu. This automatically created an Adjustment layer, masked to color the selected area, and displayed the Gradient Map dialog. At this point Gordon left the Gradient Map dialog unchanged, with the Black, White gradient chosen, and went on to add the next Gradient Map layer.

Once all the Gradient Map Adjustment layers had been created, Gordon made an additional mask for coloring the areas that surround the public lands: He held down the Shift key as he Ctrl/⌘-clicked the thumbnails of all of the placed Illustrator artwork layers; then he inverted the selection (Select > Inverse) and clicked the ⊘ button again to add another Gradient Map Adjustment layer, masked for this surrounding area. Finally, he deleted each of the Illustrator artwork layers by Ctrl/⌘-clicking all their thumbnails and Alt/Option-clicking the 🗑 button at the bottom of the Layers panel.

Now he was ready to begin coloring each Adjustment layer. He double-clicked a Gradient Map thumbnail in the Layers panel to reopen its

Gradient Map dialog and clicked the gradient bar to open the Gradient Editor. Previewing his changes in the document window as he worked, he began designing his custom gradients. He wanted each gradient to start with a dark brown color for terrain shadows, then progress into the distinctive color chosen for the particular class of public land, and end with a pale tint of that color for the highlights. To do this, he clicked below the gradient preview bar to create a third color stop in the gradient. Then he double-clicked each of the three Color stops in turn and entered numbers in the "Select stop color" dialog to mix the colors he needed. Gordon could slide the color stops as he previewed the gradient's effect on the terrain image. When he was satisfied, he typed a name into the Name field of the Gradient Editor and then clicked the "New" button to add the gradient to the current Gradient preset picker.

Gordon followed much the same procedure for all the public land areas. When he completed the terrain image, he saved a flattened copy of the file as a TIFF and placed it in Illustrator, where he added type, symbols, and line work to complete the map.

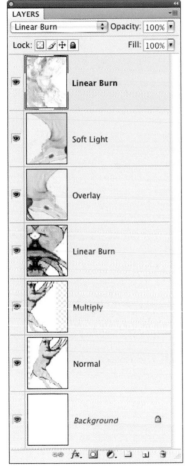

FIND OUT MORE

▼ Transforming
page 67

▼ Tinting with Color
Balance **page 205**

In the Layers panel at the left, we've renamed **Laurie Grace's** layers to show the blend mode used for each layer in *Intrusion 38*. This Photoshop composite retains the gesture of the strokes and the blended color of the art media Grace used in her original paintings.

She started a new file with a white *Background,* to define the size she wanted for the final image. From there her process was a fluid, experimental one of arranging, scaling, duplicating, flipping, and merging layers, all the while experimenting with blend modes.

She copied and pasted a dog from a scanned watercolor **A** and scaled it,▼ until it was "cropped" in a way she liked for a design element.

The second layer was a copy of the first (Ctrl/⌘-J), dragged to one side with the Move tool ▶⊕ and put in Multiply mode (set in the upper left corner of the Layers panel), so the combination of the two layers **B** repeated the lines of the dog element.

The third layer is composed of two more copies of the dog, one flipped horizontally (Edit > Transform > Flip Horizontal) and dragged to the side to form a symmetrical combination of shapes. With the upper of the two layers active, the two were merged (Ctrl/⌘-E), and the merged element flipped vertically and offset to one side, then scaled, and tinted▼ **C**. In Linear Burn mode this layer both darkens and intensifies color.

The next two layers in the stack are from a scanned oil pastel drawing **D**. Like the dog, this imported element is larger than the frame of the document, and Grace flipped one of the copies and then offset the two a little differently. Applying one layer in Overlay mode and the other in Soft Light increased contrast and lightened the developing image **E**.

The last layer **F** was another combination of two copies of the dog image, with one copy flipped vertically this time, merged with a scan from another painting.

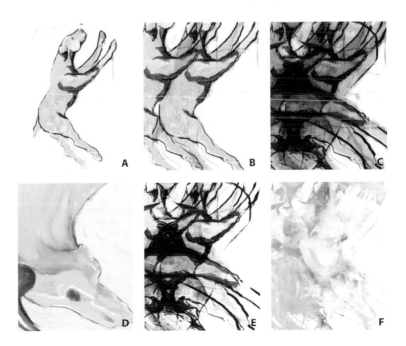

Enhancing Photos

5

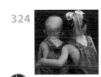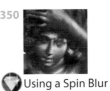

Using the Rectangular Marquee ⬚ and the Image > Crop command trims away edges without resampling the photo. Your file's dimensions are reduced, but its resolution stays the same.

To allow a soft or decorative edge on a crop made with the Rectangular Marquee ⬚, you can make the rectangular selection, create a layer mask from it, and modify the mask with Select > Refine Edge and with filters, as in "'Framing' with Masks" on page 268.

PHOTOSHOP HAS A WEALTH OF TECHNIQUES for enhancing photos — from digital versions of traditional camera and darkroom techniques such as soft focus and vignettes, to retouching and hand-tinting. But much of the day-to-day production work done with Photoshop involves simply trying to get the best possible reproduction of a photo — a crisp and clear print or on-screen image, with the fullest possible range of accurate tone and color. Many photos will need cropping, and some will need correction for camera lens distortion or for the digital noise typical of photos taken in low-light conditions. Many can also benefit from overall ("global") adjustments to tonality and color, selective ("local") touch-up, and sharpening to repair any "softness" introduced in the scan or the photo-editing process.

If the photo you start with was taken in a camera's raw format or in JPEG or TIFF, you can crop and straighten, adjust color and contrast, sharpen, and reduce noise in the Camera Raw interface. If your photo is in the 32 Bits/Channel mode,▼ you can still crop, adjust exposure,▼ and use a limited set of Photoshop's tone and color adjustments and filters, taking advantage of the extra color and tone information in the file before you convert it to 16 Bits/Channel or 8 Bits/Channel for further work or output.

FIND OUT MORE

▼ 32 Bits/Channel mode **page 169**

▼ The Exposure adjustment **page 251**

CROPPING

Cropping can improve composition, remove something distracting, or reduce the work involved in repairing a damaged photo. As usual, Photoshop provides several ways to do the job.

The Crop & Trim Command

Two commands in the Image menu are designed for simple cropping:

- Make a selection of the area you want to keep with the Rectangular Marquee ⬚ and then choose **Image > Crop.** The advantage of this method is that it's very **simple and straightforward**. **To change the size or proportions of the crop** after you've made the selection but before choosing Image > Crop, choose Select > Transform Selection, adjust the size of the selection, and double-click to complete the transformation.

- Choose **Image > Trim** and make choices in the Trim dialog box. This method is ideal for **cropping images with soft edges,** to crop them as close as possible without accidentally clipping off part of the soft edge. You can choose to trim away

Using the Trim command is a good way to avoid abruptly cutting off the outer part of a soft edge.

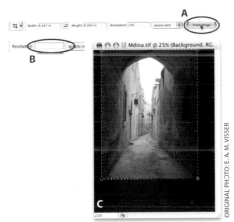

To keep the relationship between the height and width of your cropped image the same as it was in the original, choose the Crop tool 🔲 and click the "Front Image" button in the Options bar **A**; to crop without resampling, delete the value in the Resolution field **B**, and drag with the Crop tool to reframe the photo **C**.

any or all of the four edges of the image. The trim will be based on "cutting off" pixels from the edge inward, and it can be set to trim transparent pixels (you have to turn off visibility for any background layers before using this option), or pixels that are the same color as the top left or bottom right pixel.

- Or choose the **Crop tool** 🔲 (described next) and make choices in the tool's Options bar.

The Crop Tool 🔲

Once you drag the **Crop tool** 🔲 across your image to define the area you want to keep:

- **It's easy to adjust the size or proportions of the cropping frame** simply by dragging on a corner handle. To keep the ratio of height to width constant as you change size, Shift-drag on a handle.

- **You can change the orientation of an image** as you crop it by dragging around just outside a corner handle to **rotate the frame**. This function lets you **straighten a crooked scan**, **level the horizon** in an image that was taken at a tilt, **or simply reframe an image in a different orientation**.

- Turning on the **Perspective** and adjusting the individual corner points lets you **correct for keystoning** in a photo of something that's tall or that was photographed at an odd angle.

- **It's possible to crop** *and* **resize** the image in a single step by setting the Height, Width, and Resolution values you want for the cropped image in the Options bar before you drag to make the crop. (If you set the Height and Width in pixels, there's no need to set Resolution.) *Note:* A disadvantage of using the Crop tool is that it's possible to *unintentionally* resample an image as you crop it. **To avoid unintentional resampling**, make sure that in the Options bar either the dimension fields are empty, or the Resolution field is empty and the dimensions are not set in pixels.

- **To maintain the original aspect ratio of your photo** (so it isn't apparent whether the image was framed in the camera when it was shot or whether it was cropped

CROPPING NEAR THE EDGE

With the **Snap** option turned on (in the View menu) the Crop tool 🔲 snaps its cropping frame to the edges of the image when you drag the cursor close to them. To be able to crop near — but not at — the edge, open the View menu and turn off Snap, or choose Snap To and turn off Document Bounds.

Dragging the Crop tool ⊞ outward beyond the edges of the image (top) added more canvas for building a still life.

afterwards), before you crop, click the **"Front Image"** button in the Options bar. This sets the Crop tool to the Height, Width, and Resolution of the original image. **If you don't want to resample the image,** select and delete the value in the Resolution field before you drag with the Crop tool.

- **You can enlarge** the **"canvas"** around your image, with full control of how much is added at each edge of the photo. First make more space in the working window for expanding the crop (drag outward on the working window's lower right corner, or type Ctrl-Alt-hyphen in Windows or ⌘-Option-hyphen on the Mac). Then use the Crop tool ⊞ to drag across the entire image. And finally, drag a corner handle of the cropping frame outward to the proportions you want for the enlarged canvas (Shift-drag to maintain proportionality, Alt/Option-drag to enlarge the crop from the center, or combine these keys to do both at once).

Once you drag to frame the crop, the Crop tool's Options bar changes. You can now choose to **Shield** the cropped-out portion with the color and Opacity you choose, and move the Crop box around until you have the crop you want. If your image isn't flattened — that is, if it doesn't consist of a *Background* alone,

CONTROLLING THE CROP TOOL

In the Options bar that appears when you choose the Crop tool ⊞, you can set the dimensions and resolution you want for the cropped image. The entries you make will determine whether the image is resampled.

To crop the image to fit in a smaller space without changing its resolution, set the **Width** and **Height** in units other than pixels and leave the **Resolution** setting at its current value, or select and delete its value.

To base the Height, Width, and Resolution on the currently active image, click **Front Image**.

To clear the Height, Width, and Resolution so you can operate the Crop tool freely and without resampling, click **Clear**.

To keep the same crop dimensions but switch from horizontal to vertical format or vice versa, click this button.

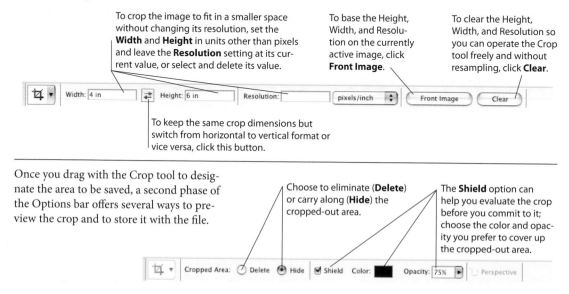

Once you drag with the Crop tool to designate the area to be saved, a second phase of the Options bar offers several ways to preview the crop and to store it with the file.

Choose to eliminate (**Delete**) or carry along (**Hide**) the cropped-out area.

The **Shield** option can help you evaluate the crop before you commit to it; choose the color and opacity you prefer to cover up the cropped-out area.

ORIGINAL PHOTO: GENEA SULLAWAY

To protect the dog and the seal from being compressed when we applied the Content-Aware Scale command, we first made an alpha channel by clicking the ▣ button at the bottom of the Channels panel. Then with that black-filled alpha channel and the RGB channel visible 👁 and the alpha channel targeted, we painted with white to set up the areas to be protected. We chose Edit > Content-Aware Scale, chose our alpha channel from the Protect menu in the Options bar, and dragged on the right side handle to narrow the image and bring the dog and seal closer together, then pressed Enter to complete the scaling.

with no other layers — you can also choose whether to **Delete** the area you're about to crop out or **Hide** it (keeping the cropped-out edge areas outside the image frame but still available). Hiding allows flexibility — you can later decide to change the "framing" of the image. And it can be useful in animation — the cropped image defines the size of the "stage" area, and the frames of the animation can be created by dragging the image across the stage with the Move tool ▸⊹ in small steps, and capturing each move as a frame. But hiding may also cause trouble, as described in the "Caution: 'Hidden' Crop" tip below. To complete the cropping operation, click the ✔ button in the Options bar to "commit" the crop, or click the ⊘ button to cancel it (double-clicking and pressing the Escape key are the respective shortcuts).

ACCOMMODATE ALL

The **Image > Reveal All** command enlarges the canvas to a size just big enough to include all of the "off-stage" parts of the file — even those on layers whose visibility 👁 is turned off.

CAUTION: "HIDDEN" CROP

When you use the Crop tool 🃋, if you choose Hide rather than Delete, the areas outside the crop are retained in the file. If you forget that there are "hidden" image edges, certain operations will produce results that are different than you expect. For instance, Photoshop continues to use the entire image (including the "off-stage" cropped-out parts) for such operations as adjusting Levels or Curves, or filling with a pattern (which starts at the upper left corner of the image), or applying a displacement map when you run the Displace filter (the map aligns with the upper left corner and tiles or stretches to fit), or adding a vignetted edge with the Lens Correction filter (the vignette is applied to the hidden edges and may be cropped off; in CS4 you can apply the vignette to the cropped area rather than the hidden edges, by cropping in Camera Raw, as described in Post-Crop Vignetting on page 280).

CONTENT-AWARE SCALING

Photoshop CS4 has a new and amazing way to change the size and shape of an image. In a sense, it's like an "internal crop." The purpose of the Content-Aware Scale command is to resize an image, maintaining the important elements while seamlessly scaling the less detailed background. For many images, you can do a remarkable job just by choosing Edit > Content-Aware Scale and dragging any of the handles on the Transform frame; you can see an example on page 8. In other cases, you may need to protect the important areas of the image — use the built-in protection for skin tones in the Options bar, or create an alpha channel as shown at the left and in Mark Wainer's *Hamaroy Lighthouse* on page 419.

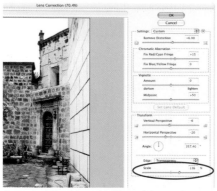

Correcting distortion with Filter > Distort > Lens Correction often leaves "empty" areas at the edges of an image. The Lens Correction interface has its own cropping function, allowing you to enlarge the image from the center until transparent edges are "pushed" outside the frame (see page 277). Or you can exit the Lens Correction interface and use one of Photoshop's standard cropping methods.

JHDAVIS

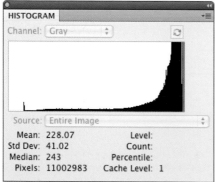

In this high-key black-and-white portrait conversion, the histogram is skewed to the right (see page 232).

CORRECTING FOR CAMERA DISTORTION

The **Lens Correction** filter (Filter > Distort > Lens Correction) is designed specifically for correcting camera-related distortion of both geometry and color. "Compensating for Camera-Related Distortion" on page 274 demonstrates the Lens Correction filter at work.

ADJUSTING TONE & COLOR

Once your image is cropped, you'll often want to make tone and color changes to the entire image or to selected areas. You can apply these changes either by choosing commands from the **Image > Adjustments** submenu or by adding an **Adjustment layer** (almost always a better option). As you work with tone and color adjustments, remember that for your final image to match the preview that your screen shows you, your monitor and output system need to be calibrated and matched, as described in "Getting Consistent Color" in Chapter 4.

The Histogram & Color Samplers

The **Histogram** panel can sit open on-screen so you can monitor your tone and color changes "live" while you make adjustments. The Histogram's graph shows what proportion of the image's pixels (indicated by the relative height of each vertical bar) is in each of 256 tones or *luminance values* (spread along the horizontal axis, from black on the left to white on the right).

The distribution of tones in the Histogram for an unadjusted photo often just reinforces what you can already see by looking at the image. The Histogram can't answer preference questions — should you increase contrast? lighten the photo overall? The Histogram simply reflects the state of the image:

- For an image that's **dark** overall, the Histogram shows more of its pixels on the left side of the graph than on the right. A **light** image shows more pixels on the right. Your photo may be under- or overexposed and you may want to correct for this. Or the image may simply be dark or light because of its content or because of intentional changes you've made.

- An image with **low contrast** overall lacks bars at either end, while a **high-contrast** image can show tall spikes at one or both extremes. In many cases you may want to improve a low-contrast image by spreading its tones over the entire tonal range, as described in "Levels & Curves" on page 246.

- If you expand the Histogram panel (by choosing **All Channels View** from the panel menu ▾≡) you can look at the distribution of tones in each of the color channels for the

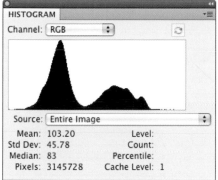

The photographer felt that the original low contrast, reflected in the histogram that doesn't reach the left or right end, recalled the mood of the location and the gray misty day.

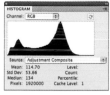

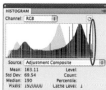

When an adjustment causes a peak to build up at either end of the Histogram, it indicates that highlight or shadow detail is being lost as the lightest or darkest tones are pushed to white or black. Before the adjustment (top) there are not spikes at the ends. Making this adjustment (bottom) would cause the loss of some highlight detail. Spaces in the Histogram indicate that the tonal range you've set holds more potential tones than are expressed in the image.

image. It may help you identify a color cast and see what to do to correct it.

The Histogram can be very helpful in monitoring changes in contrast (tonal range) or shadow and highlight detail as you make adjustments. For any tone or color adjustment dialog box that has a Preview option — such as Curves, Hue/Saturation, Color Balance, and many others, the Histogram will compare the current version of the image with what will be the adjusted version if you make the adjustment that's currently set up in the dialog box. (When you use an Adjustment layer, choose **Adjustment Composite** from the Histogram's Source menu to see both the "before" and the "after" graphs.) As you make color and tone adjustments, if either end of the Histogram spikes as you adjust tone and color, it can mean that you're losing detail in the highlights or shadows as contrast increases and more of the lightest or darkest tones are pushed to white or black. If one of the colors in the expanded Histogram shifts farther left or right than the others, a color cast may be developing (or diminishing).

Just as the Histogram panel can be useful for monitoring overall changes in tone and color, **Color Samplers** provide a great way to monitor changes in specific areas. Use the Color Sampler tool ✎, which shares a spot in the Tools panel with the Eyedropper ✎ and other information tools, to place up to four Samplers, and then read the data in the Info panel. ▼

FIND OUT MORE

▼ Color Sampler ✎
page 177

Working with Adjustment Layers

Because they provide so much flexibility, **it's almost always worthwhile to use an Adjustment layer** for adjusting tone and

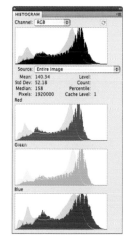

When you try out changes in a dialog box with a Preview option, the Histogram shows the distribution of tones before (lighter graph) and after the proposed change. Here we've chosen All Channels View and Show Channels in Color from the Histogram panel's menu.

In the Info panel for an RGB file, higher "after" numbers overall for Color Samplers indicate lightening, and lower numbers indicate darkening (just the opposite is true for a CMYK file). A disproportionate increase in one or more of the component colors indicates that color is shifting.

For this example from page 307, adding an Adjustment layer provided more flexibility than using a command from the Image > Adjustments menu would have. For example, we could paint a layer mask to restrict the adjustment **A**. It was also easy to go back later and reduce the Adjustment layer's Opacity to only partially desaturate the two men **B**. And we could turn off visibility for the layer mask (by Shift-clicking its thumbnail) so the adjustment applied to the entire photo **C**.

color in an image rather than choosing the same command from the Image menu. With the adjustment in a separate layer, you can later change the settings for the adjustment itself, or change its strength by reducing the layer's Opacity. You can also target the adjustment to a particular area using the built-in layer mask.▼ Or target a particular tonal range or color family with the "Blend If" sliders.▼

You add an Adjustment layer by clicking the "Create new fill or adjustment layer" button ◐ at the bottom of the Layers panel and choosing the type of adjustment you want from the pop-out menu. You'll find many examples of using Adjustment layers in this chapter and throughout the book.

In Photoshop CS3 each tone or color adjustment, whether applied as an Adjustment layer or through the Image > Adjustments menu, has its own **modal dialog box**. When you add an Adjustment layer, the dialog box opens and stays open until you finish your adjustment and click "OK." Having a dialog box open restricts your Photoshop activity almost entirely to that dialog box. An improvement in CS4 is the **Adjustments panel.** When you add an Adjustment layer, the appropriate dialog opens in the Adjustments panel. But the open dialog doesn't prevent other Photoshop operations while it's open: If you've forgotten to turn on visibility for a layer that's important for assessing your adjustment, or you want to change the Opacity of the Adjustment layer and then change the settings in the dialog some more, you can do that. (Adjustments applied through the Image > Adjustments menu still open modal dialog boxes, as in CS3.)

We'll start with two of the most generally useful adjustments — Levels and Curves. Then short descriptions of other adjustments will point out the special talents of each one, with references to where in the book you can find more information. In addition, "Quick Tone & Color Adjustments" on page 281 provides a "how-to catalog."

Levels & Curves

The **Levels** dialog is excellent for **overall tone (and sometimes color) adjustment**. Using the **Input Levels** sliders, you can increase contrast (by moving the black and white sliders in) or make the image lighter or darker overall but still keep black black and white white (by moving the gray midpoint slider). By moving the **Output Levels** sliders, you can lighten or darken all the tones in the image and reduce contrast.

FIND OUT MORE

▼ Using layer masks **page 61**

▼ Using Blending Options **page 66**

In the **Curves** dialog you can make all the same overall tone adjustments you can in Levels *and* you can adjust specific tonal ranges in your image without making the image lighter or darker overall. For instance, you can lighten shadow tones to bring out detail as shown on page 342. Curves can also be used for special color effects such as solarization or to create the look of iridescence.

Auto adjustments. The Levels and Curves dialog boxes both have **"Auto"** buttons for automated correction to tone and color. Holding down the Alt/Option key and clicking Auto opens a dialog with other automatic correction choices. "Quick Tone & Color Adjustments" starting on page 281 includes several step-by-step examples of applying and adapting these "instant fixes." If an "Auto" adjustment to Levels or Curves doesn't work, you can undo it (by holding down Alt/Option to turn the "Cancel" button into "Reset," and clicking it); then try adjusting "by hand" instead, as described next.

Adjusting Levels or Curves by hand. You can set the black point and white point, lighten or darken the midtones, and neutralize color by hand with either Levels or Curves. We'll cover both together, so it's easy to see how their settings correspond.

1 The first step is to expand the range of tones in the image.

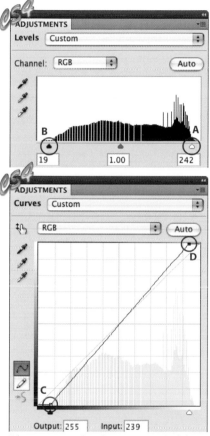

When you move the white Input Levels slider inward **A**, you increase contrast. You're telling Photoshop that you want all pixels lighter than this value to become white. Likewise, moving the black point slider inward **B** says that you want all pixels darker than this value to be black. The same thing is accomplished in the Curves dialog by moving the endpoints of the Curve horizontally **C**, **D**. A steeper Curve, which results from moving the endpoints inward, indicates more contrast.

Using Levels. To improve contrast, in the Levels dialog drag the **black point** slider and the **white point** slider for Input Levels to a point just a little inside where the graph's bars start at the left and right ends of the graph, respectively. If you watch the changes in the Histogram panel, contrast will be at its (technical) optimum when the graph indicates that there are some white and some black pixels. But stop your contrast adjustment before the black and white bars get disproportionately taller, because that will mean you're losing shadow or highlight detail as dark and light pixels get pushed all the way to black or white.

Sometimes you can identify a narrow "hump" at the extreme left or right end of the original histogram that may come from extraneous very dark or very light pixels. In that case you may get better results by dragging the black or white point slider inward to a position just barely inside the hump.

Using Curves. The "curve" in the Curves dialog box represents the relationship of tones before and after you make adjustments. It starts out as a straight line, until you add points and move them to reshape the line into a curve. With

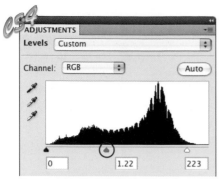

Dragging the gamma Input Levels slider in the Levels dialog box lightens or darkens the image overall without changing the black or white point.

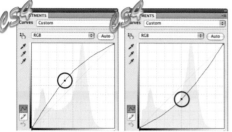

Dragging the middle of the Curve up or down will lighten or darken the image. Because you can also drag left or right, you have more control of overall tonal adjustments when you use Curves than when you use the gamma slider in Levels.

By allowing you to make an S-shaped curve, the Curves dialog offers more control of what happens to the darkest and lightest tones than Levels does.

An "S" Curves adjustment increases contrast in the midtones (see page 342 for the process).

A modified "M" Curves adjustment can also be used to increase contrast. See page 342.

the Curves dialog set up so the dark ends of the tone bars are at the bottom and left, you can increase contrast by moving the black corner point horizontally along the axis until the bars in the Histogram panel reach the far left end; move the white point horizontally along its axis until the Histogram panel shows bars at the far right end, being careful not to overdo it, as described earlier for Levels.

In either Levels or Curves you can click in your image to pick the black point (any tones darker than this will become black) with the **Set Black Point** eyedropper, and set the white point (any tones lighter than this will become white) with the **Set White Point** dropper.

2 Once you've made the Levels or Curves adjustments in step 1, you'll have a full range of tones from black to white. But the photo may still be too dark overall (underexposed) or too light overall (overexposed).

In the Levels dialog, you can remedy this by moving the gray (gamma, middle) Input Levels slider left or right to lighten or darken the image overall.

In the Curves dialog, the same correction can be made by dragging the midpoint of the curve. By default in RGB, to lighten the image, drag up. To darken the image, drag down (by default in CMYK the light-dark axes are just the opposite). An advantage of Curves over Levels is that by dragging different points on the curve, you can "bow" the curve downward or upward to control which part is steep and which is shallow. Where the curve is steep, the tones are being stretched farther from each other, increasing the contrast between them. This contrast can create sharpness and an illusion of detail because the eye is attuned to finding edges, and the increased contrast can help us see the edges. Conversely, where the curve is shallow, the number of tonal steps is reduced, decreasing contrast and sharpness.

3 Even with overall contrast and exposure adjusted, there may be an unwanted color cast in the image. To attempt to correct a color cast, choose the gray eyedropper in the Levels or Curves dialog (the **Set Gray Point** dropper) and click it on a color in the image that should be a neutral middle-tone gray. Page 286 shows an example. (If you can't find a spot that works, see "Other Tone & Color Adjustments" on page 250, or try one of the Average methods on pages 286 and 287.)

4 You can adjust particular parts of the tonal range using the Curves dialog; for instance, you can bring out shadow detail without affecting other parts of the range, or you can increase

WHY LEVELS?

If the Curves dialog can do all that Levels can do, and more, why have a Levels dialog? The answer may lie in Photoshop's history. For many versions of the program, before there was a Histogram panel, the Levels dialog was the only place with a graph of the distribution of tones in the image. The Levels histogram made it easy to see how to adjust the black point and white point without clipping (losing tones in) the highlights and shadows.

Then the Histogram became a palette/panel of its own, and finally (in version CS3) the Curves dialog gained a histogram of its own. So now it's just as easy to adjust black point and white point accurately in Curves. By now, however, many of us are used to the simpler Levels dialog for overall adjustments, have worked it into workflows and Actions, and would miss it if it disappeared.

CLARITY IN CAMERA RAW

The **Clarity** adjustment in Camera Raw can be ideal for increasing contrast in the midtones to bring out texture or fine detail. Use the **Clarity slider in the Basic tab** for a global adjustment. Or use the **Adjustment Brush** to add Clarity in a specific location. You can get a "double hit" of global Clarity by setting the slider on the Basic tab to 100% and then using a very large brush tip on the Adjustment Brush to paint more Clarity over the entire image.

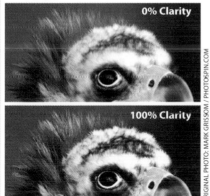

0% Clarity

100% Clarity

ORIGINAL PHOTO: MARK GRISSOM / PHOTOSPIN.COM

contrast in the midtones. If you move the cursor out of the Curves dialog, it turns into an eyedropper. (In CS4, select the Targeted Adjustment tool in the dialog first, or tap "I" on the keyboard to get the Eyedropper tool.) Clicking on a particular value in the image shows the position of that tone on the curve, or **Ctrl/⌘-clicking automatically adds the point to the curve**. Once you've identified the part of the tonal range you want to affect, you can click to anchor the curve at other points, beyond which you don't want the contrast to change. Then you can lighten or darken your targeted part of the tonal range by dragging your sampled point to reshape the section between the anchors. *Note:* If you move points to create more extreme curves than a gentle "M" or "S," you can run into trouble. Anything more than a subtle move can cause solarizing of the image (inversion of some tones).

THE PARAMETRIC CURVE

The **Parametric Curve** that occurs in Camera Raw is a somewhat "blunter instrument" than the Point Curve, familiar from Photoshop and also available as an alternative in Camera Raw. The Parametric interface divides the curve into four sections: highlights, light midtones, dark midtones, and shadows. With the four sliders you can make the tones in each section lighter (by moving the slider right) or darker (by moving left). You have less pinpoint control than with the Point Curve, but because of the way the sliders are integrated with one another, the curve stays smooth, avoiding unintended sharp breaks or odd fluctuations in tone and color that can happen with the Point Curve.

In addition to the four sliders, there are three markers on the horizontal axis of the Curve diagram. By moving these you can redefine the four parts of the range, throwing more tones into the range controlled by the Darks setting for instance, or fewer in the Highlights or Lights.

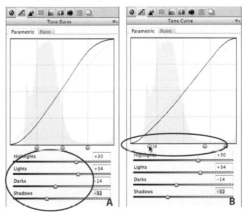

Use the Highlights, Lights, Darks, and Shadows sliders to shape the curve **A**. Then fine-tune the contrast by using the sliders on the horizontal axis **B** to change the percentages of tones affected by the four settings. Here the Shadows have been reduced from the darkest 25% of the tonal range to the darkest 18%.

The six sliders of the Black & White Adjustment layer provide a wide variety of conversion options. We were easily able to create two different black-and-white conversions, one with Auto, and the other by adjusting the sliders to create a more extreme, "gritty" look.

A Black & White Adjustment layer was applied to enhance contrast in the leaves, then masked to focus attention on the green fruit.

Other Tone & Color Adjustments

The short descriptions that follow point out the special abilities of each of the commands found in the Image > Adjustments menu. Most also occur as Adjustment layers, though some are applied as Smart Filters instead. ▼ They're listed here alphabetically.

FIND OUT MORE
▼ Smart Filters
pages 72

Black & White. New in Photoshop CS3, the Black & White adjustment has become the most effective way to **translate color images to black-and-white**. In the Black & White dialog you'll find presets, sliders, and a scrubber, all for determining how the six different color families will be mapped to shades of gray. You can push the colors to build contrast, or to reduce it. You'll find examples in "From Color to Black & White" on page 214.

Brightness/Contrast. The Brightness/Contrast adjustment was improved in Photoshop CS3. It can now operate in the old (legacy) manner or in a new way that works better for most Brightness and Contrast adjustments you might want to make to photos. In Use Legacy mode, which is an option you can check in the Brightness/Contrast dialog, the whole range of tones in the image is equally affected when you move the Brightness or Contrast slider. It's easy to push light tones to white and darks to black, "clipping" off some of the potential range of tones available for the image. With Use Legacy turned off, the black point and white point remain unchanged as you move the sliders. The Brightness slider works like the gamma (gray) slider in Levels or like raising or lowering the middle of the curve in the Curves dialog (see page 248), lightening or darkening especially in the midtones. The Contrast slider works like an "S" curve in the Curves dialog to increase contrast (see page 342), or like a

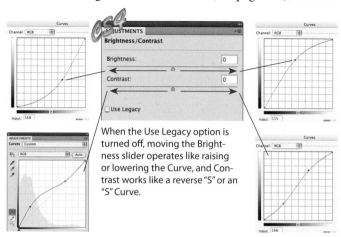

When the Use Legacy option is turned off, moving the Brightness slider operates like raising or lowering the Curve, and Contrast works like a reverse "S" or an "S" Curve.

One way to remove a color cast is by adding the opposite of what you have too much of. Here a greenish-blue cast from light coming through the tent was removed by adding red, yellow, and a little magenta to the midtones.

Before

After

The Equalize command is helpful for seeing if the edge of a soft shadow has been trimmed away and thus flattened. To prevent cropping a soft edge too close in the first place, use the Image > Trim command (page 240).

backwards "S" curve to decrease contrast. Again the midtones are most affected. *Note:* Actions or layered files that include the old Brightness/Contrast adjustment will automatically invoke the less sophisticated Use Legacy mode.

Channel Mixer. The Channel Mixer lets you adjust color in an image by **adding to or subtracting from the individual color channels**. You'll find an example in "Quick Tint Effects" on page 211.

Color Balance. Color Balance lets you **change the colors of the highlights, midtones, and shadows separately**, although the three ranges overlap somewhat. To get rid of a color cast in a photo, you simply find the slider that controls the color you have too much of (such as Red) and drag toward the opposite end of the line (Cyan). Color Balance can also be useful for tinting an image (see "Tinting by Tonal Range" on page 205).

Desaturate. The Desaturate command is one way to "remove" color, producing a grayscale look but leaving the *capacity* for color, so color can be added back. But you can do the same thing better with a Black & White adjustment, which gives you much greater control.

Equalize. The Equalize command **exaggerates the contrast between pixels that are close in color** so you can see where stray specks are or where soft edges end.

Exposure. The Exposure adjustment was designed to stand in for Levels, Curves, and other adjustments in versions of Photoshop before it was possible to apply these adjustments to files in 32 Bits/Channel mode. There are three sliders in the Exposure dialog box. Moving any slider to the right brightens the image, and moving it left darkens the image, but each slider behaves a little differently, affecting some parts of the tonal range more than others.

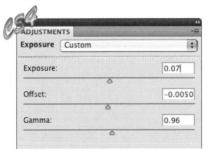

In the Exposure dialog, moving the Exposure slider to the right increases brightness throughout the image but affects the shadow areas more slowly than the highlights. Moving the Offset slider to the left darkens the shadows faster than the highlights. The Gamma slider affects the midtones faster than the extreme darks and lights, lightening them if you move the slider to the right, darkening them if you move it left.

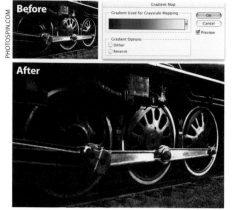

A Gradient Map Adjustment layer replaces different levels of gray with the colors of a gradient, as shown here and on page 208.

The family of colors you want to target — for instance, oranges — may not be listed in the Edit menu of the Hue/Saturation dialog. In that case, in Photoshop CS3 (shown here) just choose one of its neighboring color families — Yellows or Reds in the case of orange. Then click or drag the "+" dropper in the image to expand the range of targeted colors. Use the "–" dropper to remove colors (such as reds that aren't "orangey") from the range. For a more gradual transition between the colors that change and those that don't, drag the small white triangles outward to enlarge the light gray "fuzziness" bars; drag inward for sharper transitions.

In Photoshop CS4 you don't have to choose a color family before targeting a color in your image. Just click the 🖑 in the Adjustments panel and then click in the image to sample; or drag the 🖑 cursor left or right in the image to decrease or increase the Saturation of the starting color; Ctrl/⌘-drag to shift the color left or right along the color spectrum.

Gradient Map. The Gradient Map adjustment **replaces the tones of an image with the colors of a gradient** you choose. It offers flexibility for trying out a variety of creative color solutions simply by clicking to choose a different gradient, or by clicking the gradient bar to open the Gradient Editor, where you can change the colors in the gradient. You can invert the order in which the original tones are remapped to the gradient's colors by clicking the "Reverse" box. Examples of Gradient Map can be found in "Quick Tint Effects" on page 208 and "Exercising Gradients" on page 197.

Hue/Saturation. The Hue/Saturation dialog is packed with options for making a targeted color change. Instead of changing color overall, which this dialog can also do, you can target any of the six color "families" independently (Reds, Yellow, Greens, Blues, Cyans, or Magentas), with separate control of hue (shifting color around the color wheel), saturation (making a color more intense or more neutral, or grayish), and lightness (pushing the color closer to black or white). You can sample from your image the color family you want to target for change. You can expand or reduce the range of colors in the family, and control how sudden or gradual the transition is between the colors that are affected and those that aren't. You'll find examples of general and targeted Hue/Saturation changes in "Quick Tone & Color Adjustments" starting on page 281. With Hue/Saturation you can also tint the image with a single color by checking the Colorize box, as shown in "Quick Tint Effects," on page 204.

Invert. The Invert adjustment **changes colors and tones to their opposites**. Besides creating a "negative" look, it can be very useful for making an "opposite" layer mask, such as the ones shown below, which are used to apply different adjustments to the foreground and background of an image. You can use the Invert command to make a background mask from a foreground mask, or vice versa. (If you're working on a layer mask, you'll have to use the Invert command or keyboard shortcut [Ctrl/⌘-I]

We duplicated the masked Hue/Saturation Adjustment layer that had been added to adjust the color of the sky. Then we inverted the mask and changed the Hue/Saturation settings to adjust cloud color.

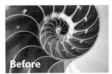 

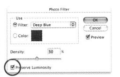

In Normal mode, an Invert Adjustment layer produces a negative of both color and luminosity. In Luminosity mode, tonality (light/dark) is inverted but color (hue and saturation) is not.

To apply a Photo Filter Adjustment layer to an RGB file without changing the exposure or contrast, leave the Preserve Luminosity box checked. The Density slider controls the strength of the tint, simulating the different densities of filters available for camera lenses.

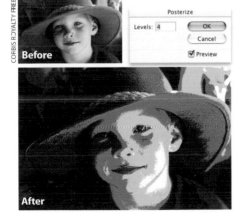

Posterizing can help simplify images for the web, for artistic effect, or for starting a painting from a photo, as shown on page 388.

rather than an Invert Adjustment layer, since Adjustment layers work on the layer content itself, not on the mask. In Photoshop CS4 you can accomplish the same thing with the "Invert" button in the Masks panel.)

Match Color. The Image > Adjustments > Match Color command lets you **modify the color of an image to match the color of another image**. For the image you're changing or the one you're matching it to, you can base the color match on the entire image, or pick out a particular area that has the colors you want Photoshop to consider. It can be useful for matching a number of photos in a series or matching the parts of a panorama before using Photomerge. You can find an example in "Quick Tone & Color Adjustments" on page 290. Match Color **isn't available as an Adjustment layer or a Smart Filter**.

Photo Filter. The Photo Filter Adjustment layer **simulates the effect of a colored filter on a camera lens**. Photo Filter works the same way whether you choose Filter or Color in the dialog, but the Filter option gives you a list of presets that correspond to common lens filters, such as Warming and Cooling filters. You can see more Photo Filter adjustments in action in "Quick Tone & Color Adjustments" on page 288 and in "Quick Tint Effects" on pages 209 and 210.

Posterize. The Posterize adjustment **simplifies an image by reducing the number of colors** (or tones in a grayscale image). It can provide a good start for reducing the palette of an image for the web, to reduce file size and thus download time. Sometimes you get fewer and bigger blocks of color if you blur the image slightly before you Posterize (Filter > Blur > Gaussian Blur or Filter > Noise > Despeckle).

Replace Color. In the Replace Color dialog box you can make a selection based on sampled color and then change the hue, saturation, or lightness, all in one operation, and in CS4 you can add or subtract localized color clusters. But Replace Color doesn't provide flexibility for making changes later — there's no way to save the selection so you can bring it back, and Replace Color **can't be applied as an Adjustment layer or a Smart Filter**.

Selective Color. Selective Color is designed for adding or subtracting specific percentages of cyan, magenta, yellow, and black. You can target these changes to any of six color families (Reds, Yellow, Greens, Blues, Cyans, or Magentas) as well as Black, White, or Neutrals. Selective Color can be ideal for **making adjustments to a CMYK file based on a color proof** that

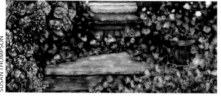

SUSAN THOMPSON

Selective Color can be a great way to make separate color adjustments to individual color families — making the reds yellower but the blues bluer, for instance. In this detail from *Summer in Arcata,* we see some of the adjustments Susan Thompson made in the Selective Color Options dialog box (see page 370 for more).

CORBIS ROYALTY FREE

Before

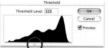

After

Move the slider in the Threshold dialog to control which tones become black and which become white.

Experimenting with Variations can help you figure out what kind of color adjustment is needed and then apply it. Variations can't be applied as an Adjustment layer, but it can be used as a Smart Filter.

shows that you aren't getting the color you want. If the printer says you need to add a certain percentage of one of the primary ink colors, you can do it with Selective Color. But Selective Color can also be very useful for adjusting color in RGB mode, especially if you're used to thinking in terms of inks.

Shadows/Highlights. The Shadows/Highlights adjustment is designed to bring out detail in underexposed or overexposed areas of an image, by brightening the shadows and adding density in the highlights. At its default settings, which are designed for photos with backlit subjects, it acts on a wide range of shadow tones but not on highlights. Clicking the "Show More Options" button opens up the dialog box as shown on page 255 so you can control how Shadows/Highlights decides what pixels are "dark" or "light," and how much it brightens or darkens them. Shadows/Highlights **can be applied as a Smart Filter.**

Threshold. The Threshold command **converts each pixel in an image to either black or white**. A slider in the Threshold dialog lets you control where in the tonal range of the image the black/white divide occurs. It can be useful for creating single-color treatments of photos or for simulating line drawings. It **can be applied as an Adjustment layer.**

Variations. The Variations command has a dual appeal: It can handle a **wide array of color adjustments** — hue, saturation, and lightness, each controlled independently for highlights, midtones, and shadows; and you can **preview several different options at once** so you can choose the direction you like. (You can see Variations in operation in "Quick Tone & Color Adjustments" on page 281.) Experimenting with Variations may suggest color adjustments that hadn't occurred to you. For instance, you may be thinking that an image needs more red, but the Variations window may show you that increasing magenta would do a better job of achieving the color you want. Variations can't be applied as an Adjustment layer, but it **can be applied as a Smart Filter.**

Vibrance. Vibrance, new in Photoshop CS4, is the sister of Saturation. It increases or decreases the intensity of color (as the Saturation setting in the Hue/Saturation dialog does), but it protects colors that are already almost as intense (pure hue) as they can get from increasing in intensity to the point where the subtle differences in saturation are swamped and no longer distinguishable. It's also designed to protect skin tones. The Vibrance dialog includes a Saturation slider also, as these two controls can often be effectively balanced to improve color.

SHADOWS/HIGHLIGHTS

The Shadows/Highlights command has separate controls for lightening shadows and darkening highlights. For each pixel, Shadows/Highlights decides whether to treat it as a shadow, a highlight, or neither. Then it determines how much to brighten it (if it's a shadow pixel) or darken it (if it's a highlight pixel). Three sliders for Shadows and three for Highlights work together to achieve the final result.

Tonal Width determines how dark or how light a pixel has to be in order to be considered shadow or highlight. A higher Tonal Width puts more pixels into the shadow or highlight category. At the default 50% for Tonal Width, anything darker than 50% gray is considered a shadow pixel and anything lighter is considered a highlight pixel. But read on, it's just a bit more complicated than that.

Instead of just using the value of each pixel itself to determine if it falls within the Tonal Width for shadows or highlights, the Shadows/Highlights command compares each pixel to the average of the pixels in its "neighborhood." The **Radius** determines how big this neighborhood is — that is, how far around each pixel the Shadows/Highlights command looks when it figures this average. So, for instance, since most shadow pixels have other dark pixels in the immediate neighborhood, the smaller the Radius, the darker this average will be, and the more likely it is that the pixel will be considered to be within the Tonal Width for Shadows and will be brightened. As the Radius gets bigger, the neighborhood includes more lighter pixels, so the average is lighter, and it's less likely that the pixel will fall within the Tonal Width for Shadows, so it won't be brightened.

The **"Save"** and **"Load"** buttons allow you to save and reuse settings for specific problems, such as backlighting (the default settings are actually designed for this), overflashing, bright sun, and deep shade.

The **Color Correction** slider increases saturation (or decreases it with a negative setting) in areas that Shadows/Highlights has brightened or darkened. (Grayscale images have a Brightness slider here instead.)

The **Midtone Contrast** slider can be used to fix contrast in the midtones, without having to use a separate Curves adjustment.

Increasing the **Black Clip** or **White Clip** pushes more of the 256 tones to full black or full white, increasing contrast. But pushing too many tones to the extremes causes a loss of detail in shadows and highlights and can even cause posterization (stepped tones rather than smooth transitions) as there are fewer remaining values between the extremes.

Once the Tonal Width and Radius settings have determined that a pixel is shadow or highlight, the **Amount** setting comes into play. Amount determines how much a shadow pixel will be brightened or a highlight pixel darkened. The darkest (or lightest) pixels within the Tonal Width are brightened (or darkened) the most. The higher the Amount setting, the greater the lightening or darkening effect at the extremes and the faster the effect falls off as the midtones are approached. With a lower setting, the effect at the extremes is less and the fall-off is slower.

A Vibrance Adjustment layer intensifies the neutral green of the couch, the tan floor, and the pastel colors in the art on the wall, without oversaturating the blue pillows or area rug.

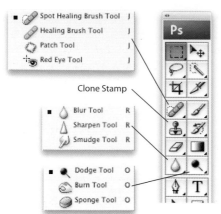

Tools commonly used for retouching and repair include the Healing Brush, Spot Healing Brush, Patch tool, Red Eye tool, and Clone Stamp. You'll find examples of these tools at work in the two "Quick Retouching" sections (page 312 and page 314) and in "Quick Cosmetic Changes" (page 316). The Blur, Sharpen, Dodge, Burn, and Sponge tools, while sometimes useful for a quick touchup, can be tricky to use with photos. Often you can get better results with a blur or sharpen filter applied as a masked Smart Filter, or with a "dodge-and-burn" layer.

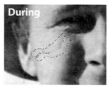

The Patch tool, which automatically blends the edges of its repairs, is great for repairing tears or major scratches in photos (see page 312). The Patch doesn't have a Sample All Layers option, so it's a good idea to use it on a duplicate image layer.

RETOUCHING PHOTOS

With Photoshop's retouching tools you can "hand-paint" repairs to an image. But if you use these tools directly on an image layer, it can be difficult to go back later and correct a several-stroke mistake. Here are some ways to do retouching so you don't risk damaging the original image if you make a mistake, and so individual corrections can be easily identified so you can remove or repair them. You'll find step-by-step examples of using the retouching tools in the "Quick Retouching" sections on page 312 and page 314.

- The **Spot Healing Brush** and **Healing Brush**, ideal **for fixing a few small blemishes,** both automatically blend their repairs with the surroundings. The Spot Healing Brush also automatically chooses the source of the repair material — you just click it on the blemish you want to hide and it makes the repair. With the Healing Brush, you Alt/Option-click to sample a source of repair material before you click on the spot you want to hide; it requires an extra step, but it allows you, instead of Photoshop, to make your best guess about a good repair source.

- One quick way **to remove a lot of dust and small scratches** — enough that it would be a nuisance to remove the marks one by one — is to turn the image into a Smart Object and run the Dust & Scratches filter as a Smart Filter. Then fill the Smart Filter mask with black to hide the entire filtered image, and finally paint the mask with white where you need the filtered image to hide the blemishes. This method is described step-by-step in "Quick Retouching Techniques for Problem Photos" on page 312. You can also use Dust & Scratches as a "pretreatment" before using the **Healing Brush**, as described in "Quick Retouching for Sky" on page 314.

- **To remove larger blemishes or to cover up a distracting element in the background of a photo,** use the **Patch Tool** or the **Clone Stamp**. The Clone Stamp can work on a transparent "repairs" layer above the image if you first set the tool to Sample All Layers in the Options bar. The Clone Stamp, which doesn't automatically blend the repair edges with the original as other healing tools do, depends on brush tip characteristics for blending. It works especially well in non-aligned mode with a medium-soft brush tip, with short dabs rather than long strokes, to avoid an obvious repetition of image material. Alt/Option-click to pick up neighboring image detail, and click to deposit it over the area you want to hide. With the repairs on a separate layer, you can change your fixes at any time.

The Healing Brush 🖌 can be set to "heal" by using a pattern, rather than by sampling color and texture from an image. This makes it possible to quickly remove fine lines such as telephone wires against the sky by using the Dust & Scratches filter on a copy of the image, and then using this blurred copy as the Pattern for the Healing Brush. See "Quick Retouching for Sky" on page 314 for the method.

REPAIRS ALONG LINES OR CURVES

To make a straight-line repair, such as hiding taut telephone wires against the sky, click once at the beginning of the wire with a retouching tool such as the Healing Brush 🖌, Spot Healing Brush 🖌, or Clone Stamp 🖫, and Shift-click again at the end. If your repair has to follow a curve — because the wire is sagging, for instance — draw a path that follows the curve, ▼ and then choose your repair tool (and define the source if necessary), and stroke the path. ▼

- **To camouflage large scratches or tears in a photo,** the **Patch tool** ○ can be a good solution. The Patch works on the current layer only, unlike the tools that can sample from all visible layers and make repairs on a separate, empty layer. For more flexibility, before you use the Patch tool, duplicate the layer that needs fixing (Ctrl/⌘-J will do this), and work on this copy, leaving the original layer intact. The Patch tool uses the same edge-blending and tone-matching technology as the Healing Brush, but it can also work "backwards" — you can first select the area to be repaired and then drag to choose the source material to replace it with.

- For both the **Clone Stamp** 🖫 and the **Healing Brush** 🖌, you can **load more than one repair brush at a time**, using different parts of your image (or even other images) as sources in the Clone Source panel, new in Photoshop CS3.

- **To scale or angle your repairs** as you apply the source material to your image — for instance, if the material you need to use for the repair is in the foreground of your image, and the repair itself needs to be done in the background — you can choose those options for the **Clone Stamp** 🖫 and **Healing Brush** 🖌 in the **Clone Source panel**. (Another option is to automatically shrink the repair material proportionally by using the Stamp tool that you'll find inside the **Vanishing Point** filter's interface.) ▼

FIND OUT MORE

▼ Drawing a path
page 448

▼ Stroking a path
page 457

▼ Vanishing Point
page 612

- **To increase the contrast, brightness, or detail of particular areas of an image,**

ORIGINAL PHOTO: KAVRAM / PHOTOSPIN.COM

To turn a garden from dull to blooming, we chose a source image with flowers (not shown) and used the Clone Source panel to store three different flowers (you can have as many as five clone sources). We chose the Clone Stamp 🖫 and we made sure "Sample" was set to Current Layer and "Align" was not checked. We set the brush tip size large enough to encompass a flower; we Alt/Option-clicked in its center to set our first clone source, and adjusted the Width (W), which is linked to Height (H) to constrain the scaling proportionally, to make the flower the size we wanted for the closest blooms. We repeated the source-setting process for two more flowers. We enabled Show Overlay so we could preview the scaled cloned material before we actually painted it onto the image, so we could visually match it to the scale of the plants at different distances in the destination image. With Auto-Hide and Clipped (CS4 only) chosen, we could limit the preview to the shape of the cursor as we painted. After cloning at one size, to scale again, we simply reset the Width for each Source. The Source point is maintained even as the size is altered. We kept the flowers on four layers according to the distance in the image, reducing the layer Opacity more with the distance, to blend them with the green arches.

The Vanishing Point filter ▼ has its own Stamp tool 🖈 that works according to the grid you set up for your image. Here this tool is being used to clone leaf litter and grass from near the bottom of the image to hide distracting elements near the top. See page 372 for the details of the process.

FIND OUT MORE

▼ Using Vanishing Point **page 612**

Enabling **Protect Tones** with either the Dodge tool 🔍 or Burn tool ◎ causes the tool to reduce its effect as its target approaches pure black or white. Throughout the range of tones, Protect Tones also attempts to protect the hue, so your colors don't become more neutral as you alter their luminance. These improvements (new in Photoshop CS4) have made the two tools more effective for local tone corrections, though they still must operate directly on the image layer they are adjusting.

add a layer above your image, putting this new layer in Overlay or Soft Light mode and filling it with 50% gray, which is neutral (invisible) in these modes. Then work on this layer by using black paint (to burn, or darken), white paint (to dodge, or lighten), or shades of gray, with a soft Brush ✐ with or without Airbrush mode 🖌 turned on in the Options bar; set Pressure or Opacity very low. (If oversaturation occurs in Overlay mode, try changing the blend mode of this gray-filled "Dodge & Burn" layer to Soft Light.) This dodge-and-burn method is shown on page 339. ***Note:*** The Dodge tool 🔍 and Burn tool ◎ can also target adjustments to contrast, brightness, and detail. Although these tools have been improved in Photoshop CS4, using them on a photo can still be a bit confusing. First, you have to contend with three different Range options for each tool (Highlights, Midtones, or Shadows) set in the Options bar. And second, when you hand-paint with the tools, you don't really know that you've reached the optimal result until you've overshot it and gone too far; then you have to undo and redo until you get it right. Also, you can't isolate your changes on a separate "repairs" layer. So it still often works better to use the "dodge and burn layer" method, described above.

- **To increase or decrease color saturation of certain areas in an image,** add a Hue/Saturation or Vibrance Adjustment layer and make a Saturation or Vibrance adjustment that cures the particular problem — for the moment, ignore what happens to the rest of the image. Fill the Adjustment layer's built-in mask with black, which will completely mask the saturation change. Finally, use a soft Brush ✐, with or without the Airbrush function 🖌 turned on in the Options bar, to paint with white in the problem areas; the lightened areas of the mask will allow the saturation changes to come through. ***Note:*** The Sponge tool ◉ can also be used for saturating or desaturating (in Photoshop CS4 it has a Vibrance option as well as Saturation), but it can be difficult to make the saturation changes you want without also changing contrast or affecting more of the image than you intended. So using a masked Adjustment layer often works better than using the Sponge. Also, the Sponge can't be used on a separate "repairs" layer.

Turning on **Vibrance** (new to the Sponge tool in Photoshop CS4) both protects skin tones from becoming unnaturally saturated, and protects saturated colors from becoming more saturated as quickly as duller colors do. As a result, when the Sponge is in Saturate mode with Vibrance turned on, saturation is added more smoothly and without oversaturation.

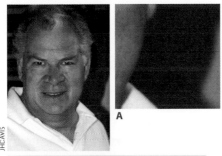

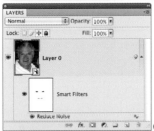

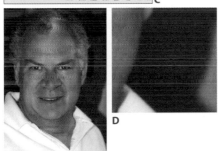

In an image with obvious digital noise **A**, you can even out the color by turning the image into a Smart Object (Filter > Convert for Smart Filters) and running the **Reduce Noise filter** as a Smart Filter (Filter > Noise > Reduce Noise). We balanced **Strength** and **Preserve Detail** settings to reduce luminance noise without softening details. Since most of the noise was random color pixels, we set **Reduce Color Noise** at its maximum. We used only a low **Sharpen Details** setting for the portrait. Here a Reduce Color Noise setting high enough to subdue the noise to suit us also tinted the teeth and eyes **B**, so we painted the Smart Filter mask with black to restore them **C, D**.

NOISE REDUCTION

The Reduce Noise filter can smooth out the fine-grained color irregularities (**noise**) in a digital photograph, particularly one that has had dramatic tone and color adjustments. This method can also be useful for fixing a color fringe (chromatic aberration). An example of the Reduce Noise filter technique is shown at the left, and another example, addressed with noise-reduction functions in Camera Raw, can be found in step 3 of "Bringing Out Detail" on page 334. There are also Photoshop methods you can use if you know at the time you take your photo that it's likely to be noisy — if you're shooting in dim light, for example, and can shoot the image more than once, you can use a multi-shot noise-reduction approach (see page 325).

SHARPENING

Sharpening, like adjusting contrast, is partly a matter of preference. But running the **Unsharp Mask** filter or the **Smart Sharpen** filter almost always improves a scanned photo or a photo stored in a camera's raw format. Likewise, transforming or resizing an image can "soften" it, although the Bicubic Sharper option available in the Resample Image menu in the Image Size dialog box may provide enough sharpening in some cases.▼ You can find step-by-step examples of sharpening, both with the sharpening filters and with other methods, in "Quick Ways To Bring Out Detail" on page 337. Usually sharpening is the last thing that should be done to an image before it's prepared for the press or for viewing on screen, because otherwise the synthetic effects of sharpening can be magnified in other image-editing processes, such as increasing the color saturation.

FIND OUT MORE

▼ Transforming **page 67**

▼ Painting masks **page 84**

▼ Blending Options **page 66**

To sharpen particular parts of the image, convert the image layer to a Smart Object, then apply the Unsharp Mask or Smart Sharpen filter as a Smart Filter. Fill the Smart Filter mask with black and use the Brush 🖌 and white paint to reveal the sharpening where you want it.▼ You can also target sharpening to particular tonal ranges using the "Blend If" sliders▼ or the built-in controls in the Smart Sharpen interface; see page 338.

SHARPENING LUMINOSITY

Sharpening can cause color changes as the contrast is increased. The more intense the sharpening, the greater the changes. To minimize color changes, apply Unsharp Mask or Smart Sharpen as a Smart Filter. Then right-click/Ctrl-click on the Smart Filter "layer" in the Layers panel to open a context-sensitive menu; choose Edit Smart Filter Blending Options, and change the blend mode to Luminosity.

After Francois Guérin painted a still life of fruit in Corel Painter (left), he opened the file in Photoshop and sharpened the parts of the pear closest to the viewer (right) to enhance depth and form.

If you take more than one exposure, you have several options for combining them into a single image that shows the detail you want in shadows, midtones, and highlights.

When you can't get a clear shot photographing in a public place, take two or more photos and use Auto Align; see page 327.

MULTI-SHOT TECHNIQUES

If you can anticipate the challenges ahead when you're photographing under less than ideal conditions, and understand how Photoshop can address those, you open up a world of possibilities. A perfect example is photographing for a panorama — if you understand how to set up the shots and you understand how to use Photomerge (covered in Chapter 9 since it's about putting pieces together into a composite), you can take the series you need to get the panorama you want. But there are other mutiple-shot techniques as well, and if you can take your photo several times instead of just once, you'll be able to merge the shots for a better result than you could get with a single image.

Combining Exposures: Merge to HDR & Other Methods

If you're photographing in a situation where there's a broader dynamic range from the lightest to the darkest tones in the scene than a single shot can capture, make a series of exposures that can then be combined. Depending on the workflow you prefer, the Merge to HDR command (available from Photoshop or Bridge) may produce an image that's ready to fine-tune. Combining exposures into 32 Bits/Channel color, which has a much broader dynamic range, you can pick and choose where you want to assign tones, maintaining detail in highlights from a darker image, midtones from a medium exposure, and shadows from a lighter image if you like, as you convert back to an 8 Bits/Channel image that can be printed or posted on the web. "Combining Exposures" on page 292 provides an example of the Merge-to-HDR method, along with a process using luminosity masks, and page 366 shows still another way to combine exposures.

The Perfect Group Shot

To get the group shot you want — all participants smiling, with eyes open — mount your camera on a tripod and tell everyone to look good and hold perfectly still while you shoot at least two photos in rapid succession. Most people will move a little, but you'll be able to pick a "best" shot and substitute parts of the other(s) to get the best expressions all around. In Photoshop, stack the files (File > Scripts > Load Files as Layers), with the best one on top and any others with parts you want to substitute below that. Then target all the layers you need and align them (Edit > Auto-Align Layers), and you'll be able to mask out the less-than-optimal parts of the top layer, allowing other parts from the next layer to show through. ▼ Work down the stack, masking to reveal the pieces you need. Use healing and cloning techniques as needed to blend the parts into the whole. ▼

FIND OUT MORE

▼ Layer masks
page 62

▼ Healing & cloning
page 256

To reduce noise in this evening photo of the train station, four shots, each quite noisy like the one shown here **A**, were stacked as layers in a single file and "averaged" **B** to smooth out the random flecks of color; see page 325. You can do your averaging "by hand," or if you have Photoshop Extended, automate the process.

Removing Foot Traffic

When you're photographing at a public event or a popular venue, you may not be able to control traffic through the shot you want to take. As long as your subject stays still as the traffic moves through, and you can take enough photos to get every part of your subject clear in at least one shot, you can blend the shots to eliminate the extra guests. "Creating Solitude" on page 327 tells how. Photoshop Extended's File > Scripts > Statistics, with Median chosen as the Stack Mode can sometimes automate the entire process.

Extending Depth of Field

When you want the close-up precision you can get only by focusing on a small part of your subject, combine several shots focused at different distances to get a composite that has your entire subject in focus. "In Focus" on page 344 will amaze you with Photoshop's ability to analyze the series, automatically blending the in-focus parts into a sharply focused whole that would have been impossible as a single shot.

Averaging Out Noise

The electronic noise that becomes part of a photo taken in low-light conditions is a random distribution of color specks. If you know you'll be photographing in low-light conditions — inside a cave, museum, or secret fort with no flash allowed or in the almost-dark evening light, you can take exactly the same shot several times and then "average" them together to smooth out the variation and get rid of the specks (see page 325 for the method).

REPURPOSING PHOTOS

There are times when a photograph is *almost* what you want to use in a project, but not quite — the camera has stopped the motion just as the photographer intended, but now you want to emphasize the energy in the shot; the photographer didn't notice (or couldn't control) distracting detail in the background, and it's generalized so you can't crop or successfully retouch it out; or the lighting doesn't work for the way you want to use the photo. Here are some ideas for those kinds of photos:

- **To hide unwanted detail in a dark subject against a bright background,** apply a Levels Adjustment layer, moving the black point slider for Input Levels to the right as far as necessary to silhouette the subject or at least remove the unwanted foreground detail. Depending on the image, you may need to select the subject before making the adjustment, or use the "Blend If" sliders to restrict the Levels adjustment to

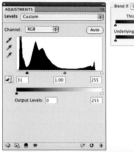

To silhouette the children, we moved the black point slider for Input Levels inward to hide the detail in their clothes. The "Blend If" sliders were used to restrict the darkening to the darkest colors. ▼

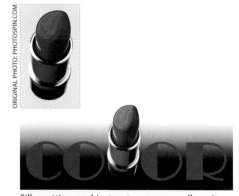

Silhouetting a subject on transparency allows it to be placed in an Adobe InDesign layout without its background, so you can layer it with other elements on the page.

the darkest tones, ▼ or even paint over lighter areas of the darkened subject with black.

FIND OUT MORE

▼ Using the Blend If sliders **page 66**

- **To suppress unwanted detail in a background,** select the background and blur it as described in some of the examples in "Quick Attention-Focusing Techniques," starting on page 301. "Exercising Lens Blur" on page 309 shows several other ways to alter depth of field, by using the Lens Blur filter.

- **To remove a background altogether,** duplicate your image file (so you have a copy), and then select the background and delete it. (If your image consists of a *Background* layer you'll have to convert it to a regular layer before deleting: Double-click the *Background* entry in the Layers panel.)

- **To shrink or stretch a background** without disturbing the subject, use Edit > Content Aware Scale (see page 243).

- To **replace the background with a different image,** first remove the background, and then copy-and-paste or drag-and-drop the new background into the subject file, or vice versa. Chapter 2 covers methods for selecting the subject, and "Quick Integration" on page 624 has pointers for making it at home in the new background.

- **To simplify and stylize an image,** use a filter such as **Cutout** (Filter > Artistic > Cutout) to create a posterized effect. You can choose the number of colors or shades of gray you want to use, and you can also control the smoothness and fidelity of the color breaks. The Cutout filter produces smoother, cleaner edges and more color control than you can get with

Here we duplicated the image layer and turned off the new layer's visibility, then turned the *Background* into a Smart Object (Filter > Convert for Smart Filters) and applied the Smart Blur filter (Filter > Blur > Smart Blur with Radius 10, Threshold 30, Quality High, and Mode Normal). Smart Blur was then also applied to the duplicate layer (with its visibility turned on again), but this time in the filter's Edge Only mode, and the filtered copy was inverted to make a black-on-white image (Ctrl/⌘-I). The blend mode of this layer was changed to Multiply to make the white disappear, and layer Opacity was reduced to blend the lines with the color. (We didn't simply add the second Smart Blur in Edge Only mode as another Smart Filter on the *Background* because we wouldn't have been able to invert the result to produce black lines.)

 Puppies.psd

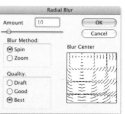

The Unsharp Mask filter can be used with extreme settings for special color effects. Here the settings were Amount 500, Radius 50, Threshold 50. (Images with large expanses of very light colors, such as sky, are usually not good candidates.)

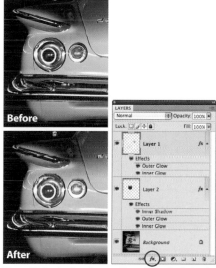

Before

After

The taillights in the photo reflected the flash (top). To brighten them up even more, we selected each one in turn with the Elliptical Marquee ◯ and copied it to a new layer (Ctrl/⌘-J). Then we clicked the *fx* at the bottom of the Layers panel to add a Layer Style consisting of an Inner Glow (set to Center so the light would spread outward from the center rather than inward from the edge) and an Outer Glow. For the larger light we also used a red Inner Shadow in Screen mode as an additional glow component.

 Valiant.psd

the Posterize command or with a Posterize Adjustment layer. Or try Filter > Blur > **Smart Blur**.

- For **special artistic effects**, try one of the filters found in the **Artistic, Brush Strokes,** or **Sketch** submenus of the Filter menu. Many of the Sketch filters use the Foreground and Background colors to create their effects, so choose the colors before you run them. Another approach is to **oversharpen** with the Unsharp Mask filter. Appendix A shows examples of these and the other Photoshop filters, and step 4 of "'Framing' with Masks" on page 269 tells how to combine filters using the Filter Gallery.

- Some of the Blur filters (Motion Blur and Radial Blur) can put the **energy and motion** of a scene back into a stop-action photo, as shown below.

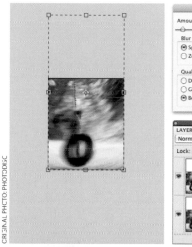

Before a Spin blur was applied to enhance the motion of the swing (Filter > Blur > Radial Blur), extra height was added by expanding the canvas with the Crop tool ⌐ (as described on page 242) so the blur center could be defined above the image, where the chain is fastened. With the blurred layer (*Background*) underneath, the original sharp image (Background copy) was masked to allow the chain and the boy's face and "leading edge" to be in sharp focus. The photo was then recropped to remove the extra canvas.

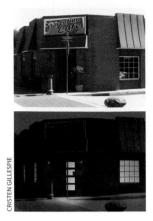

One treatment with the Lighting Effects filter lit the windows. Another created the two lamps beside the door and the light spilling out onto the walls and pavement. See a similar example of "Turning Day Into Night" on page 357.

CRISTEN GILLESPIE

- **To change the lighting in a photo,** you can add light with a **Layer Style** using one or both of the Glow effects (as shown on the previous page). Or try the **Lighting Effects** filter (Filter > Render > Lighting Effects; its dialog box is shown below). Lighting Effects can spotlight an area of an image to focus attention there (page 308). Or use it with a Negative Intensity setting to darken a corner of a scene to add mystery. Apply the same lighting to several layers to help put all the parts of a composite image into the same space (see page 626). Unify several fairly different images in a printed or online publication by applying the same lighting scheme to all of them. Or even turn day into night, as shown on page 357. *New*

LIGHTING EFFECTS

The **Lighting Effects filter** can be used as a miniature lighting studio, working on an entire layer or a part you've selected. You can set up both ambient lighting and individual light sources. Ambient light is diffuse, nondirectional light that's uniform throughout the image, like daylight on an overcast day. And it may have an inherent color, like daylight underwater. The ambient light will affect the density and color of "shadow" areas that are unlit by any individual light sources you set up.

The three varieties of individual light sources are **Omni**directional, which sends a glow in all directions, like a light bulb in a table lamp; a **Spotlight**, which is directional and focused, making a pool of light like a real spotlight; and **Directional**, which has a definite direction but is too far away to be focused, like bright sunlight or moonlight.

To save a lighting scheme so you can apply it to another layer or file later, click the "Save" button and name the style. Your new style will be added to the Style menu.

To control the direction, size, and shape of a Spotlight, drag one of the four handles on its ellipse. To change the angle only, Ctrl/⌘-drag a handle. To change the shape only, Shift-drag a handle.

To move a light source, drag its center point. **To duplicate a light source,** Alt/Option-drag its center point.

To add an individual light source, drag the light bulb icon into the Preview area.

To turn a light source off temporarily, click to turn off the "On" check mark.

To remove a light, drag its center point to the 🗑 icon below the Preview area.

To set the color for an individual light or ambient light, click the appropriate color swatch and choose a color.

The **Properties** section controls the ambient lighting and other overall properties of the environment.

The more positive the **Ambience** setting, the stronger the ambient light will be relative to the individual light sources set in the top sections of the dialog box, so the less pronounced will be the shadows produced by those lights.

The **Texture Channel** can serve as a bump map that interacts with the light sources for an image, tricking the eye into perceiving dimension or texture. The Texture Channel list includes all of the color channels (including any Spot colors) and alpha channels (if any) in the file, as well as the transparency mask and layer mask of the layer you're working on.

Lighting Effects dialog

Style: Default
Save... | Delete | OK | Cancel

Light Type: Directional / Omni / ✓ Spotlight
☑ On
Intensity: Negative — 3 — Full
Focus: Narrow — 81 — Wide

Properties
Gloss: Matte — 0 — Shiny
Material: Plastic — 69 — Metallic
Exposure: Under — 0 — Over
Ambience: Negative — -22 — Positive

Texture Channel: None
☑ White is High
Height: Flat — 50 — Mountainous

☑ Preview

Styling a Photo

YOU'LL FIND THE FILES

in 🔵 > Wow Project Files > Chapter 5 >
Styled Photo
- Styled Photo-Before.psd (to start)
- Styled Photos-After (to compare)
- Wow-Watercolor Salt Overlay.pat
  (a Pattern preset)

OPEN THIS PANEL

(from the Window menu, for instance):
- Layers

OVERVIEW

Convert *Background* to a regular layer
• Add a Color Overlay effect in a Layer
Style • Add edge effects and a surface
pattern as part of the Layer Style

ORIGINAL PHOTO: MARY LANE / PHOTOSPIN.COM

Start with an
image in RGB
Color mode, with
the *Background*
converted to a
regular layer.

AN EASY AND FLEXIBLE WAY TO TINT AN IMAGE is to use the Color Overlay effect in a Layer Style. You can get a traditional sepiatone or cyanotype look, for instance — or allow some of the original color to come through, as shown above.

Thinking the project through. With the tint stored in a Style, you can incorporate other effects also, such as a glow, a border, a drop shadow, and even a surface finish, creating a combination that can then be instantly applied to other photos.

1 Preparing the photo. Whether you start with a black-and-white or a color image, your file will need the potential for color so you can add the tint. So if your file is in Grayscale mode, convert it to color (Image > Mode > RGB Color). A *Background* can't accept a Layer Style, so if the Layers panel shows that your image is a *Background,* turn it into a regular layer by simply Alt/Option-double-clicking on the *Background* name **1**.

2 Adding the tint. At the bottom of the Layers panel, click the "Add a layer style" button *fx* and choose **Color Overlay** from its menu. When the Layer Style dialog box opens to the Color Overlay section, set the Blend Mode to **Color.** With this setting, the Style you create will control the color of the photo, but without covering up the light-and-dark picture information. Click the color swatch in the Color Overlay section to open the color picker. Use the vertical spectrum slider to choose a color family (orange is good if a sepiatone is your goal), and then click in the large color square to choose a color **2a**. Click "OK" to close the color picker, but keep the Layer Style box open. You can experiment with the brown tint effect by changing the Opacity in the Color Overlay section of the Layer Style dialog **2b**. If you

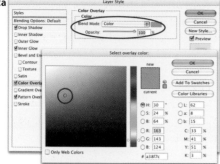

2a

Clicking the *fx* at the bottom of the Layers panel and choosing Color Overlay opens the Layer Style dialog box to the Color Overlay panel, where you can click the swatch to open the color picker. Because the Color Overlay will be in the Color blend mode, the luminosity of the color (how high up the color square you click) is not important.

2b

At 100% Opacity the sepia Color Overlay effect hides the original color in the photo.

2c

The Opacity of the Color Overlay effect is reduced to 60% in the Color Overlay section of the Layer Style dialog box.

3

An Inner Glow is added to the Layer Style. In Screen mode, light colors have a strong lightening effect. And the higher the Choke setting, the more solid the edge color.

started with a color image, reducing the Opacity will allow some of the original color to blend with the tint **2c**.

3 Adding an edge effect. While you're in the Layer Style dialog box, you can add a light edge. In the list of effects on the left side of the box, click **Inner Glow** (the name, not the checkbox) to open that panel. We used the default pale yellow, but you can change the color by clicking the square color swatch and choosing a color as in step 2. For our other Inner Glow parameters we used the settings shown in figure **3**. The **Size** setting determines how far the glow extends inward from the edge. A low **Choke** setting makes a glow that softly fades; a higher Choke setting makes a denser, more "solid" edge. When you have the glow you want, click "OK" to close the Layer Style dialog.

4 Adding a drop shadow. To add a shadow that extends outward from the edge of the image, you'll need to enlarge the image canvas to make space for it; you can do that with the Crop tool ⊥. First give yourself some extra space for your image to expand into: Press Ctrl-Alt-minus (Windows) or ⌘-Option-minus (Mac) to shrink the image but not the window. Choose the Crop tool and select the entire image by dragging diagonally from one corner to its opposite. Then drag out a little on the corner handles of the cropping frame to add more canvas **4a**; press the Enter key.

Adding a layer of white below the image will give you a better look at the shadow as you develop it. At the bottom of the Layers panel, Ctrl/⌘-click the "Create a new layer" button ⊡ (adding the Ctrl/⌘ key puts the new layer *below* the current one). Then fill the new layer with white (Edit > Fill, Contents: White).

Go back into the Layer Style dialog (click *fx* and choose Drop Shadow) and set up the Drop Shadow as you like; our settings are shown in figure **4b**. Leave the Layer Style dialog open.

5 Adding a surface finish. Click the "Pattern Overlay" name in the list of effects on the left side of the Layer Style dialog to open the **Pattern Overlay** panel. Click the **Pattern swatch** to open

4a

The Crop frame is stretched beyond the edges of the image to add more canvas for a Drop Shadow effect.

4b

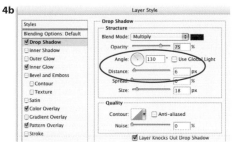

The Distance setting controls the Drop Shadow's offset. The direction of the offset is controlled by the Angle setting.

5a

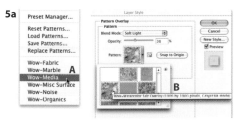

If you've already installed the Wow Patterns presets, choose Wow-Media Patterns **A** and then click on Wow-Watercolor Salt Overlay **B**. Alternatively, you can choose Load Patterns and load **Wow-Watercolor Salt Overlay.pat** from the files provided for this project.

5b

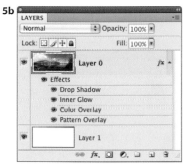

The "styled" photo over the white-filled backing layer. The component effects in the Layer Style are listed below the layer in the Layers panel.

6

With these settings, the Trim command removes the white edges. Because the shadow is a different color than the pure white edges, the trim won't flatten the soft edges of the shadow by cutting into it.

the Pattern picker; then click the ▶ button to open the picker's menu. If you've installed the Wow Patterns presets, you'll see the **Wow-Media Patterns** listed as a choice; click on it. In the warning box, click "Append," and then click the **Wow-Watercolor Salt Overlay** thumbnail in the picker **5a**. On the other hand, if you don't see the Wow-Media Patterns in the menu, choose Load Patterns from the menu and navigate to the **Wow-Watercolor Salt Overlay.pat** file supplied with the files for this section, load it, and click its thumbnail. You can regulate the effect of the pattern by changing the Opacity, Scale, or Blend Mode **5b**.

When you've developed a Layer Style you like, you can add it to the Styles panel so it's easy to apply it to other photos, and you can save it permanently with the Preset Manager. ▼

FIND OUT MORE

▼ Saving Layer Styles
page 82

6 Trimming the edges. To remove any extra white space at the edges, choose Image > Trim. In the Trim dialog box, for "Based On," choose Top Left or Bottom Right. Make sure all four "Trim Away" options are turned on **6**. Then click "OK." The image will be trimmed right up to the edge of the shadow, without clipping the shadow itself, which would create an unnatural flat edge.

Experimenting. To try different colors or patterns, double-click the name of an effect you want to change in the Layers panel and make your changes; then you can choose other effects from the list on the left side of the Layer Style dialog to make changes to them. To get the result shown below, we changed the Color Overlay to blue and its Blend Mode to Color Burn, and chose a light blue for the Inner Glow effect.

For other tinting techniques or edge treatments, see "Quick Tint Effects" on page 203, "'Framing' with Masks" on page 268, and "Filtered Frames" on page 272. *Wow!*

Starting with the Style shown at the top of page 265, we changed the Color Overlay and Inner Glow to get a different look. See Appendix C for other Wow Layer Styles designed especially for photos.

"Framing" with Masks

1a

ADRIAN BROCKWELL / PHOTOSPIN.COM

The original image

1b

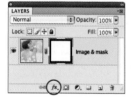

The *Background* is changed to a regular layer, and a layer mask is made from a rectangular selection.

IT'S EASY TO CREATE CUSTOM EDGE TREATMENTS for photos, starting with a layer mask that defines the area you want to frame, then softening the edges of the mask to blend the photo into the page. As shown above, you can also create a well-defined dark edge for the image within the soft vignetting.

Thinking the project through. If we use Refine Edge to feather the mask, we'll have a great interactive preview of the developing soft edge. It would be nice if we could use a Smart Filter to customize the edge, but here we'll be filtering the mask, and Smart Filters work only on Smart Objects, not on masks.

1 Creating the layer mask. Open **Frame-Before.psd** or a photo of your own **1a**. If your image consists of a *Background* layer, give it the option for transparency so it can have a layer mask: In the Layers panel, double-click the *Background* label. In the New Layer dialog box, name the layer if you'd like, and click "OK"; we named ours "Image & mask."

To add the layer mask, first choose the Rectangular Marquee tool ⬚ and drag to select the part of the image you want to frame; be sure to leave room at the edge for the soft vignetting you'll create in step 2. The border on our 1000-pixel-wide image was about 65 pixels all around. Turn your selection into a layer mask by clicking the "Add layer mask" button ⬛ at the bottom of the Layers panel **1b**. Before you soften the mask in the next step, store the frame shape for safekeeping: In the Channels

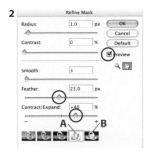

2

A

B

The mask is feathered 23 pixels, and expanded 40% using Refine Edge. The default preview method "On White" is used first **A**, but the far right preview "Mask" is a good check that edges aren't being cut off **B**.

3

We added a layer with a dark-green-filled rectangle the same size as the original frame selection, in between the image and the white background. This clearly defines the frame without eliminating the soft edges.

panel drag the *Layer Mask* name to the "Create new channel" button ◳ at the bottom of the panel.

2 Softening the edges. Adding a white-filled layer below the image layer will give you a better look at the frame edges as you develop them: To create and name a new layer *below* the current one, Ctrl-Alt-click (Windows) or ⌘-Option-click (Mac) the "Create a new layer" button ◳ at the bottom of the Layers panel. Then fill the new layer with white (type D for "default colors" and then Ctrl/⌘-Delete to fill with the Background color).

To soften the edges, click the layer mask's thumbnail in the Layers panel and choose Select > Refine Edge (in CS4 you can click the "Mask Edge" button in the Masks panel instead if you like). In the Refine Edge/Refine Mask dialog, enable Preview, using On White for the viewing method **2**. Use the Feather slider to soften the mask edge and the Contract/Expand slider to shrink or enlarge the framed area. Be careful not to let the feather grow until it reaches the hard edge of the image, which will cut off the softness abruptly. To make sure, you can switch to the Mask preview method in the dialog and look to see that your blurred edge remains well within the solid black edge. Click "OK" to accept the settings.

3 Adding a dark background to define the frame. For a well-defined frame in combination with the soft edge treatment **3**, you can add a backing layer that shows through the softened edge.

In the Layers panel create another new layer, between the white background and the masked image layer (click the ◳ button). Then activate the same selection you used to make the mask (if you haven't made a selection since creating the mask, you can choose Select > Reselect or use its shortcut, Ctrl/⌘-Shift-D; otherwise, in the Channels panel Ctrl/⌘-click the thumbnail for the alpha channel you made in step 1). Fill the selection with a dark color sampled from the photo as we did (click the Foreground color swatch in the Tools bar and then click in the image), or with black (type D, then Alt/Option-Delete); deselect (Ctrl/⌘-D).

To soften the transition between sharp frame and soft edge, you can blur the backing layer slightly. Turn the new layer into a Smart Object (right/Ctrl-click in the image and choose Convert To Smart Object), then choose Filter > Blur > Gaussian Blur; we used a Gaussian Blur with a Radius of 2 pixels for the result at the top of page 268. With the blur as a Smart Filter, you'll be able to change the edge later if you like.

4a

Targeting the layer mask and choosing Filter > Brush Strokes > Sprayed Strokes opens the Filter Gallery to the controls for this filter, with a preview on the left side of the box. You can click on the ▼ button next to "OK" to close the filter preview icons panel. Stroke Length was set at 12, Spray Radius at 20, and Stroke Direction at Right Diagonal.

4b

Here the Sprayed Strokes filter alone has been applied to the mask, using the settings in figure 4a; visibility for the dark layer is turned off by clicking its 👁 in the Layers panel.

4c

In the Filter Gallery, clicking ▣ in the bottom right corner of the dialog duplicates the filter "layer" you've been working with, and you can then replace this copy by choosing a different filter. You can click any filter in the stack and change its settings, or drag a filter up or down in the stack, effectively changing the order in which the filters are applied. To completely remove the effect of one of the filters in the stack, click on its name and then click the 🗑 button.

4 Filtering the edges. Now to experiment with some custom edge effects. In the Layers panel, click on the mask thumbnail in the "Image & mask" layer. Then make a choice from the Filter menu; we chose Filter > Brush Strokes > Sprayed Strokes. This opens the Filter Gallery dialog, with an initial "layer" for Sprayed Strokes already created **4a**. Filtering will change the edge of the mask, which will change the "frame." Click "OK" to close the Filter Gallery and see the result **4b**.

A big advantage of the Filter Gallery is that you can work interactively to combine filters **4c, 4d**. To try a different filter instead, first undo the Filter Gallery (Ctrl/⌘-Z). Then apply the Filter Gallery again by choosing the first item in the Filter menu or pressing Ctrl-Alt-F (Windows) or ⌘-Option-F (Mac) to open the last filter dialog used, in this case the Filter Gallery, so you can make changes. To keep the effect you have but also add another, click the "New effect layer" button ▣ near the bottom right corner of the dialog box, and then click on a sample thumbnail in the center section of the Filter Gallery, or choose from the pop-up alphabetical list (under the "Cancel" button). Paint Daubs, Rough Pastels, and Stamp produce interesting interactions with Sprayed Strokes. (You can see these combinations and others in "Quick Filtered Frames," starting on page 272.)

5 Trying an "all over" filter. To try a different approach, first undo the Filter Gallery (Ctrl/⌘-Z) to restore the unfiltered soft-edged mask. In the Layers panel duplicate the "Image & mask" layer (Ctrl/⌘-J), so you can work on the new layer and still have the original "Image & mask" layer with its blurred mask intact. Turn off visibility for the original "Image & mask" layer

4d

Here Mosaic Tiles was applied (Tile Size 10, Grout Width 2, Lighten Grout 10); then a Glass "layer" was added by clicking on the ▣ button at the bottom of the panel (Distortion 2, Smoothness 5, Texture: Tiny Lens, Scaling 100%). Several other examples of Filter Gallery combinations are shown on page 273.

5a

The Texturizer filter is applied to the mask (Texture Canvas, Scaling 125%, Relief 10, Light Top); visibility for the dark layer is turned off.

5b

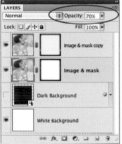

To reduce (but not completely eliminate) the texture in the image area, visibility for the "Image & mask" layer is turned on but its Opacity is reduced to 70%; this allows the "White background" layer to show through only a little.

by clicking its 👁. Then click on the new layer's mask thumbnail to make the mask active.

Now try a filter that affects the white area of the mask as well as the blurred gray, such as one of the Texture filters; we chose Filter > Texture > Texturizer. This "texturized" both the image and the "frame" **5a**. We liked the edge, but we wanted to remove most of the texture from the image itself. So we turned on visibility 👁 for the "Image & mask" layer and worked with its Opacity **5b**. Its image shows through the "holes" created by the mask on the filtered layer and smooths the photo. The result is shown at the top of page 268.

Experimenting. With a filtered mask, a blurred mask, a black or color backing, and a white background, you can try out a wealth of framing possibilities, just by turning on and off visibility for different layers as you test a variety of filters. The next two pages show other examples of filtered edge treatments. 🖌

SAVE THAT FILTER COMBO!

The Filter Gallery doesn't have a "Save" button, but it's easy to capture your filter combinations so you can apply them again. Develop the combination you like, and click "OK" to apply it. Then click Ctrl/⌘-Z to undo the Filter Gallery. In the Actions panel, click the "Create new action" button 🔲, and in the dialog box, name the Action and click "Record." Press Ctrl/⌘-F (to apply the previous Filter Gallery settings); then press the "Stop playing/recording" button ⬛ at the bottom of the Actions panel. Your Action has captured the settings for all the effects in the Filter Gallery.

FIND OUT MORE

▼ Saving and playing Actions
pages 124 & 125

OUTSIDE THE GALLERY

Using the masking and layering techniques described in "'Framing' with Masks," you can also get some great framing effects with filters that aren't included in the Filter Gallery. The process involves making a layer mask for the image, blurring the mask's edges, applying a filter to modify the blurred part of the mask, and then applying another filter to modify it further. See page 272 for filter combinations.

IMAGE SWAPPING

Once you have a framing file set up, it's easy to experiment with the same frame and another image of similar size: Start by targeting the image-and-mask layer, and then drag-and-drop your new image into the file. Press Ctrl-Alt-G (Windows) or ⌘-Option-G (Mac) to make a clipping group of the new image layer and the masked layer below.

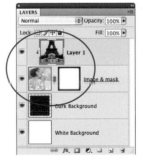

Filtered Frames

The examples on these two pages were made by running filters on a blurred layer mask in an 800-pixel-wide image, like the one created in "'Framing' with Masks" on page 268. White and black were used as the Foreground and Background colors when the filters were run.

Each of the images at the top of these two pages was made by applying a single filter. Each of the images at the bottom was made with two filters:

- For the two-filter images on this page, one filter was chosen from the Filter menu and applied, and then the other, since both weren't available in the Filter Gallery.

- For the examples on the next page, we chose Filter > Filter Gallery, clicked the "New effect layer" button ⬓ (near the bottom right corner of the dialog box), and chose from the alphabetical pop-up menu (near the top of the right side of the box). We adjusted the settings, then clicked the ⬓ button again, picked another filter from the list, and chose its settings.

The examples on these pages were made with the mask targeted. Smart Filters wouldn't work here, because the filtering is done to the mask rather than the image content of the layer.

YOU'LL FIND THE FILE
in (wow) > Wow Project Files >
Chapter 5 > Filtered Frames

Halftone Pixelate > Color Halftone (Max. Radius 5, all Screen Angles 45)

Twirl-Mild Distort > Twirl (Angle 400°)

Confetti-Crisp Pixelate > Color Halftone (default settings); then Pixelate > Crystallize (Cell Size 10)

Comb Edges Distort > Wave (Sine, Generators 5, Wavelength Min. 10 Max.11, Amplitude Min. 5 Max. 6, Scales 100); then Blur > Lens Blur > Alt/Option-click "Reset" (default)

Sketch Sketch > Graphic Pen (Stroke Length 15, Light/Dark Balance 25, Stroke Direction: Right Diagonal)

Twirl-Strong Distort > Twirl (Angle, 999°)

Confetti-Soft Brush Strokes > Spatter (Spray Radius 25, Smoothness 5) then Pixelate > Crystallize (Cell Size 10)

Zigzag-Soft Distort > Ripple (Amount 250, Size: Large); then Noise > Median (Radius 15)

Grainy Texture > Grain (Intensity 85, Contrast 75, Grain Type: Enlarged)

Ripples Distort > Ocean Ripple (Ripple Size 1, Ripple Magnitude 12)

Spatter-Soft Brush Strokes > Spatter (Spray Radius 15, Smoothness 5)

Border-Stepped Pixelate > Mosaic (Cell Size 25)

Mosaic-Organic Pixelate > Crystallize (Cell Size 25)

Water Paper Sketch > Water Paper (Fiber Length 50, Brightness 60, Contrast 75)

Dithered Filter Gallery > Smudge Stick (Str. Length 1, Highlight Area 15, Intensity 10) on the bottom; Grain (Intensity 25, Contrast 50, Grain Type: Speckle) on top

Splash Filter Gallery > Spatter (Spray Radius 15, Smoothness 5) on the bottom; Paint Daubs (Brush Size 10, Sharpness 10, Brush Type: Sparkle) on top

Border-Inline Filter Gallery > Stamp (Light/Dark Balance 25, Smoothness 5) on the bottom; Chrome (Detail 1, Smoothness 10) on top

Cut-out Filter Gallery > Ocean Ripple (Ripple Size 7, Ripple Magnitude 15) on the bottom; Stamp (Light/Dark Balance 25, Smoothness 5) on top

Glass Filter Gallery > Glass (Distortion 5, Smoothness 5, Texture: Frosted, Scaling 85) on the bottom; Sumi-e (Stroke Width 10, Stroke Pressure 5, Contrast, 0) on top

Reflections Filter Gallery > Glass (Distortion 10, Smoothness 5, Texture: Frosted, Scaling 100) on the bottom; Sumi-e (Stroke Width 10, Stroke Pressure 5, Contrast 30) on top

Compensating for Camera-Related Distortion

1

RICK WORTHINGTON

The original photo shows a complex mix of rustic stonework, modern masonry, angled planes, and different kinds of camera-related distortion. Our goal is to arrive at a more "comfortable" view.

THE LENS CORRECTION FILTER WAS designed as a "one-stop" solution for correcting much of the camera-related distortion that can happen when a photo is taken. Like so many of Photoshop's amazing operations, Lens Correction is firmly based in science and engineering, but using it is an art. Before you begin, you might want to check out its mechanics in "Exercising Lens Correction," a section from an earlier edition of the book, which is included as a PDF on the Wow DVD ROM (🔵Wow Goodies > Chapter 5 > Outtakes > Exercising Lens Correction).

Thinking the project through. Part of the beauty of Lens Correction is that you can work back and forth among its controls, adjusting the corrections interactively until you have a pleasing combination (there isn't necessarily one "right answer"). Then when you finally click "OK" to leave the dialog box, all the changes are applied at once, with only one resampling of the image, leaving it crisper than if you had made the changes separately. And when you apply Lens Correction as a Smart Filter, it's easy to go back later and make changes if you like.

1 Analyzing distortion. To start, open the **Camera Distortion-Before.psd** file or a file of your own. For our obviously distorted photo **1**, we can't completely rely on perfectly straight edges to

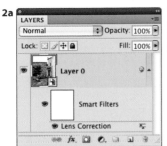

2a The Lens Correction filter is applied as a Smart Filter.

2b The Lens Correction dialog box itself, the grid, and the Preview magnification can all be resized to suit any level of precision required. ("Fit in View" resizes the image to fit in the Preview if you resize the dialog box smaller than full-screen.)

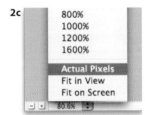

2c

800%
1000%
1200%
1600%
Actual Pixels
Fit in View
Fit on Screen

80.6%

Fit in View is the default opening view; In this case the magnification is 80.6%. Click on the number box in the lower left corner to pop up a list of magnifications to choose from, or click the "+" or "−" button. Actual Pixels gives an accurate view of details.

2d

☑ Preview ☑ Show Grid Size: 40 Color:

Click on the **Color swatch** to bring up the Color picker, and select a color that contrasts with your image. Then change the grid size (as described next) so you have enough grid lines for easy comparison with horizontal and vertical elements in your image, but not so many lines that they interfere with seeing the photo. For **Size**, use the pop-out slider, or drag-select the number and type a new one, or position the cursor over the word "Size" and scrub (make a series of short drags left or right).

guide us, but we can pick a few horizontals and verticals that were probably reasonably straight and use Lens Correction's grid to guide us in making corrections. Because the stones in the back wall were probably about the same size on each side of the wall, we can conclude that the lens and camera angle caused much of the slant in the roofline, and the image will look better if we place this wall directly opposite our viewpoint, aiming to make its roofline horizontal. These corrections will make a big change to all the other angles in the image, so we'll tackle them first.

The wall on the right side, with its more obvious geometry, is a good place to check for barrel or pincushion distortion, and we can see barreling. We can also see bright colors along some high-contrast edges, especially on the left edge of the tower, which indicates that we'll need to correct for chromatic aberration. Although we'll want to crop the image for composition, we'll do the Lens Correction work first, since the filter is designed to work on images as they come from the camera rather than after cropping.

2 Setting up Lens Correction. From Photoshop's main menu choose Filter > Convert for Smart Filters, then Filter > Distort > Lens Correction **2a**. By default Lens Correction opens with the image set to "Fit in View" **2b**, and a neutral gray grid with Size set to 16. The first thing to do is to choose a magnification for viewing your image. Actual Pixels (100% magnification, at the bottom left of the dialog) will give you an accurate pixel-for-pixel view **2c**. Then, at the right, choose a grid color that contrasts with the image and a size that makes it easy to compare horizontal and vertical lines in the image with the lines of the grid **2d**.

As we work, we'll use the Move Grid tool 🖑 by dragging to line up the grid with the elements we're trying to straighten, often zooming in (Ctrl/⌘-+) and panning with the Hand tool 🖑 to get a better look. Using the Move Grid tool, put some of the grid lines on or next to the roofline, for instance, or the vertical lines of the wall on the right.

3 Pivoting the image and adjusting for camera tilt. In order to make other adjustments easier, we can begin our correction with what appears to be the biggest change we'll want to make: swinging the back wall around to face us and making the roofline horizontally straight.

In the Lens Correction dialog box, begin by moving the Horizontal Perspective slider to the left to swing the wall **3a**. This pivots the image around a vertical axis, moving the left side of the

3a

Horizontal Perspective   −20

Pivoting the wall by changing the Horizontal Perspective

3b

Angle: 357.40 °

Straightening the horizon

3c

After pivoting the viewpoint and straightening the back wall roofline

4a

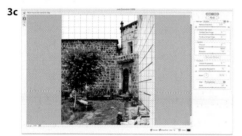

The back wall appears to bow upward, indicating barreling.

4b

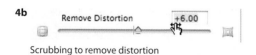

Remove Distortion   +6.00

Scrubbing to remove distortion

wall closer to us. With very little to guide us in this adjustment, we can "eyeball" our correction as we play with the slider until the blocks on the left and right sides of the wall seem to be the same size; we settled on a setting of −20. This corrects much of the roofline slant, but it looks like the camera might have been tilted a little to the right when the photo was taken. (To better see the change, readjust the size of the grid and use the Move Grid tool 🖐 as needed.)

To adjust for the tilt, highlight the number box to the right of the Angle diagram and use the ↑ or ↓ arrow key (with Shift for greater increments) until most of the important vertical and horizontal lines closely follow the grid. If you prefer to use a mouse, "scrubbing" over the word "Angle" can be equally precise (move the cursor into position over the word and when the scrubber icon appears, make short, quick drags for slight changes). We finally settled on 357.40 for the Angle **3b**. The screen preview at "Fit in View" magnification shows how far we've come toward fixing the image **3c**. (You can compare your current version with the "before" image by toggling the preview off and on with the checkbox at the bottom of the dialog box.)

4 Correcting for barreling. With the horizontal perspective and the angle adjusted, our image now clearly shows barreling (bulging) in the back wall's roofline as it curves up from the left, as well as in the newer wall on the right **4a**. We can concentrate on the roofline as we scrub the Remove Distortion slider with short drags to the right until the roofline no longer bulges upward in the middle. An amount of +6 reduced the barrel effect without disturbing our other corrections **4b**, **4c**.

5 Adjusting vertical perspective. The tower and the high wall on the right appear to narrow or lean as they go up. To straighten these elements, start by carefully moving and resizing the grid so the grid lines match a vertical element you can use as a benchmark; we set our grid to match the width of the tower window. We then moved the Vertical Perspective slider slightly to the left (−6) to straighten the edges of the window,

4c

After the Remove Distortion adjustment to diminish barreling

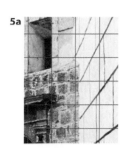

5a

Matching the grid size to the tower window, we moved the Vertical Perspective slider until the straight vertical elements were parallel with the lines of the grid.

5b

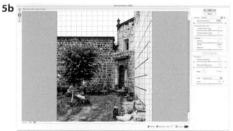

After correcting for barrel distortion and vertical tilt. The corrections have distorted the image from its rectangular shape, leaving transparency at the right edge.

6

A fringe of color is visible at several spots on the tower. Adjusting the Fix Red/Cyan Fringe slider to +15 reduces the color fringing.

7

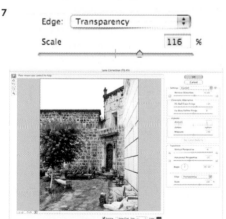

A Scale setting of 116% (shown above) was the smallest enlargement that eliminated transparency from the edges. We decided to leave the Scale set at 100% instead, and click "OK."

watching our earlier corrections to see that they weren't disturbed by this one **5a**, **5b**.

6 Subduing the color "fringe." Some photos show a "bloom," or fringe, of color along edges of high contrast. This *chromatic aberration* can come from a combination of factors, such as the way the lens bends the different wavelengths (colors) that make up white light and the way the color sensors in a digital camera respond to bright light. The Lens Correction filter can often help remove these color outlines, if not completely, at least enough so they aren't obvious when the photo is printed. In this photo, the tower is dark against a white sky. By zooming in, we can see the color fringing **6**. As you move the Fix Red/Cyan Fringe slider to the right, notice that some bands of color become more neutral, but if we move it farther, more bands pop out someplace else. In many pictures you can reduce the fringe to the point where you don't see it when you view the image at print size; we settled on a setting of +15, which reduces the color fringe on the edges of the tower somewhat without creating a noticeable fringe in other places. If the color fringe is still too obvious after you use the "Fix" sliders, you can try neutralizing it with another Photoshop method after you leave the Lens Correction dialog box; see page 336.

7 Cropping the image. The Edge and Scale features in the Lens Correction dialog box are there to help if your corrections have distorted the normal rectangular shape of the image, as our corrections have. The default Edge setting is Transparency, with the Scale slider at 100%. By increasing the Scale, you can enlarge the image to fill the frame, without any transparency at the edges, while maintaining the original photo width-to-height ratio **7**. Like the other adjustments in the Lens Correction dialog box, Scale works from the center, so if you want a crop that's centered differently, or one that doesn't necessarily maintain the original width-to-height ratio, you can leave the Scale at 100% as we did, click "OK" to close the dialog box, and do the cropping outside.

There are several ways to crop the image. ▼ We chose the Crop tool ◫ and pressed the "Clear" button in the Options bar so we wouldn't resample the image in the process. We dragged the Crop tool diagonally to frame the image. Then with Shield turned on and Perspective turned off in the Options bar, we could drag the handles to resize the Crop frame and drag inside the frame to move it; pressing the Enter key completed the crop. The result is shown at the top of page 274. *new*

FIND OUT MORE

▼ Cropping **page 240**

Vignetting

A *vignette* is an image that shades off gradually at the edges. In the camera, vignetting that darkens the edges can be *mechanical*, caused by a lens hood creating shade, or *optical*, caused by shading within the lens system. Vignetting can also result from a natural drop-off of light from the center to the edges when the aperture is small. In digital cameras, a stronger signal is produced by light hitting a sensor at a right angle than if it hits at oblique angles; this kind of vignetting is usually more pronounced in a raw-format image, since many digital cameras remove or reduce it when a photo is converted from raw format to JPEG or TIFF.

In Photoshop there are many ways to fade the edges. The method you choose will depend on the effect you want to achieve, whether you want subtle or dramatic, and what fits into your workflow. Some easy, elegant solutions can be found in the Wow-Vignettes Styles (see page 755). Here we look at some other quick vignetting options:

- simulating a mechanical or optical vignette
- automating a vignette
- creating an asymmetrical vignette to guide the eye
- vignetting an image with a "live" crop
- vignetting that blends a background color into the image itself

YOU'LL FIND THE FILES
in > Wow Project Files > Chapter 5 > Quick Vignetting

ELIMINATING VIGNETTING

Should you want to *counteract* a vignette rather than create or emphasize one, try Photoshop's Lens Correction filter▼ or the Lens Vignetting functions on the Lens Corrections tab in Camera Raw. Also, in CS4 the panorama-piecing function (File > Automate > Photomerge, or you can approach it through Bridge's Tools > Photoshop > Photomerge) offers an automatic vignette-removal feature, designed to lighten dark corners to prevent a "scalloped" look when you combine a series of images in a panorama.

☑ Blend Images Together
☑ Vignette Removal
☐ Geometric Distortion Correction

Simulating a Camera Vignette

DENISE FORTADO / PHOTOSPIN.COM

DARKENED EDGES CAN SUBDUE distracting detail and help guide the eye inward to the center. One way to create a vignette in Photoshop is to use the Lens Correction filter: Convert the image to a Smart Object (Filter > Convert for Smart Filters) and then choose Filter > Distort > Lens Correction. In the Vignette section of the Lens Correction dialog, set the Amount (negative values darken the edges) **A**, and set the Midpoint (how far in toward the center of the image the effect extends) **B**. We painted the filter's mask to partially remove the vignette from the hands near the bottom corners; "Painted Ghosting" on page 304 describes the masking method. You'll find other techniques for custom vignettes at the right and on pages 280 and 302.

 Vignette.psd

FIND OUT MORE
▼ Lens Correction filter **page 274**

A Vignetting Action

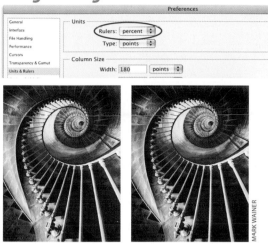

MARK WAINER SUBTLY "BURNED THE EDGES" of *Stairway #59, Isle de Re* (shown above), to help draw the viewer into the scene. Because he uses vignetting often, he developed a Photoshop Action that would do the job on any size image, either vertical or horizontal format. The key to the Edge Burn Action's flexibility is that before he recorded it, Wainer set the **units to Percent** (Photoshop > Preferences > Units & Rulers). At the bottom of the Actions panel he created a new action ⬛ and clicked "Record" in the New Action dialog. He chose the Rectangular Marquee tool (Shift-M), set the Feather in the Options bar, and dragged diagonally, from a point 10% in and down from the top left corner to a point 90% in and down, near the bottom right corner. Recording the selection in percentages rather than pixels is what allows the Action to work on files of different sizes.

Wainer's vignetting Action next inverts the selection (Ctrl/⌘-Shift-I), then adds a Levels Adjustment layer; the active selection makes a built-in layer mask, and the Input Levels gamma (middle slider) is reduced to make the edges even darker than Wainer typically wants. Then in the Layers panel the Levels layer's Opacity is reduced to 50% and the blend mode is set to Multiply.

To run the Action, double-click its icon on your desktop to add it to your Actions panel; then click its name and click the Play button ▶. After you run the Action, you can darken or lighten the vignette by changing the Opacity of the Levels layer. In CS4 you can also use the Masks panel to modify the vignette, as in step 2 of "'Framing' with Masks" (page 269). To reduce the vignetting in light areas such as sky, use a soft brush to paint that region of the mask with black.

 **EdgeBurnAction.atn**

Vignetting with Gradients

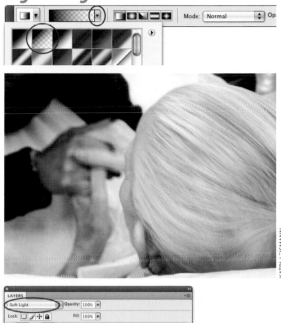

WHEN KATRIN EISMANN WANTED TO DIRECT the viewer's eye to the hands in this photo, taken at a Greenwich Village senior citizens' home, she "burned down" the areas of less importance, creating an asymmetrical vignette effect, by using the Gradient tool this way: Target the top layer in the layers panel, add an empty layer above it (Ctrl/⌘-Shift-N) and change its blend mode to Soft Light. Then choose the Gradient tool ⬛ (Shift-G); in the Options bar, choose the Linear option and choose the Foreground to Transparent gradient from the pop-out palette of swatches; choose black as the Foreground color (type D, for default colors). Make sure Reverse is turned off and Transparency is turned on. Then wield the Gradient tool like a brush, clicking near the edge and dragging inward to where you want the burning to end, near the center of attention. Repeat this "sweeping" motion from various points on the edge; then reduce the layer's Opacity in the Layers panel, if needed, to create the effect you want.

Post Crop Vignetting

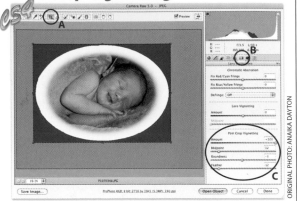

Post Crop Vignetting on the Lens Corrections tab in Camera Raw 5.0 offers a wonderful interface for creating a soft romantic look with a feathered edge all the way around. You can work with the crop and the vignetting interactively, for incredible flexibility in shaping and softening the edge. For our portrait, in **Bridge** we navigated to our JPEG photo, clicked its thumbnail, and chose File > Open in Camera Raw. Once your photo is open, click on the Crop tool ⊐ (in the toolbar at the upper left of the Camera Raw interface) **A**, or type C. Drag diagonally across the image to choose the part you want to vignette; if you want to angle your crop, drag outside the cropping frame to rotate it. Click on Camera Raw's Lens Corrections tab **B** and set up the character of the vignette in the **Post Crop Vignetting** section **C**: Set the opacity of the vignetting (take the **Amount** all the way to +100 to fade the edges to solid white, as we did, or all the way to –100 to fade to solid black). Set the shape of the vignetted image (the **Roundness** setting goes from rectangular at the left to circular on the right). Determine how much of the cropped image is included (move the **Midpoint** slider). Determine how abruptly the edge fades (increase the **Feather** for a softer, more gradual fade). Before you finalize the vignetting, make sure you can see the clipping color *all the way around* the vignetted part of the image — by default the clipping color is red if you're vignetting to white, or blue if you're vignetting to black; this looks garish in the Camera Raw interface, but making sure it's visible all the way around the vignetted image will keep the soft edges from being cut off and flattened. The Crop frame is still "live" anytime the Crop tool is chosen, so you can change the size, shape, or angle of the crop, or drag inside the frame to adjust the part of the image that's included, while you're adjusting the edge character of the vignette.

Patch Tool Vignettes

Strictly by serendipity and experimentation, we found that the Patch tool ◇ can be used to blend a brightly colored image (like this detail from a photo of flowers at a market stall) into a background color for a dreamy pastel look. First define the image as a pattern (Edit > Define Pattern). Then add a new layer (Ctrl/⌘-Shift-N), and fill the layer with the color you want for the background (one way is to choose Edit > Fill > Color and make a choice from the "Choose a color" dialog). Make a selection; we used the Elliptical Marquee ◯ (Shift-M), holding down the Shift and Alt/Option keys and dragging outward from the center of the circular area we wanted to vignette, and dragging within the selection boundary to adjust the position of the circle **A**. Feather the selection so the image will have a soft edge (we chose Select > Feather and used 20 pixels for the Feather Radius). Now choose the Patch tool ◇ (Shift-J until you get it); click the pattern swatch in the Options bar, and choose your new pattern from the bottom of the Pattern picker **B**. Click the "Use Pattern" button and wait patiently for the "Healing" to be completed.

🔴 **Patch Tool Vignettes.psd**

Tone & Color Adjustments

Photoshop offers many ways to make a less-than-perfect photo look good, or a good photo look great. In most cases you'll be looking for a solution that saves time, produces top-quality results, and leaves you with a file that's flexible, in case you need to make further changes. The "quick fixes" on these 10 pages are presented with that in mind. In some cases a quick fix may not get you all the way to your goal, but it can give you a big head start.

Most of the adjustments on these 10 pages are available as editable Adjustment layers, by clicking the "Create new fill or adjustment layer" button ◑ at the bottom of the Layers panel or by clicking one of the rectangular buttons on the Adjustments panel in Photoshop CS4.

Other adjustments, such as Shadows/Highlights and Variations, aren't available as Adjustment layers, but they *can* be applied as Smart Filters, so they're still editable.

Still other adjustments, like Match Color, are available only through the Image > Adjustments menu, so they don't remain "live."

YOU'LL FIND THE FILES
in ⓦ > Wow Project Files > Chapter 5 > Quick Tone and Color

Variations

ROHIT SETH / PHOTOSPIN.COM

THE **VARIATIONS** COMMAND provides an array of tone and color adjustments — hue, saturation, and lightness are controlled independently for highlights, midtones, and shadows. Variations also lets you preview and compare several different options at once. You can set Variations to make finer adjustments, and you can turn on Show Clipping, to alert you so you won't produce colors that may be outside the color gamut you're working in. Variations can't be applied as an Adjustment layer, but in CS3 and CS4 it *can* be applied as a Smart Filter. We converted the photo to a Smart Object (Filter > Convert for Smart Filters, or right/Ctrl-click the photo's thumbnail in the Layers panel and choose Convert to Smart Object from the context-sensitive menu). We first lightened the midtones by clicking on the Lighter preview image, then removed a little red by adding its opposite, first setting the Fine/Coarse control on the finest setting and then clicking the More Cyan preview (each opposite-color pair lies on a straight line that goes through the Current Pick).

 Variations.psd

Shadows/Highlights

Before

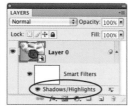

After

THE **SHADOWS/HIGHLIGHTS** COMMAND can increase or reduce contrast where it's needed at the same time it brightens or darkens.▼ Its default settings (shown above) can so often do wonders that it's almost always worth trying on an image with shadow problems, like this photo with the baby's face in shadow. Since the **Shadows/Highlights** correction isn't available as an Adjustment layer, but *is* available as a Smart Filter, our first step was to turn the image layer into a Smart Object by right/Ctrl-clicking on the image thumbnail in the Layers panel and choosing Convert to Smart Object from the context-sensitive menu. Then we chose Image > Adjustments > Shadows/Highlights and clicked "OK" to accept the default settings, which brightened up the face without losing the sense of bright sunlight and shade. To experiment, double-click Shadows/Highlights in the Layers panel and click Show More Options.▼

FIND OUT MORE
▼ Using the Shadows/Highlights command **page 254**

 **Shadows-Highlights.psd**

Masking an Adjustment

THIS PHOTO HAD THE SAME PROBLEM as the one at the left, but because more of the image was in shadow, more of it lightened up when Shadows/Highlights was applied. To try another option — lighting up the girls but keeping other shaded areas dark — we used the Smart Filter **mask** to restrict the effect of Shadows/Highlights. We targeted the mask by clicking its thumbnail in the Layers panel, then filled it with black (typing D with a mask targeted makes black the Background color; then Ctrl/⌘-Delete fills the mask with black. With white as the Foreground color, we chose the Brush tool ✏, picked a large, soft brush tip from the Options bar, and took about 20 seconds to paint the mask with white where we wanted the adjustment to take effect.▼ Because the mask's edges are soft, the adjusted areas blend smoothly into the unaltered surroundings. Shift-clicking the mask's thumbnail in the Layers panel toggled the effect of the mask off and on, allowing us to compare the masked version of the correction with the unmasked version.

Masking Adjustment.psd

FIND OUT MORE
▼ Painting a layer mask **page 84**

Auto Levels or Curves

IF A PHOTO SEEMS TO LACK CONTRAST, simply applying an "Auto" CORRECTION often markedly improves the overall color and tone. To do this, click the "Create new fill or adjustment layer" button ◑ at the bottom of the Layers panel and choose a Levels or Curves Adjustment layer from the pop-up list, or if you're working in CS4, an alternative is to open the Adjustments panel (Window > Adjustments, for instance) and click ▦ or ▦. ▼ In the dialog, click the "**Auto**" button. This correction finds the darkest tones in the image and darkens them to black, and lightens the lightest tones to white, spreading the intermediate tones over the entire tonal range to improve contrast. Because it balances contrast for each color channel independently (the Red, Blue, and Green channels in this RGB image), this option can remove an unwanted color cast (or add one, as in the image at the right).

Auto Correx.psd

FIND OUT MORE

▼ Using Levels or Curves **page 246**

Auto Options

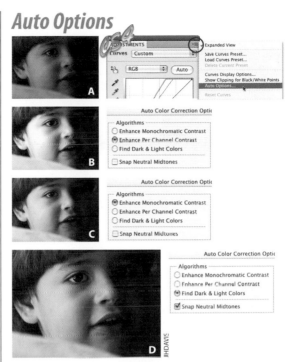

THERE'S MORE THAN ONE "AUTO" choice for Levels or Curves. If you click the "Options" button instead of "Auto," Photoshop applies the Auto adjustment (described at the left) but also opens another dialog box with more choices. (If you're using Levels or Curves through CS4's Adjustments panel as we are here, you won't see an "Options" button; instead, click the panel's menu button ▾≡ and choose Auto Options.) When you have an image that needs color and contrast adjustment **A**, it's easy to click through the three options in the Auto Color Correction Options dialog and try them out, with and without Snap Neutral Midtones:

• The default **Enhance Per Channel Contrast** option is what you get when you click the "Auto" button; for this image it adds an unwanted color cast **B**.

• The **Enhance Monochromatic Contrast** option balances contrast without changing color balance **C**. It applies the same correction as choosing Image > Adjustments > Auto Contrast.

• The bottom choice, **Find Dark & Light Colors**, with **Snap Neutral Midtones** turned on **D**, is the same as choosing Image > Adjustments > Auto Color.

Snap Neutral Midtones brings any close-to-neutral midtones in the newly adjusted image to true neutral, with equal amounts of the primary colors.

Auto-Options.psd

Selecting & Auto

An Auto or Options correction often works better if you first **select** the area that's most important for Photoshop to "look at" when it adjusts the contrast. For instance, in this photo **A**, we clicked the "Auto Options" command in the Curves dialog pop-up menu, and chose Enhance Per Channel Contrast with Snap Neutral Midtones. But the result was too dark because Photoshop found the pure white border area and used that to set the white point for the entire image **B**. So we clicked the "Cancel" button and dragged with the Rectangular Marquee tool ⬚ to make a selection that excluded the white border and some of the portrait edge to make a balanced selection of important tones. *Then* we added the Curves Adjustment layer, and the result was much better **C**. Making a selection also creates a mask for the Adjustment layer, but to extend the adjustment to the entire image, simply delete the mask (drag its thumbnail to the Layers panel's 🗑 button).

wow Selecting-Auto.psd

Auto Corrections in Camera Raw

CAMERA RAW CAN ALSO AUTO-CORRECT images with the click of a button. When you open a raw file in Camera Raw, it automatically applies a Default for initially viewing the image. But you can also use Camera Raw with JPEG and TIFF files. In that case, the Default setting is no "correction" at all. You'll view the image exactly the same as if you had opened it in Photoshop. Here we brightened the image by clicking on Auto, which increased the Brightness and Contrast settings in the Basic tab.

Raw files will open in Camera Raw if you simply double-click on them in Bridge or on the desktop, or if you use File > Open in Photoshop. To open your JPEG or TIFF in Camera Raw from Bridge, right-click/Ctrl-click on the image in Bridge and choose Open in Camera Raw from the context-sensitive menu, or use the keyboard shortcut Ctrl/⌘-R.

To open from Photoshop, choose File > Open, navigate to your file and click on its name. *Then* choose Camera Raw from the Format menu in the Open dialog, and click the "Open" button.

Auto & Luminosity

WITH AN ADJUSTMENT LAYER, you aren't limited to "full-strength" (100% Opacity) or to Normal mode. For this sepiatone **A**, the Auto correction improved the contrast but removed the color **B**. We clicked the "Options" button in the Levels dialog (or in CS4's Adjustments panel menu ▾☰, choose Auto Options) and tried Enhance Monochromatic Contrast; this made the color too intense **C**. The Find Dark & Light Colors option also overcorrected the color. So we went back to the default **Enhance Per Channel Contrast**. To maintain some of the color **D**, we changed the blend mode of the Levels layer to **Luminosity**; to reduce the contrast, which the Levels layer had overcorrected, we reduced Opacity.

Auto-Luminosity.psd

Levels/Curves & Multiply

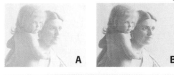

To RESTORE DENSITY TO A PHOTO that's severely "washed out" because it's overexposed or faded **A**, add a Curves Adjustment layer in **Multiply** mode (by Alt/Option-clicking the "Create new fill or adjustment layer" button ⊘ at the bottom of the Layers panel and choosing Curves from the pop-up list). In the New Layer dialog box, choose Multiply for the mode and click "OK." In the Curves dialog, click "OK" without making any adjustment. If this "blank" Adjustment layer in Multiply mode hasn't improved the range of tones enough **B**, you can duplicate it (by pressing Ctrl/⌘-J) **C**. If the image still lacks contrast, try adding a Curves layer in Normal mode to apply the adjustment using the "Auto" button. Reduce the Opacity of this top layer if the effect is too strong **D**. Now if you want to change the effect in only part of the tonal range (as you might in the shadows here), you can go back into the Curves dialog to do that (by double-clicking the top Curves thumbnail in the Layers panel). ▾

FIND OUT MORE

▾ Adjusting Curves **page 247**

Curves-Multiply.psd

Set Gray Point

Before

After

PAUL K. DAYTON, JR.

THE SET GRAY POINT EYEDROPPER, which is found in both the Levels and Curves dialogs, can be useful for correcting a color cast like the one in this discolored transparency. (The dropper is found in the lower part of the Curves dialog and in the lower right corner of the Levels dialog in CS3, but in CS4's Levels dialog, shown here, it's in the upper left.)

By clicking the dropper on the image, you tell Photoshop that the spot you've clicked on is supposed to be a neutral gray, and Photoshop makes an overall adjustment to the color balance of the image to make that happen. Here clicking on the rock fixed the color. If you don't get the change you want on your first try, click on another spot that might be neutral. Of course, if your image doesn't include anything that should be neutral gray, this method won't work, because you'll actually be adding a color cast each time you try to force some color to neutral. In that case you might try the Average method at the right, or take the time to adjust Color Balance. ▼

 **Set Gray Point.psd**

FIND OUT MORE
▼ Adjusting Color Balance **page 251**

Average Filter

A

B

C

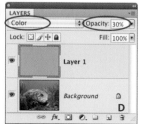

D

ORIGINAL PHOTO: KEIVAN DEHGHANPISHEH / PHOTOSPIN.COM

E

IF YOU TRY THE "SET GRAY POINT" METHOD on an image (as described at the left) but the color just switches wildly from one tint to another, Photoshop's **Average** filter is worth a try. We wanted to reduce the strength of the blue in this image **A** and restore some of the color of the turtle and the corals. We duplicated the photo to a new layer (Ctrl/⌘-J) and chose Filter > Blur > Average **B**. The filter "averaged" the duplicate layer to a solid greenish-blue **C**. We then inverted the color (Image > Adjustments > Invert, or Ctrl/⌘-I), which changed the blue to its opposite salmon color. By applying this opposite-color layer in Color mode **D** (or Hue mode for a slightly different effect), you can adjust Opacity to get the more neutral coloring that you want. We reduced the Opacity of the layer until we had the neutralizing effect we wanted at 30% **E**. *Note:* For this method, using Average as a Smart Filter wouldn't have worked. Although you can change the Opacity and blend mode of a Smart Filter, inverting the color is not an option.

 Average Filter.psd

Average & Auto

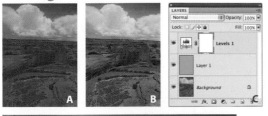

D

MONA DAYTON

USING THE AVERAGE FILTER can also be a good place to start in recovering a badly discolored photo. We opened this scan of a color transparency of Canyon de Chelly from the 1940s **A.** We tried the "Set Gray Point" method (see page 286), but because the clouds were reflecting the red earth when the photo was taken, we couldn't find a spot in the image that should be a neutral gray. Instead we duplicated the image to a new layer (Ctrl/⌘-J) and chose Filter > Blur > **Average** (the same as for the sea turtle image on page 286). The Average filter turned the duplicate layer a solid pink. We then inverted the color (Image > Adjustments > Invert, or Ctrl/⌘-I), which changed the pink to its opposite greenish blue. We changed the blend mode of this layer to Color and adjusted the layer's Opacity to balance the color as closely as possible to what we wanted **B**. Now that we had more realistic color to work with, we could add a Levels Adjustment layer **C** and click the "**Auto**" button as the next step **D**. The image was on its way to recovery.

 **Average-Auto.psd**

Color Balance

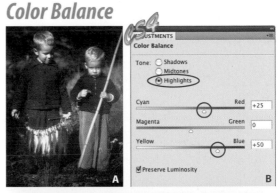

C

PAUL K. DAYTON, JR.

A **COLOR BALANCE** ADJUSTMENT LAYER (click the ◐ button and choose) can target a color change to the highlights, midtones, or shadows separately. You simply add the opposite of the color you have too much of. This RGB image showed a yellow cast in the highlights **A**. To remove the yellow, the Highlights option was chosen in the Color Balance dialog and the Yellow-Blue slider was moved toward Blue. To bring back a little warmth, the Cyan-Red slider was moved slightly toward Red **B**, **C**. We kept Preserve Luminosity checked to ensure we changed only the color and not the tonal values.

 **Color Balance.psd**

Warming

Cooling

TRADITIONALLY, photographers have used warming filters on their camera lenses to absorb the excess blue and achieve warmer tones when shooting outside in the shade or with an electronic flash — or just to "warm up" the color in a photo, especially a portrait. You can get similar results with Photoshop's Warming "filter layers." To warm this photo, we clicked the ⊘ button at the bottom of the Layers panel and chose **Photo Filter**; in CS4 another option is to click the ⊕ button in the Adjustments panel (opened by clicking Window > Adjustments, for instance). Then we chose **Warming Filter** (85) from the Filter menu in the Photo Filter dialog. For all the Photo Filters, the default Density of 25% mimics the effect of the most widely used traditional filters, but you can adjust it to suit your image; we used 35%. ▼

FIND OUT MORE
▼ Using Photo Filter **page 253**

Warm.psd

TO INCREASE THE COOL FEELING of a seascape or a snow scene, for instance **A**, you can use one of the Cooling "filter layers." Here we clicked the ⊘ button at the bottom of the Layers panel and chose **Photo Filter** from the pop-up list; in CS4 another option is to click the ⊕ button in the Adjustments panel (opened by clicking Window > Adjustments, for instance). We chose **Cooling Filter (80) B**, **C**. ▼

FIND OUT MORE
▼ Using Photo Filter
page 253

Cooling.psd

Hue/Saturation

A   B

C

D

SOME IMAGES JUST NEED A SATURATION BOOST to restore color — either generally or in a specific range of colors. For this image **A**, we added a Hue/Saturation Adjustment layer by clicking the ⬤ button and choosing from the list. In the Hue/Saturation dialog, we moved the **Saturation** slider slightly to the right to generally brighten up the color **B**. Then, to emphasize the overalls, tricycle, and flowers, we chose the **Reds** color family to edit and boosted its **Saturation** separately as well **C, D**.

🅦 Hue-Saturation-Reds.psd

Boosting CMYK

A

B

C

AN RGB IMAGE WHOSE COLORS LOOK INTENSE and lively can sometimes lose some of its punch when converted to **CMYK** mode for printing **A**. In that case a subtle change applied in a Hue/Saturation Adjustment layer in the CMYK file may help restore some of the vibrancy of the color overall, or of a particular color range. Here we clicked the ⬤ button, chose Hue/Saturation, and increased the **Saturation** overall (with the default Master chosen as the color range to edit) **B, C**.

🅦 CMYK Boost.psd

Vibrance

THE **VIBRANCE** ADJUSTMENT is designed to boost color saturation while protecting colors that are nearly saturated already. We used it to intensify the color of the beads in plastic sacks in this photo from a Beijing market. In Photoshop CS4 we opened the Adjustments panel (Window > Adjustments) and clicked the "Vibrance" button ▼ to open the very simple Vibrance dialog. If you experiment with the two sliders, you'll see the difference between Vibrance and Saturation, which affects all colors, already saturated or not. We increased Vibrance to 90. Although Vibrance has built-in protection for skin colors as well as nearly saturated colors, you may find that skin gets a little "hot" if you increase Vibrance very much. In that case you may want to paint the Vibrance layer's mask with black or gray. Or, as we did, reduce Saturation slightly in the Vibrance dialog. *Note:* Photoshop CS3 itself doesn't have a Vibrance adjustment, but you can find it near the bottom of Camera Raw's Basic tab.

FIND OUT MORE
▼ Using Camera Raw
page 141

 Vibrance.psd

Match Color

A SERIES OF IMAGES TAKEN at the same time and place can differ in color and contrast simply because they were taken at different angles to the light source, or with different camera settings. The **Match Color** command can help bring these color and tone differences into agreement. Open both the image whose color you want to change **A** and the one whose color you want to match **B**. Working on the image that needs changing, first duplicate it to a new layer to protect the original; then choose Image > Adjustments > Match Color. In the pop-up **Source** menu in the Match Color dialog, designate the image you want to match **C**. You can now use the sliders to adjust the color: **Luminance** for brightness; **Color Intensity** for saturation; **Fade** to reduce the change overall, blending it with the original color. Turn on **Neutralize** if needed to remove a color cast. For this image we used only Fade and Neutralize **D**.

 Match Color 1.psd & **Match Color 2.psd**

Mark Wainer Discovers a "Digital Polarizing Filter"

WHEN LIGHT REFLECTS off glass or water surfaces or water droplets in the air, the reflected light waves cause glare or haze. A polarizing filter attached to a camera lens can block out about half the light waves and direct the other half, darkening the sky, allowing us to see through the surface of the water to what's below, even reducing the shininess of vegetation and painted surfaces so we can see more color. In exploring the HSL / Grayscale controls of Lightroom, Mark Wainer discovered an after-the-fact polarizer, for times when the sun's at the wrong angle for the on-camera polarizer to work, or when you just don't have it handy. Exactly the same technique can be used in Camera Raw.

FIND OUT MORE
▼ Using Camera Raw
page 141

The first step in optimizing the landscape Mark shot near Ramberg, Norway was some basic tone and contrast adjustment in Camera Raw.▼ On the Basic tab Mark expanded the tonal range by increasing both the Exposure (+0.54) and the Blacks setting (+7), and recovered the shadows by increasing Fill Light (+17). He used Clarity (+46) to bring out detail in the midtones.

Before turning to the "polarizer," he also used the Lens Correction tab. He moved the Fix Red/Cyan Fringe slider to +35 and the Fix Blue/Yellow Fringe slider to −8, and turned on Defringe: Highlight Edges. "It's important to correct chromatic aberration and noise," Mark notes, "because the HSL adjustments that come next — the 'digital polarizer' — can intensify the chromatic aberration." (If necessary, you can also go back to the Lens Correction tab *after* polarizing.)

Mark's polarizer can be found on Camera Raw's HSL / Grayscale tab, specifically on the Luminance tab. He finds that lowering the Luminance of the Blues, in this case all the way to −100, brings color to the sky, takes the glare off the water, and cuts through the haze. "You can also use the Aquas or Purples to alter the sky," he says. He set Aquas at −50.

To brighten the green vegetation in the photo, he raised the Yellows value (+50). (In Camera Raw's HSL / Grayscale tab and Photoshop's Black & White adjustment, foliage is often affected more by changes to the Yellows slider than the Greens.) Mark brightened the red buildings by increasing the Reds setting (+40).

Though he didn't do so for this photo, Mark points out that the sky can be made even darker by increasing the Blues setting on the Saturation tab.

The original photo

Tonal range and contrast improved, and chromatic aberration corrected

Color intensified with Mark Wainer's "digital polarizer"

MARK WAINER

Combining Exposures

YOU'LL FIND THE FILES

in (wow) > Wow Project Files > Chapter 5 > Combining:
- Combining-Before files (to start)
- Luminosity-After.psd and Merge-After.psd (to compare)

OPEN THESE PANELS

(from the Window menu, for example):
- Layers • Channels • Adjustments

OVERVIEW

Luminosity: Align the three exposures as layers in a single file • Make a highlights mask for the underexposed layer and a shadows mask for the overexposed layer Merge to HDR: Use the Merge to HDR command • Convert to 8 Bits/Channel

THE HUMAN VISUAL SYSTEM can do a much better job than a digital camera when it comes to seeing detail in a scene with a wide span of lights and darks. Standing inside the cliff dwelling and looking at the scene above, photographer Loren Haury could see detail in the brightly lit entrance, the floor, and the walls, as well as the very dark ceiling and interior rooms. Knowing that his camera couldn't get it all in one shot, he took three, keeping aperture and ISO the same. The first shot was exposed according to the camera's metering at $\frac{1}{2}$ sec. He then took an underexposed shot at $\frac{1}{4}$ sec and an overexposed shot at 2.5 sec. Haury later combined them using an intuitive and effective method described on page 366. Here, with his permission, we use smaller versions of his three shots to look at two other combining methods that are more technical. One uses **luminosity masks** and the other uses **Merge to HDR**. All three approaches have their advantages: The luminosity mask method can be quicker than selecting or masking by hand, and it's a logical, easy-to-remember technique. Merge to HDR can be more automatic and smooth (thanks to working in 32-bit mode), but using all the options and controls to best advantage takes more practice and experience than either of the other methods. The goal of all three methods is the same — to get more detail than you could from a single original.

2a

Layers are stacked in working order and the top layer's visibility is turned off. Then a luminosity mask for the highlights is made from the underexposed image (where the highlights received the best exposure).

LUMINOSITY MASKS

Thinking the project through. In the Channels panel the RGB (composite) thumbnail at the top of the stack shows the image as you currently see it on-screen in the document window. Ctrl/⌘-clicking this thumbnail in the Channels panel loads a selection of the light areas of the image. If you then click the add a layer mask button ◰ at the bottom of the Layers panel, the selection becomes a layer mask on the targeted layer. A mask like this that's a grayscale version of the image is called a *luminosity mask*. By using a luminosity mask on the underexposed image, and the inverse of a luminosity mask on the overexposed image, we can combine the three versions of the image to distribute the tones available just the way we want them.

1 Stacking the layers. (See the tip "Auto-Loading Files into Layers" at the left.) Open all three **Combining-Before** photos, or a bracketed-exposure series of your own. If you're not opening them as suggested in the tip, and prefer to open them individually and then organize them all yourself, you'll find it easier to see what you're doing if you choose Window > Arrange > Float All in Windows. With all your images visible, choose the Move tool ⊹ (Shift-V) and Shift-drag the underexposed shot onto the medium shot. Then Shift-drag the overexposed shot onto the top of the stack. Shift-dragging will center the imported images, and thus perfectly align them, since all three have exactly the same pixel dimensions. Haury used a tripod, and nothing moved in the scene during the 3 seconds he was photographing, so he was certain they would align perfectly. If you're using your own series and you didn't use a tripod, or you have any doubts about whether the layers align perfectly, target all three layers in the Layers panel by clicking the top thumbnail and Shift-clicking the bottom one; then choose Edit > Auto Align Layers, choosing Auto in the dialog box.

2 Making a "highlights" mask. We'll first add the light areas of the underexposed image to the medium (0EV) exposure in order to gain detail in the highlights — in the entrance, for example. Turn off visibility for the overexposed layer (click its ◉ in the Layers panel) so you're looking at the underexposed layer. In the Channels panel, Ctrl/⌘-click the RGB channel's thumbnail. Then target the underexposed layer by clicking its thumbnail in the Layers panel, and click the "Add layer mask" button ◰ at the bottom of the panel **2a**. The light areas of the mask allow the underexposed image to show through and combine with the 0EV image underneath; the dark areas of the mask hide the dark areas of the underexposed layer.

Since the tonal regions you want to affect are in the 0EV image (called "Medium" here), you might prefer to make your luminosity masks directly from that image. To do so, turn off the other layers and Ctrl/⌘-click on the RGB composite channel. If making a highlights mask, target the underexposed layer (don't restore visibility yet) and click on the "Add a layer mask" icon. Target the "Medium" layer again, Ctrl/⌘-click once more on the RGB channel thumbnail, and invert this selection (Ctrl/⌘-Shift-I). With this selection active, target the overexposed layer and create a layer mask. Now turn on the visibility for both these layers to see the effect of the luminosity masks on the Medium exposure.

4a

Turning a layer with a luminosity mask into a New Group lets you add another mask to the same image layer, keeping the luminosity mask intact, but also refining its effect.

4b

Adding Adjustment layers and a Dodge and Burn layer allows you to fine-tune the details while retaining complete flexibility in the tone and color adjustments.

3 Making a "shadows" mask. In the Layers panel turn on visibility for the overexposed layer by clicking to the left of its thumbnail. Now the RGB channel in the Channels panel shows the overexposed image. Ctrl/⌘-click on the RGB thumbnail to load the highlights as a selection. To select the shadows instead of the highlights, invert the selection (Select > Inverse or Ctrl/⌘-Shift-I). Turn the selection into a layer mask (click ▢). This grayscale mask will allow any dark areas of the overexposed layers to contribute to the composite.

4 Fine-tuning. You can now target either layer mask by clicking its thumbnail in the Layers panel, and use a soft-tipped Brush ✐ (Shift-B) and white or black paint to alter it. Or another way to change the masking, keeping your changes separate from the original mask, is to turn a masked layer into its own one-layer Group (by targeting it in the Layers panel and choosing New Group from Layers from the panel's menu ▾≣). Then add a layer mask to the Group and paint the mask **4a**.▼ You can also add a Curves layer▼ to make final tone adjustments, a Hue/Saturation Adjustment layer as Haury did (page 367) to tone down the colors,▼ or a dodge-and-burn layer to bring out detail where you need more▼ **4b**.

MERGE TO HDR

Thinking the project through. Photoshop's File >Automate > Merge to HDR command combines several exposures to create a single 32-bits-per-channel file that offers enough brightness levels to contain the whole range of tonal information from the three exposures in a single file. Once all that information is collected, you can save the 32-bit file if you work with 3D and video projects that can use it, or you can convert it back to an 8- or 16-bits-per-channel image in order to view it on-screen or print it, which can't be done directly with a 32-bit image. After conversion, it will still contain detail in both highlights and shadows, and you can further manipulate it in Photoshop with more tools and commands than you can use on a 32-bit image.

1 Merging the files. You can get to the Merge to HDR function in Photoshop or from Bridge. In order to map tones accurately when you convert from 32-bit to a lower bit depth, **the images must have a color profile assigned**,▼ such as ProPhoto RGB or Adobe RGB, so the first step will be to make sure that's the case:

FIND OUT MORE
▼ Masking groups **page 620**
▼ Using Curves **page 246**
  ▼ Using Hue/Saturation **page 252**
▼ Making a dodge & burn layer **page 359**
▼ Color Profiles **page 190**

1a

Attempt to Automatically Align Images is checked by default when adding files to Merge to HDR.

1b

When merging, you can see the EV values of the images. If you want to exclude an image now, you simply uncheck the box beneath it. If you move the exposure slider under the histogram to preview the highlights without any clipping, the image often appears very dark, but you'll have more opportunities to affect the tones later on.

2a

Converted using Exposure and Gamma

2b

Converted using Highlight Compression

- **In Bridge**▼ choose the files you want to merge and **look for the Color Profile in the File Properties section of the metadata panel (Window > Metadata Panel). If you see a Color Profile listed**, choose Tools > Photoshop > Merge to HDR. On the other hand, **if you don't see a Color Profile listed**, double-click one of the files to open them all in Photoshop and enter Merge to HDR from there, as described next.

FIND OUT MORE
▼ Using Bridge
page 133

- **In Photoshop**, open the files you want to merge. You can check to see if a file has an assigned profile by choosing Edit > Assign Profile; if the Don't Color Manage This File option is chosen, no profile has been assigned, and you need to assign one. Then choose File > Automate > Merge to HDR. Choose the bracketed exposures you want to merge, so that only their names show in the Use window **1a**.

When the Merge to HDR dialog box opens, you'll see a slider for the Set White Point Preview in the upper right corner. If you're going to convert to a lower bit-depth immediately, as we are here, you can simply accept the preview "as is." If you plan to work in 32-bit color, lighten the preview as much as possible without losing any important detail in the highlights **1b**. The slider controls only the preview; it doesn't change the pixels in the file. Click "OK" to close the dialog and open the 32-bit image. Notice that you still have access to the Exposure slider for preview purposes (in the lower left of the status bar).

2 Converting back to 8 Bits/Channel mode. If you're planning to save your file in 32-bit mode for another program, you can make further adjustments to the image in Photoshop. Many of Photoshop's commands will work. Or to map (compress) the tones to a lower bit-depth instead, choose Image > Mode > 8 Bits/Channel (or 16 Bits). The HDR Conversion dialog box opens with a menu of four conversion methods at the top. Try them out, keeping in mind that your goal is to get as much data as you can into the compressed version. Results are often going to be flat, lacking the localized contrast that an image needs, but you can then edit the converted image using all of Photoshop's available tools and commands:

- If you succeeded in getting an image you like in 32 bits, the **Exposure and Gamma** option, without any adjustments, may make a good conversion **2a**.

- If your image has highlights that are much brighter than the rest of the image, **Highlight Compression** (no adjustments are possible) may work **2b**.

2c

Converted using Equalize Histogram

2d

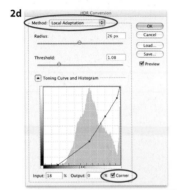

Converted using Local Adaptation and creating a curve with Corner points

3a

The final version using Local Adaptation for the conversion, and additional layers for fine-tuning

- If the histogram shows several distinct peaks (figure 1a shows that ours really didn't), **Equalize Histogram** may work (again, no adjustments are possible) **2c**.
- The fourth choice offers the most control when reducing (mapping) the dynamic range to fit into 8 or 16 bits per channel, and tends to produce results that show the greatest amount of contrast, depending upon the Curve you create. **Local Adaptation** gives direct control of the tone Curve. The **Radius** defines the size of the local region around each pixel where Local Adaptation looks for local contrast to enhance; **Threshold** controls how different the pixels in that region must be from each other in order to have their contrast enhanced. The tone **Curve** allows you to specify where in the tonal range many tones should be assigned (where there's lots of detail to bring out) and where fewer tones can be used (because there's not much in the way of important detail).

If you use Local Adaptation, you can try to balance Radius and Threshold, and then drag the black and white points inward along the bottom and top axes to match the ends of the histogram. In this image the white end of the histogram extended all the way to the white end of the curve, so we made no changes to the white point slider. But we moved the black point slider in. Click on the curve to create anchor points where you want them, and move the points to make the curve **steeper** (to assign more tones to that range) or **flatter** (to assign fewer tones). Click in the image to see where on the curve a particular tone occurs, so you can adjust the curve in that range. For any point you add, you can click the **Corner** checkbox to create straight segments that will make it easier to add or reduce contrast between tones, because you can create very flat or very steep segments without affecting the rest of the curve. Segments defined by corner points act with greater independence from the shape of the curve around them **2d**.

When you have a result you like, click "OK" to close the HDR Conversion dialog and open the 8-bit (or 16-bit) file.

3b

The final Layers panel

3 Fine-tuning. As we did in the earlier luminance-masking example (step 4 on page 294) and as Haury did in his composite, we added Adjustment layers and a dodge-and-burn layer to our Local Adaptation conversion in order to complete the image **3a**, **3b**.

CRISTEN GILLESPIE

Adjusting Tone & Color in Camera Raw

YOU'LL FIND THE FILES
in <WOW> > Wow Project Files > Chapter 5 >
Camera Raw:
  • AdJust Tone-Before.nef (to start)
  • Adjust Tone-After files (to compare)

OVERVIEW
Use Camera Raw defaults and custom settings to process a raw file for basic tone and color • Create variations from the basic image with the HSL/Grayscale and Split Tone tabs • Save variations as individual DNG files as you go

WHEN RAW FILES ARE PROCESSED through Camera Raw, often default settings or presets can do the job quickly. But some images, especially those with tricky exposures, make it worth the time and effort to customize. Raw files provide flexibility — in Camera Raw we can reduce the exposure by more than an f-stop without posterizing the image because too little data is left for smooth transitions. This photo taken at dusk was overexposed on purpose. Without a tripod, the photographer used a high ISO to capture the low light. When a high ISO is used, noise in the shadows can become pronounced, especially if you try to lighten the shadows later, so it's usually better to start with lighter shadows (too light an exposure), while taking care not to blow out all the highlights (the camera's histogram showed no high spike at the right end, so the photographer could tell that the highlights hadn't been blown out).

Thinking the project through. Starting with an overexposed image often means you won't be able to process it with default settings or presets. But we can explore the defaults as a starting point and go from there. The image might also work well as a black-and-white or split-toned image, or even with a tint effect, so we'll process it in stages, saving our variations in DNG format

1a

Opening the image with
Camera Raw Default settings

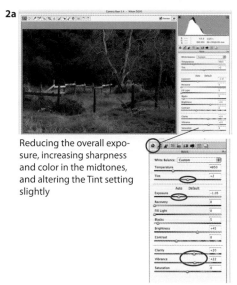

1b

The Auto option boosted contrast but took the
image in a direction we didn't want to go.

2a

Reducing the overall exposure, increasing sharpness
and color in the midtones,
and altering the Tint setting
slightly

as we go along, so we won't have to leave the Camera Raw dialog
while we experiment.

1 Trying the presets. To follow along with what we did, open
Adjust Tone-Before.nef; we opened it from Bridge, right-clicking/
Ctrl-clicking its thumbnail and choosing Open in Camera Raw
from the context-sensitive menu.▼ The image will open with
the **Default** preset **1a**. If you've saved a new Default preset other
than the one Camera Raw shipped with, your image will look
different from ours. If you want to make it look the same, open
the panel menu, choose Save New Camera Raw Defaults if you
want to be able to restore your current settings later, and then
choose Reset Camera Raw Defaults. With Default settings, our
image is still way too light and has too little contrast. We clicked
on "Auto," which increased contrast, but made both tone and color
too harsh **1b**. We clicked back on "Default" so we could more
gently adjust the image to show off the evening light.

2 Bringing back the evening light. In this intentionally overexposed image, we can reduce overall **Exposure** by more than an
f-stop **2a**. The lighted fence rails still have detail, so we can leave
the Recovery slider at 0. Because our image was overexposed,
we don't need to lighten shadows with Fill Light, and we can
leave Blacks at the default, but reducing **Brightness** by a small
amount improves the image.▼ We zeroed the Contrast slider,
which tends to be a blunt instrument compared to Curves, which
we'll use instead next, to add more contrast (and a little more
saturation). If you're working with Camera Raw 4.2 or later,▼
Clarity can add sharpness to the midtones. **Vibrance** can bring
out the evening color. Finally, liking the color that Vibrance
was bringing out, we moved the **Tint** slider at the top from −4
(slightly green) to +2 (more magenta).

To finish our basic tone and color adjustments, click on the **Tone
Curve** tab. The first tab is the **Parametric curve**▼ with all the
sliders set to 0 by default. In the second tab, the default setting
for the **Point curve** is Medium Contrast — almost every raw file
needs at least this minimal increase in contrast at some point in
its editing. We can still use a Parametric curve to increase the
contrast more **2b**.

3 Saving your work in progress. In Camera Raw there are
several ways to save current settings when we have a result we
like, so we won't lose it when we go on experimenting. One
way is to save a preset by clicking on the ▣ icon at the bottom
of the Presets tab. If you're prepared to name your settings carefully, and to later delete unwanted presets, this can be a good

2b

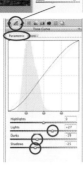

Adding a Parametric curve to deepen exposure and enhance contrast. The default Point curve (Medium Contrast preset) had already added some contrast. (Curves in Camera Raw can also increase saturation. If you don't want that, you can compensate with negative Vibrance or Saturation on the Basic tab, or by using the Saturation sliders on the HSL/Grayscale tab to tone down individual colors.)

3a

Saving Camera Raw settings as a preset

3b

Saving variations in DNG format to preserve your Camera Raw settings and to keep them editable. Using the original document name plus a letter (or number) makes it easy to find the original again.

4a

The Graduated Filter can apply tone and color corrections locally. To use it, choose the tool from the bar at the top of the Camera Raw dialog and drag in the image from where you want your tone or color correction to be applied in full force to where you want it to be faded out entirely. Then adjust the sliders to control tone and color. To leave the Graduated Filter and return to the main tabs, choose any of the first four tools in the bar, or press H for the Hand tool, for instance.

method **3a**. Another way to save editable variations as you go is to use the "Save Image" button in the bottom-left corner of the Camera Raw dialog; choose DNG for the format and choose a location, naming the individual files. This has the advantage of having files ready to open again in Camera Raw or in Photoshop without having to open the original, apply the preset, and then open or save the file again **3b**. (In later versions of the Camera Raw that comes with Photoshop CS4, you can also save "snapshots," ▼ to compare and preserve your customized settings, but there's no indication in Bridge that you saved these snapshots, so it's easy to forget they're there.)

4 Localized Corrections. In CS4, you can apply localized edits to those parts of your image where you want more than just the global alterations. You can select either the Adjustment Brush ✐ (see page 300) or the Graduated Filter ▣, which works very much like a linear masking gradient on an Adjustment layer in Photoshop. We used the **Graduated Filter 4a** to drag over the bright lower-left corner of the image, and chose settings to darken and soften it, so it wouldn't detract from the central subject **4b**. The settings, angle, and extent of the gradation can be altered directly, by dragging either of the two end points, without having to create a new gradient.

5 Creating variations. After saving the adjusted version of our image with the "Save Image" button (the result is shown at the top of page 297), we decided to see how it would look in black-and-white. Simply clicking on the HSL/Grayscale tab and clicking the **Convert to Grayscale** checkbox starts the experiment. To get closer to the same brilliant contrast we had in the color version, we moved the orange and red sliders to the right to lighten the fence and trees, while moving all the rest of the sliders except yellow to the left to darken the meadow and shrubs **5a**. (If you have Camera Raw version 5.2 or later, you can use the **Targeted Adjustment tool** instead of the sliders, dragging in the image window on the areas whose tone you want to alter. All the sliders that make up the color beneath the TAT will be selected at once. We dragged the TAT down to darken the meadow. ▼ (You can find the latest version of Camera Raw at www.adobe.com/downloads/updates, choosing Camera Raw from the Product list.) We saved our custom black-and-white version as a DNG file (as in step 3).

Next we decided to try a split-tone on the black-and-white version. On the **Split Tone** tab, we chose a saturated yellow-orange for the highlights (the color won't

FIND OUT MORE

▼ Camera Raw snapshots **page 144**

▼ Targeted Adjustment tool **page 145**

4b

Dragging inward from the corner with the Graduated Filter tool applies changes as if through a gradient mask.

5a

On the HSL/Grayscale tab, click the Convert to Grayscale option, and then adjust the lightness or darkness of the individual original colors. Or if your version supports it, use the Targeted Adjustment tool (TAT) to drag over the areas you want to change.

5b

Split-toning a black-and-white version of the image

appear without setting at least some Saturation) and a moderately saturated deep blue for the shadows. We wanted the image to be warm, so we moved the **Balance** slider to the right, which colors more tones with the yellow-orange, the Highlights color **5b**.

After saving the Split Tone version, we tried a "tinted black-and-white," with all the colors desaturated except the reds, oranges, and yellows of the evening light: In the Split Tone tab we set all the parameters back to 0. In the HSL/Grayscale tab we disabled Convert to Grayscale and moved the Saturation sliders for all the other colors to the far left **5c**.

ZEROING IN CAMERA RAW

To reset all fields to 0 on one of Camera Raw's tabs, you can select the number in the top field, set it to 0, and type Tab-0 repeatedly to move from field to field until you've zeroed all fields.

PAINTING & ERASING BASIC ADJUSTMENTS

Camera Raw's **Adjustment Brush** can apply the same changes you apply globally through the Basic tab, but targeted exactly where you want them. (Camera Raw uses a masking interface that's the opposite of the default masking in Photoshop proper. In Camera Raw the red overlay shows where the effect is applied, and the clear areas are protected from change.) Sometimes it makes sense to paint the effect only where you want it, and sometimes it's better to paint it everywhere and then erase the few spots where you *don't* want it. To make our baby vulture **A** look even softer, we used the Adjustment Brush and set the Clarity slider at −100 for maximum softening. We "painted" the entire image with this adjustment. To bring back sharp detail on the eye and beak, we used a harder, smaller brush tip to erase **B** (choose Erase at the top of the Adjustment Brush panel, or hold down Alt/Option while you paint).

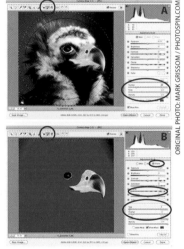

5c

Returning to the color version (from step 4) we tried desaturating all but the warm highlight colors. This kind of tinting can often produce a great result, but we decided that this one wasn't something we wanted to save.

Attention-Focusing Techniques

Blurring, desaturating, or tinting the background of a photo — or even using a combination of the three techniques — can be very effective at making the subject pop. It can be a great way to focus on the bride and groom in a crowded wedding scene, for instance. Although some of the examples on these eight pages require selecting the subject carefully to isolate it from the background, many of the examples don't require a precise selection. Start by analyzing your photo and thinking about what you want your image to convey, and then "think like Photoshop," to see if a quick method will do the job:

- Can you get the desired result without having to precisely select the subject?

- Is the area around the subject fairly neutral in color? If so, some of the quick "ghosting" methods can be successful (see page 304).

- Can you isolate the subject with a rectangular selection? One of the "stripping" methods may do the trick (pages 306 and 307).

- Is the subject a different color than the background and other elements in the photo? If so, then "Desaturating Particular Colors" on page 307 may work.

YOU'LL FIND THE FILES

in 🥏 > Wow Project Files > Chapter 5 > Quick Attention-Focusing

---

CROPPING WITHOUT THROWING ANYTHING AWAY

Once you've dragged to create the crop with Photoshop's Crop tool ⌗ (Shift-C), you can choose Hide (rather than Delete) in the Options bar. This hides, but keeps, the cropped-out material, rather than removing it permanently, so it's easy to change the crop later. However, you have to remember that any effects applied to the edges of the layer may be applied to the *whole* layer rather than the cropped edges. In CS4 there's a third option: cropping in Camera Raw (see page 302). Another option — the oldest one in the history of Photoshop, and one that doesn't leave any hidden edges to contend with — is to duplicate the image file before you crop, so you have the original to go back to, and then in the duplicate, go ahead and use the Delete option for the Crop tool.

Cropping

CORBIS ROYALTY FREE

ORIGINAL PHOTO: CORBIS ROYALTY FREE

CROPPING IS AN OBVIOUS WAY to help focus attention on a subject, by trimming off distracting elements or simply by allowing the subject to occupy a bigger fraction of the image space. After duplicating the photo **A** (Image > Duplicate), we chose the Crop tool ⌗ (Shift-C) because it would make it easy to look at different cropping options by hiding the cropped-out parts of the image as we experimented. In the Options bar we clicked the "Clear" button **B** to ensure that we wouldn't accidentally change the resolution of the file in the process of cropping it. We dragged diagonally in the image to make a cropping rectangle for the boy and his breakfast. We dragged inside the cropping box to move it around and dragged on its handles to change its size and shape, then pressed the Enter key to complete the crop **C**.

The cropped image above is the starting point for the **Ghost-Tint-Halos.psd** file used for the techniques on the next two pages.

In Photoshop if you crop a photo using the Crop tool's ⌖ Hide option (see "Caution: 'Hidden' Crop" on page 243), and then try to apply a vignette with the Lens Correction filter, the vignette will follow the edges of the original image, including the hidden part, rather than following the edges of the crop. The same is true in the version of Camera Raw that comes with Photoshop CS3. But in Camera Raw 5.0, which comes with Photoshop CS4, the Lens Corrections panel offers the option of "Post Crop Vignetting." All the cropped-out parts of the image are preserved so you can get them back later, as they always are when you crop in Camera Raw and open in Photoshop as a Smart Object, ▼ but you also have the option of making the vignette follow the cropped edge rather than the original edge.

By default, Photoshop CS4's Camera Raw displays a cropped image with the cropped-out areas screened back but still visible, just as the CS3 version does.

But in Camera Raw 5.0, you can see the cropped version (without the screened-back cropped-out areas around it) simply by clicking on a tool other than the Crop tool, such as the Hand 🖑 (H is the keyboard shortcut). You also have the option of Post Crop Vignetting — darkening the cropped edges, as shown here, rather than the original edges. This lets you "have your cake and eat it too" in a way that the "Hide" feature of Photoshop's Crop tool does not. Post Crop Vignetting also lets you control the degree of Roundness at the corners of the vignette and the softness (Feather) of the vignette edge.

Post Crop Vignetting	
Amount	-16
Midpoint	38
Roundness	-44
Feather	41

"Ghosting"

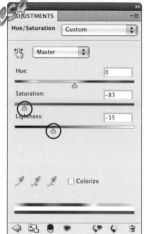

WHETHER YOU HAVE TO MAKE A DETAILED SELECTION, as shown here, or use one of the masking or stripping techniques on the pages that follow, the Hue/Saturation dialog box can provide "one-stop shopping" to desaturate, darken, and tint the surroundings. Starting with the cropped photo from page 301, we selected the subject, reversed the selection (Ctrl/⌘-Shift-I), and then clicked the "Create new fill or adjustment layer" button ● at the bottom of the Layers panel and added a Hue/Saturation Adjustment layer. In the Hue/Saturation dialog, we moved the Saturation slider to the left to take out most of the color and moved the Lightness slider to the left also, to darken the background to contrast with the subject.

 Ghost-Tint-Halos.psd

"Ghosting" & Tinting

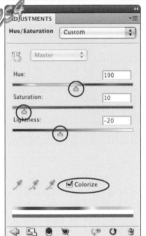

To ADD A TINT to the darkened background, we used the Colorize function in the Hue/Saturation dialog. To preserve the ghosted effect we developed in "Ghosting" on page 302, we duplicated the Hue/Saturation Adjustment layer (Ctrl/⌘-J), then turned off visibility of the original Hue/Saturation layer and used the copy. In Photoshop CS4, the Adjustments panel automatically was open to the Hue/Saturation dialog because that layer was the active (targeted) layer. In CS3 it's necessary to double-click the Hue/Saturation layer's thumbnail in the Layers panel to reopen the dialog box. In the Hue/Saturation dialog, we clicked the Colorize checkbox and adjusted the Hue slider, also readjusting the Saturation and Lightness sliders until we got the balance we liked.

Adding a Dark "Halo"

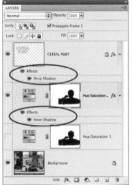

IF YOU MAKE A PRECISE SELECTION of your subject, and then ghost and tint it (as at the left), but you want even more emphasis, try adding a "dark glow" by applying a Layer Style to the Hue/Saturation layer. When you apply a Style, by default any edge effects in the Style follow the edges of the mask. The Hue/Saturation layer's mask is for the *surroundings,* not the subject. So to put the dark glow *around* the subject, we can't use a Drop Shadow effect, which would spread the shadow effect onto the subject. Instead, use the Inner Shadow: Click the "Add a layer style" button *fx* at the bottom of the Layers panel and choose Inner Shadow from the list of effects. Set the Distance at 0 so the shadow won't be displaced off-center. Increase the Size to spread the shadow out from the edge; increase the Choke to make the shadow denser.

Any type or graphics you add can have a matching dark glow. Add a Layer Style, but this time choose Drop Shadow from the pop-out list of effects. Again set the Distance to 0; match the Size you used for the Inner Shadow, and match the Spread to the Choke value you used. (In our file we rasterized the type.)

 **Ghost-Tint-Halos.psd**

Vignette "Ghosting"

Before

A

B 75

60

After

C

COLOR IS COMPELLING. To spotlight one of the rafters in this photo, we chose the Elliptical Marquee tool ⬭, set the Feather at 10 in the Options bar to soften the edge of the selection we would make, and dragged the cursor in the image to select the rafter; then we inverted the selection (Ctrl/⌘-Shift-I) to select everything *but* the rafter. We added a Black & White Adjustment layer to affect the selected area (click the "Create new fill or adjustment layer" button ◑ at the bottom of the Layers panel and choose from the list, or in CS4 you can click ▨ on the Adjustments panel instead **A**). ▼ Starting with the Default settings in Black & White, we dragged the Reds slider slightly to the right **B** to arrive at a conversion we liked (in CS3 click "OK" to close the dialog). Our inverted selection became a mask **C** that protected the color of the rafter. To return some of the color to the rest of the image, reduce the Black & White layer's Opacity (we used 85%).

 Vignette Ghosting.psd

FIND OUT MORE

▼ Black & White
Adjustment layer
page 250

Painted "Ghosting"

Before

After

Black & White 1

Background

FOR THIS PHOTO WE WANTED to highlight the daughter with more than a simple geometric vignette like the one at the left. Thinking that a loosely painted mask would do the trick, we added a Black & White Adjustment layer as described at the left, choosing the Default settings for the conversion.

Next we chose the Brush tool ✎ and picked a large, soft brush tip from the pop-up Brush Preset picker in the Options bar. With the Adjustment layer targeted in the Layers panel, we painted with black to mask the effect and restore the girl's color. (This photo's neutral background makes it ideal for this technique; you don't have to be precise in painting, as you would if the background were more colorful.) We reduced the size of the brush tip and lowered the Opacity in the Options bar, then painted with white to remove color that had spilled over onto the mother's hand.

Painted Ghosting.psd

Framing with Focus

Before

After

PHOTOSPIN.COM

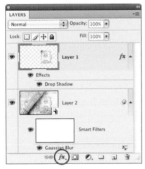

A QUICK AND EASY WAY to focus attention on one particular area of a photo starts with selecting the area you want to emphasize (we used the Rectangular Marquee tool ⬚ to make a selection) and copying the selected area to a new layer (Ctrl/⌘-J). Now blur the layer below: Choose Filter > Convert for Smart Filters and then Filter > Blur > Gaussian Blur; a Radius setting of 1.0 worked well to slightly blur this low-resolution image.

To further emphasize the separation between the sharp and blurred regions, add a "dark glow" around the sharp area: With the sharp layer targeted, click the "Add a layer style" button ⨎ at the bottom of the Layers panel, and choose Drop Shadow from the list of effects. In the Layer Style dialog box, change the Drop Shadow's Distance setting to 0 pixels, to make the shadow extend equally on all sides.

 **Framed Focus.psd**

Masking a Blur

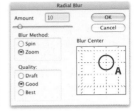

E. A. M. VISSER

Before

B

After

HERE'S AN EASY WAY to keep the subject in sharp focus and create a stylized out-of-focus effect to subdue background detail, especially if you want to imply or enhance motion. Start by blurring the image; we applied a Zoom blur: Choose Filter > Convert for Smart Filters and then Filter > Blur > Radial Blur; click the "Zoom" button, move the Blur Center so it matches the location of your subject **A**, and set the Amount of blur you want (we used 10); click "OK."

In the Layers panel, click the thumbnail for the new Smart Filters mask. Then choose the Gradient tool ▭ and in the Options bar choose the "Black, white" gradient and click the "Radial Gradient" button **B**. Center the cursor over the subject, and drag outward, stopping where you want the blur to be fully in effect. The filter effect will be masked (hidden) where the mask is dark.

 **Masked Blur.psd**

Isolating a Strip

Before

PHOTOSPIN.COM

After

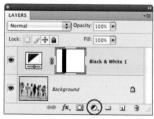

SOMETIMES A SIMPLE "STRIP SELECTION" can do a great job of highlighting one person in a group or one "slice" of a busy scene. Here we used the Rectangular Marquee ⬚ to select a strip that included the woman we wanted to spotlight. We reversed the selection so everything outside the strip was selected (Select > Inverse, or Ctrl/⌘-Shift-I). With your strip selection active, click the "Create new fill or adjustment layer" button ⬤ at the bottom of the Layers panel and choose Black & White (or in CS4 you can click the ◼ on the Adjustments panel). Experiment with presets or custom settings in Black & White if you like; we liked the conversion we got by clicking the "Auto" button; in CS3 it's necessary to click "OK" to close the dialog.

The layer mask made from the inverted strip selection will protect the color of the strip.

FIND OUT MORE
▼ Black & White Adjustment layer
page 250

 **Isolated Strip.psd**

Stripping a Silhouette

CORBIS ROYALTY FREE

A   **B**

C

IF YOU START WITH AN IMAGE in which several subjects are silhouetted **A**, you can target a single member of the group by changing the color in a strip around that subject. Here we used the Rectangular Marquee ⬚ to make a strip selection of one of the figures. Then we clicked the "Create a new fill or adjustment layer" button ⬤ at the bottom of the Layers panel and chose Invert (in CS4 you have the option of clicking ◼ on the Adjustments panel). This added an Invert Adjustment layer that made a color negative of the strip **B**. By changing the blend mode for the Invert layer to Color, ▼ we could keep the silhouette black **C**. (For some silhouetted images, it may work better to keep the subject in its original background and instead change the color of the rest of the image. In that case, reverse the selection — Ctrl/⌘-Shift-I — before adding the Invert layer.)

For other color options for the strip, instead of Invert, you could add a Hue/Saturation layer and move the Hue slider to change the background color, or use a Solid Color Fill layer and choose the color you want for the strip.

FIND OUT MORE
▼ Blend modes
page 181

Stripping a Silhouette.psd

Modifying a Strip

PHOTOSPIN.COM

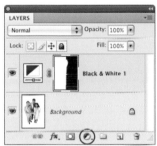

A STRIP SELECTION can be an effective way to start isolating a subject, even if you know it won't do the job completely. Here we used the Rectangular Marquee [ ] to make a strip selection of the woman. We reversed the selection (Ctrl/⌘-Shift-I), clicked the ⬭ button at the bottom of the Layers panel, and added a Black & White Adjustment layer (in CS4 you have the option of clicking ◥ on the Adjustments panel). Then it was a simple matter to use the Brush tool ✐ to paint the mask with white where one man's head and the other man's clipboard were included in the strip of color, and to paint a vertical stroke along the left edge of the strip, to soften the transition between the almost neutral colors of the man's clothing and the fully neutral Black-&-White-adjusted image. (To view image and mask together, Alt/Option-Shift-click on the mask thumbnail in the Layers panel.)

(wow) Modified Strip.psd

Desaturating Particular Colors

PHOTOSPIN.COM

IN AN RGB IMAGE **A**, people's skin tones, regardless of ethnicity, typically include much more red than blue or green, a fact we can sometimes use to "pop" the subject with very little work. We clicked the "Create new fill or adjustment layer" button ⬭ at the bottom of the Layers panel and added a Hue/Saturation layer. (In CS4 you have the option of clicking on ▦ in the Adjustments panel.) In Hue/Saturation we chose Green, Blue, and Cyan in turn from the menu of color groups, and moved the Saturation slider all the way to the left **B** to desaturate these colors. Leaving Reds, Yellows, and Magentas unchanged left color in the girl's skin, hair and shirt **C**. To remove patches of yellow-green in the upper left corner, you can move the left-hand vertical marker for the Greens a bit to the left, toward yellow **D**; likewise, extending the Blues range to the right, toward magenta, removes most of the purple under the slide **E**. In CS4 you have the option of simply clicking on Hue/Saturation's ☝ in the Adjustments panel and scrubbing to the left on a patch of color to reduce Saturation.

(wow) Desaturating Colors.psd

Replacing with Red

CORBIS ROYALTY FREE

Before

After

THE HUMAN EYE IS ATTRACTED TO RED, even in small patches. In this photo we first duplicated the image to a new layer (Ctrl/⌘-J) so we would have an untouched original in reserve. We zoomed to a close-up view (press Ctrl/⌘-+ to zoom in), then clicked the Foreground color square in the Tools panel, chose a red in the Color Picker, and clicked "OK." We chose the Color Replacement tool ✍ (Shift-B cycles through the tools that share that position in the Tools panel). We set parameters in the Options bar: With **Mode** set to Color, the tool would change the hue and saturation of the boy's shirt as we painted, but the original lights and darks would remain. **Sampling** was set to Continuous, and **Tolerance** was set to 30% to start. The **Limits** option was set to Find Edges so the green of the shirt would help limit the area of color change. As the cursor moved, the tool replaced the color under the crosshairs, as well as any close shades and tones within the tool's footprint, with red. We reduced brush tip size and Tolerance as needed to work on small areas of green in this low-resolution image.

 Replacing with Red.psd

Spotlighting

GAREN CHECKLEY

Before

A

B

C

After

ONE WAY TO GUIDE THE VIEWER'S EYE is to spotlight the center of attention. This method works well for photos that show many people or lots of activity, that can also stand to be darkened overall so the spotlighted area stands out. We started by choosing Filter > Convert for Smart Filters (so the filter we applied would remain "live" and editable). Then we chose Filter > Render > Lighting Effects. The Lighting Effects filter's preview is small **A** — it was hard to see exactly what was going on as we changed the settings. But we modified the Default Spotlight to produce lighting that we knew would be more extreme than we wanted, because we knew we could reduce the effect later if we wanted to; to repeat our settings: Drag the spotlight's handles in the preview to make the lighted area smaller, more vertical, and lit from the top, and change the Ambience setting to 28; click "OK" to close the dialog.

In the Layers panel, double-click the ☰ in the Lighting Effects entry **B**. Now experiment with the blend Mode▼ and Opacity of the filter effect; we decided on Overlay mode at 40% Opacity **C**. Click the – and + zoom buttons to change you view, and click "OK" when you have the effect you want.

FIND OUT MORE
▼ Blend modes
page 181

 Spotlight.psd

E X E R C I S I N G

Lens Blur

Traditionally, photographers have used a shallow depth of field to blur a distracting environment while keeping the subject sharp. Photoshop's Lens Blur filter can quite realistically simulate a shallow depth of field, even shaping highlights in the background into out-of-focus points of light. Proceed through the examples on these three pages for an introduction to tapping the power of Lens Blur.

If your goal is a realistic simulation, here are some things to keep in mind about a shallow depth of field:

- To take a photo with a shallow depth of focus, the photographer often sets the lens wide open (a low f-stop produces a shorter in-focus span) and gets close to the subject, either actually or through the use of a telephoto lens. So close-ups are good candidates for Lens Blur.

- With a shortened depth of field, the span that's in focus is about one-third in front of the in-focus subject and about two-thirds behind it.

- An extremely blurry foreground, whether it looks "camera-realistic" or not, can be distracting.

An easy way to work with Lens Blur is to use a grayscale mask stored in an alpha channel. By default, black in the channel tells Lens Blur to keep the corresponding parts of the image in sharp focus. Areas that correspond to white parts of the channel will be the most out-of-focus (you can switch to the opposite by clicking the Invert checkbox in the Lens Blur dialog). The more gradually the mask goes from black to white, through intermediate shades of gray, the more gradual the change in focus will be.

PRESERVING THE ORIGINAL

Lens Blur is one of the filters that aren't available as Smart Filters. So to keep your options open, duplicate your image to a new layer (Ctrl/⌘-J) so you can run the Lens Blur filter on a copy and preserve the original. Another advantage of the second layer is that you can reduce its Opacity to blend the filtered and original versions for a less pronounced effect.

YOU CAN FIND THE FILES
in 🔵 > Wow Project Files > Chapter 5 > Exercising Lens Blur

FIND OUT MORE
▼ Making an alpha channel from a selection **page 60**

Foreground Subject

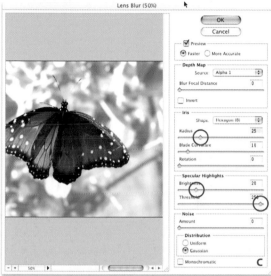

Lens Blur (50%)

A credible blur is easiest to manage if the subject of the photo is the closest thing to the viewer, extending off one edge of the photo, typically the bottom. That way there's an obvious gap between the in-focus plane, where the subject is, and the out-of-focus background, and you don't need to craft the transition between what's blurred and what isn't. Another instance that doesn't require a fall-off in focus is a photo such as the butterfly above **A** whose subject is in mid-air, with nothing else between it and the viewer.

To put the background out of focus, you'll need a sharp mask for the subject. **Lens Blur Butterfly.psd** has a mask already stored in an alpha channel (Alpha 1), which you can see if you open the Channels panel (Window > Channels) **B**.▼ To create or enhance a background blur, choose Filter > Blur > Lens Blur **C**; restore the filter's default settings by Alt/Option-clicking the "Cancel" button. Then experiment with the **Radius** slider to set the amount of blur; the **Iris** and **Specular Highlights** settings control the character of the out-of-focus highlights.

 **Lens Blur Butterfly.psd**

Focus Fall-off

To keep only *part* of the subject in focus, such as part of the face in this portrait **A**, the alpha channel mask used with the Lens Blur filter needs to show a gradual transition. You can paint such a mask by viewing both image and alpha channel together as you paint the channel: With the Channels panel open, add an alpha channel by clicking the "Create new channel" button at the bottom of the panel. With your black channel visible, turn on visibility for the image as well (tap the tilde key ~); you'll see the image, completely covered with a color overlay that represents the alpha channel mask. For our portrait, we changed the mask color to green (by double-clicking the alpha channel's thumbnail, clicking the Color swatch, and choosing a new color) **B**. We would use the green to represent the out-of-focus areas.

We painted the alpha channel using the Brush tool with white paint, with a soft brush tip and 50% Opacity chosen in the Options bar **C**, to clear the mask in the area of sharp focus and partly clear it to make the transition from sharp to blurred **D**.

With the mask painted, we targeted the image layer again (Ctrl/⌘-~ in CS3, but Ctrl/⌘-2 in CS4; then click the image thumbnail in the Layers panel) and turned off visibility for the alpha channel (clicking its 👁 in the Channels panel). We chose Filter > Blur > Lens Blur; we chose **Alpha 1** as the **Source**, but because the mask was white where we wanted the image to remain sharp, we turned on the **Invert** option. Then we moved the **Radius** slider to get the degree of blurring we wanted (we used a setting of 30), and clicked "OK." The effect seemed stronger than we wanted, so we reduced it. One way is to choose Edit > Fade Lens Blur and reduce the Opacity **E**, **F**.

Lens Blur Portrait.psd

Midground Subject

For an in-focus subject that *isn't* at the front of the image — the bike riders here **A** — the surface where that sharp subject stands will also need to be in-focus, but it will go out of focus both in front and behind. We started an alpha channel to use with Lens Blur (clicking at the bottom of the Channels panel) and also turned on visibility for the image (tap ~). To establish the "in focus" zone on the grass, we chose the Gradient tool and in the Options bar chose the **Black, White** gradient, **Normal** mode, **Linear** style, and the **Reverse** option **B** (to start our gradient with white). To mask the foreground, we held down the Shift key (to keep the gradient vertical) as we dragged the Gradient tool from where we wanted the front edge of the in-focus zone, down to where we wanted the maximum blur to start. To mask the background, we chose **Darken** for the Gradient tool's Mode in the Options bar to protect the existing gradient. Then we Shift-dragged from where we wanted the back of the sharp zone to be, upward to where the image was as out-of-focus as it was going to get; to maintain the illusion, the gradient had to end on the grassy surface rather than extending into the vertical trees at the horizon **C**.

Now all that was left was to "unmask" any part of the subject that extended above the clear area and into the mask; we used the Brush with a fairly hard brush tip (Hardness 80%) and high Opacity to paint with white. Tapping ~, we could toggle to a mask-only view **D**.

We targeted the image (Ctrl/⌘-~, but Ctrl/⌘-2 in CS4; then click the image thumbnail in the Layers panel), chose Filter > Blur > Lens Blur and Alt/Option-clicked the "Cancel" button to reset. We turned on the **Invert** option, and adjusted the **Radius** (we used 8 for this small image) **E**.

Lens Blur Bikes.psd

Masking Other Elements

IF YOUR SUBJECT isn't the only thing that "stands up" in your photo, adding a convincing Lens Blur may require a more complex mask. In our photo of chess pieces **A**, we wanted to focus on the bishop, with the rook, knight, and king out-of-focus and the queen in the transition zone.

We added an alpha channel and used the Gradient tool ▣ to create the "in-focus" zone as in "Midground Subject" on the previous page **B**. We also added the bishop to the mask **C**, using the Pen tool ✎ to trace it, ▽ then clicking the "Load path as selection" button ⊙ at the bottom of the Paths panel, and filling it with white — typing X once or twice makes white the Foreground color and Alt-Backspace (Windows) or Option-Delete (Mac) fills the selection. The knight was standing in the out-of-focus foreground, so it needed to be masked to match the black out-of-focus areas of the channel. We used the Pen tool ✎ to select the part of the knight that intruded into the in-focus area and in the alpha channel filled the selection with black (type X and delete).

Next we selected the rook, and with the alpha channel still targeted, we used the Eyedropper tool ✐ to sample the mask next to its base; we filled the selection with this sampled dark gray Foreground color. We repeated the selecting, sampling, and filling for the queen, using a lighter gray sampled from where she stands in the transition zone. The Alpha 1 channel of the **Lens Blur Chess. psd** file holds the resulting mask **D** (viewed alone in **E**).

Now we chose Filter > Blur > Lens Blur, turned on the **Invert** option, set the **Radius** (we used 25), and clicked "OK" to complete the effect **F**.

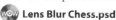

Flat Subject

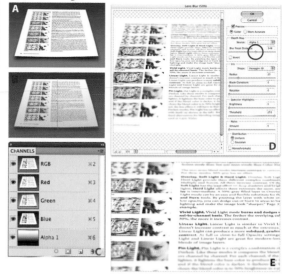

IF THE SUBJECT ITSELF RECEDES into the distance — like the page above **A** — it's really easy to put the band of sharp focus where you want it to be. To establish the focus on our page, we added an alpha channel (clicking the ▣ button at the bottom of the Channels panel) and turned on visibility for the image also (tapping ∼). We chose the Gradient tool ▣, and in the Options bar chose the **Black, White** gradient, **Normal** mode, and **Linear** style. Holding down the Shift key, we dragged from the top edge of the page in the image to its bottom edge to establish a gradient **B**, **C**.

We targeted the image again (Ctrl/⌘-∼ in CS3 or Ctrl/⌘-2 in CS4, and click the layer thumbnail in the Layers panel) and chose Filter > Blur > Lens Blur, then chose our **Alpha 1** channel for the **Source**, with **Invert turned off**. In the working window, we clicked where we wanted sharp focus, on the words "**Vivid Light**" near the middle of the page; the **Blur Focal Distance** slider moved automatically **D**, and the rest of the image went out of focus gradually both in front of and behind the point we had clicked. We could easily experiment, changing the focus by clicking at a different point. When you click, the gray in the gradient-filled alpha channel that corresponds to the point you've clicked becomes the in-focus tone, and all the lighter or darker shades in the gradient become progressively out-of-focus. Each time you click, you set a new "in-focus" gray. By changing the **Radius**, you can change the maximum blur-ring. We chose 20 for the Radius, returned to the original in-focus point, and clicked "OK" **E**.

FIND OUT MORE

▽ Operating the Pen tool ✎ **page 454**

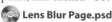

Retouching Techniques for Problem Photos

Photoshop's retouching tools are used in projects throughout this chapter. But here we tackle the repair of an old and worn but treasured family photo. The goal is to analyze the damage in the "problem photo" and choose an approach that will do the job efficiently, using a combination of retouching tools (Patch⬡, Healing Brush 🖊, and Spot Healing Brush 🖊) and filters.

If your damaged photo suffers from significant patches of missing image, the Clone Stamp 🔲 may also be helpful (using the Clone Stamp is demonstrated on page 315).

YOU'LL FIND THE FILE
in 🔵 > Wow Project Files >
Chapter 5 > Retouching Photos

MONA DAYTON

1 Analyzing Problems

THE PHOTO OF THE MAN in the hat has at least three kinds of problems needing repair. On the jacket, neck, and hat are some angular tears where the emulsion has been scraped or flaked away and the white paper is exposed, as in a tear. There are also three distinct but much smaller white spots on the jacket, and a sprinkling of small specks over the entire image.

We'll start with the biggest problem — the angular tears — then tackle the spots, and finally the specks. The **Patch tool** ⬡ is really good at repairs like the angular tears, which are too big to be dabbed over with the Spot Healing Brush 🖊 or the Healing Brush 🖊, two tools that will be ideal for fixing the smaller spots. For the hundreds of specks, we can make use of the Dust & Scratches filter.

SELECTING FOR PATCHING

With the Patch tool ⬡ you aren't limited to selecting with the Patch itself. You can make your selection with another tool or command, or a combination, ▼ and then choose the Patch; make sure the Options bar for the Patch is set the way you want it, move the cursor inside the selection boundary, and drag.

FIND OUT MORE
▼ Making selections
page 48

2 Patching

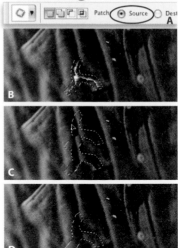

CHOOSE THE **PATCH** TOOL ⬡, and choose **Source** in the Options bar **A**, so you can start by selecting the *source of the problem.* The Patch doesn't have a Sample All Layers option; it has to work directly on the image layer, rather than on a separate layer added to hold repairs. So duplicate the image to a new layer to work on (Ctrl/⌘-J), preserving the original underneath in case you mess up and need to go back to it.

The Patch tool ⬡ can be operated like the Lasso ⟲ (by dragging to "draw" the selection boundary freehand) or like the Polygonal Lasso ⟲ (by Alt/Option-clicking to construct the boundary quickly from straight segments). We began with the large "three-arm" tear on the jacket, Alt/Option-clicking around it **B**. With your selection made, move the cursor inside the selection boundary and drag to an area that has the right texture to fill in the tear; we dragged up until all the white had disappeared from the original selection **C**. Releasing the mouse button completes the patch **D**. We used the same technique for the tears on the neck, cheek, and hat. After the last repair, type Ctrl/⌘-D to deselect.

3 Spot Healing

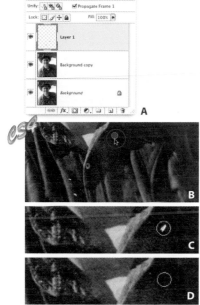

A

B

C

D

FOR THE THREE SMALLER SPOTS, using the Healing Brush 🖌 and Spot Healing Brush 🖌 would be quicker than selecting and repairing them with the Patch tool. Both tools have a Sample All Layers option so you can isolate repairs on a separate layer. Add a new layer for the repairs (Ctrl/ ⌘-Shift-N) **A**. The Spot Healing Brush 🖌 is ideal for hiding a spot that's completely surrounded by fairly uniform material that can be drawn in to cover it up. The white mark just below the collar is such a spot. Choose the Spot Healing Brush, turn on Sample All Layers, and put the cursor over the spot. Adjust the diameter of the brush tip to make it just a little bigger than the spot; you can do this by using one of the bracket keys ([or]) to make the brush tip smaller or bigger in preset steps, or in CS4 with OpenGL enabled▼ right-Alt-drag (Windows) or Ctrl-Option-drag (Mac) right or left **B**, **C**; then click once to make the repair **D**.

4 Healing Brush

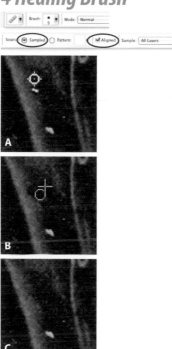

A

B

C

THE OTHER TWO SIZABLE SPOTS on the jacket have a range of tones around them; so using the Spot Healing Brush would be likely to pull highlighted material into a shadow area. The **Healing Brush** 🖌 works better in a case like this because you control where it samples from. Choose the Healing Brush, and in the Options bar set it to **Sample** and turn on **Aligned**. For each spot, make the brush tip just a little bigger than the spot (as described at the left for the Spot Healing Brush). Then Alt/Option-click on a similarly shaded area nearby (we chose an area just above the spot) **A**, release the Alt/Option key, and click or drag to paint over the spot **B**; release the mouse button to complete the healing **C**.

FIND OUT MORE
▼ OpenGL **page 9**
▼ Painting masks **page 84**

5 Dust & Scratches

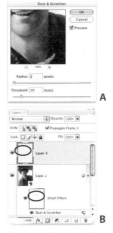

A

B

USE THE DUST & SCRATCHES filter for the hundreds of tiny specks. First make a composite layer for the filter to work on: Ctrl-Alt-Shift-E (Windows) or ⌘-Option-Shift-E (Mac). To keep the Dust & Scratches filter "live," so you have the option of making changes later, right/Ctrl-click on the new layer's name to open a context-sensitive menu and choose **Convert to Smart Object**. Then choose Filter > Noise > **Dust & Scratches** and adjust the **Radius** (to hide the specks) and **Threshold** (to retain the grain of the emulsion) **A**; for this small image (640 by 838 pixels) we used Radius 2 pixels and Threshold 20 levels.

The catchlights in the eyes are small enough so the filter has removed them. And the spot below the right eyebrow is large enough so the filter didn't completely take care of the problem. To restore the catchlights, in the Layers panel, target the mask that was automatically added when you ran Dust & Scratches, choose the Brush tool 🖌 with a soft brush tip, and paint over the eye with black to hide the unwanted "repair." To fix the spot below the eyebrow, add a new "repairs" layer at the top of the stack (Ctrl/⌘-Shift-N), and use the Healing Brush 🖌 (as in step 4) **B**.

Retouching for Sky

With or without clouds, the tonal changes across a sky can make it hard to seamlessly "clone" over a mark that spans any distance, such as the power lines in this image. However, the **Healing Brush** ✎, when used with the **Dust & Scratches** and **Add Noise** filters, makes it easy to remove wires. This approach uses the Healing Brush in **Pattern** mode.

JHDAVIS

YOU'LL FIND THE FILE
in (wow) > Wow Project Files > Chapter 5 > Retouching Sky

FIND OUT MORE

1 Making a Pattern for the Healing Brush

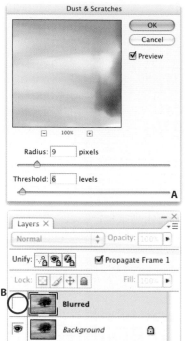

START BY DUPLICATING the image to a new layer (Ctrl/⌘-J). The wires are relatively fine, like scratches, so start by choosing Filter > Noise > Dust & Scratches **A**. We blurred the image enough (Radius 9 pixels) to eliminate even the thick wires; we set the Threshold at 6 to bring back the "grain" of the image and clicked "OK" to close the dialog box.

With the wires eliminated in the blurred duplicate image, the next step is to define this duplicate as a pattern by choosing Edit > **Define Pattern**. Then turn off visibility for the blurred layer (by clicking its 👁 in the Layers panel **B**) so you can see the wires.

2 Healing with Pattern

ADD A NEW EMPTY LAYER for making repairs (click the ⬚ button at the bottom of the Layers panel) **A**. Now choose the **Healing Brush** ✎. In the Options bar **B**, choose **Pattern** as the Source. Also choose **Replace** as the tool's Mode (this will prevent the "smearing" that can happen when you work with the Healing Brush in Normal mode near contrasting elements, such as the tree and pole in this image). Turn on the **Aligned** option. Make the brush tip a little bigger than the wire thickness; we used 6 pixels (use a bracket key — [or] — to make the brush tip smaller or bigger in preset steps, or in CS4 with Open GL enabled▼ right-Alt-drag (Windows) or Ctrl-Option-drag (Mac) left or right). Then simply click at one end of a wire to start a stroke **C** and Shift-click at the other end of the wire to paint a straight stroke between the two points **D**. Continue the click-then-Shift-click routine to cover all the wires (for sagging wires, of course, you could drag the cursor instead of Shift-clicking), or draw a path that follows the curve of the sagging wire,▼ and stroke the path.▼

3 Matching the Grain

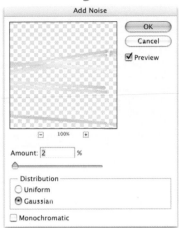

WHEN ALL OF THE WIRES are hidden, apply the Noise filter to restore the grain to the Healing Brush strokes on the repairs layer: Choose Filter > Noise > **Add Noise**; we adjusted the filter settings, checking the result at 100% magnification (View > Actual Pixels, or Ctrl/⌘-1 in the working window), until the repairs, made with the blurred image as the source, matched the grain in the photo at Amount 2%, Gaussian.

Note: In steps 1 through 3 our goal was to get rid of the wires, seamlessly. Unlike sharpening an image, where we might want to change the settings for different output, or applying a special-effects filter that we might decide later was too mild or too strong, here we only wanted to eliminate the wires and make the repairs match the rest of the image. We could easily and accurately evaluate our success as we applied the filters, so we knew we wouldn't be revisiting those tasks. Therefore, we kept our layer organization simple and direct, protecting our original image by making a blurred copy and a repairs layer, instead of using Smart Object layers with Smart Filters.

4 Spot-Healing

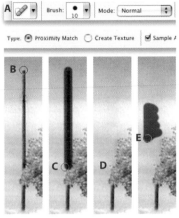

TO REMOVE THE POLE, the **Spot Healing Brush** ✎ can do most of the job. (If you find it frustrating to get the Spot Healing Brush in exactly the right starting spot, the Clone Stamp, described in "Cloning" at the right, also works.)

Because the Spot Healing Brush pulls image material from its surroundings to fill in the spot, it's important to start the stroke in a place (and drag in a direction) that pulls sky in to hide the pole. Choose Normal in the tool's Options bar **A** and choose a brush size a little bigger than the width of what you want to cover (the pole in this case; we used 10 pixels). Position the cursor so it encompasses some sky above and on both sides of the pole **B**; then drag downward **C** to pull in sky to replace the pole; we held down the Shift key to move the cursor in a straight line down the pole to the leaves, where we stopped. As you drag the cursor down, the new sky you're creating will contribute to covering up the next part of the pole. Release the mouse button to see the repair **D**.

Zoom in and out to check your work in several views. If you see any telltale edges or smudges, you can fix them by crisscrossing the area with the Spot Healing Brush **E**.

5 Cloning

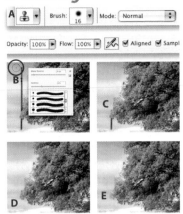

THE CLONE STAMP ♣ (instead of the Spot Healing Brush) can be used to remove the pole. For the top of the pole, we turned on the Aligned feature in the Options bar **A**, so the Clone Stamp would always pick up sky just to the left of where the cursor was, even if we had to restart the stroke; we also turned on Sample All Layers so we could continue to work on our repairs layer. We got good results with a brush tip about twice the diameter of the pole (16 pixels) with Hardness set at 30% **B**; this was soft enough to blend the edges of the cloned material. (Choosing Photoshop > Preferences > Display & Cursors and turning on Full Size Brush Tip lets you see the full diameter of the tip, including soft edges, as shown above.) We Alt/Option-clicked to sample sky close to the pole, but not close enough for the Clone Stamp to sample the pole itself. We moved the cursor onto the pole and dragged down, stopping when we came to the tree leaves **C**.

For the bottom of the pole, with the Clone Stamp set to Aligned (as described above), we Alt/Option-clicked the sky to the left of the pole, then moved the cursor over and dragged down over the pole to cover it **D**. Finally we Alt/Option-clicked to sample some sparse leaves and "dabbed" them over the pole **E**.

Cosmetic Changes

The process of improving a photo usually works best if you start with overall tone and color corrections▼ and *then* proceed to specific retouching tasks, such as meeting the "cosmetic challenges" covered on the next seven pages. In most of the fixes, we've kept the correction separate from the original image. That way, if you need to correct the correction, you won't run the risk of degrading the original image by working and reworking it. Some of Photoshop's image-fixing tools, such as the Healing Brush, can make their corrections on a separate, transparent layer above the photo. For tools that don't offer this option, you can duplicate the image (or part of it) to a new layer and work on the duplicate. For even more flexibility, you can change the duplicate layer's blend mode, lower the Opacity, or add a layer mask, for a rich variety of options in "mixing" the changed copy with the original.

LOADING THE WOW-IMAGE FIX BRUSHES

Some of the "Quick Cosmetic Changes" involve **Wow Image Fix Brushes** from the **Wow DVD-ROM**. "Installing Wow Styles, Patterns, Tools & Other Presets" on page 4 tells how to load the **Wow Image Fix Brushes** along with all the other Wow presets. Or load them from the Wow DVD-ROM by navigating to Wow Project Files > Chapter 5 > Quick Cosmetic Changes, then double-clicking the icon for **Wow Image Fix Brushes.tpl**.

BRUSH SIZE

You can use the bracket keys to resize brush tips. Tapping the ⟨⟩ key enlarges the brush tip in preset increments; tapping ⟨⟩ makes it smaller. In CS4 with OpenGL enabled, scaling brush tips is even more convenient: To change sizes "on the fly," release the mouse button, then hold down Ctrl-Option (Mac) or right mouse button–Alt (Windows) and drag left or right for continuous scaling of the brush tip; release the keys (and right mouse button) to continue painting.

YOU'LL FIND THE FILES

in  > Wow Project Files > Chapter 5 > Quick Cosmetics

FIND OUT MORE

▼ Tone & color adjustment **page 244**

▼ Brush tip settings **page 71**

Whitening Teeth

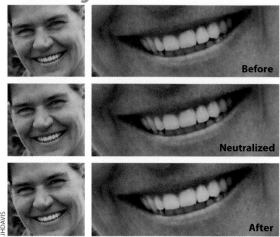

Before

Neutralized

After

JHDAVIS

An easy way to whiten teeth (or eyes) is to first take the color out of any stains, and then brighten the teeth overall. Use the Brush tool ✎ (Shift-B) with the Wow-White Teeth Neutralize and Wow-White Teeth Brighten tool presets (see how to load them at the left), or set up the Brush tool yourself with the Options described below.

First copy the entire image to a new layer (Ctrl/⌘-J), or make a loose selection of the mouth (with the Lasso ⟨⟩, for instance) and copy the selected area (Ctrl/⌘-J).

Choose the Brush tool ✎ (Shift-B). To use the Wow presets, at the far left end of the Options bar, click the ✎ to open the Tool Preset picker, and double-click the **Wow-White Teeth-Neutralize** brush (the first click targets the preset, and the second click closes the picker). The Options bar shows that the brush has a soft tip.▼ The Mode is set to Color, to neutralize the stains without changing surface detail. Opacity is set low so the neutralizing won't happen too fast to control. The Airbrush feature ✎ is chosen so the brush will keep working as you hold it in one place. The white color is built into the preset (if you're using the Brush tool with your own settings, set white as the Foreground color — type D, then X). Resize the brush tip as needed (see "Brush Size" at the left). Avoiding the gums and lips, dab the teeth to remove stains. Copy this layer (Ctrl/⌘-J) for brightening.

Next choose the **Wow-White Teeth-Brighten** preset, or change the Options bar settings to Soft Light mode and a lower Opacity. Brush over the teeth. In the Layers panel, check the whitening by toggling the white-teeth layer's visibility on and off (click the layer's 👁 icon). If the whitening seems too dramatic, lower the layer's Opacity (in the upper right corner of the Layers panel).

🔵 **White Teeth.psd**

Adding Color to Lips

Before

After

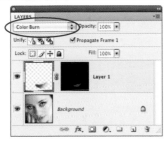

To GIVE PALE LIPS a bit more color and definition without blowing out the highlights, try blending a copy of the lips in **Color Burn** mode at low Opacity. The highlights in the lips will change only slightly, but the midtones will darken fairly dramatically.

To start, copy the image to a new layer (Ctrl/⌘-J), or make a loose selection of the lips and a little of the area around them (we used the Lasso tool ⌇), and make a new layer from the selected area (Ctrl/⌘-J). In the upper left corner of the Layers panel, choose Color Burn from the pop-up list of blend modes. Then add a black-filled ("hide all") layer mask by Alt/Option-clicking the "Add a layer mask" button ▢ at the bottom of the Layers panel or in CS4 the "Add a pixel mask" button ▣ in the Masks panel. (Adding the Alt/Option key makes the mask black.)

Then choose the Brush tool ✐ (Shift-B) and white paint (with a mask active, typing D, for "default," makes white the Foreground color). In the Brush tool's Options bar set the Mode to Normal and set the Opacity low (we used 25%). Click the "Brush" footprint and choose a soft brush at a size small enough to maneuver within the lip area. Now paint (you'll be painting the mask) to reveal the intensified color of the lips. If the color isn't strong enough, paint over the lips again to "thin" the mask. If it's too intense, lower the Color Burn layer's Opacity in the top right corner of the Layers panel. Or switch to black paint (typing X will make black the Foreground color), lower the Brush tool's Opacity even more (in the Options bar), and paint the mask to reduce the effect.

Brightening Eyes

Before

After

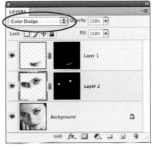

To ADD SPARKLE TO EYES, try Color Dodge mode. When a copy of the eyes in **Color Dodge** mode is combined with the original, light colors are lightened more than dark colors. If you select and duplicate only the iris and pupil of the eyes, for instance, Color Dodge will lighten the color while enhancing the contrast, giving the eyes more sparkle.

Duplicate the image, or just the eyes, to a new layer, as described for the lips (at the left). Here we started with the file with the lips already colored. We targeted this original image by clicking on the *Background* thumbnail in the Layers panel, and then we selected the eyes and surrounding area with the Lasso tool ⌇ (Shift-L) and duplicated them to a new layer (Ctrl/⌘-J).

Just as for the lips at the left, add a black-filled (hide-all) layer mask to the new layer by Alt/Option-clicking the ▢ button at the bottom of the Layers panel or in CS4 the "Add a pixel mask" button ▣ in the Masks panel. In the Layers panel, choose Color Dodge for the blend mode.

Paint the mask, using the Brush tool and white paint to reveal the eyes, the same as for the lips, except that you'll need to set the Opacity in the Brush tool's Options bar higher (we used 80%). If the highlights in the eyes were "burned out" in the process, you can calm them down by dabbing the mask with black; we did this with 40% Opacity set in the Options bar.

WOW Lips and Eyes.psd

Fixing "Red-Eye"

PHOTOSHOP'S RED EYE TOOL is designed to take care of the red-eye problem in one quick click. Choose the Red Eye tool (Shift-J) and Shift-drag diagonally to make a square that surrounds the red plus a little margin outside it **A**; then release the mouse button **B**. Defining a square in this way, instead of just clicking, seems to do a better job of keeping the black from "blooming" outside the pupil and iris, or shifting off-center. If you don't get results you like on the first try, undo (Ctrl/⌘-Z), change the Pupil and Darken Amount settings in the Options bar, and try again. For **B** we used the default 50% and 50%. Lowering these settings (we used 1% and 1%) reduces the extent and density of the black **C**; increasing them (100% and 100%) has the opposite effect **D**.

 Red-Eye.psd

ABOUT RED-EYE

Red-eye can happen because the subject, with pupils open wide for better vision in the dim surroundings, is looking directly at the flash when the camera takes the photo. This happens with many compact cameras because the flash unit is very near the lens, so when subjects "look at the camera," they're also looking right at the flash. The retina at the back of the eye, with its rich blood supply, is lit up by the light coming through the wide-open pupil, producing red-eye.

Cameras with red-eye reduction solve this problem by "pre-flashing." The eyes respond to this early light, so when the real flash goes off, the pupils are small. Less light gets to the retina, and less retina is exposed to the camera. Thus, no red-eye. Red-eye reduction has its price, though. The pupils look as if it were broad daylight instead of a low-light ambience. Also, the "pre-flash" forces the subject to pose longer, pretty much eliminating any natural facial expression. So there are times when you may prefer to *turn off* red-eye reduction, take the photo, and fix up any red-eye in Photoshop. Or avoid red-eye by using an offset flash, or by having the subject look somewhere other than straight at the camera.

Fixing "Eyeshine"

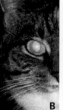

SIMILAR TO RED-EYE, "eyeshine" **A** in cats, dogs, and some other animals comes from an extra reflective membrane in the eye. The first step in removing eyeshine is to neutralize the color. Choose the Brush tool (Shift-B). In the Options bar, click the "Brush:" footprint; set the Hardness at 50 and use Master Diameter to adjust the cursor to a comfortable size for painting the pupils. In the Options bar, set Mode to Saturation and Opacity to 100% and turn off the Airbrush option (is the toggle). With black paint (type D to make black the Foreground color), paint over each pupil **B**. In Saturation mode, the Brush will apply the saturation of the black paint (0, so no color), without eliminating detail.

Add an empty layer by clicking the "Create a new layer" button at the bottom of the Layers panel. Working on the new transparent layer, change the Brush tool's Mode to Normal in the Options bar and apply black paint so the pupils are solid black, with the soft edge of the brush strokes extending just beyond. When you can see that the black is solid, with soft edges, change the layer's blend mode from Normal to Soft Light (in the upper left corner of the Layers panel); Soft Light increases contrast, to restore washed-out detail in the light eye. To build the density, duplicate the layer several times (Ctrl/⌘-J), until the pupils are darker than you want. We used a total of three layers of painted eyes **C**.

Now refine the restoration by working on the top copy. For instance, we applied Filter > Blur > Gaussian Blur to help the high-contrast pupils blend in with the rest of the eye **D**. Though we didn't, you can also lower the top layer's Opacity, or add a layer mask and paint it with black to selectively reduce the effect.

 Eyeshine.psd

Opening Eyes

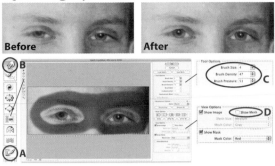

Before   **After**

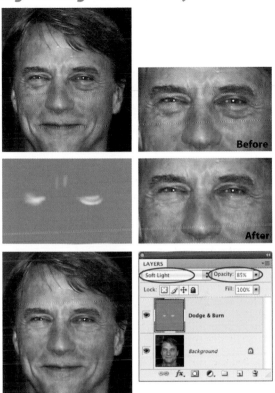

WHEN SOMEONE IN THE GROUP PHOTO has eyes half-closed or squinting, you can sometimes find another photo in the series with "good eyes" to copy and paste for the repair. But if you don't have any good eyes to substitute, the **Liquify** filter and a gentle hand can sometimes open the original eyes enough to be convincing.

Select the area around the eyes, duplicate it to a new layer (Ctrl/⌘-J), and choose Filter > Liquify. Begin by protecting most of the area you don't want changed by painting it with the Freeze Mask Tool 🖌 (type F) **A**. (Eyebrows and eyelids sometimes need to be left unfrozen so you can do a bit of "surgery" on them as well.) Next select the Forward Warp Tool 🖌 (type W) **B** and adjust the Size, Density, and Pressure of the brush **C**. (You can resize brush tips in the Liquify dialog by using the square bracket keys, just as in the main Photoshop interface; see "Brush Size" on page 316.) We left the Brush Density near the default setting of 50, but cut the Pressure in half, reducing the strength to keep from forming "waves" in our eyelids. To gradually open the eyes, make several short strokes from the center of the pupil outward, from the iris outward, and from the top of the iris up and around the new pupil area; also expand the whites of the eyes as needed, while keeping the eye shape generally intact. (Turn the mesh on and off as you work **D**, to confirm that you're not rippling the eyelids.) Patience and short, gentle strokes are the keys to "cosmetic surgery" with the Liquify filter. Check the image after each stroke, and undo if you make a mistake (Ctrl/⌘-Z); when you've finished, click "OK" to leave the Liquify dialog. Make any additional changes needed to the image; we selected the highlight from the Liquified left eye with the Lasso and copied it to a new layer (Ctrl/⌘-J), then dragged it into place over the right eye with the Move tool ▶➕ (Shift-V) and rotated it slightly (Edit > Transform > Rotate, and drag outside the Transform box).

 **Liquify Eyes.psd**

Lightening Under the Eyes

Before

After

LIGHTEN UP DARK OR PUFFY AREAS UNDER THE EYES with a "Dodge & Burn" layer. Open your image and Alt/Option-click the "Add a new layer" button 🔲 at the bottom of the Layers panel. When the New Layer dialog box opens, choose Soft Light for the Mode, click the checkbox for "Fill with Soft Light–neutral color 50% Gray," and click "OK." The gray will be invisible in Soft Light mode.

Start by typing D, then X to make white the Foreground color. Choose the Brush tool 🖌. In the Options bar click the "Brush:" footprint and set the Hardness at 0, for a soft brush; set a Master Diameter appropriate for the area you want to fix; for this small image, we started at 18 px and would later use the [key to reduce the brush as small as 6 px for finer lines. Reading left to right on the Options bar, the Mode should be Normal, since Soft Light is already set as the blend mode for the layer; set Opacity low (we used 10%); and turn off the Airbrush feature so the white won't build up too fast. Now brush over the areas you want to lighten. Make the maximum correction you think you will want, and then experiment with the layer's Opacity in the upper right corner of the Layers panel to get just the right amount of lightening.

Under Eyes.psd

Dodge & Burn Collagen & Botox

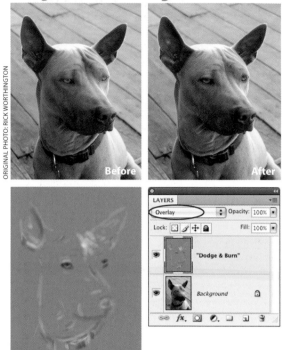

PROMINENCES ON A FACE typically catch the light, and consequently they also shade the areas below them. With a little more contrast than was used in "Lightening Under the Eyes" on page 319, you can create a dodge-and-burn layer to "sculpt" the features of a face by adding fairly concentrated light and shadow. Here we created the "Dodge & Burn" layer in Overlay mode (Alt/Option-click ▣); in the New Layer dialog box we turned on "Fill with Overlay-neutral color 50% Gray" and clicked "OK." In Overlay mode, light and dark tones lighten and darken more intensely than in Soft Light mode. We painted on this layer with white to create a ridge above each eye and to reduce the "worry lines" in the forehead, and with black to create shaded areas on the eyelids and below the eyes. We did similar sculpting with white to soften the muzzle and the neck, and used white again to enhance the backlighting of the ears.

 Sculpting.psd

Removing Spots

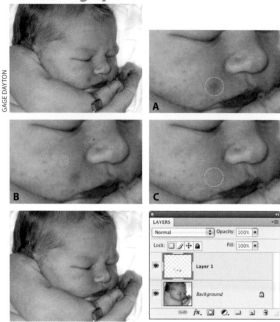

THE HEALING BRUSH AND SPOT HEALING BRUSH are almost magical for removing spots and blemishes. Start by opening your image and adding a new layer for the repairs (click the "Add a new layer" button ▣ at the bottom of the Layers panel). Move the cursor to the first spot you want to fix. Tap the ⌊ or ⌋ key to shrink or enlarge the cursor until it comfortably surrounds the spot **A**. Then do the following:

- If the area immediately around the spot has the tone and color you want for the repair, choose the Spot Healing Brush (Shift-J until you get it). Make sure Proximity Match and Sample All Layers are turned on and Mode is Normal; then simply click the spot.

- If you don't find the tone and color you want immediately around the spot, choose the Healing Brush (Shift-J until you get it). In the Options bar, make sure Mode is Normal, Source is Sampled, and Sample All Layers is chosen. Move the cursor to a nearby area that looks the way you want the spot area to look when it's fixed **B**. Hold down the Alt/Option key and click to sample. Now release Alt/Option and move the cursor back to the blemish and click to make the magical repair **C**.

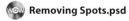 **Removing Spots.psd**

Smoothing Complexions 1: Surface Blur

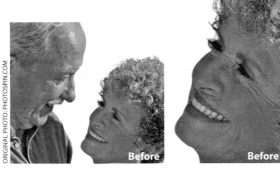

ORIGINAL PHOTO: PHOTOSPIN.COM

Before

Before

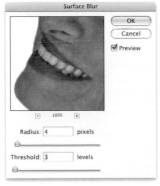

After

THE **SURFACE BLUR** FILTER preserves high-contrast edges while blurring detail (see "Using Surface Blur" at the right). Use Surface Blur "cosmetically" when you want to preserve some skin detail but hide pores and smooth out fine wrinkles and color inconsistencies. First turn the image layer into a Smart Object (Filter > **Convert for Smart Filter**) to protect the original photo when you run the filter.▼ Then choose Filter > Blur > Surface Blur. Adjust **Radius** and **Threshold**, watching the areas you want to smooth and the facial features you want to keep sharp, until you see the result you want. For this image a Radius of 4 and a Threshold of 3 act together to slightly smooth out the man's skin color, without making him look made up. These settings also smooth the woman's skin slightly and get rid of the noise that results from her being in the shade. Notice that hair and other details remain sharp.

 **Smooth Skin.psd**

FIND OUT MORE

▼ Using Smart Filters
page 72

USING SURFACE BLUR

The **Surface Blur** filter works by detecting edges — areas of strong contrast or color difference — and protecting those edges while it blurs the smaller, less contrasty details, or texture. It can be useful for smoothing skin while preserving facial features. And you can do this without losing the highlights in the eyes, teeth, and hair. On the other hand, it doesn't allow you to preserve the finest detail while smoothing slightly larger marks as the Dust & Scratches filter's Threshold slider does.

Blurring is a color-averaging process. When you choose Filter > Blur > Surface Blur, the Surface Blur dialog box opens. The Radius setting controls how widely Photoshop looks when it computes an average color for each pixel; so the bigger the Radius, the more blurred things become. The Threshold setting determines how different pixels have to be in order to be considered an edge; the higher you set the Threshold, the more different they have to be, and the fewer "edges" Photoshop will see and the more blurring will occur. With a low Threshold setting, only the finest details are blurred; with higher settings, higher-contrast differences are blurred also.

Using Surface Blur as a Smart Filter (by turning the image into a Smart Object before filtering) allows you to fine-tune the effect by trying other settings later if you like, or by varying the Opacity or blend mode of the filter effect.▼

BLACK MASK OR WHITE?

Anytime you add a layer mask, you have a choice to make: Use a black mask that completely hides the layer and paint with the Brush 🖌 and white to reveal parts of it? Or use a white mask and paint with black?

For example, on page 313 Dust & Scratches was used as a Smart Filter to hide hundreds of unwanted specks throughout the image, and the filter's effect needed to be masked in only a few spots (to restore the catchlights in the eyes). In a case like that, use a white mask to reveal the filter effect everywhere and paint with black in the few spots where you want to hide the effect.

In contrast, on page 322, where Dust & Scratches is used cosmetically, a good approach is to apply the filter to the maximum extent you might want, fill the Smart Filter mask with black to hide the effect so you can again clearly see the features you want to hide. Then paint the mask with white, varying the Brush's Opacity to smooth as much or as little as you want.

Smoothing Complexions 2: Dust & Scratches

Before

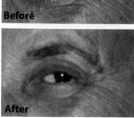

After

THE **DUST & SCRATCHES** FILTER can smooth the skin in a way that doesn't look heavily retouched, because small-scale texture, such as pores, are still visible The viewer's impression? "If the tiny pores are visible, the rest of the skin must really be as smooth as it looks."

First turn the image into a Smart Object (Filter > **Convert for Smart Filters**). Then choose Filter > Noise > Dust & Scratches. Set the Radius and Threshold as low as possible, and then increase the Radius until the spots and wrinkles disappear, to the maximum extent you might want. We settled on a Radius setting of 4, which smoothed away dark spots and toned down "hot spots" by blurring surrounding color into them. To bring back pores and the "grain" of the photo, raise the Threshold until the blemishes you've hidden just begin to reappear, then lower the Threshold just until they disappear again; we used 14. (Don't worry if important details such as highlights in the eyes, teeth, or hair are lost.)

In the Layers panel, experiment by double-clicking the ⬚ on the Dust & Scratches entry in the Layers panel. In the Blending Options dialog box, lower the Opacity of the filter effect while you look at the skin, until you get the right blend between smoothing and character; we settled on 80% Opacity. Then hide the filter effect by clicking the Smart Filter mask thumbnail in the Layers panel, typing D to set the default colors, and then pressing Ctrl/⌘-Delete to fill with black (see "Black Mask or White?" on page 321). To bring back smoothing where you want it, choose the Brush tool ✏ with a fairly soft-edged brush tip at an appropriate size (we used 35 pixels) and white paint. Paint the mask in areas where you want to soften the skin. You can reduce Opacity in the Options bar to control how much the brush reveals or hides.

 Soft Skin.psd

Smoothing Complexions 3: Clarity

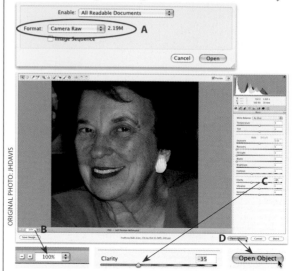

ORIGINAL PHOTO: JHDAVIS

THOUGH IT'S OFTEN USED TO *SHARPEN* DETAILS, the **Clarity** slider on **Camera Raw's Basic tab** can be used cosmetically with **negative settings**, to make details like wrinkles and pores *less* apparent. ***Note:*** If you're using Photoshop CS3, you won't have Clarity in Camera Raw, unless your Camera Raw version is 4.2 or later. See step 1 and also "Update Your Camera Raw" on page 332 to find out how to tell what version of Camera Raw you have and how to update it if needed.

Here we used the **Soft Skin-Before.jpg** file. To open the file in Camera Raw from Bridge, navigate to the file and choose File > Open in Camera Raw (in CS4 you can use the ◉ button at the top of the Bridge interface instead of the command). To open the file in Camera Raw from Photoshop, choose File > Open, navigate to the file, and click on its name or thumbnail; then choose **Camera Raw** from the **Format** menu **A** near the bottom of the Open dialog box. When the file opens in Camera Raw, in the "Select zoom level" box in the lower left corner, choose the 100% view **B**. On the Basic tab, move the Clarity slider left until you achieve the effect you want **C**. We found that a setting of –35 smoothed the skin, adding a "glow," and also lightened the shadows on the neck. If you don't see the "Open Object" button in the lower right corner of the Camera Raw interface, hold down Shift or Alt/Option to make it appear; click the button **D** to open the file as a Smart Object in Photoshop. You may want to add an empty layer and use the Healing Brush ✏ to lighten the shadows more and to soften the "hot spot" on the nose. (You can use the same settings as in "Softening Shadows" on page 323.)

 **Soft Skin-Before.jpg**

Softening Shadows

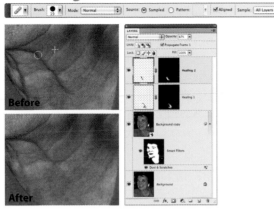

Before

After

The harsh shadows on the neck, created by the flash, are not fine enough to eliminate with Dust & Scratches and are too dark to be softened as much as we might like by Camera Raw's Clarity slider (both on page 322). To remove the shadows, try the Healing Brush 🖌. Here we've used **Soft Skin.psd** from the Dust & Scratches example on page 322 as the starting point. To start, Alt/Option-click the "Create a new layer" button 🔲 at the bottom of the Layers panel, naming the layer as you create it.

In the Options bar for the Healing Brush, choose a **hard-edged brush tip** that's just a bit wider than the mark you want to cover. Set the Healing Brush's Mode to **Normal**. Make sure **Sampled** is chosen so the healing texture will be picked up from the image. Turn on **Sample All Layers** so the Healing Brush can sample from the composite image and paint on the new empty layer. Turn on the **Aligned** option. That way, each time you start a stroke, the Healing Brush will sample from a spot parallel to your stroke, rather than starting again from the exact spot you originally sampled.

Now move the cursor to a point near the top of the right-hand shadow line, and Alt/Option-click and release to set the starting point for sampling. Move the cursor onto the shadow line itself and use short strokes to "paint over" the line. If you need to, Alt/Option-click again to sample a new source. Now add another new layer (Alt/Option-click the 🔲 button) and use the Healing Brush on the other shadow, keeping the brush tip small and avoiding the shirt so you don't pick up blue. To blend the Healing Brush strokes into the photo, adjust the Opacity of each healing layer and add a mask to "fade" parts of the marks if you like. ▼

 **Soft Shadows.psd**

FIND OUT MORE

▼ Painting masks
page 84

Taking the Heat Out

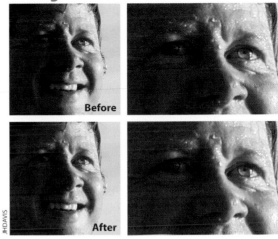

Before

After

To TAKE THE HEAT OUT of sunburn or other generalized skin redness, you can use a soft, low-opacity Brush in Hue mode to reduce the red without covering up detail or shading. Copy your entire image to a new layer above the original (Ctrl/⌘-J), or make a selection that includes more than the area you want to fix (with the Lasso 〰, for instance) and copy it (Ctrl/⌘-J).

Choose the Brush tool 🖌 (Shift-B) and then near the left end of the Options bar click the "Brush:" footprint to open the Brush Preset picker, where you can adjust the Master Diameter and Hardness. For this image, a 40-pixel brush seemed to suit the areas we wanted to fix; Hardness set to 0 produced the softest brush, for blending the change with the original color. Choose Hue from the Mode list so when you paint, it will change the hue of the skin but the detail and shading won't be covered up. Setting Opacity at 50% will give you better control as you "build" the color change. To load the brush, hold down the Alt/Option key and sample color by clicking in an area of the face that shows normal skin color; we clicked on the midtones in the chin. Release the Alt/Option key and paint over the red areas to tone down the color. When you've finished, if you want to restore some of the red "glow" overall, in the Layers panel simply reduce the Opacity of the altered layer, allowing some of the original color to blend in.

 **Reducing Red.psd**

It's What You *Don't* See . . .

"ONE OF THE THINGS I LIKE MOST about Photoshop," says photographer Mary Lynne Ashley, "is the freedom it gives me in the studio." Knowing that she can clone out extraneous elements afterwards in Photoshop, she can set up situations that would be hard to manage otherwise.

For *Who's That Guy?* (below) Mary Lynne used a black backdrop with the baby sitting on a mirror on the floor and a black drape covering the edges of the mirror. After taking the photo, she selected the baby, the reflection, and some of the surrounding background, reversed the selection (Ctrl/⌘-Shift-I), and filled it with a black sampled from that surrounding edge. She could also clone out any unwanted reflections in the mirror edge around the baby.

"I frequently use the Clone Stamp," Mary Lynne says, "to clone out parents' hands when they are 'spotting' a baby for a photo. In other words, the hands are right there in case the child slips," but there's no evidence of them in the final print.

Keeping children relaxed, happy, and still can become exponentially more challenging as the number of children increases. When she wanted to shoot *Now They Can't See Us* from behind the children, Mary Lynne had the children's mother blowing bubbles in front of them. The bubbles held their attention while Mary Lynne photographed them, and she used the Clone Stamp to remove them later in Photoshop, sampling her "repair" material from the backdrop.

To develop the color she copied the photo to a new layer (Ctrl/⌘-J) and reduced the saturation of the copy.▼ Then she made another copy of the original photo layer, dragged its thumbnail to the top of the stack in the Layers panel, and turned it into a sepiatone.▼ She added a mask to the sepia layer and painted it with black to protect the overalls from the sepia.▼ (The Image > Adjustments > Hue/Saturation dialog in Photoshop CS4 offers presets for Old Style, which is partial desaturation, and Sepia.)

FIND OUT MORE

▼ Partial desaturation **page 206**

▼ Sepia toning **pages 203 & 204**

▼ Painting a layer mask **page 84**

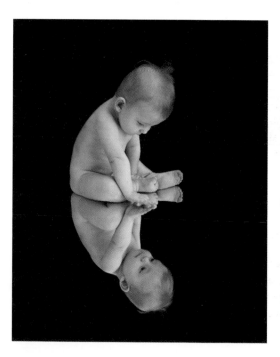

Averaging Out Noise

YOU'LL FIND THE FILES

in **wow** > Wow Project Files > Chapter 5 >
Averaging Noise
   • Noise-Before (four JPEG files to start)
   • Noise-After (two PSD files to compare)

OPEN THIS PANEL

(from the Window menu, for instance):
   • Layers

OVERVIEW

Layer and align several shots of the same
noisy image • Blend the layers by adjusting
their Opacity or with Photoshop Extended's
Mean command • Correct perspective with
Free Transform • Sharpen, masking to avoid
sharpening any noise that remains

1

Loading the files into a stack so noise can be
"averaged"

2a

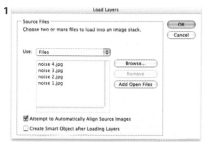

Low light
conditions
can result
in noisy
photos, as
shown in
each of the
photos in
this series.

2b

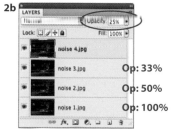

Four layers are stacked at diminishing Opacity settings, so that each ultimately contributes 25% of
the composite to "average" away the random noise.

ORIGINAL PHOTOS: GAREN CHECKLEY

Capturing the warm glow of the train station and the evening
blue of the sky required a relatively long exposure, and with no
tripod, the potential for blur was high — the image would need
sharpening. Because of the low-light conditions, the photo was
likely to be noisy also, so we'd want to remove as much of the
noise as we could, or the sharpening would make it worse. The
photographer took several shots, and we chose four with the
least blur to combine.

Thinking the project through. The digital noise we see in images shot in low light is a random electronic phenomenon. So it
stands to reason that if we can average the color values for each
pixel in three or four shots that are identical except for the noise,
the random colors and tones will neutralize each other and the
real colors will persist. This averaging can be done by layering
the shots and then controlling what percentage of the whole each
layer contributes. **In Photoshop** this is done by controlling the
Opacity for each layer. **In Photoshop Extended** it can be done
automatically with the Statistics command.

1 Preparing, stacking, and aligning the photos. In Photoshop or in Bridge, choose three or four files from your shoot that
show as little blurring as possible, so that when they're combined
they'll produce the sharpest image you can get. Then:

If your images are open in Photoshop, choose **File > Scripts >
Load Files Into Stack,** click the "Add Open Files" button **1**, target
any other open files that are listed but aren't in the series, and
click "Remove." Then make sure the Attempt to Automatically
Align Images option is checked; click "OK."

2c

After averaging with stacked layers, the noise is noticeably reduced.

2d

The Statistics script in Photoshop Extended does the averaging automatically.

2e

With a layered file open in Photoshop Extended, you can access the Mean command by converting the layers to a Smart Object and choosing Layer > Smart Objects > Stack Mode > Mean.

3a

Using Free Transform to correct for lens distortion. Holding down the Ctrl/⌘ key lets you drag each corner handle independently.

3b

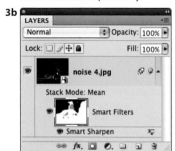

To sharpen the image, we used Smart Sharpen. You can see the settings we used for Smart Sharpen by clicking the Smart Sharpen entry in the Layers panel in the **Noise-After** files.

Or from Bridge CS4, you can target the photos you want to open,▼ and choose Tools > Photoshop > Load Files into Photoshop Layers. In Photoshop choose Edit > Auto-Align Layers.

2 Blending the layers. This next step depends on whether you're in Photoshop or Photoshop Extended, and in CS4, whether you've started in Bridge. **In Photoshop,** to watch the noise reduction as it happens, in the Layers panel, turn off visibility for all layers except the bottom one (click their 👁 icons) and zoom in (Ctrl/⌘-+) on an area with lots of noise **2a.** Then click the thumbnail of the next layer up, turn on its visibility, and set its Opacity to 50%. The composite image you see now is a blend — half contributed by the second (50%) layer and the other half by the bottom layer showing through to make up the other 50%. Notice that this blend has reduced the noise.

Turn on visibility for the next layer up and reduce its Opacity to 33%. Since this layer is contributing a third, the average of the other two layers below is now contributing two-thirds; you should see even less noise. If you have a fourth layer, turn on its visibility and set its Opacity at 25% **2b, 2c.**

When you've completed the averaging process, in the Layers panel, target all the layers (click the top one and Shift-click the bottom one) and turn them into a Smart Object (for sharpening later; right-click/Ctrl-click on one layer's name and choose Convert to Smart Object from the context-sensitive menu).

Or in Photoshop Extended, choose **File > Scripts > Statistics**, and in the Image Statistics dialog, for the **Stack Mode** choose **Mean 2d.** The noise reduction will be done automatically.

Or if you started in Bridge, in the Layers panel, target all the layers, and turn them into a **Smart Object** (choose Layer > Smart Object > Convert to Smart Object). Finally, average the layers (Layer > Smart Objects > **Stack Mode > Mean**) **2e.**

3 Finishing. As a quick fix for the lens distortion in the image, we turned on the Grid (View > Show > Grid) and used Free Transform (Ctrl/⌘-T),▼ Ctrl/⌘-dragging on the upper corner points to straighten the light poles **3a** and pressing the Enter key to complete the Transform. To crop, we selected with the Rectangular Marquee⬚ and chose Image > Crop.▼ We chose Filter > Sharpen > Smart Sharpen,▼ adjusted the settings, and painted the mask to direct the sharpening **3b.**▼ 〰

FIND OUT MORE

▼ Using Bridge **page 133**

▼ Free Transform **page 67**

▼ Cropping **page 240**

▼ Smart Sharpen **page 338**

▼ Painting masks **page 84**

Creating Solitude

YOU'LL FIND THE FILES

in **wow** > Wow Project Files > Chapter 5 >
Solitude
- Orchid Show-Before (to start)
- Orchid Show-After.psd (to compare)
- Sculpture-Before (to start)
- Sculpture-After.psd (to compare)
- Statue-Before (to start)
- Statue-After.psd (to compare)

OPEN THIS PANEL

(from the Window menu, for instance):
Layers

OVERVIEW

Stack a multi-shot series of photos as
layers in a single file • In Photoshop
remove the unwanted elements from each
layer and then align and blend the layers,
or in Photoshop Extended try the File >
Scripts > Statistics (Median) command •
Crop and retouch as needed

1a

The two photos from the **Orchid Show-Before**
folder

PHOTOS: SUSAN HELLER

IN EARLY PHOTOGRAPHY, when it took several minutes to expose
the emulsion, you could take a photo of a street corner with
people passing by and not see any people in the final photo,
because they weren't in the scene long enough to be recorded.
Photoshop's automatic stacking, aligning, and blending functions can accomplish the same sort of removal of unwanted foot
traffic or other moving elements. The image above is an example.
The Orchid Show was crowded and the aisles were narrow. The
photographer shot from the hip, knowing Photoshop could help
her get a photo of the flowers alone. In two other cases that follow this example, the stacking, aligning, and blending made a
good start, but some retouching was needed.

Thinking the project through. When you intend to remove
distractions by combining two or more photos from a multi-shot
series, it can be helpful to remove the unwanted elements *before*
you align. That way Photoshop's Auto-Align Layers command
won't be trying to align elements that you don't even want in
the final image anyway. Once the photos are aligned, they can
be seamlessly blended. And if you have Photoshop Extended,
its Statistics command may be able to automate much of the
aligning and blending processes, eliminating the need to select
and delete the distractions.

AN EASY ONE

1 Stacking the photos. Start with the two photos of the
Orchid Show **1a** or with a multi-shot series of your own. You
can choose your files in Bridge CS4 (by clicking one thumbnail
and Ctrl/⌘-clicking others) and stack them from there (**Tools** >

1b

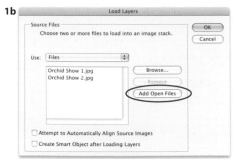

Setting up the Load Layers dialog

2a

The stacked layers with the people removed

2b

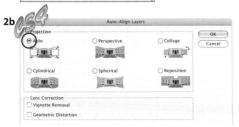

The Layout options in the Auto-Align Layers dialog are the same as for the Photomerge command. ▼

2c

After applying the Auto-Align Layers command

3

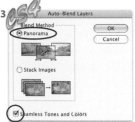

Photoshop CS4's Auto-Blend Layers dialog, set to seamlessly fit the two parts together

Photoshop > **Load Files Into Stack**). Or in Photoshop, choose **File** > **Scripts** > **Load Files Into Stack**. In the Load Layers dialog **1b**, click the "Browse" button and locate and open your files. Or if the files are already open, click the "Add Open Files" button; from the list of open files, select any that you don't want to use in this project (by Ctrl/⌘-clicking their names) and click the "Remove" button to eliminate them. At the bottom of the dialog, leave the "Attempt to Automatically Align Source Images" and "Create Smart Object after Loading Layers" boxes unchecked — the auto-aligning will be done later — and then click "OK" to close the Load Layers dialog.

2 Aligning the layers. Before you align the layers, remove the unwanted parts: For our two layers, it's easy to target the top layer (click its thumbnail in the Layers panel), use the Rectangular Marquee ⬚ (Shift-M) to drag-select the visitor (selecting as little extra as possible) and press Backspace/Delete. Then turn off visibility for the top layer (click its 👁), target the bottom layer, and select and delete the visitor on this layer also **2a**. Next target both layers (Ctrl/⌘-click the top layer's thumbnail to add it), turn on the top layer's visibility again, and choose **Edit** > **Auto-Align Layers**. In the Auto-Align Layers dialog **2b**, choose the Auto option; since we don't see any effects of lens distortion in these two photos, leave CS4's Lens Correction options unchecked; click "OK." Because our original photos were so similar to each other in tone and color, the result looks good even without blending **2c**.

3 Blending the layers. To see if the Auto-Blend Layers command will offer an even better option, with both layers still targeted, choose **Edit** > **Auto-Blend Layers**. In Photoshop CS4's Auto-Blend Layers dialog, choose Panorama and turn on Seamless Tones and Colors **3** (in CS3 these choices are made for you automatically). When you click "OK," Photoshop will create a mask for each layer and if necessary adjust the tone and color of the two images where the unmasked parts meet. For our image, the only changes we noticed were some differences in the lighting of the central flowers and leaves.

Cropping. To trim the edges where the aligning process has left transparency, choose the Rectangular Marquee ⬚ (Shift-M). Drag diagonally across the image to make a selection that doesn't include the transparent edges, and then choose Image > Crop (the result is shown on page 327).

The three original photos of the sculpture

In Photoshop Extended **Median** is chosen as the Stack Mode in the Image Statistics dialog.

In Photoshop Extended, after running the Statistics (Median) script

The Gaussian Blur filter is applied as a Smart Filter.

ANOTHER APPROACH (PHOTOSHOP EXTENDED)

1 Stacking and aligning the photos. The **Sculpture-Before** folder holds three shots of Bill Reid's *The Spirit of Haida Gwaii*, photographed in the airport in Vancouver, British Columbia **1a**.

- **In Photoshop,** you can simply follow the instructions for steps 1 and 2 in "An Easy One," starting on page 327 to load the files into a stack and align them; but use a more precise selection tool to remove the man in the green jacket, and his reflection on the floor, from the scene, since the Rectangular Marquee might remove too much of the image (we used the Quick Selection tool ✎, but the selection didn't need to be precise).▼ Then target all three layers in the Layers panel and turn them into a Smart Object (Filter > Convert for Smart Filters) to get ready for the next step.

FIND OUT MORE

▼ Quick Selection tool
✎ **page 49**

- If you have **Photoshop Extended**, try something different. Instead of steps 1 and 2 of "An Easy One," in Photoshop Extended, choose **File > Scripts > Statistics.** In the Image Statistics dialog **1b**, for the **Stack Mode** choose **Median**, and turn on the **Attempt to Automatically Align Source Images** option; use "Browse" or "Add Open Files" (and "Remove" if needed) to list your source images and click "OK." The median in a series of numbers is the middle value. For removing distractions from an aligned photo stack, choosing Median means that if each part of the subject is clear and unobscured in more than half of the source images, it will appear clear and unobscured in the composite (see "More About Median" on page 330). When we used Median with "Attempt to Automatically Align Source Images" turned on, it completely and seamlessly removed the traveler who was walking around the sculpture **1c**, but not the person in the lower left corner, who had been present in every shot and thus hadn't been removed by Median. The Statistics command produced a Smart Object.

2 Subduing the background. Once that visitor had been removed, we cropped the photo, partly to eliminate the amount

2b

Changing the blend mode and Opacity of the filter effect

of fix-up required, using the Rectangular Marquee ⬚ as in "An Easy One." To reduce the distraction from elements in the background, we applied a blur as a Smart Filter (Filter > Blur > Gaussian Blur) to the Smart Object **2a**. In the Layers panel we double-clicked the ⇶ symbol for the filter, changed the blend mode to Screen, and lowered the Opacity **2b**. We clicked on the Layers panel thumbnail for the Smart Filter's mask and painted the mask with the Brush tool 🖌 (Shift-B) and black paint to remove the blur from the sculpture itself.

We added a new layer (by clicking the ⬒ button at the bottom of the Layers panel), chose the Clone

2c

The final image, **Sculpture-After.psd**

2d

Final Layers panel

The **median** is the middle value in a series of values. For instance, in the series **2**, **2**, **3**, **97**, **210**, the median (or middle value) is **3**.

In removing unwanted traffic from a multi-shot series in Photoshop Extended, the median values of the pixels can be useful. You may be able to use the File > Scripts > Statistics (Median) command to arrive at a traffic-free composite, without having to select and remove the visitors by hand. As long as every part of your **subject is unobstructed** (no traffic hiding it from view) **in more than half of the layers** in the stack, the color values from the subject will be used in the composite (for instance, if the subject's value is **3** in the series above, the value in the composite will be **3**). So sometimes all you have to do to clear away any interlopers is to use the Statistics (Median) command **A**.

However, there are a couple of potential complications. First, if your series has an even number of photos instead of an odd number like the series above, there will be no single middle value to use as the median **B**, so Photoshop will compute the median by averaging the two middle values. In the series **2**, **2**, **3**, **3**, **97**, **210**, the median will be **3**, because $(3 + 3) \div 2 = 3$. But in the series **2**, **2**, **3**, **97**, **97**, **210**, the median will be 50 (a number that doesn't even occur in the series) because $(3 + 97) \div 2 = 50$.

The other complicating factor is that Photoshop Extended's Median is computed channel by channel. In other words, for each pixel in an RGB image, separate median values are computed for the Red, Green, and Blue channels, and this combination can also lead to a color in the final composite that didn't really occur in any of the source photos **C**.

Nevertheless, for a series of three or more photos shot with the idea of removing traffic, Statistics (Median) can often save some time and effort.

A

For this three-shot composite, using Photoshop Extended's **Median** option successfully removes the visitor.

B

For a composite made from an even number of layers (here 2), if we applied the Statistics (Median) command, we would get this "averaged" result (compare it to the result on page 327).

C

Photoshop Extended's Statistics (Median) command is applied to each color channel separately. This can produce some strange artifacts, as shown at the left when the three images above are combined.

1a

The three Statue-Before photos

1b

After loading the files into a stack, removing the people from each photo, and aligning, small transparent areas would need repair.

1c

The Statistics (Median) script produced a result that would need quite a bit of clean-up work.

2a

Cropping the combined image

Stamp 🛆 (Shift-S), chose Sample All Layers in the Options bar, and cloned out the person in the lower left corner, the white paper on the floor at the base of the sculpture, and a "ghosted" shoe at the lower right **2c**, **2d**.

MORE OF A CHALLENGE

1 Stacking, aligning, and blending the photos. The three shots in the **Statue-Before** folder **1a** have more people in them. In some cases the same spot is occupied in more than one of the three shots. This means that if we follow the procedure for Photoshop in steps 1 through 3 of "An Easy One," selecting and removing the people from all three layers, we end up with some transparency, wherever we've removed image material from the same spot in all three of the stacked photos **1b**. This requires a repair, which we'll do in step 2.

In Photoshop Extended, the Median approach described in "Another Approach" on page 329 was worth a try, but perhaps because Median computes pixel colors channel-by-channel, it left a lot of clean-up work **1c** (see "More About Median," on page 330). So instead, we closed the file without saving it and used the Photoshop method just described.

2 Cleaning up. We cropped the image, this time using the Crop tool 🛆 (type C). We dragged the cursor across the image, and then moved the cursor outside the Crop frame, where it turned into a curved double-arrow. We dragged to rotate the frame until its bottom edge was parallel to the steps **2a**; pressing the Enter key completed the crop. We added an empty layer at the top of the stack and used the Clone Stamp 🛆 as in step 2 of "Another Approach." Finally we added a Curves Adjustment layer to brighten the image and bring out detail in the dark statue by clicking the "Auto" button in the Curves dialog and then lightening the shadow tones and putting the layer in Luminosity mode to avoid a color shift. **2b**. 🖋️

2b

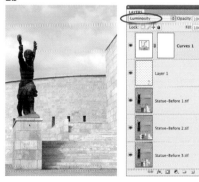

The final image, with a repairs layer to cover the "hole" and a Curves layer to adjust exposure and contrast

Bringing Out Detail

YOU'LL FIND THE FILES
in (wow) > Wow Project Files > Chapter 5 > Bringing Out Detail:
- Bringing Out Detail-Before.jpg (to start)
- Bringing Out Detail-After.psd (to compare)

OPEN THIS PANEL
(from the Window menu, for instance):
- Layers

OVERVIEW
Open a JPEG in Camera Raw • Use Recovery and Fill Light to bring back detail to the highlights and bring out shadow detail • Remove digital color noise and eliminate color fringing • Save the file to preserve the Camera Raw settings • In Photoshop soften the "flash shadow"

PHOTOSHOP OFFERS MANY WAYS to bring out detail in an image, and with Camera Raw, there are even more ways. The goal is always to do the job efficiently and preserve the maximum opportunity for making changes later.

Thinking the project through. Camera Raw has excellent easy-to-use controls for highlight recovery, shadow fill, and eliminating the color fringing that can be found at high-contrast edges. Camera Raw can open JPEG and TIFF files, as well as raw, so we can start enhancing our JPEG there. Then, to soften a harsh shadow caused by the flash, we can take the image into Photoshop. ("Quick Ways To Bring Out Detail," starting on page 337, has different approaches for other situations.)

1 Getting into Camera Raw. If you're working in Photoshop CS3, read the tip at the left. If you have a version of Camera Raw earlier than 4.2, you'll need to install Camera Raw 4.6 from the Wow DVD-ROM in order to use Clarity in step 2, but using Clarity is optional. To open the JPEG file from Bridge, right-click/ Ctrl-click on the file and choose Open in Camera Raw from the

1a

Opening **Bringing Out Detail-Before.jpg**
from Bridge

1b

Opening **Bringing Out Detail-Before.jpg** from
Photoshop

2a

Original photo

RICK WORTHINGTON

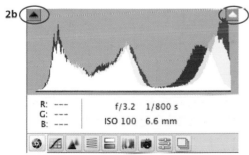

2b

The histogram in Camera Raw with a full range of
values. The triangles are clipping indicator buttons.

context-sensitive menu **1a**. Or to open from Photoshop, choose File > Open, target the file on your disk and choose Camera Raw from the Format menu, and then click "Open" **1b**.

2 Subduing highlights and opening up shadows. In this digital photo **2a** the color looks accurate, so in Camera Raw's **Basic** tab we'll leave the White Balance, Temperature, and Tint unchanged.

The light-dark balance in the image is striking, but we want to lighten the shadowed section of the back wall and tone down some of the brightest areas on the steps. The photo has a full range of tones, from black to white, as Camera Raw's **histogram** shows **2b** — the bars in the histogram reach the ends of the graph on both the left and the right. The two small triangles in the top corners of the histogram are **clipping indicators**. If you click each one to turn it on, you'll see red where there's pure white in your image and blue where there's pure black. In this image we can see a small amount of red on the stone in the foreground and some blue along the edge of the overhang. Since we know we have some pure white in the image, we can skip the **Exposure** slider (which sets the white point) and go on to **Recovery**, which is designed to bring out detail in the highlights.

Hold down the **Alt/Option** key and click on the **Recovery** slider. Your preview will turn solid black except for some white and primary-colored areas. These are the areas of the image where the brightness value in at least one of the RGB channels is "maxed out" at 255 — as light as it can get. White spots are maxed out in all three channels — there's no image data there to recover, and if you try, you'll just turn the white areas of the image a uniform gray. The colored areas show that there's some image data in one or two of the RGB channels **2c**; Camera Raw can do a good job of recovering detail with only that information. Alt/Option-drag the slider slowly to the right just until the entire preview turns black. When all colored pixels are removed, no highlights are being pushed to pure white. Notice in the histogram that when you use Recovery, the right (highlights) end of the graph is being affected much more than the left.

Next, drag the **Fill Light** slider to the right to lighten the shadows and bring out detail on the back wall. There is no modifier key to change your preview, so just keep dragging until you see enough detail in the shadows. If the histogram shows that there's now a little room at the far left, you can drag the **Blacks** slider a little to the right **2d**, just enough to increase contrast a bit, without causing a bar to spike up the far left side.

2c

Detail from the Recovery preview while holding down the Alt/Option key. Spots of color show where highlights details can be recovered.

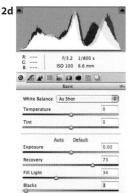

2d

Note that after using Recovery, the right side of the histogram is no longer flat against the right, but leans away from it. Fill Light lightens the shadow tones, and raising Blacks by just a little will take the darkest tones all the way to black.

2e

The photo after Basic tab adjustments

(Optional; you won't have a Clarity slider if your Camera Raw is an earlier version than 4.2.) Moving down the Basic tab, Clarity is helpful for increasing contrast (and the appearance of sharpness) in the middle tones. You can check the histogram or Alt/Option-click the Recovery slider again if you want to make sure your Clarity correction hasn't pushed the highlights too far. Vibrance adds color saturation, but not as strongly as Saturation does. We liked the color we had achieved at this point **2e**, so we skipped Vibrance and Saturation and went on to our next problem areas—color noise and color fringing.

3 Removing color noise. Now zoom to 100% view (Ctrl-Alt-0, Windows or ⌘-Option-0, Mac) or higher (Ctrl/⌘-+) and look at the darker neutral areas, like the shaded faces of the large steps. There we can see color noise, not very pronounced, but with red, green, and other specks of color **3**. In the Noise Reduction section of the Detail tab, moving the Color slider to the right neutralizes the color noise. We didn't use the Luminance slider since light-dark noise didn't seem to be a problem, and we didn't want to blur the contrast in the "grain" of the rock.

4 Removing color fringe. In this photo you'll see a "purple fringe" along the diagonal shadow on the wall at the left and sharper fringing color in several places along shadows on the steps **4a** and also near the upper right corner of the image. There are two common sources of color fringing. One is *chromatic aberration*, which can happen because the lens bends different wavelengths of light different amounts, separating the component colors of white light. This kind of fringing is a result of lens characteristics; it tends to appear more often in wide-angle shots and in the corners rather than the center of a photo. Another source of color fringing is electronic "spillover"; sensors responding to very bright light are overwhelmed and some of their electrical charge spills over to nearby sensors. The **Lens Corrections** tab has controls for correcting both kinds of fringing.

3

In the Noise Reduction section, you can minimize both luminance noise and chromatic (color) noise. Color noise appears as colored "confetti" in solid, often dark, areas.

4a

4b

Here you can see purple fringe along the highest-contrast areas.

When Defringe: All Edges is applied, much of the purple fringe disappears.

4c

Removing the last of the color fringe

5

When you leave Camera Raw (coming up in step 6), whether you save first here or not, your Camera Raw settings will be included as metadata (instructions rather than pixels) with the JPEG. However, if you're working in Camera Raw for CS3, you may be headed for confusion. When the JPEG is reopened, by you or by someone else (depending on what method, what program, what Preference settings, and so on are used to open it), it can open as the Camera Raw-altered version or as the original version. So it's a good idea to save the altered file from Camera Raw so you have a file that will look the same every time it's opened. One way is to save the file as a JPEG; this embeds the Camera Raw changes in the pixels. Save under a different name (so you don't overwrite the original), such as *filename*-CRadjusted.jpg. Or save in Digital Negative (.DNG) format.

In order to see clearly and to use the modifier keys to help locate and correct chromatic aberration, you need to zoom in to 100% or more, if you aren't still zoomed in from the beginning of step **3**. With the Hand tool 🖑, pan to a section of the steps in the middle of the image, where the contrast is high. From the **Defringe** menu, choose **All Edges 4b**. If this results in gray lines where the color fringe used to be, choose Highlight Edges instead.

Next work with one or both **Chromatic Aberration** sliders. Hold down the Alt/Option key and click on the Red/Cyan slider. The display will change to only red, cyan, and neutral grays; this helps you locate the deeper red or cyan edges — the red edge in the upper right corner, for instance. Drag the slider to the right or left to eliminate them; the fringe will get more intense as you move in the wrong direction, less intense as you drag in the right direction. Keep an eye on when the fringe disappears, and stop dragging so that its opposite doesn't suddenly start to appear **4c**. If needed, repeat this Alt/Option-drag process for the Blue/Yellow slider, checking to see if any change there reduces more of the fringe.

Correcting in one spot can cause the fringe to "pop out" in another. So when you think you've eliminated the color fringe in one area of the image, pan around to make sure you haven't made matters worse somewhere else in the image. In readjusting the Chromatic Aberration sliders, you may need to compromise.

5 Saving the altered file. Camera Raw doesn't offer layers, blend modes, or many other features Photoshop has for fine-tuning and precisely correcting an image. But before taking the file into Photoshop, especially if you're working in CS3, where there can be some confusion caused by the way Camera Raw–processed JPEGs and TIFFs are handled by your computer system and by programs other than Photoshop, it's a good idea to save the processed file. Click the "Save Image" button at the bottom left of the Camera Raw interface; choose a location, name, and file type for the file **5**. Click the Save Options dialog's "Save" button.

6 Softening the "flash shadow." Now click on the "Open Object" button to bring the image into Photoshop (if you see "Open Image" instead of "Open Object," hold down the Shift key to change it). In Photoshop, to soften the shadow without losing detail in the wall, start by adding a new, empty layer for the "shadow repair" you're about to make. Using the Layers panel's menu of blend modes, put this layer in Darken mode to

The Blur tool ◊, like any other tool that uses brush tips, can be operated in a straight line. Click at the point where you want to start the straight stroke, then move the cursor to the point where you want to end the stroke and Shift-click.

expand the shadow as it softens. Now choose the Blur tool ◊. In the Options bar choose a brush tip (we used the "Soft Round 13 pixels" tip), set the Strength (we used 100%), and turn on the Sample All Layers option. "Paint" along the outer edge of the shadow (see the tip at the left); the new layer will now hold a blurred version of the edge **6**. The blurring has made some pixels lighter and some darker. But with the layer in Darken mode, only the darker pixels will contribute, spreading and softening the shadow edge without creating a light halo. Save the layered file in PSD format (File > Save As). *Wow!*

6

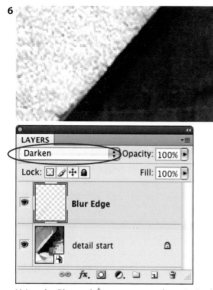

Using the Blur tool ◊ on a separate layer in Darken mode softens the edge of the shadow slightly.

WHEN CHROMATIC ABERRATION IS TOO STRONG FOR CAMERA RAW

Sometimes fringing can be so strong that the controls in Camera Raw's Lens Corrections tab (or in Photoshop's Lens Corrections filter, see page 277) can't fix it. In that case, you might want to try this method: Click the ◉ button at the bottom of the Layers panel and add a Hue/Saturation Adjustment layer. Click on "Master" to open a list of colors, and choose the color you want to eliminate; use the Hue/Saturation Eyedropper tool 🖉 to select the exact color in the image. Now if you make a big move with the Hue slider (all the way to the left, for instance), you can tell, from the areas that change color, how much of your image is going to be affected when you use the Saturation slider to reduce the color fringing. Experiment by dragging the triangles in the color bar closer together and rechecking by moving the Hue slider, until only the color you want to reduce is targeted. Restore the Hue slider to 0 and drag the Saturation slider to the left just far enough to make the color fringing blend with its environment. And if the color of your fringe happens to occur in other areas as part of the image, you can choose to paint the Hue/Saturation layer's mask with black to reduce the effect in those areas.

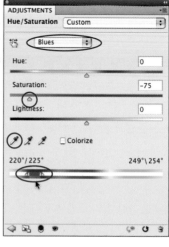

Ways To Bring Out Detail

"Bringing Out Detail" on page 332 uses a combination of Camera Raw and Photoshop methods to bring out detail that's "hidden" in an image, and Camera Raw's Clarity control is introduced on page 249. Here are some other methods — quick and easy — for enhancing small differences in color and tone:

- Using a filter, such as **Unsharp Mask**, **Smart Sharpen**, or **High Pass**, that identifies "color edges" in the image and increases contrast between the two sides of an edge

- Layering a copy of the image above the original and applying one of the **"contrast" blend modes** chosen from the menu at the top left corner of the Layers panel (Overlay mode, for example)

- Making a **Shadows/Highlights adjustment** or a painted **"dodge and burn" layer** in a contrast blend mode to increase contrast in the shadow tones and highlights

- Adding a Curves Adjustment layer, with an **S-shaped or M-shaped curve**

It pays to keep the changes separate from the original — by using a Smart Filter, an Adjustment layer, or a duplicate image layer — so you'll have the maximum range of options for fine-tuning your "detail boost":

- You can **compare various "contrast" blend modes**.

- **To reduce the effect**, you can simply lower the Opacity (in the Layers panel) of the filter or layer you added, to blend it with the original.

- **To target your changes** to a particular place in the image, paint a layer mask to reveal the enhancement in the areas where you want it and to hide it elsewhere.

- If you've arrived at a way to enhance certain details perfectly, but you want **to protect some tones or colors** from change, try the "Blend If" sliders in the Blending Options section of the Layer Style dialog box.

- Since the amount of change you need may depend on how the file will be output, keeping your alterations "live" and editable will allow you to **adjust for different output options**.

For any image, you aren't limited to one way of bringing out detail or one way of targeting the effect. The "mix and match" possibilities are endless.

YOU'LL FIND THE FILES FOR MOST EXAMPLES in > Wow Project Files > Chapter 5 > Quick Detail

Sharpening with Unsharp Mask

RICK WORTHINGTON

Before sharpening

After sharpening

When the success of the image depends on increasing contrast in the details, the Unsharp Mask filter can be a good option. For the digital photo above we started by converting the image so we could apply a Smart Filter (right-click/Ctrl-click the name of the image layer in the Layers panel and choose Convert to Smart Object). Then we chose Filter > Sharpen > Unsharp Mask and set the parameters in the Unsharp Mask dialog box. A practical approach is to start with the Threshold set at 0 temporarily (Threshold controls how different the colors at an edge have to be for the filter to recognize it as a color edge and sharpen it; 0 means that *all* differences are seen as edges). Then adjust the Amount (how much the contrast at a color edge is enhanced by the filter) and the Radius (how far in from the color edge the increased contrast will extend) until the important details are as sharp as you want. Next raise the Threshold as high as you can without losing the sharpening of this detail. Raising the Threshold keeps the filter from sharpening very small differences in tone or color such as grain or noise.

Detail-Unsharp Mask.psd

EVALUATING SHARPENING

Degree of sharpening is a matter of preference, but too much sharpening can give a photo an artificial look. You don't want to overdo it, but if you're preparing an image for the printed page, keep in mind that sharpening tends to look much "stronger" on-screen than it will when the image is printed at a much higher resolution on a press.

Using Smart Sharpen

RICK WORTHINGTON

Before Smart Sharpen

A

B

After Smart Sharpen

THE SMART SHARPEN FILTER can produce a realistic "sharp focus" result. Like Unsharp Mask (on page 337), Smart Sharpen looks for color edges and sharpens them, but it tends to produce less "halo" at the edges. You can choose to have the filter counteract a Gaussian Blur (which is the same calculation method the Unsharp Mask filter uses); a Lens Blur (a better choice if the image was shot a little out of focus), or Motion Blur (the one to try for "camera shake" or if the subject moved). With the Advanced setting turned on, you can protect the Shadows or Highlights from sharpening, which can also contribute to a more realistic result.

To bring out detail in this photo, we turned the image layer into a Smart Object (right-click/Ctrl-click the name of the image layer in the Layers panel and choose Convert to Smart Object) and then chose Filter > Sharpen > Smart Sharpen. We got the sharpening we wanted with settings of Strength 100%, Radius 1.9 px, and Remove Lens Blur **A**. With the Advanced option chosen, we could experiment to fade the oversharp "bright white" look in Highlight areas (Amount 15%, Tonal Width 80%, Radius 1) and to fade the sharpening in Shadow areas slightly (Amount 4%, Tonal Width 20%, Radius 5) **B**.

 Detail-Smart Sharpen.psd

High Pass in a "Contrast" Mode

ANAIKA DAYTON

Before

A

B

C

After

PHOTOSHOP'S HIGH PASS FILTER SUBDUES color and contrast in non-edge areas, but preserves the contrast in "edge" areas, where colors abut. When you apply this effect in one of the "contrast" blend modes (Overlay and those right below it in the pop-up blend modes list in the top left corner of the Layers panel), you have a powerful tool for sharpening detail.

The first step is to convert your image layer to a Smart Object (right-click/Ctrl-click the name of the image layer in the Layers panel and choose Convert to Smart Object). Then choose Filter > Other > High Pass and click "OK." Now double-click the icon to the right of the High Pass entry in the Layers panel **A** to open the Blending Options dialog **B**, choose Overlay for the Mode, and click "OK," so you'll be able to preview the effect of High Pass on your image as you experiment with the filter's settings. Double-click the filter's name in the Layers panel to reopen the High Pass dialog box. Experiment with the Radius setting. In the square preview inside the High Pass dialog **C** and in the image window, you'll see the combined effect of the filter and the blend mode.

Detail-High Pass.psd

Using Shadows/Highlights

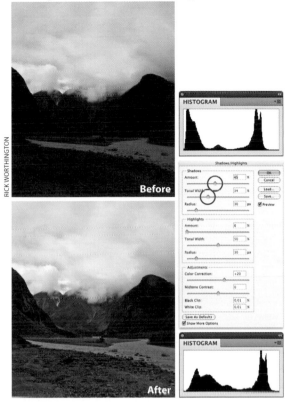

Before

After

The Shadows/Highlights command, which can add contrast where detail is washed out by bright lighting or subdued by shading, isn't available as an Adjustment layer, but it *can* be applied as a Smart Filter. For this photo, the Histogram (opened by choosing Window > Histogram) showed a peak in the shadows, suggesting that spreading out the darker tones might bring out detail in the terrain. We turned the image layer into a Smart Object (as described on the previous page), chose Image > Adjustments > Shadows/Highlights and clicked the checkbox for "Show more options." We left most of the settings at their defaults, changing only the Amount and Tonal Width in the Shadows section at the top of the box. The default 50% Tonal Width treats anything darker than 50% gray as a shadow and therefore lightens it. This setting meant losing some of the detail in the clouds, since they were dark enough to fall in the Shadows range. To avoid the loss, we reduced the Tonal Width so that only the darkest 34% of the tonal range would be changed. We experimented with the Amount until we got the result we liked best at 45%. The Histogram showed the resulting redistribution of shadow tones.

 Detail-Shadow Highlight.psd

Adding a "Dodge & Burn" Layer

Before

"Dodge & Burn" layer

Before

After

With a "dodge and burn" layer it's easy to increase contrast in exactly the areas where you want it, toning down or brightening up the detail. To try it, open the image file and Alt/Option-click the "Create a new layer" button at the bottom of the Layers panel. When the New Layer dialog box opens, set the mode to Overlay, click the checkbox for "Fill with Overlay Neutral (50% gray)" and click "OK." Your image won't look any different on-screen since 50% gray is neutral (invisible) in Overlay mode. But now you can paint black and white onto this layer with a soft Brush (with or without the Airbrush option turned on in the Options bar) with Opacity and Flow set low. This builds up the paint slowly enough so you can control it as you bring out the detail you want.

 Detail-Dodge and Burn.psd

MANAGING A DODGE & BURN LAYER

As you paint a "dodge and burn" layer in Overlay mode, if your image starts to look oversaturated — that is, the colors become too intense — try changing the blend mode of this layer to Soft Light.

Duplicating in a "Contrast" Mode

ANAIKA DAYTON

SOFT LIGHT IS A BLEND MODE that enhances contrast mainly in the midtones. Besides bringing out detail, it also tends to increase color intensity somewhat. So it works well for images like this one that are concentrated in the midtones and have unsaturated colors that can benefit from a color boost. (If you work with images that are colorful, it's easy to push colors out of the printable gamut with Soft Light, even more so with Overlay. So you run the risk that the color differences you see on-screen may disappear when the image is printed.)

To try out the effect of Soft Light, simply duplicate your image to a new layer (Ctrl/⌘-J) or add an "empty" Levels Adjustment layer as we did (the method and rationale are described in the "'Lightweight Copies' of Image Layers" tip below). Change the blend mode for the added layer to Soft Light by choosing it from the pop-up menu in the upper left corner of the Layers panel.

 Detail-Soft Light.psd

"LIGHTWEIGHT COPIES" OF IMAGE LAYERS

You can get the same effect as you would by duplicating your image to a new layer and changing its blend mode — but without increasing the file size the way a second image layer would. The trick is to use an "empty" Adjustment layer. Simply click the "Create new fill or adjustment layer" button ⬤ at the bottom of the Layers panel and choose Levels (actually, any of the choices from the "Levels" grouping in the pop-up menu will work). When the dialog opens, in CS3 just click "OK" to close it. In the Layers panel change the blend mode for this new layer. An added advantage of this method is that if you make a change to the image itself, you won't have to remake the "copy."

Reducing Opacity

RICK WORTHINGTON

SOMETIMES A DUPLICATE LAYER or an Adjustment layer produces the right *kind* of effect, but the result is just too strong overall. To reduce the effect of the filter, blend mode, or adjustment, you can simply reduce the Opacity of the Smart Filter or added layer, reducing its contribution to the blended image.

Our goal for this image was to bring out detail in the rocks, both above the water and under it. In the original photo **A** the colors were quite neutral and the tones we wanted to enhance were midtones, so we decided to use a duplicate image layer in Soft Light mode **B**, as described in "Duplicating in a 'Contrast' Mode" at the left. The midtone detail was improved, but the greens were more saturated than we wanted. And even though Soft Light works mainly on midtones, it had also affected the deeply shaded areas and the light snow and sky, so we had lost detail in both of these ranges. Setting the Soft Light layer's Opacity to about 50% produced a result we liked better **C**.

 **Detail-Opacity.psd**

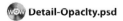

Protecting Tones with "Blend If"

A

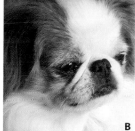
B

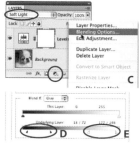

C

F

D   **E**

FOR THIS PORTRAIT **A**, an "empty" Levels Adjustment layer in Soft Light mode (as described in "Duplicating in a 'Contrast' Mode" on page 340) did exactly what we wanted for the brown hair, increasing contrast in the midtones to add richness by enhancing color detail **B**. But in an image that starts out with a full tonal range, as this one did, Soft Light can also muddy the shadows or blow out detail in the highlights. Here the darkest and lightest parts of the dog's coat had lost some of their detail. In a situation like this, the "Blend If" sliders in the Layer Style dialog box can often help.

With the Soft Light layer targeted in the Layers panel, we opened the Blending Options section of the Layer Style dialog box by right/Ctrl-clicking on the Adjustment layer's thumbnail and choosing Blending Options from the context-sensitive menu **C**. Moving the black point for "Underlying Layer" to the right **D** lightened the shadows, because the dark tones of the image — the tones represented to the left of the black point — were now protected from the Soft Light layer. To make a smooth transition from the protected tones to the exposed tones, you can split the black point by holding down the Alt/Option key and dragging the left half of the slider back to the left. A similar adjustment to the white point protects the light tones of the dog's coat **E**, **F**.

 Detail-Blending Options 1.psd

Because the Linear Light blend mode intensifies colors as it increases contrast, it can be great for bringing out detail in the sky — whether it's light blue with clouds (the sky will get bluer) or a sunset or sunrise (the colors will get more intense). The effect can be just what's needed for the sky itself, or for its reflection on land, snow, or water.

To try out Linear Light, add a Levels Adjustment layer with no changes: Click the "Create new fill or adjustment layer" button ◑ at the bottom of the Layers panel, choose Levels, and in CS3 click "OK" without making any changes. You'll see that the addition of the "empty" Adjustment layer has no effect on the image. Then put this new Adjustment layer in Linear Light mode by clicking the blend mode menu in the upper left corner of the Layers panel and choosing Linear Light from the group of "contrast" modes. For most images, the result will be a lot stronger than you want, as shown immediately below.

Reduce the Linear Light effect by using the Opacity slider near the top right corner of the panel.

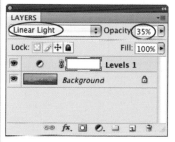

For our mountain image, an Opacity of 35% for our "empty" Levels layer in Linear Light mode cut through the haze to bring out the detail and color as the photographer remembered it, without losing the soft mistiness of the scene.

 **Detail-Linear Light.psd**

Using an "S-Curve"

A

A

LAYERS

Curves 1

Background

B

C

D

D

An "S-curve" adjustment can improve an image (or part of an image) with little contrast in the midtones and no very light or very dark tones, such as the hay field in this photo **A**. To bring out detail in the rolled hay, we clicked the "Create new fill or adjustment layer" button ⊘ at the bottom of the Layers panel **B** and chose Curves from the pop-up menu. In the Curves dialog box **C**, we clicked the midpoint on the line to anchor it in place, since we didn't want to lighten or darken the midtones overall. Then we clicked the three-quarter-tone point and dragged down a little; and finally we clicked the quarter-tone point and dragged up a little to complete the "S." In tonal ranges where the curve was now steeper (closer to vertical), contrast had been increased. And conversely, where the curve was flatter (closer to horizontal), contrast was reduced. The S-curve brought out detail by pushing some of the midtones into the high and low tonal ranges **D**.

Notice that the Curves adjustment that brought out detail in the hay also changed the sky, the trees, and the hills. If you don't like these changes, you can use a loosely painted layer mask to hide the adjustment in these areas. ▼

wow **Detail-S Curve.psd**

FIND OUT MORE
▼ Painting masks **page 84**

Using an "M-Curve"

A

B

C

D

E

E

If you want to bring out detail in the midtones in an image that also has some very dark tones **A**, a slightly M-shaped Curves adjustment is more likely to be useful than is an S-curve. To bring out the carving on the stone in the image above, we added a Curves Adjustment layer by using the ⊘ button as described at the left. Once the Curves dialog was open, we moved the cursor into the image window and dragged it around the face of the carved stone **B**. By watching the movement of the little circle that appeared on the diagonal line in the Curves dialog **C**, we could see that most of the rock face — both the carving and the surface — had tones in the upper midtone range. To bring out detail, we wanted to increase contrast in these tones, and we could do that by making the curve steeper there. We started by dragging the midpoint down and to the right to darken the stone a little overall. Then we clicked near the upper end of the curve and moved this new point to the left and up a little, making the curve steeper between the midpoint and this point and creating the first "hump" of the "M." We completed the "M" by clicking near the lower end of the curve and again dragging up and to the left to lift the curve here **D**. This restored the shadow detail **E** that had been "flattened" when we moved the midpoint. (In CS3 it's necessary to click "OK" to complete the adjustment.)

wow **Detail-M Curve.psd**

Targeting with a Layer Mask

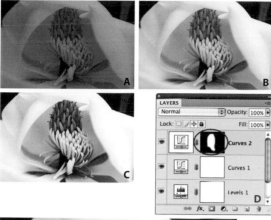

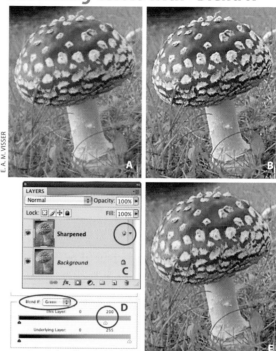

CHRISTINE ZALEWSKI

E. A. M. VISSER

TO TARGET A DETAIL-ENHANCING EFFECT to just one area of your image, you can add a "hide all" layer mask to the enhancing layer and then paint it with white to reveal the effect. Christine Zalewski often targets the effect of the S-shaped Curves she uses to enhance detail in her botanical portraits. In the magnolia shown here, she targeted the changes to the center structure of the flower, to help draw the viewer's eye there. Starting with an original photo **A**, she finished most of her preparation with a Curves Adjustment layer **B**, and then applied another Curves layer with an S-shaped curve ("Using an 'S-Curve'" on the previous page describes how to do this). She adjusted the curve until the flower's center had the "punch" she wanted **C**. Then she filled the Adjustment layer's built-in mask with black to completely hide the Curves effect (if black is the Foreground color, this can be done by typing Alt/Option-Delete; or if black is the Background color, by typing Ctrl/⌘-Delete). Zalewski chose the Brush tool ✐; in the Options bar she picked a large soft brush tip from the Brush Preset picker, which pops out when you click the brush footprint icon, and lowered the Opacity setting. She made white the Foreground color (type X if necessary) and painted the mask with white over the center of the flower **D**, **E**.

Protecting Colors with "Blend If"

THE "BLEND IF" SLIDERS in the Layer Style dialog box can protect certain tonal ranges, as seen in "Protecting Tones with 'Blend If'" on page 341. But these sliders can sometimes be helpful for protecting certain *colors* also. In the small photo of the toadstool above **A**, Unsharp Mask was applied as in "Sharpening with Unsharp Mask" on page 337 (Amount 200, Radius 2, Threshold 1) **B**, **C**. At these settings the sharpening emphasized detail in the red-and-white cap, but also in the surrounding grass, enough so it was a little distracting. Because the grass and the toadstool cap were so different in color, we thought we might be able to use the Green "Blend If" sliders to take some of the contrast out of the grass without reducing the sharpening very much in the cap.

We clicked the ▾☰ button in the upper right corner of the Layers panel and chose Blending Options from the fly-out menu. In the "Blend If" section of the Blending Options panel, we chose Green from the pop-up "Blend If" menu so we could make changes to the Green channel only. Working with the "This Layer" slider, we moved the "white" point at the bright green end of the bar to the left. This reduced the contrast in the grass much faster than it reduced sharpening in the mushroom cap. We settled on a setting of 200 **D**, **E**.

Detail-Blending Options 2.psd

In Focus

YOU'LL FIND THE FILES

in 🅦 > Wow Project Files > Chapter 5 > In Focus

• Focus-Before (six JPEG files to start)
• Focus-After.psd (to compare)

OPEN THIS PANEL

(from the Window menu, for instance):

    Layers

OVERVIEW

Load and align the series of photos as layers in a single file • Use Auto-Blend Layers; as needed, paint with black to hide the out-of-focus parts of each layer

1

PHOTOS: GAREN CHECKLEY

Shown here are the first and last of the six shots of the focus series. The first is focused on the front of the head (top) and the last on the raised tail.

BRIDGE CS4 CAN SAVE A LITTLE RAM

If the files in your focus series are large, consider opening them from Bridge to save Photoshop's RAM. Select them in Bridge and choose Tools > Photoshop > Load Files Into Photoshop Layers. In the resulting layered file, target all the layers and choose Edit > Auto-Align Layers; then go on to Edit > Auto-Blend Layers.

TO EXTEND THE NORMALLY SHALLOW FOCUS of a close-up, you can take a series of photos, each focused at a slightly different distance, and then blend the photos together. In Photoshop CS4 this can be an amazingly successful automatic process. **Note:** In CS3 it takes some hand work — for an image like the one above with the table surface extending away from the subject in all directions, it may be too much work to be worthwhile, whereas for a composition like Katrin Eismann's *Horse Mackerel Beauty* (page 648) it's a much more reasonable task.

Thinking the project through. If you're working in CS4, virtually all of the thinking happens when you take the series of photos, focusing at a different distance for each one, keeping both the camera and the subject still, and being certain to get every bit of the subject in focus somewhere in your series of shots. The rest is easy — Photoshop CS4 will do it for you.

1 Taking the photos. Garen Checkley shot six photos of Sophie, the Australian bearded dragon, who held very still. (Not many animals will behave this way, but the technique can be ideal for a product shot or a still life.) **1**. Checkley shot the six images of the focus series with a Canon EOS Rebel XTi on a tripod. He used an 18–55 mm lens, f/4.5, and ISO 200, indoors with daylight coming through the windows and a floor lamp for added light. He focused manually and shot all six shots within about 5 seconds.

2 Stacking and aligning the photos. Open the files in Photoshop. Choose File > Scripts > Load Files Into Stack. In the Load Layers dialog, click the "Add Open Files" button to see a list of all your open files **2**. If you have files open other than the ones in your focus series, select them (by Ctrl/⌘-clicking their names in the list) and click the "Remove" button to eliminate them from

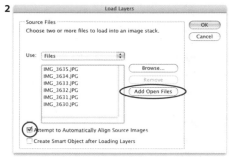

2

Setting up the Load Layers dialog

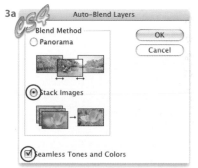

3a

Photoshop CS4's Auto-Blend Layers dialog offers the Stack Images option, which automates the process of blending a focus series.

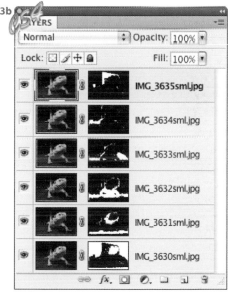

3b

The layer masks created by Photoshop CS4's Auto-Blend Layers command

this project. To align the photos so it will be possible to then get a good blend of the images at step 3, click the checkbox for "Attempt to Automatically Align Source Images" and then click "OK" to close the Load Layer dialog.

3 Blending the layers. When the stack-and-align process is complete, it's time to blend the layers. Here's where there's a big difference between CS3 and CS4:

- In CS4, the bottom layer will be targeted in the Layers panel after the stacking, To target all the layers, Shift-click the thumbnail for the layer at the top. Then choose Edit > Auto-Blend Layers. In the Auto-Blend Layers dialog, for the Blend Method choose Stack Images, and check the box for Seamless Tones and Colors **3a**. Then just sit and wait for the astonishing result. Photoshop compares all areas of all layers, looking for areas with sharp contrast in the details and masking each layer to allow these areas to contribute to the composite. Out-of-focus areas, which are characterized by less detail contrast (they're blurry), are masked out **3b**.

- In CS3 the Auto-Blend Layers function doesn't know about blending for a stack. It tries to make a panorama out of the layers, realizes it can't, and adds a white mask to one layer and black masks to the others. Blending the images by hand is a lot of work, as you can imagine if you look at the masks in the Layers panel in figure 3b. To blend the images, target the top layer's mask (by clicking its layer mask thumbnail in the Layers panel), and make sure its layer mask is white (reveal all); if it's black, invert its color Ctrl/⌘-I. Now use the Brush tool ✐ with black paint (typing X once or twice with the mask targeted will make black the Foreground color) to hide the out-of-focus areas in the layer. Repeat the process for the other layers, moving down the layer stack, painting with black on a white mask, until all of the image is in focus.

Finishing touches. Now you can add an Adjustment layer ▼ if needed to adjust color and contrast (we did not). We did use the Crop tool ⛏ ▼ to trim off transparency at the edges, created by Auto-Align Layers. To sharpen the image we added a composite layer at the top of the stack (Ctrl-Shift-Alt-E in Windows, ⌘-Shift-Option-E on the Mac) and chose Filter > Sharpen > Unsharp Mask (Amount 90, Radius 1.5, Threshold 6). ▼ 𝒲𝑜𝓌!

FIND OUT MORE

▼ Adjustment layers **page 245**

▼ Using the Crop tool ⛏ **page 240**

▼ Sharpening **page 259**

Softening the Focus

YOU'LL FIND THE FILES
in (wow) > Wow Project Files > Chapter 5 >
Soft Focus:
- Soft Focus-Before.psd (to start)
- Soft Focus-After.psd (to compare)

OPEN THESE PANELS
(from the Window menu, for example):
- Layers • Layer Comps

OVERVIEW
Blend a blurred copy with a sharp original
• Control the effect by changing Opacity
and blend mode, or limiting the tonal
range in which the two versions can
interact • Mask the blurred layer to further
limit the effect

SINCE THE END OF THE 19TH CENTURY, photographers have been using soft-focus and haze effects to impart an appealing, romantic quality to their images, sometimes covering their lenses with fabrics or gels to soften the focus. Today, using Photoshop, you can blend a blurred copy with a sharp original, adjusting the soft focus areas to taste.

Thinking the project through. For a soft, smooth blur overall, we can use Gaussian Blur. Since different blending modes and opacities will affect the softened look, we'll try several different combinations, preserving the successful ones as Layer Comps for easy review. The Layer Comps panel can record changes to layer Opacity, blend mode, and other blending options, but it can't record changes to Smart Filters. So instead we'll run the filter on a duplicate of the image and blend the filtered and unfiltered versions together.

1 Duplicating the image on a new layer. Open the **Soft Focus-Before.psd** file or an image of your own, and copy it to a new layer — Ctrl/⌘-J, or Layer > New > Layer Via Copy **1**.

The original photo is duplicated to a second layer.

The top copy of the photo is blurred.

2 Blurring the duplicate layer. To start the "haze," choose Filter > Blur > Gaussian Blur **2**. The Radius setting will determine the amount of halo or softening you can achieve; we used a Radius of 10 pixels for our 1000-pixel-wide image. If you double-click the layer's name in the Layers panel, you can change it to help recall the filter setting.

3 Adjusting blend mode and Opacity. To turn the blur into a romantic glow, choose Lighten from the pop-up menu of modes at the top left of the Layers panel **3a**. Also try Screen mode **3b**. Both of these modes allow the light pixels of the blurred image to lighten the pixels underneath, while the dark pixels in the blurred image have little or no effect. In the blended image, this limits most of the softening to the highlights, leaving some of the sharp detail in the midtones and shadows.

Notice that Lighten doesn't "blow out" the highlights or lighten the midtones as much as Screen does. In Screen mode all pixels in the top layer are used to lighten the pixels underneath, with the lightest ones lightening the most. As a result, the entire blended image, except the darkest areas, gets significantly lighter.▼

FIND OUT MORE
▼ Blend modes
page 181

4 Making layer comps. Before you experiment further, make layer comps for both the Lighten and Screen options so you can compare them to other options later: With the mode for the blurred layer set to Lighten in the Layers panel, turn your attention to the Layer Comps panel and click the "Create New Layer Comp" button ▣ at the bottom of the panel. In the Layer Comp Options dialog box, make sure the "Appearance (Layer Style)"

3a

The blur is turned into "atmosphere" by putting the top layer in Lighten mode.

3b

Putting the top layer in Screen mode lightens and brightens the photo even more.

4a

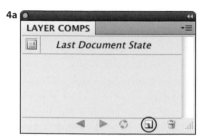

Clicking the "Create New Layer Comp" button ▣ opens the Layer Comp Options dialog box. To record the Opacity and blend mode in the Layer Comp, the "Appearance (Layer Style)" option is turned on.

4b

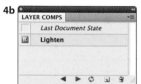

Clicking "OK" in the New Layer Comp dialog box records the comp in the Layer Comps panel.

4c

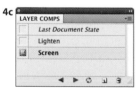

Another layer comp, named to reflect the blend mode of the blurred layer, is added to the list in the Layer Comps panel.

4d

Reducing the Opacity of the blurred layer in Screen mode produces a gentler glow.

option is turned on **4a**. (You'll be experimenting with Opacity and blend mode, both of which are recorded in layer comps if you have the Appearance option turned on.) Give your layer comp a name ("Lighten," for instance) that will help you identify your changes, and click "OK" **4b**. Then change the blend mode to Screen and make another comp ("Screen") **4c**.

Now experiment with the Opacity and with more blend modes, making layer comps for the results you like. We found that 60% Opacity in Screen mode produced a result we wanted to save **4d**, so we made another comp. Overlay mode at 60% Opacity **4e** and also Soft Light at 60% **4f** added drama to the image — results we also saved as comps.

5 Blending based on tone. Screen mode looked promising if we could keep its full glow in the highlights but prevent it from affecting the darker areas. Try this: In the Layers panel double-click the image thumbnail for the blurred layer to open the Layer Style dialog box. In the General Blending section of the Layer Style box, set the Blend Mode to Screen and the Opacity to 80%. In the "Blend If: Gray" section, hold down the Alt/Option key and on the "This Layer" bar, drag the right half-triangle of the black slider to the right **5a**. (The Alt/Option key lets you split the slider.) The slider bar represents the full tonal range, from black to white. The tones to the right of the slider you moved (the lighter tones) will contribute their full effect to the composite. The tones between the two halves of the black slider (the darker tones) will contribute partially. If there are any tones in the dark end beyond the leftmost black triangle, they won't contribute at all. By eliminating much of the contribution

APPEARANCE (LAYER STYLE)

With the "Appearance (Layer Style)" option turned on in the Layer Comp Options dialog box, the layer comp will record everything that can be set in the Layer Style dialog box. That includes Blend Mode and Opacity, even if you actually set them in the Layers panel.

4e

Putting the blurred layer in Overlay mode at 60% Opacity brightens the light areas and darkens the dark parts of the image.

4f

Soft Light mode at 60% Opacity also exaggerates lights and darks, but with less contrast than Overlay mode.

5a

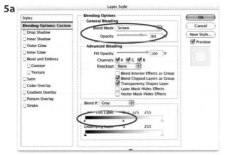

By splitting the "This Layer" black slider, you can control how the dark tones in the blurred image contribute to the composite. Besides providing the Advanced Blending options, the Blending Options section of the Layer Style dialog box also allows you to reset the Blend Mode and Opacity.

5b

The "This Layer" settings limit the effect of the blurred layer mainly to the highlights and light midtones.

6

In the Layer Comps panel, clicking the "Apply Next Selected Layer Comp" button advances through the stack.

of the darkest pixels of the blurred layer, you soften the image overall and still maintain most of the detail contributed by the darker tones in the sharp layer below. Splitting the slider makes for smooth transitions between contributing and noncontributing tones **5b**. Try different positions for the "Blend If" triangles. Whenever you get a result you like, click "OK" and then make a new layer comp. Because the Appearance option is turned on in the New Layer Comp dialog box, the layer comp will record the "Blend If" settings.

6 Choosing a comp. To review the comps you saved, click the "Apply Next Selected Layer Comp" button ▶ at the bottom of the panel to advance through them, stopping at the one you like best **6**. We chose "Screen 80% Adv Blend."

SELECTING COMPS

To review some, but not all, of the layer comps you've made, in the Layer Comps panel Ctrl/⌘-click on the names of the comps you want to look at, and then use the ▶ button to advance through them.

7 Masking the effect. Now, with a quickly and loosely painted layer mask, you can direct the "romance" to just the areas of the image where you want it. Add a layer mask by clicking the "Add layer mask" button ⬚ at the bottom of the Layers panel. Choose the Brush tool and a large, soft round brush. Make black the Foreground color (with the mask active, if black isn't already the Foreground color, typing D or X will do the trick). In the Options bar set the Brush's Opacity low (we used 15%) and paint the mask with black in the areas where you want to reduce the glow. If you overdo it, switch to white paint (type X to switch), set an even lower Opacity in the Options bar, and paint over your strokes. To emphasize the pastries, we partially masked the effect on the glass, pitcher, and spoon **7**. (If you cycle through your layer comps now, all will show the masking.)

7

A painted layer mask directs the glow — already controlled with blend mode, Opacity, and Advanced Blending — to highlight the pastries. The resulting image is shown at the top of page 346.

FROM COMPS TO FILES

You can make separate files from your layer comps (for a client to view side-by-side, for example). After making your layer comps, choose File > Scripts > Layer Comps to Files. Follow the dialog's instructions to create and save individual files.

Using a Spin Blur

ON THIS PAGE ARE TWO SPIN BLUR EXAMPLES. One was done entirely in the camera as a way to avoid problems arising from a low-light environment. The other was applied in Photoshop after the photo was taken, in order to put the action back into a stop-action photo.

 The **Spin Blurred.psd** file on the Wow DVD-ROM shows the layering and masking of the filtered image used to accentuate the motion in the photo of the dancer. Look for it in the Wow Goodies folder.

KATRIN EISMANN

"Real" (mostly). The image was cropped, so the "sharp center" is now off-center, higher than it was when the photo was taken.

ORIGINAL PHOTO: CORBIS ROYALTY FREE

Photoshop (mostly). Some of the motion we see results from strobe lighting used for the original photo.

"Real": Visiting Lisbon's Coach Museum, which doesn't allow flash photos, photographer Katrin Eismann decided to take control of the blur instead of trying to avoid it. Using a high ISO setting (800) for the low-light environment, she still needed an exposure of a half-second to capture enough light. Rather than fight the wobble that would be almost inevitable on a long handheld exposure, she rotated the camera while shooting, starting the movement first and then pushing the shutter button. Turning the camera smoothly creates a blur that's most extreme at the outside edges of the photo. The center of the lens stays in the same place, so the middle part of the image is relatively sharp. "To shoot like that you have to shoot a lot," says Katrin, "and have some luck on your side!" If you crop the image later in Photoshop, the "sharp center" doesn't have to be the actual center of the final image.

Photoshop: Photoshop's Radial Blur filter seemed promising for accentuating the swirl in this photo of a dancer in motion. So that we could later combine the filtered and unfiltered versions of the image, we turned the image into a Smart Object (Filter > Convert for Smart Filters). ▼ Then we chose Filter > Blur > Radial Blur to open the Radial Blur dialog box. ▼ We chose the Spin option for the Blur Method and dragged the spin center slightly to the right in the Blur Center diagram, to a position corresponding to the dancer's left hip (the place where the skirt fabric seemed to be anchored and thus where the spinning motion would be centered). Since the Radial Blur dialog box has no Preview option, we set the Quality to Draft for a quick result, tried an Amount setting, and clicked "OK." To try another setting, we double-clicked the Radial Blur entry in the Layers panel and changed the Amount setting, until we got the motion we wanted, with Amount set to 10. We double-clicked the Radial Blur entry one more time, reapplied the filter with Quality set to Best, and clicked "OK."

Throughout the blurring process, we had ignored the blur everywhere but in the skirt because we knew we could clear it later with the Smart Filter's built-in mask. We filled the mask with black to hide the blurred image entirely (with a mask targeted in the Layers panel, typing D and then Ctrl/⌘-Delete fills the mask with black). To add spin to the skirt, all we had to was paint the mask with a soft Brush ✎ with white as the Foreground color in the areas where we wanted the blur to show, varying the Opacity setting in the Options bar when needed. ▼ If the white painting revealed too much of the filtered image, we could paint with black on the mask to hide it again.

FIND OUT MORE

▼ Smart Filters **page 72**

▼ Using Radial Blur **page 263**

▼ Painting layer masks **page 84**

Hand-Tinting a Black & White Photo

YOU'LL FIND THE FILES

in > Wow Project Files > Chapter 5 > Hand-Tinting:

- Hand Tint-Before.psd (to start)
- Wow Tints.aco (a Swatches preset)
- Hand Tint-After.psd (to compare)

OPEN THESE PANELS

(from the Window menu, for instance):

- Layers • Swatches

OVERVIEW

Start with a black-and-white photo in RGB Color mode • Paint a separate layer in Color mode for each color and adjust its Opacity • Organize layers in Groups • Create a "dodge-and-burn" layer

1a

The original RGB scan file was duplicated so we could store one copy for safekeeping as we worked on the other copy.

1b

After color is neutralized, tonality adjusted, and damage repaired, this is **Hand Tint-Before.psd**.

From the earliest days of photography, artists hand-tinted black-and-white photos with a variety of paints and dyes. Today the look is back, in a variety of styles.

Thinking the project through. Using a separate layer in Color mode for each tint will give a great deal of flexibility in controlling how each color interacts with the black-and-white image. We can make the tinting process quite detailed — for the face of this portrait, for instance — or keep it simple and loose, for elements like the dress and background. To maintain flexibility in our tinting, we will add a new layer for each tint — sometimes more than one layer per tint so we can use a color differently in different parts of the image. We'll apply one stroke of color at full opacity (maximum tint), then reduce the layer's Opacity until we get the degree of tint we want, and then continue to paint. That first stroke can be a little startling because the color is sometimes intense, but once the layer Opacity is adjusted so the color looks right, the painting process feels quite natural and goes quickly. (For a variety of other tinting methods that don't involve hand-painting, be sure to check out "Quick Tint Effects" on page 203.)

TINTING IN COLOR MODE

In tinting a black-and-white photo, when you paint a layer whose blend mode has been set to Color, it can be hard to predict exactly how a particular color will interact with the range of grays in a layer below it. Here we applied a fully saturated spectrum gradient to a transparent layer in Color mode over a layer that holds a full range of tones from black to white.

You can see that the tints don't affect black or white at all. Also, the tints are most intense in the midtones, but the tonal range that accepts the most tint varies from color to color. Notice that if something is very light gray, you won't be able to tint it bright red with this method. And if something is dark gray, you won't be able to successfully tint it yellow.

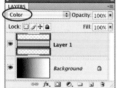

A gradient on a layer in Color mode tints the grays on the layer below.

1 Preparing the photo. The process starts with a "black-and-white" photo that has the potential for color. If your photo is a Grayscale file, start by converting it to RGB (Image > Mode > RGB Color). The photo's appearance won't change, but it will now be "tintable." If your photo is a color file to start with **1a**, the most controlled way to neutralize the color in preparation for tinting is to use a Black & White Adjustment layer, but there are alternative quick conversion methods also.▼

To get a full range of grays to tint, use a Levels or Curves Adjustment layer if needed,▼ or apply Shadows/Highlights as a Smart Filter.▼ Do any clean-up that's necessary, using the Healing Brush, Spot Healing Brush, Patch, or other tools **1b**.▼

2 Setting up your colors. Choose a few colors to use in the tinting process. We chose 10 colors and isolated them in the Swatches panel, as described in "Collecting Your Colors" below. If you want to use the same colors we used, load the **Wow Tints.aco** file (a set of Swatches) by clicking the Swatches panel's menu button ▾≡ and choosing from the list at the bottom of the pop-up menu **2**. If you haven't yet loaded the Wow Presets,▼ this set won't appear in the list. In that case, choose Load Swatches and navigate to the **Wow Tints.aco** file (see "You'll Find the Files" on page 351) to add it to the panel.

COLLECTING YOUR COLORS

To make a limited set of colors easy to pick out as you work, store them together at the end of the Swatches panel: For each color, click on its swatch in the panel (or otherwise make it the Foreground color). Move the cursor to the empty space at the end of the panel, where it will turn into a Paint Bucket. Click to "pour" the Foreground color to make a new swatch.

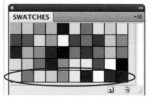

Wow Tints.aco includes a variety of skin, hair, and eye colors and accents, as well as environmental colors useful for tinting. We sampled or mixed the colors we would use for "Hand-Tinting a Black & White Photo" and poured them as 10 swatches at the end of the **Wow Tints** presets, following the black swatch.

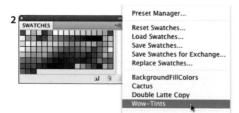

Wow-Tints appears in the Swatches panel's menu if the Wow presets have already been loaded. Otherwise, choose Load Swatches, higher up in the menu, to add Wow-Tints to the current panel.

Preset Manager...

Reset Swatches...
Load Swatches...
Save Swatches...
Save Swatches for Exchange...
Replace Swatches...

BackgroundFillColors
Cactus
Double Latte Copy
Wow-Tints

COLOR NAMES

To see the Swatches panel as a list of names and swatches rather than as swatches alone, click the panel's ▾≡ button and choose Small List.

SWATCHES
Warm Brown Skin
Warm Skin Accents
Cool Brown Skin

FIND OUT MORE

▼ Converting color to black-and-white **page 214**

▼ Adjusting tonal range **page 244**

▼ Using Shadows/Highlights **page 254**

▼ Repairing photos **page 256**

▼ Loading the Wow Presets **page 4**

3a

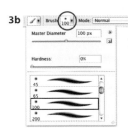

A new layer is added and put in Color mode.

3b

A soft brush tip is chosen for the Brush tool. Opacity and Flow are set at 100%. The size is set at 100 pixels, which seems like a comfortable size to use on the girl's arm.

4a

The first stroke, with the layer at 100% Opacity.

4b

Reducing the layer's Opacity to 75% produces a pleasing tint.

4c

The color on the "Basic Skin" layer, erased over the eyes and teeth. (The painted color is shown at the left, alone and at 100% Opacity.)

3 Setting up layers and brushes. Start by adding a layer above your image by clicking the "Create a new layer" button ▣ at the bottom of the Layers panel. When the layer appears in the panel, choose Color from the panel's pop-up menu of blend modes **3a**. Putting the tinting layers in Color mode will maintain the original luminosity (darks and lights) of the image as we add the tints. That way we won't end up with any opaque-looking patches of color.

Choose the Brush ✐ from the Tools panel. From the pop-up Brush Preset picker in the Options bar **3b**, pick a soft-edged brush tip, choosing a size that fits within the area you want to color first. Set the Opacity and Flow at 100%. At full Opacity and Flow, you can apply the color evenly, without developing streaks if you overlap your strokes.

4 Starting with skin tones. To begin painting with the Brush ✐ on your Color layer, click on a color in the Swatches panel and make one stroke; we started on the girl's arm with the "Light Skin" color **4a**. Then adjust the layer's Opacity in the Layers panel until the tint looks the way you want it; we reduced the layer's Opacity to 75% **4b**. (If you can't get the tint you want by adjusting Opacity, choose a different color from the Swatches panel. Or click the Foreground square in the Tools panel and choose another color in the Color Picker; when you get a color you like, save it in the Swatches panel by clicking in the empty space after the last color.)

As you paint, you can use the bracket keys ([and]) to make the brush tip smaller or larger in preset steps; or in CS4 with OpenGL Drawing enabled, ▼ for a continuous increase or decrease in size, hold down the right mouse button and Alt key (Windows) or Ctrl-Option (Mac) and drag the Brush cursor right or left, releasing when the size is right. Don't worry about perfect edges — in traditional hand-tinting, the dyes weren't applied perfectly either. We painted the girl's arms and face, making no attempt to avoid her eyes and mouth. With the Eraser ⌫ set in Brush mode at a low Opacity so it would take away a little of the tint at a time, we used a small, soft brush tip to erase any spill of skin color into other areas. We erased the eyes but not the lashes or brows, and erased the teeth but not the lips. The color in the lips serves as a base for later coloring.

FIND OUT MORE
▼ Brush tips & OpenGL Drawing **page 71**

At this point, in the Layers panel we double-clicked on our tinting layer's name and typed in "Basic Skin" so we could easily identify the layer later if we wanted to make changes **4c**.

5a

The "Light Skin Accents" color is applied on a new layer in Color mode at 20% Opacity. (The painted accents are shown at the left, alone and at 100% Opacity.)

5b

The same "Light Skin Accents" color is used for the "Lips" and "Gums" layers, with layer Opacity set to 20% for "Lips" and 35% for "Gums."

5c   **5d**

The "Light Brown Hair" color is applied to the "Basic Hair" layer (shown here alone), with layer Opacity left at 100%.

Highlights are added with strokes of "Hair Highlights 1" and "Hair Highlights 2" on another layer. The layer is shown here alone at 100% Opacity, but in the file its Opacity was reduced to 15%.

5 Painting accents. The next step is to accent the places where the shape of the face catches the light. Add a new layer in Color mode, choose "Light Skin Accents" for the color, and make the Brush smaller. Try a single stroke on the cheek, and adjust the layer's Opacity until the color is right; we settled on 20%. Then continue to paint the cheeks, chin, tip of the nose, and over the brow. With a very small Brush, place a dab of color at each corner of the eyes, and stroke along the edges of the lower eyelids **5a**. If you like, accent her hands and arms.

You may want to make a separate layer in Color mode for the lips, and one for the gums. For light-skinned people, natural lips and gums are usually the same color as the skin accents, but darker **5b**. For dark-skinned people, you may want to use cooler skin tones (with more blue in them) for the lips and gums than you used for the cheeks.

Continue adding layers for hair, irises, whites of the eyes, and teeth. For the base layer of hair color, we simply picked a color that looked right for the lightest values and left the layer Opacity at 100% **5c**. Hair painted with just one color can look artificial, so we added another layer, and painted a few streaks of two accent colors **5d**. Setting the layer's blend mode at Normal and reducing the Opacity to 15% produced the result we liked.

We tinted the irises of the eyes blue. We also tinted the whites of the eyes and the teeth. In a tinted photo even a faint hint of color is more natural-looking than the original gray **5e**.

6 Organizing the layers. When we had finished painting the girl, we targeted all the painted layers and placed them in a Group so we could change the overall color intensity later, simply by

5e

The irises are tinted with the "Blue Eyes" color (layer Opacity at 25%), and the warm "White-Eyes & Teeth" color takes the gray out of the eyes (10% layer Opacity) and teeth (20%).

6a

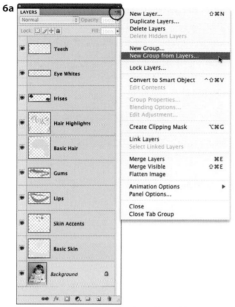

A "Girl" Group is made from the selected layers. **Note:** The Layers panel is shown here with Layer Bounds option chosen in the Panel Options dialog (choose Panel Options in the Layers panel's menu ▼≡ and then choose Layer Bounds in the Thumbnail Contents section of the dialog).

6b

After you create a Group, you can expand it in the Layers panel to get access to the individual layers. Click the tiny triangle to the left of its folder thumbnail.

7

The "Table" and "Wall" layers were tinted with two browns, the last two swatches we had stored at the end of the Wow Tints in the Swatches panel. Layers for the clothing are collected in a Group, and another Group called "Background" is created for the "Wall" and "Table" layers.

changing the Opacity of the Group itself, without changing the color balance of the related parts. To make a Group, in the Layers panel simply click the top layer you want to use in the Group, then Shift-click the bottom layer, and either choose New Group from Layers in the panel menu▼≡ **6a**, or Alt/Option-Shift-click the "Create a new group" button ▢ at the bottom of the panel to create and name it at the same time **6b**.

7 Completing the tinting. Finish painting the parts of the image that you want to color. We painted the dress, hair ribbons, and trim on separate layers, and made them into another Group. For the dress, we used the same blue as for the eyes with layer Opacity at 45%. We painted right over the trim, tinting it a very pale blue; we could have left it this way to indicate translucency in the collar's fabric, or reflection from the dress, but instead we used a small Eraser ⌀ to erase it. We also used the Eraser (at lower Opacity) to remove some of the color from the shadows, where it was too intense. We added another Color layer and painted the trim with "Pale Yellow," adjusting layer Opacity to 25%. We painted the hair ribbons with the same color as the dress, but put the layer in Overlay mode so the increased contrast would simulate the shine of the satin; Opacity was set at 50%. We painted the table and the wall on separate layers also, organizing them in another Group **7**.

8 Final touches. To balance tone and color in the final image, you can add a "dodge and burn" layer as follows: With the top layer of your file targeted in the Layers panel, Alt/Option-click the ▣ button at the bottom of the panel. In the New Layer dialog box, choose Overlay for the Mode and click the checkbox for "Fill with Overlay-neutral color (50% gray)" and then click "OK." Now use the Brush ⌀ with a large, soft brush tip and a low Opacity setting to paint with black where you want to darken the image and increase color density, and with white where you want to lighten the color **8**.

Trying other options. With each color on a separate layer and with layers grouped, you have a tremendous amount of flexibility. The two images on the facing page show the effect of starting with the file from step 8 and making some of the following changes:

- You can change the color intensity by adjusting the Opacity of single layers or of an entire Group.

- Change the blend mode of some or all layers. Use Overlay to add shine or brilliance. Or try changing the blend mode for some or all Groups from Pass Through (the default, which

8

A quickly painted "dodge and burn" layer at the top of the stack is used to balance the lighting in the image. It slightly darkens the face and sleeve on the right side of the photo, which intensifies their color, and lightens the sleeve on the left. The result is shown at the top of page 351.

simply "passes through" the modes of the individual layers in the Group) to Soft Light, for a pale tint effect.

- You can change a single color by adding a Hue/Saturation Adjustment layer, "clipped" to the layer you want to change. For instance, to adjust the color of the "Wall" you can target this layer in the Layers panel, then click the "Create new fill or adjustment layer button ⬤ at the bottom of the Layers panel and choose Hue/Saturation from the list, and in the New Layer dialog box, click the checkbox for "Use Previous Layer to Create Clipping Mask." Clicking "OK" adds a layer that affects only the "Wall" layer immediately below it. By adjusting the Hue and Saturation sliders, with or without the Colorize option turned on, you can change the color of the wall. *Wow!*

Starting with the tinted photo from step 8 (shown at the top of page 351), we changed the blend mode of the "Clothing" and "Background" Groups to Soft Light and reduced the Opacity of the "Girl" Group to 70%.

Starting with the tinted photo at the top of page 351, we added a Hue/Saturation Adjustment layer above the "Wall" layer to change the color of the background. To show that the adjustment is limited to the "Wall" layer, the name of the clipping layer is underlined in the Layers panel and the Adjustment layer's thumbnail is indented.

Turning Day into Night

OVERVIEW

Run Lighting Effects as a Smart Filter to subtract light from an image • Select and color areas that will become new light sources • Add Lighting Effect filters as new Smart Filters, to create light cast from different sources • Paint a mask that reveals the cast light where you want it and hides it everywhere else • Add finishing touches for realism

CRISTEN GILLESPIE

The original photograph, taken in the middle of a sunny day. When day becomes night, the hose will be too much a part of the shadows to bother removing it.

THE ORIGINAL DAYLIGHT in this photograph reveals the charm of an earlier era preserved in the architecture, but it also contains the elements for a very different image—one that depicts the romance and mystery of a summer's night. With Photoshop and the Lighting Effects filter, turning off the sun, lighting up the old lamp, and hinting at life indoors, is a lot easier than lugging around a tripod, flashlight in hand, hoping to find just the right nighttime atmosphere to photograph.

Thinking the project through. Begin a day-into-night image by taking note of what light you might expect to see, such as the old lamp here, light in the windows, the moon, or even the stars. We decided to light up the glass panes in the door to make it look like someone was at home, and to balance the lamp. A hint of moonlight striking the balcony would reveal more of the Victorian architecture, and also help to lead the eye through the picture. Since the Lighting Effects filter was going to play a big

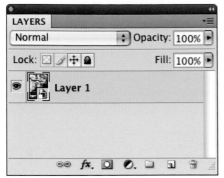

Convert the *Background* to a Smart Object layer in order to run a Smart Filter.

1b

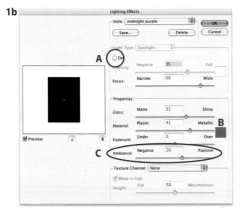

Subtract light from an image by turning lights off **A** and selecting a medium to dark color for the reflected light **B**, with a low positive Ambience setting **C** just to bring back a little detail.

2

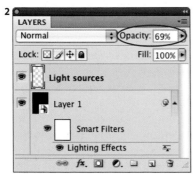

Add an empty layer, select the areas that represent light sources, and fill with an appropriate color. Reducing layer Opacity can also affect the intensity of the color you've added.

role in our ability to bring a touch of realism to our night, we wanted to use Smart Filters on Smart Object layers as much as possible. ▼ Not only could we then re-edit the filter settings as necessary, but we could easily mask the filtered results, shaping the light to the sources in our image. Our light sources were far enough apart so we would be able to use just one Smart Object layer with its single filter mask for the different instances of man-made lights and their "spill." With only one filter mask per Smart Object, if our light sources had overlapped, we would have needed separate Smart Object layers in order to have maximum masking control over shaping the spill of light from our light sources.

FIND OUT MORE
▼ Using Smart Filters
page 72

1 Adding the color of night. If you want to use our Lighting styles, copy our **Wow-Day2Night** lighting styles into your Plug-ins > Filters > Lighting Styles folder found in your Photoshop application folder. The preview for the Lighting Effects filter is too small to accurately judge your results, but using a Smart Object layer with a Smart Filter will allow you to reopen the filter and adjust the color and darkness of the night until you're satisfied with it **1a**.

Choose Filter > Render > Lighting Effects. When the dialog opens, uncheck the On box under Light Type to turn off any lights. (If you're using our styles, choose **Wow-Midnight Purple** from the Style drop-down list and look at our settings while you read on.) Pick a color for the ambient light by double-clicking on the color swatch in the Properties section to open the Color Picker and selecting a medium purple. Click "OK" to return to the dialog. For a dark night the Properties settings for Gloss and Material don't make much difference, but Ambience determines how well you can make out the structure, and how much of an effect the light sources will have on the entire image. We tried a few settings, clicking "OK" each time to view the results in the main document window, and then reopening the filter's dialog by double-clicking on its name in the Layers panel to adjust the Ambience setting again. We finally settled on 20 **1b**.

2 Turning on the lights. With the Polygonal Lasso ⊬ (Shift-L) select one of the panes of glass in the lamp: Click in a corner to start, then lift the cursor and click again on the next corner, and so on. When you're back at the starting point and the little circle appears with the cursor, click to close the path. To add to your selection, hold down the Shift key before starting to select another pane of glass. If you add too much, use the Alt/Option

2b

After adding yellow-filled panes on a separate layer

You can maintain the most flexibility in your file by "nesting" one Smart Object layer, together with its modifying layers, inside another Smart Object layer. Here the Smart Object "Layer 1" and the "Light sources" layer are selected and combined.

3b

You can add up to 16 lights in a single Lighting Effects lighting Style. Here a mere three lights does the trick. The Properties settings apply to all three lights, but the Intensity, Focus, and color of the individual lights can be adjusted separately.

key with the tool to subtract the extra area from the selection. ▼ Select all the panes in the lamp and door. You can't fill a selection on a Smart Object layer. So in order to fill selected areas with the color of incandescent light, make a new, empty layer (click the "Create a new layer" 🔲 button at the bottom of the Layers panel, name the layer, and click "OK"). With the selection still active and the empty layer targeted, double-click on the Foreground swatch to open the Color Picker and select a warm yellow. Fill the selection with the color (Alt-Backspace in Windows or Option-Delete on the Mac). Deselect. If your color seems too bright, reduce the Opacity (we lowered ours to 69%) **2a**, **2b**. This also can soften the edges.

3 Creating cast and reflected light. To make your light sources cast light over the image, independent of the purple darkness, you need to add a new Lighting Effects filter. First Shift-select the Smart Object layer to have both it and your yellow-filled layer selected, and choose Filter > Convert for Smart Filters. Nesting the two layers this way in a new Smart Object ensures that these layers will still be available to modify separately later *and* that you can use a new application of Lighting Effects on the combination of layers with the option to edit these new filter settings also **3a**.

Choose Filter > Render > Lighting Effects. Either select our **Wow-Day2Night Lights** from the Style list, or add and adjust your own lights in the dialog. To add lights, drag the light bulb icon 💡 up into the Preview window. Change the Light Type from the drop-down list. Choices are Directional (like sunlight, parallel rays from a distant source), Omni (like a bare bulb shining in all directions), and Spotlight. ▼ To select a light so you can change it, click on it in the Preview, and to delete a light, drag it onto the trash can icon. We used a Spotlight with a pale yellow color to represent the light cast on the ground by the lamp. We kept the Focus setting narrow so the light wouldn't be intense and fall-off would be rapid. We added a warm white Omni light to mimic the bright spot in the lamp where a light bulb would be. A third light, a yellow Spotlight, covered the area around the doorway, and here we widened the Focus setting to allow a more intense light to cover most of the area around the door **3b**. These lights overlap and add more light to the scene than you want, but they will be masked later. Click "OK" to apply the lights to the image and return to the main document window **3c**.

4 Adding a second Lighting Effects filter. When you add more than one light

FIND OUT MORE

▼ Making selections
page 48

▼ Lighting Effects
dialog **page 264**

3c

After adding lights for the windows and lamp

4a

When you add a separate Lighting Effects filter, you can change the Properties of the reflected light. Here Exposure and Ambience are increased to compensate for the darker blue color of the "moonlight."

source to your Lighting Effects lighting Style, you can only change the settings for the lights themselves; Properties settings relate to the overall reflected light in the scene, not the light cast by a source, so you can't change Ambience or the color of the reflected light for each source of light. If you want to change the quality of the reflected light for a given source, you need to run the filter separately for that source. You can run as many filters as you like on a Smart Object layer. The filters will all be editable, and can even be dragged into a different order of application. Each one keeps not only its own filter settings, but also its own blend mode options.

To add a light in the upper right corner that mimics pale, "silvery" moonlight, and to be able to change the reflected light, choose Filter > Render > Lighting Effects again, in order to add a separate Lighting Effects filter just for the moonlight. The moonlight can safely spill over the edges of the man-made light and interact with it, just as it would in real life, so you don't need a separate Smart Object layer — one mask can handle both types of light. You can select the **Wow-Moonlight** style from the Style list now, if you prefer. Or set up your own Spotlight with a pale, blue-gray color to keep the light cool, increasing the Exposure and Ambience to compensate for the blue being darker than yellow. It can take some experimentation to get the settings that look natural to you, but that's the advantage of running the filter as a Smart Filter. If it's not blending with the environment the way you want it to, just double-click on the filter name in the Layers

4b

After adding moonlight in the upper right corner

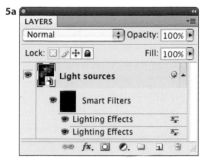

5a

We inverted the Smart Filter mask to hide the light. We could then paint in the light where we wanted it.

5b

Often it's easier to see what you're doing if you hide the light with a black-filled mask and add the light back to the image by painting the mask with white. We varied Brush Opacity, so light added to the image fell off as it got farther from the source.

5c

After painting the mask for the man-made lighting and the moonlight

panel and return to the dialog to adjust the color and Properties settings **4a**. Click "OK" to apply your moonlight **4b**.

5 Masking the filter effects. Before you can make a final decision about your lighting, you'll need to mask some of the effects, to prevent harsh, overlapping ovals and bright circles. Since most of the image won't be affected by the Lighting Effects filters, click on the Smart Filter mask and invert it (Ctrl/⌘-I) **5a**, so you'll be painting the light only where you want it.

Choose a Brush ✎ with a soft tip and a low Opacity setting in the Options bar; it's usually easier to judge the amount of light you want to show if you build up to it gradually. Change the size of the brush as you work with the keyboard shortcuts ⌊ and ⌋, and change the Opacity by quickly typing the amount on your keyboard (for example, *10* or *35*) **5b**.▼ Type "X" (eXchange) to switch between painting on the mask with White to reveal the light, and with Black to hide more of the light. It's worth it at this stage to take your time to paint a mask that mimics the nature of light — strong close to the source, and gradually falling off to nothing **5c**.

FIND OUT MORE

▼ Brushes **page 71**

6 Adding atmosphere. With your lighting in place and masked, you're nearly done. To add to the illusion of a soft night, we'll run another filter. Objects in shadow are less crisp and distinct than those in light. But if we run a Gaussian Blur filter on the same layer as our Lighting Effects, our current mask, which reveals the light, will cause the lighted areas to be blurred instead of the dark areas, so that won't work. Instead, make a merged copy of the image (Ctrl-Alt-Shift-E for Windows, or ⌘-Option-Shift-E on the Mac), and choose Filter > Convert for

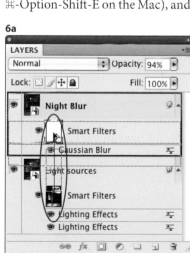

6a

Alt/Option-dragging the painted Smart Filters mask to the new Smart Filters layer. When we added the composite image layer for blurring, we renamed it "Night Blur" (by double-clicking the name in the Layers panel and typing the new name).

6b

To reveal the blur in the shadows but leave lit areas sharp, you can use a copy of the lighting mask, inverted, with some touch-up.

6c

After blurring for atmosphere and masking the blur

7a

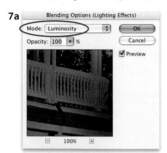

Even though all the filters on a Smart Object layer share the same mask, Blending Options for Smart Filters allow you to change the blend mode and Opacity for each filter individually.

Smart Filters. Back in the Filter menu, select Blur > Gaussian Blur and use a very low setting—between 2 and 4 pixels should be plenty. Click "OK" and check the dark areas; reduce the layer's Opacity if you think they're *too* blurry now. To prevent the blur from affecting areas clearly seen in the light, you need to mask the lit areas. Since you already have a mask that reveals the light, all you need to do is copy and invert it: Alt/Option-drag the mask (to copy it) from the Lighting Effects Smart Filter to the new Gaussian Blur Smart Filter **6a**; when Photoshop asks if you want to replace the current layer mask, say "Yes"; then Invert the mask (Ctrl/⌘-I) to protect the light from the blur. Complete the mask with a little touch-up painting to reduce still more of the blur in the lamp **6b, 6c**.

7 Finishing touches. Finally, to reduce the amount of color on the balcony caused by the purple night interacting with the moonlight color, in the Layers panel double-click on the ⊼ icon for the top (moonlight) Lighting Effects filter to open the filter Blending Options dialog; change the blend mode to Luminosity **7a**. There's also too much color at the base of the lamp. Click on the ⊘ icon to add a Hue/Saturation Adjustment layer, and lower just the Saturation amount to taste. Invert the Adjustment layer's mask to fill it with black (Ctrl-I/⌘-I), and paint the small area around the base of the lamp with white so saturation is reduced only there **7b**. The result is shown at the top of page 357.

Now that most of the work is done, you might want to experiment with the color of the night, how dark it is, or even if there are other windows lit or light sources just outside the view, spilling light into the picture. If you double-click on the Lighting Effects Smart Object thumbnail, you can return to your first

7b

A final mask on an Adjustment layer targets a small area where overlapping Lighting Effects spoil the realism by making color too intense.

Lighting Effects filter, or alter the layer that contains your basic light sources. When you save the altered Smart Object file (Ctrl/⌘-S), your edits will show up in your main image file. They can be further modified because you've used Smart Filters, masks, and Adjustment layers.

Spectacular Lens Flare

TRADITIONALLY, LENS FLARE is produced when light "bounces around," reflecting off surfaces inside a camera lens. The glaring light that becomes part of the photo as a result is often unwanted. With film cameras, other than single-lens reflex cameras (SLRs), lens flare damage is apparent only after the film is developed and the image ruined. With an SLR, either film or digital, lens flare can be previewed through the viewfinder, and thus can be avoided — or captured as a dramatic enhancement to the scene, conveying a sense of intense sunlight or adding an intriguing design element to the photo. In digital cameras other than SLRs, lens flare shows up on the LCD preview screens so it's quite easy to incorporate it into a digital shot intentionally. And, of course, if you want to add lens flare after the fact, there's Photoshop!

REAL OR SURREAL?

Photoshop's Lens Flare (Filter > Render > Lens Flare) can be a great source of glows and rays of light for special effects.

Real: Lens flare is likely to happen "in camera" when a very bright light source is part of the scene being photographed, or is just outside the frame of the photo. It's likely to happen when no hood is used to shade the camera lens, and when the lens is fairly wide open (a low f-stop value).

The arc of pentagonal reflections in this lens flare becomes one more "line" leading to the hiker crossing the bridge in this photo (top). In a cropped version of the image, the flare is a counterpoint to the silhouetted figure and balances the deep shadows on the left side of the image.

Photoshop: Photoshop's Filter > Render > Lens Flare can be used as shown here to simulate a glare and the resulting inside-the-lens reflections, adding interest to a photo.

The preview in the Lens Flare dialog box lets you watch what happens as you experiment with the type of lens and the Brightness and position of the light source. Applied as a Smart Filter,▼ the flare stays "live," so the settings, blend mode, and Opacity can be changed.

FIND OUT MORE

▼ Smart Filters
page 72

When **Cristen Gillespie** wanted to create a low-key image for **_Sleeping Woman_** from a normal, daylight photo, she decided to "go a bit grunge," using Camera Raw and the HDR Conversion dialog to both saturate _and_ selectively darken the otherwise rather dull color of the photo. In Bridge, she right-clicked/Ctrl-clicked on her file and chose Open in Camera Raw. She then adjusted the sliders on the Basic tab **A** until the image was much darker, but still held all the detail and color she wanted. Opening the image in Photoshop, she converted it to 32-bit mode (Image > Mode > 32 Bits/Channel), and then immediately converted it again

to 16 bits per channel. ▼ This opened the HDR Conversion dialog, allowing her to select Local Adaptation and begin working with the curve **B**. She preserved the highlight on the shoulder, while gradually darkening everywhere else, as if only a small

beam of light fell across the sleeping woman and her blanket. Once the highlight was established, using high Radius and Threshold settings forced the highlight to gradually spread and blend into the darker regions around it.

A

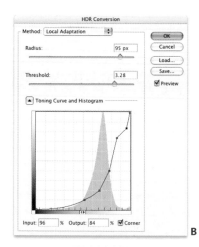

B

FIND OUT MORE

▼ Using Camera Raw and HDR Conversion for surreal color **page 212**

To create *Boston*, **Amanda Boucher** captured her nighttime photo in her Canon EOS Digital Rebel XT's raw format and went to work in Camera Raw. ▼ The biggest changes the photo needed were adjustments to exposure and contrast **A**. For a photo like this one with a full range of tones, from black to white, there's no need to adjust the Exposure or Blacks sliders if you're working in Camera Raw for Photoshop CS3 or CS4. To adjust the tones in between, Fill Light can bring out shadow detail **B**, and increasing the Brightness a lot and Contrast a little can open up the midtones; these changes cause less lightening in the highlights than simply increasing Exposure would do. Increasing Recovery can bring back detail in the highlights (in the windows here) that might have been overlightened by the Brightness increase. With the main "fixes" accomplished, Temperature and Tint could be adjusted to reduce the red but still keep the image warm **C**, **D**. Boucher also reduced Color Noise (in the Lens Corrections panel). After getting close to what she wanted in Camera Raw, she then opened the image in Photoshop and fine-tuned the color and contrast with Adjustment layers ▼ — Selective Color ▼ and Curves ▼ — to arrive at the image at the left.

FIND OUT MORE

▼ Camera Raw **page 141**
▼ Using Adjustment layers **page 245**
▼ Selective Color adjustments **page 253**
▼ Curves adjustments **page 246**

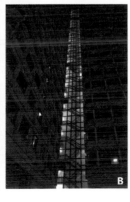

C<i>liff Dwelling</i> by **Loren Haury** is actually a composite of three photos, identical except for the exposure time. Using a tripod, Haury set up the exposure for the first photo **A**. Then he took two more shots, using the camera's aperture priority setting so the shutter speed was the only parameter that changed. He took one shot at +2 on

VARY THE TIME

When you take several exposures with the idea of combining them in a single image to get detail in both highlights and shadows, keep the aperture (f/stop) and ISO constant to keep depth of field and "grain" the same for all the shots. To change the exposure, change the shutter speed.

the camera's exposure meter **B** and the second at –2 on the meter **C**.

Haury used the Lasso ⌒ to roughly select slightly larger areas than he needed from the over- and underexposed photos, and copied and pasted these pieces into the file of the correctly exposed photo **D**. There he reduced the Opacity of the pasted layers to about 50% so he could see through them as he dragged with the Move tool ▸⊕ to align them with the <i>Background</i> image. He raised the Opacity again until he had the right blend of exposures, then used the Eraser ⌲ with a soft brush tip and low Opacity to partially erase the edges of the pasted elements ▽ to blend them seamlessly with the main image **E**. (Another way to combine the exposures would

be to Shift-drag the overexposed and underexposed versions into the file with the correct exposure. Shift-dragging would center the imported images in the file, and then targeting all three layers in the Layers panel and choosing Edit > Auto-Align Layers would perfectly align them. A "hide all" layer mask added to each of the imported layers and painted with white would reveal parts of the imported photos. This masking method is described for Haury's "dodging and burning" step, in the next paragraph. It's a "non-destructive" approach — the entire overexposed or underexposed image is still intact on the layer, and if you decide you'd like to change the layer's contribution to the image later, it's easy — just modify the mask.

The trade-off is that full masked layers produce a "bulkier" file. For *Cliff Dwelling,* for instance, the file would have been more than twice the size of Haury's cut-and-pasted version.)

Once he had assembled the pieces, Haury made a merged duplicate (Image > Duplicate > Duplicate Merged Layers Only), and went to work "dodging and burning." First he lightened the ceiling area as follows: He duplicated the image as a new layer (Ctrl/⌘-J for Layer > New > Layer Via Copy), and put the new layer in Screen mode using the menu in the upper left corner of the Layers panel. Then he added a "hide all" layer mask by Alt/Option-clicking the "Add layer mask" button ◻ at the bottom of the panel. He painted the black mask with the Brush ✐, using a soft brush tip and white paint to reveal the image only where he wanted to lighten the composite **F**.▼

He once again made a merged duplicate of the file, duplicated the image to a new layer, and added a black mask. But this time he put the layer in Multiply mode and painted the mask with white where he wanted to *darken* the image **G, H**.

To finish the image, Haury made adjustments to bring back the color of the scene the way he remembered it. He used Image > Adjustments > Hue/Saturation to reduce Saturation to neutralize the color slightly. He added a Color Balance Adjustment layer (by clicking the "Create a new fill or adjustment layer" button ⊘ at the bottom of the Layers panel) and added Cyan and Yellow to the Midtones and Shadows to balance the red. He clicked the ⊘ button again and this time added a Curves Adjustment layer **I**, setting up an "S" curve to increase contrast in the midtones▼ to arrive at the result on the facing page.

EV 0

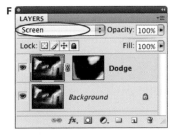

EV +2

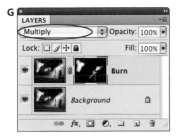

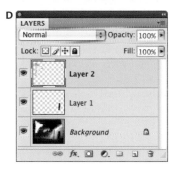

EV −2

Dodged & burned

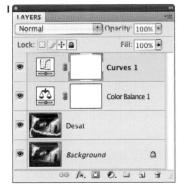

Combined

FIND OUT MORE

▼ Using the Eraser ✐ **page 380**

▼ Painting a mask **page 84**

▼ Using an "S" Curves adjustment **page 342**

Alexis Marie Deutschmann captured the original photo for *Point Loma Harbor* by setting the exposure for the blue water and using a graduated neutral-density filter to reduce the brightness of the sky **A**.

She then used Photoshop to apply Curves and Hue/Saturation adjustments to brighten the image and bring out the color. She used blend modes, Opacity adjustment, and a layer mask to mix three versions of the image, directing the increased contrast and color where she wanted them, as follows.

Deutschmann opened her image in Photoshop and duplicated it to another layer (Ctrl/⌘-J). She applied

Image > Adjustments > Curves to this duplicate layer to increase contrast **B**. ▼ Then she chose Screen from the Layers panel's blend mode menu to limit the increase in contrast to the highlights and lighter midtones. ▼ This protected the shadows and dark midtones from losing detail. Also in the Layers panel, she reduced the Opacity for the Screen layer to 60% to prevent blowing out the highlights **C**.

Targeting the *Background* again by clicking its thumbnail in the Layers panel, Deutschmann duplicated the image again (Ctrl/⌘-J) and dragged the new copy up the panel to the top of the layer stack. To intensify color in this third layer, she chose

Image > Adjustments > Hue/Saturation and moved the Saturation slider to the right **D**. She chose Saturation as the blend mode for this layer to avoid affecting brightness **E**. She also added a layer mask (by clicking the ▣ button at the bottom of the Layers panel) and used the Brush tool ✎ and black paint to protect parts of the image from the saturation boost **F**. ▼

FIND OUT MORE

▼ Using Curves **page 246**

▼ Blend modes **page 181**

▼ Painting a mask **page 84**

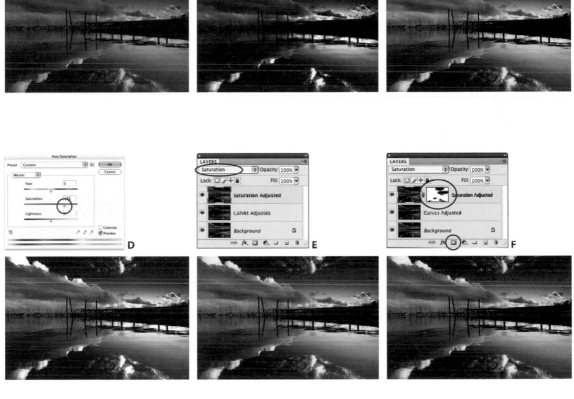

Susan Thompson began *Summer in Arcata* as a modified Polaroid SX-70 photo that she scanned into Photoshop and duplicated to a new layer (Ctrl/⌘-J) to protect the original (shown at the left). She chose View > Actual Pixels (Ctrl/⌘-1) to get the most accurate view, and scrolled through the image, removing spots and scratches with the Healing Brush and Clone Stamp. She also used the Sponge with Saturate Mode chosen in the Options bar to boost color in the hydrangeas and nasturtiums. ▼

To transform the color of the scanned and edited photo, Thompson added a number of Adjustment layers on which she made changes globally or to selected areas of the image. Working on a calibrated monitor, she experimented in the Adjustment layer dialogs until she saw the colors she wanted.

To improve color and contrast globally, she added a Curves Adjustment layer (by clicking

FIND OUT MORE

▼ Using the Healing
Brush **page 256**
Clone Stamp
 page 256
& Sponge tool
 page 258

the ⊘ button at the bottom of the Layers panel and choosing Curves). In the Curves dialog, she selected each of the color channels in turn and dragged the endpoints of the curve inward horizontally (as shown below for the Red channel). The result of adjusting all three curves was similar to (but more precise than) clicking the Curves dialog's "Auto" button, which enhances the color and contrast by adjusting each color channel separately. For the overall RGB curve, Thompson Ctrl/⌘-clicked in the image on shadow tones that she wanted to fine-tune; each click added a point to the curve, which she could then drag up slightly to lighten the targeted tones. To keep the highlights from getting too light in the process, she added another point near the top of the Curve and dragged down slightly.

Thompson also used Selective Color Adjustment layers (⊘) to deepen or shift the color of specific color families throughout the image. She started by choosing Neutrals from the Colors menu at the top of the dialog, so the changes she made next would affect primarily the neutral (near gray) colors. As shown below, she warmed the grays in *Summer in Arcata* by removing a little blue (moving the Cyan and Magenta sliders to the left) and adding Yellow, and also added a small amount of Black. Then she went on to the other color families, making the Greens more intense, for example, by reducing the opposite component (Magenta).

After making global changes, Thompson honed selected areas of the image with masked Adjustment layers. She brightened the door with a Selective Color layer and neutralized the gray steps with a Hue/Saturation layer. She often creates the masked Adjustment layers by using the Lasso tool ⌕ to select the area she wants to adjust, with the tool's Feather set to 0 pixels in the Options bar. With her selection active, she adds an Adjustment layer (⊘). The selected area automatically becomes the white area in the Adjustment layer's built-in mask, revealing the changes she makes in the Adjustment layer's dialog. To smooth the transition between the areas affected and unaffected by the adjustment, Thompson then softens the edge between the black and white areas of the mask (this can be done with the Select > Refine Edge command). She prefers the finer control of creating a hard-edged mask and then blurring the edges as she previews changes on-screen, rather than trying blindly to pick the right Feather setting when she first makes the selection.

To complete her images, Thompson often uses Nik filters (www.niksoftware.com). For *Summer in Arcata,* first she added a new composite layer at the top of the stack; this can be done by holding down Shift-Ctrl-Alt (Windows) or Shift-⌘-Option (Mac) and typing E. Photoshop automatically copied all visible artwork to the new layer. She ran the Sunshine and Skylight filters from the Nik Color Efex Pro series, and then duplicated the filtered image to a new layer (Ctrl/⌘-J) and ran a sharpening filter from the Nik Sharpener Pro series.

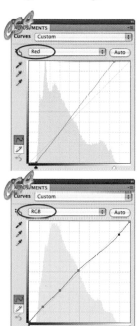

LILY DAYTON

▼ Working with Vanishing Point **page 612**

For *Afternoon in the Park, Marie Brown* duplicated Lily Dayton's photo **A** to a new layer (to preserve the original) and then chose Filter > Vanishing Point.▼ She clicked with Vanishing Point's Create Plane tool ⊞ to establish the four corners of a grid that she thought would provide the right perspective for cloning grass and leaves from the foreground to cover distractions in the background **B**. After adjusting the grid with the Edit Plane tool ▶, she alternately Alt/Option-clicked with the Stamp tool ♨ to sample near the bottom of the image and then clicked to cover up the more distant elements she wanted to hide. As she worked,

Vanishing Point's dynamic "loaded" brush tip showed how the cloning material would shrink as she moved it to the area she wanted to cover **C**.

A NATURAL FEEL FOR CLONING

Photoshop's Clone Source panel lets you preview the source material you're about to apply with the Clone Stamp ♨, and change its scale and angle. In CS3 the Clone Stamp preview can't be clipped, so you see the entire source, not just the area within the brush tip, which makes it harder to interpret what the repair will look like. So you may want to use Vanishing Point's Stamp tool instead of the Clone Stamp, even if your CS3 retouching task needs no perspective correction. In CS4, the preview can be "clipped" so it shows only within the brush footprint. But even so, when you need to scale in perspective and reset the source often to avoid creating recognizable repeats, the Stamp tool in Vanishing Point may work better than the Clone Stamp because it scales automatically.

The story of **Rod Deutschmann's** **Point Lighthouse** is about thinking of Photoshop as one more piece of camera equipment. The lighthouse, fence, and shadows were too good to pass up, even though it meant pointing the camera directly into the sun. Deutschmann took a shot, knowing he would get a lens flare, and a quick look at the captured image confirmed it **A**. The bright rays of light in the flare were interesting but too strong, the red-fringed green patch over the shadow interfered with the composition, and it would be really hard to fix all this in Photoshop. So he took the photo again, this time with his hand in front of the camera to block the sun **B**, swapping a nearly impossible Photoshop challenge for an easy one: Patch or replace the sky.

Opening the image in Photoshop, Deutschmann manufactured a "sky patch" to hide the hand. Here's one way to do it: Add a new empty layer above the image (Ctrl/⌘-Shift-N). Then choose the Gradient tool , hold down the Alt/Option key to turn it into the Eyedropper temporarily, and click the sky at the top of the image to sample this blue as the Foreground color. Typing X swaps Foreground and Background colors, and Alt/Option-clicking again, this time in the sky near the tips of the fingers, picks up the second color needed for the sky gradient.

In the Options bar click the tiny arrow to the right of the gradient swatch and click on the "Foreground to Background" option (the first choice in the picker). Holding down the Shift key and dragging up from the level of the fingertips to the top of the image, fill the layer with the sky gradient. To reveal the image again, Alt/Option-click the "Add a layer mask" button at the bottom of the Layers panel to make a "hide all" (black) mask. Now all that's left is to choose the Brush tool, pick a soft brush tip in the Options bar, and paint the mask with white to reveal the manufactured sky so it hides the hand. Deutschmann

used a lower Opacity setting in the Options bar to paint some streaks of white on the mask to help blend the real sky with the manufactured one **C**. (If the sky is hard to "patch"

— because of telephone wires or tree branches, for example — consider selecting the entire sky area, and using that selection to make the layer mask that reveals the sky gradient.)

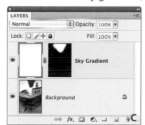

With no time for a formal portrait sitting, **Cher Pendarvis** captured a quick photo of surfer *Valentine Ching* after finishing a video interview with him at his home in Hawaii. She opened the raw-format file in Camera Raw, and made the conversion to black-and-white using the HSL/Grayscale Mix panel — she checked the "Convert to Grayscale" box and then clicked "Auto." Happy with the Auto conversion, she opened the file in Photoshop to finish editing the portrait.

Pendarvis wanted to reduce the depth of field, blurring the details in the background slightly. She duplicated the image to a new layer (Ctrl/⌘-J) and blurred this duplicate

(Filter > Blur > Gaussian Blur). She then used the Clone Stamp 🔲 to eliminate a few distractions in the background. ▼

Next she created a layer mask that would allow the sharp image of Ching himself to show through from the layer below. An accomplished painter, Pendarvis is very comfortable using a graphics tablet, so she started the mask with an outline drawn quickly with the Pen tool ✎. ▼ She converted it to a selection by

clicking the "Load path as a selection" button ◉ at the bottom of the Paths panel. Then she stored the selection in a stable pixel-based form as an alpha channel (Select > Save Selection). By clicking on the alpha channel's thumbnail in the Channels panel and also turning on visibility for the Gray (image) channel by clicking in its 👁 column, she could see both the mask (in red) and the image. She inverted the mask (Ctrl/⌘-I) so it hid Ching on that layer **A**. Using the Brush tool 🖌 and a hard-edged brush tip (Hardness 100% set in the Options bar), she painted the mask with white to "erase" its rough edges to create a better fit. ▼ If she erased too much, she could fill in again with black paint. When the mask was "tight" **B**, Pendarvis activated the selection stored in the alpha channel (by Ctrl/⌘-clicking its thumbnail in the Channels panel), and then turned this selection into a layer mask by clicking the "Add layer mask" button 🔲 at the bottom of the Layers panel. Finally, she softened the sharp edge of the mask slightly. In Photoshop CS3 or CS4 this can be done with the Select > Refine Edge command. Or in CS4 the Feather can be kept "live" and changeable if you set it in the Masks panel. ▼

FIND OUT MORE

▼ Using the Clone Stamp 🔲 **page 256**

▼ Using the Pen Tool ✎ **page 454**

▼ Painting a mask **page 84**

▼ Refine Edge command **page 58**

▼ Masks panel **page 63**

To add drama to his original late-afternoon photo of clouds **A** to create *Tampa God Rays*, **Jack Davis** first added a Levels Adjustment layer. In the Levels dialog box, he clicked the "Auto" button, which expanded the tonal range in the image from full white to full black **B**.

Next he targeted the *Background* by clicking its thumbnail in the Layers panel, duplicated it (Ctrl/⌘-J), and dragged the copy's thumbnail up to the top of the panel so it was above the Levels Adjustment layer, and put it in Overlay mode, one of the contrast blend modes.▼ To "sculpt" the clouds, adding to the feeling of dimension and space, he chose Filter > Other > High Pass. He used settings that left the filtered layer mostly medium gray, which has no effect in Overlay mode, with the edges of clouds and rays emphasized by darker gray on one side and lighter gray or white on the other **C**.

> **FIND OUT MORE**
> ▼ Contrast blend modes **page 184**

SETTING THE BLEND MODE FIRST

When you filter a duplicate layer and combine it with your original image, you can set the blend mode for the filtered layer from the beginning. For filters that have a Preview option (such as High Pass) — changing the blend mode of the duplicate layer *before* you filter allows you to see the effect on the image as soon as you begin to experiment with filter settings.

Because the filtered layer was in Overlay mode, the medium gray in the layer disappeared, since 50% gray is neutral, or transparent, in the contrast modes. The lighter and darker grays, however, acted to increase the contrast where Davis wanted it most — around existing shapes and areas of contrast, to make the light and shadows more dramatic.

A

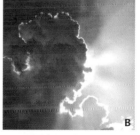

B

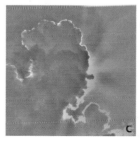

C

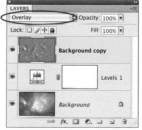

Painting

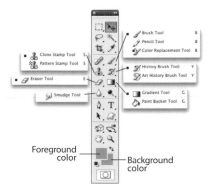

Photoshop's tools for stroking with paint and pattern are the Brush ✐, Pencil ✐, Eraser ⌫, Color Replacement ✐, and Smudge ✐. The cloning tools that are most useful for painting are the Pattern Stamp ✤ (in Impressionist mode) and the Art History Brush ✐. For restoring an earlier version of an "overworked" area of a painting, the History Brush ✐ or the Eraser in Erase to History mode ✐ can also be helpful. The Paint Bucket ✐ and Gradient ▦ "pour" color into a selected area.

Drag in the working window with CS4's Rotate View tool ↻ to angle the canvas. (Photoshop will detect whether your video card supports a new enough version of OpenGL for this to work.) Other painting improvements include smoother brush operation and brush sizing.

THERE ARE AT LEAST FOUR great ways to stroke "paint" onto "canvas" in Photoshop, running the gamut from freehand brush strokes to automated cloning:

- You can start with a blank canvas or a scanned drawing or photo and "hand paint" with the Brush tool ✐. You'll find an example in "Watercolor Over Ink" on page 389.

- Or reproduce an existing image by hand-painting with the Smudge tool ✐, as in "'Wet on Wet' Acrylics" on page 395.

- With the Impressionist option for the Pattern Stamp tool ✤, you can "clone" a photograph into a natural-media masterpiece, as described in "Pattern Stamp Watercolors" on page 403.

- Or you can use the Art History Brush ✐ to automate the process of turning a photo into a painting, as in "Art History Pastels" on page 407.

Besides these options, several methods for filling selected areas with color can be very useful for artists working in Photoshop.

Our approach in the next few pages will be to introduce the painting and cloning tools, highlight some of the amazing features of the brush tips that work with these tools, and then move on to the filling tools. We'll show how certain filters and Actions can be useful in simulating traditional art media. Finally we'll cover some interesting options for "pre-conditioning" (getting a photo ready to serve as the starting point for a painting) and "post-processing" (adding any of a series of final touches to make a digital painting look more like a traditional one).

While this chapter covers painting, Photoshop's technical drawing tools — less painterly but very precise, and resolution-independent for mechanical drawing and smooth scaling — are covered in Chapter 7.

In Photoshop the term "Brush" can refer to the **Brush tool**, shown here in the Tools panel, or to a **brush tip**, which can be used with the Brush tool or with any of the other hand-operated painting or cloning tools (or with certain healing or toning tools, which are described in Chapter 5).

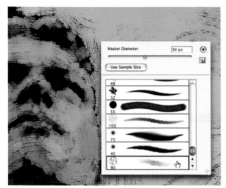

When you're working with any tool that uses a brush tip, you can choose a new brush tip without making a trip to the Options bar or Brushes panel. Simply right-click/Ctrl-click in the working window to bring up the Brush Preset picker.

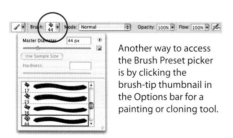

Another way to access the Brush Preset picker is by clicking the brush-tip thumbnail in the Options bar for a painting or cloning tool.

By default, the Tool Preset picker offers presets of the tool that's currently active (as shown here for the Brush tool ✐). Or you can choose to have it show you presets for all Photoshop tools.

FIRST, A FEW WORDS ABOUT TERMINOLOGY . . .

There's a bit of overlap in the terminology Photoshop uses for its painting tools and panels, particularly the term "Brush." You might want to open Photoshop and explore the interface as you read this.

The Brush & Brush Tips

"Brush" is the name of a tool — the **Brush tool** ✐ (or Paintbrush) can be chosen in the Tools panel, or by typing **B**. The term "Brush" or "Brushes" is also used to mean what in this book we call "brush tips."

Once you choose the Brush ✐, or any other painting or cloning tool, you can change its **brush tip** by choosing from the **Brush Preset picker**. Since brush tips are used with so many of Photoshop's tools, the "basics" of navigating the picker are covered in "Quick Brush Basics" in Chapter 1. The Brush preset picker can be found in three places — in a context-sensitive menu (shown at the left), in the Options bar (also shown at the left), or in the standalone **Brushes panel** (Window > Brushes; see page 382). So the **Brush Preset picker,** the **Brushes panel,** and the **context-sensitive menu** have to do with **brush tips in the generic sense**, rather than with the Brush tool ✐ itself.

Tool Presets

Tool presets are customized, saved versions of specific tools. A tool preset for the Brush tool ✐, for instance, has not only a brush tip but also a built-in blend mode, stroke opacity, and flow rate, and sometimes even color. Tool presets are available in the **Tool Preset picker** at the left end of the Options bar (shown here at the left) and in the standalone **Tool Presets panel** (Window > Tool Presets).

THE PAINTING TOOLS

Each one of the hand-operated painting tools behaves in its own unique way. In the Options bar you can set several characteristics, including the brush tip and usually the paint opacity and the blend mode (how the color you apply interacts with color that's already there). To fine-tune brush size, shape, or behavior, or to create your own elaborate media brushes, you'll need to dive into the Brushes panel, coming up on page 382.

The Wow presets for the painting and cloning tools have a wealth of built-in brush characteristics. "Exercising Wow Painting Tools" on page 413 shows how to use these presets.

Brush

By default the **Brush** lays down a smooth-edged (antialiased) stroke of color as you drag. If you click without dragging, it leaves a single "footprint" of the brush tip shape. Many of Photoshop's Brush tool presets depart from the default hard-but-smooth-edged setting and are soft, so the stroke is solid in the center but progressively more transparent toward the edges. This is controlled by the **Hardness** setting. The Brush tool's **Opacity** setting controls paint coverage; the higher the setting, the more opaque the paint can be. The **Flow** setting modifies the Opacity, reducing coverage if Flow is set at anything less than 100%.

No matter how long you hold the Brush cursor in one place, the color doesn't build up or spread out — *unless* the **Airbrush** option on the Brush tool's Options bar is turned on. With the Airbrush feature turned on, the longer you keep the cursor in one spot, the more the paint builds up. With the Airbrush on and high Flow settings, the paint flows quickly, building up until it reaches the full Opacity setting. With low Flow settings, the paint will build up to the same Opacity setting if you hold the cursor in place long enough, but it happens more slowly. The setting is a toggle, so clicking the button again turns off the Airbrush option.

Pencil

The **Pencil** operates like the Brush, but the stroke's edges can't be soft or even antialiased as the Brush's can. The advantage of using the Pencil is that Photoshop doesn't have to do the continuous calculations required for softness or antialiasing, so there's no delay between when you move the cursor and when the stroke appears on the screen, and the Pencil can seem like the most "natural" of all the tools for doing quick sketches. Lacking antialiasing, the curved or slanted edges of a Pencil stroke are

For working on a fairly small drawing, the performance difference between the Pencil and the Brush with a simple brush tip, especially in Photoshop CS4, is less obvious than it used to be when computers were slower. Cher Pendarvis used the Brush tool with the "Hard Round 5 pixels" tip, gray "paint," and a Wacom Intuos pressure-sensitive tablet to make this "pencil" sketch.

CHER PENDARVIS

HISTORY BRUSH TO THE RESCUE

The History Brush can use a previous version of your image as a source, restoring former colors and details stroke-by-stroke. What this means for painting is that, especially if you plan ahead and save History Snapshots as you paint, the History Brush can be a great way to recover if you "overwork" a part of your painting.

Loosely stroking with the Brush tool ![brush] added color to a scanned ink sketch, and dragging the Smudge tool ![smudge] over the line work "ran" the ink. A detail is shown here, and the technique is presented step-by-step in "Watercolor Over Ink" on page 389.

ORIGINAL PHOTO & PAINTING: JHDAVIS

The Smudge tool ![smudge] can automatically sample color from a reference photo as you paint. A detail of a reference photo is shown here at the top. Below it is the same detail at an early stage of painting with the Smudge. The technique is described in "'Wet on Wet' Acrylics" on page 395.

pixelated, or "stairstepped." But if your sketch is done at high resolution, or if the sketch is just for reference and won't show in the final artwork, the Pencil can be ideal.

Eraser ![eraser]

The **Eraser** ![eraser] removes pixels or changes their color. By default it leaves behind (erases to) the **Background color** if you're working on a *Background* layer. On other layers it erases to **transparency**. It can operate like a **Brush**, **Airbrush**, or **Pencil**, depending on which Mode you choose in the Options bar. (Another Mode choice is **Block**, which was the Eraser's only mode in early versions of Photoshop. It isn't as useful as other modes, though it can be helpful for erasing along a straight horizontal or vertical edge.)

The **Erase To History** choice in the Options bar lets you erase back to a previous stage of your painting. (See "Two History Brushes" on page 385 for more.)

HISTORY "ON-OFF" SWITCH
Hold down the Alt/Option key while brushing to toggle the Eraser in and out of Erase To History mode.

Smudge ![smudge]

The **Smudge** tool ![smudge] smears color as you drag it. If Finger Painting is turned on in the Smudge's Options bar, the smear starts with the Foreground color. With Finger Painting turned off, each stroke starts by sampling the color under the cursor, and the Smudge smears with that color. If the brush tip is big enough to pick up more than one color, the Smudge tool applies streaks of the sampled colors. The higher the **Strength** setting in the Options bar, the farther the Smudge tool will smear each new color it encounters. At 100% Strength the Smudge applies only the first color(s) it samples. At lower percentages the first color fades out and new ones are picked up and smeared as the cursor encounters them. At any Opacity setting other than 100%, the smearing process can be tediously slow. But at 100% it can very effectively move pixels around with a "painterly" result, as demonstrated in "'Wet on Wet' Acrylics" on page 395 and in "Watercolor Over Ink" on page 389.

Color Replacement ![color replacement]

To change the color of strokes you've painted, you can use the Color Replacement tool ![color replacement]. It samples and replaces color. For more about the Color Replacement tool, often used for seamlessly changing the color of clothing or some other product in a photo, see page 180.

With the Pattern Stamp tool in Impressionist mode, you can paint a watercolor rendition of a photo, brush stroke by brush stroke, as shown in this painting in progress. The first step was to define the entire photo as a pattern (see page 404).

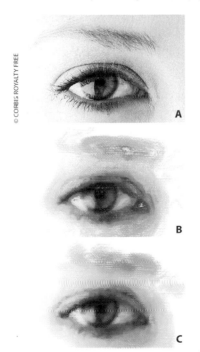

© CORBIS ROYALTY FREE

A

B

C

Starting with the same source image **A** and the same brush tip, the Art History Brush generates different results depending on the settings in the Options bar. If you change the Style setting from Tight Long **B** to Tight Short **C**, the automated brushing process more closely follows the contours of the source image — good for images with a lot of detail that you want to maintain.

THE ARTISTS' CLONING TOOLS

Photoshop's cloning tools reproduce part of the current image, or part of an earlier stage in its development, or part of a different image altogether. Of most interest for digital painting are the Art History Brush and the Pattern Stamp in its Impressionist mode. Many of the choices in the Options bar for the cloning tools are the same as for the painting tools. Other options are specific to the individual tools, as described next.

Pattern Stamp

With the **Impressionist** option chosen in the Options bar, you can use the Pattern Stamp to apply brushlike smears of color based on the colors in the original image. The trick is to turn your entire original image into a pattern, so the tool can use the pattern as a resource as you lay down each brush stroke. The technique is demonstrated in "Pattern Stamp Watercolors" on page 403. "Exercising Wow Painting Tools" on page 413 also includes examples.

Art History Brush

The **Art History Brush** paints several strokes with a single click. The strokes automatically follow the edges of color or contrast in the image source chosen in the History panel (Window > Show History); to choose a source, you click in the column to the left of either a Snapshot (one of the stored versions of the file shown at the top of the panel) or a state (one of the recent steps listed in the lower part of the panel). ▼

FIND OUT MORE

▼ Using the History panel **page 30**

Success with the Art History Brush depends on controlling the tool's automation. This is done partly by choosing the **Style** and **Area** settings in the Options bar to control how long the automated strokes are, how closely they follow the color in the image, and how many strokes are laid down with each click. The **Tolerance** setting controls how different from the source image the current version has to be in order for the Art History Brush to be allowed to paint over it. This means you can protect recently painted details that are not very different from the History you're painting from, while painting other areas. But for most painting, it works well to leave the Tolerance set at the default setting of 0, so the Art History Brush can paint over all existing strokes.

With the Art History Brush it's helpful to be able to see the original image as you paint over it, because where you click determines which of the color edges in the source will be given the most weight in determining the shape and color of the strokes that are laid down. "Art History Pastels" starting on page 407 provides

continued on page 383

BRUSH CONTROL OPTIONS

The **Options bar** offers the most often used controls for the painting and cloning tools. The standalone **Brushes panel** offers many more options, with its seven panels of controls and five additional on/off toggles. The Options bar for the Brush tool ✐ and three panels of the expanded Brushes panel are shown below.

Click to open the **Tool Preset picker** (not shown).

Click to pop out the **Brush Preset picker** as shown.

Set the **blend mode** for the paint.

Set the **maximum paint coverage**.

Click to open the **Brushes panel**; three of its control panels are shown below.

Set the rate of buildup if Airbrush is on; if Airbrush is off, settings less than 100% will reduce the coverage set in the Opacity field.

With the **Airbrush** option turned on, paint builds up as you hold the painting tool in one place.

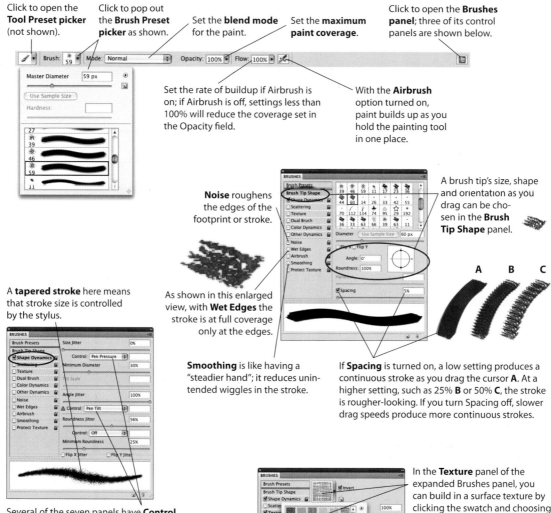

Noise roughens the edges of the footprint or stroke.

A brush tip's size, shape and orientation as you drag can be chosen in the **Brush Tip Shape** panel.

A **tapered stroke** here means that stroke size is controlled by the stylus.

As shown in this enlarged view, with **Wet Edges** the stroke is at full coverage only at the edges.

Smoothing is like having a "steadier hand"; it reduces unintended wiggles in the stroke.

If **Spacing** is turned on, a low setting produces a continuous stroke as you drag the cursor **A**. At a higher setting, such as 25% **B** or 50% **C**, the stroke is rougher-looking. If you turn Spacing off, slower drag speeds produce more continuous strokes.

Several of the seven panels have **Control** menus, where you can set the brush tip behavior to respond to stylus pressure or tilt, direction of the stroke, or other factors. Although these Control menus are often indented under **Jitter** settings (the amount of random variation that will be introduced as you use the brush tip), the Control under Size Jitter actually controls the Size itself (not the Jitter), the one under Angle Jitter controls the Angle itself, and so on.

In the **Texture** panel of the expanded Brushes panel, you can build in a surface texture by clicking the swatch and choosing from the pop-out Textures picker.

With **Protect Texture** turned on, your current Texture panel choices will apply to any brush tip you choose, overriding any built-in Texture settings the tip may have. This is an easy way to make several brush tips show the same texture, keeping a consistent "surface" for the painting.

Some of the brush tips that ship with Photoshop are great for creating "instant illustrations." For the Scattered Maple Leaves preset (top, from Photoshop's default set of brush tips), we went into the Color Dynamics panel of the Brushes panel and set the Foreground/Background Jitter amount to 100% to "give the brush permission" to randomly vary the color within the whole range between our Foreground yellow and Background orange. For the Dune Grass preset (also from the default set), the built-in Foreground/Background Jitter was already 100%, so all we had to do was to choose two shades of green for the Foreground and Background colors.

step-by-step instructions for taming this tool so the results look "painterly" rather than simply "processed." "Exercising Wow Painting Tools" on page 413 includes examples of using the Art History Brush with the Wow presets that come with this book; the Wow presets were designed to produce results that look like artists' media on canvas or paper.

CHOOSING, EDITING & CREATING BRUSH TIPS & TOOLS

Before you start working with and customizing the painting tools, be sure you've looked at "First, a Few Words About Terminology . . ." on page 378. The term *brush* is used in several ways in Photoshop, which can be confusing unless you get it sorted out early. Then read the "Brush Tips" and "Tool Presets" sections here.

Brush Tips

The **Brush Preset picker** is convenient for choosing a brush tip or changing a brush tip's size and hardness. But when you need access to more controls than the picker offers, the standalone **Brushes panel** offers a wealth of additional options; it can be

---

FADING

With Photoshop's painting tools, you can get some interesting results by choosing the Fade option. It's available for several of the Control settings in the standalone Brushes panel. For example, by setting some of the Control settings in the Shape Dynamics, Color Dynamics, and Other Dynamics panels to Fade, with a different number of steps for each, you can shrink the brush size, fade to transparency, and change the color (from the Foreground to the Background color) all at different rates, within a single brush stroke.

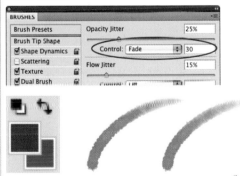

Both of these strokes were made with the Brush tool ✎. For the lefthand stroke we set the Size, the Foreground-to-Background shift, and the Opacity all to Fade in 40 steps. For the righthand stroke, we faded Size in 40 steps, but changed the color shift to fade in 15 steps and the Opacity to fade in 30 steps. The Jitter settings (such as the Opacity Jitter and Flow Jitter settings shown in the dialog box above) create variation.

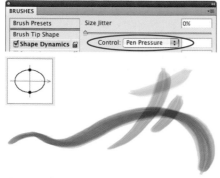

Photoshop's "Watercolor Loaded Wet Flat Tip" preset, one of the default brush tip presets for painting and cloning tools, is useful for painting details in foliage or flow lines on water with the Brush 🖌 tool. It's a Dual Brush, ▼ so its performance can be slow, but it produces great strokes when you paint methodically. To simulate the transparent look of watercolor (as shown here), try changing its blend mode to Multiply in the Options bar. When it's used with a stylus and tablet, Pen Pressure controls stroke width. The thickness of the stroke also changes when you change the orientation of the stylus, simply because the brush tip is oval rather than circular.

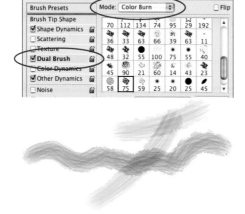

The individual bristles of the "Rough Round Bristle" (in Photoshop's default brush tip set) apply the Foreground color at different densities. The streaked bristle effect results from the Color Burn mode that's built into its Dual Brush settings. ▼ This tip is useful with the Brush 🖌 tool for laying in large areas of paint and for adding texture over existing paint. To paint semitransparent washes, in the Options bar change the blend mode from Normal to Multiply, or reduce Opacity.

FIND OUT MORE

▼ How the Dual Brush setting works **page 429**

opened by clicking the "Toggle the brushes panel" button 📄 near the right end of the Options bar or by choosing Window > Brushes.

Creating a New Brush Tip

Besides choosing a brush tip from those that are currently loaded and available to Photoshop, you can **design your own custom brush tip**:

- **Modify an existing brush tip** by choosing it and then changing any settings you want, either in the Brush Preset picker (size, hardness, or roundness) or in the Brushes panel (with more options). Add your customized tip to the Brush Preset picker: Click the 📑 button (or click the ⊙ or ▾☰ button and choose New Brush Preset) to open the Brush Name dialog box; enter a name and click "OK." Your new brush tip will be added as the last one in the Brush Preset picker.

- **Build a brush tip from scratch** and add it to the Brush Preset picker, as described in "Quick Brush Tips" on page 400.

Any brush tip you've added to the Brush Preset picker can be permanently saved, so you can load it again later. The process is described in "Quick Brush Tips" on page 402.

Tool Presets

Besides brush tip presets, there are more complex *tool presets* for individual painting tools, such as the Brush and Smudge. These are made available in the **Tool Preset picker**, which can be opened by clicking the tool icon at the left end of a tool's Options bar (shown on page 382), or by choosing Window > Tool Presets. By default, the picker shows only the presets for the current tool, but you can turn off the Current Tool Only feature to show all the other tool presets currently loaded in Photoshop as well. The presets for the painting tools include not only a brush tip but also other characteristics set for the tool. For instance, for the Brush tool it can include blend Mode, Opacity, Flow, and even color.

THE FILLING TOOLS, FILL LAYERS & OVERLAY EFFECTS

The **Paint Bucket** 🪣 and **Gradient** ▦ tools and the Fill command were originally Photoshop's only means of applying solid fills or color gradations. In recent versions of the program they've been largely superseded by the Solid Color, Pattern, and Gradient Fill layers, and by the Color, Pattern, and Gradient Overlay effects in Layer Styles (see page 502) because these are much easier

continued on page 386

To load a different set of brush tips or of tool presets, click the brush tip footprint or the tool preset icon on the Options bar. When the picker opens, click the ⊙ in the upper right corner and choose from the list. When the dialog box appears, clicking **"Append" adds** the new library to the brush tips or tools already in the picker; clicking **"OK" replaces** the current presets with the set you chose, keeping the list shorter and more manageable. If you've added or modified brushes in the set that's currently in the picker, Photoshop will know this, and you'll be warned to save the set before you replace it.

If your Brush Preset picker or Tool Preset picker gets cumbersome because it has so many entries, you can **delete brush tips** or presets one by one by Alt/Option-clicking on the ones you want to remove. **Note:** When you add custom brush tips or tool presets to the picker, be sure to save the set before you start deleting so you won't lose them permanently.

The **Erase To History** option for the Eraser tool gives you an easy way to keep two different "History brushes" ready to paint: You can choose a different brush tip for each of the two tools and quickly switch back and forth between them by using the keyboard shortcuts:

E for the Eraser

Y for the History Brush

Both tools will use the same History Snapshot or state for the source.

A pressure-sensitive tablet and stylus offer better control of painted strokes than a mouse does, not to mention putting them down faster. If you use a tablet such as the Wacom Intuos, take some time to explore the many settings available for customizing brush-tip behavior.

Within each category of Brushes panel settings (listed below) are **Control** options. **Pen Pressure**, **Pen Tilt**, and **Stylus Wheel** controls are available for:

- **Shape Dynamics** – Size, Angle, and Roundness of the brush tip
- **Scattering** – Count (how many footprints) and Scattering (how widely dispersed)
- **Texture** – Minimum Depth
- **Color Dynamics** – change from Foreground to Background color
- **Other Dynamics** – Opacity and Flow

In the driver software for the stylus itself, you may also want to:

- Set the **top rocker button** on the side of the stylus to act as **Alt/Option**-click so you can easily sample color as you paint.
- Set the **bottom rocker button** to act as the **right-click/Ctrl-click** for bringing up context-sensitive menus.
- Set the **end button** to be the **Eraser**, so you can turn the stylus upside-down and erase as you would with a traditional pencil.

Both flowers were painted with the Brush tool ✒ and a Soft Round brush tip, with Hardness adjusted to 25% and spacing to about 30%. For the one on the left (painted with the mouse) we changed the brush tip size often, using the bracket keys —] and [, or in CS4 with OpenGL enabled, right-Alt-dragging (Windows) or Ctrl-Option-dragging (Mac) to resize "on the fly." For the one on the right (painted with a tablet and stylus), brush tip size was changed only once, to paint the center; otherwise the stroke width was regulated by Pen Pressure. The biggest difference, though, was that painting with the stylus was much quicker and more natural than with the mouse.

In her painting of *Alicia*, Amanda Boucher used the Magic Wand to select areas she wanted to fill, using solid color fills for the red background and blue flowers, and then a pattern fill on another layer in Multiply mode to add the detail in the flowers. Find out more about her technique on page 420.

The Rainbow was "painted" onto this photo with the Gradient tool. The technique is described in "Exercising Gradients" on page 198.

THE "UNFILL" TOOL

The **Magic Eraser**, which shares a space in the Tools panel with the Eraser, is like a Paint Bucket that "pours" clear transparency instead of color. Like the Paint Bucket, it can "fill" Contiguous or noncontiguous color areas and have Anti-aliased edges or not. It can base its fill region on the composite color or on the color in just one layer.

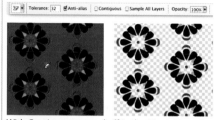

With Contiguous turned off in the Magic Eraser's Options bar, one click removes the color you click on, throughout the entire layer, leaving transparency behind.

to edit later if needed. However, for some artists the original "click-and-fill" tools still have a certain hands-on appeal.

Paint Bucket

The **Paint Bucket** can apply a solid color or a pattern. It chooses the area to fill by sampling the color where you click — either the composite color of all layers (if **All Layers** is turned on in the Options bar) or of only the layer that's targeted in the Layers panel. The **Tolerance** setting determines how closely other pixels have to match the sampled color before they'll be replaced. Sometimes it can be tricky to set the Tolerance low enough so the Paint Bucket doesn't change too wide a range of colors but high enough to change the antialiasing pixels, to avoid a lingering "fringe" of the old color at the edges of the new. With the **Contiguous** box checked, clicking with the Paint Bucket replaces pixels that are the same color as *and continuous with* the pixel that you click with the tool's hot spot. With Contiguous turned *off*, all pixels of the sampled color throughout the entire layer or selection will be replaced with the color applied by the Paint Bucket. The edges of the new fill can be **Anti-aliased** (partly transparent, to blend with the surrounding colors) or not.

Gradient

The **Gradient** tool fills an entire layer or a selected area with a color gradation. The center and direction of the gradient is controlled by where you drag the tool. In the Options bar you can choose a preset color blend and specify what type of gradient geometry you want — **Linear**, **Radial**, **Angle**, **Reflected**, or **Diamond** (examples are shown on page 175). You can also choose whether to **Reverse** the order of the colors, whether to **Dither** (jumbling the pixels slightly at the color transitions to prevent the gradient from appearing as distinct bands of color when it's printed), and whether to take advantage of any **Transparency** that's built into the gradient or simply ignore the transparency and apply the colors as opaque. "Exercising Gradients" on page 196 shows several ways to set up and apply gradients.

Other Fill Options

Besides the Gradient and Paint Bucket tools and the Edit > Fill command, there are two other ways to apply fills:

- You can add a **Fill layer** by choosing from the top of the list when you click the "Create new fill or adjustment layer" button at the bottom of the Layers panel. Depending on which kind of Fill layer you choose, the entire layer is assigned a **Solid Color, Pattern,** or **Gradient.** The layer includes a layer mask you can modify to control where the fill shows up.

To change the color of a filled or painted area on a transparent layer, in the Layers panel, target the layer you want to change and lock its transparency at the top of the panel. Then refill with the Paint Bucket 🖾 or Gradient ⬛. Or choose the Edit > Fill command. Any partial transparency will be maintained, and none of the original color will be left behind.

Before (top) and after locking transparency and refilling. No residue of the first color remains.

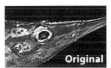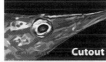

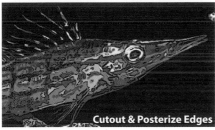

Detail of a print made by posterizing an image with the Cutout filter and then outlining with the Posterize Edges filter (see page 432 for more)

Some of the Actions on the Wow DVD-ROM are designed to apply painterly treatments to turn photos into illustrations (see page 415).

- Still another way to fill an area is to use a **Color, Pattern,** or **Gradient Overlay effect** as part of a **Layer Style.** This makes it easier to control how the Fill interacts with other effects in the Style, such as glows, drop shadows, and bevels. The Overlay effects are introduced in "Overlays" on page 502 and are used in techniques throughout the book.

"PAINTING" WITH FILTERS & ACTIONS

Some of Photoshop's filters can be great for stylizing images as artwork. Choosing Filter > **Filter Gallery** opens up several sets of filters especially designed for this purpose, such as the **Artistic, Brush Strokes,** and **Sketch** sets. Try using these filters as a starting point, combining them in the Filter Gallery, adding painted details, or combining a filtered image with the original. The **Smart Blur** filter can also be useful, as shown on page 262. You'll find examples of the Photoshop filter effects, along with tips on using them, in "Appendix A: Filter Demos."

For painterly treatments more complex than filter combinations alone, recording an **Action** provides a way to save a process as you develop it, so you can easily apply it to other images. "Quick 'Painting' with Wow Actions" starting on page 415 provides examples of "painterly" effects you can achieve with Actions supplied on the Wow DVD-ROM, and "Actions" on page 120 tells how to record an Action of your own.

"PRE-CONDITIONING" & "POST-PROCESSING"

Painting in Photoshop is a creative, expressive process. When you start with a photo, the program offers some image-preparation capabilities that can be helpful:

- **Change the composition** by selecting some parts of an image and moving, stretching, or shrinking them (page 419), or copy and paste elements from other images.

- Add a semi-transparent **"tracing paper"** layer (page 404) to make it easy to sketch from your photo and to distinguish your painted strokes from the original, or to see where to start a stroke with the Art History brush.

- Add a **Posterize** Adjustment layer to simplify the forms in the image.

- A **Hue/Saturation** Adjustment layer with the Saturation slider moved to the right can boost the intensity of the colors. Or use **Vibrance** to intensify moderately saturated color more than highly saturated color, and to protect skin tones.

CHER THREINEN-PENDARVIS

To explore possibilities for color and form in a painting based on a photo, start with the original **A** and try one of these techniques: posterizing **B**, increasing color saturation **C**, drastically adjusting Levels **D**, or oversharpening **E**. From the simplified image you can sample colors for a custom set of Swatches (page 402) or use "tracing paper" (step 3 on page 404) to sketch the simplified shapes.

- Add a **Levels** Adjustment layer and move the Input Levels black-point and white-point sliders close to the center to both intensify color and help simplify forms.

- Apply the **Unsharp Mask** filter using high Amount and Radius settings to intensify color and experiment with glowing light effects (at the left).

- To generate **bristle marks** when you use the Smudge tool, add noise to the image before you start to paint (page 395).

Another, almost magical, advantage of painting in Photoshop is the ability to warp time. You can paint first and *then* choose what kind of canvas you want. You can apply the paint and decide after the fact how wet the watercolors and the paper were, or how thickly the oils or acrylics were applied. Here are some examples:

- Use the **Photocopy filter** to "pool" the pigment in a watercolor (page 406) or to bring out texture and detail in a chalk drawing.

- Use the **Emboss filter** to thicken the paint by making brush strokes more apparent (page 398).

- Use a **Layer Style** (page 406) or the Burn tool 🖐 (page 393) to add canvas or paper texture to complement the texture that's built into the brushes you used in the painting.

- **Sharpen** to bring out the canvas or paper texture or even to create the "paper white" edges typical of watercolor.

- Add "salt staining," "paper white," or other treatments to watercolors (page 427).

Some of these "post-processing" techniques have been automated in the **Wow-Paint Enhance Actions**; you can find demonstrations starting on page 415.

Some Wow Actions are designed to enhance paintings, either produced digitally or painted with traditional media and scanned (see page 417).

Watercolor Over Ink

A QUICK ILLUSTRATION STYLE that simulates watercolor over an ink drawing can start with a hand-drawn sketch, as in this case, or with line art created in Illustrator or Photoshop, or with clip art. For this example, Frankie Frey started with a scan of an original felt-tip pen drawing

Thinking the project through. To develop the painting, this method puts the line work layer on top (so the colors won't obscure it) and in Multiply mode (so the white background of the line work is transparent and won't obscure the colors) with the paint on layers beneath it. A "paper" layer below the paint layers hides a spare copy of the cleaned-up drawing, kept on hand just in case.

Like most other artists' media in Photoshop, watercolor is much more flexible and forgiving than the traditional materials. For one thing, you can warp time, separating parts of the painting process that would occur simultaneously, or changing the order of the steps. You can apply the paint, feeling the watercolors flowing onto the paper, and *then* decide how much you want the ink to run. And you can choose the color for your background wash *after* the foreground colors are in place.

1 Preparing the drawing. Scan a drawing and do any cleanup work that's necessary, ▼ or open a clip-art or drawing file **1a**. Duplicate the drawing layer (press Ctrl/⌘-J). Add a white "paper" layer between the new layer and the original by clicking on the *Background* thumbnail in

FIND OUT MORE

▼ Scanning and
cleaning up line art
pages 103 & 108

1a

The grayscale scan was opened in Photoshop and converted to color (Image > Mode > RGB Color).

1b

As the painting develops, a copy of the drawing is in Multiply mode above the transparent painting layers. A Solid Fill "paper" layer hides a spare copy of the drawing.

USING THE WOW WATERCOLOR PRESETS

You can make a brush larger or smaller. ▼ With a pressure-sensitive tablet, applying more **pressure** will enlarge the stroke.

To control the amount of paint, in the Options bar reduce **Opacity** to decrease the maximum amount of color that can be applied in a stroke; decrease the **Flow** to slow down the rate at which the color builds up to the maximum Opacity. Flow and Opacity for these brushes also increase with **stylus pressure**.

For **overlapping strokes** whose edges show, make a stroke and release the mouse button (or lift the stylus), and then depress the mouse button or stylus and stroke again.

For a **continuous wash** — to build up color without internal stroke marks — use one continuous stroke, rather than starting and stopping.

Results vary with the **colors** used (light colors tend to show texture less) ▼ and with **painting style** (if you paint quickly, you might want to set the Flow higher than if you paint slowly).

FIND OUT MORE

▼ Loading the Wow presets **page 4**

▼ Sizing brush tips **page 71**

▼ Texture in brush tips **page 401**

---

the Layers panel and clicking the "Create a new fill or adjustment layer" button ◕ at the bottom of the Layers panel; choose Solid Color from the list, choose white in the Color Picker, and click "OK" to close the Picker.

To leave the ink black but make the white in the top drawing layer appear transparent, so the colors you add next will show through it, click on the top layer's thumbnail to target it, and then choose Multiply from the pop-up list of blend modes in the upper left corner of the Layers panel. Add a transparent layer below this drawing layer to hold the first of the paint (Ctrl/⌘-click the "Create a new layer" button ▣ at the bottom of the panel; the Ctrl/⌘ key will make the new layer come in *below* the target layer instead of above it) **1b**.

2 Painting. Now choose the Brush tool ✎ from the Tools panel, (or Shift-B). At the left end of the Options bar, click the brush icon to open the Tool Preset picker and double-click one of the **Wow-BT Watercolor** presets **2a**; Frey started with **Medium**. (If you haven't yet loaded the **Wow-Art Media Brushes** presets, the **Wow-BT Watercolor** presets won't appear in the list of tools to choose. ▼ You can load just the **Wow-BT Watercolor** tools you need for this project by clicking the menu button ◉ in the top right corner of the picker, choosing Load Tool Presets, and locating the **Wow BT-Watercolor.tpl** file on the Wow DVD-ROM, in Wow Project Files > Chapter 6 > Watercolor Over Ink.)

Like traditional watercolor brushes, the **Wow-BT Watercolor** presets are designed to let color flow onto the paper as you hold the brush in one spot, and to build color as you stroke over previously applied paint; they also simulate the pigment buildup at the edges of wet strokes. The interaction with the paper texture is built into the brushes, so the texture will appear as you paint. Choose a color (one way is to click the Foreground swatch in the Tools panel and use the Color Picker).

Begin painting loosely, modifying the brush as needed, keeping in mind the painting tips in "Using the Wow Watercolor Presets" at the left. For maximum flexibility, add a new layer for each new color. For this painting Frey started with the **Wow-BT Watercolor-Medium** preset, making it slightly smaller and reducing the Opacity and Flow in the Options bar to make the color thinner and to control the buildup **2b**. As she painted, she switched to other sizes of Wow-BT Watercolor brushes, changed Opacity and Flow, and added more layers **2c**, **2d**. With elements on different layers, you can make the paint more transparent by reducing a layer's Opacity. Or to make the paint denser, duplicate

2a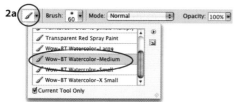

Choosing the medium-size **Wow-BT Watercolor** Brush from the Tool Preset picker

2b

Reducing the Opacity in the Options bar (to about 50%) while keeping the Flow high (100%), Frey could paint smoothly, building color by layering strokes, as in the pink flower on the left. In contrast, with Flow reduced (25%) and Opacity high (100%), the paint pools, and the texture is more obvious, as in the flower on the right.

2c

For the watering can and the plaid on the couch, Frey reduced Opacity in the Options bar somewhat (75%), keeping the Flow low (25%); she painted the blue stripes on one layer and the pink stripes on a layer above.

the layer (Ctrl/⌘-J) and then reduce the Opacity of this extra layer to get exactly the color density you want. Where strokes of different colors overlap, you can load your brush with the mixed color as described in "Sampling Color" below.

3 Collecting layers. To reduce the working file size, you can combine some layers. Where colors overlap (as in the plaid on the sofa), it's a good idea to keep the layers separate so you can control the colors independently in case you want to make changes. But where elements don't overlap, you can combine them, because if you need to change something later, you'll be able to isolate each element with a selection.

To combine layers, target all of the layers you want to combine by clicking the thumbnail of one of them in the Layers panel and then Ctrl/⌘-clicking to target additional layers one by one **3**. (Ctrl/⌘-click is a toggle; so using it on an already targeted layer releases the layer from targeting.) Choose Layer > Merge Layers (or press Ctrl/⌘-E) to combine the selected layers into one.

2d

For the clothing, she used a medium Opacity (around 50%) and a low Flow (25% or less).

3

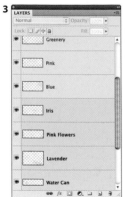

Renaming the layers helps keep track of the elements of the painting (double-click the name in the Layers panel and then type a new one). To reduce working file size, target layers whose elements don't overlap and merge them.

4

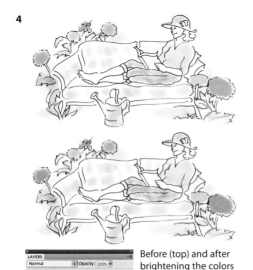

Before (top) and after brightening the colors with a masked Hue/Saturation Adjustment layer

5

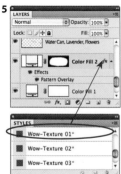

A masked Solid Color layer creates a background wash. The **Wow-Texture 01*** Layer Style applies a texture similar to the one in the Wow-BT Watercolor Brush presets.

4 Brightening the color. If you want to adjust some or all of your colors, add an Adjustment layer. To brighten the color, Frey targeted the top paint layer (just below the ink drawing layer) by clicking its thumbnail in the Layers panel, and then clicked the ⬤ button at the bottom of the panel and chose Hue/Saturation. In the Hue/Saturation dialog box she moved the Saturation slider to the right (to +30) and clicked "OK." Then, since the shirt now seemed too bright, she chose one of Photoshop's default soft brush tips (from the picker of brush tips that pops up when you click the "Brush:" button in the Options bar) to paint the Hue/Saturation layer's built-in mask with black to hide the effect in the shirt area **4**. (When a mask is active, you can make black the Foreground color by typing D for "Default" and then X for "eXchange.")

5 Adding a background wash. To put in a background wash of color, add another Solid Color layer above the white paper: In the Layers panel, target the white layer near the bottom of the layer stack. Click the ⬤ button, and choose Solid Color; choose a light, fairly neutral color from the Color Picker and click "OK." (This color will "fill in" all white areas; if you want to leave some areas white, you can mask them as described below.) Now add paper texture to match the texture in the brush strokes on the paint layers: In the Styles panel, click the menu button ▼≡ in the upper right corner, choose **Wow-Grain-Texture Styles** from the list, and then click on **Wow-Texture 01*** in the picker **5**. (If you haven't yet loaded the Wow presets, ▼ an alternative is to load just the texture you need for this painting: Choose Load Styles from the Styles panel menu and navigate to **Wow Texture 01.asl**, located in the folder with the other files for this project.) **Wow-Texture 01*** is like the pattern that's built into the **Wow-BT Watercolor** brushes and will match the painted strokes. To give the wash a soft, irregular shape, we chose the 100-pixel soft tip from the brush-tip picker (right-click/Ctrl-click on your painting to open it) and painted the edges of the built-in mask with black.

FIND OUT MORE

▼ Loading the Wow Presets **page 4**

6 "Running" the ink. To create the "bleed" for the water-soluble ink, in the Layers panel click on the "Background copy" layer's thumbnail to target the layer. Then choose the Smudge tool 👆 and choose a soft brush tip from the "Brush:" picker; we chose the 17-pixel soft brush and reduced its Strength to about 50% in the Options bar. Make sure the "Use All Layers" and "Finger Painting" options are turned *off*. To make it easier to "bleed" a wider segment of the line with a single stroke, you can flatten

6a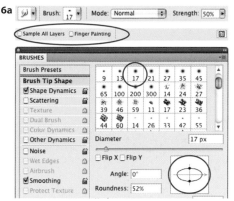

Setting up the Smudge tool for running the ink

6b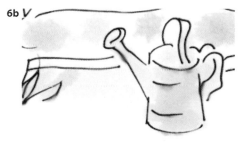

Dragging downward on the line work with the Smudge tool 🖐 with **Finger Painting turned off** in the Options bar creates the impression of blurred ink. Starting on the line smears black, the line color, but the line persists.

the brush: In the Brushes panel, click on "Brush Tip Shape" in the list on the left and in the shape diagram, drag down on the top handle to a Roundness of about 50% **6a**.

In the painting, look for an area where the paint touches or crosses the line work. Touch the cursor to the line and drag downward to "run" the ink. If you start on the line rather than above it, the black ink will bleed but the line itself will remain. If you start above the line and drag down through it, the line will be smeared away. If the result of your first "running" experiment is too strong or not strong enough, undo (Ctrl/⌘-Z); then adjust the Strength, brush tip size, or brush roundness, and try again. Run the ink at other points on the line-work layer as well **6b**. The completed painting is shown at the top of page 389.

Enhancing the painting. Even after the painting is complete, there are many ways to experiment with changes. **To increase the density of the line work,** in the Layers panel unlock the *Background* by double-clicking its name and clicking "OK"; then drag this original line work you saved for just such a purpose to the top of the stack, put it in Multiply mode, and adjust layer Opacity to taste. You can **paint details** on additional transparent layers. Or **change the color of the wash** by double-clicking the Solid Color layer's thumbnail in the Layers panel and choosing a new color. You can even **bring out the paper grain in some areas** as described in the tip below. 🎨

ADDING CANVAS OR PAPER TEXTURE EXACTLY WHERE YOU WANT IT

Want to bring out the canvas texture at certain spots in your painting? Copy the painting you've made using brushes with built-in texture, such as the **Wow-BT Watercolor** presets (Image > Duplicate, Merged layers only) and then:

Choose the painting tool you used, the one with the built-in texture, and open the Brushes panel (Window > Brushes). Click the word "Texture" on the left side of the panel **A**. The Pattern swatch near the top of the panel shows the texture built into the tool **B**. Although it's in the *tool*, it may not be in the *Pattern picker* that's accessible from everywhere in Photoshop; but you can put it there: Click the little "Create a new preset from the current pattern" button 🔲 **C**; note whether Invert is checked **D**.

Now choose the **Burn tool** ✋ from the Tools panel. In the Brushes panel, click the box to the left of the word "Texture" **E**; click the Pattern swatch **F**, and when the Pattern picker opens, click on the texture you just saved (the last swatch in the picker); click the Invert box if appropriate **G**.

Drag the Burn tool over the area where you want to emphasize the texture. In the Options bar **H** try reducing Exposure or choosing the "wrong" Range setting; for instance, if the color you're brushing over is a Midtone, try choosing Shadows for a subtler effect. Experiment with turning on and off the "Texture each tip" option in the Brushes panel **I**.

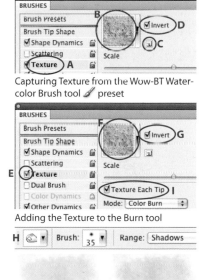

Capturing Texture from the Wow-BT Watercolor Brush tool ✏ preset

Adding the Texture to the Burn tool

Before (left) and after "burning"

We Apply a Quick Color "Wash" Over Line Work

WHETHER YOU START WITH A SCAN, as we did, or with black-and-white Il-lustrator line work or clip art, here's a quick way to add color over the lines. Like watercolor or artist's markers over ink, it creates areas of loose tint around the line work itself. Generated in the Refine Mask dialog, the amount and character of the ink can be adjusted to taste. And once you've added one color, it's easy to add more if you like.

The **Color Wash.psd** file is pro-vided on the Wow DVD-ROM (in the Wow Goodies folder).

FIND OUT MORE
▼ Cleaning up a scan **page 108**
▼ Color Picker **page 170**
▼ Painting a mask **page 84**

1 Open a cleaned-up scan,▼ or draw or import black-and-white line art in an RGB file.

Corinna Buchholz of piddix.com made an RGB scan of John Tenniel's illustration of Hatter and Hare dunking Dormouse, from *Alice's Adventures in Wonderland* by Lewis Carroll (Charles Dodgson). Corinna cleaned up the RGB scan (you can find a method on page 108), gave it an "antique" background color, and flattened the file to a single *Background* layer.

2 To set up a color layer to do the tinting, open the Channels panel (Window > Channels). Ctrl/⌘-click on the composite (RGB) channel's thumbnail to load its luminosity (light areas) as a selection, and then invert the selection (Ctrl/⌘-Shift-I) so the line work is selected rather than the light background. At the bottom of the Layers panel (Window > Layers) Alt/Option-click the "Cre-ate new fill or adjustment layer" button ◯ and choose Solid Color from the list. When the New Layer dialog box opens, choose Multiply for the Mode and click "OK" to

close the dialog and open the Col-or Picker, where you can choose a color▼ and click "OK."

At this point the mask on the Solid Color layer simply puts color on top of the black lines, making the line work look richer.

3 To expand the color to a "wash," make sure the Solid Color layer mask is still targeted in the Layers panel. Choose Select > Refine Edge to open the Refine Mask dialog. Make sure Preview is turned on, and click the leftmost (Standard) view icon. If you see "marching ants," you can hide them by typing Ctrl/⌘-H.

Set all the sliders in the Refine Mask dialog to 0. Then use Radius,

Feather, and Smooth, along with Contrast and Expand, to adjust the color to your liking.

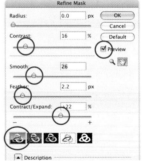

These settings in the Refine Mask dialog produced the coloring shown above. With the Standard view and the selection boundaries hidden, you can watch the coloring as you adjust the Refine Mask sliders.

Y ou needn't stop there. By duplicating your masked Solid Color layer as many times as you like (Ctrl/⌘-J), changing the col-ors, and painting the masks with black or white,▼ you can target different colors to different parts of the art.

"Wet on Wet" Acrylics

OPEN THESE PANELS

(from the Window menu, for instance):

  • Tools • Layers • Brushes

OVERVIEW

Adjust color and crop • Add a noise
pattern layer in Overlay mode, a "ground"
canvas layer, and an empty layer for
painting • Paint with the Smudge tool 👋
• Add an embossed copy of the painting in
Overlay mode • Add more brush texture
with a Pattern Fill layer

WHEN PAINTERS WORK "WET ON WET" in oils or acrylics, their brushes pick up color from previous strokes, and the colors mix. Wet-on-wet painting tends to be informal and quick, as the artist seeks to capture the light in a landscape or the expression of an informal portrait. The paint stays wet during the painting process, and in order to keep the colors pure, it has to be put on thick.

Thinking the project through. Photoshop's Smudge tool 👋 will be a responsive "brush," and the painting experience can be spontaneous, as long as you have a powerful enough computer and you work with the Smudge tool *at 100% Strength*; lower Strength settings require the computer to do even more calculation, and the painting will lag behind your brush strokes. A pressure-sensitive tablet and stylus also make the process more like traditional painting, giving the strokes more personality as the pressure you apply to the stylus scales each stroke on the fly.

1 Preparing an image for painting. Choose an image and adjust the color and crop to taste, or open **Wet Acrylics-Before. psd 1a**. To variegate the "paint" so your brush strokes will show bristle marks, add a Pattern Fill layer with one of the **Wow-**

1a

The original photo

1b Alt/Option-clicking the "Create new fill or adjustment layer" button ◉ opens a menu, where you can choose Pattern.

1c Putting the Pattern Fill layer in Overlay mode

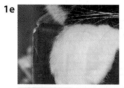

1d The **Wow-Reticulation Blotched** pattern is chosen as the Pattern Fill.

1e

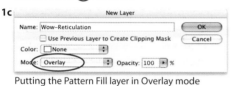

Before (left) and after adding **Wow-Reticulation Blotched** in the Pattern Fill layer in Overlay mode

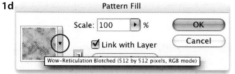

2 The canvas (or "ground") and paint layers added to the file, with the ground layer's visibility turned off during painting

Media Patterns presets (as described in the next paragraph). We used the **Wow-Reticulation Blotched** preset as the pattern, but others, such as the Wow-Noise Small Strong Gray (from the Wow-Noise Patterns presets) also work well; or if your image has a lot of small-scale color variability, you may not need to add to it.

To add a pattern-filled layer to introduce color variability, Alt/Option-click the "Create new fill or adjustment layer" button ◉ at the bottom of the Layers panel and choose Pattern from the pop-up list **1b** (the Alt/Option key will cause the New Layer dialog box to open as the layer is added). In the New Layer dialog **1c** choose Overlay for the Mode. When you click "OK" in the New Layer dialog, the Pattern Fill dialog will open **1d**. Click the triangle next to the pattern swatch to open the Pattern picker. Then click the picker's menu button ◉ and choose the **Wow-Media Patterns** from the pop-up menu. (If you haven't yet loaded the Wow presets,▼ an alternative is to choose Load Styles and navigate to **Wow-Wet Acrylics.pat** (in Wow Project Files > Chapter 6 > Wet Acrylics); this file has several Noise and Media patterns and some impasto patterns for step 6. Choose **Wow-Reticulation Blotched** (or another media or noise pattern) from the picker **1e**.

> **VIEWING PATTERN NAMES**
> If you don't see names in the Patterns panel — only swatches — you can display the names also by clicking the button ◉ in the upper right corner of the panel and choosing Small List.

> **FIND OUT MORE**
> ▼ Loading the Wow presets **page 4**

2 Preparing the canvas and paint layers. At the bottom of the Layers panel, click the "Create a new layer" button ◙ and fill this new layer with the color you want for your canvas. For example, open the Swatches panel (Window > Swatches), and click black as we did, or white, or a color that contrasts with the colors in your image (or you might want to use the Eyedropper tool 𝒫 to sample color from the image). Then press Alt/Option-Delete to fill the layer. We renamed the layer by double-clicking on its name in the Layers panel and typing "Ground."

Click the ◙ button again. Leave this new layer empty. It will hold the brush strokes you paint. Turn off visibility for the "Ground" layer by clicking its 👁 icon at the left edge of the Layers panel **2**. (If you didn't do this, the Smudge tool, which you'll be using to paint, would sample the canvas color instead of the image-and-noise composite underneath; you'll make the canvas visible again later.)

3a

Setting the options for the Smudge tool

3b

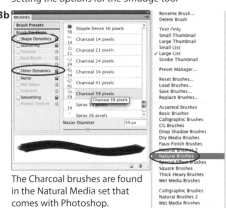

The Charcoal brushes are found in the Natural Media set that comes with Photoshop.

4a

A detail of the painting in progress. With visibility for the "Ground" layer turned off (left), gaps in the paint don't show, since the original image shows through from below. With the "Ground" layer's visibility turned on, it's easy to see the gaps.

4b

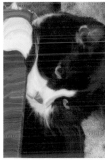

Getting ready to rough in the background with the canvas rotated to make stroking easier. The detail is shown here with visibility of the "Ground" layer turned off (left) and turned on.

3 Setting up to paint. Choose the Smudge tool 👉 from the Tools panel. In the Options bar leave Normal as the Mode, set the Strength at 100%, and turn *on* the Sample All Layers option **3a**; this will let you paint on the transparent top layer, but sample color from all the visible layers below. Also make sure that "Finger Painting" is turned *off*. In the expanded Brushes panel (Window > Brushes), make some changes **3b**: Click the ▾≡ button in the upper right corner of the panel, and choose a set of brushes to use; we chose the **Natural Brushes**. A Caution box will open. If you click the "Append" button, this set of brush tips will be added to the current menu of brush tips; if you click "OK," they will instead replace the current brush tips. Now choose a fairly large brush tip from the Natural Brushes; we chose **Charcoal 59 pixels**. In the list at the left, click **"Shape Dynamics"** — the name, not the checkbox — to open that section of the panel. If you have a pressure-sensitive tablet and stylus, for the top **"Control:"** option (it controls **Size**) choose **Pen Pressure** (strokes will get bigger as you apply more pressure); if you don't have a tablet, you can choose Off. Next, in the list at the left, click on "Other Dynamics" and for the bottom "Control:" (for **Strength**) choose **Pen Pressure** (the paint smear will be more dense with more pressure); again, if you don't have a tablet, choose Off.

4 Painting. Check "Tips for Painting with the Smudge Tool" below, and then drag with the Smudge tool to paint. As you paint, turn on the "Ground" layer's visibility from time to time by clicking in its 👁 column; this temporarily hides the original image and noise so you can check the progress of your painting **4a**, **4b**. If you added tonal variation with a Pattern Fill layer (in step 1 on page 395), the variation in color created by the pattern shows up very well as bristle marks in the midtones. But it doesn't show

---

TIPS FOR PAINTING WITH THE SMUDGE TOOL

- To make the best use of the color and shapes in the source image, **keep your strokes short** so that you sample color frequently.

- To add detail, **switch to smaller brushes** in the set you've chosen.

- You may find it easier to make more natural gestural movements if you **rotate the canvas** (in CS3 or CS4 use Image > Rotate Canvas > 90° CW or 90° CCW). This rotates the entire image — all layers at once. And because the changes are in multiples of 90°, the image won't be degraded. In CS4, if your video card supports OpenGL Drawing, you can rotate the canvas at any angle with the new Rotate View tool 🖐 without degrading the image.

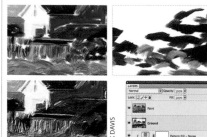

In this detail from a painting, you can see the intentional gaps in the Paint layer (viewed alone top left). When accent colors were applied to the "Ground" layer (viewed alone top right), they showed through the gaps (combined view, bottom).

4c

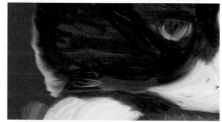

The blend mode for the "Wow-Reticulation" layer was temporarily changed to Screen to introduce color variation in the cheek and body of the cat. Opacity was reduced to around 15%. The detail is shown here with visibility of the "Ground" layer turned off (top) and turned on.

up in the lightest or darkest areas of the image. You can fix this if you temporarily reduce the Pattern Fill layer's Opacity or **change its blend mode** to Multiply when you paint highlights or Screen for the shadows. When you finish the very light or dark areas, be sure to return the Pattern Fill layer to Overlay mode and raise its Opacity again. We used this Screen method on the most solid black areas of the cat, refining the brush strokes after restoring the Pattern Fill to Overlay and 100% Opacity **4c.**

5 Adding an "impasto" effect. You can make your paint look like it was thickly applied (using an impasto technique) by making a copy of your finished painting and using it to "emboss" your brush strokes, as follows: Target the paint layer (click on its thumbnail in the Layers panel) and add a new combined copy above it by using these four-fingered keyboard shortcuts — hold down Ctrl-Shift-Alt -E (Windows) or ⌘-Shift-Option-E (Mac). Desaturate the layer (Image > Adjustments > Desaturate) and set the blend mode to Overlay. For maximum flexibility, choose Filter > Convert for Smart Filters so you can choose different filter settings later on if you want to. Then run the Emboss filter (Filter > Stylize > Emboss) **5a, 5b.** In Overlay mode the 50% gray in the layer is invisible, and the darker and lighter tones of the embossing will "raise" the brush strokes, giving them an impasto look. You might want to experiment with the embossed look. Try changing the layer's blend mode or Opacity. If you ran Emboss as a Smart Filter, you can double-click on "Emboss" and try different settings in the filter dialog.

6 Enhancing the impasto. Embossing the paint strokes in step 5 added realism to the painting **6a,** but you can further

5a

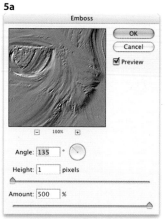

Running Filter > Stylize > Emboss on a desaturated combined copy of the image

5b

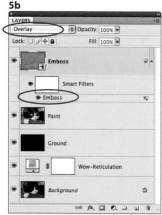

Overlay mode makes 50% gray invisible and raises the brush strokes. Applying Emboss as a Smart Filter maximizes future edibility.

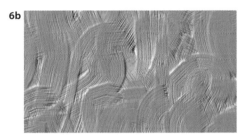

6a

A close-up of the painting, with the embossed "Impasto" layer in Overlay mode at 100% Opacity, before adding the canvas texture

6b

A Pattern Fill layer of thickly painted strokes (a detail is shown here alone) is added in Overlay mode, to provide more brush detail.

6c

A detail of the finished painting at the top of page 395. The Pattern Fill layer in Overlay mode adds texture. Its built-in mask is painted with black to hide the pattern of brush strokes in some areas.

enhance the impression that this has been hand-painted by adding even more painterly texture. Create another Pattern Fill layer in Overlay mode (as in step 1) and fill with one of the Wow patterns designed to add canvas or brush texture. Some of these seamlessly repeating patterns were made from scans of real brush strokes on real canvas, while others, such as the one we used here, were created in Corel Painter. ▼ We used **Wow-Dry Bristle 6b**. (You can choose from the **Wow-Wet Acrylics** patterns from step 1, or load **Wow-Media Pattern**s.)▼ In the Layers panel, experiment with the Opacity slider for the layer to get the degree of texture you like. If you don't like the way some of the strokes in the pattern fall on your image, just paint with black on the built-in mask for the new Fill layer, using the same kind of brush used for your image **6c**. (When a mask is active, you can make black the Foreground color by typing X for "eXchange" once or twice.) If you think there are some places where horizontal brush strokes would look better than vertical, create another Pattern Fill layer, fill with **Wow-New Acrylics Brush 2 Overlay**, and mask to taste.

7 Making final assessments. We decided at the end that the blue of the cushion was too strong and drew attention away from the cat. We targeted the "Paint" layer, then used Select > Color Range to select just the blue **7a**.▼ With our selection active, we added a Hue/Saturation layer at the top to reduce the blue color's saturation and to darken it slightly **7b**. 𝘞𝘰𝘸

7a

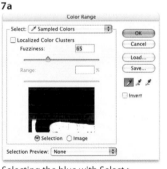

Selecting the blue with Select > Color Range

7b

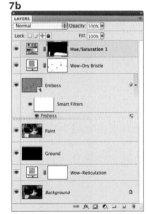

Adding a Hue/Saturation Adjustment layer to reduce saturation and luminance

FIND OUT MORE

▼ Making seamless patterns **page 560**

▼ Loading the Wow presets **page 4**

▼ Selecting with Color Range **page 51**

Brush Tips

Can't find the perfect brush for the job? Here's a method for making your own very simple brush tip and using it to make a Brush tool 🖌 preset. For more variation in the stroke, experiment with the Jitter settings in the various Brushes panel sections as you design the brush tip (steps 1–4). And if you have a pressure-sensitive tablet, try building in some Control settings that can take advantage of the stylus.

MAKING SEVERAL SIZES

When you make a brush tip, consider making a "matched set" in two or three sizes. Even if you don't need them now, having a complete set may come in handy in the future.

It's easy to enlarge or shrink a single brush tip as you paint (in the Brush Preset picker or with the square bracket keys — [and]), or in CS4 by right-Alt-clicking (Windows) or Ctrl-Option-clicking (Mac) as you paint. But when you do that, not only do you change the footprint size (which is what you want to happen), but if you enlarge the brush tip quite a bit, it can begin to look pixelated, and if you shrink it a lot, it can lose its bristle detail.

When you save the related brush tips, group them together in the panel, so you can easily cycle through them with the < and > keys.

It's easier to make three sizes of related brush tips all at once than to make one and then try to match it in a different size later.

1 Making a Footprint

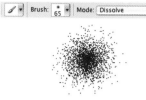

TO START A BRUSH from scratch, open a new Photoshop file with the default white *Background*. Choose the Brush tool 🖌 and one of the **soft round brush tip** presets (click the icon next to "Brush" in the Options bar to open the Brush Preset picker; we used the 65-pixel tip). Also in the Options bar set the Mode to **Dissolve**. As you'll see when you click in the working window, Dissolve mode turns the soft, semitransparent brush tip into a scattering of dots. These will become the bristles of your new brush tip. Click the Foreground color square in the Tools panel and click on a dark gray in the Color Picker. Then click once in the working window. Repeat the process for as many sizes of brush tips as you want to make; we made additional footprints with the 21-pixel tip and the 45-pixel tip.

2 Editing the Tip

"SOFTEN" THE FOOTPRINT (Filter > Blur > **Gaussian Blur**; we used a Radius of 0.5). To reshape the footprint, **remove some of the bristles** with the Eraser 🖌 — in the Options bar choose Brush for the Mode and choose a small brush tip (you can pop out the Brush Preset picker from the Eraser's Options bar). Try different Hardness and Opacity settings for the Eraser to vary the type of basic footprint you're making.

3 Capturing the Tip

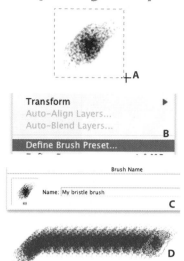

WHEN YOU'VE FINISHED designing your brush tip, **drag-select** the brush footprint with the Rectangular Marquee tool ⬚ **A**. Then choose Edit > **Define Brush Preset B**. In the Brush Name dialog box, give your creation a name **C**. The new brush tip will be added as the last one in the Brush Preset picker. **Deselect** (Ctrl/⌘-D).

Now if you **choose a painting tool**, such as the Brush 🖌, you can **access your new brush tip** from the presets picker in the Options bar or the Brushes panel, or by right-clicking/Ctrl-clicking in the working window. Click its name or thumbnail to choose it. **Choose a color** (one way is to click the Foreground swatch in the Tools panel and use the Color Picker). Change the Mode in the Options bar back to **Normal**, and paint to **test the stroke D**.

4 Refining the Stroke

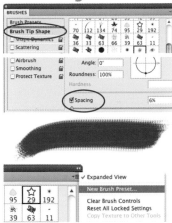

If the stroke isn't as smooth or brushlike as you want, open the Brushes panel (one way is to click the "Toggle the **Brushes** palette/panel" button 🗐 on the Options bar). Click **Brush Tip Shape** in the list on the left side of the panel. For a smoother stroke, **lower the Spacing** setting, but keep in mind that the lower the setting, the slower the brush will operate. This can cause a delay between when you paint the stroke and when it appears on-screen, which interferes with the "natural media" feel of painting. We settled on a setting of 6%.

To save the modified spacing as part of the brush tip, click the panel's menu button ▾≡ and choose **New Brush Preset** from the menu, give the preset a new name, and click "OK."

Now that you have one variation of your basic footprint, you might like to try some of the other sections of the Brushes panel. Rather than starting a new brush tip from scratch, vary the **Angle** and **Roundness** (in Brush Tip Shape) for a more calligraphic brush, or experiment with **Color Dynamics** or the **Airbrush** toggle. Be sure to save any result you like as a New Brush Preset.

5 Adding Texture

With built-in texture the stroke reveals the surface of the "canvas." Click on the word **Texture** in the Brushes panel's list of panels, and click the pattern swatch to open the Pattern picker. Click the picker's ⦿ button to access more pattern sets. We chose **Wow-Media Patterns** to replace the current patterns, and chose the **Wow-Canvas Texture 02** texture from the panel. (If you haven't yet loaded the Wow presets,▼ you won't see the Wow-Media Patterns in the panel's list of choices.)

Paint a stroke with the texture you've added. Then experiment in the Texture panel with the **Scale**, the "**Texture Each Tip**" toggle, and the **Mode** and **Depth** settings; we used a Scale of 50%, with "Texture Each Tip" turned off, Subtract for the Mode, and Depth set at 30%.

FIND OUT MORE

▼ Loading the Wow presets **page 4**

MAKING A "PICTURE" BRUSH

Photoshop's brush tips aren't limited to imitating traditional painting tools. You can make a custom tip that lays down multiples of a symbol or picture instead of a continuous painting stroke.

Photoshop's Scattered Maple Leaves brush tip distributes its symbols according to the settings in the **Scattering** section of the Brushes panel. Size Jitter, Angle Jitter, and Roundness **Jitter** settings in the **Shape Dynamics** section create the variation in size, orientation, and shape. **Hue Jitter** in the **Color Dynamics** section creates the color variation.

For a "dotted line" brush, we used the Brush tool 🖉 and a hard round brush tip chosen from the Brush Preset picker. In the Brush Tip Shape section of the Brushes panel we set **Spacing** to 200%. We painted on a transparent layer and applied **Wow-Gold** from the **Wow-Metal Styles** to the layer.▼

To paint a trail of arrowheads, we used Photoshop's **Custom Shape** tool 🔊, first clicking the "Fill pixels" button in the Options bar, to make a mark on the *Background*. We drag-selected the mark with the Rectangular Marquee ⬚ and chose Edit > Define Brush Preset. In the Brushes panel we set Spacing at 120%, and in the **Shape Dynamics** panel we chose **Direction** for **Angle Control** so the arrows would point in the direction of the stroke. We painted on a transparent layer and applied **Wow-Clear Red** from the **Wow-Plastic Styles.**

FIND OUT MORE

▼ Using Layer Styles **page 80**

6 Saving Brush Tips

A

B

To PERMANENTLY PRESERVE a brush tip as part of a set (or library) of brush tips that you can choose and reload later, you have two options:

- **To save a set of all** of the brush tips currently in the Brush Preset picker, choose Save Brushes from the Brushes panel's menu ▾☰ and give the set a new name if you like. Click "Save" to complete the process. To make the brush tips easy to find and load later, save the set in Photoshop's Brushes folder **A** so its name will be listed in the Brushes panel menu.

- **To save only some** of the brush tips that are currently in the Brushes panel, choose Brush Presets from the list on the left of the Brushes panel, then click the panel's ▾☰ button and choose Preset Manager from the menu. In the Preset Manager dialog **B**, Shift-select or Ctrl/⌘-select any brush tips you want to save as part of the set, and click Save Set; give the set a name, and click "OK."
Note: To save time, if you want to save more of the brush tips in the current set than you want to delete, select the few you want to delete, click the "Delete" button, and then Select All of the remaining ones (Ctrl/⌘-A) and click "Save Set."

7 Saving Tool Presets

A **TOOL PRESET** for a painting or cloning tool can include other characteristics besides the brush tip. As an example, we can save the brush tip we built in steps 1 through 5 in a Brush tool ✎ preset.

With the Brush tool chosen, make choices in the Options bar for the default Mode, Opacity, and Flow, and set the Airbrush toggle ✈ on or off, testing the stroke as you experiment. We reduced the Flow to 40% to show the bristle marks and turned on the Airbrush feature so paint could build up.

When you have a tool you want to save, click the icon at the far left end of the Options bar to open the **Tool Preset picker**, as shown above. Click the "Create new tool preset" button 🗋 and give the preset a name; if you want to "preload" your Brush with the Foreground color, use the checkbox to turn on that feature. The current Foreground color will be built into the tool. (The Background color will also be included if your brush tip uses Foreground/Background Jitter.) When you click "OK," the new preset will appear in the Tool Preset picker, alphabetically by name. To save a set of custom tools permanently, use the **Preset Manager** as in step 6, but choose Tools instead of Brushes.

Open a copy of an image and try out other tools that use brush tips. If your new brush tip makes an interesting Clone Stamp 🖈 or Eraser ✐, for instance, save it as a preset for that tool also.

To save a customized set of colors — perhaps for a series of related paintings or illustrations — open the Swatches panel (Window > Swatches) and clear out the colors you don't want: Hold down the Alt/Option key to bring up the Scissors cursor, and click on each unwanted swatch.

To add a swatch, choose a color:

- Choose the Eyedropper tool 🖋 and click to sample a color from any open Photoshop file.

- Or click the Foreground swatch in the Tools panel and choose from the Color Picker.

- Or use the Color panel (Window > Color) to mix a color with the sliders or sample from the spectrum bar.

After choosing a color, add it to the Swatches by moving the cursor into the empty space beyond the last swatch in the panel (the cursor will turn into a Paint Bucket ⬛). Click to "pour" a new swatch (or Alt/Option-click to skip the naming dialog box).

With CS4's kuler panel (Window > Extensions > Kuler) you can add the swatches of a color theme to the Swatches panel (see page 172).

When you've added all the colors you want, save the custom Swatches set: Click the ▾☰ button and and choose Save Swatches from the menu.

Cher Threinen-Pendarvis started with Photoshop's default Swatches panel and deleted all swatches except black, white, and several grays. To build her custom set of colors, she sampled from a color-enhanced photo reference (shown on page 388).

Pattern Stamp Watercolors

YOU'LL FIND THE FILES

in Wow Project Files > Chapter 6 >
Pattern Stamp Watercolors:

- Pattern Stamp Painting-Before.psd
  (to start)
- Wow-PS Watercolor.tpl
  (a Tools presets file)
- Wow-Texture 01.asl
  (a Styles presets file)
- Pattern Stamp Painting-After.psd
  (to compare)

OPEN THESE PANELS

(from the Window menu, for instance):

- Tools • Layers • Styles

OVERVIEW

Prepare a photo for cloning by
exaggerating the color • Define the image
as a source pattern for painting with
the Pattern Stamp 🖐 • Create a "canvas"
surface • Add a transparent layer and paint
on it • Enhance the painting with a Layer
Style and the Photocopy filter

1a

The original "before"
image

1b

The image was straight-
ened (Ctrl/⌘-T) ▼ and
then cropped a little on
the left, using the Rect-
angular Marquee ⌷
and the Image > Crop
command and cropped
again to add canvas.
This is **Pattern Stamp
Painting-Before.psd**.

FIND OUT MORE

▼ Transforming **page 67**

DONAL JOLLEY

WATERCOLOR IS A RICH MEDIUM with many techniques for
working with the paint. For instance, in some techniques, the
painter purposely leaves white space in the painting — by applying a resist, by painting carefully so that colors don't touch,
or by erasing or scratching off paint afterwards.

Thinking the project through. To turn a favorite photo into a
believable watercolor, we'll use the Pattern Stamp tool 🖐. One
of two "painterly" cloning tools, the Pattern Stamp provides
more control than the other cloner, the Art History Brush. With
specially designed watercolor presets for the Pattern Stamp, you
can paint stroke-by-stroke, pulling color, but not detail, from the
source image, and painting carefully to leave white space.

1 Preparing the photo. Choose the photo you want to turn into
a painting — use Don Jolley's **Pattern Stamp Painting-Before.psd**
from the Wow DVD or use an RGB photo file of your own **1a**. If

2a

Naming the pattern

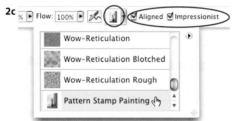

2b

Choosing the Pattern Stamp tool

2c

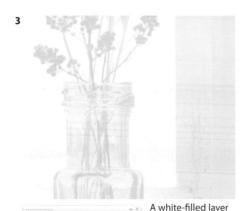

"Loading" the Pattern Stamp tool with the pattern

3

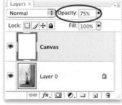

A white-filled layer is added to act as the canvas, and its Opacity is reduced. Naming the layers according to what they will hold can help organize the painting file. (Double-clicking a layer name in the Layers panel selects it so you can type a new name.)

you start with a photo of your own, here are some changes you might want to make, besides straightening and cropping:

- If you want bright colors in your painting, exaggerate the color and contrast in your photo. For instance, use a Hue/Saturation adjustment to increase Saturation. Or in CS4 use a Vibrance adjustment (Vibrance and Saturation both increase color intensity, but Vibrance protects already saturated colors from becoming overblown; it also protects skin tones).

- If you want your painting to have an "unfinished edges" look, add a white border: Type D for "default colors" to make white the Background color. Then choose Image > Canvas Size (or press Ctrl-Alt-C in Windows, or ⌘-Option-C on the Mac) and increase the Height and Width **1b**.

2 Loading "paint" into the brush. To make the photo the source for painting with the Pattern Stamp, define the entire image as a Pattern by choosing Edit > Define Pattern. In the Pattern Name dialog box, type in a name and click "OK" **2a**.

Now set up your new Pattern as the cloning source for the painting: Choose the Pattern Stamp 🎨 from the Tools panel (or type Shift-S; it shares a space with the Clone Stamp 🖊) **2b**. In the Pattern Stamp's Options bar, click the little arrow to the right of the Pattern swatch to open the Pattern picker; then find your new pattern's thumbnail as the last swatch in the picker, and click it **2c**. Also in the Options bar, make sure the **Aligned** and **Impressionist** options are both checked.

3 Making a "canvas" (or painting surface) layer. This step will add a surface layer above your image to make a foundation for your painting and to serve as a visual barrier between the photo and the painting layer, so you'll be able to see your brush strokes clearly as your painting develops. One way to add the canvas layer is to type D (for default colors), then add a new layer (Ctrl/⌘-Shift-N), and fill (Ctrl/⌘-Delete). When the new layer appears in the Layers panel, reduce its Opacity using the panel's Opacity slider, so you can see the photo through it **3**.

4 Preparing a paint layer and painting. Click the "Create a new layer" button 🗔 at the bottom of the Layers panel to add a transparent layer for painting. Then, with the Pattern Stamp 🎨 still chosen, at the left end of the Options bar, click the Tool Preset picker **4a** and double-click one of the **Wow-PS Watercolor presets** ("PS" stands for "Pattern Stamp"); we started with the **Medium** version of the tool. If you haven't yet loaded the **Wow-Pattern Stamp** presets, the **Wow-PS Watercolor** presets won't appear in the list of

4a

Choosing a **Wow-PS Watercolor** preset to start the painting

4b

The painting in progress, shown with the white layer's Opacity set at 100%

5a

Duplicating the paint layer increases the density of the paint.

FIND OUT MORE

▼ Loading the Wow presets
page 4

tools to choose; ▼ you can load just the **Wow-PS Watercolor** tools you need for this project by clicking the ⊙ button in the top right corner of the Picker, choosing Load Tool Presets, and navigating to the **Wow PS-Watercolor.tpl** file on the Wow DVD-ROM (in Wow Project Files > Chapter 6 > Pattern Stamp Watercolors).

Begin painting, keeping these pointers in mind:

- In general, start with a larger brush tip and then paint with smaller ones as you add finer details.

- Make brush strokes that follow the color and shape contours of the original. Just as in a real watercolor, if colors touch, the details will blur as the "paint" colors run together. If you need to keep some of the edges especially "crisp," you might paint that section on a separate layer.

- To imitate a single-color watercolor wash, use one continuous stroke over an area, rather than starting and stopping.

- If paint builds up too much, so the paper texture doesn't show as much as you'd like, try reducing the Flow in the Pattern Stamp's Options bar.

VARYING THE BRUSH SIZE

A pressure-sensitive tablet with a stylus definitely gives you a better feel and more options for controlling a brush than if you use a mouse. But even with a mouse, you can increase the brush size in steps (tap ⟨] ⟩) or decrease it (tap ⟨ [⟩). In CS4 with OpenGL, enlarge or shrink the brush tip by holding down the right mouse button and Alt key (Windows) or Ctrl-Option (Mac) and dragging right or left.

From time to time, temporarily increase the Opacity of the white canvas layer back to 100% to hide the photo completely so you can see how the painting is developing **4b**.

5 Enhancing the painting. When the painting is complete, you may want to try one of these techniques to further enhance the natural media effect:

- To increase the density of the color, target the paint layer by clicking its thumbnail in the Layers panel, and then duplicate it (Ctrl/⌘-J) **5a**. This extra layer will build up any strokes that are partially transparent, so it's especially effective for watercolor paintings. If the color is now too strong, you can reduce the Opacity of this top layer. (If you want still stronger color, use Ctrl/⌘-J again.) When you have the color intensity you want, you can merge the paint layers together (click and Ctrl/⌘-click thumbnails in the Layers panel to target the layers you want to merge, and press Ctrl/⌘-E).

5b

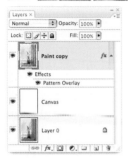

The **Wow-Texture 01*** Layer Style is applied to the merged paint layer. The Style uses Overlay mode to apply a canvas pattern. (To see the pattern that's at work here, in the Layers panel double-click the Pattern Overlay entry for your merged paint layer.)

- To make the paper texture more apparent, apply the **Wow-Texture 01*** Style to the paint layer **5b**. This Style uses the same tiling watercolor paper pattern that's built into the custom **Wow-PS Watercolor-Medium** tool preset (and all the other Wow Watercolor presets — it's a matched set!). If you've already loaded the Wow Styles, ▼ target the paint layer in the Layers panel, and in the Styles panel click the menu button ▾≡ in the top right corner; choose **Wow-Texture Styles** from the menu, and click on the **Wow-Texture 01*** Style in the panel. If you haven't yet loaded the **Wow-Texture Styles,** as an alternative you can load just the **Wow-Texture 01*** Style that you need for this project by clicking the ▾≡ button, choosing Load Styles, and navigating to the **Wow-Texture 01.asl** file on the Wow DVD-ROM.

FIND OUT MORE

▼ Loading the Wow presets **page 4**

- Make the edges of the colors darker and more distinct by running the Photocopy filter on a merged copy of the file. Target the top layer in the Layers panel, and then hold down Ctrl-Shift-Alt (Windows) or ⌘-Shift-Option (Mac) and type E. Choose Filter > Convert for Smart Filters **5c**, so you can keep the Photocopy filter "live"; that way, you can adjust it later, or simply go back and see what your filter settings were, in case you want to use the same settings as a starting point for applying the effect to another painting. Be sure the Foreground and Background colors are set to black and white (press D). Then choose Filter > Sketch > Photocopy; adjust the settings (for this painting, Detail was set at 10 and Darkness at 7) and click "OK." **5d**. In the blend mode list in the upper left corner of the Layers panel, choose Color Burn **5e**.

The final painting is shown at the top of page 403.

5c

Turning a merged copy of all the painting layers into a Smart Object in preparation for applying the Photocopy filter

5d

Running the Photocopy filter on the Smart Object layer produces dark edges.

5e

The Photocopy layer is put in Color Burn mode so the black increases color intensity and the paint pools at the edges of the colors.

Art History Pastels

PHOTOSHOP'S ART HISTORY BRUSH 𝒮 "looks at" an image and
lays down strokes — several with each click of the mouse — to
reproduce that image as a painting. Depending on the choices
you make in the Options bar, the result can be wildly abstract to
fairly photorealistic. With carefully chosen settings, you can turn
a photo into a "hand-crafted" painting or drawing — especially
if you add detailing with other painting tools.

Thinking the project through. Our approach to using the
Art History Brush involves enhancing the source photo, making
a History Snapshot, adding a color "paper" layer to frame the
painting and show through the brush marks, roughing in color,
and then painting more details. But painting is a fluid process.
Especially with an "automated" tool like the Art History Brush,
you may find you want to make mid-course corrections in your
approach. There are things you can do in your set-up to make
changes easier later.

1 Preparing the photo. Open Don Jolley's **Art History Pastels-
Before.psd** file from the Wow DVD-ROM, or use a photo of
your own, saved under a new name (File > Save As) to protect

1a

Original photo, 2745 pixels wide.

1b

Greens in nature are really very yellow. By altering the colors that make up Yellows in the image, reducing the amount of Magenta and increasing the amount of Yellow, Jolley was able to eliminate the reddish-brown tint that was dulling the greens and golds. He also adjusted the Blues and Cyans to make the sky and skirt colors more vivid.

1c

A border of dark "paper" color was added.

the original file **1a**. Adjust the colors to those you want to see in your painting. Jolley used a Selective Color Adjustment layer to make the grass more uniformly green, to increase the intensity of the blue, and to shift the color of the hair and the cornfield in the distance **1b**. ▼ Retouch the image if it needs it, removing anything you don't want. ▼

The plan for this "pastel sketch" is to start with "colored paper," which will provide contrast around the edges of the image and in the small spaces between marks made with the pastels. Jolley dragged with the Rectangular Marquee tool 🔲 to select most of the picture, leaving the outer edges unselected, and then chose Select > Inverse to switch the selection to the edges. With the Eyedropper tool 🖊 set to Sample All Layers, he clicked to sample a dark green from the trees, added a new layer above the Selective Color layer (Ctrl/⌘-Shift-N) and filled the selection with Green (Alt/Opt-Delete fills with the Foreground color). Then he deselected the border area (Ctrl/⌘-D) **1c**, **1d**.

2 Setting up the History source. Once your starting image looks the way you want it, take a **merged Snapshot** of the photo: On the History panel, click the menu button ▾≡ in the upper right corner to open the panel menu, and choose New Snapshot. In the New Snapshot dialog box **choose Merged Layers 2a**; you can also type in a name for the Snapshot; then click "OK."

When the new Snapshot's thumbnail appears in the top section of the History panel, click in the box to the left of it to make it the source for the painting you'll be doing later **2b**.

3 Setting up the paper and pastel layers. To give yourself maximum control and flexibility, you can set up a "Paper" layer filled with the color you want for your background and another separate layer to paint on. Begin in the Layers panel by Alt/Option-clicking the "Create a new layer" 🔲 button, naming

1d

Creating the border on a separate layer above the Adjustment layer gives you the freedom to make more color adjustments to the photo if you find you need them when you start painting (in step 4), without changing the border color. This is the Layers panel for **Art History Pastels-Before.psd**.

FIND OUT MORE

▼ Selective Color adjustments **page 253**

▼ Covering up unwanted elements
page 256

2a

Making a merged Snapshot

2b

Designating the new Snapshot as the source for painting. (Once you start painting, at step 5, you may find that you need to adjust the color of your source image in order to get the painted color you want. If so, you can make a new Snapshot from your adjusted image at that point, and target the new Snapshot in the History panel.)

3

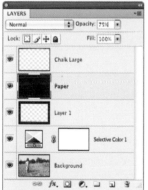

A contrasting "Paper" layer at 75% Opacity allows a view of the image beneath. The "Chalk Large" layer is added to start the painting.

the layer "Paper," and clicking "OK." Then press Alt-Backspace (Windows) or Option-Delete (Mac) to fill the layer with the same Foreground color you used to fill the outer-edges selection in step 1. In order to place your strokes intelligently, you'll need to be able to see through your "Paper" layer to the image below; so at the top of the Layers panel, reduce the layer Opacity (Jolley used 75%). Finally, make another new layer above the "Paper" layer for holding the first of the pastel markings **3**. Jolley named this layer "Chalk Large."

4 Choosing, operating, and modifying Art History presets.

Next choose the Art History Brush 🖌 (Shift-Y), which shares a space in the Tools panel with the History Brush, and pop out the Tool Preset picker by clicking the 🖌 button at the left end of the Options bar. Click the Tool Preset picker's ⊙ button to pop out a menu, and choose **Wow-Art History Brushes** if it's available. If you haven't loaded the Wow presets,▼ an alternative is to choose Load Tool Presets, navigate to the **Wow Chalks.tpl** file (supplied with the files for this project), and click the "Load" button. At this point you might want to read to the end of this step, exploring the Wow-AH Chalk presets, before you do any painting.

FIND OUT MORE

▼ Loading the Wow presets **page 4**

Choose Wow-AH Chalk-Large in the Tool Preset picker **4a**, and examine the settings in the Options bar:

- The blend **Mode** is set to Normal. Later, for detail strokes, you may want to change the mode to Lighten or Darken to add more dramatic highlights and shadows.

- **Opacity** is set at 100%. If you use a tablet and stylus, a light touch will produce thinner applications of pastels.

- The **Style** is set to Tight Short **4b**. The Style controls how closely the strokes follow the color contours in the source image (Tight or Loose) and also the length and shape of the strokes.

- The **Area** is set at 20 pixels (see 4b). At this small Area setting, each click of the Art History Brush will generate only a few

STYLE SETTINGS FOR THE ART HISTORY BRUSH

To imitate a painting technique with the Art History Brush 🖌, you might use Tight Long strokes for roughing in color and then switch to Tight Medium or Tight Short later to paint details. Applied overall, styles other than Tight Long, Tight Medium, and Tight Short can produce something that looks much more mechanical than a hand-painted effect.

4a

Jolley chose Wow-AH Chalk-Large in the Tool Presets picker.

4b

Wow-AH Chalk-Large paints with Tight Short strokes in a small Area.

4c

In the Shape Dynamics section of the Brushes panel, the top Control (it controls size) is set to Pen Pressure for the Wow-AH Chalk presets.

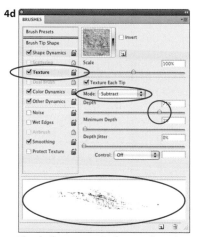

4d

The chalk-on-paper look comes from the pattern that's used as a Texture in Subtract mode.

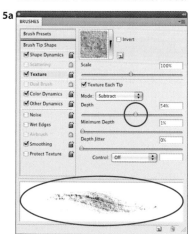

5a

Changing the Depth of the Texture to increase coverage for Jolley's pastels

quick, short strokes. The lower the setting, the more closely the strokes will follow the cursor as you move it, and the less delay there will be before the strokes appear on the screen.

- **Tolerance** is set at the default 0%, which lets you freely paint over strokes you've applied before.

The Wow-AH Chalk presets are set up for using a **pressure-sensitive tablet** for painting, which we highly recommend. The stylus controls are set in the expanded Brushes panel, which pops out if you click the 🔲 button on the Options bar.▼ On the left side of the Brushes panel, click on **Shape Dynamics** and you'll see that the Control for size (nearest the top of the panel) has been set to **Pen Pressure 4c**. With this setting, heavier pressure will produce both a larger brush tip and longer strokes.

FIND OUT MORE

▼ Setting Brush controls for pressure sensitivity
page 385

With the Brushes panel open as described above, Jolley prowled around in the settings to discover what makes the Wow Chalk presets work. He found the **Texture** option especially interesting (click on it on the left side of the Brushes panel) **4d**. Notice that a coarse pattern called "Wow-Watercolor Texture" has been loaded, and its Mode has been set to Subtract. The rough pattern was made by fine-tuning a scan of real watercolor paper. Combined with the Subtract setting, this pattern gives the tool its "dry medium over rough surface" look.

5 Painting. Before you start painting, take a look at "Art History Brush Tips" below. At this point, double-check the History panel to make sure the 🖌 icon appears to the left of the Snapshot you

---

ART HISTORY BRUSH TIPS

When you use the Art History Brush 🖌:

- There are at least three ways to operate the tool — you can click, hold, or drag: **Click** each time you want to apply a series of strokes. Or **hold** down the mouse button (or stylus) and watch the strokes pile up until you have the result you want. **Drag** the brush to set down several sets of strokes.

- In general, use **Tight** strokes (set in the Style section of the Options bar), for the reasons explained in the "Style Settings for the Art History Brush" tip on page 409.

- It's helpful to "anchor" your strokes by clicking the cursor in an area of color or contrast that has a clear edge, so the strokes will follow the detail that you want to emphasize.

- Each time you change the settings in the Options bar, try a quick experiment — click once with the cursor to see if you like the results. If not, undo (Ctrl/⌘-Z), change the settings, and try again.

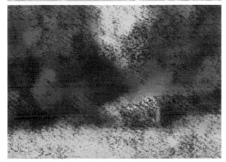

5b

Roughing in color with the **Wow-AH Chalk-Large 2.**
The strokes are shown alone on their transparent
layer (top) and over the "Paper" layer at 100%
Opacity.

5c

Adding detail with the **Wow-AH Chalk-Medium 2.**
The strokes are shown alone on their transparent
layer (top) and over the "Chalk Large" layer and the
"Paper" layer at 100% Opacity.

created in step 2. And check again that the empty painting layer
is targeted in the Layers panel (it's easy to accidentally start painting on the "Paper" layer if you've been adjusting its opacity).

As Jolley began to rough in color with the Wow-AH Chalk-Large
preset and his tablet, he realized that he wanted more coverage
from the Art History Brush to get the particular look he wanted;
this preset was showing a little too much of the paper for his taste.
So he made some adjustments: He changed the Style setting in
the Options bar to Tight Medium, which put down strokes more
quickly as he moved the cursor. And in the Texture section of
the Brushes panel **5a** he lowered the Depth setting from 75% to
54%. As he worked with his new settings, he realized he would
want to use this modified Art History Brush
again, so he saved the preset,▼ naming it
Wow-AH Chalk Large 2.

FIND OUT MORE

▼ Saving tool pre-
sets **page 402**

To get the kind of coverage found in the Chalk Large layer of
the final **Art History Pastels-After.psd** file, shown on page 407,
choose Wow-AH Chalk-Large 2 from the Tool presets panel
and begin painting loosely all over to rough in color, using a
fairly light touch if you use a stylus; to get the same result with
a mouse, try reducing the Opacity setting in the Options bar.
Now and then, check to see how your painting is progressing:
Activate the "Paper" layer (by clicking its thumbnail in the Layers panel) and restore the Opacity to 100%, to completely hide
the original photo **5b**; after you've had a look, set the Opacity
back to 75% or so.

Next, for maximum flexibility in case you later change your
mind about some of the strokes you're about to add, click the
thumbnail for your top layer and make a new layer above it
(Alt/Option-click the ▣ button) before you choose the Wow-
AH Chalk-Medium 2 from the Tool Preset picker, as in step 4.
(Jolley created this smaller preset by modifying the Wow-Art
History Chalk-Medium, this time changing only the pattern
used for the texture, again to provide more complete coverage.)
Use **Wow-Art History-Medium 2** to add detail **5c**. With a stylus,
use less pressure for finer, shorter strokes; with a mouse, vary
the Opacity setting in the Options bar.

For still finer detail, at the top of the stack add another new layer
(Alt/Option-click ▣) and paint with Wow-AH Chalk-Small. For
almost photorealistic detail (many small brush strokes that follow the History Snapshot faithfully), let the stylus tip just "feather
touch" — almost float above — the tablet. For fine-tuning that

5d

Jolley added final details with the **Wow-BT Chalk-Small** and a native Photoshop brush. The strokes on these two layers are shown alone (top) and in combination with all the other painted strokes over the "Paper" layer at 100% Opacity.

5e

This detail shows all the paint layers along with the partly transparent "Paper" layer (45% Opacity).

5f

All the paint layers, the "Paper" layer at 45% Opacity, and the source image showing through to fill in fine detail and create a "film" of pastels.

can't be finessed with the automated Art History Brush, don't forget to do some hand-detailing with the regular Brush tool ✎ on still another layer **5d**. Choose the Brush ✎ (Shift-B) in the Tools panel, and in the Tool Preset picker choose the Wow-BT Chalk-Small or Wow-BT Chalk-X Small ("BT" stands for "Brush Tool") to get the same "dry medium" look as the Wow-AH Chalk presets. Jolley used the Wow-BT Chalk Small, reducing the stroke size by using a light touch, and also one of the small soft Brush presets that ship with Photoshop.

When you've finished painting, restore the Opacity of the "Paper" layer to 100% to completely hide the original photo so you can check your painting. If you want to make changes, activate the appropriate "Chalk" layer, then choose the preset you used on that layer, and paint more strokes. Use the Eraser tool ✐ if you need to remove strokes. Jolley decided he liked the subtler effect of making the paper partly transparent, simulating a thin film of chalk, even in the "empty" spaces, so he reduced the Opacity of the "Paper" layer to 45% **5e**, to let the enhanced photo layer show through to combine with the paper color and create the "film" **5f**.

6 Finishing up. To reduce file size but still keep your painting somewhat "live" in case you want to make changes later, you can combine the three bottom layers (photo, Adjustment layer, and border): Ctrl/⌘-click the layer names and then press Ctrl/⌘-E, for Layer > Merge Layers **6**. Another file-size-reducing tactic would be to combine the paint into a single layer.

6

The Opacity of the "paper" layer is reduced, and the source image layers are combined.

Experimenting. Once you get the feel of creating with the Wow-AH Chalk presets, try (and perhaps modify) the other Wow-AH presets▼ for media effects ranging from Oils and Sponge to Stipple and Watercolors. *wow!*

FIND OUT MORE

▼ Examples of other Wow presets for the Art History Brush **page 414**

Wow Painting Tools

The **Wow-Tools** (in the PS Wow Presets folder on the DVD-ROM that comes with this book) include presets for three painting tools — the Brush ✐, Art History Brush ✐, and Pattern Stamp ✐. ▼ They share brush tip settings, so you can start a painting with the automated Art History Brush or Pattern Stamp and then hand-paint the finishing details with a small Brush. These Wow painting tools simulate chalk, dry brush, oil, pastel, sponge, stipple, and watercolor. Strokes for the seven kinds of Wow-Brush Tool presets (shown below) have pressure sensitivity built in. Strokes painted with mouse (top) and stylus are shown for comparison. Presets for each medium come in several sizes, just as traditional brushes do.

All of the Wow painting tool presets have surface texture built in, either to emphasize the character of the paint or to reveal the paper or canvas as the paint interacts with it. The **Wow-Grain & Texture Styles** (shown in Appendix C and in **"Quick 'Painting' with Wow Actions"** on page 415) are designed to emphasize paper or canvas texture, or to add to the paint — either the thick strokes of impasto or the pooling or clumping of watercolor pigment.

The layered file for "Wow Brush Tool Presets" at the right is provided on the Wow DVD-ROM so you can examine its structure. Its *Background* is the original photo, used for the experiments with the **Wow-Art History Brush** and **Wow-Pattern Stamp** presets shown on page 414.

FIND OUT MORE
▼ Loading the Wow presets **page 4**

Wow-BT Chalk   Wow-BT Dry Brush   Wow-BT Oil

Wow-BT Pastel   Wow-BT Sponge   Wow-BT Stipple

Wow-BT Watercolor

YOU CAN FIND THE FILE
in 🔵 > Wow Project Files > Chapter 6 > Exercising Wow Painting

Wow Brush Tool Presets

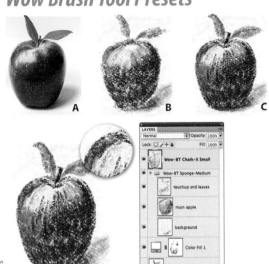

A   B   C

D

JHDAVIS

THE SEVEN KINDS OF WOW-ART MEDIA BRUSHES presets are for Photoshop's Brush tool ✐ ("BT" stands for "Brush tool"). With these tools you lay down strokes one by one, as you would with traditional artists' media.

One way to use these tools is to start with the original photo **A** and add a "canvas" layer above it (click the "Create new fill or adjustment layer" button ◐ at the bottom of the Layers panel, choose Solid Color, and pick the color you want for your canvas; we used white). Then add an empty layer for painting (click the "Create a new layer" button ◻ at the bottom of the panel). Temporarily turn off visibility for the canvas layer by clicking its 👁 icon so you can sample color from the photo (Alt/Option-click with the Brush), building a custom set of Swatches if you like. ▼ Make the canvas partially transparent for a "tracing paper" effect by toggling the 👁 on again and reducing the layer's Opacity. Rough-in the image with the largest brush tip that makes sense for your particular photo (here we used **Wow-BT Sponge-Medium**); restore the canvas layer to full opacity periodically to check your painting **B**. Add more layers for parts of the image you'd like to be able to control separately, such as the background or the smaller strokes **C** applied here with **Wow-BT Chalk-X Small**. For the finished painting, you can leave the canvas layer at full Opacity or reduce its Opacity to allow the original photo to contribute somewhat; or paint its layer mask with black or gray **D** to partially reveal the photo. ▼

FIND OUT MORE
▼ Making a custom set of Swatches **page 402**
▼ Painting layer masks **page 84**

🔵 **Wow Brush Painting.psd**

Wow Pattern Stamp Presets

Wow-PS Watercolor +
Wow-Texture 01*

Wow-PS Oil +
Wow-Texture 03*

Wow-PS Dry Brush +
Wow-Texture 02*

Wow-PS Chalk +
Wow-Texture 07*

WITH THE **WOW-PATTERN STAMP** PRESETS (they have "PS" in their names), you hand-paint each cloning stroke with the Pattern Stamp tool 🎨. The PS presets have the same brush tips as the corresponding Wow-Brush Tool presets on page 413, and the Impressionist mode (important for "clone painting") is included in the tool preset.

The samples above were painted using the techniques described in "Pattern Stamp Watercolors" on page 403. (Also, "Using the Wow Watercolor Presets," a tip on page 390, has pointers specifically for watercolor painting that apply to the Pattern Stamp as well as the Brush tool.) Using the method in "Pattern Stamp Watercolors," we captured the original photo as a pattern, and set up each sample's file with a "canvas" layer like the one described for "Wow Brush Tool Presets" on page 413 and with several painting layers that we added and then combined.

After painting we applied one of the **Wow-Texture Styles** to the combined paint layer by clicking the layer's thumbnail in the Layers panel, clicking the "Add a layer style" button *fx* at the bottom of the panel, and choosing the Style from the Wow-Texture Styles presets we had previously loaded.▼ (Examples of all of the Wow-Texture Styles can be seen in Appendix C.)

FIND OUT MORE

▼ Loading the Wow presets **page 4**

Wow Art History Brush Presets

Wow-AH Watercolor +
Wow-Texture 01*

Wow-AH Oil +
Wow-Texture 02*

Wow-AH Chalk +
Wow-Texture 07*

Wow-AH Stipple +
Wow-Texture 10*

Wow-AH Pastel +
Wow-Texture 01*

Wow-AH Sponge +
Wow-Texture 09*

THE **WOW-ART HISTORY BRUSH** PRESETS (with "AH" in their names) are set up to apply strokes that automatically follow the contrast and color features of the source image. Because the Art History Brush 🖌 lays down several strokes at once, it clones much faster than the Pattern Stamp, but the automation makes creative control of the Art History Brush more difficult. ("Art History Brush Tips" on page 410 has pointers for controlling the tool.)

We painted the samples above using the techniques described in "Art History Pastels" on page 407. Files were set up with a "canvas" layer like the one described for "Wow Brush Tool Presets" on page 413 and with several painting layers that we then combined and "styled" with one of the **Wow-Texture Styles** as described at the left.

"Painting" with Wow Actions

On the **Wow DVD-ROM** that comes with this book you'll find several Actions▼ that apply "painterly" treatments to photos, and several more that are designed to enhance paintings, whether done on the computer or painted in traditional media and photographed or scanned. Try out any of these Wow "miniprograms" and see what happens.

Open the Actions panel (Window > Actions). If you've loaded the Wow Actions, click the panel's menu button ▾☰ and choose the **Wow-Photo Enhance** set from the bottom of the panel's menu to add it to the panel. Do the same for the **Wow-Paint Enhance** set. If you *haven't* yet loaded the Wow Actions, you might want to do that now;▼ or simply click the Actions panel's ▾☰ button, choose Load Actions, and load the **Wow-Painting.atn** file provided with the files for this section.

To run an Action, click its name in the Actions panel and click the "Play selection" button ▶ at the bottom of the panel. (If your Actions panel is set to Button Mode in the panel's menu, simply click the Action's button to start running it.) **As the Action runs, it's important to read** and respond to the directions in any "Stop" message, and then click the "Continue" button in the dialog box.

YOU'LL FIND THE FILES
in > Wow Project Files >
Chapter 6 > Wow Paint Actions

FIND OUT MORE

▼ Working with Actions **page 120**

▼ Loading Wow presets **page 4**

Wow-Filtered Watercolor

Original photo

Wow-Watercolor 1

Wow-Watercolor 2

Wow-Watercolor + Linework (Threshold 215)

TRY THE **WOW-WATERCOLOR** ACTIONS to set the style for a series of illustrations or even to "save" a poorly taken photo.

Watercolor Actions.psd

Wow-Linework

Original photo

Wow-Linework Alone (Threshold 248)

Wow-Stippled Linework-Colored Anti-aliased (Threshold 130)

Wow-Stippled Linework-Gray (Threshold 130)

THE **WOW-LINEWORK** ACTIONS work especially well on photos with simple, easy-to-recognize forms. Each of these Actions includes a Stop so you can choose the setting for the Threshold command that determines how dense the lines or stippling will be. Each of the **Wow-Linework** Actions produces two line-work layers — one with and one without antialiasing.

Linework Actions.psd

ADDING A SIGNATURE

If you have a standard brush-stroke signature that you like to use on your digital paintings, you can store it as a Custom Shape preset. ▼ When you finish a painting, just use the Custom Shape tool ☁ to add it. In an "impasto" painting, where you want to emphasize the brush strokes by embossing, be sure to add the signature, then make any coloring or opacity changes you want to its layer, and merge it with the painting (press Ctrl/⌘-E for Layer > Merge Down) *before* you create the impasto layer. ▼

JHDAVIS

FIND OUT MORE
▼ Making a custom Shape preset **page 453**
▼ Adding an impasto layer **page 398**

Combining Effects

Wow-Linework Alone (Threshold 248) over original

CREATIVE POSSIBILITIES INCREASE as you layer one **Wow-Linework** treatment over another or over the original photo. Each Wow-Linework Action protects the original image by creating a duplicate layer or a separate file to work on, leaving the original intact. If the Action creates a separate file, you can combine treatments (or treatment and original) by Shift-dragging the processed layer from one file into the other file. (Using the Shift key aligns the two perfectly.) In the Layers panel, change the blend mode or Opacity of the imported layer.

Here we ran the **Wow-Linework Alone** Action. Since this Action creates a new layer for the line work rather than an entirely new file, when the Action was finished running, all we had to do to combine the antialiased line work with the original was to change the line-work layer's blend mode to Overlay, reduce its Opacity to 60%, and turn off visibility for the other line-work layer by clicking its 👁. (Try a line-work layer in Multiply mode for an ink-and-paint look; see page 415.)

Wow-Paint Enhance

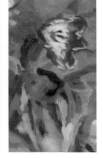

Original Art History Brush painting

Wow-Paint Edge Enhance Subtle

Wow-Paint Edge Enhance Extreme

Wow-Impasto Emboss Extreme

Wow-Impasto Emboss Subtle

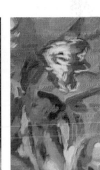

Wow Impasto Emboss Subtle w/Canvas

FOR THESE EXAMPLES the **Wow-Paint Enhance** Actions were run with their default settings on a painting done with the Art History Brush 𝒟, using a method like the one in "Exercising Wow Painting Tools" (page 413). If you find that the Action creates a darkening or embossing effect that's too strong, you can reduce it by lowering the Opacity of the enhancing layer.

The two **Wow-Paint Edge Enhance** Actions apply effects that are especially good for watercolors, like those in "Pattern Stamp Watercolors," step 5 on page 405, and in this chapter's "Gallery" on page 426.

Paint-Enhancing Actions.psd

Turpentine or Photoshop?

PAINTER DAREN BADER HAS TRANSLATED his painting techniques from oils and acrylics to Photoshop, but he hasn't put away his traditional brushes. Although for Daren, there's still nothing quite like holding a one-of-a-kind finished oil painting in his hands, he also enjoys the advantages that digital brushwork offers.

When he works on the computer, Daren prefers to display his developing painting either at its final printed dimensions (for small images) or at the largest size he can fit on-screen and still see the entire painting. He avoids zooming in, so he doesn't get lost in the details and end up painting with more precision than suits the style. He looks forward to the day when digital paintings are routinely displayed illuminated, just as they appear when the artist is painting them. In the meantime, you can see small versions of Daren's work illuminated at www.darenbader.com.

Daren finds that sometimes a combination of traditional painting and Photoshop techniques is the best way to get the job done.

When a painted book cover illustration needed revisions, the client emailed Daren a scan of the painting he had submitted; Daren opened the scan in Photoshop and made the required changes, then emailed it back. This eliminated the time that would have been spent sending the painting by courier both ways — not to mention the drying time for the paint!

Daren Bader's *Forest Rangers* was painted with traditional artists' tools and materials — in oils, directly over a pencil sketch on a treated cold press board.

Viking was painted entirely in Photoshop, as described on page 430.

This cover illustration for R. A. Salvatore's book *Paths of Darkness* was started in oils, then scanned and finished in Photoshop, which made the work go much faster. Daren modified Photoshop's Chalk brushes so his digital strokes would match the traditional ones.

You can see more of Daren Bader's paintings — oil, acrylic, and digital — reproduced in print in *The Art of Daren Bader*. If you don't look at the captions, you won't be able to tell which are paint and which are digital.

Mark Wainer created his "painterly" *Hamaroy Light-house* from his original digital capture. It was only after he had finalized the "painting" **A** that he decided to create an "improved" composition. With Photoshop CS4's Content-Aware Scale it was easy.

Wainer wanted to pull the red building on the right closer to the other buildings, confining all the "compression" to the area between the red building and the next one over. Since the buildings themselves, the boat, and the large rocks had expanses of nearly solid color, he would need to protect them in order to keep them from being scaled. He used the Rectangular Marquee [ ] to select the area between the buildings, then inverted the selection (Ctrl/⌘-Shift-I) to select everything *but* that area, and saved this selection as an alpha channel (Select > Save > Selection), naming the new channel "area to protect" **B**.

Before scaling the image, Wainer made a merged copy of the file (Image > Duplicate). As it does by default whenever a file is opened or created, Photoshop made a History Snapshot of the file **C**, which could serve as a source of "repair material" if needed after the scaling.

Wainer chose Edit > Content-Aware Scale. From the Options bar's Protect menu he chose his alpha channel **D,** and then he dragged the right side handle of the Transform frame inward until the buildings were as close as he wanted them. The white areas of the alpha channel protected most of the image, compressing only the area between buildings. After scaling, Wainer checked for any artifacts in the sky, water, and rocks caused by the compression **E**. With the ✄ symbol to the left of the "Duplicate file" thumbnail in the History panel, he then used the History Brush ✄ to smooth away the artifacts.

FIND OUT MORE

▼ Using History **page 30**

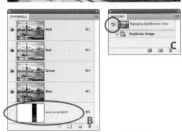

Inspired by the *art nouveau* painting and posters of Alfons Mucha and others, **Amanda Boucher** began her thoroughly modern and exuberant *Alicia* with a photograph **A**. She turned a copy of the digital photo to a light blue using a Hue/Saturation adjustment layer with the Colorize feature turned on, then printed it and used a Micron pen with black ink to draw on the print. She was careful to close the lines in areas she would fill with flat colors or patterns in Photoshop, so she would be able to select these areas efficiently.

Boucher scanned the drawing and then captured the black line work, without the blue, on a transparent layer of its own.▼ With a layer of white added below it in the layer

stack, she could use the line work as reference as she painted on transparent layers that she added between the line work and the white.

Using a tablet and stylus, she developed the portrait in Photoshop much as she does with traditional media, painting the image in sections, but also taking advantage of Photoshop's layers to build up the color. She painted with the Brush 🖌 and the Smudge tool 🖐,▼ using several brush tips to apply and blend the colors **B**. She used her original photo file for reference and to sample color (Alt/Option-clicking with any painting tool samples the color at the click-point).

As she worked, she could use Adjustment layers to experiment with color changes, overall or in selected areas. For the final painting she filled background areas with an intense red for contrast and excitement, and filled the flower shapes with blue and white. Then she used another layer to fill the flowers again with Photoshop's Strings pattern, putting the layer in Multiply mode at a lowered Opacity to blend the pattern with the flower color. (The Strings pattern can be found in the Patterns library, available from the pop-out menu of the Patterns panel anywhere patterns are used in Photoshop.) To select the areas to fill she Shift-clicked with the Magic Wand 🪄 with Contiguous turned on, to limit the selection, and Antialias turned off, to prevent partially selected pixels at the edges that wouldn't completely fill with color.

To soften the black line work in some areas, Boucher erased some parts of the lines and painted other parts with color **C** (clicking the ☒ button near the top of the Layers panel protects the layer's transparency, limiting color to already painted areas). Introducing another *art nouveau* element, she used the Pen tool ✒ to draw bold black-filled "outlines" on some edges.

ADVANTAGES OF FILL LAYERS

Depending on how you like to work in Photoshop, Fill layers may be perfect for trying out a range of options in developing artwork with solid colors, gradients, or patterns. First select the area you want to fill, and then add a Solid Color, Gradient, or Pattern Fill layer by clicking the "Create new fill or adjustment layer" button ◑ at the bottom of the Layers panel and choosing from the top of the pop-out list.

Here are some advantages of using a Fill layer rather than filling a selected area on a regular layer:

• **To choose a different fill,** you can simply double-click the Fill layer's thumbnail in the Layers panel; then choose a new color, gradient, or pattern.

• **To reposition a gradient or pattern** without leaving any unfilled space at the edges, **drag in the working window.**

• In CS3, but not in CS4, if you decide **to change the fill type** — from solid color to gradient, for instance — just choose **Layer > Change Layer Content** and choose the other kind of layer.

If you want to use a tool or filter that works only on a pixel-based layer, choose **Layer > Rasterize > Fill Content.** (After rasterizing, the layer no longer has its special Fill layer properties, of course.)

Bruce Dragoo created *Faru & Mom* (above) and *Sleeping* *(on the facing page)* as sketches, to develop the characters and an illustration style for a children's book. He started each of them with a sketch in graphite, his favorite medium, then scanned the sketch and added color and lighting in Photoshop.

He put the sketch layer in Multiply mode over a white-filled layer that would provide a base for viewing the developing color. He drew a path with the Pen tool ✎ ▽ to outline the combined shape formed by the characters in the sketch. He loaded the path as a selection, ▽ and used the Gradient tool ▢ to fill it with color on a layer between the sketch and the white base. ▽ The Pen path followed the combined shape of the animals established by the pencil sketch but allowed the freehand pencil lines at the edges to extend beyond the color to maintain the hand-drawn nature of the outer edge. Dragoo layered painted highlights (and in *Sleeping*, the color for the oxpecker's bill) above the gradient-filled shape.

Dragoo's use of gradients for backgrounds, lighting, and atmosphere is detailed on page 231. He built up the environment from layers of plants, each one painted and scaled to fit the illustration. ▽ In *Sleeping*, the foreground landscape was composed of three painted layers — a

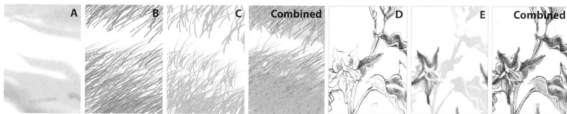

| A | B | C | Combined | D | E | Combined |

base layer of roughed-in color **A**, painted with the Brush tool ✏ with a soft tip, ▼ and two layers of grass painted with variations of Photoshop's Dune Grass brush tip. Dragoo customized Dune Grass to paint long, supple purple grass on one layer **B**, and drier, stiffer-looking grass on another **C**, with more variability in the size, angle, and color built into the brush tip. ▼

The large plant in the right foreground and the grass behind the

sleeping animals each began as a sketch in Multiply mode **D** over a painted layer **E**. Twelve other layers of painted and scaled plants were assembled to complete the scene.

When he works in Photoshop, Dragoo tries to stay in an intuitive, creative mode, and to avoid becoming absorbed in the technical aspects of the program. "The sketch is the source," he says. "I work fast to avoid getting lost in the technical detail."

FIND OUT MORE

▼ Drawing with the Pen tool ✎
page 454

▼ Loading a path as a selection
page 451

▼ Using the Gradient tool ▬ **page 174**

▼ Scaling layers **page 67**

▼ Setting Hardness for brush tips
page 71

▼ Customizing Dune Grass **page 88**

Mark Wainer creates limited-edition prints of his painterly street scenes, landscapes, and waterscapes developed from his own original photography. His goal is to simulate traditional artists' media so well that his images don't easily reveal their computer heritage. Shown here is ***Boats in Fog, Northhampton***.

Wainer made initial adjustments to tone and color in Camera Raw, ▼ then opened the image in Photoshop **A**. (Shift-clicking Camera Raw's "Open" button toggles between "Open Image," which opens the file as a standard *Background*, and "Open Object," which opens it as a Smart Object, maintaining a link back to Camera Raw as an option for further editing; Wainer used "Open Image.")

He added a Curves Adjustment layer by clicking on the ◕ button at the bottom of the Layers panel and choosing from the pop-up list. In the Curves dialog he reshaped the curve by clicking on it to add anchor points and moving these points to darken the shadows and increase contrast in the midtones, which held the detail that would become the brush strokes **B**, **C**, **D**.

Wainer's next step was retouching, removing elements from the photo that he didn't want to include in the painting. He used the Healing Brush 🩹 to hide small elements, sampling nearby areas by Alt/Option-clicking and painting over the features he wanted to hide. ▼ For larger elements he used the Clone Stamp 🧰 in the same way. ▼

Once he had the tone, color, and composition the way he wanted them, he used two filters to create the brush strokes. First he duplicated the adjusted and retouched image to a new layer (Ctrl/⌘-J), then applied the Topaz Simplify2 filter (www.topazlabs.com) **E**. One of the presets for Simplify mimics the effect created by the buZZ Simplifier filter, which Wainer also uses, but which is no longer updated or supported; he finds Topaz Simplify 2 an excellent replacement, and the filter's BuzSim preset a good starting

FIND OUT MORE

▼ Working with Camera Raw **page 140**

▼ Using the Healing Brush 🩹 **page 256**

▼ Using the Clone Stamp 🧰 **page 256**

point. The filter reduces the amount of detail in the image to produce "patches" of flat color.

Once he had run the filter, Wainer reduced the Opacity of the filtered layer to bring back as much of the original detail as he wanted **F**. He sometimes also applies a layer mask at this point to limit the amount of detail in different areas of the image. In this case he set the Opacity at 80% and did not use a mask.

Wainer then added a new layer that was a merged copy of the layered composite (Ctrl-Shift-Alt-E in Windows; ⌘-Shift-Option-E on the Mac) and "sharpened" the image, making edges more distinct, by applying the Dry Brush (Filter > Artistic > Dry Brush). For some images, Wainer further sharpens edges by applying Dry Brush more than once or by duplicating the image on a new layer and applying the High Pass filter (Filter > Other > High Pass), then changing the blend mode of this layer to Soft Light, which increases contrast in the midtones especially.▼

To complete the artwork, Wainer "burned in" some areas of the image by adding a Curves layer in Multiply mode **G**. The unadjusted Curves layer acts like a duplicate of the image below it; in Multiply mode it darkens the image. The black-filled "hide all" layer mask hides the effect of the Curves layer, but painting with white allows its effect to come through and darken the image. (To add an Adjustment layer with a black-filled layer mask, Alt/Option-click the ◑ button at the bottom of the Layers panel.)

A

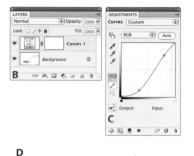

B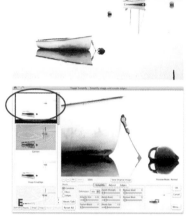

C

D

E

F

G

FIND OUT MORE

▼ Blend modes **page 181**

SMART THIRD-PARTY FILTERS

Some third-party (non-Adobe) filters, including Topaz Simplify 2, are adapted to work as Smart Filters in Photoshop. Their settings can remain "live" — if you turn a layer into a Smart Object and apply one of these filters, its name appears under the Smart Object's name in the Layers panel, and clicking on the name opens the filter dialog with the settings as you applied them. If you then change the settings, it's as if you returned the Smart Object layer to its prefiltered state, then applied the filter with your new settings. You can also change how the filtered version blends with the original — click the ⬛ icon and change the blend mode or opacity of the filtered version.

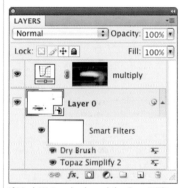

If Mark Wainer had used the Smart Filter approach to his *Boats in Fog, Northampton,* the Layers panel would have looked like this (the actual Layers panel is shown at the left). An advantage of using Smart Filters is that you can easily recall and modify the filter settings. But if you want to target filter effects with a layer mask, all the filters you apply are limited by the same mask. Wainer's method for being able to control blend mode and opacity, and for getting back to each prefiltered state was to duplicate the image as a new layer at each step before filtering. This also offered the option for separate masking for each filter, though he didn't do any masking in *Boats in Fog.*

A

B

C

D

For **Moorea Canoe**, **Jack Davis** started by creating a rough collage from his photos of the landscape, canoe, and clouds. He used Image > Adjustments > Hue/Saturation to intensify the colors, as shown in this detail **A**, and made the brightened image into a Pattern (Edit > Define Pattern). This Pattern would become the source for the cloned painting when Davis used the Pattern Stamp tool 🖌 and its Impressionist setting, chosen in the Options bar.

Working as described in "Pattern Stamp Watercolors" on page 403, Davis painted on a transparent layer, following the contours of the original collage below **B**.

To create the look of watercolor over an ink sketch, Davis duplicated his original collage layer and used Filter > Stylize > Find Edges, followed by Image > Adjustments > Threshold to create the "ink" **C**. He moved this layer above the completed painting layer and set its blend mode to Multiply **D**.

Davis then applied a Layer Style with a Pattern Overlay of "salt stain" (**Wow-Texture 09***; see Appendix C) to the finished paint layer to produce the final painting (opposite), and enhanced the details of the painting using the Photocopy filter (see page 406).

The **Wow-Linework Alone** Action (Wow Presets > Wow-Photoshop Actions > **Wow-Paint Enhance Actions.atn**) creates an "ink drawing" from a photo, as shown in **C** above.

BERT MONROY

Master of photorealism **Bert Monroy** takes neon signage way beyond the "Quick Neon Type" shown on page 551. Bert builds his neon tubes for street scenes such as *Spenger's* by first drawing a path with the Pen tool ◊ and then stroking it several times with the Brush ✐, adding a new layer for each kind of stroke. After drawing a path and choosing the Brush and the Foreground color he wants, Monroy turns to the Paths panel and clicks the "Stroke path with brush" button ○ at the bottom. ▼

Typically, he lays the strokes down in this order, from bottom to top:

Using a soft round brush tip, he paints an outer glow, usually in white or a lightened version of the color of the background behind the neon.

The tube itself is painted in three layers. He starts with a relatively intense color, painted with a hard, round brush tip, then applies a lighter, narrower version with a softer, smaller brush tip and finally an even thinner white stroke, also with a soft, smaller brush.

For the neon light that reflects off the sign base, he duplicates the layer that has the colorful stroke that defines the neon tubing, puts the new layer in Hard Light mode, ▼ drags its thumbnail in the Layers panel to a position below the tubing but above the sign base, and blurs the new layer (Filter > Blur > Gaussian Blur). He uses the Move tool ▶♦ to offset the reflection behind the neon. Using this "layer sandwich" approach, he can bring down the Fill Opacity of the individual colors or erase color at key spots as he builds up dimension and lighting for the tubes.

Monroy has developed a set of custom "grunge" presets for the Brush tool, for adding "a light touch of urban grime" to his neon. Working in the Brushes panel, he incorporates Jitter in the Size, Scatter, and Angle settings for the grunge brush tips he builds. He also uses the Brushes panel's Dual Brush option to mask the grunge inside a hard, round brush tip, adjusted to the same size as the brush he used to define the tubes. When he uses a grunge brush to stroke a path, the grunge marks build up somewhat randomly along the tubes because of the Jitter settings, but the Dual Brush keeps them from extending beyond the edges of the neon.

In the pink neon shown below, the colored reflection was made by duplicating the layer with the red stroke that defined the neon tube, blurring the duplicate in Hard Light mode, offsetting the layer, and reducing its opacity.

For the white neon Monroy used a soft stroke of light blue for the outer glow, a hard-edged stroke of darker blue to define the tube, and a lighter blue and white for the interior. To capture the wear and tear on the tubes, he partially erased the white and light blue layers and also added grime with one of his "grunge" brushes.

To add the black masking on the tubes (in the "G" below, for instance), Monroy loaded the tube outline as a selection by Ctrl/⌘-clicking in the Layers panel on the thumbnail for the layer with the hard-edged bright green stroke. He added a new layer and used the Brush with black paint to add the black material and then used the Eraser ⬘ to wear it away in some places.

FIND OUT MORE

▼ Drawing & stroking paths
pages 454 & 457

▼ Blend modes **page 181**

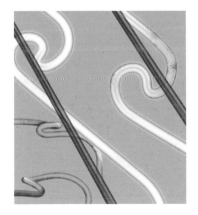

DAREN BADER

Daren Bader starts his digital paintings, such as *Viking* (above), by making a pencil sketch and scanning it. Then he starts a new file at the size and resolution he needs for the final painting. With the scan file also open in Photoshop, he drags-and-drops the scan into the new file to serve as a reference. He enlarges the scan to fit, using Edit > Free Transform and Shift-dragging a corner handle of the Transform box to keep the drawing in proportion.

If necessary, Bader uses an Adjustment layer to get sharp black line work (page 105 describes a method). He puts the scan layer in Multiply mode, which makes the white appear clear, so he can see both the line work and the painting he will be doing on layers below.

Bader adds one transparent layer at a time, painting on it with the Brush tool with "chalky" brush tips like the default Chalk brushes shown at the right. He sets his controls so the stylus pressure he applies on his Wacom Intuos tablet controls the Opacity and Size of the strokes.

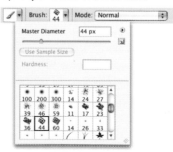

DAREN BADER / © KOSMOS GAMES

DAREN BADER / © KOSMOS GAMES

DAREN BADER / © KOSMOS GAMES

Daren Bader often starts a new illustration by sampling color from a previous one. He then mixes more colors by using the Brush tool ✎ to overlay low-opacity strokes of color on top of existing color, Alt/Option-clicking to sample from the color this produces.

He starts by roughing in color and then adds detail, checking his progress by clicking the 👁 icon to turn visibility on and off for the layer he's currently painting. When he's pleased with his progress on a layer, he merges it into the earlier work (Ctrl/⌘-E, for Layer > Merge Down). On the other hand, if he finds that the painting on the most recent layer has taken off in a direction he doesn't like, it's easy to delete it (by dragging it to the "Delete layer" button 🗑 at the bottom of the Layers panel). "I sometimes have the same epiphany when I'm working with oils or acrylics," says Bader, "but with paint, it's harder to fix," because repainting can "muddy" the colors.

By merging layers as he works, Bader reduces file size, which keeps brush performance high so his painting flows freely. Eventually he paints on and merges the scanned sketch, but

not before he duplicates the original sketch layer (Ctrl/⌘-J) for safekeeping, hiding the layer by turning off its visibility.

Bader keeps the entire image in view on-screen as he works. He zooms in only when he needs to add detail to draw attention to something, as shown below in a detail from **Helitos** (above left), one of a series of 32 illustrations Bader was commissioned to paint for a deck of cards for a fantasy game.

FIT ON-SCREEN

To size an image so it will fit, as large as it can, on your computer screen, press Ctrl/⌘-0 (that's the number zero).

For this series Bader was given a template for the card layout that showed the location and dimensions of the text boxes. He dragged this layer into each of his painting files and put it in Multiply mode so he could see the "live" and "dead" space as he developed his illustration.

To draw the first of the tattoos, seen here in **Kabukat** (above center) and **Silentosol** as well as *Helitos,* he set up a separate layer and used the Pencil tool ✏ so he could draw quickly. Then he blurred the layer a little to smooth the edges (Filter > Blur > Gaussian Blur). He worked out the blend mode and Opacity for the tattoo layer that made a perfect blend of the tattoo's color with the shading on the skin (Hard Light at 83%). He could then drag-and-drop an existing tattoo layer into a new illustration file, select the contents of the layer (Ctrl/⌘-A), press the Delete key to remove the old tattoo, and paint a new tattoo on this layer with the blend mode and opacity already set up.

DEEANNE EDWARDS

For her **Marine Life Impressions**, which are artistically re-created in Photoshop from her underwater photos, **Deeanne Edwards** starts by "cleaning up any messy, confusing background." To do this she often selects and darkens the background as she did for *Moray Eel, Baja California, Mexico* (the original is shown below), or she selects and blurs it.▼

Edwards then uses a combination of filters to posterize the image, simplifying it to a few colors, and to add "ink" lines. She finds that the Cutout, Dry Brush, Ink Outlines, and Poster Edges filters work especially well to get the effect she wants.

Any of the filters Edwards uses can be applied as Smart Filters by targeting the image layer in the Layers panel, choosing Filter > Convert for Smart Filters, and then choosing Filter > Filter Gallery; in the Filter Gallery dialog, click the "New effect layer" button 🔲 in the bottom right corner of the Filter Gallery dialog box **A**, and choose from the pop-up alphabetical list of filters (located below the "Cancel" button) **B**.

To arrive at the combination used for the portraits shown on the facing page, Edwards applied the Cutout filter first, then clicked the 🔲 button again and chose Poster Edges. With the two "effects layers" listed at the bottom right corner of the dialog box **C**, she could click the name of either one and change its settings, thus working with the two filters interactively to arrive at the look she

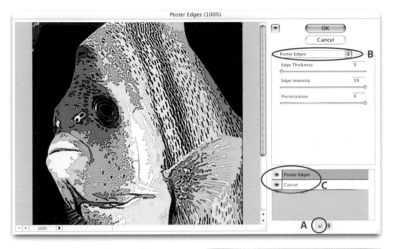

Poster Edges (100%)

wanted. When the Filter Gallery is applied as a Smart Filter, it can be re-opened (by double-clicking its entry in the Layers panel), and its settings can be interactively readjusted if you want to change the look later.▼

FIND OUT MORE

▼ "Subduing" a background **page 262**

▼ Smart Filtering **page 72**

▼ "Subduing" a background **page 262**

▼ Smart Filtering **page 72**

A BIGGER PREVIEW

Clicking the 🔽 button at the top of the Filter Gallery dialog box toggles the sample thumbnails of filter effects on (so you can choose a filter by clicking one) or off (so you have more room for the preview).

THE "SMART FILTER GALLERY" AS A STARTING POINT

When you set out to create a coordinated series of stylized images using filters, as Deeanne Edwards did in her *Marine Life Impressions*, each image may require slightly different settings. But with the Filter Gallery applied as a Smart Filter, once you work out a filter treatment for one image, you have an easy-to-adapt "starting point" for others.

First apply the Filter Gallery to your first image as a Smart Filter (choose Filter > Convert for Smart Filters, and then Filter > Filter Gallery), and choose the filters in the Filter Gallery dialog and adjust their settings to suit. Then, in your new image file, target the image layer you want to filter (by clicking its thumbnail in the Layers panel) and turn it into a Smart Object (Filter > Convert for Smart Filters). Then drag-and-drop the Filter Gallery entry from your filtered file's Layers panel onto your new image file. The Filter Gallery settings will be applied instantly, and you can then double-click the Filter Gallery entry in the new file's Layers panel to open the Filter Gallery dialog, where you can "tweak" the settings to suit your new image.

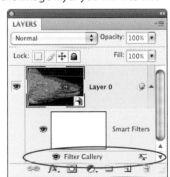

Type & Vector Graphics

7

Type
Shape
Pixels

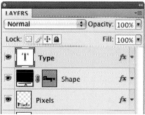

Photoshop's type and vector-based graphics are resolution-independent. When printed, they can produce smooth outlines, no matter what the native resolution of the image file. In this demo illustration the resolution of the file was set very low, at 38 pixels/inch, to produce exaggerated pixelation in the image. Type was set on three layers. The "Type" layer was left as it was (live type), the "Shape" layer was converted from type to Shapes, and the "Pixels" layer was rasterized (converted to pixels). The file was saved in Photoshop PDF format. In print, the "Pixels" layer shows the stairstepped edges we would expect at this resolution. But the outlines of the "Type" and "Shape" layers are smooth. The interior effects of the Layer Style, which provide the color and pattern here, also conform to these smooth edges. But the pixel-based pattern and drop shadow built into the Style are coarse, produced at the file's native 38 pixels/inch.

PHOTOSHOP HAS AN IMPRESSIVE ARRAY of typesetting and vector-based drawing capabilities. They rival some of the best features of PostScript drawing and page-layout programs, such as Adobe Illustrator and Adobe InDesign. Type and vector-based graphics can be scaled, rotated, and otherwise manipulated without any "softening" or deterioration of edges. With Photoshop you can produce:

- **Type** (with spell-checking and advanced spacing and formatting controls) that can be set **on** or **inside a** *path* (defined next). Type can remain "live," editable, and crisp-edged all the way to the output device.

- **Paths**, which are resolution-independent curves or outlines that aren't necessarily associated with any particular layer in a file. They can be stored and activated for making selections, for serving as a baseline or an enclosure for type, or for silhouetting when a file is output.

- **Vector masks** for sharp-edged silhouetting of individual layers or Groups. ▼

- Vector-based **Shape layers**, which are layers of color, each with a vector mask that controls where the color is revealed.

Vector-based type and graphics are efficient (you can easily reshape them) and economical (they add less to file size than pixel-based layers do). This chapter tells how to use Photoshop's "vector power." It also suggests when it's better to rely instead on dedicated PostScript-based illustration programs such as Adobe Illustrator, and how to move your work smoothly between Illustrator and Photoshop.

FIND OUT MORE

▼ Masks **page 61**

▼ Groups **page 583**

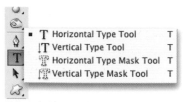

Although there are four Type tools, most type is set with the Horizontal Type tool **T**. In most instances it's more efficient to use the "live" Type tools and then make any necessary masks from the type itself, than to use the Type Mask tools.

You can use a path as a baseline for type. Center-aligned type (shown here) spreads out in both directions from the point where you first click on the path.

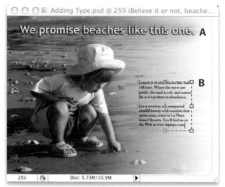

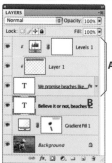

The type in a live type layer can be "filled" with an image and still maintain its editability. This can be done with a clipping group **A**, as in this developing layout. The headline was set as point type, but the body copy **B** was set as paragraph type to fit within a defined space.

TYPE

Photoshop uses a sophisticated type engine, with access to the special features of Open Type (fonts that use a single font file for both Windows and Mac and that provide advanced typographic controls such as automatic substitution of special characters, or *glyphs*, such as ligatures). Because you can also set type on or inside a path, you can often do all the typesetting you need for an image-based single-page document right in Photoshop.

Under most conditions, you can maintain type as "live" (editable) and still be able to control its color, opacity, special effects, and how it blends with other layers in the file. For instance, you can add special effects with Layer Styles and Warp effects. And images can be masked inside of type by using a clipping group ▼ with the type as the base layer.

FIND OUT MORE

▼ Clipping groups **page 65**

Photoshop has four **Type tools**, as shown at top left, but for most jobs the **Horizontal Type tool** (the default **T** in the Tools panel) is the one to use. When we refer to "the Type tool," that's the one we mean. The **Vertical Type tool** works like the Horizontal one, but by default it stacks the characters in a column instead of stringing them out horizontally.

Starting Out

To cover the basics of type, we'll start with a quick "executive summary" of working with type, and then move on to specific type controls. It's rare to set type perfectly on the first try, so we'll then cover how to move type exactly where you want it to be, and how to fit it to the space available. Because type-on-a-path requires specialized ways of working, it's treated separately, starting on page 442. Next we'll take a quick look at how to come back and edit type later. We'll look at scaling type judiciously or warping it for special effects, and finally we'll consider when and how to work with type as a Smart Object.

Here's a quick summary of how to work with type:

- **To add your first type** to a Photoshop file, all you need to do is to choose the Type tool **T** (type Shift-T to choose it), click or drag in the working window, and begin typing. If you **click** (rather than drag) the type will be *point type* — it will continue in a single line unless you tell it to start a new line (the tip "Multi-Line Point Type" on page 437 tells how to do this). If you **drag** with the Type tool instead of clicking, Photoshop will set up a rectangular bounding box, and when you type, the text will automatically "wrap" to start a new line

Type-inside-a-path is a special kind of paragraph type. When a closed path is active and you move the Type tool's cursor inside the path, it becomes the type-inside-a-path cursor shown here. Any typing you do now will be paragraph type that uses the path as a bounding box. This makes it possible to constrain the type inside spaces that aren't necessarily rectangular.

MULTI-LINE POINT TYPE

To set type on several lines, without being constrained by a bounding box, you can use point type. Start a **new paragraph** with the **Enter/Return** key, or a **new line** with **Shift-Enter/Return**.

• A **new line** is simply that. The cursor moves into position to start another line of type. Photoshop uses the current alignment, (left, right, or center, set in the Options bar or Paragraph panel) and the current leading (space between lines, set in the Character panel).

• A **new paragraph** also starts a new line, but in addition to the current alignment and leading, there may be additional space before the new paragraph, or the first line may be indented. These paragraph characteristics are established in the Paragraph panel.

CHOOSING FONTS

Here are two quick ways to try out fonts. Choose the type tool T (Shift-T); then:

• To **cycle** up or down through the list, trying out different fonts, first drag-select your type, then click in the "Set the font family" field in the Options bar and use the ↑ and ↓ arrow keys. Adding the Shift key gets the first and last fonts in the list.

• To quickly get to the part of the list where a **particular font** is found, click in the "Set the font family" field in the Options bar and start typing the name of the font you want.

each time it encounters the edge of the box; this automatically wrapping text is called **paragraph type**.

Point type is ideal for headlines and labels. It also works well for several lines of type when you want to control exactly where the lines break or you don't want to be constrained by operating within a bounding box. **Paragraph type** is great for fitting type within a set space, because you can establish the bounding box first to exactly fit the space available, and then type into it.

• **Type specifications** — such as **font**, **size**, **alignment**, and a number of **spacing** characteristics — are set in the Options bar, Character panel, and Paragraph panel, shown on pages 440 and 441. You can set the specifications as soon as you choose the Type tool — before you click or drag to begin typing — or you can type first and *then* set the specs. "The Scope of Your Settings" (below) tells how to apply type specs to just *some* of the type on a layer or to *all* of it.

THE SCOPE OF YOUR SETTINGS

The settings you choose in the Options bar or in the Character or Paragraph panel can be applied to selected characters, to a whole type layer, or even to more than one layer. In each case, you start by targeting the type layer (clicking once on its name in the Layers panel). Then:

• **To affect just *new* type** that you will add to your type layer, choose the Type tool T (Shift-T) and click to put the insertion point where you want it. Choose your settings, and type.

• **To change just *some* of the existing type** on a layer, choose the Type tool T and select the type you want to change — by drag-selecting, for example. Then change the settings.

• **To change *all* of the type on a layer**, choose the Type tool T, and *without clicking in the working window,* change the settings.

• **To change several type layers at once**, you can simply Shift-click or Ctrl/⌘-click the other type layers in the Layers panel to select them, choose the Type tool T, and choose your settings.

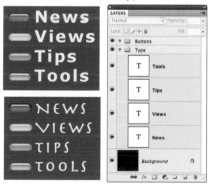

Using the color swatch in the Type tool's Options bar, you can change the color of type without changing the Foreground color in the Tools panel.

Right-clicking/Ctrl-clicking with the Type tool T when a type layer is active opens a context-sensitive menu that can save you a trip to the menu bar.

Paragraph type has more options for type specifications than point type does. These include **justification** (the ability to make both sides of the text block straight with the edges of the text box), **hyphenation** (whether and how words are broken at the end of a line in order to make the text fit within the box), **hanging punctuation** (punctuation marks such as quotes and commas can extend slightly outside the edges of the text block for better visual balance and alignment), and access to many more sophisticated controls with **Adobe Composer** (there's more about these controls on page 440).

• Whether you set point type or paragraph type, Photoshop will set up a **type layer**, where the type is isolated from other elements in the file, so it can be manipulated separately and it can remain "live" for editing later. When you've finished typing and you're ready **to get out of the type layer** and go on to something else, one way is to click the "Commit any current edits" button ✔ on the Options bar (or the "Cancel any current edits" ⊘ button). Typing Ctrl-Enter (Windows) or ⌘-Return (Mac) is the keyboard shortcut for "Commit"; pressing the Escape key is the equivalent of "Cancel."

• **To come back and edit your type later,** choose the appropriate Type tool, click once on your type layer's name in the Layers panel, and you're in! You can start selecting text and making changes as described in "Going Back To Edit Type" on page 444.

• It can be tricky **to start another, separate type layer** in a file that already has type in it, without accidentally clicking into an existing type layer. A foolproof way is to add a new transparent layer (Ctrl-Shift-Alt-N in Windows or ⌘-Shift-Option N on the Mac) and then type, to turn the new layer into a type layer.

Type Controls

Once you select a Type tool, all of Photoshop's **type controls** can be found on the Options bar, including access to the **Character panel** (for type controls on a character-by-character basis) and the **Paragraph panel** (for controls such as paragraph indents and extra space before and after paragraphs). "Type Options" on pages 440 and 441 shows these controls and tells what they do. "Exercising Type Layers" on page 464 covers kerning and other character-level controls, as well as keyboard shortcuts that can be used to speed up your work. Another timesaver is the **context-sensitive** menu that opens if you right-click/Ctrl-click in the working window when a type layer is active. The menu offers slightly different choices if the type cursor is active.

Scrubbing the "Select font size" icon to increase or decrease type size

Lorem ipsum dolor sit amet, consectetuer

Dragging a handle of the dotted-line text box for paragraph type will resize the box and redistribute the type accordingly. (Note the hanging punctuation used here, an option chosen in the Paragraph panel's fly-out menu.)

Roses are red and violets are blue. Sugar is sweet and so are you.

Roses are red and violets are blue. Sugar is sweet and so are you.

Whether paragraph type or type-inside-a-path is left-, right-, or center-aligned, it will start as close as it can to the top of the text box or closed path. If this creates an awkward break (top), you can move the type down by typing Enter/Return (to create an "empty" paragraph) and then "scrubbing" the icon for "Add space before paragraph" in the Paragraph panel.

Making Type Fit

To quickly and dynamically experiment with fitting point type or paragraph type into the space available, with the Type tool **T** chosen you can change the type's overall size by selecting all (Ctrl/⌘-A) and "scrubbing" the font size setting in the Options bar or Character panel (opened by clicking the ▤ near the right end of the Options bar). For other type-fitting settings, such as tracking (changing the letter spacing overall), use the scrubbers in the Character panel. Except as a last resort, avoid type-fitting by changing settings in the Character panel that actually distort the type itself, such as the height or width of the characters (see "Avoiding Type Distortion" on page 445 for the reasoning behind this advice).

Paragraph type offers more options for fitting type, one of which is enlarging the text bounding box. If you type more text than will fit in the text box you defined by dragging with the Type tool, Photoshop will "hold" the extra text and put an "x" in the lower right handle of the text box to alert you that there's more text stored. Dragging on any handle will reshape the box. As you enlarge the text box, the stored text appears inside it. If you don't have the option of stretching the bounding box because space for the text is limited, "Type-Fitting" on page 593 offers more suggestions for fitting paragraph type.

Fitting type that you've set **inside a path** works the same way as fitting paragraph type in general — you can grab a handle and drag to make more room so the additional type can appear, reshaping the path in the process.

Fitting **type-on-a-path** is covered on page 443.

Moving or Tilting Type

To move your entire setting of point type, paragraph type, or type-inside-a-path, make sure the type layer is targeted (click its thumbnail in the Layers panel) and that a Type tool is chosen (**T** or ↓**T**). Then click inside the type, hold down the Ctrl/⌘ key so the cursor becomes an arrowhead, rather than an I-beam, and drag. To tilt the type, again hold down the Ctrl/⌘ key, move the cursor outside the bounding box to get the curved-arrow cursor, and drag to rotate. *Caution:* With the Ctrl/⌘ key held down, **dragging a *handle*** of the solid-line bounding box will distort the type itself along with the bounding box (see "Avoiding Type Distortion" on page 445).

continued on page 442

TYPE OPTIONS

Photoshop's sophisticated controls for creating and editing text with the Type tool are spread among the Options bar, the Character and Paragraph panels, and several dialog boxes. The Options bar offers **font**, **size**, and **alignment** choices. More extensive options are offered in the Character and Paragraph panels (see below and on the facing page).

Clicking the **"Create warped text"** button opens a dialog box that lets you fit type inside one of 15 preset envelopes that you can choose from its Style menu and then modify.

The Type tool's **Options bar** offers the opportunity to set type **horizontally** or **vertically**, with a button that toggles between the Type tools.

Three **alignment options** are available in the Options bar for the Type and Type Mask tools.

Click the **color swatch** (here or in the Character panel) to set Type color independently of the Foreground color in the Tools panel.

The **"Toggle the character and paragraph panels"** button opens the Character and Paragraph panels.

The default Sharp **antialiasing** is a good option for most type; Crisp is a little less sharp. For small on-screen type, it may be better to choose Strong (to make the type heavier) or Smooth (to smooth it), or even None (when jagged edges are preferable to blurry edges, or if significant extra file size is added by the colors required for antialiasing).

The **"Cancel any current edits"** and **"Commit any current edits"** buttons are added to the Options bar as soon as you click with the Type tool in the working window. Clicking the "Cancel" button is equivalent to pressing Escape on the keyboard; it gets you out of typesetting without including any changes you've made in the current typing or editing session. The "Commit" button is equivalent to pressing Ctrl/⌘-Enter to accept the changes and exit typesetting.

Many of the options in the **Paragraph panel** (such as indents and spacing between paragraphs) are available only for paragraph type, including type-inside-a-path. But the **"Justify All"** button can also be useful for spacing type on a path, as shown on page 444.

Roman Hanging Punctuation (shown here in the bottom paragraph) lets opening or closing punctuation such as quotation marks, hyphens, and commas extend just beyond the limits of the text box. Since these marks are small, the type can look "indented" if they are aligned and justified with the bigger characters (as shown in the top paragraph).

"What she did," he said to his long-time friend.

"Yeah, I know," said his friend, putting his drink on the table.

In the **Justification** dialog box, acceptable ranges are set for the spacing in justified text. You can control letter and word spacing, and even the horizontal scaling of type. You can also specify what multiple of type size to use for **Auto leading**, which is chosen in the Character dialog box.

In the **Hyphenation** dialog you can choose whether to automatically hyphenate standard text and capitalized words. You can specify how many letters of a hyphenated word can be alone on a line, how many lines in sequence can end in hyphens (**Hyphen Limit**), and how far from the right margin a word can start and still be eligible to be hyphenated (**Hyphenation Zone**; this applies only to type that isn't justified and when the Single-line Composer is used).

The difference between **Single-line Composer** and **Every-line Composer** is clear in the paragraphs below. **Single-line** attempts to fix unattractive spacing by choosing the best spacing option for each line separately. It adjusts word spacing first, then hyphenation (if it's allowed, which it wasn't in this case), then letter spacing, with compressed spacing being preferable to expanded spacing. **Every-line Composer** can change spacing in the entire paragraph, if necessary, to solve a spacing problem in any one line. Keeping the spacing even throughout the paragraph is given the highest priority, which often makes it a better choice than Single-line.

Single-line
Pellentesque laoreet ligula sit amet eros. In neque mauris, sodales in, pharetra vel, condimentum sit amet, massa. Aenean lacinia ligula sit amet.

Every-line
Pellentesque laoreet ligula sit amet eros. In neque mauris, sodales in, pharetra vel, condimentum sit amet, massa. Aenean lacinia ligula sit amet.

The **Character panel** lets you **kern, track, adjust the baseline**, and set other type specifications character by character.

The **language** you choose determines which dictionary Photoshop relies on when you choose Edit > Check Spelling.

You can turn off **Fractional Widths** to ensure that characters set in small sizes for on-screen display don't run together.

With **System Layout** turned on you can see how your text will appear in an interface design displayed with your operating system's default text display. Turning on System Layout automatically sets antialiasing to None in the Options bar.

You can select a word or series of words that you don't want to break at the end of a line (**No Break**).

The **Reset Character** command quickly returns text formatting on the targeted layer to the program default. Part of the default is for the Foreground color to control the text color. If your Foreground color is green, for instance, Reset Character will make your text color green. Note that *paragraph* characteristics, such as justification, are not restored to the default with Reset Character but with the Reset Paragraph command in the Paragraph panel.

LOREM IPSUM DOLOR SIT AMET, CONSECTETUER

Lorem ipsum dolor sit amet, consectetuer

The **Change Text Orientation** option lets you switch between type set vertically and horizontally. **Standard Vertical Roman Alignment** stacks characters one above the other (**A**, below); turning it off gives a result like setting type horizontally and then rotating the entire setting 90° clockwise (**B**, below).

CHARACTER

Hypatia Sans ... | Light
10.5 pt | 11.5 pt
0
100% | 100%
Color:
English: USA | Crisp

Change Text Orientation
Standard Vertical Roman Alignment
OpenType ▶
Faux Bold
Faux Italic
All Caps
Small Caps
Superscript
Subscript
Underline
Strikethrough
✓ Fractional Widths
System Layout
No Break
Reset Character
Close
Close Tab Group

✓ Standard Ligatures
✓ Contextual Alternates
Discretionary Ligatures
Swash
Oldstyle
Stylistic Alternates
Titling Alternates
Ornaments
Ordinals
Fractions

VERTICAL TEXT B

VERTICAL TEXT A

Most of the styles in this part of the menu (also found as icons at the bottom of the Character panel) are generated by Photoshop rather than being part of the font. **Small Caps** will either use the small caps included with the font or generate them if the type designer didn't include them.

LOREM IPSUM dolor sit amet, consectetuer adipiscing elit.

Type that has **Faux Bold** applied can't be converted to Shapes or paths. But Faux Bold and **Faux Italic** can be useful when you plan to use Layer Styles or filters, rasterizing the type in the finished image. For most fonts that include real Bold and Italic styles, the Faux Bold and Faux Italic look different from these.

Bold   **Faux Bold**
Italic   *Faux Italic*

Not all **Open Type** fonts contain alternate or additional glyphs (characters). Although an Open Type font can include as many as 65,000 glyphs, many contain only the standard 256 characters they had in their PostScript or True Type format. To access any alternates in an Open Type font, simply choose from the fly-out menu. If any item on the list is grayed out, the current font doesn't include that alternate.

On the 3rd Tuesday of this month, the meeting of the Guard committee was held at 17548 Banyon Street. They agreed to fulfill their contract to keep Platform 9 3/4 a secret.

On the 3rd Tuesday of this month, the meeting of the Guard committee was held at 17548 Banyon Street. They agreed to fulfill their contract to keep Platform 9¾ a secret.

To draw an invisible path for type-on-a-path, you can use the Pen ✒ or one of the Shape tools, with the **Paths** option chosen in the Options bar.

When the type-on-a-path cursor appears, any typing you do will follow the path.

When this cursor appears, you can Ctrl/⌘-drag the beginning marker of type-on-a-path to reset the starting point and move the type along the path.

When this cursor appears, you can drag the end marker to reset the ending point and move the type along the path.

For center-aligned type, you can move the center point to move the type. One of the two end markers will also move.

The text overflow marker shows that there's more type being held. Move the marker outward from the type to reveal the extra.

Type-on-a-Path

Type-on-a-path is point type that uses a path as its baseline, rather than simply setting up horizontally (or vertically if you use the Vertical Type tool ⏷T). The path can be open (with two ends) or closed (continuous, with no loose ends). To keep the type easy to read, it's usually best to use paths and shapes that are gently curved and fairly simple.

To set type on a path, you can activate an existing path (by clicking its thumbnail in the Paths panel), or activate a Shape layer (by clicking its thumbnail in the Layers panel). Or draw a new path: For a **hand-drawn path**, select the Pen tool ✒; in the Options bar, click on the "Paths" button ▨, and begin drawing. For a **preset path (or shape)**, select any of the Shape tools (pressing Shift-U toggles through them); in the Options bar click on the "Paths" button ▨, and then draw your shape. ▼

FIND OUT MORE

▼ Using drawing tools **page 448**

Once you have a path, set your type specifications in the Options bar, including alignment. Then move the cursor onto the path until you see the angled path mark through the cursor ⌇ and click on the path — click where you want to **start your left-aligned type**, or where you want to **end your right-aligned type**, or where you want to **center your center-aligned type**.

When you click to begin putting type on a path, be patient. Photoshop may take a little while to display the flashing insertion cursor. A new type layer will be formed and will appear in the Layers panel. Along with the insertion cursor, two **end markers** — "x" and "o" — will appear on the path to mark the extremes of where the type can go. Photoshop does its best to put these points where you want them:

- For **left-aligned**, the "x" is where you click and the "o" is at the end of the path.

- For **right-aligned**, the "o" is where you clicked and the "x" is at the beginning of the path.

- **Center-aligned** is more interesting. First, you get an additional marker — a diamond (◇) to mark the center. Then, whichever end of the path is closer to where you clicked gets one of the end markers; the other end marker goes an *equal distance on the other side* of where you clicked — it has to, because otherwise your type wouldn't be centered around your center point.

When you start to type, the characters will start at the appropriate marker. If you type more than will fit between the end

When you use a Shape layer as a path for type, a new type layer is added and the separate Shape layer is also retained. To set type along opposite sides of a closed path, it's often more convenient to set the type on two different layers, as shown here. The title type was set with the Horizontal Type tool T and a negative baseline shift (set in the Character panel) to put the type below the path. The author's name was added with the Vertical Type tool ↓T.

CONTROLLING TYPE-ON-A-PATH

Especially on a closed path, it can be hard to figure out what's happening as you Ctrl/⌘-drag the Type cursor over an end marker and the type starts to disappear or flip around. This series of pictures may help you "decode" what's happening and fix it.

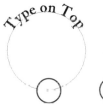

On a closed path the end markers overlap, so it's important to pay close attention to which marker you've selected.

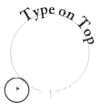

Splitting the end markers by dragging in the correct direction moves the type along the path.

If you accidentally cross the end markers over each other, the type will flip and may partly disappear. But you can fix it by dragging back again.

If you drag the cursor perpendicular to, or across, the path, the type flips upside down and backwards. Drag back across the path to right the type.

---

markers, Photoshop will "hold" the extra text, and a "+" inside the "o" end marker will show that there's more text waiting.

At any time you can move any of the markers to change the span the type can cover: With the Type tool active, click somewhere in the type (anywhere — it doesn't matter where you put the insertion point for this). Then hold down the Ctrl/⌘ key and "hover" the cursor over the marker until the cursor turns into an I-beam with one or two thick arrows — ⫟, ⫠, or ⫲; then drag in one direction or the other to move the marker along the path. A couple of warnings here:

- First, if Photoshop thinks that you're dragging the thick-arrowed cursor *perpendicular* to the path rather than along it (even though you may not think so), the type will jump to the other side of the path and flip upside down and backwards. To fix this, simply hover over a marker again to get the thick-arrowed cursor and drag back across to the other side of the path.

- Second, if at some point you change alignment by making another choice from the Options bar or Paragraph panel, *the end markers won't automatically move.* In many cases, you'll want to move them, as just described above, to work with the new alignment.

Fitting type-on-a-path. To adjust the size or tracking of type-on-a-path, you can use the same methods described for point, paragraph, and "in-path" type on page 439. But with type-on-a-path you also have another type-fitting option. If you click the ▯ button in the Options bar to open the Paragraph panel, you'll find that, way over on the right side, the "Justify all" button is active, which isn't true for other point type. If you click this button, Photoshop will spread your type from one end marker of the type-on-a-path to the other. If the text consists of a single word (no spaces between the letters), Photoshop increases letter spacing to spread out the characters. But if the text is more than one word, the type is justified by increasing the space *between words.* For more control, see the "Spreading Type Along a Path" tip on page 444.

To make more space for type along the path, you can move one or both end markers, as described earlier. Or tweak the path itself by choosing the Direct Selection tool ▹ and dragging one of the path's control points or segments.▼ (While you have the Direct Selection tool active, the thick-arrowed cursors — ⫟, ⫠, and ⫲ — will also be available. This means you don't have to switch to the

FIND OUT MORE

▼ Editing paths
page 455

When you set type along a path that has strong curves or angles, the type will almost always need *tracking* (adjusting space overall) or *kerning* (adjusting space between a pair of letters). Watch out for special type features that may interfere with these spacing adjustments.

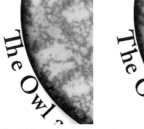

The "Th" pair didn't respond to tracking or kerning (left) because the Ligatures option was selected in the Character panel's menu. When this option was toggled off, tracking and kerning worked (right).

To spread type evenly from one end marker of the type-on-a-path to the other, type the entire text string as a single word — that is, with no spaces between words **A**. Then choose the "Justify All" alignment option from the Paragraph panel **B**. To insert the spaces between words but still keep the type spread out, click where a space should go, and in the Character panel set the kerning to a large positive value **C**, using additional kerning or tracking where needed.

A

B

C

Type tool to move the markers, but it also means you should be ready to deal with flipped type, as described on page 443.)

Moving or tilting type on a path. Besides sliding type along its path, you can also move the whole path and the type along with it. To move or tilt the path, use basically the same method as described for moving point type (page 439) — with the Type tool active, hold down the Ctrl/⌘ key, move the cursor far enough from a marker so it becomes an arrowhead rather than an I-beam, and drag.

Going Back To Edit Type

If you've moved on to something else and then find that you need to come back and make changes to the type you set earlier, simply click once on the type layer's name in the Layers panel, and choose the Type tool T (Shift-T). Now:

- **To change all the type on the layer,** *don't click or drag anywhere.* Without a cursor in the type, simply make changes to settings in the Options bar or Character and Paragraph panels.

- **To target your changes to specific characters or to refit, move, or tilt the type,** *first click in the type to get the insertion point, or drag to select some type,* and then make your changes.

If you have a lot of text, you may want to use Edit > **Find and Replace** to help you locate a misspelled company name, for instance; but don't expect a full-featured search-and-replace dialog box such as those in InDesign or Microsoft Word.

Resizing or Reshaping Type

We've covered the process of reshaping a text box or a path in "Making Type Fit" and "Type on a Path." It's also possible to

When the Type tool T is chosen and a type layer is targeted, the Check Spelling command is available in the Edit menu. It's a good idea to leave the **"Check all layers" option turned on** in the "Check Spelling" dialog box. Otherwise, Photoshop checks spelling only on the currently targeted layer. The setting is a persistent preference, and there's no warning if you haven't checked *all* your layers.

Because live type is vector-based, resizing won't affect the edge quality. But it *can* affect the type's aesthetics. That's why, unless you're going for a special distortion effect, it's important to get the size and spacing close to what you want using the settings in the Options bar and Character panel, rather than stretching or shrinking the characters themselves. For one thing, big changes in type size require adjustment in the spacing relationships between characters in order to look good. Also, drastically scaling a block of type horizontally or vertically to make it fit a certain space can differentially distort the thick and thin strokes, ruining the proportions designed into the characters.

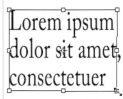

With the Type tool **T** chosen and the Ctrl/⌘ key held down, a solid-line box appears around the type. Dragging on any handle of the solid box not only resizes the box but also distorts the type.

Steven Gordon set four lines of left-justified point type with tight leading (little space between lines) and then used a Twist warp to make it flow (see the completed work on page 494).

resize or distort the type itself by using one of the Transform commands or the Warp Text function, as described next.

Transforming. Any time there's an insertion point in the type, all the point or paragraph type on a type layer can be **scaled**, **skewed**, **rotated**, or **flipped** by holding down the Ctrl/⌘ key as you make changes using the handles on the bounding box around the type. **Transforming the type is an all-or-none process** — you can't select and transform just *some* of the type on a layer. If you transform type on or inside a path, the path is transformed along with it. To make other changes to the path — adding or deleting points or reshaping the curve — use the path-editing tools nested with the Pen tool ✎. ▼

FIND OUT MORE

▼ Editing paths
page 455

If you start to Ctrl/⌘-drag on a handle and *then* add the **Shift key**, the change will be **constrained** — with a corner handle, proportionality will be maintained; for other handles, the drag will be constrained to vertical or horizontal motion. If you're using the curved double-arrow cursor for rotation, the turning will be constrained to 15° steps.

Warping type. Any type can be reshaped using the **Warp Text** function, which bends, stretches, or otherwise distorts type to fit within an "envelope." When a type layer is active, the Warp Text dialog box can be opened by clicking the "Create warped text" button ⍧ on the Type tool's Options bar, or by choosing Layer > Type > Warp Text. In the Warp Text dialog box you can choose a type of envelope from the Style list, and then set parameters for bending and distorting.

- The **Style** shows you the general shape of the envelope — for instance, an Arc.
- The **Bend** controls the *degree* to which the type is distorted into that shape. For instance, is it a shallow arc (a low setting) or a more pronounced arc (a higher setting)?
- And the **Horizontal** and **Vertical Distortion** settings control where the effect is centered — left or right, up or down.

The **warping stays "live,"** so you can come back later, choose Warp Text again, and reshape the existing envelope, or even pick a new envelope style.

Like rotating, skewing, or scaling, **warping is applied to the entire type layer;** you can't select and warp individual characters on a layer. Nor is there any way to reshape the envelope as you could a path, editing the outline point-by-point. For more

When you warp type that's set on or inside a path, the warping envelope distorts the path as well as the type, and then the path seems to disappear. But you can get it back later if you need it — for instance, if you want to alter the bounding box or baseline path later to try a different effect: Duplicate the warped type layer (Ctrl/⌘-J) and click the 👁 for the original warped layer to hide it so you can see what you're doing. Then click the "Create warped text" button 🏦 in the Options bar and choose None as the Style. The type will "unwarp" and the original path will return! You can see it if you click in the type layer with the Type tool **T** or click the path's thumbnail in the Paths panel.

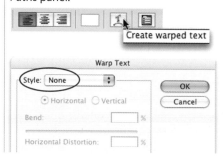

FOOTBALL PHOTO: PHOTOSPIN.COM

kick

Live type can mask an image and can accept a Layer Style. But to rotate individual characters or edit a character's shape, first convert the type to a Shape layer (Layer > Type > Convert to Shape). Then use the Edit > Transform Path command and the path-editing tools, as we did here to rotate each letter separately and to extend the leg of the "K" by Shift-selecting its control points and moving them.

sophisticated warping effects, convert the type to shapes or to a Smart Object (see "When To Convert Type," below).

Saving Type

For greatest flexibility, save any files that include type in **Photoshop PDF** format. For flexibility, choose to preserve the Layers, and choose Preserve Photoshop Editing Capabilities. That way it will be possible to open the file with Adobe Reader with the resolution-independent type outlines intact and the type accessible for copying as text, even if the fonts you used aren't present on the system where the file is opened. You can also reopen the PDF in Photoshop if you ever need to edit the type further.

The **Photoshop EPS** format, with the Include Vector Data option turned on when you save, can retain the vector information for the printer, but the type can't be edited — either outside of Photoshop or inside if the file is reopened, because it will have become a flattened, single-layer file, without type layers.

When To Convert Type

Keeping Photoshop type "live" and editable as long as possible provides a great deal of flexibility. And with clipping groups, Layer Styles, Smart Objects, and the ability to save in PDF and EPS formats, you rarely have to rasterize the type or even convert it to a Shape layer for output. However, there are some exceptions:

- **To edit the shape or tilt** of individual characters in a type block, you can first convert the type to a Shape layer (Layer > Type > Convert to Shape) and then select and manipulate the individual character outlines, using the Direct Selection tool ▸ or the tools nested with the Pen tool ▵. ▼

- Although you can transform live type, ▼ the Distort and Perspective functions aren't available, and warping is limited. For more control you have two options: (1) converting the type to a Smart Object, which keeps the type live and gives you access to finer warping control with the Edit > Transform > Warp command, or (2) converting the type to a Shape layer, in which case the type is no longer live and editable but you have access to Edit > Transform > Distort and Perspective as well as Warp.

- **To run a filter** on type, the type layer has to either be turned into a Smart Object (Filter > Convert for Smart Filters) or be rasterized (turned into a pixel-based layer).

FIND OUT MORE

▼ Editing paths
page 455

▼ Transforming
page 67

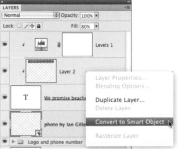

To turn a type layer into a Smart Object, simply right-click/Ctrl-click on the layer's name and choose Convert to Smart Object. This accomplishes the same thing as targeting the layer in the Layers panel and choosing Filter > Convert for Smart Filters or Layer > Smart Objects > Convert to Smart Object.

- If your type has **to exactly match** a Shape version of the same type, or a rasterized version (in a Spot Color channel or a mask, for instance), it's safer to convert your live type to a Shape layer. That's because even slight variations in the name or tracking values of the font on the system where the file is output can cause a mismatch between the live type and the channel or mask. You'll find an example of using type with spot color in "Adding Spot Color" on page 226.

- **To be sure that a file with display type will open and print as expected**, whether or not the font is present on the next system that handles the file, you can convert the type to Shape layers (Layer > Type > Convert to Shape). The type retains its smooth outlines, but without font complications.

Moving Type Between Illustrator & Photoshop

Adobe Illustrator, Adobe In Design, and QuarkXPress have additional text facilities — such as the ability to define Character and Paragraph styles — that make certain projects easier to do in these programs than in Photoshop alone. For complex, text-intensive single-page layout projects, such as menus or book jackets, it often makes sense to place your Photoshop

When warping or transforming type doesn't do exactly what you want, you can convert type to a Smart Object to get more control of the warp. With a Smart Object you can also apply filters and still keep the type live. "Carving" this type into the sand is described on page 593.

Photoshop rarely does anything "destructive" without warning you first. If you try to run a filter on a type layer, it will ask if you really want to rasterize the type. Often a better option is to convert the type to a Smart Object so that it remains live and can be edited later.

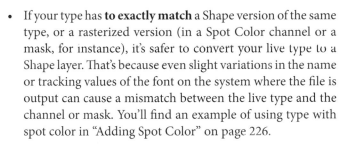

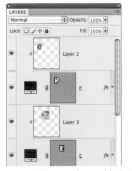

John Odam set each letter of his type on a separate layer so he could tilt them independently before he masked a photo inside each one. Designing the cover is described on page 493.

When all kerning, tracking, and other adjusting is complete, converting display type to Shape layers avoids font complications (see page 468).

Illustrator has more "styles" of type on a path than Photoshop's one kind. When you save an Illustrator file in Photoshop (PSD) format, all of the type on a path is preserved. Both the type and the path can be edited in Photoshop, and the type keeps its orientation to the path, so the file can serve as an editable source for alternative approaches to type-on-a-path in Photoshop, even if you don't have Illustrator on your computer.

 Path Type.psd

artwork in Illustrator (or InDesign or QuarkXPress) and add the type there.

In other cases — if you want to add a Photoshop Layer Style to the type, for instance, or incorporate the type into an image — you may want to create type in Illustrator and bring it into Photoshop. If you think you might need to edit the text in Photoshop, either copy and paste the Illustrator text, which will convert it into plain text, or export the file as a PSD file with both PDF Compatibility and Preserve Text Editability enabled. If you need to preserve any effects, but also want to be able to edit the text later, consider pasting it as a Smart Object. ▼ If you don't need to edit the text, treating it as an image will ensure that you preserve the text's appearance.

FIND OUT MORE
▼ Working with Smart Objects
page 75

DRAWING

Compared to painting, which is pixel-based, vector drawing has the advantages of being resolution-independent and often easier to change cleanly. When vector graphics are printed on a Postscript-based device, their smooth lines are retained regardless of the resolution or size of the output. This makes Photoshop's vector-based drawing tools — the Pens and Shapes — ideal for creating sharp, smooth-edged graphics.

Starting Out

There are three essential choices to make each time you start drawing in Photoshop:

1 **Which drawing tool do you want to use?** Choose one of the Pen or Shape tools nested in the Tools panel — use a **Pen** to create your own curves from scratch; use a **Shape** tool to start with a preset shape.

2 **What kind of element do you want to make?** Using the "mode of operation" buttons at the left end of any drawing tool's Options bar, you can choose to make a **Shape layer** or a "bare-wire" **Path** (no layer, just a wire-frame outline that can be stored in the Paths panel). A path can then be used to make a selection, a baseline for type, or a filled or stroked element on a pixel-based layer. A third choice (for Shape tools only) is to step outside the realm of vector art and draw an area filled with **pixels** on an existing regular (transparent) layer or on the *Background*.

Note: **The "mode of operation" setting persists** from the last time you used a Pen or Shape. In your eagerness to begin

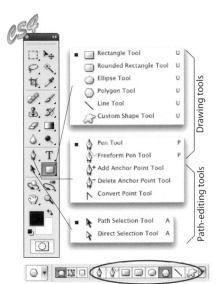

Photoshop's tools for drawing and editing vector-based graphics include the Shapes, Pens, and path-editing tools, some of which share a Tools panel space with the Pens. When any Shape or Pen tool is chosen, the Options bar includes buttons for all the Shapes and Pens. To switch tools, just click your choice.

drawing after choosing a tool, it's easy to forget to check this setting. But it's worth getting into the habit. It's disappointing — not to mention time-consuming — to expect to make a Shape layer, do your drawing, and then find that you've accidentally created a *Work Path* instead. You can turn a path into a Shape layer (as described in the "Convertibility" tip on page 456), but it isn't instantaneous.

3 Do you want to start a new Shape layer or path, **or modify the currently targeted one?** This choice is made by clicking one of the buttons farther to the right on the Options bar (see "Combining Options for Drawing Tools" (below).

Besides these options, you can also choose to incorporate a Layer Style or a specific color as you draw (see "Style & Color Options for Drawing Tools," on page 450).

In addition to the choices common to all vector drawing tools, each tool has its own additional tool-specific options — for instance, the number of sides produced when you draw with the Polygon tool. "Options for Specific Drawing Tools" on page 452 tells about these choices.

DRAWING TOOL MODES OF OPERATION

The **Shape** and **Pen** tools have the modes of operation shown here for originating vector graphics or modifying the currently targeted graphics.

For all Pens and Shapes, the **Paths** option produces a resolution-independent path. The path is stored in the Paths panel (see page 451), where it can be activated to create a Shape layer, a baseline for type, or a filled or stroked area on a pixel-based layer.

For all Pen and Shape tools, the **Shape layers** option creates a color layer with a vector mask that defines exactly where this color is revealed and where it's hidden.

Fill pixels (for Shape tools but not Pens) is a quick way to draw pixel-based graphics that you can paint on; but these graphics aren't resolution-independent. When the *Background* or a regular (transparent) layer is active and this option is chosen, you can set the blend Mode and Opacity for the fill; you can also choose whether the edges will be antialiased (smooth) or not (pixelated).

COMBINING OPTIONS FOR DRAWING TOOLS

To start a Shape layer or path, use the "New" button. Then you can use any of the other buttons to add to it or subtract from it; or start another one by choosing "New" again.

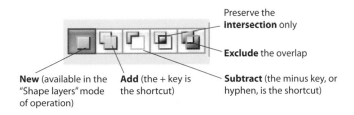

Preserve the **Intersection** only

Exclude the overlap

New (available in the "Shape layers" mode of operation)

Add (the + key is the shortcut)

Subtract (the minus key, or hyphen, is the shortcut)

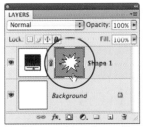

To add to or subtract from a Shape layer, the mask for the layer has to be targeted in the Layers panel. To do this, click once or twice on the mask thumbnail; a double border will show that the mask is active.

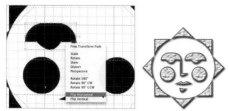

"Exercising Drawing Tools" on page 471 is a quick vector drawing and editing tutorial.

PATH PARTS

The paths produced by the Pen and Shape tools in Photoshop are defined by *anchor points* (which can be *smooth points* or *corner points*) and by *direction lines*.

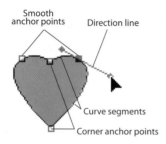

Smooth anchor points

Direction line

Curve segments

Corner anchor points

STYLE & COLOR OPTIONS FOR DRAWING TOOLS

When you draw a Shape layer, you can add a Layer Style or color as you draw; or change the Style or color after drawing. You can also save a drawing tool preset that includes a built-in Style and color (see page 453).

When this button is **darkened** (as shown), any changes to the Style or color will be applied to the **currently active Shape layer**. When the button is **light**, the Style and color won't be applied until you draw the **next Shape layer**. To set a Style or color for the next Shape layer without changing the current layer, click the button until it's light, and then make Style and color choices.

Path Terminology

Paths, Shape layers, and vector masks can all be described by the more generic term *paths*. A *path* is made up of *path segments* that stretch between *anchor points*. An anchor point can be a smooth point (where the curve continues smoothly through the point) or a corner point (which makes a corner or cusp where the path abruptly changes direction).

How each segment bends between its two anchor points is determined by one or two *direction lines*, which are "levers" located at the anchor points. The amount of tension a direction line puts on the wirelike segment it controls is what determines how steep or flat the curve of the segment is; the tension can be changed by adjusting the lever. The **direction line for a smooth point** operates as a continuous rod that pivots around the smooth point. Moving one end of the direction line also moves the other in the opposite direction, controlling both segments of the curve that come into that point and maintaining the smoothness of the curve. A **corner point's two direction lines** are moved independently of each other, so you have separate control of the two segments coming into the point.

A path can include more than one *component path*, or subpath. A component path is produced when you end one series of segments and then start a separate one without starting a new Shape layer, vector mask, or path.

Rather than opening the Styles panel, you can choose a **Layer Style** for your Shape layer from the pop-out **Style picker**.

The **Color** of Shape layers can be controlled independently of the Foreground color by clicking this swatch and choosing a color.

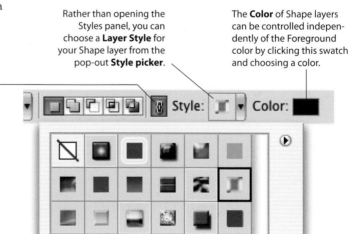

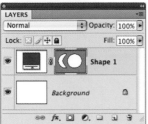

A component path can be selected and manipulated independently of other components in the path.

The Paths Panel

The Paths panel (see below) provides everything that's needed for storing, filling, and stroking paths; converting selections to paths and vice versa; and making clipping paths for exporting silhouetted areas.

The Shape Tools

The Shape tools — Rectangle ▭, Rounded Rectangle ▢, Ellipse ◯, Polygon ◯, Line ╲, and Custom Shape 🐾 — are all nested in a single space in the Tools panel, as shown on page 449. The Shape tools are operated by dragging. By default, you drag from corner to diagonally opposite corner of your shape. For many of the tools, though, you have the option of drawing the shape outward from its center. Other options are described in "Options for Specific Drawing Tools" on page 452.

continued on page 454

CYCLING CUSTOM SHAPES

As they can with so many preset pickers, the bracket keys — [and] — can cycle through the Custom Shape tools in the Options bar. Press] for the next Custom Shape in the picker or [for the previous one. Adding the Shift key cycles to the end (Shift-]) or the beginning (Shift-[) of the picker.

THE PATHS PANEL

Each entry in the Paths panel represents a **path**, which may include **component paths**. A path can be designated as a **clipping path** to silhouette a subject.

SAVING THE WORK PATH

The current *Work Path* will be eliminated if you click in an empty area of the Paths panel and then start to draw again. To avoid accidentally eliminating the *Work Path*, double-click its name in the Paths panel to open the Save Path dialog box.

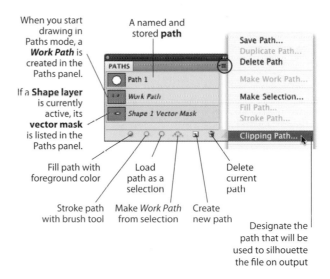

When you start drawing in Paths mode, a **Work Path** is created in the Paths panel.

If a **Shape layer** is currently active, its **vector mask** is listed in the Paths panel.

A named and stored **path**

Fill path with foreground color

Load path as a selection

Delete current path

Stroke path with brush tool

Make *Work Path* from selection

Create new path

Designate the path that will be used to silhouette the file on output

OPTIONS FOR SPECIFIC DRAWING TOOLS

In addition to the Options bar settings available for all the Shape or Pen tools, each specific tool has its own options, available in the bar itself or in the "Geometry options" that become available when you click the ▾ button to the right of the tool buttons. If you set a Layer Style or a color in the Options bar, it will appear as you draw.

The only option in the panel for the **Pen** tool ✒ is **Rubber Band**, which lets you "preview" the next segment of the path as you draw, before you click to set an anchor point.

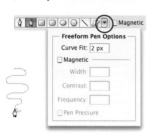

The Options for the **Freeform Pen** ✒ include the **Curve Fit** (to determine how closely the path will follow the movement of the cursor). In the Freeform Pen's Options bar you can also access the **Magnetic Pen** ✒ (see page 454).

The **Polygon** tool ⬡ can draw both **polygons** and **stars**, with the number of sides or arms specified in the **Sides** field. Without a specific **Radius** setting, size is determined by how far you drag. Unlike the other shapes, the Polygon is always drawn from the center; it has a fixed width-to-height proportion, and the direction you drag controls the orientation of the figure. You can choose **Smooth Corners** or sharp (as here), and for a **star** you can choose how much to **indent** the sides and whether the indents are **Smooth** (as here) or sharp.

Custom arrowheads can be applied to either or both ends of a line as you draw it with the **Line** tool ╲. **Width**, **Length**, and **Concavity** are set as percentages of the line's **Weight**. A negative Concavity stretches the base of the arrowhead away from the tip, as in the two arrows above on the right. The arrow on the far left was made by clicking with the Line tool to place the starting arrowhead and then dragging *toward* the tip rather than away from it.

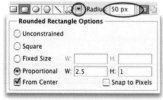

For the **Rectangle** ▭ and **Rounded Rectangle** ▢ (shown here), you can constrain the shape to a **Square**; the **Ellipse** ○ can be constrained to a **Circle**. You can choose **Fixed Size** or a **Proportional** relationship between Width and Height, rather than controlling this by dragging. You can also choose to draw from the **Center** outward. For the Rounded Rectangle, you can set the **Radius** of the round corners as well.

For the **Custom Shape** tool ✐ you can choose the shape you want to draw from the **Custom Shape picker** (above) with shapes that have been stored as presets; the picker is opened by clicking the ▾ button to the right of the Shape thumbnail in the Options bar. Using the "Geometry options" pop-out (left), you can choose to constrain the shape to its original **Defined Size** or **Proportions**, specify a **Fixed Size**, or draw from the **Center**.

Graphics that are often used in a particular color or Layer Style can be stored in a way that lets you draw them with the Style and color already in place. This can be ideal for a logo in a corporate color, a digital signature for photos or artwork, or any other graphics that you might want to incorporate into Photoshop files. Here's how you can do that.

1 Once you've created a **Shape layer** with your graphics, add it to the Shapes that can be drawn with the Custom Shape tool: Target the layer's **vector mask** in the Layers panel and choose **Edit > Define Custom Shape** ("Defining & Saving" on page 474 has an example).

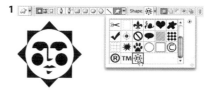
1

When the Custom Shape preset is defined, it will be stored as a black graphic, even if it already has a Layer Style or color applied. But it *is* possible to store Style and color with the graphic if you then go on to define your shape as a ***Tool preset***:

2 Choose the **Custom Shape** tool, click on the **"Shape layers"** mode of operation near the left end of the Options bar **A**, and in the **Custom Shape picker** click on your stored shape to choose it **B**. Add the Style and color you want (one way is to use the **Style picker C** and **Color swatch D** in the Options bar). Scale the Style if needed.▼

> **FIND OUT MORE**
> ▼ Scaling Styles
> **page 81**

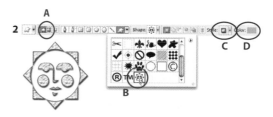
2

3 **At the left end of the Options bar**, click the tool icon **A** to open the **Tool Preset picker**. When it opens, click the "Create new tool preset" button **B**. In the New Tool Preset dialog box, name the tool, make sure the **Include Color** box is checked **C**, and click "OK."

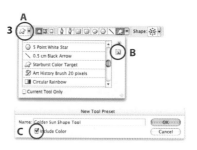
3

4 Choose **Edit > Preset Manager**, and in the Preset Manager dialog box, choose **Tools** (*not* Custom Shapes) from the menu of Preset Types **A**. In the array of tools, click on your new tool **B** and then Shift-click or Ctrl/⌘-click to add any other tools that you want to include in the set with it. Click the "Save Set" button **C**. In the Save dialog box **D**, name the set and click the "Save" button; then click the "Done" button to close the Preset Manager dialog. A Tool presets file will be created with your new tool and any others you specified.

Now your set will be available to load from the menu of the Tool Preset picker; click the ⊙ button and choose Load Tool Presets. If you saved your preset file as described in step 4, the set will appear in the list at the bottom of the Tool Preset picker's ⊙ menu.

4

A

Clicking to make
a corner point

B

Dragging to make
a smooth point

C

Adding a path
segment with a
single bend

D

Adding a path seg-
ment with a double
(S-shaped) bend

E

Closing a path

F

Ending a compo-
nent path without
closing it

G

Clicking to continue
a path

DRAWING ON THE GRID

Photoshop's Grid can be a tremendous
help for drawing symmetrical curves. To
make the Pen tool ✎ follow the Grid as
you draw a path, mapping anchor points
and direction lines to the Grid, choose
View > Show > Grid and View > Snap To >
Grid.

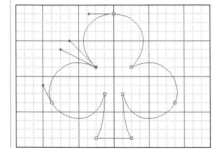

The Pen Tools

With the tools in the Pen family, you can create your own paths
by clicking and dragging. If you're new to the drawing process,
you might want to turn on the Rubber Band option for the Pen
tool (see page 452) as you practice.

Operating the Pen ✎. You can draw with the Pen tool ✎ (Shift-
P), complete your path, and then go back and edit, or you can
make adjustments to the path as you place each anchor point.
Here are the drawing maneuvers ("Editing Shapes & Paths" on
page 455 covers the adjustment process):

A **To set a corner point,** for a corner, or cusp, where the path
abruptly changes direction, just click.

B **To place a smooth (curve) point**, click where you want to
put the point, and then shape the curve by dragging in the
direction you want the next segment of the curve to go.

C **To draw a path segment with a single bend** (more or less
C-shaped), click where you want to end the segment and
drag in a direction opposite the direction line you can see
on your previous anchor point.

D **To draw a "torqued" path segment, with a double** (or
S-shaped) **bend,** click where you want to end the segment
and **drag in about the same direction** as the direction line
you can see on your previous anchor point.

E **To close the path**, move the cursor close to the starting point
and click when you see a little circle next to the cursor ✎.

F **To end a component path without closing it** so you can start
another, unattached, component path, hold down the Ctrl/⌘
key and click somewhere off the path.

G **To add to a path,** continuing from an open endpoint, move
the cursor toward the end of the path until you see ✎ or ✎, and
click on the endpoint; then continue to draw by placing your
next anchor point.

Operating the Freeform Pen. You operate the **Freeform
Pen** ✎ as if you were drawing with a pencil; anchor points are
placed automatically to create the path. In the Options bar's
pop-out, you can set the **Curve Fit** (between 0.5 and 10 pixels),
which determines how closely the path will follow your movement of the cursor. With lower settings the curve will follow
more closely, placing more anchor points.

The **Magnetic** choice in the Freeform Pen's Options bar turns
this tool into the **Magnetic Pen** ✎, which was designed to create

Though it won't have the precision or "snap to" properties of Photoshop's native grid, you can make a perspective grid to use as a guide for drawing. In your file, add a new empty layer (Ctrl/⌘-Shift-N) or duplicate the white-filled Background (Ctrl/⌘-J). Then choose Filter > Vanishing Point and set up the perspective grid(s) you want.▼

Click on the menu button ▾☰ in the upper left corner and select Render Grids to Photoshop, then click "OK." Your grid will appear on the layer you added. To use the guide for drawing on another layer, change the layer's blend mode or Opacity to suit, and zoom in if you like.

(In CS4 Extended, the New 3D Postcard from Layer command provides another option for putting a grid in perspective.)▼

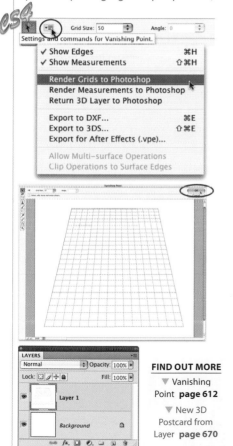

FIND OUT MORE

▼ Vanishing Point **page 612**

▼ New 3D Postcard from Layer **page 670**

a path by automatically following color and contrast differences in an image. To operate the Magnetic Pen, you click the cursor somewhere on the edge you want to trace and then "float" the cursor along, moving the mouse without pressing its button, or guiding the stylus without touching it to the tablet surface. To control the Magnetic Pen, you can set Curve Fit as you can for the Freeform Pen. You can also set the **Width** (the area where the tool looks for the edge as you float the cursor along), the **Contrast** (how much difference the tool looks for when deciding whether a change in color constitutes an "edge"), and the **Frequency** (the distance between "fastening points," which "tack down" the curve as you draw it, to determine how far back the path will "unravel" if you press the Delete key). To stop drawing, press the Enter/Return key. The Magnetic Pen is tricky to use, and in real-world projects you may find it more efficient to use the Pen and Freeform Pen as described in "Tracing Edges," next.

Tracing Edges

Used together, the Pen ✎ and Freeform Pen ✎ can be especially useful for tracing edges from photo reference, especially when your goal is nicely shaped details rather than a perfectly faithful outline. You can toggle between the Pen ✎ and Freeform Pen ✎ by typing Shift-P; if the Magnetic option is turned on in the Options bar, Shift-P toggles between Pen and Magnetic Pen. To make a path by tracing an element with some smooth and some detailed edges, use the Pen for the smooth edges, then type Shift-P and continue with the Freeform Pen, dragging to follow the edge. When you come to a smooth section again, type Shift-P to toggle back to the Pen. Follow the edges as carefully as you like, but rather than adjust each anchor point and segment as you draw, finish the path and then zoom in (Ctrl/⌘-+) to find areas that need fixing, and use the techniques in "Editing Shapes & Paths" (next) to quickly make adjustments.

EDITING SHAPES & PATHS

With Photoshop's path-editing tools you can edit the outlines already created with the drawing tools. Some of the editing tools are nested with the Pen tools:

A Click on a path segment with the **Add Anchor Point** tool ✎⁺ to add a point for more control in reshaping a path.

B Click on an anchor point with the **Delete Anchor Point** ✎⁻ tool to reduce the complexity of a path.

A

B

Clicking on a path segment adds a point.

Clicking on a point deletes it.

C

Clicking on a smooth or corner point turns it into the opposite type.

CONVERTIBILITY

You can duplicate a Shape layer as a path and vice versa. And both Shapes and paths can be rasterized (converted to or duplicated as pixels):

• The active Shape layer can be duplicated as a saved Path by double-clicking its name in the Paths panel.

• The active Shape layer can be converted to pixels by choosing Layer > Rasterize > Shape.

• A saved Path or the Work Path can be duplicated as pixels by first making sure that a transparent layer or the *Background* is the active layer, then clicking the path in the Paths panel, and clicking or Alt/Option-clicking the "Fill path with foreground color" button ● or the "Stroke path with brush" button ○ at the bottom of the panel.

To duplicate a saved Path or the Work Path as a Shape layer, click the name of the path in the Paths panel, then click the "Create new fill or adjustment layer" button ● at the bottom of the Layers panel and choose Solid Color from the pop-up menu. The result will be a Shape layer — a Color layer with a vector mask.

C Click or drag on an anchor point with the **Convert Point** tool ⊾ to change it from a smooth point to a corner point or vice versa.

Two other path-editing tools — the Path Selection tool ▶ and the Direct Selection tool ▶ — share a space above the Pens.

To work on path segments, use the **Direct Selection tool** ▶:

• **To reposition an anchor point or a straight path segment,** drag it with the ▶.

• **To make a curved path segment steeper or flatter,** use the ▶ to drag the center of the segment.

• Another way **to reshape a curved path segment** is to click with the ▶ on an anchor point and **drag one or both ends of its direction line(s).** Or **to convert the anchor point** from a corner to a smooth point or vice versa **and reshape the curve,** Alt/Option-drag a direction-line endpoint with the ▶.

To work on an entire path or component path, rather than a path segment, use the **Path Selection tool** ▶:

• **To move a path or component path,** drag it with the ▶.

• **To duplicate a path or component path,** click it with the ▶ once or twice (until the anchor points show), hold down the Alt/Option key, and drag. (Shift-click or drag to select more than one component path at a time.)

• **To invert the nature of a Shape layer** so the solid area becomes a "hole" and vice versa, activate the vector mask component of the Shape layer (by clicking its mask thumbnail in the Layers panel once or twice, until the double border appears around it). Then, in the working window, use the ▶ to click the particular component path you want to invert, and click the Add ▣ or Subtract ▣ button on the Options bar (shown on page 449).

• **To combine closed component paths** into a single component path or a single path, you should first make sure the positive and negative

AUTOMATED EDITING TOOLS

With **Auto Add/Delete** turned on in the Options bar, the Pen ◊ automatically turns into the **Add Anchor Point** tool ◊⁺ when the cursor moves onto a path segment. The Pen becomes the **Delete Anchor Point** tool ◊⁻ when the cursor moves onto an anchor point.

SELECTING A SUBPATH

There are several ways to select a component path, but the following way always works: In the Paths panel, click the name of the path. Then use the Direct Selection tool ▶ or the Path Selection tool ▶ to click the component path in the working window. To select additional subpaths, Shift-click them.

Use the Path Selection tool ▸ (Shift-A) to move, duplicate, or combine paths or component paths; to change a Shape layer from a shape on a transparent background to a "hole" in a solid background, or vice versa; or to align or distribute component paths.

Use the Move tool ▸ to align or distribute Shape layers with one another or with other layers.

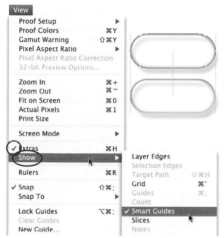

To use Smart Guides to align paths, Shape layers, and other elements, choose View > Show > Smart Guides. For the Smart Guides to show up, the Extras option in the View menu must also be turned on.

attributes for all the component paths are set the way you want them. To reset these attributes, click a component path with the ▸ and then click the appropriate button in the Options bar — Add ▣, Subtract ▣, Intersect ▣, or Exclude ▣. When the attributes are set correctly, select the component paths you want to combine permanently, and click the Options bar's "Combine" button.

ALIGNING PATHS & SHAPE LAYERS

Photoshop's precise alignment capabilities can be applied to paths and Shape layers:

- **To align component paths or distribute them evenly,** Shift-click them with the Path Selection tool ▸ and click an Align or Distribute button in the Options bar.

- **To align or distribute Shape layers**, target one by clicking its thumbnail in the Layers panel. Then Shift-click or Ctrl/⌘-click to target additional layers. Now choose the Move tool ▸ and click one of the alignment buttons in the Options bar.

You can also align elements "on the fly" by using the Smart Guides. If you choose View > Show > Smart Guides to turn on this option, guidelines will appear whenever the centers or edges of elements line up with one another.

TRANSFORMING PATHS

When a path or Shape layer is targeted, the Edit > Free Transform command becomes Edit > Free Transform Path. Choosing this command (or using its shortcut, Ctrl/⌘-T) gives you a Transform box, and you can scale, distort, or move the targeted path, component path, or path segment. ▼

FIND OUT MORE
▼ Transforming
page 67

STROKING & FILLING PATHS

Photoshop offers a wide range of options for **filling** and **stroking** paths. A path can be filled or stroked with pixels on a ***Background***, a **regular (transparent) layer**, or a **layer mask**; these kinds of layers and masks are the only ones that will accept a pixel-based fill or stroke. With the layer or mask targeted, target the path you want by clicking its thumbnail in the Paths panel. (If you want to fill or stroke *some* components of a path but not all, click or Shift-click them in the working window with the Path Selection tool ▸.) Then:

A single path can produce a variety of different fill effects, depending on which options are chosen in the Fill Path dialog box. Open the dialog by Alt/Option-clicking the leftmost button ⊙ at the bottom of the Paths panel, and choose a fill, blend mode, opacity, and amount of feather.

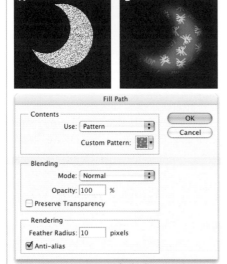

The same path was used for both examples. The path was filled with the Foreground Color in Dissolve mode (with reduced Opacity) **A** and with a pattern in Normal mode with a feathered edge **B**.

- **To simply fill with the Foreground color,** click the "Fill path with Foreground color" button ⊙ at the bottom of the Paths panel.

- **To fill with a color you choose** (independent of the Foreground color) **or with a pattern,** Alt/Option-click the ⊙ button to open the Fill Path dialog box, where you can choose a fill color or a pattern; you can also specify the blend Mode and Opacity for the fill, and even a Feather setting to soften the edges of the filled area.

- **To stroke a path with the Foreground color,** in the Tools panel click on the painting or toning tool you want to stroke with, set its characteristics in the Options bar, and click the "Stroke path with brush" button ○ at the bottom of the Paths panel. (If the current tool isn't one of the tools that can stroke, the stroke will be made with the current settings for the Brush tool 🖌 or with the current settings for the last painting tool you selected in this work session.)

- **To choose from a menu of all the tools that can stroke a path,** open the Stroke Path dialog box by Alt/Option-clicking the Stroke Path button ○. The tool you choose will use its most recent settings to make the stroke; you won't be able to see or change its settings once the Stroke Path dialog is open.

"SOFTENING" VECTOR ART

Beyond stroking and filling paths, there are other methods of adding texture and more complex color to vector art. "Coloring Clip Art" on page 482 adds color, shading, and dimension to

You can stroke and restroke a path with different tools, brush sizes, or colors to layer the "paint."

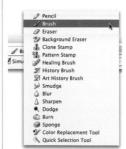

The Stroke Path dialog box, opened by Alt/Option clicking the "Stroke path with brush" button ○ at the bottom of the Paths panel, has a menu of all the tools that can be used to stroke a path.

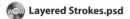 **Layered Strokes.psd**

On a transparent layer the moon path was stroked with the Brush tool 🖌 using a Flat Bristle brush tip (from Adobe's Thick Heavy Brush presets) with Diameter reduced to 60 px, Roundness reduced to 40%, Size control set to Off instead of Pen Pressure, and Noise turned on **A**. Then on another layer it was stroked with the Crosshatch 4 brush tip from Adobe's Assorted Brushes presets, with Diameter at 60 px, Spacing at 180% to separate the "stars," and Angle Jitter at 10% **B**. Layer Styles were added to the two layers **C**.

With the Simulate Pressure option turned on in the Stroke Path dialog, any Pen Pressure controls built into the brush tip you're using will be expressed. The stroke will be applied as if Pen Pressure started out low, increased, and then tapered off to low again.

Filters and textures can be used to "soften" vector graphics (see page 475).

black-and-white art, and "Organic Graphics" on page 475 and "Quick Filter Treatments" starting on page 479 suggest ways of using Photoshop's filters to stylize flat-color artwork.

USING PHOTOSHOP WITH ADOBE ILLUSTRATOR

Photoshop can exchange graphics and type with Adobe Illustrator. (Type exchange was covered earlier in the chapter, on page 447.)

Illustrator's Unique Drawing Abilities

Despite all of Photoshop's typographic, vector-drawing, and layout tools, Illustrator is better at some vector-drawing tasks than Photoshop is. If you have Illustrator, here are some capabilities you might like to know about. If you don't have it, this section may help you decide whether you need it:

- Illustrator's **Spiral** tool — with control over the number of turns, the radius, and the decay rate — gives you more kinds of spirals than you get with Photoshop's Custom Shape spiral.

- If you hold down the Alt/Option key, Illustrator's **Star** tool can automatically draw stars with arms whose edges are aligned, as shown on page 460. You can control the number of arms as you draw or control the depth of the indent on the fly (after you start drawing, hold down the Ctrl/⌘ key).

- The two **Grid** tools (Rectangular and Polar) are great for quickly drawing the precisely aligned paths for these forms.

- The **Flare tool**, demonstrated on page 460, produces a vector-based lens flare with more controls than Photoshop's Filter > Render > Lens Flare.

- When you need a series of related shapes or an intermediate between two shapes, the **Blend** tool or command can morph one vector path or shape into another, with the number of in-between shapes you specify.

Here are a few of the many styles of stars and spirals easily created with Illustrator's interactive Star and Spiral tools.

The two stars on the right have arms whose edges are not aligned — these stars are easy to draw in Photoshop with the Polygon tool ⬡ in Star mode (see below). The star on the left has arms whose edges *are* aligned, which can be done automatically in Illustrator. In Photoshop you can align the edges of the arms if you know the right "Indent Sides By" value, but this number changes with the number of sides on the star. (For a five-pointed star, the magic number is 50%.)

This star was drawn with Photoshop's Polygon tool ⬡ with the Star and Smooth Indents options chosen. Illustrator doesn't have an equivalent option.

The Flare tool is one of Illustrator's vector drawing tools. You can adjust the diameter, length, and angle of the flare simply by dragging on it.

Illustrator's Object > Blend command was used to create the three intermediate shapes between the star and the circle. A blend can be made with a specified number of steps (as this one was) or a specified distance *between* steps. The example on the bottom was created from a star with no fill. For the one at the top, the star had the same green fill as the circle but with the fill's Opacity set to 0%.

- Use vector **Art brushes** to mimic watercolors, charcoal, or calligraphic pens. Or use **Pattern brushes** to quickly create complex lines and borders.

- The **Symbol Sprayer tool** can "spray" symbols (vector or pixel artwork from Photoshop or Illustrator) onto the canvas. You can then interactively manipulate their size, shape, distribution, color, and transparency.

- In Illustrator you have more options for **aligning individual points** of shapes and paths, making it easier, for instance, to create a symmetrically zigzagging path.

- The **Live Trace** command automatically traces images as vector graphics, with interactive controls for simplifying an image for tracing.

- The **Live Paint** makes working with vector graphics much more like working with traditional artists' drawing and coloring tools. Live Paint treats all paths as if they were on a single flat surface, dividing the surface into areas that can be filled with color. When the paths are edited, the color adapts to the reshaped areas.

Moving Artwork Between Photoshop & Illustrator

In some cases, type and vector artwork can be transferred between Photoshop and Illustrator with font information or paths intact. In other cases the vector-based artwork has to be rasterized first, or at least simplified, to make the trip. The way you move artwork between the two programs will depend on what sort of artwork you're moving and which of its properties are most important to preserve. Because each program can produce such a wide range of type and vector art, it's hard to come up with a set of hard-and-fast rules for making the transfer. With as many exceptions as rules, exact results can be hard to predict. But here's a generalized list of options for moving artwork (see page 447 for type options):

Drag-and-drop (for paths and shapes). By default, Illustrator artwork will be rasterized when it's dragged from Illustrator and dropped into Photoshop, but you can keep editable paths if you hold down the Ctrl/⌘ key as you drag. In the other direction, Photoshop paths and shapes retain their vector character and editability when you drag-and-drop them into Illustrator.

Copy and paste (for pixels, paths, and shapes). With Preferences set correctly (as described in "Pasting from Illustrator" on page 461), when you copy an Illustrator object to the clipboard and paste it into a Photoshop file, the Paste dialog will offer you

In Illustrator CS3/CS4, the AICB option must be checked in the File Handling & Clipboard section of the Preferences dialog box in order to paste "live" shapes or paths into Photoshop.

Then when you paste from the clipboard into Photoshop, the Paste dialog box will let you choose to rasterize the clipboard contents (turn it into pixels), or bring it in as a path, or import it as a Shape layer or as a Smart Object, with the option for further editing in Illustrator later.

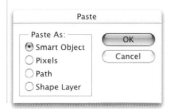

Of course, Illustrator isn't the only Post-Script drawing program that produces files Photoshop can handle. For instance, CorelDraw files can be rasterized and exported as Photoshop files or saved in Adobe Illustrator format and processed through Illustrator to Photoshop. Translation of a complex file from CorelDraw to Illustrator may not be completely accurate, though.

the choice to paste as Pixels, a Path, a Shape Layer, or a Smart Object, which maintains a link back to Illustrator for editing, and automatic updating of the Photoshop file.

Going from Photoshop to Illustrator, simply select and copy the element you want in Photoshop, and then paste it into your Illustrator document. Its pixel or vector character will be retained.

Files (for shapes and multiple layers). To move an **Illustrator file to Photoshop**, choose Photoshop (PSD) in Illustrator's File > Export dialog box. In saving in PSD format, Illustrator tries to retain as much editability as possible (live type and layer structure, which keeps objects separate and easy to select in Photoshop) without sacrificing appearance.

To move **Photoshop files to Illustrator**, for paths, choose File > Export > Paths to Illustrator. For Shape layers, save the file in Photoshop (PSD) format, and then open it in Illustrator (File > Open). When Illustrator's Photoshop Import Options dialog opens, choose "Convert Photoshop layers to objects and make text editable where possible" and click "OK."

When you Open or Place (embed) a PSD file in Illustrator, choosing the "Convert Photoshop layers to objects. . ." option preserves as much of the layer structure as can be done without compromising the appearance of the document. The rules governing which layers are merged (and what parts of the artwork are rasterized) are complex, but in general, layers with features that Illustrator doesn't support will be merged into other layers.

continued on page 463

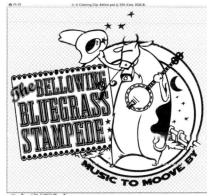

The logo was drawn in Illustrator, with elements organized on layers according to how they would be used in Photoshop, and saved in PSD format, which preserved the layers. In Photoshop the layers were further organized into groups for convenience.

We can think of every Smart Object as having two parts: **contents** that can be edited, and a **"package"** (or bounding box) that's established when the Smart Object is created and can't be changed later. When you create artwork in Illustrator **A** and paste it into Photoshop as a Smart Object **B**, the package is the smallest rectangle that can contain the art.

If you later double-click the Smart Object's thumbnail in Photoshop's Layers panel and edit the artwork in Illustrator, making it bigger than the original bounding box, Illustrator will seem to be enlarging the package **C**, but when you save the edited file, Photoshop will scale as necessary (often disproportionately) to fit the edited contents within the *original* Smart Object bounding box **D**.

This scaling is rarely desirable. To avoid it, there's something you can do when you first create the Illustrator artwork, to ensure that Photoshop will create a bigger package that can then accommodate more changes without distorting the art.

In Illustrator, after you've created the art, add an invisible (no-stroke, no-fill) bounding box shape that's bigger than the artwork itself **E**. Align the center of this object with the center of the artwork, so that if the Smart Object is rotated or scaled in Photoshop, it will be transformed correctly around the center of the graphics.

If you later edit the Smart Object contents in Illustrator, you can add elements anywhere inside the "oversize" bounding box without having the artwork distorted in Photoshop when you save your Illustrator edits **F**.

(When you edit the artwork in Illustrator, you may want to realign the center of the edited artwork with the center of the unchanged bounding box. Do this if you want Photoshop to use the new center of the graphics when the Smart Object "remembers" previous transformations in the Photoshop file.)

A The original graphics in Illustrator

B Pasted into Photoshop as a Smart Object, with a Layer Style added for color and texture

C Edited in Illustrator

D Updating the Photoshop file causes distortion.

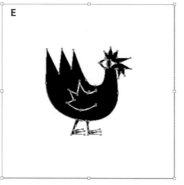

E Adding an invisible rectangle when the graphics are first created, to establish a larger "package" for the Smart Object

F If the graphics are edited within the oversize bounding box, the edited artwork isn't distorted when the Illustrator file is saved and the Photoshop file is automatically updated.

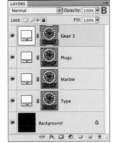

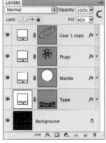

The original Illustrator art **A** was imported as a Shape layer, which was duplicated three times **B**. Then different subpaths were deleted from each layer **C** and Layer Styles were applied **D**. The finished file is included on the Wow DVD-ROM (in Wow Goodies > Outtakes) so you can examine its construction or borrow its Styles.

 Separated graphics.psd

The original Illustrator artwork was pasted into Photoshop as a Shape layer, and a Layer Style was applied **A**, **B**. Then some of the component paths were selected, cut, and pasted into new Solid Color layers with vector masks added, so the color of the neon could be changed **C**, **D** by copying the pink neon Style to all the new layers and then changing the colors for the effects that make up the Style. This file is included on the Wow DVD-ROM (in Wow Goodies > Outtakes) so you can examine its construction or borrow its neon Styles.

Neon. psd

Importing complex graphics. One often used workflow is to construct a complex graphic in Illustrator and then bring it into Photoshop to apply Layer Styles, coloring, or other enhancements to individual components. The goal is to separate all the elements that need different Styles, colors, or treatments onto their own layers in Photoshop, keeping the elements in register as in the original graphic. One approach is described in "Coloring Clip Art" on page 482. A layered Illustrator file is saved in PSD format, with the elements sorted onto layers according to how they will need to be treated in Photoshop.

A second approach, used in the Caffein[3] illustration shown at the left, is to select and copy the desired artwork to the clipboard in Illustrator, and then paste it into a Photoshop file as a single Shape layer; next duplicate this Shape layer as many times as you need for separate treatments, and then delete the unwanted elements from each layer.

Here's a third option, used in the Neon.psd file at the left. Once you've copied the artwork from Illustrator and pasted it as a single Shape layer, in your pasted layer, select any path that you want to put on a layer of its own and cut it to the clipboard. Then add a Solid Color Fill layer (via the "Create new fill or adjustment layer" button at the bottom of the Layers panel), add a vector mask (by Alt/Option-clicking the "Add vector mask" button at the bottom of the Layers panel), and paste (Ctrl/⌘-V). The path will appear in the new layer in exactly the same position where it was when you selected and copied it.

And finally, you can create the artwork in Illustrator (see the tip "Designing Illustrator Artwork for Smart Objects" on the facing page), copy it to the clipboard, and paste it into Photoshop as a **Smart Object**. ▼ You can then treat it like any regular layer in Photoshop, applying a Style or transforming it repeatedly without deterioration; its Smart Object status protects it. If you want to edit the artwork, double-clicking the Smart Object's thumbnail in Photoshop's Layers panel reopens the file in Illustrator, where you can make changes. Saving the edited file in Illustrator automatically updates the Photoshop file.

FIND OUT MORE
▼ Working with Smart Objects **page 75**

EXERCISING

Type Layers

Lance Jackson designed the artwork below for a holiday card for the *San Francisco Chronicle* newspaper, using the Electra font (www.linotype.com). Here, with his and the *Chronicle's* permission, we use it as a model to explore the kinds of typesetting that can be done within a single type layer in Photoshop, as well as other type tasks that require separation of the characters onto more than one layer.

Managing type in Photoshop depends partly on understanding the typesetting controls, most of which are available through the Options bar. But there are also some important tricks to learn about working with type *layers*, such as:

- How to make global changes to an entire type layer
- How to make character-by-character changes
- How to start a new type layer (rather than typing into an existing one)
- How to make a mask for type
- How to finish working on a type layer (see "'Escaping' from a Type Layer" at the right)

We've used the Georgia font for our example (at the bottom) because it's "native" to both Mac and Windows Systems.

LANCE JACKSON /
SAN FRANCISCO CHRONICLE

AFTER LANCE JACKSON,
WITH PERMISSION

THE FINISHED TYPE CAN BE FOUND
in 🅦 > Wow Project Files > Chapter 7 > Exercising Type Layers

1 Setting Type

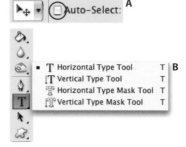

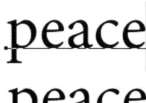

Before pressing Ctrl/⌘-Enter

After pressing Ctrl/⌘-Enter

To FOLLOW OUR EXAMPLE, start a Photoshop document (File > New) 6 inches wide by 3 inches high, at a resolution of 225 pixels/inch, in RGB mode with a white background. Before beginning to set type, choose the Move tool ▸⊕ and in the Options bar, ***turn off the Auto Select Layer option* A**. This will make it easier to manage the type layers.

Choose the Horizontal Type tool (T) **B**. (We'll call it simply the Type tool.) Without worrying about the settings in the Options bar, click in the working window and type the word "peace," using whatever font and size your Options bar is set at; we typed ours in a Minion font at 24 pt size.

Now ***press Ctrl/⌘-Enter***. The Type tool will still be chosen, but the blinking *insertion point cursor* and the baseline indicator will have disappeared from the line of type, as shown above. When there is no insertion point in the type, the choices you make in the Options bar (as you will in a moment) will affect *all the type on the layer.*

"ESCAPING" FROM A TYPE LAYER

When you've finished making changes to a type layer:

- To accept the changes, press Ctrl/⌘-Enter.
- To move on without making the changes, press the Escape key or type Ctrl/⌘-period.

2 Changing the Layer's Type Specs

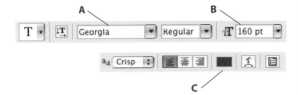

peace

Click the ● button next to the font name near the left end of the Options bar, and choose Georgia **A**. (If you don't have Georgia, you might try Arial.)

One way to make the type bigger than the sizes offered by the Options bar's pop-up size menu is to put the cursor over the ᵀT symbol to the left of the "Set the font size" field, and "scrub," dragging to the right to increase the size (we used 160 pt) **B**. Don't worry if the type extends beyond the edge of the working window. Just hold down the Ctrl/⌘ key to toggle to the Move tool ▶⊕, drag on the type to move it into position, and release the Ctrl/⌘ key to toggle back to the Type tool.

Next, change the color: Click the color swatch in the Options bar **C** to open the "Select text color" box to display the Color Picker, click on a bright red, and click "OK" to close the picker.

CHANGING SEVERAL TYPE LAYERS AT ONCE

To change the color, font, or other characteristics of more than one type layer at a time, first target one of the layers by clicking its thumbnail in the Layers panel. Then Shift-click or Ctrl/⌘-click thumbnails to target the other layers. With the Type tool chosen but no insertion point (if the insertion point is visible, pressing Ctrl/⌘-Enter will turn it off), make the changes you want in the Options bar.

3 Trying Other Fonts

peace **Minion Pro**

peace **News Gothic Std**

peace **Nueva Std**

peace **Georgia**

If you want to try out other fonts for your type at this point, it's easy. With the type layer targeted (highlighted in the Layers panel) and the Type tool chosen, but with no insertion point active, you can change the font for all the type on the layer by choosing a different font from the pop-up list in the Options bar. To try out all the fonts in this menu, one after another, use the method in "Automated Type Showings" below.

If you choose a font other than Georgia, the kerning values suggested later in this exercise may be different than the ones you will need to use.

AUTOMATED TYPE SHOWINGS

It's easy to try out a whole series of different fonts for your type. Make sure your type layer is targeted in the Layers panel. Choose the Type tool **T** but make sure the insertion point is *not* present (if you see it, press Ctrl/⌘-Enter to turn it off). In the Options bar, click in the "Set the font family" entry field. Now press the up or down arrow on the keyboard (↑ or ↓) to step through the available fonts.

Holding down the Shift key as you press the ↑ key will change the font to the one at the top of the pop up list; Shift ↓ will change to the last font in the list.

4 Adding a Stroke

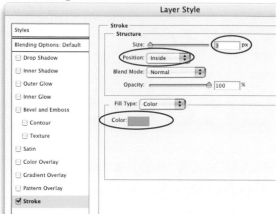

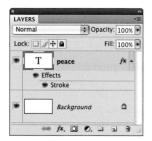

To ADD A STROKE to all the type in a Photoshop layer, you can use a Layer Style. With the type layer targeted in the Layers panel, click the "Add a layer style" button *fx* at the bottom of the panel and choose Stroke from the pop-up menu. When the Layer Style dialog box opens, click the color swatch to choose a stroke color (we chose a bright green). Then experiment to arrive at a Size and Position; we chose a narrow stroke (3 px) and chose Inside (so the stroke wouldn't fatten the type). When your stroke is in place, click "OK" to close the Layer Style dialog box.

5 Changing an Individual Letter

SO FAR, WE'VE MADE ALL OF OUR CHANGES to the entire type layer. Now we'll change the color, as well as the position, of a single letter. When some of the type is selected, any changes made in the Options bar apply to the selected type only. With the Type tool active, click between the "p" and the "e" and drag right to select the "e." Using the color swatch in the Options bar, change the color to black. Don't press Ctrl/⌘-Enter yet. Notice that the Stroke is still present.

HIDING THE HIGHLIGHT

When you select characters on a type layer, a highlight box shows what's selected. But the inverted colors in the selection highlight can make it hard to evaluate your type changes. To hide the highlight, press Ctrl/⌘-H. Pressing Ctrl/⌘-H again restores the highlight.

It can be hard to interpret the type characteristics of selected type (left). To keep the type selected but hide the selection highlight (right), press Ctrl/⌘-H.

6 Rotating a Character

p**e**ace **A** p**a**ce **B**

p**e**ace **C**

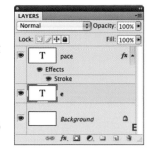

p**e**ace **D** **E**

IN PHOTOSHOP, you can *transform* an entire layer of type (resize, rotate, or skew it), but you can't select and transform only *some* of the characters. So to rotate the "e," we'll put this letter on a type layer of its own.

With the "e" selected (as we left it in "5 Changing an Individual Letter"), cut it from the current layer (Ctrl/⌘-X); then press Ctrl/⌘-Enter to complete the change. Now start a new type layer for the "e": **Hold down the Shift key** and click where the "e" used to be. Since you pressed Ctrl/⌘-Enter to turn off the insertion point, and since you held down the Shift key before clicking with the cursor, a *new type layer* will be added when you paste the "e" (Ctrl/⌘-V); don't worry if the "e" isn't in the right spot **A**. (Notice that the stroke didn't come with the cut-and-pasted letter. A Layer Style disappears in transit when an element is cut and pasted to a brand-new layer. This is fine for the "e" in Jackson's design. We'll see how you can keep a Style if you want to in "8 Overlapping & Restoring a Style" on page 468.)

To rotate the "e" and move it into place, first press Ctrl/⌘-Enter to let Photoshop know you're finished with typesetting. To turn the letter around, choose Edit > Transform > Rotate 180° **B**. Hold down the Ctrl/⌘ key to toggle to the Move tool, and drag the letter where you want it **C**. (For his "peace" design Jackson used a font whose "e" has a higher bar than the Georgia font used here. So we moved the "e" down a bit to allow for the interweaving to come.)

To continue to build Jackson's design, we'll need to move the "e" behind the other characters: Drag its thumbnail down below the "pace" layer in the Layers panel **D, E**.

7 Kerning

p**e**ace **A**

B

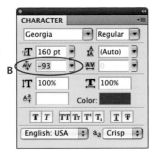

p**e**ace **C**

NOW THAT THE "e" HAS BEEN MOVED to another layer and rotated, we can adjust the spacing of the "p" and "a" so we can intertwine them with the "c." In the Layers panel target the "pace" layer by clicking on its thumbnail. With the Type tool chosen, click in between the "p" and the "a" **A**.

On the Options bar, click the ▣ button to open the Character panel. Now tighten the space between the two letters as much as possible without overlapping them. You can do this by entering a negative number in the **kerning** field and pressing Enter **B**. We zoomed in to the 100% view; this can be done by pressing Ctrl-Alt-0 (Windows) or ⌘-Option-0 (Mac; that's a zero). Then we experimented with bigger negative numbers until the outlines of the two characters seemed to be touching at 93. (To change the kerning, you can use the "scrubbing" method described for the font size in "2 Changing the Layer's Type Specs" on page 465. But for precise control, drag-select the number in the kerning entry field and type in a new number; then press Enter to complete the kerning operation.) Notice that if you kern too tightly, the two characters merge and the stroke disappears where they overlap. That's because the Stroke effect in the Layer Style follows the outline of the *layer contents,* and when you merge the two characters, the outline changes and the Stroke reflects this.

When you've pressed Enter to complete the kerning, press Ctrl/⌘-Enter to let Photoshop know you've finished editing **C**.

8 Overlapping & Restoring a Style

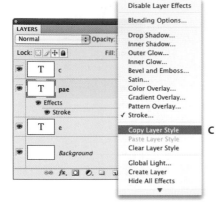

9 Interweaving the Type

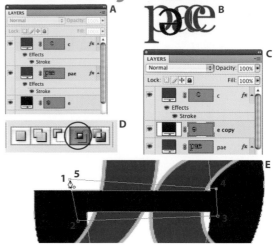

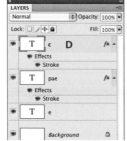

To PULL THE "a" AND "e" TOGETHER and put the "c" on top, drag the insertion point across the "c" to select it and cut it (Ctrl/⌘-X); then click between the "a" and "e" and kern the "ae" pair **A** as in "7 Kerning" on page 467; we used a kerning value of –129. Finally, **press Ctrl/⌘-Enter and then Shift-click** with the Type tool to start a new type layer. Paste the "c" (Ctrl/⌘-V) and then press Enter again. Toggle to the Move tool ▶ by holding down the Ctrl/⌘ key, and drag the "c" into position **B**.

Like the "e" in "6 Rotating a Character" on page 467, the "c" has lost its stroke in transit. But we can restore it. In the Layers panel, copy the Layer Style from the "pae" layer by right/Ctrl-clicking on the *fx for the layer* and choosing Copy Layer Style from the context-sensitive menu that pops up **C**. Then right-click/Ctrl-click in about the same position on the "c" layer's entry in the Layers panel and choose Paste Layer Style to add the Style to the "c" layer **D, E**.

Now THAT WE'VE MADE FINAL ADJUSTMENTS to the spacing, we'll convert the type to Shape layers. By converting, we can be sure to avoid any font complications when the file is output on a system other the one that originated it. To make the conversion, start by targeting the type layers: Click the top type layer and Shift-click the bottom type layer to target the entire stack of them. Then choose Layer > Type > Convert to Shape **A**.

To bring the bar of the black "e" in front of the "p" and "a," we'll put a duplicate of the black "e" above the red "pae" layer and hide all but the bar. Click the black thumbnail for the "e" layer and type Ctrl/⌘-J to duplicate the layer. Drag the thumbnail for the new layer up the Layers panel until it's between the "c" and "pae" layers. Now make sure the vector mask for this layer is active (click the mask thumbnail in the Layers panel once or twice — until the double border appears around it) **B, C**.

To hide all of the "e" except the bar, choose the Pen tool ◊, and in the Options bar **D** click the "Intersect shape areas" button ⬚ so that when you draw a shape with the Pen, only the intersection of the "e" and the new shape will show. Zoom in (Ctrl/⌘-+) and click from point to point with the Pen, to make a path that surrounds the bar **E**; it's OK to include some of the body of the "e" within the path, as long as you don't include any that should be hidden by the overlapping "p" and "a." When you click on your starting point to complete the path (a tiny circle ◊ will indicate that clicking will close the path), most of the "e" will disappear, leaving the bar to complete the interweaving effect. Our final "peace" model is shown at the bottom of page 464.

Type on a Circle

YOU'LL FIND THE FILES

in (wow) > Wow Project Files > Chapter 7 > Circle Type:
- Circle Type-Before.psd (to start)
- Circle Type-After.psd (to compare)

OPEN THESE PANELS

(from the Window menu, for instance):
- Tools • Layers

OVERVIEW

Draw a circle around the central element • Set type on the circle, centered at the top • Duplicate the type layer • Replace the type on the duplicate layer • Lower the baseline • Rotate both type layers to move the type around the circle

DONAL JOLLEY

1a

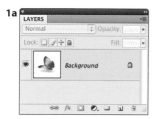

The **Circle Type-Before.psd** file consists of a butterfly image on a white background.

1b

Choosing the Paths mode for the Ellipse tool

1c

The circular path, centered on the butterfly

2a

Setting up the type specifications, including "Center text." Jolley used Schneidler Initials.

HERE'S A QUICK, RELIABLE METHOD for putting type around a circle — some at the top, some at the bottom, and both settings reading left to right.

Thinking the project through. Photoshop can't really set type on a path in two directions on a single layer — clockwise for the quotation and counterclockwise for the author's name. For that you need two type layers. In this example the quotation is set using a circular path as the baseline. The author's name is dropped below the baseline on the same circle but on a different layer.

1 Drawing the circle. Start with the **Circle Type-Before.psd** file **1a**, or with an image of your own. Use the Ellipse tool ⬭ (Shift-U) with the Paths option 🔲 chosen in the Options bar **1b**, to draw a circle: Put the cursor approximately at the center of the element you want to surround with type and start to drag outward; then depress the Shift and Alt/Option keys to draw a perfect circle centered at the starting point **1c**. (If you need to move the circle a little as you draw in order to get it centered right, don't release the mouse button or the helper keys, but press and hold the spacebar and drag; release the spacebar to draw.)

2 Setting the top type. Now choose the Type tool (T). In the Options bar, choose the "Center text" option and choose the font, size, and color you want **2a**. Click on the top of the circle (you'll see the type on a path cursor) **2b** and type the text you want there. As the text is typed, it spreads out from the top of the circle **2c**. Press Ctrl/⌘-Return or Enter to commit the type.

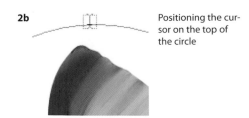

Positioning the cursor on the top of the circle

2c

The finished type layer. The type has spread out in both directions from the initial cursor position.

3 Setting the bottom type. To get a second circular path that's exactly the right size and centered in the same place as the first, duplicate the type layer (Ctrl/⌘-J). Then choose Edit > Transform Path > Flip Vertical **3a**. Now you have a copy of your top type at the bottom of the circle, right-side up and facing the right direction, but inside the circle rather than outside. Before moving the type outside, replace it with the text you want on the bottom: Select All (by putting the cursor in the type and pressing Ctrl/⌘-A) **3b**. Then type the new text **3c** and press Ctrl/⌘-Return or Enter to commit the type.

4 Lowering the type. To put the type outside the circle where it belongs, all you have to do is lower the baseline: Select all the type and enter a negative number in the baseline shift field of the Character panel (Window > Character) **4**. Experiment with the setting until you get it right. You may want to track and kern the type also.▼ When finished, press Ctrl/⌘-Return or Enter.

FIND OUT MORE
▼ Tracking **page 439**
▼ Kerning **page 467**

5 Rotating the type. Moving the type around to the left is easy. Rotate the two circles together: In the Layers panel click the thumbnail for one type layer and Ctrl/⌘-click the thumbnail for the other **5**. Then choose the Move tool (Shift-V), type Ctrl/⌘-T, and drag around outside the Transform frame to turn the type; press Enter. The finished type is shown on page 469.

3a

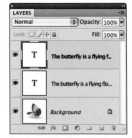

The type layer is copied and the new layer is flipped, which puts type on the bottom of the circle but inside rather than outside.

3b

Selecting the text for replacement

3c

After typing the new text

4

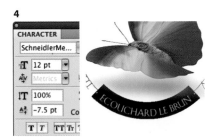

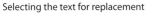

Besides changing the baseline, Don Jolley added bullet characters and spaces. Then he drag-selected the type and changed its color.

5

Targeting the two layers before rotating the type

EXERCISING

Drawing Tools

With Photoshop's drawing tools — the Shapes, Pen, and path-editing tools — you can create vector-based elements that you can then stretch or otherwise reshape with no deterioration of the edge quality.

The aim of this exercise is to create a sun figure like the one below, all in one Shape layer so you can save it as a Custom Shape. You'll learn how to:

- Work with a Grid, Guides, and the Transform command.
- Set up the Options bar to make a new Shape layer or modify an existing one.
- Draw with the Shape tools and the Pen.
- Modify and combine shapes.
- Copy shapes.
- Define a Custom Shape so you can use it again later.

Read the tips as you go along!

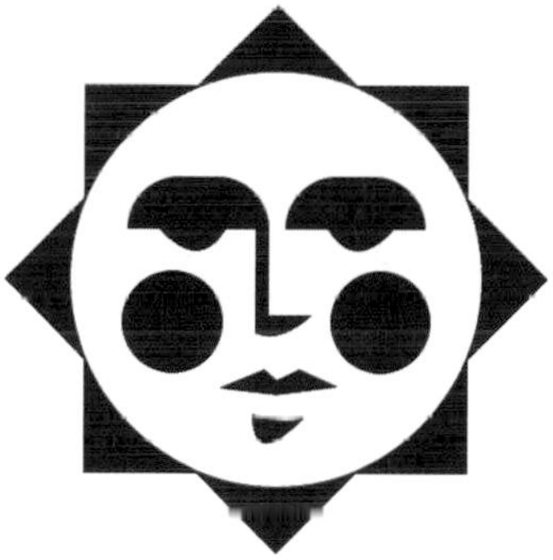

YOU'LL FIND THE FILE

in WOW > Wow Project Files > Chapter 7 > Exercising Drawing Tools

1 Setting Up to Draw

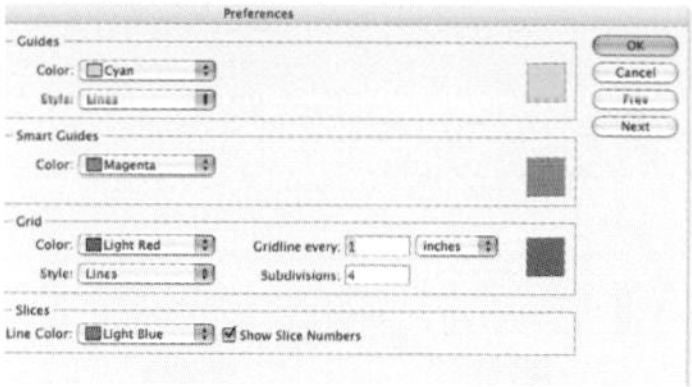

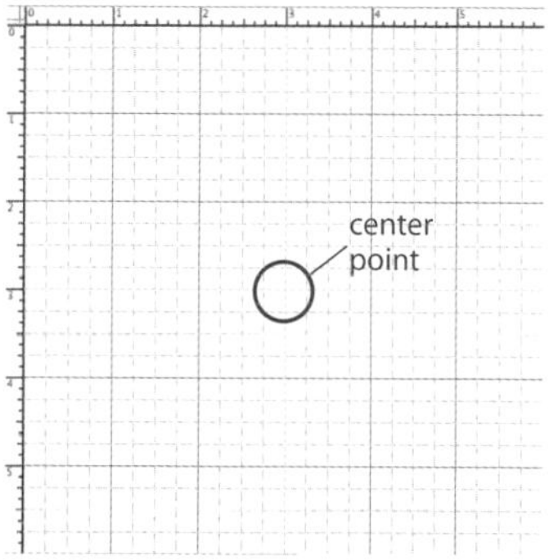

START A NEW SQUARE FILE (File > New; ours was 6 by 6 inches; because we're working with resolution-independent shapes, file size is unimportant, so we chose 72 pixels/inch for a nice-sized on-screen view at 100%). To set up a Grid, open the Preferences dialog box (type Ctrl/⌘-K) and choose Guides, Grid & Slices from the top menu; we used a Gridline every 1 inch, with 4 Subdivisions; click "OK." Make sure View > Show > Grid is on.

Also in the View menu, make sure Snap has a check mark (if not, click Snap to turn it on). Choose View > Snap To and turn on Grid and Guides. This will make the Grid (and the Guide lines you'll add next) "magnetic," so they'll attract the cursor when it gets close, making it easier to draw with geometric precision.

Now in your working window, set a center point: Press Ctrl/⌘-R to display the rulers. Set a vertical Guide by dragging from the left-hand ruler to a point near the center, and set an intersecting horizontal Guide by dragging down from the top ruler. The intersection will be your center.

2 Drawing a Shape

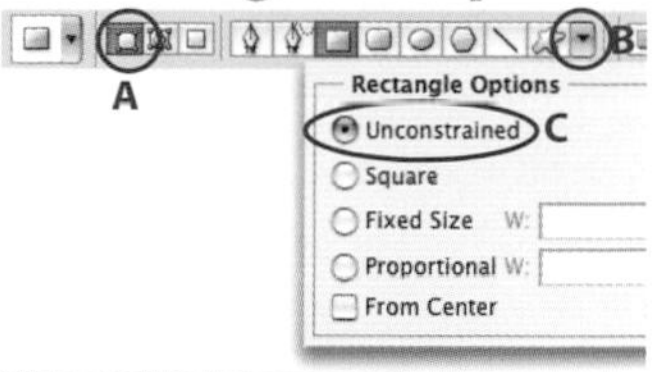

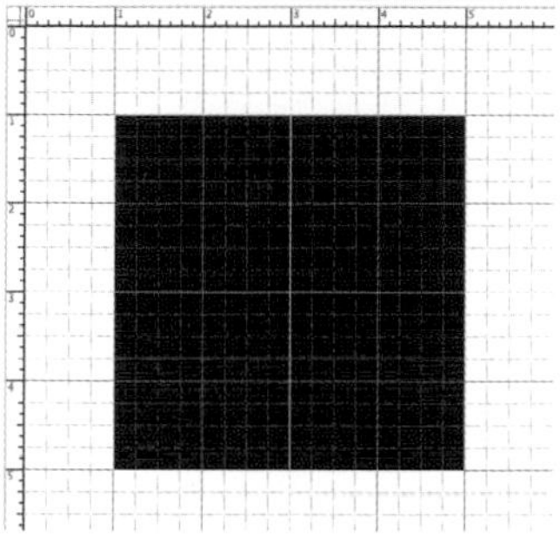

CHOOSE THE RECTANGLE TOOL (Shift-U). Make sure the Options bar is set to create a Shape layer **A**. Click the Geometry Options button **B** and make sure "Unconstrained" is the only option checked **C**. This will allow you to use modifier keys to change how the shapes are drawn while you're drawing them (see the Tip below). If the color swatch isn't black, click it and choose black from the Color Picker.

Put the cursor on the center point, and drag outward, pressing and holding down the Shift and Alt/Option keys once you get started. The Shift key will constrain the shape to a square; the Alt/Option key will cause the shape to be drawn outward, using your starting point as the center.

MODIFIER KEYS FOR DRAWING

Start to draw with a Shape tool and ***then* press**:

- **Shift** to constrain to a 1:1 ratio of width to height.
- **Alt/Option** to draw from the center.
- **Spacebar** to move the path; then release the spacebar to continue drawing.

3 Adding to a Shape

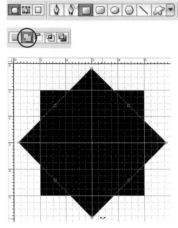

To ADD A SECOND, rotated, square to complete the sun's corona, click the "Add to shape area" button ⬚ in the Options bar. To copy the square and rotate the copy 45°, all at once, press **Ctrl-Alt-T** (Windows) or ⌘-**Option-T** (Mac) and drag around outside the Transform frame to rotate 45°, pressing the Shift key once you get started. (Adding the Alt/Option key creates a copy to transform, and the Shift key constrains the rotation to certain angles, including 45°.) Double-click inside the Transform frame (or press the Enter key) to complete the transformation.

4 Subtracting a Shape

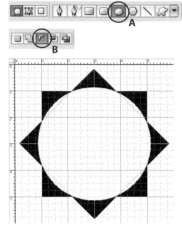

Now IN THE VIEW > Snap To menu, turn off the Grid, so it won't be magnetic and you'll have more freedom to choose where the circle you draw next cuts the squares; but leave Guides turned on so that your center point will still "snap." To choose the Ellipse tool ⬭ quickly, click its button in the Options bar **A**, or press Shift-U twice; also click the "Subtract from shape area" button ⬚ **B**. Draw a circle outward from your center point, again pressing Shift and Alt/Option once you get started to center the shape at the starting point. Make the circle extend all the way out to the "joints" of the corona.

5 Duplicating a Path

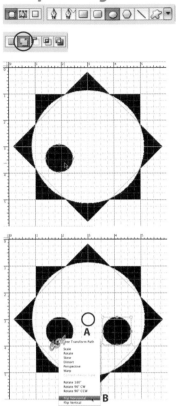

To ADD THE CHEEKS, click the "Add to shape area" button ⬚ in the Options bar, hold down the Shift key, and drag the Ellipse tool ⬭ to make one of the circular cheeks. Then hold down the Ctrl/⌘ key to toggle to the Path Selection tool ▸ and drag the cheek into position where you want it.

Make the second cheek by duplicating the first: Press Ctrl-Alt-T (Windows) or ⌘-Option-T (Mac). In the Transform frame, drag the center point of the circle onto the vertical Guide **A**. Then right/Ctrl-click in the window to open a context-sensitive menu, and choose Flip Horizontal **B**. Double-click inside the Transform frame to complete the move.

NOTHING BUT NEW!

You may find yourself working on a Shape layer and wanting to add to or take away from it, but "Create new shape layer" ▪ is the only one of the five drawing mode buttons available. This may be because you accidentally "detargeted" your Shape layer's mask. To remedy the situation, in the Layers panel, click the vector mask thumbnail once or twice, until you see the double-line frame around it.

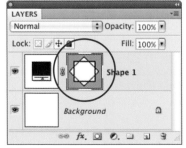

A double border shows that the Shape layer's built-in vector mask is active.

6 Pen Drawing 1

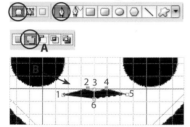

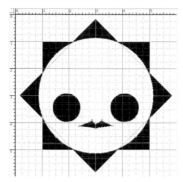

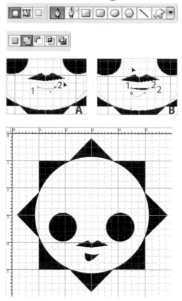

To ADD THE UPPER LIP, made from a series of straight segments, choose the Pen tool 𝆕 (Shift-P) and make sure "Shape layers" ▱ and "Add to shape area" ▱ are chosen in the Options bar **A**. Then click from point to point, without dragging (you can follow the numbers above **B**), finishing by clicking the starting point again.

If you want to reshape the lip, choose the Direct Selection tool ▸ (Shift-A; it shares a space in the Tools panel with the Path Selection tool ▸). Shift click the points you want to move, and drag them. We dragged points 2 and 4 up.

RESHAPING A PATH

To reshape a path, select the Direct Selection tool ▸ (Shift-A). Then:

- Drag a path segment to reshape it.
- Click or drag-select a point (it will look solid while the other points look empty) and then drag the point to move it.

7 Pen Drawing 2

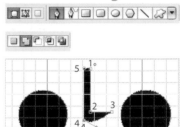

To MAKE THE SHADOW that defines the lower lip, you might want to read these directions all the way through, and then start, but here's the "executive summary": Click at 1, click-drag at 2, Alt/Option-click point 2, click-drag at point 1.

To start, choose the Pen 𝆕 (Shift-P, with "Shape layers" ▱ and "Add to shape area" ▱ chosen) and click to make the first point (1), then click and drag up and to the right a little to make the next point (2), using the drag motion to shape the curve between points 1 and 2 **A**. Since this last segment was a curve, Photoshop thinks you're going to go on drawing curves, so it makes the new point (2) a curve point. But to define the lower lip, you want point 2 to be a sharp cusp, or "hinge." To change point 2 to a cusp, hold down the Alt/Option key (a tiny "convert point" icon ▸ will be added to the Pen cursor) and "re-click" point 2. Then click at point 1, and drag out a handle (a little up and to the left) to shape this curve segment and complete and close the path **B**.

8 Pen Drawing 3

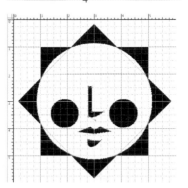

To MAKE THE NOSE, follow the numbers as you draw it as described below, centered around the vertical Guide. (To work close to the Guide without snapping to it, you may want to zoom in — press Ctrl/⌘-+.)

Start by clicking with the Pen 𝆕 to make the point at the top of the right side (1). Shift-click below the first point to make the tip of the nose (2). Shift-click to the right to make the outside corner of the nose (3). Then click and drag (4) to make the bottom curve. Since this last segment was a curve, you need to tell Photoshop that you want point 4 to be a cusp instead of a curve point. So hold down the Alt/Option key and re-click point 4. Now when you click at the top (5), you'll get a straight segment. Click point 1 again to close the path.

CLOSE ENOUGH TO CLOSE

When you draw with the Pen, the cursor signals you with a little "o" 𝆕ₒ when it's close enough to the first point to close the path.

9 Combining Paths

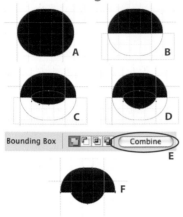

Bounding Box | Combine **E**

F

You could use Photoshop's Pen and Grid to create a symmetrical eyelid shape, but another option is to build it with Shape tools: In the Options bar choose the Rounded Rectangle tool ⬜, with "Shape layers" ⬜ and "Add to shape area" 🔲 chosen, and set the Corner Radius (we used 40 px). Drag to make a shape as wide as you want the eye to be, and twice as high **A**.

Now subtract the bottom half of the figure you drew: In the Options bar choose the Rectangle tool ⬜ and click the "Subtract from shape area" button 🔲, and then drag over the bottom half of the rounded rectangle **B**.

To add the eyeball, in the Options bar choose the Ellipse tool ⬭, click the "Add to shape area" button 🔲 in the Options bar, and then drag to make an ellipse overlapping the eyelid shape **C**. If you want to adjust the shape of the eyeball, as we did, choose the Direct Selection tool ➤ (Shift-A) and drag the bottom point down **D**.

To combine eyelid and eyeball into a single shape, choose the Path Selection tool ➤ (Shift-A), then Shift-click the three paths, and click the "Combine" button in the Options bar **E**, **F**.

10 Finishing up

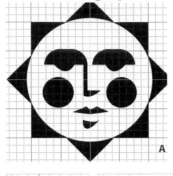

A

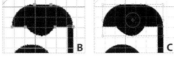

B   **C**

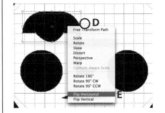

D

E

F

To adjust the position of the eye, drag with the Path Selection tool **A**, **B**, zooming in (Ctrl/⌘-+) for finer control. To make the other eye, press Ctrl-Alt-T (Windows) or ⌘-Option-T (Mac) to make a copy and bring up the Transform frame **C**, as you did for the cheeks. As before, reposition the Transform center point over the vertical Guide **D**. Then right/Ctrl-click in the window to open the context-sensitive menu, and choose Flip Horizontal **E** to finish the eyes **F**. Double-click inside the Transform frame to commit the transformation.

11 Defining & Saving

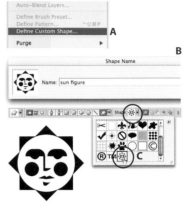

A

B

C

To add your new sun figure to the Shapes that can be drawn with the Custom Shape tool, make sure its vector mask thumbnail is still targeted, and choose Edit > Define Custom Shape **A**. Name the shape and click "OK" **B**. Now if you choose the Custom Shape tool 🔷, you can find your new shape at the bottom of the fly-out Custom Shape picker **C**. When you draw, Shift-drag to keep the figure in proportion. (For safekeeping, it's a good idea to use the Preset Manager ▼ to save a set that includes any new shape you create.)

FIND OUT MORE

▼ Using the Preset Manager **page 82**

STYLING AS YOU DRAW

With the path-drawing tools (Shapes and Pens) you can add a Layer Style *as you draw* a Shape layer: In the Options bar, make sure the 📎 isn't depressed (it should be light rather than dark). Open the Style picker, and choose a Style. Now every new Shape layer you draw will automatically include that Style.

Organic Graphics

OPEN THESE PANELS

(from the Window menu, for instance):

- Tools • Layers

OVERVIEW

Starting with graphics (black and flat colors on white), make a duplicate layer in Multiply mode and shade the edges with the Photocopy filter • Separate the black and colors to two layers • Add a patterned background and a texture layer and adjust the texture layer's blend mode

The original Adobe Illustrator artwork is duplicated to a new layer.

OFIGINAL ARTWORK: 4P GRAPHICS / PHOTOSPIN.COM

The Photocopy filter is run on the Smart Object. (Here we've hidden the filter thumbnails by clicking the arrow button to the left of the "OK" button, to make the preview window bigger.) Detail is set at 10, and Darkness at 8.

THERE ARE TIMES WHEN YOU WANT to take a crisp vector-based graphic out of its slick-lined, flat-colored environment and bring it into a space with a little more texture and a different personality. The step-by-step process presented here allows you to treat line work, color, and background separately. (For a quicker though less sophisticated approach to customizing clip art, see "Quick Filter Treatments" on page 479.)

Thinking the project through. This method calls for filtering, in which case a Smart Object has some advantages. ▼ For instance, filtering a Smart Object allows you to change the filter settings later if you like. So after you've made other adjustments to the file, you can go back and see how changes in the filter settings would interact with the other effects. Or drag and drop a filter treatment from the Smart Object to another file.

When you use only one filter per Smart Object (as we do in this project), setting the Opacity and blend mode for the filter "layer" produces exactly the same result as setting Opacity and blend mode for the whole Smart Object layer. We decided to control these factors through the Smart Object layer, just for simplicity and clarity — that way the settings are out in the open at the top of the Layers panel, and we can see them at a glance and change them very easily.

1 Importing the PostScript artwork.
Open, place, or paste your PostScript artwork into Photoshop in a single layer. ▼ We opened an Illustrator file (File > Open), rasterizing it at about 1000 pixels wide **1**. Our artwork was on a white background,

FIND OUT MORE

▼ Smart filtering
page 72

▼ Importing Post-
Script artwork
page 460

When you work with pixel-based graphics with high-contrast edges, starting with a file that has a resolution of two to three times the value of the halftone screen you will print with, or for web images, twice the size you want to end up with, can reduce the impact of artifacts created by filtering or transforming the art.

2b

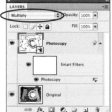

The filtered layer is put in Multiply mode, which makes the white parts transparent. We also experimented with the layer's Opacity, but we left it at 100%.

3a

Using the Magic Wand ✦ to select the black on a second copy of the original artwork. Here we've turned off visibility for the Photocopy layer to better show the selection made from the Colors layer.

which can be important, since some filters work differently on transparency than on white. (An approach for enhancing Post-Script art using a layered file with transparency is presented in "Coloring Clip Art" on page 482.)

Start by duplicating the artwork (one way is to press Ctrl/⌘-J, for Layer > New > Layer Via Copy). We renamed the layers at this point, "Original" below and "Photocopy" for the new layer above. To rename a layer, in the Layers panel double-click on the layer's name and type the new name.

2 Shading the edges. Target the "Photocopy" layer (click on its name in the Layers panel) and convert it to a Smart Object for filtering (Filter > **Convert for Smart Filters**). Make sure black and white are the Foreground and Background colors by typing D (for default). Then instantly turn your graphics into a shaded black-and-white version of the art by running the Photocopy filter (Filter > Sketch > **Photocopy**; we used Detail 10, Darkness 8) **2a**. To let the color show through the black-and-white filter effect, change the "Photocopy" layer's blend mode to Multiply (at the upper left corner of the Layers panel) **2b**. If you want to soften the effect, you can also reduce the Opacity (we did not).

3 Separating the black from the colors. The next step is to isolate the black artwork on one layer and the colors on another so you can easily treat them separately. In the Layers panel, click on the thumbnail for the "Original" layer and duplicate this

Here's what the Photocopy filter (Filter > Sketch > Photocopy) does to graphics:

- Photocopy has no effect on **white** areas; it leaves them white.

- For **black** elements, the filter turns the middle of the shape white and creates black shading extending inward from the edges. However, if the original black shape is narrow — as in type, for instance — the shading from the edges may extend all the way to the middle, so little or no white shows.

- **Colors** and **grays** respond according to how light or dark they are compared to their surroundings. Where they are next to a lighter color or white, the filter treats them more like black, creating shading that extends inward from the edges. But where they are next to a darker color or black, the filter treats them more like white, producing little or no shading. A color shape will show stronger shading if it doesn't have a black outline.

- The **Detail** setting for the Photocopy filter controls how far the shading extends inward from the edges. The **Darkness** setting determines how dense the shading is.

3b

Cutting the selected black artwork to a new layer (Ctrl/⌘-Shift-J) also leaves the color on a layer of its own. Here each new layer is viewed alone.

4a

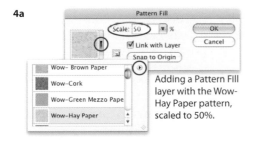

Adding a Pattern Fill layer with the Wow-Hay Paper pattern, scaled to 50%.

4b

The Pattern Fill layer provided an organic background. The Black layer's Opacity was reduced to 70%, and the Colors layer was put in Multiply mode. (This produces a nice-looking result, even without proceeding further.)

layer (Ctrl/⌘-J). We renamed this new layer "Colors," which is what it would soon contain. In this new "Colors" layer, select the black, using the Magic Wand ✸ with these Options bar settings **3a**: **Tolerance** set to 0, so that only 100% black will be selected when you click on a black pixel; **Anti-alias** turned on, for a smooth edge; and **Contiguous turned off**, so that all black will be selected, whether or not it's connected to the pixel you click on; **Sample All Layers turned off,** so the Wand doesn't consider the black in the Photocopy layer. With these settings the Magic Wand selection won't be perfect — it will be slightly smaller than the original black art overall, leaving behind thin dark edges around the color areas. But this won't be a problem because the "Photocopy" layer above will help define the black edges. After clicking on black to make the selection, separate the black onto its own layer by choosing Layer > New > Layer Via Cut (or use the shortcut, Ctrl/⌘-Shift-J) **3b**. We named this new layer "Black."

4 Adding a background. Putting a new background in place now will help you see the "organic" treatment as it develops. One way to add a background is to use a Pattern Fill layer. In the Layers panel, target the "Original" layer by clicking its thumbnail in the Layers panel. Then click the "Create new fill or adjustment layer" button ◉ at the bottom of the panel and choose Pattern from the pop-up list. In the Pattern Fill dialog box **4a**, click the triangle to the right of the pattern swatch to open the picker, and click on one of the available patterns. We chose **Wow-Hay Paper** from the **Wow Organic Patterns** set and adjusted the Scale to 50%. If you haven't yet loaded the Wow presets from the DVD-ROM that comes with this book, ▼ click the ◉ button to the right of the pattern menu, choose Load Patterns, and navigate to the **Wow Organics** (see "You'll Find the Files" on page 475). In the Caution box, click the "Append" button to add the Wow Organic Patterns set to the currently available swatches.

Target the "Colors" layer and put it in Multiply mode to let the Pattern Fill show through. At this point you can experiment by adjusting Opacity; we left the Opacity of the "Colors"

FINDING PATTERNS BY NAME

Looking for a particular pattern? Wherever the Patterns preset picker occurs in Photoshop, you can see all the pattern names as well as the swatches by choosing Large List from the picker's pop-up menu. But even without using one of the List modes, if you have Show Tool Tips turned on in Preferences > General (Ctrl/⌘-K is the shortcut), you can see the name of a particular pattern by pausing your cursor over the swatch.

FIND OUT MORE
▼ Loading the Wow presets
page 4

layer at 100%, but reduced the Opacity of the "Black" layer to 70% to get a look that we liked **4b**.

5 "Airbrushing." For a soft, subtle airbrushing effect, target the "Colors" layer, turn it into a Smart Object (Filter > Convert for Smart Filters) and blur it (Filter > Blur > Gaussian Blur) **5**; we set the Radius to 3 pixels to get the degree of blurring we wanted; because we used "smart filtering," we could adjust the setting later if we wanted to.

6 Adding texture. To add an overall texture to the graphics, try the Stucco pattern from the Patterns 2 presets file that comes with Photoshop: In the Layers panel click on the "Photocopy" layer (the top layer) to target it. Then click the "Create new fill or adjustment layer" button ◕ and choose Pattern. In the Pattern Fill dialog box, click the little triangle to the right of the swatch to open the Pattern picker; then click on that panel's ▶ button and choose Patterns 2 from the list. In the Caution box that pops up, click "Append." The Patterns 2 set will be added at the bottom of the list of swatches, and you can choose Stucco **6a**.

Now change the blend mode of your new gray-stucco-filled layer to Overlay or one of the other modes immediately below it in the list. We chose Vivid Light because it brightened the background color and intensified the texture **6b**. The result is shown at the top of page 475.

Experimenting. With your texture and background in Pattern Fill layers, it's easy to try out other textures. Double-click the thumbnail for the Pattern Fill layer and choose other patterns. You can also experiment by turning on and off visibility or changing Opacity for various layers, or by double-clicking a filter name in the Layers panel and changing the filter settings. 〰

5

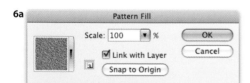
Blurring the "Colors" layer for a softer "airbrushed" look produces another nice-looking result.

6a

Choosing the Stucco pattern from Adobe's Patterns 2 set, for the texture layer

6b

Setting the texture layer's blend mode to Vivid Light brightens the graphics.

Filter Treatments

Some of the options in Photoshop's Filter menu are especially good for quickly turning flat-color artwork into something that looks more organic, textured, or dimensional.

To create any of the effects shown here, go to Photoshop's Filter menu and choose Convert for Smart Filters. ▼ Then choose a filter and make the choices shown in the caption.

Note: In the Tools panel the Fore ground and Background colors were set to the default black and white (by typing D) before the filters were run.

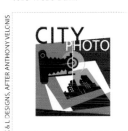

We started with this logo, 1000 pixels square including the white border.

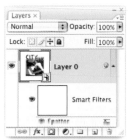

We chose Filter > Convert for Smart Filters and applied one or more filters.

YOU'LL FIND THE FILE
in 🄦 > Wow Project Files > Chapter 7 > Quick Filters

FIND OUT MORE

▼ Smart Filters **page 72**

Roughening the Lines

The following filter treatments act on the quality of the lines and edges.

Brush Strokes > Spatter (Spray Radius 5, Smoothness 10)

Distort > Glass (Distortion 3, Smoothness 5, Texture: Frosted, Scaling 100)

Artistic > Poster Edges (Edge Thickness 2, Edge Intensity 6, Posterization 2)

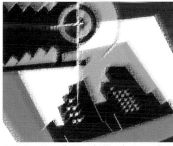

Artistic > Rough Pastels (Stroke Length 6, Stroke Detail 4, Texture: Canvas, Scaling 100, Relief 20, Light: Top Left)

Pattern & Texture

The filters shown here add pattern to the artwork.

Artistic > Sponge (Brush Size 0, Definition 25, Smoothness 1)

Distort > Diffuse Glow (Graininess 10, Glow Amount 5, Clear Amount 10)

Pixelate > Color Halftone (Max. Radius 6, Default Angles)

Texture > Grain (Intensity 30, Contrast 50, Grain Type: Contrasty)

Monochrome Effects

Most of the filters in the Sketch menu render artwork in the current Foreground and Background colors.

Sketch > Chalk & Charcoal (Charcoal Area 6, Chalk Area 6, Stroke Pressure 1)

Sketch > Halftone Pattern (Size 1, Contrast 10, Pattern Type: Line)

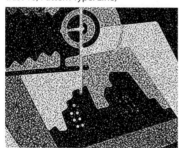

Sketch > Reticulation (Density 12, Foreground Level 15, Background Level 5)

Sketch > Conté Crayon (Foreground Level 11, Background Level 7, Texture: Canvas, Scaling 100, Relief 4, Light: Top Right)

Dimensional Effects

Some filters simulate light and shadow to add thickness to graphics.

Render > Lighting Effects (Style: Default, Texture Channel: Green, Height 100)

Artistic > Plastic Wrap (Highlight Strength 20, Detail 7, Smoothness 7)

Sketch > Note Paper (Image Balance 20, Graininess 5, Relief 10)

Sketch > Plaster (Image Balance 29, Smoothness 1, Light: Top Right)

Lighting

Photoshop's built-in lighting studio (Filter > Render > Lighting Effects) and other filters can light up your graphics.

Render > Lighting Effects (Style: Triple Spotlight, Intensity 100)

Sharpen > Unsharp Mask (Amount 400, Radius 75, Threshold 0)

Render > Lens Flare (Brightness 100, Flare Center moved, Lens Type: 50–300mm Zoom)

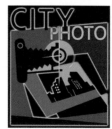

Artistic > Neon Glow (Glow Size 5, Glow Brightness 20, Glow Color yellow-green)

Artistic > Neon Glow (Glow Size –5, Glow Brightness 20, Glow Color yellow-green)

Distorting the Artwork

To distort an entire graphic without having the distortion "flatten out" at the edges, you need empty space around the artwork, as in our example, shown on page 479.

Distort > Twirl (Angle −30)

Distort > Pinch (Amount 50)

Distort > Spherize (Amount 100, Mode: Normal)

Blending the Filter

Produce eye-catching effects by changing the blend mode or Opacity (double-click the ⟱ to the right of the filter's name to open the Blending Options dialog box.)

Render > Fibers (Variance 16, Strength 64) in Overlay mode at 50% Opacity

Blur > Average in Hue mode at 100% Opacity

Stylize > Find Edges in Multiply mode at 100% Opacity

Layering Filters

For other interesting combinations, choose a second filter to treat the Smart Object, at reduced Opacity or in a different blend mode.

Other > High Pass (Radius 30); then Sketch > Photocopy (Detail 7, Darkness 8) in Overlay mode at 100% Opacity

Other > High Pass (Radius 30); then Sketch > Halftone Pattern (Size 1, Contrast 10, Pattern Type: Line) in Color Burn mode at 100% Opacity

Artistic > Plastic Wrap (Highlight Strength 20, Detail 7, Smoothness 7); then Artistic > Neon Glow (Glow Size 5, Glow Brightness 20, Glow Color yellow-green) in Normal mode at 60% Opacity

DONAL JOLLEY

Coloring Clip Art

YOU'LL FIND THE FILES
in (wow) > Wow Project Files > Chapter 7 >
Coloring Clip Art:
- Coloring Clip-Before.psd (to start)
- Checkered.pat (a Pattern presets file)
- Coloring Clip-After.psd (to compare)

OPEN THESE PANELS
from the Window menu, for instance:
- Tools • Options • Layers • Channels

OVERVIEW
Divide the artwork into the layers you'll
need for treating elements separately
• Create layers with line work only and
white-filled base layers • Add color on new
layers in Multiply mode • Add a Pattern
Fill layer • Apply Layer Styles to add
dimension

START WITH YOUR OWN ARTWORK created in a PostScript
drawing program, or take advantage of the zillions of clip art
files out there just waiting for the kinds of coloring and special
effects that Photoshop can do so well. We started with a logo
designed by Don Jolley in Adobe Illustrator. Use artwork of
your own choosing, or open **Coloring Clip-Before.psd** and
follow along.

Thinking the project through. The exact step-by-step coloring
process will depend on the complexity of your original artwork
and how it was created. But several concepts covered here can
be useful regardless of the file you start with:

- If you might want to use some elements of your clip art
  separately, set up your file so the pieces are easy to isolate.

- Like many clip art files, Jolley's original PostScript artwork for
  "Bellowing Bluegrass Stampede" consisted of stacked black-
  filled and white-filled shapes. But in our Photoshop file one
  goal is to isolate the black "line work" on its own transparent

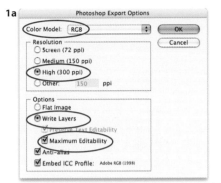

1a

Exporting the file in Photoshop format from Adobe Illustrator

1b

The layered file opened in Photoshop, with Groups created to help organize the layers for the three main parts of the art — the cow, the sign, and the background.

layers so we can apply Layer Styles to add a little dimension to it. The "cleanest" approach starts with using the luminosity of the artwork itself to select the lines.

- We want to replace the white with color, in a way that doesn't produce gaps between the color and the line work. We can use flat colors on a transparent layer in Multiply mode, and then enhance these layers with Photoshop's brush-based tools.

- A Pattern Fill layer is a great way to construct the patterned border, because it will allow us to scale and move the pattern to get exactly the effect we want.

1 Preparing the art. Jolley had set up the Illustrator file as an RGB document (File > Document Color Mode). In Illustrator we sorted the objects that made up the file into layers, using as few layers as we could that would still isolate the areas that would need independent color fills, painting, or different Layer Styles. We ended up with six layers — from bottom to top, a layer for the background elements, four layers for the marquee and lettering, a layer for the cow, and a layer for the stars, moon, and wheat straw. We decided to keep the cow, the marquee and its lettering, and the background elements separate — essentially as three different pieces of clip art. That way we could layer them and adjust their spatial relationships, and we could also use the cow and marquee alone as spot illustrations.

We exported the file (File > Export) and selected Photoshop (psd) from the Save As dropdown list, choosing RGB for the Color Mode in the Photoshop Export Options dialog **1a**, setting the Resolution at High, and clicking the checkboxes to turn on Anti-alias (for smooth edges) and Write Layers (to translate the Illustrator layers directly into Photoshop layers). The resulting file, opened in Photoshop, kept the same layer names. We made a Group for each of our three sections — Cow, Sign, and Background **1b**. ▼

FIND OUT MORE
▼ Setting up Groups
page 583

2 Making black-on-transparent artwork. To isolate the black line work, load the luminosity of the artwork layer as a selection (start with the "Cow" layer in this case), as follows: First turn off visibility for all layers except the one you want to make lines from, by Alt/Option-clicking the 👁 icon for that layer **2a**. Then in the Channels panel, Ctrl/⌘-click on the RGB composite channel's name to load its luminosity as a selection **2b**. This will select all the white areas in the layer completely, leave the black unselected completely, and partially select the gray pixels, such as the ones in the antialiasing that smooths the edges of the lines;

2a

2b

Making only the "Cow" artwork layer visible

Ctrl/⌘-clicking on the composite color channel to load the luminosity of the "Cow" layer as a selection

2c

The selection is filled with black on a new transparent layer to make artwork that can be acted on by a Layer Style later. Part of the new "Cow Lines" layer is viewed alone here.

3a

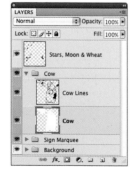

Part of the finished white base layer for the cow, shown above as it would look if viewed alone

lighter grays will be more fully selected than darker ones. Invert the selection (Ctrl/⌘-Shift-I) to select the black instead of the white. Now add a new transparent layer above the artwork layer (in our example, Alt/Option-click the "Create a new layer" button at the bottom of the Layers panel, or type Ctrl/⌘-Shift-N, to open the New Layer dialog box so you can name the layer as you create it; we named ours "Cow Lines"). In this new layer, with black as the Foreground color (type D for default colors), press Alt-Backspace (Windows) or Option-Delete (Mac) to fill the selection with black; partially selected pixels remain partially transparent. Then deselect (Ctrl/⌘-D) **2c**. (By selecting and filling on a new transparent layer, rather than simply cutting or copying the selected line work to a new layer, you avoid bringing along any whitish fringe from the antialiasing at the edges of the lines.)

3 Making a white base layer for the art. Now the black line work is isolated on its own new "Cow Lines" layer, and the black-and-white art is on the original "Cow" layer below. The process of adding color to the artwork (in step 4) depends on using Multiply mode so the solid color will extend all the way into the black "lines," to avoid rough edges on the color or a "fringe" of gray antialiasing between the color and the black. But for Multiply mode to work, there has to be something opaque underneath for the color to affect. So we need a white-filled shape to go below the color layer we'll add.

To turn the original black-and-white artwork into a white base for the color, target the layer by clicking its thumbnail in the Layers panel; we targeted the "Cow" layer. With white as the Background color in the Tools panel (type D if needed) and no selection active, press Ctrl-Shift-Backspace (Windows) or ⌘-Shift-Delete (Mac) to fill all the nontransparent areas on this layer with white **3a**. (Including the Shift key in the keyboard shortcut temporarily turns on the "Lock transparent pixels" function, which can also be set with a button at the top the Layers panel. This way the transparent areas stay transparent and all partially transparent pixels, in the antialiasing in this case, are recolored white but with their partial transparency maintained for a smooth edge.)

To ensure that a white fringe doesn't peek out from behind the black line work in the layer above, we can trim off the edges of the white layer: Ctrl/⌘-click the white layer's thumbnail to load its outline as a selection. Then choose Select > Modify > Contract (1 pixel) to shrink the selection **3b**. Invert the selection (Ctrl/⌘-Shift-I) to select the surrounding transparency and the

We contracted the selection of the white base layer by 1 pixel all around (above). Then we inverted the selection and deleted the 1-pixel edge.

3c

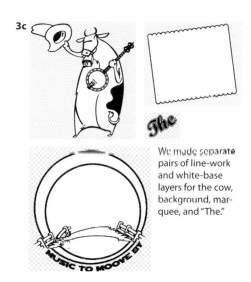

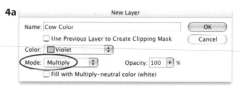

We made separate pairs of line-work and white-base layers for the cow, background, marquee, and "The."

4a

Starting a new layer to hold the color

4b

Setting up the Magic Wand to select filled areas on the color layer only

slightest edge of the white, and press the Backspace/Delete key to trim; then deselect (Ctrl/⌘-D).

For each element repeat the process of isolating the line work and making and trimming a white backing; we created additional black line work and white base layers for the "Background Elements" layer, the "Marquee" layer, and the word "The" **3c**.

4 Coloring the artwork. For each pair (line-work layer and base layer), you'll need a layer above for the color. Target a line-work layer (click its thumbnail in the Layers panel); we started with the "Cow" layer. Then add a new layer above it (Ctrl/⌘-Shift-N; in the New Layer dialog box, choose Multiply for the new layer's blend mode) **4a**.

The next step is to select and color each enclosed shape in the artwork. With the Magic Wand chosen, in the Options bar **4b** turn on both **Contiguous** and **Sample All Layers**, turn **Anti-alias off**, and set the **Tolerance at 254**.

- The **Contiguous** setting will limit the selection to the single black-line-enclosed area you click with the Wand.

- The **Sample All Layers** setting will let you work on your new transparent layer, so you can fill with color there, while allowing the Wand to "see" the artwork in all layers to make the selection.

- Turning **Anti-alias off** will make a selection that will fill entirely with color, rather than adding partial transparency at the edges. This will prevent the edge from getting messy if you select and reselect, fill and refill a selection as you experiment with color. The rough edges won't show because they will blend with the black line work, as described next.

- Setting the **Tolerance at 254** (1 less than the maximum 255 tones) means that if you click on a white area, all pixels except solid black ones will be included in the selection — in other words, the selection will pick up the antialiasing pixels along with the solid white. This makes the color-filled area overlap the black line work slightly, "trapping" the color-and-line interface so there's no gap between them.

In the Layers panel, turn on visibility (the icons) for the line-work layer and the base layer you'll be working with; we wanted to work on the cow first, so we turned on visibility for the "Cow Color," "Cow Lines," and "Cow" layers, and turned off visibility for the other layers. Click each black-line-enclosed area with the Magic Wand, Shift-clicking if you want to add another area to

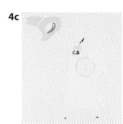

4c

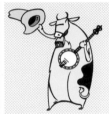

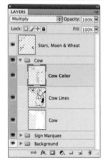

The "Cow Color" layer with all the basic fills in place, viewed alone (top left) and with the "Cow Lines" and "Cow" white base layer (top right). (You can temporarily switch the color layer from Multiply to Normal mode — in the list at the upper left of the Layers panel — to see how the edges of the colors overlap the black lines.)

5a

Setting up the Gradient tool's ⬛ options to color the sky in the "Background Elements Color" layer

5b

Color fills and gradient in place for the Background Elements

6a

The Marquee Color layer with the "Marquee," "Marquee Lines," and two "Lettering" layers visible

be filled with the same color. Then choose a Foreground color (click the Foreground swatch in the Tools panel to open the Color Picker, and choose a color); then press Alt-Backspace or Option-Delete to fill the selection **4c**. (The reason we used the Magic Wand and then filled, rather than using the Paint Bucket at the same settings mentioned, is that we could "multiselect" areas to fill, as described above, and the marching ants would show us which areas were about to be filled, *before* we filled them.)

5 Coloring with a gradient. When the "Cow Color" layer had all its color fills, we turned off visibility for the "Cow" Group and turned on visibility for the "Background" Group. We added a new transparent layer in Multiply mode to hold the colors for this Group. We used the same technique for coloring the fence and grass in the "Background Elements" color layer as we had for the cow. To fill the sky with a blue gradient, we Shift-selected the areas that made up the sky and chose two shades of dark blue as Foreground and Background colors (to set the Foreground or Background color, click its swatch in the Tools panel and choose a color). We used the Gradient tool ⬛ (Shift-G) with the Foreground to Background Linear gradient **5a**, dragging from top to bottom of the selection.▼ We left the circular border uncolored **5b**; we would apply a pattern to this area later (at step 8).

FIND OUT MORE
▼ Working with gradients
page 174

6 Adding a slanted stripe of color. For the sign marquee, we used the same selecting-and-filling technique from step 4 to color the sign yellow. In addition to our line-work, base, and color layers for the Marquee, we turned on visibility for the lettering layers so we could see exactly where to build a green band behind the word "BLUEGRASS" **6a**. We needed to make a tilted rectangular selection in order to fill the band. Here's one way to select a tilted rectangle: To figure out the tilt angle, choose the Ruler tool 📏 (Shift-I) and drag it along one edge of the sign — for instance, position the cursor near the bottom of the right edge of the sign and drag up the edge **6b**. This draws a nonprinting line, and the "A" value in the Options bar and Info panel reports the line's angle; make a note of this number, because you'll need it in a minute. Choose the Rectangular Marquee [_] and drag to select a rectangle of any dimensions. Choose Select > Transform Selection and in

RECALLING MEASUREMENTS

It's easy to recall the length, width, origin, and angle values for the most recent line you've drawn with the Ruler tool 📏. Simply choose the tool again (Shift-I) and read the values in the Options bar or Info panel.

6b

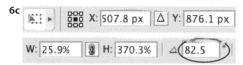

Using the Ruler tool ✐ to find the tilt angle for the sign marquee

6c

Entering the negative of the angle measurement after choosing Select > Transform Selection

6d

The tilted rectangular selection

6e

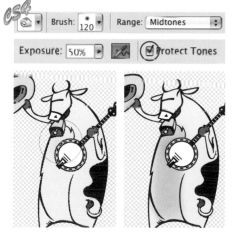

After choosing a green for the Foreground color and pressing Alt-Backspace (Windows) or Option-Delete (Mac) to fill the selected stripe with color

7a

Locking transparency for the color layer

---

the Options bar, type into the "Set rotation" field a value *equal to but opposite* the value you noted for the Ruler tool **6c**; in other words, if the value was –82.5, you would type 82.5; or if the value was 50, you would type –50. Then use the handles of the Transform frame to stretch or shrink the selection to fit the area you want to color **6d**. Complete the transformation (press Enter/Return, or double-click inside the Transform frame) and then fill the selection with color **6e**.

7 Refining the color. To "tune" the color on each color layer, you can use the Dodge tool ✦ (Shift-O) for highlighting and the Burn tool ✊ (Shift-O) for shading, or add highlights or shadows with the Brush tool ✐ (Shift-B) with Airbrush mode ✐ turned on in the Options bar. First, lock the transparent pixels for the color layer (by clicking the ⊡ button near the top of the Layers panel) **7a** to prevent "coloring outside the lines." If you need a selection to fill, use the Magic Wand ✦ (Shift-W) again to select the individual color patches, **but this time turn *off* Sample All Layers** in the Options bar **7b**, so the Wand will only "look at" the active layer — the color layer in this case — as it makes selections. Leave **Contiguous turned on** and leave the **Tolerance at 254** so that each click of the Wand selects *all* the color that's inside the clicked area and surrounded by the transparent gaps — even if you've previously filled the clicked area with a gradient or modified the color with other shades and tones. Select and tone, paint, or refill as you like. We used the Burn tool ✊ (Shift-O) with a soft brush tip to darken various areas of the cow

7b

Setting up the Magic Wand ✦ for selecting patches of color to fine-tune

7c

We used the Brush ✐ to paint the hooves and tail, and the Burn tool ✊ to tone the cow's body and hat. For the body we started with a large soft brush tip (left), made a vertical stroke downward to "burn" the color, and then reduced both the size of the brush tip and the Exposure, and painted to tone the edges of the area. (In CS4 you can turn on **Protect Tones** to prevent pushing a very light or very dark color too far, and to help protect the original hue.)

7d

The "Background Elements Color" layer is fine-tuned by using the Brush tool with the Airbrush option turned on to spray the fence rails and posts with a lighter brown for highlighting.

8a

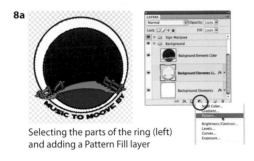

Selecting the parts of the ring (left) and adding a Pattern Fill layer

8b

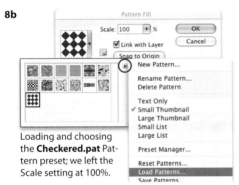

Loading and choosing the **Checkered.pat** Pattern preset; we left the Scale setting at 100%.

8c

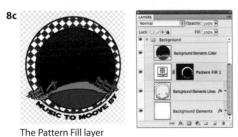

The Pattern Fill layer in place

8d

After turning on visibility for the "Cow" Group, we adjusted the position of the Pattern slightly within the ring.

and the hat **7c**. We also used the selection of the cow to contain the gray paint as we used the Brush (Shift-B) to paint the hooves and the brown paint for the tail. We used the Brush with Airbrush turned on in the Options bar to highlight the fence rails and posts **7d**.

8 Using a Pattern Fill layer. For the ring that frames the sky and ground, we wanted to use a checkered pattern. Instead of simply selecting and filling the ring on the color layer, we used a Pattern Fill layer for more control of the positioning and scale of the pattern. Here's how to do it: Target the "Background Elements" layer and use the Magic Wand (Shift-W) with settings as in step 4 (Sample All Layers turned on), Shift-clicking to select all parts of the ring. Once the selection is complete, click on the "Create new fill or adjustment layer" button at the bottom of the Layers panel and choose Pattern **8a**. In the Pattern Fill dialog, click the tiny triangle next to the pattern swatch to open the Pattern picker **8b**. Then click the button and choose Load Patterns from the menu. Load **Checkered.pat** (supplied with the other files for this section) and watch the working window as you move the pattern (by dragging in the working window) or adjust the size of the squares with the Scale slider **8c**; scale by a factor of 2 (50% or 25%, for example) to prevent "softening" of the pattern. (If you decide later that you want to change the scale or position of the pattern, you can simply double-click the Pattern layer's thumbnail in the Layers panel to reopen the Pattern Fill dialog) **8d**.

9 Coloring some of the black artwork. We wanted to color the stars, moon, and wheat, the "Bellowing Bluegrass Stampede" (the "Inner Lettering" layer), the marquee lights and stars, and the word "The," all of them parts of the black artwork. To repeat what we did:

- For the stars, moon, and wheat, target the layer and lock its transparency (click the button). Paint with the Brush tool (Shift-B) with a hard round brush tip and 100% Opacity **9a**, sampling colors by Alt/Option-clicking the colors already used for coloring the art. Shade the moon with the Burn tool as described in step 7; page 482 shows the result.

- On the "Inner Lettering" layer, choose the color and with transparency locked (click), press Alt-Backspace (Windows)/Option-Delete (Mac) to fill the lettering, the round marquee lights, and the three stars with color all at once **9b**. Then change the color of the lights and stars to white by using the Brush tool , white paint, and a hard round brush tip **9c**: With a brush tip larger than the circles, click to the left of the top row of lights, then Shift-click past the right end; repeat

9a Lock:

Painting the stars

9b

We locked transparency for the "Inner Lettering" layer and filled it with color.

9c

With transparency still locked, we painted over the dots and stars with white.

9d

Setting up options for the Paint Bucket

9e

With Contiguous turned on, we could click to fill the lettering with red while preserving the black outline.

the process for the bottom row of lights and (top to bottom) for the three stars.

- To color the word "The" red, but preserve its black outline, lock transparency for "The Lines" layer and choose the Paint Bucket tool ⬦ (Shift-G). In the Options bar set **Tolerance** to **254** and turn **Contiguous on 9d**; it took three clicks on different parts of the lettering to turn all the black pixels red, including those that were partly transparent for antialiasing **9e**. The black outline, though, shouldn't change, since it isn't touching (contiguous with) the central parts of the lettering that have been clicked.

10 Adding Layer Styles. When you think the coloring is complete — because of the way you've constructed the color layer, you can always go back and recolor later — add dimensionality to the black lines with Layer Styles. To "emboss" the "Cow Lines" layer, we added a subtle bevel by targeting the layer, clicking the "Add a layer style" button *fx* at the bottom of the Layers panel, and choosing Bevel and Emboss **10**. To copy and paste a Style, in the Layers panel, first right/Ctrl-click on the *fx* icon for the "styled" layer and choose Copy Layer Style from the context-sensitive menu. Then, to paste a copied Style to several layers at once, Shift-click or Ctrl-click the layers' thumbnails to multitarget them, and then paste to one of the targeted layers: Right-click/ Ctrl-click to the right of the layer's name and choose Paste Layer Style. We pasted the Style to the "Background Elements Lines" and "Marquee Lines" layers and also to the colored line work in the "Stars, Moon, and Wheat" and "Inner Lettering" layers.

To complete the illustration on page 482 with a subtle layered look, we added a Style with only a Drop Shadow to the white base layers for the cow, marquee, and background. The Drop Shadow becomes more obvious when the artwork is placed against the background of a page, as at the top of page 482. 🐄

10

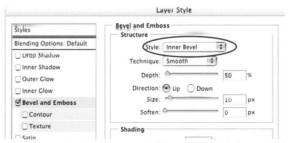

When the Bevel and Emboss panel of the Layer Style dialog opened, we used the default Smooth Inner Bevel, adjusting the Depth and Size to give the line work just a slight "bump."

Black & White Graphics

Photoshop's **Black & White** adjustment can be useful for translating graphics from color to grayscale. Add a Black & White Adjustment layer by clicking the "Create new fill or adjustment layer" button ⬤ at the bottom of the Layers panel, or in CS4 the ▬ button on the Adjustments panel. If you don't like the default conversion, try the "Auto" button, and if that isn't what you want, use the sliders or "scrub" right or left in the image to lighten or darken the shade of gray that represents the color that was at that spot in the original. When you have the conversion you like, choose Image > Mode > Grayscale to convert the image for printing in a single color.

With an illustration it can be a little harder than with a photo to remember the original colors once you've added the Black & White Adjustment layer. But you need the color information so you can scrub in the right place or move the correct slider. If the graphics are fairly simple, a large thumbnail in the Layers panel may be enough of a color reference. From the Layers panel menu, choose Palette Options/Panel Options and choose the largest thumbnail. For a more complex illustration (like the maps at the right), you may want to duplicate the artwork (Image > Duplicate > Duplicate Merged Layers Only) in its own floating window.

FIND OUT MORE

▼ Black & White
adjustment **page 214**

YOU'LL FIND THE FILES
in wow > Wow Project Files >
Chapter 7 > Quick Black & White

Converting Graphics

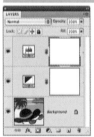

ORIGINAL GRAPHICS: FANATIC STUDIO / PHOTOSPIN.COM

AFTER EVALUATING the default and Auto settings for the Black & White Adjustment layer, we decided to "scrub" in the image. In Photoshop CS3 simply "dab" left or right. In CS4 you'll need to click the Scrubber button 🖑 before you start. Experiment with lightening and darkening this way until you get the balance you want. If you find that you're close, but not really getting closer by experimenting, add a Levels or Curves Adjustment layer (click ⬤ on the Layers panel and choose, or in CS4 click ⬛ or ⬛ on the Adjustments panel). Use the "Auto" button or adjust by hand to fine-tune.

wow **BW Graphics.psd**

Saving a Preset

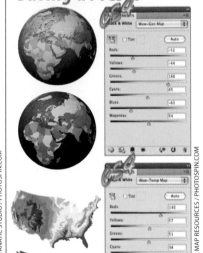

ORIGINAL GRAPHICS: MAP RESOURCES / PHOTOSPIN.COM

WHEN YOU DEVELOP Black & White settings that might be useful again, it's easy to save them. For instance, geopolitical maps are often colored with four pastel colors to separate the countries or states. Although the colors are quite distinct, when converted to grays they can be hard to tell apart. And climate maps often use a range of cool to hot colors that don't translate automatically to a useful progression of grays. If you're converting a series of maps, graphs, or other illustrations, it makes sense to save your Black & White settings as a preset and apply it to the entire series. But even if you're converting only one map now, the preset you develop may be a good starting point for other maps in the future.

We tried the default and Auto, then developed a conversion for the globe, mainly by scrubbing. For the climate map we made a progressive arrangement of the color sliders. Again, you can add a Levels or Curves layer for fine-tuning.

wow **BW Presets**

Alicia Buelow mixed many images and techniques in developing *No. 9, The Escape*. She used a scanned photo of concrete as a background, selected an area at the top with the Rectangular Marquee ⬚ and colorized it with Image > Adjustment > Hue/Saturation with Colorize turned on.

She made the bottom section of the inner rectangle by scanning a paper collage, opened the scan in Photoshop, and reversed the color (Ctrl/⌘-I), making a negative, before colorizing it with Hue/Saturation in the same way she had done the top.

Buelow scanned a broad brush stroke made with black ink, copied and pasted it into the working file and put it in Multiply mode. She

made long rectangular selections of a scanned texture and applied them in Color Burn mode to make the frame. To complete the background, she colorized it gold and layered over it a scan of a 19th-century map.

To create a "calligraphic" outline, she first used the Pen tool ✒ to draw the bird. Then with white as the Foreground color, she clicked the "Fill path with Foreground color" button ● at the bottom of the Paths panel (the white fill is shown in red at the right so it's easier to see). Next, she Ctrl/⌘-clicked the bird layer's thumbnail in the Layers panel to load it as a selection; then she made the selection a little smaller (Select > Modify > Contract) and Alt/Option-clicked the "Add a layer mask" button ⬚ at

the bottom of the Layers panel. This made a black mask that hid all but the very edge of the bird graphic. She unlinked the mask from the graphic by clicking the 🔗 between them in the Layers panel. Now, with the Move tool chosen, she could target the mask by clicking its thumbnail in the Layers panel and then drag in the image to offset the mask, creating an irregular outline.

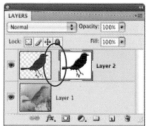

PERSUASION: RECEPTION AND RESPONSIBILITY

JOHN ODAM

Charles U. Larson 10th Edition

In developing the cover illustration for *Persuasion: Reception and Responsibility, Tenth Edition*, by Charles U. Larson (Wadsworth), designer **John Odam** used type to mask photos. He started by setting the Futura Extra Bold type, one letter per layer, in black. Many of the changes Odam planned to make to the type — scaling the characters and changing their baselines, for instance — could have been done with a single type layer. But to tilt (rotate) the letters individually, overlap them in any order, and add a separate drop shadow to each letter, even when letters overlapped, he had to put his characters on different layers.

Odam didn't need the type to remain editable — the title of the book wasn't going to change at this point, and by eliminating the live type he could avoid any font problems during output. Converting it to a Shape layer would preserve the sharp letter outline, even if the file was resized, so he clicked its thumbnail in the Layers panel and chose Layer > Type > Convert to Shape from the main menu.

After converting the type and targeting one of his letter layers by clicking its vector mask thumbnail in the Layers panel, Odam transformed the individual black letter (by pressing Ctrl/⌘-T for Edit > Free Transform Path and dragging — outside a corner to rotate, or on a corner handle with the Shift key held down to scale proportionally, or inside the Transform box to reposition.

When the layout was complete **A**, he began to add photos; some he shot himself with a digital camera and some were purchased as stock photography. He opened the photo files and then clicked in the working window of the layout file to activate it. If you target a letter layer, and then drag the photo you want to mask with that layer into the file, the photo becomes a layer just above its

letter. Then by Alt/Option-clicking on the line between the photo and letter layers in the Layers panel, you form a clipping group that masks the photo inside the letter **B**. Using the Move tool ▶₊, you can drag in the working window to move the photo until the part of the image you want shows in the letter.

When all the photos had been clipped inside letters, Odam targeted one of the letter layers and added Photoshop's default drop shadow by clicking the "Add a layer style" button *fx* at the bottom of the Layers panel, choosing Drop Shadow from the list of effects, and clicking "OK" to close the Layer Style dialog box. Then he duplicated the drop shadow to the other letter layers (see "You Have Three Choices . . ." below)

A finished file composed of clipping groups and Layer Styles offers a great deal of flexibility, because you still have separate access to each of the photos, letter shapes, and effects.

When Odam had finished his illustration, he made a single-layer copy of it (Image > Duplicate, choosing Duplicate Merged Layers Only),

saved it in TIFF format, and placed it in a page layout file, where he added type for the title and author.

A

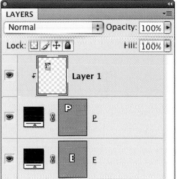

B

THE
SEASONS
OF A SOUL
RHYME
WITH
HOT
WARM
COOL
AND
COLD.

To create the abstract background for his type in *Seasons of the Soul,* **Steven Gordon** opened a photograph **A** and turned it into a pattern (Edit > Define Pattern). He closed the photo file and created a new document at 72 pixels/inch. Gordon chose the Pattern Stamp tool 🖌, clicked the Tool Preset picker at the left end of the Options bar, and chose the **Wow-PS Dry Brush-Large** preset from the **Wow Pattern Stamp Brushes** set of presets. ▼ In the Options bar he lowered the brush's Opacity to 50%, but he kept the pattern Aligned and kept Impressionist turned on. On the canvas Gordon painted short, overlapping strokes **B**. Because the source image was larger than the document on which he was painting, only the upper left corner of the source contributed to his Pattern Stamp strokes.

When he finished painting, Gordon added a Hue/Saturation layer (clicking ◐ at the bottom of the Layers panel) and increased the Saturation to make the colors more vibrant. He increased the document's resolution to 288 pixels/inch (Image > Image Size, with Resample Image checked) and used Unsharp Mask to sharpen the definition of the brush marks. ▼

To create the four-seasons type, Gordon selected the Horizontal Type tool T. In the Options bar's font list he chose Cancione, an all-capitals font designed by Brenda Walton (www.itcfonts.com). To make a solid block of type that would hold together well as he warped it, he clicked the Options bar's "Toggle the Character and Paragraph panels" button and set the font size and leading the same, which would leave little space between the lines of type. He clicked in the working window, automatically creating a new type layer, and keyed in the text, beginning with "WINTER" and pressing the Enter/Return key at the end of each word. When the type was set, he clicked the "Create warped text" button in the Options bar, and chose the Twist style in the Warp Text dialog box **C**. He adjusted the Bend and Distortion controls until he had the geometry he wanted **D**. In the Layers panel, Gordon changed the blend mode for the layer to Overlay so the background colors of the painting affected the color of the type. Finally, he set off the type by clicking the fx button at the bottom of the Layers panel and adding a Drop Shadow, changing its color to white, its Mode to Normal, and its Opacity to 30%. To fade the type on the right side, he added a layer mask by clicking the button at the bottom of the panel and applied a gradient to it. ▼

For the verse, Gordon used paragraph type: He dragged with the Type tool T to create a rectangle for the type, then moved the cursor outside a corner of the type box and dragged counterclockwise to rotate the box to the angle he wanted for the verse. In the Options bar he chose the OpenType Lithos Pro font and the right-aligned option. In the Character panel he chose type size and Auto leading, and typed the verse, pressing Enter/Return whenever he wanted to start a new line **E**, **F**.

 You'll find a low-resolution version of Steven Gordon's **Seasons.psd** file in Wow Goodies so you can inspect its construction and experiment with the type.

FIND OUT MORE

▼ Loading the Wow presets **page 4**

▼ Using Unsharp Mask **page 337**

▼ Masking with Gradients **page 84**

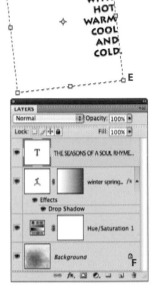

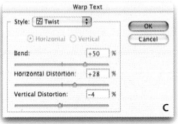

Special Effects for Type & Graphics

8

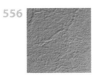

If you haven't worked extensively with Styles and you haven't yet absorbed "Exercising Layer Styles" (pages 80–83), you might want to look at that section now, as a quick introduction to the subject. It includes some important tips for applying, copying, and saving Styles.

"Honoring a Style's 'Design Resolution'" on page 83 tells how to keep a Wow Style looking the way it was designed to look, even if you apply it to a file whose resolution is very different from the file in which the Style was designed. Knowing this little secret can make the difference between the result on the left (the Wow-Clear Orange Style applied to a file at 72 pixels/inch) and the one on the right (with the same Style applied to a file at its design resolution of 225 pixels/inch).

Turning a flat graphic or type into a translucent dimensional object is just one of the things you can accomplish with a Layer Style. The Layer Style used for the type above is described in "Anatomy of Clear Color" on page 525.

Most of the special effects in this chapter are designed to simulate what happens when light and materials interact — from a simple drop shadow to the complex reflections and refraction of chrome, brushed metal, or glass. Photoshop's Layer Styles excel at creating "live" special effects for graphics and type.

WORKING WITH LAYER STYLES

With Layer Styles you can create entire dimensional lighting and color schemes wherever you want them. Because Styles are such a powerful component of Photoshop's bag of tricks, they were introduced in Chapter 1 in "Exercising Layer Styles" (page 80). But here's a brief recap of some of the important features.

A Layer Style (or simply Style) is a collection of effects — such as glows, shadows, dimensional edges, and textures. It can be added to any layer that isn't completely locked — that is, any layer that doesn't have a solid black 🔒 symbol next to its name in the Layers panel. And you can edit and re-edit the effects — changing the lighting direction or the shape of a beveled edge — without degrading the element you've "styled."

The Layer Style is applied to or contained within an edge that's determined by the "footprint" of the layer's pixels, type, or Shape — the demarcation between what's transparent and what's opaque on a layer. The edge may be modified by a **layer mask** or **vector mask**. ▼ As the default, both of these masks help define the edge for the Layer Style.

FIND OUT MORE
▼ Using masks
page 61

A Layer Style can consist of as many as 12 different component **effects**, along with the **Blending Option**s that govern how the effects interact with the layer's content and how the layer itself interacts with other layers in the file. Most of the effects (and the Blending Options) have several parameters you can change, and there are *millions* of possible combinations of settings.

Photoshop comes with collections of **preset Styles** that can be loaded for use by choosing from the Styles panel's pop-out menu ▾≡. The bottom part of the menu lists all the preset files that are currently in the Styles folder (created inside the Presets folder in your Photoshop application folder when you install the program). You can choose Load Styles to find and load others.

To **develop your own custom Styles**, you can start by applying an existing Style and then edit it in the Layer Style dialog box. Or build a Style from scratch by targeting any unlocked and

THE LIST IN THE LAYER STYLE DIALOG

All the effects that you can incorporate in a Layer Style are listed at the left side of the Layer Style dialog box.

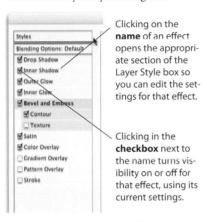

Clicking on the **name** of an effect opens the appropriate section of the Layer Style box so you can edit the settings for that effect.

Clicking in the **checkbox** next to the name turns visibility on or off for that effect, using its current settings.

"unstyled" layer in the Layers panel and clicking the "Add a layer style" button *fx* at the bottom of the Layers panel and choosing an effect from the pop-up menu (or use one of the other methods in "Getting Inside the Box" on page 500). In the Layer Style dialog box adjust the settings for the effect you chose, and then choose another effect, if you want, from the list on the left side of the box. You can go on this way, choosing effects and setting parameters for as many effects as you want in your Style.

Once a Style is applied, it can be copied, with all its component effects, to other layers or other documents — it can even be named and saved as a **preset** for future use. When you apply these portable Styles to other layers, they can be **scaled to fit** the new elements you apply them to, with a single easy scaling operation that adjusts all the component effects at once.

continued on page 501

APPLYING A PRESET STYLE

"Exercising Layer Styles" on page 80 provides a quick but thorough introduction to working with Styles. But here's a summary of how to simply apply a Style from the Styles panel. With both the Layers panel and the Styles panel open (they're available through the Window menu):

1 Target any unlocked layer (click the layer's thumbnail in the Layers panel).

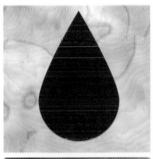

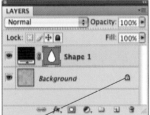

A Style can't be applied to a *Background* or to any fully locked 🔒 layer.

2 Click the Style of your choice in the Styles panel, which holds Styles that you've loaded and any new ones that you've saved. (Page 4 tells how to load the Wow Styles.)

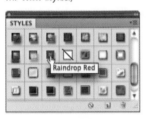

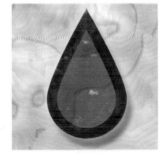

3 In the Layers panel, right-click/Ctrl-click on the *fx* for the "styled" layer and choose Scale Effects from the context-sensitive menu. Experiment with the Scale slider to get the best "fit." Styles that include patterns should be scaled with care (see page 81).

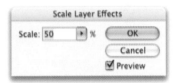

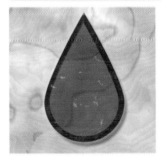

COPYING A STYLE FROM ANOTHER LAYER

You can copy a Style from another layer in the same file or from another open file:

1 In the Layers panel right-click/Ctrl-click on the *fx* for the "styled" layer and choose Copy Layer Style from the context-sensitive menu.

2 Right-click/Ctrl-click to the right of the unstyled layer's name in the Layers panel and choose Paste Layer Style.

3 If you like, open the Scale Layer Effects dialog and experiment with the scale of the Style, as described in step 3 on page 499.

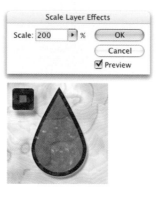

GETTING INSIDE THE BOX

There are several ways to open the Layer Style dialog box. Once you're "inside the box," you can use the list on the left side (as shown on page 499) to move from effect to effect or to set up the Blending Options.

For a layer that already has a Style applied to it, double-click the *layer's fx icon* in the Layers panel (this method opens to the **Blending Options** section).

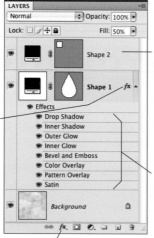

Click the "Add a layer style" button *fx* at the bottom of the Layers panel and choose an **effect** you want to work on.

Double-click in the space to the right of a layer's name in the Layers panel (this method opens to the **Blending Options** section of the Layer Style dialog box).

In the Layers panel, in an **expanded list of effects** for a layer that already has a Style applied to it, double-click the Effects line (this opens the Layer Style dialog to the **Blending Options**), or double-click a specific **effect line** to open that section.

Choose Layer > Layer Style and choose an **effect** you want to work on, in order to open the Layer Style dialog box to that section.

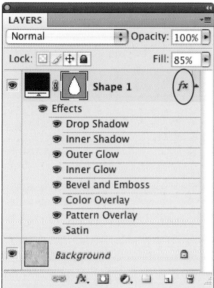

An *fx* icon to the right of a layer's name in the Layers panel means that a Layer Style has been applied to the layer. By clicking the little triangle next to the *fx*, you can display the list of effects used in that particular Style, as shown here. The "jewel" above was developed by adding a Layer Style to a dark gray shape.

 **Styled Shape.psd**

UNDERSTANDING STYLES

The next few pages show how the component effects of Photoshop's Layer Styles work. The "Anatomy" sections of the chapter provide examples of exactly how the effects in a Style work together to create different materials, dimensionality, and lighting. The layered-and-styled "Anatomy" files on the Wow DVD-ROM offer a compact, interactive, and interesting way for you to pick up the details of what constitutes a Layer Style. All of a Style's different effects and Blending Options interact with one another, and a slight difference in the combination can make the Style turn out very different than you expect. If one or two little settings are left unmodified, or if your Blending Options are set up differently, instead of translucent blue glass, you could end up with slick black plastic!

The step-by-step special-effects techniques in the chapter show how to develop these highly tactile dimensional treatments even further with additional image layers and Adjustment layers. When you start one of these step-by-step techniques, you may want to **open not only the "before" version** of the artwork from the Wow DVD-ROM, **but also the "after" file**, so you can refer to it as you work. Also, if your goal is simply to *use* a particular Style from the "after" file rather than learning exactly how it's put together, you can apply the Style by copying and pasting from the file, as described on page 82.

Exploring the Layer Style Dialog Box

One way to learn about how the settings work in a Shadow or Glow or any other effect is to make a type or Shape layer, then open the Layer Style dialog box and for each effect that you want to explore, click its name in the list on the left side of the dialog box to open its section of the box. Then set Opacity to 100%, Blend Mode to Normal, and all other parameters to their minimum settings. Experiment by changing the settings one at a time and in combination, seeing what each one does and how it interacts with the others.

Taking a Style Apart

Another interesting experiment is to set up several effects to create a Style, as we have in the **Styled Shape.psd** file shown at the left, and then rasterize the effects (right-click/Ctrl-click the layer's *fx* icon and choose Create Layers from the context-sensitive menu). Each effect will be separated into a layer of its own, as shown on the next page — some effects may even need two layers. Notice where the new layers fall in the Layers panel — some will be above and some below the layer you applied

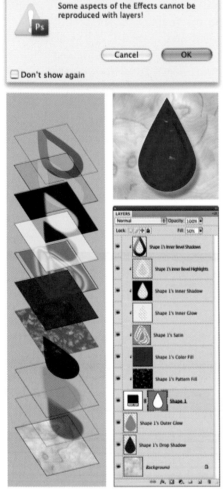

Adobe Photoshop

Some aspects of the Effects cannot be reproduced with layers!

Cancel   OK

☐ Don't show again

LAYERS

Normal ▾   Opacity: 100% ▸

Lock: ▨ ✎ ✛ 🔒   Fill: 50% ▸

Shape 1's Inner Bevel Shadows

Shape 1's Inner Bevel Highlights

Shape 1's Inner Shadow

Shape 1's Inner Glow

Shape 1's Satin

Shape 1's Color Fill

Shape 1's Pattern Fill

Shape 1

Shape 1's Outer Glow

Shape 1's Drop Shadow

Background

The Create Layers command renders the effects in a Layer Style as separate layers. As shown here for the **Styled Shape.psd** file shown on page 501, sometimes with a Layer Style the whole is greater than the sum of the parts, and the combination of effects you can create with a Style can't be successfully rasterized into separate layers. The "jewel" has lost some important characteristics in the translation from Style to separate layers.

the Style to. The order of the layers can be enlightening. The "effects" layers that are above the original "styled" layer will be included in a clipping group ▼ with your original layer serving as the base (as shown in the Layers panel at the left), so the effects show only *inside* the outline created by the original layer. If you now Alt/Option-click in the Layers panel on the border between the original layer and the one just above it in the Layers panel, the layers will be released from the clipping group, and you'll be able to see what the clipping group was accomplishing. Now experiment by clicking the 👁 icons for individual layers.

FIND OUT MORE

▼ Clipping groups
page 65

LOST IN TRANSLATION

When you choose the **Create Layers** command, a Caution box will warn you that some aspects of the Style cannot be reproduced with layers. For safekeeping, save your Style before you Create Layers: Click the "Create new style" button ⬜ at the bottom of the Styles panel, name the Style if you like, and click "OK." It will be added to the Styles panel.

LAYER STYLE COMPONENTS

Many of the individual components of a Layer Style are named for the specific effects they were designed to create — Drop Shadow, Inner Shadow, Inner Glow, Outer Glow, and so on. Examples of these effects are shown in "Layer Style Options" on page 503. But a *brightly colored* Drop Shadow can also be put to work as part of a glow (as in the Wow-Neon & Glows set shown on page 767), and a *dark* Inner Glow can help build realistic shadows (as in "Anatomy of Clear Color" on page 525). If you can get beyond the names and understand how each effect can interact with the others, you'll greatly expand the creative potential that Styles offer.

Another important aspect of Styles is lighting — what direction the light comes from, whether it's directly overhead or more oblique, and how strong it is. Let's start with the simplest of the effects — the Color, Gradient, and Pattern Overlays, then explore lighting, and the effects in which lighting plays a role.

OVERLAYS

The three **Overlay** effects provide an easy, flexible way to add a solid color, pattern, or gradient, with complete freedom to change it at any time. The Overlays interact as if they were stacked in the same order they occur in the Layer Style dialog's list: Color Overlay (a solid color fill) is on top, then Gradient,

continued on page 504

LAYER STYLE OPTIONS

A Layer Style can be made up of any of the effects shown here: There are three **Overlays** for coloring the surface, two **Shadows** and two **Glows**, a **Satin** effect, and a **Stroke**. The **Bevel And Emboss** effect has five different kinds of bevel structures, as well as a **Contour** to shape the bevel. The structure and lighting in the Bevel and Emboss effect also control the "bump mapping" added by the **Texture** effect.

 Style Samples.psd

Inner Shadow

Bevel And Emboss: Inner Bevel

Outer Glow

Bevel And Emboss: Outer Bevel

Color Overlay

Inner Glow: Edge

Bevel And Emboss: Emboss

Gradient Overlay (Solid, 90°, Reflected)

Inner Glow: Center

Bevel And Emboss: Pillow Emboss

Gradient Overlay (Noise, 27°, Linear)

Satin

Bevel And Emboss: Stroke Emboss

Pattern Overlay

Stroke: Color

Bevel And Emboss with Contour

Drop Shadow

Stroke: Shape Burst Gradient

Bevel And Emboss with Texture

A shadow created with the Drop Shadow component of a Layer Style can be separated from its graphic element and rendered as a layer of its own (one way is to choose Layer > Layer Style > Create Layer). Then it can be distorted with the Free Transform command (Ctrl/⌘-T) ▽ to produce a cast shadow. Another Layer Style, including a Drop Shadow, can then be added to the graphic element to create dimensionality and surface characteristics that remain "live" and editable.

FIND OUT MORE

▽ Free Transform command **page 67**

A Layer Style was used to add a **Drop Shadow** to the "Home icon" layer. Then the Style was separated to create an independent shadow layer that could be manipulated to make a cast shadow. A new Style, including a Drop Shadow with its Distance set to 0 to make a "dark halo," was added to the "Home icon" layer to build dimensionality, lighting, and surface characteristics.

then Pattern. With **Color Overlay** you can darken a recessed element, as if it were in a shadow created by carving it into the surface; the two **Wow-Carved** Styles (shown in Appendix C) are examples. Or store color information that you want to apply often — the corporate color for a logo, for instance — so you can apply this Color Overlay wherever you need it.

For the **Gradient Overlay** if the **"Align with Layer"** box is **checked, the gradient starts at the edge of the layer content**. With the box checked it's as though the entire gradient is "poured into" the opaque part of the layer, and if you move the layer content after closing the Layer Style dialog box, the gradient will move with it. With the box **unchecked, the gradient will be aligned with the edge of the *document***, and it may be that only part of the gradient will fall within the layer content. (The edge of the document may be outside the canvas if any layers are oversized or have been moved partly "offstage.") **Angle** sets the direction of the color changes, and **Style** offers the five gradient types (these are demonstrated on page 175). The **Scale** slider can be used to compress or expand the gradient. When the Scale is less than 100%, the end colors extend to fill the edges. Anytime the Layer Style dialog is open to the Gradient Overlay section, you can adjust the gradient's position just by dragging in the image window.

For the **Pattern Overlay** if the **"Link with Layer"** box is **checked** when you apply the effect, the pattern starts at the upper left corner of an imaginary bounding box around the **layer content**. With the box **unchecked**, the pattern starts at the upper left corner of the **document** instead. *After* you apply the pattern, however, checking or unchecking the "Link with Layer" box doesn't by itself shift the pattern's position. You have to uncheck the box, and then click the "Snap to Origin" button. You can also change the pattern's position by dragging in the image window. Checking the "Link with Layer" box also binds the pattern to the layer. If you move the layer content around (after closing the Layer Style box), the pattern will move along with it. The **Scale** slider lets you shrink or enlarge the pattern without resizing the layer content.

Note: Since patterns are pixel-based rather than instruction-based like most of the other effects in a Layer Style, a Pattern Overlay can "soften" with scaling. This is also true for both the Texture effect and a patterned Stroke. ▽

FIND OUT MORE

▽ Scaling Styles that include patterns **page 81**

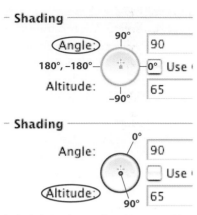

In the lighting diagram found in many of the effects in the Layer Style dialog box, the compass direction around the circle determines the direction of the light source (Angle). The distance from the center of the circle determines the height of the light source above the surface of the styled type or graphic (Altitude), with the center (90°) being highest and around the edge of the circle being at "ground level" (0°).

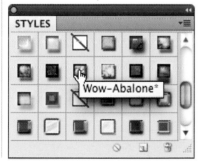
LIGHTING IN LAYER STYLES

To understand lighting in a Layer Style, imagine that the little circle you see in the lighting setup for many of the layer effects (as shown at the left) represents a half-sphere dome sitting over your image. The **Angle** setting determines where around the circle the light is positioned. The **Altitude** determines how far up the dome the light is hung — from 0° (at "floor level") to 90° (at the top of the dome).

Global Light

Every Photoshop file that can accept Layer Styles — even a brand-new empty file you just created — has built-in **Global Light** settings for Altitude and Angle. The **Use Global Light** option, found in the Drop Shadow, Bevel and Emboss, and other sections of the Layer Style dialog box, was designed to make it easy to coordinate lighting for all of the effects in a Style and for all Layer Styles in a file, so the light will seem to come consistently from a single direction.

When you apply a Layer Style to a file, if Use Global Light is already turned on for any of that Style's effects, these effects *automatically take on the Global Light settings that already exist* in the file. These could be Adobe's default settings (Angle, 120° and Altitude, 30°), or they could be custom settings. You can see what the Global Light settings are, or customize them, by choosing Layer > Layer Style > Global Light.

If Use Global Light is turned on for any effect in any Layer Style in your file and then you change the Angle or Altitude for this effect, *your new Angle and Altitude settings become the new Global Light values, affecting all other effects in the file that have Use Global Light turned on.* Since "on" is the default state for Use Global Light in the Layer Style dialog box, *it's easy to accidentally reset the lighting for your entire file as you experiment with settings for one effect on one layer.* (See "Lighting: Global or Not" on page 506 for tips on working with lighting.)

Other Lighting Controls

Besides Altitude and Angle settings and whether Global Light is turned on, there are other settings that change the lighting for the effects in a Layer Style. These are the color, Blend Mode, and Opacity settings for the Shadow and Highlight controls for individual effects, as well as Gloss Contour. These parameters are described in the effects sections that follow.

LIGHTING: GLOBAL OR NOT?

Turning on **Global Light** works well for coordinating the lighting Angle for all Styles in a file, but it can ruin the **material characteristics** that can be simulated with the **Altitude** setting. For instance, a shiny surface that depends on a high Altitude setting in the Satin effect can become dull if the Global Light setting forces it to use the same Altitude setting as in the Bevel and Emboss effect.

Let's say you design a Layer Style that takes advantage of Global Light. You run the risk, using it in another situation, that the Global Light already built into that file could produce different material characteristics than you want, since only one Global Light is allowed per file, and the file's existing Global Light setting will "take over" the Layer Style. To protect your Altitude settings, your best bet is to **turn off the Global Light option** before you experiment with the settings for any single effect.

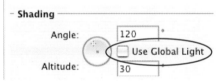

A yellow Stroke was added to the green type. To create the hard-edged black shading, the Inner Shadow's Choke was set to 100 (one way to keep a hard edge). To harden the edge of the Drop Shadow, whose Size had been increased to 8 to thicken the shadow, we increased the Spread almost to 100%. For details, see page 544 in "Anatomy of Bevels."

SHADOWS & GLOWS

Like most of the effects in a Layer Style, both Shadow and Glow effects work by duplicating the outline of a layer's contents — whether pixels, vector outline, or a combination created by masking (the expanded Style shown on page 502 can help you visualize this). The duplicate is then either filled with color (for a Drop Shadow, an Outer Glow, or an Inner Glow from the Center) or used as a hole in an overlay that's filled with color (for an Inner Shadow or an Inner Glow from the Edge); the copy is usually resized and blurred somewhat. Once you visualize the blurred copy as the starting point, you can begin to look at the differences between Shadow and Glow effects. The two main differences between Shadow effects and Glow effects are:

- A **Shadow can be** *offset*, but **a Glow radiates evenly** in all directions.
- A **Glow** can use a *gradient* or a solid color; a Shadow can only use a solid color.

Distance & Angle

The **Distance** setting in a **Shadow** effect determines how far the shadow will be offset in one direction. You can change the Distance setting by using the slider, typing a value into the box, using the arrow keys on the keyboard (↑ and ↓), or simply dragging in the working window while the dialog box is open.

You can individually set the **Angle** that determines where the light source is located for each Shadow effect and for other effects in your Style, such as Bevel and Emboss. Or you can turn on **Global Light**, which will **apply the same lighting Angle to all of the effects**. See the tip at the left for pointers.

Glows cannot be offset. If you choose any of the Glow effects in the list on the left side of the Layer Style dialog box, you'll see that there's no Distance setting and no Angle, and they aren't subject to Global Light.

Blend Mode, Color & Gradient

We think of shadows as dark and we think of glows as light, but both Shadow and Glow effects can be *either* dark or light, depending on the color and Blend Mode setting you choose. By default, Shadows are set to dark colors and are in Multiply mode, and Glows are light colors in Screen mode. But you can reverse that if you want to, or use other modes.▼ A light-colored Shadow in Screen mode with a Distance setting

FIND OUT MORE
▼ Blend modes
page 181

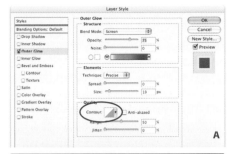

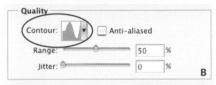

A straight line Contour Λ is the default for a Shadow or Glow effect. But the Contour setting can be used to "remap" the colors or tones, as shown for this Outer Glow **B**.

 **Glow Contour.psd**

of 0 creates a glow. A dark-colored Outer Glow in Multiply mode becomes an evenly radiating shadow or "dark halo."

What **Glows** lack in offset ability, they more than make up for in their capacity for using **gradients**. Instead of simply offering a color swatch (as in the Shadow sections), the Glow sections also offer a gradient choice, which, with the right combination of colors and transparency in the gradient, can be used for some great multicolor radiant effects. There are three additional controls for **Gradient glows**. **Noise** introduces a random pattern of light-dark variation that can prevent the obvious banding that sometimes happens when gradients are reproduced in print. **Jitter** mixes up pixels of the colors in the gradient so the color transitions are less well-defined. If you push the Jitter slider all the way to the right, you'll reduce the gradient to a mixture of color sprinkles. The **Range** setting determines what part of the gradient is used for the Glow.

The Difference Between Inner & Outer

Logically enough, the outer effects (Outer Glow and Drop Shadow) extend *outward* from the edge of the layer content you apply them to. You can think of them as filled and blurred duplicates of the outline, placed *behind* the layer — that is, below it in the layer stack.

Inner effects (Inner Shadow and Inner Glow) happen *inside* the edge. The **Inner Shadow** and the **Inner Glow** with **Edge** as the Source radiate inward from the edge, getting thinner toward the center. The **Inner Glow** with **Center** as the Source radiates color from the center outward; the color gets thinner as it extends toward the edge.

Size, Spread & Choke

In shadows and glows the **Size** determines the **amount of blur** that's applied to the color-filled copy that makes the shadow or glow. The greater the Size setting, the more the shadow or glow is blurred into the surroundings, so at higher Size settings, the shadow or glow is more diffuse — it's thinner and it spreads out farther.

Spread and Choke interact with the Size setting. Increasing the **Spread** of an outer shadow or glow, or the **Choke** of an inner one, makes the effect denser, or more concentrated, by controlling where and how abruptly the transition is made from dense to transparent within the range established by the Size.

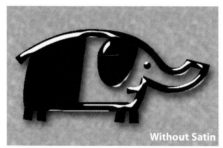

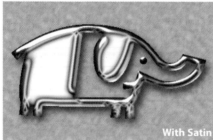

The interior lighting added by the Satin effect can be subtle (top) or dramatic. Shown here are two examples of "styled" graphics before and after the Satin effect was added to the Layer Style.

 Satin.psd

Contour

A **Contour** setting is like a Curves setting. It **"remaps" the intermediate tones** that are created by the blur used to make a Shadow or Glow. If the default **Linear** (45° straight-line) Contour is chosen, the tones or colors stay the same as when they were generated by the blur, proceeding from opaque to transparent as they extend away from the outline — either inward or outward (except for the Inner Glow with Center as the Source, which is more opaque in the center and gets "thinner" as it goes from the center to the outline).

If you choose a Contour other than the default, the intermediate tones are changed according to the Curve. By applying a Contour with several extreme peaks and valleys, you can get some fairly wild "striping" in a Glow or Shadow (see page 507).

SATIN

The **Satin** effect is created by the intersection of two blurred, offset, reflected copies of the outline of the layer content. It can be useful for simulating **internal reflections** or a **satiny finish**. **Size** controls the amount of blur as in other effects. **Distance** controls how much the two blurred and offset copies overlap, and **Angle** determines the direction of offset. As in other effects, the **Contour** remaps the tones created by the blurring according to the Curve you choose.

To get an idea of what's happening when you change the settings for the Satin effect, try this:

1 Choose the Ellipse tool ⬭, choose the "Shape layers" option in the Options bar, and drag the cursor to create a layer with a filled circle or oval.

2 Double-click to the right of the layer's name in the Layers panel to open the Layer Style dialog box to the Blending Options section. In the Advanced Blending area, make sure the Blend Interior Effects As Group box is *not* checked, and set the Fill Opacity to 0. (The filled circle will disappear.)

3 Open the Satin section of the Layer Style dialog box by clicking the Satin entry in the list at the left side of the box. Experiment with the Size (blur), Distance (amount of overlap), and Angle. Pop open the Contour picker by clicking the little triangle to the right of the Contour swatch, and try different Contours. For some fun, watch what happens when you choose a really complex Contour, such as Ring-Double (one of the presets that come with Photoshop) and vary the Distance.

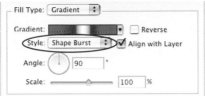

These two glowing bulbs were created by reducing the Fill Opacity of the white graphic shown on the left to 0, and adding a Stroke made with a Shape Burst Gradient. The difference between the two bulbs on the right is the color of the gradients and the Inner and Outer Glows.

 **Neon Stroke.psd**

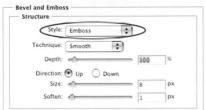

The Emboss style of the Bevel and Emboss effect builds the bevel partly inward and partly outward, letting the color from the layer below show through as well as the color of the current layer. Here the Emboss was applied to the layer with the type, but the beveling also changes the look of the layer below. You'll find a layered example on page 763.

STROKE

For the **Stroke** effect, the **Size** sets the width of the stroke that outlines the layer content. The **Position** determines whether the stroke is built from the edge outward or inward, or is centered on the edge. The Stroke's width is filled according to the **Fill Type** you choose: solid color, pattern, or any of the usual five gradient styles (Linear, Radial, Angle, Reflected, or Diamond). There's also one more gradient form that occurs nowhere else in Photoshop — the **Shape Burst** gradient. With a Shape Burst gradient the colors follow along the outline, which can create a quick neon effect (shown at the left), an inline/outline effect for type (see page 198), or a multicolor glow if the gradient includes transparency at the outer edge. Patterns and gradients can be scaled within the Stroke width. A solid-color Stroke effect can be useful for filling in an Outer Bevel when you don't want the layer below to show through it, as illustrated on page 543.

BEVEL AND EMBOSS

The **Bevel and Emboss** dialog box is complex, but if you remember the filled, blurred duplicate idea, it can be easier to grasp how it works. To create the highlight and shadow effects that simulate the bevel shading, Photoshop offsets and trims blurred light and dark duplicates. Because of the blur, the highlights and shadows are partly transparent, even when you set the Opacity at 100%, so they blend with the color underneath, creating the illusion of the bevel.

Like the Shadows and Glows, the Bevel and Emboss effect has tremendous potential beyond what its name implies. Some of its possibilities are explored in "Anatomy of Bevels" on page 542. Experiment in the Structure panel of the Bevel And Emboss section. Then move on to the Shading section, which controls the lighting.

Structure

When you start to experiment with Bevel and Emboss, an obvious place to begin is with the **Direction**: The default **Up** raises the object from the surface; **Down** sinks it into the surface.

Then choose the **Style:** The **Inner Bevel** builds the beveled edge *inward* from the outline of the layer content, so the element itself appears to get slimmer, and the highlight and shadow the bevel generates will blend with the element's own color. The **Outer Bevel** builds the beveled edge *outward* from the outline and blends with whatever is "beyond" the layer content. The material that's beyond the outline can be supplied by the layers

In the graphics used for "Anatomy of Bevels" on page 542, the Layer Style for the small central star uses Smooth for the Technique in the Structure section of the Bevel and Emboss panel in the Layer Style dialog. For all other elements — the large star, plain ring, and ring of spokes — the Technique is set to Chisel Hard.

A high Altitude setting (70°, used in the Bevel and Emboss effects on both the frame and lens layers for the glasses on the right) can add thickness and can simulate a strong reflection from the surface. The Bevel and Emboss effects for the glasses on the left use Photoshop's default Altitude setting, 30°.

 Altitude.psd

The Gloss Contour in the Bevel and Emboss section of the Layer Style dialog box was important in creating the dark and light "reflections" that make the surface of the Chrome look shiny and curved, as described in "Anatomy of 'Shiny'" on page 537.

below, or it can be a band of color created by the Stroke effect. In the **Emboss** Style, the bevel "straddles" the outline, building the bevel half outward and half inward to create the kind of bevel seen in license plates and street signs. **Pillow Emboss** is a kind of double bevel, with a bevel extending away from the outline in both directions, like a quilted effect. If you've added a Stroke effect, the **Stroke Emboss** builds the bevel using only the width of the Stroke.

The **Technique** sets the "character" of the edge. **Smooth** creates the smoothest, hardest-looking edge; **Chisel Hard** simulates an edge worked in a hard material; and **Chisel Soft** simulates an edge worked in softer material.

Size, which again is the degree of blurring used to create the effect, determines how far inward or outward the bevel goes — that is, how much of the shape or the background is consumed by the bevel. **Soften** controls what happens to the edge that's away from the outline — whether this edge is abrupt and angular or rounded. A higher Soften value makes it rounder.

Depth determines how steep the sides of the bevel are. A greater Depth setting increases contrast between the tones used for the highlights and shadows and makes the beveled element appear to stick up from the surface farther or sink into it more.

Shading

The **Angle** setting operates the same way as for the Shadows. It determines the direction of the light. By increasing the **Altitude**, you can move the "bevel highlight" farther onto the front (top) surface of the element to which the Style is applied. The result is that surfaces seem more polished with the harder highlights created by higher Altitude settings.

Gloss Contour remaps the tones in the bevel highlight and shadow to make the surfaces seem more or less glossy and reflective. The Gloss Contour can be useful for imitating highly polished surfaces with multiple highlights.

The **Color**, **Mode**, and **Opacity** settings let you control the characteristics of highlighted edges and shadowed edges independently. So if you like, you can use them to simulate two different-colored light sources as shown in the colorful type at the top of page 511, rather than simulating a single highlight and a shadow.

Contour

Indented just below Bevel and Emboss in the list on the left side of the Layer Style dialog box you'll find **Contour**. This

The type was colored with a red Color Overlay and then "lit" with a Bevel and Emboss effect. In the Bevel and Emboss section of the Layer Style dialog box, yellow in Screen mode was used for the bevel highlights and purple in Color Mode for the shadows, to simulate two colored light sources shining on the red type. See page 544 for details.

Contour has to do with the Structure of the bevel. It defines the shape of the bevel's "shoulder." To explore its effect, you can start with a gray Shape, such as the one in **Bevel Contour.psd,** shown on page 512. Then add the default Bevel and Emboss, and increase the Size to make the bevel wider. Click Contour in the list at the left side of the box and make choices from the Contour panel that pops out when you click the little triangle to the right of the Contour swatch. You'll be able to see that the Contour changes the cross-section of the bevel. Experiment with the **Range** slider, which controls how much of the bevel is "sculpted" by the Contour — in other words, how much of the bevel is consumed by the "shoulder." Low Range settings make the "shoulder" smaller and move it away from the outline created by the layer content.

SETTINGS FOR BEVEL AND EMBOSS

The **Style** setting of **Bevel and Emboss** determines where the bevel will be built — inside, outside, or overlapping the outline of the layer content.

The **Technique** controls the smoothness of the bevel walls. The Smooth setting produces the smoothest walls, and the Chisel Soft produces the most gouged.

Depth controls the contrast between the highlighted and shaded walls of the bevel. The greater the Depth setting, the greater the contrast, and therefore the steeper the walls will look.

The **Direction** setting determines whether the beveled element seems to rise from the surrounding surface (Up) or sinks into it (Down).

Size controls how wide the bevel is.

Soften controls the rounding/sharpness of the edge of the bevel that's away from the layer content's outline.

Angle controls the direction of the lighting that causes highlights and shadows. **Altitude** controls how high above the surface the light source is. The **Use Global Light** option unifies the lighting in all effects that use Angle or Altitude in all Layer Styles throughout the file, which has its pros and cons (see pages 505 & 506).

Gloss Contour controls the shininess of the surface, from matte to highly polished, by remapping the tones in the bevel highlights and shadows.

Mode, **Color**, and **Opacity** settings can be controlled independently for the bevel highlights and shadows.

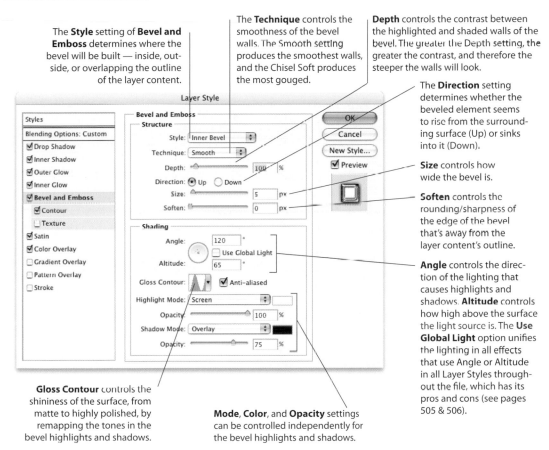

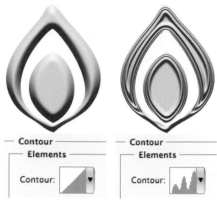

The Contour of the Bevel and Emboss effect can be used to shape the bevel "shoulder." Here the default Linear Contour is shown on the left and a custom Contour on the right.

🔵 **Bevel Contour.psd**

When you add **Texture** to a Bevel and Emboss effect, the Style setting within the Bevel and Emboss section of the Layer Style dialog determines where the texture shows up, as shown above. Only the bottom example has an added Stroke effect, so that the Stroke style of Bevel and Emboss will work and the Texture will appear on the Stroke.

Texture

Below Contour in the effects list is **Texture**. The Texture effect embosses the pattern you choose from the **Pattern picker** in the Texture section of the Layer Style dialog box. This picker is like the one in the Pattern Overlay section of the dialog box except that here the patterns appear in grayscale. That's because Photoshop uses only the lights and darks of the pattern — to simulate bumps and pits in the surface. By using the same pattern for the Pattern Overlay and the Texture, you can match the surface texture to the surface patterning.

For an **Inner Bevel** the embossed pattern goes inside the outline of the layer content (and so does the Pattern Overlay). For the **Outer Bevel** the embossed pattern goes outside, so the texture appears on whatever is in the image below the layer with the Style. For **Emboss** and **Pillow Emboss** the embossed pattern extends both inside and outside, and for **Stroke** it appears only within the stroke width. The "embossing" of the pattern is affected by the Depth and Soften settings for Bevel and Emboss and by all the settings in its Shading section.

BLENDING OPTIONS

The **Blending Options** section of the Layer Style dialog box (shown on page 513) governs how the layer interacts with other layers. In the **General Blending** section at the top of the box you can change the Blend Mode and the Opacity. These changes are reflected in the **Blend Mode** and **Opacity** settings at the top of the Layers panel and can also be controlled there. ▼

FIND OUT MORE
▼ Using blend modes
page 181

Advanced Blending

Also reflected in the Layers panel is the **Fill Opacity**, the first of the **Advanced Blending** settings. It allows you to reduce the Opacity of the layer's "fill" without reducing the opacity of the entire layer. That means, for instance, that you can make the layer content partly or completely transparent but leave the shadows or glows around it at full strength.

The other settings in the **Advanced Blending** section are a bit more complex. The two checkboxes under the Fill Opacity slider control whether certain inner effects are considered part of the Fill for purposes of adjusting Fill Opacity. With the **"Blend Interior Effects as Group"** box checked (see the illustration on the next page), the Inner Glow, any interior bevel highlights and shadows, the three Overlays, and the Satin effect — all of which fall within the layer content's outline — are considered part of

BLENDING OPTIONS

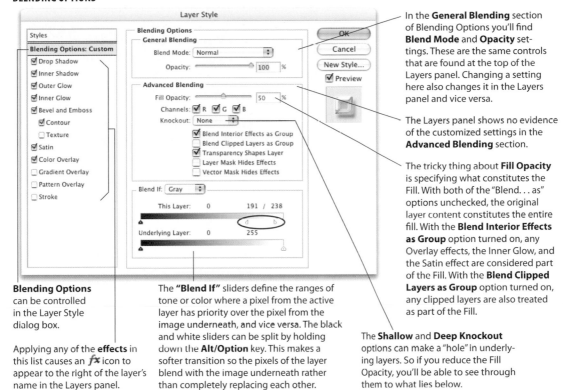

In the **General Blending** section of Blending Options you'll find **Blend Mode** and **Opacity** settings. These are the same controls that are found at the top of the Layers panel. Changing a setting here also changes it in the Layers panel and vice versa.

The Layers panel shows no evidence of the customized settings in the **Advanced Blending** section.

The tricky thing about **Fill Opacity** is specifying what constitutes the Fill. With both of the "Blend...as" options unchecked, the original layer content constitutes the entire fill. With the **Blend Interior Effects as Group** option turned on, any Overlay effects, the Inner Glow, and the Satin effect are considered part of the Fill. With the **Blend Clipped Layers as Group** option turned on, any clipped layers are also treated as part of the Fill.

Blending Options can be controlled in the Layer Style dialog box.

Applying any of the **effects** in this list causes an fx icon to appear to the right of the layer's name in the Layers panel.

The **"Blend If"** sliders define the ranges of tone or color where a pixel from the active layer has priority over the pixel from the image underneath, and vice versa. The black and white sliders can be split by holding down the **Alt/Option** key. This makes a softer transition so the pixels of the layer blend with the image underneath rather than completely replacing each other.

The **Shallow** and **Deep Knockout** options can make a "hole" in underlying layers. So if you reduce the Fill Opacity, you'll be able to see through them to what lies below.

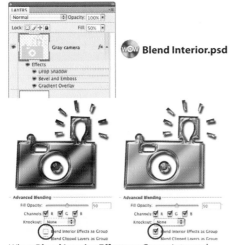

WOW **Blend Interior.psd**

When **Blend Interior Effects as Group** is turned **off** (left), only the original color's opacity is reduced when Fill Opacity is reduced to 50%; we don't see any reduction because the Gradient Overlay in the Style covers it. When **Blend Interior Effects as Group** is turned **on** (right), the opacity of both the Gradient Overlay and the original color are reduced.

the fill when the Fill Opacity is reduced. (The Inner Shadow isn't considered an Interior Effect for purposes of blending, probably because it results from an *outside* light source.)

The **"Blend Clipped Layers as Group"** checkbox controls whether any layers that are part of a clipping group with the "styled" layer as the base are treated as if they became part of the layer *before* or *after* the Layer Style was added. With this option *turned on*, it's as if any clipped layers became part of the fill *before* the Layer Style's effects are applied. So a Color Overlay, Gradient Overlay, or Pattern Overlay (see page 502) will hide or change the clipped image. Blend modes of the various layers also play a role, of course, and it gets complicated quickly.

If you want a layer to cut a hole in the layers below, you can reduce the Fill Opacity to 0% and choose the appropriate option for **Knockout**:

* If you choose **Deep**, the knockout can go all the way down to (but not through) the *Background* at the bottom of the layer stack, or to transparency if there is no *Background*.

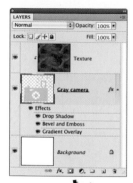

Here the tortoise shell image is "clipped" by the graphic. With **Blend Clipped Layers as Group** turned **off** (left), it's as if the tortoise shell surface goes on top of the Gradient Overlay and hides it. If **Blend Clipped Layers as Group** is turned **on** (right), it's as if the tortoise shell surface became part of the original graphic first and then the Gradient Overlay was added.

 Blend Clipped

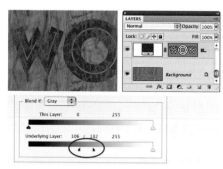

If your background has a mix of light and dark tones, it's easy to "distress" type or graphics by eliminating the active layer's contribution in either the light or the dark areas. Here the "Blend If" sliders are set so the black graphics don't cover the dark areas of the woodgrain. Splitting the sliders (by holding down the Alt/Option key as you drag) makes a smooth transition.

 **Style Samples.psd**

- If the **Shallow** option is chosen, the knockout goes only as far as the first logical stopping point — through the bottom of the clipping group or Group of layers, for instance. If there is no clipping group or Group, then the knockout goes all the way to the *Background* or transparency, just as Deep does.

- If the Knockout setting is the default **None**, then no hole is made in the layers below.

The results of the Knockout settings are modified by the settings in the two **"Blend. . . as"** checkboxes and by whether the layer set is in Pass Through mode, not to mention the blend modes of the individual layers or whether there are nested Groups. Again, it's very powerful, but it gets complicated quickly!

The "Blend If" Settings

At the bottom of the Blending Options dialog are the **"Blend If"** sliders, which provide a way to blend a layer with the image formed by the layers below. ▼ With these sliders you can control which tones and colors in the active layer contribute to the composite, and which will act as if they are

FIND OUT MORE

▼ Using the "Blend If" sliders **page 66**

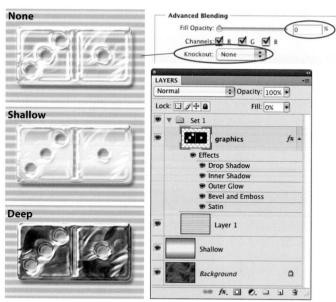

With **Knockout** set to **None**, the striped surface in Layer 1 shows behind the styled "glass" graphic. With Knockout set to **Shallow**, the graphic knocks out through the striped surface since it's included in the Group with the graphic, but it doesn't knock out the gradient beneath the Group. With Knockout set to **Deep**, the graphic knocks out all the way to the *Background*.

 Knockout.psd

transparent, allowing the image underneath to show through. These controls provide a great way to "distress" or weather type or graphics applied to a patterned or textured surface.

ENHANCING LAYER STYLES

Once you have a Layer Style in place, it may be easier to make a color or lighting change by adding an Adjustment layer or using the Lighting Effects filter than to "remix" all the effects in the Style. For highly polished surfaces created with Layer Styles you can also add "environmental" reflections by using Distort filters to bend a reflected image to fit the styled element. Filters can also be useful for roughening the edges of a graphic to which a Style with texture has been applied, for a more realistic look.

Adjustment Layers

In some cases Levels, Curves, Color Balance, and Hue/Saturation can be varied through Adjustment layers to change the color or brightness of a layer to which a Style has been applied, without the need to go back into the Layer Style box and make changes (examples are shown at the left). You can set the Adjustment layer to affect just the interior of the styled element, or the interior and exterior effects, or the interior, exterior, and all visible layers below. Just be sure that the two "Blend. . . as" checkboxes in the Blending Options panel of the Layer Style box are set up so the Adjustment layer will act on the interior effects and clipped layers if that's what you want:

- **If the Adjustment layer is made part of a clipping group** with the styled layer serving as its base, the Adjustment Layer will **act only on the interior of the element**. If "Blend Interior Effects as Group" is turned on, it will affect any Overlay, Inner Glow, or Satin effects along with the original fill.

- **If the Adjustment layer is not "clipped,"** it will affect not only the **interior** of the element but also any **exterior effects**, such as Drop Shadow or Outer Glow, as well as any **other layers** that are visible below it.

- You can set up your file so **the Adjustment layer affects a number of consecutive layers, even if they are not at the bottom of the layer stack and are not clipped.** To do this, make a Group, with the Adjustment layer as the top layer in the Group, and set the blend mode of the Group to Normal. To make a Group, simply target all the layers you want in the Group by Shift-clicking or Ctrl/⌘-clicking, and then choose New Group from Layers from the panel's menu ▾☰.

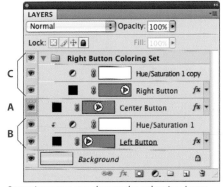

Sometimes you can change the colors in a Layer Style without editing the individual effects. The middle graphic **A** shows the original color of all three graphics. To change the color of the left graphic, a Hue/Saturation Adjustment layer was made part of a clipping group with the graphic layer as the "clipper" **B**. Notice that the color of the "shadow" hasn't changed, since it's outside the graphic. To change the color of the right graphic **C**, we used a Hue/Saturation Adjustment layer with the same settings, but it was included in a Group of layers whose mode was changed from the default Pass Through to Normal. Notice that in this case, since the Adjustment layer is not clipped by the graphic, it also changes the color of the shadow.

 **Color Adjustments.psd**

A landscape photo was treated with the Glass filter and layered above the styled graphic in this chrome treatment. The techniques are described in "Custom Chrome" (page 530) and "Custom Glass" (page 539).

The initial "carving" of the rock was done by applying a Layer Style to graphics on a transparent layer, using Bevel and Emboss, Shadow, and Overlay effects. The "styled" layer was modified with the Displace filter to make the beveled edge follow the features of the rock surface. The Lighting Effects filter was used to add a spotlight. (These Style, Displace, and Lighting Effects techniques are presented step-by-step in "Carving" on page 545.)

In this corroded metal effect, after the same **Wow-Rust** Layer Style was applied to both the chicken graphics and the background shape, two Adjustment layers were used to brighten and "neutralize" the color of the chicken. Then the Spatter filter was applied to a matching layer mask to "roughen" the edge so it matches the surface corrosion that had been applied by the Style. An "environment" image was added to further "weather" the metal. The technique is described step-by-step in "Adding Dimension, Color & Texture," starting on page 517.

Lighting Effects

With the Lighting Effects filter you can create pools of light exactly where you want them by adding Spotlights. A flexible way to use the Lighting Effects filter, introduced in CS3 with Smart Filters, allows you to keep the filter "live," so it's easy to improve on your lighting if the filter's small preview doesn't allow you to "tune" it exactly as you like on the first try. You can change the direction, intensity, color, or any other aspect of Lighting Effects by double-clicking on the name of the filter in the Layers panel to reopen the dialog with your settings intact, and then alter them as necessary. You can change the blend mode and Opacity of the Smart Filter layer, and even mask the effects if you choose. You'll find an example on page 547.

Other Filters

The **Glass** filter (Filter > Distort > Glass) can be extremely useful in distorting environmental images to look like reflections in polished metal or glass surfaces, as shown at top left. You can find examples on pages 530 and 539 in this chapter. The **Displace** filter, also in the Distort "family," can augment carved and chiseled effects by distorting the layer content to make it conform to the textured surface you want to "carve" into, as shown at the left.

Other filters, such as **Spatter**, can be used to modify the edge of a graphic so its texture matches the roughness introduced by the Texture effect in a Layer Style, as in "Adding Dimension, Color & Texture," starting on page 517. And the **Texturizer**, **Add Noise**, **Clouds**, **Fibers**, and other filters can be very useful for producing backgrounds, textures, and patterns for styled type or graphics, as shown in "Quick Backgrounds & Textures" on page 556 and "Quick Seamless Patterns" on page 560. *Wow!*

DONAL JOLLEY

Adding Dimension, Color & Texture

USING LAYER MASKS WITH VECTOR-BASED ARTWORK, along with the Overlay and Bevel and Emboss effects in Layer Styles, allows for a tremendous amount of flexibility in creating realistic-looking surfaces and edges, as in this "weathered metal."

Thinking the project through. Don Jolley prepared the plain black "chicken" graphics for this project in Adobe Illustrator, where he converted the type to paths to avoid problems that can arise with live type. ▼ The first decision in the Photoshop part of this project (at step 1) is whether to bring the graphics into Photoshop as a shape layer or as a Smart Object. ▼ Both are resolution-independent (their edges stay smooth and crisp even when they're reshaped and scaled repeatedly). A plus for the Smart Object approach is that it would make it easy to go back into Illustrator if we wanted to make changes to the chicken graphics at any point in the project, Photoshop would then automatically apply to the new art all the Photoshop work we had done to the old art up to that point.

But changing the Illustrator artwork — a logo — was unlikely. We opted for a Shape layer to keep file organization obvious in the Layers panel. We'll create our color and texture with Layer Styles, which are very quick and easy to apply.

FIND OUT MORE

▼ Converting type **page 446**

▼ Illustrator art as Smart Objects **page 462**

1a The artwork was drawn in Adobe Illustrator, selected, and copied to the clipboard.

1b Pasting the artwork into Photoshop as a Shape layer

1c Adjusting the size of the artwork in the Photoshop file

1d Setting Options for the Rounded Rectangle tool

1e The file with the imported artwork and the added plaque shape

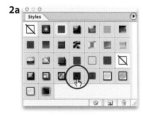

2a Choosing **Wow-Rust** from the Wow-Metal presets in the Styles panel to add color, thickness, and texture to the graphics

1 Setting up the file. In Illustrator our artwork was selected **1a** and copied to the clipboard; then we pasted it into Photoshop as a Shape layer **1b**. We scaled it to fit; to scale proportionally while keeping the pasted element centered, type Ctrl/⌘-T (for Edit > Transform) and Alt/Option-Shift-drag a corner handle **1c**.

In Photoshop, we added a skewed plaque behind the logo: First we targeted the *Background* by clicking on it, so the Shape layer we were about to add would be between the *Background* and the imported graphic. We chose a Shape tool (Shift-U), and in the Options bar **1d** made sure the Shape Layers option ▢, the Rounded Rectangle option ▢, and the Create New Shape Layer option ▢ were all chosen; we set the corner Radius to 30 px and then clicked the color swatch and chose a medium gray. Dragging in the working window created a rectangle. Then we typed Ctrl/⌘-T (for Edit > Free Transform) and dragged around outside the Transform box to rotate the shape. We reshaped the rectangle by holding down the Ctrl/⌘ key and dragging the individual corner handles of the Transform box to distort the plaque. We dragged inside the box to move the shape into position and then double-clicked inside the box to complete the transformation **1e**.

2 "Rusting" the logo and plaque. To follow along using the rusty chicken artwork, open the **Rusted-Before.psd** file, which has both shape layers already in place. Or start your own RGB Photoshop file with a white *Background* (File > New) and add type, draw vector graphics, or import graphics as in step 1.

To add color, surface texture, and a bevel to both layers, you can use the **Wow-Rust** Style. ("Anatomy of 'Bumpy'" on page 522 shows how the individual effects in **Wow-Rust** work together to produce the Style.)

To "style" both layers at once, click the thumbnail for the logo layer and then Shift-click the thumbnail for the plaque layer. In the Styles panel click the ▾≡ button near the top right corner and choose **Wow-Metal** Styles. If you haven't yet loaded the Wow presets,▼ the **Wow-Metal** Styles won't appear in the menu. To load just the two Styles associated with this project, choose Load Styles and navigate to **Wow-Rust Project.asl** in Wow Project Files > Chapter 8 > Rusted. Once you've loaded one or the other of these sets of Styles, just click on the **Wow-Rust** thumbnail **2a** to apply the Style **2b**. If you're using your own graphics, you may then need to scale the Style to fit.▼

FIND OUT MORE

▼ Loading the Wow presets **page 4**

▼ Scaling a Style **page 81**

2b

The Wow-Rust Style is applied to both graphics layers. You can make the Layers panel more compact, as shown here for the top layer, by clicking the little arrow next to the *fx* for the layer to hide the list of effects.

3a

Ctrl/⌘-clicking the vector mask thumbnail for the Shape layer **A** and then clicking the "Add layer mask" button **B** created a matching layer mask **C**.

3 Eroding the edges of the logo. The next step is to roughen the edges of the logo. An effective way to do that, without actually doing any damage to the artwork itself, is to add a pixel-based layer mask to the Shape layer and erode the edge of this layer mask. The Layer Style that we added at step 2 will then apply the bevel, drop shadow, and other effects to the shape defined by a combination of the layer mask and the layer's built-in vector mask.

To add a layer mask, make sure the logo layer is targeted (click its thumbnail in the Layers panel). Then load the outline of the artwork as a selection: In the Layers panel, Ctrl/⌘-click the vector mask thumbnail **3a**. Then click the "Add a layer mask" button at the bottom of the panel.

To roughen the edges of the new layer mask, apply the Spatter filter (Filter > Brush Strokes > Spatter). In the Spatter dialog box **3b**, first set the lower slider (Smoothness) at the maximum (15) so you can get a rough but not crumbly edge, and then adjust the Spray Radius until you get the edge effect you want (we used 8; with higher settings the thin lines and sharp points on the chicken began to break up). As you look at the preview in the Spatter dialog, you won't be seeing exactly what will happen to the edge outline of your graphic or type. That's because *two* masking elements — the roughened layer mask and the hard-edged vector mask that's built into the Shape layer will work in concert to define the edge. Where the filter "eats *into*" the edge of the layer mask, its effects will show in the final artwork. But anywhere the filter spreads the edge of the mask *outward*, the layer mask edge *won't* have an effect, because the hard edge of the vector outline will mask out these protrusions **3c**. This works well for our degrading effect — when a metal edge erodes, it's eaten away, not splattered outward. Click "OK" to close the dialog. If you need to rerun the filter with a different setting, type Ctrl/⌘-Z to undo and then Ctrl-Alt-F (Windows) or ⌘-Option-F (Mac) to reopen the Filter Gallery so you can change the settings.

Repeat the masking and filtering on the plaque layer.

3b

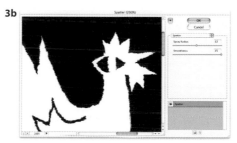

Running the Spatter filter on the layer mask for the logo graphics layer. Choosing Filter > Brush Strokes > Spatter automatically opens the Filter Gallery.

3c

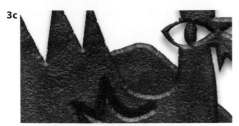

The roughened edge of the layer mask was "clipped" by the vector mask, to give the styled graphic an "eaten-away" look.

4a

Adding a Hue/Saturation Adjustment layer clipped to the logo below it in the layer stack

4b

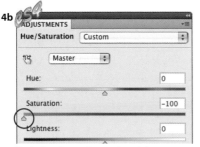

Reducing Saturation to the minimum removes the color from the logo.

4c

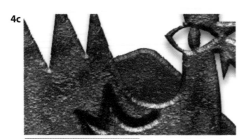

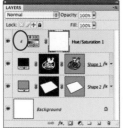

Because the Hue/Saturation Adjustment layer is "clipped" by the logo layer, it doesn't affect the color of the plaque. The indent and downward arrow in the Layers panel show that the layer is clipped.

4 Changing the surface characteristics. With both graphics elements styled, it's easy to experiment with the texture and color of either layer. To turn the rusted logo into pitted (but not rusted) metal, you can remove the color in the logo layer and increase its contrast to emphasize the texture, as described next. To remove the color, target the logo layer in the Layers panel; then create a Hue/Saturation Adjustment layer above it:

- In either CS3 or CS4 you can Alt/Option-click the "Create new fill or adjustment layer" button ⬮ at the bottom of the Layers panel and choose Hue/Saturation from the menu. Using the Alt/Option key opens the New Layer dialog box **4a**, where you can choose "Use Previous Layer to Create Clipping Mask" so the Hue/Saturation adjustment will affect only the logo layer, not the layers below it in the stack. Click "OK" to close the New Layer box.

- In CS4 there are other options. You can click on the Hue/Saturation button ▤ in the Adjustments panel to open the Hue/Saturation dialog. And you can clip this new Adjustment layer to the layer below by clicking on the "clip to layer" button ⬤ at the bottom of the panel.

In the Hue/Saturation dialog reduce the Saturation to –100 (the minimum setting) and click "OK" **4b**, **4c**.

Now increase the contrast with another Adjustment layer:

- In either CS3 or CS4 you can Alt/Option-click the ⬮ button again to add another Adjustment layer, this time choosing Levels, and again choosing "Use Previous Layer to Create Clipping Mask" to add the Levels layer to the clipping group so it won't affect the plaque shape.

- In CS4 you can instead click the "return to Adjustment list" button ◀ at the bottom of the Adjustments panel; then click the Levels button ⬤ to add a Levels Adjustment layer, and finally click on the clipping mask button ⬤ at the bottom of the Adjustments panel.

In the Levels dialog, move the Input Levels white point slider to the left to increase the contrast until you have some true white highlights **4d**.

5 Adding "atmosphere." A hint of "environment" can add to a weathered look. (If needed, it can also help disguise the repeat in a texture pattern applied with a Layer Style.) Copy-and-paste or drag-and-drop ▼ a blurred environment photo

FIND OUT MORE
▼ Drag & drop between tabbed documents **page 23**

4d

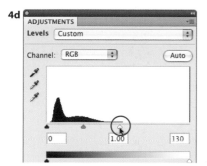

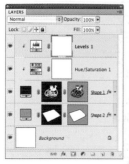

Moving the white-point slider in a Levels Adjustment layer brightens the highlights in the metal. If you like, you can also move the black point slider to the right a little to bring back some internal contrast.

5a

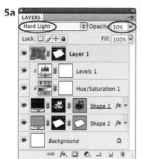

A carefully masked blurred photo is added in Hard Light mode at 30% Opacity to add more weathering. A "composite" layer mask hides the photo except on the logo and plaque. The finished image is shown at the top of page 517.

5b

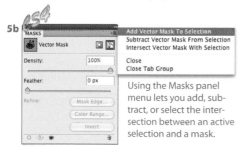

Using the Masks panel menu lets you add, subtract, or select the intersection between an active selection and a mask.

above the graphics; the **Rust-After.psd** file includes such a layer. Change this layer's blend mode (we used Hard Light), and reduce its Opacity (we used 30%).

Creating the mask for the environment layer was a tricky but logical process:

- The method we used works in CS3 or CS4. We Ctrl/⌘-clicked the *logo layer's vector mask* thumbnail to load the mask's outline as a selection. The next step in developing the mask was to Ctrl-Alt-Shift-click (Windows) or ⌘-Option-Shift-click the *logo's layer mask* thumbnail (this changed the selection to the intersection of the layer mask and vector mask, eliminating any parts that extended outside the overlap of the two). Finally we Ctrl/⌘-Shift-clicked the *plaque's vector mask* thumbnail (this added the plaque outline to the selection). With this combined selection active, we clicked the thumbnail for the photo layer and clicked the ◻ button at the bottom of the Layers panel to add a layer mask **5a**.

- Using CS4's Masks panel, you can target the masks and choose from the panel's menu to select the intersection of two masks or add them together **5b**. ▼

FIND OUT MORE
▼ Masks panel
page 63

Experimenting. Here are two more options to try on your styled graphics:

- To take away the rust color entirely, release the Adjustment layers from the clipping group so the Saturation and Levels adjustments will affect both the logo and the plaque. (You can release a layer from its clipping group by Alt/Option-clicking on the boundary between it and the layer below in the Layers panel; any layers above it in the clipping group will also be released.)

- For the look of hot, glowing metal, turn off visibility for the photo layer and Adjustment layers by clicking their 👁 icons in the Layers panel. Then Shift-click to target both graphics layers, and click **Wow-Hot Metal** in the Styles panel. *Wow!*

Releasing the Adjustment layers from the clipping group allows the Adjustment layers to work on both graphics layers.

The Wow-Hot Metal Layer Style heats up the metal.

"Bumpy"

In the **Wow-Rust** Layer Style shown here and used in "Adding Dimension, Color & Texture" on page 517, the component effects create a weathered metal surface texture. To explore how the effects combine to make this Style, open the **Bumpy.psd** file, then open the Layers panel and double-click the *fx* symbol to the right of the "Graphic" layer's name to open the Layer Style dialog box. **In the list on the left side of the Layer Style box**, click on the name of each individual effect as you read its description here, to open that section of the dialog so you can take a look.

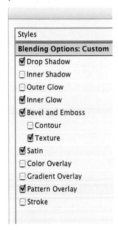

YOU'LL FIND THE FILE
in 🟢 > Wow Project Files > Chapter 8 > Anatomy of Bumpy

Layer Content

W E   S T A R T E D   W I T H   A R T W O R K copied to the clipboard in Illustrator and then pasted into a Photoshop file (Edit > Paste > **Paste As Shape**). You also have the additional choice of pasting from Illustrator as a Smart Object. This gives you the option of returning to Illustrator to make changes to the original artwork later and then automatically updating the Photoshop file to reflect the changes. (For tips on getting the results you expect when you edit a Vector Smart Object in Illustrator, see page 462.)

SMART OBJECT OR NO?

One thing to consider when choosing whether to Paste As Shape Layer or Paste As Smart Object is that if you Paste As Smart Object, someone opening the file in a version of the program before CS2 will be able to import it only as a pixel-based layer, not as a vector-based Shape Layer.

The warning that appears in Photoshop CS when you open a file containing a Vector Smart Object from a newer version of Photoshop isn't as dire as it may seem. Clicking "OK" doesn't discard the pasted element itself; it simply rasterizes it, eliminating its Vector Smart Object qualities.

Color & Pattern

THE **PATTERN OVERLAY** EFFECT provides the surface color and pattern in the **Wow-Rust** Style. We added it next because with the Pattern Overlay in place, it would be easier to see how the other effects were developing later. We turned on the Pattern Overlay by clicking its *checkbox* in the list on the left side of the Layer Style dialog box; to see the settings, click its *name*.

We clicked the **Pattern** swatch and chose the **Wow-Rust** pattern from the Pattern picker (**Wow-Rust** is part of the **Wow-Misc Surface Patterns** set from the DVD-ROM that comes with this book.)▼

We left "Link with Layer" checked (the default setting).▼

FIND OUT MORE
▼ Installing Wow presets **page 4**
▼ Link with Layer **page 504**

Blending Options

WHAT WE DID NEXT had no immediate effect on the artwork, but it would make a big difference in the Style's versatility. Clicking **"Blending Options"** in the list on the left side of the Layer Style dialog box opened that section. We used these settings in **Advanced Blending**:

- We turned **"Blend Interior Effects as Group" on** so the Pattern Overlay we were using in the Style would replace the styled layer's "native" coloring.

- We turned **"Blend Clipped Layers as Group" off**. That way we could use an Adjustment layer in a clipping group to modify the color of the Layer Style, as described in step 4 of "Adding Dimension, Color & Texture" on page 520. (If "Blend Clipped Layers as Group" were turned on, any Adjustment layers we might include in a clipping group would affect the native coloring of the layer *before* the Layer Style could come into play — so the effect of the Adjustment layers wouldn't show, because it would be "covered" by the Pattern Overlay.)

Drop Shadow

TO ADD TO THE ILLUSION of a solid object, we clicked **"Drop Shadow"** in the list and adjusted its settings so it looked like a metal cutout was casting a shadow onto the white surface:

- We moved the cursor into the working window, grabbed the shadow with it, and dragged straight down. We ended up with a 90° **Angle** (this made it look as if the light was positioned at 12 o'clock) and a **Distance** of 10 px. We turned Use Global Light off, for reasons having to do with the bevel▼ (the next effect we would apply).

- We reduced the **Opacity** to 60%, and increased the **Size** setting to 10 px. Both of these settings softened the shadow a little — the larger the Size setting, the more diffuse the shadow.

The combination of Distance, Angle, Size, and Opacity helps characterize the ambient light.

Bevel Structure

TO ADD DIMENSION, we clicked on **"Bevel And Emboss"** and in the **Structure** section of the panel set up an **Inner Bevel** in the **Up** direction. This starts the bevel at the edge of the graphic and raises it inward from there.▼ We chose **Chisel Hard** for Technique to create subtle chisel marks in the edge. (The Smooth Technique doesn't produce chisel marks, and Chisel Soft makes the marks more pronounced, as if the edge were being chiseled in softer material.) We raised the **Depth** to 300% for a larger bevel.

At this point the Shading section of the Bevel and Emboss section was still set to its defaults. But we would change that next.

FIND OUT MORE

▼ Turning off Use Global Light **page 506**

▼ Bevel structure **pages 509 & 542**

Bevel Shading

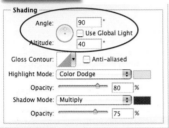

STILL WORKING in the **Bevel and Emboss** panel of the Layer Style dialog box, we turned to the **Shading** section. For the **Highlight** we chose a yellow by clicking the color swatch and choosing from the "Select highlight color" dialog when it opened. Putting the yellow Highlight in Color Dodge mode and raising the Opacity to 80% created warm lighting.

To keep the lighting consistent, we used the same 90° **Angle** that we had used for the Drop Shadow. Increasing the **Altitude** to 40° moved the light farther up onto the surface of the graphic, as if the light were higher overhead. We turned **Use Global Light off**. If Use Global Light had been on, whenever the Style was applied to a different file, the existing Altitude setting for the file — often Adobe's default 30° — would have changed the character of the bevel.

For the bevel's **Shadow** we clicked the color swatch and then clicked on the patterned surface of the graphic to sample a dark brown for the shaded faces of the bevel.

Surface Texture

BESIDES THE EDGE, the **Bevel and Emboss** effect also controls the "embossing" of surface texture. In the list in the Layers panel, we clicked on **"Texture,"** one of the subcategories under "Bevel and Emboss."

We used the **Wow-Rust** pattern from the Texture panel's Pattern picker. The swatch showed the pattern in grayscale because only the brightness (or luminance) information — not the color — is used to create the Texture.

We were embossing the same pattern used in the Pattern Overlay, so we left the **Scale** at 100% to match the default 100% used there. And we left **"Link with Layer"** checked, as we had for the Pattern Overlay, so the embossing would align with the Pattern Overlay. (If you wanted to break up the pattern with a different texture, you could uncheck the "Link with Layer" box and drag in the working window until the texture interrupted the pattern as you wanted it to.)

The **Depth** slider controls how deeply the texture is embossed; our +50% setting produced a fairly shallow emboss.

Edge Definition

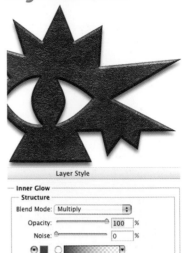

AN **INNER GLOW** of a dark yellow-gray in Multiply mode added shading inside the edge to increase contrast and improve edge definition.

Shading & Weathering

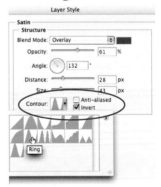

THE **SATIN EFFECT** completes the Style (see the bottom of page 522). Using a complementary color, Overlay mode, and an Angle we arrived at by experimenting, Satin creates tonal variation that's based on the **Contour.** Like a Curves setting, the Contour "remaps" the tones in a blurred copy of the layer content. Satin can change the surface lighting in a way that adds weathering here and helps hide repetition in the Pattern Overlay and Texture.

Clear Color

The Layer Styles we used for the **Clear.psd** file (shown below) are variants of **Wow-Clear Blue.** To explore the component effects that work together to turn type or graphics into the dimensional, translucent objects shown, open the **Clear.psd** file, then open the Layers panel and double-click the *f͓x* **symbol to the right of the "O" layer's name** to open the Layer Style dialog box. **In the list on the left side of the dialog,** click on the name of each individual effect as you read its description here, to open the appropriate section of the Layer Style dialog so you can look at the settings.

YOU'LL FIND THE FILE
in 🅦🅦 > Wow Project Files > Chapter 8 > Clear Anatomy

Layer Content

WE STARTED by typing the letter "O" in the BeesWax font above a striped *Background*. The Layer Style could have been applied directly to the live type. But in the **Clear.psd** file, all the type has been converted to Shape layers, so you can explore the Layer Style without encountering a Caution box if you don't have the BeesWax font installed on your system. ▼

Taking Over the Color

WHEN YOU PUT TOGETHER a Layer Style, it's good to start with the effect that will bring about the biggest change. Then you can watch the Style develop as you build it up by adding the subtler effects.

In this case we started by applying color using the **Color Overlay** effect. We clicked "Color Overlay" in the list on the left side of the Layer Style dialog box, then clicked the color swatch and chose a light blue from the "Select overlay color" dialog. By applying the effect in Normal mode at 100% Opacity, we could ensure that the Style would always produce the light blue color, completely replacing the original color of the type or graphics we would apply it to.

FIND OUT MORE

▼ Converting type to Shape layers
page 446

Blending

SINCE WE WOULD BE BUILDING a Style that included several interior effects — Color Overlay, Inner Glow, and Satin — we made sure that **"Blend Interior Effects as Group"** was turned on in the **Blending Options** section of the Layer Style box. With this choice, the Blending Options settings, such as Fill Opacity, would act on the interior of the "O" as a blended unit, applying to all the interior effects combined. For instance, **reducing the Fill Opacity** to 85% to make the "O" partially transparent also makes the Color Overlay, Inner Glow, and Satin partially transparent. Without the "Blend Interior Effects as Group" setting, the Color Overlay, for instance, would stay at its 100% Opacity setting, making the "O" a solid blue even if Fill Opacity for the layer was reduced all the way to 0%! (We also turned on the **"Transparency Shapes Layer"** option; it would make no difference in applying the Style to a Shape layer, but is necessary for the Style to work with a regular layer or Type layer.)

Color Drop Shadow

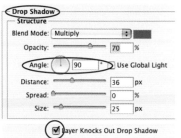

THE **DROP SHADOW** was a good next step, to start creating dimensionality by making a blurred offset copy "behind" the "O." We could use the Drop Shadow to contribute to the illusion of transparency by making it look as if light is passing through the blue "O" and coloring the shadow. We clicked the color swatch and chose a darker, less saturated blue in the "Select shadow color" dialog. To light the "O" from the top, we set the Drop Shadow's **Angle** at 90°. It would have been convenient to turn on Use Global Light so this Angle would automatically carry over to all other effects that use a lighting Angle setting. But Use Global Light is risky when the Altitude setting is important in creating a shiny surface (see "Lighting: Global or Not?" on page 506). At the bottom of the Drop Shadow panel, we made sure the default **Layer Knocks Out Drop Shadow** was turned on, so the shadow wouldn't darken the partly transparent "O."

Shading the Edge 1

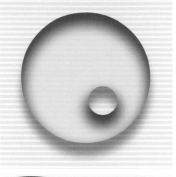

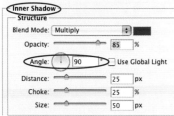

THE **INNER SHADOW** EFFECT, a blurred offset copy that's created *inside* the edge, was used here to help round the edges of the "O." We made a soft transition for a gentle rounding (the **Size** setting controls how soft, or diffuse, a blurred effect will be). So that it would darken the color already established by the Color Overlay, we left the Inner Shadow in its default Multiply mode, though we chose a slightly brighter blue for the color. We set the **Angle** at 90°, the same as for the Drop Shadow. (The Inner Shadow is often used for a cutout or carved-in, effect. But because a drop shadow was already in place making the "O" look like it was floating above the background, the Inner Shadow didn't create that illusion.) *Note:* Consistent with its nature as a shadow, **the Inner Shadow does *not* blend with other interior effects** (Overlays, Inner Glow, and Satin) even when the "Blend Interior Effects as Group" option is turned on.

Shading the Edge 2

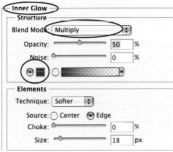

WE USED THE **INNER GLOW** to enhance the rounding of the edge that had been started with the Inner Shadow. We changed the Blend Mode from the default Screen to **Multiply** and used approximately the same blue as for the Inner Shadow. In Multiply mode the dark Inner Glow darkens the shading already established inside the "O" by the Inner Shadow. But unlike the Inner Shadow, the Inner Glow is not an offset effect, so its dark "halo" applies evenly around the edges, also darkening the edge areas that were not shaded by the Inner Shadow — for example, the lower edge of the "O."

Adding a Highlight

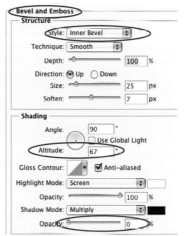

HERE WE USED the **Bevel and Emboss** effect, not so much for bevelling but to add reflective highlights on the surface of the "O." We used **Inner Bevel** for the Style and the default white in Screen mode for the Highlight. But because we had used the Inner Shadow and Inner Glow to control the shading, we didn't need the bevel's Shadow, so we could effectively turn it off by setting its Opacity at 0 (using the bottom slider in the section). Changing the **Altitude** setting to 65° was very important, because it pulled the highlight off the top edge of the plastic "O" and onto the front surface. Again we set the **Angle** at 90° to keep the lighting consistent with the Drop Shadow and Inner Shadow.

Refining the Shine

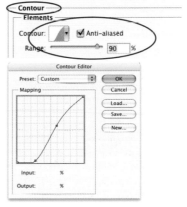

IN THE LIST OF EFFECTS at the left side of the Layer Style dialog box and just below Bevel and Emboss, we clicked on **Contour**. In the Contour section we clicked the Contour thumbnail and customized the curve in the Contour Editor box as shown above. We also changed the Range to 90%. These changes sharpened and narrowed the highlight and pulled it farther up onto the front surface and off the edge of the "O," so it looked even more like a reflection on a hard surface.

Mottling

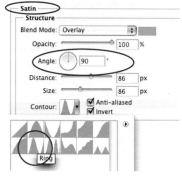

To ADD THE LOOK of subtle streaks and spots to the color, we applied the **Satin** effect in light blue in Overlay mode, creating an offset, manipulated copy of the "O." The **Distance** setting scaled the copy, reducing it vertically because of the 90° **Angle** setting, which determines the angle of distortion of the Satin duplicate. A 90° setting squashes the duplicate vertically, making it shorter and fatter. As in the other sections of the Layer Style box, the **Size** setting controls the amount of blur, making the effect subtler by blurring the copy. We clicked the triangle to the right of the Contour thumbnail and chose a Contour ("Ring" from Adobe's default set) that provides light-dark-light variation in the blurred, squashed duplicate, making it look as if light is bouncing around inside the plastic.

Creating Refraction

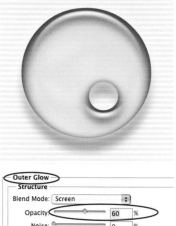

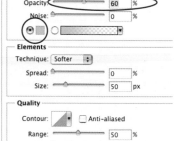

FINALLY, the **Outer Glow** effect in light blue was applied in its default Screen mode. We used **Softer** for the Technique for a more diffuse and irregular look than the alternative Precise setting would have produced. Because the glow is in Screen mode, it affects only the parts of the shadow that are darker than itself, and it affects the light background only slightly. As a result, it lightens and colors the Drop Shadow close to the edge of the "O." This makes it look as if light is being focused through the plastic, brightening the shadow beneath. The degree of brightening was controlled by adjusting the glow's **Opacity**.

CONTROLLING TRANSPARENCY

To reduce the opacity of an element without reducing the opacity of the Drop Shadow, Inner Shadow, or Outer Glow, **reduce Fill Opacity** rather than Layer Opacity. Both of the Opacity controls can be found at the top of the Layers panel and in the Blending Options section of the Layer Style dialog. Changing the setting in one of these places also changes it in the other.

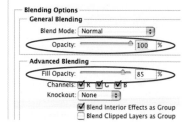

CHECKING SCALE

When you apply a Layer Style, it's a good idea to check the scale, to see if you're getting the best "fit" for the element you're applying it to. One way to open the Scale Layer Effects dialog is to choose Layer > Layer Style > Scale Effects. Once the box is open, pop out the Scale slider and try out various settings.

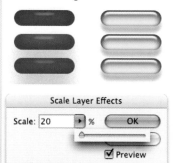

The **Wow-Clear Blue** Style looks very different (top left) until it's scaled down to fit the graphics (top right).

Scaling the Style

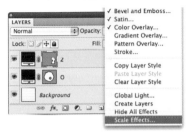

To add a second character, we duplicated the first (Ctrl/⌘-J), used the Type tool **T** to change the "O" to a "2," and also changed the type size in the Options bar. Then we used the Move tool ▶⊕ to drag the "2" into position approximately where we wanted it to be.▼ (Remember, in the **Clear.psd** file all the type has been converted to Shape layers to avoid font conflicts, so you'll see Shape layers rather than live type.)

To better fit the style to the smaller character, we right-clicked/Ctrl-clicked the *fx* icon for the layer, chose Scale Effects from the pop-up menu, and moved the Scale slider to the left until the style fit the "2."

FIND OUT MORE

▼ Using the Type tool **T**
page 436

Adjusting Color

We added another character, again targeting and duplicating the "O" layer, and this time changing the duplicate to a "C." We wanted to change the color of the "C," but didn't want to have to adjust settings in each of the effects in the Layer Style. So we added a Hue/Saturation Adjustment layer immediately above the "C" layer by clicking the "Create new fill or adjustment layer" button ◐ at the bottom of the Layers panel and clicking Hue/Saturation in the list of choices. In the Hue/Saturation dialog, we turned on the Colorize option and adjusted the Hue and Saturation sliders. Then we experimented with the best way to restrict the color change to the "C" *and* its shadow and glow (see "Recoloring a 'Styled' Element" at the right).

To make the mottling more apparent in the "C," in the Layers panel we double-clicked "Satin" in the list of effects for the "C" layer to open that section of the Layer Style dialog, and changed the Satin effect's Blend Mode to Hard Light (see the result on page 525).

A Hue/Saturation Adjustment layer provides a way to change the color of a "styled" layer without having to go into the Layer Style dialog and individually adjust all the effects that make up the Style. But once the Hue/Saturation layer is in place and adjusted, you'll need to find exactly the right configuration for the color change:

• Making a **clipping group** (by Alt/Option-clicking on the border between the two layers) will restrict the color change to the one styled layer, but the Drop Shadow, Outer Glow, Outer Shadow, and Inner Shadow won't be affected.

• Putting the Hue/Saturation layer and the "C" in a **Group** passes the color change through to any layers below.

• But if you change the blend mode for the Group from the default Pass Through to **Normal**, the two layers contribute to the composite image as if the Group were a single merged layer.

Custom Chrome

YOU'LL FIND THE FILES

in (wow) > Wow Project Files > Chapter 8 > Reflective Chrome:

- Shiny Chrome-Before.psd (to start)
- Wow Chrome Project.asl (a Style presets file)
- Cloud Reflection.psd (for creating the reflection)
- Shiny Chrome-After.psd (to compare)

OPEN THESE PANELS

(from the Window menu, for instance):

- Tools • Layers • Channels • Styles

OVERVIEW

Prepare an RGB file with a background image and a graphics layer • Apply the Wow-Chrome 03 Layer Style to add shine and dimension to the graphics • Build a displacement map from the graphics • Use the displacement map with the Glass filter to apply a reflected image onto the surface of the graphics • Touch up the chrome surface • Create a dimensional surface for the graphics to sit on • Apply and modify a Style for this surface

THE CHALLENGE IN IMITATING THE uniquely shiny surfaces of chrome is to get the reflections right — to re-create the complex distortion of the environment that's mirrored in the rounded, curving surfaces of the polished object.

Thinking the project through. The project starts with graphics already created in Adobe Illustrator, then copied and pasted into a Photoshop document consisting of a background layer. The first question we face is whether to paste the graphics as pixels, a Shape layer, or a Smart Object. In this situation a Smart Object probably won't give us much advantage, since if we swap out the graphics, the displacement map (the device that distorts the reflected environment) will still have to be remade, and that can't happen automatically, even with a Smart Object. So we'll paste the graphics as pixels to keep the file simple.

We'll apply a Layer Style to start the chrome. ("Anatomy of 'Shiny'" on page 536 dissects this chrome Style and tells how it works. And "Chrome" in Appendix C shows 19 more chrome variations you can apply instantly.)

Once the pasted graphics are "styled," we'll use the Glass filter with a displacement map made from the graphics to warp a blurred "environment photo" so the outside world seems to be mirrored in the shiny chrome surface. For this part of the project, we'll convert the environment photo into a Smart Object once it's in place, and then apply Gaussian Blur and Glass as Smart Filters. This will keep the filters "live" in case we want to make adjustments later, or use the same filter settings on other "chromed" graphics.

1

The Cooper Bold Italic type and the ellipse were created in Illustrator, copied to the clipboard, and pasted-as-pixels into the marble file.

2a

Choosing the **Wow-Chrome 03** Style

2b

When the **Wow-Chrome 03** Style is applied, its component effects are listed under the "Orbit logo" layer in the Layers panel.

3a

Ctrl/⌘-clicking the "Orbit logo" layer's thumbnail in the Layers panel and choosing Select > Save Selection to start the displacement map file

1 Preparing the file. Open a color file that you want to use for the background behind your chrome object, or open the **Shiny Chrome-Before.psd** file provided. If your file isn't in RGB Color mode, convert it now (Image > Mode > RGB Color), since the Glass filter won't work in CMYK. Import the graphics or type you want to turn into chrome, or create them in Photoshop. We started with a 1000-pixel-wide scan of marble that had been colored blue▼ and added the "Orbit" logo, which had been created in Illustrator, copied to the clipboard, and pasted into the Photoshop file (Edit > Paste > Paste As: Pixels)▼ **1**.

2 Adding the chrome. Click on the thumbnail for your graphics layer to target it. In the Styles panel click the ▼≡ button near the top right corner and choose **Wow-Chrome Styles**. (If you haven't yet loaded the Wow presets,▼ the **Wow-Chrome Styles** won't appear in the menu. To load just the Styles associated with this project, choose Load Styles and navigate to **Wow-Chrome Project.asl** in Wow Project Files > Chapter 8 > Reflective Chrome.) Once you've loaded one of these sets of Styles, click on **Wow-Chrome 03** in the panel **2a**, **2b**. (If you're using a file other than **Chrome-Before.psd,** you may need to scale the Style after you apply it;▼ in the Layers panel, right/Ctrl-click on the *fx* icon for the layer where you applied the Style, choose Scale Effects from the pop-up menu, and adjust the slider until the Style looks good.)

VIEWING STYLE NAMES

If you don't see names in the Styles panel — only swatches — you can display the names also by clicking the ▼≡ button in the upper right corner of the panel and choosing Large List.

3 Building a displacement map. To reflect an "environment" in the chrome, we need to warp the environment photo onto the surface of the chrome object. The first step is to make a *displacement map* (a separate file) from our graphics, to be used with the Glass filter to accomplish the distortion. The Glass filter, like the Displace filter, moves image pixels a given distance depending upon the luminance (or brightness) of the corresponding pixel in the displacement map. Any image in Photoshop format (**.psd**), except one in Bitmap mode, can serve as a displacement map. When you use a grayscale file, white pixels move their corresponding pixels in the filtered image the maximum distance in one direction, black pixels produce the maximum displacement in the opposite direction, and grays produce intermediate displacement, with 50%

FIND OUT MORE

▼ Colorizing an image **page 203**

▼ Pasting from Illustrator **page 460**

▼ Loading the Wow presets **page 4**

▼ Scaling Layer Styles **page 81**

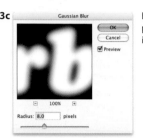

3b

The Save Selection command opens a new file with the graphics in black-and-white.

3c

Blurring the displacement map image

3d

The displacement map, shown here, must be saved as a Photoshop file (remember where you put it!) before it can be used with the Glass filter.

4a

ORIGINAL PHOTO: JHDAVIS

The imported clouds image is positioned and stretched (top), then cropped to the size of the image canvas restored to full Opacity, and converted to a Smart Object for filtering.

brightness producing no displacement at all. The Glass filter also adds the highlights that characterize shiny objects.

To make the displacement map, make an active selection from the outline of the original graphic by Ctrl/⌘-clicking the thumbnail for the "Orbit logo" layer in the Layers panel. Save the selection as a new file by choosing **Select > Save Selection** and choosing **New** in the Document menu of the Save Selection dialog box, naming the file (we called ours "Orbit displacement map"), and clicking "OK" **3a**, **3b**. Deselect (Ctrl/⌘-D) the original selection. The displacement map has to have a soft transition from black through grays to white to produce smooth, rounded edges. To produce the gray tones, blur the new file (Filter > Blur > Gaussian Blur); a good rule of thumb is to use a Radius that's half the Size setting for the Inner Bevel of the chrome Layer Style. Since the Size setting for **Wow-Chrome 03** is 16 pixels, we used an 8-pixel Radius **3c**. (You can check the bevel size setting in a Style by double-clicking "Bevel and Emboss" in the list of effects in the Layers panel to open the Layer Style dialog box.) Now save the displacement map file, since it can't be used with the Glass filter until it's saved (File > Save As, Format: Photoshop) **3d**.

4 Adding the reflection. In this next step, when you add the image you want to use as the reflected environment, it's important that it end up exactly the same pixel size as the canvas of the developing chrome file, in order for the Glass filter to work correctly. Open the image you want to use (we used the **Cloud Reflection.psd** file from the Wow DVD-ROM) and drag with the Rectangular Marquee ⬚ to select the part you want to use, or select all (Ctrl/⌘-A); and then copy (Ctrl/⌘-C). Target the graphics layer in the chrome file by clicking on its thumbnail in the Layers panel, and paste (Ctrl/⌘-V); your pasted image will

---

ALIGNMENT IS IMPORTANT

When you apply a filter that uses a displacement map, such as Displace or Glass, Photoshop aligns the displacement map with the **upper-left corner of the layer** you apply it to. It can cause problems if your layer is oversize and extends above or to the left of the canvas, or if it falls short of the corner. In that case the displacement map will line up differently than you expect when you run the filter. For instance, if you've made the displacement map from a graphic in the file and you run it on a layer that's bigger or smaller, the distortion the filter produces won't align with your graphic. To avoid the problem, trim away excess on a layer before running the filter: Select all (Ctrl/⌘-A) and choose Image > Crop. For a layer whose pixels don't fill the canvas, fill in the empty space or select all (Ctrl/⌘-A) before running the filter.

4b

Blurring the clouds image slightly

4c

Running the Glass filter on the blurred clouds layer

4d

The clouds layer at full opacity after running the Glass filter

4e

A clipping group allows the clouds to show only on the chromed graphic. Opacity of the clouds layer is reduced until the reflection is the right strength.

5a

Before (left) and after using the Blur tool ○ to smooth a pixelated color break

come in right above the graphics layer in the layer stack. In the Layers panel, reduce the Opacity of the new layer so you can see the "styled" graphics through it.

Choose Edit > Free Transform (or press Ctrl/⌘-T) so you can make your photo larger or smaller, to fit the reflections to your graphics as you like. Next make sure you can see enough extra space (gray by default) around the image to show the entire Free Transform box: In CS3 grab the lower right corner of the document window and drag outward to enlarge the window. In CS4 you can use this same method if you're working in a floating window. Or if you're using the new Application frame instead of a document window, you can reduce your view by choosing View > Zoom Out. Once you can see the entire bounding box, drag on a handle to enlarge or reduce it. Make sure it's larger all around than the document itself, and position it (by dragging inside the Transform box) **4a**; double-click inside the Transform box to complete the transformation.

To trim off the parts of the environment image layer that extend beyond the canvas, select all (Ctrl/⌘-A) and choose Image > Crop. Deselect (Ctrl/⌘-D). (This step — cropping the photo — is important in order for the Glass filter to work correctly.)

When the image is in place and trimmed, restore its Opacity to 100% and turn it into a Smart Object (Filter > Convert for Smart Filters). Then choose Filter > Blur > Gaussian Blur; blurring minimizes distractions and prevents a pixelated result when the Glass filter is run. For the soft image of clouds that we used, we set the Gaussian Blur Radius to 4 pixels, which made the edges of the clouds even softer and hid the film grain **4b**.

Now run the Glass filter (Filter > Distort > Glass) **4c**. For the Texture, choose Load Texture from the pop-up menu, locate the displacement map you made at step 3, and click "Open." We used the maximum setting (20) for Distortion and 6 for Smoothness. Lower Smoothness settings produce sharper edges, but may also produce pixelated breaks in the image; higher settings make smoother distortions, but the edges are softer. We left Scaling at 100% and Invert turned off. When you have a result you like, even if there are a few small areas of pixelation, click "OK" to apply the filter **4d**. We can touch up those few spots in step 5.

To limit the distorted environment image to the graphic itself, make a clipping group: In the Layers panel, Alt/Option-click on the border between the last bottom filter for the Smart Object image and the graphics layer. Because of the way the Blending Options have been set in the **Wow-Chrome 03** Layer Style, the

5b

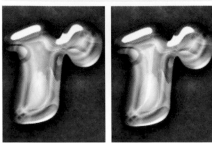

Before (left) and after using the "Blend If" settings to bring back some of the sharp specular highlights that had been reduced by overlaying the clouds image

6a

Setting up the Magic Wand ✺ to select the empty space inside the oval on the "Orbit logo" layer

6b

Hold down the Shift key as you use an appropriate selection tool to add to the selection.

6c

A new layer is added, and the oval selection is filled with blue.

clipped image will interact with the edge effects applied by the Style of the graphic layer below **4e**. ▼ Experiment with reducing the Opacity of the image layer to arrive at the right blend of the image and the light/dark "striping" created by the Satin effect; we settled on 60% Opacity.

FIND OUT MORE
▼ Blending Options
page 512

5 Touching up. To smooth pixelated spots in the reflected image — for example, in the dot of the "i" in our example, add a new layer above the image (Ctrl/⌘-Shift-N), choose the Blur tool ◊ (Shift-R in CS3; no assigned shortcut in CS4, as R is assigned to the Rotate View tool). In the Options bar click the "Brush:" swatch and choose a small, soft brush tip and reduce the Strength (we used a 13-pixel tip and 80% Strength); turn on Sample All Layers. Make short strokes in the pixelated area to eliminate rough edges **5a**.

If you want to keep the cloud image from dulling the brightest specular highlights in the chrome, you can click the cloud layer's thumbnail in the Layers panel to target the layer, then click the *fx* at the bottom of the panel to open the Blending Options dialog box. Then Alt/Option-drag the left part of the white point slider of the "Underlying Layer" to the left slightly **5b**. With a setting of 251/255, the whitest highlights are partially protected from the clouds image.

6 Adding an internal surface. At this point we'll add a stone surface inside the chrome oval and behind the "Orbit" lettering: With the Eyedropper tool 🖋, click on the blue background to set that as the Foreground Color Swatch.

Next select the oval: We chose the Magic Wand ✺ and targeted the "Orbit logo" layer. We turned off the visibility icons for the Shadow effects. With Sample All Layers turned **off** in the Options bar **6a**, we clicked once inside the oval, but outside the lettering. To add to the selection, we held down the Shift key, chose the Polygonal Lasso ⋎ (Shift-L), and clicked to begin encircling the letters **6b**. You don't have to keep the Shift key depressed after you begin selecting. When the selection is complete, add a new layer *below* the "Orbit logo" layer by Ctrl/⌘-clicking the "Create a new layer" button ▣ at the bottom of the Layers panel, and fill the selection with your blue color by pressing Alt/Option-Delete, the shortcut for filling with the Foreground color; then deselect all (Ctrl/⌘-D) **6c**.

7 Modifying a Style. Next we'll create a patterned, polished surface for the stone by applying the **Wow-Red Amber** Style and changing its settings to keep the intricate patterning but eliminate the red-orange color. Click the **Wow-Red Amber**

7a

The **Wow-Red Amber** Style is applied to the blue oval.

7b

Turning off the Color Overlay effect **A,** changing the Pattern Overlay to Luminosity mode **B,** and lowering the Altitude slightly for Bevel and Emboss **C** produces the polished stone effect shown at the top of page 530.

The displacement map for the modified logo

swatch in the Styles panel; it's found in the **Wow-Gems** Styles and also in the **Wow-Chrome Project** Styles (from step 2) **7a**. (If you notice that the shadow outside the chrome oval gets a bit denser, it's because Wow-Red Amber's Drop Shadow has Distance, Size, and Spread settings large enough so the shadow shows around the edges of the graphic.)

Now to change the settings for the Style: In the Layers panel, double-click the Color Overlay listing for the Style you just added to the blue oval; this opens the Layer Style dialog to the Color Overlay section. We can see that the red color comes, at least in part, from this Color Overlay. Since our oval is already the blue we want it to be, we don't need the Color Overlay. Click on the check mark next to **Color Overlay** in the list on the left side of the dialog box to turn **off** this effect.

Turning off Color Overlay doesn't remove the red entirely. Since the Pattern Overlay is now the only overlay effect that's turned on, we can deduce that the color is probably coming from there. In the list on the left side of the dialog box, click Pattern Overlay (the name, not the checkbox). We can see by looking at the swatch that the red-orange color is built into the pattern; to change it would be a project that we don't need to tackle. Instead, since we have the blue color we want in the layer itself, we can simply change the Blend Mode to Luminosity, so the pattern will contribute its light-and-dark detail but not its color **7b**.

One more change: To flatten the top of the gemstone so the chrome letters rest on it comfortably, we can move the bevel highlight a little farther toward the edge. Click "Bevel and Emboss" in the list of effects, and reduce the Altitude setting slightly; we used a setting of 58°.

Variations. The "environment" image you choose can make a big difference in the way your chrome looks. The examples below were made from the "negative" version of the Orbit logo graphics with the **Wow-Chrome 03** Style applied. A displacement map made from the new graphics was used with the Glass filter to distort the environment photo in step 4. The only difference between the two examples is the environment image. **WOW**

The same clouds image used in step 4, but with the layer at 100% Opacity

A photo of the Arc de Triomphe (by E. A. M. Visser) used as the environment image

The file called **Reflections.psd** on the Wow DVD-ROM (Wow Project Files > Chapter 8 > Reflective Chrome) includes these custom chrome treatments.

CUSTOM CHROME **535**

"Shiny"

The next three pages examine the **Wow-Chrome 03** Layer Style, looking at how the component effects interact in this and other shiny Styles. The goal is to show you how to create or modify a Layer Style that adds both dimension and shine. To follow along, you can open **Chrome Anatomy-Before. psd** and build the Style step-by-step, or open **Chrome Anatomy-After.psd** and examine the effects as they're described.

"Custom Chrome" on page 530 tells how to add an environmental reflection to this chrome using a photo. And "Chrome" in Appendix C shows all 20 of the chrome Styles on the Wow DVD-ROM.

WITH THE LAYERS PANEL OPEN (Window > Layers), we targeted the "Orbit logo" layer by clicking its thumbnail, and then clicked the "Add a layer style" button *fx* at the bottom of the panel. In the Advanced Blending section of the Layer Style dialog, we turned **"Blend Interior Effects as Group" on** and **"Blend Clipped Layers as Group" off**. These settings give us the option of adding an image to be reflected in the chrome, as described in step 4 of "Custom Chrome" on page 532. Without these settings, the reflection wouldn't show up.

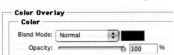

Although the "Orbit logo" graphic is already black, we used a **Color Overlay** effect to set the color for our Layer Style, to build a Style that could be applied to type or graphics of *any* color without surprises. From the effects listed on the left side of the Layer Style dialog, we chose **Color Overlay**. We left the Blend Mode set at Normal and Opacity at 100%. But we clicked the color swatch and clicked on black in the "Select overlay color" dialog as the basis for the Style.

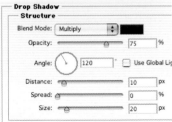

TO START THE ILLUSION of physical objects in a space, we chose **Drop Shadow** from the list in the dialog box. We entered a setting of 10 pixels for the **Distance** (how far the shadow is offset) and 20 pixels for the **Size** (how far the shadow extends out from the edge), leaving the **Spread** at 0. The Spread setting controls whether the shadow is soft and diffuse (a low setting) or dense and sharp-edged (a high setting).

We left the **Angle** at the default 120° but turned **Use Global Light off** so our lighting angle would be independent of any other Layer Style in the file. It works like this:

When you turn on Use Global Light for an effect in a Layer Style, the Angle setting you then choose will reset the lighting for any other Layer Styles already in the file that have Use Global Light turned on. Likewise, if you later add to your file another Style that has Use Global Light turned on, the lighting angle will be reset again, to match the newly introduced Angle.

Before

After

YOU'LL FIND THE FILES

in (wow) > Wow Project Files > Chapter 8 > Shiny:

- Chrome Anatomy-Before.psd (to build the Layer Style from scratch)
- Wow-Chrome.shc (a Contours file)
- Chrome Anatomy-After.psd (to inspect the finished Style)

Adding Thickness

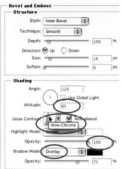

To CREATE A ROUNDED EDGE for the chrome, we clicked on **Bevel and Emboss** in the list of effects. In the Structure section we chose Smooth for the **Technique**. For the bevel **Style** we chose Inner Bevel, to build the bevel inward from the edge of the graphic, and we increased the **Size** to 16 pixels. In the Shading section we again turned **Use Global Light off**. We chose a high **Altitude** setting of 65° to position the highlight up on the "shoulder" of the bevel, and selected our own custom contour (Wow-Chrome) for the Gloss Contour. This contour makes the highlight bright and sharp. (If you're building the Style, click the arrow next to the Contour swatch to open the Contour picker. Click its ● button, load **Wow-Chrome. shc**, and click Wow-Chrome in the picker.)

We changed the **Highlight Opacity** to 100% and the **Shadow Mode** to Overlay. The Mode makes no difference now, but when we add the Satin effect, using Overlay for the Shadow will increase the contrast of the light/dark banding the Satin creates.

Shaping the "Shoulder"

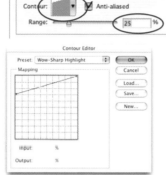

We NEXT CLICKED on the **Contour** option, under **Bevel and Emboss** in the list on the left, to open its panel. This Contour interacts with other bevel characteristics to control the shape and lighting of the edges. In this case, we customized the contour by clicking on the Contour thumbnail to open the Contour Editor and dragging up on the left end of the curve. The **Contour Editor** has a live preview, so we could see the effect of the new curve as we created it. After adjusting, we clicked "OK." Back in the Contour panel, we reduced the **Range** percentage in order to increase the complexity of the highlight and to let some of the highlights "pop up" on the shaded side of the object

GRID SCALE

To switch between a coarse and a fine grid in the Contour Editor anywhere you encounter it in the Layer Style dialog, Alt/Option-click in the Mapping box. (This also works in Photoshop's Curves dialog box.)

Creating Reflections

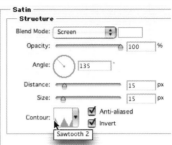

NOW WE WERE READY to use the **Satin effect** to do the magic of the reflections. We chose white for the **color** and Screen for the **Blend Mode**, in order to lighten the object overall. We used 100% **Opacity** for the fullest lightening effect we could get. For the **Contour**, we chose Sawtooth 2 in order to get the light/dark striping that's characteristic of multiple light sources reflected in a polished, curved surface. We experimented with the **Angle** of the effect, changing it from the default of 19° to 135° to position the brightest highlights where we wanted them. We wanted to use Satin's full potential for interacting with the shape of the graphic it's applied to, so we also experimented with **Distance**. We kept the setting low enough (15 pixels) to get well-defined repeats of the graphic's shapes inside the letters and the oval ring, and sharp specular highlights on the letters. We increased the **Size** enough to nicely blur the repeats (also 15 pixels), without blowing them out entirely.

Deepening Reflections

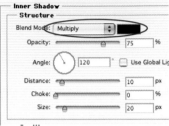

WE EXPERIMENTED with the Inner Shadow and Inner Glow to increase the complexity of the highlights and shadows in the chrome, and to enhance the edge definition.

For the **Inner Shadow** we left the **Angle** at 120° and again turned **Use Global Light off**. The Distance and Size settings were adjusted until the interaction of these two characteristics with the Satin had restored some of the gray in the metal, and had further defined but also softened the bands the Satin effect had created. We settled on 10 pixels for **Distance** and 20 pixels for **Size**.

Enhancing Roundness

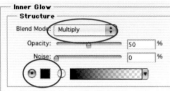

UNLIKE THE INNER SHADOW, which is applied at an angle so that some aspects are darkened and others are not, the Inner Glow is applied evenly, extending inward from the edges of the graphic. Though the defaults for the Inner Glow are set to produce a light glow, we chose black for the **color** and set the **Blend Mode** to Multiply. We chose a moderate **Opacity** setting of 50% — just enough to throw the edges into shadow, enhancing the illusion of roundness in the object as the edges fall away from the light.

Additional Shading

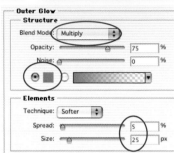

FINALLY, TO MAKE THE CHROME look more like it's sitting on the surface of the stone rather than floating above it, we added an **Outer Glow**, using a medium gray in Multiply mode. (By using gray rather than black, we gave ourselves finer control of the shadow density through the Opacity slider.) With Size reset to 35 and Spread to 5, the Outer Glow created a diffuse darkness around the graphics, defining the shiny forms even more and creating the interacting shadows between pairs of solid letters and between the letters and the rim. At this point, our chrome Style was complete, so we clicked "OK" to close the Layer Style dialog box.

BUILT-IN "REFLECTIONS" FOR SHINY STYLES

In a Layer Style, the three Overlay effects interact with one another as if they were "stacked" in the order they appear in the list in the Layer Style dialog box, with Color on top, then Gradient, then Pattern. So when a Pattern or Gradient Overlay is added to create reflections in a shiny style, the Opacity or Blend Mode of the Color Overlay is typically adjusted to allow the gradient to show.

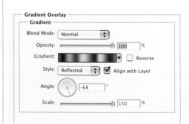

In the **Wow-Chrome 05** Style a reflected environment is simulated with a Gradient Overlay. The white Color Overlay's Opacity is reduced to let the steel-blue gradient "beneath" contribute to the look.

Don't miss the other Style-based chrome treatments shown in "Chrome" in "Appendix C: Wow Layer Styles." You can apply any of them to your own type or graphics with one click in the Styles panel, or by copying and pasting from Appendix C's **Wow-Chrome Samples.psd** file as explained on page 500.

Custom Glass

YOU'LL FIND THE FILES

in (wow) > Wow Project Files > Chapter 8 >
Custom Glass:
- Custom Glass-Before.psd (to start)
- Displace.psd (a displacement map for the Glass filter)
- Earth.psd (for the reflection)
- Custom Glass-After.psd (to compare)

OPEN THESE PANELS

(from the Window menu, for instance):
- Tools • Layers

OVERVIEW

Apply the **Wow-Chrome 03** Style to graphics • Add, clip, and distort a copy of the background image • Adjust the Layer Style • Add glare and a reflected image

1

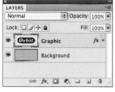

The graphics, treated with the **Wow-Chrome 03** Layer Style, over a background image

The GLASS PLAQUE SHOWN HERE is produced using a variation of the "Custom Chrome" technique on page 530.

Thinking the project through. The main difference in construction between chrome and this glass is the addition of a distorted copy of the background image, clipped by the logo, which makes it seem as if we're seeing the background through a transparent object. Also, the Opacity of the "environment" photo reflected in the surface is lower than with chrome, since glass is not as reflective. A few strategic changes to the Layer Style complete the character of the glass.

1 Setting up the file. Open the file you want to use as the background behind your glass object. On another layer create or import graphics. Our **Glass-Before.psd** file is a 1000-pixel-wide background with a logo on another layer. To build your new glass Style, you can start by applying the **Wow-Chrome 03** Style on your graphics layer as described on page 531. Or open the **Custom Glass-After.psd** file and copy the Style from there. ▼ You may need to scale the Style to fit your graphics; right-click/Ctrl-click the *fx* for the styled layer, choose Scale Effects, and adjust the slider until the chrome surface looks right **1**; you don't need to be concerned about the exterior shadows, since they'll be changed in step 3.

FIND OUT MORE

▼ Copying a Layer
Style **page 500**

2 Making the object transparent. In the Layers panel, duplicate the background image — click its thumbnail to target it, and then type Ctrl/⌘-J. Drag the new layer's thumbnail up in the panel so it's above the graphics, and Alt/Option-click the border between this copy and the graphics layer below it, to "clip" the "Background copy" inside the graphics shape. For the next step, choose Filter > Convert for Smart Filters **2a**.

2a

A copy of the background image is clipped by the graphics and converted to a Smart Object so a Smart Filter can be applied.

2b

Running the Glass filter on the "Background copy" layer distorts the image as if it were being viewed through the rounded glass logo. Running it as a Smart Filter lets you change the slider settings or the Texture image later on.

To distort the background as seen through the glass, you'll need a displacement map made from the graphics, as described in step 3 of "Custom Chrome"; our displacement map is the file **Displace.psd**. Use the displacement map with the Glass filter (Filter > Distort > Glass) to "glassify" the "Background copy" layer, clicking the ▾≡ button in the Glass dialog, choosing Load Texture, and loading the displacement map file; we used Distortion and Smoothness settings of 20 and 5 respectively **2b**.

3 Adjusting the Style. To make the graphics more glasslike, make these changes to the Style on the graphics layer:

- In the Layers panel, if you don't see the list of effects for the styled layer, click the tiny arrow next to the layer's *fx* icon. Double-click the **Inner Shadow** entry to open the Layer Style dialog to that panel. Change the Inner Shadow's Blend Mode to **Overlay**. This will brighten the edges of the glass graphic **3a**, because Overlay darkens less than Multiply does. We liked the results for Overlay, but you might also try Soft Light or another of the contrast-enhancing modes grouped with Overlay in the Blend Mode list. ▼

  FIND OUT MORE
  ▼ Using blend modes **page 181**

- In the list of effects at the left of the Layer Style dialog, click on the name **Outer Glow** (not the checkbox). To change the Outer Glow from a "dark halo" to a glow that simulates light being refracted through the glass to light up the surface beneath, click the color swatch and change the color to white; change the Blend Mode to **Overlay**, which lightens, but not as intensely as Screen would; and experiment with reducing the Size setting; we reduced the Size to 20 pixels **3b**. Even with the Outer Glow lightened, the glass graphics will still cast a slight shadow, thanks to the Drop Shadow. This helps with the illusion of a clear but solid material.

3a

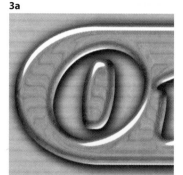

After modifying the Inner Shadow

3b

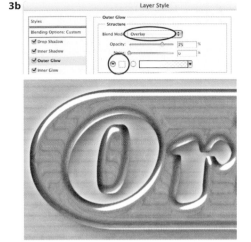

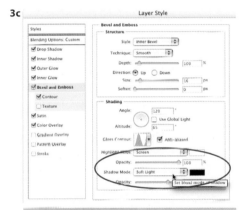

Changing the Outer Glow

3c

Changing the Bevel and Emboss Shadow

- Depending on your background image, your glass may look too much darker or more saturated than the background. If so, click on **Bevel and Emboss** in the list at the left and reduce the Opacity of the **Shadow** in the Shading section of the Bevel and Emboss panel, or change the Mode from Overlay to **Soft Light**; we changed the Shadow Mode to Soft Light and left the Opacity at 75% **3c**.

4 Creating glare. You can "reflect" diffuse light from the surface of the glass graphics by lowering the Opacity setting for the glassified background copy; we settled on 85% Opacity for the "Background copy" layer **4**.

5 Reflecting an environment. To reflect an image on the glass, target the "Background copy" layer by clicking its thumbnail; then open a photo file and drag and drop the image; we used the **Earth.psd** image. Choose Filter > Convert for Smart Filters. Then add this new layer to the clipping group by Alt/Option-clicking its lower border in the Layers panel. We renamed our imported image layer by double-clicking its name in the Layers panel and typing "Reflection."

Before you "glassify" this layer, *be sure to crop off any excess* from the layer so the displacement map will line up correctly (type Ctrl/⌘-A to Select All, and choose Image > Crop). To use the same filter settings you used on "Background copy," hold down the Alt/Option key and drag the Smart Filter layer from "Background copy" to the "Reflection" layer **5**. Reduce the Opacity of "Reflection" until the reflection is at the strength you want; we used 10% for the result shown at the top of page 539.

4

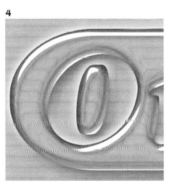

Reducing the glassified "Background copy" layer's Opacity creates a slight surface glare.

5

A photo for reflection is added and modified with the Glass filter.

Bevels

Photoshop's Bevel and Emboss is one of the most valuable effects in a Layer Style for turning type and graphics into tangible objects. It plays a role in most of the special effects in this chapter, contributing everything from a smooth and rounded look to a rough and angular appearance. The essential tools for beveling are found in the Bevel and Emboss section of the Layer Style dialog box, and in the related Contour and Texture sections. But the Stroke effect is also very useful for building bevels.

The fundamentals of Bevel and Emboss are covered starting on page 509, along with their relationship to Contour (which shapes the "shoulder" of a bevel; page 510) and Texture (which adds an embossed surface, the location of the texture being determined by the type of bevel; page 512). This "Anatomy of Bevels" section explores the potential of some Bevel and Emboss nuances that aren't covered elsewhere in the chapter.

In the Layer Styles applied to the four graphics layers that make up **Star.psd**, the Bevel and Emboss effects are key to creating the illusion of solid, dimensional objects. Use this file to explore the importance of bevel position and Stroke in establishing a beveled look. And plan to come back and refer to this file when you need to create, modify, or "borrow" a bevel.

 Star.psd

YOU'LL FIND THE FILES

in wow > Wow Project Files > Chapter 8 > Anatomy of Bevels

Bevel Position

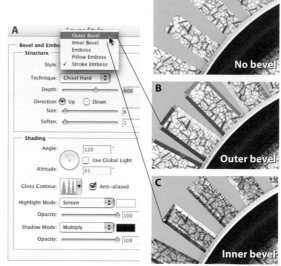

IN THE BEVEL AND EMBOSS PANEL of the Layer Style dialog box **A**, you can set the **Style**, or position, of the bevel in the **Structure** section. The choice you make determines where the bevel will be built relative to the edge of the layer content. The Inner Bevel and Outer Bevel extend inward and outward, of course; Emboss straddles the outline, and so does Pillow Emboss; the position of a Stroke Emboss depends entirely on the position of the Stroke (as shown in "Bevels & Strokes" on page 543).

Below are some things to consider when choosing a bevel's position. To follow along, turn off visibility for the Stroke effect for the "Spokes" layer (click the Stroke's 👁 in the Layers panel); for a simpler view, also turn off visibility for the Shadow and Glow effects, as shown here.

- An **Outer Bevel extends** outward **B**, so you may need to add extra space between characters if you use it on type. Also, the **Outer Bevel** is **semi-transparent** and allows whatever is below it in the Layer stack to show through the bevel (as the yellow does here). But this can change if you use the Outer Bevel with a Stroke effect, as described on page 543.

- The **Inner Bevel** takes its characteristics (such as color or pattern) from the beveled element itself, so it **creates a solid edge** that doesn't let a background show through **C**. An Inner Bevel "consumes" part of the shape it's applied to, which can be a problem if you use it on a delicate shape or on type.

- An **Outer Bevel is rounded** around any sharp points, while an **Inner Bevel has sharp corners**. An **Emboss** bevel creates **intermediate rounding**.

Bevels & Strokes

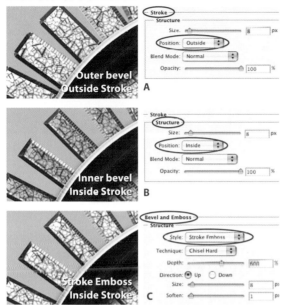

THE COMBINATION of a Bevel and Emboss and a Stroke can help tailor the edge profile and lighting for a bevel:

- An **Outer Bevel**, which is otherwise semi-transparent, can be filled in by adding a **Stroke** with **Outside** chosen as the Stroke's Position. Notice that with a Stroke in place **A**, the yellow background no longer shows through as it does for the Outer Bevel on page 542. For a good fit between bevel and Stroke, try **matching the Size** setting of the Stroke to the Size setting for the Bevel and Emboss and then adjust as needed. (Another option for a solid outer bevel is to use the **Stroke Emboss with an Outside Stroke**.)

- For an **Inner Bevel**, adding an **Inside Stroke** creates a cleanly "cut" edge by keeping any Overlay effects (Color, Gradient, or Pattern) from "spilling over" onto the bevel **B** (to see the effect, compare **B** here to the Inner Bevel on page 542, in which the Overlay effects extend from the top surface onto the bevel). A **Center Stroke** can be used in the same way for an **Emboss** or **Pillow Emboss** bevel. (Note that a Stroke *doesn't* hide a *Texture* effect applied with Bevel and Emboss.)

- For an Inner Bevel the settings in the Shading section of the Bevel and Emboss panel also affect the "top surface" of the element you apply the bevel to; for instance, in **B** the Bevel and Emboss Shadow darkens the surface. But if you use the Inside Stroke with a **Stroke Emboss**, instead of an Inner Bevel, you get the same bevel effect without the shading on the top surface **C**.

Bevels & Lighting

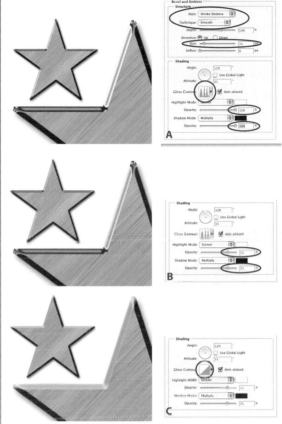

THE LIGHTING FOR BEVELS is set up in the Shading section of the Bevel and Emboss panel, using the Gloss Contour and the Mode, Opacity, and colors of the highlights and shadows. With the Stroke Emboss and Stroke (as described at the left), the characteristics of the bevel and the top surface are independent of each other. You may want to turn off visibility for the Satin effect (as we did here) as you "deconstruct" the Bevel and Emboss for the "Small Star" layer, which has a **Stroke Emboss** (15 pixels) backed up with a **Center Stroke** (10 pixels).

The **highly reflective edge** with alternating high-contrast lights and darks results in part from choosing a **complex Gloss Contour** with multiple ridges, such as Adobe's Ring-Triple **A**. Also, with **Highlight Mode** and **Shadow Mode** set to their default Screen and Multiply, using higher **Opacity** settings makes the beveled edges **more reflective** — shinier. See the difference by reducing both Opacity settings to 75% **B**, and then also compare the effect of using the default Gloss Contour **C**.

Bevels & Color

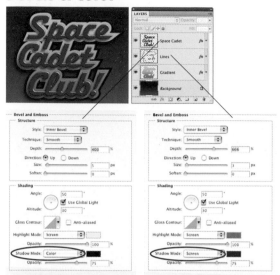

You can use the Bevel and Emboss effect not only to add thickness and lighting direction to type or graphics but also to set the *color* of the lighting. Two examples are shown here; the type and border were created on separate layers so that each could have its own Layer Style:

• With an **Inner Bevel** chosen for the "Space Cadet" layer, we used yellow for the Highlight and a bright purple for the Shadow. We put the Shadow in Color mode to override the color on the shaded edges of the bevel, to make it look as if a purple light source was shining from below.

• For the black outlines that make up the "Lines" layer, the **Inner Bevel** was used with a magenta Highlight in Screen mode and a violet Shadow, also in Screen mode, again to simulate additional light sources.

(Using a higher Size setting for the Bevel and Emboss effect on the "Space Cadet" logotype — 5 instead of the 3 used for the "Lines" layer — makes the logotype look thicker, as if it stands up higher from the background.)

 Space.psd

A Bevel That Isn't a Bevel

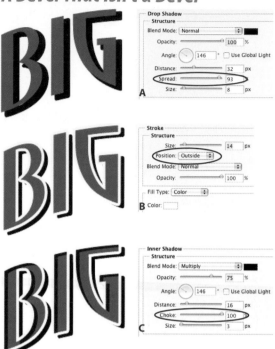

When is a bevel not a bevel? With the "multiple-stroke" approach described here, you can create an old-fashioned dimensional look, with "square" bevels, without using Bevel and Emboss. We started with graphics colored with a green Color Overlay effect.

• We added a **Drop Shadow.** Its **Distance** setting determines the offset, and the **Size** setting adds to its width. We set the **Spread at 93%** to harden the softened edge created by the Size setting **A**.

• To start the bevel, we added a light-colored **Stroke** effect **B**; it creates the flat top surface of the square bevel. In the Structure section of the Stroke settings, the **Outside** choice for Position **thickens the letters.**

• The **Inner Shadow** turns the Stroke into a built-up edge **C**. In the Structure section, we set the **Choke to 100%**, which is one way to keep the shadow hard-edged.

• We made sure to use the same **Angle** for the Inner Shadow and Drop Shadow, to keep lighting consistent. (If you toggle the 👁 for the Drop Shadow effect, you'll see how important the Drop Shadow is in establishing the letters as solid objects. Also notice that even though the "cast shadow" illusion isn't perfect at the corners, the dimensional impression works!)

 Big.psd

Carving

YOU'LL FIND THE FILES

in (wow) > Wow Project Files > Chapter 8 >
Carving:
- Carve-Before files (to start)
- Wow-Carve.asl (a Style presets file)
- Carve-After files (to compare)

OPEN THESE PANELS

(from the Window menu, for instance):
- Tools • Layers • Styles

OVERVIEW

Add a Layer Style to a graphic to "carve"
it into a plain background • Use the
Lighting Effects filter to enhance the
dimensionality of the carving • Switch
to a smooth, patterned background
image; offset a copy of this surface image,
masked with the graphic, to add to the
Illusion of depth • Switch to a textured
background image; make a displacement
map from the background image, and use
the Displace filter to roughen the carving

SOMETIMES ALL YOU NEED in order to create the illusion of the
third dimension is an edge defined by highlights and shadows
that can make a shape look carved or cut-out. In Photoshop an
excellent way to accomplish this is to use a Layer Style.

Thinking the project through. The **Bevel and Emboss** effect
raises or depresses edges, creating the initial cut, while an **Inner
Shadow** will add depth to the carving, and **Color Overlay** can
control the overall shading of the recessed areas. The **Lighting
Effects** filter can enhance the realism. Running the filter on a
separate layer offers flexible results you can change with Opacity
and blend modes, and running it as a Smart Filter lets you access
the lighting settings to change them later if you need to.

The combination of Layer Style and Lighting Effects may be all
you need if the carved surface is smooth and plain. But if the
surface has distinct color markings such as wood grain, you
can add to the illusion by **offsetting** the interior of the carving.
This creates an obvious "jump" in the markings that adds to the
appearance that the carved area is recessed.

For a textured surface like the rock above, the **Displace** filter,
used with a displacement map made from the surface image, can
"disrupt" or bend the edges of the carved graphic to conform
to the surface texture.

The **Carve Smooth-Before.psd** file consists of graphics on a transparent layer over a smooth surface that was created by applying a Layer Style to a color-filled layer.

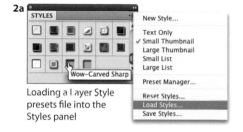

Loading a Layer Style presets file into the Styles panel

In the **Wow-Carved Sharp** Style, a black Color Overlay replaces the native color of the element it's applied to (in this case the graphics were black already anyway, so it made no difference); the reduced Fill opacity (25%, also built into the Style) makes the black graphics partly transparent, so the effect is to shade the recessed areas of the carving.

2c

In the Bevel and Emboss section of the Layer Style dialog box, we changed the Style to Emboss and the Technique to Smooth.

1 Preparing to carve a smooth surface. Open or create an image of a smooth surface, without distinct markings or texture. Add the graphics you want to carve, as a transparent layer in this file; you might copy-and-paste or drag-and-drop the artwork from another file, or create it with Photoshop's drawing tools. ▼ Or open the **Carve Smooth-Before.psd** file **1**. The red surface is created with a variant of a Layer Style (**Wow-Red**, one of the **Wow Plastics** Styles shown in Appendix C) adjusted for this graphic; the graphics are old-fashioned clip art, scanned, modified, and isolated from the white background.▼

2 Adding a Layer Style to the graphics. To carve the graphics into the surface, we began by targeting the graphics layer (by clicking its thumbnail in the Layers panel) and applying the **Wow-Carved Sharp** Layer Style from the **Wow Halos & Embossing** Styles on the DVD-ROM that comes with this book; "Anatomy of Bevels" on page 542 tells how the effects in this and other Styles work together to create dimensional edges. To apply the Style, you can either click on it in the Styles panel (if you've installed the Wow presets as explained on page 4), or you can choose Load Styles **2a** from the panel's menu ▾☰ and load the **Wow-Carve.asl** file from the folder with the other files for this project; once it's loaded into the Styles panel, click on the **Wow-Carved Sharp** Style to apply it **2b**.

Depending on the size and type of graphics you're using, you may want to scale the Style overall (we did not),▼ or you may want to modify some of its effects. We didn't change the Inner Shadow (which creates the shadow cast by the carved edge) or the Color Overlay (which darkens the recessed areas overall). But the Bevel and Emboss effect seemed too heavy for our graphics on this surface, so in the Layers panel we double-clicked the Bevel and Emboss listing for the graphics layer and made some changes **2c**: We changed the Outer Bevel, which builds the carved edge outward from the black graphics, to **Emboss**, which creates half the width of the edge by building outward, and half by building inward. We also changed the Chisel Hard setting to Smooth for a "machined" look **2d**. (If you want to experiment with the Inner Shadow or the Color Overlay, click its name in the list on the left side of the Layer Style dialog box; the check

2d

The carved graphics after the change in the Style

FIND OUT MORE

▼ Using the drawing tools **page 448**

▼ Isolating graphics on a transparent layer
page 483

▼ Scaling Styles **page 81**

3a

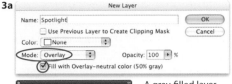

A gray-filled layer in Overlay mode was added for the lighting. Choosing Filter > Convert for Smart Filters turned the new layer into a Smart Object.

3b

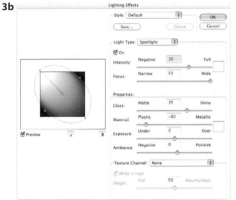

Setting up a spotlight

3c

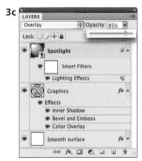

The lighting in place; the result is shown on page 545.

4a

The **Carve Pattern-Before.psd** file, with the **Wow-Carved Sharp** Style applied to the graphics

marks indicate which effects are turned on and contributing to the Style, but you'll need to click the *name* of the effect to get to the right section of the dialog box to make changes.)

3 Making a "lighting" layer. To liven up the carved image, we applied a Spotlight with the **Lighting Effects** filter,▼ but we kept it on a separate "lighting" layer for greater control of the effect: With the graphics layer targeted, add a new layer in Overlay mode by Alt/Option-clicking the "Create a new layer" button ▣ at the bottom of the Layers panel; using the Alt/Option key opens the New Layer dialog box, where you can choose **Overlay** for the Mode and click the checkbox for **"Fill with Overlay-neutral color (50% gray)" 3a**. Since the gray is neutral (invisible) in this mode, your image won't change when you click "OK" to close the box, but you'll see the gray-filled thumbnail in the Layers panel.

FIND OUT MORE

▼ Using Lighting Effects **page 264**

To create the Spotlight, first choose Filter > Convert for Smart Filters, so you can alter the lighting settings easily later on. Next choose Filter > Render > Lighting Effects and set up your lighting **3b**. We started with the Default lighting, reoriented the light so it was most intense in the upper left corner, and made it closer to circular by dragging inward on the bottom handle. The Lighting Effects preview will show only the gray layer, and you won't be able to preview the effect on your image in the working window, but you'll be able to modify the Smart Filter at any time. In the Layers panel you can experiment by choosing other blend modes for the spotlight layer (such as Soft Light or Hard Light) or by reducing the Opacity setting to decrease the spotlight effect. You can also double-click the name of the Filter to adjust the filter's settings, as we did. We decided to decrease the Intensity to 30 and change Gloss to 35 and Material to –80. In the Layers panel we kept Overlay for the layer's blend mode but reduced the Opacity to 85% **3c**.

4 Carving a patterned surface. To carve a patterned surface, either open your own image file and add graphics (as in step 1), then apply the **Wow-Carved Sharp** Style (step 2), and add lighting (step 3). Or open the **Carve Pattern-Before.psd** file; we've already applied the **Wow-Carved Sharp** Style (we found that this Style worked well for the wood carving without changes), and we copied the "Spotlight" layer from the first carving and changed the Material setting to 30 (double-clicking on the filter name in the Layers panel reopened the Lighting Effects dialog so we could make that change) **4a**.

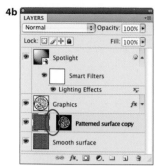

4b

The duplicate patterned layer with a layer mask applied and unlinked

4c

Before

After

Offsetting the masked duplicate layer slightly to create a "jump" in the pattern

5a

The **Carve Rough-Before.psd** file, with the **Wow-Carved Smooth** Layer Style applied to the graphics layer. Some of the leaves in the foreground are "caught" in the carving, but that will be fixed in step 7.

To shift the recessed area to enhance the illusion of depth, **create a masked duplicate** of the surface image: Target the surface image in the Layers panel and press Ctrl/⌘-J to duplicate it; then load the graphics layer as a selection by Ctrl/⌘-clicking the graphics layer's thumbnail, and click the "Add a layer mask" button at the bottom of the panel. **Unlink the mask** in this duplicate layer (by clicking the icon between the layer's image thumbnail and its mask thumbnail) **4b**. This will allow you to move the wood image while the mask stays right in place: Target the image rather than the mask; choose the Move tool and nudge the image by tapping the arrow keys on the keyboard until the image is shifted as much as you like **4c**.

5 Carving a textured surface. If the surface you're carving has some roughness to it, there's something else you can do to add to the illusion. To follow our example, open the **Carve Rough-Before.psd** file **5a**, or if you're using your own image and graphics, follow steps 1 through 4, but in step 2 instead of using the Wow-Carved Sharp Style, you may want to try **Wow-Carved Smooth**, to make the carving look "rounder" as if worn with age **5b**. We changed the copied Lighting Effects Smart Filter settings again so Gloss was now set to 0 and Material to 85.

> **LAYERING TWO MATERIALS**
>
> When you "carve" a patterned surface, the mask you create (in step 4 of "Carving") can be used not only for shifting the recessed surface, but also for *replacing* it with a different material (we used a layer filled with the **Wow-Wood 06** pattern, shown in Appendix C). You can do that as follows: Target the layer that has the mask by clicking on it in the Layers panel. Open the image file you want to use for the second surface, and with the Move tool drag-and-drop it into the carving file; it will come in as a layer above the masked layer. Now "copy the mask" to your new layer by Alt/Option-dragging the mask thumbnail up the Layers panel to the imported layer.

5b

In the Bevel and Emboss section of the Layer Style dialog box, a higher Size setting (16 for Wow-Carved Smooth, instead of the 9 used for Wow-Carved Sharp) and the Smooth setting for Technique make a softer, rounder edge on the bevel.

6a

The carving file, with only the rock image layer visible, is duplicated to start making the displacement map.

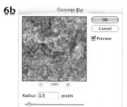

6b

After converting the displacement map file to grayscale, we blurred it slightly to smooth out differences in the tone in the rock that had nothing to do with surface texture.

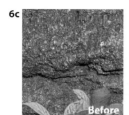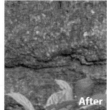

6c

The effect of blurring the displacement map

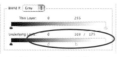

6d

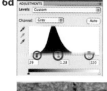

Using a Levels Adjustment layer and the "Blend If" sliders to increase contrast in the darkest tones, to emphasize the dark crevices without exaggerating the "grain" of the rock. (Right-click/Ctrl-click the Adjustment layer's thumbnail to open to Blending Options.)

6 "Roughening" the carving. For the rough surface, the next step is to create a displacement map to use with the Displace filter to make the carving look like it's affected by the depressions (dark areas) and rises (lighter areas) in the surface topography. The Displace filter works on an image by "pushing" pixels up or down and right or left. For each pixel the direction is decided by whether the corresponding pixel in the displacement map is dark or light, and the relative amount of displacement is affected by the degree of darkness or lightness. ▼

At this point, in case there might be any layers that extend beyond the canvas, select all (Ctrl/⌘-A) and choose Image > **Crop**, so the displacement map you're about to make is sure to match up with the surface image when you apply the Displace filter. Then in the Layers panel, temporarily turn off visibility for all but the surface image layer (Alt/Option-click its 👁 icon), choose Image > Duplicate, and check the Duplicate Merged Layers Only option **6a**.

To make it easier to see how the contrast in the new image will work as a displacement map, convert the duplicate file to Grayscale (Image > Mode > Grayscale). Then you may want to get rid of unwanted detail by blurring **6b**, **6c**, and increase the contrast to exaggerate the light/dark differences in major features of the surface; we used a Levels Adjustment layer to increase contrast ▼ and then used the Blend If sliders to restrict the increased contrast to the dark tones in the cracks **6d**. ▼ **Save the file in Photoshop (PSD) format**, since the Displace filter requires a saved Photoshop file.

To "roughen" the carving, back in your developing carving file, target the graphics layer in the Layers panel and turn on its visibility (click in the Visibility column in the Layers panel to bring back its 👁 icon). Choose Filter > Convert for Smart Filters in order to be able to alter your settings later if needed **6e**. Next choose Filter > Distort > Displace. In the Displace dialog box, put in values for the Horizontal and Vertical Scale (we used 6 for both) **6f**, and click "OK" to close the box; navigate to the displacement map you just made, and click "Open." If you decide to change the result after running Displace, double-click on the filter name to reopen the dialog and adjust the settings to get a more or less pronounced effect, and click "OK" to reapply the filter.

7 Bringing foreground elements in front of the carving. Whether your carved surface is smooth, patterned, or

FIND OUT MORE

▼ How the Displace filter works **page 575**

▼ Using Levels **page 246**

▼ Using Blend If **page 66**

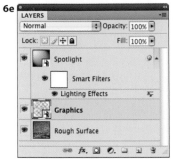

6e

The graphics layer is converted to a Smart Object layer for the Displace filter.

6f

Applying the Displace filter distorts the carved graphics to match the surface.

7

A Levels adjustment targeted to the Green channel increases color contrast between the leaves and the rock, which makes it easier for the Magnetic Lasso to follow the edge.

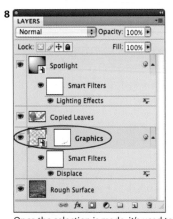

8

Once the selection is made, it's used to copy the foreground elements to a separate layer above the graphics. The extra Levels layer is deleted, and a mask is added to the Graphics layer to tone down the highlight in some areas.

textured, if there is a subject in your surface image that needs to appear in front of the carving, you can make that happen by selecting the subject and duplicating it to a new layer.

Use a selection method appropriate to your subject. ▼ To keep our selecting work to a minimum, we selected only those few leaves that overlapped the carving. Because of the variation in the leaves and the speckled nature of the stone, it would be hard to select with the Quick Selection tool, the Magic Wand, or the Color Range command. We decided to use the Magnetic Lasso ⬡, operating the tool magnetically wherever the edge was distinct enough by "floating" the cursor along without depressing the mouse button, ▼ and then clicking or Alt/Option-dragging where the tool needed our help to follow the edge. But before we started, we increased the color contrast between the leaves and the rock to make it easier for the Magnetic Lasso to "see" the edges: We turned off visibility for all layers except the image layer. We clicked the "Create new fill or adjustment layer" button ⬤ at the bottom of the Layers panel and chose Levels. Sometimes increasing overall contrast with the Levels Input sliders is all that's needed. In this case, however, we decided to use the fact that we had green leaves on a neutral background. We chose Green from the Channel menu at the top of the Levels dialog and moved the black slider inward, turning the rock a dark magenta **7**, which provided better contrast with the green leaves. When the selection was finished, we deleted the Levels layer, targeted the image layer again, selected the leaves, and copied them to a new layer (Ctrl/ ⌘-J). Then it was just a matter of dragging the leaves up the stack in the Layers panel until they were in front of the carving, and turning on visibility for the other layers again.

8 Finishing touches. To tone down the bevel highlight at the bottom of the carving where the rock is undercut, we added a mask to the Graphics layer (by targeting the layer in the Layers panel and clicking the "Add a layer mask button" ⬜ at the bottom of the panel). We painted the mask with black, using the Brush ✎ with a soft tip and low Opacity **8**.

If your image has a color cast in the shadows, for any shadow effect in the Layer Style dialog box, click the color swatch and click in a shadowed area of the image to sample color. If you wish to further exaggerate displacement of some elements, make a flattened copy of the file (Image > Duplicate, Duplicate Merged Layers Only), and try Liquify. ▼ *wow*

FIND OUT MORE

▼ Choosing a selection method
page 47

▼ Operating the Magnetic Lasso ⬡
page 55

▼ Using Liquify
page 575

Neon Type

Page 429 shows how Bert Monroy, master of photorealism, hand-crafts his neon, complete with the "grunge" of the city environment. And **Crafting a Neon Glow. pdf** presents a tutorial that appeared in previous editions of this book, but that has now been moved to the Wow DVD-ROM to make room for new pages. It tells step-by-step how to construct a neon sign using a Shape layer, make it glow with a Layer Style, and finally add details like pinches in the tubing and supports to hold it to the wall. Here we see some simpler examples of quick neon styling for type.

The **Quick Neon Type** files include all the examples shown here (with the type rasterized) so you can easily explore the settings for the Layer Styles (in the Layers panel simply double-click on the *fx* for a layer to open the Layer Style dialog box). The Quick Neon Type files can also serve as a source of neon for copying a Style, which you can then paste into another file.

YOU'LL FIND THE FILES

in > Wow Project Files > Chapter 7 > Quick Neon Type, and Wow Goodies > Outtakes > Crafting a Neon Glow

---

VIEWING CHARACTERS

How do you know what the characters in a particular font look like? Here are some ways to find out:

• The font menu in the Type tool's Options bar includes a **"Sample" column** that gives you a peek at these six characters in every font.

• Both Windows and Mac provide ways to look at font content. **Windows's Character Map** utility (found in the **Start, Accessories,** or **System Tools** menu in different versions) lets you see all the characters of a font, and copy and paste them into a Photoshop type layer. In **Mac OS X** the **Character Palette** shows all the characters in a particular font, or the same character in all the fonts in your System. Choosing **Edit > Special Characters** from the Finder menu opens the palette. Or include it in the **"flag"** menu near the right end of the menu bar by choosing > **System Preferences > International > Input Menu** and checking the box next to Character Palette.

"Made-for-Neon" Fonts

CERTAIN DISPLAY FONTS, such as **Eklektic** (used for "space bar" above) and MiniPics **Confetti** (an icon font, used for the swirl), are ideal for simulating neon tubing. Their characters are formed with a single monoweight stroke (neon tubes have a consistent diameter) and with rounded ends. Lighting up such a font is simply a matter of typing the text (choose the Type tool T, click in the working window, and type) and then applying a Layer Style like any of those in the Wow-Neon & Glows set (page 767), scaling the Style if necessary (Layer > Layer Style > Scale Effects).

In this case we drew a path with the Pen tool and set type on the path by clicking on it with the Type tool and typing the word "space." Then we duplicated the type-on-a-path layer (Ctrl/⌘-J). On the new layer we held down the Ctrl/⌘ key and used the Move tool to drag the new type layer down. We selected the type by dragging the cursor over it and then typed "bar." On both layers we positioned, tracked, and kerned the type.▼

We added a new empty layer (Ctrl/⌘ Shift-N, or add the Alt/Option key to bypass the New Layer dialog box) and turned it into a third type layer by typing on it — a symbol from the MiniPics Confetti font. Then, to fit this swirl with the two lines of Eklektic, we resized and rotated the swirl (by pressing Ctrl/⌘-T, Shift-dragging on a corner handle to resize, and then dragging around outside a corner handle to rotate).

FIND OUT MORE

▼ Adjusting type along a path **page 442**

 Made for Neon.psd

KERNING & TRACKING

To **kern**, put the Type tool T cursor between two characters, hold down Alt/Option, and use the → or ← key to widen or narrow the space. To **track**, drag the Type tool T cursor over the type you want to affect, hold down Alt/Option and use the → or ← key.

Almost "Made-for-Neon"

"Outlining" with Neon

MANY OTHER MONOWEIGHT TYPEFACES, though not quite perfect, can still successfully suggest neon. In the examples above:

- The **Pump Tri D** font (used for "zebra room"), **Harpoon** (for "city deli"), and **Chunky Monkey** are practical candidates even though they have square rather than round ends on their strokes.

- For "Motel 5" we used the **Balloon** font, pairing sizes (36-point Bold and 80-point Light) that gave a visually consistent diameter to the neon tubing. In this font family the strokes have round ends. The characters lack the breaks between strokes that you would see in real neon, but for suggesting neon, the font works.

- The **Circle D** font used for "joe's" is monoweight with round ends. But it was too thin by itself to make neon tubes. So after setting the type and pressing the Enter key, we thickened the strokes: We clicked the ▣ toggle on the Type tool's Options bar to open the Character panel, then clicked the ▾≡ at the top right corner of the panel and chose Faux Bold from the fly-out menu; the tubes gained the weight we wanted, and the type was still live.

- The rainclouds icon is from **Inkfont Dingbats**. To get the purple color we added a Hue/Saturation Adjustment layer above this type layer (by clicking the "Create new fill or adjustment layer" button ◑ at the bottom of the Layers panel and moving the Hue slider). This recoloring method changes both the Inner Glow and the Outer Glow. It's successful in this case, even without a clipping group, because the rainclouds layer is below all the other type layers and because the *Background* is black (it has no hue), so none of these other layers is affected by the Hue/Saturation layer.

Almost Made for Neon.psd

YOU CAN BEND NEON TUBING to fit type outlines by using a Layer Style that includes a gradient Stroke effect. Choose a bold font without sharp points, and type your text; use any color — the Layer Style will hide the fill. Click the "Add a layer style" button *ƒх* at the bottom of the Layers panel and choose **Blending Options** at the top of the pop-up list. When the Layer Style dialog box opens, in the Advanced Blending section set the **Fill Opacity** to **0**, to make the type transparent. Also make sure the **Blend Interior Effects As Group** option is *not checked*. This will ensure that for the Stroke (which we'll add next), the part that falls inside the body of the type will show, even though the Fill Opacity is 0.

From the list on the left side of the Layer Style box, click on the word "Stroke." In the Stroke panel, for the **Position** choose **Center** so the Stroke will straddle the edge and won't make the characters too fat or too thin. For the **Fill Type** choose **Gradient** and for the **Style** choose **Shape Burst**. You'll need a gradient that goes from a light color or white in the center to the same bright color at each end. To get the tubes to glow just right, experiment with the Stroke's **Size** slider. For the glow around the tubing, we added Inner Glow and Outer Glow effects, both in Screen mode.

- For "crow bar" we used the **Fluf** font.

- We typed "blue" and "hippo" in the **BeesWax** font and used the **Animal** font for the outline of the hippo. The dots are type-on-a-path (the period character) with the Justify All option turned on in the Paragraph panel to space them evenly from one end of the path to the other, and with a Style like those in "Almost 'Made-for-Neon.'"

- The first character of "ink" is from the **Hygiene** font, and the "nk" is set in **BubbleSoft**.

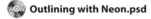
Outlining with Neon.psd

FX: Wow Actions

The **Wow-Graphix Enhance Actions** are "miniprograms" designed to give type or graphics a "special effects" treatment that's more complex than you can achieve with a Layer Style. **Each Action produces a layered file,** so you can customize the results.

If you haven't yet installed the **Wow Actions,** do that now (see page 4). Then open the Actions panel (Window > Actions) and open the panel's menu ▼≡ and choose the **Wow-Graphix Enhance Actions** set.

To run an Action, click its name in the Actions panel and click the "Play selection" button ▶ at the bottom of the panel. (If your Actions panel is set to Button mode, simply click the Action's button to start running it.) **Whenever a "Stop" message appears during an Action, read and follow its instructions.**

FX.psd is one kind of file the Wow-Graphix Enhance Actions are designed to work with — graphics or type on a top layer above an image layer on the bottom. We've included it so you can experiment with the Actions to get the results shown on the next three pages.

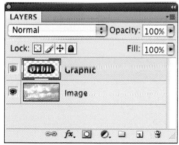

** FX.psd**

YOU'LL FIND THE FILES in 🔴 > Wow Project Files > Chapter 8 > Quick FX

Wow-Silvery
Wow-Golden

IN THE **WOW-SILVERY** and **Wow-Golden** Actions, the Lighting Effects filter creates the initial play of light and uses a blurred copy of the graphics to add dimension. A Color Balance layer fine-tunes the color, and a Layer Style adds thickness and gleam.

After you try out the settings built into the Action by running it on the **FX.psd** file or a file of your own, you might want to choose File > Revert and run it again, this time making some changes when the Lighting Effects dialog opens — such as rearranging the lights (by dragging their center points) to change which parts of the graphics are highlighted.

In the finished layered file, try changing the blend mode or Opacity of the "Graphic Wrapped" layer,▼ or the Color Balance settings. ▼

FIND OUT MORE
▼ Blend modes **page 181**
▼ Using Color Balance **page 251**

Wow-Streaked
Metal

IN THE **WOW-STREAKED METAL** Action, Lighting Effects and a Layer Style provide the lighting and dimensionality. A "burnished" metal surface with rounded edges is added by a layer in Overlay mode, filled with Overlay-neutral 50% gray. Running the Noise filter on this gray-filled layer adds the raw material that the Motion Blur filter then turns into streaks.

To create a sense of environment, a wildly bent Curves Adjustment layer adds mottled lighting. ▼ The Curves layer's reduced Opacity keeps reflections subtle.

FIND OUT MORE
▼ Adjusting
Curves **page 246**

PAY ATTENTION TO PIXELS

Some of the **Wow-Graphix Enhance Actions** use Photoshop filters whose parameters are set as **numbers of pixels.** If your graphics are much larger or smaller than ours (at 1000 pixels wide), the Actions may produce different results. "Examining an Action" on page 555 tells how to adapt the filter settings to your file.

Wow-Streaked Steel
Wow-Oily Steel

IN THE **WOW-STREAKED STEEL** and **Wow-Oily Steel** Actions, Lighting Effects and a Layer Style provide the lighting and dimensionality, as in Wow-Silvery and Wow-Golden, and the Noise and Motion Blur filters add the streaking, as in Wow-Streaked Metal. Added to Wow-Streaked Steel and Wow-Oily Steel is a sharply cut bevel — the surface color and streaking don't extend into the beveled edges.

As in Wow-Streaked Metal, a wildly bent Curves adjustment creates the "environment" that seems to be reflected in the surface of the streaked steel. A similar Curves adjustment is used for the oily steel, with a higher Opacity setting and a more colorful surface to act on.

Wow-Chromed
Wow-Crystal

THE **WOW-CHROMED ACTION** uses the "image" layer to create a reflection on the surface of the chrome, producing a result like the examples in "Variations" on page 535. The **Wow-Crystal** Action simulates both reflected light at the surface and refracted light inside the crystal object.

In both Actions, when the Glass filter's dialog box opens, you're asked to load the **Displace.psd** file (which the Action will have made for you) as the Texture.

In Wow-Chromed, the "Bkg Blurred" layer and the "Hue/Saturation I" Adjustment layer that colors it are used simply to make a dark contrasting background for the chrome. The color was chosen to match highlight and shadow colors in the chrome Layer Style.

In Wow-Crystal, to change the material characteristics of the crystal, change the blend mode of the "Reflection" layer.▼ Or reduce the Fill opacity of the "Wow-Crystal" layer to make the object more translucent without reducing the glow at the edges.

FIND OUT MORE
▼ Blend modes **page 181**

CHANGING THE BACKGROUND

After you run a Wow Action, you may want to change the background for your enhanced graphics or move the graphics into a different file. Here are some ways to make those kinds of changes:

• Change the background image by targeting the bottom layer of your file (clicking its thumbnail in the Layers panel) and then dragging and dropping a different background into the file.

• If you "package" the layered results of your Action by enclosing them in a Group, you can duplicate the Group into another file. To make the Group, in the Layers panel Ctrl/⌘-click the names of the layers you want to include; then open the panel's menu ▾☰ and choose New Group From Layers. Now you can simply drag and drop the entire folder to move the "package" to another file.

• Instead of moving the layered result, you can merge a copy of the Group to one layer before dragging and dropping. With the Group targeted in the Layers panel, duplicate it (so you'll still have the separate layers in the original Group) by right-clicking/Ctrl-clicking on the Group's entry in the Layers panel and choosing Duplicate Group from the context-sensitive menu. Then type Ctrl/⌘-E to merge the Group into a single layer.

Wow-Distressed

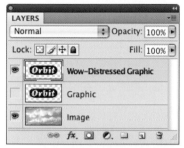

THE **WOW-DISTRESSED** ACTION can be used to "roughen" type or graphics before applying a Layer Style, such as **Wow-Heavy Rust** from the **Wow-Metals Styles**.

SLOWING THE PACE

By default Photoshop runs Actions faster than it can show you what's happening. But if you want to see each step as it happens, open the Actions panel's menu ▾≡, choose **Playback Options**, and set the Performance to **Step by Step** or **Pause For** 1 or 2 seconds.

Wow-Fire

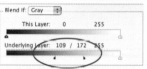
FX2 files

THE **WOW-FIRE** ACTION adds stylized flames around the edges of the type or graphics. Here we've also run it on a black "i" shape. To bring some flame in front of the "i," after running the Action we double-clicked the thumbnail for "Layer 1" in the Layers panel and worked with the "Underlying Layer," holding down the Alt/Option key to split the black slider. ▼ We also increased the Size and Spread of the Inner Glow.

Wow-Fire is an interesting Action to observe step-by-step for its use of filters (see "Slowing the Pace" at the left).

EXAMINING AN ACTION

To play an Action one step at a time so you can explore what each step does before going on to the next one, first expand the list to show all the steps by clicking the tiny arrow in front of the Action's name in the Actions panel. Then target the first step by clicking on it; hold down the Ctrl/⌘ key and click the "Play selection" button ▶ at the bottom of the panel. The single step will be carried out, the next step will be targeted, and the Action will stop and wait. Continue to Ctrl/⌘-click the ▶ button to carry out each step. You can see the settings for any step that has a tiny triangle in front of its name by clicking the triangle to expand the list of settings.

If you'd like to change the settings inside the dialog box for a step you just played, type Ctrl/⌘-Z to undo the step, then click in the "Toggle dialog on/off" box for that step, if needed, to add a dialog box icon for that step.

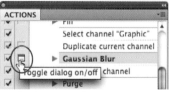

At the bottom of the panel, Ctrl/⌘-click the ▶ button again, and the dialog box will open. Any changes you make inside the dialog will be carried out in this run of the Action, but the Action itself won't incorporate the changes for future use. To do that, you need to edit the Action by recording the changes. ▼

FIND OUT MORE

▼ Working with "Blend If" **page 66**

▼ Editing Actions **page 124**

Backgrounds & Textures

Photoshop gives you a magician's kit of filters, patterns, and Layer Styles — all great places to start when you're looking for some "raw material" to support a concept or extend an image. With these tools you can invent patterns and textures out of thin air. Then use them to develop backgrounds, to turn plain flat type or graphics into believable solid objects, or with Photoshop Extended to apply a surface to a 3D object.

On the next few pages are some examples to get you started. ("Legacy Backgrounds & Textures," which describes examples from previous editions of the book, all updated for Photoshop CS3/CS4, is provided as a PDF on the Wow DVD-ROM.) Before you begin working with the new "Backgrounds & Textures" examples, be sure to load the **Wow Presets** (at least the Patterns and Gradients) as described on page 4.

In addition to the methods shown here, using a pattern in a Layer Style — as both the Pattern Overlay effect and the Texture for the Bevel and Emboss effect — can generate some great surface textures. "Anatomy of 'Bumpy'" on page 522 shows exactly how that works.

YOU'LL FIND THE FILES in > Wow Project Files > Chapter 8 > Quick Backgrounds

Legacy Backgrounds & Textures

Brushed Metal (Add Noise, Motion Blur & Lighting Effects)

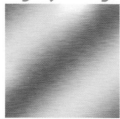

Mixed Metals (Adobe Metal gradients)

Color Blends (Gradients in Color Channels)

Color Blends & Wave (Sine Mode)

Color Blends & Wave (Square Mode)

Color Blends, Twirl & Glass

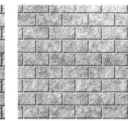

Brick Surfaces (Wow-Brick pattern, Wow-Misc. Surface patterns, Lighting Effects & Blending Options)

Carpet/Nubby Fabric (Fibers)

Wood Surface 1 (Fibers)

Wood Surface 2 (Fibers & Liquify)

THE MANY METHODS for producing backgrounds and textures that have appeared in past editions of *The Photoshop Wow! Book* are still excellent solutions. But in order to make space in the book for some new ones, we've included the "legacy" versions as a PDF on the Wow! DVD-ROM that comes with the book. Each method in the PDF has been updated for Photoshop CS3/CS4.

Legacy Backgrounds.pdf

Legacy Backgrounds & Textures (continued)

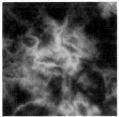

Marble (Clouds)

Rough Rock (Clouds & Lighting Effects)

Paper/Wall (Add Noise, Gaussian Blur & Emboss)

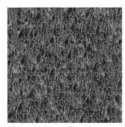

Plaids (Noise Gradient & Unsharp Mask)

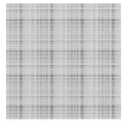

Weave (Fibers & Blending Options)

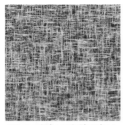

Weave Pattern (Fibers, Blending Options & Pattern Maker*)

Textures from Photos (Pattern Maker*)

Surface Relief (Texturizer filter)

* The Pattern Maker filter is no longer installed with Photoshop CS4, but it's available in the Optional Plug-ins and Presets.▼

FIND OUT MORE

▼ Optional Plugins & Presets **page 120**

TEXTURES TO GO

The Textures files that Adobe supplies make good "bump maps" for creating surface relief for the Texturizer filter to act on. (Textures are installed in the Presets folder in your Photoshop folder in CS3/in CS4 you'll find them in the <language>/Goodies/Presets/Textures folder on the Photoshop installation disc, or download the Optional Plug-ins and Presets from adobe.com.)▼ Some of the files in the Textures folder are already in the **.psd** format required by Texturizer. Others are in **.jpg** format, but to be able to use them with Texturizer (as well as Displace and other filters that use .psd files for creating and enhancing textures), all you have to do is open them in Photoshop and resave them in .psd (Photoshop) format.

To use Textures with Texturizer (as in the "Surface Relief" example shown above), choose Filter > Texture > Texturizer, click on the ▼≡ button next to the dialog box's Texture menu, and choose Load Texture. Navigate to the Textures folder (or whatever folder you have that contains suitable files in .psd format), choose a texture, and click the "Load" button.

CLOUDY SKIES

By itself, Filter > Render > Clouds isn't necessarily convincing for creating sky. But to add clouds to the sky in a photo, try running the Clouds filter on a layer above the image, using as the Foreground color a blue that you sample from the sky in your photo, and using white as the Background color. If you first make a mask to reveal the sky area only (for instance, by clicking on the blue sky with the Magic Wand ✳ and then clicking the "Add a layer mask" button ▣ at the bottom of the Layers panel), you can "audition" different sky backgrounds as you type Ctrl/⌘-F to rerun the filter to generate a new array of clouds each time. You can also change the blend mode and Opacity of the clouds layer. Or paint the mask with black to diminish the clouds: Choose the Brush tool ✐ (Shift-B), black paint, and a large, soft brush tip, set at low Opacity in the Options bar.

Before

After

PETER CARLISLE

Painting a Backdrop

THIS "STUDIO BACKDROP" starts with a brush tip made from a captured image. You can modify the brush tip, as we did, both by altering a single brush "footprint" and by adjusting the settings in the Brushes panel (see "A Brush Tip from an Image" at the right).

To paint the backdrop, create a new document (Ctrl/⌘-N) the size and resolution you want. Click your Foreground swatch in the Tools panel and click on the basic color you plan to use (we used a medium blue here); fill the document with this color (Alt/Option-Delete). Add a transparent layer (Ctrl/⌘-Shift-N) and paint it randomly, using the Brush tool ✎, the brush tip you made, and the same Foreground color; resize your brush tip if necessary; remember, the [and] keys, or in CS4 the dynamic method — right-drag/Alt-drag (Windows) or Ctrl-Option-drag (Mac). The built-in Color Dynamics Jitter settings in our brush tip introduce some related colors. You can adjust the opacity of the painted layer or use the Eraser ✐ to remove some of your painting to create the texture you want. When you have a backdrop you like, choose Layer > Flatten Image.

⦿ **Painted Background files**

A BRUSH TIP FROM AN IMAGE

To make an abstract brush from an image-based brush, create a new document (Ctrl/⌘-N), using White for the Background Contents and making it slightly larger than you want the brush to be. We wanted our brush to be at least 200 pixels, so we created a document that was 300 pixels square.

Set the swatches to the default black and white (type D) and choose the Brush tool ✎. In the Options bar open the Brush Preset picker and choose a captured-image brush tip; we chose Large Roses with Chroma from the Special Effect Brushes installed with Photoshop.

Resize the brush tip if needed, using the [or] key, and click once in the document to place a single "footprint" of the brush image. It's this image that will be modified.

Reduce the Opacity of the layer. Using the Eraser tool ✐ in Brush mode (set in the Options bar) with a moderately soft brush, erase uneven "chunks" from the edges of the image to distress the edges. Lower the opacity of the Eraser and lightly dab the interior to further break up the image.

Now adjust some of the settings in the Brushes panel (below). If you use a graphics tablet, you can choose a feature of your pen, such as Pen Pressure or Direction, as the Control for any of the settings, but even with a mouse you can vary enough settings to create an all-over randomized texture. For instance, try one, some, or all of these: Set **Angle Jitter** to a high amount in Shape Dynamics. Add a small amount (10–15%) of change in **Hue, Saturation** or **Brightness Jitter** settings in Color Dynamics. Two other settings that randomize the brush are

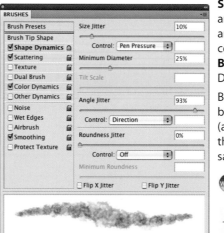

Size Jitter (Shape Dynamics) and **Scatter** (Scattering), and you can add even more color with **Foreground/Background Jitter** (Color Dynamics).▼

Before you use your new brush to paint a background (as in "Painting a Backdrop" at the left), you might want to save your new brush tip.▼

⦿ **BackgroundBrush.abr**

FIND OUT MORE
▼ Saving brush tips **page 402**

Adding Lighting

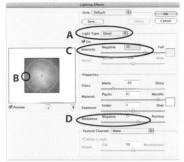

USE THE LIGHTING EFFECTS FILTER to help a subject stand out from your background. Lighting Effects can even modify the colors in your backdrop. And you can keep the filter settings live and editable. In the Layers panel, target the backdrop layer and turn it into a Smart Object (Filter > Convert for Smart Filters). Then choose Filter > Render > Lighting Effects. In the Lighting Effects dialog, set the Light Type to Omni **A**, for a light like a bulb that shines evenly in all directions. Use one of the four handles on the circular perimeter of the light to stretch it to nearly fill the backdrop **B**. Use a low Intensity **C** with a slightly increased Ambience setting **D**. Click on the color swatch for the light (the upper swatch) and select a color. When the preview looks the way you want it, click OK to close the Lighting Effects dialog. (To go back to the unlighted look, click the 👁 for the Lighting Effects "layer" in the Layers panel.)

Adding Texture

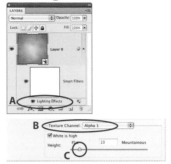

IF YOU MAKE A BACKDROP using Lighting Effects as a Smart Filter (as in "Adding Lighting" at the left), in the future you can change any of the filter settings, creating a new backdrop from the old. ▼ Here we added a subtle texture.

In the new file, open the Channels panel (Window > Channels) and click the "Create new channel" button at the bottom of the panel. Choose Edit > Fill and Use: Pattern. We chose **Wow-Rice Paper White** from the **Wow-Organics** patterns. ▼

Double-click the name of the Lighting Effects "layer" in the Layers panel **A** to reopen the dialog box. Then choose your alpha channel as the Texture Channel **B**. Set the Height very low for a soft paper texture (we used 10) **C**. Click "OK" to close the box.

FIND OUT MORE
▼ Smart filtering **page 72**
▼ Loading the Wow patterns **page 4**

Changing Color

TINT A BACKGROUND by adding a Hue/Saturation Adjustment layer above it: Click the "Create new fill or adjustment layer" button ⬤ at the bottom of the Layers panel. Now move the Hue slider to see different color ways for your background for a soft paper texture. Adjust Saturation and Lightness as you like.

For a single-color pattern (the dark red one above), click the Colorize box (not shown here) near the bottom of the Hue/Saturation dialog.

Seamless Patterns

With all the ways you can use patterns in Photoshop, it's good to know how to generate your own. If you want to turn an image (such as one of those from "Quick Backgrounds & Textures" on page 556) into a seamlessly tiling pattern, you need to first assess the seams that would be generated if you simply defined the whole image as the pattern tile. Then, if necessary, choose a method for hiding the seams.

Some kinds of pattern images will be seamless automatically. For instance, the plaid shown on page 557 consists of lines that extend straight from left to right and from top to bottom, so the edges automatically line up perfectly when the pattern tile is repeated. Another example is the "Joy" pattern and its "relatives," assembled from graphic elements (page 75 and page 568). Most pattern material, however, even with fine-grained textures, requires some editing to hide the seams between tiles.

Once you've looked for seams as described at the right, use one of the three methods on the next two pages (healing, spot healing, or patching) to remove them. Then recheck for seams and do further hiding if necessary. Finally, define the altered image as a pattern tile, as in "Defining & Applying Patterns" on page 562.

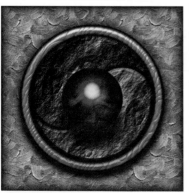

To make this illustration, patterns were applied to graphics layers as the Pattern Overlay and Texture components of Layer Styles. Open the file to explore the patterns or to capture them for your own use, as described on page 563.

Seamless.psd

YOU'LL FIND THE FILES
in (wow) > Wow Project Files > Chapter 8 > Quick Seamless Patterns

Assessing the Seam

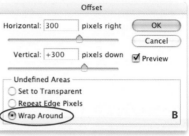

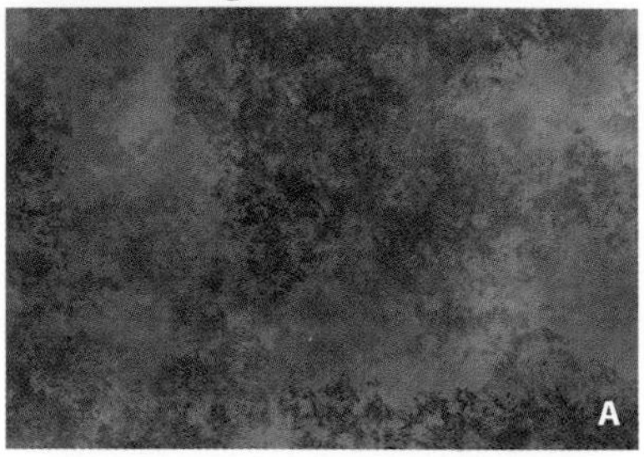

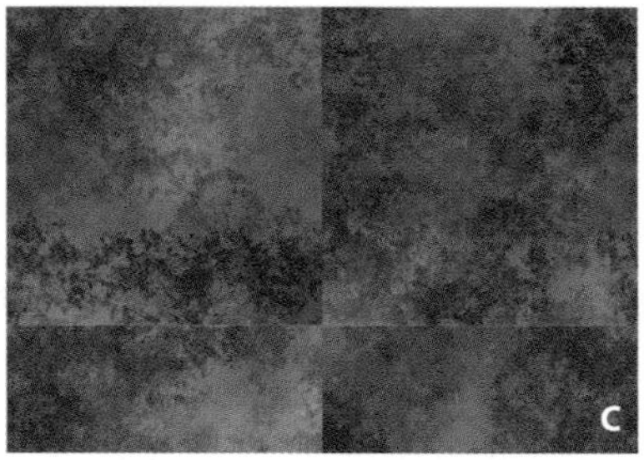

To MAKE A PATTERN TILE, you'll need a **single-layer file** that includes only the area you want to use for the tile; here we've used a 450-pixel-high file **A**. If your file is multilayer or if you want to use less than the entire image as your pattern tile, duplicate the file (Image > Duplicate, turning on Duplicate Merged Layers Only if it's available); in the duplicate file, you can use the Crop tool ⌷ to crop to just the section of the image you want.

Next use the **Offset filter** to find out how bad the seam would be if you did nothing to hide it **B**: Choose Filter > Other > Offset and enter pixel dimensions for Horizontal and Vertical that are roughly half the width and height of your file; set the Undefined Areas to Wrap Around and click "OK" to run the filter. Any unmatched "seams" will now be shifted to the interior and will be plainly visible near the middle of your image **C**. If you don't see any seams, you can go directly to "Defining & Applying Patterns" (page 562). Otherwise, choose one of the seam-removal methods on the next two pages, depending on the nature of your developing pattern tile. For this pattern we chose the Spot Healing Brush method (shown on page 561).

"Healing" the Seam

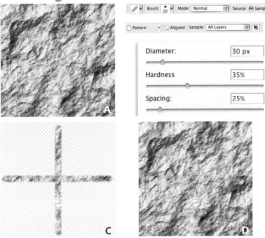

If THE TEXTURE in your image is quite random and "fine-grained" without a lot of large contrasting areas, after running the Offset filter **A** (page 560) you can probably hide the seam by "healing" it. To make it easier to fix any mistakes you might make in the seam-hiding process, add an empty "repairs" layer (Ctrl/⌘-Shift-N). Choose the Healing Brush ✐ and in the Options bar **B**, set the Mode to Normal, and turn on Sample All Layers. Open the Brush picker (click the tiny triangle to the right of the brush footprint); for our seam we used a 30-pixel brush with Hardness set at 35%.

To sample and paint, hold down the Alt/Option key and click somewhere away from the vertical seam and near (but not right at) the top edge of the image to "load" the tool with "source" image material; then release the Alt/Option key and click on the vertical seam at about the same height as you sampled. Shift-click on the seam near (but not right at) the bottom edge to "paint" a straight stroke that covers the seam. Repeat the process for the horizontal seam. Inspect the repairs for obvious edges or repeating elements (the repairs layer is shown alone in **C**, in place in **D**. You can use the Eraser ✐ to remove a mistake, or simply use the Healing Brush ✐: Alt/Option-click away from the seam to sample, and then click on the seam to "dab" over the problem area.

Flatten the file (Layer > Flatten Image), run the Offset filter again with the same settings as in "Assessing the Seam" on page 560, and again check for seams in the middle (there shouldn't be any if you were able to sample away from the edges). If any subtle corrections are needed, use the Healing Brush ✐ on another repairs layer to make them, and again flatten the image. When the image is "seamless," proceed to "Defining & Applying Patterns."

Spot Heal the Seam

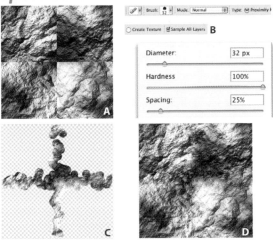

If THE TEXTURE in your image is random but there are big differences in tone or hue of adjacent areas, after running the Offset filter **A** (page 560) you can usually hide the seam with the Spot Healing Brush. The empty repairs layer you used in "Healing the Seam" works well here, too. Choose the Spot Healing Brush ✐ and in the Options bar **B** set the Mode to Normal, and turn on Sample All Layers. We picked a moderate Brush size of 32, and because the Spot Healing Brush has a built-in feather, we left the Hardness setting at 100%.

To hide the seam, drag the Spot Healing Brush at angles over the seam, moving from light values into dark and vice versa. Vary the length of your strokes and watch that both texture and tone are carried randomly between sections **C**. Make sure your strokes cover the seam almost up to, but not over, an edge; if you touch the edge, you might make a new seam. If an area isn't blending well, try varying the size of the Spot Healing Brush (press the] key to enlarge, [to reduce), or just click (dab) instead of dragging. Inspect for edges that are too blurred or too sharp, or for repeating elements. If you see any, you can use the Eraser ✐ to remove a mistake or make more dabs with the Spot Healing Brush.

Flatten the file (Layer > Flatten Image), run the Offset filter again with the same settings as in "Assessing the Seam" on page 560, and again check for seams in the middle (there shouldn't be any if you were able to stay away from the edges) **D**. If any subtle corrections are needed, use the Spot Healing Brush to make them on another repairs layer, and again flatten the image. When the image is "seamless," proceed to "Defining & Applying Patterns."

Copying Bits & Pieces

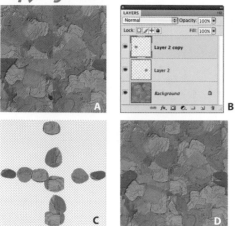

If your image is a texture that's fairly coarse or filled with discreet objects **A**, the best way to cover the seam may be to select, copy, and overlay parts of the image. This method often works well for photos of discrete items, from pebbles to cherries, clouds, or brush strokes. Start by selecting a feature; for this painted "canvas," made with Corel Painter's Auto-Painting function, we used the Lasso ⌁ to select a section to overlap the seam area we wanted to cover. Then copy the selected element to a new "patch" layer (Ctrl/⌘-J). Use the Move tool ⯈ to drag the patch over the seam. Use the Free Transform command (Ctrl/⌘-T) if you need to flip or rotate the patch ▼ (try to keep your patch from touching an edge of the image where it may create a hard edge instead of a seamless one). When transforming, be careful not to change the apparent direction of the light for the copied element in a way that would clash with the lighting in the original image; press the Enter key to complete the transformation.

You can now duplicate this element (Ctrl/⌘-J) and move and transform the new copy to cover another part of the seam. If you use the same selected element too many times, the repair will be obvious and the element can become blurred from repeated transforming. So instead you can target the original image layer again by clicking its thumbnail in the Layers panel, then make another selection, copy it to a new layer, and so on **B**. When your seam is hidden **C**, **D**, flatten the file (Layer > Flatten Image) and run the Offset filter again with the same settings as in "Assessing the Seam" on page 560 to check for new seams. If necessary, create more "patches," and flatten the file again. Then proceed to "Defining & Applying Patterns."

FIND OUT MORE
▼ Free Transform
page 67

Defining & Applying Patterns

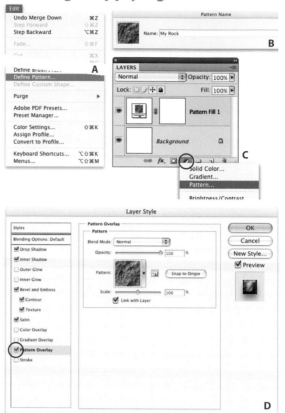

Once you've prepared an image for use as a pattern tile, choose Edit > **Define Pattern A**, name it in the Pattern Name dialog box **B**, and click "OK." Your new pattern will appear as the last pattern swatch in the Pattern picker anywhere it appears in Photoshop.

You can now apply the pattern as a **Pattern Fill layer C**, an effect in a **Layer Style D**, the "paint" for the Pattern Stamp tool 🖌, or a fill for a regular layer or a selection (with the **Edit > Fill** command). You can find more about making and using patterns in Appendix D.

SAVING A PATTERN

To save a pattern permanently, along with other patterns of your choice that are currently in the Pattern picker, choose **Preset Manager** from Photoshop's Edit menu or from the Pattern picker's menu ⊙. In the Preset Manager dialog box, choose Patterns for the Preset Type. Shift-click or Ctrl/⌘-click to select all the patterns you want to save together in a new Patterns preset file, and click the "Save Set" button.

To make a pattern with an obvious repeat:

1 Create your pattern element on a transparent layer. Then select it with the Rectangular Marquee `[⁀]`, with half as much space around it as you want between the repeating elements of your pattern; choose Image > Crop to trim away excess space.

2 Choose Edit > Define Pattern; in the Pattern Name dialog box, name the pattern and click "OK." You can stop there, or build a more complex pattern as described in steps 3 through 5.

3 To set up the pattern so elements in alternate columns are offset, do this: Start a new file that's twice as wide and twice as high as your pattern element with its surrounding space from step 1 (choose File > New, with Transparent chosen in the Background Contents section of the New dialog box). Fill with the pattern you defined in step 2 (Edit > Fill).

4 In your pattern-filled layer use the Rectangular Marquee `[⁀]` to select one column of your pattern, and choose Filter > Other > Offset (with Undefined Areas set to Wrap Around). Set the Horizontal Offset at 0 and use the up or down arrow key (↑ or ↓, with the Shift key held down for bigger steps) to offset the pattern elements as much as you like.

5 Deselect (Ctrl/⌘-D) and choose Edit > Define Pattern. Now you can apply your pattern over any background; to change its color, you can also use a Color Overlay effect in a Layer Style or an Adjustment layer, as shown here.

Altered Repeat.psd

Any pattern that's used in a Pattern Fill layer or a Layer Style can easily be "captured" and added to the Pattern picker for use elsewhere. To capture a pattern, the first thing you have to do is to find it: In the Layers panel, double-click the thumbnail for the Pattern Fill layer, or double-click on the Pattern Overlay, Texture, or Stroke (wherever the pattern is used) in the list of effects in a Layer Style. When you see the swatch of pattern you want to capture, click the little "Create a new preset from this pattern" button ⬚ that's right next to the swatch. The pattern is added to the Pattern picker, available anywhere in Photoshop that patterns are used.

from far away she looked like jesus

wild mane of hair
crown of thorns
from far away she looked like jesus
crucified, suffering
now close I can see
she is an angel
her disguise translucent as tissue paper
laid in wet strips over her breaking heart
the pain of her possession
how much she wants to have it

comfort comes only
in the shape of a lover
the size of the earth
who sees the beauty of sadness
who sees love inside fear
who pushes through her like the ocean
and changes the tide forever

this cocoon falls away
I can see what I've been seeing
hear what I've been hearing
touch what I've been touching
lavish heart
perfect beauty
turning everyone inside out
her music still resonating
within me

Fig. 97

For the CD cover ***From Far Away She Looked Like Jesus***, **Alicia Buelow** used a scanned photo of a stucco wall to lend an organic feel to the background. Next, she used the Move tool ▶♣ to drag and drop photos of a tree and roots into her working file, blending their layers into the background by choosing the Color Burn blend mode at 50% Opacity for the trees, and Luminosity at 90% for the roots. ▼

To make the central ghostly figure, Buelow used three images — photos of a child's head and a youth's body, and a scan of her own hand. She inverted the color of the head and body images (Ctrl/⌘-I). Then for each of the three subjects in turn, she made a feathered selection and used the Move tool ▶♣ to drag each selected part into the working file. She set the blend mode for the head and body to Screen and the hand's blend mode to Luminosity. She further blended the three together by adjusting the layers' Opacity settings and using layer masks (added by clicking the "Add layer mask" button ◻ at the bottom of the Layers panel, and then painted with the Brush tool ✎ with a soft tip, black paint, and a low Opacity setting chosen in the Options bar).

Using an image of a wing from Getty Images, Buelow dragged it into the working file, copied this wing layer, and flipped the copy to compose the matching pair. She then duplicated each wing layer and blurred the bottom copy of each (Filter > Blur > Motion Blur).

Drawing a white cube in Adobe Illustrator, Buelow copied it to the clipboard and pasted it into Photoshop as pixels. ▼ She set the cube layer's blend mode to Overlay, then clicked the "Add a layer style" button ƒx at the bottom of the Layers panel and chose the Outer Glow effect, using the default light yellow color but setting the effect's blend mode to Overlay and its Opacity to 80%.

To complete the illustration, Buelow selected the Type tool T and typed numbers and words on several layers, blurring some layers slightly (Filter > Blur > Gaussian Blur). For the drop shadow behind the block of text on the left, she duplicated the type layer, and chose a dark gray for the lower layer by clicking the color swatch in the Type tool's Options bar. After using the Move tool ▶♣ to drag the shadow layer down and to the right, she applied a strong blur with the Gaussian Blur filter and set the layer's blend mode to Color Burn. Because the shadow was a layer of its own rather than a Drop Shadow effect on the original type

COPY & TRANSFORM

To copy a layer and transform the copy at the same time, hold down the Alt/Option key as you transform — for instance, by choosing Edit > Transform > Flip Horizontal.

layer, she could add a layer mask and paint it with black to obscure parts of the shadow, giving it an eroded appearance.

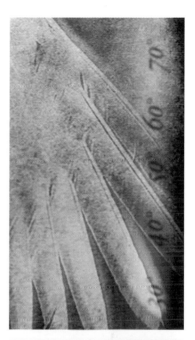

FIND OUT MORE

▼ Using blend modes **page 181**

▼ Copying & pasting from Adobe Illustrator **page 460**

The depth and color of **Don Jolley's** striking editorial illustration *Behavior* were achieved with layered photos and Adobe Illustrator artwork, masks, blend modes, and Adjustment layers. The one Layer Style in the file is there not to create a dimesional effect but as a solution for a design challenge that arose as the image developed.

To create his composition, Jolley layered a filtered copy of his photo of a friend over the original **A**, and added several copies of a photo of a brain model **B**. He dragged in images from his own texture library (described on page 161) and added transparent layers, which he painted with the Brush tool ✐, and masked Adjustment layers ▼ for tweaking color **C**. From Illustrator he brought in a page of text, as well as a dynamic spiral element made by drawing a 20-arm star and applying Illustrator's Filter > Distort > Twist to the figure; in Photoshop he added layer masks to mostly hide the text and spiral where they overlapped the man's face **D**. ▼

Jolley also pasted in a grid of lines and circles that he had drawn in Illustrator to highlight four areas of the brain **E**; he had used a flattened version of his developing composition as a template in Illustrator in order to put the circles and lines where he wanted them. With the grid in place, he added a series of geometric selections filled with color as well as copies of parts of the grid.

To highlight each of the four regions of the brain with color, Jolley needed to select a circular area larger than the circles imported from Illustrator, but centered at the same spot. In order to do that, he found

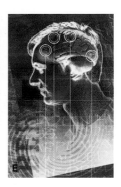

A   **B**   **C**   **D**   **E**

the center of each existing pair of concentric circles so that he could then draw a selection outward from that center. Here's a way to do it that takes advantage of the Transform frame's center point, which "attracts" Guides: He turned on the Rulers (Ctrl/⌘-R) and dragged a Guide from the vertical ruler to line up with the "stalk" of the pair of circles **F**. Next he used the Rectangular Marquee 🔲 and his new Guide to draw a selection from the top of the outer circle to its bottom (the width of the rectangle didn't matter, just the height). Pressing Ctrl/⌘-T brought up the Transform frame **G**. With the Snap feature turned on in the View menu, he dragged a Guide down from the top ruler until it snapped to the center of the frame **H**. At this point he could escape from the Transform frame (Ctrl/⌘-period) and the selection (Ctrl/⌘-D), leaving only the new Guides, which intersected at the center of the circles.

With the center of the circles marked by the intersection of the Guides, Jolley chose the Elliptical Marquee tool ⭕ and Alt/Option-Shift-dragged outward from the intersection to make a circle the size he wanted **I**. Then he clicked the "Create new fill or adjustment layer" button ⬤ at the bottom of the Layers panel and chose Hue/Saturation. He turned on the Colorize option in the dialog box and adjusted the Hue slider, also increasing the Lightness.

His circular selection became a mask for the Hue/Saturation change.

For the additional highlights, Jolley added more masked Hue/Saturation layers. Drawing intersecting Guides to find the center of each pair of circles as he had for the first pair, he then recalled the circular selection (in the Layers panel, Ctrl/⌘-click on the thumbnail for the Hue/Saturation layer's mask) and, with a selection tool chosen, moved it into position on another pair of circles **J**; the selection boundary automatically snapped into place, centered on the intersection of the Guides.

With the Hue/Saturation layers in place, Jolley decided he needed a stroke around each of these larger circles. This is where the Layer Style came in. He targeted one of the Hue/Saturation layers and clicked the "Add layer style" button *fx* at the bottom of the Layers panel, choosing Stroke from the list of effects; the Stroke automatically followed the edge of the layer mask. He could experiment with Size (he chose 10 pixels for this 1700-pixel wide image), Position (he chose Outside), and Color until he had exactly the look he wanted **K**, **L**, **M**. He could then copy the Style and paste it to the other Hue/Saturation layers. ▼

FIND OUT MORE
▼ Adjustment layers **page 245**
▼ Masks **page 61**
▼ Copying & pasting Styles **page 500**

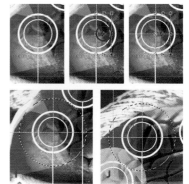

I   **J**

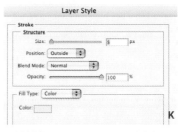

Layer Style

Stroke

K

L

M

When **Cristen Gillespie** developed *Lady with a Harp*, the second piece in the *Joy of Music* series, it was important to maintain a visual relationship between the illustrations, but she didn't want to use identical patterns. Because she had used Smart Objects when creating the patterns for the first illustration (above left) and had saved the .psd pattern development file with layers and Smart Objects intact, all she had to do to make new but related patterns was to change a few elements in this file. (For the "how to" of making the original patterns, see "Exercising Smart Objects" on page 75.)

Gillespie decided to make the new patterns on transparency, so they could be applied over any background. She opened her pattern development file (**Exercising SO-After.psd** from page 75) and turned off visibility for the *Background* and the Solid Color Fill layer by clicking their 👁 icons in the Layers panel. To make the new pattern for the harp, she wanted independent control of the "JOY" type and the dancing figures. She decided she would actually make two separate patterns, one with "JOY" and another with the dancers, that would look like a single pattern when used together. To start with "JOY" she also turned off visibility for the "Leaping Lady" Smart Object, leaving only "JOY" visible **A**.

She made changes to the Layer Style for the "JOY" Smart Object, adding a Color Overlay and a Satin effect. ▼ To capture the pattern, she Ctrl/⌘-clicked on the Solid Fill layer's mask to load it as a selection (this mask had been designed as the square tile for defining the pattern, as described on page 76) **B**. With the selection active, she chose Edit > Define Pattern, and saved and named the pattern.

Gillespie next changed the dancing figures part of the pattern **C**: She restored visibility to the "Leaping Lady" Smart Object and turned off visibility for "JOY." She double-clicked the thumbnail for the "Leaping Lady" Smart Object to open its .psb file and then also double-clicked one of the Smart Object instances nested within that file. When that second .psb file opened, she added a new layer with a different character rasterized from the Pedestria PictOne font and turned off the 👁 icon for the layers below. Using Ctrl/⌘-T for Free Transform, she resized the new character to fit within the document so its edges wouldn't be cropped off; she added a Layer Style with a Gradient Overlay effect to color the new character.

Then she worked backwards to update the nested Smart Objects: When she saved the Smart Object file (Ctrl/⌘-S) all instances of the dancing couple character in the "super" Smart Object file were automatically updated. Happy with how the characters looked as a group, she also saved this "super" Smart

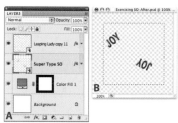

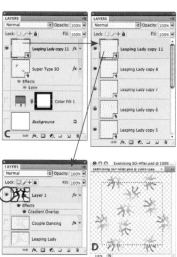

Object file (Ctrl/⌘-S) to update it. She defined a pattern with the dancing figures on transparency by using the same method she had used for the "JOY" pattern **D**.

To define a pattern with the leaping lady on a transparent background, Gillespie opened nested Smart Objects until she got to the one where she could turn on visibility for that figure only **E**, then saved the file for automatic updating. To substitute the leaping lady for all of the pattern elements, she had to do this series of operations twice — once to substitute the leaping lady in the "Leaping Lady" super Smart Object and once to substitute it in the "JOY" super Smart Object. Back in the main pattern development file with visibility turned on for both of these Smart Objects and turned off for all other layers, she could capture a "leaping ladies" pattern on transparency **F**.

Now Gillespie could apply the new patterns to her *Lady with a Harp* illustration. Targeting the *Background* of the image, she used the Magic Wand 🪄 with Contiguous unchecked to select all of the blue background. ▼ She Alt/Option-clicked on the "Create new fill or adjustment layer" button ⊘ at the bottom of the Layers panel, and chose Pattern Fill. In the Pattern Fill dialog box **G** she chose the new "leaping lady" pattern she had just made, scaled it to 50%, and clicked "OK." The wallpaper seemed too bright, so she reduced the Opacity of the Pattern Fill layer to 80%.

Targeting the *Background* again, Gillespie clicked and Shift-clicked with the Magic Wand 🪄 to make a selection that included all three parts of the golden harp. Then she made another Pattern Fill layer, choosing the "dancing figures" pattern. She duplicated this layer (Ctrl/⌘-J) and double-clicked the new duplicate layer's thumbnail in the Layers panel to reopen the Pattern Fill dialog box. There she chose

the "JOY" pattern. Because Photoshop defaults to starting each pattern at the upper left corner of the document, the "JOY" and "dancing figures" pattern layers aligned with each other perfectly, to give the impression of a single pattern. The benefit of having them separate, though, was that Gillespie could change the blend mode of the "JOY" layer independently of the dancing figures, putting it in Hard Light mode for a more interesting blend.

Finally, to balance the patterns and subdue the grayish streak in the Lady's hair, Gillespie added another Pattern Fill layer to fill the streak with the "leaping lady" pattern scaled to 25%. She used Luminosity as the blend mode (so the pattern's color had no effect), and reduced the layer's Opacity to mute the pattern even more **H**.

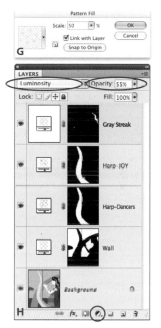

FIND OUT MORE

▼ Layer Style components **page 502**

▼ Using the Magic Wand 🪄 **page 50**

YOU'LL FIND THE FILE
in 🔵 >Wow Goodies > Chapter 9 > Lady with Harp.psd

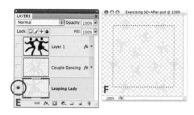

Putting It All Together

9

We promise beaches like this one.

Believe it or not, beaches like this still exist. Where the waves are gentle, the sand is soft, and marine life is everywhere in abundance.

For a vacation in unsurpassed natural beauty with wonders that never cease, come to La Playa Island Resorts. You'll find us on the Web at www.laplaya.com.

1.800.555.2323

"Adding Type to an Image" on page 587 demonstrates Photoshop's versatile masking and blending techniques for combining images, type, and graphics. This file is also used as an example of how the components of a Photoshop file work together to produce a composite result (see page 34).

Using the File > Place command brings in the image (here the silhouetted photo of the little girl) as a Smart Object, ready to scale and move into position to fit the composition.

WITH PHOTOSHOP'S EXTRAORDINARY ability to combine elements, you can create any kind of combination — from a seamless "faked" photo to an obvious montage or a page layout. In this chapter the skills and techniques covered in earlier chapters are brought together to combine photos with each other and with nonphotographic elements.

COMPOSITION METHODS

Of prime importance in Photoshop's compositing process are the **selections, masks, clipping groups**, and **blending options** covered in Chapter 2, as well as the **blend modes** covered in Chapter 4 and the **Adjustment layers** detailed in Chapter 5. Many of these and other combining functions can be set up and organized through the Layers panel, as shown in the illustration on page 573.

The following Photoshop tools and commands are among the most useful for making composites:

- The **Quick Selection tool** and the **Filter > Extract** and **Select > Refine Edge** commands excel at making clean selections of elements with difficult organic edges, such as hair, so they can be seamlessly combined with a new background. You'll find examples of selection methods in Chapter 2 and of ways to blend selected elements into a new background on page 624.

- To get images from other files into your composite, you can use the **Edit > Copy** and **Edit > Paste** commands, though this ties up memory because the copied element is stored on the clipboard. Or you can arrange your windows so you can see your source and its destination, and use the **Move tool** to drag and drop an image into your composition, adding the Shift key if you want to drop the image precisely in the center. Another way to bring in an image file is to use the **File > Place**

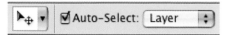

When **Auto Select Layer** or **Auto Select Group** is turned on in the Move tool's ▶⊕ Options bar, clicking in the document window automatically targets the uppermost layer or Group with content under the cursor, as long as that layer's Opacity is 50% or more. Check pages 583 and 620 for more about layer Groups.

WHAT AUTO SELECT LAYER "SEES"

A layer may be invisible because of its blend mode, but the Move tool's ▶⊕ **Auto Select Layer** option can still see it, as long as its visibility 👁 is turned on in the Layers panel. Auto Select Layer doesn't "see" a layer if its Opacity is less than 50%. But if you can **regulate transparency with Fill opacity** instead of Opacity, the Auto Select Layer option *will* see the layer.

The kinds of components typically used in a composite like the one above are identified and explained in the Layers panel on the facing page. The layout was assembled with masks, clipping groups, layer Groups, and a Smart Object, with Filter Gallery filters applied as a Smart Filter.

command. This brings the image in as a Smart Object. The placed image comes in centered and ready to scale, and its Smart Object status will protect it (see below) while you scale or otherwise transform it to suit your composite.

- With the **Move tool** ▶⊕ you can slide layers around until you're happy with the composition. Photoshop even preserves the parts of layers that you move outside the margins of the canvas. So if you change your mind, the entire element will still exist and you can move it back into the image frame. You can also set the Move tool's Options to automatically target the layer or Group that's under the pointer where you click.

- In conjunction with the Move tool, **Smart Guides** will help align elements as you compose. And the **Align** and **Distribute** commands in the Layer menu (and in the Move tool's ▶⊕ Options bar) can arrange several elements at once.

- The **Edit > Transform** and **Free Transform** commands are often essential in resizing or distorting elements to fit into the overall picture. ▼ And turning a component into a **Smart Object** allows you the freedom to experiment as you build a composition. With a Smart Object you can transform several times if needed, with no more reduction in image quality than a single transformation would cause. ▼

- The **Patch Tool** ◇, **Clone Stamp** 🔖, and **Healing Brush** 🖊 can copy image material from one part of the composite and repeat it in another area. The **Clone Source panel** will store up to five different sources for the Clone Stamp and Healing Brush to clone from, and it provides a way to control the size of the cloned material and the angle at which it's applied.

- To make one image conform to a surface depicted in another image, the **Liquify** filter (page 599), the **Displace** filter (page 595), and the **Edit > Transform > Warp** command (page 603) are important resources. Another tool for molding elements to fit is Warp Text (page 445).

- The **Photomerge** command helps with piecing together a panorama from a series of images shot for that purpose. Its operation is described on page 576, and its use is demonstrated in "Exercising Photomerge" on page 630. (In addition, the three functions that make up Photomerge are now available separately, in the **Load Files Into Stack** command in the File > Scripts menu and the **Auto-Align Layers** and **Auto-Blend Layers** commands in the Edit menu; their use in combining multiple shots of the same subject — to extend focus, remove

continued on page 574

FIND OUT MORE
▼ Transforming **page 67**
▼ Smart Objects **page 75**

ELEMENTS IN A PHOTOSHOP FILE

Each layer or Group has a **blend mode** that determines how the color of that layer's content affects the color of layers below.

A **layer mask** is a pixel-based, grayscale mask that reveals some parts of a layer and hides others. A layer mask can be applied to any layer (including the "folder" for a Group) except the *Background*.

A **vector mask** is a path-based mask whose shape reveals part of a layer and hides the rest. A vector mask can be applied to any layer (including the "folder" for a Group) except the *Background*.

You can use **color coding** to show that certain layers are related.

Visibility can be toggled on and off for including all or just some of the file's layers in a composite.

If you turn one or more layers into a **Smart Object**, you can scale, rotate, skew, or otherwise transform it, making changes repeatedly without causing deterioration of layer content. Likewise, filters can be applied "live" as **Smart Filters** so you can change their settings "nondestructively" whenever you like.

A **Layer Style** is a set of editable effects that are applied to the layer. Some layer effects, such as the Drop Shadow, can be very useful in combining images.

The **Background** is a non-transparent bottom layer that establishes the canvas size (boundaries) for an image. It can't have masks or a Layer Style.

Link related layers to make it easier to multitarget them again in the future.

Reducing the **Opacity** of a layer or Group allows the image below to show through.

For individual layers, the **Fill** percentage allows you to reduce the opacity of the layer content without reducing the strength of a Drop Shadow or other "exterior" effects of an applied Layer Style.

Four toggle buttons in the **Lock** line allow you to protect a layer from change. From left to right, they lock transparent pixels, image pixels, position, and "all of the above."

Collapsible layer **Groups** can be useful for keeping the panel manageable as the number of layers grows. Masks on a Group affect all the layers in the Group.

A **Type** layer, plain or warped, is "live" and editable.

A **Shape** layer consists of a solid fill with a built-in vector mask.

A **clipping group** consists of a bottom layer that "masks" the other layers in the clipping group so they are revealed only within the "footprint" of the image and masks of the clipping layer.

An **Adjustment layer** contains instructions for changing the color or tone of layers below it. Its effect can be targeted with masks, and it can be part of a clipping group. Adjustment layers can help unify color and lighting in a composite image.

A **Fill layer** applies a solid color, pattern, or gradient. It has a built-in layer mask.

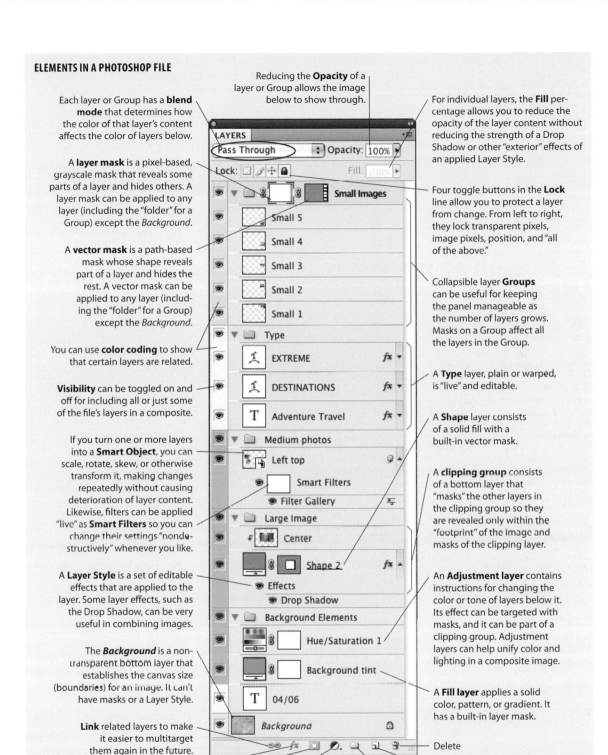

Add a layer style | Add layer mask/vector mask | Create new fill or adjustment layer | Create a new group | Create a new layer

Delete

In the **Vanishing Point** interface, you can start by clicking with the Create Plane tool ▦ to set the four corners of a perspective plane, which then generates a grid. With the grid in place and adjusted, pasted elements such as the sign graphics above can be dragged onto the grid to automatically fit the perspective. With Vanishing Point you can also paint and clone in perspective. "Exercising Vanishing Point" on page 612 shows how to get the most from Vanishing Point's set of tools.

noise, or eliminate distracting elements passing through the scene — are covered in Chapter 5.)

- The **Vanishing Point** filter allows you to automatically paste an element into the perspective of the image you add it to. "Exercising Vanishing Point" on page 612 takes you through this process step-by-step.

- The **Image > Variables** command allows you to make a template that will automatically substitute alternate sets of images and text into the same layout.

CHOOSING & PREPARING COMPONENTS

One requirement for creating a successful "seamless" photo montage, when that's your goal, is choosing component images that match one another in several key respects. For example, the light should be coming from the same direction, the color and amount of detail in the shadows and highlights should be about the same, and the "graininess" of the images should match. Some of these factors are more important than others:

- **Highlight and shadow detail can be manipulated** by using the Image > Adjustments > **Shadows/Highlights** command, which can be kept "live", by applying it as a Smart Filter, ▼ or with **Curves** or **Levels**, both of which are especially effective as Adjustment layers. ▼

- A **color cast** — in a shadow, for instance— can be identified with the RGB or CMYK readings in the Info panel (you can choose Window > Show Info to open it, or use the F8 default keyboard shortcut). ▼ It can also be identified in the Histogram. ▼ Then the color cast **can be adjusted** — with Curves, Levels, Color Balance, or Match Color. ▼ There's an example of using the Match Color command for this purpose on page 625.

- **Changing the direction of the light can be much more challenging** than managing shadow detail or a color cast. If the elements you want to blend are fairly flat (like pictures on a wall), you may get good results with the Lighting Effects filter or a Layer Style's Bevel and Emboss, Drop Shadow, or Inner Shadow effect, or a combination of these (see page 626). If the final effect you're looking for will tolerate it, you may be able to "overpower" the varied "native" lighting of the elements of a composite image by applying the same lighting effect to all the parts (see page 626). You can also dodge and burn to create highlights and shadows. ▼ But if quick Lighting Effects or dodging-and-burning fixes won't work, you may get better results if you continue your search for photo elements

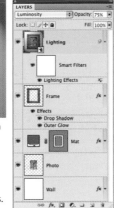

A spotlight created with the Lighting Effects filter helps to unify this composite, adding to the lighting provided by Layer Styles on the "Mat" and "Frame" layers. For more about the construction of the image, see page 626.

When Don Jolley applied the sign graphics to the wall and aged the sign in place, the Displace filter played a role in "painting" the graphics onto the bricks. The techniques he used are presented step-by-step in "Applying an Image to a Textured Surface" on page 595.

whose lighting matches, rather than trying to make further adjustments to correct the lighting direction.

- **Film grain or digital noise can be simulated** to match the grain of other image components by using the Lens Blur filter or one of the Wow Noise patterns (as described in "Quick Integration" starting on page 624).

FITTING AN ELEMENT TO A SURFACE

When you want an image to take on the contours or surface texture of another image below it in the layer stack, Photoshop offers three main methods for distorting the image to fit. These are the Displace and Liquify filters and the Warp command.

Displace

The **Displace filter** (Filter > Distort > Displace) requires a third image, called (appropriately enough) a *displacement map,* to distort the upper layer to fit the image below it. The displacement map uses differences in brightness to determine the amount of shifting that should take place in various parts of the applied image. Dark pixels in the displacement map will push the image pixels down and to the right; light pixels will push them up and to the left. In many cases a displacement map made from the surface image itself will successfully distort the applied image so it appears to dip where it goes over crevices and indentations, which are dark because they are in shadow; likewise the image will appear to rise where it goes over raised, highlighted areas. This won't work right, of course, if there are pronounced lights and darks on the surface that have nothing to do with depth changes — patterns or cast shadows, for instance. In a case like that you can paint your own grayscale displacement map, brushing in the dark dips and highlighted "hills" for the image to follow.

Rasterized type, familiar shapes, or bold patterns with strong vertical or horizontal motifs are great choices for images to apply with the Displace filter, because they show distortion so effectively. In contrast, busy images or patterns may not show displacement well. "Applying an Image to a Textured Surface" on page 595 shows an example of combining images with the Displace filter.

Liquify

Unlike Displace, which has no preview, **Liquify** employs a warping process that's completely visible while you work. Using Liquify, you mold the upper image to the contours of the lower by "fingerpainting," warping the image to the picture below to whatever degree you like. You can set up the filter to preview

The Liquify command is great for "massaging" an image or graphics to fit organic contours. The process is presented in "Liquifying a Tattoo" on page 599.

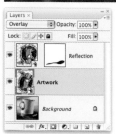

The Warp command is great for smooth geometric distortions. Here we distorted the artwork to fit the mug and used Overlay mode to apply it to the surface. A masked reflection enhanced the illusion. See page 603 for more.

both the warped image and the rest of the composite, so you can watch the combination. Though the on-screen preview shows the changes to the image, no changes will actually be made to the "Liquified" layer itself until you click "OK" to close the Liquify dialog box. This means that the pixels won't suffer from being worked and reworked as you use the filter.

As you work, you are actually distorting the Liquify *mesh,* which then distorts the image itself. Liquify is applied to a single layer at a time. But saving the mesh before you close the Liquify dialog and then reloading it for use on another layer provides a way to bend several components to match the same surface.

Warp

The **Edit > Transform > Warp** command is ideal for applying graphics or images to shapes that are curved and geometric or nearly so. Unlike the Displace and Liquify filters, which can be used on pixel-based layers only (the filters will offer to rasterize any other kind of layer you try to apply them to), the Warp command can be used on pixel-based or Shape layers and on Smart Objects. Used on a Smart Object, the Warp command offers a kind of "surface template" that allows you to quickly substitute different images or graphics as surface art, as in "'Warping' Graphics to a Surface" on page 603.

Combining Techniques

For the most realistic blend of an image over complex topography, when it matters that the warping appears real and the image and topography are one, it often makes sense to start with the Displace filter, or even Warp or Warp Text, and then use Liquify to "touch up" the image to help some of the contours show up more clearly.

CREATING PANORAMAS

The **Photomerge** command (from Photoshop's File > Automate menu or Bridge's Tools > Photoshop menu) opens a dialog box where you can choose the images you want to blend together into the panorama. "The Photomerge Interface" on page 577 shows the choices you can make in the Photomerge dialog box. "Rules of Thumb," starting on page 578, provides a directed approach for arriving at the panorama you want. "Photomerge Options" on page 580 explains how the Photomerge Layout options work, with the idea that if you understand what each option does, it may help you save time in picking the best option for a panoramic series you've shot. And "Exercising Photomerge" on page 630 shows examples of some Photomerge choices in operation.

When you shoot photos for a panorama, here are some things you can do to make the eventual merging process easier:

- Check to see if your camera has a special setting for shooting for a panorama.

- If not, set the exposure manually if you can, setting it once and leaving it at that setting for the entire series.

- Keep the camera in one spot if you can, turning it rather than moving it around. And keep it level, both side-to-side and front-to-back. A tripod can be a big help.

- Shoot for an overlap of at least 25%. More may require too many photos, but less might not be enough overlap for merging.

- For the typical horizontal panorama, shoot "taller" than you think you'll need. Allow plenty of top and bottom edge space, so you won't have to crop off or clone in something important at the top or bottom of your panorama when photos are moved up or down or distorted in order to align them. One approach is to shoot in portrait (vertical) orientation.

When you assemble a panorama, your goal may be to recall as closely as you can what the scene looked like to you. Or your aim may simply be a believable, pleasing result, or even a unique combination of real and unreal like Allen Furbeck's work on page 636. As Photomerge overlaps the images to fit them together into a panorama, it can arrange them in a straight line (adjusting an image up or down a little if the camera was moved accidentally between shots), or it can transform the individual photos (rotate, scale, or distort them) or arrange them along a curve to make them fit together better. If a rectangular image is your goal, when Photomerge has finished, you'll need to crop off or patch some blank spaces at the edges of the composite.

Photomerge doesn't throw anything away. If it can't make some images fit into your panoramic layout, it includes them anyway, building a larger document to contain them, rather than discarding them. Here an accidentally included image was placed into the document above the pieced-together panorama.

THE PHOTOMERGE INTERFACE

Photomerge Layout options are a little different in Photoshop CS3 and CS4. See page 580 for descriptions of what the Layout options do.

Choose a **Layout** for your panorama here. See the text and illustrations in "Rules of Thumb," starting on page 578, for pointers on choosing a layout.

Click **"Browse"** to choose files to include in the panorama.

All files listed in the Photomerge dialog box will be used for the panorama, so before you click "OK" to run Photomerge, target any extra files (Shift-click or Ctrl/⌘-click to multi-select) and click the **"Remove"** button.

Click **"Add Open Files"** to add all of your open files to the list of files to be included in the panorama.

The **Blend Images Together** option tells Photomerge to create layer masks and make tone and color changes where images meet, in order to make seamless transitions from each photo to the next. In Photoshop CS4, **Vignette Removal** lightens dark edges to avoid a "scalloped" appearance when the images are pieced together. **Geometric Distortion Correction** attempts to correct lens distortion. (Geometric Distortion Correction and Vignette Removal are not available in Photoshop CS3.)

The three original images, shot hand-held with Auto exposure. Photomerge can often do a good job even if your original series of photos violates most of the rules for shooting for a panorama.

When we chose File > Automate > Photomerge, the Auto layout (with Blend Images Together) bent the horizon and reduced the depth of the sky.

We got a better result with the Cylindrical layout, again with Blend Images Together turned on.

To be able to transform and rearrange the components and edit the composite, we ran Photomerge with the Cylindrical layout but this time with Blend Images Together turned off.

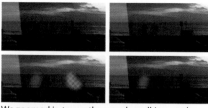

We zoomed in to see the people walking on the beach and the silhouetted sign. We reduced the Opacity of the top (center image) layer so we could see the left image through it. We liked the trio on the left image better, so we erased the people from the top layer using the Eraser tool ⌫, then targeted the left image layer and erased the sign. We targeted the top layer and restored it to full Opacity.

Rules of Thumb for Choosing Photomerge Options

Photomerge offers many options for exercising your creativity; you can see some inspiring examples on pages 636–637. But when your goal is to piece together a panorama to match your memory of the scene you photographed, the following approach may give you a head start toward reaching that goal:

1 If you don't know how broad an angle your panorama spans, try **Auto** first, with **Blend Images Together** turned on (it can often do a good job); if you think from looking at the photos that lens distortion (from a wide angle or fish-eye lens, for instance) or vignetting (darkening at the edges) is a factor, turn on Geometric Distortion Correction or Vignette Removal before you click "OK." (In CS3, where the Geometric Distortion Correction and Vignette Removal are not offered, you may want to remove vignettes in Camera Raw ▼ or with the Lens Correction filter ▼ before you Photomerge.)

2 If Auto produces a Perspective-like (bow-tie) result that will require a great deal of hand-tweaking to get it into a usable form, try running Photomerge again. This time choose **Cylindrical**, again with **Blend Images Together** turned on and the lens correction options as needed. Many panoramas cover a fairly wide angle, making Cylindrical a good choice.

3 What you do next will depend on whether or not Auto or Cylindrical produced a result that's close to what you want.

If you're close but the pieces need a little reorientation or retouching (for instance, to remove someone walking through the scene, appearing in a different place in one of the component images than in another), run Photomerge again with the Layout you prefer, but this time with Blend Images Together turned off. You'll get the benefit of automatic alignment but without masking and color blending. (Both the masks and the color blending can present obstacles when you want to customize the alignment or content of the pieces.)

If you're not close with either Auto or Cylindrical, try Interactive Layout (in CS3) or Reposition or Collage (in CS4), with Blend Images Together turned off. Photoshop CS3's Interactive Layout repositions your photos as well as it can, and gives you the tools to rotate, scale, and apply perspective. It temporarily makes the overlapping images partly transparent as you move them around, to make it easier to see how the image content matches up.

After Photomerge delivers the layered file, use Edit > Free

FIND OUT MORE

▼ Camera Raw vignettes **page 280**

▼ Lens Correction filter **page 278**

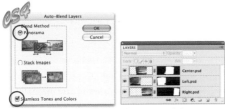

Choosing Edit > Auto-Blend Layers and choosing Panorama with Seamless Tones and Colors checked produced the masks and color blending needed to complete the sunset panorama.

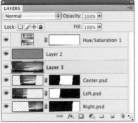

We made a merged copy on a new layer, selected a small area and made a minor Transform adjustment. We cropped the image with the Crop tool 🔲 and then selected a small sliver near the bottom right corner and used Edit > Content Aware Scale to stretch it to fill the vacant corner. We added a dodge-and-burn layer to lighten a small area slightly, and added a Hue/Saturation Adjustment layer to increase the saturation of Reds, Cyans, and Yellows.

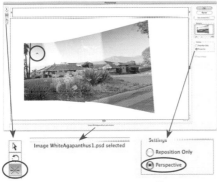

Photoshop CS3's Interactive Layout allows you to designate which of the images in the panorama should be considered the one photographed "head on." Here the photographer was facing the house most directly when the middle image of five was shot, but the perspective was shifted to the leftmost image.

Transform on the individual layers to do any alignment you like, adjusting layer Opacity so you can see to align. Holding down the Ctrl/⌘ key lets you move the individual corners of the Transform frame independently to distort the image to match up with the one next to it in the series. If you want to remove a moving element from a layer, target the appropriate layer in the Layers panel and use the Eraser tool 🩹 with a soft-edged brush tip. After you've adjusted angles and removed unwanted elements, **make sure Opacity is returned to 100%** for all layers; target all the layers; and choose Edit > Auto-Blend Layers; in CS4 use Auto-Blend's Panorama option with Seamless Tone and Color chosen (in CS3 these options are chosen for you automatically).

4 Once your panorama is pieced together, take advantage of other Photoshop tools to complete the image. To fill in gaps in the image, add a new empty layer at the top of the stack (Ctrl/⌘ Shift-N) and use the Clone Stamp 🩹 (or the Healing Brush 🩹 for small spots) with Sample All Layers turned on. If you want to use the Free Transform command or the Lens Correction filter to "undistort" the image, first make yourself a single layer that has the entire panorama in it by adding a merged copy: Target the top layer in the Layers panel and press Ctrl-Alt-Shift-E (Windows) or ⌘-Option-Shift-E (Mac). Before you use Free Transform (don't forget the Warp option for straightening out curves) or the Lens Correction filter (to correct barreling, a tilted horizon, or horizontal or vertical perspective distortion), turn the new layer into a Smart Object so you can transform or filter repeatedly and nondestructively as you see things you'd like to adjust. Add a dodge-and-burn layer if you like, or fine-tune color or contrast with an Adjustment layer. To crop off the rough edges, use the Crop tool 🔲.

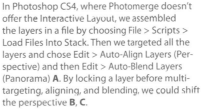

In Photoshop CS4, where Photomerge doesn't offer the Interactive Layout, we assembled the layers in a file by choosing File > Scripts > Load Files Into Stack. Then we targeted all the layers and chose Edit > Auto-Align Layers (Perspective) and then Edit > Auto-Blend Layers (Panorama) **A**. By locking a layer before multi-targeting, aligning, and blending, we could shift the perspective **B**, **C**.

PHOTOMERGE OPTIONS

In piecing together a panorama, each Photomerge Layout option takes a different approach. But the common goal is to "reverse" the distortion the camera introduced when it recorded a three-dimensional real-world scene as a series of two-dimensional rectangular image files. To get an idea of what Photomerge does, imagine you have three photos that you took for your panorama. And imagine that you're going to combine the three shots by projecting the photos, each one from its own projector, onto a movie screen so the three photos will overlap and align where the content is the same. The Layout options offered in the Photomerge dialog provide different ways of projecting, overlapping, and aligning. Knowing what kinds of distortion to expect when Photomerge's different Layouts are applied can help you choose which options to try.

Auto. If you choose **Auto**, Photomerge does its best (which can be amazingly good) to put together the panorama, based on what it can tell from the image data in your three files. It uses some variation of Perspective or Cylindrical.

Perspective. To get an idea of what **Perspective** does, imagine that all three of your projectors sit in the same spot on a table a few feet back from your flat movie screen — it isn't possible for three projectors to occupy the same space, of course, but we can imagine it. The projector with the middle photo in the series is aimed straight at the screen. The projector with the lefthand image is aimed enough to the left so its projected image overlaps the middle one only partly, just enough to align the image content, and the rest of its image extends off to the left. The third projector, with the righthand image, is aimed a bit to the right.

Remember this about projectors — the farther the projector is from the screen, the larger the projected image will be. For the left-aimed and right-aimed projectors, the distance from the lens to the screen is farther on the outer edge than the inner edge, so the picture spreads out, getting larger as it extends away from the middle. The result is the "bow-tie" arrangement you see in a Perspective Photomerge. The Perspective choice is best for panorama photos that were taken with the camera in one spot, and where the panorama spans a fairly small angle (otherwise the bow-tie flare will become too extreme).

Cylindrical. The **Cylindrical** choice is appropriate for panorama photos that were taken with the camera in one spot but that span a bigger angle than you'd use Perspective for, since Cylindrical doesn't stretch out the images as much as Perspective does (Adobe suggests using Cylindrical for spans of more than 120° — that's one-third of a full circle around the camera position).

Your three projectors still sit in the same spot on the table. The left-aimed and right-aimed projectors are turned even more than before. But now the screen is a large cylinder, with the projectors inside the cylinder, at the center of it. Now the inner edge of each photo is the same distance from the screen as the middle and the outer edge, since the screen wraps around. Thus there's no bow-tie flare. But the curvature of the lens may create a bulge at the top and bottom of each projected image. Now, let's say the projected images are magically imprinted onto the cylindrical screen, and the cylinder is unrolled and flattened. The result is like Photomerge's Cylindrical projection.

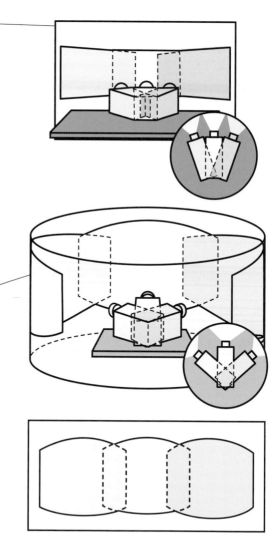

Spherical. To get an idea what CS4's **Spherical** option does, imagine that your three projectors are centered inside a sphere instead of a cylinder, and then the sphere, like the cylinder in the Cylindrical example, is "unwrapped" and flattened. A Spherical projection is designed for situations in which the photographer has shot a full 360° around the horizon and may also have shot a series above the horizon and another below the horizon.

Reposition Only/Reposition. If you choose **Reposition Only** (in Photoshop CS3) or **Reposition** (in CS4), Photomerge will only slide your images around to overlap and align them — it won't rotate, scale, or distort them. It's as if your three projectors were projecting onto a flat screen, but now the projectors are spaced apart (not all in the same spot anymore) so that each one faces the screen straight on, projecting an undistorted rectangular image. A projector may be raised a bit — but there's no bow-tie stretch and no cylindrical bulge. The Reposition options work well for photos that were taken as the camera moved along parallel to the scene being photographed, or for photomicroscopy, where the slide was moved from one side of the microscope stage to the other under the lens as the series of images was snapped.

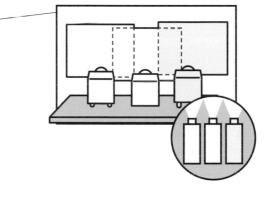

Collage. Photoshop CS4's **Collage** choice can move the component images as the Reposition choice does. But it can also rotate and scale the photos to try to bring them into alignment to make the panorama. It's as if the projectors are spaced apart, each directly facing the flat screen (as they were for the Reposition options), but now each projector can be tilted sideways a little (so the rectangular photo is angled a little clockwise or counterclockwise). And a projector can be moved closer to the screen or farther away, so the rectangular projected images may also vary in size. The images aren't distorted from rectangular, though, because each projector still faces the screen directly. (There's no equivalent to Collage in CS3.)

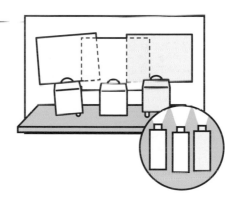

Interactive Layout (CS3 only). Photoshop CS3's **Interactive Layout** provides a nice interface for positioning elements by hand, with a "lightbox" above and a work area below it, providing the space and the tools to adjust the position and perspective of the elements (see page 579). There's no equivalent in Photoshop CS4, but you can do much of the same work in Photoshop proper by stacking the images as layers in a single file, then using Edit > Auto-Align Layers, customizing the layout with the Move tool 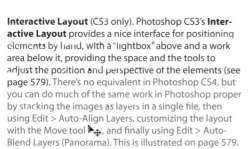, and finally using Edit > Auto-Blend Layers (Panorama). This is illustrated on page 579.

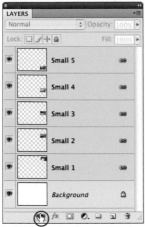

To link layers, "multitarget" the layers you want to link (by clicking the thumbnail of one in the Layers panel and Shift-clicking to select all layers between the first click and the Shift-click, or Ctrl/⌘-click to add single layers). Then click the "Link layers" button 🔗 at the bottom of the panel. To unlink, select any thumbnails whose layers you want to remove from the "linkage" and click the 🔗 at the bottom of the panel.

Layer Groups provide an easy way to "tidy up" the Layers panel. Groups also provide a way to apply the same layer mask or vector mask to more than one layer, or to provide extra masking options for a single layer.

FIND OUT MORE

▼ Drag & drop layers
pages 22 & 23

▼ Copying & pasting Layer Styles
page 82

Photomerge doesn't have a "Draft" mode, so if you think you might be trying lots of options, it can be helpful to make smaller copies of your images to experiment with, so that Photomerge can run faster. Then once you arrive at what you think your Photomerge options should be (make a note of them), run Photomerge on the full-size images. A potential disadvantage is that in scaling down, you could lose detail that Photomerge would find helpful in aligning and blending, but this is less likely than the advantage you gain in time savings in this experimental phase of the project.

OPERATING ON SEVERAL LAYERS AT ONCE

Some of Photoshop's operations can be carried out on more than one layer at a time. To work on two or more layers together, you can **multitarget** them in the Layers panel by Shift-clicking or Ctrl/⌘-clicking their thumbnails. Associate them more permanently by **linking** them or collecting them into a layer **Group**.

"Multitargeting"

When you multitarget layers:

- Dragging one targeted layer, from the *document window* or the Layers panel, and dropping it into another document drags the other targeted layers along. ▼

- You can **lock or unlock** all the multitargeted layers at once by choosing Lock Layers from the Layers panel's menu ▼☰ or the main Layer menu.

- You can also paste the same **Layer Style** to multitargeted layers by copying the Style from a layer, then pasting to one of the targeted layers. ▼

Although layer Groups offer certain advantages over multitargeted layers, multitargeting has an advantage of its own — you can target layers even if they aren't stacked consecutively in the Layers panel, while a Group's layers have to be consecutive.

Linking

Linking is a more permanent sort of multitargeting. It's useful especially if you want to associate layers that aren't right together in the layer stack and thus can't be grouped (grouping is covered on page 583). To link layers, multitarget them and then click the "Link layers" button 🔗 at the bottom of the Layers panel. Now you can recover the multitargeting anytime later by right-clicking/Ctrl-clicking one of the layers with the 🔗 symbol on the right side and choosing Select Linked Layers from the context-sensitive menu.

Here a single-layer Group provides a way to add a second layer mask. The mask on the layer itself silhouettes the boy and his raft. The mask on the Group allows him to be "tucked in" between the girl and the water on the *Background* layer. See page 620 for more.

One way to group layers is to Shift-select them in the Layers panel and then either choose New Group from Layers from the panel's menu ▾☰, or Shift-click on the "Create a new group" button ☐ at the bottom of the panel.

MOVING A LAYER GROUP

To reposition all the layers in a Group at the same time, turn on the Auto Select option and choose Group from the menu; then drag in the working window to move the Group.

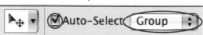

Groups

The **layer Group** is a great way to organize layers that occur together in the Layers panel. You can hide several layers inside a single "folder," making the Layers panel more compact. By clicking the little triangle to the left of the folder icon in the Layers panel, you can collapse or expand the Group, hiding or showing the thumbnails of all the layers in the Group. In a file with many layers, closing a folder (collapsing a Group) can make it easier to find other layers in the Layers panel.

You can start a layer Group "from scratch" (by clicking the Create a new group" button ☐ at the bottom of the Layers panel) or quickly make one from multitargeted layers: Multitarget the layers as described in "Multitargeting" or in "Linking" (page 582); then choose New Group From Layers from the Layers panel's menu ▾☰. Once a Group is established, you can add more layers by dragging their thumbnails to the Group's folder, or directly to the spot where you want the layer to be in an expanded Group. And you can add a brand-new layer to a Group by targeting the folder in the Layers panel and then clicking the "Create a new layer" button ☑ at the bottom of the panel.

GROUPING SHORTCUTS

To quickly group multitargeted layers into a "folder" ☐, type Ctrl/⌘-G. To disband a group and delete the folder but keep the layers, type Ctrl/⌘-Shift-G.

A folder can't have image content of its own, but it lets you control certain layer attributes for the entire Group at once, and it can have a layer mask, a vector mask, or both. With the ability to nest Groups within other Groups, you can do some complex masking and blending. See "Anatomy of Masked Groups" on page 620 for more.

The Opacity and blend mode for the folder don't *replace* the settings for the individual layers; they *interact* with them:

- **The folder's Opacity is a multiplier** for the Opacity of each layer in the Group. At 100%, the folder's Opacity setting makes no change to the look of the composite. Below 100% the folder's Opacity reduces the opacity of the layers proportionally. So, for instance if you have a Group with some layers at 50% Opacity and some at 80%, if you reduce the folder's Opacity to 50%, the cumulative effect is that some layers are now only 25% opaque (50% of 50% is 25%) and some are 40% opaque (50% of 80% is 40%).

Quickly open or close all layer Groups by right/Ctrl-clicking the tiny arrow to the left of a folder ⬜ in the Layers panel and choosing from the context-sensitive menu.

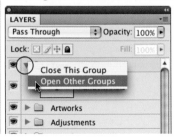

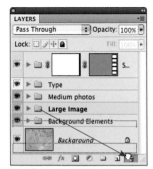

Targeting a layer Group and then clicking the "Delete" button 🗑 at the bottom of the Layers panel opens a Caution box where you can choose to remove the "Group and Contents" or disband the "Group Only," keeping the layers. Alt/Option-click the 🗑 to delete everything without the Caution box popup.

Dragging a Group's thumbnail to the "Delete" button 🗑 is often the quickest way to remove it from the file; Photoshop doesn't stop you to ask if you really mean it. Ctrl/⌘-drag to merely disband the Group, removing the folder but leaving the layers in place.

- **The folder's default blend mode is Pass Through,** which simply means that each layer in the Group keeps its own blend mode, the same as if it weren't in a Group. If you choose any other blend mode for the folder, the result is as if you had merged all the layers in the Group (with their existing blend modes) into a single layer and then applied the folder's blend mode to that merged image.

Not everything you can do to a layer can be done to a Group. For instance, you can't apply a Layer Style to a folder. Also, a folder's masks aren't subject to the Layer Styles of any layers in the Group. And a folder can't be part of a clipping group.

You can remove a layer from a Group by dragging its thumbnail to a position above or below the Group in the Layers panel. You can remove an entire Group from the file by dragging its ⬜ icon to the "Delete" button 🗑 at the bottom of the Layers panel. To delete the folder, releasing the layers from the Group but not deleting the layers themselves, hold down the Ctrl/⌘ key as you drag the ⬜ to the 🗑 button. *Note:* When you disband a Group, any layer mask or vector mask it had is discarded without being applied.

Color Coding

You can color-code layers in the Layers panel, assigning the same color to layers that are somehow related. Color coding has no effect on the layers or folders you apply it to — it's simply a visual organizing tool for the panel.

Here are some ideas for using color coding:

- You might color all the members of a **Group** with the same color, to help you quickly see where Groups begin and end when they are expanded in the panel.

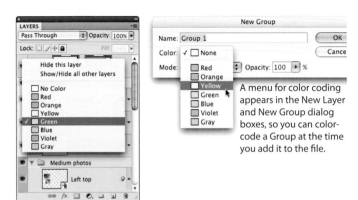

A menu for color coding appears in the New Layer and New Group dialog boxes, so you can color-code a Group at the time you add it to the file.

Right-click/Ctrl-click on a layer's or Group's visibility icon to change the color coding for this layer or Group.

Several options for merging visible layers are available in the Layers panel's menu and in the main Layer menu. Others are available elsewhere, as noted below. The same keyboard shortcut (Ctrl/⌘-E) works for many of them.

- When the "folder" of a layer Group is targeted in the Layers panel, **Merge Group (Ctrl/⌘-E)** combines all the visible layers of the group, **discarding any hidden layers.**

- **Merge Down (Ctrl/⌘-E)** combines the targeted layer with the very next layer below it in the stack; the bottom layer of the "merge" has to be a pixel-based layer.

- **Merge Visible (Ctrl/⌘-Shift-E)** combines all visible layers and also **keeps all the hidden layers.**

- The **Image > Duplicate** command offers the **Merged Layers Only** option, which makes a merged copy of the file, ignoring invisible layers.

- **Edit > Copy Merged (Ctrl/⌘-Shift-C)** makes a copy that includes the selected area of all visible layers, as if they were a single layer. Then Edit > Paste (Ctrl/⌘-V) can be used to turn the copy into a new layer.

- Unchecking the Layers box in the **Save As** dialog box saves a merged copy of the file.

- **Merge Clipping Mask** merges all the layers in a clipping group. For this command to be available, the base (clipping) layer has to be targeted, and it must be a pixel-based layer.

- **Flatten Image** discards invisible layers and merges all visible layers into a *Background*, filling any transparent areas with white.

- Or use a color to identify all the layers that were duplicated from a single **original layer or Smart Object**. (When a layer is duplicated, the new copy keeps the same color code.)

- Or use the same color to identify **related elements** in several different files; for instance, you might routinely make all "live" type layers yellow so you can see them quickly if you want to simplify your file by converting them to Shape layers or rasterizing them.

You can color-code a layer or Group at the time you create it or afterwards:

- When you create a layer or Group, hold down the Alt/Option key as you click the ▣ or ▢ button at the bottom of the Layers panel, to open a dialog box where you can choose a Color.

- To color-code an existing layer (or Group), choose Layer > Layer Properties (or Layer > Group Properties), or use the context-sensitive menu as shown on page 584.

- When you color-code a Group, you automatically color-code all the layers in the Group. But when you move a layer into a Group, the layer keeps its own color if it has one, or takes on the Group's color if it hasn't yet been color-coded.

REORDERING LAYERS

To change the stacking order of layers in your file, you can drag their thumbnails up or down the Layers panel. Or use keyboard shortcuts: **Ctrl/⌘-[** moves the targeted layer **up** one position in the stack, and **Ctrl/⌘-[** moves it **down**. Move a layer to the **top or bottom** of the entire stack (not displacing the *Background*, though) by typing **Ctrl/⌘-Shift-[** or **Ctrl/⌘-Shift-[**.

MERGING & FLATTENING

Merging combines two or more visible layers into a single layer. Several merging options appear at the bottom of the Layer menu. You might want to merge a series of layers when you've finished working on them and you no longer need to keep them separate and "live." Since merging reduces the number of layers, it also reduces the amount of RAM needed for the file. When you merge layers, any Layer Styles and masks are applied and then discarded, and type is rasterized. The new combined layer takes its blend mode and opacity from the bottom layer of the merged series; it becomes a *Background* only if the bottom layer of the merged series is a *Background*.

Certain file formats require a *flattened* file — a single-layered file with the capacity for transparency won't do. Flattening (**Layer** >

SHARON STEUER

LAYER COMPS

	Last Document State
	bleached w/lines
	Woodcut
	mezzotint stipple
▣	**Mottled**
	mezzotint
	marker stipple
	Woodcut#3
	poster1
	poster2
	Mottled dark
	Seurat
	aquatint

The Layer Comps panel provides a way to save alternate versions of multilayer compositions such as Sharon Steuer's *Oil Spirit,* shown here. Starting with a photo of her original sculpture (top left), Steuer duplicated the image several times, and applied filters and other effects, using blend modes and masking to combine the results. As she developed an alternative composite, Steuer generated and named a new layer comp. This made it possible to go back later and, with one click, turn on visibility for all the layers and masks that make up a particular version of the image.

Flatten Image) combines all visible layers into a *Background*. A Caution box warns that hidden layers will be discarded, giving you a chance to reconsider. Any transparency in the combined image is filled with white. Alpha channels are kept.

LAYER COMPS

For a many-layered, complex file with masks and Layer Styles, **layer comps** can be invaluable for keeping track of alternatives for the final composition. A layer comp is a "snapshot" of the current state of the file, as reflected in the Layers panel. Make a layer comp by choosing New Layer Comp from the Layer Comps panel's menu ▾≡, or by clicking the "Create New Layer Comp" button ▣ at the bottom of the Layer Comps panel. Your new layer comp captures the position, visibility and masking, opacity, and blend mode of each layer. Also, it captures anything that can be set in the Layer Styles dialog box — blend mode, "Blend If" settings, and other blending options, as well as the effects in a Layer Style. Once you capture a layer comp, if you make changes to any of these properties, your existing comp won't change. You can try out options by changing visibility, position, or effects, then making another comp, and so on. To bring back the state of the file represented by any comp, you simply click in the column to the left of that comp's name in the Layer Comps panel.

A layer comp *doesn't* freeze image *content*. So, for instance, if you add or take away pixels, edit Shape layers, move a layer up or down the stack in the Layers panel, or change the text in a type layer, these changes *will* also be made to any existing comp that includes the layers you changed. Of course, there's a way to change content without changing your comps. You simply make your changes in a new layer — for instance, duplicate a type layer in the Layers panel, turn off visibility for the original type layer, and change the copy — and then use the Layer Comps panel to make another comp.

A comp can be modified (updated) by clicking on its name in the Layer Comps panel, then adjusting visibility, layer position, or effects, and clicking the "Update Layer Comp" button ↻ at the bottom of the panel.

Assigning meaningful names to layer comps can be helpful later, when you want to quickly find a particular comp. Assign the name when you make the comp, or double-click a comp's name in the Layer Comps panel and type a new name. The use of layer comps is shown at the left and is covered step-by-step in "Softening the Focus" on page 346. *wow!*

We promise beaches like this one.

Believe it or not, beaches like this
still exist. Where the waves are
gentle, the sand is soft, and marine
life is everywhere in abundance.

For a vacation in unsurpassed
natural beauty with wonders that
never cease, come to La Playa
Island Resorts. You'll find us on
the Web at www.laplaya.com.

1.800.555.2323

photo by Ian Gillespie

Adding Type to an Image

WITH TYPE ON A PATH and within a path, combined with Photoshop's expert typesetting engine, it's easy to design an ad, from logo to body text, without ever leaving Photoshop.

Thinking the project through. A photo like this one with a background that's fluid, organic, and without a pronounced grain is an ideal candidate for "reproportioning" to slightly different dimensions, especially in Photoshop CS4 with its Content-Aware Scale command. With large areas of background without important detail, it's easy to add type, whether the background gets "screened back" to allow normal type to be easy to read, or the type itself gets a change in tone and a drop shadow to separate it from the background. For smaller type, sampling a dark color from the image can help coordinate the piece, and a Bevel and Emboss effect can make type look carved into the sand.

1 Choosing a photo. We began our ad by choosing a photo that suited our theme and that we could adapt to accommodate the text, headline, and logo we wanted to use **1**. As often happens, the layout of the photo didn't quite fit with the way we wanted to use it. We had more photo on the left than we needed, less

1

The original photo

2a

This is **Add Type-Before.psd**. A file has been created for the small ad. The photo has been dragged into position and the file has been cropped.

2b

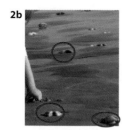

The small or indistinct groups of shells in the image can be stretched without looking obviously distorted. And some stretched shells can be eliminated. But we want some, such as the ones marked here, to remain, unstretched.

2c

With the photo layer targeted in the Layers panel (as shown in figure 2a), the top of the image is selected and stretched to the top of the canvas.

on the right, and a bit too little at the top of the image to fit the headline well.

2 "Reproportioning" the image. We opened our photo file and also started a new RGB file at the size we wanted for our small ad (File > New, at 7.2 inches wide by 5.5 inches high and 225 pixels/inch). We used the Move tool ⊹ to drag the photo into our new file and offset it to the left. (If it had been necessary to resize the image to fit the ad file, we would have done it at this point ▽, but it wasn't needed.) To tidy up the file, we selected all (Ctrl/⌘-A) and cropped (Image > Crop), which trimmed away the extra image beyond the canvas **2a**.

FIND OUT MORE

▼ Resizing **page 70**

Before you stretch some areas of your image layer, you may want to preserve certain features in their original proportions **2b** so you can use them to replace or eliminate any obviously stretched elements later. One way to do this is to duplicate the image before stretching (**Image > Duplicate**) so you'll have a clean source to clone from.

Now for the stretching. In your developing file, drag with the Rectangular Marquee ⬚ to select the top of the photo, above the child's head. (The taller the selection, the less you'll have to stretch it, but obviously, you don't want to select anything below the area you want to stretch; in this image, stay above the hat.)

Then stretch the selected area to the top of the canvas, as follows:

- In CS3 press Ctrl/⌘-T (for Edit > Free Transform)
- In CS4 choose Edit > Content-Aware Scale (it may do a better job of stretching).

Drag up on the top center handle of the Transform frame to fill the top of the canvas with image **2c**; press the Enter/Return key to complete the transformation.

Next select as much of the right side of the image as you can without selecting the child, and transform that area, stretching until it reaches the right side of the canvas, again using Ctrl/⌘-T in CS3, Content-Aware Scale in CS4 **2d**. In CS3 details like those in figure 2b will be stretched unacceptably. When we used CS4, two of the three pairs of shells were unaffected by the content-aware scale, but the top pair was stretched.

3 Repairing the details. Add a "repairs" layer so the repairs you will make can be edited if necessary without disturbing the main image (Ctrl/⌘-Shift-N). Now, to remove shells that

The image after the top and right side have been stretched. In CS3 (top) the shells have been stretched. In CS4, the largest pairs of shells have maintained their original shapes.

Using the Clone Stamp to remove an obviously stretched detail in CS3

Details are added back as needed with the Clone Stamp, cloning from the duplicate image made in step 2. The "footprint" preview in CS4 (shown here) previews the part of the image being cloned before you click on the image to place it.

Setting up the Options bar for typing the headline

are obviously stretched but that you don't need to keep, use the Clone Stamp tool (Shift-S)▼ with a soft brush tip (so the repairs blend in) and Sample All Layers turned on in the Options bar: Alt/Option-click to sample an area of beach that's similar in tone and color, and then release the Alt/Option key and paint over the stretched shells **3a**. To replace the large stretched shells from figure 2b (three pairs in CS3 and just the one pair needed in CS4), add another repairs layer (Ctrl/⌘-Shift-N), and use the Clone Stamp again, this time using a soft brush tip a bit larger than the shells you want to clone. Sample from the duplicate file you made before stretching, and then paint the cloned shells onto your new layer in the stretched image **3b**. Now check for obvious signs of manipulation. If you see any, you can add a third repairs layer and then use the Healing Brush, the Spot Healing Brush, or the Clone Stamp, with Sample All Layers turned on in the Options bar.▼ Finally merge all the layers into the *Background* (Ctrl/⌘-Shift-E).

4 Typing and "styling" the headline. For the headline, select the Type tool **T**. In the Options bar choose a bold font (we used Trebuchet MS Bold at 28 pt for our small ad), set the Alignment option to Center text, and click the color swatch to choose a color that's easy to see against the image (we used white) **4a**. For **centered point type**, click once where you want the line to be centered (in our case, halfway across the image) and type. When you finish typing, hit Ctrl/⌘-Enter **4b**. With the Type tool still selected, you can adjust the position of the type if necessary by holding down the Ctrl/⌘ key (to turn the Type tool into the Move tool ▶⊕ temporarily) and dragging.

To help the type stand out, you can add a Layer Style, building it *before* fine-tuning the spacing of the headline, since it may change the way the spacing looks. Click the "Add a layer style" button *fx* at the bottom of the Layers panel and choose Drop Shadow. Turn off "Use Global Light"▼ and set the Angle (we used 45° to cast the shadow to the left and down) and the Distance (we offset the shadow 13 px). Adjust the Size (to determine how far the shadow extends; we used 12 px) and Spread (to determine how dense the shadow will be; we used 23%). We left the Blend Mode and Opacity at their default settings, Multiply and 75%. Click "OK."

Now that you can see how the Layer Style affects the spacing of the type **4c**, you can interactively fine-tune the headline if you

FIND OUT MORE

▼ Using the Clone Stamp **page 256**

▼ Using the Healing Brush **page 256**

▼ Using the Spot Healing Brush **page 256**

▼ The "Use Global Light" option **page 505**

4b Headline type set

4c Drop shadow added

5a

Drawing a rectangular selection big enough to include the type

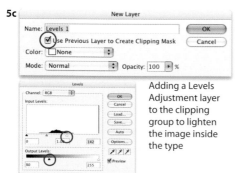

5b

Making a clipping group to mask the image inside the type. Since the masked image and the background are identical, only the Drop Shadow effect defines the characters at this point.

5c

Adding a Levels Adjustment layer to the clipping group to lighten the image inside the type

think it needs it. Click to make an insertion point between two letters whose spacing needs adjusting (kerning), or drag-select several characters if you want to change their spacing overall (tracking). Hold down the Alt/Option key and hit the → or ← key for more or less space, respectively. Or use the Character panel (click the ▣ button in the Type tool's Options bar if you need to) to type in an amount, or to "scrub" to make the change. ▼ When you're satisfied with the spacing, type Ctrl/⌘-Enter to commit the type.

FIND OUT MORE
▼ Scrubbing **page 24**

5 Filling the headline. The next step is to fill the headline with the background image. With the Marquee tool ⬚, drag a rectangle around the type **5a**. Then in the Layers panel, turn off visibility for the type layer by clicking its 👁 and target the *Background*. Copy the selected area (Ctrl/⌘-C), and then target the type layer and paste (Ctrl/⌘-V); because the type layer is targeted, the copied selection will be pasted as a layer just above it. Now restore the type, which has been hidden by the pasted layer: In the Layers panel, Alt/Option-click on the border between the type and the pasted layer to make a clipping group, which allows the pasted layer to show only inside the type **5b**.

The area you selected and clipped inside the headline type is identical to the background, but lightening it will make the type stand out more. One way to do it (in either CS3 or CS4) is to Alt/Option-click on the "Create new fill or adjustment layer" button ◐, choose Levels, and in the New Layer dialog box check the box for "Use Previous Layer to Create Clipping Mask" so that only the image that's clipped inside the type will be affected by the Levels adjustment. Click "OK" to close the New Layer dialog. In CS4 you can instead open Levels by clicking the 👑 button in the Adjustments panel and then click the panel's ● button to form the clipping group. We moved the Input Levels

5d

In the clipping group the type layer is the base that masks both the image rectangle and the Levels adjustment.

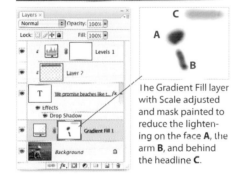

6a

Setting up the gradient for the Gradient Fill layer

6b

The Gradient Fill layer with Scale adjusted and mask painted to reduce the lightening on the face **A**, the arm **B**, and behind the headline **C**.

7a

A text box for paragraph type is defined by dragging with the Type tool T. If necessary, the box can be adjusted to fit the text better later.

white point slider left to brighten the type by both lightening it and boosting contrast, and moved the Output Levels black point slider to the right to lighten the type even more without further increasing contrast **5c, 5d**. In CS3 you'll need to click "OK" to close the Levels dialog.

6 Preparing an area for text. A Gradient Fill layer is a flexible way to lighten part of the photo so it's easier to read dark text over it, and to provide the kind of effect we want here. ▼ Select white as the Foreground color (you can do this by typing D and then X). Again target the *Background* and click on the "Create new fill or adjustment layer" button ⊘ at the bottom of the Layers panel and choose Gradient from the pop-up list. In the Gradient Fill dialog, make sure the gradient shows white to transparent (if it doesn't, click on the gradient and in the Gradient Preset picker, click on the Foreground to Transparent swatch). Then set up the gradient this way **6a**:

FIND OUT MORE
▼ Gradient Fill layers
page 175

- For a simple left-to-right transition from clear to white, select Linear as the Style and set the Angle at 180°.

- With the Gradient Fill dialog box still open, you can move the gradient and adjust its density to make the background right for the type, as follows: Move the cursor into the image window, where it automatically becomes a temporary Move tool ▶⊕, and drag the gradient to the right in the image window until the lightening begins just over the child's cheek (you can remove the gradient from the child's face and arm later).

- Adjust the Scale in the Gradient Fill dialog (we used 75%) to make the gradient go from clear to white over a shorter distance, creating a light enough background for the type.

When you're satisfied with the gradient's position and scale, click "OK." You can leave the blend mode for the Gradient Fill layer at Normal since the gradient is white, but if you were using a color instead, you might try Screen or Lighter Color.

You can take advantage of the automatic mask created with the Gradient Fill layer to fix areas that are lightened too much. In our image, for instance, the edge of the child's face and her arm seemed too light. We chose the Brush tool ✐, clicked on the brush footprint in the Options bar, and picked a soft brush tip from the Brush Preset picker; also in the Options bar we lowered Opacity to 50% (for more control in building density), and changed the Foreground color to black (type X if needed). We painted on the mask just over the face and arm to remove

7b

Specifying type in the Options bar

7c

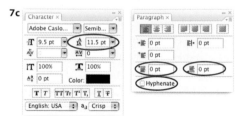

Using the Character and Paragraph panels to add to the type specs

7d

The body text is typed into the text box. Although it's possible to set interparagraph spacing in the Paragraph panel, we simply pressed the Enter/Return key to add space between paragraphs.

most of the lightening effect. We also brushed the area behind the right end of the headline type, for more contrast between the lightened type and the background **6b**.

7 Typing the text. For **paragraph type** aligned with the right edge of the headline, turn on the rulers (Ctrl/⌘-R) and drag a guide from the ruler on the left, lining it up with the last letter of the headline. With the guide in place, select the Type tool **T**. Start at the guide and at the level of the child's eyes, and drag left and down to make a box to hold the text **7a**; if you need to move the box, hold down the Ctrl/⌘ key and drag.

In the Type tool's Options bar, select a typeface for the body that's bold enough to show up against the background (we chose Adobe Caslon Pro Semibold); we chose 9.5 pt for the Size, clicked the "Left align text" button, and chose black for the color **7b**. Set leading in the Character panel (we chose 11.5 pt) **7c**. In the Paragraph panel we made sure that Hyphenate was unchecked and that both "Add space before paragraph" and "Add space after paragraph" were set to 0 because we preferred to separate the paragraphs of our text with a full line space. Type the body text **7d**. If you want to check spelling, now is a good time, before you fine-tune the spacing (see the "Spell-Checking" tip at the left). If the text doesn't fit the text box, adjust the spacing as described in the "Type-Fitting" tip on the next page.

8 Adding a stored logo. The next step is to add the logo, which has been stored as a Custom Shape preset and will be added as a Shape layer. Choose the Custom Shape tool ⬡. Click the "Shape" icon in the middle of the Options bar to open the Custom Shape Preset picker **8a**, where you can then click the ▶ button to open the picker's menu. Choose Load Shapes and load the **Wow Sun Logo.csh** file from the **Add Type** folder of files for this project. Now you can find the Wow Sun Logo listed at the bottom of the open picker; click on it. Click the "Shape layers" button ⬚ at the left end of the Options bar. Click the color swatch in the Options bar and choose a color; we sampled a dark warm brown by clicking a shadow on the child's leg. To position the logo, we added a horizontal guide in line with the bottom of the child's lower sandal. Now Shift-drag the Custom Shape tool to draw the logo at the size you want (adding the Shift key ensures that the logo's proportions will be maintained as you draw). With the Ctrl/⌘ key held down to temporarily access the Move tool ▶⊕, you can reposition the logo **8b**.

We added a drop shadow to the logo to pop it off the page a bit. To construct this Style, click the "Add a layer style" button *fx* at

8a

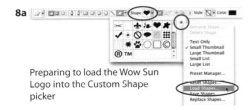

Preparing to load the Wow Sun Logo into the Custom Shape picker

8b

The scaled logo in place, aligned with the bottom of the child's foot.

TYPE-FITTING

Here's a series of adjustments you can make to get paragraph text to fit better in the space available for it:

1 Photoshop uses a sophisticated type engine. With the **Adobe Every-line Composer** selected from the Paragraph panel's menu ▼☰, Photoshop can adjust spacing anywhere in a paragraph to solve a spacing problem in any one line. When your design allows you the flexibility to **make the text box a bit larger or smaller,** you can often get professional-looking typesetting simply by adjusting the size of the box and letting the Adobe Every-line Composer reflow the type.

2 If you still don't like the way the type is set and can't adjust the text box any more, you can **change the font size or leading** in the Character panel to help the type fit the box; the size and leading boxes accept numbers to two decimal places.

3 Turn on **Hyphenate** if your project allows you to use it.

4 As a last resort, in the Character panel manually adjust **tracking** and **kerning.**

---

the bottom of the Layers panel and choose Drop Shadow. Turn off Use Global Light and set the parameters for the shadow; we used Angle 45°, Distance 3 px, Spread 1%, and Size 7 px **8c**.

9 Adding type on a circle. To set the type around the logo, first make a circular path: Choose the Ellipse tool ⬭ and click on the "Paths" button ▦ near the left end of the Options bar. Starting at the center of the logo shape, begin to drag outward. Then hold down the Shift and Alt/Option keys to draw a perfect circle centered at your starting point; if you notice that the circle is forming off-center, add the spacebar to the keys you're holding down, drag to reposition the circle, and then release the spacebar so you can continue drawing the circle.

Choose the Type tool **T** and set your type specs. In the Options bar we chose Trebuchet MS Bold at 11 pt and clicked the "Center text" button. We clicked the color swatch and clicked on the logo to sample color. We also clicked the Character panel's "Small Caps" button and chose a value of +25 from its menu for tracking. Move the Type tool cursor to the center of the top of the path; when it turns into the **type-on-a-path** icon, click and type the company name. Type Ctrl/⌘-Enter to commit the type **9**. Adjust type size in the Options bar if necessary for fit.▼

FIND OUT MORE

▼ Using the Type tool **T** page 436

To "style" the type to match the logo, in the Layers panel right/Ctrl-click on the **fx** for the logo layer and choose Copy Layer Style. Then right-click/Ctrl-click in the same area of the panel's entry for the type layer and choose Paste Layer Style.

You may need to do some more tracking or kerning at this point to make the type fit around the circle better, using the same method as with the headline. If you need to reposition the type around the circle after kerning, choose the Path Selection tool ▸, hover the cursor over the top center of the type circle until it turns into the •|• cursor, and then drag. (If you need to reposition the entire circle of type relative to the logo, you can do it by dragging with the Move tool ▸⊕.)

The phone number was set as **point type** in Trebuchet MS Bold, 10 pt, using the guide as the baseline. We clicked the color swatch in the Options bar and clicked on the logo to sample color.

10 "Carving" type into the sand. Next we added a photo credit, distorted to suggest that it was drawn in the sand: Choose the Pen tool ◊ and click the "Paths" button ▦ in the Options bar; then click and drag to draw a path that curves below the child's right foot **10a**.▼ Choose the Type

FIND OUT MORE

▼ Using the Pen tool ◊ page 454

8c

A Layer Style consisting only of a Drop Shadow effect is added to the logo.

9

Using capital letters will make the circling "band" of type more uniform. Choosing small caps kept the letter height in proportion to the sun without reducing point size and decreasing legibility. Positive tracking (here +25) often improves the look of type set on a circle.

10a

A path is drawn for the type.

10b

The type is set on the path.

10c

The rasterized type is flattened onto the sand with the Distort command.

tool **T** again, setting the type specs in the Options bar: We chose Trebuchet MS, Bold, 9 pt, and "Left aligned"; we clicked the color swatch and sampled a dark wet-sand color from the image. Click on the path, type the photographer's name, and press Ctrl/⌘-Enter **10b**.

To distort the type, we would use the Distort command, which we found easier to control than Warp Text or Edit > Transform > Warp. Distort is one of the Transform commands that can't be used on live type, so first convert the type to pixels (Layer > Rasterize > Type). Then choose Edit > Transform > Distort and drag the individual handles of the Transform frame to spread the type out on the sand; double-click inside the Transform frame to complete the distortion **10c** (if your distortion goes awry and you want to start over, instead of double-clicking, type Ctrl/⌘-period or tap the Escape key, and then use Edit > Transform > Distort again).

Next we used the Ripple filter to distort the letters slightly and a Layer Style to add shading to create depth. Choose **Filter > Convert for Smart Filters**, then **Filter > Distort > Ripple**; set the parameters (we used Small for the Size and 70% for the Amount) **10d**, and click "OK." Then click the "Add a layer style" button *fx* at the bottom of the Layers panel and choose Bevel and Emboss; choose Inner Bevel and Smooth, and turn off Use Global Light; choose **Down** for the **Direction** and set the parameters so the shadows inside the type match the shadows caused by small lumps of sand in the image (we used 35° for the Angle, 16° for the Altitude, a Depth of 50%, and Size and Soften settings of 0); click "OK." In the Layers panel we reduced the Fill opacity for this "carved" layer to 80%, which lightened the letters without affecting the bevel shadows and highlights of the Style as much as if we had reduced the overall layer Opacity **10e**. 🌀

10d

Adding a slight ripple to the lettering

10e

The "drawn in the sand" look, after applying the Ripple filter, adding a Layer Style, and reducing the Fill opacity

DONA JOLLEY

Applying an Image to a Textured Surface

OPEN THESE PANELS

(from the Window menu, for instance):
  • Layers • Channels

OVERVIEW

"Apply" graphics on one layer to a surface
image in another layer, using the luminance
of the surface layer to distort the graphics
to conform to the surface • Adjust blend
mode and opacity • Add masks as needed

BENDING, SUBTLY DISTORTING, AND "AGING" an image so it
appears to be part of a textured surface in another image can
create a unified visual illusion that can be very powerful in
presenting a concept.

Thinking the project through. The Liquify filter, so successful
for "massaging" one image to fit the organic contours of another,
as on page 599, couldn't begin to do the precise, practical work
needed to paint the graphics onto the deteriorating bricks and
mortar of this image. Nor could the Warp command (page 603).
Besides requiring the right blend mode, transparency, and masking to let the character of the wall show through, this project
calls for the use of the Displace filter with a *displacement map*
made from the main image to subtly mold the graphics to the
wall. Where the displacement map is dark, the graphics will be
"pushed" into the surface of the wall; where the displacement
map is light, the graphics will be "pulled" up onto the surface
of the bricks. The Displace filter has no preview, so we'll turn
the graphics into a Smart Object to make it easy to experiment,
rerunning the filter with new settings if needed.

1a

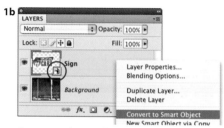

Applying Image-Before.psd,
with the sign pasted in position

1b

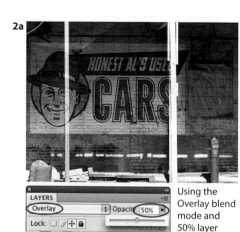

Converting the sign layer to a Smart Object

2a

Using the Overlay blend mode and 50% layer Opacity to apply the sign

1 Assembling the elements. Open your main image and import the image or graphics you want to apply to it. Or open the **Applying Image-Before.psd** file, which includes Don Jolley's sign graphics layered over his photo of a shaded, deteriorating brick wall behind brightly lit posts **1a**. Jolley copied and pasted the sign art into the photo file, dragging it into place with the Move tool ▶₊ and sizing it to fit the space available. ▼ Turn the imported layer into a Smart Object to preserve the original: right-click/Ctrl-click the graphics layer's entry in the Layers panel and choose Convert to Smart Object from the context-sensitive menu **1b**.

FIND OUT MORE
▼ Scaling **page 67**

2 Blending. In the pop-out blend mode list at the top left of the Layers panel, choose Overlay, and try reducing the Opacity (at the top right of the panel) until the graphics and the main image blend as you want; we liked 50% Opacity **2a**. (For the moment, ignore the parts of the main image that should be in front of the applied element — here the two posts; we'll deal with them in step 5.) You may want to experiment with other Opacity settings and blend modes, such as Multiply, Soft Light, Hard Light, or Color for different visual effects. We tried Soft Light, which lightened and faded the sign **2b**, and Multiply, which darkened and faded it **2c**, but we liked Overlay at 50% the best, so we restored these settings.

3 Making the displacement map. The next step is to prepare a grayscale displacement map from the main image. You'll use it with the Displace filter in step 4 to distort the graphics so it looks like they're affected by the surface topography (in this case the goal is to make them seem to dip into the shaded mortar troughs between the bricks and into the chips and dents in the brick itself). *Note:* If your graphics extend beyond the edges of your main image, you'll need to trim away any excess now in order for the displacement to work right in step 4. To trim, select all (Ctrl/⌘-A) and then choose Image > Crop. And once you've made the displacement map, the file should not be cropped again or resized — at least until after you've run the Displace filter.

To make a grayscale displacement map from the main image layer, in the Layers panel Alt/Option-click this layer's 👁 icon to make it the only visible layer. Then choose Image > Duplicate, check the "Duplicate Merged Layers Only" option in the Duplicate dialog box, and click "OK." In the new file, choose Image > Mode > Grayscale. To make the grayscale image work better as a displacement map, you may want to get rid of the finest detail by blurring (although we didn't for this image, since the mortar

2b

The sign layer in Soft Light mode at 65% Opacity

2c

The sign layer in Multiply mode at 100% Opacity

3

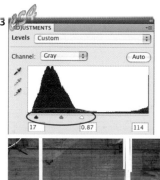

The file, with only the background photo visible, is duplicated and converted to Grayscale. Then a Levels adjustment increases contrast between the mortar lines and the bricks.

4a

Running the Displace filter. For a higher-resolution file or for more displacement, you would use higher Scale settings.

lines themselves were quite small and our displacement would be subtle). You might also want to increase the contrast to exaggerate the light/dark differences (we used Image > Adjust > Levels), moving the black and white Input Levels sliders inward and the gamma slider to the right **3**. (Although we didn't need to here, you may also want to paint over with gray any especially dark or light marks that aren't part of the surface texture, so they won't have any effect.) When your grayscale image is adjusted, **save** (Ctrl/⌘-S) **in Photoshop (PSD) format**, since the Displace filter uses only saved Photoshop-format files.

4 Applying the displacement map. Back in your composite image, before you do anything else, turn on visibility for the graphics Smart Object layer (click its 👁 column in the Layers panel) and target it (click its layer thumbnail). Then choose Filter > Distort > Displace. In the Displace dialog box **4a**, choose values for the Horizontal and Vertical Scale of the displacement; the higher the numbers, the farther the pixels of your graphics will be nudged by the corresponding dark and light pixels in the displacement map file. Since we needed only subtle nudges to "push" the paint into the troughs of the mortar and "pull" it onto the surface of the bricks, we used small values — Horizontal 2 and Vertical 1. (In the Displace dialog, the Displacement Map setting is irrelevant because the displacement map is exactly the same dimensions as the main image file. And Undefined Areas is irrelevant because the displacement is very small.) Click "OK," locate the displacement map file you just made, and click the "Open" button. The filter will displace the graphics **4b**.(If you don't like your Displace results, right-click/Ctrl-click on the filter's entry in the Layers panel and choose Edit Filter Settings.)

5 Masking the graphics. To put the graphics "behind" any elements in the image that are supposed to appear in front, you can use a layer mask. Target the main image layer and select the forward elements, in this case the two wooden supports. ▼ One way is to use the Quick Selection tool 🖌, turning off Sample All Layers in the tool's Options bar (so the tool will be "looking at" the photo only, not the sign graphics) and sizing the brush tip so it fits entirely within the width of the large post (you can use the bracket keys — [and] — to resize the brush tip). ▼ Click or drag repeatedly to add more of the white areas of the posts to the selection, sizing the brush down to click in the narrower parts of the posts **5a**. Rather than try to add the shaded area of the large post with the Quick Selection tool, which also would select some of the brick wall,

FIND OUT MORE

▼ Using the Quick Selection tool 🖌 **page 49**

▼ Resizing brush tips **page 71**

4b

Before (left) and after running the Displace filter

5a

Setting up the Quick Selection tool

5b

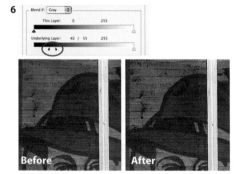

The Quick Mask is clear over the posts. Jolley also erased the mask over a few small fixtures on the wall.

6

The black point slider is moved inward for the Underlying Layer so the darkest marks on the wall show through the sign more, adding to the worn and stained look. Holding down Alt/Option splits the slider to make a smooth transition in these areas.

7a

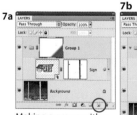

Making a group with a mask to fade the lower right corner of the sign

7b

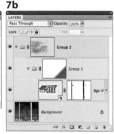

The masked folder is nested inside another group, which is masked to "erode" the sign so more of the wall shows through.

---

switch to Quick Mask mode at this point (by clicking the "Edit in Quick Mask mode" button near the bottom of the Tools panel). Use the Brush with a hard round tip (we used 9 pixels) and white paint (type D, then X) to erase the mask in the shaded area of the larger post **5b**; click the "Edit in Standard Mode" button to go back to an active selection. With your selection made, in the Layers panel target the graphics layer and Alt/Option-click the "Add layer mask" button at the bottom of the panel to make a mask that "pops" the posts in front of the sign.

6 Experimenting with Blending Options. To try "wearing away" parts of the applied graphics, in the Layers panel, right/Ctrl-click the thumbnail for the graphics layer to open a menu where you can choose Blending Options to open the Layer Style dialog box; then adjust the "Blend If" sliders **6**. ▼

7 Adding a "lighting" mask and a "grunge" mask. Putting your graphics layer in a Group, ▼ as Jolley often does, will give you a way to add a second layer mask: Shift-click the "Create a new group" button at the bottom of the Layers panel (this is the shortcut for the New Group from Layers command). Then target the new folder and add a mask by clicking the button at the bottom of the panel. Use a gradient mask to fade the bottom right corner of the sign: With Foreground and Background colors set to black and white in the Tools panel, click the black Foreground swatch and choose a medium gray instead; then choose the Gradient tool (Shift-G), choose Foreground to Background from the Gradient picker in the Options bar, position the cursor well inside the lower right corner and drag diagonally up for a short distance **7a**. ▼

Nesting this Group inside another one and adding a layer mask to the new outer folder gives you still another separate masking opportunity, which can be used to apply some "grunge" to the sign. With the first Group targeted, Shift-click the button again. Stored in an alpha channel in the **Apply Image-Before.psd** file is a photo from Jolley's texture collection. You can turn it into a mask for the new Group: In the Channels panel, Ctrl/⌘-click on the "Alpha 1" thumbnail to load the luminosity of the channel as a selection. In the Layers panel, target the new folder and click the button. To control how much this mask "erodes" the sign, use Image > Adjustments > Levels to adjust Input or Output Levels. With the "grunge" mask in place **7b**, you may want to brighten the sign; we increased Opacity to 80% to get the result on page 595.

FIND OUT MORE

▼ Using the "Blend If" sliders **page 66**

▼ Layer Groups **page 583**

▼ Masking with gradients **page 84**

Liquifying a Tattoo

YOU'LL FIND THE FILES

in (wow) > Wow Project Files > Chapter 9 >
Liquify a Tattoo:
- Tattoo-Before.psd (to start)
- Tattoo-After.psd (to compare)

OPEN THESE PANELS

(from the Window menu, for example):
- Tools • Layers

OVERVIEW

Add a line drawing in Multiply mode to
an image of a person • Use Free Transform
to scale the line drawing to fit • Duplicate
the layer to preserve the original drawing
and mask the copy to fit the model • Use
the Liquify filter to shape the tattoo to
the body, and save the mesh • Use Layer
Opacity and a Pattern Fill layer to help the
tattoo blend in more naturally

SOMETIMES THE PERFECT PHOTO YOU envision for an ad or an
editorial illustration comes with "some assembly required." To
embellish this model's back with a big, bold tattoo, the Liquify
filter is just the tool for creating some subtle, organic shaping.

Thinking the project through. Getting a line drawing to
fool the eye into seeing it as a tattoo is going to take more than
a simple warp effect with the Transform command. Using the
Liquify filter, we can shape the Liquify mesh to the body and let
the intricate drawing flow with the mesh. Multiply mode will
blend the "ink" with the skin. And if we make the tattoo appear
to extend to hidden areas, it won't look "stamped on."

1 Performing the initial fit between images. In **Tattoo-
Before.psd,** the dragon drawing has been dragged and dropped
into place over the model's back using the Move tool ▸⊕, ▾ and
the new layer has been given a descriptive
name for future reference. (To rename a
layer, double-click its name in the Layers
panel and type the new name.)

FIND OUT MORE
▾ Drag-and-drop in
tabbed documents
page 23

To drop out the white background and see just the black lines in
the drawing, put the tattoo layer in Multiply mode **1a**. To resize

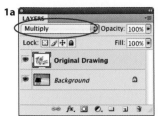

1a Putting the drawing layer in Multiply mode eliminates the white background.

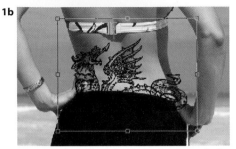

1b Using Free Transform to scale the drawing to fit the model with just a little bit of overlap

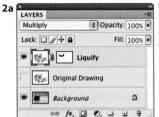

2a The drawing layer is duplicated, and the duplicate is masked.

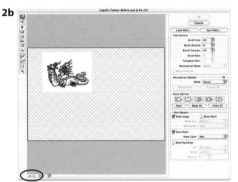

2b The default opening view in the Liquify dialog. Buttons in the lower left corner allow zooming.

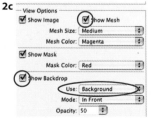

2c Liquify offers many options for viewing the area you're warping.

the drawing, press Ctrl/⌘-T for Free Transform. Holding down both the Shift and Alt/Option keys, drag on a corner handle to scale the drawing both proportionally and from the center until it extends only slightly beyond our model's torso **1b**. This way, when you use Liquify to mold the drawing to the body, the filter will have some extra drawing around the edges to pull from, so you won't get holes or gaps along the edges. Double-click in the Transform frame to complete the resizing.

2 Preparing to warp the tattoo. Now duplicate the tattoo graphics layer (Ctrl/⌘-J is a quick way), in order to preserve your original drawing in case you decide you want to change something later, such as the size or position of the dragon, and you want to start over from scratch; we renamed our new layer "Liquify." Turn off visibility for the original drawing layer. On the new layer, use the Lasso tool to quickly select the part of the drawing that extends beyond the model's back, including the area that overlaps her shorts, and Alt/Option click on the "Add layer mask" button at the bottom of the Layers panel to make a mask that hides the selected area **2a**. Use the Brush tool with a light feather and black paint to add her thumbs to the mask; use white paint to tidy any edges where the mask overlaps the torso. ▼

FIND OUT MORE
▼ Masking **page 61**

Make sure the duplicate drawing layer is still targeted and choose Filter > Liquify **2b**. You'll notice that the entire tattoo drawing shows in the Liquify dialog, as if there were no layer mask. By default, neither the Liquify mesh nor layers other than the active layer are visible. But since it's often easier to judge fine distortions by looking at the how the mesh is warped, turn on Show Mesh. Choose a mesh size and color that are easy to work with.

SETTING UP THE BACKDROP

The **Backdrop** in Liquify lets you see other layers in addition to the one you're Liquifying. You can choose to see one layer besides the layer you're Liquifying, *or* you can choose **All Layers** to view a composite of all visible layers in your file. If you choose **All Layers**, you also will see the layer you're Liquifying in its original state, which can make it difficult to clearly see the results of the warp you're creating. To "fool" Liquify into showing you all the layers you want to see, before you choose Filter > Liquify, turn off visibility for any layers you don't want to see in the Backdrop, including the layer you intend to Liquify, and make a merged copy of the remaining layers: Ctrl-Alt-Shift-E (Windows) or ⌘-Option-Shift-E (Mac). Then target the layer you want to Liquify, make it visible, and choose Filter > Liquify. In the Liquify dialog, choose your merged copy as your Backdrop. You'll see what you're Liquifying and a composite view of your layers.

3a

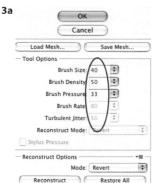

Tool Options and Reconstruct Options in the Liquify Filter dialog. Not all the Tool Options apply to every tool. The three shown here are available for the Forward Warp tool 🖉.

3b

Warping the mesh to fit the body

3c

Turning off the mesh for an unobstructed view of the warp effect

3d

Viewing the Mesh with **All Layers** chosen from the Use menu shows both the original state of the layer being Liquified, and the Liquify effect itself.

A fine mesh is good for intricate modeling to a detailed "terrain," while a large mesh works best for big features; we used Medium. In order to see what you're modeling the drawing to, click the Show Backdrop checkbox and turn on the layer (or layers) that contains your subject (see "Setting Up the Backdrop" on page 600); we turned on Background, and we left Opacity at the default 50% **2c**. But try different settings to see which you prefer; you can also change the settings as you work if you like.

3 Using Liquify for a subtle, organic effect. Make sure the Forward Warp tool 🖉 is selected. Since the area for the tattoo is only about 300 pixels wide and the drawing has a lot of detail, reduce the Brush Size so it will affect only a small section at a time (we chose 40 pixels), and reduce the Brush Pressure (we used 33) so each brush stroke will distort only a little **3a**. Brush Density "feathers" the amount of distortion the brush applies—more at the center than at the edge, with higher settings producing a more solid brush.

For a noncritical distortion like this one, it will be easy to use Forward Warp to push the pixels back and forth by small amounts. Try using the Bloat tool ✦ right around the thumbs, to emphasize the depression the thumbs make pressing against the skin. The Bloat tool will distort the image more the longer you keep the mouse button depressed, so use short "clicks" to just barely distort the tattoo. Keep working until you're happy with the result **3b**. It's easier to slowly *add* distortion than it is to *remove* just some of it if you go too far. Using the Freeze Mask tool 🖉 to paint a protective mask can help you control the effects of the warp tools (see "Mask = Freeze," below). Also, Liquify responds to Photoshop's Edit > Undo command (by default, Ctrl/⌘-Z) for a single undo, or Edit > Step Backward to undo multiple strokes (by default, Ctrl-Alt-Z on Windows or ⌘-Option-Z on the Mac). But if you find that you want to reduce the distortion in a way that freezing or stepping backwards won't accomplish, use the

---

MASK = FREEZE

The "Mask" functions in the Liquify window let you specify which parts of your image are "frozen" (protected from the effects of Liquify's tools), and which parts are "thawed" (exposed to the changes). You can create a mask while in the Liquify dialog by using the Freeze Mask tool 🖉, or by selecting an existing mask in the Mask Options section. Black parts of the mask protect, and white parts expose. You can alter the mask with the Freeze Mask and Thaw Mask 🖉 tools. (*By default, a layer mask has no effect within the Liquify filtering process.* But you *can* use it for freezing by choosing Layer Mask from any of the pop-up menus in the Mask Options section of the Liquify dialog box.)

3e

After Liquifying the dragon drawing. Note that the layer mask takes effect again when you leave the Liquify dialog.

4a

After reducing the Opacity of the tattoo layer

4b

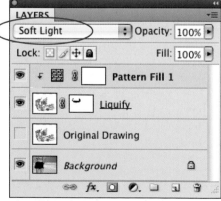

After adding a Pattern Fill layer to add a little "skin" texture, giving the tattoo that lived-in look.

Reconstruct tool ✎ with a low Brush Rate for the most "hands-on" control over local reconstruction. For overall change, rather than local corrections, you can use the Reconstruct Options: use the "Reconstruct" button to partially or fully restore the image; the Mode settings control the nature of the reconstruction. Or use the "Restore All" button to remove all warping. Especially if your distortion is complicated, you might want to freeze some areas you've warped before you attempt to reconstruct other areas that are nearby. For a last touch, turn off the mesh to view the warped image without any distraction **3c**. Turning on the All Layers view lets you compare "before" and "after" versions of the graphics **3d**. If you're now satisfied with the way it looks, click on the "Save Mesh" button. When the dialog opens, give the mesh a descriptive name, save it to the same folder as your image for easy retrieval, and click "Save." Click "OK" to apply the filter and return to the main document **3e**. This tattoo seems a little too dark and smooth. A couple of easy changes will blend it further with the model.

4 Adding final touches. First reduce the Opacity to taste (we chose 56%) **4a**. Now the tattoo doesn't seem quite so new, and it looks as if it's lightened naturally by the strong sunlight. To "wear" it even further, add a Pattern Fill layer by Alt/Option-clicking on the "Create new fill or adjustment layer" button ◑ at the bottom of the Layers panel. Choose Pattern from the menu, and from the dialog that opens, enable "Use Previous Layer to Create Clipping Mask." For Mode, choose Soft Light. We used the Wax Crayon on Vellum pattern from the Artist Surfaces set that ships with Photoshop, but any fine-grained grayscale texture will break up the solid outlines of the tattoo. Try different ones, if you like; then click "OK" to apply the pattern **4b**. 🖌

SAVED MESH — WHAT'S IT GOOD FOR?

When you've taken the time to create a Liquify mesh to fit one image to the surface of another — a dragon tattoo on a torso, for instance — be sure to save the mesh before you leave the Liquify dialog box. If you decide you want to make a few changes in the way the dragon fits, it's safer to go back to your original graphics (or a duplicate of the original layer), choose Filter > Liquify, and click the "Load Mesh" button to import the saved mesh. Then make your minor adjustments and click "OK." Starting over in this way, even for small adjustments, avoids the damage that can come from working and reworking the graphics.

If you want to switch to other graphics — swap the dragon for a butterfly, for instance — you can add a butterfly-graphics layer to your file, choose Filter > Liquify, and load the saved mesh. Instantly, the mesh molds the butterfly to the body, and then you can make any changes needed to adjust for the different graphic.

"Warping" Graphics to a Surface

YOU'LL FIND THE FILES

in [wow] Wow Project Files > Chapter 9 > Warping Graphics

- Warp Mug-Before.psd (to start)
- Warp Graphics files (to apply)
- Warp After files (to compare)

OPEN THIS PANEL

(from the Window menu, for instance):

- Layers

OVERVIEW

Draw a grid • Turn it into a Smart Object • Scale, position, warp, and blend it • Open the Smart Object file, add graphics, and save to update the main file • Duplicate the main file and fine-tune the copy

PHOTOSHOP'S WARP COMMAND CAN BE the perfect tool for applying artwork to the smoothly curving surfaces of something in a photo, like a bottle, a car, or a coffee mug, especially if you're working in Photoshop rather than Photoshop Extended with its 3D capabilities, or if you can't find a 3D model that fits your image. (For a method of graphics application using Extended's 3D functions, see "Exercising 3D Tools" on page 672.)

Thinking the project through. For top quality and efficiency, we'll use the Warp command and a Smart Object to mock up three mugs, and we can use blend modes and masks to reinforce the illusion. To also add the graphics to the mug's reflection, we'll use a copy of the Smart Object, so that replacing the graphics on the mug will also replace the graphics in the reflection. We can use one file to set up the warping and reflection but then "spin off" each individual mug design as a separate file to apply the finishing touches to that particular design.

1 Creating a Smart-Object grid. Open the file with the object you want to apply graphics to, or use the **Warp Mug-Before.psd** file **1a**. This mug is basically a cylinder, but slightly pinched in at

1a

The **Warp Mug-Before.psd** file

CORBIS ROYALTY FREE

1b

Choosing the Grid from the Tiles set in the Custom Shape picker

1c

Draw the Grid by Shift-dragging. To help make the Layers panel easier to interpret, we renamed the layer by double-clicking its name in the panel and typing "Artwork."

1d

Turning the Grid graphics into a Smart Object puts an identifying mark on its thumbnail in the Layers panel.

2a

Rotating, scaling, and positioning the Grid with the Edit > Free Transform command

the "waist." To get a good sense of the geometry of the warping and the size of the area where the graphics will be applied (the side facing us), start by fitting a reference grid element to the object: Choose the Custom Shape tool 🔾. At the left end of the Options bar, click the "Shape layers" button ▱. Click the tiny arrow to the right of the "Shape:" label in the Options bar to pop out the Custom Shape picker, and choose the Grid shape that comes with Photoshop **1b** (it's in the Tiles set available from the picker's ⊙ menu). To make a square Grid, begin dragging, then press the Shift key as you drag to make a square figure almost as tall as the mug **1c**.

Before you fit the Grid to the surface, turning it into a **Smart Object** ▽ will protect the graphics from deteriorating as you experiment with transforming them, and will also let you substitute different graphics for the grid without having to repeat the warping steps: In the Layers panel right-click/ Ctrl-click on the name of the Shape layer to open a menu **1d** where you can choose **Convert to Smart Object**.

FIND OUT MORE
▽ Smart Objects
page 18

2 Warping the Smart Object. To fit the Grid to your object (in this case the mug), choose Edit > Free Transform (Ctrl/⌘-T). Start with the big, general adjustments and move to the finer ones. For instance, for the mug, we'll first orient and scale the Grid, and then warp it to the cylindrical shape, then "pinch the waist," and finally fine-tune the warp.

To get the left side of the Grid into position **2a**, start by dragging inside the Transform frame to move the Grid. Drag outside a corner of the Transform frame (the cursor turns into a curved, double-headed arrow) to rotate the Grid to match the tilt of the object. If necessary, Shift-drag on a corner handle to adjust the size. To bend the Grid, switch from the Transform frame to the Warp mesh (right-click/Ctrl-click inside the Transform frame to open a menu where you can choose Warp **2b**, or click the "Switch between free transform and warp modes" button ⚟ in the Options bar).

The Warp mesh is anchored by control points at all four corners of the mesh. The two handles attached to each control point are designed to work as levers to bend the curve between these points and reshape the mesh. Feel free to make adjustments as you go, or come back and adjust later. The Smart Object will "collect" all the transformation info and apply it without degrading the image any more than if you had done it in a single Transform/Warp session.

2b

Switching from Transform to Warp, using the Transform frame's context-sensitive menu

2c

Moving the control points for the two right-side corners

2d

Using the horizontal handles for the corner points to curve the top and bottom edges of the mug

2e

"Pinching" the left and right sides by dragging the vertical handles for the corner points

Here's how we warped the mesh and Grid to the mug:

- Drag the two right-side control points into position where you want them on the mug **2c**.

- To make the top and bottom of the Grid follow the top and bottom curves of the mug **2d**, drag down on each of the two handles on the top line of the mesh (also drag the handles a little outward toward the side edges if needed). Then also drag down (and slightly outward) on each of the handles on the bottom line of the mesh.

- To "pinch the waist," drag inward just a little on the two handles on the left edge of the mesh. Then also drag inward on the two handles on the right edge **2e**.

- The middle "column" of the mesh is closest to us and the two side columns are receding as the surface of the mug curves away. Drag each of the top horizontal handles a little outward, so the center column becomes a little wider than the side columns. Repeat with the bottom horizontal handles.

- Since the middle "row" of the mesh is "pinched" away from us, make it slightly shorter than the top and bottom rows — on each side, drag the top handle down a little and the bottom handle up.

- At this point we dragged on the internal spaces and lines of the mesh to finalize the shaping **2f**. We wanted to keep the center column of squares aligned directly above one another (allowing for the tilt of the mug, of course).

When the mesh and Grid look about right to you, look at the Grid figure without control points and handles for a clearer view **2g**: Make the mesh invisible by choosing View > Extras or typing Ctrl/⌘-H (it's a toggle, and you may have to use it twice). When we did this, we decided the upper left corner needed to be moved a little to the left, which we could do by dragging the corner, even though the mesh was invisible.

When the Grid looks right, press the Enter key (or click the "Commit transform" button ✔ in the Options bar). The mesh will become an invisible template that will scale, orient, and warp any other graphics that you substitute in the Smart Object (coming up in step 5). But the Warp mesh will also remain live, so you can reactivate it later to adjust it if needed.

3 Blending the applied graphics into the surface. Now you can experiment with the blend mode and Opacity for the "Artwork" layer, to allow the character of the object's surface (noise, grain, texture, or lighting) to show through, making the artwork

2f After adjusting by dragging inside individual cells of the Warp mesh

The view of the mesh is turned off and a final adjustment is made to the upper left corner.

3

Changing the "Artwork" layer's blend mode to Overlay and reducing Opacity to 90% brings the glare onto the graphics, blending the Grid into the surface of the mug.

4a

The Smart Object is duplicated, and the copy is flipped vertically; we renamed the new layer "Reflection."

4b

The duplicate Grid is dragged downward

look like it's part of the surface finish rather than "pasted on" **3**. We used Overlay mode and reduced the Opacity to 90%.

4 Adding a reflection. To extend the illusion that the artwork is printed on the mug, we can also add the artwork to the mug's reflection. If we make the reflection from a duplicate of the Smart Object, then the reflection will change automatically when we change the main graphics for the mug. To add the reflection, duplicate the Smart Object layer (Ctrl/⌘-J); rename the new layer if you like; we called it "Reflection." Flip the layer vertically (Edit > Transform > Flip Vertical) **4a**. Then reorient the reflected copy by dragging it down **4b** and rotating it. Adjust the mesh to reshape at least the visible part of the Grid reflection **4c**.

To hide the reflected Grid where the spoon handle blocks our view of it, add a layer mask: Click the "Add a layer mask" button 🔲 at the bottom of the Layers panel. To mask the handle, we painted the mask with the Brush tool 🖌 and black paint (press X if necessary to make black the Foreground color) using a round brush tip with Hardness set to 50% and Opacity at 100% in the Options bar. ▼ For less contrast in the reflection, we put the "Reflection" layer in Soft Light mode and reduced its Opacity **4d**.

> **FIND OUT MORE**
> ▼ Painting layer masks **page 84**

5 Substituting graphics in the Smart Object. We can now experiment with substituting graphics for the Grid. In the Layers panel, double-click on the thumbnail for either copy of the Smart Object ("Artwork" or "Reflection") to open the Smart Object

4c

The warping is changed to match the mug's reflection. Pressing Ctrl-Alt-hyphen (Windows) or ⌘-Option-hyphen (Mac) shrinks the window so you can reach parts of the mesh that extend below the bottom of the image.

4d

A layer mask is added to the "Reflection" layer to bring the spoon handle in front of the reflection. The blend mode for the layer is changed to Soft Light, and the Opacity is reduced to 40%.

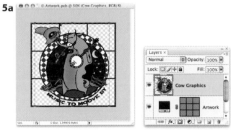

5a

The Cow Graphics imported into the Artwork.psb file and scaled. Viewing the Grid at the same time helps with positioning the graphics.

5b

The .psb file, with the new graphics scaled and Grid visibility turned off, is ready to Save.

5c

After you save the .psb file, clicking in the working window of the main file automatically replaces the Grid with the Cow Graphics in both copies of the Smart Object layer.

6

Duplicating the developing mug file before fine-tuning the Cow Graphics design

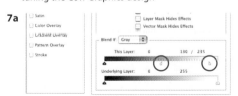

7a

Using the white point slider for "This Layer" to "drop out" the white from the "Artwork" layer in the Warp Cow file. The same change is applied to the "Reflection" layer.

"subfile" (**Artwork.psb**). Then add graphics; we opened the first of the three files of artwork for the mug — **Cow Graphics.psd**. Use the Move tool ▸⊕ to drag the artwork into the .psb file **5a** (if you're working in tabbed view, see page 23 for drag-and-drop instructions). As long as you scale the artwork (Ctrl/⌘-T and Shift-drag a corner) to fit entirely within the "canvas" that the Grid element has established, the graphics won't be cropped when applied to the mug.

With the new art in place in the .psb file, turn off visibility for the Grid layer by clicking its ● icon in the Layers panel **5b**, and save the .psb file (Ctrl/⌘-S). Then simply click in the working window of the main file. The new artwork will replace the Grid — automatically warped to fit both the mug and the reflection **5c**.

6 "Spinning off" a separate file. The fine-tuning needed for the "Cow Graphics" is likely to be different than what's needed for the "Horses" photo or the "Indifferent" graphics. So it makes sense to save a copy of the "Cow Graphics" version of the file separately to do the final tweaking that may not apply to the other designs. A quick, safe way to "spin off" a version of the file — keeping the Smart Object layers live — is to copy the file (Image > Duplicate, *without choosing Duplicate Merged Layers Only*) **6**; we named the file "Warp Cow."

7 Fine-tuning the applied graphics. In the Warp Cow file, we can see that the white in the artwork is too bright for the shading on the mug. To make it look like the white in the artwork has simply been left unprinted so the surface of the mug shows through, try this: With the "Artwork" Smart Object targeted in the Layers panel, choose Blending Options from the panel's ▾≡ menu. At the bottom of the dialog box in the "Blend If" section **7a**, move the white-point slider for "This Layer" a little to the left, until the white in the checkered pattern and in the banjo disappears except at the edges of the white areas; we stopped at a setting of 235, which told Photoshop that any pixels in this layer lighter than 235 (bright white is 255) should be blocked from contributing to the image. Then hold down the Alt/Option key and drag farther left on the left half of the white point slider to remove the white fringe; we used a setting of 130. Splitting the slider allows a partial contribution from pixels that are light but not bright white, such as the antialiasing at the edges of the whites, for a smooth (rather than abrupt) transition. To remove white from the "Reflection" layer, repeat the "Blend If" adjustment on that layer **7b**. These adjustments have made the light colors in the graphics paler than we'd like, but we can address that next.

7b

The lightest tones in the "Artwork" and "Reflection" layers are dropped out with "Blend If," to allow the "white" of the mug to show through.

8a

To change the colorful background but not the neutral mug, a Hue/Saturation Adjustment layer is applied in Hue mode.

8b

Moving the Hue slider to recolor the abstract background

8c   **8d**

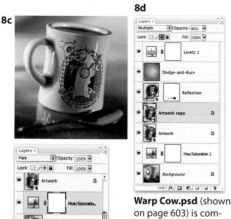

The recolored background

Warp Cow.psd (shown on page 603) is completed with a duplicate "Artwork" layer in Multiply mode, a dodge-and-burn layer, and a Levels Adjustment.

8 Finishing the first mug file. To complete the mock-up, we can change the background color to pick up color in the graphics. We can also restore color density that suffered when we dropped out the white, and we can light up the graphics a bit where they're in the shadows. To change the background color, we used a Hue/Saturation Adjustment layer in Hue mode because it would change the colorful background without affecting the grays of the mug (neutral colors aren't affected by adjustments in Hue mode). ▼ In the Layers panel, Alt/Option-click the "Create new fill or adjustment layer" button ⊘ and choose Hue/Saturation. (In CS4 an alternate approach is to Alt/Option-click the ▬ button in the Adjustments panel.) When the New Layer dialog box opens, choose Hue for the Mode **8a** and click "OK." In the Hue/Saturation dialog box **8b**, move the Hue slider to the right (we stopped at +158) to change the background from green to blue; click "OK" **8c**.

To build up the graphics on the mug, we first targeted the "Artwork" layer and duplicated it. We put the duplicate layer in Multiply mode and reduced its Opacity to 40%.

We added a gray-filled "dodge-and-burn" layer in Overlay mode by Alt/Option-clicking the "Create a new layer" button ⊡ at the bottom of the Layers panel, choosing Overlay mode in the New Layer dialog, checking the "Fill with Overlay-Neutral Color (50% gray)" box, and clicking "OK." Where we wanted more light, we painted the new layer loosely with the Brush tool ✐ with a large soft brush tip and white paint (pressing D then X makes white the Foreground color), with a low Opacity set in the Options bar; for deeper shading around the edges we used black paint. ▼ To improve contrast and complete the mock-up shown on page 603, we clicked the ⊘ button at the bottom of the Layers panel, chose Levels, and clicked "Auto" in the Levels dialog **8d**. ▼

When you've applied the final touches, save the file (File > Save As) in Photoshop format; its own Smart Object "subfile" (.psb) will be saved as part of the file. If in the future you want to make changes to the warping, blending, or tone and color, or even the Smart Object graphics, you can do so without affecting your original working file (the developing **Warp Mug-Before.psd** in this case). If you want to change the graphics, clicking on one of the Smart Object layers in the **Warp Cow.psd** file will open the Smart Object file with the Grid and Cow Graphics layers.

9 Using a photo for the second mug.
To apply a photo, go back to your main

FIND OUT MORE

▼ Using blend modes
page 181

▼ Making a dodge & burn layer **page 339**

▼ Using Auto Levels
page 247

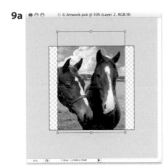
9a

The photo from **Horses.psd** is dragged into the .psb file and scaled. In scaling and positioning the photo, we allowed some of the image to extend beyond the top and bottom edges of the Grid; this would crop the photo when it was automatically applied to the mug.

9b

Saving the .psb file automatically applies the photo to the mug in the developing .psd file.

9c

Stretching the photo sideways in the Warp Horses file to fill more of the available space. The stretching becomes part of the "single" transformation stored in the Smart Object layer.

9d

Tinting the mug and background with the Colorize function in a Hue/Saturation Adjustment layer

working file as you left it after step 5 (in this example, it's the developing **Warp Mug-Before.psd** file). In the Layers panel, double-click the thumbnail for the "Artwork" or "Reflection" layer; either will open the Artwork.psb file. Open the file that holds the photo you want to apply; we used **Horses.psd**. Drag the photo into the .psb file and scale it (Ctrl/⌘-T) **9a**. Turn off visibility for all layers except the photo, and save the .psb file (Ctrl/⌘-S); then click in the working window of the developing **Warp Mug-Before.psd** file to see the photo on the mug and in the reflection **9b**.

Duplicate the **Warp Mug-Before.psd** file (as in step 6; Image > Duplicate); we named our duplicate file "Warp Horses." To fine-tune this mug design:

- With the photo in place on the mug, we wanted to widen it to fill more of the surface. We could stretch the photo by typing Ctrl/⌘-T (for Edit > Free Transform) and dragging the right-side middle handle outward **9c**. (This is an example of fine-tuning that's better done in a "spun-off" file; it will change the Horses image, which can be stretched slightly without looking distorted, without changing the fit of the Cow Graphics.) We stretched the "Reflection" layer also.

- We simulated applying the photo to a tan mug by tinting the background image with a Hue/Saturation layer in Normal mode with Colorize turned on **9d**.

- We liked the result we got for blending the photo into the mug surface when we changed the blend mode for the Horses layer to Soft Light and restored the Opacity to 100%, then duplicated this layer (Ctrl/⌘-J) and put the copy in Multiply mode at 40% Opacity **9e**. We left the white parts opaque as if white had been "printed" onto the mug.

- We added a Levels Adjustment layer as in step 8, but not a dodge-and-burn layer; the result is shown on page 603.

10 Making the "Indifferent" mug. We went back to the developing **Warp Mug-Before.psd** file from step 5 and double-clicked the "Artwork" layer to open the .psb file. We brought in the converted type from the **Indifferent.psd** file **10a** by dragging the entire group ⬚ from its Layers panel into the working window of the .psb file (in tabbed view, drag from the document window; see page 23). Scaling it to fit the Grid, we purposely let the "t" in "Different" extend a little beyond the right edge so it would appear to curve out of sight around the mug **10b**. Once again, saving the .psb file and clicking in the working window of the main file updated the composite image.

9e

Two layers — in Soft Light and Multiply modes — are used to blend the photo with the "colorized" mug.

We spun off the third version of the file (File > Save As), naming it "Warp-Indifferent." Targeting the "Artwork" layer, we used the Move tool ➤⊕ to reposition the graphics, and adjusted the layer's Opacity (85%). To reinforce the subject matter in this illustration, we added a Hue/Saturation Adjustment layer above the photo layer and reduced Saturation to dull the background. We left the face of the mug in shadows, but added a Levels Adjustment layer at the top of the stack and clicked "Auto" to improve contrast; the result is shown at the top of page 603. *WOW*

10b

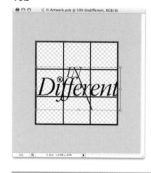

Positioning the graphics in the **Artwork.psb** file so the type would appear to curve out of sight

10a

To build **Indifferent.psd** we set, tracked, and kerned two layers of type ("IN" in red and "Different" in black), and converted them to Shape layers (Layer > Type > Convert to Shape). ▼ The "not" symbol (from Photoshop's Symbols set of presets) was added with the Custom Shape tool ✿; the blend mode for this Shape layer was changed to Color Burn so the slash would disappear where it crossed the black dot, seeming to cross behind it. All three parts of the design were targeted by clicking and Shift-clicking their thumbnails in the Layers panel and were collected in a group by choosing New Group from Layers from the panel's ▼☰ menu.

FIND OUT MORE

▼ Working with type **page 436**

APPLYING LABELS TO GLASS

To mock up a label on a glass container, you can add details that make the transparency of the glass more photorealistic:

- Using two layers, construct a label with a solid-filled label shape in one layer and another layer above it with the type. Reduce the Opacity of the label shape layer until you get the translucent effect you want, with the image below showing through. Then with the type layer targeted in the Layers panel, merge it with the layer below (Ctrl/⌘-E), combining the partial transparency of the label shape and the full opacity of the type.

- If there's something inside the container, a drop shadow on the contents adds to the illusion: Click the "Add a layer style" button *fx* at the bottom of the Layers panel and choose Drop Shadow from the pop-out list. In the Drop Shadow section of the Layer Style dialog box, click the color swatch and sample a shadow color from the image. Choose the Opacity, Spread (density), and Size (softness) to match the light in your photo; experiment with Distance and Angle by dragging in the image to move the shadow, creating the appropriate physical space between the label and the material it falls on.

The label was made with type in one layer and a label shape in a 70%-opaque layer below (left). The two were merged, the merged layer was warped, and a Drop Shadow was added.

Warp-Extra.psd

Reflections

REFLECTIONS can lend serenity or elegance to a scene. Simulated in Photoshop, reflections can also make a composed image more photorealistic and three-dimensional by integrating the subject into its environment. Here are three approaches to "capturing" reflections.

Rod and Robin Deutschmann are distilling the camera artistry they teach in their classes into a series of books on "absolutely Photoshop-free" creative techniques for digital photographers. *Off-Camera Flash* is the first in the series.

Real: One way to capture a gorgeous and convincing reflection is to hike 20 miles in and 10,000 feet up, sit down, point your camera, and take the shot.

This method registers a high serenity factor.

Photoshop: Another approach is to duplicate and flip an image of your subject, hiding part of the flipped copy with a layer mask, as described in "'Warping' Graphics to a Surface" on page 603.

The layer mask hides the part of the "reflection" where the spoon would cover it up. The layer mask is unlinked from the reflection so the reflection can be moved without moving the mask out of position.

"Real": A third way is to carry your lake, ocean, or mist in your pocket in the form of a mirror. Rod Deutschmann teaches this third approach. Used with or without a polarizing filter, a mirror — flat, with no bevels at the edges — is held perpendicular to the lens. With a digital camera it's easy to preview the image in the LCD screen as you tilt the camera and the mirror to get the composition you want.

The first step is to find the image in the broader scene.

With a friend supplying the third hand to hold the polarizer, Deutschmann worked out the right combination for the camera, polarizer, and mirror positions, previewing the shot on his LCD screen.

A structure takes on a new geometry.

Deutschmann chose the tops of the palms.

The image with reflections. To create the slight "motion blur" in the "water," Deutschmann had used a citrus-based cleaner to partially remove the silver from some areas of the back of the mirror.

Mirror work enhances the St. Louis skyline.

Vanishing Point

Photoshop's Vanishing Point "megafilter" allows you to paste, paint, and clone in perspective. Once you create a perspective grid to work on, the grid stays with the file, so you can work back and forth between Vanishing Point and Photoshop, returning to the grid when you need it.

This project demonstrates the basics of Vanishing Point. We'll set up grids, paste a new sign in place, repaint an existing strip of wood trim and extend it to another wall, remove the alarm bell, perform a variety of clean-up operations, and paint a sign "around a corner" to produce the composite below.

Vanishing Point can be run on empty layers, so you can protect the rest of your file from changes and keep your Vanishing Point edits separate and available for further changes in Photoshop. Vanishing Point also allows for multiple undo's (type Ctrl/⌘-Z to step backwards through your edits).

As you work, it's a good idea to make changes on separate layers and name your layers according to their content (to rename a layer, double-click its name in the Layers panel and type the new name).

YOU'LL FIND THE FILES in 🌟 > Wow Project Files > Chapter 9 > Exercising Vanishing Point

🌟 **VP-After.psd**

1 Assemble the Components

A

B

🌟 **VP-Before.psd
Sunrise Bakery.psd**

GRAPHICS: DONAL JOLLEY

C

OPEN THE **VP-BEFORE.PSD** and **Sunrise Bakery.psd** files. You'll see that we've done some advance preparation to the **VP-Before.psd** file **A**. We removed the existing logo to create a blank signboard. We also isolated the green leaves in front of the sign by making a Rectangular Marquee selection of the area where the plants appear in front of the sign, and then running the Select > Color Range command on the selected area; we copied the selected leaves from the *Background* to a new layer (Ctrl/⌘-J) **B**. Now all of our Vanishing Point changes can be made on other layers that we'll add between the two. In the Layers panel we can turn visibility for the "Plants" layer off and on as needed by clicking its 👁 icon.

The new sign graphics were designed in Adobe Illustrator to fit the estimated measurements of the actual sign space so we wouldn't have to stretch the artwork out of proportion to fit it onto the signboard. The file was saved in EPS format and opened in Photoshop at the same resolution as the photo (225 ppi) and close to the size of the sign in the image (almost 3 inches by a little over 1 inch) **C**. That way, when we copied and pasted it into the image in Vanishing Point, it would come in at a size that would be easy to manage.

2 Establish the Perspective Plane

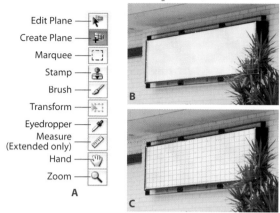

Edit Plane
Create Plane
Marquee
Stamp
Brush
Transform
Eyedropper
Measure
(Extended only)
Hand
Zoom

A

B

C

IN **VP-BEFORE.PSD** open the Vanishing Point interface (Filter > Vanishing Point). Everything that happens in Vanishing Point begins with a grid you draw, called the *perspective plane*. The image-altering tools **A** automatically change the proportions of any editing you do to match this perspective. To create a grid, start by placing an anchor on each of four corners of something that you believe is rectangular and represents the image perspective, such as a door or window, or the signboard in our image. Then adjust the corner positions as needed. Before you begin to place the points, read "Grid Gymnastics" at the right for some insight into the process.

Success depends on drawing and adjusting the grid. As you use the **Create Plane tool** to place the corner anchor points, holding down the **X key temporarily zooms** in so you can see more precisely (the X shortcut also works when the other Vanishing Point tools are active). As soon as you place the fourth point and release the cursor, you'll see a red, yellow **B**, or blue grid **C**. Although you can use the tools on red or yellow, the color warns you that Vanishing Point might not accurately scale and proportion elements on it; a **blue grid** is what you're aiming for. Setting the fourth anchor automatically chooses the **Edit Plane tool**, and you can move the anchors to adjust the grid. In **VPoint-Before.psd**, we could see that the sign wasn't badly distorted by perspective, so we chose and then edited the position for the fourth point to generate a grid whose cells weren't very distorted from square (the blue grid shown here). To make it easier to see how elements in your image relate to the Vanishing Point perspective plane, you can change the **Grid size** (at the top of the Vanishing Point interface) and use the Edit Plane tool to **align the grid** by dragging on a grid line. With the grid established, click "OK" to return to the main Photoshop interface.

If we were to create a Vanishing Point perspective plane on a surface that was facing us directly, it would consist of square cells **A**.

The more skewed the surface is, the more pronounced the perspective distortion is, and the more distorted the squares become. For instance, with a wall that instead of facing us is sharply angled, the cells are distorted into tall skewed rectangles as the grid is foreshortened **B**.

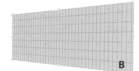

A

B

As shown below, when you create a perspective plane in Vanishing Point, a very small difference in the placement of a single point can make a big difference in the grid and in the results you get when you use it.

Placing the four anchors precisely on the corners of your rectangular element is less important than making sure they generate a grid that makes sense for the image, even if this involves some creative tweaking of the anchor positions. Some reasons that you and Vanishing Point might generate a grid that needs tweaking in order to work right are:

- Despite your best efforts, you may have positioned one of your points a little off the exact corner of your rectangular element.

- The "rectangle" you're using might actually have been not-quite-rectangular in real life.

- The camera lens may have caused distortion.

- Any combination of the above factors could be at work.

3 Paste in Perspective

To bring in the new sign, in the **Sunrise Bakery.psd** file, select the entire sign graphic (Ctrl/⌘-A) and copy it to the clipboard (Ctrl/⌘-C). In the **VP-Before.psd** file, target the *Background* by clicking its thumbnail in the Layers panel, and then add a new layer above it (Ctrl/⌘-Shift-N). This layer will hold the sign when you paste it into the file in Vanishing Point.

With the new layer active, reopen Vanishing Point (Ctrl-Alt-V on Windows; ⌘-Option-V on the Mac) and paste the copied sign graphics (Ctrl/⌘-V). The pasted element will appear in the upper left corner **A** and Vanishing Point's Marquee tool will be active. Drag inside the pasted element to move it into the plane — its perspective will change to match **B**. *Note:* If your grid is different from ours, you'll get a different result than you see here. You can tweak the pasted sign (see "'Cheating' a Little" at the right) and expect that your results from here on might be slightly different from ours. Or you can open the **VP-with grid.psd** file, open Vanishing Point, paste the sign graphics, and follow along from there.

Now choose Vanishing Point's Transform tool to adjust the pasted and moved logo graphics. As with Photoshop's Transform function, Shift-dragging inward on a corner handle of the Transform box will shrink the logo proportionally. Putting the cursor inside the Transform box and dragging will reposition the logo. We reduced the graphics just enough so they weren't taller than the sign space (see the "Crop or No Crop" tip at the right), and we moved them until we had a balance of white space on the two sides of the graphics **C**. With the sign completed, go on to step 4 without leaving Vanishing Point.

"CHEATING" A LITTLE

If you need to, in many cases you can tweak the proportions of a pasted element slightly without the distortion being obvious. Drag a side, top, or bottom midpoint handle to scale horizontally or vertically. Add the Alt/Option key to make the resizing happen evenly around the center.

If you have to cheat *a lot* to get the pasted element to fit the way you think it should, you might want to redraw the grid.

CROP OR NO CROP

With the Clip Operations to Surface Edges option turned on (the default) in Vanishing Point's menu ⊙, when you paste something into the Vanishing Point dialog and drag it onto a plane, the pasted element will appear cropped within the plane. You may have to drag the pasted element around a bit to find the handles needed for scaling the pasted element to fit.

An alternative is to turn off Clip Operations to Surface Edges. In that case, when you paste an element and drag it onto a plane, the entire pasted element will show. It won't appear cropped, and it will be easier to scale because none of the handles will be hidden. But the pasted element may then hide the edges of the plane.

A rule of thumb might be to keep Clip Operations turned on if you're pasting a "solid" element, and just deal with the inconvenience of the "disappearing" handles. But if you're pasting type or graphics that have a transparent background and thus won't hide the plane from view, turn "Clip Operations" off.

Clip Operations "On"

Clip Operations "Off"

4 Expand the Perspective Plane

ONCE YOU'VE CREATED THE PERSPECTIVE PLANE in Vanishing Point (as you did in step 2), you can use the Edit Plane tool 📐 at any time to adjust or expand it. Editing the plane doesn't change the perspective of any changes you've already made, only those that you make afterwards.

In our image the perspective for the sign is probably just slightly different from the perspective of the wall it's on and from that of the wall on the left side, which is set farther back. But the perspectives are close enough so that we can probably use the same grid for all three surfaces rather than make separate but overlapping grids, which can be a little harder to manage than a single one.

To expand the plane to cover the wall surfaces, drag each midpoint handle outward. To zoom out to see the entire image, type Ctrl/⌘ 0 (that's zero); to zoom in increments, use Ctrl/⌘-hyphen to zoom out and Ctrl/⌘-+ to zoom in. Expand the grid beyond the edges of the image in order to be able to make selections beyond the edges.

With your grid established and expanded as shown above, click "OK" to leave Vanishing Point. In Photoshop proper, set up a new empty layer for painting the strip of wood trim (Ctrl/⌘-N). Then go back into Vanishing Point (Ctrl-Alt-V or ⌘-Option-V).

5 Brush To Paint

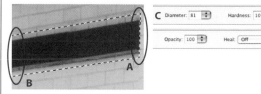

WHEN YOU PAINT, if you need to keep the paint from spilling over an edge like the one at the right side of our blue strip of wood trim, it's easiest to first make a selection with Vanishing Point's **Marquee** tool 🔲 to limit the paint; we used the default Feather setting (1 pixel). The Marquee can leave pixels at the edge of the image partly unselected if you don't select a bit beyond the document bounds. If you're already zoomed in and can't select beyond the document bounds (the left edge in this case), marquee more on the opposite side than you want, then place the cursor inside the selection, and drag until the edge of the selection boundary lines up with the edge you want to preserve **A**. The other end of the marquee will "disappear" into the document edge **B**, indicating that the selection now extends beyond the edge.

Setting the color for the Brush tool 🖌 to use for painting works a little differently in Vanishing Point than in Photoshop proper. If you want to sample a color to use with Vanishing Point's Brush, you do it *before* choosing the Brush tool. Choose the **Eyedropper** 💧 and click on the red in the word "Bakery." Then choose the **Brush** 🖌. To completely cover the blue, use **Heal:Off** and leave Hardness set at 100% **C**. Put the cursor at the point where you want to begin to paint, and set the Diameter — use the left and right bracket keys ([and]) and watch the footprint "preview" to get close to the size you need. (For finer adjustment, scrub over the word "Diameter" or drag-select the number and change it.) We started at the left end of the wood trim with the Diameter set at 81 (your diameter may be different, depending on your grid). The brush will automatically adjust its size to match the perspective plane as you paint. Click where you want to start painting **D**, and Shift-click at the other end (the Shift key constrains the Brush to straight lines) **E**, **F**. Type Ctrl/⌘-H to turn off "Show Edges," hiding the selection marquee so you can see the right edge. If you need to try again, type Ctrl/⌘-Z to step backwards.

Vanishing Point's **Marquee**, **Stamp**, and **Brush** tools, when you operate them in **Heal:Off** mode, will copy, clone, or paint much the same as the tools with the same names in Photoshop proper. But they can also operate in two other modes — **Heal:On** and **Heal: Luminance**. With these options, Vanishing Point's Marquee operates as a combination Marquee and Patch tool, the Stamp as Stamp plus Healing Brush, and the Brush as Brush plus Spot Healing Brush.

The **Brush** tool 🖌 paints. In **Heal:Off** mode it paints with the chosen color, covering up whatever is below it. In **Heal:Luminance** mode, the brush paints with the chosen color, but it uses the luminance of the area it covers (the brush footprint "preview" is also shown here). In **Heal:On** mode, the brush ignores the chosen color and instead samples color and luminance from the area you're painting.

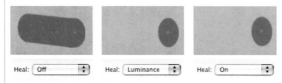

In **Heal:Off** mode the **Marquee** ⬚ (shown below) and **Stamp** ♣ cover the image by cloning the source you designate. The Opacity and the amount of Feather (Marquee) or Hardness (Stamp) control how completely the image is covered. With **Heal:Off** the Marquee and Stamp copy the selected material (here a part of the brick wall) to hide the area you copy into. With **Heal:Luminance** checked, these tools preserve the luminance of the area you copy into. With **Heal:On**, they use the source area for the details, but blend it with the color *and* the luminance of the area you copy into.

While the Stamp tool requires you to set a source first, the Marquee tool has two **Move Modes** — Destination and Source. We find it easiest to leave the Move Mode set to Destination and use helper keys to change the mode of operation — Ctrl/⌘-drag to copy material from outside *into* the selection, or Alt/Option-drag to copy the selected area to another place in the image.

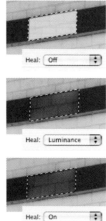

6 Marquee to Copy

THE NEXT STEP is to copy the red strip to the right-hand side of the wall and also add a bit to the left side by the sign. If you turned off "Show Edges" in step 5, turn it back on now (Ctrl/⌘-H). Starting with the copy for the far right, and using the default settings for the **Marquee** tool ⬚ (Feather 1, Opacity 100, Heal:Off), select most of the strip on the left, including the shadowed bottom edge. Then hold down the Alt/Option key (to make a copy) and begin dragging to the right (to move the copy). As you drag, also depress the Shift key (to keep the copy aligned with the original strip). The strip will grow proportionally larger as you move the copy along the wall **A**. You'll cover part of the alarm, but that's fine because we'll be removing it anyway. Align the left edge of the copied strip with the sign (use Ctrl/⌘-H to check), and release the mouse and keys to "commit" the copy — but don't deselect it yet.

To extend the strip, rather than copy again (which might leave a mark where the copies join), you can stretch your copy, since there isn't any texture or detail to worry about. With the copy still selected, choose the Transform tool ⛶, grab the midpoint anchor on the right side, and drag just beyond the right edge **B** (zoom out with Ctrl/⌘-hyphen if necessary to get beyond the edge).

To copy the original red strip into the area just to the left of the sign, use the Marquee tool ⬚: Drag with the Marquee around the small area you want to replace, offsetting this selection just a little upward to hint that the two sections of the wall are separate, and including enough room in the selection marquee for the shaded bottom edge of the strip. Then Ctrl/⌘-drag into the original strip to clone into the selection **C**. If necessary, type Ctrl/⌘-H and use the Transform tool ⛶ to adjust **D**. With the red strips completed, click "OK" **E**.

7 Stamp to Remove an Object

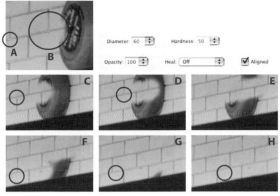

BACK IN PHOTOSHOP, add another new empty layer and reopen Vanishing Point. To remove the alarm bell, we'll cover it with bricks. The Marquee tool would seem to be a natural for copying bricks from another area. However, the only area large enough to fill a selection that will cover the alarm is brighter than the bricks near the alarm, and because the alarm is very dark, neither Heal:Luminance nor Heal:On will work.

Instead, to match the bricks around the bell, choose the **Stamp** tool, hold down the Alt/Option key, and line up the crosshairs with an intersection of a vertical and a horizontal mortar line in the bricks just to the left of the alarm **A**; this way you'll avoid the lighter bricks to the right and the shadow near the edge of the sign.

Because you can't get a footprint "preview" of the Stamp's "loaded" brush tip **B** until you Alt/Option-click on your source point, it's easier to size the brush after setting the source. Set the Size to cover an area large enough to make it easy to line it up with the existing bricks, but small enough so that you don't pick up any of the alarm bell; we used a Diameter of 60. We also chose a soft brush (Hardness 50%), which would make it easy to see how the cloned bricks were blending with the original, and would prevent any telltale hard edges; and we chose Aligned to automatically resample as we moved the cursor along.

Once the Stamp is loaded, move the cursor to the right to the next "mortar intersection" and click. A few more clicks to the right **C**, **D**, **E** will cover the middle of the alarm. Because you started sampling at the left, working left-to-right should ensure a "clean" dab source each time you click. Then you can repeat the left-to-right process for the top and for the bottom **F**, **G**, **H**. If you get some smudges nevertheless, you can even out the tone by setting a new source to the right and cloning back over the "smudgier" areas. Then click "OK" and return to Photoshop.

8 Marquee & Stamp To Cover Up

TO REMOVE THE MARKET BASKET, add another layer and open Vanishing Point. Since we have several straight edges to work with (the document edge on the left, the edge of the sign's wall on the right, and the top of the planter wall at the bottom), we decided the Marquee tool might be a quick way to start the cover-up. We could then use the Stamp for details if necessary.

With the **Marquee**, select the area you want to replace, extending the selection outside the document to make sure all edge pixels are included **A**. To copy from another area into your selection, hold down the Ctrl/⌘ key while dragging the cursor to the bushes you want to use to replace the basket; adding the Shift key as you drag will constrain the move to follow the perspective grid, which will make it easier to keep the planter edge lined up. When you like the way the basket is covered in the "preview," release the mouse to set the "clone" **B**. If you want to undo and try again, you need to also step backwards (Ctrl/⌘-Z) an extra time, until Move Mode is no longer grayed out. When you've finished, type Ctrl/⌘-D to deselect.

The Stamp tool works well to clone small areas over the hard edges or over repeating elements that are a dead giveaway that we've been cloning. Select the Stamp, Alt/Option-click to "load" it, and click to add new bits and pieces of shrubbery and bricks, "reloading" as needed; use a small, hard-edged brush tip to clone the bush where it meets the bricks, and a larger, softer brush to tidy up any areas within the bush or bricks that look cloned and unnatural **C**. If needed, use Ctrl/⌘-Z and try new options until you're comfortable that your cover-up of the basket no longer looks fake. When you've finished, click "OK."

9 Cleanup

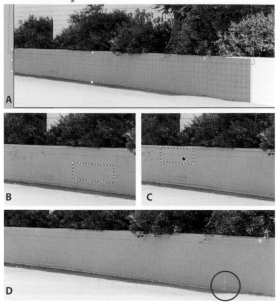

AGAIN ADD AN EMPTY LAYER and reopen the filter dialog. The planter wall is marred, but the **Marquee** tool ⬚ will make quick work of cleaning up large spaces, as you can select and drag clean areas over marred ones. Any textures will automatically be scaled to fit the perspective.

If you use the Edit Plane 🛠 tool to drag the bottom middle handle of the grid down, you can see that the original grid doesn't fit the perspective of the planter wall. For the kind of clean-up we want to do here (a blank wall with some texture), the existing grid would probably work anyway. But since, in general, this situation might call for a new plane, let's create one for the planter wall; use the Create Plane tool 📐 to set the anchors and the Edit Plane tool to adjust the grid **A** (as in step 2).

To remove the marks from the wall without losing the luminosity and color of the original, we used the **Marquee** ⬚ with **Heal:On**, selecting a clean area **B** and then Alt/Option-dragging repeatedly to cover up the worst of the marks in other areas **C**. After deselecting (Ctrl/⌘-D) we used the **Stamp** tool 🖈 with a soft tip, small size, and 60% Opacity with **Heal:On** to work at the bottom of the wall without allowing the nearby shadow on the sidewalk to darken our repairs **D**. When the touch-up is finished, click "OK."

"REDO"

In Vanishing Point, if you undo a change and then decide you want it back, press **Ctrl-Shift-Z** (Windows) or **⌘-Shift-Z** (Mac) to undo the undo.

10 Turn a Corner in Perspective

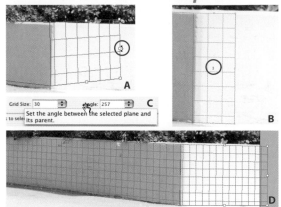

IN ORDER TO "PAINT" OUR SIGN on the planter's wall so that it wraps around the corner, we'll take advantage of a big change to Vanishing Point that came with version CS3 — the ability to get a grid to "turn the corner" at any angle you need, not just 90°, and to wrap a pasted element around a corner. Here we'll create grids for the small bevel at the corner of the low wall, and for the part of this wall on the right.

The method for adding a grid at any angle you like is to add it at a 90° angle and then operate it like a hinged door, "opening" or "closing" it to the angle you want. To add a new grid, hold down the Ctrl/⌘ key and use the Edit Plane 🛠 tool to drag the right-hand middle handle of the existing plane to the right. This generates a new plane at a right angle **A**. To get the new section of the grid to match the actual angle in the photo, on the new grid you just generated, hold down the Alt/Option key while hovering over the center handle of the edge away from the "hinge" where the two grids meet. When your cursor turns into a curved, double-headed arrow ⟲ to show rotation, click and drag up or down until the grid is aligned with the edges of the bevel at the corner of the wall **B**; when you have a match, let go. Now move the right side handle to the left to narrow the grid to the bevel.

Next make a grid for the brightly lit part of the wall: Ctrl/⌘-drag the right middle handle of the narrow bevel grid, and then adjust the grid's angle as you did for the narrow bevel. Or, if you prefer, you can drag the grid beyond the edge of the image, then "scrub" the Angle in Vanishing Point's Options bar until the grid matches the wall's perspective **C, D**. Drag on the midpoint handles to more closely fit the area, if necessary, but allow the grid to extend slightly beyond the image as you did in step 4.

11 Wrap Around the Corner

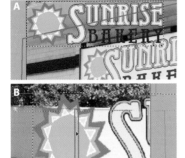

Wall Sign.psd

Now OPEN **Wall Sign.psd**, select all (Ctrl/⌘-A) and copy it to the clipboard (Ctrl/⌘-C). Add a new layer to your developing **VP-Before.psd** file, and reopen Vanishing Point. Type Ctrl/⌘-V to paste the sign into Vanishing Point **A**. Then drag the sign over the planter — you'll see the sign adjust to each perspective plane it traverses. Drag the sign partly onto the plane on the side wall, so it wraps around the corner. When the sign is roughly where you want it **B**, use the Transform tool 🔣 to move it into position and, with the Shift key held down (to scale proportionally), drag a corner to resize the sign to fit **C**. Click "OK" to return to Photoshop.

12 Add Finishing Touches

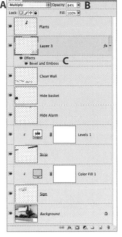

FIND OUT MORE

▼ Using Adjustment layers **page 245**

▼ Using Layer Styles **page 80**

▼ Using Fill layers **page 174**

BECAUSE YOU'VE KEPT your Vanishing Point edits on separate layers, you can now refine them further in Photoshop proper. Open the **VP-After.psd** file to examine our final result (shown on page 612). To finish this image, we used a Levels Adjustment layer in a clipping group to darken the red strips.▼ We put the sign that turns the corner on the planter wall in Multiply mode **A** and reduced the layer's Opacity **B**. We also added a Layer Style to simulate the wall's texture on this painted sign **C**.▼ The larger sign on the signboard seemed too sharp and bright for the image, so we added a Solid Color Fill layer in a light gray sampled from the brick wall, formed a clipping group from the sign graphics layer and the gray layer to restrict the dulling effect to the sign graphics alone, and reduced Opacity to 20%.▼

WORKING WITH MORE THAN ONE PLANE

After you use the Create Plane and Edit Plane tools to make the first perspective plane in Vanishing Point, you can either build other related planes or start completely new ones. Tools will automatically work in the perspective of the plane the cursor is in.

To start a new plane, click with the Create Plane 🔲 tool to make four new corner anchors, and adjust them with the Edit Plane tool 🔳 to make the plane.

To create a secondary plane that turns a corner, use the Edit Plane tool 🔳 to Ctrl/⌘-drag on a midpoint handle. Then drag with the scrubber on the Angle setting until your grid matches the angle perspective of the plane, or use Alt/Option-drag when the cursor turns into a double-headed arrow (near the mid-point handle) to manually adjust the grid's angle. Any art you want to place on the grid can now reside on either plane, *or* partly on each plane, wrapping the corner.

If you want to have more than one grid selected at once, **Shift-click 🔳 to add a grid** to the selection. **Ctrl/⌘-click to deselect it**. Secondary planes are treated as separate grids.

If you've created overlapping perspective planes, you can **activate the plane you want** by repeatedly Ctrl/⌘-clicking 🔳 inside it, activating planes in the "stack" until you get to the right one.

To delete a plane, click with the Edit Plane tool 🔳 to highlight it and then press Backspace/Delete.

ANATOMY OF

Masked Groups

In Photoshop a group of layers is more than just a "housekeeping" feature. It's true — collecting several layers inside a single "folder" does make the Layers panel more compact and organized. But Groups, especially combined with masking, can do a lot more than that. Let's look at a few examples, all of which start with making a Group.

To create a Group, in the Layers panel just target the layer or layers you want to group (click on the thumbnail for the first layer and then Shift-click or Ctrl/⌘-click to add the other layers you want in the Group). Then Shift-click the "Create a new group" button 🗀 at the bottom of the panel. When your new Group appears in the panel, you may need to click the little triangle to the left of it to show thumbnails for the individual layers.

To add a layer mask to the Group, use the same process as you would for a mask on a standard layer: With the Group targeted in the Layers panel, simply click the "Add layer mask" button ▣ at the bottom of the panel. Now you can build the mask in any of the ways you would a standard layer mask. ▼

YOU'LL FIND THE FILES
in 🔘 > Wow Project Files > Chapter 9 > Masked Groups

FIND OUT MORE
▼ Layer mask basics **page 61**
▼ Gradient-filled masks **page 84**

Masking Several Layers

WITH A MASK ON A GROUP you can apply the same mask to several layers, like the gradient mask▼ used here to fade the bottoms of three aligned photos **A**. You can use an individual layer mask to reveal or hide part of any layer in the Group, and also apply a Group mask that affects all the layers **B**. A Group's mask not only hides the layer content but also masks the effects of any Layer Styles applied to the individual layers. Here it hides part of the Inner and Outer Glow effects **C**.

🔘 **Group Mask.psd**

Separate Masks, Separate Functions

COMBINE THE EFFECTS of a layer mask and a Group mask to silhouette a subject from one photo and put it in between the foreground and background of another photo. By keeping the silhouetting mask **A** separate from the compositing mask **B**, you leave yourself the freedom to reposition and scale the silhouetted layer. Here the mask for the layer isolates the boy and his raft from its own background. Turning that layer into a single-layer Group meant that a mask could be added to the Group to hide boy and raft where they would otherwise overlap the girl in the main image, situating the boy between the girl and the background. With this setup it was possible to adjust the size and position of the boy relative to the girl and to position him simply by dragging the "BOY" layer (and its linked layer mask) with the Move tool ▸⊕.

ORIGINAL PHOTOS: PHOTOSPIN.COM

JHDAVIS

Masks on Nested Groups

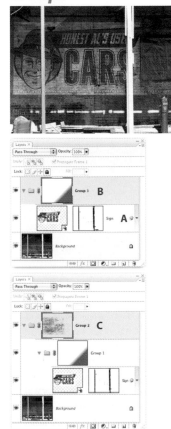

You don't have to stop at one Group mask and one layer mask. Nest a Group within a Group to give yourself a third mask. And so on. Don Jolley used a layer mask to put the posts in front of the sign he applied to the wall **A**. He put the sign in a Group of its own and used a layer mask on the Group to fade the lower right corner of the sign **B**. Then he nested that Group inside a new Group and added a layer mask with a texture to "erode" the sign to show more of the original wall **C**. The file is provided with "Applying an Image to a Textured Surface" (see page 595) and this masking process is detailed in step 7.

Avoiding Stacked Masks

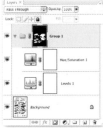

If you need to apply the same layer mask to two or more layers that are together in the layer stack, a single mask on a Group can do a cleaner job. Otherwise, semi-transparent areas of the stacked copies of the mask, including anti-aliased edges, will build in density. The result will be to hide more of the edges in the upper layers than in the lower, which can create a light, dark, or tinted "fringe."

To illustrate a talk on marine conservation, we started with a scanned poster of fishes in Southern California kelp beds and "ghosted" the species now rarely seen. We grouped a Levels layer (used to reduce contrast) and a Hue/Saturation layer (used to remove color). We added a black-filled mask on the Group, and painted it with white where we wanted to show the effects of the two Adjustment layers.

Linking a Mask to a Smart Object in CS3

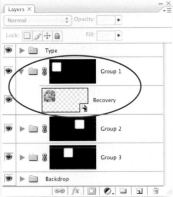

One thing that can be frustrating about using a Smart Object in Photoshop CS3 is that if you add a layer mask, you can't link the image and its mask, so you can't reposition the layer and its mask together. But you can solve this problem by creating a one-layer Group and masking the Group. Make sure folder and mask are linked (if you don't see the 🔗 icon between their thumbnails in the Layers panel, click in that spot to add it). Now use the Move tool 🡥 with **Auto Select Group** turned on in the Options bar, to move the Group — both the Smart Object and its mask. *Note:* In CS4, layer masks on Smart Objects can be either linked or unlinked. ▼

FIND OUT MORE

▼ Masks on Smart Objects **page 64**

 Smart Object Group Mask.psd

Derek Lea Splits the Difference

DEREK LEA IS A MASTER of splitting highlights from shadows and isolating tone or texture from color, as he piles up color and contrast adjustments to get exactly what he wants. *Voodoo*, which he created for the cover of *Pharmacy Practice* magazine to illustrate the topic of joint pain, provides a wealth of examples.

The raw material for *Voodoo* came from a photo of the doll itself, along with pins created in Strata 3D CX5, and textures from the library of materials Derek keeps on hand for building his images. He first created the doll — from rough cloth, stuffing, buttons, and thread — then set it on the floor, leaning against a door. He lighted the scene and photographed it. In Photoshop he made some repairs to the wood with the Clone Stamp 🖊. He built up the doll by selecting and copying patches of its "skin," pasting them to a new layer, rotating the copies into position, and painting layer masks with soft brush tips and black paint to blend the edges into the surrounding cloth.

Much of the story of how Derek completed his composite can be read in the Channels, Layers, and Paths panels. Here we've named the components to help describe what they do.

The original photo

Splitting subject from background. He drew a path around the doll with the Pen tool 🖊 and saved it as an alpha channel: To do this, click the "Load path as a selection" button ⦿ at the bottom of the Paths panel and then choose Select > Save Selection.

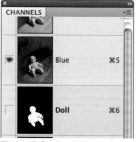

The path for the doll was also saved as an alpha channel.

Now he could load the alpha channel as a selection to target the effect of an Adjustment layer to the doll alone (by clicking the "Create new fill or adjustment layer" button ◐ at the bottom of the Layers panel). Or by Ctrl/⌘-clicking the ◐ button, he could produce the opposite mask to isolate the effect to the background, protecting the doll.

Here one Adjustment layer was applied to the background and several others to the doll. The "Doll 1" Curves layer was applied twice, in two different blend modes and Opacity settings, to build just the effect Derek wanted.

Splitting highlights from shadows. Starting with his "Doll" channel, Derek could make the other masks he needed to isolate the doll's highlights or shadows for change. Creating a mask that would target the highlights of the doll could easily be done in the Channels panel: Ctrl/⌘-click the thumbnail for the "Doll" channel to load it as a selection. Then Ctrl-Alt-click (Windows) or ⌘-Option-click (Mac) the RGB thumbnail, to load the luminosity of the photo as a selection, but only where it coincides with the selection that's already active. Save this combination as another alpha channel (Select > Save Selection; New Channel).

Then he could easily make a "Doll shadows" mask for targeting changes to the darker tones in the doll. One way to do this is to duplicate the "Doll highlights" channel by dragging its thumbnail to the "Create new channel" button ▣ at the bottom of the Channels panel, then load the doll outline as a selection again by Ctrl/⌘-clicking its thumbnail in the Channels panel, and finally invert the tones (Ctrl/⌘-I) within the selected area.

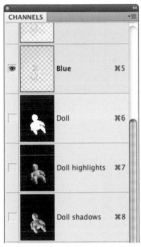

The stored masks for the doll, the doll highlights, and the doll shadows

Splitting texture from color.

For each of the textures he used to create a kind of vignette edge for the image, Derek made a new alpha channel, opened a file from his texture library, selected all and copied, and then pasted into the new channel. Now he could add a new layer, load the texture channel as a selection, and fill the selection with exactly the color he wanted.

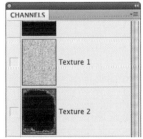

Pasting a texture image into an alpha channel stores the texture without its associated color.

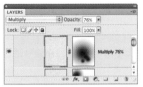

A texture stored in an alpha channel can be loaded as a selection, filled with a color of your choice on a new layer, and masked to appear where you want it.

Splitting contrast from color.

Adding a copy of the image as a layer in Soft Light mode increases contrast, especially in the midtones. But it can also cause an unwanted color shift. If you put this layer in Luminosity mode instead, the color problem is solved, but the contrast boost is lost. With the layer in Soft Light mode and the color removed (Image > Adjustments > Black & White is one way), you can keep the contrast without the color change. In a way, you're getting the benefits of both

Luminosity mode and Soft Light mode in a single layer.

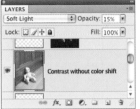

A black-and-white version of the image in Soft Light mode at a low opacity adds just a touch of contrast in the midtones.

The photo was used as a backdrop in Strata 3D so the pins could be created to fit it. Back in Photoshop Derek imported the pins and fine-tuned their contrast and color. He created closed curved paths (see the facing page) to use as selections to contain shadows applied with the Gradient tool on a layer in Multiply mode.

The finished image for the magazine cover. You can see more of Derek Lea's approach to Photoshop in his books *Creative Photoshop CS4* and *Creative Photoshop* (for CS3).

FIND OUT MORE

▼ Using the Pen tool ✎
  page 454

▼ Alpha channels **page 60**

▼ Loading channels as selections **page 61**

▼ Contrast blend modes
  page 184

▼ Using Gradients
  page 174

Integration

No matter how carefully you choose and isolate the elements you use in a composite, and no matter what methods you use to select and assemble them, there are sure to be times when you need to provide a little extra help to make the elements look "comfortable" together in the same space. These six pages provide some suggestions that can be helpful, singly or in combination. These methods are based on how the color of light interacts with the surfaces it falls on, how shadows interact with surfaces and with one another, and how reflections work.

ANOTHER SOLUTION FOR REFLECTIONS

"Reflections: At an Angle" on page 629 shows how to put a subject and its reflection into perspective. In Photoshop CS4 Extended, the 3D > New 3D Postcard from Layer command provides an easier, and geometrically different way of doing that. So if you have CS4 Extended, check page 670 in Chapter 10.

RESTORING GRAIN IN BLURRED AREAS

The technique presented in "Adding Atmosphere: Noise & Grain" on page 628 can be useful not only for unifying a composition of elements from several different sources, but also for restoring grain in photos in which the background has been blurred to increase the depth of field (page 309) or to focus attention on the subject (page 305). Another option for keeping blurred areas from becoming too slick is to use the Lens Blur filter's Noise adjustment. ▼

YOU'LL FIND THE FILES
in 🔵 > Wow Project Files >
Chapter 9 > Quick Integration

FIND OUT MORE
▼ Lens Blur filter
page 309

Spilling Light Over the Edges

Before blur

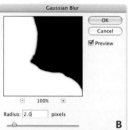

After blur

ORIGINAL PHOTO: LILY DAYTON

TO HELP A MASKED SUBJECT look at home in its new background, you can blur the interior of the mask edge to allow the background's color to spill over onto the subject. The subtle result can be quite effective. In the Layers panel Ctrl/⌘-click on the layer mask to load it as a selection **A**. The selection will restrict the blur you're about to apply so it extends inward from the edge but not outward. Target the layer mask by clicking its thumbnail, and hide the selection boundary (Ctrl/⌘-H) so that when you choose Filter > Blur > **Gaussian Blur**, you can watch the color spill onto the edges of the subject as you increase the Radius **B**. If your subject extends beyond the image frame, as ours does at the bottom, drop the selection (Ctrl/ ⌘-D) and use the Brush tool 🖌 and white paint to whiten that edge of the layer mask.

🔵 **Spilling Light.psd**

Neutralizing a Color Highlight

ORIGINAL PHOTOS: CORBIS ROYALTY FREE

A

B

C

Border Selection

Width: 10   pixels

OK

Cancel

E

LAYERS

Normal   Opacity: 100%

Unify: Propagate Frame 1

Lock: Fill: 100%

Color Balance 1

Background copy

F

ADJUSTMENTS

Color Balance

Tone: ○ Shadows
       ○ Midtones
       ● Highlights

Cyan   Red   +10

Magenta   Green −23

Yellow   Blue   0

D

G

YOUR SUBJECT MAY BRING WITH IT a fringe of its original background color **A**, **B**. To remove the green tinge on the forehead, the eyelashes, and to a lesser degree the hair, we Ctrl/⌘-clicked on the Layers panel thumbnail for the silhouetted portrait to load its silhouette as a selection. Then we chose Select > Modify > Border, using a Width of 10 pixels in the Border Selection dialog **C** and clicked "OK." With the selection active **D**, we clicked the "Create new fill or adjustment layer" button ⬤ at the bottom of the Layers panel and chose **Color Balance**.

The selection made a layer mask that restricted the Color Balance adjustment to the edges **E**. To neutralize a highlight within the border selection, click the Color Balance **Highlights** button, then find the slider that has the color you want to neutralize and move its pointer toward the opposite end. We moved the Magenta/Green slider toward Magenta and the Cyan/Red slider toward Red **F**, **G**. To add more highlights areas to be adjusted, paint the layer mask with white. To reduce the color adjustment in particular spots, paint the mask with black at a low opacity.

Neutralizing.psd

Matching Color

Match Color

Destination Image

Target: Swapping-Before.psd (B..., RGB/8)

☐ Ignore Selection when Applying Adjustment

Image Options

Luminance   100

Color Intensity 100

Fade   75

☐ Neutralize

Image Statistics

☐ Use Selection in Source to Calculate Colors

☐ Use Selection in Target to Calculate Adjustment

Source: Swapping-Bef...

Layer: Sunset

Load Statistics...

Save Statistics...

A

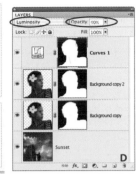

LAYERS

Luminosity   Opacity: 10%

Lock: Fill: 100%

Curves 1

Background copy 2

Background copy

Sunset

D

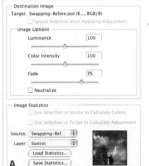
B

C

E

THE MATCH COLOR COMMAND can work well for integrating a silhouetted subject into a background with intensely colored lighting. To change the subject's color to match the light in the new background, duplicate the subject layer for safekeeping (there's no Adjustment layer or Smart Filter option for Match Color, so it has to be applied "destructively," directly to the image). Turn off visibility for the original layer. Then choose Image > Adjustments > **Match Color.** At the bottom of the Match Color dialog **A**, for the **Source** choose the name of the current file. Then in the **Layer** list, choose the layer that holds the new background. The color of your subject will change dramatically **B**. Use Match Color's **Fade** slider to reduce the new color to a level that looks right (we used a Fade setting of 75) **C**, and click "OK." Now turn on visibility for the original subject layer 👁 and experiment with the blend mode and Opacity of the color-matched layer. (For a subtler background image than this sunset, you might want to restrict the color matching to the shadows or highlights. For managing that kind of change, see examples of using the "Blend If" sliders on page 66, or Derek Lea's masking methods on pages 622.)

Our subject would naturally appear in shadow against the bright sky. We applied a masked Curves layer in Luminosity mode **D**, **E**. If your subject's edge needs better blending, try the method in "Spilling Light Over the Edges" on page 624.

Matching Color.psd

Suggesting Light with Layer Styles

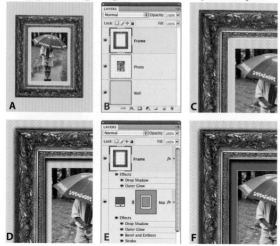

THE SHADOW AND BEVEL EFFECTS in Layer Styles, with the Use Global Light option turned on, can help unify assembled components by establishing the direction of the lighting. Into our background file we dragged and dropped the photo we wanted to frame as well as a photo of a frame, which had been isolated on a transparent layer **A**, **B**, **C**. The lighting on the frame was quite direct and the gilt reflected the light in different directions, so the lighting of this element was adaptable. We clicked the "Add a layer style" button *fx* at the bottom of the Layers panel and chose **Drop Shadow**. Leaving the Angle at the default 120°, we also left **Use Global Light** turned on. Before leaving the Layer Style dialog, we added dimension to the scene with even, narrow shading around the entire frame, clicking **Outer Glow** in the list at the left side of the dialog and changing the color to a dark brown sampled from the frame image and setting the blend mode to Multiply **D**.

For the mat, we targeted the photo, added a layer above it (Ctrl/⌘-Shift-N) and used the Rectangle tool ▢ with Shape layer ▢ chosen in the Options panel. We reduced the Opacity of the Shape layer so we could see the photo through it, and used the Rectangle tool again choosing "Subtract from shape area" mode ▢ in the Options bar to make the opening in the mat. We made the cut edge of the mat by adding a Layer Style: a **Drop Shadow** to establish thickness, a **Stroke** effect for the interior of the mat board exposed by the cut, and a **Bevel and Emboss**, set to **Stroke Emboss** with **Use Global Light** turned on, to match the direction on the frame layer. An Outer Glow was used in the same way as for the frame **E**, **F**.

"Swamping" the Lighting

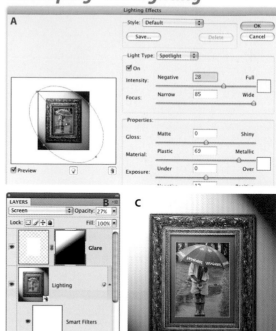

STRONG LIGHTING applied to all the elements of a composite can help put them all "in the same space." But rather than apply the same Lighting Effects filter settings to each layer separately, we can make a merged copy to light. With visibility turned on in the layers panel for the layers you want to include, target the top layer by clicking its thumbnail and pressing Ctrl-Alt-Shift-E (Windows) or ⌘-Option-Shift-E (Mac) to add a layer containing a merged copy. Turn this layer into a **Smart Object** (right-click/Ctrl-click its name in the Layers panel and choose Convert to Smart Object). Then choose Filter > Render > **Lighting Effects**. We applied a **Spotlight** to light the image from the upper left, consistent with the lighting established by the Layer Styles **A**.

As another way to unify the composition, we added a slight "glare" layer to put glass in the frame. We added a new layer (Ctrl/⌘-Shift-N), used the Rectangular Selection tool ⌗ to select an area the size of the photo and mat, and filled it with white. We put the layer in Screen mode and reduced its Opacity. We clicked the "Add layer mask" button ▢ at the bottom of the Layers panel and used the Gradient tool ▭ with the Black, White gradient chosen in the Options bar **B**, **C**.

 Lighting.psd

Cast Shadows: Simple

A

B

C

D

A CAST SHADOW can help a silhouetted photo look like a three-dimensional object and can also help define the surface the object sits on. Simply target the subject layer by clicking its thumbnail in the Layers panel and apply the shadow by clicking the "Add a layer style" button *fx* at the bottom of the panel and choosing **Drop Shadow**. Adjust the **Spread** and **Size** to get the kind of edge that indicates either focused light (a sharper edge) or diffuse light (a softer edge).▼ Click "OK" to finish the Drop Shadow **A, B** and close the Layer Style dialog. In the Layers panel, right-click/Ctrl-click the *fx* symbol to the right of the styled layer's name and in the context-sensitive menu choose **Create Layer**. Now target the shadow layer and skew, scale, and distort it to put the shadow where you want it and to narrow it as it extends behind the subject. One way to do this is to use separate commands (Edit > Transform > **Skew** and drag the top center handle sideways, then Edit > Transform > **Scale** and drag the top center handle down, and finally Edit > Transform > **Distort** to operate the Transform handles one at a time). Another way is to use Free Transform (Ctrl/⌘-T) and use helper keys to change from a simple Scale to a Skew or Distort.▼

To fade the shadow as it extends into the distance, add a layer mask (click the "Add a layer mask" button ▢ at the bottom of the Layers panel) and use the Gradient tool ▢ on the mask **C, D**.▼ To dissipate the shadow more, you can turn the shadow layer into a **Smart Object** (Filter > Convert for Smart Filter) and choose Filter > Blur > **Gaussian Blur**, using a gradient in the **Smart Filter** mask.▼

 **Shadows-Atmosphere.psd**

Cast Shadows: Complex

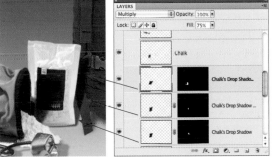

IF ONE ELEMENT'S SHADOW falls across more than one surface in your composite image, you'll need more than one copy of the shadow layer (made as described at the left). For instance, the chalk bag's shadow falls on the "floor," the red strap, and the body of the backpack. That means we'll need three copies of the shadow rotated to three different angles. The shadow will be at a steeper angle as it falls on the more vertical surface of the strap, and the still more vertical surface of the pack. Mask each of the three shadow layers to limit it to the surface it falls on.

OVERLAPPING SHADOWS

When soft shadows in Multiply mode overlap in Photoshop, the shadow gets darker in the overlap. But this isn't the way things work in the real world. So some masking may be needed to eliminate the overlap.

FIND OUT MORE

▼ Drop Shadow effect **page 506**

▼ Keyboard shortcuts for transforming **page 67**

▼ Gradient masks **page 84**

▼ Smart Filters **page 72**

Adding Atmosphere: Average

Before

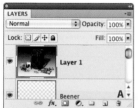
A

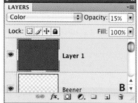
B

After

To CREATE A SHARED "ATMOSPHERE" for your assembled image components, you can unify the color and reduce color saturation. Add a new layer with a **merged copy** (Ctrl-Alt-Shift-E in Windows; ⌘-Option-Shift-E on the Mac) **A**. Then apply the Average filter (Filter > Blur > Average), put the layer in Color mode, and adjust Opacity **B**.

Adding Atmosphere: Noise & Grain

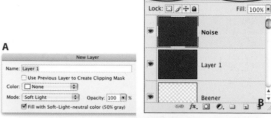

A

C

D

A SHARED DIGITAL OR FILM GRAIN provides another way to unify assembled parts of an image. Add a gray-filled layer in Soft Light mode treated with the Add Noise filter: In the Layers panel, target the top layer of the file. Ctrl/⌘-Shift-N opens the **New Layer** dialog **A**, where you can choose to put the new layer in **Soft Light** mode and fill it with **Soft Light-neutral 50% gray**; click "OK." Choose Filter > Noise > **Add Noise** and adjust the Amount to add more **Monochromatic** "grain" than you want. Then reduce the Opacity of this layer until the grain is as you like it **B**, **C**, **D**.

WOW Shadows-Atmosphere.psd

Reflections: Straightforward

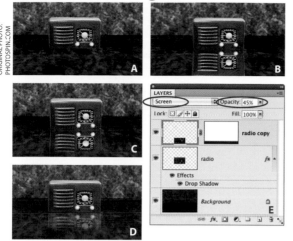

LIKE SHADOWS, reflections help put transplanted subjects firmly in their new environment. Here we added a silhouetted photo of a radio **A**, and duplicated the layer. We chose Edit > Transform > **Flip Vertical** and used the Move tool ▸⊕ to drag the reflection thus created into place below the subject **B**. We clicked the "Add layer mask" button ◘ at the bottom of the Layers panel, and used the Gradient tool ▭ to apply a gradient to the mask, to fade the reflection into the surface **C**. We also put the reflection layer in Screen mode, reduced its Opacity, and added a narrow Drop Shadow at an Angle of 90° to the original photo layer to provide a bit of a shadow beneath the radio **D**, **E**.

GOOD CANDIDATES FOR REFLECTION

It's easy to make reflections for elements photographed straight-on, not from an angle above or below, or from the side. If the item is photographed from slightly above, like the radio shown here, you may still be able to create a credible reflection by masking out the troublesome part of the reflection that wouldn't appear in a real life reflection — in this case the top surface of the radio. A good subject for reflection has a fairly flat front, without protuberances, and sits flat on the surface, rather than being raised above it on legs for instance. That's because if anything sticks out or is raised up, a real reflection would show the bottom surface, which doesn't actually appear in the photo.

 Reflections-Straight.psd

Reflections: At an Angle

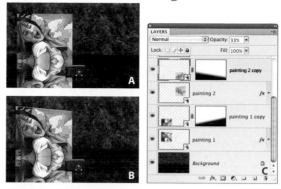

IF YOU'RE PLANNING to bring in a flat element, put it in perspective, and add a reflection, consider putting the reflection step ahead of the perspective, so you can put both the subject and the reflection into perspective together. Otherwise, you may need to do some fairly fiddly work to get the bottom of the reflection to match up with the bottom of the subject while keeping the vertical edges vertical.

Here we dragged and dropped a painting, and as at the left, duplicated the layer, flipped it vertically, and moved it into position **A**. Then we targeted the painting layer (by clicking its thumbnail in the Layers panel) and the reflection layer (by Ctrl/⌘-clicking its thumbnail). We chose Edit > Transform > **Perspective** and dragged the bottom right-hand corner up; we chose Edit > Transform > **Scale** and dragged the left side handle in to foreshorten both the painting and the reflection **B**; and we chose Edit > Transform > Skew and dragged the left side handle down a bit to slant the bottom edge. We faded the reflection with a layer mask and reduced Opacity (as at the left). We added a second painting, making a reflection and applying Perspective, Scale, and Skew, this time from the opposite direction. When everything was in place, we used a **Drop Shadow** and **Bevel and Emboss** to add thickness to both painting layers **C**, **D**.

Photomerge

Improvements to **Photomerge** in Photoshop CS3 and CS4 have made it much easier to piece together a series of overlapping images into a panorama. And its three main functions have also been made available separately — first assembling a series of images in a single file (**Load Files into Stack**), then aligning the images (**Auto-Align Layers**), and finally blending them together with layer masks and adjustments to tone and color (**Auto-Blend Layers**). This separation can make these commands more useful not only for panoramas but also for other multiple-shot techniques, as shown in "Averaging Out Noise," "Creating Solitude," and "In Focus," all in Chapter 5.

Another advantage of using the separate commands is that it allows you to intervene between the aligning and blending processes, in case you want to tweak alignment in some places. Tweaking alignment *after* blending can lead to problems with masking and with color matching at the joins between images.

Still another advantage of separating the steps is that breaking the task into parts can make it faster (or make it possible) to work with more or larger component photos than Photomerge could otherwise handle efficiently (or at all), given the RAM and processing speed available to you.

Pages 576 through 582 provide an introduction to Photomerge and some examples of its use for piecing together typical panoramas. In this section we'll look at some other options for using Photomerge and its "component" commands. If you need more detail about the Photomerge functions described here, refer to the introductory material on pages 576 through 579. For more info about other techniques referred to here, check the Find Out More box below.

YOU'LL FIND THE FILES

in (wow) > Wow Project Files > Chapter 9 > Exercising Photomerge

---

FIND OUT MORE

▼ Match Color command **page 253**

▼ Layer masks **page 62**

▼ Painting layer masks **page 84**

▼ Transforming **page 67**

▼ Healing Brush tool , Spot Healing Brush tool ,

Clone Stamp tool **page 256**

Color Matching

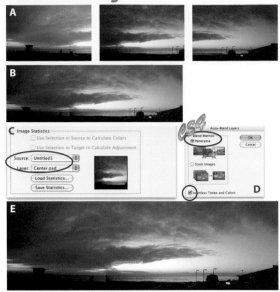

THE PHOTOS FOR THE SUNSET PANORAMA example on pages 578 and 579 were taken at varying exposure settings, which caused the color to vary from image to image as the camera was aimed closer to the setting sun or farther away **A**. Photomerge did a good job of blending the colors **B**. But if you want to shift the color of an entire panorama you're about to make toward the color in one particular photo, you can do it with the **Match Color** command, ▼ using commands from the Edit menu instead of Photomerge. In Photoshop, choose File > Scripts > **Load Files into Stack**, and in the Load Layers dialog choose "Browse" or "Add Open Files" to load the image files for the panorama (or from Bridge CS4, select the images you want and choose Tools > Photoshop > **Load Files into Photoshop Layers**). In the resulting Untitled file, target the layer whose color you want to change; in our series it's **Left.psd**. Choose Image > Adjustments > **Match Color**. In the Match Color dialog **C**, for the Source choose the same **Untitled** file, and choose the Layer whose color you want to match; we chose **Center.psd**. Click "OK" to close the dialog box. Now do any editing you want to the layers (as shown on page 578, for example). Then target all the layers in the file (by clicking the thumbnail for the top layer in the Layers panel and Shift-clicking the bottom thumbnail) and choose Edit > **Auto-Align Layers**; we chose the Cylindrical option. Choose Edit > **Auto-Blend Layers** with **Panorama** chosen for the Method in CS4 **D**, and **Seamless Tones and Colors** turned on, and click "OK" **E**.

 **Match Color Panorama**

An Action Series Montage (CS3)

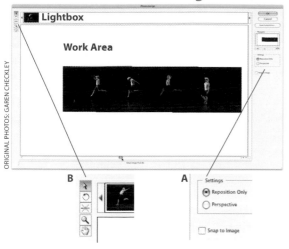

In Photoshop CS3, Photomerge's Interactive Layout option provides a "stage" for arranging images. Here we assembled five photos of dancer Adam Gauzza rehearsing. We started in Bridge, selecting our five images and choosing Tools > Photoshop > **Photomerge**. In the Photomerge dialog, we chose **Interactive Layout** and turned off **Blend Images Together**, because it can produce unexpected results for a montage that isn't really panoramic. We would blend the images with layer masks by hand in Photoshop after running Photomerge.

In the **Interactive Layout** interface you can store images in the "lightbox" at the top until you want to drag them to the work area to build your "panorama." Choosing the **Reposition Only** option **A**, rather than Perspective, and turning off **Snap to Image** gives you complete freedom to line up the photos the way you want them in the work area. Tools are provided **B** for dragging to reposition and rotate the photos. There are also tools for changing the view (and).

When you drag an image, it becomes partly transparent where it overlaps another image, so it's easy to align the photos according to their content. Here we dragged the photos to adjust the spacing between the dancer images and to align the floor from one image to the next.

Clicking "OK" returned a layered file. We added layer masks and painted them with black at reduced Opacity where we wanted to blend the background from one image to the next. We used Free Transform (Ctrl/⌘-T) to reduce the size of the image on the left. Finally, we used the Rectangular Marquee (Shift-M) to drag-select the area we wanted to keep and chose Image > Crop.

An Action Series Montage (CS4)

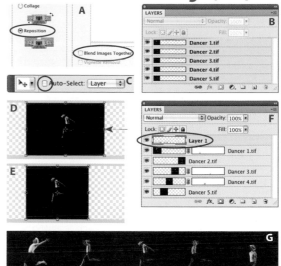

In Photoshop CS4, Photomerge doesn't have the Interactive Layout. But Photomerge can still provide the advantage of layering your images in a file wide enough to accommodate all of them. If you start in Bridge, select your images and choose Tools > Photoshop > **Photomerge**. In the Photomerge dialog, choose **Reposition, turn off Blend Images Together A**, and click "OK." The result will be a wide stack of layers, all with the images at the left end **B**. Choose the Move tool (type V), and **turn off Auto Select** in the Options bar **C**. For each layer, target it by clicking its thumbnail in the Layers panel, then drag in the document window to move the layer into the position where you want it. To align it with layers below, reduce layer Opacity temporarily in the Layers panel so you can see through. Transform and mask the images as needed, as described at the left. In addition to Free Transform, CS4 offers Edit > **Content Aware Scale,** which can often do a great job of condensing or expanding a plain background, without disturbing the subject of the photo; drag a frame handle in or out to reduce or expand the background **D, E**.

If you want to retouch your composite — for instance, to remove white specks from the floor, or clone out another dancer's leg that appears in one of the shots — target the top layer in the file by clicking its thumbnail in the Layers panel, then click the "Create a new layer" button. Use the Healing Brush, Spot Healing Brush, or Clone Stamp on this new top layer, with **Sample All Layers** chosen in the Options bar **F, G**.

 **Dancer Montage**

After you create a panorama, either through Photomerge or by using the Auto-Align Layers and Auto-Blend Layers commands, some work often remains if you want to produce a flawless composite. For some of these adjustments, it can be more efficient to make a single-layer copy of your composition to work with. You can make such a **merged copy** by pressing **Ctrl-Alt-Shift-E** in Windows, or ⌘-**Option-Shift-E** on the Mac.

Besides making global adjustments, with a merged copy you can select an area of the image to transform without having to identify and target the component photos involved. And if you select the area of the copy that you want to transform, then duplicate that area to a separate layer before you transform it, you can blend your transformed section with the merged copy, by targeting both layers and choosing Edit > Auto-Blend Layers. Remember that you can move the center point of the Transform frame to change the center of rotation.

After using the Spherical layout in Photomerge, we wanted to lower the two ends of this 360°-plus panorama. We made a merged copy in a new layer and used the Rectangular Marquee ⸬⸬ to select the left end of the image **A**.

We copied the selected area to a new layer (Ctrl/⌘-J) and pressed Ctrl/⌘-T. We dragged the center point of the Transform frame to the right end of the lake **B**. When we then moved the cursor outside the frame and dragged to rotate the left end down, the image rotated around the moved center point **C**.

We targeted the merged layer and the transformed part, and used Edit > Auto-Blend Layers to blend them seamlessly **D**, **E**.

A Collage of Prints: 1 Setting Up the Images

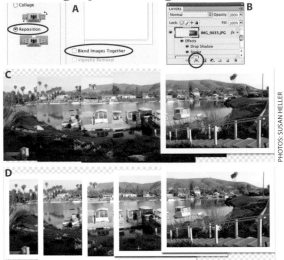

PHOTOS: SUSAN HELLER

Your goal in using Photomerge doesn't have to be a seamless panorama. For these paddle boats on Lake San Marcos, for instance, we wanted to communicate a sense of the space in the scene but also to introduce a "summer vacation" feel, dividing the expanse among a few casually arranged photo prints. We started in Bridge with five images from a panoramic series. We chose Tools > Photoshop > **Photomerge**. In the Photomerge dialog, we chose **Reposition Only/Reposition** and **turned off the Blend Images Together** option **A**, then clicked "OK." The result was a layered file with images overlapped but not rotated or scaled.

Targeting one of the layers in the new panorama file, we created a Layer Style to add a white edge and a drop shadow **B**, **C**: We clicked the *fx* button at the bottom of the Layers panel and chose **Stroke**, clicking the color swatch and choosing white in the Color picker; we set the Stroke **Position** to **Inside** (for sharp corners) and the **Size** to **30 px**. Next we clicked **Drop Shadow** in the list at the left of the Layer Style dialog and added a shadow with settings that produced a shadow we liked: We set the **Angle** at 120°, the **Distance** (offset) at 8 px, and the **Size** (softness) at 8 px also. Now we could copy the Layer Style (by right-clicking/Ctrl-clicking the *fx* icon for the "styled" layer in the Layers panel and choosing **Copy Layer Style**) and then paste it by multi-targeting all the other layers (by Shift-clicking or Ctrl-clicking their thumbnails in the Layers panel), then right-clicking/Ctrl-clicking the spot where the *fx* would be for one of the layers, and choosing **Paste Layer Style D**.

A Collage of Prints:
2 Finessing the Arrangement

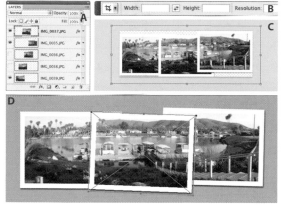

Once you have all of your images arranged, with borders added, you may want to remove some photos and rearrange the remaining ones. We turned off visibility for two of the layers in the "panorama" and dragged the center image of the remaining three to the top of the stack **A**.

Create some working space around the assembled images by holding down the Alt/Option key as you zoom out (Ctrl/⌘-hyphen). Then choose the Crop tool ⊡ and clear the Width, Height, and Resolution settings in the Options bar **B**, so the Crop frame can be sized freely. Drag the Crop tool's cursor diagonally from the top left corner of the entire assemblage to the bottom right corner; now drag outward on the corner handles of the Crop frame until you have as much space as you want in the file (to allow for the shadows and any rearranging you might want to do) **C**, and press Enter to complete the crop.

For a background, we added a new layer at the bottom, first targeting the current bottom layer by clicking its thumbnail in the Layers panel and then Ctrl/⌘-clicking the "Create a new layer" button ▣ (using the Ctrl/⌘ key adds a new layer *below* the current layer). We used the Eyedropper tool ⌖ to sample a tan color from the image and filled the new layer with this Foreground color (Alt-Backspace in Windows; Option-Delete on the Mac).

Now you can rearrange the photos to improve the panorama or just to make a more interesting composition. Target each layer in turn and use Edit > Transform > Rotate to reorient the photo **D**; drag inside the Transform frame to move the rotated photo.

 **Collage Panorama**

A Collage of Prints:
3 Adding Depth

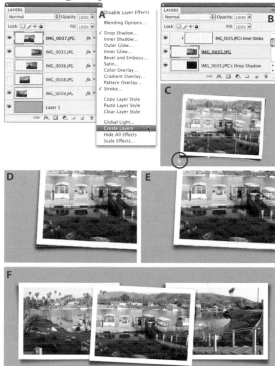

When the layout is as you like it, you can add dimension to the "pile." Start by separating each photo's shadow from the photo itself so you can manipulate the shadow separately. For each of the photo layers in turn:

First right-click/Ctrl-click its *fx* in the Layers panel and choose **Create Layer** from the context-sensitive menu. You can ignore the warning dialog, and click "OK." Both the Stroke and the Drop Shadow "translate" perfectly when layers are created from a Style **A**, **B**.

Next target the shadow layer by clicking its thumbnail, choose Edit > Transform > Warp, and drag one or more of the corners to distort the shadow slightly, making the corner of the shadow seem farther from the corner of the photo **C**. This creates the illusion that the photo corners are curling up slightly. To soften the shadow more (another way to create the illusion of distance between the photo and the surface the shadow falls on), you can blur the shadow layer (Filter > Blur > Gaussian Blur) **D**, or use the Blur tool ⌀ on a corner of the shadow, or reduce the Opacity or Fill Opacity of the shadow layer **E**, **F**.

To compose **Addie's Artwork**, **Melissa Au** combined a photo taken in the warm light of late afternoon with two of the child's marker drawings. With her composition in mind, she created a new file the size she wanted (File > New, 8 x 10 inches at 300 ppi). In a duplicate of the photo file, she selected the girl with the Quick Selection tool ▽, cleaning up the edges by hand (one way is to use Quick Mask),▼ and then used Select > Refine Edge to smooth the edge of the selection and feather it slightly so her subject would blend smoothly with the white background of the composite file.▼ Au reversed the selection (Ctrl/⌘-Shift-I) and deleted the background, then used Adjustment layers (Hue/Saturation and Curves) to lighten and cool the color.▼ She merged the layers (Ctrl/⌘-Shift-E), returned to the composite file, and placed the silhouetted photo (File > Place), positioning and scaling it and pressing the Enter key to complete its placement as a Smart Object.

She also placed the two scanned drawings the same way. With all the elements positioned and sized, she targeted all the Smart Objects in the Layers panel and rasterized them (right-clicking/Ctrl-clicking a layer's name opens a context-sensitive menu where you can choose Rasterize). She used the Lasso ⌁ to select the little man from the sunshine drawing and then cut him to a layer of his own (Ctrl/⌘-Shift-J) and positioned him under the sun using the Move tool ▶. She duplicated the photo layer (Ctrl/⌘-J), blurred the copy (Filter > Blur > Gaussian Blur), and put the blurred copy in Overlay mode at reduced Opacity; the blur kept Overlay mode from sharpening the photo as it livened up the color and contrast.▼

FIND OUT MORE

▼ Quick Selection tool **page 49**
▼ Quick Mask **page 60**
▼ Refine Edge command **page 58**
▼ Adjustment layers **page 245**
▼ Overlay blend mode **page 184**

Working with photos taken more than 30 years ago, Marv Lyons produced ***Woman Waiting in Papeete*** (above) and ***Three Girls*** (right) by scanning and layering them. In each case Lyons combined the original photo with an image of palm trees overhead, which he had photographed through a chandelier prism. Lyons often takes "ambience" photos like the one of the palm trees and uses them to add atmosphere to photos taken in the same location. He developed his original compositing technique in the darkroom, and later "translated" it to Photoshop, layering scanned images with varied blend modes and opacities.

In ***Woman Waiting*** the "Palm Trees" layer is in Overlay mode at 100% Opacity. Lyons manufactured a "warming filter" by choosing a gold as the Foreground color, adding an empty layer, and filling it with color (Alt-Backspace in Windows; Option-Delete on the Mac). He put the layer in Multiply mode and reduced its Opacity to 17%.

For ***Three Girls***, Lyons used the "Palm Trees" layer twice, once in Overlay mode at 100% and again above that in Multiply mode at 41%.

Each of these two cityscapes by **Allen Furbeck** began as a series of photos taken with a hand-held Canon EOS 1D Mark II with a wide-angle zoom lens (16–35 mm). For *24th Street & Seventh Avenue* (this page) "I shot 17 images," says Furbeck. "For *23rd Street & Seventh Avenue* I shot 26, a full 360 degrees around the intersection, but I used only 22 of them."

Furbeck typically photographs his cityscape series in a back-and-forth pattern, shooting either up-to-down to form a column of shots, then over a bit and down-to-up, and so on, or left-to-right to form a row, then

down a bit and back across from right to left. He sometimes rotates the camera, rarely holds it parallel to the horizon, and often varies the focus or exposure for the shots in the series. "I know the rules for taking panoramas," he says. "Set the exposure and focus manually and shoot them all the same. Hold the camera parallel to the horizon, and use a tripod." So much for the rules. He describes his photo shoots as "dancing with the scene and the camera, all together. If I frame each shot so it's interesting by itself, it seems to produce a better combined image," he notes.

Furbeck keeps Photoshop's capabilities clearly in mind as he photographs. As he shoots a series, he often anticipates using a particular Photomerge layout. But when he gets back to his studio, he tries other layout options, enjoying the surprise of how Photomerge stitches the parts together. Also, removing one or more shots from the series before (or even after) running Photomerge sometimes produces a very different-looking result.

Furbeck, who studied photography in college but pursued painting as a career instead, got back into

photography when Photoshop came out. He started stitching photos together in order to get the print size and detail using digital cameras that he had been getting for his more traditional landscape photos, shot with medium- and large-format film cameras. He was photo-merging in Photoshop — using the Edit > Transform command, Adjustment layers, and masking – well before Photomerge appeared on the scene.

In Photoshop CS3 and CS4, improvements to Photomerge and the addition of the Auto-Align Layers and Auto-Blend Layers commands▼

make it possible to separate the two parts of the stitching process — aligning and blending. Photomerge can be run with the Blend Images Together option turned off, and then the alignment can be tweaked with the Transform command▼ before the images are blended with Edit > Auto-Blend Layers. (In CS4 Photomerge and Auto-Align Layers can also stitch with or without correcting geometric distortion caused by the camera lens.)

For both of these images, Furbeck used Photomerge. He chose the Auto layout for *24th Street,* and he produced the "lobes" of asphalt

in *23rd Street* with the Cylindrical layout. He likes the uncropped, nonrectangular results he gets in his cityscapes. "The shape doesn't confine the image," he says. Unlike photos, especially panoramas, that are constrained within the rectangular format, each of his cityscapes emphasizes the connection between the image and the wider world beyond the edges.

FIND OUT MORE

▼ Using Photomerge **page 576**

▼ Auto-Align Layers & Auto-Blend layers
page 630

▼ Transforming **page 67**

For the 40th Anniversary Commemorative Issue of *Footprints*, the newsletter of Adventure 16 Outdoor & Travel Outfitters, **Betsy Schulz** designed the cover and inside spreads as layered Photoshop files. For each spread she set up a full-size RGB file in Photoshop (22 x 12 inches) at the resolution she wanted for printing (300 pixels/inch). Using Photoshop's File > Import command, she scanned various photo and drawing files, and then dragged-and-dropped them into the layout file. She tinted some of these layers▼ and used Edit > Free Transform (Ctrl/⌘-T) to reduce them to the appropriate sizes, rotate them, and move them into position.

For the *Footprints* nameplate on the cover **A**, she dragged and dropped a stock image of rusted metal. She used the Pen tool ◊ to draw a path for the shape she wanted for the plate, first making sure to select the "Paths" ▥ and "Add to path area"▢ settings in the Options bar.▼ Then she made a selection from the path (one way is to right-click/Ctrl-click in the document window and choose Make Selection from the context sensitive menu) and clicked the "Add a layer mask" button ▢ at the bottom of the Layers panel to create

a layer mask (with an active selection, clicking ▢ adds a mask that hides all but the selected area). With the layer mask active, she "knocked out" the type: First she used the Horizontal Type Mask tool ⊤ to set the type, pressing Ctrl/⌘-Enter to complete the setting.▼ Then she pressed Backspace/Delete to fill the type with black (when a mask is active, black is the Background color by default, and pressing Backspace/Delete fills the selection with black).

She created a shadow for each photo **B** by clicking the *fx* at the bottom of the Layers panel and adding a Drop Shadow effect, then rendering the shadow onto a separate layer so she could modify it. (To render the effects in a Layer Style, you can right-click/Ctrl-click on the *fx* for the layer in the Layers panel and choose Create Layers.) With each shadow on a separate layer, she could distort it (Edit > Transform > Distort), to create the

optical illusion that the snapshot was curled slightly.

For the pieces of paper that would hold the text **C** (to be set later in the page layout program), Schulz scanned a textured sheet and added a Drop Shadow effect. For each piece of paper she needed, she duplicated this paper layer, sometimes tinting the duplicate. Then she used the Pen tool to draw a path that defined the shape of the piece of paper she needed. As she had done for the *Footprints* nameplate, she made a selection from the path and added a layer mask that revealed the image only in the selected area. The Drop Shadow automatically conformed to the shape defined by the mask.

Schulz saved each completed file in Photoshop EPS format and imported it into her QuarkXPress file, where she added logos and other graphics to the pages and set the type in fonts from the VTypewriter family by Vintage Type (www.vintagetype.com).

B

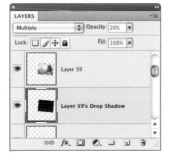

C

FIND OUT MORE

▼ Tinting images **page 203**

▼ Using the Pen tools **page 454**

▼ Using the Type tools **page 436**

A

While traveling in Tasmania, **Katrin Eismann** learned that about 40 percent of the island is a National Park with very strict access regulations. "I noticed how much the people loved nature and their country," says Eismann. "Then I noticed how clean everything was and I wondered about what they did with their garbage. And that led me to the Hobart city dump."

She set up a mini studio **A** and spent the day photographing the interesting objects she found there. Two of the series of compositions that resulted, *Bathroom Scales* and *Paint Can Lids*, are shown above.

"Before the garbage is dumped into a landfill," says Eismann, "paid workers sort through it to take out anything that's usable. This material (wood, furniture, flower pots, the things I photographed) is sold in a

type of thrift shop near the entrance to the dump, where anyone can come and buy (very cheap) materials for arts, crafts, or home projects."

Eismann imported the day's photos, shot with a Hasselblad 503cxi with a Phase P25+ back and a 120 Macro lens and strobe, into Lightroom. There she selected the photos she wanted to use for each composite image. After processing the files in Lightroom (with the same photo-optimizing engine used in Adobe Camera Raw),▼ she opened the files in Camera Raw, and from there opened them as Smart Objects in Photoshop. It's possible to open a file as a Smart Object in Photoshop directly from Lightroom 2, but you can't determine the size at which the file will open. In Camera Raw, on the other hand, you can click the link at the bottom of the window **B** and choose from a menu of several different resolutions. Eismann's original photo files were 128 MB each; it was important to reduce the size going into Photoshop so she could mask and freely arrange the six or eight components for each composite. From Camera Raw she opened the files as Smart Objects at 6 to 8 MB — a meaningful difference in file size.

For her first composite, Eismann created a new Photoshop file big enough to fit all six bathroom scales, arranged in a grid formation. With the Move tool ▶⊕ she dragged and dropped each Smart Object from its own file into place as a separate element in the composite file **C**.

Eismann needed to "crop out" parts of the background of each photo.

She added Guides to mark where she wanted the boundaries between her scales,▼ then added a layer mask to each Smart Object and used black to mask out the edges **D**.▼

She used the Pen tool ⌀ (Shift-P) to create a path around each of the scales and then used these paths to make layer masks for the Curves, Hue/Saturation, and Selective Color Adjustment layers that she used to match the "white" backgrounds to one another.▼ To restrict the adjustments to each scale image, she made a clipping group with the scale photo as the base **E**.▼

Eismann applied the Smart Sharpen filter to each of her Smart Objects.▼ She limited the sharpening to each bathroom scale (not its background) by loading her path as a selection, then inverting the selection, and filling the selected area of the Smart Filter's built-in mask with black **F**.▼

After much tweaking "and lots of coffee," says Eismann, the backgrounds still didn't match one another perfectly. "I needed something more to define the grid" **G**. One way to draw a grid is to target the top layer of the composite and use

the Line tool ╲ (Shift-U); click the "Shape layers" button ▱ in the Options bar and set the Weight for the line width you want; then Shift-drag vertically or horizontally, click the "Add to shape layer (+)" button, and Shift-drag to place each additional grid line where you want it.

She could then duplicate the file (Image > Duplicate) and scale the duplicate (Image > Image Size) to make whatever print size she wanted.▼ Since the sharpening had been applied to Smart Objects, she could reopen the Smart Sharpen dialog and adjust the sharpening if necessary for the different print sizes.

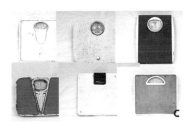

ProPhoto RGB; 8 bit; 3072 by 2304 (7.1MP); 240 ppi

B

C

ORIGINAL PHOTO: SIMONE MUELLER

A

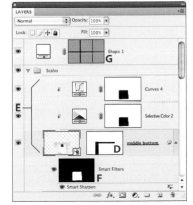

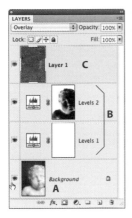

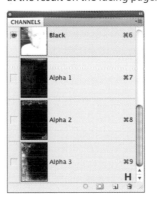

To create his *Afraid* image, **Derek Lea** started with a cherub from the 13th-century St. Mary's church in Berkeley, England, which he photographed out-of-focus **A**. He added two Levels Adjustment layers **B**, one to increase contrast and darken overall, and another to darken the shadow tones▼ (a technique for making a layer mask to target shadow tones is described on page 622). In a layer above that, he added a "texture" scan in Overlay mode **C** to "antique" the cherub and color it **D** to match the skin around the eyes he would add next.

He used the eyes from a photo of an elderly man, selecting each eye and copying and pasting it onto its own layer, scaling each one and rotating it into place **E**. Lea selected the irises of the eyes and added a Levels Adjustment layer; the active selection became a layer mask for the Levels layer, so the lightening effect was limited to the irises alone. He added a Selective Color Adjustment layer▼ with the same mask,▼ adding Magenta and Yellow to the Neutrals and removing Cyan and Black **F**, which moved the color toward the color of the cherub **G**. To unify his composite, he duplicated his texture layer, Alt/Option-dragging on its thumbnail to make a copy and move it up the Layers panel into position above the eyes.

Lea added other textures from his collection to his layered image. For each one, he added a new alpha channel to his developing *Afraid* file (by clicking the "Create new channel" button ▣ at the bottom of the Channels panel), then copied and pasted from his texture file into the alpha channel **H**. For instance, in one channel he used a scan of a rusted cookie sheet and in another a "scratches" texture he had made as follows: He made a photocopy with the lid of the copier wide open, which produced a page covered with black toner; he sandpapered the page, crumpled and uncrumpled it several times, and scanned the result. By storing each texture in an alpha channel he could load the texture as a selection (by Ctrl/⌘ clicking the channel's thumbnail in the Channels panel) and fill it with color on one or more transparent layers, whose blend modes and opacities he could then adjust to arrive at the result on the facing page.

FIND OUT MORE

▼ Using Levels
page 246

▼ Selective Color
adjustment **page 253**

▼ Copying layer
masks **page 361–362**

Layer Styles ▼ and blend modes ▼ play important roles in developing the rich color of **Jack Davis's *Grace*** image. Davis started his composition with a black background, and then layered photos of an antique book cover **A** and a wooden box over it **B**, each one selected from its background and isolated on a transparent layer. ▼ On the box layer he added a Layer Style consisting of a Drop Shadow effect and an Outer Glow, both dark and both in Overlay mode so they intensified the color and contrast where they fell on the book cover layer below.

Next he added a layer with wings, with a black Drop Shadow in Multiply mode, so it darkened the image underneath but didn't change the color saturation. To complete the basic composition **C**, he added a layer with overlapping chambered nautilus shells, again with a Drop Shadow in Multiply mode.

Next Davis added a complex texture image with darkened edges **D**. A "texture photo" in the right blend mode can add richness, and at the same time can unify the parts of a composite image, helping to "put them all in the same space." Soft Light mode will increase contrast and saturate colors **E**. Color mode unifies hue and saturation **F**. Davis decided on Difference mode, which turned colors to their opposites and turned shadows to glows **G**.

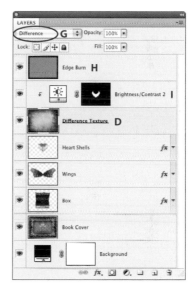

To "burn" the edges of his composition, he added a new layer **H** in Overlay mode, filled with 50% gray, which has no effect in Overlay mode. He then darkened the edges. (One way is to make a selection with the Rectangular Marquee tool [ ], then use Select > Refine Edge ▼ to feather the selection, and finally invert the selection [Ctrl/-Shift-I] and fill it with black [Edit > Fill > Black]. In Overlay mode the black darkens and saturates.)

Looking at the nearly final image, Davis wanted to brighten the nautilus shells, so he added a Brightness/Contrast adjustment layer **I** ▼ and clipped it to his texture layer, so it would affect only that layer. ▼ After increasing the Brightness, he inverted the color of this adjustment layer's built-in layer mask, turning it black (Ctrl/⌘-I). The black-filled mask hid the Brightness adjustment, and then he painted the mask with white ▼ to reveal the Brightness

exactly where he wanted it, in the area where it would brighten the shells, as shown in the final artwork on the facing page.

FIND OUT MORE

▼ Layer styles **page 80**
▼ Blend modes **page 181**
▼ Refine edge **page 58**
▼ Adjustment layers **page 245**
▼ Clipping groups **page 65**
▼ Painting layer masks **page 84**

ORIGINAL PHOTOS: BEVERLY GOWARD

For each of a series of ***Wedding Keepsake Prints*** for the members of the bridal party, photographer **Beverly Goward** wanted to assemble a portrait of the bride with four candid shots. Working with Goward's photos, **Marie Brown** approached the project with Photoshop's Picture Package, starting with the page for the flower girl. ***Note:*** Picture Package is installed automatically with Photoshop CS3, but in CS4 it has to be installed as an optional plug-in (see page 120).

 The **Bridal Party layout** is included on the Wow DVD-ROM, along with **Creating a Mat.psd**, a smaller file that shows the construction of the beveled mat.

In Photoshop Brown began by choosing File > Automate > Picture Package, then clicking the "Choose" button to choose a photo. She navigated to a folder that contained the main portrait of the bride, cropped to a 5 x 7 horizontal format. ▼

In the Picture Package window, Brown set the Page Size at "8.0 x 10.0 in" **A** and the resolution at 300 pixels/in **B**. She chose the "(1)5x7 (4)2.5x3.5" option from the Layout menu **C** — it was closest to the layout she wanted. Each of the five zones in the Layout displayed the portrait **D**.

The Picture Package routine is designed to place repeats of an image, maximizing image coverage on the output page. But Brown and Goward wanted a different result — a balanced arrangement with space between the images so a "mat" could be added to the print. Before substituting the four photos of the flower girl, Brown modified the layout. She clicked the "Edit Layout" button **E** to open the Picture Package Edit Layout dialog.

In the upper left corner of the Edit Layout dialog, Brown named her layout "Bridal Party" **F** and set the Units to "inches" **G**. To make it easier to resize and align the zones, she turned on the Snap To function **H** to display the "magnetic" grid; she set the grid Size to 0.25 in, the smallest division **I**.

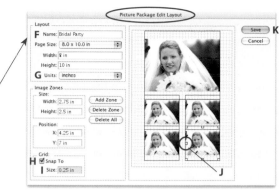

She dragged the side handles of the large zone to reduce it so there was space around it. Then she put the cursor inside the image and dragged to center the zone near the top of the page. Next she used the side handles to reduce the smaller zones, and then dragged inside each one to align its outside edge with a side edge of the large photo **J**. With the side edges aligned, she could drag the zones up or down, using the white space at the tops and bottoms of the zones (rather than the zone boundaries themselves) as the predictors of how much space there would be between photos.

"I noticed some interesting behavior in Picture Package," says Brown. "First, if I wanted to both edit the layout *and* replace some of the photos, it was important to **do the editing *before*** I substituted the photos, because if I did things in the reverse order, the substitutions would be lost as soon as I clicked 'Edit Layout.'

"Second, resizing a zone in Picture Package works differently than scaling with Photoshop's Transform command. In Picture Package, no matter which handle you drag, the photo is always resized proportionally. But if you use a mid-side handle, then the width seems to become the critical dimension, and empty space is added at the top and bottom of the photo to fill the zone. I

use mid-side handles when I want the side edges of photos to align. Using a center top or center bottom handle makes height the critical dimension, and space is added at the sides; so if I want to align top or bottom edges of photos, I resize the zones using the center top or bottom handle."

When Brown clicked the "Save" button **K** and the "Enter the new layout file name" dialog box opened, she named the layout and clicked "Save." The main Picture Package dialog opened again, showing the new layout; its name also became available in the Layout menu so she could use it for other prints in the series.

To substitute for the small photos, Brown went back to the folder that held photos of the flower girl. These had been cropped to a 5 x 7 horizontal format, which is the same aspect ratio as 2.5 x 3.5. "It's important to have your images cropped to the right aspect ratio in advance," says Brown.

She clicked on one of the images and dragged it into the Picture Package dialog and onto the zone where she wanted it, repeating the process until she had all the photos in place **L**. (An alternative to drag-and-drop is to click one of the Picture Package zones to open the "Select an image" dialog, and navigate to the photo you want.)

With the Flatten All Images option chosen in the Document panel of the dialog box, Brown clicked "OK" and watched as Photoshop built a file named "Picture Package 1," with all the photos in place on a single transparent layer above a *Background*.

To this file she added a mat. Targeting the file's *Background* in the Layers panel, she clicked the "Create new fill or adjustment layer" button ⬤ at the bottom of the panel and chose Solid Color, then sampled a color by clicking on one of the assembled photos.

To "cut" the mat, she targeted the photo layer again by clicking its thumbnail in the Layers panel, then clicked the "Add a layer style" button *fx* at the bottom of the panel and chose the Bevel and Emboss effect. Setting up an Outer Bevel, she built a semi-transparent rise from the edge of each photo *outward,* so the mat, rather than the photo, seemed to be beveled.▼

FIND OUT MORE

▼ Cropping **page 240**
▼ Building bevels **pages 509 & 542**

Katrin Eismann's *Mackerel Beauty* (above) is optically impossible as a single photo. To get sharp focus for both the extreme close-up of the fish and the far-away sky required taking a "focus series" of four photos and then blending them together with layer masks to preserve the sharply focused areas of each.

Eismann set up her photo on the balcony of her home using a tripod to steady her camera just a few inches above a market fish she had set on a mirror. Aiming the camera at this still life, she focused at infinity to get a clear picture of the mirrored sky **A**, knowing that for the image reflected in the mirror, she would need to set the focus based on how far away the sky was from the mirror rather than for the short distance between the mirror and the camera.

After taking the sky photo, Eismann focused her macro lens on the skin of the fish. Since the lens

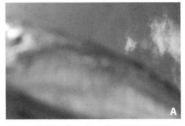

has a very shallow depth of field when used close up, she took three photos, each focused at a slightly different distance, to capture detail on the back **B**, fin **C**, and belly **D**.

She layered the four shots in a single file, and then painted layer masks with black on all but the sky layer to

hide the out-of-focus areas of each layer. The result was a "photo" with everything in focus (see "In Focus" on page 344 for an alternate automated method). To complete the image, she brought out color and detail by adding Adjustment layers and manipulating blend modes.

Sharon Steuer's line of *Steuer Bags* features reproductions of her art collages, printed onto fabric and stitched into tote bags. Steuer often develops her collages at least partly in Photoshop, using layering methods and layer comps as described for the *Oil Spirit* series shown on page 586; some of the elements used in *Oil & Rain* (above) are from that series. She also scans paintings done with traditional media as another source of artwork.

To arrive at the final collages for her bags, Steuer prints her art on paper using an inkjet printer and then uses a method taught by Jonathan Talbot (talbot1.com): She coats the printed pieces on both sides with clear acrylic gloss gel. After the gel dries, she cuts out the pieces she wants and arranges them. When she's sure of a position, she places a sheet of nonstick unbleached parchment paper on top and uses a small tacking iron to fuse the acrylic gel and attach the pieces

together. Because both sides of each printed piece have been coated, the overlapping parts will attach in any arrangement she chooses.

At this point Steuer often enhances the collage with watercolor pencils, as she did for *RainySeason* (top right) and *giraffes*. Then she digitally photographs the collage, retouches as needed in Photoshop, and moves the project into InDesign, where she finds it easier to arrange and crop the files to fit a layout (bottom right) that will print the parts for four bags to a yard of fabric. The company that prints the custom fabric (spoonflower.com) prefers to receive the art as TIFF files in Lab color mode. So Steuer exports a PDF from InDesign, opens it in Photoshop, converts it to Lab color, and resaves it as a TIFF. Once the fabric is printed, it's cut and sewn into bags (jajajapurses.com), and the bags are marketed through steuerbags.com.

3D, Video & Animation

GPU Settings
Detected Video Card:

NVIDIA Corporation
NVIDIA GeForce 8600M GT
OpenGL Engine

☑ Enable 3D Acceleration

Adobe Photoshop

Ps   Your video card does not meet the requirements for hardware-accelerated 3D rendering. All 3D will be rendered with software only.

OK

To work at all comfortably (or at all) with 3D in Photoshop Extended, you need to have a computer with a video card that supports OpenGL ▼ and with 3D acceleration enabled in the GPU Settings section of Preferences (Ctrl/⌘-K) > Performance (top). Without OpenGL you'll see a warning (bottom) when you try to work with 3D functions.

FIND OUT MORE

▼ OpenGL   **page 9**

MUCH OF THIS CHAPTER applies to Photoshop Extended only. It's only in the Extended versions, for instance, that we find the tools, commands, and panels for working with 3D models, and the ability to edit video with other than a frame-by-frame approach. The Frames mode of the Animation panel exists in both Photoshop and Photoshop Extended, but with the new Timeline mode of the panel in the Extended versions, much more complex animation is possible. 3D, video, and motion graphics can be combined to produce some exciting results, even if your goal is not so much to move into 3D or video as to draw on what these fields have to offer for enhancing still 2D images and graphics. This chapter will give you a look at what's possible and provide a foundation for experimenting and for using other expert resources for 3D, video, and animation.

3D

Photoshop has always had a role to play in 3D. Images and patterns created in Photoshop have long been imported into 3D programs to be used as texture maps (surface color and pattern) or bump maps (surface relief). Photoshop also imports images rendered from 3D programs, so they can be included in Photoshop compositions. One typical Photoshop–3D workflow involves creating a background image in Photoshop, saving the image, and then opening it in a 3D modeling program, where a model is developed to fit into the background image. When the model is rendered and saved in the 3D program (often with an alpha channel to silhouette it), it can then be opened in Photoshop and combined with the original Photoshop image. You can find some inspiring examples of this kind of work in this chapter's "Gallery," starting on page 703. But now it's also possible to work more directly with 3D in Photoshop Extended, especially in CS4. This new access to 3D is somewhat limited in its usefulness. People who are experienced with 3D are likely to

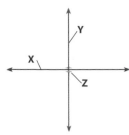

3D space is defined in terms of X, Y, and Z directions, at right angles to one another. X (red here) goes side to side, Y (blue) goes up and down, and Z (green) goes front to back. (Since the Z axis points straight at us here, we can see only the arrowheads.)

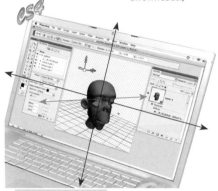

In Photoshop Extended's 3D space, the X, Y, and Z axes go side-to-side, up-and-down, and in-and-out relative to the plane of the computer screen. But the X, Y, and Z axes for the 3D Axis widget in CS4 Extended relate to the original orientation of the model rather than the screen.

Original

Object rotated

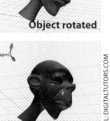

Camera rotated

If you turn on visibility for the **ground plane** in Photoshop CS4 Extended, it's easier to see the difference in the results you get when you manipulate the model and when you move the camera. Without the ground plane as a reference, the two kinds of manipulations can seem to produce almost the same result.

MODEL: DIGITALTUTORS.COM

take a look at its implementation here, find it still too limited for their needs, and go back to their favorite 3D programs. People who have never worked in 3D before will find themselves in strange territory, without the vocabulary or experience to get a lot out of Help in some cases. Still, there are some interesting things designers and illustrators can do with this capability, and that's where we place the emphasis here.

The 3D World & Its Vocabulary

In Photoshop Extended, a 3D model is a ***scene*** consisting of an **object**, a ***ground plane*** (a floor, or reference for moving objects in 3D space), and **lighting**; a **camera** provides our view onto the scene. Each object consists of a ***mesh*** with one or more associated ***materials***. The mesh, the "bones" of the object, defines the object's shape in three dimensions. The materials are like the "skin" over the mesh. A mesh (a cube is a really simple example) can have several materials (one for each of the six faces of the cube, for instance), each applied to a different part of the mesh. Another example would be a model of a head, with different materials for the face, hair, and eyeballs. Each material can have up to nine different kinds of characteristics, or ***textures***. For instance, there can be a texture for surface color or pattern (called *Diffuse*), for surface texture (called *Bump*), and for shininess.

The 3D tools and dialogs for controlling the object, camera, and lights operate in a space defined by **axes** in three directions, as shown at the left. As you look at your computer screen, the X axis runs left and right, the Y axis runs up and down, and the Z axis runs back and forward, directly perpendicular to the screen.

CS4 Extended's **3D Axis widget** (its operation is explained on page 656) has its own X, Y, and Z axes. These are the axes as they were when the model was saved or exported. But the widget's axes will be reoriented along with the model if you move the model in Photoshop Extended. You use Photoshop Extended's 3D tools to move and scale the model, or move and zoom the camera, in 3D space. Use the widget to move and scale the model in its "native" space, the orientation it was saved or exported in.

The 3D Interface

The 3D interface is quite different in Photoshop CS3 Extended than in Photoshop CS4 Extended. In CS3 Extended the tools and other functions for repositioning or scaling the model and repositioning or zooming the camera are available through pop-outs on the Options bar that appears when Layer > 3D Layers > Transform 3D Model is chosen. In CS4 Extended the 3D functions are easier to get to — 3D has its own menu, and the two sets of 3D tools appear in the Tools panel. In addition there's a four-part 3D panel, opened by choosing Window > 3D. The parts of Photoshop CS3 Extended's 3D interface are shown on page 654, and the CS4 Extended interface is shown on pages 655–656.

Working with 3D Models

Both Photoshop CS3 Extended and CS4 Extended can open a number of 3D file formats (you'll find a list on page 668) so you can work with them right in Photoshop Extended, moving, scaling, and rotating the meshes; editing the textures; changing the lighting; or moving the camera within the 3D space to get

continued on page 657

When you're working in 3D, it's easy to switch between the 3D Rotate Object tool ⚬ and 3D Roll Object tool ⚬ or between the 3D Orbit Camera ⚬ and 3D Roll Camera ⚬ tools. Just hold down the Alt/Option key to make the switch.

3D OBJECT TOOLS

The **3D Object tools** move, rotate, or scale the model. They change only the model's position or size, not your viewpoint, and not the position of the lights in the scene. Instead of using the tools, you can enter numeric values in a drop-down dialog from the Options bar in CS3, or right on the Options bar in CS4.

3D Slide lets you move the model anywhere on the horizontal (XZ) plane — side-to-side, closer or farther away. But hold down the **Shift** key to limit the motion to either the X or the Z direction.

3D Scale changes the size of the model proportionally. But to compress or expand the model in only one direction, changing its shape, hold down **Shift** and drag left or right to scale it only in the X direction, up or down to scale it only in the Y direction; to scale it only in the Z direction, hold down **Alt/Option** (instead of Shift) as you drag.

3D Rotate rotates the object around a vertical (Y) axis if you drag left or right. If you drag straight up or down, it rotates the model around a horizontal (X) axis. Dragging at an angle rotates in both directions at once, but holding down the **Shift** key limits the rotation to one direction.

3D Roll rotates the object around a Z axis, which goes near-to-far, into and out of the screen; drag right to rotate clockwise, left for counterclockwise.

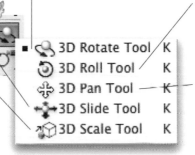

3D Drag/Pan lets you move the model anywhere on the vertical XY plane — side-to-side, up or down. Hold down the **Shift** key to limit the motion to either the X or the Y direction.

3D CAMERA TOOLS

The **3D Camera tools** change only the camera's position or zoom setting, changing your viewpoint. The object itself doesn't move relative to the ground plane or the lights. As it does for the comparable 3D Object tools, adding the **Shift** key constrains movement to one direction for the **Orbit**, **Pan**, and **Walk** tools. Instead of using the tools, you can enter numeric values in a drop-down dialog from the Options bar in CS3, or right on the Options bar in CS4.

3D Orbit revolves the camera around the model in a circle, either horizontally or vertically.

3D Roll View revolves the camera around a Z axis.

3D Pan View moves the camera left and right, up and down, in the XY plane.

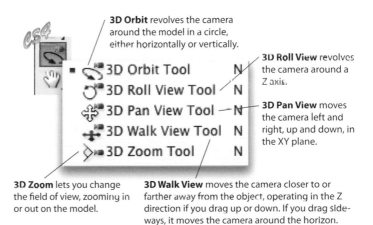

3D Zoom lets you change the field of view, zooming in or out on the model.

3D Walk View moves the camera closer to or farther away from the object, operating in the Z direction if you drag up or down. If you drag sideways, it moves the camera around the horizon.

3D IN PHOTOSHOP CS3 EXTENDED

With Photoshop CS3 Extended you can import 3D objects and manipulate their position and scale. You can make some basic decisions about lighting and whether to display (render) the object in a solid, shaded form, or in one of the wireframe or cross-section views. You can also modify the textures that make up the "skin" of the model.

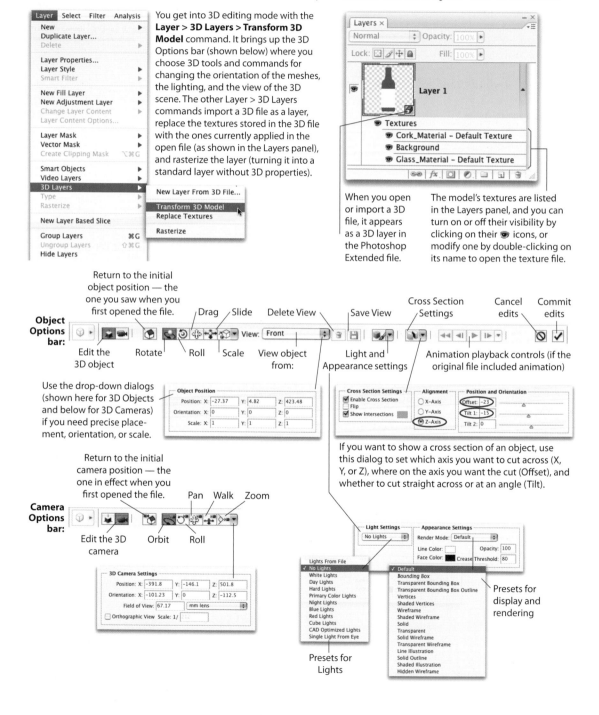

You get into 3D editing mode with the **Layer > 3D Layers > Transform 3D Model** command. It brings up the 3D Options bar (shown below) where you choose 3D tools and commands for changing the orientation of the meshes, the lighting, and the view of the 3D scene. The other Layer > 3D Layers commands import a 3D file as a layer, replace the textures stored in the 3D file with the ones currently applied in the open file (as shown in the Layers panel), and rasterize the layer (turning it into a standard layer without 3D properties).

When you open or import a 3D file, it appears as a 3D layer in the Photoshop Extended file.

The model's textures are listed in the Layers panel, and you can turn on or off their visibility by clicking on their 👁 icons, or modify one by double-clicking on its name to open the texture file.

Object Options bar:

Return to the initial object position — the one you saw when you first opened the file.

Drag Slide Delete View Save View Cross Section Settings Cancel edits Commit edits

View: Front

Edit the 3D object Rotate Roll Scale View object from: Light and Appearance settings Animation playback controls (if the original file included animation)

Use the drop-down dialogs (shown here for 3D Objects and below for 3D Cameras) if you need precise placement, orientation, or scale.

If you want to show a cross section of an object, use this dialog to set which axis you want to cut across (X, Y, or Z), where on the axis you want the cut (Offset), and whether to cut straight across or at an angle (Tilt).

Camera Options bar:

Return to the initial camera position — the one in effect when you first opened the file.

Pan Walk Zoom

Edit the 3D camera Orbit Roll

Presets for Lights

Presets for display and rendering

3D IN PHOTOSHOP CS4 EXTENDED

With CS4, 3D in Photoshop Extended gained its own panels for editing objects in a scene without diving into the menus. It also added an extensive menu of commands that help with creating, modifying, and exporting 3D objects. Although Photoshop's ability to create 3D models remains very limited, it nevertheless can create some basic models from image layers, as shown in "Quick Sources of 3D Material" on page 668. You can then paint on or otherwise modify the textures of these models.

Create:

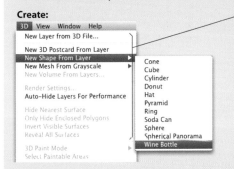

The first half of the 3D menu contains the commands for creating simple 3D objects and for viewing objects.

The second half of the menu contains commands for painting textures on the objects and for rendering and exporting your objects or scenes.

The last command in the menu takes you online to Adobe's resource site for 3D-related materials.

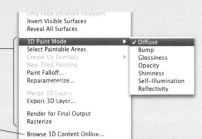

Edit:

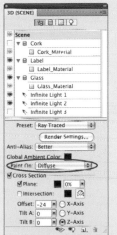

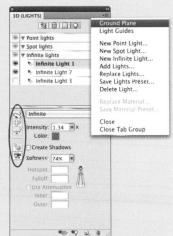

The **3D (Scene)** panel lists all the elements in your 3D scene. Here you choose your rendering options, whether or not you want to set a cross section, and which texture will be painted if you simply start to paint on the 3D object rather than choosing a texture first; the default texture is Diffuse.

The base of each panel holds the buttons (left to right) to show the **ground plane**, show **light guides** (with the type, angle, and fall-off of each light), **create a new light**, and **delete a light**.

The **3D (Mesh)** panel lets you target each of the meshes that make up your model. The same 3D Object tools available in the Tools panel and Options bar are available here for the mesh being previewed. This lets you see and manipulate a mesh without any other distracting elements.

In the **3D (Materials)** panel you can access any of nine textures (properties of a material) to edit them. You can choose a different file as the texture source, or create a new texture file; click on the button to the right of each property to open a menu of choices. In this panel you can also change the color of the ambient lighting.

The **3D (Lights)** panel controls all the sources of light except ambient light and self-illumination, both of which are controlled in the 3D (Materials) panel. You can determine the position of each light in the scene, its intensity, whether it casts shadows, how far the light extends, how fast its intensity falls off, and what type of light it is — Point, Spot, or Infinite. Here you can add lights, delete lights, or change one type of light to another. The tools on the left side of the panel are available according to the type of light chosen, and are specifically for moving lights.

continued on page 656

continued from page 655

Output:

The **3D Render Settings** dialog replaces the Appearance Settings dialog from CS3 (shown on page 654). You can open the dialog by choosing 3D > Render Settings or by clicking the "Render Settings" button in the 3D (Scene) panel (shown on page 655). Any options you chose in the 3D (Scene) panel are reflected in the 3D Render Settings dialog, but you can also change them here. As long as your video card supports it, you can choose to render your model in a variety of ways and with several different options within each method.

The typical render is a solid **Face Style**, with options for how to render a solid object and what properties to render.

Edge and **Vertex** styles determine whether and how the wireframe (mesh) is displayed and rendered.

Volume Style is primarily used for DICOM renders, and **Stereo Type** is designed to be used when special glasses or a lenticular lens will be used for viewing.

Save preset   Delete preset   Cross Section toggle

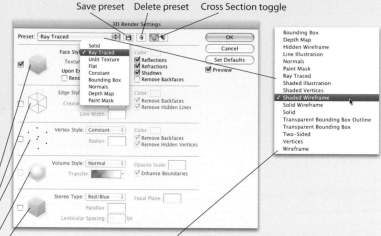

Choose a **preset** in the 3D Render Settings dialog, or in the 3D (Scene) panel. Then set properties appropriate to the type of render you want to do. An advantage of using this dialog rather than the 3D (Scene) panel is that you can save your customized presets for the types of rendering you do often. If you've created a cross section, you can also set different render settings for each side of the dividing plane, using the buttons at the top of the dialog to toggle between sides.

THE 3D AXIS WIDGET

Photoshop CS4 Extended's **3D Axis widget** (View > Show > 3D Axis) is shown below. It represents the object's original orientation and rotates with the object. You can also use it instead of the 3D Object tools. The cursor becomes a different tool as you hover over each different part of the 3D Axis, letting you scale, rotate, or move the object. The red arm represents the X axis, the blue represents the Y axis, and the green (almost invisible here since it's pointing directly away from us) is the Z axis. The active part of the widget — arrowhead, ring, bar, or center cube — will turn yellow to show that it's active.

When you start to use the widget, a gray bar appears above it. Drag the gray bar to reposition the widget so it's handy but not in the way. Click at the left end of the bar to minimize the widget, or click on the right end and then drag to shrink or enlarge the widget (dragging left shrinks, right enlarges).

Drag on the **white cube** to scale the object — drag up to make it larger, down to make it smaller.

Drag in or out on a conical **arrowhead** to move the object along that axis.

Hover over the small **bar** until it turns yellow, and then drag inward (toward the cube) to compress the object along that axis. Drag outward (away from the cube) to expand the object.

Drag clockwise or counterclockwise on a **ring segment** to show the entire yellow ring and rotate the object. A wedge of color shows the angle you've rotated through.

Move your cursor between two axes and near the white cube in the center to show a **yellow square** with an "I" cursor. The square represents the flat plane formed by the two axes (here the XY plane). Now you can drag with the cursor to move your object anywhere on that entire two-dimensional plane.

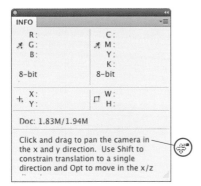

If you need help remembering how a 3D Object or 3D Camera tool works, open the **Info panel**. If you don't see a description of the currently selected 3D tool, choose Panel Options from the panel's menu ▾≡ and check the box at the bottom for Show Tool Tips.

different views of the model. "Quick Sources of 3D Material" starting on page 668, tells how to open or import 3D models and how to generate some very simple models within Photoshop Extended.

Modifying textures. Photoshop Extended can't add new materials to a 3D model. But any material that already exists as part of the model can have any of its existing textures modified, and in CS4 Extended, other texture files can be loaded in place of the existing ones, and new textures can be added (a new 2D file is opened, in which you can create a new texture). You can use the standard Photoshop painting and adjusting tools to edit the textures. In Photoshop CS3 Extended editing is done by double-clicking on the name of a texture in the Layers panel to open up the texture file, and then editing it or painting it with the Brush tool ✎ as you might any other Photoshop file.▼ That

continued on page 659

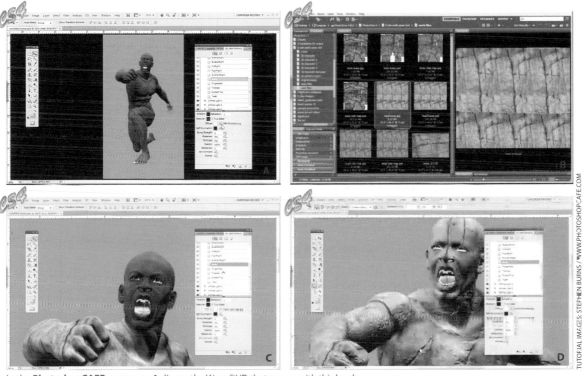

In the **PhotoshopCAFE_poser.mp4** clip on the Wow DVD that comes with this book, Stephen Burns shows how he used Photoshop CS4 Extended to replace and add to the textures of the body and head materials of a model **A** he had created in the Poser 3D-modeling program. Using Bridge, he explains how the files for surface pattern and surface texture were created **B**. He uses Photoshop Extended's 3D (Materials) panel to load the Diffuse and Bump textures and to set the strength with which the Bump textures are applied **C, D**. In the "Gallery" (on page 708), you can see how Burns developed this model into a finished image.

🔴 **PhotoshopCAFE_poser.mp4**

FIND OUT MORE
▼ Using the Brush tool ✎
page 71

TUTORIAL IMAGES: STEPHEN BURNS / WWW.PHOTOSHOPCAFE.COM

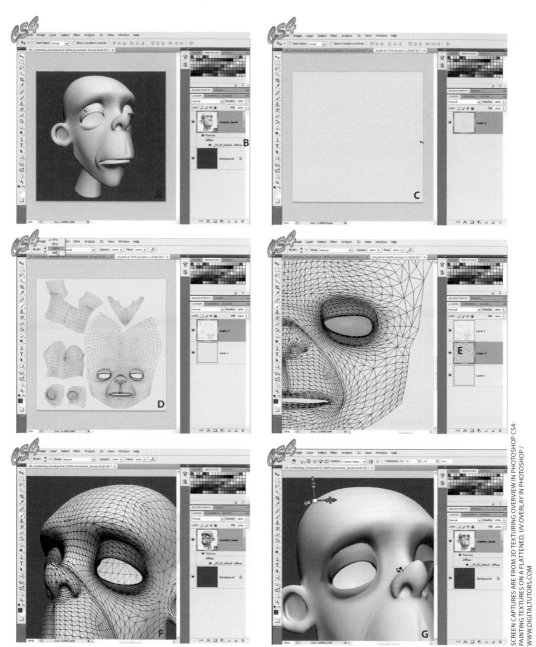

In a model like this one **A** it can be difficult to get full, even coverage if you paint directly on the 3D layer in Photoshop Extended because the details of the geometry, such as the creases above the eyes, can get in the way of the brush. But if you open the Diffuse texture file (by double-clicking on its entry in the Layers panel) **B**, it's impossible to tell where to paint on the flat pink layer **C** in order to color the eye area. To see where the eyes are on the 2D texture file, you can choose **3D > Create UV Overlays**. This adds a separate overlay layer to the 2D texture file, which clearly shows what part of the texture surrounds the eyes **D**. You can then add a new transparent layer to paint on **E**; since you're painting on a flat image, there are no creases to get in the way when you paint. Saving the texture file (Ctrl/⌘-S) without first turning off visibility for the UV overlay carries the overlay back to the 3D layer **F**. But if you turn off the UV layer's visibility before saving, the overlay won't show in the 3D layer **G**. *Note:* Whatever layer is targeted in the 2D texture file when you save it, will remain the active layer. So if you add a new empty layer to the 2D texture file, save the file, and then paint directly on the 3D layer, this painting will be applied to the empty layer, and will be separate from other layers in the 2D texture file. That way you can remove or edit the layer later if you change your mind.

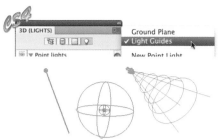

If you turn on the Light Guides option in the 3D (Lights) panel menu ▼☰ in Photoshop CS4 Extended, you can see the orientation and extent of the lighting. Shown here left to right are Infinite, Point, and Spot lights.

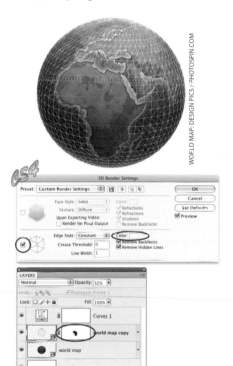

WORLD MAP: DESIGN PICS / PHOTOSPIN.COM

In this print illustration, a flat world map in a 2:1 width-to-height ratio was applied to a sphere in Photoshop CS4 Extended (3D > New Shape from Layer > Sphere) and the sphere was reoriented with the 3D Rotate ⟳ and 3D Roll ↻ tools to show the part of the world we wanted. We duplicated the 3D layer (Ctrl/⌘-J) and changed the Render Settings for this copy from the default Solid preset to the Wireframe preset but then chose white as the wireframe color. We added a layer mask to the wireframe layer and painted the mask with black to remove the lines from the African continent and Madagascar. Finally, we reduced the opacity of the wireframe layer and added a Curves Adjustment layer to lighten the image. See Derek Lea's *Biorhythms* on page 704 for an elegant example of the combination of two renderings.

option is also available in CS4 Extended, but another option is to load a different texture directly into the 3D layer.▼ You can also paint directly onto the 3D layer itself, without opening a texture. Another improvement is the UV overlay, a guide to help you know where on the 2D texture file to paint. In order to put the paint where you want it on the model, choose **3D > Create UV Overlays** to add a layer with a UV map (by default it's a wireframe) that helps you see how the texture file fits the model. (If you're not used to operating in 3D environments, you might not know that UV has nothing to do with ultraviolet lighting; it has to do with axes for mapping textures to the geometry of a model.) Once you've added the overlay, if you save the 2D texture file, the overlay will also become part of the 3D layer, unless you turn off visibility for the overlay layer, or delete it, before you save the texture file.

Lighting

In Photoshop CS3 Extended your choices for lighting are limited to a list of presets (popped out from the Options bar, as shown on page 654). In CS4 Extended, you can open the list of presets by choosing Add Lights from the 3D (Lights) panel's menu ▼☰. But you can also modify an existing light or build a new one and even save it as a preset. Photoshop Extended CS4's 3D has three kinds of lights, similar to the three kinds in the Lighting Effects filter.▼ In 3D they're called **Point** (it's like a bulb that sends light in all directions, like Omni in Lighting Effects), **Spot** (a focused, directed light; it's like the Spotlight in Lighting Effects), and **Infinite** (a faraway light source that has a direction but not a point source like that of a spotlight; it's like Directional in Lighting Effects). Besides position, you can set the intensity and color of each light, decide whether it will cast shadows, and set other characteristics, depending on what type of light it is.

Rendering, Rasterizing, Saving & Exporting

To *render* is to convert the mesh, materials, lighting information, and camera position into the image you see on the screen. You can choose the type of rendering you want, either in CS3 Extended's Appearance dialog (popped out from the Options bar, as shown on page 654) or in CS4's 3D Render Settings dialog (page 656), which can be opened by choosing 3D > Render Settings. Rendering can be done at less than optimal quality and detail in order to reduce the amount of processing power and time needed to display the changes you make. In addition to the settings available in the 3D Render Settings

---
FIND OUT MORE

▼ Creating textures in Photoshop **page 556–562**

▼ Lighting Effects **page 264**

Before · **After**

When you convert a video frame for print or Web purposes, besides converting to square pixels, you'll want to get rid of any visible **interlacing**. Photoshop's **Filter > Video > De-Interlace** can do the job. See page 680 for more about interlacing and deinterlacing.

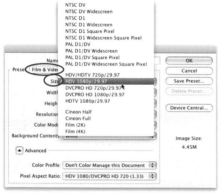

Photoshop offers a variety of formats for designing for broadcast video. Choose File > New and choose **Film & Video** from the Preset menu, and finally, choose from the **Size** menu.

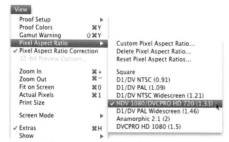

To switch between a scaled and an unscaled view of a video-format file you're working on in Photoshop, choose **View > Pixel Aspect Ratio** and choose the format. Then toggle **Pixel Aspect Ratio Correction** on and off.

dialog, there's a "best" setting that's applied if you choose 3D > Render For Final Output.

When you've completed a file with a 3D layer, you can save it in Photoshop format for full access to all the 3D layers and functions in the future (File > Save As, with Photoshop chosen for the Format; turn on Maximize Compatibility). If you choose a format that doesn't support the 3D layers (such as JPEG), Photoshop will save a copy of the file in that format (the new file will be saved closed), leaving the layered file open. Or export only the 3D layer as a 3D model that can be opened in a 3D program (3D > Export 3D Layer). (In CS3 Extended you can't export a 3D file or save it in a 3D format, but you *can* permanently change the model file you opened by choosing Layer > 3D > Layer > Replace Textures.) If you no longer need access to the 3D properties of the 3D layer and you want a standard pixel-based layer instead, choose 3D > Rasterize.

VIDEO

In Photoshop, you can capture a frame from video and convert it for use in print or on the Web. You can also prepare a still image to be incorporated into a video clip. In Photoshop Extended you can incorporate an entire video clip as a video layer in a Photoshop file, enhance it with tone and color adjustments, even turn it into a Smart Object and filter it, then save it in video format again. We'll start (below) with the kinds of video work that can be done in either Photoshop or Photoshop Extended, and then move on to the kinds of video editing that are limited to Photoshop Extended (page 662).

Pixel Aspect Ratio

Video can be digitally encoded in a number of different file formats, and many of these formats use nonsquare pixels. Photoshop can manage the oblong pixels of many video formats, making it possible to take a frame from video and turn it into a still image for print or the Web (page 678), or to create a still image for video in Photoshop, complete with nonsquare pixels if needed (page 681).

Designing for Video

When you design an image in Photoshop to be used for video, it's good to be aware of some differences between designing for video and designing for print or for the Web:

- To produce a file to incorporate into existing video for broadcast, you need to know which **broadcast standard** your video

In Photoshop's scaled view of your video frame (with pixel aspect ratio corrected, shown here on the left), you can draw a circle by holding down the Shift key and dragging with the Ellipse tool ⬭ and it will look like a circle. In the unscaled view, it will look stretched (right), but either way, when it's displayed on TV, it will be decoded as a circle, and that's how the audience will see it.

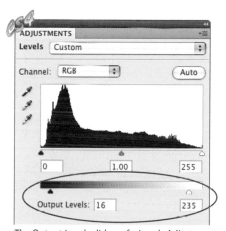

The Output Levels sliders of a Levels Adjustment layer can be moved inward as shown here to bring contrast (and sometimes color saturation) into a video-safe range. The standard of no color darker than 16 or lighter than 235 is a conservative one.

Photoshop's Filter > Video > NTSC Colors command "subdues" certain colors to prevent color from "bleeding" across the scan lines of broadcast TV.

has to adhere to. There are several, with variations on each. The most commonly used broadcast standards are NTSC (the North American standard), PAL (the primary format in Europe, Japan, Australia, and New Zealand), SECAM (the French standard), and now HDTV and HDV.

- When you start a new file in a video format, Photoshop provides guides for keeping type and important parts of the image within **"safe" areas** of the video frame, so they won't be cropped out or distorted at the edges, as described in "Respecting the Guides" on page 681.

- Horizontal lines thinner than 2 pixels and fine serifs on type can show an unwanted **flicker** when displayed. You may need to make graphics and type more "robust" than you would for print or for the Web, or limit yourself to sans serif type.

- **Contrast & color.** Color for video goes through a conversion process when it's broadcast that doesn't allow the kind of precision that we ask of print media. For example, analog video reserves pure black for special keying purposes and dulls bright whites so the signal doesn't "bleed" into the audio track. To keep **black-and-white contrast** within a safe range, you can use the very conservative standard of a black no lower than 16 and a white no higher than 235, set in the Output Levels sliders in the Levels dialog as shown at the left. Or investigate the limits for the specific broadcast standard you're working with and use those settings.

  Even the sharp contrast in a heavily sharpened image can create a problem. Try **Filter > Blur > Motion Blur** at an angle of 0° to add enough intermediate tones so the image won't vibrate when broadcast, or cause audible noise. For rasterized type or graphics, use antialiasing to avoid sharp contrast at the edges.

- Even after contrast is adjusted, your image may still include highly saturated (intense) colors — the bright red in a shirt, for instance — that can "bleed" onto their surroundings. To **reduce saturated colors to broadcast-safe,** you have three options: Use **Filter > Video > NTSC Colors** (which is conservative and may dull the color more than you need); or convert from your working RGB color space to your broadcast color space with **Edit > Convert to Profile**; or keep the file in your **working RGB color space**, save it with that profile (check the Embed Color Profile option in the Save As dialog box), and make the conversion in your video-editing program.

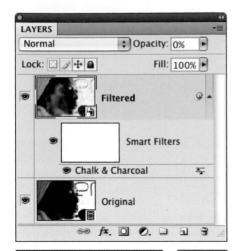

For the beginning of a music video, we opened the QuickTime movie clip as a video layer in Photoshop Extended. We duplicated the layer and then, in order to apply a filter to all of its frames, we turned the duplicate into a Smart Object. The two video layers were blended by using the "stopwatch" **A** and play head **B** to set keyframes **C** in the Animation (Timeline) panel to control the Opacity of the filtered layer, so that in the final clip, the image started out as filtered, and then the filter effect faded, leaving the original clip to lead into the rest of the video (the process is explained step-by-step, starting on page 684).

Saving an Image for Video

To save your video-ready image, you need to know which file formats will work with the video-editing software that will handle the file next. Some programs (such as Adobe After Effects and Adobe Premiere Pro) can read layered Photoshop (PSD) files, and some can even accept live Photoshop Layer Styles. Other programs can take only a flattened file, with a *Background* alone.

"Round-trip" Video Editing in Photoshop

Even in Photoshop — not the Extended version — there are a number of ways to work on video frames. You can export the frames of a video clip from your video editing program as individual files, then enhance and resave the files in Photoshop, and assemble them again in your video-editing software. For a "round trip" like that above, you won't want to convert the video frames to a square-pixel aspect ratio and back, but you may want Photoshop to correct the preview, so you can avoid the "stretched" look while you're working.

A PERFECT PLACE FOR AN ACTION

If you're working in Photoshop rather than Photoshop Extended, and you're importing a video clip for editing in Photoshop, with each frame as a separate file, and then resaving the files to be reassembled into video again in a video-editing program, you can save time by recording an Action.▼ Record as you process the first image, and then use File > Automate > Batch to apply the same processing to the other files.

FIND OUT MORE

▼ Recording & playing Actions **page 120**

An essential part of a video-to-Photoshop-to-video process is knowing what Photoshop-compatible formats your video editor can use to export frames, and what file formats it can accept on the return trip. For a series of frames, you'll also need to know what naming conventions to follow in order to make the transition work right. Look for that information in your video editor's Help resource.

A Photoshop Extended Video-Editing Workflow

Photoshop Extended can work with an entire video clip to enhance its color and contrast, filter it, combine it with 3D or animation, and render it as video again in any of several different formats.

1 Open a video file in Photoshop Extended. It will appear as a video layer in the Layers panel, and you'll see its duration bar in the Animation (Timeline) panel. (The Timeline mode of the Animation panel is described on page 666.)

By default, a set of three **"Unify" buttons** and a **Propagate Frame 1** checkbox automatically appears at the top of the Layers panel whenever the Animation panel is open in Frames mode. (You can choose to have them showing all the time or never instead, by choosing Animation Options from the Layers panel's menu ▾≡.)

The **"Unify"** buttons control what happens in your animation frames when you change a layer's **Position** (moving the content with the Move tool ▸⊕, for example), **Visibility** (turning the layer's 👁 on or off), or **Style** (changing the effects in a Layer Style, or the Warp Text settings for a type layer).

When a Unify function is turned **on** (by clicking its button), the current state of the layer is applied to all frames, and when you make any subsequent changes to the layer, these are also applied to all frames. (If instead of unifying a layer's Position, Visibility, or Style for *all* frames, you want to unify just *some* frames, you can click the button to turn off the Unify function, and then select just the frames you want in the Animation panel: Click to select the first frame you want to change, and then Shift-click to select a contiguous range of frames or Ctrl/⌘-click to select noncontiguous frames. Then make the change.) **Note:** Visibility, controlled by the 👁 in the Layers panel, is not the same as Opacity, which is regulated through the Opacity slider. With "Unify visibility" turned on, you can still control Opacity for individual frames, and you can also tween the Opacity. ▼

FIND OUT MORE

▼ Tweening **page 664**

2 Drag the Timeline's **current time indicator (play head)** to view the video so you can locate the section you want to work on first. Move the Timeline's two **work area indicators** into position at the beginning and end of this section. Photoshop Extended will render only this section, and no processing power or time will be wasted on frames beyond those points.

3 Make the changes you want:

To make **color and tone adjustments**, you can simply add an Adjustment layer above the video layer; you'll find examples in "Quick Video Techniques" on page 687.

If you want to apply one of Photoshop's **filters** to a video, you'll need to turn the video layer into a Smart Object (Filter > Convert for Smart Filters). "Animating a Video Clip in Photoshop Extended" on page 684 shows how to combine filtered and unfiltered video.

You can also do **rotoscoping,** painting or cloning image material into the video. You can paint or clone right onto the video layer, nondestructively — if you change your mind about the edits, you can restore the original video, as it was when you opened it, by choosing Layer > Video Layers > **Restore Frame** (for changes to a single frame) or **Restore All Frames**. But for the most flexibility in changing your rotoscoping later, add a new layer (or layers) above the video and do your rotoscoping there. To add a new video layer, choose **Layer > Video Layers > New Blank Video Layer**.

4 Render the video (**File > Export > Render Video**). (Page 686 has information on exporting.)

ANIMATION

Animation, or motion graphics, consists of a series of still images called *frames*. Usually each frame is only slightly different from the frame before, with just a small change applied. Playing all the frames in sequence, if you have enough of them and you swap them fast enough, creates the illusion of motion. In Photoshop Extended the **Animation panel** has two modes, **Frames** and **Timeline**; in the standard Photoshop versions, the Animation panel exists in Frames mode only.

Frame Animation

In its **Frames** mode, the Animation panel shows a series of frames, each one a "snapshot" initially made from all visible layers at the time the frame was added; it's possible to go back later and edit a frame by targeting the frame and then changing the visibility and content of the layers. You can control the speed of motion in the animation by adjusting the time that each frame remains on the screen as the animation is played.

Three ways to animate. There are three approaches to frame animation in Photoshop:

- In **frame-by-frame animation**, you create a single frame, then copy the frame and make changes to the artwork (adding a new layer for new content) so this new frame now looks slightly different. Then copy this new frame to make the next one, make more changes, copy again, change again, and so on. There's an example on page 694.

- Another option is to create the artwork for all of your frames ahead of time, as separate layers in your Photoshop file. Then use the **Make Frames from Layers** command from the Animation panel's menu ▾☰. The "SPIN" animation on the facing page is an example.

- Instead of hand-crafting every frame, for some kinds of animation sequences you can make the starting and ending frames for an animation sequence and then let Photoshop automatically generate the intermediate action. This automated way of making frames is called *tweening* (short for "in-betweening"). Three kinds of properties of each layer can be tweened: **Position** of the artwork on the layer, layer

THE ANIMATION PANEL (FRAMES)

With the Animation panel in **Frames mode,** you can create GIF animations by using layers and tweening to generate changes and motion over time.

When a "**Unify**" button is clicked, a change to that property of the targeted layer will be made throughout all the frames. Unify works with three layer properties: **Position**, **Visibility** (not the same as Opacity), and **Style**.

Check **Propagate Frame 1** if you want a change to the Position, Opacity, or Style of Frame 1 to affect the other frames in the animation.

Changes in a layer's visibility, Opacity, and Style are reflected in any frame(s) currently targeted in the Animation panel. If you change the content of the layer, it will be changed in all frames for which that layer is visible.

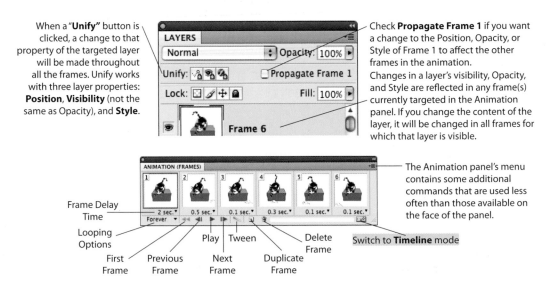

The Animation panel's menu contains some additional commands that are used less often than those available on the face of the panel.

Frame Delay Time

Looping Options

First Frame

Previous Frame

Play

Next Frame

Tween

Duplicate Frame

Delete Frame

Switch to **Timeline** mode

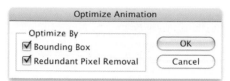

	OK
☑ Bounding Box	Cancel
☑ Redundant Pixel Removal	

Optimize By

The two options offered in the Optimize Animation dialog can dramatically reduce the number of pixels in a frame, which cuts file size without affecting image quality. **Bounding Box** effectively crops the frame to include only the area that has changed since the previous frame. **Redundant Pixel Removal** makes transparent all pixels that are the same as they were in the preceding frame.

Opacity, and **Effects** (the effects in a Layer Style as well as text warp on type layers). You'll find an example of tweening on page 700.

Timing. Once you've created your frames, you can set the timing and looping options in the Animation (Frames) panel, and then use the panel's Play button ▶ to preview the animation so you can adjust the timing (see page 698 for an example).

Optimizing and saving animations. From Photoshop you can save animations in GIF format: Choose Optimize Animation from the Animation panel's menu ▾≡, turn on both options, and click "OK." Then choose File > **Save for Web & Devices**. In the Save for Web & Devices dialog (shown on page 666), do the following to reduce file size and thus loading time:

1 At the top of the panel, choose **GIF** for the format.

2 In the **Image Size** section reduce the dimensions of the file if your design allows it.

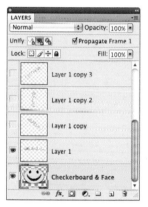

Spin.psd

Thinking smart and using keyboard shortcuts, Geno Andrews produced his "SPIN" animation in Photoshop almost as quickly as if he could have tweened it (but transforming, such as the rotation and perspective applied to the word "SPIN," isn't tweenable). He typed "SPIN" above his image layer and chose **Layer > Type > Rasterize**. Then he duplicated this "SPIN" layer and rotated the copy 45° all in one step using the shortcut for copy-and-transform: **Ctrl-alt-T (Windows); ⌘-Option-T (Mac)**. He used **Filter > Blur > Radial Blur (Spin)** to blur the word. Then he copied and rotated the blurred result six more times, each time using the shortcut for copy-and-transform-again: **Ctrl-Alt-Shift-T (Windows); ⌘-Option-Shift-T (Mac)**. In the Layers panel he Shift-selected all the "SPIN" layers and distorted them (**Edit > Transform > Perspective**, and **Scale**) to fit the spin into the face. This had to be done *after* the rotation to be tilted correctly. **Make Frames from Layers** from the Animation panel's ▾≡ menu made the frames. Finally, he clicked on the thumbnail for the layer with the face, made sure it was visible 👁, and clicked on the **"Unify layer visibility" button** 🔒 to add the face and background behind the "SPIN" in each frame. He then deleted the very first frame (the one made from the face layer alone) and adjusted the timing for the frames so the spinning would stop briefly after each full rotation.

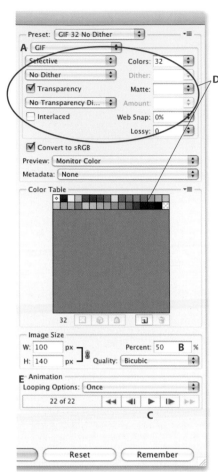

To save an animation, choose GIF as the format **A**, and reduce the dimensions of the file **B**. Use the playback controls **C** to choose a frame for optimizing color, and then set color options **D**. Set the animation to play as many times as you like with Looping Options **E**. Then preview and save the animation.

3 Using the playback buttons in the **Animation** section of the dialog, review the frames and choose one with the most complex color in the animation. Then set color options in the top part of the panel.▼

FIND OUT MORE
▼ Optimizing a GIF file **page 152**

4 Set the number of times you want the animation to *loop*, or replay.

5 Use the **"Preview in browser"** button to review the final animation, and then click the **"Save"** button.

Timeline Animation

In Photoshop Extended with the Animation panel in **Timeline mode** (shown on page 667), you have a "movie-making" apparatus that can combine 2D and 3D graphics (still or moving), and video. Instead of showing individual "snapshots" as the Frames mode does, the Timeline shows a **duration bar** to represent each layer in the file, with one exception: The *Background* is fixed in place and so can't be animated; it doesn't appear in the Timeline. By adjusting the length of a duration bar, you determine when the layer appears in the movie. A **current time indicator (play head)** lets you "scrub" through any part of the movie to view it. **Keyframe indicators** can be added for the individual layers, to control changes in the course of the movie — for instance, keyframes can be used to establish starting and ending positions for graphics that move, to establish when a video layer starts to fade out or has faded completely, or to set the start or end of a 3D model's rotation or zoom. For each layer the same properties that can be tweened in the Animations panel's Frames mode — Position, Opacity, and Style (in Frames mode it's called Effects) — can be keyframed. In addition, for 3D layers, object and camera position can be "tweened" with keyframes, which adds zooming and spinning effects that aren't possible without 3D. As you work, you can turn on **onion-skinning** if you want to see a ghosted version of the frames that come just before or after the one you're working on, to see how your changes will fit into the movie.

From Photoshop Extended, you can save as an animated GIF (as described on page 665) or use **File** > **Export** > **Render Video** to save as a QuickTime movie, an AVI (Windows) movie, MPEG-4, 3G, or other formats (you'll find the process on page 686). *Wow*

THE ANIMATION PANEL (TIMELINE)

Using the **Timeline** in Photoshop Extended, you can create, edit, and render movies consisting of 3D, video, and motion graphics.

The **Timecode** shows the point where the play head is positioned, measured in hours:minutes:seconds:frames from the beginning of the movie. Hold the Alt/Option key and click on the numbers to toggle to the **frame counter**.

The **Frame Rate** is displayed in parentheses next to the units display.

The **current time indicator**, or **play head**, can be "scrubbed" to render a section of the movie, or positioned for setting a keyframe.

Cached Frames Indicator (thin green line) shows which parts have been rendered and stored.

The two **work area indicators** can be dragged to shorten or lengthen the section of the Timeline that is rendered for preview or for export.

Add **Comments** by using keyframes

3D objects have several properties to animate, in addition to the three basic properties of other layers.

Click the **stopwatch** so you can set a keyframe for that property by dragging the play head.

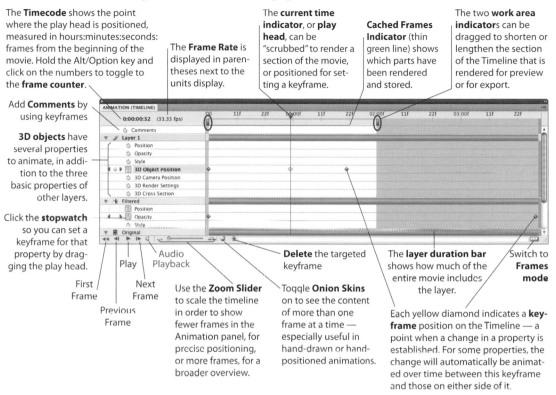

First Frame

Previous Frame

Play

Next Frame

Audio Playback

Use the **Zoom Slider** to scale the timeline in order to show fewer frames in the Animation panel, for precise positioning, or more frames, for a broader overview.

Toggle **Onion Skins** on to see the content of more than one frame at a time — especially useful in hand-drawn or hand-positioned animations.

Delete the targeted keyframe

The **layer duration bar** shows how much of the entire movie includes the layer.

Switch to **Frames mode**

Each yellow diamond indicates a **keyframe** position on the Timeline — a point when a change in a property is established. For some properties, the change will automatically be animated over time between this keyframe and those on either side of it.

With 3D layers, video layers, Smart Filters, and keyframing, you can construct some impressive motion graphics in Photoshop Extended. If you decide you'd like to learn more about motion graphics in Photoshop, we recommend *Adobe Photoshop CS3 Extended: Photoshop in Motion*. Corey Barker starts with the basics of the Animation (Timeline) panel, works through some very practical title animations, and builds up to animating masks and zooming with Layer Styles. He works with Smart Objects, Smart Filters, and nested animation to create fire, and he designs swooping curls and sparkles of light with Layer Styles, Smart Objects, the Warp command, and painting in Dissolve mode.

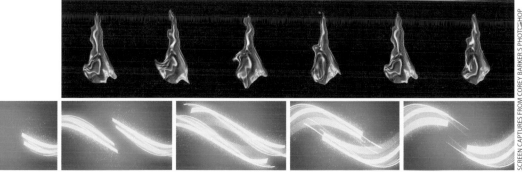

Sources of 3D Material in Photoshop Extended

Photoshop CS3 and CS4 Extended can't generate 3D models from scratch. But here are some ways to get material into the 3D environment so you can take advantage of 3D space. You'll find more applications of the 3D environment in "Quick Video Techniques" on page 687.

We'll start with the two ways to bring in 3D models created by other programs (at the right). Both options are available in both CS3 and CS4, and both bring in the model as a 3D layer, a "package" whose components can be accessed individually, edited, and saved to update the model. Then we'll move to a number of ways to generate very simple models within Photoshop Extended.

3D FORMATS

Photoshop CS3 and CS4 Extended can open or import 3D models in the formats listed below. In CS4 Extended, you can also export models in the U3D, OBJ, DAE, and KMZ formats using the 3D > Export 3D Layer command.

- U3D (a universal standard compressed format)
- 3DS (3D Studio Max)
- OBJ (Alias/Wavefront)
- DAE (Collada digital aspect exchange, a format designed for passing 3D files between applications)
- KMZ (a compressed format; Google Earth 4)

A word of warning, though: The fact that a file is in one of those formats doesn't guarantee that Photoshop Extended can open that particular file.

WHERE TO GO FROM HERE

If you want to use Edit > Transform or any of the choices from the Filter menu on a 3D layer, convert the layer to a Smart Object▼ (Filter > Convert for Smart Filters)▼, or copy the layer (Ctrl/⌘-J) and rasterize the copy (Layer > 3D Layers > Rasterize in Photoshop CS3 Extended, or 3D > Rasterize in CS4 Extended).

YOU'LL FIND THE FILES
in (wow) > Wow Project Files > 3D Sources

FIND OUT MORE
▼ Smart Objects **page 18**
▼ Smart Filters **page 72**

Open a Model

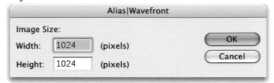

CHOOSE **FILE > OPEN** and locate the model you want to open. In the dialog box that pops up for your model in Photoshop CS3 Extended (above), indicate how big you want the file to be. The larger the Image Size, the more computer power it will take to work with the file, and large files may slow your computer down significantly. CS4 Extended doesn't offer the dialog box.

Import a Model

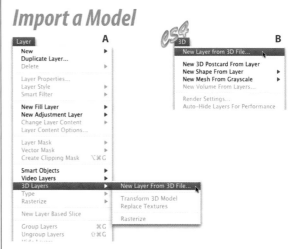

TO IMPORT A 3D MODEL into an RGB file that's already open in Photoshop Extended, use the **New Layer From 3D File** command. In Photoshop Extended CS3 you'll find this command in the **Layer > 3D Layers** menu **A**; in CS4 it's in the **3D** menu **B**. The model will automatically be sized to fit your open file. (The critical dimension of the open file seems to be Height.)

3D from Vanishing Point

When you need an establishing shot to "set the scene" for a movie, but have no budget for on-location filming or intricate 3D modeling, **Vanishing Point**, in conjunction with **After Effects**, can come to your rescue. Pick a photograph that's representative of the location and that has a clear path for your After Effects camera to follow, such as this one of a Hong Kong alley. In Vanishing Point, ▼ draw connecting grids in perspective that cover all the relevant planes above, below, and to either side of the imaginary path, as well as the "end" of the path, where the camera can travel no farther (three of our grids are shown selected). When the grids are drawn, choose **Export for After Effects (.vpe)** from Vanishing Point's menu. Photoshop will export a .png image file for each grid, along with a .3ds and a .vpe document containing instructions for After Effects to reconstruct your 2D image now as a 3D model. Inside After Effects are several controls for positioning the view properly and moving the camera through its 3D world, allowing you to create video footage from a photograph.

IN VANISHING POINT you can capture a surface that's in perspective in a photo, turn it into a 3D layer, and use the 3D Rotate 🔄 and 3D Roll 🔄 tools to transform it to something closer to a straight-on view. Open your image **A**, choose Filter > Vanishing Point, and create a grid for the surface you want to capture **B**. ▼ Select the grid (click on it with Vanishing Point's Edit Plane tool 🔲) and choose **Return 3D Layer to Photoshop** from the menu ▼≡ near the upper-left corner of the dialog **C**; then click "OK." This creates a flat (2D) image of the area covered by the grid, as a 3D layer **D**. You can then manipulate this plane in 3D space with the 3D tools **E**, **F**. For final tweaking, you may want to convert the layer to a Smart Object and use Edit > Transform. ▼

FIND OUT MORE

▼ Using Vanishing
Point **page 612**

▼ Transforming **page 67**

^{CS4} 3D Postcard

A

C

D

New 3D Postcard from Layer in Photoshop CS4 Extended turns the currently targeted layer(s) into a 2D surface in 3D space. Distorting type, graphics, or an image in 3D space can be easier and more intuitive, at least as a start, than trying to accomplish a realistic perspective distortion with the Edit > Transform commands. Target the layer you want to put into 3D space; ours was a PDF exported from InDesign and opened in Photoshop Extended **A**. Choose **3D > New 3D Postcard from Layer B**, wait while Photoshop Extended creates the 3D layer, and then use any of the 3D tools to manipulate the "postcard" **C**, **D**.

A 3D postcard can also be useful for animating type or graphics (see page 691) or as a way to zoom in or out of a photo (page 690). *Note:* For fitting an image, type, or graphics into the particular perspective of a photo, Vanishing Point (page 612) or Edit > Transform (page 67) seems to work better, perhaps because the camera lens distorts the perspective of the background image.

^{CS4} 3D Postcard: Reflections

A **B**

C

D **E**

A 3D "postcard" can be useful for putting images and their reflections into perspective. Here we opened our image file **A** and duplicated it to a new layer (Ctrl/⌘-J), then flipped the duplicate by choosing Edit > Transform > Flip Vertical. We added enough canvas to hold the reflection (Ctrl-Alt-C in Windows, ⌘-Option-C on the Mac to open the Canvas Size dialog, and then set the Height to 200 percent, with the added territory at the bottom of the image) **B**. With the Move tool ▸₊ we Shift-dragged the flipped image down and reduced the Opacity of this layer **C**, just until it was the maximum intensity we might want for the reflection (we could always fade it more with a layer mask once it was in place). Then we Shift-clicked the other layer in the Layers panel so that both layers were targeted, and chose **3D > New 3D Postcard From Layer D**. We used the 3D Rotate tool ⟲ to orient the image and its reflection **E**, and it was ready to drag into our background image. *Note:* Page 629 has a 2D approach to reflections that doesn't require CS4 or the Extended version of Photoshop.

^{CS4} Volume

The 3D > New Volume From Layers command is designed to assemble a series of DICOM medical images, such as sonograms or MRI captures, into a 3D volume. Photoshop CS4 Extended's Help tells how to use the command for this purpose. People who work with other kinds of cross sections, such as histology or pathology series, may also find this command useful. With your cross sections stacked up in order on separate layers, target the layers you want to include and choose 3D > New Volume From Layers. In the **Convert To Volume** dialog, if you change the X or Y setting, the cross sections will be distorted. If you change the Z setting, you change the thickness of the sections that will be generated. **To make your new volume more opaque**, choose 3D > Render Settings and increase the Opacity in the volume section.

CS4 Shapes

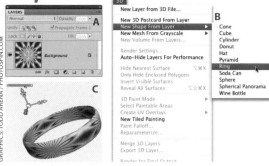

GRAPHICS: TODD ARENA / PHOTOSPIN.COM

NEW SHAPE FROM LAYER applies the contents of a targeted layer **A** to one of the 11 models supplied with Photoshop CS4 Extended. You simply target the layer that holds the image, choose this command from the 3D menu, and choose the shape you want **B**. The image on the layer will become the Diffuse texture (surface color and pattern) of one of the meshes in the model **C**. If the model has more than one mesh, you don't control which mesh the layer is applied to, but once the model is open in Photoshop Extended, you can choose other meshes and load new textures for those. Ring, shown here, as well as Hat and Donut, have only one mesh, but the shapes in "Shapes & Sizes," below, have additional meshes.

Shapes.psd

SHAPES & SIZES

For some of the 11 shapes offered by the 3D > New 3D Shape From Layer command, a square document will serve well as the "generator" for the new 3D Shape. It will become the Diffuse texture for the default Material of the new shape, with little or no distortion by stretching. (By "default Material" we mean the Material to which your layer is applied when you choose 3D > New Shape From Layer.) By experimenting, we found that a **square document** (far left) works for these 3D Shapes: Cone, Cube, Soda Can, and Wine Bottle. (For Soda Can and Wine bottle, the image repeats on the back.)

And a **2:1 rectangular document** works for the Cylinder and Sphere.

CS4 Mesh from Grayscale

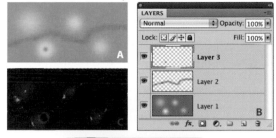

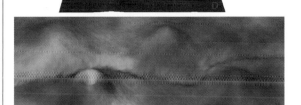

NEW MESH FROM GRAYSCALE makes a 3D mesh from a 2D image, with light tones becoming high spots and dark tones becoming low spots in the 3D mesh. When you use this command, you may be able to start with a recognizable photo (an aerial photo of a landscape, for instance), copy it and blur the copy, and then choose 3D > New 3D Mesh From Grayscale. If you can use your original sharp photo as the Diffuse texture, you now have a 3D version of the image.

Instead of starting with a photo, we manufactured the topography for a simple imaginary landscape. We started a new file (File > New) and filled with medium gray (Edit > Fill > Use: 50% Gray). We dabbed with the Brush tool 🖌 with white paint, a soft brush tip, and low Opacity to paint spots for mountains. Then we added another layer and used a dark gray with the Brush in Dissolve mode to paint a canyon; we blurred the layer (Filter > Blur > Gaussian Blur) and reduced its Opacity. On a third layer we painted a crater in one of the hills **A**. In the Layers panel we targeted all three layers **B**, then chose 3D > **New Mesh From Grayscale** with **Plane** as the mesh choice to produce a 3D layer **C**. We used the 3D Rotate Object tool 🔄 to tilt the plane. To make it look more real, we could reduce Glossiness and Shininess **D**. We added Diffuse and Bump textures (see page 657) and edited the Ambient color and the lighting. We copied the layer and rasterized the copy, then used the Blur tool 💧 to smooth out some rough areas. We duplicated this layer (Ctrl/⌘-J) and put the copy in Hard Light mode at 50% Opacity **E**.

 Landscape.psd

3D Tools

The 3D functions in Photoshop Extended, especially in CS3, have to do with importing 3D objects, replacing or changing their surface textures, and relighting them; in CS4 you can also export them again as 3D objects. Here we explore the operation of the menus, tools, and panels of the 3D interface in Photoshop Extended. But we'll use the model in a way that a graphic designer or illustrator might, taking advantage of Extended's 3D abilities without getting too deeply involved in 3D. (For a fairly simple project like this one, you might want to compare the 3D process presented here with the Warp process used on page 603. Each one has its advantages — the 3D can produce a more accurate result in fitting the label to the bottle, and once you've done it, you can easily adjust it for a bottle photographed in a different position, for instance. But using the Warp process doesn't require learning an unfamiliar interface if you don't have experience with 3D, and it's easily adapted to bottles or other objects that are not quite cylindrical.)

YOU'LL FIND THE FILES

in **WOW** > Wow Project Files > Chapter 10 > Exercising 3D Basics:

- WinePhoto-Before.psd (to start)
- LabelGraphics.psd
- 3DWineBottle.obj
- WinePhoto-After CS3 (or CS4).psd (to compare)

The original photograph, ready to have the 3D label applied. The shadows in the photo show that the studio lighting is soft and multi-directional. Some light comes from behind the objects, casting shadows in front of them. But some light also seems to come from the front right, illuminating the background and also casting a soft shadow of the wine glass on the bottle. The wine glass was selected and copied to a layer above, so we could put it in front of the label being developed on a layer in between.

Where the Model Came From

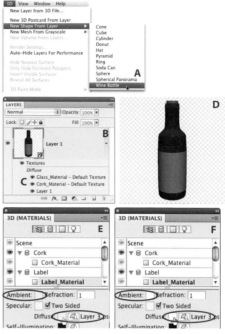

We wanted to start this exercise with the same model, whether you were using CS3 or CS4, so we manufactured and exported **3DWineBottle.obj** from Photoshop CS4 Extended. Here's how we did it: We opened a new file (File > New) 800 x 800 pixels (about the height of the bottle in our photo, and square because we had determined that a square was the best shape to use; see page 671) with Background Contents set to Transparent. From the 3D menu, we chose New Shape From Layer > Wine Bottle **A**. Photoshop Extended created a wine bottle to fit our document, turning the empty layer into a 3D layer **B**. The Layers panel showed that the Wine Bottle had three textures — one each for Glass Material, Cork Material, and Layer 1 **C**. Our empty "Layer 1" had been added to the Label texture for the bottle.

We opened the 3D panel (Window > 3D). The 3D (Scene) panel lists all the materials in the scene. Clicking on the name of one of them changes the panel heading to "3D (Materials)." The default color for the label in the wine bottle model is pink **D**. When we clicked on Label Material in the 3D (Scene) panel, we could see pink color swatches for Ambient and Diffuse **E**. We clicked on the Ambient and Diffuse swatches in turn, changing the color of these two to white **F**. Our label now showed the white paper it would be printed on. To export the model, we chose 3D > Export 3D Layer and saved the model as **3DWineBottle.obj**.

1a Importing a Model in CS3

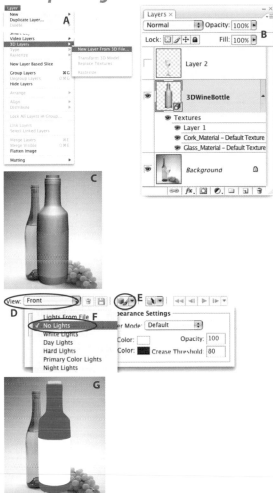

OPEN **WINEPHOTO-BEFORE.PSD** in Photoshop CS3 Extended and then choose **Layer > 3D Layers > New Layer From 3D File A** to bring in **3DWineBottle.obj**. The bottle is imported as a 3D layer, sized to fit the height of the photo. The Layers panel **B** shows a list of Textures for the 3D layer.

Lights often don't translate from a program that exports the object, and the gray model you see is typical of this **C**. But we'll set the model up so the label graphics will be facing us, and we'll restore the white of the label. Choose Layer > 3D Layers > Transform 3D Model, and in the Options bar choose **Front** from the View list **D**. To get the color back, click the "Lighting and Appearance Settings" button ⚪ **E** and choose **No Lights** from the Light Settings menu **F** to restore the native color **G**.

1b Importing a Model in CS4

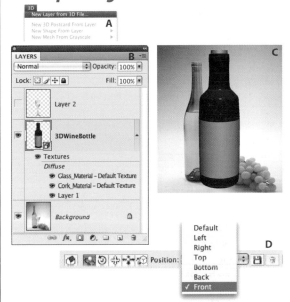

OPEN **WINEPHOTO-BEFORE.PSD** in Photoshop CS4 Extended and then choose **3D > New Layer From 3D File A** to bring in **3DWineBottle.obj**. The bottle is imported as a 3D layer, sized to fit the height of the photo. The Layers panel **B** shows a list of Textures for the 3D layer.

Lights often don't translate perfectly from a program that exports the object **C**, but in this case we decided the lighting was acceptable for fitting the label; we would adjust the lighting after the label graphics were in place (at step 6). But we'll set the model up so the label graphics will be facing us. Choose a 3D Object tool (K is the shortcut for 3D Rotate ⟳), and choose **Front** from the Position menu in the Options bar **D**. *Note:* If you want to get the brighter white of the label back, in the 3D (Scene) panel, with Scene targeted at the top of the panel, click the Global Ambient color swatch and choose a gray, or even white, to restore the color.

2 Modifying a Texture

IN EITHER CS3 OR CS4 EXTENDED, in the Layers panel double-click on "Layer 3" to open the texture file for the label of the bottle model. It opens in the .psb format like a Smart Object layer. ▼ Open **LabelGraphics.psd A**, and with the Move tool ▶₊, drag the graphics from the document window into the Layer 3.psb file.

To make the label take up less vertical space on the bottle, we won't fill the entire height of the label file with our graphics, leaving some room at the top to trim off some of the original label material. Type Ctrl/⌘-T for Free Transform, hold down the Alt/Option and Shift keys to transform proportionally from the center, and drag to scale it. (In the model the label wraps nearly half-way around the bottle. To keep the graphics from going right to the label's edge, scale to about 80% **B**.) Drag with the Move tool ▶₊ to center the graphics near the bottom of the document **C**, and click the ✓ in the Options bar to finalize the transformation. Save the file (Ctrl/⌘-S) to automatically update the "Layer 3" texture in the 3D layer in the main file **D**.

3 Hiding Parts of the Model

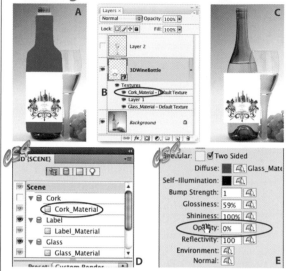

AS WE ADD THE LABEL to the wine bottle in the photo, we'll want only the label from the bottle model, and not the glass or cork. After using the Move tool ▶₊ to drag the model over the bottle in the photo **A**, our next step is to make the glass and cork "disappear." To do this, you need to make their materials transparent:

• In CS3, in the Layers panel double-click on the Cork Material entry **B**. When the .psb file opens, double-click on the *Background* to turn it into a standard layer. Reduce the layer's Opacity to 0%. Save the .psb file (Ctrl/⌘-S) and return to the main document. Your cork will no longer be visible. Repeat for the Glass Material **C**.

• In CS4 you don't have to leave the main model file to make the cork and glass invisible: Open the 3D (Scene) panel 🔲 and click on the name of the material you want to disappear ("Cork Material" in this case) **D**. The 3D (Scene) panel changes to 3D (Materials). Below the list of materials, find the Opacity setting and change it to 0% **E**. Repeat for the Glass Material.

FIND OUT MORE
▼ Smart Objects
page 75

4 Scaling and Rotating the Label

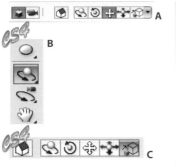

SINCE OUR BOTTLE IS FACE-FORWARD, upright, and almost the size we want, we won't have too much work to do to match the perspective and scale in the photo. Use the Move tool ▶✛ to adjust the 3D label's position on top of the bottle in the photo to begin the matching process. In CS3 choose Layer > 3D Layers > **Transform 3D Model** to access the tools in the Options bar **A** for positioning and scaling. In CS4 if you choose one of the 3D tools near the bottom of the Tools panel, they will all also appear in the Options bar **B**, **C**. Starting with the **3D Scale** tool ⬭, drag downward to make the label smaller, or upward to make it larger. Use the **3D Drag/3D Pan** tool ✛ to move the label up or down the bottle, or to move it from side to side. The **3D Slide** tool ✛ lets you move the object front to back in 3D space. The bottle in the photograph isn't sitting perfectly straight. Choose the **3D Roll** tool ↻ to tip the label very slightly to the side, so the label matches the sides of the bottle at both the top and the bottom. The camera's perspective isn't absolutely level with the bottle, but is looking down slightly. To match that, choose the 3D Rotate tool ◔ (or just press Alt/Option to turn the Roll tool into the Rotate tool). The Rotate tool easily rotates the model in any combination of back-and-forward or side-to-side directions, and it can be difficult to control. To make it easier to handle, begin very slowly to drag in the direction you want (in this case, drag down to tilt the label downward), and immediately depress the Shift key to constrain the movement to the direction you've chosen. Drag to bring the curve of the top of the label to resemble the curve of the wine level in the bottle. Scaling and positioning the label is a little finicky, but by working in very small increments with the various tools, you'll be able to match the size and perspective in the photo, and your label will retain its 3D appearance throughout **D**.

5a "Trimming" the Label (CS3)

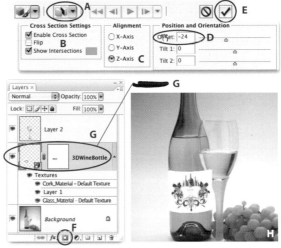

NEXT WE'LL REMOVE THE EXTRA LABEL area above the graphics. In Photoshop CS3 Extended, click on the "Cross Section Settings" button ⬎ **A** to open the Cross Section Settings dialog. Choose **Enable Cross Section** and **Show Intersections B**. Being able to see the intersections (the line where the plane cuts the model to make the cross section) makes it much easier to distinguish the front from the back of the label, which you'll need to do in order to mask the back part (below). The cross section is made perpendicular to one of the axes. To make it cut off the top section of our label, we need to choose the **Z axis C**. The **Offset** determines where the cross section is established in relation to the center of the 3D object (the whole bottle, not just the label). Use the Offset slider to place the cross section where you want it (–24 in our example) **D**. Click the ✔ to apply your transformation **E**.

With the 3D layer still targeted, click on the "Add layer mask" button ▣ at the bottom of the Layers panel **F**. With a slightly soft-edged brush, ▼ paint with black to conceal the back edge **G**. ▼ Turn off Show Intersections after painting the mask, once it's no longer needed to demarcate the label edges **H**; you'll need to choose Layer > 3D Layers > Transform 3D Model to do this.

FIND OUT MORE

▼ Adjusting brush tips **page 71**

▼ Painting masks **page 84**

5b "Trimming" the Label (CS4)

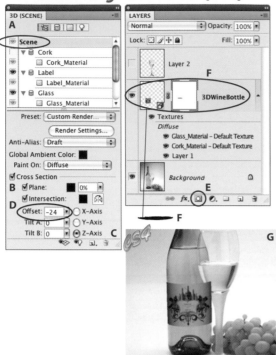

To REMOVE THE EXTRA LABEL area above the graphics in Photoshop CS4 Extended, use the 3D (Scene) panel (Window > 3D). Choose **Scene A**, and in the lower part of the panel choose **Cross Section**, **Intersection**, and, if you like, Plane (you can set the Opacity of the plane that cuts through the model to make the cross section) **B**. Being able to see the intersections (the line where the plane cuts the model) makes it much easier to distinguish the front from the back of the label, which you'll need to do in order to mask the back part (below). The cross section is made perpendicular to one of the axes. To make it cut off the top section of our label, we need to choose the **Z axis C**. The **Offset** determines where the cross section is established in relation to the center of the 3D object (the whole bottle, not just the label). Use the Offset slider to place the cross section where you want it (–24 in our example) **D**.

With the 3D layer still targeted, click on the "Add layer mask" button ▣ at the bottom of the Layers panel **E**. With a slightly soft-edged brush,▼ paint with black to conceal the back edge **F**.▼ Turn off Intersection after painting the mask, once it's no longer needed to mark the label edges **G**.

FIND OUT MORE
▼ Adjusting brush tips **page 71**
▼ Painting masks **page 84**

6a Using Lighting Effects in CS3

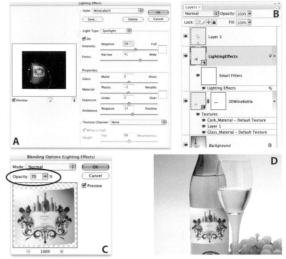

PHOTOSHOP CS3 EXTENDED offers some preset 3D lighting schemes — you saw the list when we set the lights to No Lights in step 1. Go ahead and try them out, but for this label comp we decided to use the Lighting Effects filter for more control in matching the lighting in the photo. Turn on the top layer's visibility now, so you can work out the shading on the label created by the wine glass. To set up your file to apply Lighting Effects to just the label, duplicate your 3D layer (Ctrl/⌘-J). In the Layers panel, double-click the name of the copy and rename it "Lighting Effects." Right-click/Ctrl-click on the layer and choose Rasterize 3D from the context-sensitive menu. Next, from the same menu (right-click/Ctrl-click again), choose Convert to Smart Object. The Lighting Effects filter has a small preview, and it often takes several tries to get the lights adjusted just the way you want, so using a Smart Filter here can be helpful.▼

Choose **Filter > Render > Lighting Effects** to open the dialog.▼ Start with the default Spotlight, adjusting the size, angle, Intensity, and Focus to match the lighting in the photograph **A**. A second, very faint Spotlight fills in some of the shadow the first light created, and a final Omni light with a very slight negative Intensity brings a little shadow to the left side of the label where it curves away from the front. (You can open the Lighting Effects dialog by clicking the Lighting Effects entry in the Layers panel in **Wine Photo-After CS3.psd** to see the settings.) After clicking "OK," we decided to double-click on the filter's ⬆ icon **B**, and in the Blending Options dialog, reduce the filter's Opacity to 70% **C**, **D**.

FIND OUT MORE
▼ Lighting Effects Filter **page 264**
▼ Smart Filters **page 72**

6b Setting Up 3D Lighting in CS4

A

D

E

F

7 Saving the File

A

B

C

CS4 ALLOWS YOU TO CREATE, move, and adjust lights in 3D space. In the 3D (Lights) panel ♀, click on the "Toggle lights" button ☜ at the bottom of the panel **A**. Blue-headed "pins" appear in your image representing the lights that are included with your model (in this case, three **B**. With just a few tools, housed on the left side of the 3D (Lights) panel, you can interactively move your lights around. You can adjust settings and see the results in your document window in real time. Turn on visibility for the wine glass in the top layer now, so you can account for any shadows the glass would produce as you set up your label lighting.

Click on the first name in the lights list (Infinite Light 1) and click its ☜ to turn on the light **C**. In the properties list below, you can change the type of light (we didn't), and with Infinite lights, you can move the light to the camera position by clicking on the ☞ icon on the left-hand side (we did). Next click on the Rotate Light tool ☜ **D** and drag in the image over the lights. Only the light that is currently targeted will move. Rotate the light to match the general direction of light and shadow in the photograph. Then adjust the Intensity to bring the brightest part of the light to the level you need, being careful not to blow out the highlights, and click on the color swatch to match the general (warm) color of the photo. The lighter the color you choose, the lighter the label. If you want the light to cast shadows, you can choose it here (we didn't). Repeat the lighting procedure for each light **E**. We used two Infinite lights to warm and light the label **F**.

ONCE THE WINE LABEL COMP is complete **A**, save a layered version in .psd format. This way, you'll be able to make any changes easily, by once again substituting a new texture for the old, as in "2 Modifying a Texture." In CS3, with Lighting Effects as a Smart filter, you can copy it to a new layer that holds a fresh copy of the modified label, so you won't have to set up your lights again. You can also always add Adjustment layers in the .psb file to modify a label's color, as we did when we added a Hue/Saturation layer in Color mode to switch from golds to greens **B**.

You can also change a texture in a model by painting on it **C**. In CS3 you'll need to open the .psb file and do your painting on the flat version of the texture. In CS4 you can also paint in the 3D view: In the 3D (Scene) panel choose Paint On: Diffuse, then select a painting tool and paint directly on the label.▼

When you're ready to show your designs to others, create flattened versions of the image and save in an easy-to-exchange format such as JPEG or PDF.

FIND OUT MORE

▼ Painting in 3D
page 657

Video: Stills From Video

If you want to select a single video frame and repurpose it for the web or for print, simply save the frame in your video-editing software in one of the many file formats that Photoshop can open, such as the .tif format we used for the **Stills from Video-Before.tif** file in this exercise. (You can see a list of formats Photoshop can open by choosing File > Open and clicking to open the Enable menu.) If the frame you want to capture is the first frame of the video, or if you have Photoshop Extended, there may be no need to go through a video-editing program (see the tip below).

OPENING VIDEO DIRECTLY IN PHOTOSHOP

In some cases you can work directly with any video file format that Photoshop can open (such as the QuickTime .mov format) instead of going through video-editing software to pick out the frame and save it in .tif or another still format. For instance, you can open the **first frame** of a QuickTime video simply by using the File > Open command. The first frame is all you'll get, but if the first frame is what you want, you're set. In the Layers panel simply right/Ctrl-click on the name of the layer to open a context-sensitive menu where you can choose **Rasterize Layer**.

If you have **Photoshop Extended**, you're not limited to the first frame. For a QuickTime video, for instance, use the File > Open command to open the file; it will open as a video layer. If the Animation panel isn't already open, open it now (Window > Animation; it will open to the Timeline version of the panel), and drag the **Current Time Indicator** (play head) until the frame you want to capture is showing in the document window. Then click the **"Convert to frame animation"** button ▦ at the bottom right of the Animation panel. The Frame version of the panel will appear, and only the frame you selected will be available. Right/Ctrl-click on the name of the layer to open a context-sensitive menu where you can choose **Rasterize Layer**.

YOU'LL FIND THE FILES

in ⊚ > Wow Project Files > Chapter 10 > Exercising Video > Stills from Video:

• Stills from Video-Before.tif (to start)

• Stills from Video-After.tif (to compare)

1 Opening the Video Frame

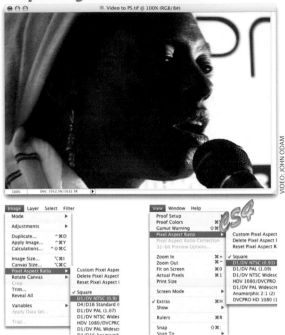

VIDEO: JOHN ODAM

OPEN THE VIDEO FRAME (**Stills from Video-Before.tif**, shown at the top) in Photoshop (File > Open). If you have Photoshop Extended, you could instead open Stills from Video-Before.mov (see the tip at the left; you'll find the frame we've used here at around 3:10). Photoshop assumes that an image has square pixels unless you tell it otherwise. So a non-square-pixel image will look out-of-proportion when you open it. To correct the on-screen view, let Photoshop know that this image was *not* created as a square-pixel document — choose **Image > Pixel Aspect Ratio (in CS3, above left)** or View > Pixel Aspect Ratio (in CS4, above right) and choose the aspect ratio that's built into your video frame, such as D1/DV NTSC (0.9) for the image above.

MISSING ASPECT RATIO?

If you open a video file in Photoshop and its aspect ratio isn't listed in the Image > Pixel Aspect Ratio menu (or View > Pixel Aspect Ratio in CS4), you can create a custom setting (Image, or View > Pixel Aspect Ratio > Custom Pixel Aspect Ratio). If you don't know the aspect ratio of your video frame, try the default options or create a custom aspect ratio, experimenting to find one that makes the image look right on your computer screen.

2 The Corrected View

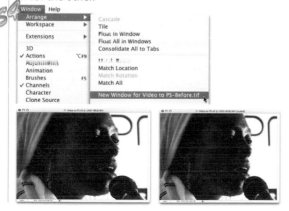

WHEN YOU CHOOSE AN ASPECT RATIO, Photoshop will scale the on-screen display so the image appears on your computer screen with the same height-width proportions as it would on TV (top). The "scaled" label in the title bar tells you that you're now looking at the corrected view.

The toggle for switching between the corrected (scaled) view and the uncorrected view is **View > Pixel Aspect Ratio Correction**. This is automatically turned on (to the corrected view) when you tell Photoshop, as you just did, that your image is a non-square-pixel file.

TWO VIEWS AT ONCE

To see both the uncorrected and corrected views of your file on-screen at once, choose Window > Arrange > New Window for..., and turn on View > Pixel Aspect Ratio Correction for one window and turn it off for the other.

3 Converting the File

ONCE YOUR VIDEO FILE IS OPEN in Photoshop and you can see what it really looks like because of the Pixel Aspect Ratio Correction, you still need to actually *convert* the image to the square pixels you need for the web or for print. So far, you've only corrected Photoshop's computer-screen *view*; you haven't changed the pixel shape in the file.

You can create the square-pixel image you need by simply copying the video image to the clipboard and pasting it into a new square-pixel file, as follows: Select all (Ctrl/⌘-A) and copy (Ctrl/⌘-C). Then start a new file (File > New). Photoshop assumes that you want to create a file the right size to hold the clipboard contents — good assumption! At the bottom of the **New** dialog, you'll see that Photoshop also assumes you want the file to be the same Pixel Aspect Ratio as the clipboard contents — a reasonable assumption, but not the one you want this time. Choose **Square** instead. Click "OK" to close the dialog box, and then paste the clipboard contents into the new file (Ctrl/⌘-V).

You'll notice extra white space along some edges of the image in your new square-pixel document. How much space and which edges will depend on the aspect ratio of the video file you started with. We'll get rid of the extra space shortly (in step 5).

4 De-Interlacing

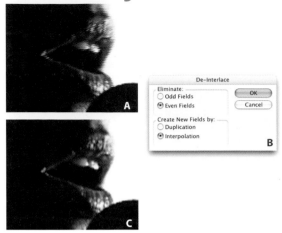

FOR SMOOTH MOTION, some video cameras record *interlaced* frames **A**. Each frame is recorded as two separate *fields*, each field consisting of half the horizontal *scan lines* used to display the image. These smaller files allow for recording at a faster frame rate than if each one were a full frame, and a faster frame rate produces smoother motion. One field has the odd-numbered lines used for display, the other the even-numbered ones. For print or web purposes, you'll want to get rid of any visible interlacing. Photoshop's De-Interlace filter can do the job, and now is a great time to do it, *before* you make any changes to the file — such as resizing, smoothing, or sharpening — that will disrupt the interlacing and "confuse" the filter. (Other digital video cameras record *progressive* frames rather than interlaced; in that case, no de-interlacing is required.)

To de-interlace for a better still image, choose **Filter > Video > De-Interlace**. The filter smooths the image by eliminating either the odd- or even-numbered rows of pixels. To fill in, you can choose whether to simply double the remaining lines, or interpolate between them **B**. You may need to try one group of settings, then undo and try others until you see which ones work best for your image; we used the settings shown above **C**.

"SIZING UP" FOR PRINT

If you need to make your converted video image file bigger for printing, use Image > Image Size with Resample Image turned on and Bicubic Smoother chosen. After scaling up, the image will likely need sharpening to bring out detail, and the Unsharp Mask or Smart Sharpen filter may sharpen other features too much. If so, try one of the techniques in "Quick Ways To Bring Out Detail," starting on page 337.

---

5 Trimming, Resizing & Sharpening

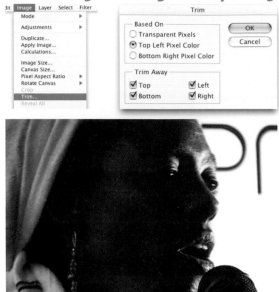

TO REMOVE THE EXTRA WHITE SPACE at the edges of your image (from step 3), choose **Image > Trim**, set the "Based On" option to "Top Left Pixel Color," turn on all of the "Trim Away" options, and click "OK."

To make the image the right size for your web or print purposes, use the **Image > Image Size** command, with Constrain Proportions and Resample Image turned on. We sized our image to a Width of 3 inches at 300 pixels/inch; we liked the look of the enlargement we got when we chose Bicubic Smoother from the pop-up Resample menu. Click "OK" to complete the resizing.

De-interlacing and resizing can soften the image, so sharpening will probably be needed. ▼ You may also need to boost color and contrast; one way is to add a Levels or Curves Adjustment layer. ▼

If your output process requires a flattened image, save the layered file in PSD format and then make a flat copy (Image > Duplicate, Duplicate Merged Layers Only, and if needed Image > Flatten Image) and save it in the format needed.

FIND OUT MORE
▼ Sharpening **page 337**
▼ Using Levels or Curves
page 246

Video: From Photoshop to Video

If you want to create a file in video format from a standard square-pixel Photoshop file, the first step is to create a new file for the video frame, using the correct size and pixel aspect ratio. Then you'll move the layer(s) you need from your standard Photoshop file into this new video file, add any new material you want, and save the video file, to be passed on for work in a video-editing program.

YOU'LL FIND THE FILES

in 🟣 > Wow Project Files > Chapter 10 > Exercising Video > From Photoshop to Video:

- PS to Video-Before.psd (to start)
- PS to Video After.psd (to compare)

RESPECTING THE GUIDES

When you create a new video-format file, Photoshop provides two sets of guides. The outer guides set the limits for the *action-safe* area of a TV screen, and the inner guides define the *title-safe* area. Some TVs can't show all of a standard video frame, so the outer guides are there to help you keep important detail within the action-safe area. Furthermore, on some TVs the signal becomes increasingly distorted at the edges of the screen, so the title-safe area ensures that text will remain clear and readable. In newer TVs this is less a problem than it used to be, so you may not lose anything if you choose to ignore the guides. But if you're working for a client, the default is to respect the guides.

If the Guides won't show up well enough against the image you want to develop, choose Edit > Preferences (in Windows) or Photoshop > Preferences (on the Mac) and choose Guides, Grid & Slices, and choose a different color for Guides.

1 Starting a Video-Format Document

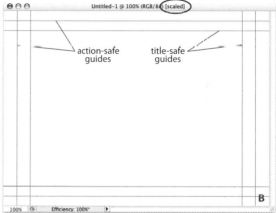

To START THE VIDEO-FORMAT DOCUMENT, choose File > New. In the New dialog box, choose **Film & Video** for the Preset, then choose your video format from the Size list. For our example **A**, we chose NTSC DV.

If the Advanced section at the bottom is open, you can see that Photoshop has already chosen the Pixel Aspect Ratio that matches the Preset you chose — in this case D1/DV NTSC (0.9/0.91, a slightly more accurate conversion factor, supplied with Photoshop CS4). Click "OK"; if a warning box pops up, click "OK" again.

The blank document **B** will have two sets of guides (if you don't see them, choose View > Show > Guides). The "Respecting the Guides" tip at the left explains why they are there. Notice also that the "scaled" label appears in the title bar, to let you know that the on-screen preview will be "normalized" to look good in Photoshop's standard square-pixel view, although the document will actually be in the format you chose in the New dialog box.

2 Importing an Image

To CONVERT AN IMAGE for your video document, open the source file **A**, in this case **PS to Video-Before.psd**. Choose the Move tool ▸₊; if your source image file has more than one layer, target the layer you want to move by clicking its thumbnail in the Layers panel, and make sure **Auto-Select is** *off* in the Options bar. Drag the image from its document window onto the new video window **B**, holding down the Shift key if you want to center it in the new window. If your documents are displayed in CS4's tabbed view rather than floating windows, drag onto the tab of your empty video document, and when the tab is highlighted, drag down into the document window.

MOVING MORE THAN ONE LAYER

If you want to add more than one layer from a source file to your video document, in the Layers panel Shift-click the layers you want (or Ctrl/⌘ click noncontiguous layers). Choose the Move tool ▸₊ (make sure **Auto-Select is** *off* in the Options bar) and drag or Shift-drag the targeted elements into the working window of your new video document. If you are in CS4's tabbed mode, be sure to drag from the document window, not the Layers panel; drag to the tab until it's highlighted, and then drag down into the window.

3 Scaling the Image

PHOTOSHOP DOESN'T AUTOMATICALLY resize the image to fit the video file. Since our source image is bigger than the new video document, we'll need to scale it to fit. Type Ctrl/⌘-T (for Edit > Free Transform). If you can't see all four corner handles of the Transform frame in your working window, press Ctrl/⌘-0 (that's zero) to expand the window to show the entire Transform frame **A**. Once you can see the entire Transform frame, Shift-drag on a corner handle of the frame to resize the image to fit; or Alt/Option-Shift-drag to resize from the center **B**. ▼ Our image will scale to fit exactly, but if it didn't, you could drag the image around until it was framed the way you wanted it within the "safe" areas indicated by the guides. When you're satisfied with the size and position, double-click inside the Transform frame to complete the transformation, or press the Enter key.

FIND OUT MORE
▼ Transforming
page 67

PRE-SCALING

If you know that your Photoshop source file is a lot bigger than the video file you're constructing, it may be easier to duplicate the image file (Image > Duplicate) and reduce the duplicate (Image > Image Size with Resample Image turned on and Bicubic Sharper chosen) before you import it into the video file — rather than doing all the transforming once it's imported.

4 Working on the Video File

IF YOU LIKE, you can toggle off the View > Pixel Aspect Ratio Correction command to see the unscaled view of the video file **A**; then toggle it back on **B**. Or to see both views at once, open a second window for the document (Window > Arrange > New Window for. . .), and toggle its View.

Now you can add to the image if you like, within the limits of your video format.▼ As you work, Photoshop will show you the result correctly in either view. For instance, if you hold down the Shift key and drag with the Ellipse tool to draw a circle,▼ it will look circular in the "scaled" window but oblong in the one that isn't scaled.

5 Saving the File

THERE ARE TWO THINGS to do before you save a video document: First, for future use, save the file in PSD format with any layers intact. Second, check your video-editing software to find out which file formats it can work with (and which features within a file format; for instance, it may accept .tif files, but not with layers). Photoshop has all the major file formats covered, and some of the obscure ones as well, so you should be able to find one that will work. To be conservative, you can merge your imported image and any additions you've made with the *Background* (Layer > Merge Visible). This will also trim away any of your imported image that extends outside the limits of the video format.

At this point you could make sure the color is within the gamut of the video format you are using (see "Contrast and color" on page 661), or leave the file in your working RGB profile, as we did, and make the change in your video editor.

To save the file, choose File > Save As, choose a format your video editor can use, and click the "Save" button. If you save in .psd format, be sure to choose the "Maximize compatibility" option if it's offered (if you've set your Preferences for File Handling to Always maximize compatibility, it will happen automatically without asking).

FIND OUT MORE

▼ Designing for video
page 660

▼ Using Shape tools
page 451

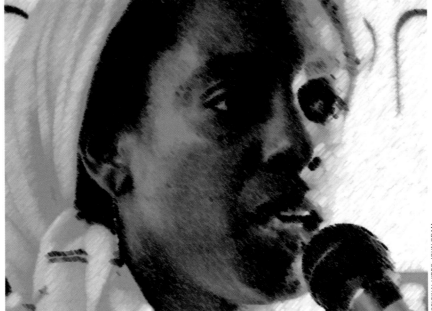

Animating a Video Clip in Photoshop Extended

YOU'LL FIND THE FILES
in WOW > Wow Project Files > Chapter 10 >
Animating a Video Clip:
- Video-Before.mov (to start)
- Video-After.mov (to compare)

OPEN THESE PHOTOSHOP EXTENDED PANELS
from the Window menu:
- Layers • Actions • Animation

OVERVIEW
Open a video file • Duplicate the video
to a new layer • Convert the duplicate
to a Smart Object • Run an artistic filter
on the Smart Object • Use keyframes to
interpolate the Opacity of the filtered layer

VIDEOGRAPHER JOHN ODAM wanted an animation to crossfade as an introduction to his video. So he exported a clip from Adobe Premiere in QuickTime (**.mov**) format, and we went to work in **Photoshop Extended,** applying one of the Sketch filters. We used a 4-second clip (about 120 frames) at full size (720 x 480 pixels). To follow along with the filtering process, you can use any QuickTime movie clip you have, or use a reduced version of Odam's clip, **Video-Before. mov**, provided on the Wow DVD-ROM.

Thinking the project through. When you open a video file in Photoshop Extended, it comes in as a video layer. If you apply a filter to a video layer, only the first frame will be filtered. But if you convert the video layer to a Smart Object and *then* apply the filter, the filter will act on the entire clip. Photoshop Extended's Animation (Timeline) panel allows you to blend video layers together, so you can create a transition, or crossfade, between the filtered video and the original.

1 Importing the video. Open the video clip (File > Open). The pixel aspect ratio of the clip makes the images look like they're stretched horizontally. (We won't worry about this, since we'll be exporting the filtered and cross-faded clip back out to the same video format. But if you plan to output to a different format, you may need to "square up" the file. "Exercising Video: Stills from Video" on page 678 tells how to do it.) In Photoshop Extended's Layers panel you'll see a video layer **1a**, which will also show

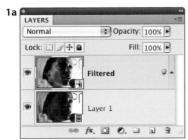

1a

The video clip opens as a video layer.

1b

In the Animation (Timeline) panel you'll see the video layer's name and a green bar stretching across the panel for the duration of the video.

2

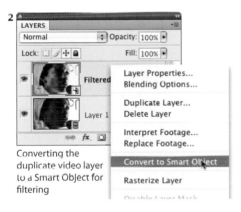

Layer Properties...
Blending Options...

Duplicate Layer...
Delete Layer

Interpret Footage...
Replace Footage...

Convert to Smart Object

Rasterize Layer

Converting the duplicate video layer to a Smart Object for filtering

3a

The Sketch filters use the current Foreground and Background colors. You can reset to black and white by typing D.

3b

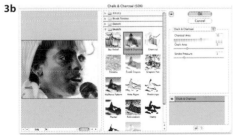

Applying the Chalk & Charcoal filter (The settings are for Odam's full-size video clip. You may prefer other settings for the reduced clip or for another video file.)

up in the Animation (Timeline) panel as a green bar spanning the length of the panel **1b**.

2 Setting up the Smart Object for filtering. Now duplicate the video layer (Ctrl/⌘-J), rename it by double-clicking the name and typing a new one (we called ours "Filtered"), and turn this new video layer into a Smart Object: In the Layers panel, right-click/Ctrl-click anywhere to the right of the new video layer's thumbnail and choose Convert to Smart Object from the context-sensitive menu that opens **2** (another way to make the Smart Object is to choose Filter > Convert for Smart Filters).

3 Filtering. Before you start experimenting with artistic filters, set your Foreground and Background colors to the ones you want to use; we set the default colors (black and white) by typing D (for "default") **3a**. Now open the Filter Gallery (choose Filter > Filter Gallery) and begin experimenting. Choose a filter by clicking its sample thumbnail in the Filter Gallery's middle panel, or choose from the alphabetical pop-up list of filters in the right panel **3b**. We tried Charcoal and Chalk & Charcoal (from the Sketch set) and Colored Pencil, Neon Glow, and Palette Knife (from Artistic). We settled on Chalk & Charcoal. Click "OK" to complete the filtering **3c**.

4 Crossfading. If you now click the "Play" button ▶ at the bottom of the Animation panel, you'll see your filtered video clip. To create the transition between the filtered and the original, in the Animation panel click the arrow to the left of the filtered video's name (here "Filtered") to open the list of layer properties you can change **4a**. To make the transition from filtered to original, we can fade the filtered layer's Opacity from 100% at the beginning of the clip to 0% at the end. To do that, put the Current Time Indicator (also called the play head) at the beginning of the clip (drag it as far left as it will go). Then click the little stopwatch button ⏱ to the left of the Opacity listing, that will add a *keyframe* (indicated by a little yellow diamond ◆), which establishes the Opacity as it is currently set (100%) **4b**. A keyframe is the point in time (and the frame) at which a value is recorded for the property. Photoshop uses these values to interpolate (or tween) these properties automatically, from one keyframe to the next.

Now drag the play head to the end of the video clip, at the right side of the Animation panel. To establish another keyframe there, all you have to do now is reset the layer's Opacity; we set it to 0%. Photoshop Extended knows you're still working on Opacity (the Opacity stopwatch is still targeted in the Animation panel) and

3c

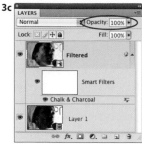

The Layers panel after filtering. Since the filtered layer is at 100% Opacity, playing the video (with the ▶ button at the bottom of the Animation panel) will show only the filtered version.

4a

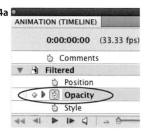

Opacity is one of the properties whose change over time can be set with keyframes in the Animation (Timeline) panel.

4b

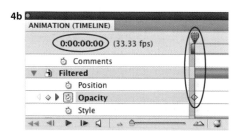

The first Opacity keyframe. The time set for the keyframe is indicated in the upper left corner.

4c

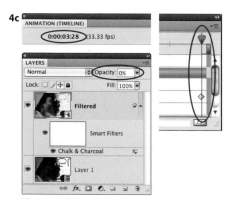

The second Opacity keyframe, set by dragging the play head into position on the timeline and changing the Opacity in the Layers panel

that you've moved the play head to the time when you want to set a new Opacity value, so as soon as you set the Opacity, the keyframe is added **4c**. Now if you return the play head to the beginning of the clip and click the Play button ▶, you'll see the filtered version crossfade to reveal the original.

To fine-tune the timing of the crossfade, you can move (drag) the second keyframe to start or end the fade at some other point on the timeline. Or, to make the crossfade go faster in some parts of the timespan than others, drag the play head to a point in between the two keyframes and adjust the Opacity (to 50% for instance) to add another keyframe. Now by moving this middle keyframe left, you can make the first half of the fade go faster; by moving it right, make the second half go faster. By adding more keyframes, you could control the fade even more closely.

5 Exporting the clip. When the crossfade result looks promising, save the file in Photoshop (.psd) format to keep your editing alive, and also export the video (File > Export > Render Video). In the Render Video dialog box **5**, give the file a new name. In the File Options section choose QuickTime Export and choose from the menu of file types beside it; we chose QuickTime Movie (for more about choosing export settings, choose Help > Photoshop Help and search on "Specify Quick Time Movie settings" or "Export video"). If the "Settings" button is active for the format you've chosen, click it to choose options; we clicked the "Settings" button and then also clicked "Settings" in the Movie Settings dialog box that opened and chose Odam's original DV/DVCPRO-NTSC format in the Standard Video Compression Settings dialog box; click "OK" to close the dialogs. Now you can play the filtered movie with its correct timing in the Animation panel, or play it with QuickTime player (QuickTime Player for Mac or Windows can be downloaded free of charge: **www.apple.com**.) Frames from the beginning, middle, and end of the crossfaded clip are shown at the top of page 684. *Wow!*

5

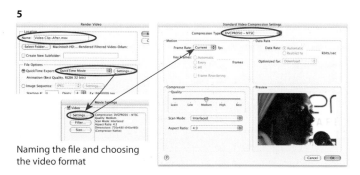

Naming the file and choosing the video format

Video Techniques in Photoshop Extended

Here are a few simple improvements or additions that can be made to video in Photoshop Extended, some of them suggested to us by filmmaker and Photoshop trainer Geno Andrews, others inspired by the work of documentary filmmaker Ken Burns. We'll start with the really easy ones and build up. If you need more information about making a 3D Postcard or operating the 3D tools (for "Zooming with 3D" on page 690), see pages 651–660. For more about Pattern Overlays (for "Zooming with a Pattern Overlay" on page 689), see pages 502–504. "Image Stabilization" on page 691 is still fairly "quick" in terms of your making choices and applying changes, but it's nevertheless processor-intensive, requiring significant computer power or time for Photoshop Extended to do its work. Except as noted, for these examples we imported the video with the File > Open command with QuickTime Movie or All Readable Files chosen in the Open dialog's Enable menu.

We don't mean to suggest that Photoshop can substitute for a video-editing program for serious video work, but if you just need to improve a short clip now and then, consider these techniques.

YOU'LL FIND THE FILES

in > Wow Project Files > Chapter 10 > Quick Video

DON'T FORGET SHADOWS/HIGHLIGHTS

"Animating a Video Clip in Photoshop Extended" on page 684 shows how to filter a video clip using a Smart Filter. Remember that Shadows/Highlights and Variations (both from the Image > Adjustments menu) are available as Smart Filters. Says filmmaker Geno Andrews, "By converting the video to a Smart Object and using Shadows/Highlights, I was able to compensate for extremely hot lighting that no filter in the video-editing program we used for *Cold Play* could come close to."

DON'T FORGET WARP TEXT

Style is one of the properties of a layer that can be interpolated with keyframes in the Animation (Timeline) panel. Besides the effects listed in the Layer Style dialog, don't forget that Style also includes **Warp Text** (⌐ on the Type tool's Options bar, or Layer > Type > Warp Text), so it can be used for animating titles added to a movie.

DEINTERLACE FIRST

If your video is interlaced,▼ it's a good idea to deinterlace it before you start manipulating it in Photoshop. If you don't deinterlace before you transform it, filter it, or otherwise modify it, you run the risk that the artifacts caused by deinterlacing will be magnified by your changes.

If you're not sure whether your clip is interlaced, zoom to 200% (Ctrl/⌘-+ to zoom in) and look for the interlacing lines. If you still can't tell, the video probably isn't interlaced. One way to be sure is to deinterlace and see if edges in the image get smoother-looking: Turn the video layer into a Smart Object (Filter > Convert for Smart Filters) and then apply the De-Interlace filter (Filter > Video > De-Interlace). If the edges get rougher instead, it wasn't interlaced; in that case, undo the deinterlacing filter step (Ctrl/⌘-Z).

ORIGINAL VIDEO: V DEOMETRY / PHOTCSPIN.COM

Experiment with the settings In the De-Interlace dialog to see what combination of Odd or Even Fields and Duplication or Interpolation works best.

FIND OUT MORE

▼ Interlaced video **page 680**

An Instant "Film" Look

Before

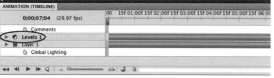

After

 **Film Look.psd**

To make the color and contrast of almost any video clip more dramatic, put an **"empty" Adjustment layer** above it in **Soft Light mode**: With your video layer targeted in the Layers panel, click the "Create new fill or adjustment layer" button 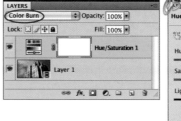 at the bottom of the panel and choose Levels, but don't make any changes to the Levels settings. In CS3, click "OK" to close the dialog. Now put the Levels layer in Soft Light mode, and watch your video pop. If the boost is too much, reduce the Levels layer's Opacity in the Layers panel to adjust the blend.

Tinted or Black & White Video

Before

After

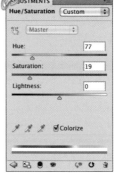

Tinted Video.psd

Change the color of an entire video clip with one of the methods in "Quick Tint Effects" (page 203) or "From Color to Black & White" (page 214) that uses a Fill or Adjustment layer but doesn't involve masking it (though if you want to try masking to target the effect, see the technique in "Geno Andrews Conjures a 'Horror' Effect" on page 692). With the video layer targeted, click the "Create new fill or adjustment layer" button 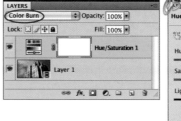 at the bottom of the Layers panel. Here we added a **Hue/Saturation Adjustment layer** to a time-lapse video. We clicked the **Colorize** checkbox in the Hue/Saturation dialog, moved the Hue slider to arrive at a green tint, and moved the Saturation slider a little to the left. (In CS3 we'd need to close the dialog box.) We changed the blend mode for the Adjustment layer to Color Burn.

Vignetting

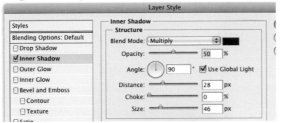

To DARKEN THE EDGES of a video, in order to imitate a lens shade or simply for a special effect, you can use one of the methods in "Quick Vignetting" (starting on page 278). Or try the following method, which uses the settings in the Layer Style dialog: With the video layer targeted in the Layers panel, click the **"Add a layer style" button** *fx* at the bottom of the panel and choose **Inner Shadow** from the list of effects. When the Inner Shadow section opens, to shade from the top, set the **Angle at 90°** and adjust **Distance, Size,** and **Choke** to taste. With Distance at 0, the shadow will be about even all the way around the edge. The bigger the Distance, the more the shade seems to be at the top of the frame. Size affects the inward reach and softness of the shadow, and Choke increases density. Adjust **Opacity** to suit. (You can see examples of this kind of vignetting for video on pages 710–713.) Since Style is one of the things that can be interpolated, you can change the vignette over time by setting keyframes. ▼

FIND OUT MORE

▼ Using keyframes **page 685**

▼ Scaling patterns in Layer Styles **page 81**

▼ Rendering video **page 686**

Zooming with a Pattern Overlay

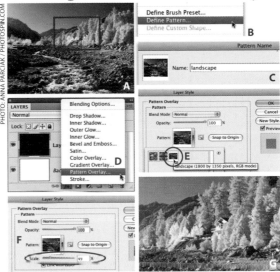

YOU CAN CREATE THE ILLUSION of zooming by using a still photo as a Pattern Overlay effect in a Layer Style. (If you have Photoshop CS4 Extended, "Zooming with 3D" on page 690 produces a sharper zoom.) Open the still photo **A** (a larger photo makes a sharper zoom), **select all** (Ctrl/⌘-A), and choose **Edit > Define Pattern B, C**. In your movie file, add a layer (Ctrl/⌘-Shift-N) and fill it (Ctrl-/⌘-Delete); the fill can be any color, because we're going to cover it up. Add a Style to the filled layer by clicking the *fx* **button** at the bottom of the Layers panel and choosing **Pattern Overlay D**. When the dialog opens, click the **Pattern swatch** and choose the pattern you just made **E**. Reduce the **Scale** to the zoomed-out size you want **F**; ▼ choosing something other than 50% or 25% makes the entire zoom softer, but it keeps the first frame of your zoom from being obviously sharper than the rest. Reach into the document window and drag to the part of the photo you want to zoom. Click "OK."

Drag the play head to the point in the timeline where you want the zoom to begin and click the stopwatch ⊙ for **Style** to add a keyframe. Then move the play head to the point where you want to be fully zoomed in. Double-click the Pattern Overlay listing in the Layers panel to reopen the Layer Style dialog. Once again adjust the position and Scale of the Pattern Overlay **G** (avoiding 25%, 50%, or 100% keeps the image from getting suddenly sharper at the end of the zoom); click "OK." Render the movie (File > Export > Render Video; use QuickTime Export ▼). Then open the .mov file in Photoshop Extended and sharpen it there (Filter > Convert for Smart Filters, and then Filter > Sharpen > Unsharp Mask or Smart Sharpen) and render.

Zooming with 3D

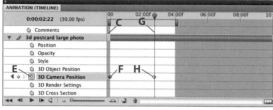

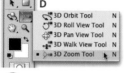

Panning-Zooming

In Photoshop Extended CS4 if you want type, graphics, a still photo (as in this example), or even a video to appear far away at first and then have the camera travel into the scene, you can do it with a 3D Postcard and 3D Camera tools. To avoid magnifying to the point where the image gets "soft," start with a photo that won't have to be enlarged for your full zoom. If your working document is 720 x 480 at 72 ppi, for instance, the zoomed-in area should be at least that big. With the image layer **A** targeted in the Layers panel, choose **3D > New 3D Postcard From Layer** to put the layer into 3D space **B**.

In the Animation (Timeline) panel move the play head to the point where you want the zoom to begin **C**. Scale the image to the zoomed-out size you want by using the **3D Zoom tool** ⇥ (one of the 3D Camera tools **D**), dragging up to zoom out, or down to zoom in; use the **3D Pan View tool** ⊕ if you need to reposition the image to get the zoom you want. To set a keyframe for the zoom, click the tiny twirl-down arrow for the 3D Postcard layer to open the properties that can be keyframed. Click on the stopwatch icon ⏱ for **3D Camera Position E, F**. Now move the play head to the point in the timeline where you want to be fully zoomed in **G**, and drag down with the 3D Zoom tool to zoom into the image; this sets another keyframe (again, use the 3D Pan View tool if you need to) **H**. Now when you render and play the clip, the effect will be to zoom into the image **I**. See "Finer Control of Pan or Zoom" at the right for more options.

Panning

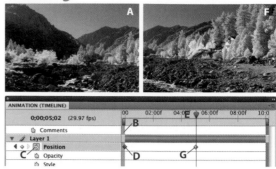

To create the illusion of moving *across* a landscape, rather than zooming in, you can start with a landscape and pan across it. This can be done with a **Pattern Overlay**, as described on page 689, using keyframes but simply moving the pattern while the Layer Style dialog is open to the Pattern Overlay section, rather than scaling it. It can also be done with a **3D Postcard** as described at the left, dragging with the **3D Pan View tool** ⊕ rather than 3D Zoom.

If all you want to do is pan, without zooming, there's no need to bother with a Pattern Overlay or a 3D Postcard. You can simply add a photo layer and interpolate its **Position**, as shown above. With the Move tool ▸⊕ drag the new layer until you see the area where you want to start the pan **A**. In the Animation (Timeline) panel, move the play head to the point in the movie where you want the panning to start **B**. Twirl the tiny arrow next to the new layer's name downward to open the list of properties that can be keyframed. Click the stopwatch icon ⏱ for **Position C**. This sets the first keyframe **D**. Now move the play head to the point on the timeline where you want the panning to end **E**. Use the Move tool ▸⊕ (with the Shift key held down if you want straight horizontal motion) to drag the photo layer until you see the area where you want the panning to end **F**. Another keyframe will be added automatically **G**.

FINER CONTROL OF PAN OR ZOOM

Depending on the photo you use and the kind of pan or zoom you're trying to accomplish, you may want more control than just two keyframes can give you. In that case, set two more keyframes in between the start and end of your pan or zoom, one at about a third of the total pan or zoom and the other at about two-thirds. ▼ Now you can drag the two intermediate keyframes to slow down or speed up the pan or zoom as you like.

FIND OUT MORE

▼ Setting keyframes **page 685**

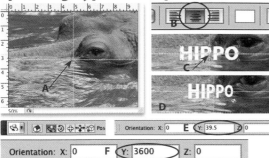 Spinning Type or Graphics

HERE'S A WAY TO ADD spinning type or graphics to your movie clip. With your video layer targeted, choose the Move tool ▶⊕, and in the Options bar turn on **Show Transform Controls**. Then bring up the rulers (Ctrl/⌘-R), drag a Guide in from the ruler on the left side until it lines up with the center point of the transform box, and drag another down from the top until it also lines up **A**. The intersection of the two guides marks the center of the video layer. Now choose the Type tool T. In the Options bar, choose font, size, and color, and choose the **Center Text** option **B**. Put the cursor on the intersection of the Guides and type your text; commit the type (one way is to press the Enter key). Choose the Move tool and drag the type if needed to align the center mark of the type bounding box with the intersection **C**. Now choose **3D > New 3D Postcard From Layer**. This will turn the type into a 3D layer that can be manipulated with the 3D Object tools. And because you centered the type on the "postcard," when you rotate the postcard, the type will rotate around its own center.

In the Animation (Timeline) panel, move the play head to the point where you want the spin to start. Twirl down the tiny arrow to the left of the type layer's name and click the stopwatch ⏱ for **3D Object Position**. Choose the **3D Rotate tool** ⟳ as we did for a horizontal spin, or the 3D Roll tool ⟳. We'll use the tool to start the rotation, and then enter the rotation value we want in the Options bar. Move the play head to the point where you want the rotation to finish. Hold down the Shift key as you drag to the right a little to start to turn the type **D**. When you stop dragging, notice which value in the Options bar has changed **E**. Drag-select that field, and type in a multiple of 360° **F**, since 360° is a full rotation and we want the type to end up in its original position; the biggest number you can enter is 3600, or 10 full rotations; press the Enter key. Return the play head to the first keyframe and click the "Play" button ▶ to see the spin. Use the Move tool to drag your type anywhere you want it in the frame.

Image Stabilization

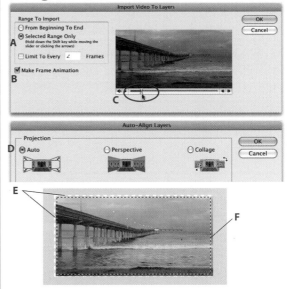

EVEN WITH THE VIDEO CAMERA's image-stabilization function turned on, you may see unwanted movement in your handheld video. To "stabilize the camera" after the fact for a short clip, try this: First choose **File > Import > Video Frames to Layers**, choosing **Selected Range Only A** and **Make Frame Animation B**; Shift-drag the slider from where you want to start the clip to where you want to end it **C**; click "OK." A layered file will open in Photoshop Extended, with a layer for each frame. **Target all the layers** (in the Layers panel the bottom layer should be targeted already, so just Shift-click the top layer's thumbnail). Then choose **Edit > Auto-Align Layers**, choose the **Auto** option **D**, and click "OK." Now have a cup of tea while the layers are aligned. After alignment you'll see transparent borders on one or two sides of your image **E**; you can assume that all edges have the bigger amount of transparency on some frames. Use the Rectangular Marquee ⬚ to make a selection inside the transparent edges **F**, and choose **Image > Crop**. Play the movie (click the "Play" ▶ button at the bottom of the Animation panel) and watch to make sure the transparency is gone. To restore your movie to its original dimensions (in this case 360 x 180) use **Image > Image Size** with Constrain Proportions turned off. Then render the movie: File > Export > Render Video, choosing the QuickTime format. Play your movie with the QuickTime player, and if it seems to need sharpening (because you resized it), open the .mov file in Photoshop Extended and sharpen it (Filter > Convert for Smart Filters, then Filter > Sharpen > Smart Sharpen or Unsharp Mask).

 **Image Stabilizing**

Geno Andrews Conjures a "Horror" Effect

EVEN IF YOU NEVER need to turn a charming child into a monster for a fleeting moment, you can learn a lot from the way Geno Andrews went about it, combining an edited video with the original and limiting the edits to one particular area of the scene. A close examination of the Layers panel and the Animation (Timeline) panel will show how he did it. The secret is in the clipping group.

FIND OUT MORE

▼ Smart Objects **page 18**
▼ Smart Filters **page 72**
▼ Clipping groups **page 65**
▼ Using Adjustment layers **page 245**
▼ Hue/Saturation adjustment **page 252**
▼ Curves adjustment **page 246**

To experiment with his idea for a special-effects flash of "monster" lighting, Geno opened a 32-second video clip in Photoshop Extended (File > Open). The clip appeared as a video layer in the Layers panel and was also represented by a duration bar in the Animation (Timeline) panel. He dragged the Timeline panel's play head to scan the video and choose a short segment. He dragged the two work area indicator bars to frame that part of the clip in the Timeline so rendering would be limited to that section of the video and no time would be wasted rendering the parts of the clip he wasn't working on.

For his special-effects lighting, Geno wanted to apply the Plastic Wrap filter and a Hue/Saturation adjustment to the image, and to limit the effect to the boy's face. He wanted to fade the effect in and out quickly but smoothly. At the same time he was lighting up the face, he would darken the rest of the frame to contrast with the lighting. "Animating a Video Clip in Photoshop Extended" on page 684 tells step-by-step how to combine filtered and unfiltered versions of a video clip. Briefly, you duplicate the video layer and filter the duplicate — but only after turning the duplicate into a Smart Object▼ (Filter > Convert for Smart Filters),

because if you apply a filter directly to a video layer, the filter affects the first frame only. Geno applied Filter > Artistic > Plastic Wrap as a Smart Filter▼ and then brightened up the effect by also applying Filter > Sharpen > Unsharp Mask.

To limit the effect to the boy's face, he could have filled the Smart Filter mask with black and then painted with white where he wanted the filter effects to show. But that would have given him no way to make the smooth transition he wanted, since he couldn't control the opacity of a Smart Filter mask with keyframes in the Timeline. To make a "mask" whose Opacity he *could* control with keyframing, he would use a clipping group.▼ He added a layer below the filtered video layer and turned it into the base of a clipping group. On this layer ("Layer 3") he painted with the Brush tool 🖌 and a soft brush tip with black paint (it could have been any color) to define the area where he wanted the clipped contents to show. Then he Alt/Option-clicked the border between this layer and the filtered layer to clip the filtered layer. He also added a Hue/Saturation Adjustment layer▼ above the filtered video, turned on the Colorize option, and set the sliders to add a blue cast to the horror lighting.▼ He Alt/Option-clicked the Hue/Saturation

layer's border with the video layer to add it to the clipping group. To darken the surroundings, he added a masked Curves layer.▼

With all the elements in place, Geno went to work in the Timeline. He set keyframes for the Opacity of "Layer 3," the clipping layer, at 0%, 100%, 100%, and 0% over a span of ⅔ of a second, or 20 frames. These keyframes for the clipping layer would control both the filtered video and the Hue/Saturation adjustment, so he didn't have to set keyframes for those two layers. He also set matching keyframes for the Curves adjustment layer, since he wanted the rest of the scene to darken at the same time the face flashed. To copy a set of keyframes from one layer and apply them to another, click the stopwatch ⏱ for the layer with the keyframes, choose Select All Keyframes from the Timeline panel menu, and then choose Copy Keyframe(s). Use one of the arrow buttons to the left of that stopwatch to move the play head to the first of the keyframes you just copied. Then find the name of the layer you want to add the keyframes to (here "Curves1"), click on the property you want to control for that layer (in this case Opacity), and choose Paste Keyframe(s) in the Timeline panel's menu. He added another keyframe between the second and third.

◇ **Layer 3: 0%**
◇ **Curves1: 0%**

◇ **Layer 3: 100%**   ◇ **Curves1: 100%**
◇ **Curves1: 50%**

◇ **Layer 3: 100%**   ◇ **Layer 3: 0%**
◇ **Curves1: 50%**   ◇ **Curves1: 0%**

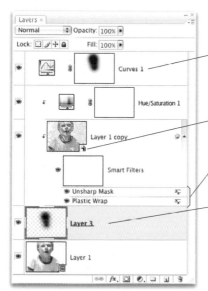

A Curves Adjustment layer was masked to protect the face as the rest of the scene was darkened.

A duplicate of the video layer was turned into a Smart Object so all frames of the video could be filtered.

Smart Filters were applied to the Smart Object that contained the duplicate video layer.

A clipping group was formed, with "Layer 3" as the clipping mask and the video and Hue/Saturation layers clipped, in order to "mask" the filtered video in a way that would allow the Opacity of the mask to be controlled with keyframes in the Timeline.

Four keyframes were used to regulate the Opacity of "Layer 3" (and thereby the filtered video and the Hue/Saturation adjustment, which were clipped within that layer's "footprint" so that they changed only the face). The same four keyframe positions, plus one more that Geno added, were used to regulate the Opacity of the Curves layer that was masked to darken the rest of the image at the same time the filter lighted the face.

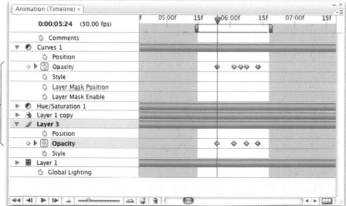

Animating Frame-by-Frame

YOU'LL FIND THE FILES

in 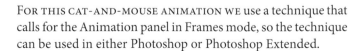 > Wow Project Files > Chapter 10 > Frame-by-Frame:
- Catanimation-Before. psd (to start)
- Catanimation-After. psd & Catanimation. gif (to compare)

OPEN THESE PANELS

(from the Window menu, for instance):
- Layers • Animation (Frames)

OVERVIEW

Compose the frames of an animation by moving, transforming, and editing components • Adjust timing • Create a layer for each frame • Duplicate each layer, filter the copy, and combine with the original • Optimize and save the animation

FOR THIS CAT-AND-MOUSE ANIMATION WE use a technique that calls for the Animation panel in Frames mode, so the technique can be used in either Photoshop or Photoshop Extended.

Thinking the project through. While there are certainly more sophisticated ways of animating for the web (vector-based Flash animation, for example), a simple "hand-crafted" animation exported in GIF format can be viewed by any browser that supports graphics. Here we'll start with hand-drawn elements that we'll assemble, modify, and animate to produce a six-frame "cartoon." In order to have some flexibility in the final size of our animation, we'll start working at about 200% of what our final frame dimensions will be. We can add a little dimensionality and subtle motion with the Photocopy filter.

There are many ways to control the timing of the motion in an animation. To see the animation in **Catanimation.gif**, open it in a browser and notice the timing:

- The speed of the white mouse varies as it runs across the stage. The variation comes mostly from **moving** the little animal farther in some frames than others. Similar speed effects are achieved by turning the cat's head, paw, or tail through a greater or smaller arc from one frame to the next. These changes were made as the frames were composed and captured one by one.

- A long pause occurs before the mouse appears, and there's a short pause when the cat bats at the mouse. These were accomplished after all the frames were made, by increasing the **timing** setting for these two frames.

- The "small motion" of the muscles comes from applying the **Photocopy filter** to the finished art for each frame, varying the setting slightly for one of the frames.

1 Preparing the graphics. Open a file with the essential graphics for your own animation, or use the **Catanimation-Before. psd** file **1a**.

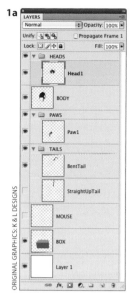

In the **Catanimation-Before.psd** file, layer visibility is set up to show the image that will appear in Frame 1. If you're working with a file of your own, use the 👁 column in the Layers panel to turn each layer's visibility on or off, depending on whether or not you want that layer to show up in the first frame.

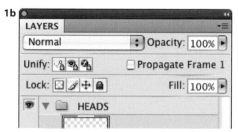

In the Layers panel the Propagate Frame 1 option is turned off so the first frame can be edited later without having the changes "ripple" through the other frames that will be added.

Clicking the "Duplicates selected frames" button 🔲 copies Frame 1 as a start for Frame 2. Any changes you make to your image now will be reflected in Frame 2.

Our file includes the cat's head, its body, a paw, two versions of the tail (bent and straight up), a mouse, the box the cat sits on, and a white background, each on its own layer, and with layer Groups set up to keep like parts together as we develop the animation. The body and box will remain visible for all frames and won't change position. You can duplicate and change the other elements as needed, and turn visibility on and off to set up the frames to create motion.

Before you begin to make frames, turn off Propagate Frame 1 near the top of the Layers panel **1b**. (If you don't see that option, open the Layers panel's menu ▾≡, choose Animation Options, and choose Automatic; now anytime the Animation panel is open, these options will be available in the Layers panel.) With Propagate Frame 1 off, if you find yourself returning to Frame 1 to edit it, you won't accidentally change the other frames as well. (Make sure you turn off Propagate Frame 1 whenever Frame 1 is active, unless, of course, you want to add something to all frames of your animation; then you can turn the "Propagate" option back on temporarily.) Also turn off New Layers Visible in All Frames in the Animation panel's ▾≡ menu.

To preserve your "scene" as the first frame, create a second frame that will then become the active one: **Click the "Duplicates selected frame" button 🔲 at the bottom of the Animation panel 1c**. Now your first frame won't change as you rearrange and modify your artwork and change layer visibility to set up the second frame.

2 Animating by transforming: Frame 2. Now transform the components of your artwork as needed to create the frames of the animation. The changes in **Frame 2** of *Catanimation* are the appearance of the mouse and the movement of the head, as the mouse catches the cat's attention. In the Layers panel, turn on visibility for the "MOUSE" layer by clicking in its 👁 column. Click on the thumbnail for the "Head1" layer and duplicate it (Ctrl/⌘-J) **2a**. Rotate the head counterclockwise to look at the mouse at the right, by pressing Ctrl/⌘-T (for Edit > Free Transform) and dragging the curved double-headed arrow cursor counterclockwise outside the Transform frame **2b**; then double-click inside the frame to close it, and turn off visibility for "Head1" (click its 👁). We used the Brush ✏ to paint changes in the eyes **2c**, holding down Alt/Option to sample colors as needed. ▼ With the second frame complete, **click the 🔲 button in the Animation panel** to move on to the third frame **2d**.

FIND OUT MORE

▼ Using the Brush tool ✏ **page 378**

2a

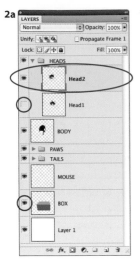

For Frame 2, visibility is turned on for the "MOUSE" layer. The "Head1" layer is duplicated, and the copy is renamed (by double-clicking the layer name and typing "Head2"). Visibility for the original "Head1" layer is turned off.

3 Animating by transforming: Frame 3. In Frame 3, use the Move tool ▶₊ to drag the "MOUSE" layer a little farther to the left **3a. Click ▣ at the bottom of the Animation panel** to start the fourth frame **3b.**

4 Animating by transforming: Frame 4. For this frame, use the Move tool ▶₊ to drag the mouse directly in front of the cat. Target the original "Head1" by clicking its thumbnail in the Layers panel, duplicate it (Ctrl/⌘-J) to make the "Head3" layer, turn on visibility ● for this copy, and turn off visibility for "Head2." Rotate your new "Head3" and paint the eyes to look down at the mouse. Turn off visibility for the "BentTail" layer and turn on visibility for "StraightUpTail" **4a.**

To extend the paw, duplicate the "Paw1" layer to create "Paw2," turn off visibility for "Paw1," and type Ctrl/⌘-T to open the Transform frame. Drag the center of rotation (the little "target" in the middle of the Transform frame) to the shoulder area, where the limb would be articulated **4b**. Now when you drag counterclockwise outside the frame to rotate until the paw is pointing down, the shoulder will be the pivot point for the swiping motion. After rotating the paw, drag the center bottom handle to stretch it down to touch the mouse. This completes Frame 4, so **click ▣ at the bottom of the Animation panel** to start the fifth frame **4c.**

2b

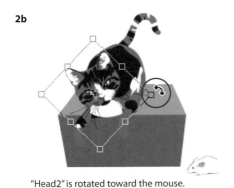

"Head2" is rotated toward the mouse.

2c

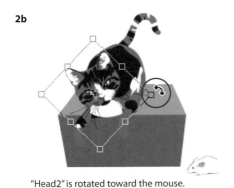

The eyes are repainted to look at the mouse, using color sampled from the artwork.

2d

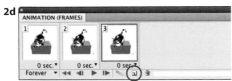

After completing Frame 2, duplicate it to start Frame 3.

3a

In Frame 3, the "MOUSE" layer is moved slightly.

3b

Duplicating Frame 3 to start Frame 4

4a

In Frame 4, the mouse moves a longer distance, the cat's head rotates, the eyelids are lowered, and the "StraightUpTail" layer is visible.

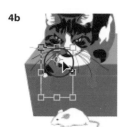

4b

In the "Paw2" layer, move the center of rotation to the shoulder (top left). Then rotate the layer (top right), and stretch the paw down to reach the mouse.

4c

A new frame is added to start Frame 5.

5a

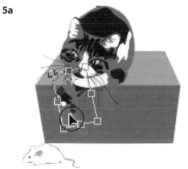

It's easier to position "Paw3" between the paw's other positions if you use a form of "onion-skinning."

5b

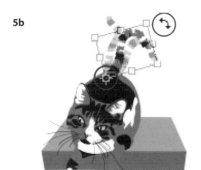

The "BentTail" layer is duplicated to make "BentTail copy," and the copy is rotated.

5 Animating by transforming: Frame 5. Move the mouse a little farther along. Turn off visibility for "Head3" and turn on visibility for "Head1," the head's original position.

Make another copy of "Paw1"; turn on visibility for this new "Paw3" as well as the "Paw1" and "Paw2" layers but reduce the Opacity for "Paw1" and "Paw2" so you can do some "onion-skinning," looking at related frames while working on the current frame. With the "Paw3" layer targeted, open the Transform frame (Ctrl/⌘-T), move the center of rotation to the shoulder again, and rotate the limb to a position between the angle of "Paw1" and the stretched "Paw2"; drag inside the Transform frame to move the limb down slightly **5a**. Restore Opacity for "Paw1" and "Paw2" (for later) and turn off their visibility.

To swish the tail, turn on visibility for "BentTail" and duplicate it. With the new layer targeted, type Ctrl/⌘-T, move the center of rotation to the base of the tail where it attaches to the body, and rotate the tail to a position between its original and the "StraightUpTail" **5b**. Then use Edit > Transform > Flip Horizontal **5c** and drag to adjust the tail's position if necessary. Restore Opacity for "BentTail" and "StraightUpTail," turn off their visibility, and in the Animation panel, create a new frame ▣ **5d**.

6 Animating by transforming: Frame 6. In this frame the mouse moves farther left, to the edge of the frame. Duplicate the "BentTail copy" layer from step 5, move the center of rotation, and rotate it farther to the left **6**. Adjust visibility.

5c

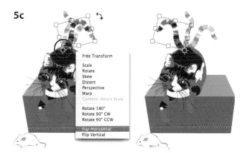

Flipping the "BentTail copy" layer. While the Transform frame is open you can right-click/Ctrl-click and choose Flip Horizontal from a context-sensitive menu.

5d

Duplicating frame 5 to start Frame 6

6

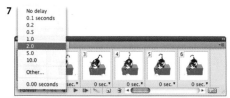

Frame 6 completes the motion as the mouse escapes.

7

Changing the timing for Frame 1

8a

Making a single layer from each frame

8b

After choosing Flatten Frames Into Layers but before targeting the layer corresponding to Frame 1

7 Testing the animation and setting the timing. At this point, click the "Play" button ▶ at the bottom of the Animation panel to play the action frame-by-frame. Click the ■ button to stop it, and change the timing for some of the frames as needed: Click the tiny arrow in the bottom-right corner of the frame and choose from the menu; we used 2 sec for Frame 1 (a long pause) **7**, 0.5 sec for Frame 2, 0.1 sec for Frame 3, 0.3 sec for Frame 4 (a slight hesitation for the strike), and then back to 0.1 for Frames 5 and 6 (for the quick escape).

Now check the timing: Choose File > Save For Web and use the "Play" button ▶ in the Animation section at the bottom right of the dialog. Also look at the animation in a browser by clicking the "Preview" button at the bottom of the dialog box. To leave the dialog box and get back to Photoshop, click the Cancel button.

At this point you can adjust the timing in the Animation panel if needed, preview again, and so on until you're happy with the motion. If you want to change the artwork in a frame, click the frame in the Animation panel, arrange position and visibility to your liking in the working window and Layers panel, and preview again.

8 Adding a little dimension. The Photocopy filter can add shading and edge definition. Because you can't run a filter on a frame — you need a layer — make a layer from each of your frames by choosing Flatten Frames Into Layers from the Animation panel's ▾≡ menu **8a**. At the top of the layer stack, a new layer will be added for each frame in the animation **8b**.

Modify each of these new layers in turn with the Photocopy filter as described next. But first choose the Move tool ▸⊕ so you can control the blend mode with a keyboard shortcut (with the Move tool or any selection tool chosen, Shift-+ steps through the blend modes for the active layer). Also, reset the Foreground and Background colors (type D for "Default"). If you had many frames in the animation, recording an Action would speed the process of filtering, ▼ but because we had just a few frames, we simply used keyboard shortcuts instead.

FIND OUT MORE
▼ Recording an Action
page 122

Before beginning the filtering process, make sure Propagate Frame 1 is turned off in the Layers panel. Then click on the first frame in the Animation panel. In the Layers panel, visibility for the corresponding layer (called Frame 1) will be turned on automatically, but you'll still need to *target* the layer in the Layers

8c

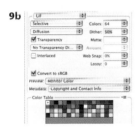

Running the Photocopy filter on a copy of the "Frame 1" layer (top). In Multiply mode, the filtered layer adds shading.

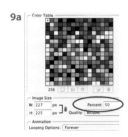

9a Reducing Image Size to 50% in Photoshop's Save for Web & Devices dialog. Pressing the Enter key reduces the size for the GIF that will be saved but doesn't permanently change the size of the .psd file.

9b We used the Selective reduction method, 64 colors, Diffusion Dither at 50%, and a Lossy setting of 0.

9c

| Size/Download Time (9600 bps Modem) |
| Size/Download Time (14.4 Kbps Modem) |
| Size/Download Time (28.8 Kbps Modem) |
| Size/Download Time (56.6 Kbps Modem/ISDN) |
| Size/Download Time (128 Kbps Dual ISDN) |
| ✓ Size/Download Time (256 Kbps Cable/DSL) |
| Size/Download Time (384 Kbps Cable/DSL) |
| Size/Download Time (512 Kbps Cable/DSL) |
| Size/Download Time (768 Kbps Cable/DSL) |
| Size/Download Time (1 Mbps Cable) |
| Size/Download Time (1.5 Mbps Cable/T1) |
| Size/Download Time (2 Mbps) |

The changes made in the Save for Web & Devices dialog reduced the download time to 2 sec at 256 Kbps.

panel to make it the active one — click its thumbnail. Duplicate the layer (Ctrl/⌘-J). Then choose Filter > Sketch > Photocopy and set the Detail (we used 6) and Darkness (we used 2); click "OK" to leave the filter dialog; if you don't like the result, undo (Ctrl/⌘-Z), reopen Photocopy (Ctrl-Alt-F in Windows or ⌘-Option-F on the Mac), change the settings, and click "OK." After filtering, put the copy in Multiply mode (to get from Normal to Multiply hold down Shift and type +++) **8c**. Then press Ctrl/⌘-E to merge the Photocopy layer with the original; the corresponding animation frame is updated automatically.

Advance to the next frame (you can do that by clicking the "Select next frame" button ▶ at the bottom of the Animation panel) and target that frame's layer in the Layers panel, then use the keyboard shortcuts: Ctrl/⌘-J duplicates the layer, Ctrl/⌘-F repeats the filter, Shift-+++ puts the filtered layer in Multiply mode, and Ctrl/⌘-E merges the filtered and original layers. We repeated the process for Frame 3 but departed from this routine for Frame 4; at the filtering step we used Ctrl-Alt-F (Windows)/⌘-Option-F (Mac) to open the Photocopy dialog so we could change the settings to Detail 10, Darkness 2 to emphasize the strike at the mouse. When filtering the next frame's layer copy we used Ctrl-Alt-F/⌘-Option-F again, to restore the Detail 6, Darkness 2 settings; then we used Ctrl/⌘-F to keep these settings for the last frame.

9 Optimizing and saving. Choose Optimize Animation from the animation panel's ▾≡ menu, and make sure both Bounding Box and Redundant Pixel Removal are checked. Beyond that, optimizing this GIF animation is much like optimizing any GIF, described on page 153. Choose File > Save for Web & Devices and start by reducing the dimensions of the file (recall that the artwork had been designed twice as big as we wanted it) in the Image Size section (near the lower-right corner of the Save for Web & Devices dialog) **9a**.

For color reduction, use the frame with the most color complexity — the most colors and the most broken-up distribution of the color patches. In *Catanimation*, the colors don't vary much, but we used Frame 4 because it included the mouse and had more shading at the edges **9b**, **9c**.

When you've optimized the file, previewed it in a browser, and decided it's ready, click the "Save" button. In the Save Optimized As dialog, choose Images Only for the Format and click "Save." *Voilà!*

Tweening & Tweaking

YOU'LL FIND THE FILES

in 🎨 > Wow Project Files > Chapter 10 >
Tweening & Tweaking:
- Bounce-Before.psd (to start)
- Bounce-After.psd & Bounce-After.gif
  (to compare)

OPEN THESE PANELS

(from the Window menu, for instance):
- Layers • Animation (Frames)

OVERVIEW

Compose the frames of an animation by
moving the components, turning layer
visibility on and off, and changing layer
Opacity and Style • Adjust timing

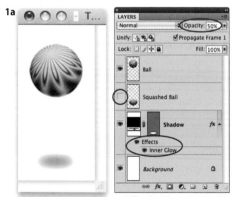

In the **Bounce-Before.psd** file, the "Squashed Ball"
layer (its visibility is turned off here) is a duplicate of
the "Ball" layer, flattened somewhat with the Edit >
Transform > Scale command. ▼ The "Shadow" layer
was made with the Ellipse tool ◯ ▼ and scaled the
same way as the "Squashed Ball" layer.

FIND OUT MORE

▼ Transforming **page 67**

▼ Drawing with the Shape tools **page 451**

FOR MANY GIF ANIMATIONS you can save a great deal of time
with *tweening*, letting Photoshop automatically create the intermediate frames between the start and end of an animation
sequence. Here's a simple example.

Thinking the project through. To animate a bouncing ball, we
want to drop the ball to the floor, distort it briefly on impact, and
bounce it back up. We also want to change the density, size, and
position of the shadow as the ball gets closer to or farther away
from the floor. Layer properties that can be tweened are **Position** of the layer's content, **Opacity**, and **Effects** (controlled in
the Layer Style dialog). We can easily move the ball by tweening
Position. And we can use tweened Opacity to lighten the shadow
and a tweened Inner Glow effect to shrink it. The "squashed"
ball will be added as a frame of its own, since transformations
(scaling or changing shape) can't be tweened.

1 Examining the first frame. Open the **Bounce-Before.psd**
file, a four-layer Photoshop file **1a** that includes a "Ball" layer;
a "Squashed Ball" layer, which is a duplicate of the "Ball" layer
but with the ball compressed vertically (this layer's visibility is
turned off for now); a black Shape layer for the "Shadow"; and
a white *Background*. A Layer Style consisting of an Inner Glow
from the Edge has been applied to the "Shadow" layer.

The first frame in the Animation (Frames) panel automatically
reflects the current state of the file. The round ball is positioned
high in the frame. Since the ball is high above the floor, in the
Layers panel the Opacity of the "Shadow" layer has been reduced
to 50%. If you double-click the Inner Glow entry in the Layers
panel to open the Layer Style dialog **1b**, you'll see that the Size
of the glow is set to 20 pixels to soften the edge of the shadow.
Click "Cancel" to close the Layer Style dialog.

In the Animation (Frames) panel, use the drop-down menu in
the bottom-right corner of the first frame to set the timing at

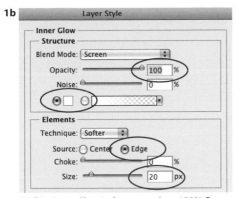

1b

A white Inner Glow in Screen mode at 100% Opacity with the Edge option chosen can be sized to make the Shadow look softer.

2a

The first frame is duplicated to make the second.

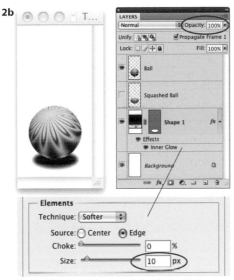

2b

The ball is moved down and the shadow's density is increased. Reducing the size of the Inner Glow hardens the edge of the shadow.

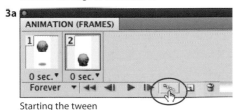

3a

Starting the tween

"No delay," or 0 seconds. This timing will carry over to all other frames made from this one.

2 Making the second frame. Copy the first frame by clicking the "Duplicates selected frame" button ▣ at the bottom of the Animation panel **2a**. Then change the graphics for the frame **2b**: Click on the "Ball" layer in the Layers panel to target it, and use the Move tool ▶₊ to drag the ball down to the "floor" level. Target the "Shadow" layer and move it down a bit also. Make the shadow denser by increasing the Shadow layer's Opacity in the Layers panel, and open the Layer Style dialog (double-click the Inner Glow entry in the Layers panel) and reduce the Size of the Inner Glow to 10 pixels.

3 Tweening. Now make the in-between frames by clicking the "Tween" button ⁕ at the bottom of the Animation panel **3a**. In the Tween dialog box **3b**, for **Tween With**, choose **Previous Frame**, and enter 5 in the **Frames to Add** field. Choose all three properties at the bottom of the dialog box. We'll be tweening the Position to move the ball, the Opacity to increase the Shadow density, and the Effects to harden up the shadow's edge by reducing the size of the Inner Glow. Click "OK" to close the dialog. Photoshop will add the five intermediate frames **3c**.

4 Distorting the ball. When the tweening is done, the last frame will still be targeted. Duplicate this frame (click the ▣ button). Now turn on visibility for the "Squashed Ball" layer (click in the Layers panel in its ◉ column) and turn *off* visibility for the Ball layer **4**.

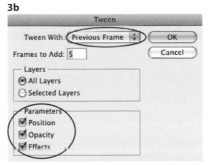

3b

Setting up the Tween dialog. (If you were to target two frames in the Animation panel instead of one, the Tween With choice in the dialog would change to Selection, so that the selected frames would be tweened.)

3c

After tweening

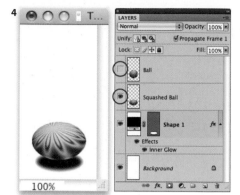

4

100%

Visibility is turned on for the "Squashed Ball" layer and turned off for the "Ball" layer.

OTHER PROPERTIES THAT CAN BE TWEENED

Besides the individual layer effects themselves, the **Angle of the Global Light**, set in the Layer Style dialog, can be tweened to imitate a moving light source.

Bolt Bulb.psd & .gif files

And although it isn't controlled in the Layer Style dialog, **warped text** is among the things that can be tweened when Effects is chosen in the Tween dialog.

Type Warp tween.psd & .gif

5 Tweening the bounce. To start the bounce back up, in the Animation panel, copy the last round-ball frame (the one before the squashed-ball frame) by Alt/Option-dragging it beyond the squashed-ball frame. This makes the start of the bounce back up **5a**. Now click the Tween button again and in the Tween dialog, leave all settings as they are, except change the **Tween With** choice to **First Frame**. This will add five more frames, returning the ball to the high point **5b**.

6 Adjusting the timing. To roughly imitate the acceleration and deceleration of a real bounce, you can change the timing of some of the frames. We set a delay of 0.2 second for the first frame; 0.1 for the second frame, the "Squashed-Ball" frame, and the last frame; and 0.05 (by choosing Other) for the third frame and the next-to-last frame **6**. In the bottom-left corner of the Animation panel, choose a looping scheme. If you don't want Once, 3 times, or Forever, choose Other and enter a number in the Play field.

Saving & exporting. Save the Photoshop file, and optimize and export the animation as a GIF, using the Optimize Animation command from the Animation panel's menu and then File > Save for Web & Devices, as described on page 699.

5a

Duplicating the "down" frame

5b

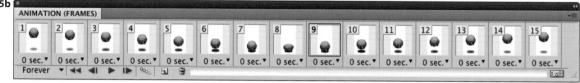

After tweening to make the upward bounce

6

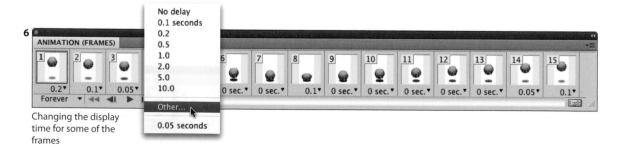

Changing the display time for some of the frames

Hands reaching into and out of the image to support a mutually held object illustrate **Web Services,** the Internet services and applications that allow remote users to share resources. **Rob Magiera** started in the 3D program Alias Maya, where he created the hands and central object. He constructed a patterned line for the outer rings in Adobe Illustrator, opened the file in Photoshop, and saved it as a TIFF for import into Maya. Magiera created a texture image in Photoshop that conveyed the idea of "data," imported it into Maya, and applied it to the central object.

He rendered each form as a separate file so he could add special effects and masks to combine them in Photoshop. Maya automatically generated an alpha channel for each file during rendering, which Magiera could load as a selection in Photoshop in order to delete the background (this process is described on page 706).

After Magiera had opened the rendered files in Photoshop and dragged and dropped each one into his working file, he added layer masks (by clicking the "Create a layer mask" button at the bottom of the Layers panel) and painted them with black to make some elements appear to be partly in front of and partly behind others.

To make the glow of the outer rings, Magiera duplicated the layer with the rings (Ctrl/⌘-J), blurred the copy (Filter > Blur > Gaussian Blur), and set the blurred layer's blend mode to Screen. ▼

To unify the image, he then scaled up a copy of the texture he had used for the central object (by pressing Ctrl/⌘-T for Edit > Free Transform and dragging a corner handle) and layered it over the image. To confine the texture to the outer edges of the illustration, he added a layer mask and filled it with a black-to-white radial gradient. ▼

To complete the dimensional "atmosphere," Magiera filled a layer with a pattern of blue vertical stripes (Edit > Fill > Pattern) that he then blurred. After reducing Opacity and adding a layer mask, he customized a large airbrush ▼ and painted the mask with black to block out the stripes in the center and corners.

FIND OUT MORE

▼ Blend modes **page 181**

▼ Masking with gradients **page 84**

▼ Creating brushes **page 363**

Derek Lea's *Biorhythms* illustration for an article in *Cancer Nursing Practice* magazine includes components from three different 3D programs. With his composition in mind, Lea started a Photoshop file and created the outer-space sky: Adding an alpha channel (by clicking the "Create new channel" button at the bottom of the Channels panel), he set the Foreground and Background colors to black and white (typing D, then X will do this), and ran the Clouds filter in the channel (Filter > Render > Clouds). He then loaded the channel as a selection (Ctrl/⌘-click its thumbnail in the Channels panel), and used the Gradient tool to apply a gradient through this selection on a separate layer. He stippled the stars on other layers with the Brush tool, changing the brush tip's size and hardness. In Bryce he created a sky with a bright sun, and copied and pasted the sun into his Photoshop file.

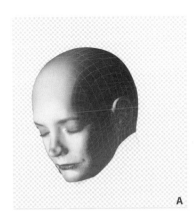

A

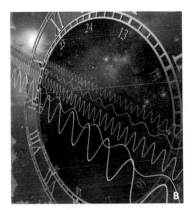

B

He added his own photo of a woman's face, duplicated the layered file, flattened the copy to a *Background*, and saved it as a TIFF. He could then open his flattened comp in the Poser 3D figure-design program, where he modeled a woman's bald head to match the photo, rendering the head to match the skin color from the photo and the lighting from his comp. He rendered the Poser model a second time, in wireframe mode.

He dragged and dropped the realistically rendered head into his developing Photoshop file. He copied the wireframe rendering and pasted it into another alpha channel, so that he could load it as a selection and fill the selected wires with color on a new layer (Edit > Fill > Color). He used layer masks to blend the three versions of the head and used Hue/Saturation, Levels, and Selective Color Adjustment layers

to change color and contrast **A**. Lea often desaturates first,▼ then uses a Levels adjustment to get the tonal composition the way he wants it,▼ and then adds a Selective Color layer to color the Blacks, Whites, and Neutrals.▼ He typically uses many layers, targeting his toning and coloring with layer masks.

The metallic clock elements and the sine waves were drawn in Adobe Illustrator as paths and imported into Strata 3D for extrusion and rendering, with another flattened copy of the developing comp used as a background for orientation. The rendered graphics were incorporated into the Photoshop file, layered above the background **B** and below the head. The waves were then partially masked to blend into the background in places, and the head layers were grouped, masked, and assigned blend modes to

blend the head with the waves and background.▼

When an illustration is destined for print, as *Biorhythms* was, Lea often starts his file in CMYK mode. He's well aware of the wider gamut that can be achieved by working in RGB, but "I have never seen the advantage of using a range of colors that will not reproduce accurately," he says. "It is an old habit rooted in simply predicting the outcome accurately." At each stage he meticulously modulates the details of tone and color to develop the illustration. He typically doesn't use the Photoshop filters and commands that work only in RGB mode, so he doesn't miss them when working in CMYK. And he can keep his adjustment options open right to the end, because he doesn't have to flatten a copy of the file before converting, to prevent layer blend modes from changing their effect as they can when a file is converted from RGB to CMYK or vice versa.▼

For illustrator **Rob Magiera,** the acorn-to-oak metaphor was the perfect expression of the sprouting of hundreds of acronyms that have accompanied the growth of the Internet. Magiera began *Seeds of Internet Growth* in the 3D program Alias Maya and then used standard Photoshop tools and commands (not the Photoshop Extended 3D interface) to complete the scene. Working in Maya, Magiera painted key parts of the image with Maya's Paint Effects tools. He benefited from the software's option to generate an alpha channel when rendering, which made it easy to isolate the trees in Photoshop. He could load the alpha channel as a selection (Select > Load Selection), then invert the selection (Ctrl/⌘-Shift-I), and press

the Delete key to remove the black background. To remove all remaining traces of black from the edges of the trees, Magiera used Photoshop's Layer > Matting > Remove Black Matte, which replaces any black at the edges with transparency. (He had chosen black for the background in Maya with this command in mind.)

To get the image of the ground, Magiera threw a scoop of dirt on his flatbed scanner and scanned it, having first stretched a piece of clear plastic wrap over the glass to avoid scratches and make cleanup easier. For the sprouted acorn, he opened a stock image in Photoshop, painted roots on it, and added a shadow by clicking the "Add a layer style" button *fx* at the bottom of the Layers panel and choosing Drop Shadow.

Magiera next opened the rendered main tree file and copied and pasted the other trees, the acorn artwork, and the dirt scan. To help keep track of his various elements, he created a Group for the far trees and also one for the near tree. (To collect layers into a Group, target one layer by clicking its thumbnail in the Layers panel; then Ctrl/⌘-click or Shift-click the other layer thumbnails; finally, Shift-click the "Create a new group" button 🗀 at the bottom of the panel.)

To make the acronym text, Magiera selected the Type tool T and dragged a rectangle larger than the main tree to create paragraph type. (Photoshop automatically creates a type layer when you click or drag with the Type tool with a layer targeted that already contains non-type artwork.) He set the font, size, and color in the Options bar and began typing. He added a Layer Style to make the type glow, clicking the *fx* button at the bottom of the Layers panel and choosing Outer Glow from the pop-up list. To light up the type and its glow, he put the layer in Screen mode, using the blend mode pop-up menu in the upper left corner of the Layers panel.

Magiera duplicated the type layer (Ctrl/⌘-J) and dragged the copy's thumbnail in the Layers panel to a position above the layer with the far trees. He reduced the size of the duplicate type (by pressing Ctrl/⌘-T for Edit > Free Transform, and then Shift-dragging inward on a corner handle of the Transform frame). He rasterized the type layers so the font wouldn't be needed for output.

With all of the elements assembled in Photoshop, Magiera began modifying them, using layer masks and clipping groups and adding Adjustment layers, to preserve as much editability as possible. He masked the acorn root and a painted

shadow at the base of the tree inside the dirt layer by creating a clipping group with the dirt as its base, so the parts of the shadow and root that extended above the dirt surface were hidden. Also in this clipping group was a Hue/Saturation layer that brightened the dirt around the acorn. (To create a clipping group, target the layer you want to use as the mask and then Alt/Option-click the border between this clipping layer and the next one above it. If you like, you can continue up the layer stack, masking consecutive layers inside the "footprint" of the clipping layer.)

He added a layer mask to each of the type layers so the type would show up only on the trees' leaves. Layer masks worked better than clipping groups in these cases, because he could modify the masks — blurring the edges slightly and painting with black to hide the type in some places, allowing the branches and trunk to show. He made each mask by Ctrl/⌘-clicking the thumbnail for the tree, then targeting the type layer and clicking the "Add layer mask"

button 🔲 at the bottom of the Layers panel. In Photoshop CS3 Select > Refine Edge allows you to feather the edge of a mask, previewing the change in the composite as you work.▼ In CS4 you can use Refine Edge or use the Feather setting on the Masks panel; the latter keeps the feather "live" so you can change it later if you like.▼ By clicking the link icon 🔗 between the layer thumbnail and mask thumbnail in the Layers panel, Magiera could decouple the type and the mask, so he could move the type around until he got the placement he wanted.

Magiera used several layers to create the atmosphere in his image, starting with a gray-filled layer at the bottom of the stack. He put a white-filled layer at reduced opacity between the far trees and the near tree to create atmospheric fog that adds depth. He added a Hue/Saturation Adjustment layer to colorize the fog and a gradient-filled layer in Overlay mode to change the green at the top of the image, using layer masks to protect the near tree from the color.

To add more atmosphere immediately around the near tree, Magiera created a softened, dark green copy of the tree by adding a Drop Shadow to the layer (as described earlier for the acorn) and then separating the shadow to its own layer (Layer > Layer Style > Create Layer), where he adjusted Opacity.

FIND OUT MORE

▼ Refine Edge command **page 59**

▼ Masks panel **page 63**

To create this illustration for *The Art of Poser and Photoshop*, **Stephen Burns** developed the character model in Poser and the background image in Photoshop. He used the background photo to generate the lighting for the model in Poser, and rendered the character in Poser. He then composed the scene in Photoshop, blending the model with photos of tree trunks and roots to make a single integrated form, and enhancing color and contrast. Here's how he did it.

Starting with the Kelvin G2 figure from Poser's figure library, Burns set Endomorph and Mesomorph values in Poser's FBM (Full Body Morph) menu to give the figure a muscular body. In the Main Camera menu he set the Focal and Perspective values at 31 mm for an exaggerated depth of field. Using the Head Camera parameters, he made the eyes squint, opened the mouth, and set the lips for a snarling yell **A**. With Poser's Advanced Texture panel, he

applied a brick image as the Diffuse Color (surface color and pattern) and Bump (surface texture) properties. (For an alternative method of applying surface color and texture to this model in Photoshop Extended, see page 657. For this image, though, all 3D work was done in Poser.)

In Photoshop Burns started with a series of eight photos of a sunset and blended them into a panorama with Photomerge, using the Auto setting **B**. ▼ He duplicated the

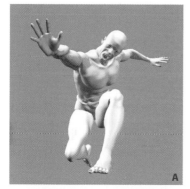

layered panorama as a single-layer file (Image > Duplicate, Duplicate Merged Layers Only) and used Edit > Transform (Ctrl/⌘-T), dragging in on a side handle to compress the image, exaggerating the perspective for the clouds and the sun's rays **C**. He blurred the image using a Smart Filter so he could readjust the blur later. ▼

Burns copied and pasted from four photos of tree roots and trunks **D** into his developing image file. He used Edit > Transform commands, including Warp, ▼ along with layer masks, to shape and blend the tree parts to create the foreground and background "floor" of the image. ▼ To add drama, he enhanced color and contrast with a Curves Adjustment layer above the developing image **E**. ▼

Burns used a flattened copy of the background image in Poser to create

the lighting for his model. He applied the image in the background's Color channel, which brought it into the scene as the background. He used Poser's Image Based Lighting option to light the character with the colors and intensity of light from the background image, regulating the Light Properties as he would for any Spot, Infinite, or Point light in Poser.

He rendered the character at 300 pixels/inch at a size to fit with the background image **F**. He opened the rendered file in Photoshop and dragged it into his image file. By Ctrl/⌘-clicking on the Layers panel's thumbnail for his character, he could load its outline as a selection. Then he targeted a tree layer and added a layer mask. Made from the active selection, the mask hid the tree everywhere except where it overlapped the

body. After doing the same for other tree layers, he could paint the layer masks with black or white to blend the tree elements as he wanted.

Burns also added color and texture-filled layers with black-filled layer masks. By choosing the right blend modes (Overlay and Lighter Color, for instance) ▼ and painting the layer masks with white, he could warm the highlights, cool the shadows, or enhance the surface texture exactly where he wanted these changes.

FIND OUT MORE

▼ Photomerge **page 576**

▼ Smart Filters **page 72**

▼ Transforming **page 67**

▼ Blending with layer masks **page 84**

▼ Curves Adjustment layers **page 246**

▼ Blend modes **page 181**

Geno **Andrews** did much of the editing of the feature-length *Cold Play* in Apple Final Cut Pro, but added finishing touches in Photoshop Extended. After exporting this establishing shot from Final Cut as a QuickTime movie, he opened it in Photoshop Extended **A** and added two type layers, one with "BUENOS AIRES" in white and the other with "AEROPUERTO INTERNACIONAL" in gold to match the front of the portico **B**. Both type layers were rotated and scaled slightly to fit in their positions on the building.

Next, for each type layer, Andrews targeted the layer by clicking its name in the Layers panel, and with the Type tool T chosen, clicked the "Create warped text" button in the Options bar. He chose the Arch for the warp Style and used the three Bend sliders **C** to fit the type to the curvature of the building **D**.

In the Layers panel he changed the blend mode of the "BUENOS AIRES" layer to Soft Light mode **E**, to create the illusion that the type was etched on the inside of the window.▼ He added an Inner Shadow effect▼ to

the "AEROPUERTO INTERNACIONAL" type to make it appear chiseled into the metal **F**.

"You might be tempted to go overboard and create an inner bevel — which for a still image would be great," says Andrews. "But even the resolution of high-def video gets soft when compressed to standard digital video. So in this case the basic Inner Shadow worked fine."

A layer mask was added to each type layer and painted▼ to hide the type behind the tree leaves in the foreground **G**, **H**.

To add a plane landing at what was now the airport, Andrews started with a still photo of a plane and removed its identifying marks. He extracted the plane from its background with the Background Eraser tool , dragged it into his video file, and scaled it to fit the image using Ctrl/⌘-T for Edit > Transform, and Shift-dragging a corner handle inward to reduce the size proportionately.▼

With the plane on a transparent layer, Andrews used the Animation (Timeline) panel▼ to put it on final

approach for landing. He used the Move tool to put the plane just "offstage" to the right. In the Animation panel **I** he clicked the ▶ to the left of the "Airplane" layer entry to open the list of characteristics that can be interpolated over time. He moved the Current Time Indicator (play head) to the starting position and clicked the stopwatch icon for Position. This created a keyframe (marked by a small yellow diamond ◇) establishing the plane's position at that time. He added another keyframe by repositioning the play head, then dragging the plane to the left with the Move tool until it completely overlapped the building **J**.

Now all that was left was to mask the plane layer so the plane appeared to fly behind the building instead of in front of it. Andrews selected the sky with the Select > Color Range command and clicked the "Add layer mask" button at the bottom of the Layers panel. He painted over the windows in the mask with the Brush tool and black paint **K**. Now when he played the video clip, the plane appeared in the sky only, gliding behind the building.

A

B

Warp Text

Style: Arch

OK

Cancel

Horizontal   Vertical

Bend: +2   %

Horizontal Distortion: -4   %

Vertical Distortion: -1   %

C

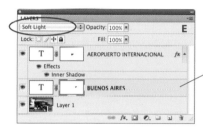

D

LAYERS

Soft Light   Opacity: 100%

E

Lock: Fill: 100%

T   AEROPUERTO INTERNACIONAL   fx

Effects

Inner Shadow

T   BUENOS AIRES

Layer 1

F

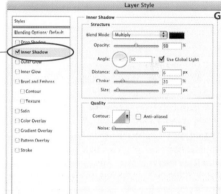

Layer Style

Styles

Blending Options: Default

Drop Shadow

Inner Shadow

Outer Glow

Inner Glow

Bevel and Emboss

Contour

Texture

Satin

Color Overlay

Gradient Overlay

Pattern Overlay

Stroke

Inner Shadow

Structure

Blend Mode: Multiply

Opacity: 50   %

Angle: 30   °   Use Global Light

Distance: 6   px

Choke: 20   %

Size: 9   px

Quality

Contour: Anti-aliased

Noise: 0   %

G

H

ANIMATION (TIMELINE)

0:00:04:00   (30.00 fps)

00   15f   01:00f   15f   02:00f   15f   03:00f   15f   04:00f   15f

Comments

Airplane

Position

Opacity

Style

T   AEROPUERTO INTERNACIONAL

T   BUENOS AIRES

Layer 1

Global Lighting

FIND OUT MORE

▼ Blend mode **page 181**

▼ Inner Shadow effect **page 506**

▼ Painting layer masks **page 84**

▼ Transforming **page 67**

▼ Animation panel **page 667**

J

K

I n this scene from **Cold Play,** Indigo (Vanessa Branch) meets with her koi broker (Jacklyn Blomker) to buy some fish. The film's budget didn't allow for paying for the location, and time was limited (the entire movie was shot in 16 and a half days). So the tourists who were also enjoying the public pond **A**, would later be edited out of the 5-second establishing shot, filmed with the camera locked down. "Shoot your actors with some separation from civilians," says actor-director-editor **Geno Andrews**. "A wide shot is helpful as establishing, but consider punching in closer and framing out the unwanted talent **B**. You'll have more variety in your shots and less post work ahead of you."

With the video for the wide shot open in Photoshop Extended, Andrews went to work to make a separate layer that could sit on top of the video layer, hiding the tourists. There was enough unobstructed lattice and railing **C** so he could select with the Lasso tool ⌒ and Rectangular Marquee ⸾⸾⸽ and do a copy-and-paste reconstruction of the boathouse, merged on a regular Photoshop layer **D**. On the same layer he used the Clone Stamp ♣ with

a soft-edged brush tip and Sample All Layers chosen in the Options bar to paint in some of the bushes and blend edge details. Once he had that fixed layer sitting on top of the layer of footage **E,** he chose File > Export > Render Video, and Photoshop Extended merged the two layers to produce a new movie without the guests.

The vignette effect shown here and on the facing page were applied as the Inner Shadow effect in a Layer Style on the video layer as described on page 689.

I n this shot of a Malibu hotel from *Cold Play,* filmmaker **Geno Andrews** didn't have permission to use the hotel's name. There was also the problem of the big white van parked in the scene **A**, not to mention the traffic passing by.

In Photoshop Extended Andrews used the Rectangular Marquee tool ▢ with a Feather set in the Options bar to copy a rectangular section of the wall to the left of the name and paste it several times to cover the name cleanly. He merged the pasted layers to make one layer that could then sit on top of the video for the entire shot (to merge layers, target them in the Layers panel and press Ctrl/⌘-E for Layer > Merge Layers). Andrews then used a type layer with a Layer Style to carve the new name on the building **B** (see page 710 for the method).

To remove the van, he used the same method as for the sign, copying and pasting the highway on top of it **C**. "The trickiest part," says Andrews, "was keeping the bush in the fore-ground." He painted a mask on the patch layer around the yellow flower, because although the camera was locked down, the flower still moved in the wind. In the final shot, the

flower bends in the wind and partly disappears briefly when it bends into the layer mask. "On screen," says Andrews, "no one would ever notice. It's good to remember when you're doing clean-up work like this that it's video. People won't stare at it like they would a photograph. It goes by so quickly. Also, compression can ac-tually help to hide the rough details in your work. So don't kill yourself trying to make your touch-up work photorealistic."

There were several options for paint-ing out the traffic. "The thing you *don't* want to do," says Andrews, "is paint it out frame by frame." The solution he chose was to let the tape roll for 5 minutes, knowing that somewhere in that footage there would be a relatively traffic-free frame. He located a frame with just two cars, and painted out those cars and some red cones across the street with copied selections and the Clone Stamp ⚒. Another option would be to export a number of relatively traffic-free frames as files and use File > Scripts > Statistics with Median chosen in the Choose Stack Mode menu to remove parts that aren't in half the frames or more (see page 327).

SHOOTING BOTH WAYS

Filmmaker Geno Andrews sug-gests, "If you have doubts as to whether your shot of a building or crowd will present legal problems for a distributor, consider shooting once with standard camera move-ment and once with the camera locked down. If you have to make changes, the locked-down version will make post-production work in Photoshop much easier."

www.freedomfriesart.org

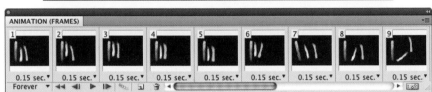

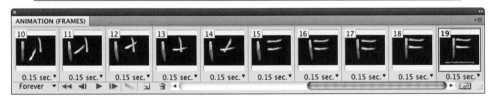

For the ***animated Freedom Fries Art Collective logo***, **Sharon Steuer** raided the refrigerator and took a Claymation-like approach that works in either Photoshop or Photoshop Extended. Like Claymation, her process involved setting up the elements of the scene, then rearranging them to make each new frame. But instead of photographing the scene anew for each frame, she made only one photo and did the rest of the arranging in Photoshop using Smart Objects and the Animation panel in Frames mode (in Photoshop, Frames mode is the only option for the Animation panel; in Photoshop

Extended, if the Animation panel opens in Timeline mode instead, open the panel's menu and choose Convert to Frame Animation).

Steuer started by placing the three french fries to make the "F" logo on a white background and photographing them with a digital camera. In Photoshop she opened a new document (File > New) in RGB color at 640 by 480 pixels with a black *Background*.

After saving a copy of her intact photo (File > Save As, choosing the "As a Copy" option), she used the Magic Wand ✎ with Contiguous turned off in the Options bar to click on the background and thus select all the white in the image. Switching

to Quick Mask mode (using the ▣ button near the bottom of the Tools panel), she tidied up the selection with the Brush and black and white paint;▼ then she switched back to Standard mode ▣ and pressed the Backspace/Delete key. This left the three fries on a transparent layer. She selected all (Ctrl/⌘-A), copied (Ctrl/⌘-C), then clicked in the working window of the black document, and pasted (Ctrl/⌘-V). To scale the pasted-in "F" to the size she wanted **A**, she used the Free Transform command (Ctrl/⌘-T), Shift-dragging on a corner of the Transform frame.

Steuer then made a loose selection of one of the fries with the Lasso tool ⌀ and copied it to a separate layer (Ctrl/⌘-J). She repeated the selecting and copying process for a second french fry, and then the third. She turned each of the three fries layers into a Smart Object of its own by right/Ctrl-clicking its name in the Layers panel and choosing Convert to Smart Object from the context-sensitive menu **B**. This Smart Object "packaging" would protect the fries from deteriorating as she repeatedly rotated them into new positions to make the frames of the animation.

Steuer turned off visibility for the "F" layer, by clicking its 👁 in the Layers panel. Now it was time for the Clay-mation-like process. With the Auto Select: Layer and Show Transform Controls options turned on in the Options bar **C**, the Transform frame appeared automatically when she clicked on a french fry to target its layer. She dragged inside the Trans-form frame with the Move tool ▸₊ to change the position of each french fry and dragged the double-headed curved-arrow cursor outside the frame to rotate it as needed **D**, pressing the Enter key to complete the transformation. When she had lined up all the fries in the starting position for the first frame of the

animation, she opened the Anima-tion panel (Window > Animation), and the starting image appeared in Frame 1. At this point in the process it's important to preserve the trans-formations already made as you go on to make more transformations for the next frame. Here's a way to do it:

Before moving on to the next frame, target the top layer of the file by clicking its thumbnail in the Layers panel. Add a layer that's a merged copy of everything currently vis-ible (Ctrl-Alt-Shift-E in Windows, ⌘-Shift-Option-E on the Mac). Then add another frame by clicking the "Duplicates selected frame" but-ton ⎘ at the bottom of the Anima-tion panel. Now turn off visibility for the merged-copy layer in the layers panel, and move and transform each of the Smart Objects again to make the arrangement you want for the second frame.

Steuer continued adding frames and rearranging fries. To add the web site address to the last frame, she first opened the Animation panel's menu (clicking the ▾≡ button does it) and made sure the "New Layers Visible in All Frames" option was turned off **E**, so the text she was about to add

would appear only in the currently targeted last frame. Then she chose the Type tool T, added the address, and converted the type to pixels (Layer > Rasterize >Type).

Steuer had designed the animation assuming the same uniform timing for all the frames. After setting the Animation panel's looping options to Once (in the lower-left corner of the panel), she previewed the ani-mation by clicking the panel's Play button ▸. To set the timing, she se-lected all the frames by clicking the starting frame and then Shift-click-ing the end frame. She clicked the tiny triangle to the right of the frame delay value at the bottom of one of the frames, chose Other from the pop-out menu, and entered a value of 0.15 sec in the Set Delay field.

Steuer exported the animation in QuickTime format (File > Export > Render Video, choosing the Quick-Time Export: QuickTime Movie option and clicking the "Render" but-ton) **F**. Jeff Jacoby used Apple Final Cut Pro to incorporate the QuickTime animation with voice-over, music, and other video into a QuickTime video trailer, which can be seen at www.freedomfriesart.org/pages/ viewtrailer.html.

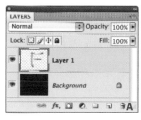

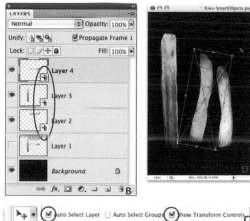

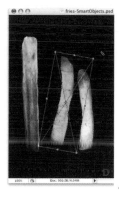

FIND OUT MORE

▼ Quick Mask
page 60

Measurement & Analysis

PHOTOSHOP & SCIENTIFIC RESEARCH

As Photoshop has become established as the standard for improving the appearance of digital images, many scientific journals have developed rules for how Photoshop may and may not be used to enhance published images, or to collect or analyze data. If you work in science, it's worthwhile to check the image-editing standards for the journals in your field. As examples, here are excerpts from the current standards for two cell biology journals:

From *Nature Cell Biology*, "Guide to Authors, Editorial and Publishing Policies, Digital Image Integrity and Standards" (www.nature.com/authors/editorial_policies/image.html):

"Authors should list all image acquisition tools and image processing software packages used. Authors should document key image-gathering settings and processing manipulations in the Methods. . . . The use of touch-up tools, such as cloning and healing tools in Photoshop, or any feature that deliberately obscures manipulations, is to be avoided. Processing (such as changing brightness and contrast) is appropriate only when it is applied equally across the entire image and is applied equally to controls. Contrast should not be adjusted so that data disappear. Excessive manipulations, such as processing to emphasize one region in the image at the expense of others . . . is inappropriate, as is emphasizing experimental data relative to the control."

From *Journal of Cell Biology*, "Instructions for Authors, Editorial Policies, Image Manipulation" (http://jcb.rupress.org/misc/ifora.shtml):

"No specific feature within an image may be enhanced, obscured, moved, removed, or introduced. . . . Adjustments of brightness, contrast, or color balance are acceptable if they are applied to the whole image and as long as they do not obscure, eliminate, or misrepresent any information present in the original, including backgrounds. Non-linear adjustments (e.g., changes to gamma settings) must be disclosed in the figure legend."

You can find Photoshop Extended's tools and commands for measuring and for recording measurements in the Analysis menu.

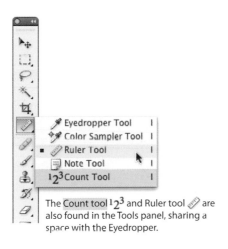

The Count tool 1 2 3 and Ruler tool ✐ are also found in the Tools panel, sharing a space with the Eyedropper.

FROM ITS BEGINNINGS, Photoshop has been an impressive storehouse of data. For every color image, it keeps track of the location and three or four channels' worth of color data for every pixel. With versions CS3 and CS4, Photoshop Extended has made some first steps toward "mining" this data with measurement and analysis tools. This chapter tells how Photoshop Extended can help with counting particular features in an image, setting a measurement scale, and measuring the linear dimensions, areas, and other parameters of selected features. It gives a brief introduction to the functions in Photoshop Extended's Analysis menu and Measurement Log, as well as other aspects of Photoshop that may be of use to those collecting and analyzing data from photos or using photos to present their work. Two tutorials show what the counting and measuring functions can do, so you can see if they could be useful, given any other tools you have available.

COUNTING & MEASURING

The Analysis menu and expanded Tools panel at the left and "The Measurement Tools" on page 718 show the components of Photoshop Extended's measuring apparatus:

- The **Measurement Log panel** (Window > Measurement Log) records counts made with the Count tool 1 2 3 as well as measurements made with the Ruler tool ✐, or you can make a selection and it records the area and other parameters of each part of the selection. The kinds of data are listed across the top of the Measurement Log panel as column headings, and the measurements are entered as rows in the table. You can rearrange the space in the Measurement Log, and you can delete rows or columns. To preserve the measurements in the Measurement Log panel as a separate text file, select the rows you want to include and click the "Export selected data" button ✎ at the top right of the Log panel.

THE MEASUREMENT TOOLS

The **Analysis menu** (shown on page 717) provides access to the **Measurement Log panel,** where data are recorded; the **Select Data Points dialog**, where you choose which data to record in the Measurement Log panel; and the **Measurement Scale dialog**, where you establish a scale for your image or series of images.

Your choices in the **Select Data Points** dialog determine which parameters will be included in the Measurement Log panel. Even if you delete a column of data in the Log, the measurements for that parameter will continue to be recorded unless you make the change in the Select Data Points dialog. By default, all options are on.

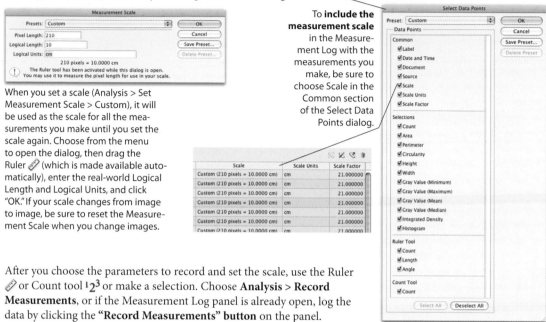

When you set a scale (Analysis > Set Measurement Scale > Custom), it will be used as the scale for all the measurements you make until you set the scale again. Choose from the menu to open the dialog, then drag the Ruler (which is made available automatically), enter the real-world Logical Length and Logical Units, and click "OK." If your scale changes from image to image, be sure to reset the Measurement Scale when you change images.

To **include the measurement scale** in the Measurement Log with the measurements you make, be sure to choose Scale in the Common section of the Select Data Points dialog.

After you choose the parameters to record and set the scale, use the Ruler or Count tool 1**2**³ or make a selection. Choose **Analysis > Record Measurements**, or if the Measurement Log panel is already open, log the data by clicking the **"Record Measurements" button** on the panel.

Click the "Record Measurements" button to add the current measurement (count, Ruler measure, or selection measurement) to the Measurement Log.

In the column headings, drag the dividers left or right to widen or narrow the columns.

The Measurement Log panel has no Undo function. If you make a mistake in selecting areas to measure, for instance, and don't discover it until after you record the measurements, you can remove the unwanted measurements by selecting those rows and clicking the "Delete selected measurements" button.

Delete selected measurements. To delete, click on the column heading to select a column or click anywhere in a row to select that measurement, and click the Delete button.

Select all measurements   Deselect all measurements   Export selected measurements

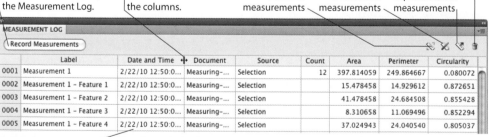

By default, measurements are listed in order by date and time. But you can sort by other criteria. Double-click any column heading to use that parameter for sorting. A tiny triangle will appear to the right of the column heading; click it to toggle between ascending and descending order.

To move a column to a different position in the Measurement Log layout, click the column heading to select the column, release the mouse button, and then depress the button again and drag left or right to reposition the column. (You can select more than one column by dragging over adjacent column titles, instead of clicking just one; or click one and then Shift-click or Ctrl/⌘-click others.)

The Measurement Log, which records data from counts and measures, is not stored in your image file. So it's a good idea to store the .txt file that the Log can export together with the image files in one folder.

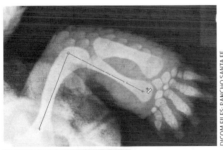

You can set the color of the Count tool's markers to contrast with the features you're counting. In Photoshop CS4 you can also set the dot size and type size, and you can make separate counts for different kinds of features, such as the green jelly beans and white jelly beans here.

PHOTO: PHOTOSPIN.COM

DICOM FILES: RANCHO SANTA FE VETERINARY HOSPITAL

When you use the Ruler tool ✐, the length of the measuring lines (L, or L1 and L2) and the angle (A) appear in the Info panel, expressed in the units set in Preferences (Ctrl/⌘-K) > Units & Rulers and computed based on the Resolution in the Image Size dialog. But the measurement recorded in Photoshop Extended's Measurement Log will be based on the scale set in the Measurement Scale dialog. For a single measuring line, the angle is measured from horizontal (0°); for a "protractor," the angle between the two lines is measured.

Note: The Measurement Log starts over with each Photoshop Extended session — *not* each time you open a document or each time you set the measurement scale, but each time you start Photoshop Extended. This allows you to collect data from several images in the same Log, with separate scales for the images as needed. It also means that if the program hangs up or your computer crashes, all data for the current Photoshop Extended session can be lost. To avoid losing data, you can export the Measurement Log periodically.

- To determine which measurements, calculated values, and statistics are recorded in the Measurement Log, choose **Analysis > Set Data Points > Custom**. In the Select Data Points dialog, choose what data to record for the Count tool, Ruler tool, and selections, as well as some general data, such as date and document name.

- Using **Analysis > Set Measurement Scale**, you can set a scale for how many pixels in the image represent how many inches, centimeters, or another unit of measure in the real world.

Counting

Counting particular features in an image file is a simple matter of clicking with the Count tool ₁₂³ to mark each one. To record the total count after you've completed it, choose **Analysis > Record Measurements** or click the **"Record Measurements" button** in the Measurement Log panel. For each count, the record in the Measurement Log can include the total count, the name of the document, and the date and time the count was made. Since the Measurement Log is not linked to a particular document, you could, for instance, count the same feature in a series of photos, capture all the counts to the Measurement Log, and export the Log (as a .txt document with tab-delimited fields), with all the counts from all of your photos in a single text file for comparison in a spreadsheet. Photoshop Extended's system for counting improves significantly between versions CS3 and CS4. A method for keeping count data with the image file so you can always identify which features were counted is described in "Counting" on page 724.

Measuring

Besides counts, Photoshop Extended can collect location, distance, and angle measurements made with the Ruler tool ✐ and additional measurements made by selecting features of interest and computing various measurements from the selection.

The Ruler tool ✐. In either Photoshop or Photoshop Extended, the Ruler can be used to pinpoint a location, or measure a linear distance or an angle. To measure a distance, drag with the ruler

To the photo of fields, we added an empty layer in Photoshop Extended to "catch" the measurements we would make, and then we chose Filter > Vanishing Point.

After drawing a perspective plane, ▼ we dragged with the Measure tool 📏 along the length of the tractor, which we knew was about 15 feet long, and entered that value for Length.

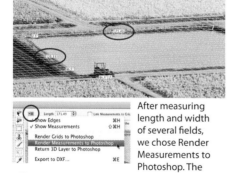

VP Measure.psd

After measuring length and width of several fields, we chose Render Measurements to Photoshop. The measurement markers were recorded on the empty layer we had added at the beginning.

tool from one end of the feature to be measured, and click again at the other end. A measuring line will mark the distance measured, and the distance and the angle (with horizontal at 0°) will appear in the Options bar and the Info panel, along with other data. To measure an angle between two measuring lines rather than between a measuring line and horizontal, Alt/Option-drag from one end of the existing measuring line to create a second measuring line, creating what Photoshop calls a *protractor*.

In Photoshop Extended, the Ruler 📏 is also useful for setting a scale of measure for an image so that when you then select features for Photoshop to measure automatically, the measurements will be expressed in the units of the scale you've set. The Ruler can also be especially useful if you have a series of images in which you have to measure one feature in each image for comparison. When you open each file, reset the Measurement Scale if necessary, drag with the ruler to make a measurement, and click the "Record Measurements" button at the top of the Measurement Log panel. To be preserved as part of the Measurement Log, each Ruler measurement has to be recorded before the Ruler is used again.

Your Ruler measurements are listed in the Log as Ruler 1, Ruler 2, and so on, from the first measurement of the session to the last. Since entries in the fields of the Log can't be edited, there's no way to make more explicit what you've measured. The Measurement Log panel doesn't associate a Ruler measurement with the particular feature that was measured. And no permanent distance marker remains in the file. Each Ruler measurement removes the previous marker. So if you make several Ruler measurements per image, it can be difficult (or impossible) to reconstruct which measurement went with which feature. For these reasons, you may not find the Ruler useful for measuring more than one feature per photo.

Measuring in Vanishing Point. Photoshop's Vanishing Point filter has a Measure tool 📏 that can set a scale, in perspective, and then measure according to that scale. To set the scale, on a perspective grid in Vanishing Point, ▼ drag with the Measure tool over a distance whose measurement you know, and then enter the distance in the Length field at the top of the Vanishing Point window. For instance, if we want to find the approximate sizes of some of the agricultural fields in the photo at the left and we know that the Caterpillar D4 tractor in the picture is about 15 feet long including the blade, we can measure the approximate length and width of

FIND OUT MORE

▼ Using Vanishing Point
page 612

If you'd like to keep your measurements with the file, indicating which feature each measurement goes with, you can do that with Vanishing Point's Measure tool ✐, even if your image is a straight-on view that doesn't require correcting for perspective. Before entering Vanishing point, choose the Rectangle tool ▢ and click the "Shape layers" button ▢ in the Options bar, then drag to draw a rectangle. Next add a new empty layer to your file (one way is to click the ▣ button at the bottom of the Layers panel).

Choose Filter > Vanishing Point. Draw your grid with the Create Plane Tool ▦, placing the four corner nodes of the perspective plane at the corners of the rectangle you added. When your grid appears, it should be a rectangle made up of blue squares. Choose the Measure tool, set the scale, and make your measurements. From Vanishing Point's menu, choose Render Measurements to Photoshop. The measuring lines and the numbers that go with them will be collected on the empty layer you added.

each field. Accuracy of the measurements you make in Vanishing Point will depend not only on the accuracy of the scale you draw but also on the accuracy of your perspective plane.

Any measurements you make with Vanishing Point's Measure tool are retained when you save the file and will be available any time you enter Vanishing Point in this file. You can also render the measurements to the main Photoshop file as markers that will be kept with the file, by choosing Render Measurements to Photoshop from Vanishing Point's menu ▾≡ (found in the upper-left corner of the dialog box). Vanishing Point measurements will not be recorded in Photoshop Extended's Measurement Log, but the markers and their measurements will remain with the file.

Measuring selections. You can use any of Photoshop's selection methods to select the parts of an image that you want to measure, and in the Selections section of the Select Data Points dialog, you can set which data you want to record in the Measurement Log. If the features you want to measure can be successfully selected by color — with Select > Color Range, for instance — that's the most efficient way to make the selection. But for images in which the features of interest are broken up by highlights and shadows, or are composed of many parts, like a tree made up of leaves and branches, selecting by color may not work. "Measuring in Photoshop Extended" on page 728 works through an example of measuring from a selection.

DICOM

Besides the features of the Analysis panel, Photoshop CS3/CS4 Extended also has the ability to work with DICOM files, the standard for medical digital imaging systems such as x-rays and PET scans. Choosing File > Open and then choosing one or more DICOM files opens a dialog where you can choose to import multiple files as layers in a single Photoshop file or as several images tiled on a single layer. (If, for some reason, the files won't open as layers in a single file, try File > Scripts > Load Files Into Stack.) If you open the files as layers in a single file, you can then produce an animation by choosing Make Frames From Layers from the Animation panel's menu ▾≡,▾ useful for a range-of-motion series, for instance. You can turn a series of DICOM-format sections into a 3D object that can be manipulated with the 3D tools and commands (File > Open; in the Frame Import Options choose Import As Volume). DICOM is also one of the file formats, along with JPEG and others, that can be opened with Photoshop Extended's Image Sequence function (page 723).

A series of DICOM files can be opened as layers or tiles in a single file, as a 3D volume, or as an Image Sequence.

FIND OUT MORE
▾ Animation panel
page 664

Even for those who don't work in science, the ability to handle DICOM files may be of interest as a source of imagery. The texture above was derived from a mammogram, and the skeletal overlay at the left from an x-ray.

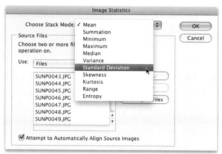

The File > Scripts > Statistics command loads files as stacked layers, aligns the layers if you choose, makes a Smart Object of the layers, and performs the statistical analysis you choose in the Image Statistics dialog.

SIDE-BY-SIDE COMPARISONS

For ease in comparing several open files to one another, choose Window > Arrange > Tile to display them all without overlap. Choose the Zoom tool 🔍 and in the Options bar choose Zoom All Windows. Choose the Hand tool ✋and in the Options bar choose Scroll All Windows. Now as you move around one image, all others are scrolled to that location also, and if you zoom, all will zoom. You can do all of your panning and zooming with a single tool if you choose the Hand tool ✋ and then use keyboard shortcuts to turn it into the Zoom tool (Alt/Option to zoom out, Ctrl/⌘ to zoom in).

MATLAB

If you're already counting and measuring features in photos using MATLAB, the widely used technical scripting environment for analysis and visual presentation of data, you may find it useful to set up Photoshop Extended and MATLAB so that MATLAB command lines can call certain Photoshop functions directly, with no need to take the file out of MATLAB, into Photoshop, and back. But the process isn't necessarily seamless in versions CS3 and CS4. In the MATLAB folder that's installed in your Photoshop folder is the **MATLAB Photoshop Read Me.pdf** file. It tells how to install the MATLAB–Photoshop link, test the installation, and use Photoshop from inside MATLAB. Also in this folder is a list of the Photoshop Extended commands that MATLAB can call (see page 13).

STATISTICS

Photoshop Extended can compute a number of Statistics values by comparing color values from layer to layer, channel by channel, for each pixel location in a stack of layers. These computed values are then represented by colors and tones in the image file. "Averaging Out Noise" on page 325 tells how to use one of these Statistics, the Mean, for removing noise, and "Creating Solitude" on page 327 uses the Median value to remove features that appear in fewer than half of the images layered in a stack. The Statistics functions can be used for comparing images that are almost alike but may show slight differences, and to look at where in the image the differences are greatest from image to image. You can apply these comparisons by opening the files as a stack of layers, aligning the layers based on content, and then applying the Statistics. One way to do this is to choose **File > Scripts > Statistics**, and in the Image Statistics dialog identify the files you want to stack; at the top of the dialog choose a **Stack Mode**; at the bottom of the dialog, turn on **Attempt to Automatically Align Source Images** (to line up features for comparison from layer to layer). When you click "OK," Photoshop Extended will produce a file with a Smart Object▼ consisting of a layer for each image; the image you see is the result of computing the statistic you chose as the Stack Mode. Since the entire stack of layers is a Smart Object, you can change your choice of statistic (choose Layer > Smart Objects > Stack Mode and choose a different option), or you can remove layers from the calculation if you like by double-clicking the Smart Object thumbnail in the Layers panel to open the .psb file and turning off visibility for layers you want to eliminate; when you save the .psb file (Ctrl/⌘-S), the statistic will be recomputed in the main document.

FIND OUT MORE

▼ Smart Objects **page 75**

IMAGE SEQUENCES

Opening a sequentially numbered series of files as an Image Sequence can be useful for compiling time-lapse photography, automatically turning the time-series photos into a video layer. Collect all the files of the series in a single folder. Choose **File > Open** and in the Open dialog, select the first file in the series, check the **Image Sequence box** near the bottom of the dialog, and click "Open." Choose a frame rate in the Frame Rate dialog (if you guess wrong here, you'll be able to adjust the rate later). The series of images will open as a video layer, which you can then play by clicking the "Play" button ▶ in the **Animation (Timeline) panel**. To change the frame rate if you'd like, choose Document Settings from the Animation (Timeline) panel's menu ▼≡, make the change, and click "OK." All or part of the movie can be rendered as video, as described on page 686.

SOME OTHER USEFUL FUNCTIONS

Here are a few other Photoshop and Photoshop Extended functions that can be useful for analyzing or presenting images in scientific and technical fields:

- The **Slideshow** function in Bridge (see page 139) can be an excellent way to review large numbers of photos, such as time series, to search out those with interesting content.

- **Zoomify** can be ideal for presenting histological slides on the Web, for instance, or for any situation that requires zooming in to several locations on a large-scale photo for close examination (see page 12 and page 130).

- As shown below, Photoshop Extended's **Place Scale Marker** command provides a way to show scale in an image.

- A **Black & White Adjustment layer** can help in converting color photos, graphs, and charts for publication in black-and-white (see page 214 for photos, page 490 for graphics).

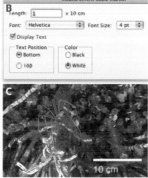

The deep-submergence vehicle Alvin has a laser system that provides a measurement scale for its photos and videos. The two red dots **A** indicate a distance of 10 cm. For this snapshot taken at a methane seep 1000 meters deep in the Pacific Ocean, we set the scale in Photoshop Extended by choosing **Analysis > Set Measurement Scale** and then chose **Analysis > Place Scale Marker B.** The type layer in the scale marker, part of a layer Group that also includes a standard layer with the mark itself, is live and can be edited. The entire Group was repositioned to show scale in this close-up **C** showing worm tubes, a pycnogonid "sea spider," and a small shrimp.

ORIGINAL PHOTO: LISA LEVIN

Counting in Photoshop Extended

OPEN THESE PANELS
(from the Window menu, for instance):
  • Layers • Measurement Log

OVERVIEW
Mark and automatically count elements
in your image file, and capture the count
data as part of the file • Choose which
information to record in the Measurement
Log • Record the count in the Log • Make
and record any other counts you want of
elements in the image

OUR FICTITIOUS STUDY of mallard ducks in mixed flocks on
the shore of Port Dover Harbour includes counts from photos
taken at four different points on the shore, at monthly intervals,
to estimate the changing composition of the flocks. To look at
the ratio of male to female mallards and the ratio of mallards to
gulls, we made three counts per photo — male mallards, female
mallards, and gulls. Photoshop Extended's Count tool 1_2^3 allows
us to make and record the counts digitally and store this raw
data as part of the photo files.

Thinking the project through. When making a count from a
photo, it would be ideal to be able to make more than one count
per file and to retain the count markers with the image file, so
you could always go back and see exactly what you counted.
In Photoshop CS4 Extended you can make multiple counts
per image, and the markers placed by the Count tool 1_2^3 are
automatically retained with the file even after you close the file.
In CS3 Extended, with its single count and no automatic count
retention, you have to work a little harder to produce the data-
rich image file you want, but a screen capture utility can help.

1 Setting up for counting. Open your image file in Photoshop
Extended, or use our **Counting-Before.jpg 1a**. Make a plan for

1a

The original image, **Count-Before.jpg**

1b

CS3 Extended's Count tool Options bar offers a color choice for the count markers.

1c

CS4 Extended adds choices for marker size **A** and type size **B** as well, and you can add more Count groups **C**.

2a

Each click with the Count tool's "+1" cursor places a numbered point.

2b

In CS4 Extended, you can rename a Count group.

2c

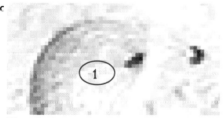

When the Count tool's "+1" cursor is over a marker, the "+" sign gets bigger. Then holding down the Alt/Option key turns the "+" to a "–" and clicking will remove the marker.

3a

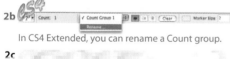

The count is tracked in the Options bar. CS3 Extended can keep track of the Total Count only.

counting; we decided to start counting at the top left, counting generally downward and to the right. Although you can count in any order you like, having a systematic method may make it less likely that you'll miss counting something.

Choose the **Count tool** ₁₂³. In the Options bar **1b**, **1c**, choose a convenient color (one that contrasts with the items you want to count in your photo); we used the default cyan color. In CS4 Extended you can also choose a size for the dot that serves as the counting marker and choose the type size of the number that goes with each dot.

2 Making the first count. In the image window, click on each item you want to count **2a**. In CS4 Extended, as soon as you start counting, Count Group 1 is created, and you can choose Rename from the menu in the Options bar **2b** and type in a more descriptive group name; we used "Male Mallards."

When you think you've finished counting, you might review the image, making sure you haven't missed something or counted something twice. When you've finished, save the file; we used File > Save As, calling the new file **Count-After.psd**. If you make a mistake, hover the Count tool cursor over the point you want to remove until the "+" gets bigger; then hold down the Alt/Option key (the "+" turns to a "–") and click **2c**. Any higher-numbered count points will be automatically renumbered when the point is removed.

3 Recording the count data. The current count appears in the Options bar **3a**, **3b**. When you finish counting, you can check the total count and make a note of it by hand (if you have a standard written log you want to maintain, for instance). Or use Photoshop Extended's Measurement Log to record it. First choose **Analysis > Select Data Points > Custom**; in the **Common** section of the Select Data Points dialog **3c**, choose the identifying items you want to include in your recorded data: **Label** (the word "Count" and a number that indicates the order of this count in the counts that have been done since Photoshop was opened for the current session); **Date and Time** (when the count was recorded); **Document** (file name); and **Source** (how the data will be collected, in this case with the Count tool). In the **Count Tool** section at the very bottom of the list in the Select Data Points dialog, make sure Count is checked **3d**.

Now choose **Analysis > Record Measurements** so the count will be stored as an item in the Measurement Log **3e**. (Remember that the Measurement Log records any measurements you've

3b

CS4 Extended's Options bar keeps both a total count (the number on the left), and the count for the selected group (in parentheses on the right).

3c

Each item you choose in the Select Data Points dialog will become a column in the Measurement Log.

3d

Checking the Count option at the bottom of the Select Data Points dialog creates a column for the Count tool data.

3e

The count is recorded in the Measurement Log.

4a

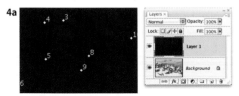

A detail (near the upper-left corner) of the image as it appears in CS3 Extended after a black-filled layer is added.

4b

Aligning the screen-captured image of the counts with the upper-left corner of the photo in CS3 Extended. At this point you can see both the pasted-in numbers and the "live" count numbers.

---

told it to *during the current session*. To preserve the data records, you'll need to export the contents of the Log before quitting Photoshop; step 6 tells how.)

4 Storing the count data in the file. (If you're working in CS4 Extended, your count data will automatically be stored with the file, so you can go on to step 5.) CS3 Extended doesn't automatically store the count data with the file. But here's a way to do it: With your image layer targeted in the Layers panel, make the entire image visible on-screen; Ctrl/⌘-0 (that's zero) makes the view as large as will fit on-screen. Now add a layer (Ctrl/⌘-Shift-N, or click the ▣ button at the bottom of the Layers panel). Fill the new layer with either black or white, whichever contrasts better with the count color you chose at step 1; pressing the D key sets the Foreground and Background colors to black and white, and then Alt-Backspace (Windows) or Option-Delete (Mac) fills with black, and Ctrl-Backspace or ⌘-Delete fills with white. You'll now see your count dots and numbers against a solid black or white background **4a**.

Use a screen-capture utility (for instance, SnagIt for Windows or SnapzPro for Mac, or the utility that comes with your operating system), to capture just the black or white area with its numbered dots, if possible, to the clipboard. The native screen-capture for Windows is the Alt-PrtScreen key combination; Mac has the Grab utility, installed in the Applications > Utilities folder. In Photoshop Extended, paste the screen capture into the counting photo (Ctrl/⌘-V). With the Move tool ▸₊, move the new layer so the upper-left corner of the black or white area (not including any window frame) aligns with the upper-left corner of the counting image (not including any window frame) **4b**; press Ctrl/⌘-T (for Free Transform) and scale the pasted image up or down as needed, to align with the lower-right corner of your document (Shift-drag the lower-right corner handle of the Transform frame to resize proportionally) **4c**; complete the transform (for instance, press Enter).

In the Layers panel, first turn off visibility for the black- or white-filled layer you added to the file before making the screen capture. Then click the thumbnail for the layer you just added; click the "Add a layer style" button *fx* at the bottom of the Layers panel and choose Blending Options. In the This Layer slider near the bottom of the Layer Style dialog, move the black or white point inward just until the background color disappears, leaving the numbers **4d**. ▼ The pasted numbers

FIND OUT MORE

▼ "Blend If" This Layer
page 66

4c

Scaling the screen capture to match the photo in CS3 Extended puts the count markers in the right positions.

4d

If you store the count markers in a layer in the CS3 Extended file, you'll be able to see their positions even after the Count is cleared (in the Options bar) or the file is closed and reopened. Before clearing, the counters may seem "doubled" (as shown here), depending on how much your screen capture had to be scaled to fit the image.

5a

Total Count: 42   Label Color: Clear

In CS3 Extended, click the "Clear" button in order to start a new count.

5b

Count Group Name

Count Group Name: Female Mallards   OK   Cancel

In CS4 Extended you can add a new Count group by clicking the ▢ button in the Options bar, without losing previous counts. Choose **Rename** from the menu to bring up the Count Group Name dialog in order to give your group a descriptive name. Click the color swatch to change the marker color, so your new Count group can be distinguished from the first one.

6

Clicking the "Export selected measurements" button ✍ produces a tab-delimited text file. You may want to open the file in a text editor and edit the names of the Count groups to make them more descriptive. Here "Count 1" has been changed to "Male Mallards," and "Count 2" is selected and ready to change.

will be preserved even if the count is cleared in order to count something else (in step 5) or if you quit Photoshop Extended. Save the file again to preserve the count in the layer.

5 Making additional counts. (If you don't have anything else you want to count, go on to step 6.) To make another count, you may want your original count numbers visible, or you may not. If you don't want to see them:

- **In CS3 Extended, in the Layers panel** click the ◉ for the layer with the numbers.
- **In CS4 Extended,** in the Count **Options bar** click the ◉.

To add a new count:

- **In CS3 Extended,** in the Options bar click the "Clear" button to remove the markers for your first count **5a**; the count info you recorded will remain in the Measurement Log, and your layer with the screen grab will also remain.
- **In CS4 Extended,** in the Options bar click the "Create a new count group" button ▢ and name the new group; we named ours "Female Mallards" **5b**.

Choose a new color for the second count; we used yellow. Repeat the counting, recording, and clearing processes in steps 1 through 4 (in CS3 Extended you won't need to add another black-filled layer; just turn on visibility for the one you added at step 4). *Note:* In CS4 Extended, when you get to the point of recording the count data in the Measurement Log, turn off visibility for any counts other than the one you currently want to record; otherwise all visible counts will be added together and stored as a single Count. (This can actually be helpful if you want to get the sum of the counts after all counts have been recorded separately.) Make as many additional counts as you want. We made a third count, of the gulls, changing the color to red. The result is shown at the top of page 724.

6 Exporting the Measurement Log. To export the contents of the Measurement Log (a good idea, since the Log data will disappear when you quit Photoshop), select the lines in the Measurement Log that you want to export (multi-select by Ctrl/⌘-clicking or Shift-clicking, or use the "Select all measurements" button ✍ near the top right corner of the Measurement Log), and then click the "Export selected measurements" button ✍. The data will be exported as a tab-delimited text (.txt) file **6**. ✍

Measuring in Photoshop Extended

PHOTOSHOP EXTENDED'S MEASUREMENT LOG can record data about active selections and export it as a text file for use in other programs. For a fictitious study of Pacific Northwest tidepools, we wanted to use archival photos to estimate the percent cover of the sea anemone *Anthopleura xanthogrammica* (as a measure of its success in competition with several species of brown algae, pink coralline algae, and other encrusting species for space on the rocky surface). We also wanted to record information about size variability (as a measure of age structure in the population).

Thinking the project through. We want to select the area occupied by each anemone. The open sea anemones are distinctly different in color from the surrounding coralline algae and the overlying kelp fronds. But this photo shows some common problems with selecting by color. One problem is keeping each feature as a separate selection; anemones that touch each other will blend into a single selected area. Second, some of the anemones are closed, and the amount of exposed blue-green color doesn't indicate the size. Third, for some anemones the blue-green area is divided and partly obscured by kelp fronds that overlie them but are not anchored to the rock in the area of the photo. Given the amount of hand work that would be needed in this case to edit a selection by color, we will instead do all the selecting by hand. We'll set up a measurement scale

1

For making measurements from selections, set the data points for **Common** (include **Scale**) and **Selections**. The kinds of data that are recorded from measurements are found at the top of the Selections list.

2a

Dragging with the Ruler tool to measure the length in pixels of an item of known size in the photo

2b

The Ruler-measured Pixel Length is automatically entered in the Measurement Scale dialog box **A**. You then enter the known "real-world" measurement **B**, **C**.

3a Click the button at the bottom of the Tools panel to toggle between Quick Mask and an active selection.

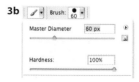

3b Setting brush-tip size and hardness for painting the Quick Mask

for each photo so we can get real-world measurements, and so we can compare measurements from several photos.

1 Deciding what measurements will be recorded. Open the **Measuring-Before.jpg** file and choose **Analysis > Select Data Points > Custom** to open the Select Data Points dialog, where you can check the boxes for the data you want to include, and uncheck the ones for data you don't want **1**. For measuring from selections as we will be doing here, the sections of the dialog to pay attention to are **Common** (at the top) and **Selections**. We turned on all the options in the Common section. In the Selections section we kept all choices that had to do with measurement, but turned off those that had to do with pixel color — from Gray Value (Minimum) to the end of the list.

2 Setting the measurement scale. Choose **Analysis > Set Measurement Scale.** When the Measurement Scale dialog opens, choose the Ruler tool in the Tools panel (or type Shift-I until you get it), and drag it along the length of the 10 cm ruler in the photo **2a**. Enter 10 in the **Logical Length** field, and enter cm in the **Logical Units** field **2b**. Now when we select and measure the animals and record the measurements, they will be recorded in cm and cm^2.

3 Selecting the anemones. Given that we can't actually see the attachment of the anemones to the rock, our estimate will be just that — an estimate. To use the method we used, at the bottom of the Tools panel click on the **"Edit in Quick Mask mode"** button ▢ **3a**. ▼ Choose the Brush tool ✎ (Shift-B), and in the Options bar choose a hard, round brush tip at a size that won't take too many strokes to paint over an anemone; we chose 60 pixels to start **3b**. You can always change brush-tip size if you need to, with the bracket keys — [and] — or dynamically if you have OpenGL drawing enabled. ▼ Type D to make black the Foreground color. We know that the size of the anemone's open oral disc is a good indicator of the amount of surface the animal occupies on the rock. Paint over the anemones **3c**. Use the Eraser tool ✎ with a smaller hard brush tip to erase thin strips of the red mask if you need to, so that each anemone is separate **3d**.

When you've painted over all the anemones **3e**, convert the Quick Mask to an active selection by once again clicking the ▢ button. By default, the red in Quick Mask represents the *unse*-lected areas, so we need to **invert the selection** (Ctrl/⌘-Shift-I) to select the anemones. Then immediately go on to step 4 to save the selection.

FIND OUT MORE

▼ Using Quick Mask
page 60

▼ Sizing brush tips **page 71**

3c

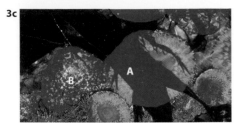

In painting the Quick Mask over the anemones, we can paint right over kelp fronds that cross an anemone **A** because we know that the anemone occupies that space on the rock. We can also paint the closed anemones in the photo, as shown by the cursor near the lower left here **B** (they can be identified by the bits of shell sticking to their outer surface).

3d

The Eraser tool ✐ with a small, hard brush tip was used where necessary to quickly separate adjacent anemones so that an individual selection would be created for each one.

3e

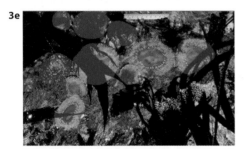

After painting over all the anemones in Quick Mask mode

4

After the Quick Mask is converted to a selection and the selection is inverted, the inverted selection is stored as an alpha channel.

4 Saving the selection. It's really easy to save the work you've put into your selection: Choose **Select > Save Selection**, choose **New Channel** for the Operation, name the alpha channel you're about to make if you like, and click "OK" **4**. Now you'll have a permanent record, stored with the file, of the areas selected to be measured. So if you ever wanted to go back and check on exactly what was selected and measured, you could.

5 Recording the measurements. To record the measurements you chose in step 1, simply click the **"Record Measurements" button** on the Measurement Log panel **5**. By default, recorded measurements are in order by date and time, from oldest (at the top of the panel) to newest (at the bottom).▼ Whenever you record a measurement based on a multi-part selection (like the one in this example), the first measurement row in the Log will hold the sum of measurements for all the parts. After that, the individual selections and their measurements will be listed as Feature 1, Feature 2, and so on.

FIND OUT MORE
▼ The Measurement Log panel **page 718**

6 Recording total area. To be able to compute percent cover of anemones, we'll need to know not only the area occupied by anemones, but also the total area that was considered. So before we move on to make measurements in another photo, record one more measurement in this photo: Select All (Ctrl/⌘-A), then switch to Quick Mask mode again and paint with black any areas that are hidden by floating kelp fronds that are large enough to effectively hide what species occupies the rock underneath **6a**. Click the ▢ button again to make an active selection, save the

5

	Label	Date and Time	Document	Source	Count	Area
0001	Measurement 1	2/22/10 12:50:0...	Measuring-...	Selection	**A** 12	397.814059 **B**
0002	Measurement 1 - Feature 1	2/22/10 12:50:0...	Measuring-...	Selection		15.478458
0003	Measurement 1 - Feature 2	2/22/10 12:50:0...	Measuring-...	Selection		41.478458
0004	Measurement 1 - Feature 3	2/22/10 12:50:0...	Measuring-...	Selection		8.310658
0005	Measurement 1 - Feature 4	2/22/10 12:50:0...	Measuring-...	Selection		37.024943
0006	Measurement 1 - Feature 5	2/22/10 12:50:0...	Measuring-...	Selection		76.145125
0007	Measurement 1 - Feature 6	2/22/10 12:50:0...	Measuring-...	Selection		29.519274
0008	Measurement 1 - Feature 7	2/22/10 12:50:0...	Measuring-...	Selection		64.133787
0009	Measurement 1 - Feature 8	2/22/10 12:50:0...	Measuring-...	Selection		14.335601
0010	Measurement 1 - Feature 9	2/22/10 12:50:0...	Measuring-...	Selection		51.916100
0011	Measurement 1 - Feature 10	2/22/10 12:50:0...	Measuring-...	Selection		19.854875
0012	Measurement 1 - Feature 11	2/22/10 12:50:0...	Measuring-...	Selection		37.807256
0013	Measurement 1 - Feature 12	2/22/10 12:50:0...	Measuring-...	Selection		1.809524

The first row of a series of measurements made from selected areas gives the sum of all the selected areas. The **Count** is the total number of separate areas selected **A**. Here the 12 sets of measurements correspond to the 12 selected anemones. The first **Area** measurement **B** is the total area occupied by the anemones, and the individual measurements (**Feature 1, Feature 2,** and so on) are for each of the 12 anemones.

6a

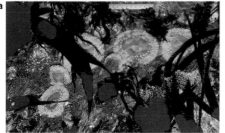

We painted over some parts of the floating kelp fronds to subtract hidden and thus "unknowable" areas from the total area of the photo. This time we were painting the areas we did *not* want to select, so when we toggled to an active selection, we didn't need to invert the selection before saving it as an alpha channel.

6b

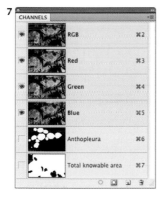

0011	Measurement 1 - Feature 10	?		19.854875	1
0012	Measurement 1 - Feature 11	?		37.807256	2
0013	Measurement 1 - Feature 12	?		1.809324	
0014	Measurement 2		2	1236.163265	20
0015	Measurement 2 - Feature 1	?		2.417234	
0016	Measurement 2 - Feature 2	?		1233.746032	19

Measurements were recorded for the total area of the rock surface that can be seen in the photo. The first row of this measurement is the total selected area. The two other rows are measurements for the small space at the upper-left corner (see figure 6a) and the rest of the selected area.

7

The saved .psd file includes the two alpha channels, documenting our selections in case we ever want to recheck our measurements.

	CHANNELS		
◉		RGB	⌘2
◉		Red	⌘3
◉		Green	⌘4
◉		Blue	⌘5
		Anthopleura	⌘6
		Total knowable area	⌘7

8a

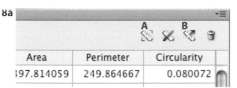

	A	B	
Area	Perimeter	Circularity	
97.814059	249.864667	0.080072	

Buttons are provided in the top right corner of the Measurement Log panel to select all data **A** and to export selected data to a tab-delimited text file **B**.

selection as another alpha channel (as in step 4), and click the "Record Measurements" button **6b**.

7 Saving the measured file. Save your image file in Photoshop (.psd) format (File > Save As), maintaining the alpha channels **7**.

Measuring other images. At this point, if you had other photos to measure, you could open another file, reset the measurement scale to match the new photo (step 2), and repeat steps 3 through 6, continuing this way until you had recorded data in the Measurement Log panel for all of your images.

8 Exporting the Log. After you've made and recorded all the measurements you need, select all the data in the Measurement Log panel by clicking the **"Select all measurements"** button 🔲 at the top of the panel, and then click the **"Export selected measurements"** button 🔲 **8a**. (Be sure to export the Log before quitting Photoshop Extended, because the measurements will not be preserved once you quit.) In the Save dialog, navigate to the folder that includes your saved .psd photo files, so the exported text file **8b** and the photos that include the alpha channels will be stored together.

Analyzing the data. The text file from the Measurement Log can be imported into a spreadsheet program or MATLAB for analysis. For each photo, we can divide the total area covered by anemones (the first record in the first set of measurements made from our selection of the anemones) by the total available area (the area of the entire photo minus the "unknowable" areas under the kelp fronds). We can analyze the Area values of the individual anemone selections to determine size variability. The Circularity measurement may even be of interest. As anemones become crowded, their shapes become "squeezed" and less circular in cross section. So comparing average Circularity of anemones between photos might provide interesting insights about local habitats. 🐚

8b

"Label"	"Date and Time"	"Document"	"Source"	"Count"	"Area"	"Perimeter"	"Circularity"	"Height"	"Width
"Measurement 1"	"2010-02-22T13:00:47-08:00"		"Measuring-After.psd"	"Selection"	"12"	"397.814059"		"249.864667"	
"Measurement 1 - Feature 1"	"2010-02-22T13:00:47-08:00"		"Measuring-After.psd"	"Selection"				"15.470458"	
"Measurement 1 - Feature 2"	"2010-02-22T13:00:47-08:00"		"Measuring-After.psd"	"Selection"				"41.478458"	
"Measurement 1 - Feature 3"	"2010-02-22T13:00:47-08:00"		"Measuring-After.psd"	"Selection"				"8.310658"	
"Measurement 1 - Feature 4"	"2010-02-22T13:00:47-08:00"		"Measuring-After.psd"	"Selection"				"37.024943"	
"Measurement 1 - Feature 5"	"2010-02-22T13:00:47-08:00"		"Measuring-After.psd"	"Selection"				"76.145125"	
"Measurement 1 - Feature 6"	"2010-02-22T13:00:47-08:00"		"Measuring-After.psd"	"Selection"				"29.519274"	
"Measurement 1 - Feature 7"	"2010-02-22T13:00:47-08:00"		"Measuring-After.psd"	"Selection"				"64.133787"	
"Measurement 1 - Feature 8"	"2010-02-22T13:00:47-08:00"		"Measuring-After.psd"	"Selection"				"14.335601"	
"Measurement 1 - Feature 9"	"2010-02-22T13:00:47-08:00"		"Measuring-After.psd"	"Selection"				"51.916100"	
"Measurement 1 - Feature 10"	"2010-02-22T13:00:47-08:00"		"Measuring-After.psd"	"Selection"				"19.854875"	
"Measurement 1 - Feature 11"	"2010-02-22T13:00:47-08:00"		"Measuring-After.psd"	"Selection"				"37.807256"	
"Measurement 1 - Feature 12"	"2010-02-22T13:00:47-08:00"		"Measuring-After.psd"	"Selection"				"1.809524"	
"Measurement 2"	"2010-02-22T17:19:14-08:00"		"Measuring-After.psd"	"Selection"	"2"	"1236.163265"		"208.944439"	
"Measurement 2 - Feature 1"	"2010-02-22T17:19:14-08:00"		"Measuring-After.psd"	"Selection"				"2.417234"	
"Measurement 2 - Feature 2"	"2010-02-22T17:19:14-08:00"		"Measuring-After.psd"	"Selection"				"1233.746032"	

The text file exported from the Measurement Log can be used by applications, such as spreadsheets and MATLAB, that accept tab-delimited data.

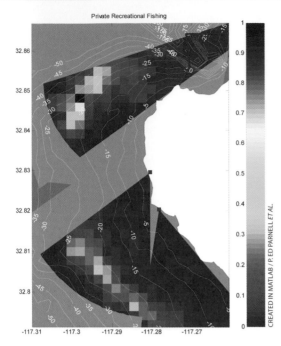

Private Recreational Fishing

CREATED IN MATLAB / P. ED PARNELL ET AL.

Daytime

Glare

Nighttime

ACTIONS
Ed's Actions
▶ Levels–Sharp
▶ Lessen Glare
▶ Night
▶ Production

Photoshop played a role in the preliminary analysis of photos by **P. Ed Parnell _et al._** in their study **_"Spatial Patterns of Fishing Effort Off San Diego: Implications for Zonal Management and Ecosystem Function"_** in _Ecological Applications_ (in press). This project was one of a series of studies involved in choosing the best sites for a proposed nearshore marine protected area off the Southern California coast. The goal of the studies was to arrive at a proposal for protecting biodiversity, the number and variety of animal and plant life that occurs naturally in the area; a second objective in siting the reserve was to minimize interference with ongoing recreational and commercial fishing. Other studies in the series had looked at the species present and their abundance, and at the different kinds of habitats in the area (based on local circulation of ocean water, water depth, and type of bottom, such as sand or rock). For species that seemed in danger of disappearing from the area, Parnell _et al._ took a closer look, to identify habitats that are critical for different

stages in the life histories of the locally endangered organisms. For instance, a "turf" of algae might be required for larvae of some species to settle and develop into adults.

In this particular study, however, the goal was to identify the areas most heavily used by various fishing interests. As part of a survey that also included dockside interviews of fishermen and a review of fishing logs, five Nikon Coolpix 8700 cameras were placed in waterproof housings on shore, aimed to cover areas of particular interest based on years of habitat study and observation of fishing patterns. Cameras were controlled by DigiSnap 2100 camera controllers (www.harbortronics.com), programmed to take photos at 15-minute intervals — a compromise between providing adequate vessel information and limits on camera memory and photo analysis time. Fishing effort was to be quantified by the presence of boats associated with different types of fishing and by "boat behavior" — for instance, boats of any type that appeared in just one photo were considered to be just passing through and weren't counted.

Early in the project, Photoshop was used to enhance the photos taken under various conditions so that types of boats could be recognized. Actions were recorded to sharpen daytime photos (an example is shown above), to reduce glare for late afternoon images, and to brighten the nighttime shots. Photoshop Droplets were made to automate batch processing of the photos.

Once Parnell _et al._ had established with Photoshop that the types of boats could be identified, they used MATLAB's Image Processing Toolbox for the rest of the project, to adjust the exposure and contrast, to transform the images to account for perspective in order to accurately plot the positions of the boats, and to divide each photo into sections for convenient on-screen analysis at 100% view to identify types and locations of fishing activity. By mapping the results for private recreational fishing (above), charter recreational fishing, and commercial sea urchin and lobster fishing, the researchers were able to identify and recommend sites where habitat could be protected with minimal interference with fishing.

Appendixes

Appendix A: Filter Demos

YOU'LL FIND THE FILE
in > Wow Project Files > Appendixes > Filter Demo-Before.psd (to start)

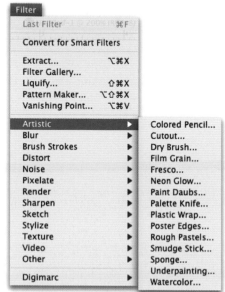

The filters shown on these pages can be chosen from the list in the lower part of Photoshop's Filter menu. In CS4 this list is the same, although the "megafilters" list at the top of the menu is different: Extract and Pattern Maker have been removed. They can be added back with the Optional Plug-ins found in the Goodies folder on your installation disc or at **adobe.com** (we found them for Macintosh at **www.adobe.com/support/downloads/ product.jsp?product=39&platform=Macintosh** and for Windows at **www.adobe.com/support/ downloads/product.jsp?product=39&platform =Windows**.

THIS "CATALOG" demonstrates most of the filters that Adobe supplies with Photoshop. (Not included are the "megafilters" from the top of the Filter menu.) The filters shown are applied to the photo and drawing above. The drawing was made by creating paths with the Pen tool, stroking them with the Brush on a transparent layer, and adding a Layer Style consisting of a white Outer Glow. This drawing layer was stacked over a scan of wood in the layer below and the file was flattened.

The filters in this catalog follow the grouping and order of the Filter menu. When settings were altered from the default for effect, they are listed in the order they appear in the filter's dialog box. If the default settings were used, no values are shown.

The sample image on which the filters were run is 408 pixels square. Many of the filter settings are in pixel units, so to evaluate the effect of a setting, you have to relate the setting (not exactly but generally) to the size of the image. For an image whose dimensions are approximately twice as big as our sample (800 by 800 pixels, for instance), you might need a setting of 40 pixels to get the same effect that a 20-pixel setting produces in the sample.

Many of the filters shown on these pages are also available by choosing Filter > Filter Gallery▼ and

FIND OUT MORE
▼ Filter Gallery **page 270**

selecting from the alphabetical list in the Filter Gallery dialog box. And all of the filters on these pages, including the Filter Gallery, can also be applied as Smart Filters, which keep your filter settings "alive" and editable. This important improvement, new with Photoshop CS3, adds Photoshop's filters to the list of nondestructive changes you can make. ▼

FIND OUT MORE
▼ Smart Filters **page 72**

In addition to the filters in the Filter menu, two commands from the Image > Adjustments menu can also be applied as Smart Filters: the Variations command, which lets you compare a spectrum of color and tone shifts on-screen before you choose one of them, and the Shadow/Highlight command, a very useful "filter" with controls that were designed to pull subjects out of the shadows or restore blown-out skies in the background or both.

To be able to come back and edit the settings after you've applied a filter, first turn the image into a Smart Object (if it isn't one already): In the Layers panel, target the layer you want the filter(s) to affect, and choose either Filter > Convert for Smart Filters (as shown above), or Layer > Smart Objects > Convert to Smart Object. Both commands do exactly the same thing. Or use the **shortcut**: Right-click/Ctrl-click on the layer's name in the Layers panel and choose Convert to Smart Object when the **context-sensitive menu** opens.

The Shadows/Highlights and Variations commands can also be applied as Smart Filters.

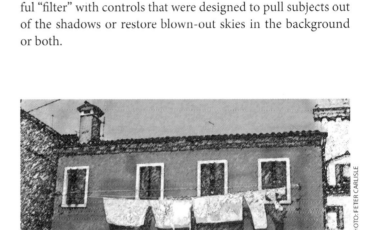

ORIGINAL PHOTO: PETER CARLISLE

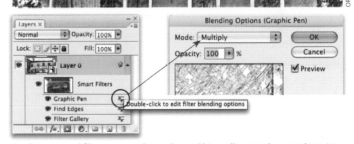

Applying several filters separately to a Smart Object allows each one to have its own blend mode and Opacity setting. In contrast, when you apply several filters to a Smart Object via the Filter Gallery, the filter effects are combined as one Smart Filter, and only one blend mode and Opacity setting can be applied to the combination. Here the Dry Brush filter and then the Charcoal filter (both from the Artistic filters) were applied in red and white through the Filter Gallery. Then Find Edges was applied separately, and Graphic Pen was also applied separately in black and white. The Graphic Pen's blend mode was then changed to Multiply. Painting the Smart Filters mask limited the effects of all the Smart Filters.

Artistic

The Artistic filters are available through Photoshop's Filter Gallery (indicated here by "FG"). Most of the Artistic filters simulate traditional art media. But the Plastic Wrap filter provides highlights and shadows that can add dimension and a slick surface texture.

8 Bits/Channel mode only

Colored Pencil — FG

Cutout — FG

Dry Brush — FG

Film Grain — FG

Fresco — FG

Neon Glow — FG

Paint Daubs — FG

Palette Knife — FG

Plastic Wrap — FG

Poster Edges — FG

Rough Pastels — FG

Smudge Stick   FG

Sponge   FG

Underpainting   FG

Watercolor   FG

NOT ALL FILTERS WORK IN ALL COLOR MODES

If you need to produce your Photoshop file in CMYK, Grayscale, or Indexed Color for the output process you'll use to publish it, it's still a good idea to do your creative work in RGB mode and then make the color mode conversion afterwards. One reason is that all of Photoshop's filters can be run in RGB mode, but in other color modes the choice narrows dramatically. For instance, Lens Flare and Lighting Effects work only in RGB mode. **In CMYK mode you lose the Filter Gallery** and all the individual filters in it, as well as the Vanishing Point "superfilter."

Blur

The Blur menu includes a range of filters, some designed for fairly specific uses: Average, for filling a selected area with a single color, arrived at by averaging the colors of all pixels within that area; Lens Blur, for camera depth-of-field effects; Box Blur and Shape Blur, for special effects; Smart Blur, which can be precisely controlled, and which can also trace the edges as lines; and Surface Blur, for smoothing out small differences in tone or color without blurring the image overall. All can be used as Smart Filters except Lens Blur.

8 & 16 Bits/Channel, except as noted

Average (32 Bits/Channel also)

Blur

Blur More

Box Blur (20) (32 Bits/Channel also)

Blur (continued)

Gaussian Blur (10) (32 Bits/Channel also)

Lens Blur (not available as a Smart Filter)

Motion Blur (45/30) (32 Bits/Channel also)

Radial Blur (Spin/10) (32 Bits/Channel also)

Radial Blur (Zoom/20) (32 Bits/Channel also)

Shape Blur (10/ Tiles: Tile 3) (32 Bits/Ch. also)

Smart Blur (3/25/Normal) (8 Bits/Ch only)

Smart Blur (3/25 Edge Only) (8 Bits/Ch only)

TESTING A BLUR

For the Radial Blur filter use a Quality setting of Draft (quick but rough) to experiment with the Amount and the blur center; then undo (Ctrl/⌘-Z) and use Good or Best for the final effect. Equivalent settings for Smart Blur are Low, Medium, and High.

Surface Blur (15/15) (32 Bits/Channel also)

Surface Blur (15/35) (32 Bits/Channel also)

Brush Strokes

The Brush Strokes filters are all available through the Filter Gallery (indicated here by "FG"). They simulate different ways of applying paint.

8 Bits/Channel mode only

Accented Edges · FG

Angled Strokes · FG

Crosshatch · FG

Dark Strokes · FG

Ink Outlines · FG

Spatter · FG

Sprayed Strokes · FG

Sumi-e · FG

RECORDING FILTER SETTINGS

Coming up with the right filter settings or the right combination of filters for a special effect can involve a lot of trial and error, and the steps and settings are easily forgotten. To avoid having to do the work over:

- Some of Photoshop's filters, especially newer ones, have "Save" buttons in their dialog boxes, so you can save your settings. Giving the settings file a descriptive name will help you find it later.

- If you used the Filter Gallery, you can save your settings in an Action▼ after the fact and play it back on other files (see page 271).

FIND OUT MORE

▼ Creating Actions **page 120**

Distort

Most of the Distort filters add special effects and textures to an image. The Displace filter "bends" the image based on the light and dark areas in a *displacement map* (a separate image that acts like the texture or "topography" of a surface to which the image is applied). When the displacement occurs, some edge pixels may be pulled inward from an edge, leaving a gap, and others may be pushed off the opposite edge. You can specify that the filter should fill the gap with the pixels pushed off the opposite side (Wrap), or that the pixels closest to the edge should be stretched to fill the gap (Repeat Edge Pixels). A few of the Distort filters (marked here with "FG") appear in the Filter Gallery.

8 Bits/Channel mode, except as noted

LENS DISTORTION

The Lens Correction filter typically removes distortion (as shown in "Compensating for Camera-Related Distortion" on page 274). But it can also be used to add distortion for special effects. See "Exercising Lens Blur" on page 309 for more about Lens Blur.

MORE DISPLACEMENT MAPS

Adobe provides two sets of files to use with Filter > Distort > Displace. The Displacement Maps set is in the Plug-ins folder, and Textures is in the Presets folder. More files can be found in the Textures For Lighting Effects folder. If they're not installed with CS4, you can find them at adobe.com (see page 734 for the URL). You can also create your own displacement maps, as in step 6 of "Carving" on page 549 or step 3 of "Applying an Image to a Textured Surface" on page 596.

Diffuse Glow   FG

Displace (Honeycomb 10/Repeat Edge Pixels)

Displace (Random Strokes 25/Wrap)

Displace (Snake Skin /Repeat Edge Pixels)

Glass (Frosted)   FG

Glass (Blocks)   FG

Lens Correction (Chromatic Aberration
–100/+100; Scale 70; Edge Extension)
(16 Bits/Channel also)

Lens Correction (Vertical Perspective +50)
(16 Bits/Channel also)

Ocean Ripple   FG

Pinch (100%)

Pinch (−100%)

Polar Coordinates (Polar to Rectangular)

Polar Coordinates (Rectangular to Polar)

Ripple

Shear

Spherize (100%/Normal)

Spherize (−100%/Normal)

Twirl

Wave

Zigzag (Pond Ripples)

Noise

The Add Noise filter can be used to "roughen" the texture of an image, and the other four Noise filters (Despeckle, Dust & Scratches, Median, and Reduce Noise) are used for smoothing, or eliminating irregularities. Reduce Noise can be used for eliminating digital camera noise, as well as film grain and JPEG artifacts, but you may get better results from Camera Raw, ▼ the Lens Correction filter, or Photoshop Extended's Statistics command. ▼

8 & 16 Bits/Channel
Add Noise is 32 Bits/Channel also

FIND OUT MORE

▼ Reducing noise in Camera Raw
page 334

▼ Noise reduction with Statistics
page 325

▼ Converting to black-and-white
page 214

Add Noise (Gaussian/50%/Monochromatic) | Add Noise (Uniform/50%)

Despeckle | Dust & Scratches (5/25)

Median (5)

REMOVING CHANNEL NOISE

The Reduce Noise filter can operate on individual color channels. So, for instance, if the Blue channel is noisy and the Green channel shows most of the contrast for fine detail, the noise can be reduced by filtering the Blue channel without blurring the details in the Green channel. This can improve the color image overall or improve the Blue channel as a source for converting from color to black-and-white. ▼

Clicking the "Advanced" button and choosing the Per Channel panel in the Reduce Noise dialog box allows you to reduce noise in individual channels, as shown here for the Blue channel. A detail of the Blue channel before reducing noise is shown at the right for comparison.

Reduce Noise (10/0)

Pixelate

Most of the Pixelate filters turn an image into a pattern consisting of spots of flat color. For all but Facet and Fragment, you can control the size of the spots, producing very different effects depending on the size settings.

8 Bits/Channel only

Color Halftone

Crystallize (10)

Facet

Fragment

Mezzotint (Coarse Dots)

Mezzotint (Medium Lines)

Mosaic

Pointillize (white Background color)

NAVIGATING FILTER DIALOGS

A typical Photoshop filter interface includes a preview box with an enlarged preview, one or more sliders and number fields for setting the filter's parameters, zooming buttons (the "+" and "–" under the preview), and the ability to move a different part of the image into the preview by simply dragging in the preview window (the Hand tool cursor appears automatically) or by clicking a particular place in the document window.

REAPPLYING A FILTER

To repeat the last filter you used, with exactly the same settings as before, type **Ctrl/⌘-F**.

To choose the last filter applied, but with the dialog box open so you can change the settings if you like, press **Ctrl-Alt-F** (Windows) or **⌘-Option-F** (Mac).

Note: If you're repeating a **Smart Filter, the dialog box will re-open** even if you use Ctrl/⌘-F.

Render

The Render filters create texture or "atmosphere." Two of them act independently of the color in the image: Clouds creates a sky, and Fibers can create a range of fibrous textures. (Holding down the Alt/Option key while choosing the Clouds filter produces a "sky" with more contrast.)

8 Bits/Channel, except as noted

Clouds, without (left) and with Alt/Option (16 & 32 Bits/Channel also)

BLUE SKY

When you run the Clouds filter, it produces clouds in the Background color and "sky" in the Foreground color. Using blue as Foreground and white as Background can create a realistic sky.

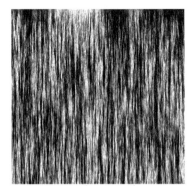

DAPPLED LIGHT

Create dappled light by running the Clouds filter on an empty layer above the photo and putting the Clouds layer in Multiply, Screen, or Soft Light mode, masked and at reduced Opacity.

Difference Clouds (16 & 32 Bits/Channel also)

Fibers (16 Bits/Channel also)

Lens Flare (16 & 32 Bits/Channel also)

Lighting Effects (Default)

Lighting Effects (Soft Direct Lights: both white)

Lighting Effects (Flashlight)

Lighting Effects (Flashlight: Texture Ch. Green)

Sharpen

Although there are five Sharpen filters, the ones you'll use most are Unsharp Mask and Smart Sharpen, because they are the only ones that let you control the sharpening. Smart Sharpen lets you control the amount of sharpening in the highlights, midtones, and shadows independently. See pages 337 and 338 for more about Unsharp Mask and Smart Sharpen.

8 & 16 Bits/Channel, except as noted

Sharpen

Sharpen Edges

Sharpen More

Smart Sharpen (Sharpen 50, 1.0) (32 Bits/Channel also)

SPECIAL-EFFECTS SHARPENING

Oversharpening can produce some interesting graphics effects. For example, convert to Lab mode (Image > Mode > Lab

Color), click the Lightness channel's name in the Channels panel, and run Unsharp Mask (Amount 500, Radius 20, Threshold 0).

Unsharp Mask (32 Bits/Channel also)

OTHER FILTERS FOR SHARPENING

It's sometimes difficult to sharpen areas of contrast with enough strength without also sharpening areas that you want left smooth, such as skin. Two other filters that can be used for sharpening edges without sharpening texture details are High Pass (see page 338) and Emboss (page 398).

Sketch

The Sketch filters, available through the Filter Gallery, include a number of artistic effects. Some of them imitate drawing methods, while others simulate various dimensional media. Except for Water Paper, the Sketch filters use the current Foreground and Background colors. The effects shown here were produced using black and white.

8 Bits/Channel mode only

Bas Relief   FG

Chalk & Charcoal   FG

Sketch (continued)

Charcoal FG

Chrome FG

Conté Crayon FG

Graphic Pen FG

Halftone Pattern (Dot) FG

Note Paper FG

Photocopy FG

Plaster FG

Reticulation FG

Stamp FG

Torn Edges FG

Water Paper FG

Stylize

Among the Stylize filters you'll find a diverse collection of edge treatments and other special effects. One of the Stylize filters (Glowing Edges) appears in the Filter Gallery.

8 Bits/Channel, except as noted

Diffuse

Emboss (16 & 32 Bits/Channel also)

Extrude (Blocks)

Extrude (Pyramids)

Find Edges (16 Bits/Channel also)

Glowing Edges   FG

Solarize (16 Bits/Channel also)

Tiles

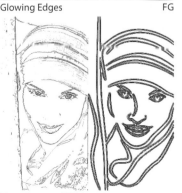

Trace Contour (50/Upper)

Wind (Wind)

NEUTRAL EMBOSSING

To eliminate the color from an image that has been treated with the Emboss filter, keeping only the highlights and shadows, use

Image > Adjustments > Desaturate.

Texture

Most of the Texture filters create the illusion that the image has been applied to an uneven surface. But Stained Glass remakes the image into polygons, each filled with a single color. All of the Texture filters can be found in the Filter Gallery (FG).

8 Bits/Channel mode only

Craquelure   FG

Grain (Sprinkles)   FG

Grain (Stippled)   FG

Grain (Vertical)   FG

Grain (Speckle)   FG

Mosaic Tiles (25/2/4)   FG

Patchwork   FG

Stained Glass (3/1/1)   FG

Texturizer (Brick)   FG

Texturizer (Canvas)   FG

Texturizer (Sandstone)   FG

Video

The De-Interlace filter (not shown here but see page 680) "repairs" images captured on video, replacing either the odd or the even interlaced lines in a way that smooths the image. The other Video filter, NTSC Colors, prevents color "bleed" by restricting colors in the image to those acceptable for television.
8, 16 & 32 Bits/Channel

NTSC Colors

Other

The Other submenu houses an eclectic collection of filters. The Maximum and Minimum filters can be used to thin and thicken line art, respectively. With the Custom interface you can design your own filters. You can save an effect you like so you can load it later and use it again.
8, 16 & 32 Bits/Channel, except Custom

Custom (8 & 16 Bits/Channel only)

High Pass (10)

Maximum (1)

Minimum (1)

Offset (100/100/Wrap Around)

Digimarc

Choosing Filter > Digimarc > Embed Watermark opens a dialog box that lets you embed a recognizable noise pattern in your image, to deter unauthorized use of your work.
8 Bits/Channel mode only

Embed Watermark (4)

Appendix B:
Wow Gradients

YOU'LL FIND THE FILE
in 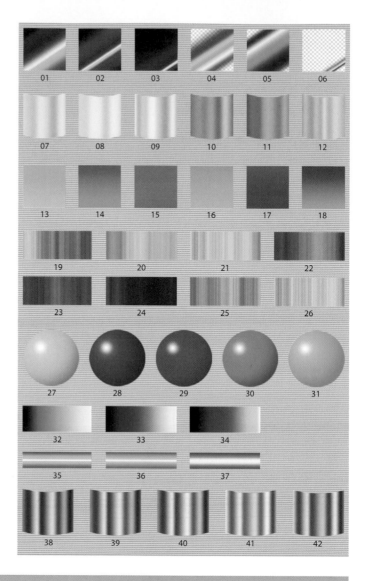 > Wow Project Files > Appendixes > Wow Gradients

ONCE YOU'VE LOADED THE Wow Gradients,▼ they become available anywhere in Photoshop that the Gradient picker appears — in the Options bar for the Gradient tool ▣, the dialog boxes for Gradient Fill and Gradient Map layers, for some effects in the Layer Style dialog, and in the Preset Manager.

The "classic" **Wow Gradients** fall into the following categories:

01–06 are spectrum gradients (see page 198).

07–12 and the shinier-looking **38–42** simulate highlights on a curved surface.

13–18 are simple two-tone gradients for backgrounds or for tinting (page 207).

19–26 are Noise gradients, excellent for making streaked surfaces.▼

27–31 are designed for "rounding" (see the "Masked Gradients" tip below). These gradients are

FIND OUT MORE

▼ Loading the Wow presets **page 4**

▼ Noise gradients **page 197**

MASKED GRADIENTS

A Gradient Fill layer includes a mask that can be used to shape the gradient. Use the Elliptical Marquee ◯ to make a selection and then click the "Create new fill or adjustment layer" button ◑ at the bottom of the Layers panel and choose **Gradient** from the list. In the Gradient Fill dialog choose **Radial** for the Style, click the tiny triangle next to the gradient bar to open a palette of swatches, and click on one of the **Wow Gradients 27–31**. Position the highlight by dragging inside the working window. Experiment with the Scale setting to control the shading, and click "OK."

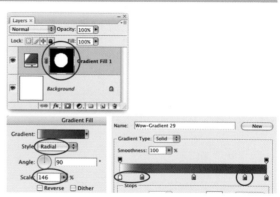

more complex than a simple white-to-color blend. In order to make a sharp highlight for each gradient, the Color Stops for the transition from white to a light version of the color are close together, to make this transition more abrupt than the other color changes, and a shadow tone is inserted near the right end of the gradient.

32–34 are designed to be used in Gradient Maps (see an example on page 208) or as special-effects glows or Shape Burst Stroke effects (page 198).

35–37 can serve as the basis for a neon Layer Style, as in "'Outlining' with Neon" on page 552.

The new **Wow Gradients** (43–77) are of two kinds:

43–54 are designed to be applied as a Gradient Fill layer at reduced Opacity or in Color or Hue mode, to enhance color in landscapes. Of these, **43–47** include transparency, to allow some of the original color of the subject of the photo to come through, while the gradient tints the background (at the top of the photo, often the sky) and the foreground in front of the subject (at the bottom of the photo). You can move or scale the transparent areas to fit a particular photo (take a look at "Gradient Tints for Landscapes" on page 207 for an example).

55–77 are designed to be used in a Gradient Map Adjustment layer. Many of them, especially **62–77**, imitate antique darkroom processes. (On page 208 see "Using a Gradient Map Layer" for a sepia-toning process, and "Creating a Mock 'Split-Tone'" tells how to use Wow Gradient 65 for "split-toning" a photo.

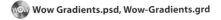 **Wow Gradients.psd, Wow-Gradients.grd**

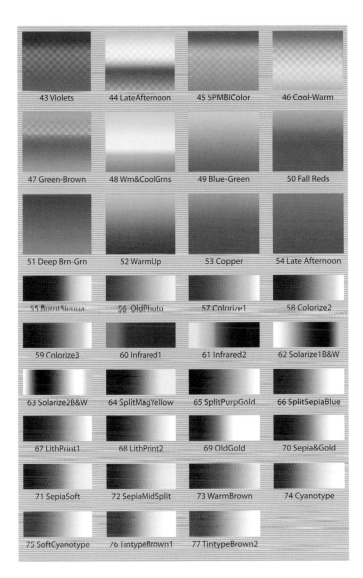

43 Violets   44 LateAfternoon   45 5PMBiColor   46 Cool-Warm
47 Green-Brown   48 Wm&CoolGrns   49 Blue-Green   50 Fall Reds
51 Deep Brn-Grn   52 WarmUp   53 Copper   54 Late Afternoon
55 Burnt Sienna   56 OldPhoto   57 Colorize1   58 Colorize2
59 Colorize3   60 Infrared1   61 Infrared2   62 Solarize1B&W
63 Solarize2B&W   64 SplitMagYellow   65 SplitPurpGold   66 SplitSepiaBlue
67 LithPrint1   68 LithPrint2   69 OldGold   70 Sepia&Gold
71 SepiaSoft   72 SepiaMidSplit   73 WarmBrown   74 Cyanotype
75 SoftCyanotype   76 TintypeBrown1   77 TintypeBrown2

Appendix C:
Wow Layer Styles

PHOTO: BEVERLY GOWARD

The **Wow Styles** for photos were designed with print images in mind, at 225 pixels/inch. In our catalog we've applied them to images that are 1000 pixels in their greater dimension (height or width). If you want to see the Drop Shadow that's built into several of the Wow-Edges-Frames Styles (such as **Wow-Edge Color**, shown here), there has to be some empty, transparent space around the image for the shadow to extend into. To add empty space at the edges, choose Image > Canvas Size and increase the Width and Height.

The **Wow Styles** for type and graphics, also designed at 225 pixels/inch, can be applied through the Styles panel or copied from the **Wow-Sampler** files.▼

The **Wow-Button Styles** were designed at 72 pixels/inch, to look good when applied to small on-screen navigational elements.

STYLING A *BACKGROUND*

If you try to apply a Style to a *Background*, nothing will happen. Double-click *"Background"* in the Layers panel to turn the layer into one that can accept a Style.

FIND OUT MORE
▼ Installing the Wow Layer Styles **page 4**
▼ Applying Styles to files at resolutions other than 225 or 72 pixels/inch **page 83**
▼ Copying & pasting a Style **page 500**

THIS APPENDIX IS A "CATALOG" of examples of the **Wow Layer Styles**, those instant solutions that you'll find on the Wow DVD-ROM that comes with this book. Once you install the Wow Styles,▼ you can apply them through Photoshop's Styles panel. The Wow Layer Styles include:

- Styles for photos and other images such as paintings (pages 753–759), for framing them, adding surface texture, or enhancing their color and tone

- Styles that work magic on flat graphics and type, adding color, dimension, and light (pages 760–767)

You'll also find pointers on how some of the effects work and how you can start with a Wow Style and develop your own — you may want to change a color, substitute a pattern, or scale down a glow without changing the relative size of a bevel effect. Learn more about using, modifying, and developing Styles in "Exercising Layer Styles" on page 80 and in the techniques and "Anatomy" sections in Chapter 8.

Whether you apply a Wow Style to a file that matches the Style's "design resolution" (225 pixels/inch for the photo and graphics Styles, and 72 pixels/inch for the button styles) or to a file at some other resolution,▼ we suggest that you open the Scale Effects dialog box as soon as you apply it. (One way to do that is to choose Layer > Layer Style > Scale Effects.) Experiment with the Scale to see if you want to adjust it for the size of your image or the "weight" of your graphics.

Any Wow Style whose name includes the * symbol uses a built-in pattern. In a file whose resolution is 225 pixels/inch (or 72 pixels/inch for the Wow-Button Styles), the Scale factors 25%, 50%, 100%, and 200% will scale the Style without degrading the pattern. If you scale to some other percentage, or if you use the Style on a file at some other resolution, you may want to zoom in and monitor the quality of the pattern as you scale.

Edges & Frames

The **Wow-Edges-Frames Styles** provide a great start for making your own Styles for framing images on the page.

In **Wow-Soft White** a soft white Inner Shadow makes the edges of the image disappear. The Distance for the Inner Shadow is set to 0 so the fade is even all the way around the image. A white Inner Glow in Saturation mode fades the color at the edges. If you don't want to lose the color, click the Inner Glow effect's 👁 icon in the Layers panel to turn it off.

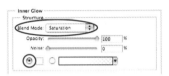

Wow-Soft White

Wow-Edge Color also uses a white Inner Shadow and Inner Glow, but the Inner Glow is applied in Difference mode, so it turns the colors at the edges to their opposites. In addition, this Style includes a Drop Shadow, which you'll be able to see if there's extra (transparent) space beyond the edges of your image.

Wow-Edge Color

Wow-Modern creates a darkened stippled edge. The stippling comes from the black Inner Shadow's Noise setting (100%), and its sharp edge comes from the 100% Choke setting, which "hardens" the shadow. A black Inner Glow adds shading at the outer edges.

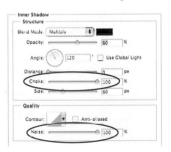

Wow-Modern

Three "traditional" framing Styles — **Wow-Wood Frame**, **Wow-Wood&Mat**, and **Wow-Fabric&Mat** — use the Stroke effect and Bevel and Emboss to make the **frame** itself. For the Bevel and Emboss, the Style is set to Stroke Emboss. The Contour helps shape the molding of the wooden frame. For the Stroke, the Fill Type is set to Pattern. You can change the material by clicking the pattern swatch and choosing a different pattern.

Wow-Wood Frame*

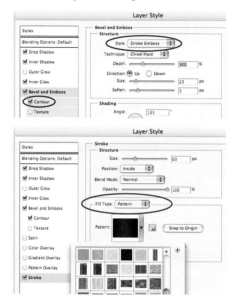

Wow-Wood&Mat*

The **mat** in **Wow-Wood&Mat** and **Wow-Fabric&Mat** is an Inner Glow. The Choke is set at 100% and 90% respectively, to harden the "glow" into a solid stripe. You can remove the mat by turning the Inner Glow effect off (click its 👁 icon in the Layers panel). Or change its color by clicking the color swatch and choosing a new color (for a mat that matches your image, click in the image to sample a color).

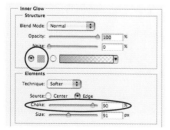

Wow-Fabric&Mat*

Vignettes

The **Wow-Vignette Styles** simulate effects traditionally achieved with lenses and filters, either on the camera or in the darkroom. They focus attention on the center of the image by darkening the edges and in some cases brightening, warming, or cooling the center.

Wow-Top&Bottom creates its effect with a Gradient Overlay. A Reflected black-to-transparent gradient is used, and the Reverse option is checked, to put the clear part in the center with the black on the outside. The Angle for the gradient is set at 90° (vertical), which puts the two dark edges at the top and bottom. The gradient is applied in Overlay mode, and the intensity of the effect can be adjusted by changing the Gradient Overlay's Opacity.

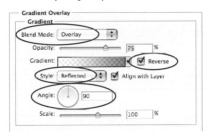

The **Wow-Vignette 1** and **Wow-Vignette 2** series of Styles all include a black Inner Shadow in Soft Light mode, with Distance set at 0 so the darkening is even all around. One difference between the Vignette 1 and Vignette 2 series is the Opacity of the Inner Shadow — it's 75% in the Vignette 1 Styles and 100% in the Vignette 2 series, so the Vignette 2 Styles darken more.

The other component of the **Wow-Vignette 1** and **Wow-Vignette 2** Styles is a light Inner Glow in Overlay mode (Overlay brightens the highlights more than Soft Light would). With Center (instead of Edge) chosen for

Wow-Top&Bottom

Wow-Vignette 1

Wow-Vignette 1 Warm

the Source, the Inner Glow brightens most at the center.

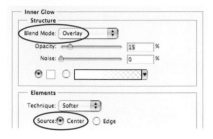

The Size for both the Inner Shadow and Inner Glow is set at the maximum 250 px and Choke at 0, to make both effects as soft and diffuse as possible. So the light spreads out from the center, and the dark spreads in from the edges.

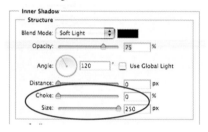

To change the balance between the lightening from the center and the darkening from the edges, you can simply change the Opacity of the Inner Shadow and Inner Glow.

The **Wow-Vignette 1** and **Wow-Vignette 2** Styles vary in the color and Opacity of the Inner Glow. **Wow-Vignette 1 Warm** (its settings are shown below) and the two **Wow-Vignette 2** Styles use a light yellow-to-orange color, so these Styles combine the effects of vignetting and a warming filter. **Wow-Vignette 1 Cool** uses a light blue for the Inner Glow.

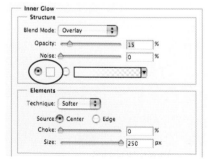

Wow-Vignette 1 Cool

Wow-Vignette 2 Warm

Wow-Vignette 2 Warmer

Tints

The **Wow-Tint FX Styles** apply or remove color, some with edge treatments and overall textures. Edge treatments are created by the Inner Shadow and Inner Glow effects.

Wow-Sepia 1 uses a Color Overlay to apply a warm brown in Color mode. The Opacity of the Color Overlay is reduced to 60% to allow some of the original color to show through.

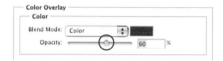

In **Wow-Sepia 2** the Opacity for the Color Overlay is set higher (at 95%). But another important difference from Wow-Sepia 1 is that the brown used here is a more neutral color and so produces a cooler sepia tint. Built into **Wow-Sepia 2** is an overall surface texture, applied with the Texture feature of Bevel and Emboss. To allow the Texture to show up over the entire image, the Style for Bevel and Emboss is set to Inner Bevel, but an unusual Contour prevents beveling of the edges (for another way to emboss texture without creating a bevel, see the "Pattern, Texture & Bevel" tip on page 765).

For variations on the two **Wow-Sepia** Styles, try adjusting the Opacity to show more or less of the original color, and try changing the Blend Mode for the Color Overlay to Hue to protect neutral colors in the original from being tinted.

Wow-Black&White applies a black Color Overlay in Hue mode (Color or Saturation mode would have worked equally well).

Wow-Subdue applies a white Color Overlay in Normal mode at 80% Opacity, so the image can be used as a background for text or other elements.

Wow-Gradient Tint applies its gradient in Color mode. This Style can be useful for landscapes, since it intensifies the color of sky at the top of the photo and grass below. By choosing a different gradient, you can modify the Style to enhance sunset colors.

Original photo

Wow-Sepia 1

Wow-Sepia 2*

Wow-Black&White

Wow-Subdue

Wow-Gradient Tint

PHOTOSPIN.COM

Grains & Textures

Most of the **Wow-Grain & Texture Styles** use a Pattern Overlay effect to apply a grayscale pattern in Overlay or Soft Light mode. Since medium gray is "invisible" in these two "contrast" modes, only the highlights and shadows affect the image, adding surface texture. **Wow-Texture 05, 06, 07,** and **10** use the Texture component of Bevel and Emboss rather than a Pattern Overlay to add "bump" to the surface texture.

Wow-G&T 01*

Wow-G&T 02*

Wow-G&T 03*

Wow-Texture 01*

Wow-Texture 02*

Wow-Texture 03*

Wow-Texture 04*

Wow-Texture 05*

Wow-Texture 06*

Wow-Texture 07*

Wow-Texture 08*

Wow-Texture 09*

Wow-Texture 10*

Chrome

The **Wow-Chrome Styles**▼ were designed to simulate various kinds of shiny, reflective surfaces. Although many of these Styles have built-in reflections, all of them are set up so you can reflect an image using the method described step-by-step in "Custom Chrome" on page 530.

 Here the **Wow-Chrome Styles** are applied to one of Photoshop's Custom Shapes.▼ The crown shows how the Styles look on relatively thick and thin components, and on sharp and round corners. Notice also what happens to the weight of the elements and the space between them when the bevel in the Style extends outward (as in **05**, **07**, **15**, **17**, and **19**) rather than inward from the edge.

Most of the **Wow-Chrome Styles** completely replace the original color of the graphics or type. **Wow-Chrome 11** is the only one that allows some of the original color to come through. So if you start with a colorful symbol (as shown bottom right) instead of the black one used here, your chrome will show a slight color tint.

ROUND CORNERS

Chrome Styles with rounded rather than sharp bevels (such as **Wow-Chrome 11**) look especially good on graphics or type with rounded corners. You may want to choose artwork or typefaces with that in mind, or adjust some corners after applying the Style.▼

Changing corner points to curve points, and adjusting their positions, rounds the corners.

 Wow-Chrome Samples.psd

FIND OUT MORE

▼ Installing the Wow Styles **page 4**

▼ Applying Layer Styles **page 80**

▼ Custom Shapes **page 451**

▼ Editing paths **page 455**

Wow-Chrome 01*

Wow-Chrome 02*

Wow-Chrome 03

Wow-Chrome 04

Wow-Chrome 05

Wow-Chrome 06

Wow-Chrome 07

Wow-Chrome 08

Wow-Chrome 09

Wow-Chrome 10*

Wow-Chrome 11*

Wow-Chrome 12

Wow-Chrome 13

Wow-Chrome 14*

Wow-Chrome 15

Wow-Chrome 16*

Wow-Chrome 17*

Wow-Chrome 18

Wow-Chrome 19

Wow-Chrome 20

Wow-Chrome 11*
applied to red graphics

Metal

Some of the **Wow-Metal Styles**▼ have textured surfaces and others have surfaces that are patterned but smooth. "Anatomy of 'Bumpy'" on page 522 tells how a Layer Style that applies a textured surface is constructed. Another important variable is the Size of the bevel in the Bevel and Emboss effect. A large Size, as in **Wow-Cast Metal**, "consumes" more of the shape you apply it to, leaving less top surface than the other **Wow-Metal Styles**, which have lower Size settings.

ADJUSTING BLEND MODES

If the shadow or glow in a Layer Style doesn't show up against a white or black background, try changing the Blend Mode for these effects. For instance, **Wow-Hot Metal** shows a hot glow over gray (below) but not over white (right). For a similar glow over white or black, change the Drop Shadow's mode to Multiply and the Outer Glow's to Screen.

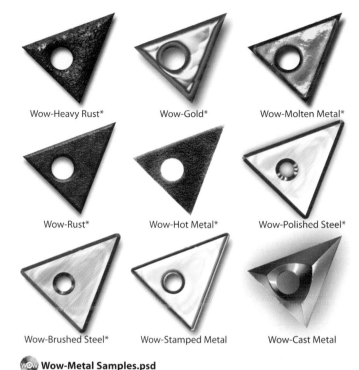

Wow-Heavy Rust* Wow-Gold* Wow-Molten Metal*

Wow-Rust* Wow-Hot Metal* Wow-Polished Steel*

Wow-Brushed Steel* Wow-Stamped Metal Wow-Cast Metal

Wow-Metal Samples.psd

Glass, Ice & Crystal

The **Wow-Glass Styles**▼ are clear, allowing an image below in the layer stack to show through. The transparency is achieved with a reduced Fill Opacity, and the background image is brightened by effects applied in Overlay mode. The bright surface reflections in **Wow-Ice** and **Wow-Clear Ice** are created by settings in the Bevel and Emboss effect. The Pattern Overlay effect provides the "inclusions" in **Wow-Crystal** and **Wow-Smoky Glass**.

SCALING TO FIT

Whenever you apply a Layer Style, especially a dimensional one, experiment by right-clicking/Ctrl-clicking the *fx* icon for the styled layer in the Layers panel and choosing Scale Effects to adjust the fit.▼

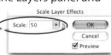

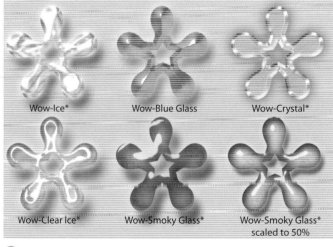

Wow-Ice* Wow-Blue Glass Wow-Crystal*

Wow-Clear Ice* Wow-Smoky Glass* Wow-Smoky Glass* scaled to 50%

Wow-Glass Samples.psd

FIND OUT MORE

▼ Installing Wow Styles **page 4**

▼ Scaling Styles **page 81**

Gems & Polished Stones

Some of the **Wow-Gem Styles**▼ are opaque, while others are transparent or translucent. The illusion of light traveling through and being magnified by the gem (in the **Wow-Gibson Opal**, **Wow-Amber**, **Wow-Tortoise Shell**, and **Wow-Clear Opal**, for instance) is created by a color Drop Shadow effect in Multiply mode and a lighter-color Outer Glow effect, either in Screen mode or Overlay mode.

Here the **Wow-Gem Styles** are applied to a Shape created with the Polygon tool , which shares a space in the Tools panel with the Rectangle ▭ and other Shape tools. In the Options bar the Polygon was set for 3 Sides and for Smooth Corners (in the Polygon Options panel that appears when you click the tiny Geometry Options triangle to the left of the Sides field).

 Wow-Gem Samples.psd

SCALING PATTERNED STYLES

In a Layer Style, a surface pattern applied with a Pattern Overlay effect (such as the surfaces of the **Wow-Wood Styles** and **Wow-Gem Styles**) is pixel-based. If you enlarge the pattern by scaling the Style too much, the pattern may "soften."▼

Wow-Turquoise*   Wow-Red Amber*   Wow-Gibson Opal*

Wow-Amber*   Wow-Jasper*   Wow-Abalone*

Wow-Light Marble*   Wow-Dark Marble*   Wow-Tortoise Shell*

Wow-Clear Opal*

Woods

Some of the **Wow-Wood Styles**▼ have raised grain, while others are polished and smooth. All of the Styles include a surface pattern, applied with a Pattern Overlay.▼

 Wow-Wood Samples.psd

FIND OUT MORE

▼ Installing Wow Styles **page 4**

▼ Scaling Styles **page 81**

▼ Pattern & texture in Styles **page 81**

Wow-Blonde Wood*   Wow-Fine Wood*   Wow-Bocote*

Wow-Rustic Wood*   Wow-Oak*   Wow-Birdseye*

Plastics

The **Wow-Plastic Styles**▼ show different degrees of translucency or transparency. "Anatomy of Clear Color" on page 525 tells how to build these qualities into a Layer Style, and how they interact with the color and dimensional effects that are also part of these Styles.

 Wow-Plastic Samples.psd

Wow-Mottled Purple   Wow-Red   Wow-Edged Swirl*

Wow-Clear Blue   Wow-Clear Orange   Wow-Clear Red

Wow-Textured Swirl*   Wow-Sign Base   Wow-Sign Emboss*

Wow-Rainbow

MORE CLEAR, COLORFUL WOW STYLES

Many of the 150 **Wow-Button Styles** (see page 767) are "plastic-like." To greatly expand your clear, colorful options, just load the **Wow-Button Styles** into the Styles panel and click one of the thumbnails to apply the Style. Be sure to scale the Style after you apply it, to get exactly the color, clarity, and dimensional look that you want.

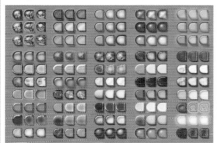

For a closer look at the **Wow-Button Styles**, complete with their ID numbers, see page 767. Most of them have color, surface reflections, and translucency similar to the **Wow-Plastic** Styles.

SIGNS & LICENSE PLATES

Two of the **Wow-Plastic Styles** (**Wow-Sign Base** and **Wow-Sign Emboss**) are designed to be used on stacked layers to create the look of a stamped and painted metal sign or plate. The **Wow-Emboss Bevel.psd** file shows how to structure a sign in two layers using these Layer Styles. This stacking of styled layers works because the **Wow-Sign Emboss** Style uses the Emboss option to build the bevel partly inward and partly outward.▼ The part of the bevel that extends out beyond the edge of the element it's applied to (the sign graphics in this case) is clear, so the color from the layer below can show through.

 Wow-Emboss Bevel.psd

FIND OUT MORE

▼ Installing Wow Styles **page 4**

▼ Scaling Styles **page 81**

▼ Bevel structure **pages 509 & 542**

Organic Materials

The **Wow-Organic Styles** ▼ take their character from seamlessly tiling patterns made from photos of natural textures. Most of the patterns used in these Styles, along with 17 other natural-materials patterns, can be found in the **Wow-Organic Patterns.pat** file of Pattern presets on the Wow DVD-ROM. The patterns are included in the Wow-Organic Styles via the Pattern Overlay effect. In some cases the same pattern is used as the Texture component of the Bevel and Emboss effect to add dimension to the surface texture.

 Wow-Organic Samples.psd

Wow-Seed Pod 1**

Wow-Seed Pod 2*

Wow-Water*

Wow-Green Mat*

Wow-Green Mezzo Paper*

Wow-Brown Paper*

Wow-Rice Paper*

Wow-Bamboo*

Wow-Green Weave*

ADJUSTING PATTERN PLACEMENT

If you apply a Layer Style with a fairly large-scale Pattern Overlay (such as those in the **Wow-Seed Pod** Styles) to a relatively small element, you may want to adjust what part of the pattern shows in the element. (This works well for Styles *without* "embossed" surface texture.) To reposition the pattern, open the Pattern Overlay section of the Layer Style dialog box (one way is to double-click the *fx* that appears to the right of the name of the layer in the Layers panel, and then click on the "Pattern Overlay" name in the list of effects). Now move the cursor into the document window and drag to reposition the pattern.

Wow-Brown Weave*

** The **Wow-Seed Pod 1** Style includes a light Outer Glow that doesn't show up against the white of this page. See the "Adjusting Blend Modes" tip on page 761.

FIND OUT MORE
▼ Installing Wow Styles **page 4**

Fabrics

The **Wow-Fabric Styles** ▼ are seamlessly repeating patterns that include subtle embossing on the surface. The edges are beveled, but the bevel can be turned off, as described in the "Pattern, Texture & Bevel" tip on page 765, if you simply want to use the pattern as a background. The 6 patterns used in the **Wow-Fabric Styles** and 39 more fabric patterns can be found in the **Wow-Fabric Patterns** presets, shown on page 769.

 Wow-Fabric Samples.psd

Wow-Butterfly*

Wow-Violet*

Wow-Black Geometric*

Wow-Pineapple*

Wow-Yellow Ikat*

Wow-Flowing Triangles*

Rock & Masonry

The **Wow-Rock Styles**▼ have patterned, textured surfaces and beveled edges. For many of these Styles, the same pattern is used as a Pattern Overlay for the surface pattern and as the Texture component of the Bevel and Emboss effect for the surface texture. In **Wow-Veined Stone** the pattern has been inverted in the Texture component, so the dark veins appear to be carved *into* the rock instead of raised from the surface.

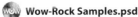

🎨 **Wow-Rock Samples.psd**

Wow-Bricks*

Wow-Green Rock*

Wow-Brown Rock*

Wow-Purple Rock*

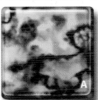
Wow-Granite*

Wow-Iron Rock*

Wow-Veined Stone*

Wow-Weathered Wall*

Wow-Stucco*

FIND OUT MORE
▼ Installing the Wow Styles **page 4**

PATTERN, TEXTURE & BEVEL

In a Layer Style with a textured surface, such as the **Wow-Veined Stone** Style (shown above), the surface texture is usually applied through the Texture component of the Bevel and Emboss effect. But you can turn off the texture while keeping the bevel in place, or vice versa. Start by opening the Layer Style dialog box (you can do this by double-clicking the *fx* icon to the right of the "styled" layer's name in the Layers panel). Then work with the list of effects on the left side of the dialog box, clicking "OK" when you've made the changes you want:

- To eliminate the embossed texture but keep the beveled edge, simply click the checkbox for Texture (under Bevel and Emboss) to remove the check mark **A**.

- To eliminate the bevel but keep the surface texture, it won't work to just turn off Bevel and Emboss, since the Texture is part of it and will disappear along with the bevel. Instead, in the list of effects in the Layer Style dialog box, click the name "Bevel and Emboss" (the name, not the check mark) to open the Bevel and Emboss panel of the dialog box. Note the Size setting in the Structure section. Drag the Size slider all the way to the left to set the Size at 0. The bevel will be gone, but since Bevel and Emboss is still turned on, the Texture effect can be restored. Click the name "Texture" in the list of effects and increase the Depth setting to bring back the surface texture **B**.

Unchecking the "Texture" effect eliminates texture but keeps the bevel.

With both "Bevel and Emboss" and "Texture" checked, reducing the bevel's Size to 0 and raising the Texture's Depth to the Depth of the bevel plus the original Depth of the Texture (here 481 + 6), eliminates the bevel but keeps the texture.

Halos & Embossing

Like some of the Styles in "Neon & Glows" on the next page, the **Wow-Halo** Styles ▼ create dark or light edge effects, both inside and outside the graphics you apply them to. Here we've applied the Styles to red graphics. Some Styles include a Color Overlay of black or gray, and some include reduced Fill opacity. In the two "Carved" Styles, a black Color Overlay combined with reducing the Fill opacity (but not all the way to 0) creates a shaded effect for the entire recessed surface.

FIND OUT MORE

▼ Installing Wow Styles **page 4**

 Wow-Halo Samples.psd

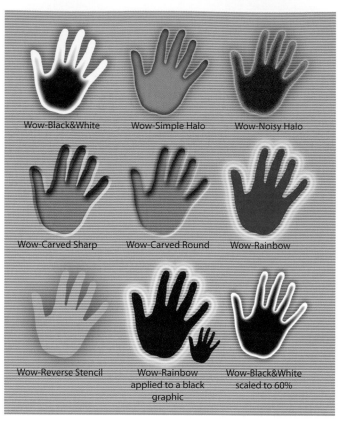

Wow-Black&White

Wow-Simple Halo

Wow-Noisy Halo

Wow-Carved Sharp

Wow-Carved Round

Wow-Rainbow

Wow-Reverse Stencil

Wow-Rainbow applied to a black graphic

Wow-Black&White scaled to 60%

Strokes & Fills

Most of the **Wow-Stroke** Styles ▼ include a Stroke effect. You can replace a Stroke or other effect with one from another Style by Alt/Option-dragging as described in "Copying a Single Effect" on page 83. The Position of the Stroke determines whether or not the Style will "fatten" the type or graphics you add it to (by adding thickness at the edges).

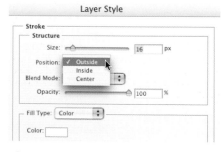

 Wow-Stroke Samples.psd

Wow-Hot Plasma*

Wow-Circus

Wow-Darks

Wow-Fuzzy*

Wow-Mottled Fill*

Wow-Banded Fill*

Wow-Comix

Neon & Glows

Most of the **Wow-Glow** Styles▼ use a Fill opacity of 0% to make the type or graphics disappear, and a Gradient-based Stroke effect to add a glow that follows its outline. Some of the **Wow-Glow** Styles work best when you apply them to type or graphics used against dark or middle-tone backgrounds that contrast with their glowing light. Others look like neon tubes in the "off" state or aglow in the daytime. You can change the color of a **Wow-Glow** Style by opening the Layer Style dialog for a layer to which the Style has been applied and adjusting the colors used in the individual layer effects.

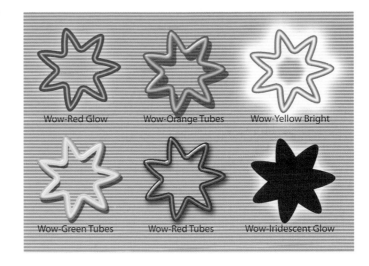

Wow-Red Glow   Wow-Orange Tubes   Wow-Yellow Bright

Wow-Green Tubes   Wow-Red Tubes   Wow-Iridescent Glow

 **Wow-Glow Samples.psd**

Button Styles

Shown on this page are 150 Wow Button Styles, designed to work with 72-dpi files, especially for use in turning graphics into on-screen buttons.▼ The **Wow Button Styles.psd** file (shown at the right) includes 150 individual button layers with Layer Styles — 50 sets with three Styles in each set. The top three rows of each column are different color variations of five Styles.

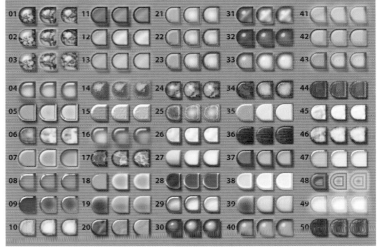

 **Wow Button Styles.psd**

The 150 Wow Button Styles shown above can be loaded into the Styles panel of Photoshop by choosing from the Styles panel's pop-out menu ▾ ☰ and selecting the Wow-Button Styles. Then the Styles can be applied to a 72-dpi file by targeting a layer and clicking the Style's thumbnail in the Styles panel. Or you can copy and paste the individual styles from the Wow Button Styles.psd file, shown above.

FIND OUT MORE

▼ Installing Wow Layer Styles **page 4**

▼ Using Layer Styles **page 80**

Appendix D: Wow Patterns

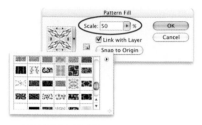

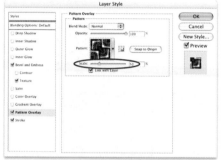

When you apply a pattern in a **Pattern Fill layer** (top) or a **Layer Style**, you can scale it (as shown here) and also adjust its position by dragging in the document window.

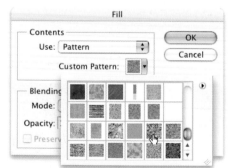

Using the **Edit > Fill** command to apply a pattern doesn't offer the scaling, positioning, and substitution options of a Fill layer or Layer Style. But it provides a way to use a pattern in a layer mask or an alpha channel.

FIND OUT MORE

▼ Installing the Wow Patterns **page 4**

ON THE NEXT FIVE PAGES are printed swatches of the **Wow Patterns** supplied on the DVD-ROM that comes with this book. Some of these patterns started with a rectangular selection in a scan or digital photo. The **Wow-Marble** and **Wow-Media** patterns were started this way, for example. The rectangle was then turned into a seamlessly repeating pattern using one of the methods described in "Quick Seamless Patterns" on page 560.

Photoshop has several ways to apply patterns:

- A Pattern Fill layer

- One or more effects in a Layer Style, where patterns can be used as a Pattern Overlay (for surface pattern), as the Texture component of the Bevel and Emboss effect (for adding "bump" to the surface), or as a Stroke (for adding pattern around the edges of the layer's content)

- The Edit > Fill command

- The Pattern Stamp tool 🖐

Wherever patterns can be used in Photoshop, you'll find a Pattern picker with a menu that lists all the patterns currently in Photoshop's Presets > Patterns folder.▼ You can also load patterns stored outside this folder by choosing Load Patterns from the picker's menu, opened by clicking the ▶ button.

Fabric

The **Wow-Fabric** patterns are ideal for backgrounds and fills. Used as the Pattern Overlay effect in a Layer Style, the same pattern can also be applied as the Texture component of the Bevel and Emboss effect to slightly emboss the surface pattern. The **Wow-Fabric Styles** (page 764) are constructed this way. Change the pattern in any of these Styles by substituting one of these **Wow-Fabric** patterns for the Pattern Overlay and Texture in the Style.

Many of the Wow-Fabric patterns shown here have been scaled to 50% to better show the repeating pattern.

Wow-Fabric 01 (50%)

Wow-Fabric 02 (50%)

Wow-Fabric 03 (50%)

Wow-Fabric 04 (50%)

Wow-Fabric 05 (50%)

Wow-Fabric 06 (50%)

Wow-Fabric 07 (50%)

Wow-Fabric 08 (50%)

Wow-Fabric 09 (50%)

Wow-Fabric 10 (50%)

Wow-Fabric 11 (50%)

Wow-Fabric 12 (50%)

Wow-Fabric 13 (50%)

Wow-Fabric 14 (50%)

Wow-Fabric 15 (50%)

Wow-Fabric 16

Wow-Fabric 17

Wow-Fabric 18

Wow-Fabric 19 (50%)

Wow-Fabric 20 (50%)

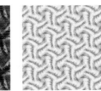
Wow-Fabric 21

Wow-Fabric 22

Wow-Fabric 23 (50%)

Wow-Fabric 24 (50%)

Wow-Fabric 25

Wow-Fabric 26 (50%)

Wow-Fabric 27 (50%)

Wow-Fabric 28 (50%)

Wow-Fabric 29 (50%)

Wow-Fabric 30 (50%)

Wow-Fabric 31

Wow-Fabric 32

Wow-Fabric 33 (50%)

Wow-Fabric 34 (50%)

Wow-Fabric 35

Wow-Fabric 36 (50%)

Fabric (continued)

Wow-Fabric 37

Wow-Fabric 38 (50%)

Wow-Fabric 39 (50%)

Wow-Fabric 40

Wow-Fabric 41 (50%)

Wow-Fabric 42 (50%)

Wow-Fabric 43 (50%)

Wow-Fabric 44 (50%)

Wow-Fabric 45 (50%)

FIND OUT MORE

▼ Working with gradients **page 174**

▼ Adding texture with Layer Styles
page 512

Marble

The **Wow-Marble** patterns make fine backgrounds "as is," or alter them with an Adjustment layer, added by clicking the ◑ button at the bottom of the Layers panel. Use a Hue/Saturation layer with Colorize turned on; set the Adjustment layer's blend mode to Color in the Layers panel to maintain any black and white in the pattern but tint the grays. Or use a Gradient Map layer; click the gradient sample bar to open the Gradient Editor and move the Color Stops or change their colors to get just the effect you want.▼ To generate your own marble-like backgrounds, try the Clouds filter. An example is shown on page 557.

Wow-Marble B&W 01

Wow-Marble B&W 02

Wow-Marble B&W 03

Wow-Marble B&W 04

Wow-Marble B&W 05

Wow-Marble Purple

Wow-Marble Brown

Wow-Marble Green 01

Wow-Marble Green 02

Wow-Marble Gold 01

Wow-Marble Gold 02

Misc Surface

The **Wow-Misc Surface** patterns are great for creating either smooth and polished or textured surfaces. Some of them are used in the **Wow-Rock Styles** (page 765), and you can make similar Styles of your own by applying one of those Styles to a layer and then substituting a **Wow-Misc Surface** pattern for the Pattern Overlay effect and the Texture component of the Bevel and Emboss effect.▼

Wow-Abstract 01

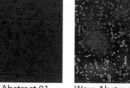
Wow-Abstract 02

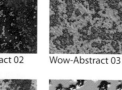
Wow-Abstract 03

Wow-Abstract 04

Wow-Abstract 05

Wow-Abstract 06

Wow-Abstract 07

Wow-Abstract 08

Wow-Abstract 09 | Wow-Abstract 10 | Wow-Abstract 11 | Wow-Blurred Bump | Wow-Brick (50%) | Wow-Brown Rock

Wow-Brushed Metal | Wow-Brushed Stucco | Wow-Bump | Wow-Chrome Spaghetti | Wow-Corrosion | Wow-Granite 01

Wow-Granite 02 | Wow-Inferno 01 | Wow-Inferno 02 | Wow-Inferno 03 | Wow-Inferno 04 | Wow-Light Rust

Wow Rock Textured | Wow-Rust | Wow-Sandstone | Wow-Streaked Gold | Wow-Stripes (200%) | Wow-Styrofoam

Organic

The **Wow-Organics** patterns are photo-based, seamlessly repeating backgrounds. If you apply a pattern as a Pattern Fill layer or as a Pattern Overlay effect in a Layer Style, while the dialog box is open you can move the pattern by dragging in the document window. This is especially useful for positioning patterns that have large components, such as the three **Seed Pod** patterns.

Wow-Brown Paper | Wow-Cork | Wow-Green Mezzo Paper | Wow-Hay Paper

Wow-Rice Paper Black | Wow-Rice Paper White | Wow-Seed Pod Cover 01 (50%) | Wow-Seed Pod Cover 02 (50%)

Wow-Seed Pod Spine

Wow-Weave 01 (50%)

Wow-Weave 02 (50%)

Wow-Weave 03

Wow-Weave 04 (50%)

Wow-Weave 05

Wow-Weave 06

Wow-Bamboo Wall

Wow-Tortoise Shell

Wow-Abalone 01

Wow-Abalone 02

Wow-Wood 01 (50%)

Wow-Wood 02 (50%)

Wow-Wood 03

Wow-Wood 04 (50%)

Wow-Wood 05 (50%)

Wow-Wood 06

Noise

Most of the **Wow-Noise** patterns were designed to simulate film grain or digital noise, either overall for artistic effect, or in specific areas that have been blurred and now look "too smooth" to match the rest of the image. They can be effective when applied to a layer as a Pattern Overlay effect in a Layer Style, or as a Pattern Fill layer, targeted with a layer mask if needed. The **Wow-Noise** patterns are gray in order to be applied in Overlay or other "contrast" blend modes (see "Media" on page 773).

Wow-Noise Big Soft Color

Wow-Noise Big Soft Gray

Wow-Noise Big Hard Color

Wow-Noise Big Hard Gray

Wow-Noise Small Strong Color

Wow-Noise Small Strong Gray

Wow-Noise Small Subtle Gray

Wow-Noise Small Subtle Color

Media

The **Wow-Media** patterns imitate painting surfaces and paint. Many are gray because they were designed to be applied in one of the "contrast" blend modes — those grouped with Overlay in the blend mode menus found in the Layers panel, the Layer Style dialog, and elsewhere in Photoshop's interface. In these modes 50% gray is invisible, and the darker and lighter tones create shadows and highlights to "texturize" your image, whether you apply the pattern alone or emboss it (one way is with Filter > Stylize > Emboss).

Wow-Canvas
Background

Wow-Canvas
Texture 01

Wow-Canvas
Texture 02

Wow-Canvas + Brush
Overlay-Large

Wow-Canvas + Brush
Overlay-Medium

Wow-Canvas + Brush
Overlay-Small

Wow-Watercolor
Background

Wow-Watercolor
Texture

Wow-Watercolor
Overlay

Wow-Watercolor
Salt Overlay

Wow-Cracked Paint

Wow Coquille
Board 01

Wow Coquille
Board 02

Wow-Pebble Board
01

Wow-Pebble Board
02

Wow-Reticulation

Wow-Reticulation
Blotched

Wow-Reticulation
Rough

Wow-Dry Bristle

Appendix E: Artists & Photographers

Geno Andrews 665, 692, 710, 712, 713
www.genoandrews.com
www.photoshopbasics101.com

Mary Lynne Ashley 324
Ashley Photography
Colorado Springs, CO 80903
719-329-0396 (voicemail)
MaryLynne@aol.com
www.ashleyphotography.com

Melissa Au 634
Dandelion Dreams Photography
San Diego, CA
858-349-5846
melissa@dandeliondreamsphoto.com
www.dandeliondreamsphoto.com

Daren Bader 418, 430, 431
Daren.Bader@rockstarsandiego.com
www.darenbader.com

Corey Barker 667

Amanda Boucher 365, 420, 629
amanda_lynn@comcast.net
www.mondarlynn.blogspot.com

Marie Brown 88, 372, 646

Corinna Buchholz 107, 108, 156, 157, 394
Portland, Oregon
503-776-0099
piddix@gmail.com
www.piddix.com
www.etsy.com/shop/piddix
www.instantcollagesheets.com

Alicia Buelow 491, 564
415-522-5902
alicia@aliciabuelow.com
www.aliciabuelow.com

Stephen Burns 657, 708
San Diego, CA
chrome@ucsd.edu
www. chromeallusion.com

Peter Carlisle 557

Garen Checkley 261, 308, 311, 325, 344, 631
GarenCheckley@gmail.com
www.GarenCheckley.com

Jack Davis, JHDavis 110, 115, 118, 131, 153, 179, 198, 232, 259, 282, 283, 314, 316, 322, 323, 339, 375, 377, 380, 398, 413, 417, 426, 610, 620, 630, 644
www.adventuresinphotoshop.com

Anaika Dayton 245, 338, 340

Gage Dayton 282, 320

Lily Dayton 372

Mona Dayton 287, 312

Paul Dayton 611, 632

Paul K. Dayton, Jr. 286, 287, 288, 289

Alexis Marie Deutschmann 368

Rod Deutschmann 116, 373, 611
www.iflcsandiego.com

Bruce Dragoo 44, 231, 422, 423
brucedragoo@yahoo.com

Deeanne Edwards 432
info@marinelifephoto.com
www.marinelifephoto.com

Katrin Eismann 112, 279, 350, 640, 648
Katrin@photoshopdiva.com
www.katrineismann.com

Frankie Frey 389

Allen Furbeck 636, 637
508–526 W. 26th Street
Studio 7D
New York, NY 10011
212-807-7594
mail@allenfurbeck.com
www.allenfurbeck.com

Cristen Gillespie 100, 212, 264, 297, 357, 364, 368, 568

Ian Gillespie 34, 588
ian_gillespie@mac.com

Louis Glanzman 107, 108

Steven Gordon 234, 494
Cartagram, LLC
136 Mill Creek Crossing
Madison, AL 35758
www.cartagram.com

Beverly Goward 210, 241, 634, 646, 752
bevgoward@gmail.com

Laurie Grace 98, 236
860-659-0748
lgrace@lauriegrace.com
www.lauriegrace.com

F. W. Guerin 107

Francois Guérin 260

Loren Haury 260, 292, 366
www.lorenhaury.visualserver.com

Susan Heller 63, 88, 131, 196, 197, 205, 206, 327, 632
hellersd@yahoo.com

Lance Hidy 42
2 Summer Street
Merrimac, MA 01860
lance@lancehidy.com
www.lancehidy.com

Jeff Irwin 96, 97
jeff.irwin@gcccd.net
www.grossmont.edu/jeffirwin

Lance Jackson 464
noirture design
925-253-3131
lancejjackson@earthlink.net
www.lancejackson.net

Jeff Jacoby 715
Broadcast & Electronic Communication Arts Department
San Francisco State University
jeff@jeffjacoby.net
www.jeffjacoby.net

Donal Jolley cover, 132, 160, 403, 407, 469, 482, 517, 542, 566, 595, 612
10505 Wren Ridge Road
Johns Creek, GA 30022
don@donaljolley.com
www.donaljolley.com

K & L Designs 479, 627, 694
615-870-4710
kelly@knldesigns.com
www.knldesigns.com

William Karkow 12
204D Goldthorp, U. Dubuque
1150 Algona Street
Dubuque, IA 52001
wkarkow@dbq.edu

Michael L. Kungl, Mike Kungl 37, 155
M Kungl Studios
Tustin, CA
info@mkunglstudios.com
www.mkunglstudios.com

Jeff Lancaster 242, 627
Lancaster Photographics
619-234-4325
www.lancasterphoto.com

Derek Lea 622, 642, 704
derek@dereklea.com
www.dereklea.com

Lisa Levin 723

Marv Lyons 93, 635
619-691-8776
lyons@visionsynthesis.com
www.visionsynthesis.com

Rob Magiera 703, 706
Noumena Digital
1017 W. Washington Blvd. 5F
Chicago, IL 60607
312-929-4020
rob@studionoumena.com
www.studionoumena.com

Bert Monroy 428
11 Latham Lane
Berkeley, CA 94708
510-524-9412
bert@bertmonroy.com
www.bertmonroy.com

John Odam 163, 164, 492, 678, 684
jodam@san.rr.com

Jonathan Parker book production, 163, 164, 165
Jonathan Parker Design
jmparker@cox.net

P. Ed Parnell *et al.* 732

Wayne Rankin 94
Rankin Design Group
P. O. Box 221
Warrandyte, Victoria 3113
Australia
61 [0]3 9844 4438
wayne@rankindesign.com.au
www.rankindesign.com.au

Betsy Schulz 40, 638
A Design Garden
www.adesigngarden.com

Sharon Steuer 195, 586, 649, 714
San Francisco, CA
studio@ssteuer.com
www.ssteuer.com

Genoa Sullaway 243

John Tenniel 394

Susan Thompson 370
160 North Elmwood Avenue
Lindsay, CA 93247
559-562-5155
susan@sx70.com
www.sx70.com
www.davidswann.com

Cher Threinen-Pendarvis 119, 374, 379, 388, 688
cher@pendarvis-studios.com
www.pendarvis-studios.com
www.pendo.com

Anthony Velonis 479

E. A. M. Visser 178, 253, 342, 343, 535
LilVisser@gmail.com

Mark Wainer 38, 70, 291, 419, 424
mark@markwainer.com
www.markwainer.com

Irene de Watteville 158
irenetile@roadrunner.com

Rick Worthington 320, 333, 337, 338, 339, 340, 363, 682

Tommy Yune 105
www.tommyyune.com

Christine Zalewski 343
www.zalewskiphotography.com

Index

Note: Entries in blue are specific to Photoshop CS4 only and do not apply to version CS3.
Note: If you're looking for a "palette" topic for CS3, look for "panel" instead.

Multiply blend mode, 183
  with Adjustment layers, 285
  for "dropping out" white, 45, 599
  increase image density (darken), 195, 285
  with line art, 484–485
  for shading, sampled color, 526
  for shadows, 183, 627
Multi-shot techniques
  averaging out noise, 325–326
  blending exposures, 292–296
  eliminating unwanted elements, 327–331
  extending depth of field with, 344–345
  for panoramas, 576–581
"multitargeting" layers, 582

N

Natural Media brushes, 397
Natural Scene Designer software, 235
Navigator panel, 19
neon effects, 463, 509, 767
  animated, 463
  with type, 551–552
Neon Glow filter, 736
nested Actions, 122
New Group From Layers command, 515, 554, 583, 598
nighttime, simulating, 357–362
noise, reducing, 261, 325–326, 333. *See also* Reduce Noise filter
  averaging out, 325–326
Despeckle filter, 156
Noise filters, 742
  for restoring film grain, 315, 628
  with Healing Brush, 315
  for patterns and textures, 553
Noise gradients, 175, 197
  Wow Gradients, 175, 750
Normal blend mode, 182, 203, 253
Note Paper filter, 746
Notes/ Note tool, 21, 127
NTSC Colors filter, 661
NTSC DV 720 x 480 video format, 681
NTSC (North American) video standard, 661

O

Ocean Ripple filter, 273, 741
Offset filter, 749
  for finding "seams" in pattern tiles, 560, 561
  for staggering pattern elements, 563
Omnidirectional lighting, 264, 359, 559
onion-skinning (Extended), 666, 667
Opacity, layer, controlling, 35, 512–513, 583
opaque ink previews, 230
OpenGL, 19
  "bird's eye view," 19
  Brush tip controls, 71

Open Type fonts, 436, 441
Open With Adobe Photoshop command (Bridge), 119
Optimize Animation, 665, 699
Optimizing (for web), 131, 152–154
Optimize To File Size command, 154
Options bar, 20, 22. *See also* individual tools and commands
  for 3D (Extended), 653, 654, 673, 675
Other filters, 749. *See also* High Pass filter; Offset filter
Outer Glow effect, 227, 507, 528, 540
  as shadow, 506, 538, 626, 644
out-of-gamut warning, 179
Overlay blend mode, 161, 184, 258
  blending images, 495, 596, 606
  for contrast, 340, 348, 375
  with dodge & burn layer, 258, 320, 608
  simulate satin, 355
  for adding texture, 397
Overlay effects (Layer Styles), 406, 459, 502–504, 538, 543
  for reflections, 538
Overlay-Neutral fill, 320, 339, 355, 608
  for Lighting Effects, 547
Overprint Colors dialog box, 200

P

page layout programs. *See also* Adobe InDesign
  file formats required by, 127–128
  and using type, 447–448
Paint Bucket, 386, 391, 489
Paint Daubs filter, 739
Painter. *See* Corel Painter
painting
  photos used for reference, 387–388, 407–408
  "post-processing," 387–388
  troubleshooting, 379
  with tablet and stylus, 385
  using layers, 26
  watercolor techniques, 389–393
    with Pattern Stamp, 403–406, 494
  wet-on-wet technique, 395–399
  with Wow Actions, 415–417
PAL video standard, 661
Palette Knife filter, 736
palettes. *See* panels
palettes/panels, change of name, 1, 15
panels, 23
  docking/nesting/stacking, 20, 23
  dragging and sizing, 23
  menu, 23
  Navigator, 19
  Preferences, 24
  Tools, 20
panning, 690
panorama, 328
  with Photomerge, 572, 576–581, 632
Pantone Matching System (PMS), 168

Paragraph panel
  toggle on Options bar, 440
  type specifications, 437, 439, 440
paragraph type, 436–439, 592. *See also* type
Parametric Curve, 144, 145, 249
Pass Through blend mode, 184, 514
Paste commands
  from Illustrator, 460–461
  Paste As: Paths, 461
  Paste As: Pixels, 531
  Paste As: Shape Layer, 461, 522
  Paste As: Smart Object, 16, 462, 522
  Paste Behind, 61
  Paste Into, 61
  Paste Layer Style, 82, 468, 489
Patch tool, 256–257, 312
  copying/pasting, 572
  selections, 312
  tint effects, 211
  vignettes, 280
Patchwork filter, 748
Path Selection tool, 456–457
paths, 18–19, 122, 454–457
  in actions, 122
  in Adobe Illustrator, 155, 460–461
  aligning, 457
  anchor points, 450, 455–457
  clipping paths, 451
  combining, 474
  component, 454, 456
  converting to Shape layers, 456
  duplicating, 456
  editing, 455–456
  filling, 457–458
  Fill Path dialog, 458
  hand-drawn with Pen tool, 422, 442, 622, 639, 641
  pasting, 155, 460–461
  reshaping, 455–457
  selection, loading as, 54, 155, 622
  Stroke Path dialog, 459
  stroking and filling, 429, 457–458
    layering strokes, 458
  subpaths, 450, 454, 456
  transforming, 457
  type-on-a-path, 442–444
    warping, 445–446
  Work Path, 19, 122, 449, 451, 456
Paths panel, 62, 155, 429, 451
  Work Path, 19, 122, 451
Pattern brushes (Illustrator), 460
Pattern Fill layers, 35, 77, 396, 477–478, 488, 569
  layer masks, 35, 399, 569
Pattern Maker filter, 557
Pattern Overlay effect, 176, 266–267, 427, 459, 504, 758
Pattern picker, 393, 401, 478, 768
Pattern Stamp, 122, 377, 403–405, 494
  versus Art History Brush, 403